Ruanaidh

By Art Rooney Jr.

with Roy McHugh

The story of Art Rooney and his clan

First printing: February, 2008
Limited Edition

Manufactured in the United States of America
ISBN No. Hard Cover: 978-0-9814760-2-5
ISBN No. Soft Cover: 978-0-9814760-3-2

Printed by Geyer Printing Company, Inc.
3700 Bigelow Boulevard
Pittsburgh, PA 15213

Typography by Cold-Comp
91 Green Glen Drive
Pittsburgh, PA 15227

Cover design by Kathy Rooney; illustrations by Merv Corning

For my parents, Art and Kathleen (Kass) Rooney

For my wife, Kathleen (Kay) Rooney

For all of my relatives who crossed the high seas to America
and worked in the steel mills and coal mines

"... If a book must be written about me, wait 30 years ...
for I touched all the bases."
                                    - Art Rooney (The Chief)

"Sorry, Dad, I could only wait 18 years
because I'm getting to be an old fogey myself."
                                    - Art Rooney, Jr.

Ruanaidh
(Rooney)

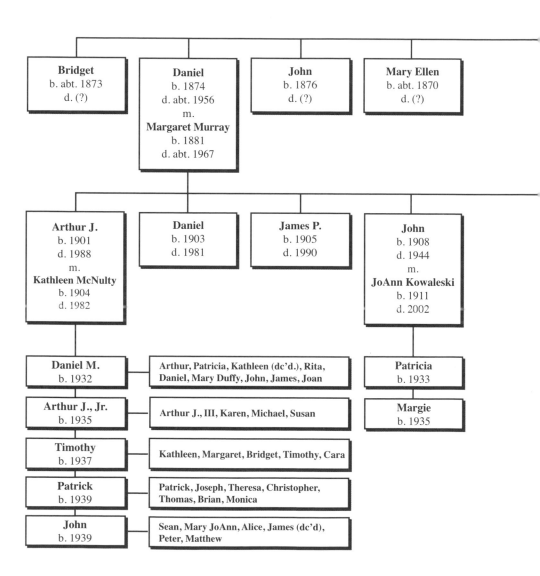

Bridget b. abt. 1873 d. (?)	**Daniel** b. 1874 d. abt. 1956 m. **Margaret Murray** b. 1881 d. abt. 1967	**John** b. 1876 d. (?)	**Mary Ellen** b. abt. 1870 d. (?)

Arthur J. b. 1901 d. 1988 m. **Kathleen McNulty** b. 1904 d. 1982	**Daniel** b. 1903 d. 1981	**James P.** b. 1905 d. 1990	**John** b. 1908 d. 1944 m. **JoAnn Kowaleski** b. 1911 d. 2002

Daniel M. b. 1932	Arthur, Patricia, Kathleen (dc'd.), Rita, Daniel, Mary Duffy, John, James, Joan
Arthur J., Jr. b. 1935	Arthur J., III, Karen, Michael, Susan
Timothy b. 1937	Kathleen, Margaret, Bridget, Timothy, Cara
Patrick b. 1939	Patrick, Joseph, Theresa, Christopher, Thomas, Brian, Monica
John b. 1939	Sean, Mary JoAnn, Alice, James (dc'd), Peter, Matthew

Patricia b. 1933
Margie b. 1935

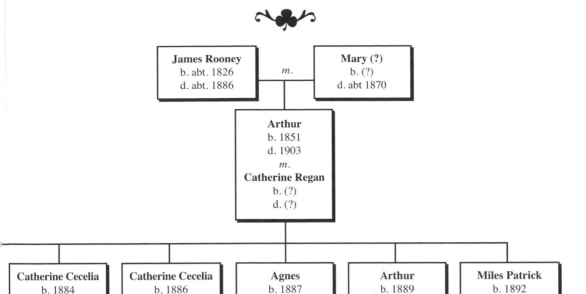

James Rooney
b. abt. 1826
d. abt. 1886

m.

Mary (?)
b. (?)
d. abt 1870

Arthur
b. 1851
d. 1903
m.
Catherine Regan
b. (?)
d. (?)

Catherine Cecelia
b. 1884
d. abt. 1886

Catherine Cecelia
b. 1886
d. abt. 1888

Agnes
b. 1887
d. (?)

Arthur
b. 1889
d. abt. 1889

Miles Patrick
b. 1892
d. (?)

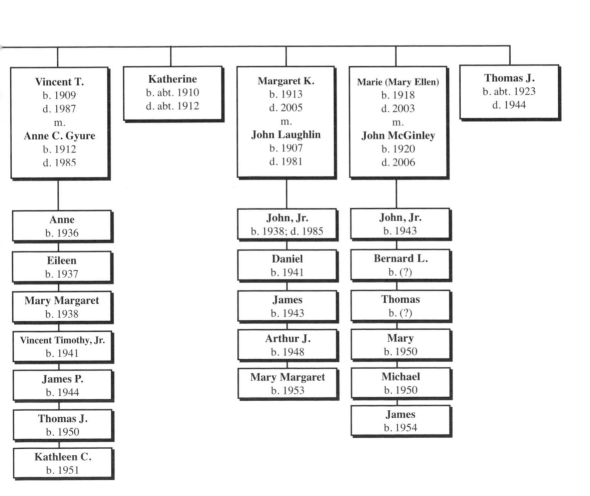

Vincent T.
b. 1909
d. 1987
m.
Anne C. Gyure
b. 1912
d. 1985

Katherine
b. abt. 1910
d. abt. 1912

Margaret K.
b. 1913
d. 2005
m.
John Laughlin
b. 1907
d. 1981

Marie (Mary Ellen)
b. 1918
d. 2003
m.
John McGinley
b. 1920
d. 2006

Thomas J.
b. abt. 1923
d. 1944

Anne
b. 1936

Eileen
b. 1937

Mary Margaret
b. 1938

Vincent Timothy, Jr.
b. 1941

James P.
b. 1944

Thomas J.
b. 1950

Kathleen C.
b. 1951

John, Jr.
b. 1938; d. 1985

Daniel
b. 1941

James
b. 1943

Arthur J.
b. 1948

Mary Margaret
b. 1953

John, Jr.
b. 1943

Bernard L.
b. (?)

Thomas
b. (?)

Mary
b. 1950

Michael
b. 1950

James
b. 1954

Acknowledgements

Contributing Artists

Merv Corning, The Preeminent Sports Artist
Dan DeBonis
George Gaadt, *www.gaadtstudio.com*
Dino Guarino, *www.dinoguarino.com*
Denny Karchner, *www.karchnerwesternart.com*
Kathy Rooney, Art Director & Cover Design, *www.krooney.net*

Support

Tula Corning (Mrs.) supplied encouragement and allowed use of Merv's art work.
Mike Fabus, Steelers Photographer, photographs
Clark Gardner, Transportation
Dee Herrod, Our secretary and #1 reason this book is a reality after 12 years.
Keith Maiden, Geyer Printing
Maureen Maier, Finance
Jim O'Brien, Self-Publishing Advisor
Joe Polk, Web Design
Mike Rooney, Interactive Telecommunications
Rob Ruck & Maggie Patterson, for sharing research from their Art Rooney book.
The Pittsburgh Steelers, for the players who gave permission to use their images.

Readers

Tom Atkins, Actor, "The Chief"
Jack Butler, #80
Larry Deer, Teammate at North Catholic High School
Sean Doherty, R.I.P.
Dr. Robert Friday, PH.D.
Carl Hughes, former *Pittsburgh Press* Sports Columnist
Kay Rooney, Invaluable support.
Kathy Rooney, Art Direction
John Troan, Editorial Assistance
Rev. Raymond Utz, Cousin
Jeff Weber, Statistics

Art Rooney and his Hope Harvey players at the Hope Fire Station, North Side

(*Drawing by Kathy Rooney*)

Roy McHugh

The spare elegance of supreme craftsmanship marked Roy McHugh's column writing for the *Pittsburgh Press* in the second half of the 20th century. McHugh is a native of Iowa and graduate of Coe College, where he cultivated a love of both sports and language. McHugh became both sports editor and columnist-at-large during the "City of Champions" era in Pittsburgh's distinguished sports history. None of the heroes of that era were any more distinguished than the quiet, meticulous columnist who chronicled their triumphs and foibles. He traveled with Muhammad Ali, contributed with distinction to national magazines, and his humanity and insight was indispensable to the dozens of American journalists who've examined the life and death of Roberto Clemente, Art Rooney, Sr., Billy Conn, and many more.

— Gene Collier, Sports Columnist
Pittsburgh Post-Gazette

Contents

Part One: The First Hundred Years

Part Two: Bit Player
1956-1965

Part Three: A Seat at the Table
1965-1969

Part Four: A New Broom
1970-1973

Part Five: Full Speed Ahead
1970-1973

Part Six: Winding Down

Preface

The idea for this book was Mort Sharnik's. A versatile and knowledgeable *Sports Illustrated* writer, Mort was doing research for a story about my father and his football team, the Steelers, the day I met him. This was in 1968, when the Steelers were still occupying outgrown quarters in the Roosevelt Hotel. I took Mort into the Sylvan Room restaurant, and there we found my Uncle Jim having coffee. His droll observations and unique way of speaking in a confidential undertone fascinated Mort. From the Sylvan Room, Mort came with me to the small, drab, windowless office from which I directed the Steelers' scouting organization, and Dr. Art Sekay, the team dentist, paid us a visit. Blunt and outspoken, he made as vivid an impression on Mort as Uncle Jim had. Later in an adjoining office, we encountered two old friends of my dad's from the North Side. Dago Sam Leone was an animated story teller, steadfast horse player, and amiable eccentric, Patsy Scanlon a battered ex-prizefighter whose flower store in the downtown business district was a front for his bookmaking operation. Their off-the-cuff reminiscences kept Mort entertained for most of the next hour.

As soon as we were by ourselves, he said, "Art, you have to write these things down for posterity, or at any rate for your children and grandchildren. Get the whole cast of characters down on paper."

I considered this good advice, but I didn't act on it. Mort kept after me. He kept after me for more than twenty years before I started to write.

Gradually it became an obsession. I attempted, as Mort had urged me, to put everything down. It would be the story, through my own eyes, of Art Rooney and his clan, the chronicle of his life and times. Off and on, with no clear notion of where I was going, I recorded memories pretty much as they occurred to me. I wrote in longhand, filling several dozen voluminous journals. My prose style, two friends who looked at samples of it told me, was stream-of-consciousness. "You write like James Joyce," they said, not intending it as flattery. They meant that in Joyce's great novel "Ulysses" there were countless digressions, and that I digress, too. We write alike in the sense that an elementary-school football team and the Super Bowl champions might both line up in the T-formation.

If any publisher was ever to see my manuscript, it needed editing, and Roy McHugh, a former *Pittsburgh Press* columnist, offered to help. "I'm not touchy about having my words changed," I told him, "so rewrite with a free hand." He preserved as much of my raconteur's voice — a blend of North Side Irish and Pittsburghese — as he could. The stories are mine, or as I heard them, but my collaborator's newspaper background and familiarity with the subject matter enabled him, in certain cases, to add details. The judgments I make and the content of the personal portraits I include are mine alone.

We pulled together several different narrative threads. There is family legend in the text, and some anecdotal history of the old North Side. There are race-track stories and football stories. It's a memoir, so a lot of it's about me. I write of the players and coaches I knew, of scouting trips and scouts, of the drafts I prepared for and the arguments they triggered.

I reconstruct long-ago conversations as I remember them or as others remembered them. Direct quotes make for easier reading, and I quote people directly when I can, but I am not about to pretend that every quote in the book is one hundred percent verbatim. That would be an impossibility, so in places where no harm would result I take some creative license. Let me state for the record, however, that my powers of recall are above average and nowhere have I intentionally changed the substance of what anybody said.

It is customary for an author to thank the people who've read and commented on parts of the manuscript, or all of it, and I do so. I did not seek permission to name them. The computer know-how of my secretary, Dee Herrod, was indispensable. One final acknowledgement: My good fortune in being Art Rooney's son is the only reason I ever could have thought of getting a project like this under way and the only reason I could finish it.

Part One: The First Hundred Years

Daniel Rooney

Margaret Murray Rooney

Chapter 1

Forebears

From the seacoast manufacturing town of Newry, in Northern Ireland, James and Mary Rooney, steerage passengers on a sailing ship, crossed the Atlantic Ocean to Canada during the Irish potato famine near the end of the 1840s. The young married couple settled in Montreal, where James Rooney, who had worked with hot metal in a Newry iron forge, became a millwright and where Arthur Rooney, an only child, was born in 1851. Over the course of the next fifty years, Arthur Rooney had a son named Daniel and Daniel Rooney had a son named Arthur. This Arthur Rooney was my father, the focus of these memoirs.

I'm indebted to his official biographers, Rob Ruck and Maggie Patterson, for what little I know about the personal history of my nineteenth-century forebears. When the first Arthur Rooney was 21, his parents returned to the British Isles, taking him along — not to Ireland, but to Wales, where the iron industry was flourishing. In a town called Ebbw Vale, father and son landed jobs in a mill. Ebbw Vale (pronounce it "Ebba") is a place of special importance to the Rooneys. It was where Arthur met and married an Irish girl named Catherine Regan and where Daniel Rooney, my grandfather, was born.

Not that Roman Catholics like the Rooneys were popular in Ebbw Vale. When they marched off to Mass, Dan Rooney in later life would recollect, their Protestant neighbors bombarded them with stones. Imminent hard times compounded the family's miseries. During a phase-out of iron production — the age of steel had begun — James and Arthur Rooney lost their jobs. Then, not long afterward, Mary Rooney died, and, for Arthur Rooney, that was enough. Back to Canada he sailed in 1876 with a family that now included one more son and a daughter. James Rooney, who had taken another wife, remained in Ebbw Vale.

Arthur Rooney's trail for the next few years is hard to follow. By 1879 he had somehow made his way to Youngstown, Ohio, and was working again at the occupation he had learned in Wales, puddling iron. Rooney folklore has it that he walked across the border and into the United States alone and without a passport. How, then, did he manage to reassemble his family? On that point, there is no information.

As a puddler and then a roller, Arthur Rooney worked ten, sometimes twelve, hours a day. He worked in debilitating heat at a job that took know-how, endurance, and strength. Puddlers and rollers supervised their own crews, crews of as many as a dozen men. By the standards of the times, they were highly paid — the aristocrats of the working class, Ruck and Patterson call them. And yet for all their specialized skills, they were no more immune than common laborers to the ups and downs of the economy. When in one town the economy tanked, Arthur Rooney would move on, and in 1884 his wanderings brought him to Pittsburgh.

He was 33. There were now four children, with two more to come. For extra money, Arthur and Catherine Rooney took in boarders. They lived on the South Side and bought property there, a lot and a house costing seven thousand dollars. They owned a smaller plot of land in Mansfield, now Carnegie. They were frugal and persevering. They believed that a penny saved was a penny earned. And they were prospering.

But then a major depression hit. Once more Arthur Rooney was jobless. His union, the Amalgamated Association of Iron, Steel, and Tin Workers, had gone on strike, and there was violence in the offing. Henry Clay Frick, the manager of Andrew Carnegie's Homestead steel works, hired Pinkerton detectives to protect the scabs who took the place of the strikers. Arriving by barge at four o'clock in the morning on July 6, 1892, three hundred armed Pinkertons attempted an amphibious landing at the mill site on the Monongahela River. The strikers resisted with rifles, revolvers, and sticks of dynamite. Ten union men and three Pinkertons lost their lives. Outnumbered, the Pinkertons surrendered, but Governor Robert E. Pattison called out the state militia. Eight thousand strong, they kept the mill open, and the strikers eventually gave in. Henry Clay Frick had broken the union.

Arthur Rooney's role in all this can only be guessed at. Between 1892 and 1896 he worked at a series of low-paying menial jobs. He sold his Mansfield property and his house on the South Side. In this second transaction, there was more than meets the eye. Michael Concannon, his daughter Bridget's husband, bought the house from Arthur for the original purchase price, seven thousand dollars, and transferred the deed to Catherine, Arthur's wife. My interpretation is that he thus shielded Arthur from his creditors.

Somehow or other, Arthur was sufficiently well off by 1896 to buy a saloon on the South Side — to be specific, on East Carson Street. (Even that far back, there was no better place to open a saloon.) His new business seemed depression-proof, for in good times or bad, men drank. But, with housing scarce — housing for immigrant steelworkers — the Rooneys continued to take in boarders. There were five altogether and they lived in a single room. They worked in shifts and they slept in shifts, making way for one another in what beds were provided or maybe even doubling up.

Four of the Rooneys' children, all but the three oldest, were still at home. Catherine Rooney did the cooking and the housework. She did the laundry, hand-scrubbing her boarders' filthy work clothes. In the daytime during the summer months, Catherine and two of her daughters fetched laundry water, cooking water, and drinking water from the polluted Mon River. They carried it to the house, several hundred yards distant, in buckets. The mills, Ruck and Patterson tell us, made such prodigal use of water during their peak hours that none was available for the taps of the South Side's resident population.

Such details are illuminating, but not much else is chronicled about these first of the Rooneys to settle in Pittsburgh. Arthur, according to Ruck and Patterson, was wiry and probably muscular. We know that he had a red beard; we know that he rode a white horse, on which he sometimes led the St. Patrick's Day parade in downtown Pittsburgh; we know that he had a nickname — Cap, its derivation obscure. Besides the beard, the horse, and the nickname, he had a shotgun, and he used it, the story goes, in a confrontation on a bridge. In the words of my uncle John, one of Arthur Rooney's grandsons, he met his adversary, "a notorious scoundrel," in the dead of night. Shots rang out. There were flashes from the guns. "Only Grandfather Rooney walked off the bridge," Uncle John would intone.

Could the "notorious scoundrel" have been a Pinkerton detective? Recall that Arthur belonged to the Amalgamated Association of Iron, Steel, and Tin Workers. One of his sons, I have heard, kept a shotgun he described to younger relatives as an heirloom, explaining, "We used this to shoot the Pinks." Was it the weapon that felled the notorious scoundrel? We'll never know.

In Uncle John's version of what happened, Western Pennsylvania was too hot for Arthur after the gun fight. Whether his enemy on the bridge lived or died, Uncle John could not say; what he did say was that, one step ahead of whatever retribution may have been coming, Arthur Rooney left the country, taking temporary refuge in Ireland. Ruck and Patterson point out that no confirmation exists for this tale. Believe it or don't; the choice is yours.

The Salt of the Earth

Arthur Rooney died in 1903 of either typhoid fever or pneumonia. He may have been 51 or he may have been 52 — for that time and place a normal lifespan. Although my knowledge of Red Beard is sketchy and for the most part undocumented, I saw his signature once on the deed to his Carson Street property. What I remembered about it was the calligraphy. His hand was unsure and he wrote in an old-fashioned script. I had the feeling that his name was the only thing he could write. His wife Catherine signed with an X. As the years went by, his sons and daughters came to believe that the property they inherited was worth a great deal of money. There were squabbles over what to do with it until Dan — my grandfather — put an end to the rhetoric by selling this piece of land for a sum he divided with the others.

It amounted to very little.

In 1903, Dan Rooney was 29. He had worked a year or two in the mills, had been a cook on a riverboat (Pittsburgh to Cincinnati and back), and, like his father before him, had opened a saloon of his own. It was in Coulter, or Coultersville, a Monongahela Valley coal patch near McKeesport. And it was there that he had married a coal miner's daughter, Margaret Murray, called Maggie — red-haired, pretty, and petite.

In their saloon, which was also a boarding house, the same as old Arthur's, Maggie did most of the work. She cooked and baked, specializing in bread — crusty on the outside, soft and white on the inside. She picked wild berries for her homemade jellies and jam. She scrubbed and cleaned for the boarders; she prepared ham sandwiches for the saloon clientele.

In a room above the bar on January 27, 1901, Arthur Joseph Rooney, my father, came into the world. Shortly afterward, Maggie's mother, who was 43, gave birth to a daughter. How unusual was it, I ask, to acquire both a son and a sister just hours apart?

Around Coultersville, alas, the coal was now all but mined out, so the Rooneys picked up and moved to Monaca. Dan and Maggie again became the owners of a boarding house and saloon, naming it the Colonial Hotel for a nearby steel mill, and in 1903, also in a room above the bar, their second son, Dan Junior, was born.

1903 must have been the year that Dan Rooney, Sr., got into trouble of some kind. The details are to this day obscure. At any rate, suddenly and mysteriously, he sold his hotel and left Monaca, sustaining himself with part of the $16,000 sales price and leaving the remainder with Maggie. His hideout, I'm guessing, was in St. Louis, or near there. I say that because my father, years later, recalled a trip to the 1904 St. Louis World's Fair with his mother and baby brother for a family reunion.

Maggie and the kids were making their home then with Catherine, Dan's mother, in a boarding house she ran in the Beaver Valley town of Crescent City, where Maggie helped with the work and gave birth in 1905 to a third son, James Patrick. The date of her husband's return is unclear, but by 1906 or 1907 the Rooneys were together once more. They lived in a rented house in the heavily Irish Pittsburgh neighborhood of Homewood. Dan Senior, struggling to pay off his debts, clerked in a paint store. Soon there were two more sons to feed and clothe — John, born in 1908, and Vincent, born in 1910. A daughter named Katherine, born in 1911, died at the age of two.

The big turning point for the Rooneys came when Maggie's parents, Mike and Mary Ann Murray, bought a three-story wood and brick building at the corner of Corey Street and General Robinson Street on Pittsburgh's North Side for six thousand dollars and sold it for the same amount to their daughter, who had learned to scrimp and save. The year was 1913. On the first floor of this building, Dan Senior, going back to the trade he knew best, opened a "bar and café." On the second and third floors were the living quarters.

In a very short time, there was still another addition to the family — a daughter named Margaret for her mother. Then along came Marie, born in 1914, and, belatedly, one last son, Thomas Joseph, born in 1919. By 1920, the rooms above the bar and café were crowded to the eaves. There was the ten-member immediate family; there was Helen Ward, an adopted daughter; there were Maggie's two sisters, Gertrude and Stella Murray. Besides these permanent residents, there were other assorted relatives, coming and going, and always a few castaways of the most helpless and pitiable kind — the orphaned children of friends.

Hygienic conditions in the early years of the twentieth century created a steady flow of orphans. And the Rooneys — Dan and Maggie — were willing when called upon to give them safe harbor.

These forebears of ours, my aunt Margaret used to say, invoking a phrase from the Bible (Matthew 5:13), were "the salt of the earth."

Maggie Rooney was notable for her strength and determination, Dan for his clear-eyed probity. "He was free of guile," a friend named George Quinlan once said, "and he called a spade a spade."

Of the men in Maggie's family — the Murrays — there were some who dug coal and others, like Maggie's father, who tested for gas, going deep into the mines' lower passages. A Murray who preferred the wide open spaces enlisted in the Army and fought in the Indian wars of the Western frontier. Wild Indians, he may have thought, were not as dangerous as coal mines. Decades after they had left Coultersville, an old-timer from the area described the Murrays as "gentlemen, all of them," and the Rooneys as "a pack of hooligans."

If the first Arthur Rooney ever worked in a mine, it was probably in Wales. His son Dan might have known, but Dan recollected next to nothing of Wales and seldom mentioned the place. Being interviewed once for an insurance policy, he was asked where he was born. "Wales," he said reluctantly. The insurance man put down his pen. "Dan," he said, "you've been telling people in Pittsburgh all these years that you're Irish. You're not. You're a Welshman."

"Look," said Dan patiently. "If you had a cat, and the cat had kittens in an oven, would you call the kittens biscuits?"

The insurance man dropped the subject.

Rooted

The First Ward on the North Side — everybody omitted the numerical designation and called it simply "The Ward" — was where Dan Rooney at last put down roots. His sons and daughters and grandchildren called him Pop. In the family quarters above the saloon, my father — AJR from now on — shared a room in the attic with his brother Dan Junior. Waking up on a cold winter morning, they would often find snow on their blankets, snow that had blown in through cracks in the walls. On the grandstand roof at neighboring Exposition Park, which had been the Pittsburgh Pirates' home field until 1909, there were ornamental steeples. One day a hard wind blew a steeple off the roof and it fell through a window into the barroom.

At least twice a year the Allegheny River would flood, sending residents of The Ward to their high and dry second stories to be rescued by skiff or rowboat. One time during a flood, AJR and his brother Dan were rowing across the site of Exposition Park in a canoe. A kid named Squawker Mullen was with them, a kid who could never sit still. When Squawker tried to move from one end of the canoe to the other, it overturned, dumping the three boys into the water. They started swimming for the unsubmerged part of the grandstand on the third-base side of the field. Squawker and Dan made it easily; AJR was wearing boots and an overcoat and only saved himself from drowning with a last desperate lunge.

There were no public swimming pools when AJR was a boy. Everybody swam in the rivers. On the banks, there were roped-off areas with bath houses — makeshift structures where people could take a shower. Swimmers who crossed from shore to shore — they did it to show off — were playing dice with their lives. Boat and barge traffic was heavy and the current was swift. Every summer, AJR often recalled, a friend or acquaintance would drown.

No women were allowed in the Rooneys' bar. Typically on Saturday night a fight would break out, with Pop in the middle of it, restoring peace. Afterward, he would drag himself upstairs and change from his torn, bloody shirt into a fresh one. The troublemakers, he always said, were the crazy Irish from Galway. "Go over there some day," Pop urged his sons, "and find out what makes them tick." To Pop, it remained a dark mystery.

When Pop was new to the North Side, people warned him about the neighborhood bully, a man they predicted would tear up the barroom and scare away all the respectable drinkers. Resolutely, Pop went into training. He shadow-boxed; he lifted weights. At last the bully appeared — and at the sight of him Pop could only laugh. "Why, you greasy bum!" he shouted, using his epithet for unsavory characters. "I've thrown you out of my other bars, and I'll do it again." The greasy bum saved him the trouble. He left without further encouragement, and the First Ward from then on regarded Pop as a man to be reckoned with.

Uncle Jim liked to talk about Pop's night watchman — a big, mean German police dog. Jim described the animal as "nobody's friend." Even the Rooney kids were careful to be in the house before Pop closed the barroom and turned the dog loose. This, of course, pleased their mother. "Anything important," she always said, "can be done before midnight, and should be. After that hour, you're up to no good."

In search of a more upscale environment for the family, Pop bought a house in Manchester, and there he came down with smallpox. The house was quarantined; Pop's bed was moved to the attic; his mother Catherine nursed him back to health. Obeying doctor's orders — up to a point — she burned all his clothes except a fine pair of woolen long johns, which she took to the back yard and soaked in boiling water. For the rest of his life, Pop's nose was heavily scarred by the pox.

The Rooneys and the Murrays, it seemed to me, were different in temperament. Rooneys tended to be outgoing and flamboyant, Murrays much less so. No one could be as outgoing as AJR, and yet in my opinion, anyway, he was more like his mother Maggie than his father. For one thing, she believed very deeply in the Roman Catholic religion, and so did AJR. He told me that once when his mother was seriously ill, he prayed for her recovery in St. Peter's Church from 6 o'clock in the morning until 7:30 or 8 at night. He was 15 years old, I think he said.

Maggie Rooney hoped fervently that AJR would be in the church choir, and from her household funds she gave him the price of a tryout — fifty cents. The trouble was that he lacked a qualification thought to be necessary: he couldn't sing. When the choirmaster conveyed this to him, AJR replied that he was not going to quit. He'd be letting his mother down and wasting her fifty cents. There was only one thing for the choirmaster to do — pay hush money. He returned the fifty cents, AJR faced the fact that he was no John McCormack, and the choir got back on key.

The performance art in which AJR excelled was not music, but sports. He was spending most of his time now at a playground in the neighborhood, punting and passing a football or in baseball season learning to hit and field. He had a natural aptitude for sports of all kinds, and sports were to be his main occupation from boyhood into maturity.

The pattern of his life had taken shape.

Fun And Games

AJR worked at sports with more determination and energy than any of the other boys from The Ward. Dan and Jim were good at sports, too, John and Vince less so. Tom, the youngest brother, born when his parents were past 40, belonged to a different era. When Tom was growing up, the family lived on Perrysville Avenue. They were still North Siders, but in those days suburban North Siders.

Baseball games between AJR's team and teams from other neighborhoods frequently turned into free-for-alls. In one such altercation, AJR and his friends got the worst of it. They were the visiting team, but a return game was scheduled in The Ward, and their opponents had the audacity to show up, or it may have been more like simplemindedness. As they trooped onto the field, AJR — perched on a fence post like Cecil B. DeMille directing a battle scene in a movie — singled out the dirtiest fighters among them. He would shout, "There's one!" or "Get that guy!" — the cue for his teammates to attack in a group. They sent the enemy home badly mauled.

AJR was one of the baseball players from The Ward who had dinner one night with Harry K. Thaw. In 1906, Harry K. Thaw, the demented heir to a Pittsburgh industrial fortune, had murdered the architect Stanford White at his table in the rooftop restaurant of Madison Square Garden, the New York landmark building White had designed. It seems that White had seduced Thaw's wife, an artist's model from Tarentum named Evelyn Nesbit. At his trial, Thaw pleaded insanity, escaping prison but not confinement to a mental institution. Now he was back home on North Lincoln Avenue, where Pittsburgh's earliest millionaires lived. His mother, still believing he could lead a normal life, had grasped at the idea that an evening's conversation with some healthy teenage athletes might be good for him. She could not have been more mistaken. Before, during, and after dinner, AJR reported, Thaw sat mute, inter-acting with no one.

As the Rooney boys outgrew their adolescence, they became interested in such gambling games as craps. A pair of dice and a blanket were all that was needed to play, and the blanket was optional. Dan, by common consent, ordinarily served as the pit boss. If the dice went off the blanket, Dan made the call.

One day an outsider organized a game. By the standards of The Ward, big money was at stake. Dan, who'd been hurt playing football, came hobbling around on crutches just to observe, and a state of tension quickly developed. The outsider, as it happened, was a "greasy bum" — in the parlance of the Rooneys a "bad guy." AJR had a way of distinguishing between bad guys and tough guys. A tough guy, he said, wasn't necessarily a bad guy. You could be a bad guy or a tough guy or both. This particular bad guy was both. He immediately let Dan know that it was "his" game — that he was making the calls. And, no matter how obviously wrong they were, the calls favored himself every time. Finally Dan said something. The "greasy bum" continued to cheat. Again Dan spoke up.

"What are you going to do about it? You're on crutches," the bum said scornfully.

So Dan let one of his crutches fall to the ground and used the other crutch to beat the hell out of the guy.

According to family friend George Quinlan, Dan could be "a one-man riot." No one in The Ward was more feared, but his brother Jim got to thinking he could handle Dan. It was arranged that they were to settle the issue at Phipps Playground. At the appointed hour, a good-sized crowd was on hand. Jim, approaching the area cleared for combat, with enthusiastic backers egging him on, began to lose confidence. The sight of Dan calmly waiting unnerved him completely. He turned around and bolted for home.

It was Dan Senior — Pop — who encouraged the boys to fight. "Do you know what he got them for Christmas?" asked Quinlan. "Boxing gloves and a punching bag. And, boy, could they punch and, boy, could they fight — even Duke, who never weighed more than 120 pounds." Duke was Vince, the No. 5 son.

AJR boxed in the amateurs. He was runner-up twice — in different weight divisions — for the National AAU championship and won an international tournament in Canada. AJR sometimes said that he qualified for the 1920 Olympic team but passed up his chance to compete in the Antwerp games in order to play baseball at Georgetown University. In researching their book, Rob Ruck and Maggie Patterson found that, though the Olympic regional trials were held in Pittsburgh, AJR did not participate. He had beaten two fighters on the team that went to Antwerp, Sammy Mosberg and Frank Cassidy, and this may have accounted for the confusion in his mind.

Art Rooney, Boxer
(Drawing by Kathy Rooney)

Mosberg, a New Yorker, was the gold medalist in Antwerp at 135 pounds. After he returned to the United States, AJR beat him again. My brother Tim suggests that the real reason AJR did not enter the trials was for fear of raising questions about his amateur status. Since the age of 15, he'd been playing semi-pro baseball for money. No such reservations kept him out of the 1921 national amateur tournament in Boston. In 1920 he had been the runner-up as a lightweight. This time he boxed as a welterweight and lost again in the title bout. Dan, a light-heavyweight, got to the semi-finals before losing.

Traveling carnivals had house fighters back then, hired professionals who would take on all comers from the audience. For every round a challenger lasted, the carnival paid him either a dollar, three dollars, or five dollars, depending on the owner's generosity. AJR's problem, and Dan's too, was making certain the house fighter lasted. "Those carnival guys could handle a farmer, all right, but they were very ordinary fighters," AJR told Myron Cope in an interview taped when he was 69 years old. Once when Squawker Mullen, a national amateur champion at 110 pounds, was getting the worst of it from a carnival guy, Dan, Squawker's second, "reached up over the ropes," said AJR, "and hit the fellow — nailed him like you'd nail a bird in the air." It started a "hey rube" — carnival terminology for a riot — and there was no more boxing that night after the tent came down.

One of the carnival boxers the Rooney brothers took on was KO Circus. KO's manager — a bit of a thief — paid him off in one-dollar bills. KO had a poor grasp of currency values and thought that five one-dollar bills were obviously worth more than one ten-dollar bill. The manager — I forget his name — parted grudgingly with one-dollar bills, ten-dollar bills, or bills of any other denomination. A dollar was all he offered to challengers from the audience for each round they lasted with KO. For AJR and Dan, keeping KO on his feet for three rounds, the maximum number permitted, hardly seemed worth the effort, but they worked at it doggedly. They returned to the carnival night after night and the dollar bills added up. KO's manager couldn't stand the sight of them.

And then, to his chagrin, they started showing up with Jim. Like AJR and Dan, Jim could punch. George Quinlan always said he could punch from any angle. "I saw him stretch a guy once when he was flat on his back," Quinlan declared. "The other guy had Jim down and had fallen on top of him, and Jim reached up and knocked him out."

With KO, Jim took it easy — his brothers had warned him not to spoil a good thing. The Rooneys were now costing KO's manager nine dollars a day instead of six. Clearly something had to be done. And cutting his losses, he decided, was the answer. In search of help, he went to Dan Senior and made him a proposition. "I'll give you six bucks a day for your boys to split up if they promise to stay away from the carnival," he said, adding, "It was bad enough when Art and Dan were going three rounds with KO every night, but now they've got Jim doing it, too. I'm paying those kids NOT to fight."

That being the case, he was willing to pay them a little bit less for not even pretending to fight, but easy money in small amounts never satisfied AJR. If his fists were to be his fortune, he'd turn professional. He joined a stable of boxers under the management of an Australian — barnstormers going through Pittsburgh. They were fighting their way across America; when they reached the West Coast they would all board a ship for Australia.

AJR didn't get far. Despite having won all his fights on the tour, he'd begun to suspect that the ring as a career was not for him. He could see himself twenty years in the future — a washed-up ex-pug with cauliflower ears, scar tissue, and brain damage. By most accounts, including his own, he fought like a bulldog, wading into his opponent and taking a lot of punches. He won on sheer persistence, wearing the other guy down. He was game; he was tough; he was strong; he packed a wallop. But others before him who'd been game, tough and strong, and could hit hard, were walking around on their heels.

Before the barnstormers reached the West Coast, a woman on the tour, the wife of the best Australian fighter, took him aside. "You come from a good family," she said. "You're educated. There'll be opportunities for you in life. Go home."

AJR listened. He took the next train back to Pittsburgh still undefeated, neither better off nor worse off than he'd been on the day he left, and without regrets.

Among themselves, the Rooneys boxed for recreation, and AJR, with his advantage in years and experience, punched the others around at will. Sometimes, though, there were sweet, heady moments of revenge. Once in later life, when AJR was standing with his hands in his pockets and a cigar in his mouth, he said to Vince, who had had several beers, "Why don't you go home? You're drunk." Vince wound up and slugged AJR, knocking him down. By the time he got up, Vince was running for his life, a block away.

AJR won his matches with Dan until Dan got to be nearly six feet tall and substantially outweighed AJR, who was maybe 5 feet 8. After that, according to George Quinlan, Dan started "lathering" AJR, who said to him finally, "Dan, it's disgraceful, two brothers fighting like this. We've got to stop." And Dan said, "I'm just now beginning to enjoy it."

Dan licked a street fighter called the toughest and meanest in The Ward. This guy was so strong the "detention boxes" used by the police to hold unruly prisoners until the paddy wagon arrived couldn't contain him. Arrested one night for drunkenness and placed in the nearest box, he knocked it over and broke the door open, but he was no match for Dan.

It surprised people to learn that Dan was religious. One time after a baseball game, a few of Dan's teammates informed him that they intended to visit a whorehouse in Steubenville, notorious for its red-light district. Dan, full of evangelical fervor, tried to talk them out of it. "You'll be committing a mortal sin," he uselessly warned them.

"That was when I knew he was going to be a priest," said the man who told me the story.

Learning The Ropes

AJR, meanwhile, was developing political skills. In Pop's saloon, he got acquainted with the ward bosses who gathered there and started running errands for them. AJR had street smarts. At first he could get small things done and then he could get bigger things done. In some ways he was strangely naive. As an old man, he said that in his younger days he'd had no idea that it was breaking the law to vote more than once in an election.

Many people in the early 1900s voted for the last person to "duke" them — which is to say give them money — as they entered the polling place. This was a time when there weren't any welfare checks, when there weren't any Social Security checks. If you needed help, you got it from your relatives, or the church, or the ward chairman. Cars and drivers were scarce, so in case of a death in the family the politicians supplied them. Thanks to the politicians, the bereaved had a ride to the cemetery.

AJR not only rounded up drivers but did some driving himself, making friends. He took care to remain on extra good terms with the family of Kathleen McNulty, his future wife, in part because the McNultys owned an automobile agency and were willing to let him have cars.

Among his regular drivers was a small-time gambler called Cocky O'Malley. As a sideline, O'Malley sold pedigreed dogs to people who wanted pets. He had an eye affliction of some kind, but could recognize quality in dogs. If he spied a valuable pooch on the way to the graveyard — dogs at that time still ran loose — he would stop, pick it up, toss it into the back seat with the mourners, and drive on. This callousness in matters pertaining to mortuary etiquette was by no means exceptional in the drivers recruited by AJR. Once the burial service was over, they would break all speed limits in their haste to be on time for the party that followed every funeral, knowing how freely the liquor would flow.

The police in The Ward respected AJR for his political clout and athletic ability, which was helpful to him sometimes when trouble occurred. On Federal Street one cloudy afternoon, he stopped to show concern for a friend who was seated on the sidewalk and holding his ankle. Two strangers were standing over him, a man and a woman, the woman tightly clutching a folded umbrella. AJR asked what had happened. His friend explained that he and the other guy had been fighting. In the midst of the fracas he'd fallen down, and he suspected his ankle was broken. AJR looked inquiringly at the other guy, who ordered him to mind his own business. "Or I'll take care of you the same way," he added.

Cheerfully, AJR invited him to try. They squared off, and at this point, lifting her umbrella, the woman brought it down on AJR's head.

"Don't do that again," he said.

And she did it again.

AJR accepted no abuse from anyone of either sex. "Well, you've had your last warning," he said. Feinting a punch at the man, he "crossed over," as he put it, "and hit the broad right on the button." Down she went. He then belted out her boyfriend.

Moments later a Black Maria pulled up and the cops jumped out. Recognizing AJR, one of them said, "Art, what's going on here?"

"These two beat up my pal," he answered, indicating the pair he had flattened. The cops threw them into the paddy wagon and gave the man with the broken leg a ride to the hospital.

Not every policeman knew that AJR rated special treatment. Once when his big new car ran out of gas on the Sixth Street Bridge, a traffic cop berated him for failing to keep an eye on the gauge.

"Maybe you could do better," AJR suggested.

"I sure could, you dumb hick," the cop said.

AJR got out of his car. "Then do it," he said, and walked across the bridge to the North Side and home.

That night he received a telephone call. The police had delivered the car, unticketed and filled with gas, to his father's saloon.

He was getting to be a man of some importance.

Oddballs

Grandma Rooney — Maggie — had a sister whose name was Stella. My mother described her as "very pretty, with fine features, a nice figure, and red hair." In the personal column of a Pittsburgh newspaper, a man with the Anglicized name of Jackson announced that he was looking for a bride, and Stella responded to his ad. The man was Slavic; he was a Communist, or perhaps a Socialist; he did not believe in a deity.

Atheism was hard for an Irish-Catholic girl like Stella Murray to swallow, but she and Jackson were married. They had children. Jackson was opposed to Catholic baptism or to any other kind of baptism, so Stella made secret arrangements with a priest. At one baptism, my Uncle Dan was the godfather. The baby, christened Anne, grew up to be a well-known stage and screen actress.

Anne Jackson's father had a great deal to say about the "pie-in-the-sky" Catholic religion, all of it negative. Returning from a family funeral one day, he ridiculed Christian burial. This was too much for Pop Rooney, who proceeded to give him hell — holy hell, Pop may have thought. "I am what I am and you are what you are, so keep your big mouth shut," Pop shouted. There are differing accounts as to what happened next. Either Jackson took a punch at Pop or Pop took a punch at Jackson. In any case, if it was Pop who threw the punch — and I believe that to be true — he had nothing but sore knuckles to show for it. In this scenario, Jackson, it seems, was in the front seat of an automobile while they were yammering at each other and Pop was standing just outside. And, unaccountably, Pop failed to notice until after he delivered the punch that Jackson had rolled up the window.

Eventually, the Jacksons all moved to New York City, where Anne got her start in the theater. Grandma Rooney, who never said anything negative about anybody, made her brother-in-law the only exception, pronouncing him "a bad one." My mother gave Jackson higher marks. She said he was kind and considerate, but my mother did not really know him.

Another relative my elders always talked about was Pop's brother Jack, a man who had money enough to sponsor amateur baseball teams. Well past middle age, he was still unmarried. He took a liking to AJR, the best baseball player in the family, and it seemed a foregone conclusion that AJR would be provided for in Jack's will. But Jack met a woman named Bobbie Smith, previously married and twenty years younger than he was, and she allowed him to sweep her off her feet. Jack proposed; they went to the altar. Not long after the wedding, Jack broke his neck in a fall down some steps. The injury was fatal, and Bobbie, of course, inherited his money.

I met Bobbie once. It was in Kaufmann's or Horne's, where I had gone with my mother to shop. A woman said hello to us and my mother said hello and they exchanged a few pleasantries. When the woman went on her way my mother said to me, "That was Bobbie Smith, who was married to Uncle Jack." The Bobbie I met in the department store that day had a bubbling, agreeable personality.

Pop's most colorful, headstrong, and irresponsible brother was Uncle Myles. Margaret Laughlin, his niece, said that whenever she saw Myles he was smiling. There were others more familiar with his serious side. One of AJR's political-minded friends told him that Myles had been a "slugger" — an enforcer of party discipline — at election time. He would punch people out if they voted the wrong way. According to family folklore, Uncle Myles mixed it up with a heavyweight champion, Jim Jeffries, during World War I. This was after Jeffries had retired undefeated and then lost a comeback fight to Jack Johnson. Myles was in the service and Jeffries was touring the Army camps. For the entertainment of the troops, he would spar with their unit's best fighter or with anyone intrepid enough to climb through the ropes. In exhibition matches, there is very little actual fighting as a rule, but Uncle Myles, the story goes, fearlessly tore into Jeffries and turned their sparring session into something that was more like a war. Anyway, that is how my father and my uncles told the tale.

Myles was a bit of a daredevil. To win a bet, he would jump off any bridge in Pittsburgh. On one of his descents he appeared to be heading for the skiff that always took him ashore. The skiff's oarsmen leaped into the water, but Myles came down with a splash, not a thunk, and lived to collect the wager he had made. How it affected his rapport with the crew of the skiff I don't know.

After the Eighteenth Amendment became law, Pop Rooney was forced to close his saloon and put his unsold liquor into a bonded warehouse. The only legal customers for it were outside the United States, and to market the stuff would take time. This gave Myles an idea. He was working then as a mail carrier and he knew that some old-model Post Office trucks were for sale. Myles bought two of them. Their colors had been changed and their insignia painted over, but Myles could use a paintbrush himself. In twenty-four hours they looked like mail trucks again, and Myles carried out his scam. He would drive to the warehouse, pick up all the booze a truck would hold — for shipment overseas, as he explained — and then return in the second truck for another load. Finding his own buyers in Allegheny County was never difficult. Perhaps inevitably, the Prohibition agents caught up with him, and Myles served time in the slammer.

He came to a sad end, partly because of his weakness for women and partly because of an unfortunate misjudgment. I happened to be in Belle Vernon once on a ticket promotion job for AJR's professional football team, the Steelers, when a friend of Uncle Jim, a man called Possum, said to me, "I know your cousin who lives here." I told him I did not have any relatives in Belle Vernon. "Well, this lady," he said, "claims to be the illegitimate daughter of a Rooney named Myles." I could only say, "I believe it." At any rate, some time after Myles got out of jail and was working in a roadhouse, a certain Joe the Barber came to see him. He accused Myles of trifling with his wife and pulled a gun. Myles took it away from him, but then made the mistake of giving it back, "You're too gutless to use it," he said. They were the last words Myles ever spoke. Gutless Joe the Barber shot and killed him.

Joe went to prison for the deed and served fifteen years before coming up for parole. Pop Rooney testified at his hearing. "Let him go," Pop said to the parole board. "He's paid his debt, and, anyway, Myles provoked him."

Myles had a son named Art (for his grandfather, the original, red-bearded Art Rooney.) The kid became an excellent football player, one of the best halfbacks in the late 1930s at North Carolina State University. On my scouting trips to Raleigh thirty years later I would sometimes be asked if I were the same Art Rooney. Apparently the other Art, in addition to being quite a football player, was pretty good with his fists. I met a shoe salesman in Palm Beach who told me that "little Art Rooney" had belted out his (the shoe salesman's) brother when they were North Carolina State classmates. Art was a World War II Army officer and made the service his career, retiring with the rank of lieutenant colonel. He was married, but had no children I ever heard of. One thing he did have, like many another Irishman, was a serious drinking problem.

The McNultys

My knowledge of the McNultys is limited. The McNultys all seemed to lead conventional lives. They were Irish for the most part, but with Scottish and German blood in the mix. My mother, Kathleen McNulty, who married AJR in 1931, belonged to the third generation.

I have a single vague memory of being alone at the bedside of my grandfather, John McNulty, in the last few days of his life. He was calling for his daughter Harriet. "Go fetch her, Artie," he begged me. I was too young to know what death was, but old enough to realize that this was no ordinary request, and I hurried to deliver the message.

One of John McNulty's relatives, a man named Free, was a city councilman. McNulty himself owned a cooperage on Herr's Island in the Allegheny River and had a permit from the city to scavenge for old or damaged barrels in a dump (today we would call it a landfill). He cleaned and repaired the barrels and then sold them. Almost every business used barrels for shipping and storage back then. Later, during Prohibition, Pop Rooney used McNulty barrels to ship out his illegal booze.

My maternal grandmother, Bridget, was a Devlin. I never knew her. She died at 38, of cancer. Radiation treatment was in its infancy then, and in my grandmother's case, according to her daughter Alice, misused. Some of the male Devlins were railroaders, and another Devlin — Chris, who went to Penn State University — was a linebacker on the football team and afterward played for the Cincinnati Bengals. No Rooney ever played beyond the college level.

A Devlin who worked on the railroad was in charge of returning wrecked trains to the track. After finishing a job, he would send his office a wire: "Off again … on again … gone again. Devlin."

Because their names were so similar, my mother and Henry McAnulty, a Holy Ghost priest and former Air Force general who was president of Duquesne University in the 1970s, believed, or pretended to believe, that they were distantly related. Father McAnulty was a man of wit, charm, and intelligence.

Like the Rooneys, the McNultys were North Siders and attended St. Peter's Church. St. Peter's had a tough old pastor who would call out from the sacristy when his assistants were giving longwinded sermons, "Come on — get it over with!" He accused them of endlessly repeating themselves.

The McNultys lived on Lacock Street in a neighborhood more upscale than The Ward. By saying yes to AJR, their daughter Kathleen, the McNultys thought, had "married down". Old John McNulty had always done well financially, but when wooden barrels gave way to steel drums he was slow to make the changeover and lost everything — his stable, his horses, and his business. Meanwhile, the Russian immigrants who had worked for him saw that steel drums were the future, went into business for themselves, and, according to Alice McNulty, my mother's sister, became rich.

The McNultys often spoke of their missed opportunities. "Any fool can make money," my mother would say. "It takes a wise man to keep it." My mother had a million of these sayings and she used every one.

Aside from his lack of business acumen, there was still another reason why John McNulty went broke. After the death of his wife he got into booze and lost his competitive spirit. When things were going good, he had helped his brother George start the first Buick dealership in Western Pennsylvania; now that it was John who needed help, George put him to work as a night watchman in the Buick garage. For my mother and her sisters, this was heartbreaking.

The North Side Buick Company, by the way, was in business for many years under the ownership of the McDonoughs, who were cousins of the McNultys.

My parents often talked about the great flu epidemic of 1918. It seems to me that my mother lost a sister, a young girl named Elizabeth; if I had listened more closely I would not be in doubt. Other families were wiped out completely. The dead would be laid out at home, my mother said, and in almost every house there would be a casket. When the Diocese of Pittsburgh called for its young male parishioners to help with the work in the cemeteries, AJR, Dan, and Jim became volunteer gravediggers. It was a time they would never forget.

Chapter 2

School Days

AJR and his brothers learned the three Rs at St. Peter's parochial school, but got their secondary educations at Duquesne Prep — Holy Ghost Academy when AJR first enrolled and later called University School. Even in the dead of winter, they made the long daily trek from the North Side to the Bluff — and back — on foot.

At University School, AJR played football, basketball, and baseball. In 1917, his junior year, the football team had a 7-1-1 record, and according to the school paper its success was in large measure due to the "wriggling, squirming, and serpentine runs" of "Halfback Rooney." This same Halfback Rooney, wrote the anonymous author of the piece, "stands head and shoulders above his companions."

Due to the influenza epidemic of 1918, even high school journalists were preoccupied with matters of more importance than football games, and Halfback Rooney's accomplishments in his senior year are lost to us now. We know that at the end of the season two or three colleges offered him athletic scholarships. And we know that these offers were not accepted. His mother, the dominant early influence in AJR's life, had ideas of her own for the oldest Rooney boy. She thought he should go to work, which as she understood it meant working with your hands. A man who worked was a coal miner, like AJR's grandfather on his mother's side, or a steelworker, like Pop Rooney's brother-in-law, Mike Concannon.

Uncle Mike Concannon, a foreman in one of the mills, pulled a few strings to get a job there for AJR. It was not the kind of job that AJR himself would have chosen. The work was hard, it was boring, it was dirty, and it made you sweat. On his first day, at lunch-time, he put a question to Uncle Mike. "How much money do you make?" Mike told him. AJR was not impressed. At the suggestion that in, oh, about fifteen years he, too, might be a foreman earning a foreman's wages, AJR had heard all he needed to hear. He was playing summer baseball, for a semi-pro team, and making more money than Mike Concannon made. With a thank-you-very-much, he picked up his lunch bucket and went home, never to return. Nor did he bother to collect the half day's pay that was coming to him. In his old age he reckoned that, with interest, the steel company owed him a sizable sum.

Unquestionably, the few long hours he spent that day in the mill were life-shaping for AJR. His mother's notion of work, it was now clear, differed radically from his own. He saw that manual labor was the deadest of dead ends. He would get where he intended to go by using his wits.

And a college education was to be the first step. He considered Notre Dame, having heard from the new football coach, a Norwegian immigrant by the name of Knute Rockne. Years later, when AJR off-handedly mentioned this to his sons, we took it with a small grain of salt. Knute Rockne by then had entered mythology. Everybody knew all the fables about winning one for the Gipper, about the Four Horsemen outlined — in Grantland Rice's imagination — against a blue-gray October sky. But a Rockne-Rooney connection? Long after Rockne's death, and shortly after AJR's, we came across proof. A footnote in a book, a biography of Rockne, revealed that in his files there indeed was a letter to AJR, or a copy of one. Would he be interested, Rockne had asked, in playing football at Notre Dame?

Penn State wanted him, too — badly enough to offer a share of the program concession on game days. The NCAA had been in existence since 1910, but essentially it had no policing powers. There were rules and regulations, but not many. In the end, though, AJR opted for Indiana Normal, now called Indiana University of Pennsylvania.

One reason may have been that he had a girlfriend there, a girl with an Irish name I don't remember. In due time they went their separate ways. Years passed. And then, unexpectedly, when AJR was famous as the owner of the four-time Super Bowl champions, the woman wrote to him. She was proud to have been his classmate, she said. Of equal importance in her life, she continued, was one other distinction she could claim. Indiana Normal had been a two-year teachers' college in her day and his, and she had taught after graduation in the local Indiana school system, where her students included a shaggy-haired, drawling home-town boy named Jimmy Stewart.

It's about even money that AJR had to be told who Jimmy Stewart was. In the 1970s friends of his in Los Angeles — Hollywood Park race-track people — introduced him to Cary Grant. Making conversation with Grant, AJR casually asked, "Do you work at Hollywood Park?" Later on when someone explained that Grant sort of worked in the movies, AJR said, "Well, if he doesn't make cowboy pictures I wouldn't know him."

Jimmy Stewart made cowboy pictures, but not the kind that AJR normally would have seen.

At Indiana, AJR played football, of course. His old associate George Quinlan described him as "a little-bitty halfback who could run like hell." Trained down to the lightweight limit, AJR was a 135-pound boxer. For football he must have weighed more — 145 pounds at the least. In the days before behemoths roamed the earth, college football players no bigger than that were commonplace. In any case, AJR was not a runt. Fully mature, he had a frame that could carry 160 pounds of mostly muscle.

At Indiana, lacking enough credits for his high-school diploma, AJR took the college preparatory course but competed on the varsity teams in football, basketball, baseball, and track while continuing to box. (After winning a tournament somewhere, he returned with two black eyes to a hero's welcome; the entire Indiana student body was waiting to greet him at the railroad station.) In all four team sports, Indiana scheduled other normal schools and the freshman teams from Pitt, Penn State, Carnegie Tech, Syracuse, and West Virginia. Dividing time between halfback and quarterback, AJR was named by the Indiana yearbook as "the individual star" of a team that won state normal championships in 1919 and 1920.

In 1920 he was also — and this is hard to believe — the individual star of the Duquesne University team. Old newspaper files contain stories that recount AJR's exploits on behalf of both schools. If it occurred to the writers of these stories that there was anything unusual about this, they kept such reflections to themselves. Perhaps there was no eligibility issue, Rob Ruck and Maggie Patterson conjecture, because at Indiana AJR was a prep student. Moreover, "questions of eligibility were not frequently raised at the time." It was the age of the tramp athlete, that much is certain.

No football player made of flesh and blood, not even AJR, could have been in two places at once, but Duquesne and Indiana did not normally play their games on the same day of the week.

Once when both teams did play on the same date – October 23, 1920 – the starting times must have differed by several hours. In any case, Ruck and Patterson tell us, AJR played for Duquesne against St. Mary's of Emmitsburg, Maryland, and for Indiana against the Penn State freshmen. Exhausted, apparently, from his earlier efforts, he could not keep Indiana from losing to Penn State by the score of 54-0.

Just as he afterward said, AJR went from Indiana to Georgetown for baseball, but also to be the boxing instructor at Georgetown Prep, where lessons in the manly art were compulsory. Besides his work with the preps, he boxed for the university team and won medals. To his lasting disappointment, he played little baseball. The coach, a man named John O'Reilly, had a veteran team returning. His lineup was set before the season ever started, and AJR sat on the bench. It was his first and only experience with failure in baseball. He was a left-handed batting, right-handed throwing outfielder whose arm did not completely measure up but who covered a lot of ground, took extra bases and stole them almost at will, and could hit.

Whatever John O'Reilly may have thought, the Boston Red Sox considered him a major-league prospect. He signed a contract with the Red Sox calling for $250 a month and could have gone to their spring-training camp. In the end, he decided to stay at home. "Playing around here," he explained, "I could make two hundred and fifty dollars in a couple of weeks." By June he had dropped out of Georgetown and in the free and easy spirit of the times was playing left field for Duquesne University. Dan, his growing baby brother, caught and batted cleanup for Duquesne Prep. Both played that summer for a touring independent team called the Pittsburgh Collegians. In previous summers, AJR had played for as many as three and four independent teams at the same time.

He was back at Duquesne in the fall, a starting halfback on the football team. His brother Dan was the Dukes' quarterback. In their opening game, a 7-7 tie with Marietta, AJR injured his shoulder and was out for the season.

Enrolled in a pre-law course, he cut most of his classes. When he bothered to show up, he argued with the professor, who suggested that they meet in private.

"You're being disruptive," the pedagogue said when they got together. "You remind me of a gandy dancer," he added.

"What's a gandy dancer?" AJR asked.

"He's the boss of a crew that works on the railroad tracks with sledgehammers. When the gandy dancer yells 'Yup' the guys with the sledgehammers drive in the spikes that hold the rails in place."

The professor then asked if AJR was in college to improve his mind and acquire knowledge or to make himself more attractive to employers.

"Either way it's OK," the professor said, "but you don't need a college degree if the only reason you're here is to get ahead. You are loaded with leadership qualities. The only thing you must learn is how to use them."

AJR took the advice to heart. He left Duquesne soon afterwards without a degree. And, just as the professor foretold, he didn't need one to be a success.

'Nobody to Fool Around With'

Tradition required that the first son born to Dan and Margaret Rooney be named for the father's father and the second son for the father himself. It's either an Irish tradition or a Rooney tradition, I'm not sure which. In any case that is how AJR and the oldest of his five brothers got their names.

Something about Dan Junior – old Dan's second son – lifted him above even AJR. Seeing them together, I felt that AJR may have held Dan in awe. Why? Not for his enviable prowess as an athlete; not for his intellect, as smart as I knew Dan to be; not for his political astuteness – he had none. No, the reason, it seemed to me, was that Dan had put aside everything else in life for the Catholic Church, which greatly impressed AJR.

Thanks to their upbringing they were both deeply religious. It was what separated them from their friends and from Jim, Red, and Duke. Faith was a gift, AJR used to say, but I knew it was more than that. You could not have faith without wanting to, without working at it.

In the fall of 1998, when both were long gone, their sister Margaret spent some time as a patient in Allegheny General Hospital. One day her nephew, Jack McGinley, Jr., stopped by to say hello. They talked for a few minutes, sitting by the window in her room. Aunt Margaret glanced out at the cityscape below and said, "Jack, we're right above the street where my brother Dan was pinched."

Jack was stunned. "Your brother Dan? The priest? Arrested?"

"Well," said Aunt Margaret, "he hadn't been ordained yet. He was still in the seminary, or about to go into the seminary. He had a summer job driving a beer truck, but it was during Prohibition and beer wasn't legal."

Technically, the cop did not arrest Dan. He listened to whatever explanation Dan may have come up with and accepted it. Anywhere on the North Side, the name Rooney carried weight with the police.

For all his piety, Dan was a tough customer in his youth — very much similar to AJR. They had spent countless hours on the playground in The Ward, wearing out most of their friends. They could box and they could fight rough and tumble. Dan was the more serious of the two — "nobody to fool around with." He had a temper, which he tried to keep in check. Once on a Steeler road trip my roommate was Uncle Jim, who'd been drinking and acting up. The morning after, he was sleeping it off. Somebody sent for Dan — Father Silas, to use his Franciscan name — and we met by accident in the lobby of the hotel. "Take me to Jim's room," he said. I tried to think of an excuse. "Look," he went on, in his usual matter-of-fact tone, "I have to have you with me or there's no telling what I might do."

All of the stories about him, I realized at that moment, were true.

AJR used to say that Dan had more knockouts than Jack Dempsey. At least once he mixed pugilism with football. Dan played fullback at St. Bonaventure University, and on this particular Saturday a guard by the name of Dave Packard kept failing to block his man, who would tackle Dan for a loss. Dan ordered Packard to start doing his job, but the missed blocks continued. Finally Dan called out from the huddle; "Man injured!" The St. Bonaventure trainer ran onto the field just as Dan hit Packard on the chin. In his billfold for years afterward, Packard carried a newspaper clipping about the only player in the history of football ever to be knocked out in a huddle.

Art Rooney, Baseball
(Drawing by Kathy Rooney)

Another time, in Frostburg, Maryland, the Rooney brothers took on a baseball team, or as much of a team as they could get their hands on. Dan and AJR played for the Wheeling Stogies in the Mid-Atlantic League, and Frostburg's bench jockeys started taunting them with anti-Catholic jibes. Dan attacked them ferociously, with AJR pitching in. They broke up the game, but that was not the end of it. The same Frostburg players wandered into the restaurant where the Stogies were eating that night, and the Rooneys went after them again.

Frostburg's city council reacted swiftly, sending an ultimatum to the owners of the Wheeling team. The next time the Stogies played in Frostburg they were to leave their catcher, Dan Rooney, and their center fielder, Art Rooney, at home. By official decree, the Rooney brothers could never set foot in Frostburg again for as long as they lived.

During their one season with Wheeling, 1924, AJR led the Mid-Atlantic League in runs scored, hits, and stolen bases and was runnerup for the batting title with a .369 average. Dan hit .359. Both had dead arms or they might have ended up in the major leagues. AJR made a swing around the National League with the Chicago Cubs, but never got into a game. A team in the Southern League offered him a contract for a salary he considered inadequate. Turning it down, he said to the manager, "I can make more money at the race track." As young as he was at the time, there were few better handicappers than AJR.

Off and on, the brothers played sandlot baseball for the Pittsburgh Collegians and the North Side Board of Trade. AJR played for a team in Michigan, Dan for a team in Cumberland, Maryland.

Dan even played in Panama for a while. Pitching to him high and inside was not prudent. Once when Smoky Joe Williams of the Homestead Grays hit Dan on the head with a fastball, Dan chased him out of the ballpark.

Dan played football at Duquesne University as well as at St. Bonaventure, and by the time he got to Olean he had probably used up his eligibility. Moreover, he had played professional baseball. These facts may explain why he was Mike Rooney, not Dan Rooney, at St. Bonaventure. When the Bonnies took the field for a game with Cornell, one of Cornell's assistant coaches looked at Dan closely and said, "Hey — I played minor-league baseball with that guy five years ago!" Repeated to the officials, his words put an end to Dan's football career.

He continued to play pool, and he was good at it, good enough to recognize a hustle when he saw one. During his years at Duquesne, he had a partner, a Fast Eddie Felson called Scarface who could blow away everybody in The Ward. Dan was his backer, or manager. Dan put up the money, Scarface reeled in the suckers. Sometimes they went on the road together. Less often, it would be Scarface alone. He was in Canton, Youngstown, or maybe New Castle when a stranger came to Pittsburgh and took up where Scarface had left off. Nobody could beat him. To make matters worse, the guy was obnoxious. The situation cried out for Scarface, but not even Dan knew where to find him.

And then, by happenstance, everyone thought, Scarface called a friend of the Rooney brothers, Sam Leone, from Akron. Sam told him, "You're needed here," and spread the word through The Ward that Scarface was on his way. Dan, in the role of backer, set up a match between Scarface and the stranger at the fanciest pool palace on Federal Street. The betting was hot and heavy. Special stands were brought in for the crowd. All of The Ward's money was on Scarface.

Dan got there late, delayed by urgent, unfinished classwork at Duquesne. To his consternation, he learned that Scarface was off his game — missing easy shots, leaving the table open for the other guy. Sam Leone couldn't understand it. "We're going to lose all our dough," he said to Dan, who did understand — immediately.

"Time out!" he called. He quietly took Scarface aside. He said, "You leave on a trip. This guy shows up and busts everybody out. You finally call Sam. And now you're missing shots you should make with your eyes closed." They were standing next to a window. "If this bum beats you," Dan said, "right through the glass you go — head first."

Scarface never missed another shot. He ran the table three times and there were no bankruptcies that night in The Ward. But Dan would have nothing more to do with him.

Visiting old friends at St. Bonaventure in his mid-seventies, he stayed at the Marriott Hotel in Buffalo. Off the lobby, in the game room, was a regulation pool table. He picked up a stick, leaned over the rail, and hesitated. He was wearing thick glasses. After a moment he looked up, put the stick down, and said, "I can't see the balls."

He studied for the priesthood at Catholic University in Washington, D. C. On the campus, the seminarians wore cassocks, and once when Dan was in a group that approached some students hanging out at a recreation area, he heard somebody say, "Here come the girls." Dan went back to his dormitory, changed into street clothes, and returned to the recreation area. 'Now do I look like a girl?" he said, and proceeded to give two of the wise guys a thrashing.

He was devoted to the Lord but quick to use his fists — characteristics that may seem incompatible. It was not until I had known him for years that I came to appreciate how kind he could be and how concerned for the welfare of others.

Chapter 3

Jimmy Coyne

James Joseph Coyne was an immigrant from Galway. Immigrants from Galway customarily settled in Oakland, and those who did not become firemen or policemen went to work for the Pittsburgh Traction Company. On streetcars back then the motorman was at one end of the car and the conductor, wearing a change belt, took fares at the other end. Jimmy Coyne got a job as a motorman. "I'm on the wrong end," he complained to his friends.

There was room on the right end in politics. Coyne worked as a sandhog, a teamster, and a mill hand before catching on with a construction firm owned by William Flinn, the Republican Party's city and county chairman. Flinn promoted Coyne to superintendent, helped him buy a saloon on Bates Street in Oakland, and made him Republican chairman of the Fourth Ward.

Rob Ruck and Maggie Patterson describe Coyne as a hulking, florid-faced man with small gray eyes, a fondness for cigars, and considerable personal magnetism. In the 1920s, long after William Flinn's death, he aligned himself with the most powerful Republican in Western Pennsylvania, William Larimer Mellon. With Mellon behind him, he won election to the State Legislature and then the State Senate and became a mighty dispenser of patronage.

On the side, he made a fortune in real estate.

AJR was his North Side lieutenant. Coyne bought property all over town and constantly urged AJR to do likewise. "Buy land, Art," he would say. "They're not making any more of it." Uninterested, AJR dragged his feet. "What do I know about real estate?" he asked. All because of a gambling debt, he ended up with thirty acres anyway.

The man who owed him the money couldn't pay. "Forget it," said AJR.

"Forget it, nothing — I'm not a deadbeat," the man replied. Almost as a favor, AJR accepted the deed to an undeveloped plot in the North Hills.

Over three or four decades, the land increased in value, and he sold it for what he said was "a nice piece of change." Speculating in the commodities market, he lost every nickel of it.

Politically liberal, AJR was more like a Democrat than a Republican. He believed, and so did Coyne, in putting his supporters on the city or county payroll, but on the North Side the patronage king was a political foe, a Republican state senator named Eisenstadt. So popular was Eisenstadt in Germantown that the infamous "Suicide Bridge" over East Street had been given his name. Everybody, of course, kept calling it the Suicide Bridge, but no matter. Not even Jimmy Coyne was powerful enough to control him.

So Coyne and AJR got their heads together. They could make trouble for Eisenstadt in the primary election, they thought, by persuading the owner of a prosperous bakery to run. He had friends, money, and a good reputation, and though his chances of winning seemed remote, he turned out to be a vigorous campaigner. Voters who considered Eisenstadt arrogant, a sizable minority, were switching their allegiance to the baker.

Election day drew near. The baker appeared to be gaining ground. And then with no explanation he suddenly dropped out of the race. Eisenstadt, unopposed, won his easiest victory, thus assuring himself of another term. In general elections back then, Republicans always beat Democrats.

Meanwhile, people wondered why the baker had quit. To AJR it was incomprehensible. And then one evening as he strolled past the North Side Market House, a chauffeur-driven limousine pulled up beside him. The man being driven — Eisenstadt — asked AJR to get in. Making small talk, they slowly circled the block. They circled it again and again until Eisenstadt at last told the driver to stop. He had taken up enough of AJR's time. They said good night, and AJR, still in the dark as to what it all meant, opened the car door and stepped down onto the curb. "By the way," called out Eisenstadt, having waited until the very last minute. "The next time you and Jimmy Coyne try to teach me a lesson; don't ask a baker who sells his doughnuts to the Pennsylvania Railroad to do it."

With those words the pieces of the puzzle fell into place. Eisenstadt, AJR remembered, was on the Pennsylvania Railroad's Board of Trustees. AJR and his teacher, Jimmy Coyne, had met their match.

In the Republican pecking order, Coyne answered only to William Larimer Mellon, one of the Mellon banking and industrial overlords, and William Larimer Mellon answered only to his uncle, Andrew Mellon, secretary of the treasury under Presidents Harding, Coolidge, and Hoover (1921-1932). AJR liked to relate a story that illustrated graphically how the table of organization worked. In a small inner room adjacent to Coyne's main office, the senator was presiding in a high-handed way at a meeting of GOP ward bosses, as AJR described the incident, when a secretary interrupted to say that he had a telephone call.

He dismissed her with an impatient gesture. "Tell whoever it is to call me later."

In less than one minute, the secretary was back. "This call," she said, "is very important."

Coyne made no attempt to hide his annoyance. "Didn't you hear me? I'm busy. Tell whoever it is to call me later. I don't care if it's the Pope himself on the line."

The secretary hesitated. Then she said quietly, "It's Mister Andrew Mellon."

Coyne was a big lumbering fellow, but he bolted out of his chair like a sixteen-year-old, recalled AJR. The side pocket of his trousers caught on the arm of the chair and ripped loose, exposing his underwear. Without pausing, Coyne rushed to the door and headed straight for the telephone.

"Everybody, including Jimmy Coyne, has a higher-up to report to," AJR would pontificate.

Politician, real estate tycoon, and country squire, Coyne was a man of many facets. He owned a hardscrabble farm and a pickup truck. Aware of his status as a rich and influential Pennsylvania state senator, he made up his mind to buy a Cadillac. He drove the pickup truck to the agency and traded it in. He was now the possessor of wheels that reflected his material worth, and he prepared to drive the Cadillac home. At this point the salesman spoke up. In the back of the truck, which now belonged to the Cadillac people, was a calf.

"We'll have it delivered to your farm," the salesman said.

Not necessary, Coyne informed him. Taking purposeful strides, he went to the rear of the truck, lifted out the calf, carried it to his shiny new car, and plopped it down in the middle of the plush back seat.

"Pig-shit Irish," someone murmured. Someone usually did when Jimmy Coyne was being himself, but never in the presence of AJR, who loved and admired the old Hibernian.

Aviator

Everybody on the North Side called Sam Leone "Dago Sam." The ethnic slur did not seem to bother him — not if whoever used it was a friend. Sam was a small-time gambler, well-liked and a good story teller. He could get himself into jams, but his friends helped him out of them. He lived by his wits — God knows how.

Milton Jaffe, called "Big Nose," was Sam's opposite — a very shrewd gambler with wits as sharp as a razor. Milton had "offices" on lower Federal Street in The Ward. Before he knew AJR, he had heard "positive things" about him, mostly from Sam. So Milton told Sam he'd like to meet AJR, and Sam "brought him around." When AJR showed up wearing a letter sweater from Duquesne, or maybe Indiana Normal, Milton dismissed him as "just another jock," or whatever athletes were called in the early years of the twentieth century. In that, Milton admitted later, he was greatly mistaken.

As Milton and others came to realize, AJR could do almost anything. One of his early interests was aviation, this at a time that was not too far distant from the Wright brothers' flight at Kitty Hawk. A friend who had played for the Pittsburgh Pirates was into flying and prevailed on AJR to take lessons. Seeing that AJR had the instincts to be a good pilot, he urged him to study navigation and aeronautical engineering in a course he taught at Carnegie Tech.

AJR was dubious. "I couldn't pass that stuff," he said. The friend advised him to show up for all the classes, take notes, and keep quiet. AJR did as he was told. But he worried. He said the star of the class, a guy who answered all the questions, made him feel like a dolt. Relax, his friend told him. Though smart as a whip and not a bad kid, the guy had no judgment as a flyer, whereas AJR was a natural in the cockpit.

At final examination time, the smart kid passed with a high score. AJR's friend counseled him to sit through the test and hand in a blank sheet of paper with his name on it. Again AJR did as he was told, and the ex-Pirate — his name escapes me — gave him a passing grade.

Now came the hands-on flying. The student who had answered all the questions crash-landed and was lucky to walk away from the wreck of his plane. He did not get a license to fly; AJR did.

His career as a pilot had its spectacular moments. On a landing one time, he bounced off the runway and over some trees and onto the Oakmont golf course. Reputedly, he flew under every one of Pittsburgh's many bridges.

Marriage to Kathleen McNulty grounded him — permanently. Flying, said his bride, was too dangerous. As the head of a family — and since husband and wife were both Irish Catholic the family was bound to be a large one — he could take no more chances in the air.

Bridegroom

AJR was 29 and Kathleen McNulty 25 when they were married — the first time. "Kass," as AJR called his wife, used to say that she had a rival, namely Imogene Coca, the gifted comedienne who became a television star in the 1950s. In the late 1920s, in partnership with Milton Jaffe, AJR owned The Showboat, a floating casino on the Allegheny River, and Imogene Coca's act was part of the entertainment.

Pittsburgh during Prohibition was a wide-open town — a "paradise," in fact, for entrepreneurs like AJR and Milton Jaffe and for scufflers like George Quinlan, who ran a wildcat brewery in Millvale. "You had to pay the police, but not the Mafia," Quinlan explained. His point of view was the same as AJR's: drinking and gambling were "illegal but not illicit."

Getting back to Imogene Coca, she was crazy about poodles. Where Imogene went, her poodles went, and when Imogene played The Showboat it was AJR's job to exercise them. "Good thing you didn't marry that woman," the woman he did marry told him. "You'd have had poodles instead of children."

The way it turned out, AJR was married twice — both times to Kass. A civil ceremony in New York City preceded their marriage at St. Peter's Church. That is my understanding, at any rate; nobody ever talked about it except Kass's three sisters, Aunt Alice, Aunt Harriet, and Aunt Mary Miller, and their conversations on the subject were private. Although the rest of us sometimes eavesdropped, we did not ask questions.

Anyway, it seems that by 1930 AJR was something of a public figure — a shy public figure. Getting married would result in unwanted attention, and Kass's wishes apparently dovetailed with his. Conscientious Catholic that he was, he went to the pastor of St. Peter's, a Father O'Shay, and notified him of their plan to elope. Father O'Shay was not pleased, but AJR had made up his mind.

He chose as his best man George Engel, a fight manager. Engel had managed Frank Klaus and Harry Greb, middleweight champions from Pittsburgh, and had worked with Gene Tunney, the heavyweight champion who took the title from Jack Dempsey. During the honeymoon, Engel and the newlyweds stayed at the same hotel. AJR made his living in those days as a gambler, and, as gamblers will, he carried a lot of cash, thousands of dollars, which he deposited in a pillowcase upon going to bed. One morning as he and Kass were having breakfast with Engel in the hotel dining room he reached for his money to pay the check and became aware that it was still in the pillowcase. Honeymooners and best man jumped up from the table and hurried to the bridal suite. They were not in time. The bed had already been stripped. AJR said with a shrug, "Forget about it. I'll send for more cash. Either that or we'll just go home." At this point Engel took over.

Careful not to show undue concern, he went to the head housekeeper. An inexpensive "brooch" of considerable sentimental value — a gift from Mrs. Rooney's "Aunt Minnie" — had been lost, Engel lied. Could she give him the name of the maid who had cleaned the room? And where did the soiled linen go before it was sent to the laundry?

Engel, remember, was a fight manager, and it is second nature with fight managers to regard everybody as a thief. "If you let those people know you're looking for a bankroll," he cautioned AJR and Kass, "they'll be in competition with you. They'll find it before we do and keep it."

From the housekeeper Engel learned that the dirty sheets and pillowcases were dropped down a chute to the basement. If he hurried, she said, he could get there before the pillowcase with the "brooch" in it was gone. Engel hurried, and so did the newlyweds. Laundry workers directed them to the proper chute and after digging through piles of rumpled bedclothes they found the right pillowcase, its contents still undisturbed.

I have to admit that the first time I heard this story I was baffled. How could AJR have been so absent-minded? To leave all that money in a pillowcase in a hotel room wasn't like him. Not until much later did the realization come to me that he and Kass must have had a big night.

The honeymoon indeed was exciting, Kass acknowledged, and the excitement had begun with their arrival at the Pennsylvania Railroad Station. Waiting to pick them up, in a bullet-proof armored car belonging to Owney Madden, a big-time Irish mobster, was Madden's lieutenant, Bill Duffy. The car had embrasures in it, Kass noticed — gun embrasures. No doubt the couple spent time at the Cotton Club in Harlem, where Prohibition was just a rumor. Madden owned it.

Kass couldn't help but be impressed. Did she also wonder, "What am I getting myself into?"

Owney Madden, an Irishman born in England, committed his first murder at the age of 17 and had racked up several more by the time he was 23. Crime reporters called him "the little banty rooster from hell." For his fifth or sixth murder, the shooting of a gangland rival named Patsy Doyle, he served his first prison term, eight years in Sing Sing — where he met Bill Duffy.

The stretch in the slammer reformed Madden a little. Turned loose in 1923, he abruptly stopped killing people and took up the profession of rum-running. When Prohibition ended, in 1933, he was wealthy enough to retire. He spent his last thirty years in the Arkansas resort town of Hot Springs, married to the postmaster's daughter and living next door to the police chief. Notable for the easy-going ways of its law-enforcement officers, Hot Springs was a mecca for horseplayers (it had a race track), card players (there were half a dozen casinos), pool sharks, and criminals on the lam.

The connection between Owney Madden and AJR is unclear. AJR was a man who "knew" people. Someone's name might come up, and he would say, "Oh, I know that guy," which could mean that they were friends or could mean that they were nothing more than speaking acquaintances. How well he knew Madden, and what he thought of him, I have no idea. It wasn't something you asked about. Certainly he and Madden did not do business together. My guess would be that they met through Bill Duffy and that AJR knew Duffy because Duffy managed fighters.

One fighter Duffy managed, with Owney Madden a presence behind the scenes, was the awkward Italian giant Primo Carnera. By arranging a long series of tank jobs, Duffy and Madden steered their 6-foot-7, 270-pound man mountain to the heavyweight championship. Carnera held the title from June 1933 to June 1934, and during that time he boxed an exhibition match in the St. Peter's school yard to raise money for North Side families being squeezed by the Depression. Duffy brought him to Pittsburgh, against his will, as a favor to AJR. Carnera had balked when Duffy told him he'd be boxing in a school yard. He growled that he wouldn't do it, whereupon Duffy — or maybe Madden — slapped him across the face. Such was their power to exploit this hapless pituitary case, for alongside Carnera they were pygmies. Carnera did come to Pittsburgh and seems to have had a good time. Dago Sam Leone took charge of him after the exhibition bout, and they socialized the night away in various North Side Italian-American haunts, with Carnera the admired guest of honor.

Carnera wasn't much of a fighter. In what was probably his first honest fight, he lost the title to Max Baer, and in his next honest fight he took a merciless beating from Joe Louis. Duffy and Madden, having no further use for Carnera, went on their way, which in Duffy's case was downhill. He served time for tax evasion and ended up broke. Carnera was penniless, too, but later made some money as a wrestling attraction. He wrestled once in Pittsburgh and paid a visit to AJR at his office in the Fort Pitt Hotel, where they reminisced like old friends about the time Carnera boxed at St. Peter's School.

AJR's honeymoon lasted a whole year. Traveling by train, the carefree couple went from New York to Hot Springs — Owney Madden had not yet taken up residence there — and from Hot Springs to San Diego, accompanied by an entourage. AJR owned race horses by then, just a few, and hired a special freight car to transport them. There were men to run errands and men to provide security. When the honeymooners stopped to visit race tracks along the way, there were men to place bets and collect winnings. The men were young, tough, and athletic. And AJR was a good captain. His subordinates ate well and slept comfortably. Too comfortably at times. They were called on to attend early Mass — AJR continued to practice his religion — and to clock the horses in their morning workouts, and getting them out of bed was never easy.

San Diego in 1930 was a quiet seaport city and naval base. The Rooney contingent stayed at the El Cortez Hotel downtown. Just across the Mexican border in Tijuana was the Agua Caliente race track. Connected to San Diego by a highway called "The Road to Hell," Tijuana was known as "Sin City." It reminded AJR of the old Wild West, he always said. "Anything went." Kass said the same thing differently: "It was 'Out of my way or a leg off.'"

In "Seabiscuit," her best-selling book about a race horse, Laura Hillenbrand tells what the Tijuana of the 1920s and '30s was like. It offered "unlimited indulgence." It had the longest bar in the world, 241 feet, jammed from end to end by Americans sick and tired of the Eighteenth Amendment. Tijuana was wide open, "every hour, every day." There were quickie divorces and quickie marriages. "Single men were steered into one of the many brothels, a cottage industry in Tijuana."

But the town's greatest tourist attraction, Laura Hillenbrand writes, was its race track. California had outlawed betting on horses in 1916 after a series of scandals involving bookmakers. Tijuana promptly opened a track which at once became a haven for American racing stables and race fans. It didn't look like much — one jockey compared it to an outhouse — and yet it had the first movable starting gates and the first photo-finish camera. Hillenbrand: "The racing was lawless and wild and the Americans loved it." In 1929 a flood washed the track away, and a new three-million-dollar park — Agua Caliente — came into existence "just down the road."

AJR and his coterie made frequent visits to Agua Caliente. At times another pair of honeymooners, Pirate third baseman Pie Traynor and his bride Eve, joined the party. Once when Pie and Eve were with the group and they were late returning, the customs people informed them that the border was closed for the night. AJR told the others not to worry. He led the way down the fence to a dark, quiet spot where illegal immigrants crossed over. One by one they squeezed through an opening and eventually found a taxi that took them to San Diego.

On a trip into Mexico by touring car, AJR observed that one of his sidekicks, Harp Vaughan, was toting a shotgun.

"What's that for?" AJR demanded.

"To protect ourselves. We're carrying a lot of money," Harp said.

"Take that thing apart," ordered AJR.

Harp took the shotgun apart. There was never any doubt as to who was the boss.

"Now give me the pieces," said AJR.

And piece by piece as they motored along, he threw them out of the car.

He said, "Harp, if you have a gun, you'll use a gun. Use your brains or your fists instead. From now on, think ahead of the play." (This was Dad's way of telling someone, "Think before you act.")

Years went by. AJR owned a football team, the Pittsburgh Steelers. There was a game in San Diego between the Steelers and the Chargers, and, for old time's sake, Kass made the trip from Pittsburgh with her husband. They drove around the city, looking for familiar places. The old hotel was still standing, but so dilapidated that no NFL team would stay there. They revisited Agua Caliente, where somebody called out their names. Two ancient horse players, befriended in the old days by AJR, had spotted and instantly recognized them.

This was half a century after the honeymoon, which continued into 1931. When it was over, finally, and the lovebirds returned to Pittsburgh, tongues were still wagging. Everybody in St. Peter's parish knew they had "run away," knew they'd been married by a justice of the peace in New York. Father O'Shay, family legend has it, summoned them to the rectory for chastisement. They had given a bad example, and so on and so on. A second marriage, this one in the church, followed soon afterward. AJR got off with a light penance. Poor Kass did not fare so well. As her sisters told the story, she was forced to kneel in prayer at the altar rail all through Sunday Mass.

It's the woman who pays. But I know that if old Father O'Shay had lived his life twice, and had spent every minute in service to the Lord, he would still not have been as good and faithful a Catholic as my mother was.

Ship Ahoy

Back from the West Coast, AJR and Kass moved into an upstairs apartment on Western Avenue. They would never again leave the North Side. In the second year of their marriage, Daniel Milton Rooney was born.

"Milton" is not a typically Irish name. The new parents conferred it on the first of their five sons as a special mark of esteem for AJR's business partner, Milton Jaffe, who was Jewish.

Milton Jaffe had kept The Showboat afloat while AJR was on his honeymoon, and now the partnership was fully restored. Milton had know-how and pizzazz. AJR had know-how, pizzazz, and, most important of all, political connections. You could gamble and drink at The Showboat, and both forms of entertainment were illegal. It was therefore essential to be on good terms with the politicians and by extension the police.

The Showboat catered to a respectable clientele. The food was good and the gambling honest. Few men in Pittsburgh or anywhere else were more familiar with games of chance than Milton Jaffe, an expert card player and craps shooter. AJR once told me that even in his old age, when Milton was still in Las Vegas running the Stardust Casino, he could beat Jimmy the Greek at cards. But, then, Jimmy the Greek, added AJR, was more of a P.R. man than a gambler. Milton Jaffe believed in a fair shake for the customers, as did AJR. On the other hand, they were quick to spot professional cheaters and knew how to deal with them. The Showboat's stated policy — stated off the record, by AJR — was: "Treat everybody as you would like to be treated yourself, but never let kindness be mistaken for weakness."

It was Milton who booked the acts, the best obtainable. Decades after The Showboat's demise, AJR and some family members were dining at Moore's Restaurant in New York City. Seeing Groucho Marx just a table away, AJR was in doubt as to whether he should speak. Groucho had played The Showboat, but appeared not to recognize him. After two or three minutes, AJR broke the ice. "Do you remember Milton Jaffe, from Pittsburgh?" he asked. With a smile, Groucho answered, "Do you guys still have that riverboat?"

Allegheny County in the 1920s and '30s was not a Mafia stronghold. The nearest power base of the mob, a term under which AJR lumped racketeers in general, was New Kensington. Two brothers from New Kensington, goes a story that may or may not be fictitious, called on Milton Jaffe at The Showboat one day and introduced themselves as his new partners. Milton advised them to check that out with AJR, on the other side of the main deck, and his response when they did so was to throw them into the river.

A more credible story has AJR telling a couple of strong-arm guys who came on board packing heat that they'd be overmatched. "I've got three hundred guys of my own with guns — and badges and blue suits. The Pittsburgh Police Department," he said.

Dago Sam Leone had his own unique method of handling gunslingers. AJR was at a table with him once in a restaurant on the North Side when two men brandishing pistols burst through the door. "Sit still!" one of them shouted at AJR. "We're after Sam — not you." But Sam was too fast on the draw. Before they could fire a shot he started throwing things at them — salt and pepper shakers, a sugar bowl, cups and saucers, plates, water glasses, knives and forks. The gunmen when last seen were running down Federal Street, fast.

Like Inspector Renault, in "Casablanca," any Pittsburgh law-enforcement officer would have been SHOCKED to discover that gambling was allowed on The Showboat and SHOCKED at the news that there were other, less conspicuous gambling operations in town — false-front places, hidden away. Aunt Margaret Laughlin told of an evening when her brother "Arthur" — she never called him Art — took a carload of Rooneys to dinner. He parked near a building that to Margaret looked like a warehouse, and they followed him to the door. A peephole opened; somebody scrutinized them. The peephole closed and they went inside. At the top of some stairs, they passed through an area where card players, dice players, and roulette players were crowded around an assortment of tables. Beyond it was an elegant dining room. Efficient waiters served them an excellent meal. AJR paid the bill and they left, never to return or to speak of the occasion again. The most vivid impression Aunt Margaret retained was that "everybody there seemed to know Arthur."

No doorman stood guard at The Showboat. It was easy to find and easy to board. Access for those who arrived late at the wharf was by speedboat. There were two of them, both high-powered. One day John and Vince Rooney, in need of a little excitement, commandeered these fast, lively boats. They raced them down the river and flew right over a flood-control dam, still at full throttle. John and Vince, by some miracle, escaped serious injury. The speedboats were totally destroyed.

Flood-control dams in the 1930s did not prevent annual floods, and a big one, carrying heavy debris, left The Showboat damaged beyond repair. By mutual agreement, AJR and Milton ended their partnership, disappointing no one at police headquarters. Times were changing by then; sooner or later, The Showboat would have been drydocked. Instead, it remained half-sunken in the Allegheny River, a blight on the waterfront, for years.

Chapter 4

She Rattled and Rolled

North Side people were either Irish or German. The Germans, for the most part, worked in the trades. They considered themselves somehow more "substantial" than the Irish in The Ward. They drank a lot of beer but were not addicted to booze, the curse of the Irish. Instead of getting drunk, they'd get depressed and commit suicide. North Siders would say on a dark, gloomy day, "Hide all the clotheslines in Germantown." One German who hanged himself was a man we knew. "The Dutch Act," everyone called it.

According to my mother, intermarriage between the Germans and the Irish was all to the good. German genes gave the Irish stability; Irish genes gave the Germans light-heartedness. My mother believed that Germans were very law-abiding. The police, she pointed out, kept busier in The Ward than in Germantown. However, H.J. Heinz lived in Germantown, and a North Side fireman boasted that back around 1900 he made a citizen's arrest of the ketchup and pickle king for driving his horse and buggy at a reckless rate of speed.

Stella Guier drove horses and wagons recklessly and could even drive wagons that were powered by nothing but gravity. Stella Guier was a teamster in the days when women stayed at home, did the housework, and looked after their kids. AJR remembered her well. He said she looked like a man and dressed like a man. He said she could outwork, outdrink, outswear, and outfight any teamster in Pittsburgh.

Whooping it up with the boys one night, in a bar at the foot of Galveston Avenue and Reedsdale Street, Stella repeated a claim she had made before. She said that in a wagon with no horses hitched up to it she could drive all the way down Galveston Avenue and onto the Manchester Bridge, which crossed the Allegheny River between the North Side and the Point. And she could do it, she said, without ever using her brakes.

This time the boys offered to bet. They knew that what Stella proposed was insane. She would literally be taking her life in her hands.

Galveston Avenue cut through Monument Hill, the North Side's answer to Mount Washington. It was not as steep or as high as Mount Washington, but steep enough and high enough to make the trip down Galveston Avenue an adventure. Even as late as the 1940s and '50s, many automobiles with brakes that failed to hold would plow into parked cars at the curbside as drivers tried desperately to halt their descent.

AJR was a witness to Stella's ride. Hundreds of spectators were there — almost everybody in The Ward — and a big majority of them had not come to cheer Stella but to see her get killed. As AJR gently put it, Stella was not a woman with countless friends.

To provide traction for horses pulling heavy loads uphill, Galveston Avenue was paved with Belgian blocks — cobblestones brought to this country from Europe as ballast in the holds of ships. With Stella hanging onto the tiller, the long, heavy pole to which the horses would have been yoked, the wagon bumped and bounced on its descent. Its steel-rimmed wheels made a deafening racket and sparks flew up from the cobblestones as if all hell had erupted. Stella leaned forward in the driver's seat, wrestling with the tiller. She was steering her horseless wagon with her hands, a feat that looked next to impossible.

But Stella managed it. She rattled and rolled to the bottom of the hill, from where momentum took the wagon onto the bridge. That night in the saloon, collecting her bets, Stella remained in character.

"Any teamster worth his salt could have done it, but not you bastards," she crowed, "because you're all too yellow!"

The Irish

The North Side Irish seem to have been an unruly lot. On the other hand, they could also be generous and likable.

Pop and Maggie Rooney, as I have said, were glad to make room in their house for down-and-out relatives and friends. Some of these transients stayed for weeks or months, with never a complaint from their hosts.

The Irish faced problems matter-of-factly and with a dash of good humor. They were proud of their nationality and strong in their Catholic faith. True, they had weaknesses — in particular a fondness for drink.

It was inbred, I think, a habit they brought from the old country. On my first trip to Ireland I stayed at a hotel in Limerick. Everywhere in the lobby there were empty glasses and bottles.

Whether or not the cause is genetic, the Irish have difficulty with booze. Before his death at 87, AJR had not touched a drop in years. "There are three types of people who can't drink," he told his sons. "The Indians, the Irish, and everyone else."

AJR's father always had a bar, and AJR's business kept him around bars, but experience taught him that alcohol is an evil. Instead of succumbing to his environment, he put it to use.

Pop's saloon was a schoolroom for AJR. He learned about politics there. He learned about human nature. As a boy, he ran errands for the ward bosses. As a young man, he made himself useful to them by driving their constituents to churches, to wakes, and to funerals. He learned how to get things done and he learned how to make things happen.

In many ways he was puritanical; in other ways, liberal. There were God's rules and man's rules, and he knew which was which.

Unlike some of his brothers, he did not have trouble with booze. Unlike many of his friends, and in common with Dan, the brother who became a Franciscan missionary, he did not have trouble with sins of the flesh.

The Little Mayor

It would not be much of an exaggeration to say that everybody on the North Side had a nickname. There were nicknames that the cultural sensibilities of today would not abide — nicknames like Dago Sam and Nigger Smitty and Big Nose Milton. On the North Side of the 1920s an ethnic or racial slur was nothing to get excited about, and physical characteristics were fair game for ridicule. A nickname like Nigger Smitty would be unthinkable today — so toxic it could not be uttered by any decent person. In what was called "polite society" when AJR was growing up, blasphemy and obscenity were the forbidden areas of speech. Words having to do with race or ethnicity rolled off the tongue almost casually. What was shocking back then was the kind of language now heard in theaters and on the air, language routinely printed in books and magazines and sometimes even newspapers — four-letter Anglo Saxon words. The revolution in attitudes that began in the 1960s changed everything. Smitty, by the way, was not black. And his name wasn't Smith; it was Schultz, or something similar. He was a white man, said to be Jewish, who came to Pittsburgh from Cleveland. He was before my time, just a little, and I have never heard anyone describe his appearance.

Somehow, nicknames for the Irish — the Vaughan brothers answered to "Big Harp" and "Little Harp" — did not offend. Sticks and stones, the Irish figured. Better to be a harp or a mick than anything else.

There were nicknames based on personal idiosyncrasies. Game Boy, for instance. Was he game in the sense of being courageous and persistent or was he someone who liked to gamble, who liked the action? I never knew Game Boy. I did know St. Francis, an ex-pug. In the ring, he was Buck Crouse, and he fought the best middleweights of his day, including Harry Greb and George Chip, who were champions. Too many punches to the head scrambled his brain. After hanging up the gloves, he changed his identity. He stopped being Buck Crouse and was now, he explained, St. Francis of Assisi.

Unlike the original St. Francis, he continued to put a value on worldly goods. Once when AJR gave him a ten-dollar bill and told him to light candles at St. Peter's Church for a seriously ill mutual friend, St. Francis spent the money on himself. Instead of lighting candles he lit kerosene lamps, which he assured AJR would make a stronger impression on the Lord.

Growing up, I never heard AJR called by any name but Mister Rooney or Art. Later, in recognition of his title – president of the Steelers – his friends in the media nicknamed him "Prez." Later still, "Prez" gave way to "the Chief." It seems that my brothers John and Pat, the twins, detected a close similarity between AJR and a television character known as the Chief. The television Chief, a newspaper editor, was bossy and demanding but at the same time big-hearted. So John and Pat started calling their dad "the Chief," and soon the football players were doing it. Then the coaches, front-office people, newspapermen, and broadcasters got in on the act, and of course the football fans, too – at first just in Western Pennsylvania, but everywhere in the country when the Steelers were piling up Super Bowl victories.

Back in the 1920s and '30s, as the unelected, unofficial political boss of the North Side, AJR had a nickname less familiar to the general public – "The Little Mayor." He never acknowledged it, and he disavowed the label of "boss." "If I'm the boss," he would say, "the North Side is in trouble." Actually, not a week went by when North Side residents by the dozen were not in trouble, and most of them came for help to The Mayor. Some people asked for money. Others wanted jobs for their kids. Some had aged parents they were trying to place in a retirement home, or mentally ill relatives they were trying to place in a hospital. Others had relatives on trial for felonies, or relatives already in prison but coming up for parole. AJR was much in demand as a character witness.

Whatever the request, he did what he could, never more successfully than in the case of the grocer's son who fell for a floozie.

He was young, inexperienced, naive – and, on the evidence, not very smart. The girl thought his people were rich. Everyone knew her game except the kid, who was blinded by love. Either he failed to see, or preferred not to see, that as soon as she got her hands on his money she would dump him for somebody else. His successor, in fact, was waiting in the wings.

When at last he wised up, he went looking for the girl and her dude. He was Italian, the hot-blooded kind, and he had a gun. He found them in West Park, holding hands. In an uncontrollable jealous rage, oblivious to the fact that there were witnesses, he shot them dead.

The district attorney charged him with first degree murder. He went to jail, and his parents, who were anything but rich, spent all their money paying lawyers' bills. In desperation, they turned to AJR. The expense of a trial, they confided, would put them in hock; they expected to lose their store.

AJR gave the problem his full attention. He liked both parents; he liked the kid. So did Kass. The kid had delivered their groceries. Tell me everything you know about the shooting, AJR said to the parents.

It had happened the way the papers reported it, they answered. Their son had no alibi. On the advice of his lawyer, they added, he was going to plead guilty.

"No, he isn't," said AJR. "Never! Let me work on this."

Wasting no time, AJR talked to the judge. He talked to the parish priest. The parish priest talked to the judge. In the end, there was no plea of guilty. Like another North Sider in the same kind of fix – remember Harry K. Thaw? – the kid pleaded temporary insanity. Also like Thaw, he did not go to prison but was sent for a short time to a mental institution. The court then released him into AJR's custody.

Eventually the kid married. His wife was a nice Italian girl. They had children. The parents kept their grocery store and left it to the kid when they died. AJR and Kass continued to trade there, receiving good service, gratitude, and nothing else, which was exactly how they wanted it.

A former cellmate of the kid's, a convicted murderer who received a life sentence, brooded on the inequities of the criminal justice system. "I had the wrong lawyer," he complained. "I should have had Art Rooney. Here's a kid who shot down two people in front of witnesses, screaming, 'Take that – if I had more bullets I'd put them into you!' and he gets off with an insanity plea. Nobody saw me do anything – I was framed – and I'm in prison for life."

AJR, as everyone in the know understood, was not called The Little Mayor for nothing.

Curly

George Quinlan used to talk about Curly Lacock. He said that Curly Lacock weighed 300 pounds, that his mother was a prostitute, and that she gave birth to Curly in a whorehouse on Lacock Street and named him Edward Lacock.

By occupation, Curly was an ironworker. In spite of his great bulk, he could ride an iron beam into the sky. On the side, he ran a whorehouse, a wildcat brewery, and a bingo game.

The bingo game was in Millvale, in a big unused stable built for brewery horses. The Catholic church in Millvale also ran a bingo game. In those days — the 1920s — bingo operators gave baskets of food, rather than money, as prizes. If the church in Millvale gave a basket with one ham in it, Curly would give a basket with two hams. When Father McSwigan, the pastor, had had enough of this, he went to the police, who raided Curly's whorehouse, brewery, and bingo game and shut them all down.

Curly was distraught. Using Quinlan as an intermediary, he pleaded his case with AJR. He believed that AJR could prevail upon Father McSwigan to go back to the police and get the charges dropped. Curly said to Quinlan, "I don't care about the brewery and the bingo game, but please ask Art to save my whorehouse."

Quinlan liked Curly, so he delivered the message to AJR. The conversation that resulted was a short one. AJR heard Quinlan out and then he exploded.

"Are you crazy?" he said. "How can I ask a priest keep a whorehouse in business?"

A painter in Millvale, a friend of Curly's, dropped dead. Curly and Quinlan and AJR got three hundred dollars together and gave it to the widow for funeral expenses. A day or two later, Curly asked the woman where her husband was laid out.

"Nowhere," she said. "I sold the body to a clinic for fifty dollars."

Curly said, "Give me my money back."

As described by George Quinlan, he was one of the North side characters who made up the environment in which AJR and his brothers learned to cope with the world's vicissitudes.

The Legend

He was known simply as Pittsburgh Phil. A gambler and horse player whose name has entered legend, he flourished from the mid-1870s to about 1915. Pittsburgh Phil Smith came from the North Side but worked the race tracks and casinos in every part of the country. Although we never knew him, my brothers and I held him in awe. There were Rooney kin who knew Smith kin, and AJR was said to be the reincarnation of Pittsburgh Phil.

Both were special; what made them so was that both took up residence in the perilous world of big-time gambling and were not destroyed by it. Even in strongly Presbyterian turn-of-the-century Western Pennsylvania, Pittsburgh Phil was considered a man of consequence.

He is buried in one of those upscale cemeteries on Brighton Road, his marker a statue of himself. He is holding a newspaper — the Racing Form, Kass always said.

Uncle Jim used to claim that after a good day at the track he would take his marked Racing Form to Phil's grave and respectfully drop it off.

Chapter 5

With Arthur

Uncle Jim reminded me of Victor McLaglen, the actor who played the title role in John Ford's classic movie "The Informer" and won an Academy Award. Like McLaglen in so many of his screen appearances, Jim was a lovable, larger-than-life, drunken-Irishman character. With his sense of timing and his deep, resonant voice, he could have been an actor himself. He was tall — a little over six feet — and distinguished looking. Roy Blount, a *Sports Illustrated* writer who spent the 1973 football season with AJR's Steelers and recorded his impressions in a book called "About Three Bricks Shy of a Load," said of Uncle Jim that he talked in "a series of asides." He talked at such times in clearly audible stage whispers, from the corner of his mouth. There was no eye contact. You had the feeling that everything Jim said was "on the Q.T.," as he put it.

Jim fancied dark blue suits, the kind that bankers wore. One shoe was built up to compensate for a short leg, the result of a serious automobile accident. Still in his twenties, Jim was making trips to New York City to see a showgirl named Polly Lux. Now and then he traveled with friends, and there came a time when the friend at the wheel, driving in snow and ice, smashed up his car on a lonely mountain road in central Pennsylvania. Forever after, Jim walked with a limp.

Everybody liked Jim. Everybody liked him for his constant good humor and his gently sardonic wit. When people who assumed that he worked for a living, but saw no evidence of it, were rude enough to ask what he did, he would answer confidentially, "I'm with Arthur." Being "with Arthur" could mean almost anything. It could mean that he was Arthur's "main man" (without portfolio) — lobbying politicians, taking care of payoffs, "setting things up." Or it could mean that Arthur paid him a salary for doing nothing, which was closer to the truth. Either way, Jim was always around, saying little. He could be wise, flippant, caustic, kindly, street-smart, trusting — but never responsible. Or sober.

Instead of attending Duquesne Prep, as his older brothers had, Jim went to Allegheny High School. Duquesne Prep was for boys only. More than a few women have told me over the years that they were Jim's one and only at Allegheny High. I didn't doubt them. Marriage, however, was not in his plans. He preferred to live at home with Mom and Pop. Jim's younger sisters, Margaret and Marie, said their mom thought of Jim as her reason for staying alive. When he was drunk, she would say he was sick.

Jim could play football, and the legendary coach Jock Sutherland recruited him for Pitt. Sutherland made it a practice to stockpile excess talent at Bellefonte Academy, a sort of football finishing school in the middle of the state, and he sent Jim there for seasoning. When Jim entered Pitt, he would be bigger, stronger, older, and more mature.

There were rich men's sons at Bellefonte and there were immigrants' sons — the coal miners and steelworkers Sutherland was stashing away, raw material for future Pitt juggernauts. Meanwhile, they were making the Bellefonte Academy team a fearsome opponent for the college freshman teams on its schedule. Bellefonte beat one freshman team so badly, Jim said, that the president of the university — it may have been Cornell — told the headmaster of the prep school that never again would such a hardened bunch of mercenaries be allowed within sight of the campus. They were tough and unpolished, these young manual laborers reeled in by Sutherland from the mines and the mills, but higher education brought out their potential. In later years, if you went down the list, you'd find there were doctors, dentists, lawyers, and businessmen among them.

John Bain Sutherland was a big, rawboned immigrant Scot who came to this country at the age of 18 and worked at any job he could find. He was walking a police beat in Sewickley when a YMCA director advised him to go to college. Courses at Oberlin Academy, in Ohio, readied him for Pitt. At Pitt, Sutherland majored in dentistry and there he discovered football. Biographers always note that he played in the first game he ever saw. Pitt lost only once in Sutherland's first year and not at all in the next three. He was an All-American guard as a senior.

His coach was Pop Warner, who had coached Jim Thorpe at the Carlisle Indian School and was one of football's accredited masterminds. Pop Warner invented the single wing, a power-blood-and-guts formation that Sutherland made his trademark. He used it at Lafayette, in his first coaching job, and when Warner left Pitt for Stanford, and Sutherland succeeded him, the transition was seamless. Actually, Sutherland's single wing put even more stress on the power-blood-and guts aspect. If you bled, his players said, he would tell you to "get back out there" and bleed some more.

Sutherland's pre-season training camp near Windber in the Allegheny Mountains was cut off from civilization and fenced in by barbed wire. The team slept in Army tents on bags filled with straw. To keep everybody dehydrated during practice, Jock put oatmeal in the water bucket. Too much water, the coaches in those days believed, made a football player sluggish. Pitt's twice-a-day practice sessions — three hours in the morning and three in the afternoon — were brutal. In the rigid Sutherland system, everything had to be done in precisely the same way every time. Running backs always took exactly three steps, no more and no less, before cutting to the hole. From the never-ending repetitions Jock demanded, they wore out the turf, Jim said, tracing a deep rut.

In the single wing, the primary running back was the tailback — Jim's position. Jim was big and fast, and he made some long runs for the undefeated 1929 team. What he did best of all, though, was punt. Jim could kick a football tremendous distances. One of his punts in a game against Duke traveled seventy yards. Five times that day, he punted out of bounds inside the 12-yard line.

On the train trip to California for the Rose Bowl game in Pasadena with Southern California, Jim's luggage consisted of a shaving kit and a pocket full of twenty-dollar bills. There were stops along the way for publicity photos, and he would take the opportunity to buy shirts, ties, socks, and underwear at the nearest clothing store. That way, he could travel unencumbered and still have a daily change of haberdashery. To get rid of the things he'd been wearing, he would stuff them into a toilet for the porter to gather up. Forty-eight hours out of Pittsburgh, a teammate, Luby DiMeolo, noticed what Jim was doing. On the spot, he became a scavenger, retrieving Jim's good-as-new discards day after day and packing them into his luggage. When the train reached Los Angeles, Luby had to buy an extra bag.

Traveling with the team at Jock Sutherland's invitation was Yutzie Pasquarelli, proprietor of the newsstand at the corner of Forbes and Atwood in Oakland. A Pitt student himself in the 1920s, he had irritated his economics professor by falling asleep every morning in class.

"Mr. Pasquarelli," the instructor said to him one day, "why can't you keep your eyes open when I'm lecturing?"

Because he stayed up all night selling papers, Yutzie explained.

"How much do you make at that job?" the professor asked.

"Around a hundred and twenty-five dollars a week."

The professor thought about that for a minute and then finally said, "Do you know what my teaching job pays, Mr. Pasquarelli? *Thirty* dollars a week. My advice to you, sir, is: drop out of school and sell newspapers full-time."

So ended Yutzie's exposure to higher learning.

He had gone to Pitt initially in the hope of playing football. Three factors worked against this ambition: he was short, fat, and slow. Humanely, Jock Sutherland kept him out of scrimmages. Appearances to the contrary, Sutherland had a heart and a conscience. In his gruff way, he was fond of Yutzie, who solidified himself further with the coach by making interest-free loans to Pitt football players. Pitt football players were chronically hard-up (all except Jim), and Sutherland, to show his appreciation, reserved a place on the Pitt bench for Yutzie at home games and road games alike, including the one in Pasadena.

AJR now requested Yutzie's help on a matter concerning Jim. He had given Jim money for the train ride, but, knowing his spendthrift habits, had held back five hundred dollars. This was cash Jim would need for the team's five days at the game site. Notoriously, the other Pitt players would be dependent on Jim's largesse. Almost to a man, they were from families that lived hand-to-mouth. Entrusting the five hundred to Yutzie, AJR outlined an installment plan for passing it on to Jim. Yutzie was to let Jim have one hundred dollars a day, and no more than that. It was good thinking on AJR's part, and, up to a point, Jim went along with the system. He accepted his allowance for the first day and spent every cent of it. On the second day, feeling deprived of what was rightfully his, he demanded all the rest of the money.

For a minute or so, Yutzie stood firm. "Your brother said one hundred dollars a day."

Jim said, "Yutzie, if you don't give me the rest of that dough I'm going to have to slug you."

"And if I do give you the rest of it," pleaded Yutzie, "your brother will slug me."

Face to face with Jim and separated from AJR by four thousand miles, Yutzie did the sensible thing. He handed Jim four hundred dollars.

For the record, AJR refrained from slugging him. Also for the record, Jim was broke at the end of the second day.

The Pitt players elected their captain every fall at a pre-season meeting in the Pittsburgh Athletic Association. Only seniors could vote. In the 1920s, the Pittsburgh Athletic Association was a bastion of the city's WASP ruling class. Sutherland himself lived there, his home for twenty-five years a single room. He took a very keen interest in the voting for captain, never more so than in Jim's senior year. On the day of the election, Sutherland sent for Jim and asked him to "help make sure" that the players chose an Anglo-Saxon Protestant as their leader. It would be best for the team and best for the university, he said. Jim replied that he would do what he could, but reminded Sutherland that most of the players had Italian, Slavic, or Irish names and were Catholic. (Jim never failed to address Sutherland as "Doctor." Although he had not practiced dentistry since getting his D.D.S., Sutherland insisted upon the title. He was "Jock" to the sportswriters, but only in print. Face to face, they dutifully called him "Doctor.")

Regardless of any promises, Jim had no intention of complying with Sutherland's request. In balloting uninfluenced by Jim or anyone else, the man with the most votes was the very Italian, very Catholic Luby DiMeolo. To appreciate how much this meant is rather difficult now, but in Luby's day it was no small honor. Keep in mind that the city did not have a professional team and that, in any case, pro football was still just a fledgling sport. The only real football was college football, and though Carnegie Tech and Duquesne had their moments, the only college football team in Pittsburgh, the only one at least in the public perception, was Pitt. And when Pitt elected a captain — his identity always revealed at a banquet the same night — every football fan paid attention.

On this occasion, as on all such occasions, the banquet, of course, was at the PAA. Alumni and various bigwigs were present. The men wore tuxedoes, the women their finest evening gowns. Waiting for the team to appear, the band leader called for "Hail to Pitt," and the diners applauded in rhythm. Behind closed doors where the players were secluded, Luby DiMeolo climbed into a huge silver hollowed-out football. Somebody closed the lid, and designated bearers picked up the contraption, Luby now hidden from view. Ceremoniously, they carried it into the banquet hall.

"Then they opened the top," Jim said, "and there sat Luby, with his dark skin and curly hair ... like he just got off a banana boat."

It was a memory Jim cherished to the end of his days.

The Senator

Jock Sutherland asked Jim to help out at spring practice when Jim was a senior, his eligibility used up. Jim coached the punters. "Got a hundred dollars for it," he said, managing to convey, by his tone of voice, a mixture of disdain and amusement. The good Doctor's reputation was that of a tightwad. No doubt he paid his assistants the going rate, but to Jim a hundred dollars was chump change.

Jimmy Coyne now induced him to run for the State Legislature. There was no need to campaign; if you were Jimmy Coyne's man you couldn't lose, and Jim's friends barely waited for the votes to be counted before they started calling him "Senator." Misnomer though it was, the title suited him. He had the looks and deportment of a senator. The fact that he actually served in the House of Representatives seemed irrelevant.

Jim went to Harrisburg unversed in the ways of politicians. The first piece of advice he received was, "Make sure there's a transom over the door in your room at the hotel so they can throw in the money." Jim knew all the rascals and he knew the reformers and he got along best with the rascals.

According to George Quinlan, Jim made two speeches as a legislator. Commenting on Vice President Marshall's assertion that what America needed was a good five-cent cigar, Jim said, "My constituents don't care about nickel cigars. What they want is a good five-cent glass of beer."

"His other speech," Quinlan said, "was when a guy got up and started preaching about honesty in government. Jim got up and said, 'Honesty is the best policy after you get yours.'"

Jim probably did say that his constituents wanted a -five-cent glass of beer. The Volstead Act was still in effect and Jim was asking the legislature to petition the United States Congress for an amendment, an amendment that would legalize four percent beer. The rest of Quinlan's story may well be apocryphal. Jim was capable of having said that honesty is the best policy after you get yours, but on the floor of the General Assembly? I think that is doubtful.

Quinlan was Jim's closest confidant. "Any bill Coyne gave him," Quinlan said, "Jim would go up and present it. He wouldn't even read it. One time he presented a bill to put school boards back in politics. The next day he woke up, and about two hundred schoolteachers were marching around with signs that said, 'Down with Senator Rooney.'"

There is one obvious misstatement here. The signs could not have misidentified Jim. Schoolteachers are better informed than that. Really they are. For another thing, there is reason to believe that Jim was nowhere near Harrisburg on the morning of the demonstration. A colleague had warned him to get out of town, and the likelihood is that he was visiting Polly Lux in New York.

Jim's proposed legislation — to make school boards elective with a salary of five thousand dollars a year for each member — was roundly assailed by newspaper editorial writers as an attempt to increase the patronage power of local and state politicians. Abandoned by Coyne, who denied being the source of the idea, Jim stopped pushing for the bill, and it never became law. Nor did a bill he introduced calling for tax money to support parochial schools. AJR said that Jim made a speech predicting a march on the state capitol by thousands of Catholic schoolchildren, all waving American flags. Nothing of the kind ever happened, and financial help for parochial schools has continued to be a lost cause.

In calling for the repeal of the Pennsylvania Blue Laws, Jim was on safer ground. By 1933, Sunday football and Sunday baseball were no longer illegal. And Jim, swept out in a great tide of anti-Republican feeling, was no longer in politics.

Cracks in the Coyne machine began appearing in 1931, when the puppet he had installed as mayor of Pittsburgh, Charles Kline, was convicted of malfeasance in office. Given a six-month suspended sentence, Kline resigned in disgrace. Coyne himself ran for county commissioner and lost. In the same election, at Coyne's behest, Jim ran for City Council and lost. Coyne's motivation was simple: there were now more patronage jobs in the county and the city than in Harrisburg.

But the course of events was against him. The Great Depression had peaked, hitting Pittsburgh and the steel industry with devastating effect. Men without jobs sold apples on street corners. Soup kitchens fed the hungry. The homeless built Shantytowns and Hoovervilles. Father James Cox of St. Patrick's parish in the Strip District led a march of the unemployed on Washington, D. C.

In Allegheny County, as in most other parts of America, blame for the Depression had settled on the Republican Party. The few Democrats in the county were led by David L. Lawrence, who was not so much a rival of Coyne as his friend and collaborator. Coyne tossed him patronage jobs that might otherwise have gone to Republicans. But Lawrence could see what was coming: the Republicans were the party of the past, the Democrats the party of the future. He therefore dissolved his marriage of convenience with Coyne. In the 1932 presidential election, a Democratic landslide, Franklin D. Roosevelt carried Allegheny County by 37,000 votes, a substantial margin. And in the Seventh Legislative District, the Democrat running on FDR's coattails beat Jim, temporarily ending his political career. He was 27 years old.

In 1933, Dave Lawrence's candidate for mayor, William McNair, easily defeated the Republican hand-picked by Coyne. Three years later, Coyne lost his Senate seat, and he was finished. For the rest of the century, no Republican could be elected to any political office in Pittsburgh or to any important office in Allegheny County. Almost alone among Jimmy Coyne's followers, AJR remained steadfast. Davey Lawrence urged him to change parties, as countless others were doing, but though AJR had the highest regard for Lawrence, and though they often were seen together at prize fights, football games, and Kentucky Derbies, he was not a turncoat.

Nor was Jim, for whatever it may have been worth. He ran again for the legislature in 1934 and won, but retired at the end of his two-year term. Politics meant little to Jim. His priorities were booze and wild times.

Of Jim's many girlfriends, the most interesting was Polly Lux. They had known each other since she lived on the North Side, and there were those who believed that Jim had serious intentions.

"Polly Lux" was a stage name. For show-business purposes, her real name, Eastern European in origin, was apparently too ethnic. She was blond and she was beautiful and she made it all the way to the Ziegfeld Follies.

Jim spent weekends with Polly in New York from time to time. Like Imogene Coca, Polly owned a poodle. And Polly's poodle, like Imogene's, had to be taken for walks. This, of course, was where Jim came in. Hadn't AJR tended to Imogene Coca's little dog? Anyway, the story is that one day when Jim was in Polly's apartment she told him to walk the dog and went into another room. Jim — the story is — took the dog to a window and dropped it onto the sidewalk, eight floors below. Returning, Polly said, "Where's my dog?" And Jim said, "He went for a walk by himself."

That's a story I have heard about people other than Jim, a story I think may be closer to myth than to fact.

Jim was lucky to be alive after the automobile accident that crippled him on March 22, 1933. Driven by a man called Ticky Tock Toth, the car in which he was riding had skidded on the icy road and slammed into a brick wall. For days Jim remained in a coma. His skull was fractured. His chest was crushed. He had a dislocated hip and a broken knee. Another passenger, fight manager Al Kane, died of similar injuries. The driver, Ticky Tock, escaped with a brain concussion and "lacerations." While Jim was in the hospital, Polly Lux came from New York to see him. All he would say to her was that he wanted his Mom. Jim could never stand pain. Polly distanced herself from him after that. In the end, she married an exiled Polish baron and lived in Florida.

Jim was not exactly heartbroken. Once his romances were over, he never seemed to give them a thought. I remember mentioning to him the name of an old girlfriend whose sister I had met. "Ah, yes," Jim said in his W. C. Fieldsian manner. "A nice girl ... Killed by a truck, ya know."

That was that. Jim wasted no time on sentiment.

Plain Speaking

As one last favor to Jimmy Coyne, who still had control of a hamstrung Republican Party, AJR agreed to run for an Allegheny County row office — register of wills — in 1936.

So discredited were the Republicans that his chances of winning looked infinitesimal. They could not, however, be completely written off, and for the candidate who ended up with the job a nice little windfall seemed possible.

In those days the register of wills received a modest percentage of each estate that was processed. Ordinarily it amounted to very little, but in this particular election year the outlook was more promising. Andrew Mellon, the owner or part owner of a bank and trust company, an oil company, a gas and coke company, an aluminum company, and a coal company — the list may be incomplete — was extremely old and frail. If he went to his reward without dawdling, the register of wills could expect to cash in.

So, after his own fashion, AJR gave it a try.

"Oh, what a campaigner he was," said George Quinlan. "He never asked anybody to vote for him and he never asked anybody for a contribution."

According to Quinlan, this was how AJR ran:

"We'd get full of beer" — AJR had not yet sworn off — "and then we'd start out, four or five of us. One night we started in Wilkinsburg. There were twenty-five people at the meeting and twenty-four of them were anti-Irish, anti-Catholic little old ladies. Wilkinsburg was a strait-laced Protestant town with nineteen churches and no saloons. Rooney got up, and do you know what he talked about? The great ability and character of the people he met in horse racing. He didn't get too many votes from that crowd."

One afternoon the campaigners pulled up at a picnic grounds, unannounced. A polka band was playing; people were dancing. At a concession stand, AJR bought some beer and some food for the crowd. Then he and his friends joined the merrymaking. AJR, circulating among the bystanders, charmed one and all and let it be known that he was running for register of wills.

"In what county?" someone asked.

"Allegheny."

"Well, gee," the questioner said. "I'd like to vote for you, but I can't. None of us can."

"Why not?"

"All of us live here in Houston. And Houston is not in Allegheny County. It's in Washington County. Where you aren't on the ballot."

AJR lost the election, done in by a forthright campaign speech which the saloonkeeper Owney McManus, his campaign manager, had warned him not to make.. "I don't know what a register of wills is supposed to do," he told a large crowd at the Syria Mosque in Oakland, assembled to hear all the candidates deliver their last pitch for votes, "and I don't even know where the office is. But if you elect me, I promise to hire people who can run the place, the very best people I can find."

The speech was in some ways a success. Everybody in the audience, and everybody who read about it, laughed. The newspapers played the story big, praising AJR on the editorial page for his candor, and even Time magazine picked up on it. The election, however, went to his opponent. In politics, as Uncle Jim supposedly said, honesty isn't always the best policy.

It was AJR's last hurrah. He was never again a candidate for anything. In fact, when Tip O'Neill, the Massachusetts Democrat who was speaker of the House of Representatives at the time, asked if he would like to be ambassador to Ireland, AJR demurred. O'Neill offered to recommend him for the appointment. Jimmy Carter was president, and the Democrats were handing out plums.

But AJR wasn't interested. "I'm too old," he said. "And not rich enough. And besides," he added, remembering his ties to Jimmy Coyne, "I'm a Republican."

Sandlot Tycoon

When AJR was in his twenties he owned, coached, and sometimes played halfback for a semi-pro football team that underwent a series of name changes. In the beginning it was known as the Hope-Harveys. Hope, as AJR once explained, was the name of the firehouse in The Ward where the players put on their uniforms and showered, and Harvey was the name of the team's doctor. Later, acquiring a sponsor, the Hope-Harveys became the Majestic Radios. Later still, in 1930, when Uncle Jim ran (so to speak) for the State Legislature, AJR re-named them the J. P. Rooneys to publicize his brother's campaign, which consisted, as I have said, of waiting for the votes to be counted.

Uncle Jim had played for the Majestic Radios, using an assumed name to protect his eligibility at Pitt, and even during his term in the legislature he played for the J. P. Rooneys. He was a triple-threat halfback who could run, pass, and kick.

AJR's playing career had by this time come to an end. He seldom spoke of it except to recall that in a game with the Canton Bulldogs he was instrumental in the Hope-Harveys' defeat. He tried a field goal; somebody blocked it; Jim Thorpe, who was ten years past his prime, picked up the ball and ran for the winning touchdown.

With AJR and Dan in the backfield, the Hope-Harveys were usually the best sandlot team for miles around. In a 1926 article, the *Pittsburgh Post* referred to AJR as "the Red Grange of the independents." Dan was even "more dominant," a straight-ahead runner with breakaway speed and a kicker in the mold of Uncle Jim.

In AJR's opinion, the Hope-Harveys, the Majestics, and the J. P. Rooneys were on a par with the teams of the National Football League. The pay was about the same — very little. If there were fences and gates, the home team charged an admission price. Otherwise, management fell back on the time-honored expedient of passing the hat. The personnel was a mixture of players like Jim — former college stars — and ordinary neighborhood guys who worked all day at their jobs and practiced football in the evening.

Game day was Sunday. Under the Pennsylvania Blue Laws, organized sports and other occasions of sin were prohibited on Sunday, but friendly constables could be induced — nobody ever used the word "bribed" — to look the other way. So the games went on, sometimes doubly disrupting the peace of the Sabbath. Often if the home team was losing, its supporters would circle the field and wait for a provocation from anyone who looked unfamiliar. Then fists would start flying, the

Hope Harvey Player
(Drawing by Kathy Rooney)

players would join in, and the game would end in a riot, which canceled all bets. Without an official conclusion, the home team technically hadn't lost.

A game at Exposition Park between the Hope-Harveys and West View ended earlier than usual — in the first quarter. Hope-Harvey blocked a punt, and a fight broke out. "Pretty soon the crowd was all over the field," recalled AJR, "and the fight turned into a riot." Playing tackle for the Hope-Harveys that day, for a promised seventy-five dollars, was ex-Notre Damer Joe Bach, an assistant coach at Duquesne University. He saw that the game wasn't going to be finished and went home. "The next day," said AJR, "I sent a guy over to pay Joe his seventy-five dollars. He wouldn't take it. 'Go ahead,' the guy told him. 'The Hope-Harveys never finish any of their games.'"

Always in the crowd there were hoodlums and petty thieves. On train trips to road games — that was how everybody traveled back then — the hoods would be in one car, the team in another. The Majestics, or it may have been the J. P. Rooneys, went by train once to Johnstown for a game, and the mayor of the city came to watch. A man named Eddie McCloskey, he was famous at the time for having marched on Washington with Father Cox's Army. Father James R. Cox was the pastor of St. Patrick's Church in the Strip. In January of 1932, disillusioned with the Hoover administration's handling of the economic crisis, he led an army of the unemployed, three or four thousand to start with, many more as the march proceeded, from Pittsburgh to the national capitol. When they passed through Johnstown, McCloskey joined them. McCloskey and AJR were good friends. They met on the field after the football game and did not part company until the Majestics (or the Rooneys) entrained for Pittsburgh, together with their fans.

Returning home, McCloskey discovered that his wallet was missing. "My pocket has been picked," he said to his wife, "but don't worry. Art Rooney will take care of this for me."

He telephoned the station master at a stop between Johnstown and Pittsburgh. There the train was sidetracked while AJR called the mayor. At the end of their conversation, he knew what to do.

Back on the train, he conferred with a few of his henchmen. "This game in Johnstown," he reminded them, "is a real big payday for us. I'd hate to blow it. Not only that, but when somebody picks the mayor's pocket it makes us look bad. So find the guy who did this. He'll be in the club car, playing cards."

Faster than you can say Oliver Twist, the search party flushed out the thief. He was where AJR had said he would be — in the club car, playing cards. He gave up the wallet without an argument. Not a dollar was missing. He apologized for failing to realize that the mayor was AJR's friend. If he'd had any notion, it never would have happened, he said. He hoped that AJR understood.

All's well that ends well. AJR called the mayor from Pittsburgh that night. When the mayor hung up, he said to his wife, "I told you I'd get that wallet back. It couldn't have been safer in my pocket."

As a matter of fact, it hadn't been nearly as safe.

Enfranchised

Given advance information that the Blue Laws would be changed to allow professional athletic contests on Sunday, AJR paid $2,500 for a National Football League franchise in time to arrange a schedule of games for the 1933 season.

If $2,500 seems like a piddling sum, bear in mind that the economics of sports were far different back then. "The pro game," as AJR put it, reminiscing some forty years later, "wasn't even a hop, skip and jump from semi-pro ball, maybe just a hop. For a hundred dollars a game, you could hire a good player. You didn't make a lot of money, but you didn't lose a lot, either."

Originally — or unoriginally — he called his new team the Pirates. There was a baseball team in Pittsburgh called the Pirates, but nobody hollered "trademark infringement." Former Pitt, Duquesne, and Carnegie Tech players, including some who had worked in the coal mines and steel mills, packed the eighteen-man roster. The quarterback was Harp Vaughan, using Hope-Harvey and Majestic Radio plays. Harp took the field with a bandanna tied to his head; it rippled in the wind when he ran. Even for the NFL of the 1930s, that was sandlot stuff. Uncle Jim would have been in the backfield, too, if not for the automobile accident that left him a permanent cripple.

For the team's first coach, AJR wanted Earle "Greasy" Neale, from Parkersburg, West Virginia. Neale, who had played college football (at West Virginia Wesleyan), professional football (with the

Canton Bulldogs), and major-league baseball (for the Cincinnati Reds), was on the verge of signing a contract with the new Pittsburgh team when an Ivy League college offered him a job as an assistant. That this would be a better career move, fantastic as it may seem to us now, was obvious. The Ivy League had prestige; the NFL was still a shoestring operation. Willingly, AJR released him from their agreement.

Neale would have been an excellent choice for the Pirates. He did eventually coach in the NFL, winning a division championship and two league championships with the Philadelphia Eagles. Like AJR, he is now in the Hall of Fame. The coach AJR ended up with, Forrest "Jap" Douds, is not. Douds played tackle for the Pirates, as he had for some good Washington & Jefferson teams. If Uncle Jim's opinion carried any weight, that must have been the extent of his contribution. "Between you and me," Jim said in one of his confidential asides after the 1933 team had passed into history, "he was no coach."

Actually, the Pirates' record of three victories, six defeats and two ties in Douds' only season wasn't at all bad for an expansion team, but AJR, convinced as he was that the Hope-Harveys or Majestic Radios were the equal of most NFL teams, had higher expectations. It may be that he underestimated the difficulty. I don't think he was wrong in believing that Western Pennsylvania football players were as tough and tenacious as they come.

The first game the Pirates ever played was on a Wednesday night at Forbes Field. They lost to the New York Giants, 23-2, and AJR wrote in his diary, "Our fans" — the paid attendance was 13,483 — "didn't get their money's worth." Two days before the team's first scheduled home game on a Sunday; AJR received a telephone call from Mayor William McNair. "Some preacher," the mayor said, was constantly reminding him that Pittsburgh's City Council had not yet ratified the amendment to the Blue Laws. Legally, therefore, the game at Forbes Field between the Pirates and the Brooklyn Dodgers could not be played.

AJR was flabbergasted. "Mayor," he said, "I never heard of this thing, ratification."

Neither had McNair, it turned out. He advised AJR to see the public safety director, a man named Harmar Denny. Typically the politician, Denny washed his hands of the affair. "I'm going away this weekend," he decided on the spur of the moment.

AJR said, "Good. You go away." He then took his problem to the chief of police, Fran McQuade. McQuade heard him out and asked for two tickets to the game.

Over the next forty-eight hours, the preacher and his followers pressed on relentlessly in their efforts to keep holy the Sabbath day, but they were spinning their wheels. They could not find Denny, who was out of town. They could not find McQuade, who had gone into hiding. Sunday came, and right up to kickoff time they looked for him everywhere except in the one place he knew they would never think of looking — Forbes Field.

The Pirates played poorly, losing by a score of 32-0. AJR's reaction is not to be found in his diary.

'Arthur, What Can I Do for You?'

What everybody remembered about Mayor Charles Kline was not the forty-seven counts of malfeasance that ended his political career, but the fact that in the middle of the Depression he bought, with public funds, an outrageously expensive Oriental carpet for his office in City Hall. Any mention of Kline as the years went by reminded AJR of the carpet.

"And they're still using it," he would say.

AJR had no dealings with Kline but on one occasion went to see his executive assistant about Pittsburgh's interpretation of the Blue Laws. A tough, prudish, anti-Catholic Protestant, this untitled deputy mayor kept AJR waiting for an unreasonable length of time and then re-scheduled the interview.

Before their next appointment, AJR happened to be talking with the biggest numbers operator in Mount Oliver and asked him how things were going. "OK," was the answer, "but this guy down at City Hall is putting the squeeze on me."

And who would that be? inquired AJR.

None other, replied the numbers writer, than Mayor Charles Kline's executive assistant.

"He's a creep," the numbers guy continued. "A creep, a phony, and a hypocrite. He's a deacon in his church, and his hands are in every racket in town."

Not long afterward, AJR's meeting with the administrator in question took place.

Predictably, the man was cold and condescending. In ways that were subtle and not so subtle, he put down the Catholic Church. AJR did not respond, but merely stated his business and listened to what the executive assistant said. The executive assistant then dismissed him.

AJR got up and went to the door. He opened it a little before turning to say, "Oh, I knew there was something else. I saw your old friend [Joe Blow] from Mount Oliver. He told me to give you a big hello."

The executive assistant straightened up in his chair. "Arthur!" he said. There was warmth in his voice. Always before, it had been "Mister Rooney." "Wait just a minute. Come back and sit down. So we share a good common friend?"

It was certainly no secret to the executive assistant that AJR had remarkably close contacts among newspapermen. With a well-placed word, he could generate unpleasant headlines.

"Arthur, what can I do for you?" the executive assistant asked.

As a result of the conversation that followed, twenty-eight young men from the North Side, for the most part Irish Catholics, went to work in the Fire Department or the Police Department, and one of those twenty-eight eventually became the city's fire chief.

Chapter 6

Growing Pains I

In their first three seasons, AJR's Pirates had three different coaches. Jap Douds made way for Luby DiMeolo in 1934 and Luby DiMeolo made way for Joe Bach in 1935.

Douds, after stepping down as coach, continued to be a starting tackle for two more years. The other tackle, Ray Kemp, disappears from the roster after 1933. Ray Kemp was not the first black player in the NFL — several others preceded him — but after Kemp's one season a de facto color line existed in both the college and professional games for too many years.

AJR was familiar with Ray Kemp because Kemp had played for his semi-pro teams and also at Duquesne University. The discrimination blacks met with back then did not come exclusively from whites. Kemp told a story, perhaps with humorous intent, about making a good hit on a running back who happened to be a full-blooded Indian. Aware that in a white man's world, Indians, for the most part, were treated no better than blacks, Kemp reached out a brotherly hand to help him regain his feet. The Indian pushed it away.

"I don't want any help from a black bastard," he said.

In 1934 Kemp did not return, and there were no more black players in professional football until 1946. It was all such a waste of talent and so unfair to a lot of good people.

Luby DiMeolo asked his former Pitt teammate, Uncle Jim, to be the backfield coach of the Pirates. Still convalescing from the automobile accident that shortened one leg, Jim was of little assistance, and the Pirates had an unsuccessful season, winning only two games. Under Luby, the team lacked discipline. He was too much one of the boys.

One afternoon in the Pirate offices at the Fort Pitt Hotel, Luby fell to arguing with AJR about a hypothetical question: in a fight between a boxer and a football player, who would prevail?

"The boxer," said AJR.

"The football player," insisted Luby.

Boxer and football player, AJR could have taken either role. It appears in this instance that he thought of himself as a boxer. Luby had only played football. "There's a way we can settle this," said AJR, and he sent for a pair of boxing gloves. Luby, a tender-hearted fellow, began to dwell on the possibility of doing his opponent serious harm.

"I'm too big and strong for you," he protested.

"Maybe," said AJR. "I'll take my chances."

The gloves arrived. They pushed the office furniture up against the wall and squared off – and Luby's size and strength were mostly wasted. AJR, much the quicker of the two, and by far the more skillful, handled him easily.

After leaving the Pirates, Luby found his calling: he became a U. S. marshal. His friendship with the Rooney family continued for as long as he lived.

Joe Bach, Luby's successor, was one of Notre Dame's Seven Mules, the linemen who blocked for the celebrated Four Horsemen in the Notre Dame-Army game of 1924, but were not, unlike the Four Horsemen, outlined against the blue-gray October sky depicted by Grantland Rice in the *New York Herald-Tribune* and did not, unlike the Four Horsemen, derive their nickname from Rice. The Seven Mules nicknamed themselves. Center Adam Walsh, who played with a broken hand, was the only Mule visible to Rice. In his lyrical game story, he mentioned no others.

AJR had sized up Joe Bach as "a take-charge guy and a top organizer." Certainly Bach took charge of the Pirates. In his second season, 1936, they had the Eastern Division championship in their grasp, but then December came, bringing disaster. They lost their last two games, which were both on the road because AJR had rejiggered the schedule as a favor to another owner, sacrificing a home date..

Consequently, Joe Bach blamed him for the Pirates' sorry finish. AJR, for his part, believed the coaching was at fault. Sure, the Pirates had shown improvement. Their 6-6 record was a big step forward. Even so, it was galling to watch them fall apart. And though AJR acknowledged that Bach had done a better job than his predecessors, take-charge guys can be irritating at times. The trouble was that Bach took charge, or tried to take charge, in areas where AJR thought that he, as the employer, was in charge. Taking charge was second nature to Bach. "If you were playing cards," said AJR, "he'd grab the deck and deal."

Tensions between them came to the surface after a 13-3 defeat at the hands of George Preston Marshall's Boston Redskins, forerunners of the Washington Redskins, in the next-to-the-last game of the season. On the train ride home, Bach complained that AJR had scheduled too many exhibition games during the regular season. They argued; owner and coach came to blows. And they fought, witnesses said, from one end of Massachusetts to the other.

Luby DiMeolo had been no competition for AJR. Joe Bach was a handful. He was almost as big as Luby and just as strong, and apparently he knew how to fight. AJR held his own – perhaps he more than held his own – but there was no satisfaction in it for him.

He had duked it out, for different reasons, with two of his first three coaches. In The Ward, that was normal behavior; that was the way differences were resolved, by duking it out. And he was still only 35, still with rough edges, still in his physical prime and full of enormous energy.

AJR respected Joe Bach, but there was no way, he thought, that Bach could stay on as coach. So after a season-ending loss to the Giants in New York, AJR let him go – and quickly regretted it. "If I'd been a little more patient," he said, looking back, "we'd have had a winner for years and years. Joe took care of details, and not many pro coaches were doing that in the 1930s."

Let the record show that AJR made amends. When Father Silas was the athletic director at St. Bonaventure University and needed a coach, AJR suggested Bach, who got the job. And when, in 1952, St. Bonaventure dropped football, AJR rehired him to coach the team that was now called the Steelers.

Saratoga

It was not too surprising that AJR, growing up in The Ward, became a horse player. Horse parlors and bookie joints were easy to find in The Ward, and horse players congregated at Pop Rooney's saloon. Pop played the horses himself, at the track in Cleveland, where he and his friends had to go because racing in Pennsylvania was forbidden by law. AJR would be with them, enhancing his education.

The Ward was a raffish, sports-centered neighborhood. Exposition Park, where the baseball team called the Pirates played its home games for many years, was just across the street from Pop's bar. There were fight shows there, too, and carnivals and football games.

One of the characters in The Ward, a woman named Nettie Gordon, was said to preside over forty-one "sporting houses," as they were called. "Oh, she made a ton of money," said George Quinlan after Nettie's demise, "and the politicians got most of it."

Maggie — Grandma Rooney — knew nothing of Nettie Gordon except that her hats, elaborate feathered constructions, were "funny looking." "But she's a very nice lady," Maggie announced, evoking a burst of laughter from Uncle John. He said, "Mom! She's a madam! She runs sporting houses!"

AJR's sister, Margaret Laughlin, often repeated a story about Nettie. "I'll never forget the day after Pop's brother Myles was shot — I mean died," she would say. "He was laid out at the Perrysville Avenue house. There were so many well-wishers. But do you know what happened? Aunt Annie, Pop's sister, had five dollars taken from her purse. The last person there who could afford to lose money. Aunt Annie was as poor as a church mouse. It was some crowd of mourners. Little Tommy" — the youngest of AJR's brothers — "had some change in a milk bottle. Pennies and nickels. He was saving up to buy roller skates. And somebody stole the change out of that milk bottle.

"Anyway, this very big floral wreath is delivered to the house. On the ribbon, it's printed, 'For Myles ... with love ... from Nettie Gordon.'

"The notorious Nettie Gordon, some would have said. But Mom" — Maggie Rooney — "never hesitated. She put Nettie's wreath in front of the casket. A few minutes later, one of Pop's sisters, she was married to a man named Brooks, moved it behind the casket. Then somebody put it in front again. And then it went back behind the casket. Back and forth, back and forth. What was the right thing to do? Obviously, Myles and Nettie had been pretty good friends. But there were members of the family who didn't think it ought to be advertised."

AJR believed that the kind of recreational facilities Nettie ran served a worthwhile purpose. They were safety valves, he thought, protecting decent young women from the kind of sexual aggression which has come to be known as "date rape." This idea goes back to the Middle Ages, when the Roman Catholic Church endorsed it. Prostitution, in the view of the Church, was the lesser of two evils. Later the Church reversed itself. AJR, who would argue the point with Catholic priests, resisted their attempts to change his mind.

None of Pop Rooney's sons worked in the family saloon. All were athletes. All attended college. All went through life without ever punching a time clock. AJR was born to play the horses, and he quickly surpassed in expertise his teachers from The Ward, the touts and bookies and racing-form readers who recognized his precociousness and took him under their wing. Betting on horses paid for his piece of The Showboat and financed his marriage and honeymoon. Then in 1936, in two days at two tracks in New York, he made a killing that people talked about for years.

Talked about and wrote about. Joseph Madden, a New York saloonkeeper with literary aspirations, was the first to record the details. They appeared in his book of memoirs, "Set 'Em Up." Under the caption "Rooney's Ride," John Lardner re-told the story in his Newsweek column. Other accounts followed, all describing how AJR picked as many as eleven straight winners in that two-day spree and won an indeterminate amount of money which may have totaled upwards of $380,000. Roy Blount, in his book about the Steelers and the Rooneys, said it was "probably the greatest individual performance in the history of American horse-playing." Nobody since has disagreed.

Rooney's Ride to Riches began on a Saturday afternoon at the Empire City track in Yonkers, which forty years later, when AJR bought it, was a harness racing track. According to Joseph Madden, who had changed his name from Penzo for business reasons — his bar clientele was largely Irish — AJR came to Empire City with $300 in his kick and ran it up to $21,000. Buck Crouse, the punch-drunk ex-fighter, was with him. When the races were over, they adjourned to Madden's saloon and steak house and set out from there for Saratoga, upstate, with Madden at the wheel of his beat-up jalopy. En route, it had "four bad coughing spells," Lardner wrote. "Mr. Rooney and Mr. Crouse," he added, "got out and pushed."

There was no racing on Sunday at Saratoga, but on Monday AJR continued to pick the right horses and won an additional sum which can only be guessed at. On an 8-to-1 shot in the fifth or sixth race, he was able to get down just $10,000 of the $15,000 he wanted to bet. (In those days, bookmakers took your action; there were no parimutuel machines.) The race was a photo finish involving four horses. Madden, who said he had "bet a few clams" himself, "nearly died waiting for the picture." AJR, unconcerned, went off to the men's room. When Madden rushed in to tell him their horse had won, he was talking football with the attendant.

Madden and Lardner wrote that AJR cleared $256,000 at Saratoga that day. AJR told me it was more, but did not say precisely how much more. A friend of his, the director of racing at our Yonkers track, put the figure at $380,000. Other estimates are higher. Whatever he won, and the officials at Saratoga offered him a Brink's armored truck to carry the money back to New York City, he won it at a time when working men were supporting wives and children on as little as twenty dollars a week.

Those two memorable days in 1936 were the foundation of AJR's fortune. When he returned home, he said to either his brother Vince or to Kass — or maybe to both — "We'll never have to worry about money again."

The story is, and I'm sure it's true, that AJR gave $10,000 of his winnings to Father Silas, who needed a roof for the mission house in China, where the Franciscans had sent him to do missionary work. Another tale — that AJR paid for his NFL franchise out of the Empire City/Saratoga money — doesn't compute. The football team had been his for three years. However, his take from that weekend paid a lot of bills and helped keep the team afloat.

One mild summer evening before the start of the hot weather, AJR took me to a movie called "Saratoga Trunk" at the Kenyon Theater on Federal Street. Afterward, walking home, we passed the Planetarium and St. Peter's School. At East Ohio Street we waited for the light to change. (AJR preached constantly against jaywalking.) As we stood on the curb, he fell to reminiscing, stimulated perhaps by the movie. He talked about Saratoga, which had been a nineteenth-century spa. "Bluebloods" from New York City went there for the waters, he said. In that small country town, hotels, casinos, and a race track were built. Decades later, the casinos had gone out of business, the hotels, though still grand, were aging — in AJR's room a coil of rope on the floor was the fire escape — and the mineral springs had lost their attraction, but still the bluebloods came in the racing season, rubbing elbows now with the proletariat.

"In my day at Saratoga," said AJR, "horse racing was king." On the Saturday he picked all those long shots, a premonition came over him. "I just felt I was going to win," he said as we walked through West Park. It had happened before and would happen again, this feeling of invincibility, but never with such forcefulness. Maybe, after all, the Irish really do have visions. I thought of Gary Cooper in the movie at the Kenyon, merely acting out a part my father had lived.

When the parimutuel system replaced bookmakers, AJR cut back on the scale of his betting. If you placed a bet with a bookie at, say, 3-to-1 odds, those were the odds he paid off on. In parimutuel betting, the odds continually change on the basis of where the money is going. Also, the state and the track take their cuts. Parimutuels, it seemed to AJR, threw the percentages way out of whack. Winning $256,000 or $380,000 in a single day would no longer be possible.

So instead of just betting on horses he took to breeding them and racing them. He bought a stud farm in Maryland and named it Shamrock Farm, which later became Shamrock Farms.. It was there that I saw something unusual one day — AJR on horseback. As much as he knew about horses, I don't think he ever had ridden one. But on this particular day, he slowly climbed onto the saddle of an old lead pony the kids used to ride. He had a cigar in the corner of his mouth and was wearing a suit, a topcoat, and a hat. He looked very serious and uncomfortable. As you might expect, the ride didn't last long. I assumed at the time, and still do, that it was something he wanted to say he had done, and for no better reason, if there is a better reason, than his own satisfaction.

'Holy God, You're a Priest!'

Upon being ordained, Uncle Dan became Father Silas, O.F.M. The original Silas was an early Christian missionary who accompanied St. Paul on his travels.

Father Silas Rooney, wearing his Roman collar, attended a baseball game at Griffith Stadium, the home of the Washington Senators. The team's manager and shortstop, Joe Cronin, had played in the Middle Atlantic League for Johnstown when Dan played for Wheeling, and from his field-level box seat the new Franciscan missionary waved a greeting. Cronin tipped his cap. At the end of the inning, on his way to the dugout, he stopped and said:

"Father, I don't know you, but you put me in mind of a tough Irishman who played in the Middle Atlantic League. His name was Dan Rooney."

"I'm Dan Rooney," came the reply.

"Holy God!" Cronin exclaimed. "You're a priest!"

The Franciscans sent Dan — Father Silas from now on — to China. He spent the early-to-late 1930s in a small provincial town, propagating the faith and running an orphanage. In view of the Chinese attitude toward unwanted female children, the orphans were sometimes the lucky ones.

Crossing a foot bridge one day, Father Silas observed a man with a bag over his shoulder. The bag was moving. Father Silas flagged him down and discovered that inside the bag there were two baby girls — twins. The man intended to drop them into the river, which was how the Chinese disposed of excess baby girls. Father Silas paid him off — he demanded a small sum of money — and took the girls to the orphanage.

Years later, during the time when AJR's Steelers had their pre-season training camp at St. Bonaventure University and Father Silas was St. Bonaventure's athletic director, a newspaper photographer posed a young rookie quarterback with two Franciscan nuns for a publicity shot. The quarterback was Johnny Unitas, a detail worth mentioning for one reason: Unitas went on to a Hall-of-Fame career with the Baltimore Colts after Coach Walt Kiesling of the Steelers declared him expendable — "too dumb" to succeed in the National Football League. The nuns — theological students at St. Bonaventure — were the sisters Father Silas had saved from a watery grave.

He protected both the orphanage girls and the town girls from the predatory warlords who ruled China's countryside. Passing through, the warlords and their men would be looking for virgins to rape. So Father Silas dispatched the virgins and maybe some non-virgins as well — he didn't discriminate — to a hiding place in the hills.

Along with the warlords, the villagers had to deal with the Japanese, who overran parts of China starting in 1938. At one of our family reunions, my brother Dan's son Jim told me of meeting a very old Chinese woman in Colombia, where he was working as a volunteer with an organization similar to the Peace Corps. She had made it out of China during the Japanese occupation, she told him. Before her escape, she added, an American missionary priest had hidden her from Japanese soldiers with rape on their minds.

"My Uncle Dan was a priest in China when the Japanese came," said Jim.

"Oh?" the woman answered. "What did you say his name was?"

"Father Silas."

"That was him!" said the woman excitedly.

No surprise.

In all of those years there was famine in China. Father Silas made his rounds on a broken-down race horse, donated to the mission by some philanthropist, and it was fated to end up in a dozen or more cooking pots.

The horse was an old plug, barely able to move. But one day something startled it. Bolting, it galloped down the principal street of a village. Father Silas could do nothing. He pulled at the reins, but the nag kept going. And then in full stride it suddenly dropped dead.

A throng of peasants voracious as buzzards instantly descended on the corpse. All of them seemed to have butcher knives, and they were fighting one another to get at the choicest cuts. Father Silas jumped to his feet and called for order. The peasants backed off. Taking charge, he organized a lottery. Numbers were drawn, civility maintained, and everybody went home with fresh meat.

In addition to famine, there was plague. Father Silas stopped a man who was poised to jump into the river. "I have nothing to live for," he said. "The plague has killed all of my children, and the famine has destroyed all my crops. All I have left is my wife, and I've never liked her."

Father Silas took the man to the orphanage and gave him a job. In time, he was baptized a Catholic. When others in the town were joining the Communist Party, this man would have none of it. Father Silas had shown him what faith was, and how could the Communists offer more?

Eight years in China left their mark on Father Silas. He fell once, into the river — the river that took the lives of infant children and suicidal men — and a microbe got into his ear. From then on he was partially deaf. After the Japanese invasion, the Franciscans sent him home. He returned with what the medical men called malaria; I know it was amyotrophic lateral sclerosis — Lou Gehrig's Disease — and eventually it killed him.

In public Father Silas rarely talked about China. A story he told at a banquet in McKeesport was uncharacteristically humorous. It involved Jake Mintz, the Rooney-McGinley Boxing Club's matchmaker, and it may or may not have been apocryphal. You must understand to appreciate the punch line that Mintz had a bashed-in nose, the result of his own years in the ring. On this night in McKeesport, with Mintz among those at the speakers' table, Father Silas told of entering a Chinese village where no Occidental before him ever had ventured. Two men were staring at him. "My God, isn't he ugly?" one of them said. They spoke a dialect Father Silas understood, and he could not let it pass.

In their own language, he said to the men, "You should see Jake Mintz."

Chapter 7

Stand-Patter

AJR never left the North Side. He lived for the rest of his life in the first house he bought — an eleven-room, two-story red brick Victorian at 940 North Lincoln Avenue that cost him five thousand dollars.

The year was 1939. Kass always called their house the smallest on the street. Perhaps at one time it was. North Lincoln Avenue had been a Millionaire's Row when fortunes were being made in the steel industry, but then as smoke from the mills sent the people who lived there to such clean-air havens as Oakland, the East End, and Sewickley, a transformation occurred. Working-class Irish and Germans moved in; they partitioned the mansions, tore down the stables, and opened mom-and-pop stores and saloons. But neighborhoods age and deteriorate. In time, the Irish and the Germans departed, and North Lincoln Avenue became heavily black.

AJR refused to join the exodus. Black or white, rich or poor, the North Side was still the North Side, and good enough for him. He was scornful of people who "put on the dog." To "put on the dog" meant to show off your money. I asked him about it once — where did the expression come from? Well, he said, when you see a woman wearing expensive clothes and parading around with a fluffy French poodle on a leash, that's the stereotype. She's putting on the dog.

"Acting like Johnny O'Donnell" was something else the Chief could not abide. Johnny O'Donnell was a North Side bricklayer who got a job buying bricks for the construction of a sewer system. He was making good money, and it went to his head. He bought a new car, a big black Cadillac, and hired a chauffeur. Dressed in full uniform, the chauffeur would drive him to work every day, and then Johnny O'Donnell would step into his coveralls, step out of the Cadillac, and go down into the sewer to oversee the laying of the bricks. So anyone guilty of ostentation, which AJR had no use for, was "acting like Johnny O'Donnell" — which was pretty hard to distinguish from putting on the dog.

North Lincoln Avenue suited Kass. She was not one to put on the dog, or to act like Johnny O'Donnell. The size of the house, she thought, was just about right. There was room for her sister Alice and their niece Trish, but not for the vagabond relatives so common back then in large extended families. Times were hard and the government unresponsive; a house could become a hotel. Aunt Alice spent her life at 940 because AJR was absent so much at night and on weekends. It had bothered Kass, being left alone, when they lived in a rented apartment, and she said so. "Look," replied AJR, "you weren't a kid when you agreed to marry me. You knew how I made my living."

The solution to the problem was Alice. At first she would come for just a night or two when AJR was out of town, and then she was coming more often, and finally when Grandfather McNulty died — Alice had been his primary caretaker — it seemed logical for her to move in and stay.

This was a rather Irish thing to do, the unmarried aunt living in and helping out with the children. "Why didn't she marry, a pretty girl like Alice?" people would ask. Because, for one thing, a lot of Irish old maids are hard to please. They don't just say yes to the first proposal — or the second, sometimes, or the third. Then, too, there is always one daughter who stays at home with the parent left alone. In the McNulty family, it happened to be Alice.

So Alice moved in, and a routine developed. Alice would be up in the morning with the kids and make a good breakfast. Then she would fix lunch, leaving Kass plenty of time to prepare the big dinner, always with a homemade dessert.

The sisters were lively story-tellers, quick to express opinions about everything that happened, and they could swear like troopers when the occasion demanded it. Alice seemed always to be calling someone a "simple son of a bitch," giving scandal, it may be, to AJR, who never was known to use even the mildest of expletives, never so much as a "hell" or a "damn." What must have pleased him, on the other hand, was the sisters' daily habit of going to Mass. These were women who lived good religious lives and placed the welfare of the family above their own.

In the early, pre-Alice days, the household included a full-time maid. Not long before he died, AJR told a story about the maid. It was a story I never had heard, and if not for the fact that AJR was 86 years old, an age when inhibitions tend to fade, I don't think we'd have heard it at all, because sex was involved. When it came to sex, the Rooneys were puritanical, AJR very much so. One day, as he related it, he suddenly told Kass, "Get rid of that maid."

Kass was nonplussed. She said, "Of course I won't get rid of the maid. The girl's a hard worker and she's good with the kids."

"I said, 'Get rid of that maid,'" repeated AJR. "Just take my word for it."

Again Kass objected. Again AJR insisted that the maid had to go.

Days went by, and nothing happened, except that AJR lost his patience.

"Kass, I told you to get rid of that girl," he said, raising his voice. "Fire her! Do you need a ton of bricks to fall on you?"

Apparently Kass did. The message, for some reason, was not getting through.

"She wants to go to bed with me!" AJR shouted, putting it into words at last. As for himself, he added, so that nothing would remain in doubt, he desired to go to bed with no one but Kass.

When she emerged from beneath the ton of bricks, Kass fired the maid. And at 940 North Lincoln Avenue, there was no further cause for domestic unease.

New Year's with Owney

New Year's Eve was like any other night as far as AJR and Kass were concerned. Curiosity once prompted me to ask why they never went out. Because the last two times they did go out, replied Kass, it was with Owney McManus and his girlfriend.

Owney McManus had a restaurant and bar on Fourth Avenue, Downtown, where the sports crowd gathered. The security system was activated by voice. When a dubious character walked in, the bartender called out, "Paul Waner at bat." If Owney said, "Pitch to him," the customer got a drink. "Walk him" was the signal for an invitation to leave.

Owney McManus was a hotheaded little guy who had boxed professionally at 118 pounds. For Billy Conn's major fights in New York — the one with Melio Bettina for the light-heavyweight championship and the two with heavyweight champion Joe Louis — Owney would charter a private car or two on a train and sell tickets. "The Ham and Cabbage Special," everyone called it, which was just a name. No ham and cabbage or anything else edible was served.

After closing his bar at two in the morning, Owney would sit down with a few favored customers and give vent to his animosities, which were numerous. To Havey Boyle, sports editor of the *Post-Gazette*, this relaxation time was "the Hour of Hate." Owney despised Franklin D. Roosevelt and he was outspokenly anti-Semitic. "One night," said George Quinlan, "I'm sitting at a table with Owney and Havey Boyle, and Owney got started on the Hebes. I said, 'Here, I'm giving Havey a ten-dollar bill, and you put up a ten-dollar bill, and for every lousy Hebe you name, I'll name a lousier Irishman.' He started off with Jake Mintz. I said, 'Splash Gallagher.' He said, 'You win.' Then Owney named another Jew he didn't like, and I named an Irishman he hated. Same result — 'You win.' See, Owney had a million enemies out in the Strip, which was all Irish then, and I knew who they were. After the fifth name, he took a punch at me, and I punched back and hit the wall and broke my right hand."

In any situation involving Owney, as you can see, there was always the likelihood of trouble.

AJR must have known that, but on a New Year's Eve after Prohibition ended he and Kass double-dated with Owney and a girl named Marie. The death of Owney's wife had left him alone with their son, Owney Junior. They lived above the restaurant — not the best environment for a child. Owney Junior was a quiet, sensitive boy, the temperamental opposite of his father. He attended Catholic boarding schools, earned a law degree at Pitt (AJR hired him to represent the Steelers), and, like his mother, died young. Marie, Kass thought, resented Owney Junior — "wasn't nice to him," as she put it. This is why Kass didn't care for Marie, but AJR and Owney Senior were friends, and so the couples from time to time socialized.

Owney and Marie liked to drink. AJR, up to the age of about 45, drank moderately. Then he quit — cold turkey. The only time I ever saw him not completely sober was on a day he had lingered too long at the Ligonier Golf Club's nineteenth hole. Driving home, he went off the road. (I should say here that AJR was an excellent golfer. He took up the game to prove he could beat Milton Jaffe, who'd been playing for some time. Without a lesson or a practice swing, he did beat Milton Jaffe. He then made a bet that before the summer was over he could beat the club pro, and that happened too. AJR was good at any game he ever tried. But as though the time had come to get rid of another bad habit, he stopped playing golf as suddenly as he had given up alcohol.) Once he was on the wagon, he delivered stern temperance lectures to his sons. None of us ever dared to lift so much as a wine glass in his presence. If Kass took a drink he remained silent — one way of showing displeasure, perhaps.

The New Year's Eve parties with Owney and his girlfriend pre-dated all this. On the first one Kass told me about, the two couples met at the Wildwood Golf Club, where AJR was a member. Probably there were drinks before dinner. Most certainly there were drinks after dinner, coming slower now for AJR and Kass, but faster for Owney and Marie. The drinks of course loosened their tongues. Owney said something that Marie didn't like, or Marie said something that Owney didn't like, and it started a fight. Quickly they were shouting obscenities at each other. Except for the combatants, the room fell silent. The New Year's Eve hum came to a stop; laughter and conversation died away. All eyes were focused on Owney and Marie, shouting at each other, on Kass, who was red with embarrassment, and on AJR, poker-faced as always. Owney's Christmas present for Marie had been a "friendship ring," a half-hearted tender of devotion, and now he demanded it back.

"Like hell you'll get it back!" yelled Marie.

Owney made a lunge for her hand. Marie, too fast for him, ran to the ladies' room. Owney galloped after her, never pausing at the door. He rushed on through, and then there were screams, muffled noises from within, and women emerging in states of disarray. Behind them came Owney, clutching his friendship ring.

A reception committee awaited him — the husbands of the women who had exited in fright. They had a few choice words for Owney, none being "Happy New Year." When somebody gave him a shove, Owney started swinging. After that, said Kass, "it was real mayhem."

To AJR, she said, "Never again," a resolution he persuaded her not to keep.

On New Year's Eve of the following year, they were celebrating once more with Owney and Marie (the friendship ring back on her finger), but at the Highland Country Club, not Wildwood. This time the party included Havey Boyle and his wife. Nothing went amiss until Owney, smoking a cigarette, spilled the ashes on Mrs. Boyle's dress. The dress was chiffon. It caught fire. Women started screaming. Men jumped around, accomplishing nothing. At last to save Mrs. Boyle from incineration, her rescuers tore off her dress.

"And that," said Kass, "is why we never went out again on New Year's Eve."

An Army of Midgets

AJR was always driving to Miami, sometimes with Kass, sometimes with Kass and the kids, sometimes with race-track friends, and sometimes alone. The family would stay in a large rented house and the friends in a room above the garage.

Sometimes Uncle Jim would make the trip. Once when Kass was in the car with Uncle Jim and two of the kids, she remarked that she needed change for a fifty-dollar bill. They were passing a bar called Mother Kelly's, and Jim said, "Stop here." He took the fifty inside and was gone for what seemed to Kass like a very long time. Reappearing, he handed her twenty-five dollars. "Jim, where's the rest of the money?" she asked. In all innocence he answered, "I couldn't go in there without setting up the house, could I?"

That was Jim. He thought of fifty-dollar bills as tip money. At The Showboat one night, Jim said to George Quinlan, "Give me a couple hundred." Quinlan produced four fifties, and Jim gave one to the hat-check girl. "And he wasn't wearing a hat," Quinlan said. Puzzled, he asked Jim, "Why did you do that?"

"She looked like a nice kid," Jim explained.

If AJR had horses that were running at Hialeah, he would drive from Pittsburgh to Miami non-stop and go directly to the race track. On one such trip he had a passenger with him. They arrived at the track in time for the first race, and AJR plunged on the daily double. When the second race tapped him out, he said to the other guy, "Come on," and led the way to the parking lot. They got into the car, and he drove back to Pittsburgh — non-stop.

In a hurry or not, AJR drove at breakneck speed. On one of his solo trips to Miami, a Georgia state trooper chased him the length of the state, or close to it, over the two-lane highways of the 1930s. Unaware he was being followed, AJR steadily put distance between them. He crossed into Florida, where no Georgia law enforcement agency could touch him, and was drinking coffee at the counter of a roadside restaurant when the trooper walked in. "Who has the car with the Pennsylvania license?" he demanded. "I do," said AJR. The trooper sat down next to him and said, "I just wanted to meet the guy who outran me."

Within minutes, AJR had learned that the trooper was Irish and a Catholic, one of only three in the ranks of the Georgia state police, and from that moment on they were kindred spirits.

When the Hialeah season was over, AJR and his companions would rent a boat and a crew in the Keys and go deep-sea fishing. They went to a place one winter where the crew members were "Conchs" — pronounced "Conks" — the part-Indian, part-English, part-Spanish, part-Negro descendants of early settlers and pirates who intermarried or interbred with the natives. Uncle Jim said they married their cousins and didn't have any sense. As AJR described them, the ones who went out with the fishermen were short, black-haired guys with dark complexions. He would have occasion before the day was over to learn something else about Conchs: they were tough, vicious, unrelenting fighters.

Besides Uncle Jim, AJR's fellow anglers, all from Pittsburgh, included Billy Conn, a future light-heavyweight boxing champion; Milton Jaffe, Conn's business manager; Walt Kiesling, the coach of the Steelers; Ed Karpowich, one of Kiesling's players; and the North Side character called Nigger Smitty. Kiesling, Karpowich, and Uncle Jim were men of imposing size. Billy Conn and AJR had the unmistakable self-confident look that accompanies success in the ring. And Smitty, you somehow sensed, was a guy who could hold his own in a free-for-all. None of which meant a thing to the Conchs.

The day began peacefully enough. All morning long the fish were biting. Afternoon came, and the boat headed back to port with a sizable catch. One of the Conchs cut up a piece of the bait and threw it overboard to the seagulls. Fighting for the scraps, the birds went wild. They would snatch them out of the air with their beaks or their claws. AJR and his friends were so impressed and entertained that they cut up the fish they had caught and tossed every piece to the gulls. They got a kick out of seeing them work for this unexpected meal. The Conchs, meanwhile, were seething with anger.

By the terms of an unwritten contract, all the fish that were caught belonged to the crew. No one, unfortunately, had explained this to AJR or Milton. When the boat reached the dock, the Conchs began calling to other Conchs at work around the waterfront. AJR and Milton, still not foreseeing any trouble, paid for the cruise and threw in a generous tip, but the Conchs became increasingly hostile, increasingly belligerent. They jabbered at the fishermen in pidgin English. No! They didn't want their tip. "Never let anyone confuse kindness with weakness," AJR used to say, and the Conchs were confusing kindness with weakness.

Exactly what they did want was not at all clear, but Karpowich, the burly football player, thought it might be a fight. Probably just to see what would happen, he picked up the nearest Conch and pitched him into the water.

Instantly, a hey rube broke out. Smitty, I like to think, may have actually shouted, "Hey rube!" — the battle cry of carnival workers when they went into combat with local yokels, as in the old days they frequently did. Smitty had been a "carnie" himself, and his experience served him well against the Conchs. He rabbit-punched, he used his knees, and he gouged a few eyes — techniques that had been effective in previous hey rubes. Above all else, he protected his back.

Karpowich, alas, did not protect his back. A Conch sneaked up behind him with a grappling hook and brought it down on his head. Karp from then on was out of commission, a serious loss to the Pittsburgh forces. He'd been flinging the Conchs around and pitching them off the dock as if they were babies.

Next, Uncle Jim went down. The Conchs were armed with fish knives, and Jim took a thrust between the ribs. That left AJR, Kiesling, and Smitty to hold off the enemy on their own. Billy Conn was with them, yes, and Conn was a great Marquis of Queensberry fighter, but hey rubes were bare-knuckle affairs. Conn was "terrified," Uncle Jim recalled, of hurting his hands, a boxer's most indispensable asset. All through the battle, he held them under his armpits. "Billy showed excellent footwork," said AJR later, striving to give Conn his due. In every other respect, Billy's usefulness to the Pittsburgh cause was limited. Milton Jaffe, a lifelong pacifist, was of no use at all. He did a marvelous job, noted AJR, of keeping space between himself and the action.

One-sided already, the odds became prohibitive when Conch reinforcements from the fishing village joined the melee. "We were up against an army of midgets," said AJR afterward. "They wouldn't stop coming and there were lots of them. Everywhere you looked, you saw blood. There were guys in the water and guys sprawled out on the ground."

In the nick of time, the sheriff and his deputies arrived. They got the outnumbered Pittsburghers safely into their cars. "Now, take off," the sheriff advised them. "These Conchs have killed people. You're lucky to be alive."

Uncle Jim and Karp recovered from their wounds in a hospital. Jim had somehow lost a jacket during the fight, and AJR resolved to go back and retrieve it, this time with an army of his own – Pittsburgh friends eager to take revenge for Jim and Karp on "those nasty little wharf rats."

But first the sheriff found out. He spoke to AJR on the telephone. "You have a jacket you'd like to pick up? That's a bad idea," he said. "I have it here in my office, and I'll drive up to Miami with it myself. Stay away from this part of the Keys. Don't come back down here – EVER."

AJR thought it over, and decided to let bygones be bygones.

Penn-Mint

K ass always said that AJR made a ton of money during the Great Depression. Not all of it came from the killing at Saratoga, which put him on Easy Street in 1936. Nor did the football team become profitable until television so greatly enhanced the NFL's sources of revenue. "Maybe you made five thousand dollars a season or maybe you lost a few thousand," AJR reminisced when Myron Cope interviewed him in 1970 for a book called "The Game That Was."

AJR did well at the race track and not all that badly in the slot-machine business. On a train trip from Pittsburgh to Chicago, Kass said, he met a man named Dan Odom, who had worked for a carnival or a circus but now was a broker of slot machines. Odom knew AJR by reputation and offered to supply him with as many slot machines as he could place.

"If you can set things up politically," Odom said, "I can guarantee you a million dollars a year."

In venues open to the public, slot machines were illegal, but the authorities allowed them, or were willing at any rate to tolerate them, in social clubs like the Elks, the Moose, or the American Legion, and in the private clubs exempt from the Pennsylvania Blue Laws. AJR had all the right political connections, and Kass always said that he did make a million dollars a year. Maybe so, but Kass was something of a romanticist, and in her marvelous stories about the old days it is not inconceivable that she indulged in poetic license now and again. Whatever AJR's take actually was, he believed that when times were tough people would find money to gamble, "looking for a way to improve their luck."

Under pressure from the reformers and the newspapers, the state passed a law requiring slot machines to pay off in candy – rolls of mints – rather than coins. There was a way, of course, to get around that. The mints could be used like chips in a poker game. If you won, you turned them in for cash.

AJR named his slot machine company Penn-Mint and put Uncle Jim in charge, which was not a judicious move. When Jim had money at his disposal, he would either give it away or drink it away. One of Jim's duties as company president was to deliver the machines to the clubs. At first he transported them in a hearse, which AJR thought was unwise. Jim then obtained a big black truck and was driving it around with no identification on the panels until AJR happened to notice.

"Jim," he shouted, "get a sign on that truck! I don't care if it reads 'Merry Christmas' or 'Happy New Year,' but get a sign on that truck."

Jim got a sign on the truck: "Penn-Mint."

In his various enterprises, AJR avoided any connection with the mob, as he called the Mafia. There were certain kinds of favors you could prudently do for a mob guy, he used to say. And then he would add, "But never, never let a mob guy do a favor for you." In any event, he did not long remain in the slot-machine business. A conversation with Mayor Dave Lawrence hastened his early departure.

"Do you think this business of yours is legal?" asked the mayor.

"Of course it is not," replied AJR.

"Then you'd better do something about it," said Lawrence.

Nothing more had to be explained.

AJR left an estate valued at two hundred million dollars. He was at one time the head of ten corporations that owned or controlled the Steelers, Yonkers Raceway, the William Penn Racing Association at Liberty Bell, Green Mountain Race Track in Vermont, and the Palm Beach Kennel Club, a dog-racing track in Florida. He owned the Shamrock Farms and bred race horses there. During the 1920s and '30s he invested heavily in the stock market, but came out a loser. He was leery of putting his cash into real estate. "I don't know about anything, only horses," he told Roy Blount. "And football. Sports. I didn't know you could go to the bank and borrow money. I thought you had to have it in your pocket."

He lived just as simply as he ran his various enterprises. His suits — he always wore one — were not expensive. The only car he ever drove was a Buick. Cadillacs and Lincolns were for showoffs. When his sons moved away from the North Side and bought houses in ritzier neighborhoods they were "putting on the dog." He permitted himself one extravagance: he smoked good cigars, constantly. Toward the end of his life he merely chewed them. A friend with the mind of an accountant once estimated that AJR had spent more money on cigars than on the college educations of his sons.

I could give you examples by the dozen of AJR's generosity. Uncle Jim practiced philanthropy on a first-come, first-served basis, shoveling out money — as long as he had money — to bartenders, hat-check girls, elevator operators, doormen, and anybody else who happened to be within reach. AJR was more discriminating, and he continued to give beyond the grave.

A provision in his will earmarked one million dollars for charitable contributions to be made by each of his five sons. Broken down, that was two hundred thousand apiece. From my share, on the last day of 1996, I sent a check for fifteen thousand dollars with my son Art III to the Little Sisters of the Poor, and the head nun told him a story. At regular intervals, she said, AJR would come into the convent and empty his pockets. Large wads of cash would fall out. The nuns of course surmised that he had had a good day at the race track.

"So we prayed that his luck would continue," Sister Madeline went on. "We felt that some of it, anyway, was coming from a source up above."

Chapter 8

Local Talent

During the 1930s AJR's team in the National Football League had a Western Pennsylvania component. Besides Harp Vaughan, there was Ray Kemp, who played at Duquesne University. There was Armand Niccolai, who also played at Duquesne. There was John (Bull) Karcis, who played at Carnegie Tech. There was Mose Kelsch, who went directly from the Pittsburgh sandlots to the NFL. There was Ed Karpowich, who played at Catholic University.

Ray Kemp, as I have said, was one of the pioneer black players in the NFL. Explaining to me once why his first season with the Pirates, 1933, turned out to be his last, he said that AJR was color blind but went along with the wishes of the other owners, who were not. In the spirit of the times, they wanted an all-white NFL, and from 1934 until 1946 that is exactly what they had. Pigmentation-wise, the contrast between then and now is enormous and speaks for itself.

I don't know how well Kemp could play. What I do know is that he *looked* like someone who could play: he had the physique. Tackles in the present era weigh 300 pounds and up. Kemp wasn't nearly that big — in the 1930s, nobody was. He was big, though, for his day, and big enough to have played in any decade before weight training, steroids, nutritional advances, and evolution changed the standards by which football coaches measure size.

Bull Karcis was the fullback on the Carnegie Tech team that won from Notre Dame in 1928. According to the *Pittsburgh Post-Gazette*, he was "as unstoppable [that day] as Niagara Falls." Although somewhat less unstoppable in the NFL, he prolonged his career until 1943, logging four years with the Brooklyn Dodgers, three with the Pirates (1936-38), and three with the New York Giants. After World War II, he coached and taught mathematics at North Catholic High School. In Bull's final season, my brother Dan played quarterback on the varsity, and I played tackle on the freshman team. Karcis was not the freshman team's coach, but both teams used his playbook. Whether he thought that North Side kids were dumb or that any play is a good one if you execute it properly, his offense was as simple as two plus two.

At the start of each season, Karcis would remind his players at a squad meeting that they represented a Catholic institution and should watch their language. Karcis was not a Catholic himself but decided to take instruction in the faith. Not long afterward, the Brothers of Mary fired him. What effect this had on his conversion to Rome I never learned.

Karcis was built like a barrel. His wife had a set of mammary glands that won her the nickname of "Iron Tits." (Kids can be cruel.) Delivering a package to the coach's door one day, a North Catholic player glanced through the window and saw the two of them — Bull and his wife — fencing. They had the face masks on and the protective clothes and were going at it with foils. For the rest of the football season their friendly little duel was the talk of the dressing room.

Mose Kelsch was a tough old semi-pro who did not wear a helmet (the rules were different then) or need one. He had a big, bald head that attracted more attention than Harp Vaughan's bandanna. Mose Kelsch and Harp Vaughan were backfield teammates in 1933, Mose's only year with the team.

Mose lived on the North Side and was said to have played football at Christian College. There's a Christian Brothers College in Tennessee. Christian College, my researchers tell me, is as mythical a place as Brigadoon. But here's a fact that may add to the confusion: Mose's first, or Christian, name was Christian.

In the 1930s AJR was the same age as some of his players, and he made it a practice to socialize with them. There were card games, there were trips to the race track. Two of his best friends on the team, Ed Karpowich and Armand Niccolai, were both from the Mon Valley. When they played for the Pirates they rented rooms or an apartment in an old brick mansion on Ridge Avenue, not far from North Lincoln, a remnant of the days when the North Side was teeming with the rich and the powerful. They called the house they lived in El Rancho Grande.

Karp and Nick were good guys. Because they spent a lot of time at our house, I knew them when I was a kid. Karp was a two-way end, Niccolai a tackle. Nick played for AJR from 1934 to 1942 and later coached football at Monessen High School, where his wife just happened to be the principal. The Niccolais often sat with the Rooneys in the owner's box at Three Rivers Stadium, and, looking back, I see that I missed an opportunity. Instead of pumping Nick for stories about the old days, I was satisfied with conventional small talk.

I recall that he volunteered a story about a game the Pirates moved from Pittsburgh to New Orleans when they were having attendance problems one year. Nick was the team captain, and for some reason he missed the train. Mortified, he at once headed South in his car. It was late November or early December; there was snow and ice on the roads, which were nothing like modern freeways; twice he was pulled out of ditches. Driving night and day, he got there in time for the kickoff —and played what was probably his worst game of the season, he said.

Vagabond Halfback

On a fall afternoon in 1933, John Victor McNally, who played football under the name of Johnny Blood for the Green Bay Packers, came to practice drunk. Attempting a punt, he missed the ball completely and fell on the seat of his pants. The Packers' coach, Curly Lambeau, traded him to Pittsburgh before the start of the next season.

After one year with the Pirates he was back in Green Bay, but Pittsburgh had not seen the last of him. In 1937, AJR decided — quixotically — that Blood was the man to succeed Joe Bach as the Pirates' coach.

His credentials for the job were obscure. Tall, gaunt, and lithe, with heavy black eyebrows and thick black hair, Blood was an exotic free spirit. The way he acquired his football name reflected his attitude toward life, which was whimsical. Having played three years at St. John's University in Minnesota, he went to work as a stereotyper for a Minneapolis newspaper. Along with a friend who was also a stereotyper, he agreed to play football on Sundays for a semi-pro team, the East Twenty-Sixth Street Liberties. Both felt they might have some college eligibility left and realized they would need false names. On the way to the field, riding McNally's motorcycle, they passed a theater marquee advertising "Blood and Sand," a bullfighting film starring Rudolph Valentino. So when the Liberties' coach asked them what names they intended to use, McNally said, "I'm Blood and this guy is Sand."

Blood/McNally became known as the Vagabond Halfback. From St. John's he had gone to Notre Dame but never played a down for the football team. Suspended for breaking curfew once too often, he left academia for the stereotyper's job and left newspaper work for a Hall-of-Fame career in the NFL. There were teams called the Milwaukee Badgers, Duluth Eskimos, and Pottsville Maroons back then, and he played for all three before moving on to Green Bay. With Blood making long runs from scrimmage and catching passes for a record number of touchdowns, the Packers proceeded to win three straight championships. It was for his deeds off the field, however, that Blood is remembered in folklore.

The Packers, like Notre Dame, enforced a curfew. Locked into his sixth-floor hotel room on the night before a game on the road — with Blood, extreme measures were necessary — he opened a window, climbed out onto the fire escape, and jumped to the ledge of a teammate's window several feet away. All it took from there was a tap on a pane of glass to set him free.

On another occasion, Blood missed a 10 a.m. train with the rest of the Packers aboard. Accompanied by the young woman with whom he had spent the night, he got into his touring car, beat the train to the nearest railroad crossing, and stopped it by parking on the tracks.

Blood coached the Pirates for two seasons and part of a third, during which AJR became gradually aware that "you couldn't depend on John a whole lot." Not that they failed to get along. "Art liked Irishmen," Blood was to reminisce, "but I think I disappointed him. He pressed me to go to confession to make me a better Roman Catholic. Let's just say I came under that heading but spell it a little differently. I was a roamin' Catholic."

He was also, as it happened, a roamin' football coach. One Sunday when the Pirates were playing the Philadelphia Eagles in Pittsburgh, he was absent without leave in Chicago, watching his old team the Packers play the Bears. To a reporter he explained that the Pirates had an open date. Just then the public-address announcer was heard from: "Scores of other games ... Philadelphia 16, Pittsburgh 7."

"On most teams," said AJR, "the coach worries about the players. On our team, the players worry about the coach."

Blood's skills had greatly deteriorated and his blazing speed was by now just a memory, but in certain situations he would put himself into a game. If the Pirates reached their opponent's 20-yard line, he insisted on going in to call the plays. Against the New York Giants one Sunday, he did that two or three times, and two or three times the Pirates' offense lost its momentum. Near the end of the game they were back in scoring position, and here came Blood once again. The captain of the team conferred with the referee.

"What happens," he said, "if I don't accept a substitute?"

The referee said, "In that case, we won't accept him, either."

So the captain sent his coach back to the bench, and the Pirates scored the game-winning touchdown.

On another day, in a punting situation, Blood went in for the team's regular kicker, Johnny Gildea. AJR, sitting on the bench — owners did that in the 1930s — shouted, "No! No! No!" It was too late. Blood was waiting for the center snap. AJR turned to Max Fiske, a second-string halfback, and said, "I don't care if he kicks the ball sixty yards and it goes out on the two-yard line. He should let Gildea punt." With the words scarcely out of his mouth, Blood kicked the ball sixty yards — out of bounds on the two-yard line. AJR turned to Fiske again and said, "What do you do with a guy like that?"

Blood saved him the trouble of deciding. After a 2-9 season in 1938 and three straight defeats at the start of the 1939 season he resigned, and Walt Kiesling, an all-pro guard the Pirates had picked up when his all-pro days were gone beyond recall, succeeded him. Kiesling began enforcing curfew and bed checks and the Pirates managed to win a game and tie one while losing the other six.

"The players all loved John," said AJR of the departed Blood. Unfortunately, their performance on the field did not reflect it.

All through my teens I had heard so many stories about Johnny Blood, stories having to do with his eccentric behavior, that when AJR told us he was coming to dinner one night I guess I expected a sideshow. Would he do something bizarre — maybe dance on the table while we ate? To my surprise, a distinguished looking man with courtly manners, graying hair, and piercing black eyes knocked at our door. He was wearing a smartly tailored conservative dark suit. He walked with a soft tread, like a cat. Blood greeted Kass with a peck on the cheek, and the evening passed uneventfully.

Over the years I encountered him several other times when he was more like the Johnny Blood of legend. AJR's sixty-fifth birthday party was a big affair at the Hilton Hotel. Tom Landry and Tex Schramm came from Dallas, Toots Shor from New York, and Johnny Blood from Minneapolis. Bishop John Wright, soon to become a cardinal, was the principal speaker. Blood looked much the same as on the night he had been our dinner guest. His hair was completely gray but still abundant, and he looked as distinguished as ever. He might have been a senator, a judge, or an aging matinee idol. Called on to address the audience, he did not go all the way to the podium, stopping instead where Bishop Wright was seated. In a deep, dramatic voice, he said, "Your Excellency. Would you kindly stand?" Puzzled, Bishop Wright got to his feet. "Ladies and gentlemen," continued Blood. "This," he said, resting a hand on the bishop's shoulder, "is a saint." He paused a few moments for effect. "I," he went on, "am a sinner." The crowd roared with delight, and Blood resumed his trip to the podium.

I saw him again at an NFL meeting in Honolulu. He was there with his (second) wife, and wherever he went in the Royal Hawaiian Hotel he carried a large palm branch in one hand, even on the dance floor. Before the night was over he had an orchid behind each ear and orchids festooning his hair.

Blood fancied himself as a philosopher and a theorist. Ruminating about the Great Depression, he put his thoughts down on paper and developed them into a book (never published) called "Spend Yourself Rich." The essence of it was that depressions are caused by a scarcity of consumers; the way to terminate one, then, is to encourage consumption. He wrote that everybody, no matter how poor, has money, if only a dollar or two, and so by not holding back we can spend ourselves rich.

His ideas impressed someone at St. John's University, and Blood taught economics there while at the same time coaching the football team. When he was 50, he resigned to take a graduate course at the University of Minnesota, later confessing that he didn't know why. Having inherited money, he could do just about as he pleased, and in 1976 he embarked on a campaign to draft Supreme Court Justice Byron White for president.

Nothing came of it. Only AJR ever drafted Byron White, and that was in 1938, when White was an All-American halfback called Whizzer (a nickname he detested) at the University of Colorado. He was also a Phi Beta Kappa who planned on going to Oxford as a Rhodes Scholar. AJR offered him a salary of $15,800, outlandish by the standards of the day, to sign with the Pirates.

No football player had ever before earned that kind of money, and the other owners were aghast. They said that AJR was destroying the salary scale. "All I'm trying to do is bring a little class to the game," he responded. Still White was dragging his feet. According to AJR, it was Blood, through his persistence, who prevailed on the Whizzer to put off going to Oxford for a year.

White took the $15,800 (in his later years AJR said he'd forgotten what the eight hundred was for) and led the league in rushing. Returning from Oxford in 1940, he led the league in rushing again, but this time for the Detroit Lions, who lost him to the Navy during World War II and subsequently to the legal profession.

White was no charmer. His face, with its high cheekbones, appeared to be made of granite. Being interviewed and photographed was distasteful to him. "You know, I've been exhibited like a freak ever since I signed with the Pirates," he complained in his rookie year to a sportswriter. Johnny Blood liked him, but White was never one of the boys. "He's cold as ice. You can freeze sitting next to him," said George Quinlan, who managed the Pirates' training camp when White was with the team. Big Ed Karpowich made $100 a game. In perverse ways, he liked to call attention to the difference between his own small salary and White's. "Come on," he would say to the serious-minded rookie, "I'll get you a two-dollar broad."

"Whizzer didn't go for that," Quinlan recalled.

The Pirates lost money during White's year with the team, and he offered to return some of his salary. AJR refused to hear of it. He said that White worked harder than anybody else the Pirates had. He said it was no accident that White led the league in rushing, because this was a player who worked and fought for every yard. White worked for, and richly deserved, every honor he achieved, and there were many, culminating in his appointment to the U.S. Supreme Court by President John F. Kennedy.

His friendship with Johnny Blood endured for as long as Blood lived. A strange relationship, I thought, but they did have something in common. Each in his own way, Johnny Blood and Whizzer White were unforgettable members of the Pirate/Steeler family.

Name Change

In 1940 the Pirates became the Steelers. AJR had grown tired of their copycat name and held a contest to pick a new one. The *Pittsburgh Post-Gazette* cooperated with him, inviting its readers to send in suggestions.

Thirty years later, AJR told Myron Cope that the winner of the contest was the girlfriend of the Pirates' business manager, Joe Carr. With a touch of wryness, he added, "There were people who said, 'That contest don't look like it was on the level.'"

Actually, there were multiple winners, Joe Carr's girlfriend (who later became his wife) being one of them. When Joe Santoni, the owner of a restaurant in Carnegie, died in 2003, the headline over his obituary in the *Post-Gazette* was: "Restaurateur who named Steelers." Santoni's sister, Norma Fayer, recalled that his prize was a pair of season tickets. That same year, as I was about to enter a church in Palm Beach, Florida, to attend Mass one Sunday, a nun introduced herself to me. "I'm from Pittsburgh," she said, "and I'm a celebrity up there. I named the Steelers." Apparently all of the winners, and there were twenty or more others, either forgot or chose to forget that the distinction of re-naming the team was a shared one. For *her* prize, the nun received a war bond, she told me.

In one respect, the Steelers were no different from the Pirates. They continued to lose. Their record in 1940 under Walt Kiesling was 2-7-2. Over the eleven-game season, the team with the new identity scored a total of 60 points.

AJR was discouraged. In his eight years as owner he had lost about $100,000. Impulsively, he sold the team to Alexis Thompson, a rich young Bostonian, and quickly regretted it. A few months later, he bought a piece of Bert Bell's team, the Philadelphia Eagles. Next, he persuaded Thompson and Bell to trade franchises. Thompson took over the Eagles and Bell took over the Steelers, with AJR and Barney McGinley as his partners. Each owned a third of the stock. Barney McGinley, as it happened, was AJR's partner in the Rooney-McGinley Boxing Club as well. They promoted almost every big fight in Pittsburgh between the mid-1930s and the early 1950s.

AJR's genius, I've always said, resided in the fact that he was able to stay in business through thick and thin.

At the start of the 1941 season Bert Bell was the Steelers' coach. Scion of a Main Line family in Philadelphia, Bell had played and coached at the University of Pennsylvania. He had coached the Eagles as well, but not before serving as publicity director, ticket manager, and general manager.

Responding no better to Bell than to any of the coaches before him, the Steelers proceeded to lose their first two games, and he voluntarily stepped down. The owners now made an incomprehensible decision. They brought in, as head coach, Aldo (Buff) Donelli, who happened to be coaching, and would continue to coach, the Duquesne University team. How could he do this? By coaching the Steelers in the morning and the Dukes in the afternoon. On Saturdays he would be with the Dukes and on Sundays with the Steelers.

Buff was a local guy from Bridgeville, one of the coal-mining towns in a soccer hotbed populated largely by European immigrants and their offspring. Soccer, in fact, was Donelli's best sport. Football coaches had not yet learned to convert soccer players into placekickers, or Buff would have excelled at that specialty. As it was, he played center and fullback on some of Elmer Layden's fine Duquesne teams in the late 1920s. Another Donelli, Buff's brother Allan, played halfback for the Steelers in 1941 and 1942. In the 1950s a third brother went to work as the team's trainer but suddenly got religion and became a full-time drum beater for the Seventh Day Adventists.

Football in those days was all blocking and tackling.. Buff put some pizzazz into the game. He was not the inventor of the box formation, the spinner series, or the wing-T, but he refined those systems and added something to them. His offense involved a lot of quick and clever ball handling. Blocks were set up by quickness and deception, with all eleven men participating at either the point of attack or farther downfield. And, more than most other coaches did at the time, he emphasized passing. My two high school coaches and my coach at St. Vincent had played for Buff at Duquesne, and all three of them adopted his methods.

AJR, for his part, felt that Buff was a bit too full of himself. Buff met with the press at Owney McManus's restaurant every week, and AJR said that he once used a blackboard to show how the British generals under Sir Harold Alexander should be maneuvering their tanks against Erwin Rommel's German army in the deserts of North Africa..

Buff's 1936 Duquesne team had upset Pitt and had beaten Mississippi State in the Orange Bowl (on a 72-yard pass play) and his 1939 team was undefeated. His 1941 team also went undefeated, but the Steelers under Buff lost five games in a row. In their sixth game with Buff as the coach they were scheduled to play the Eagles in Philadelphia; Duquesne that weekend had a game on the West Coast with St. Mary's. Unable to be in two places at the same time, Buff chose the trip to California. At that point Elmer Layden, the NFL commissioner and Buff's old coach at Duquesne, intervened. An edict was handed down from league headquarters, and Buff's dual role came to an end, leaving the Steelers once more without a coach.

Walt Kiesling, as usual, moved up from the ranks of the assistant coaches to take command. The Steelers went to Philly and tied the Eagles, and then they won a game — from Jock Sutherland's Brooklyn Dodgers, an unexpected show of strength that cost the Dodgers an Eastern Division title. Two defeats followed as the Steelers reverted to form, and another dismal season was over.

Duquesne dropped football after the United States entered the war, and when peace came Donelli did not return. He coached for a while at Boston U. and then in the Ivy League at Columbia. On a scouting trip to Boston College in the early 1970s, just before Chuck Noll turned the Steelers into a championship team, I met Buff by chance. He was not any longer in coaching. As we talked, though, he casually suggested, "Have your dad call me ... I can help him."

I reported this to AJR. Although he made no reply, I could tell from his body language and the expression on his face that he did not feel the need for Buff's assistance. If the British Army got by without it, so could Chuck Noll, he may have thought.

Chapter 9

Big Harp

There were two Harp Vaughans — Big Harp Vaughan and Little Harp Vaughan. Big Harp's first name was John. He was actually not very big —5 feet 9 or 10 at the most — but he was bigger than his brother, Little Harp, and so their friends started calling him Big Harp. They called him other things, too, that were not as complimentary.

Big Harp's background was similar to AJR's. In fact, I think they were distant relatives. Harp may not have lived in The Ward, but he came from the North Side. He was good at sports. He took an interest in politics. And he was not without Irish charm. Those were the similarities. But AJR was the genuine article and Harp an inferior copy. He was a guy, you might say, who could never quite get to the next level.

It bothers me to take such a negative view of Harp, because on the surface at any rate we were friends. He officiated football games at St. Vincent College when I played on the team there, and often he would drive me home to Pittsburgh. During one of our games, Harp called a penalty on a kid from another team who seemed to know who he was. When Harp dropped the flag, the kid said, "Gee, Mister Vaughan, I'm a Catholic too." It made him angry at the time, Harp said, but he appreciated the humor as well.

Harp was a state legislator from the late 1930s to the early 1940s. Jimmy Coyne, I suppose, had quite a bit to do with Harp's election, but after Coyne lost his Senate berth and his power to hand pick candidates, Harp kept going back to Harrisburg. In the 1960s, he held a political office that was little more than a sinecure — boxing commissioner for Western Pennsylvania. Defying Governor Raymond Shafer, who was in Nelson Rockefeller's camp, Harp supported Richard Nixon for president at the 1968 Republican national convention. Nixon, as it turned out, won both the nomination and the election, but Shafer was still governor and he lost no time in appointing a new boxing commissioner.

Harp's career as a state legislator had ended when he lost to a superior politician, Tom Foerster. Foerster, like Harp, was born on the North Side. Unlike Harp, he had issues to run on. Subsequently, he served for many years as the Democratic chairman of the county commission. Harp complained to me once that Tom supplanted him by using dirty tricks. I said, "Harp, you're mad because you didn't think of doing those things yourself."

I know I was out of line, and yet my assessment of Harp still seems accurate.

As the years went by, AJR gradually distanced himself from Harp. Whatever bond had existed between them was not the enduring kind.

Coal Heaver

John Miller, Aunt Mary McNulty's husband, was a short, tough, violent drinking man with a large beer belly. To underestimate him, though, would not have been wise. He owned a couple of coal trucks and stopped working only long enough to drink, go to the movies, eat, and sleep. Cultural activities, including sports, held no interest for him. John's brother Clarence, his partner in the coal business, drove one of the trucks. They shoveled and hauled and delivered coal from early in the morning until supper time.

John and Aunt Mary — Kass's sister — lived in an upstairs apartment on Cedar Avenue, not far from North Lincoln. On the way home from work, John would stop somewhere for drinks. After eating, he would take in a movie by himself — the only kind of popular entertainment he liked — or go off to bed.

On days when the coal business was slow, he made a few dollars by picking up scrap iron in and around the mill towns and selling it to junk dealers. This source of income dried up after the residents found out that they could pick up the stuff and sell it themselves. The Depression had not yet lifted, and unless you were rich you watched every penny. To make ends meet, the Millers scrimped and saved.

John was a bad drunk. With his snoot full of "boilermakers" — whisky and beer, in that order — he would take out all of his malice on Aunt Mary, who could always set him off with a word or two.

Miller nursed a hatred for AJR. In neighborhood bars, he denounced his wife's relative by marriage as a tinhorn gambler, "the Little Mayor of Pittsburgh." When AJR got wind of this, he made a habit of dropping in at John's usual hangouts. He would settle down with a beer at an out-of-the-way corner table and hope to catch John unawares, mouthing off. AJR figured to be more than John could handle in a bar fight, but it would not have been easy. Once when John came home looking pretty well beaten up, Aunt Mary screamed that his jacket was covered with blood. "It's from the other guy," John said. But when he stripped to his shirt he found a knife wound in his side. "Son of a bitch!" he exclaimed. "That bastard!" Galvanized into action, he flew out the door. "Where are you going?" Aunt Mary called after him. "Down to the bar," he shouted over his shoulder. "I'm gonna get that dirty bum!"

On one occasion he bit off more than he could chew. This was when Aunt Alice lived on Cedar Avenue in the apartment below John and Mary's. Arriving home from a visit to a bar, John *was* yelling and screaming and cursing his wife as he mounted the stairs. Aunt Alice came into the hall with a vase and threw it at John. Unhurt, he stumbled up a few more steps. So Alice went after him with a broom, and *whack!* She broke it over his head. Meanwhile, Alice was swearing a blue streak. Together, the vase and broom and her vocabulary succeeded in bringing John to his senses, at least temporarily.

Too much food, too much work, and too much booze were the death of John Miller. After a stroke that laid him low he survived for several years as an invalid. By that time the Millers had moved to a well-kept-up house on East Street, in the "suburban" part of the North Side.

John and Mary had a son called Jack, who went to North Catholic High School, studied engineering at Pitt, and became a man of high moral values. Eventually he was head of the Pittsburgh Water Commission. Jack's son, also called Jack, turned out equally well, ending up in the planning division of the Western Pennsylvania History and Landmarks Foundation.

After John's bad stroke he could never drink or work again. He sold the coal trucks and all of the tools that went with that job. He spent his time hobbling around his garden and house, doing what he could to stay busy. Television by then was delivering movies right to his living room. Without the booze he was greatly mellowed. At last Aunt Mary had some peace in her life.

All in all, the original John Miller, product of Depression that he was, did quite well for his family, but seemed to regard himself as just an unsuccessful rival of AJR.

Max

Aunt Harriet married Max Fiske, a halfback from DePaul University in Chicago who played in 1936, 1938, and 1939 for the Pirates and in 1937 for the Chicago Cardinals. Max was a good-looking, very personable guy with some wit and a gift of gab. He was not, unfortunately, an ideal husband, and Harriet was not a devoted wife.

A truly beautiful girl, she could hold her own with Max when it came to expressing herself cleverly. Her beauty, alas — this and the fact that her brother-in-law owned the football team — gave her a sense of entitlement. She did not take responsibility well and neither did Max.

To be fair, it was not an auspicious time for two rather young, undisciplined people to be starting a new life together. The Depression was not yet over; a world war was impending. After Max went into the Army, leaving Harriet at loose ends, the marriage disintegrated.

Almost as soon as Max got out of uniform they divorced. With football out of the question, he returned to Chicago, his home town, and opened a couple of bars. Harriet stayed in Pittsburgh, too busy gadding about to care for her young daughter, Patricia. Kass and Alice stepped in, and Trish became a member of the Rooney family at 940 North Lincoln Avenue.

Max Fiske had brothers who were good amateur athletes and successful in later life. Max himself was another Art Rooney wannabe. He tried to operate shrewdly on the edges of the law but without knowing how.

AJR eventually lost respect for Max. From time to time he would be in Chicago for a football game or a championship fight, always with friends, and frequently Max would join them for dinner. On one occasion, with a train to catch, AJR and his crew were running late. He tossed the check to Max, telling him, "Sign my name to this and put on a tip." Max may have thought he was being treated like a flunky. At any rate, the tip he put on was one hundred dollars — more money, at the time, than the waiter who had served them could expect to take home in a week. Attributing this grandstand play to spitefulness or ignorance, AJR had no use for Max from then on.

With Harriet in mind, he would say to his granddaughters, "Never marry a football player." There were football players who'd have done the family proud, but what he knew of Max Fiske had left a sour note.

Car Salesman

Kass's brother, John McNulty, was a little wiry guy whose hair had turned steel gray prematurely while at the same time retreating from the front of his head. Uncle John wore glasses; he had an artificial eye as the result of a boyhood accident. George McNulty, John's uncle, owned the North Side Buick Company and gave him a job as a car salesman. He was a sporty dresser and had a pleasing personality, but also a couple of hangups.

An addiction to booze was one of them. The other went back to the injury affecting his eye. A surgeon took it out while his mother, Bridget Devlin McNulty, held him in her arms. From then on as far as his mother was concerned he could do no wrong. Until her death at 38 she spoiled him terribly, and then his three older sisters babied him for the rest of his life.

The McNulty family was upper middle class before the bottom fell out of the wooden barrel business, and John McNulty, Sr. lost everything he had. "Johnny," he would tell his son mournfully, "when you have a good day at work you never want it to end. You could work all night long." But the good days by then were coming less often, and in time they stopped coming altogether.

As the years went by for John Junior at North Side Buick, there were more bad days than good. AJR directed customers his way, but Dortha, John's wife, was no helpmate, and he was taking their problems to work. His relatives the McDonoughs, who ran the place, gradually lost patience with him and did not attempt to conceal it. John's sisters and many of his customers — he was a popular salesman — resented this. Something else came into play. Through an inheritance, John owned stock in the company — which mattered not a bit to the McDonoughs. Only the fact that he was George McNulty's nephew kept him from being fired.

AJR never took John seriously, but saved him one day from a beating. Outside the apartment building on Western Avenue where AJR lived with Kass in the early years of their marriage, John had words with a big, mean truck driver. The guy was pushing John around, daring him to retaliate, when AJR intervened. On the ground floor of the building was a division office of Anheuser-Busch, fronted by a plate-glass window. AJR sent the truck driver crashing through it, head over heels. From that moment on, Uncle John held my dad in considerable awe. I was afraid of him myself and could understand why others might be.

John told another story that contributed to the mystique building up around the man who would one day be known as the Chief. For a trip from Pittsburgh to Miami, or, more specifically, to Hialeah race track, AJR had engaged John and two others — "rough-looking guys," John called them — as drivers. Actually, John was the driver and the rough-looking guys may have been bodyguards, because AJR always carried large amounts of cash on his person. Anyway, somewhere on the outskirts of Washington, D.C., his big Buick Roadmaster broke down. John was able to get it to a General Motors garage, and AJR asked the manager how long the repairs would take.

"Couple of days at least. Gotta get a new part."

"Couple of days?" AJR didn't like that. "I don't have a couple of days." He was hell-bent on getting to Hialeah.

They were standing in the showroom, and he glanced around quickly. Indicating another Buick, the latest model, he said to the manager, "How much for that car over there?"

The manager stated a price.

"How much with my car as a trade-in?"

The manager stated a somewhat lower price.

"I'll take it," said AJR. Then to John and the tough guys, he said, "Come on, let's get going."

Eventually, John and Dortha were divorced. John died young — in his mid-fifties — of an alcohol-related illness. Dortha, who was a registered nurse, went to work for the Allegheny County Health Department. She retired with a pension and moved to Florida.

John and Dortha had a son and two daughters. The son, John McNulty III, worked for a long time at our race tracks in Florida, New York, and Vermont. Late in life, he made the admirable decision to give up his racing connections and start an entirely new career as a counselor of mentally and emotionally disturbed children in Vermont.

John McNulty II was a good guy who could not overcome his weaknesses. Those who suffered most from the way John and Dortha's story unfolded were their three children and his sisters, Kass, Alice, and Mary.

The Pittsburgh Kid

I was never much interested in boxing. When I was in high school, playing football at North Catholic, George Engel tried to teach me the rudiments. Engel was one of the fight game's top managers. He said that I looked like the great nineteenth-century heavyweight champion, John L. Sullivan. We were all up in Ligonier for the summer, and George had some time to spare. He showed me how to move my feet and hold up my hands. But I wasn't into it, and he picked that up pretty quickly. You have to have the temperament for boxing, I guess. It was something I failed to inherit from AJR.

From the mid-1930s into the early 1950s, AJR and Barney McGinley promoted almost every big fight involving Pittsburgh champions like Billy Conn, Fritzie Zivic, Billy Soose, and Sammy Angott at Forbes Field, at Hickey Park in Millvale, or in places like Duquesne Gardens, across the street from St. Paul's Cathedral in Oakland, and Motor Square Garden on Baum Boulevard in East Liberty. In 1951 The Rooney-McGinley Club promoted the heavyweight championship fight in which Jersey Joe Walcott took the title from Ezzard Charles, knocking him out in the seventh round with a single left hook.

Before teaming up with AJR, Barney McGinley had owned a saloon and a horse room in Braddock. Barney was the silent partner, a genial white-haired man. AJR considered him a standup guy he could call on to help meet the football team's payroll. As it happened, there was never any need for Barney's cash.

Ray Foutts, who had managed middleweight champion Teddy Yarosz of Monaca, was the boxing club's first matchmaker. When he returned to his home town, East Liverpool, Ohio, Jake Mintz succeeded him. Excitable and terrier-like, Mintz had been a fighter himself, with a misshapen nose to prove it. His record in the flyweight division was perfect — three fights and three knockout defeats. As matchmaker, he shared an office in the Fort Pitt Hotel, the football team's headquarters, with Bert Bell, whose voice was so loud, and so continually at full volume, that when Mintz had to make a telephone call he would crawl under the desk they both used.

When Mintz left the organization to become the manager of Ezzard Charles, Barney McGinley's son Jack took over the matchmaking. In time, as AJR and the senior McGinley became more and more preoccupied with football, they left the boxing end of the business entirely in Jack's hands. It was Jack who made all the arrangements for the Walcott-Charles fight at Forbes Field. The crowd, more than 28,000, was a record for boxing in Pittsburgh, and still is.

Jack McGinley was a decorated veteran of World War II. After graduation from Pitt, married now to Marie Rooney, AJR's sister, he enlisted in the Navy and became the engineering officer on an LST (landing ship/tank) with the rank of lieutenant junior grade. In the North African and Italian campaigns, he was cited for heroism. And then in the hours before dawn on the morning of June 6, 1944, — D-Day — his LST shoved off for Omaha Beach with 216 men in half a dozen amphibious landing-craft vehicles. In addition, they had a load of "ducks" — floatable tanks — with troops in them. Seven miles offshore was as close as they could get. Later McGinley recalled, "It was too jammed up. We had to let the troops out."

Whether their passengers made it to the beach they never knew. The LST returned to England and boarded more troops on the night of June 8th. In the middle of the English Channel, headed for Normandy again, they took a hit and then another from a German torpedo boat and sank. It was 3 a.m.

"God only knows how many people we lost. Hundreds," McGinley said. He was tossed about in the water for the next three hours. "We had life belts," he said, "and six of us held onto one of those little rubber doughnuts. As we were leaving the ship, one fellow had said, 'We'd better take this along.'" It saved their lives. Around daybreak, a British destroyer picked up the lucky half-dozen.

Meanwhile, AJR had heard from a friend in the Navy Department that McGinley's ship had been lost with all aboard. "Get ready to break the news to the family," he was told, but then came word of the rescue. I never knew about that until I heard it from Judge Barney McGinley, Jack's son.

At the end of the war, Jack was a full lieutenant. Back home in Pittsburgh, he went to work in the family's sports conglomerate, doing whatever had to be done. His most important job was to learn the boxing business, and in just a few years he was one of the most respected promoters in the country, known by all who had dealings with him as a man of the highest character and integrity.

AJR's favorite fighter was Billy Conn. At the age of 21 he took the light-heavyweight championship from Melio Bettina in New York. After winning their return match at Forbes Field in a fight the Rooney-McGinley Club did not promote (Conn's manager, Johnny Ray, was feuding with Ray Foutts), he started looking for bigger game. Because "that's where the money is," as he said, he relinquished his light-heavyweight title and moved up into the heavyweight class.

In less than a year he had beaten all the other contenders and was ready to fight the champion, Joe Louis. As a final tune-up, he took on a nobody named Buddy Knox for the Rooney-McGinley Club. He won by a knockout, which was only to be expected, but a crowd of 27,000 came to see the fight at Forbes Field.

Conn was the original "Pittsburgh Kid" — black-haired, handsome, devil-may-care. He had fallen in love with beautiful Mary Louise Smith, the teenage daughter of Greenfield Jimmy Smith, a tough former major-league baseball player. Once when Jimmy Smith was a utility infielder with John McGraw's New York Giants, he challenged a whole bench full of Brooklyn Dodgers, shouting, "All right, you sons of bitches, I'll fight you one at a time or in groups of five." Jimmy was barely 5 feet 9, but nobody in the Brooklyn dugout moved a muscle.

Though he had introduced his daughter to Conn, Jimmy disapproved of him — disapproved of any fighter — as a son-in-law. To get her away from Billy, he sent Mary Louise off to Rosemont College, in Philadelphia. That didn't keep them from sneaking up to Brookville, in northern Pennsylvania, the day after the Knox fight, to take out a marriage license. But Jimmy Smith heard about it and stopped the young lovers from getting the knot tied at St. Philomena's in Squirrel Hill by storming into the residence of the bishop himself and telling him what would happen if Mary Louise ever married a pug.

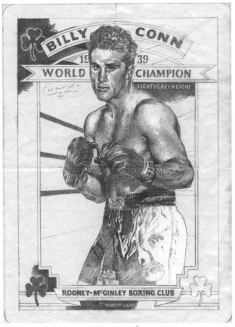

Billy Conn
(Drawing by Merv Corning)

Billy had another major distraction while training for his fight with Louis. Maggie, his beloved one hundred percent Irish mother, was dying of cancer. Fight night came — June 18, 1941 — and Billy went into the ring at the Polo Grounds in New York weighing 169 pounds. Louis weighed 201. This was seen as an embarrassment to the promotion. In the first place, no one was giving Billy a chance. With such a difference in the weights, it looked all the more like a mismatch. So the crowd of 54,487 was informed by the ring announcer that Conn weighed 174 and Louis weighed 199 ½.

Public interest in this fight, especially in Pittsburgh, was phenomenal. Owney McManus's Ham and Cabbage Special disgorged hundreds of Conn's admirers, wearing leprechaun hats, at Grand Central Station. They were waving paper shamrocks and sucking on clay pipes. At Forbes Field that night the Pirates were playing the New York Giants. Before the start of the fourth inning the umpires called time. Both teams retired to their dugouts, and for most of the next hour everybody listened to the amplified radio broadcast of the fight.

All over America people listened. Conn started slowly, as he usually did, and nervously. Skipping around the ring as Louis plodded after him, he slipped and fell. Both feet went out from under him. But after trading punches a few times, and taking Louis's best shots with no apparent ill effects, Billy gained confidence. He was quicker than Louis, quicker with his hands and quicker on his feet, and was beating him to the punch, moving in and landing fast combinations and then disengaging. By the eleventh round Conn seemed to be coming on strong. In the twelfth, he staggered Louis with a left hook. Going back to his corner, he lifted his right hand to acknowledge the cheers of the crowd.

"I've got him," he said to Johnny Ray. "I'm going to knock him out."

"Box," Ray advised him. "Stay away."

"No, I've got him," said Conn. When he answered the bell for the thirteenth, Ray called after him, "OK, then. You're on your own."

After fiddling around for half a minute, Conn tore into Louis. He threw a seventeen-punch combination, and more than half of the punches found their mark. But suddenly over a missed left hook Louis drove a murderous right. Conn was hurt, and Louis leaped to the attack. He landed twenty-five punches without a return and Conn went down. He wobbled to his feet a split second too late. Arthur Donovan, the referee, had counted him out.

In Conn's dressing room, the reporters waited for his tears to dry before one of them asked, "Billy, why did you go out there and slug with Louis in the thirteenth round? You were winning the fight." Conn's answer has gone down in ring lore. Smiling, he said, "What's the use of being Irish if you can't be dumb?"

Mary Louise had listened to the fight with her aunt at the Waldorf Hotel, or, rather, had listened to her aunt's account of it between rounds. She spent the rest of the time in the bathroom, shutting herself off from Don Dunphy's dramatic blow-by-blow description on the radio. When Billy had showered and dressed, he walked with Johnny Ray from the Polo Grounds to the Waldorf, a distance of five miles, recognized here and there on his passage through Harlem by exuberant Joe Louis fans who called out words of condolence. At the Waldorf, Mary Louise opened the door of the suite for him. Standing there alone, he told her, "I did my best." The tears were back in his eyes. "Billy," she said, "it's all right."

Billy's mother died on June 28th, ten days after the fight. She died in the large brick house he had bought for her with his ring earnings, a house on Fifth Avenue in Shadyside, where rich people lived. On Billy's last visit to Maggie's bedside, she had persuaded him against his own wishes to go ahead with a recuperative trip to the Jersey shore. "I'll see you when I get back," he promised.

"No, son," answered Maggie. "The next time I see you will be in Paradise."

Billy got the news of her death by telephone. On the day after the funeral Billy and Mary Louise eloped, having found a priest in Philadelphia who feared neither bishops nor Greenfield Jimmy Smith and was willing to marry them. Mary Louise had just turned 18.

Shortly after Pearl Harbor, both Conn and Louis went into the Army. Their return bout was scheduled for the following June, and the Army allowed them time off to train. It would be a big-money fight for everybody concerned, including the military's United Services Organization, or USO, which was guaranteed a cut of the gate receipts. In May, Conn came home on furlough for the christening of his first son, Timmy. AJR was the godfather. In the company of Milton Jaffe, Conn's business manager, he approached Jimmy Smith and talked him into patching things up with Billy and Mary Louise. Timmy was baptized at St. Philomena's Church on a Sunday, with Jimmy present, and then the guests all gathered at his house in Greenfield for a party.

Jimmy and Billy were polite to each other — at first. Late in the afternoon, they got into a mild argument over the regularity of Billy's church attendance. Jimmy told him he'd better start going to Mass more often. They were with AJR and some others in the kitchen, and Billy was sitting on the stove. He said something back; Jimmy threatened to punch him. Long afterward, AJR told the writer Frank Deford, "I can still see Billy coming off that stove."

AJR and the rest of the men jumped in to break up the fight, but not before Billy had broken his left hand on Jimmy's head, and Milton Jaffe, caught in the middle of the scuffling, had broken an ankle in a fall down the steps to the basement. There were scratches and bruises all over Billy's face; Jimmy Smith was unmarked. When Joe Louis would see Billy after both had retired from the ring and were good friends, he never failed to ask him, "Has your father-in-law beaten you up lately?"

Conn's broken hand put the return bout on hold until after the war. As was all too evident, neither Conn nor Louis had been in a real fight since 1941. Louis looked slow, but he could still punch. Conn's skills had disappeared completely. In the sorriest exhibition of his career, he lost by an eighth-round knockout.

Today that fight is largely forgotten. So is the fact that Conn fought eleven world champions twenty times and won from them all except Louis. He's remembered for one thing. In the biggest fight of his life, he was too Irish and too headstrong to be satisfied just with winning it. "I'm going to knock him out," he told Johnny Ray, and instead he was knocked out himself.

Patsy

L ike David L. Lawrence, Patsy Scanlon came from the Point, that triangular wedge of land where two rivers converge to form a third. During the early years of the twentieth century the Point was heavily Irish. In Stefan Lorant's Pittsburgh book, there's a photograph of the Point the way it looked around 1900. What you see is a slum, a wretched clutter of warehouses, freight sheds, and low-roofed buildings that squat side by side, blackened with soot. There were planing mills and grog shops and a boiler works. There were "unsightly, rickety tenements."

Uncle Jim recalled that, as kids, he and his brothers and friends would "go over to the Point and visit Patsy's mother. She'd give us tea and Irish cake." Irish cake was bread — heavy, coarse white bread with raisins in it. "The houses they lived in!" Jim said. "No carpets on the floor. No bathrooms. No hot water. There'd be a big wooden barrel under the rainspout. On winter mornings, to get a pan of water to cook in, first you had to break the ice."

Such neighborhoods were spawning grounds of fighters and politicians. Patsy Scanlon became a fighter, a good one, although never quite a champion. A gnome-like figure with a meandering nose, he had a sharp left hook, but his right was "nigh useless," as a Pittsburgh sportswriter called Jim Jab put it. Scanlon's biggest fights were with bantamweight champions Pete Herman in 1919 and Kid Williams in 1921.

The Herman fight was one-sided. Jim Jab depicted Scanlon as "a plaything in Herman's hands." Herman handed Scanlon "the worst beating doled out in moons," Jim Jab wrote. "Patrick's face," he continued, "was a sight. One lamp was just peeping out, the other was mussed." When the tenth round ended, "old friends could hardly recognize him."

Scanlon and Harry Greb *were* stablemates and sparring partners. Someone else Scanlon boxed with was AJR. Woogie Harris, a numbers writer from the Hill, saw them spar one time, and he told George Quinlan, "Art was a bulldog. He fought like Henry Armstrong, always boring in. But Patsy batted the hell out of him. He hasn't hit Patsy yet." This must have been before 1921, when AJR was an amateur, one of the best in the country but still just a kid, and Patsy was at his peak, fighting all the best men in his weight class.

When Patsy Scanlon retired from the ring, he opened a flower shop and a bookie joint, both on the same premises. I knew him later on. He was still running a book, but working out of a saloon near the Roosevelt Hotel. His once red hair was receding and had turned to pure white. He had a red complexion — beet red at times, which was due, I suppose, to the pickling effect of John Barleycorn.

At least when I was around, Patsy never talked a great deal. He appeared to be very well liked and was said to have a sense of humor.

Dad once invited Patsy, Dago Sam, Owney McManus, and Tom Bodkin, a former boxing promoter and referee who later became a theatrical agent in New York, to 940 North Lincoln Avenue for a dinner party. Mom that night was impeccably groomed and she received these guests as though they were big-shot owners from the National Football League. (That was one of the reasons people loved her; she treated everybody the same.)

Tom Bodkin had had some exposure to the good life, and even Owney McManus could play the part of a gentleman, but Patsy and Dago Sam were uncomfortable, Patsy more so than Sam, who didn't really give a damn. In any case, both had trouble deciding what fork to use and where to place the napkin when dinner was finished.

On that one memorable night, Kathleen McNulty Rooney's grand old home looked like the stage setting for a Damon Runyon Alumni reunion.

Chapter 10

Big Kies

Off and on, Walt Kiesling was AJR's head coach from 1939 until the late 1950s. The Chief had other head coaches during that time span but except for a number of years after World War II, during the Jock Sutherland-John Michelosen era, he kept his good friend Kies on the payroll as an assistant.

Kies was a quiet, somber-looking German from the upper Middle West, 6 feet 4 inches tall with a large frame. Usually he weighed more than 300 pounds. By his early thirties, he had a full, round face and a bald head.

Like Johnny Blood, Kies played college football at a small Catholic school in Minnesota — in his case, St. Thomas. He was in the NFL, as player and coach, for thirty-four years, starting out with the old Duluth Eskimos. From Duluth he went to another of the teams that shortly became extinct, the Pottsville Maroons. His all-pro years (1929-33) were with the Chicago Cardinals. In 1934 he moved across town to play for the Bears, who were undefeated that year but lost the championship playoff to the New York Giants on an ice-covered field at the Polo Grounds. For better traction, the Giants put on tennis shoes at half-time and scored twenty-seven points in the fourth quarter to win going away, 33-13.

Kies was so quick that despite his size he played guard rather than tackle, pulling out to lead the interference. Before football took up all of his time, he had been a baseball player, and a good one. His ungainly looks were deceptive. When navigating wooden steps he went about it carefully, for fear they'd collapse under his weight, but to see him dance was a revelation. He was agile and light on his feet and he could do all the ethnic dances, such as the polka.

Jack Butler, the Steelers' all-pro defensive back, described a post-game incident in the bar of a hotel on the West Coast, where the players and coaches were killing time before they were due to catch a train. Kies had been drinking beer, and now nature called, but he was seated at a table in back, cut off from the men's room by tables that were pushed close together. Squeezing through would be impossible, and in order to clear a path for him the other members of the traveling party would have to vacate their chairs. "Don't worry about it," Kies said. He stepped up onto his own chair and then up onto his table. All of these tables — Butler didn't say how many there were — had plate-glass tops. Very nimbly, this 6-foot-4, 300-pound old football player tiptoed from one table to the next all the way to the end of the row. His audience just sat there and gaped, expecting him at any minute to crash through the glass.

AJR considered him as much of a crony as a coach. Kies liked to play cards and he liked to play the horses. He would come to 940 North Lincoln Avenue every morning to pick up the boss and drive him to work. He'd arrive when we were having breakfast in the kitchen and accept an invitation to sit down and drink a cup of coffee. One day he sat in one of those cast-iron and plastic S-shaped chairs, and it collapsed, dumping him on the floor amid the wreckage. Everybody laughed — except Kies. The next morning he sat in what he took to be a different chair but was actually the same one, restored to some semblance of its former appearance by the twins. And it happened again. Down went the chair, with Kies again riding it to the floor. The hilarity, of course, was even greater than before. After that, Kies drank his coffee standing up.

Kies was very bright but had some strange ideas about football players, which I'll get into later on. His brightness was most apparent at the card table. According to AJR, at any point in the game he could remember what cards had been played and thus seemed to know exactly what cards were left in everybody's hand.

At the race track, he made some decent side money by betting on the horses that AJR had picked. In fact, to AJR's annoyance, he would sneak a big bet with a bookie, telling no one. Pretty certain of where Kies's information had come from, the bookies would bet on the horse themselves, diminishing the payoff. After Big Kies died, somebody found a shoe box full of money under his bed — money he apparently had won at the race track and at cards.

The contents of the box went to his wife, a nice, kind woman who cooked the good German food that Kies liked. On social occasions, she would not say no to a cocktail, and it loosened her up.

She told Kass one time that her husband would win more games if AJR would spend more money on better players. This happened to be true, but it was also true that there wasn't any money to spend — the Steelers in those days operated at close to the break-even level — and Mrs. Kiesling's suggestion was not well received by Kass.

Anyway, Kies was head coach in the wartime year of 1942, and the Steelers had their first winning season, finishing second in the Eastern Division with a 7-4 record. Their success was largely due to the all-around ability of the player they had made the NFL's No. 1 draft pick that year — Bill Dudley, an All-American halfback from the University of Virginia. He led the league in rushing with 696 yards — 129 more than Whizzer White had gained in 1938 — scored six touchdowns, passed for two more, and was an extraordinary defensive back. His selection as Rookie of the Year followed automatically.

I will have more to say about Kiesling, and more about Dudley, later on.

Chaplain

"St. Francis Church in New York," said George Quinlan, "was on Thirty-Fourth Street, right off Seventh Avenue. They had what was called an Actors' Mass at 2:30 Sunday morning. So on this one Sunday there was a little disturbance in the vestibule. A short, bald-headed guy was telling jokes to some people gathered around him. Everybody was laughing. A priest goes into the vestibule and takes the bald-headed guy by the arm and ushers him out onto Thirty-Fourth Street and says, 'Now get going.' On Monday a housekeeper came to the priest's room and said, 'There's a man here to see you.' It was the little bald-headed guy. He said to the priest, 'You know something, Father? You damn near broke my arm.' And he gave the priest a five-thousand dollar check. The bald-headed guy was Jimmy Durante. The priest was Father Silas Rooney."

When Father Silas went to China to be a missionary, he was big, strong, and athletic. He came back to America weighing 125 pounds and ravaged by the onset of Lou Gehrig's disease. A few years at St. Francis, his next assignment, apparently did wonders for him.

The Franciscans had ordered their missionaries to leave China when the Japanese invaded that country in the late 1930s. A Japanese cruise ship took the priests to Hawaii, and Father Silas became friendly with one of the stewards. He said the steward called his attention to the removable cabin walls. They were removable, the man explained, so that the cruise ship could be turned into a troop ship. The Japs were preparing even then for war with the United States.

Not long after Pearl Harbor, Father Silas went into the Army as a chaplain. After D-Day, he served with the troops that were fighting the Germans, but first he spent some time at a staging area in England. There was a recreation room, where one day he picked up a pool stick and got into a game with some high-ranking officers, including a general or two. The ease with which he ran the table excited a few captains and lieutenants; its effect on the generals, colonels, and majors was different.

"Where did you learn to play like that?" one of the generals asked. "There must be something in your past you don't talk about."

Father Silas was in the Battle of the Bulge. During the siege, he was pinned down in a bunker with two other chaplains. Panicking, one of them made a break for it. He was gone before the others could stop him, running across open ground while the shells and the bullets were coming. The next day the Americans found his body. Father Silas said the German soldiers who shot him must have been practicing Christians. The chaplain's corpse was laid out on a bench, with his hands crossed on his chest and the uniform cap over his face.

Before a battle, said Father Silas, the troops would give the chaplains their money to take care of. If a soldier was killed, it would be up to the chaplain to get that money to his family back home. This, said Father Silas, was one of the most difficult parts of his job.

After the Americans crossed into Germany, Father Silas was with an outfit located near a Catholic orphanage. One day he got hold of a jeep and loaded it with C-rations for the children and the nuns. As he was about to take off for the orphanage, an officer caught sight of him.

"Just where are you going with that?" he demanded.

Father Silas explained what the purpose was.

The officer said, "Leave that jeep where it is. You don't have any authority to give food to the enemy."

Father Silas was upset but obeyed orders. The officer outranked him. Forty-five minutes later, a truck full of food pulled into his area. The officer who had halted his jeep came up to him and said, "If we're going to help those orphans, let's do it right."

Years after the war, Father Silas showed up at Three Rivers Stadium with a copy of an old insurance policy. It was not for a large amount. Grandma Rooney had taken it out when he was in Europe. He could now cash it in, and he was misty-eyed.

"God bless her," he said.

Civilian

On December 11, 1941, four days after Pearl Harbor, Hitler's German Reich, as an ally of Japan, declared war on the United States. AJR was in a German restaurant in New York with Walt Kiesling the previous night and spoke to some German sailors at a nearby table who appeared to be having a good time. "They seemed like such nice guys," AJR remembered thinking. The next day in the papers he read that these same German sailors had scuttled their ship in the harbor. I was just a kid at the time, and I asked AJR what it meant to scuttle a ship.

"To pull the plug and sink it." he said.

AJR had been too young for World War I, and now he was 40 years old, but he went to the Navy recruiting office in Pittsburgh and volunteered. As a married man with children, the officer in charge informed him, he would need his wife's signature on the enlistment papers. So AJR came home with the documents, and Kass reluctantly signed. When he took them back to the recruiting office, the Navy man was extremely cordial. He watched while AJR put his own name on the papers and then a remarkable change in his manner took place.

"Well, big shot," he said, "now you're in the Navy, and you'll do what we tell you to do," etc., etc. He was waving the papers in AJR's face.

There were other volunteers waiting to sign; no one, including AJR, had been given the oath. "Are we officially in the Navy before we're sworn in?" AJR asked the recruiting officer.

"No," said the recruiter, "but that will be taken care of as soon as I get the rest of these guys signed up."

Without another word, AJR yanked his papers out of the officer's hands. He tore them to pieces, dropped the pieces on the floor, and walked out, ignoring the Navy man's cries of "Hey, wait a minute!"

Kass said that even though she never had met that sailor, she couldn't thank him enough.

As the fighting in the Pacific and in Europe heated up, AJR gave blood at the Red Cross so many times he was finally told not to come back. And he arranged for the Steelers to play a game with the profits all going to the USO. (I remember a USO canteen near the Pennsylvania Railroad Station for military men passing through Pittsburgh.)

Gasoline rationing was now in effect, but AJR had a way of getting around the regulations and continued to travel extensively. I know he had friends who owned gas stations. One place, near Ligonier, had a garden hose rigged up to a gasoline pump for favored customers. In my youthful naiveté, I couldn't figure out why the attendant was putting a water hose into our gasoline tank.

There were shortages of almost everything, but I don't recall doing without necessities. Up to a point, AJR felt that government rules were for other people to obey. There were government rules and there were God's rules, and AJR followed God's rules. He was lucky and smart and never got into trouble.

On the highway he picked up hitchhikers in uniform and would take these passengers to wherever they were headed, within reason. He hoped, as he said to Kass, that someone would do the same for his brother Tom, who was in the Marines.

Late one night with the temperature in the teens, he picked up a young Navy yeoman at the New Stanton exit on the Pennsylvania Turnpike. As the yeoman later described it, he'd been waiting thirty minutes in a razor-sharp wind, and his ears were frosting over. When a pair of headlights approached, he frantically waved his arms, only to watch the big sedan roar by.

"But whoa!" the sailor went on. "About a hundred yards beyond me, the car braked to a stop and began backing up — on the Turnpike, a real no-no. As it reached me, a door swung open and a voice boomed out, 'Hop in.' A man in the back seat extended his hand and said, 'Hi. I'm Art Rooney.'"

The sailor was momentarily flustered. He said, "Oh." Huddled in his Navy peacoat, glad to be out of the cold, he was silent for a moment. Then he said, "I'm afraid to tell you who I am."

"Why would you say that?" AJR wanted to know.

"Because I work for the *Pittsburgh Press*. And when you ran for register of wills, our paper creamed you." (As a matter of fact, the *Press* had declared AJR to be "utterly without qualifications for the office" and "the hand-picked tool of James J. Coyne.")

AJR laughed. "Best thing the *Press* ever did," he said. "I never had any business being in politics."

The sailor was John Troan. In another twenty-five years he would be editor-in-chief of the *Press*, a Steeler season-ticket holder, and one of AJR's many friends.

He said that AJR was returning to Pittsburgh from the Army-Navy football game in Baltimore (the price of admission was the purchase of a war bond). He himself was trying to get home from his Navy base near Baltimore. Of course Troan said something like, "Drop me off anywhere that's convenient for you," and of course AJR had the driver — Harp Vaughan? Walt Kiesling? — deliver him to his front door.

"Good luck," said AJR as they parted, "and look me up when the war is over."

However he did it, wherever he was, AJR could always find gasoline. On a solo trip South, deep in the boondocks of Georgia, he was flagged down for speeding and hauled off to the rustic police station. It was in a clapboard house with woods on all sides. The speed trap had netted several others, among them a young guy in a sailor suit, and they were being told they could pay their fines on the spot or wait for the judge to appear.

"How long will that be?" asked the serviceman.

"Three days."

"Three days? In three days, I report back to my ship. How much is the fine?"

"Fifty dollars."

The young sailor was in shock. He said, "But fifty dollars is all the money I have."

"Pay the fine or wait for the judge," said the cop.

AJR stepped up. He pulled a hundred-dollar bill out of his pocket. "I'm pleading guilty and that sailor is pleading guilty," he told the cop. "Here's a hundred bucks for our fines." He turned to the sailor. "Let's get out of here, kid," he said, and, together, they took off.

Randomly, in ways of his own choosing, AJR contributed to the war effort.

Red

AJR's brother John was called Red for good reason — his full head of strawberry blond hair. Red was about 5 feet 11 with a medium build. He had been an athlete at Duquesne Prep, although not of the same caliber as AJR, Dan, and Jim. However, the Rooney Reds, one of AJR's semi-pro football teams, were named for John, I am sure.

He took a pre-med course at Duquesne University but was working for AJR in the Steeler ticket office when he volunteered for the Army — or was drafted; I'm not sure which — nine months before Pearl Harbor. AJR would say, without elaborating, that Red "screwed up" at some point during the time that he served — four and a half years. When Aunt Margaret heard him talking this way, she stoutly defended Red. "He fought in all the big battles in western Europe. And he was hurt real bad in an ammunition dump explosion," she told me.

Red's job as a toxic gas handler in a chemical warfare outfit that fought in the North African campaign, as well as in Sicily, Italy, France, and Germany, was to issue high-explosive shells for 4.2 chemical mortars. The risks, more than likely, were enormous. Red earned six Bronze Stars and a medal called an Invasion Indian Arrowhead before the ammunition-dump explosion somewhere in Germany.

It is hard to separate fact from fiction where Red was concerned, but Aunt Margaret and the Chief agreed on one thing: after Red returned from the war, he was never the same man.

There were war veterans back then who suffered from what was called "shell shock." Bruce Catton, in one of his marvelous Civil War books, wrote of veterans who could only sit and stare. The war in Vietnam gave us a different term for this malady: "post-traumatic stress disorder."

Anyway, after coming home, Red did not finish college. That the government would have paid his tuition under the GI Bill of Rights made no difference. In the kitchen at 940 North Lincoln Avenue one night, Kass tried to tell him a college degree was important. Red wasn't listening. "It's too late for that," he insisted. "It's time to get on with my life."

Getting on with his life was a process lubricated by alcohol. Red was a good-looking, likable, gregarious sort of guy. He could tell a good story, extracting all the drama. I've written how the first of our ancestors to be born in North America left a "scoundrel" for dead on one of Pittsburgh's many bridges, and the words I used came from Red. "A shot rang out in the night," he would say, "and only Grandfather Rooney walked off the bridge."

Could Red have been a doctor? He was smart enough. "Red had a lot on the ball," a friend of his said, "but he wanted to be like his brother Art — a hot-shot gambler." What he lacked was the temperament and the aptitude.

He did have an air of refinement. While I was being tutored by a straitlaced old spinster called Miss Hall in AJR's offices at the Fort Pitt Hotel. Red would come in and exchange a few words with her in French. She considered him superior in looks and intelligence to the horse players, card players, and newspapermen who frequented the Fort Pitt. I heard Miss Hall tell Kass how much she admired Red. In fact, she once asked if he would like to meet her niece. "No, thanks," he replied. "I've had enough woman trouble as it is."

Which was true. Red had been married and divorced. There were two children, Margie and Patty, and both grew up to be fine young ladies. As a result, Kass said, of Red's interest in medicine, Margie became a nurse. Both girls left Pittsburgh for greener, sunnier pastures in California.

AJR put Red to work at the Steelers' pre-season camp in Cambridge Springs doing odd jobs, and he may have looked upon this as demeaning. At any rate, one of the football players — Ralph Calcagni — died of a ruptured appendix, and Red put the blame on the "brutal" training methods of Jock Sutherland, the new coach. Using this as an excuse, he immediately left camp. Back in Pittsburgh, he told family members that in Cambridge Springs the players were "dropping like flies." He said there was too much hard physical contact; the drills were too exhausting; the practice sessions lasted too long.

For all his potential, he ended up driving a Yellow Cab. On a raw winter day when I was still just a kid, Red saw me playing near the North Side Carnegie Library. Noticing that my hands were bare, he stopped his cab, called me over, and handed me a dollar. "Artie, you look cold," he said. "Take this and buy yourself a pair of gloves."

Red died at 42, another nice guy who wasted his life. The cause of death, as Jack McGinley put it, was "too much booze and too little self-esteem." Something else that contributed, at least in my opinion, was post-traumatic stress disorder, which we did not yet understand.

The Day Art Rooney Cried

Born to Irish Catholic parents who accepted the strictures of the Church against birth control, my Uncle Tom, the last of Dan and Maggie Rooney's eight children, was young enough to be AJR's son. If you were Catholic you took all the kids that God sent you.

So Tom Rooney was a gift of God, but with some deviltry in his makeup — a "wild thing," Kass said, who would "fight at the drop of a hat." Tom had red hair and fair skin. He was of medium height — maybe 5 feet 10 — but compactly built. Rip Scherer described him to me as "one of the best high school football players I've ever seen." They were teammates at North Catholic, where Tom was a halfback and Rip a freshman fullback. In years to come, Rip coached AJR's sons at North.

Uncle Tom always seemed to be somewhere nearby when you needed him. I have a boyhood memory of being locked in the bathroom at 940 North Lincoln Avenue. The door could not be opened from either the inside or the outside. I was getting desperate when here comes Tom, crawling through the window. He had found a ladder that would reach the second floor. On my part after that, there was hero worship for Tom.

When my brother Dan was 10 he came home one day with a story about a "flasher" accosting kids around the North Side park area called Monument Hill. He said the man who exposed himself was wearing a dark blue or gray business suit. Uncle Tom happened to be in the house, and he ordered Dan into the family car. Wasting no time, they drove to Monument Hill. The dark-suited man was still there.

"Is that him?" asked Tom.

"That's him."

Tom jumped out of the car, grabbed the pervert by the scruff of his neck, and gave him a tooth-rattling shake. "Keep away from those kids, you son of a bitch!" Tom shouted. "If I ever see you around here again, you're dead!"

And it was no idle threat.

When Tom was a kid he went to St. Peter's School through the eighth grade and then to Duquesne Prep, where he skipped so many classes that AJR got involved. His motivational tool was sarcasm. In a snowstorm one morning, Tom set out for the Bluff on foot, battling heavy drifts all the way. Anything to escape his oldest brother's withering tongue. Except for the headmaster, he found the place deserted. "Rooney," the headmaster said, "you don't show up when the weather is good. Today it's terrible outside – nothing is moving – and here you are. Well, you can turn right around and go home – we've canceled all classes."

On the theory that a change of environment might be helpful in some fashion, Pop and Maggie removed Tom from Duquesne Prep and sent him to North Catholic. I'm not sure how it turned out. In any event, with the European powers at war, AJR perceived that sooner or later the United States would be drawn in, and he believed he could use his political pull to get Tom appointed to the Naval Academy. The stumbling block was Tom's academic record at North, but AJR knew what to do about it. Bullis Prep, in New Jersey, made a specialty of preparing athletes with weak grades for higher education, in particular the higher education the Naval Academy offered. Thanks to AJR, Bullis Prep was the next stop for Tom. He may have lasted a semester before dropping out.

The one option left to him, AJR thought, was the military service. "It's better than being a bum," he would say. As though in agreement, Tom enlisted in the Marine Corps. Afterwards, AJR regretted having pushed him in that direction.

Once when his mother was ill, Tom all but threatened to go AWOL in persuading the company commander to grant him an emergency leave. He was home for a few days looking fit. I can still see him passing a football around at the family cottage in Ligonier ... the red hair, the fair complexion. He was wearing a Navy blue turtleneck sweater that AJR had bought in Canada. AJR told him to keep the sweater, but Tom said no, it was not regulation equipment. His wardrobe had to be one hundred percent government Issue.

He said that never in his civilian days had he imagined he could get through anything as demanding, both physically and psychologically, as boot camp at Parris Island, in South Carolina. What he talked about more than the rigorous training, though, was how the non-commissioned officers exploited the personal fears and hang-ups of the recruits. If they discovered that someone had a snake phobia, or a spider phobia, there would be snakes or spiders that night in his bed. But Parris Island was child's play, the veterans back from the Pacific all said, compared to the experience of combat against the Japs.

Tom's leave was soon over, and we never saw him again.

He fought in three major battles. Writing home after the first or second, he said that if he was fortunate enough to get out alive he would seriously consider the priesthood. I'm sure he meant it. "There aren't any atheists in foxholes" was a saying that came out of the war. But in July of 1944 when the Marines recaptured Guam, an island the Japs had held for two and a half years, Tom was killed.

Weeks passed before the family received the news. First, Tom's letters stopped coming. Then a Marine friend of Tom's, in a letter to Aunt Harriet, wrote: "Too bad about Tommy. He was a great guy." His use of the past tense prompted AJR to get in touch with some people he knew in the Navy Department, and they confirmed that Tom was a casualty of the invasion.

"I'll never forget that day," said George Quinlan. "It was the only time I ever saw Art Rooney cry."

Tom's mother was a long time recovering. His remains were sent back from Guam after the war and he was buried in the North Side Catholic Cemetery. In January of 2002, I met a pharmacist named Carl Wincalowicz who had been a Seabee. He said that for fifty-five years he had wanted to speak with somebody from the Rooney family but always held back out of reticence. Learning that Rip Scherer had kept in touch with me emboldened him. He had known Rip and Tom at North Catholic High School, and through Rip, we got together. This was the story he told: When his Seabee outfit went to Guam, once the island was secured, he had recognized a sailor from Pittsburgh. The sailor was a Fogarty, a brother of Fran, the Steelers' accountant. He told Carl where Tom was buried — up on a nearby hill — and at the cemetery, among the rows of white crosses, Carl found the one with Tom's name on it. Breaking a rule, he took a picture of the grave, and for all these years he had wanted a Rooney to have it. The moment was rather touching, as he talked of Tom, North Catholic, and the photograph.

Another time after the war — this must have been in the 1980s — I met a friend of the family who had preceded Tom into the Marines. He was driving a truck for a bakery. Tearfully, he told me that after Tom's death Grandma Rooney had refused to see him or speak to him. He said she believed that what had influenced Tom to become a Marine was the sight of this friend in his handsome green uniform. If she knew that AJR had encouraged Tom to enlist, it was something she never mentioned.

Down through the years, AJR and Kass would sometimes come across veterans of the war who had been in Tom's outfit. Tom may have thought he had a religious vocation, but their stories portrayed him as still very much a wild kid. He'd been a sergeant or a corporal but was busted to private, it seems, for "borrowing" a jeep while on liberty. Unofficially, the top brass in the Corps did not disapprove of such behavior. High-spirited Marines were the kind who excelled in combat.

There were conflicting accounts of how Tom lost his life: "killed in the water when his company stormed the beach" ... "using a flame thrower that exploded in his face." No one will ever know. On the day of the invasion, one story went, Tom was among the first to board the landing craft from the ship. Another Marine, about to climb down the netting, caught Tom's eye and gave him a thumbs-up. Smiling, Tom returned the gesture. And then quickly, with a twist of the wrist, he converted thumbs-up to thumbs-down.

During the late summer of 1944 when there was no word from Tom, something very strange and very Irish happened. Two owls appeared at our cottage in Ligonier one night. Hooting ceaselessly, they perched on a utility pole outside the second-floor bedroom occupied by AJR and Kass. They did not fly away until AJR and the kids tossed rocks and shined flashlights at them. The next night they returned and again were driven off, a routine that went on for at least a month, and then at last they stopped coming. It was not long afterward that the Navy Department confirmed Tom's death. Kass and Aunt Alice always felt that the first appearance of the owls corresponded to the date on which Tom was killed.

One more reminiscence: On a Memorial Day evening a long time after the war, my family was gathered for dinner. One of the young people at the table asked what Memorial Day signified. When the explanation was given, another young one asked, "Did anyone here ever know anyone who was killed in a war?"

I picked up my glass and quietly said, "Here's to Uncle Tommy Rooney, United States Marine Corps, 24 years old ... killed on Guam during World War II."

Home Front

With World War II, the Depression years came to an end and Western Pennsylvania's economy turned around. Pittsburgh always had been a dark, forbidding place; as the raw materials of war rolled out of the steel mills and manufacturing plants, it became even darker. Smoke and smog hung in the air, but the night-time glow of the open hearths lit up the riversides, and there was action Downtown until dawn.

The restaurants and clubs were always packed. Broadway plays and revivals came to the sold-out Nixon Theater. On a Friday or Saturday after 6 p.m., you couldn't buy a ticket to a movie. Owney McManus, who ran a thriving bar on Fourth Avenue, said the paddy wagons were full every night with petty wise-guy hoodlums from Donora, Brownsville, Ambridge, and the other surrounding mill towns. Everybody out of uniform had work; everybody out of uniform had money.

There were men the Army and Navy didn't want. Men in their thirties and forties. Men with wives and kids like AJR (who was over the age limit as well). Four-Fs like gimpy-legged Uncle Jim and one-eyed Uncle John McNulty and sickly Uncle Vince (who lived to be 75). Men with defense-related jobs like Uncle John Laughlin. And men besides these who paid off someone in politics to avoid the draft.

All things considered, the Rooneys did more than their share. Father Silas was an Army chaplain in France. Uncle John was a soldier in the ranks. Uncle Tom, a Marine, died in combat. Aunt Marie's husband to-be, Jack McGinley, had a ship blown out from under him in the English Channel. Not to mention Aunt Harriet, with a husband *and* a boyfriend in the service.

I saw the war from the perspective of a child. When the Japanese bombed Pearl Harbor I was six years old. When the Enola Gay dropped its load on Hiroshima I was ten. My brothers John, Pat, and Tim were even younger. At the cottage in Ligonier and in the back yard at 940 North Lincoln Avenue we played war games, launching attacks on one another from our fox holes. AJR brought us war toys, a scarce commodity. He kept the family supplied with the necessities of life and kept the Steelers from going out of business.

Many government functions were suspended for the duration. I knew that something called the "infrastructure" was falling apart. Bridges, ramps, and roads crumbled. Beating the enemy – the Germans and Japs – came first. In a crowded North Side bakery a woman hoped out loud that the war would go on forever: it had given her money to spend. The saleslady picked up a pie and threw it right into her face.

Jeeps and tanks, instead of new cars, rumbled off the assembly lines in Detroit. Cars, which were irreplaceable, had to last just as long as the war did, but AJR could beat the system. We were never without a car that looked and ran like new, and always there was plenty of gas. In the summer we drove to Ligonier. Or Kass would take the kids to North Park, with a stop for ice cream at the North Hills Dairy on McKnight Road.

The way to get around in the city was by streetcar. Everything that could move was on the tracks, including old wooden relics that may once have been pulled by horses. At Pennsylvania Station, railroad trains were constantly arriving or leaving. Sternwheeler riverboats paddled up and down the Allegheny, the Mon, and the Ohio.

I remember the sounds of the streetcars on a summer night, and the sounds coming into my second-floor bedroom, the one I shared with Tim, in the morning – the bells clanging, the steel wheels grinding against the tracks, the screech of the cars as they turned onto Western Avenue. In those long-ago days before air-conditioning, we slept with the windows wide open. Later, with my brother Dan married and gone, I had the back bedroom to myself, but the streetcar sounds and the whistles of the trains – the Pennsylvania's main line to Chicago ran through West Park – were my constant companions. In the late 1940s, when the houses on Millionaires' Row were coming down, I heard the whistles and horns of the riverboats, too.

Everyone had a relative in the service. You could put a star in the window for every family member in the military – gold stars for those who had died. Grandma Rooney had a gold star for Tom in her window. The radio was the great communicator. We would all sit around and listen to the "stories," and then the old folks would tune in the war news, which Gabriel Heatter knew how to dramatize. Walter Winchell mixed war news with gossip. Milton and Ruth Jaffe spent time in New York, and Ruth would return with all the scandal about the stars of stage and screen.

Rural West Virginians came here to get jobs in the war-related industries, and many of them lived on the North Side, in the nineteenth-century mansions partitioned off as rooming houses. Behind the Tiffany-glass windows they lived as they had in their mountain shacks. They tore the handcrafted woodwork from the walls and drove nails into the plaster for coat hooks. North Lincoln and Ridge avenues would never be the same again.

The last house to go on our part of the street belonged to a member of the Mellon-related Scaife family. He hired a watchman who lived in the basement and kept an eye out for intruders. Thanks to Kass, 940 North Lincoln remained in pristine condition. Anxious to keep up appearances, she poured a lot of money into the house. More than once during those years the doorbell would ring, and relatives of the original owners, introducing themselves, would tell Kass how grateful they were that she had not let the place deteriorate. One woman became very emotional, calling our house "an island in a sea of disaster."

Pop Rooney's bar was just a memory by then, but some of the old First Ward people — the McCabes, the Yuhaszes, and the Mareks — still lived in the neighborhood. They were solid citizens. For other North Siders, the war was the end of the line. There were no drugs then, but lots of booze, and lots of people who'd rather drink than take the jobs to be had for the asking.

Our neighborhood was primarily white. The First Ward School was still there. St. Peter's School was nearby, at the summit of Arch Street. It was nonetheless an unforgiving location. For every family like the McCabes, who eventually got out, there were more that sank into the muck. If you were young, all you had was one chance. You couldn't sow your wild oats and then make a second new start, or a third, or a fourth. If you flunked out of school, it was either the Army or a crummy job. The kids we hung out with were athletes, mostly. Football players and basketball players finished high school; the most skilled among them had scholarship offers from colleges and universities.

Our friend Mike Kearns lived with his mother and sister in the billiard room of a big old house on Ridge Avenue, a block from North Lincoln, broken up now into "apartments." In these gray brick and red brick Georgian and English Manor landmarks, the tenants were the poorest of the poor. Down the hall from the Kearnses, another family, a mother and several children, occupied the original pantry — sharing it, Mike said, with the chickens the woman kept for their eggs.

Mike was a bright kid, one of the brightest among the thousand or more boys at North Catholic High School, a football, basketball, and baseball star and the "end man" in the yearly minstrel show. Kent State offered him a football scholarship. After two years of college, he went into the Army — we were fighting now in Korea — and in the Army he did very well. He returned to civilian life, married, and became a devoted drunk.

With eight kids to support, all he could ever handle was a routine job making Clark bars and Teaberry gum at the Clark Candy Company, where many North Siders without his ability ended up. The marriage, strained to the utmost, didn't last, but neither did Mike's boozing. He gave up drinking after twenty years, remarried, and contributed something to society, helping other reformed drunks in Alcoholics Anonymous.

Mike's sister had a master's degree from Pitt and went into social work, specializing in children's psychology. With five kids of her own — three boys and two girls — she divorced a husband who drank. Soon afterward, she married a well-to-do Seattle lawyer, a North Sider she had known in high school. She moved to the West Coast, continued her work in psychology, and gave birth to another daughter.

Mike and Mary Jane were North Siders with talent and a mother who cared. They survived. Hundreds of others couldn't make it through the trash heap, lacking the toughness to overcome their environment. Of course the Kearnses were not the only exceptions. One North Sider I knew became a general in the Air Force. Richie McCabe became a good defensive back for the Steelers and a coach in the NFL.

AJR took these kids for what they were. Some of them he helped — the unlucky ones, the children from a family of drunks. A saloon owner's son, he hated booze and spent frequent odd moments in the last forty years of his life preaching temperance sermons to his own sons and to three of his brothers.

Mongrels

In the middle of the Depression, AJR had scraped up $2,500 to buy an NFL franchise. He kept it going through continued hard times. Now, just as the team was beginning to show promise, the Second World War subordinated all other activities, including professional sports, to the task of defeating Germany and Japan.

By 1943, the armed services had started drafting married men with children. Only 4-Fs, defense workers, and middle-aged has-beens were left to play football. The Cleveland Rams suspended operations, and the Steelers, at the suggestion of Commissioner Elmer Layden, merged with the Philadelphia Eagles to form a team officially known as Phil-Pitt but which the sportswriters called the Steagles. By going along with this idea, AJR showed his pioneering spirit and his genius for toughing it out.

The Steagles played two of their five home games in Pittsburgh and three in Philadelphia. Watching the team practice, AJR remarked to one of the sportswriters, "The name is different and the colors are different, but when you get down to it they're the same old Steelers." It was a phrase that haunted him for years after the war, appearing repeatedly in the newspapers as losing season followed losing season: "S.O.S. — Same old Steelers."

"I should have kept my mouth shut," AJR said to me more than once.

The Steagles had two head coaches, Walt Kiesling and Philadelphia's man, Greasy Neal, who despised each other and argued constantly. Players holding jobs in war plants worked by day and practiced with the team at night, from 6 to 9. Bill Dudley was in the Pacific as an Army bomber pilot. The center, Ray Graves, had one ear. A guard, Ed Michaels, had two ears but was almost deaf. Tony Bova, the team's best pass catcher, was almost blind. Jack Hinkle, a halfback, had washed out of the Air Corps, classified as "unfit for service" because of ulcers. Bill Hewitt, 34, was back in the game after four years of retirement to play end.

Before the war, people did not have money to spend on football tickets. Now there was money enough, but the manpower shortage had depleted the talent available to the teams, and crowds were still sparse. I remember that when I watched the Steagles practice one evening I was more impressed with a column of soldiers drilling in the sunset than with the football players.

Despite the animosity that existed between Kiesling and Neale, the Steagles ended the season with a decent 5-4-1 record. Frank (Bucko) Kilroy, a 240-pound rookie tackle who was still going to Temple University as a student in the Navy College Training Program, said that Kiesling and Neale could not have been less alike as coaches. Neale stressed offense, Kiesling defense. Neale was humorous, confident, and upbeat. Kiesling was serious — even, at times, glum.

For years after the war, Kilroy played for the Eagles and took pride in his reputation as one of the meanest, toughest linemen ever to wear a uniform. His off-the-field persona was different. Irish, red-haired, and full of blarney, he expressed great admiration for AJR and Bert Bell and was always very friendly toward me, a young kid. When I was grown, just in talking with Bucko, I learned a lot about what to look for as a scout.

In the mid-to-late 1970s we were trying to get a team picture from every year since the beginning and soon had them all with one exception. Missing was a photo of the 1943 Steagles. At last one turned up — standing out from all the rest because the players were not in uniform. They wore business suits. Something else about it was eye-catching as well. There were not enough men for a backup at every position. The total, as I recall it, was twenty. On game days, they must have picked up extra players to round out a squad.

In 1944 the Eagles resumed operating on their own, and the Steelers merged with the weak Chicago Cardinals, owned by AJR's good friend Charley Bidwill. Named the Card-Pitts, this team was so bad the sportswriters took to calling it the Carpets. The Carpets were coached by Kiesling and Phil (Moxie) Handler. They lost every game, ten in all, and every game was one-sided.

After a 34-7 defeat at the hands of the Bears, Kiesling and Handler fined three of their players for showing "indifference" on the field. One of the three was Johnny Grigas, a fullback from Holy Cross. Grigas that year scored nine of the Card-Pitts' sixteen touchdowns and led the team in rushing. Going into the final game of the season, in fact, he led the whole league in rushing.

That final game, a rematch with the Bears, was at Forbes Field, where two high school teams had played the day before in the rain, creating a lot of mud. Overnight the temperature fell, and the mud changed to hard, icy ridges. AJR recalled that they were "sticking out of the ground like spikes." Grigas suited up and went out on the field before the game. He looked at the ridges and tested them with his foot. They felt like concrete. So Grigas returned to the dressing room and put on his street clothes again. He called a cab. When the next train left for Boston, Grigas was on it — bound for home. The Bears beat the Card-Pitts by 42 points. Meanwhile, Bill Paschal of the New York Giants, playing on a weekend pass from the Army, ran for enough yardage that day to win the rushing title. Grigas finished second.

Phil Handler fitted right in with AJR and his crowd. During the season he got a letter from a high school coach who wanted a copy of his playbook. When AJR heard about it, he told Phil, "That guy must be nuts — we haven't won a game."

Phil had something in common with AJR, a fondness for betting on race horses. Years after the Card-Pitts were history I saw Phil at the College All-Stars' practice field the week of their annual game with the NFL champions, later discontinued. He was scouting the All-Stars for the Bears. I hardly knew Phil, but when I walked up beside him he turned and shook hands. Then he said matter-of-factly, "Tell your dad to give me a call when he has a horse running." With that, he turned back to the field and watched the rest of practice without ever saying another word to me. Somehow Phil reminded me of an old uncle I did not spend much time with but who recognized and acknowledged me when we met.

There was always a bond, I felt, between the Steelers and our partners in those wartime mergers, especially Mr. Bidwill's team. Charley's sons, Billy and Stormy, ran the Cardinals after his death, and after a falling-out between them, Billy alone was in charge. I valued them both as friends

World War II ended in August of 1945, the year the Steelers regained their name and their identity. Walt Kiesling was gone, not to return until 1954, and Jim Leonard, a Villanova guy, became the new head coach.

Earlier in the decade, Jim had been an assistant under Kies. Some of the good pre-war players were filtering back, but not quite soon enough. The Steelers ended up with a 2-8 record. Bill Dudley was available for the last four games and led the team in scoring with three touchdowns.

Jim Leonard and AJR were very fond of each other. I recall a family trip through the New Jersey countryside in the 1950s. We were on our way to a seashore resort, with a stop at the Monmouth race track, but made a detour to look for Jim, who had an asparagus farm in the vicinity. AJR wasn't sure where it was, so we covered a lot of ground on our search. Leonard by then was out of football and spending most of his time in the asparagus fields. Suddenly AJR caught sight of a man on a tractor. He tooted his horn. Climbing down from the tractor, Jim Leonard came over to the side of the road, a big smile on his face. He shook hands with all of us, and then AJR drew him aside for a private conversation that lasted about fifteen minutes.

I saw Jim again at one of our games in the 1970s and for the last time ever at AJR's funeral in 1988. Jim was an old man, but still tall and robust looking. He lived for another five or six years.

'Me?'

Chuck Cherundolo was all man. You'd have sworn he was 6 feet 6 instead of 6 feet 2 and weighed 320 pounds instead of 250. His classic Italian face looked like something carved out of marble by a Renaissance sculptor, and he had what is known as a foghorn voice. The way he walked and the way he talked reminded people of John Wayne, only with Cherundolo there wasn't any play-acting. Chuck was the real article. A child of the Depression from the tough hard-coal region of northeastern Pennsylvania, he had played college football — linebacker and center — at Penn State.

In the NFL, Cherundolo started out with the Cleveland Rams and Philadelphia Eagles, but ended his career with the rugged Steeler teams of the years just before and just after the Second World War. The Navy took him in 1943, and he was thus never stigmatized as a Steagle or Card-Pitt.

On shore leave one time and due to ship out unexpectedly, he found himself with two full bottles of high-grade whiskey he hadn't gotten around to finishing off. He might have smuggled it on board, but did not. Cherundolo was an officer, the kind who toed the line. In the lobby of the hotel where he was staying he noticed two young Navy enlisted men. They looked thirsty. "Hey, swabbies, would you like a drink?" he bellowed. The sailors seemed to take it as an order and responded with meek yes sirs.

"Come on, then," Cherundolo said, leading them to the elevator. Up to his room they went, the swabbies showing signs of uneasiness. Roughly, Cherundolo handed them the bottles. "The only reason you're getting this stuff," he said, "is that I'm shipping out right away, and I'd rather give it to you guys than waste it on officers. Now, scram." He had left the door open, but the two sailors paused before leaving. A change had come over them. They thanked Cherundolo for the bottles with unusual effusiveness and continued to thank him as they went on their way.

Cherundolo stood watching their backs, nonplussed. What had been going on in the minds of those guys? And then all of a sudden he saw the light. "Why, those little farts," he said to himself. "They came up here thinking I was queer. Me! A queer! ME!"

He told the story about the sailors in pre-season training camp one year. "Well, Chuck," a teammate said after the laughs had died away, "you never know." Cherundolo chased him out of the room.

Captain of the team, Cherundolo led the Steelers in their daily calisthenics. With his big voice, he bullied, cajoled, and encouraged, booming out the cadence, keeping an eye on the shirkers, putting hecklers in their place. "If you're gonna soar with the eagles, you can't hoot with the owls," he would roar.

Unlike some of the other players, he always had time for the water boys. Often he shot baskets with them after practice or meetings. Though his appearance belied it, he was agile and quick, and he knew enough basketball to offer the kids helpful little tips.

After the 1948 season, Cherundolo joined the coaching staff. Head coaches came and went; Cherundolo stayed on into the 1950s. He coached and scouted elsewhere for something like fifteen more years and meanwhile went into business for himself. On the roof of his bar and grill on Route 51 at the south end of the Liberty Tubes was a big neon sign in the shape of a football. Cherundolo served beer and sandwiches mostly and he entertained his customers with unscheduled showings of Steeler highlight films.

When my son Mike attended Washington & Jefferson College, he wrote a paper on AJR for one of his English courses. In doing research, he asked Cherundolo for some reminiscences. The old war horse answered in writing and ended his long account with the sentence: "I was lucky to have played in Pittsburgh for the Steelers and Art Rooney, one of the finest men I ever knew."

Chapter 11

On the Road

A JR knew all the roads and shortcuts between Pittsburgh and New York and between Pittsburgh and Philadelphia. He was a very fast driver on those two-lane highways, but he was also very sure of himself. "The best driver I ever drove with," he would say, "was me."

The narrow, dangerous mountain roads never gave him the slightest pause. He would shoot past other cars, and on the Pennsylvania Turnpike, which opened in 1940, he would even pass cars in the tunnels when there were still just two lanes, with traffic moving both ways.

When he drove he would smoke big Cuban cigars and spit the ends, chewed to mush, out the window. The tobacco juice would be blown back into the car and onto the faces of the passengers in the back seat, who were usually his sons. We sat there choking in cigar smoke and listening to static on the radio. In his ceaseless efforts to get the news or the baseball scores or the race results, AJR would be fiddling with the station selector.

Kass and his friends had gone through this experience before we did, and a generation later his grandkids had to endure it. The grandkids, more resourceful than the sons, would open the back windows a crack, make a funnel out of a newspaper — there were always newspapers in the back seat — stick one end of the funnel into the crack, and breathe through it.

On Route 30 once, Johnny Blood was with AJR, who asked him to drive for a while as they were coming out of the Allegheny Mountains toward Pittsburgh. It was three o'clock in the morning. They changed places, and AJR said to Blood, "I'm going to take a nap. Wake me up when we get to Greensburg." Some time later, jostled out of his sleep, he looked around and said, "Where are we?"

"Zelienople," answered Blood.

Zelienople is northwest of Pittsburgh. Greensburg is east of Pittsburgh.

"Why didn't you wake me in Greensburg?" asked AJR.

"I didn't see it," Blood said. "We went through some little towns, but nothing as big as Greensburg."

AJR reflected on that for a minute. Then he said, "To get where we are, we had to go through Pittsburgh, and Pittsburgh's not exactly a small town."

"It's not exactly a big town, either," said Blood, "or I'd have waked you up for sure."

Blood had a reputation for eccentricity. It was well deserved.

'Ever Been Arrested?'

There's a theory called six degrees of separation. Simply put — too simply, perhaps — it holds that everybody knows six people who each know six other people who each know six other people and so on and so on until you reach the sixth degree and have a chain that connects everybody in the world to everybody else. It sounds pretty dubious, but AJR always knew someone who knew someone who knew someone, and it helped ease his way through life. To illustrate:

On the primitive roads of the 1940s, he and Harp Vaughan were driving to Buffalo when a rainstorm blew in from Lake Erie. Dad's big old touring car skidded into a ditch and there was nothing they could do to extricate it. Somehow they located a farmer. He came with a team of horses and got them headed toward Buffalo again. It was close to 3 a.m. when they pulled up in front of their hotel. The desk clerk eyed them suspiciously — bedraggled, mud-spattered strangers climbing out of a battered, mud-spattered car.

"What can I do for you?" he asked.

"We called for a reservation," said AJR.

"Your names?"

"Rooney and Vaughan — from Pittsburgh. We had car trouble. All that rain. Needed help getting out of a ditch. Farmer pulled us out with his horses."

"Just a minute," said the clerk.

He went into a back room and called the police. "Looks like we've got a couple of hoodlums over here. They're trying to check in. I think they might be on the lam." The tourists had not moved an inch when two cops walked into the lobby.

"Who are you guys?" the cops demanded. "Can you show identification?" AJR reached into his back pocket. Empty. His side pockets. Empty. The pocket on the inside of his suit. Empty. His exertions in the ditch had dislodged his wallet.

"Ever been arrested?" asked one of the cops. "Ever been in jail?"

Quickly, AJR answered, "I haven't, but he has," indicating Harp with a nod and a gesture.

Turning from the cops to AJR and back to the cops, Harp looked perplexed, and a little hurt.

"Uh ... yeah. That's right," he said. "But only one night."

"You fellows will have to come with us," the cop said, but AJR said, "Wait a minute. Do you know Charley Murray, the football writer at the Buffalo News?"

"Sure. We've seen him around."

"Well, call Charley Murray. He'll vouch for us."

So at 3:15 in the morning, Charley Murray, sound asleep at home, was getting a telephone call from a policeman. "I know Rooney," he said. "Vaughan? I'm not sure."

"Will you come down to the hotel and identify Mister Rooney?"

Charley Murray got out of bed, put on some clothes, drove into town, and identified Mr. Rooney, which was good enough for the cops and the hotel clerk. The six degrees of separation factor had saved Harp Vaughan a trip to the police station, but one thing bothered him.

"Why did you tell that cop I'd been arrested?" he asked AJR in the elevator on the way to their room.

"I was afraid you'd tell him you hadn't been," said AJR. "And then we really would have been in trouble."

Footnote: Many years later AJR was a pallbearer at Charley Murray's funeral. Coming out of the church, he remembered something important. A horse of his was running that day at Bowie and he wanted to get a bet down — a big one. He looked around and spotted Ken Stilley, a football coach he knew very well. He caught Stilley's eye, beckoned him over, and said in an undertone, "Do me a favor. Take this end of the casket. I have to get out of here and call my bookie. Please fill in for me. Charley was our friend. He'd understand."

That was what Stilley thought, too.

Rooneyspeak

AJR and his brothers — Jim and Father Silas in particular — had their own distinctive way of talking. Much of what they said was in the form of pronouncements. They spoke as though laying down the law. They were making statements that could not be contradicted.

They would stress certain vowels or consonants, stretching them out. "Hey ... you-u-u ... big-g-g ... bum-m-m" could be a form of greeting or a protest of some kind. When AJR was annoyed with someone, he might exclaim, "Say-ie-ie ... you-u-u ... big ... sa-a-p ... star-r-t ... using ... your ... hea-a-d!" Another way to express this was "Think ... ahead ... of the ... pla-a-y!" "Wha-a-t ... a ... piec-c-c-e ... of w-wor-r-k ... he-e-e ... is!" defined an absent third party who was also a yegg or a bum.

The nearest approximation to Rooneyspeak I can think of would be the elongated syllables used for comic effect by W. C. Fields.

I never heard AJR swear either casually or in anger. He might call somebody a "bum," or a "stiff," or a "greaser," or a "rube." John and Pat, the twins, were called saps so often they looked up the word in the dictionary. The definition they found was "a dumb or stupid person who can only dig ditches" — or so they said.

AJR and his brothers had deep, challenging voices when they talked in this very assertive manner. With Uncle Jim, talking was an art form. While getting the words out, he could snicker or laugh in the same breath. I never heard these inflections in the speech of Pop Rooney or the boys' two sisters.

Another thing I noticed about AJR, Jim, and Father Silas was the way they used figures of speech. Eating, for example, was "putting on the feed bag." If you tipped a waiter, you "duked" him. And so on.

A locution that originated with Pop Rooney is still used by some of his grandchildren. When the need comes to urinate, you "go to see a man about a horse."

Think Ahead of the Play

AJR had some catchy little phrases he would lay on his sons: "Don't kid the kidder" ... "Don't be a sap" ... "You are brand new" ... "He's come a long way" ... "Kidding on the square" ... and one that he picked up in sports, "Think ahead of the play." This one may have been handed down by his long-time mentor Dick Guy, a sportswriter and manager of sandlot and minor-league baseball teams.

Dick was one of the "main gazzumboes" of the Middle Atlantic League when AJR and Uncle Dan played for the Wheeling Stogies. AJR seemed to love him. It was interesting to find out from Rob Ruck and Maggie Patterson's research that Dick Guy and others like him would use the sports pages to inform the sandlot players that there was a game on such and such a date, naming a time for them to gather at the pickup spot. The managers and promoters used the newspapers as a bulletin board. Knowing enough to look in the sports section for the information on when and where to assemble would be "thinking ahead of the play." Dick must have repeated that to youngsters like AJR and Uncle Dan again and again.

When brother Pat was putting a lot of time in on baseball, Dad would have Dick Guy work him out at Monument Hill Field. By this time Dick was up in years; he reminded me of Coleridge's Ancient Mariner. Pat would pitch, John would catch, and the rest of us would shag balls, with Dick looking on. I think he felt we were rich kids fooling around rather than dedicated athletes like Dad and Uncle Dan.

Dick was a big part of Dad's formative years. I heard many stories about him — how he could give the players "holy hell," how they tried to avoid his ire. Before every game, Dick counted the balls and bats, and afterwards he counted them again. One time when some balls were missing, the player in charge of the "poke" — the canvas bag they were kept in — told Dick that AJR was in charge of it. Dick chuckled a bit and said nothing. AJR was starting to show the leadership qualities that distinguished him later on, and, recognizing this, Dick always treated him deferentially.

"Thinking ahead of the play" carried over from the playing fields to all of your endeavors in life. "Kidding on the square" had its counterpart in Mary Poppins singing "a spoonful of sugar makes the medicine go down." It was telling the truth in such a way as not to hurt the feelings of a friend or a child. Often Dad would say, "Well, I told him what I thought was right, but I kind of kidded him on the square as I did it."

I don't doubt that Dick Guy had kidding on the square down pat, but he looked like such a stern old bird to me.

"He's come a long way" could either be sarcasm or a true compliment. Some of Dad's acquaintances who found redemption of a sort deserved it as a compliment. But if you said "He's come a long way" about a phony who had a hand in everyone's pocket it was a warning: "Watch out for this yegg. He couldn't have changed all that much."

I heard these little phrases until AJR's dying day.

Dress Code

A JR and his cronies all seemed to dress the same way. I don't remember seeing Dad in anything but a dark blue or gray suit. Perhaps he had a brown suit in his wardrobe; if so, he'd forgotten about it.

At banquets and other formal affairs he wore his dark blue suit with a snap-on black tie. On trips, he would carry the tie in his pocket, referring to it as his "tux." Until his later years, when he was often the guest of honor at testimonial dinners, he never owned a black suit, much less a tuxedo.

I remember once when I was still a young boy — it must have been in the early 1950s — that the Knights of Columbus made him a grand knight, requiring the purchase of tails, a white tie, and a plumed hat. The sword he had to carry was a gift from the K.C.'s. A cobblestone alley called Mallis Way separated their headquarters, one of the old North Side mansions, from our house on North Lincoln Avenue. On the night of the big affair, AJR got into this "get-up," as he called it, sneaked across the alley, and went through the back door of the K.C. building. At the end of the evening, he returned by the same route.

He put the sword away in the closet where he had hidden a snub-nosed pistol, but my brothers and I found it one day. We took it out of the scabbard and engaged in a series of duels. One of us would have the sword and the other the scabbard. We dueled all over the second floor of our house, and it was only by a miracle that nobody lost an eye.

When Dad was a young man he always wore a cap. In middle age he wore a fedora. In old age he went back to the cap, having developed a fondness for caps from Ireland. He said you could get into and out of automobiles and taxicabs without knocking your cap off, but not so with a hat. During the time that he wore a hat — the 1930s, '40s and '50s — a newspaperman from San Francisco wrote that nobody wore a hat with more flair than Art Rooney. Seldom did Dad buy a new one and almost never did he have his old one cleaned and blocked. The well-worn gray fedora he favored resembled a John Wayne hat with its wide turned-up brim. He wore it at a bit of a rakish angle. In spite of his efforts to keep from calling attention to himself, the cigars, his suits, and the big dark overcoat he wore all marked him as a character. In his seventies he began wearing a sport jacket, slacks, and a raincoat.

Kass tried to dress well but modestly. Her good friend Ruth Jaffe steered her to the most fashionable women's clothing stores in Squirrel Hill and Shadyside, and AJR gave her money to spend. She had a dignified figure which she chose not to show off. Once when she and my wife Kay were going to a formal dinner party, both in low-cut evening gowns, Kass stood in front of a mirror and pulled at the upper part of her dress to cover the cleavage. She sighed and said to Kay, "God! I look like a whore."

Kay thought that was hilarious. Actually, their dresses were demure for the styles of the late 1970s.

Aunt Alice inherited her sister's old clothes, which were never very old, and so she, too, was always well dressed.

I was with Mom one time when she took Dad to Larrimor's, a fancy clothing store Downtown, to buy him an overcoat as a gift of some kind. Mr. Schlesinger, the manager, brought out the best coats he had — cashmere ... wool ... cashmere *and* wool. AJR selected one that he liked and asked Mr. Schlesinger, "How much?"

"Three hundred and fifty dollars" was the answer.

AJR said, "We're looking for an overcoat, not a used car." My father was anything but a clothes horse.

Mom often dressed us kids in football shirts and slacks. We were dressed this way one night to have dinner with Mom and Dad at Poli's Restaurant in Squirrel Hill. But Dad said, "Take those shirts off the kids. I don't want it to look like I'm advertising our business." Mom's feelings were hurt. She felt that she had dressed us in perfect good taste.

Because he spent so much time in automobiles, AJR's suits were always wrinkled. In the summer months he wore broadcloth dress shirts. From early fall until late spring he favored long-sleeved cashmere polo shirts or golf shirts. Such shirts are not meant to be worn with neckties, but for weddings and funerals AJR put on a necktie.

Black dress shoes, well worn but never down at the heels, completed his ensemble. He was punctual about replacing the heels, and he would reinforce the toes with metal plates. When he walked down the aisle in church, complained Kass, his shoes made an unholy noise.

Dad never wore trench coats. If you constantly smoked cigars, as he did, you were apt to burn a hole in a trench coat. Raincoats were more resistant to that sort of thing. His habit of leaving raincoats in restaurants was unbreakable, so whenever he bought a new one he kept an embossed plastic card with his name on it in one of the pockets.

Even in old age he walked with the bounce and swagger of an athlete. He walked each day for his health, conscious of the figure he cut, though ready at all times to deny it. As boastful as he was about his modesty, he knew he had style.

We knew he knew it, too, but we never said so. To the end we were mindful of the rule that he himself always lived by: "Don't kid the kidder."

Lighting Up

Dad, Milton Jaffe, Uncle Jim, and a lot of their friends smoked fine Cuban cigars. AJR would chew tobacco or just the end of his cigar. He would tear out a sheet from a newspaper or the Racing Form and toss it into a waste-paper basket in order to be able to spit.

He continued to chew right up to the end of his life, tapering off as he aged. The cigars, of course, had become his trademark. Cigarettes, he once told me, were for girls.

To get his cigars going, Dad used matches in preference to a lighter. He kept them in his home office, which also served as the downstairs sitting room. One day my brothers and I discovered these matches, with the predictable result that we somehow set the contents of the waste-paper basket on fire and might have easily burned down the house.

All over Dad's study there were humidors, filled for the most part with the best Cuban cigars. First he would smoke a Cuban cigar and then a Marsh Wheeling or a tobey from one of the old cigar makers still doing business in Pittsburgh or Philadelphia. He liked to chew and spit out the Cuban cigars and the tobeys. He said the Marsh Wheelings tasted good but were not satisfactory chewers.

Oddly, he was a bit of a pyromaniac. After removing the cellophane wrapper from a cigar, he would twist it up and set it ablaze. His fireplace would be an ash tray. When the flames rose high, he would remove the paper ring from his cigar and toss it into the inferno. If the fire got out of hand, Mom would come rushing in from the kitchen and put it out with a wet tea towel.

There were ash trays all over the den and all over Dad's office in the Roosevelt Hotel. Many of these receptacles were gifts — fine Waterford crystal ash trays from Ireland, ash trays he brought back from the Kentucky Derby (all told, he went to about fifty Kentucky Derbies), ash trays from the Shrine of St. Anne de Beaupre in Quebec.

On the shelves above his big reclining chair were humidors made of glass or expensive wood. Next to the chair, on the floor, was a brass spittoon. More than once, the spittoon caught fire. Mary Roseboro, our white-uniformed maid, would come into the den each morning with long rubber gloves on and take the ash-laden thing to the basement for a thorough cleaning. She would polish the brass until it looked like new — a labor of love, for Mary idolized AJR. Among ourselves we would say that no one could be paid enough for this kind of work.

People sent chocolate candy, as well as ash trays and humidors, to AJR. Wearing pajamas and his cashmere robe, with fleece-lined slippers on his feet and a cashmere blanket around his shoulders, he would settle himself into his reclining chair and reach for his cigars or a chocolate or the telephone, all conveniently placed on the table at his side. Finished with the cigar, he would go outdoors and toss away the stub. Cigar stubs were "dead Indians" in his lexicon. It never troubled him to be seen outdoors in his nightclothes. He would go for the paper dressed like that, or even just to catch a breath of air, lingering to talk if a neighbor passed by.

I never saw him work on his checkbook. Fran Fogarty, the football team's accountant, kept it in balance. The bills that came to the house were paid in cash — the old horse player's way.

AJR read the New York papers and the Pittsburgh papers, the Daily Racing Form, and the Morning Telegraph. He read magazines. And of course he read his prayer book, bound in red leather and dog-eared from constant use. He never read fiction or biography or history. If he wasn't reading he was talking on the telephone. If he wasn't on the telephone he was saying the rosary. He had glass rosary beads, gold rosary beads, wooden rosary beads, plastic rosary beads. He was a man who lived his religion

His humility, although he made a great display of it, was real. Even so, he enjoyed the celebrity that came to him after the Steelers' Super Bowl years. When he was going to be on television, we would gather in his den or in the kitchen if the show had been taped ahead of time. As soon as it began he would hold up his hand, which meant: "Silence." He was always a good performer on television, confident and unflappable. Never did I know him to make a fool of himself. There would be times when his role in a panel discussion or something like that seemed inconsequential. Hardly worth the bother, we would think, but it was not wise to say so. Always, we remembered the maxim he liked to repeat: "Don't kid the kidder." Because kidders are always thin-skinned, went the unspoken corollary.

Chapter 12

Papa Bear

The National Football League goes back to 1920, and if you start at the beginning you start with George Halas, the founding father.

At the University of Illinois, where he studied civil engineering, Halas had been an end on the football team and an outfielder on the baseball team. He was good enough at baseball to play for the New York Yankees in 1919, but the Yanks sent him down to the minors and from then on football came first. When A. E. Staley, a starch manufacturer from Decatur, Illinois, asked him to organize a company team in 1920, Halas got in touch with representatives of ten other independent teams in five states. They met in an automobile showroom in Canton, Ohio, and talked into existence the American Professional Football Association, forerunner of the NFL.

In 1921 the Decatur starch factory went out of business, so Halas moved the Staleys to Chicago, his home town, and renamed them the Bears. He owned the team, coached it, and for ten seasons played end. In his forty years as coach, the Bears won eight championships.

Halas was a tough-looking Czech, reputed to be close with a buck. AJR knew how to charm sportswriters; Halas did not. One columnist wrote that he possessed all the warmth of broken bones. It may be true that he was tight and it is certainly true that he was tough, but in my opinion, anyway, he kept a lot of people who were not super producers on the payroll, and I can personally vouch for his kindness and courtesy.

After our second or third Super Bowl, when I was the Steelers' personnel director, he invited my wife Kathleen and me to have dinner with him. Assuming he meant to include the rest of the family — AJR, Kass, Dan and his wife Pat, etc. — I volunteered to notify them. The invitation, he replied, was for Kay and me — no one else. The only others present were his daughter Virginia and his son-in-law, Ed McCaskey. At the end of the evening, he asked me to pull my chair closer to his. "Kathleen," he said, calling to my wife, "you come over here, too. I want you to hear this." He then turned to me. "Arthur," he said, "you have done the best job of scouting and putting together a great football team that I have seen." From there he proceeded to ask my advice on some personnel problems his team was having. Because my head was swimming, I don't think I answered him sensibly.

So much for mean old tough-guy George Halas.

AJR liked to tell about the time back in the early days of the NFL that he agreed to change the date and location of a game with the Bears as a way of doing Halas a favor.   The new site was to be a medium-sized midwestern city, and to sweeten the deal for AJR, Halas promised him five hundred dollars "off the top." Owing to bad weather, lack of interest, or both, the game drew a pitifully small crowd. The reaction of Halas, said AJR, was bitter disappointment. When they divided the meager box-office receipts, AJR put his share in a satchel and started out the door. At that point, it occurred to him that Halas had withheld the extra five hundred dollars, which would be the difference, as things turned out, between taking a loss on the game and breaking even. He stopped and asked where it was. Halas denied having made such a deal. AJR said, "You know that's a lie. Come on, George, come across with the dough."

Halas wasn't lying, he was stalling. He glared at AJR and said, "I'll fight you for the five hundred bucks."

AJR said, "George, I don't want to fight. I just want the money."

Grudgingly, Halas coughed it up. For the second time, AJR turned to leave, and for the second time he paused in the doorway.

"Thanks, George," he said, "but don't be so sure you'd have won that fight."

Considering the status of pro football and the cost-of-living index at the time, five hundred dollars was quite a substantial sum. In not too many years it would look like chicken feed. I was present one day in 1962 when AJR said to Halas, "George, I've had an offer to play a pre-season game in Europe, but we need an opponent. It's a big payday. Would you be interested?"

"No, Arthur," replied Halas, "and neither should you. You have a good ball club this year. Don't take a chance on messing it up with a trip like that. Something bad could happen."

These were the days before fast, reliable air travel. AJR had been ready to pack his bags. Halas talked him out of it. So there was no big payday, but the Steelers that year won nine of their fourteen games. Halas had been one hundred percent right.

He was "Papa Bear" by then, the league's presiding guru. At a meeting I attended, a resolution was passed to change the football used by the NFL. Halas spoke out against it, and everybody listened. He said that in the 1930s a sporting-goods salesman promoting a new ball gave the owners a demonstration. Placing it endwise between two lead pencils, he made the ball spin. He made it spin for several minutes, and the owners were impressed. "Let's adopt it," some of them said. A ball that would spin between lead pencils would make passing easier, which would open up the game and add to the excitement. But a few less impulsive voices were raised, Halas went on. "This ball looks good," one owner suggested, "but why don't we try it out in the exhibition games before we commit ourselves?"

"So we did," Halas said, "And nobody — not even the best passers — could get a good spiral on this ball that would spin between lead pencils."

Case closed.

Halas was such a presence in the NFL that as rival coaches would have it he intimidated the officials. Jack Butler, a great defensive back for the Steelers, believed that to be true. He told of watching a Chicago Bear put a flagrantly illegal block on Pittsburgh's Ernie Stautner, a Hall-of-Fame tackle who played in nine Pro Bowls, and of watching the official toss a flag. Out on the field at a dead run came Halas, screaming and waving his arms. There was no way, said Butler, that the official could pick up the flag, but he knew what to do. "He called the penalty on Stautner — unsportsmanlike conduct for causing the other player to throw the illegal block."

The advantage his reputation gave him was not lost on Halas. Don Joyce, a scout who had been a tackle for several NFL teams, told me that when he played for the Baltimore Colts he knocked a Chicago player flat one Sunday directly in front of Halas on the bench. Instantly, Halas was in his face, pounding on his shoulder pads and pulling at his shirt. To the Chicago fans it appeared that he was tongue-lashing Joyce for a needlessly vicious hit. Not so, Joyce said. "He was yelling, 'Joyce, I love you! You're the type of guy I want for the Bears! I'm going to make a trade for you!'"

There were those who found none of this amusing, who thought that Halas threw his weight around too freely. One man seemed bent on doing him serious harm. This was Mickey McBride, the owner of the Cleveland Browns and no stranger to violence. Before the Browns came into the league in 1950, McBride had been running the taxicab business in Cleveland. He took an immediate dislike to Halas, resentful of his high-handed ways.

"How can you put up with that guy?" he said to AJR, and in the next breath was telling him of a plan he intended to carry out.

"When a bully is pushing you around, you can't go after his working stiffs. You go after the main culprit," he said. In this case, the main culprit was Halas. A game was coming up between the Browns and the Bears in Chicago, and McBride had arranged to have a dozen or so members of the private army he deployed against union organizers — real thugs who specialized in breaking arms and jaws — planted behind the Chicago bench at ground level. At the first sign of rough play on the part of the Bears, McBride would give a signal and his goons would pour out of the stands. The police, McBride thought, would stop most of them short of the bench, but two or three would be able to reach Halas. "And they'll work him over good," McBride said.

It wasn't easy for AJR to convince his friend McBride that this type of activity had no place whatever in professional football.

Halas had a son named George Junior. Everybody knew him as Muggsy. During games, he sat on the Bears' bench, frequently jumping up to shout and swear at the officials and the players. Imitating his father, he carried on to such an extent that Halas at length banished him to the stands.

Muggsy was always in evidence at meetings of the scouting service called Blesto, an acronym for Bears-Lions-Eagles-Steelers Talent Organization. Once when a disagreement could not be quickly resolved, Muggsy wanted to end the meeting and re-convene the next morning and the others wanted to work things out before adjourning. Muggsy refused to give in, so Russ Thomas of the Detroit Lions suggested that we settle the matter by flipping a coin. Muggsy objected to that too, but was voted down. So Thomas went ahead and flipped a coin, and Muggsy put on a display of hand speed and throwing accuracy that astonished us. He snatched the coin out of the air and hurled it cleanly through a crack of no more than two or three inches between the slightly raised window and the window sill.

Halas Senior and AJR outlived all their contemporaries. At NFL meetings, they would take their meals together. Very often Ed McCaskey would join them. In the 1970s and '80s Ed became a great friend of the Rooney family. He would pal around with AJR at the meetings, joining him for breakfast and lunch and to smoke cigars.

When my mother passed away, Halas came to Pittsburgh to pay his respects. He'd had a hip replacement and was very feeble but stood at the side of the grave for the last rites of the church. Not long afterward, Halas himself was dead, and the entire Rooney family attended his funeral in Chicago.

Laundryman

When George Preston Marshall owned the Boston Redskins he hired a full-blooded Indian, Lone Star Dietz, as coach. On the first day of practice the players lined up for the team picture in war paint and feathered headdresses. If any Indians took offense, Lone Star Dietz was not among them.

Marshall brought showmanship into the NFL. Deciding that Boston wasn't ready for showmanship, he moved his team to Washington, D.C., where he owned a laundry business, and entertained the fans with halftime shows and a marching band. Slingin' Sammy Baugh, the pinpoint passer from Texas Christian University, was the Redskins' No. 1 draft choice that year — 1937 — and Marshall instructed him to appear at his introductory press conference with a cowboy hat on his head and high-heeled boots on his feet. Never having worn either, Baugh had to purchase those items before leaving Texas.

Even though Marshall came from Grafton, West Virginia, there was nothing of the hillbilly in his makeup. He was a tall, well-barbered, well-tailored, gray-haired man who carried himself with an air of authority — at times with an air of condescension — and whose gravelly speaking voice commanded instant attention. He was married to Corrine Griffith, a leading lady in the films. Once when AJR was their dinner guest, Mrs. Marshall objected to his cigar smoking and later accused him of spitting tobacco juice into her fish pond with fatal consequences to the fish. Actually, AJR had deposited both his cigar butts and expectorations in a much more convenient receptacle — the pots holding her plants.

Marshall had a friend who arranged for the team to be met by a brass band on its arrival in Washington from Boston. Corrine Griffith had objected to that, too, so Marshall buttonholed the fellow and told him to knock it off. Insulted, he brought his entire band to the Marshalls' hotel suite late that night and gave the persnickety Mrs. Marshall a serenade she did not greatly appreciate.

Marshall made every effort to please Corrine. To start with, he toned down his lifestyle. Where once he had been a ladies' man, he suddenly became monogamous. It may or may not have been Corinne who persuaded him that the Far West was a good place for his pre-season training camp. Whoever was responsible, it worked out rather well. The Redskins pitched camp in Washington – the state – but played two of their exhibition games in Los Angeles and made money. Remember, there were no NFL teams on the West Coast back then. At Corrine's invitation, her pal Fred Astaire met with the Washington players and showed them his regimen of exercises to prevent sprained ankles – something they could all tell their grandchildren.

Marshall was more than just a ringmaster. He suggested and lobbied for many important structural changes in the NFL. A set schedule, two divisions with a championship playoff, moving the goal posts to the goal line (when field-goal kicking exponentially improved, they were moved again to the rear of the end zone), a slimmed-down football to facilitate passing – all of these things were the Washington owner's ideas.

In Baugh's first season the Redskins won the Eastern Division title and the playoff for the league championship, defeating the Chicago Bears. Three years later the same teams met again in the playoff. During the regular season the Redskins had won a 7-3 game from the Bears, and when the Chicago players complained about the officiating, Marshall called them "front-runners," "quitters," and "crybabies." In the championship game, using the brand new T-formation installed by Clark Shaughnessy, the infuriated Bears made him eat his words. The final score – Bears 73, Redskins 0 – still looks like a misprint.

There was one more title game between the Bears and the Redskins – in 1942, with the country at war. On the blackboard in the Washington dressing room, Coach Ray Flaherty, who would be going into the Navy the following week, wrote "73-0" in large numerals. The Redskins responded with a 14-6 victory.

The Redskins won two more division titles for Marshall but lost to the Bears again and to the Cleveland Browns in the playoffs for the championship. In 1949 Marshall decided that his coach, Turk Edwards, was too indecisive. Declaring that the Redskins needed a forceful military leader, someone who had helped win the war, he transferred Edwards to the front office and hired a retired admiral, John Whelchel, to succeed him as coach. A former coach at the Naval Academy, Whelchel was a fish out of water in the NFL. One Redskin who played for him told me that in a game the team was losing by forty points at the start of the fourth quarter, Whelchel went to Sammy Baugh, who'd been benched, and said to him, "Sam, you better get back in there before this thing gets out of hand."

Whelchel walked off the practice field one day after Marshall started telling him how to coach. He was quitting, he said, but agreed to return for one last game. The Redskins won and carried Whelchel to the locker room on their shoulders.

Throughout the 1940s there were two George Marshalls in Washington. The owner of the Redskins insisted on being known as George *Preston* Marshall to distinguish himself from George Catlett Marshall, Army chief of staff during the war and afterwards secretary of state. The story is often told of the clash between George Preston Marshall and the War Department on Sunday, December 7, 1941. The Redskins were playing the Philadelphia Eagles at Griffith Stadium in Washington – named for Clark Griffith, owner of the Washington baseball team, and not for Corrine – and AJR was in Marshall's box. A low-ranking Navy officer came in and said the Navy would like permission to make an announcement over the public-address system. Marshall refused, stating emphatically that *no one* could make an announcement over his system. The Navy man left, and Marshall said to AJR and the others that if you let one outfit in Washington get away with that kind of thing, then all the rest would be making demands. A few minutes later a much higher-ranking officer confronted him. He informed Marshall sternly that the Japanese had just bombed Pearl Harbor and that the public-address system would be commandeered in the interest of national defense. "There will be no discussion about this," he said. Then came a series of announcements – first, that all Navy personnel would immediately report to their bases; next, that all *military* personnel would report; then all State Department and embassy people, and so on and so on.

I don't believe Marshall was a racist, but he had put together a radio network that broadcast his team's games in the Deep South, and clearly for that reason he was slow to allow the signing of black players. At last the pressure of public opinion in the North compelled him to draft one — halfback Ernie Davis, the Heisman Trophy winner from Syracuse. He immediately traded Davis to the Cleveland Browns for another black player, Bobby Mitchell, an all-pro running back and receiver. Bobby told me that he was seated next to Marshall at a banquet one night when the band started playing "Dixie." Marshall nudged him, he said with a smile, and whispered, "Sing, Bobby, sing." Just to humor Marshall, Bobby lip-synched the words.

In the Redskins' front office, Marshall installed an antique wooden Indian. It remained there for years and years. At last the office staff complained that it was gathering dust and taking up space. Declaring the thing had "sentimental value" for him, Marshall "bought" it from the ball club at a bargain-basement price and moved it into his own private office. Some time later, in need of walking-around money, he had a friendly antique dealer over-appraise the Indian and sold it back to the team for much more money than it was worth. According to his lawyer, Leo DeOrsey, this got to be a routine.

A misunderstanding occurred once between Marshall and AJR over the railroad fare of a player who'd been traded from the Redskins to the Steelers. They were arguing back and forth on the telephone over fifty dollars at the most, although neither would think twice about handing out a tip for that amount. Marshall kept repeating, "Arthur, send me the dough." Finally AJR said he would do just that, whereupon Marshall hung up, feeling triumphant. As good as his word, AJR dispatched Fran Fogarty, the Steelers' accountant, to the Ritz Bakery with an order for fifty individual pieces of raw dough. Fogarty had them wrapped in gold foil and sent to Mr. Marshall in Washington.

In all the years that he knew Fogarty, and conferred with him on business matters, Marshall never learned to pronounce his name. "He'd call me Mr. Flaherty ... Mr. Flogarty ... Mr. Foglerty ... everything but Fogarty," Fran said, and he didn't exaggerate. I was with my father in the lobby of the Hotel Drake in New York one time when Marshall walked over to us and said, "Arthur, you have a good man in that Fran Flaherty."

Marshall behaved more like royalty than like a simple laundryman from Grafton, West Virginia. I saw him once at a morning NFL meeting in a silk robe or dressing gown, a pair of silk pajamas, and bedroom slippers. At other times he would wear a suit with his pajama shirt underneath. Once in the dining room of the Kenilworth Hotel in Florida, he spoke to a man whose face was familiar. "Aren't you a doctor?" Marshall asked. The man said he was, adding that they had recently met. Marshall then remarked that he was feeling a bit rundown. "Be a good fellow," he said to the M.D., "and have your nurse send a large bottle of Vitamin B-12 to my room." To my astonishment, the doctor agreed.

As the years went by, Marshall's health began to fail, and he wasted away before our eyes. I attended a scrimmage one day at Dickinson College, in Carlisle, Pennsylvania, where the Redskins trained. It was well under way when a large black limo pulled up to the edge of the field: Marshall and his entourage. He emerged from the car and waved to the spectators. Then he got back in, watched for a while, and left. Just an appearance. No doubt it took every bit of his waning strength.

At the next NFL meeting he walked into a conference, very muddled. He would stand up, say something eloquent, maybe even powerful, and then almost fall back into his seat. He was resilient, though. That winter at a meeting in New York City, my brother Tim and I saw him getting onto the elevator in the hotel. With him, on each arm, was a tall, lovely, well-dressed showgirl; they were young enough to be his granddaughters. As the elevator door closed, Marshall had a grin on his face.

His marriage to Corrine Griffith had ended some time earlier, so he was now a free agent where the ladies were concerned and attempting to be as flamboyant as ever. That same year during the football season, Tim and I left the press box in RFK Stadium, where the Redskins were playing the Steelers, to get a hot dog. An elevator door close to where we were standing slid open and there in a wheelchair, with a blanket over his knees, was Mr. Marshall, now a true invalid. Tim looked at me; I looked at him. Tim then put into words what I was thinking. He said, "Those two showgirls in New York last winter were too much for the old guy."

Marshall owned a house in Miami, where the NFL's next meeting took place, and all of his old friends, advised to do so by Commissioner Pete Rozelle, went to see him. In effect, they were saying good-bye. One of the other old-timers told AJR that George would much prefer to be caught in bed with a beautiful woman and shot in the head by her irate husband than wither away as he did. Perhaps so.

Blueblood

AJR liked to say that Bert Bell was a blueblood. He said it with facetious intent, but Bert actually did come from an old French family of aristocratic origins. His middle name, in fact, was Bienville. The Bienville-Bells had money, lived on Philadelphia's Main Line, and saw to it that Bert received a good education.

But if Bert was a blueblood, he never acted like one. Far from conforming to any High Society model, he resembled AJR in his personality and outlook on life. There were people who thought the two partners were relatives, or came from the same neighborhood. Both were open and accessible. Both wore old, rumpled, dark-colored suits and wide-brimmed fedoras. Both had a passion for football and the NFL. More truly than George Halas, George Preston Marshall, or the Maras — Tim and his two sons, Jack and Wellington — Bert was a Damon Runyon type.

He smoked cigarettes and had a loud, gravelly voice. When he co-owned the Steelers with AJR and Barney McGinley, he slept on a cot in the office he shared with Jake Mintz, the Rooney-McGinley Boxing Club's matchmaker. Given the opportunity, he would never stop talking football. I remember a time in a New York restaurant when Bert talked football through dinner, dessert, and coffee, and then on into the night, with the waiters, bartenders, and busboys all listening.

By the 1940s, Bert's family was no longer rich, and Bert himself, by living beyond his means, had run short of cash. His wife, the former Frances Upton, had been a Ziegfeld Follies girl. "Why fool around with a broken-down jock?" her show-business friends wanted to know. "You can do a lot better than that," they advised her. Hollywood beckoned, and Frances signed a movie contract for one thousand dollars a week, but soon she was back in New York, unsuited by her Catholic upbringing for the free-and- easy ways of Tinseltown. (The sexual mores of Broadway must have seemed puritanical out there.) Hurrying home, she married Bert, converted him to her faith, and became the mother of three fine kids.

AJR told a story that illustrates the influence of his conversion on Bert. An NFL meeting ran late, so Bert sent out for sandwiches. It was discovered when the time came to eat them that the only kind he had ordered was cheese. "Why aren't there any meat sandwiches?" demanded George Preston Marshall. "George," Bert reminded him, "it's Friday." For Catholics back then, Friday was a day of abstinence. "Do you think the whole world is Catholic?" roared Marshall. "Get some meat sandwiches in here!"

When Elmer Layden's contract as NFL commissioner expired in 1946, AJR and other insiders campaigned successfully for Bert to succeed him. Bert, AJR, and Barney McGinley had been equal partners in the ownership of the Steelers. A realignment now took place. Bert sold his stock to AJR, making him once again the team's majority owner. In the long run, this move had tremendous financial importance for the Rooney family. In 1946, the franchise was not worth a great deal, but its value increased significantly over the years. I hope the transfer of stock was put through with Barney McGinley's agreement and understanding.

As one of the owners, Bert had been frugal to a fault. He kept a sharp eye on expenditures, even making sure that nobody wasted any postage stamps. In Hershey, where the team had its pre-season training camp, he would stand at the head of the cafeteria line and take food off the players' trays, saying, "You are now on a diet." He slept, as I have said, in his office, on a cot. Joe Carr, the ticket manager, claimed that Bert would have the cot brought out on his visits to Pittsburgh as commissioner.

The commissioner's job was one that he took with the utmost seriousness and sense of responsibility. On the eve of the 1946 championship game in New York between the Bears and the Giants, there were rumors of a fix. Supposedly Frank Filchock and Merle Hapes of the Giants were involved. Jack Sell, who covered the Steelers for the *Pittsburgh Post-Gazette*, told me that he and some others had been out to dinner with AJR the night before the game and found Bert Bell in AJR's suite when they returned to the hotel. "He was in a terrible state," Sell said. "He told Art there'd be hell to pay, and that the scandal would ruin the NFL." AJR remained calm, Sell said, assuring Bert that "everything would be OK."

The investigation that was going on cleared Filchock, but not Hapes. For failing to report a contact by gamblers, the NFL suspended him. Filchock played against the Bears, and played well, but Chicago won, 24-14.

Bert went through another stressful period during the war between the NFL and the upstart All-America Football Conference. Attempting to outbid the rival league for players, almost every NFL team lost money. When peace came in 1950, the NFL assimilated the Cleveland Browns, the San Francisco Forty-Niners, and the Baltimore Colts of the AAFC. At the end of the season the Baltimore team, insolvent, gave up its franchise, but Bell, in a speech to the city's Advertising Club, said he would keep the Colts in the league if the fans would buy fifteen thousand season tickets and a new owner turned up.

The fifteen thousand tickets were sold within six weeks, and Bert himself hand-picked the new owner — Carroll Rosenbloom, a business executive from Philadelphia. Bert had coached him at Penn, and now they were personal friends. While he was at it, Bert selected a general manager for the Colts, Donald Kellett, and a head coach, Keith Molesworth.

As part of the deal, the understanding was that Bert would become a minority owner of the Colts when he retired as commissioner. It never happened. In 1959, still the commissioner, Bert died of a heart attack at a game in Philadelphia between the Eagles and the Steelers. He was 64.

Some time before that, he did get jobs with the Colts for his sons, Bert Junior and Upton. After Bert Senior's death, they remained with the team until 1969 or 1970, when Bert Junior left to work for a gambling casino in Atlantic City and Upton became general manager of the New England Patriots. Quickly let go, he went into radio as the host of a long-running sports talk show in Boston.

I once addressed Upton by his baptismal name, George. "Hey, Art," he said, "don't call me by that fruity name — call me by my real name, Upton." So from then on, Upton it was.

With Bert gone, AJR and some of the other old-timers made sure that Frances, the widow, and Janie, her daughter, were well taken care of. It was only proper. These were the days before pensions and bonuses, and Bert Bell had been as instrumental as anyone in keeping the NFL afloat through the war-time years and the years of competition with the AAFC. Pete Rozelle, the commissioner who followed him, gets all the credit for the television policy that has meant so much to the NFL, but Bert played a part in the early negotiations.

Jane Bell, by the way, went into the television business and became a successful producer.

Chapter 13

Lessons in Living

Mom and Dad sent all five of their sons to grade school in Oakland, at Mount Mercy Academy. It was part of Mom's plan to control our environment — Mount Mercy during the school year and Ligonier in the summer. But we were still North Side kids and could not avoid picking up some street smarts.

Our instructions from AJR were: travel in groups; keep moving; don't speak to strangers; don't act like big shots; don't attract attention. Even though there were close calls, we survived.

Walking across the Manchester Bridge from Downtown one day, I was with friends of my own age — 10 or 11. We encountered two roughnecks of 14 or so. They grabbed one of our smaller kids and, each holding a leg, dangled him from the bridge above the river. The rest of us ran. We could hear the big guys laughing and the friend we abandoned screaming bloody murder. None of us tried to help. We were anything but heroes. I ran to the end of the bridge and jumped over the railing onto a huge pile of loose, ground-up coal. There I felt safe; what I never gave a thought to was the possibility of starting a slide. I could have been suffocated.

We took the streetcar to and from school. Streetcars all over town were operated by old men. North Side kids would climb up in back of the car and ride hanging on. There were special cars for the North Catholic High School kids, who would crowd them to capacity and make the car sway by shifting their weight. Fearful it would overturn, the operator would often jump off. In response to threats from the traction company — "We'll cut off service to North Catholic" — the Marianist Brothers had to keep the kids from getting on in packs.

During World War II the site later occupied by Three Rivers Stadium was a junk yard. There were huge piles of scrap iron and slag and other raw materials and, most impressive to us kids, dozens of captured German tanks, delivered by rail and by barge. From time to time some friend of ours would find a German helmet or a Luger gun in all the debris. The scavengers included grown-ups as well. One man, I remember, gave a beautiful German pistol in a black leather holster to AJR, who let us handle it briefly before he put it away. A nice souvenir, he said, but too dangerous for kids; there were bullets that came with it. He presented the gun later to a policeman he knew.

For protection from burglars, AJR kept a snub-nosed revolver in the house. One day we found it, hidden in his underwear drawer. In another drawer we came across the bullets. We took the bullets, but not the gun, to Mount Mercy. The nuns had a fit, and at home we got a lecture we did not soon forget.

AJR believed in corporal punishment but could terrorize you just as easily with a yell or even a look. He could be very sarcastic — make you feel like a dog. Kass, for the most part, kept him in check. She never laid a hand on us herself. One day our youngest, John the twin, sneaked off to the junk pile with a kid called Johnny Blue Coat because his family was so poor he wore the same old blue rag of a coat until it seemed to be nothing but tatters. How the two of them ever made it through security John didn't say. At any rate a patrol car came along and the cops saw them wandering close to the river bank. It was spring, and the water was rising dangerously. The escapade earned John a beating from Dad. I never knew what happened to Johnny Blue Coat.

When I was seven or eight years old I wrote my name in red fingernail polish on the door of a car that belonged to a neighbor. That night he paid us a visit. The evidence against me was still on the car door — a big red ART. Frightened, I told a lie. I said that I had written the "A" but that other kids had added the "R" and the "T." I said they had egged me on; that much, at least, was the truth. AJR must have seen I was scared stiff — he let me off with nothing more than a reprimand. Just his disapproval was so intimidating I never again defaced anyone's property. Looking back, I wish I'd been brave enough to confess that I deserved all the blame.

After finishing five grades at Mount Mercy, all of us attended St. Peter's. We went back and forth on foot, and AJR was adamant about the route he wanted us to take. We liked to cross Western Avenue at the bridge over the main line of the Pennsylvania Railroad near a sharp curve where traffic came through very fast. AJR insisted that we walk up to Sherman Avenue and cross at the light. To see that we obeyed orders, he would follow us. I was never afraid to cross the street at the bridge but always afraid to cross Dad.

When he was with us we watched our manners. Once I was sent from the dinner table for burping. This happened also to my brothers. In restaurants he was especially vigilant. One time all of us made a dive for the bread and the French fries. We had to put everything back and start over, taking turns.

I never heard him tell a lie or repeat an off-color story. Girl talk was taboo. His one-time business partner, Milton Jaffe, had a brother named George who owned and operated the Casino burlesque house on Diamond Street, later Forbes Avenue, Downtown. This place of course was off-limits to all five of us, but I went there once to pick up a package. While I was waiting in the lobby I peeked at the dancers on the stage. Nothing too evil seemed to be going on. In fact, the girls were no more scantily clad than the Wild West floozies in the cowboy pictures at the Barry Theater a few blocks away. I was maybe 12 years old. My curiosity satisfied, I never went back.

Dad, Mom, and the Sisters of Mercy warned us to stay away from the Art Cinema, which specialized in "dirty movies" — actually foreign films and "art" films. I remember going there once with Uncle Jim to fetch a pal of his called "Fish," who was standing at the box office, talking with the ticket seller. Neither Jim nor Fish seemed to think of this place as a den of iniquity, but Jim used to tell us that pornography softened the brain.

"Dirty" magazines, he said, were for old men like Pop Rooney's friend, Mr. Curley. Just why he singled out Mr. Curley I never knew. Mr. Curley would come to the Steelers' training camp for a week, and all he ever did was take walks, eat in the dining hall with the players, and go to Mass. My belief is that Mr. Curley got a bum rap from Jim.

The twins, Pat and John, said they "ducked" into the Art Cinema once and were terribly embarrassed when the father of a schoolmate spotted them. Later they began to wonder what *he* was doing there and realized that his embarrassment must have exceeded their own.

At home we said the rosary together every night. Daily Mass was not uncommon. You got there early and stayed until it was over. AJR always sat in the same place at St. Peter's — on the left side not far from the altar. We went to novenas all over Pittsburgh. Our favorite was at a church in the Lower Hill called St. Benedict the Moor. If AJR was out of town, Kass and Aunt Alice would take us. I remember a big fat Italian guy who sang all the hymns off-key: "Tantum Ergo," "Holy God, We Praise Thy Name," "Oh, Blessed Mother Mary ..." He was always there and he knew every word.

Farther up the Hill was a small church presided over by Father Charles Owen Rice, who lived to be well past 90. Uncle Jim called him a Commie. Dad would just say he was "different." Father Jim Campbell, AJR's dear friend, liked Father Rice, which was good enough for Dad. Father Rice was Irish, a fine speaker and writer, a man of great spunk and learning. He was known as "the labor priest" for his activity on behalf of the steelworkers' union. But AJR said he was "different." The other priests would play cards with Dad; Father Rice never did. A priest named Francis Rooney — no relation — let me see a letter Dad wrote in which he said that priests were his heroes. The ones he brought home were OK with Kass, but she admitted they made her ass tired, as she put it — always around to be waited on.

AJR's hatred of coarse language was amusing to Kass. She'd tell him he wouldn't say "shit" if he fell in it. Kass always had a putdown for AJR. Once when her gaze lingered on him reprovingly for some reason, he asked what she was looking at. "Can't a cat look at a king?" she replied. Another time he complained that she was using the tea bags only once. "What do you want me to do?" she demanded. "Dry them and use them for snuff?" Kass was more than a match for the Chief ... unlike her sons.

The Great White Way

The big respectable movie palaces Downtown were Loew's Penn (later Heinz Hall), the Stanley Warner (later the Benedum Center), the Harris, and the Fulton. All had large seating capacities and all were grand places to see a film.

During World War II and shortly afterward there was money around, and for movies like "Red River," starring John Wayne, the theaters would be packed. I heard one old film distributor say that if you opened a can of sardines, a line to see you do it would form.

Actually, the entertainment was much better than that. Along with the movie, you could take in a vaudeville show. I remember that the non-talking Marx brother, Harpo, did a solo act before a Tarzan picture at the Stanley one week. When the movie came on, Harpo returned to the stage with a spear and used it to stick Johnny Weissmuller's pet elephant in the bum (our word back then for posteriors.)

The Barry, "catty-corner" from the Stanley on Sixth Street, had the class B action movies we liked. In a psychology course I took at St. Vincent, we were taught that you could tell something about children and adolescents by the way they reacted to the characters in movies. If they identified with the good guys, that was salutary. If they identified with the bad guys, it was cause for concern.

The Washington lawyer Edward Bennett Williams had a problem son who worked for AJR at the Shamrock Farm in Maryland one summer. Dad thought the kid was pretty normal until they spent an evening together watching television. He said the kid not only cheered for the bad guys all the time but also got violent about it. At least the Rooney brothers always cheered for the good guys.

We had a kid in our neighborhood who made the Williams kid look like an altar boy. Father Flanagan of Boys Town said there was no such thing as a bad boy, but he never met Skippy Guzik. Skippy always, I mean always, identified with the bad guy, and he laced his conversation with the foulest obscenities. One day when Tim and I were with him, Skippy made a crack about Mom. We jumped him right away, and though he got in some good licks, we fought clean. We would fight for a while, take a rest, and start in again. During one of the rest periods, Skippy pretended to drop some papers on the ground. He casually bent over to pick them up and instead grabbed a rock, which he threw in our general direction. It missed us both, and from then on Tim forgot about fighting clean. A good-sized branch from a tree — a branch the size of a club — was lying within reach. Tim armed himself with it and chased Skippy Guzik from one end of North Lincoln Avenue to the other.

Tim never fought clean again in his life, I don't think.

As for Skippy, he ended up doing time for rape and armed robbery. Detective Jack Stack described him as one of the worst kids who ever came out of the North Side or anywhere in Pittsburgh. After serving his sentence, he joined the American Nazi Party, got into another scrape, and went back to jail.

Oh, yes ... that business of dropping the papers on the ground and picking up a rock was something he learned from an old Boston Blackie movie.

We called the movies "the show," as in "Mom, can we go to the show?" And most of the shows we went to were the ones on the North Side. The two best were the Kenyon, on Federal Street, and the Garden, across West Park on North Avenue. The upper part of Federal Street was full of bars, drunks, panhandlers, and perverts, but there were always big crowds at the movies, the entertainment of the masses.

At St. Peter's Church, we had to take a pledge that we would not go to movies that were blacklisted by the Catholic Legion of Decency. I think for Irish Catholics the only real sins were sins of the flesh. If you avoided booze and sex, you'd go to heaven. On Federal Street, there was plenty of booze, and on the screen at the Kenyon and Garden no shortage of sex.

I remember how the nuns at St. Peter's warned us against movies like "Forever Amber" and "The Outlaw." Years later I saw "The Outlaw" on television; it was tame in comparison to the films of the '70s, the '80s, and the '90s. Nowadays, in fact, the television commercials are more explicit than the worst of those wartime movies.

(Speaking of "The Outlaw," condemned by the Legion of Decency because Jane Russell's cleavage was deemed an occasion of sin, I met her husband, Bob Waterfield, Hall-of-Fame quarterback for the Los Angeles Rams, on a scouting trip. He was quiet and polite. Scouting friends who met the seductive Miss Russell reported her to be a very nice lady involved in church and charity work.)

The Kenyon was the place where Chris McCormick, who weighed 350 pounds, had two seats in back remodeled into one seat. He paid for the carpenter work himself, and this giant single seat was reserved for McCormick alone.

On Friday nights the Kenyon would have a double feature for kids — a cowboy or war movie and maybe a Tarzan movie or a movie starring a dog. There would also be trailers (previews), a newsreel, and a cartoon or two. An off-duty cop would be present to keep order. Management needed extra help because some of the eighth-grade kids from St. Peter's or the public schools would be too much for the ushers to handle. My eighth-grade classmate Charley Pruett sat next to a man who put a hand on his leg one night. Charley was big for his age. He threw the guy into the aisle and gave him a pretty good thrashing. When he was finished, he took hold of the pervert by one foot and dragged him up the aisle to the lobby. "This queer," he said to the manager, "attacked me." The manager must have wondered just who had done the attacking.

The Garden, although not as upscale as the Kenyon, had an orchestra pit and vaudeville acts. In time it became a venue for Triple X-rated movies — the kind that could not have been even imagined by the nuns at St. Peter's who worried about Jane Russell's cleavage.

Seamy Side

There were two other movie houses in our neighborhood — the William Penn and the Novelty. The William Penn, a theater that belonged to the Harris family, who were pioneer motion-picture exhibitors, was on Federal Street near the Allegheny River. The William Penn was not the "dive" the Novelty was, but the admission price was the same — ten cents. Both places had third- and fourth-run films. For your dime you could see a double feature, a short subject, two cartoons, a newsreel, and lots of previews. And the Novelty would throw in a candy bar now and then.

When you went to the William Penn or the Novelty you descended to the lower end of the social ladder. Couples came in to make out, drunks to sleep off hangovers, and of course there was always a sprinkling of perverts in the crowd. Rats would be crawling underfoot, nibbling at spilled potato chips. Lice would get into your clothes and ringworm onto your scalp.

Bald-headed men were targets for smart-aleck kids like Jimmy Scanlon. Jimmy's game was to creep up behind a bald guy and slap him on top of the head. He had another favorite trick — blowing air into a paper bag and then slamming his fist into it, which created a loud bang. Once when he exploded a paper bag around the time that the war ended a man in the row ahead of him jumped up screaming. "I just got out of combat! Knock that shit off!"

Sometimes, instead of going to the rest rooms the kids would pee on the floor. As a result, both theaters smelled like a urinal. The movies were pure escape stuff, but the live, unrehearsed floor show was better entertainment if you were looking for certain kinds of realism.

AJR made sure by bringing us up in that environment that his kids saw the seamy side of Pittsburgh and did not enter adulthood with fancy ideas. Too busy becoming or being Art Rooney, he was never around much himself. He was lucky to have a wife like Kass, who was lucky to have a sister like Alice McNulty. Kass and Aunt Alice lived their lives for us kids. In turn, they were lucky to have the Mercy nuns at St. Peter's School teaching us values, because the North Side was the Barbary Coast.

When he was not out of town, AJR would usually be attending a sports event somewhere, most often a Pirate game at Forbes Field. Often he took us with him to these events. He sponsored a sandlot baseball team and a sandlot football team. He called the football team the Rooney Ninety-Eights in recognition of the fact that 98 was the number on every uniform. All the kids wanted to wear it because Don Hutson of the Green Bay Packers wore that number, and Hutson was the greatest pass catcher in football. The team bus was an old pickup truck or dump truck supplied by one of AJR's friends in the construction business.

The Rooney kids traveled to events at Forbes Field or Pitt Stadium or Duquesne Gardens in a broken-down station wagon, hauling as many of their friends as the back seat would accommodate. It had a door that would not stay closed unless we sealed it with heavy-duty tape. My brother Dan, who had just turned 16, did the driving. On the way home from Oakland he'd take a shortcut past Pitt Stadium and up Herron Hill, and one day AJR was with us. When we came to the steepest part of the grade, Dan pulled into a driveway, backed out onto the street, and proceeded up the hill in reverse. AJR thought he had gone nuts. "What are you doing?" he shouted. Patiently, Dan explained that the station wagon was so feeble and worn out it could not get to the top in forward gear.

At least we had wheels, which was more than our North Side pals ever did. Because of sports, our home life, and the family rosary, we came out of the North Side undamaged. Except for Father Silas, AJR's brothers were not so fortunate.

Rough and Tumble

The multimillionaires who lived on the North Side in the nineteenth century left one enduring legacy — the parks. These industrial barons wanted fresh milk and cream on their tables and had set aside acres and acres of grazing land for their cattle. It survived in the form of a park system ringed by stately old mansions that did not fall to the wreckers' ball until the 1950s.

The East Park swimming pool was adjacent to a bath house where the First Ward and Federal Street poor — strangers to indoor plumbing — could shower for five cents. When black kids started using the pool, the whites of the neighborhood took to calling it the Ink Well.

In the age-old tradition of Irish Catholic prudery, I thought it was something scandalous that mothers nursed their babies on the park benches. AJR viewed the parks as gathering places for bums, perverts, and Communists, but stopped short of declaring them off-limits.

By edict of the Parks Department, the grass was off-limits. That did not deter us from playing pickup football and softball games until the park police came by in their squad cars. Then we'd scatter, heading for home through the alleys and hidden walkways we knew. The cops were simply doing their job but did not get much sympathy from the residents of the neighborhood, whose attitude was: Let the kids play; it keeps them out of trouble.

One of the bigger kids in the neighborhood was Varney, nicknamed "Flat Foot Floogie" because of his slow, awkward gait. The cops had an easy time running him down, and then he would squeal on the rest of us. Once as my brothers and I were congratulating ourselves on getting home free, the cops pulled up behind us with Varney in the back seat. AJR came out of the house and conferred with them. They immediately turned Varney loose, and that was the end of it.

In West Park, up past the bronze deer and the railroad footbridge, we could play football or a game we called "rough and tumble" on a field that was all coal cinders — soft soot, actually, deposited there by the trains. "Rough and tumble" had other names, such as "fumbles." It was played like this: to start with, somebody tossed a football into the air, and the kids all jumped for it. The one who came down with the ball would run for his life through the soot. None of us wore football equipment except for an occasional pair of shoulder pads or hip pads or cleated shoes with high tops. There was fierce competition for the ball — and the privilege of being thoroughly mauled — and no interference from the cops.

I think I have said before that the Pennsylvania Railroad cut a huge path through these parks. In the early 1900s, business took precedence over ecology, and the Pennsylvania Railroad was the big boy of Pennsylvania politics. I have heard it argued that the laying of the tracks through the park system was the first nail in the coffin of Allegheny City, as the North Side was called until about 1908.

During World War II the Signal Corps took over West Park as a training ground for its short-wave radio operators. You would see them moving around with their hand-cranked generators — exciting stuff for the neighborhood kids. And then one day the trainees disappeared, all reassigned to regular Army camps.

Over by man-made Lake Elizabeth, there were wonderful old monuments dating back to the Civil War. They fell into disrepair and began to crumble. Next, the kids started climbing all over them. An arm from a statue would come off, and then a nose or an ear. When the neighborhood's racial makeup changed in the late 1950s the statues were deliberately vandalized. Beheadings would leave only the trunk and the legs and finally just the feet, immovably cemented to the base. Thus did ancient Rome fall to the barbarian tribes.

Through the years of deterioration, AJR and Kass remained steadfast North Siders. They were there to stay. For Kass, 940 North Lincoln Avenue had become a beautiful cage.

If the area we played in was a soot field, the swimming pool was even worse. In the old days, when Allegheny City was an independent municipality, there were swans and ducks on Lake Elizabeth, small wooded islands in the middle, and a boat house on the shore. By the 1940s the trees and bushes and flower beds were gone and the lake was a vast swimming pool, thickly coated with railroad soot. The Rooney kids never swam there. We had the pool at the Wildwood Golf Club and later a pool near the cottage in Ligonier. Away from the North Side, we were not apt to get polio. Money may not be everything, but it comes in handy at times.

I remember an aluminum collection for the war effort. After V-J Day, much of it went into the lake. Filled with old pots and pans and other kinds of junk and topped off with soil, the lake was now a playground on which football games were allowed. Almost always, they ended up in fights. As the years went by, it got worse: big kids crowded out little kids; teen-agers crowded out the big kids; young adults crowded out the teen-agers. Once on Thanksgiving, the Parks Department sponsored a turkey chase. Instead of chasing the turkey, the kids staged a free-for-all, piling on top of one another, but at last Charley Pruett broke free from the mob. He snatched up the turkey by its neck and kept running, too fast to be caught.

In the 1950s the city fathers tried to restore these parks to their original grandeur. Although nothing could be done about the railroad, it no longer sprayed us with soot: diesel fuel had replaced coal. The lake was dug out and the islands reappeared, trees, bushes, and flowers included. Footbridges were built, ducks put back on the water. However, the area by now was 90 percent black, and quickly the ducks vanished. At least the blacks, if they were guilty, took the ducks home for a family feast. White vandals would have killed the ducks and left them to rot.

Pete Lybock

My mom was a very saintly woman. She went to Mass each day. She said a lot of rosaries. She made novenas. She visited shrines.

When she was peeved at Dad, however, or when she was aggravated, her language was hardly fit to repeat. She could swear, as I have said, like a trooper. In the years since she left us, I have come to believe that there are other saints in heaven who could swear up a blue streak too.

Once I heard Mom calling Dad "a cheap Pete Lybock bastard."

Dad was anything but cheap, but Mom had her own way of gauging such things. What I wondered about, though, was Pete Lybock. I'd never heard of Pete Lybock. Who could this Pete Lybock be?

I put the question to Aunt Alice.

Pete Lybock, she said, was a well-known North Side miser. He lived on Ohio Street, or maybe East Street, in the heavily German part of the North Side.   Wearing   ragged   second-hand clothes, he went around with his pushcart and picked up all kinds of junk — empty bottles and cans, small pieces of scrap iron, everything of any possible use. Junk dealers higher up on the economic ladder would buy this stuff, and he pinched every penny he got his hands on.

"When he opened his purse," Alice said, "the moths would fly out."

Pete lived alone, and he lived in squalor. As he aged and became more reclusive, the neighbors began to worry about him. It was feared that he would freeze to death in the wintertime, or that his gas stove would leak and asphyxiate him. Was he getting enough to eat? people asked.

Somebody must have notified the public health authorities. In any case, investigators came knocking at his door. Pete wanted nothing to do with them. As far as he was concerned, they were trespassers. When he put up a fight they overpowered him, forced their way in, and found hiding places all over the house where Pete had thousands of dollars stashed away. Acting on a tip, they dug up the back yard, where still more cash was buried in tin cans.

The authorities now faced the problem of what to do about Pete. Had he broken any laws? No — unless it's a crime to be distrustful of banks. Was he in need of supervision or help? It didn't appear so. For an old guy with no one to look after him, Pete was in pretty good physical condition. He fed and clothed himself, after a fashion. He wasn't harming anybody.

All that could be done was to take Pete's money, put it in a trust, and allow him to get on with his life.

He did not die for many more years. When the end came, the do-gooders returned. Again they found thousands of dollars hidden away. As before, they dug up the back yard and found buried treasure. Pete hadn't changed.

For a long time after the funeral, said Aunt Alice, the neighbors would come to Pete's back yard with their shovels, hoping to turn up an overlooked tin can or two. If anyone struck it rich, she didn't tell me.

None of Alice's nephews ever had seen the old junk dealer, but "cheap Pete Lybock bastard" was an epithet we never forgot. When my brother John was living near Philadelphia, he met a guy named Lybock at his golf course one day.

"You wouldn't be from Pittsburgh, would you?" asked John.

"No," the guy said, "but my family was."

"Did you have a relative named Pete?"

"Yes, a distant relative — a great-uncle. I didn't think anybody in Philadelphia would have known about old Pete," Lybock said. "I guess you're from Pittsburgh yourself — from the North Side of Pittsburgh."

"That's right, I'm from the North Side of Pittsburgh," answered John. "And in our family your Uncle Pete was a legend!"

Commies, Perverts, and Bums

Question: How do you get to the North Side?
Answer: Drink wine.

North Side jokes were common currency in the 1950s and '60s. Allegheny Center, the Allegheny County Community College, and Three Rivers Stadium rose up on the North Side in the 1970s, but winos still populated Federal Street. West Park got the overflow. In AJR's demonology a special place was reserved for the urban planners who laid out the parks — gathering places, AJR used to say, for "Communists, perverts, and bums."

I don't know about Communists, but there were perverts and bums to be found in the Garden Theater, which had made the overnight transition from family motion-picture house to den of iniquity, showing porn films seven days a week. Next door was the notorious Apache Grill. Over on Woods Run, a bar with the ironic misnomer Cuddles attracted under-age drinkers, my cousin John McNulty among them.

When Cousin John was 15 he showed up at Cuddles with a friend the same age. They had one fake I.D. card between them. First John and then his friend presented it to the bartender. "Hey, this is something!" the bartender said. "These two guys were born on the same day." And with the same name, he might have added, but didn't. Smiling, he took their orders — beer, I suppose — and set the glasses on the bar with a hearty "Drink up!"

Cuddles' best customer was the owner of the place, who passed out one night while tending bar. With no one tending the cash register, the patrons became his guests. They helped themselves to all the booze in the place, starting with the very best stuff. They broke into the food lockers and gorged themselves. Fights broke out over the choicest take-home items, the hams. When Mr. Cuddles came to, nothing was left.

Industrial Manchester, just down the hill from North Lincoln Avenue, was a neighborhood undergoing change — in other words, a slum. Over in the Woods Run section of the North Side, people were still using outdoor privies. Teen-age boys hung out on every corner, sitting on stoops, sitting on car fenders, sitting on mail boxes — and waiting for the next street fight to begin. The Work House — "Work House" being a nineteenth-century euphemism for slammer— overlooked the Ohio River. Jokesters like Baldy Regan and Mike Kearns said there were fewer crooks behind bars in the Work House than outside its doors walking the streets.

And it may have been literally true. So many murders took place in the vicinity of Cuddles that the cops finally shut the place down, describing it officially as a public nuisance.

After that, was the North Side a haven of peace and quiet? Not exactly. But AJR was determined never to leave. Nine forty North Lincoln remained a shining jewel in a dung heap.

Mrs. Kearns

Mike Kearns's mother was a fine-looking, dignified woman, fastidious in her choice of words. She referred to her son as "Michael," never Mike, and once in my hearing, when Mike and I were children, accused him of "playing truant." I had to ask what it meant.

As I have said, the three Kearnses — mother, son, and daughter — lived on Ridge Avenue in what once had been the billiard room of a decaying old mansion converted into a rooming house after the rich people who built it had moved away.

When Mike was eight months old, his father, looking for work, had gone by himself to Chicago and never returned. The mother, left on her own, struggled to make ends meet. Despite the elegance of her speech, Mrs. Kearns lacked a formal education and was forced to take the meanest of jobs. At home, she did the housework, easing the burden when possible in ways that were sometimes ingenious.

I am thinking in particular of her garbage-disposal system. For the upper-floor tenants especially, garbage disposal was a problem in these big old rooming houses because of the great distance between the apartments and the trash cans in the alley. So Mrs. Kearns would wrap her garbage in neat, attractive packages tied with a ribbon or a string and leave them on streetcars. Invariably, they were picked up by other passengers, carried home like discovered treasure, and opened with high expectations. This arrangement worked to perfection until a cop came knocking at the door to the

Kearnses' billiard-room abode. At the station house, Mike, who was 13 at the time, gallantly took the rap for his mom, claiming to have planted the packages, but there remained the little matter of a ten-dollar fine. Somehow, Mrs. Kearns was able to pay.

In her old age, Mrs. Kearns had a well-off friend — a Mrs. McCarthy. When they were both past 80, Mrs. McCarthy acquired a brand new set of upper front teeth. Mrs. Kearns wore false uppers too, but a welfare dentist had made and installed them. They looked bad and felt bad. Time went by, and Mrs. McCarthy died. The first to discover the body was Mrs. Kearns. Since the day Mrs. McCarthy obtained her new teeth, Mrs. Kearns had admired them. What could be the harm, she thought, in switching dentures with the corpse? Mrs. McCarthy, after all, would have no further use for those teeth. The thought was the mother to the deed.

It was Mike's daughter who noticed something different about Mrs. Kearns. "Daddy," she said to Mike, "Grandma's mouth looks all swollen." Ever the dutiful son, Mike checked it out. He said he knew at a glance what had happened.

"Mom," he told his mother, "if you did what I think you did, you should be ashamed of yourself. Furthermore, the teeth don't even fit."

Mrs. Kearns put Mike in his place. "You're talking to the one who changed your diapers," she said. "Anyway, I feel entitled to those teeth. Mrs. McCarthy would want me to have them."

Some years later, Mrs. Kearns passed on. At her wake, the funeral director took Mike aside and said, "We did our best to make your mother look good, but we had a lot of trouble with that upper plate. The dentist who made those teeth for her should be put in jail!"

Chapter 14

Betting Man

In my childhood, the scene at the Fort Pitt Hotel, where AJR ran his football, boxing, and race-track businesses from a ground-floor office, was always the same: guys at a table playing cards and guys just sitting around, all of them listening to somebody on the telephone, perhaps Uncle Red, call a horse race in progress at an out-of-the-state track. Racing in Pennsylvania had not yet been legalized.

There was nothing about racing that AJR didn't know. He knew the terminology, he knew how to bet, and he understood the nuances of the parimutuel system. Before there were parimutuels he had mastered the art of betting with bookmakers. He studied the Racing Form and the Morning Telegraph for countless hours in hotel rooms.

At the track he would bet from twenty dollars to fifty dollars a race, which he considered chicken feed. But if one of his horses or a good friend's horse was going to the post, and he liked the horse's chances, he would sometimes bet thousands on it to win.

There were times when he wanted to bet at the track and bet on the same race by telephone. Often the telephone — invariably a pay phone — would be two or three miles away and he would send Uncle Jim with a driver. In order to get there quickly, Jim would first make friends with the cops who patrolled the road.

Phones were very important to AJR and his people. He could not have them tied up. When his sons started using the phone, extended conversations were forbidden. "Go to a pay phone," he would order us if we talked too long. Once when he tried to call Mom, the line was busy. He tried again. Same result. So AJR had a telegram delivered to 940 North Lincoln Avenue, asking her to get off the line.

You could not call a bookmaker from a race track, or weren't supposed to. There were ways of getting calls out to horse rooms around the country, to be sure, but the tracks all did what they could to discourage this sort of thing. Calls from the track's business office were recorded. This was before the invention of the cell phone. John the twin told me that where cell phones are concerned the tracks have had to throw in the towel; there is no way to police them.

Always there were people who wanted to tap in on AJR's expertise. They would follow him around at the track, hoping to overhear a scrap of dialogue, or hoping to see him make a bet. They would follow his friends around. As a defense against eavesdroppers, AJR would separate himself from the people who were with him. Going to the track, they would be on the same bus or train, but never seated together. They took pains to avoid speaking with one another. Some would watch the races from the grandstand, others from the clubhouse. They might even be in different parts of the grandstand or clubhouse. There were prearranged signals to deliver information picked up from a trainer or some other source. Displaying a handkerchief, opening a newspaper, adjusting or removing a hat might mean: don't bet.

When he was plunging or taking advantage of a tip, AJR liked to bet at the last minute, so that the tote board would not reflect a suspiciously large amount of "smart money" showing up on a particular horse. For the man he entrusted to get the bet down, that could be nerve-wracking. As post time neared, the line at the ticket window might be long. It might be moving slowly because a timid or inexperienced bettor was suddenly gripped by indecision.

AJR, who had nerves of steel, could time the placing of a bet to perfection. He knew how to make himself invisible. And he was always very careful to maintain a good image at his work place — i.e., the race track.

'Is Mr. Goldfarb There?'

AJR's routine on visits to Monmouth Park was always the same:
Check in at the hotel, the Berkeley Carteret in Asbury Park.
Eat dinner.
Return to hotel room with Racing Form, Morning Telegraph, and one of the local newspapers.
Tear the local paper into small pieces and use them to cover the bottom of the waste basket.
Remove shirt.
Bite off a cigar end and chew it.
Study Monmouth Park entries for following day in Racing Form and Telegraph, meanwhile spitting cigar juice into waste basket.
Pick out four or five horses to bet on — a job that required hours of deep concentration — and circle their numbers heavily with a lead pencil the size of a cigar.
Go to bed.
Up and at 'em early enough for 5 a.m. arrival at track.
Clock the horses in their morning workouts.
Eat breakfast in track kitchen.
Return to hotel, stopping on the way to attend Mass.
Clean up and get dressed for the day.
Call Steeler office in Pittsburgh to stay abreast of what's going on.
Return to race track; eat lunch.
Talk with trainers, friends, and other horse people, absorbing information — information that might or might not affect the plan of action decided upon the previous night.

It would be post time by then — as freighted a moment, for AJR, as the kickoff at the start of any Steeler game. Over the next few hours, all of his expertise, all of his preparation, would come into play, with thousands of dollars at stake.

One night about forty-five minutes before AJR turned in, a loud, alcoholic party got under way in the room adjoining his at the Berkeley Carteret. AJR expected it to taper off, but the commotion only increased. There were probably no more than three to five men in the room, he judged, but they were making enough noise for a biker's convention, shouting and laughing uproariously. Occasionally a fight would break out; sounds of cursing and scuffling would come from the room. On one thing the men all agreed. They did not like Jews, and said so in voices that penetrated the walls.

At one o'clock, AJR called the front desk and asked the night manager to send the house detective to his floor. The noise next door continued without abatement.

At half past three — his wake-up call was at four — the party ended. Finally there was silence, but for AJR it had come too late to think of sleep. He got up and put on his clothes.

The revelers, he knew, had not left the room. In all probability, they were lying stupefied on the beds and the sofa. He began calling them on the phone. Every time someone answered, he would ask for "Mr. Goldfarb," or "Mr. Bernstein," or "Mr.Rosenberg." At last one of the drunks took the receiver off the hook. AJR turned on his radio and placed it right next to the door between the rooms. He had the volume as high as it would go. With the radio blaring, he pounded on the door for several minutes.

It was time to leave for the track now, and he pounded on the door in the hallway. Whoever opened it would be greeted with his best right hook. No one did. At the front desk, he spoke to the manager, who said he was sorry the house detective's threats had gone unheeded; both he and the detective had assumed there would be no further trouble. He would not charge AJR for his room. AJR walked away from him. Before going out to his car, he gave the switchboard girl ten dollars and instructed her to call the bums who'd been making all the racket every fifteen minutes. She should ask for Mr. Cohen or Mr. Levine or Mr. Silverman.

When he was back from the race track, he stopped at the switchboard again. What effect had the calls had? he asked the operator. Enough, after an hour or so, to get the phone off the hook, she said. AJR went up to his room, stopping in the corridor to pound on the door to the room where the drunks were sleeping it off. No one answered. The radio in his room was still blasting away, and he turned it off. He pounded on the connecting door. Still no answer. He picked up his phone book and threw it against the door. He kept throwing it against the door until the binding came off and it fell apart. He did the same thing with the book containing the yellow pages. The only other missile he could find was the Gideon Bible. Sturdier than the phone book, it lasted a good long time. After slamming it against the door, he would shout, "Hey, Mr. Rubenstein," or "Hey, Mr. Shapiro," or "Hey, Mr. Horowitz."

Suddenly his phone rang. In a tired, thick voice, someone said, "I'm calling from next door. You win. All of us over here apologize. Now will you please let us get some sleep?"

AJR accepted this offer of surrender and started thinking once more about the horses he would bet on that day.

Metamorphosis

K ass, though she could swear like a trooper, was never obscene and limited her profanity to damns and goddams. Her vocabulary of invective included S.O.B., bastard, dirty bastard, old bastard, and goddam old bastard. It was truly amazing that Mom, and Aunt Alice also, could cuss like that and at the same time be so devout, attending Mass every day, saying tons of rosaries, making novenas, and praying the pages out of their prayer books.

They were not Bible quoters, and neither was Dad. In fact, we did not get a lot of preaching from Mom or Aunt Alice or from Dad until almost the end of his days. They all for the most part taught by example. Looking back on it, they were really impressive people. They had lived through world wars, the flu epidemic, and the Great Depression. The McNulty girls' mother had died when she was only 38 and Old Man McNulty lost his worldly possessions a piece at a time. As Aunt Alice put it, what all of this did was make them stronger — and stronger in their faith.

AJR came from a rough, tough environment and also grew stronger in his faith. He would give you a lot of hell for small infractions, such as keeping late hours, but was with you to the hilt when there were major problems, or so I was told by my brothers. I was always pretty dull and domesticated and did not often get into scrapes. Perhaps for this reason, AJR tried to interest me in the priesthood, but that would be years down the road.

The Second World War was over, and Pop and Grandma Rooney had lost their red-headed youngest boy in the fighting. Still, life went on. Pop was retired, but AJR — and Social Security — kept the old folks comfortably fixed. They could count on AJR for everything they would ever need. That did not suit Pop entirely. Pounding on the wall with his cane, he would say, "It's time for me to go back to work." Unhappily, there was nothing he could do. Uncle Jim had no desire to work and never did, even though Pittsburgh's economy was thriving.

The city had once seemed almost beyond repair. I remember hearing Bill Walsh, a center for the Steelers from 1949 to 1954, say that his parents — Easterners — always bypassed Pittsburgh on their way to see him play at Notre Dame, driving on old Route 40 through Washington, PA. Pittsburgh's dirt and smoke were too much for them. I know it is not a myth that on overcast winter days the street lights would be burning at high noon or that businessmen changed their shirts at lunchtime. But David Lawrence, the politician, and Richard Mellon, the financier, had brought together the forces of government and industry to clean up the rivers and the air. A Renaissance, as they called it, was under way.

As Pittsburgh changed, so did AJR's reputation. The public no longer thought of him as a colorful gambler. He was now the owner of the Steelers and a "sportsman" and becoming known, in addition, as a giving and sharing kind of guy, free with his time and his money and able to make people believe in his sincerity. After spending a few minutes with AJR, strangers instinctively felt that he was their friend, and always had been.

He was a legendary big tipper, and so was his old pal Milton Jaffe. Neither, of course, was as profligate as Jim, who thought of money as something to get rid of as soon as possible. AJR knew the value of a buck, but believed in what the nuns used to teach: "Bread cast upon the water is twice returned."

All of these people — the Rooneys, the McNultys, Milton Jaffe, and I include Dago Sam — had a ripe sense of humor, and it helped them get over the bumps we encounter in life. One thing North Siders always clung to was hope. You could be down and out one day and hit a number the next. You could win a lot of dough at the race track. When Uncle John McNulty was going through a particularly bad period, Uncle Jim told him cheerfully, "Johnny, it can't continue like this. Your luck is bound to change. And when it does change, I hope you are at the race track — and I hope I am with you."

Daily life on the North Side was somewhere between a Eugene O'Neill play on the sad side and a John Ford movie on the bright side.

For the Rooney family, old St. Peter's Church was a pivotal location. St. Peter's was the center of our lives. Situated on the threshold of beautiful West Park, it was built when Allegheny City teemed with power and money. In our time, coal smoke from the trains of the Pennsylvania Railroad had blackened the magnificent stones of the church, but the stained-glass windows and fine interior woodwork had remained as good as new.

The Sisters of Mercy ran the school. They had taught Mom and Dad and now they were teaching a second generation of Rooneys. These dedicated ladies in the long black gowns were not above handing out corporal punishment. On days when the whole class was disruptive, we lined up obediently to have our fingers slapped with a ruler, boys and girls alike. There were girls who considered this harsh and unnecessary, but the boys put on a show of indifference. If you were yelled at or hit, and told AJR, you'd be yelled at again and maybe hit again, too. "Don't give those holy women any trouble. They have offered up their lives to God and are trying to help you," he would say.

It was easy to forget that under the long black gowns the sisters were still just women, with all the problems of women. Reined in by strict rules, they could not leave the convent except in pairs or in groups; they could not shed their cowls or their starched white breastplates; they could not let their hair grow long; they could not drive a car.

When Pope John XXIII opened the windows of the church for air, loosening the grip of the vows they had taken, little wonder that some of them bolted. They had tasted freedom and liked it.

Retreat

Often Dad would go to the retreats at St. Paul's Monastery on the South Side and often he would take someone with him. His friend Havey Boyle, sports editor of the *Pittsburgh Post-Gazette*, was a talented writer with a drinking problem — among other weaknesses. Dad liked Havey a lot and thought a retreat at St. Paul's would do him some good.

The idea was not well received. Havey demurred, offered excuses, dragged his feet. But AJR was persistent and Havey at last gave in.

Retreats lasted two days at St. Paul's. They began with an assembly at which the priest in charge spoke of the subjects he would be covering. Afterward, the men who were there to listen, pray, meditate, and confess retired to their cell-like rooms.

Ten minutes had not passed before Havey, with his suitcase packed, came to AJR's room. "Arthur," he said without preamble, "I have always considered you my friend but now I know I was mistaken. You are not a true friend at all."

AJR was shocked.

"What do you mean, Havey? Why would you say that?" he asked.

"For this reason: That priest who just spoke to us was talking about the sins he was going to deal with. He named them — every one. And they were sins I've committed over and over. And all the time he was talking, he looked right at me.

"Now, who knows me better than you do, Arthur? You know all the things I've done wrong in my life. So how did that priest find out? Arthur, you must have told him. After all, you're the one who brought me here. You went to that priest and you ratted on me."

I am unable to say whether AJR could talk Havey Boyle into going through with the retreat. But whenever he repeated the story as I have told it, his eyes would light up.

Masses, Rosaries, Novenas

At a memorial Mass in St. Peter's Church on the anniversary of Aunt Alice McNulty's death, my son Art asked me to take a good look at the stained-glass windows. "Look at the names of the saints on them," he said. "They're our family names."

Sure enough. The names on the windows were Joseph, Peter, John, Matthew, Patrick, Bridget, Francis, Anthony, Michael the Archangel ... The children, grandchildren, and great-grandchildren of AJR and Kass, who went to Mass in that church for so many years, had been given all of those names. Though it's a stretch, I am tempted to add Catherine, for Kathleen.

I can't emphasize too much the importance of the Catholic Church in the lives of Dad, Mom, and Aunt Alice. As I have written before, novenas, the rosary, and daily Mass attendance were routine. Another thing the three of them were into was holy oil and holy water from the shrine of St. Anne in Quebec. Cuts and scratches could be healed with those sacred liquids and recovery from an operation could be hastened.

This belief was passed on to others in the family. My brother Pat, while he was living in Philadelphia, underwent back surgery. He was lying face-down on his hospital bed, groggy from the anesthesia, when John and his wife JoAnn came into the room. Immediately, JoAnn reached into her purse and pulled out a bottle of St. Anne's holy oil. Then she yanked up Pat's hospital gown, exposing his rear end as well as the recent incision in his back. With the holy oil she anointed the entire area. "This is just what you need to get better, Pat," she said. Pat, who was pretty much out of it, kept his thoughts to himself. My wife Kay, however, whispered to me, "Aren't you afraid that oil on an unhealed cut might cause an infection?" I shook my head. "Don't you have any faith?" I demanded. "Yes," Kay said, "but don't push it."

We made novenas for everything — novenas to St. Anne to find a good wife, novenas to St. Anthony to find a lost valuable, novenas to St. Joseph the carpenter to find a job, novenas to St. Cecilia for better eyesight, and of course novenas to St. Jude asking help for hopeless cases.

We prayed to them all, and we had a lot to pray for. Mom and Aunt Alice prayed very hard for the Steelers. On Sundays when the team had a home game, Mom took her statue of the Blessed Mother into the back yard. Mary's presence out there, she felt, would guarantee fair weather — and fair weather would bring a good crowd.

When the Rooney boys played for North Catholic High School, Mom and Aunt Alice prayed for the Trojans. When I played at St. Vincent College they prayed for the Bearcats. They prayed for the success of those teams — and the Steelers, of course — but also that no one would get hurt. Where Tim was concerned, it didn't seem to help. In a game between North Catholic and Scott High of Braddock he was knocked unconscious while making a tackle on the kickoff. Then at Kiski Prep he took a punishing blow to the testicles.

Would he be able to have children? we wondered. Who is the patron saint of virility and potency?

Following North Catholic all over Western Pennsylvania, Mom and Aunt Alice found their way to football stadiums in tough little mill towns and mining towns like Ambridge, Aliquippa, Windber, and Masontown. They were troopers. Dad came, too, if he could get away. We never minded when he couldn't; we'd be spared his words of criticism and his even more damning silences.

Mom and Aunt Alice were looking on from the stands at St. Vincent when I came off the field with a bloody mouth and a missing tooth. Simultaneously, they dived into their purses for rosary beads. My own prayers were mostly for the Steelers. I remember a promise to give up cigars if we won our first Super Bowl. God allowed us to beat the Vikings and I kept my vow — for three months.

Chapter 15

The Great Stoneface

Over fifteen seasons, the Pitt teams coached by Jock Sutherland won 111 games, lost 20 and tied 12. Three of those twenty defeats came in the Rose Bowl. Pitt lost in Pasadena to Stanford (by one point) and Southern California twice (the scores were embarrassing) before the 1936 team routed Washington. Sutherland's undefeated 1937 team was a consensus national champion; his '36, '34, '31, and '29 teams all were declared national champions by at least one of the mathematicians who had worked out the various complicated rating systems that existed back then (remember Dick Dunkel?). Uncle Jim, you may recall, was on the 1929 team that won nine of its ten regular-season games but lost to USC in the Rose Bowl by thirty-three points.

With the appointment in the mid-1930s of John C. Bowman as Pitt's chancellor, friction began to develop between Sutherland and the administration. In its simplest terms, the reason for their strained relations was a difference of opinion about football's importance in the overall scheme of things. To Sutherland, it seemed that the administration was ashamed of his success. Starting in 1932, Sutherland won so often from Notre Dame — five times in six games, with the Irish held scoreless in four of them — that Notre Dame dropped Pitt from its schedule. Then Wisconsin backed out of a two-year commitment and there were troubling allegations of "professionalism." Most Pitt players worked five hours a week at campus jobs for forty-eight dollars a month. Others simply picked up their stipends. Pitt had no dormitories or training table, so the players needed money for room and board. How was this worse, a few realists asked, than the popular alternative of under-the-table payments?

But Chancellor Bowman, uncomfortable with the whole situation, ordered cutbacks in recruiting, scholarships, and practice time. At the Pitt-Washington Rose Bowl game, Sutherland clashed openly with Athletic Director Don Harrison, a former English teacher. The issue was spending money. Each Washington player had one hundred dollars from university funds, each Pitt player seventeen dollars from the pockets of Sutherland and his staff. Confronting Harrison at the post-game dinner-dance, Sutherland accused him of "penny-pinching." Within a few months, Harrison was no longer the athletic director, but his successor, Whitey Hagan, a Pitt tailback under Sutherland in the 1920s and later one of his assistant coaches, enforced all of Bowman's restrictions as relentlessly as Harrison had. When the 1937 team voted not to accept the Rose Bowl invitation that arrived as a matter of course, and Sutherland heard about it at second hand, he felt stripped of authority. After coaching one more season, he resigned.

This was in March 1939. For days on end the story was front-page news. The *Pittsburgh Press* ran a cartoon in which Sutherland towered over the Cathedral of Learning, Pitt's 36-story classroom skyscraper. So now a real big-name coach was providentially available to the highest bidder, and AJR made his move.

Johnny Blood had coached the 1938 Pirates (two years away from becoming the Steelers), but AJR knew that he would soon have to find a replacement. The replacement he had in mind was Sutherland, who agreed to a secret late-night meeting at the Fort Pitt Hotel. Sutherland wanted no publicity. But a desk clerk leaked the story to sportswriter Jack Sell, and it appeared the next day in the *Post-Gazette*.

Sutherland was incensed. Blaming AJR, he cut off negotiations.

The offer from AJR was one of several he refused. To keep his hand in, he coached an assemblage of college "all-stars," culled for the most part from his 1938 Pitt team, against the NFL champion New York Giants in a pre-season charity game promoted by the *New York Herald-Tribune*, and the professionals won, 10-0, poking holes in the argument that major-college football was superior to the NFL brand.

Before the 1940 season, Dan Topping, the owner of the Brooklyn team in the NFL, a rich man married to Sonja Henie, the ice skater/movie star, went after Sutherland. Where AJR had failed,

Topping succeeded. Sutherland coached the Dodgers in the last two seasons before America got into the Second World War — missing out on a division title in 1941, as I have written, when Brooklyn lost to the Steelers, who did not win another game that year and whose record was the worst in the league.

Not long after Pearl Harbor, Sutherland volunteered for the Navy. While he was doing his bit for the war effort as a lieutenant commander in charge of physical-fitness centers, the Brooklyn Dodgers went out of business. And with America once more at peace, AJR made a second, more adroitly handled attempt to interest Jock in the Steelers.

He signed him to a contract for fifteen thousand dollars a year and twenty-five percent of the profits. In the Steelers' entire history there seldom had been any profits, but Sutherland's name was magic. He had kept his own list of Pitt's season-ticket holders and to each of them he wrote a personal note, promising great things from his new team. His old team, Pitt, had been going downhill. Exactly how many Pitt fans changed their allegiance is hard to say, but for 1946 the Steelers sold twenty-two thousand season tickets. In 1946 and 1947 every game at Forbes Field was played before a capacity crowd. Cash customers, for once, outnumbered the deadheads, and Sutherland gave them something to watch. Under his iron hand, a team long noted for succeeding only at failure began to win — just half of its games in 1946 (which stood for improvement), but enough the next season to tie for first place in the NFL East.

John Bain Sutherland was a formal, aloof disciplinarian who did not inspire universal love. A lifelong bachelor (though fond of the ladies), he lived in one room at the Pittsburgh Athletic Association. He allowed no summer to pass without a visit to his aged mother in Scotland. Nobody called him "Jock" except the sportswriters — and they called him that only in print. Chet Smith, sports editor of the *Pittsburgh Press*, gave him a nickname — The Great Stoneface. But even AJR addressed him as "Doctor."

He had a reputation for tight-fistedness which may or may not have been deserved. Jack McGinley recalled that Sutherland came to the Steelers' office in the Union Trust Building at the end of the 1946 season to examine the books. Having walked all the way from the PAA in Oakland, as he usually did, he came through the door wearing an overcoat and a hat, neither of which he removed. "Is Arthur satisfied with these figures?" he said to McGinley. "Yes," answered Jack. "Is Bernard satisfied?" Sutherland asked, referring to Jack's father, Barney McGinley. Again the answer was yes. "Then so am I," Sutherland said. "Just send me my check." And without another word he turned and walked out.

By 1946 almost every team in football was using the T-formation. Sutherland stayed with the old single wing he had coached for twenty-five years. To build up the Steelers' confidence he scheduled pre-season games with minor-league teams like the Richmond Rebels, the Erie Vets, and the Roanoke whatevers. They were low-scoring games which the Steelers just barely won. Nick Skorich, one of the linemen, said their offense consisted of five plays. Sutherland worked the team so hard that Frank Wydo, a tackle, claimed to be worn out by the time the regular season began. Before the last play of a game with the Erie Vets, Wydo said, he told the quarterback, "Call something simple. I'm too tired to block anyone."

At the Steelers' 1947 training camp in Cambridge Springs, Sutherland instructed the trainer, Doc Sweeney, to put Mother's Oats in the water buckets. I was a water boy that year, and I tried this concoction one day. It was like drinking puke. Once after practice when a few of the players started to pour the gooey stuff over their heads to cool off, Sweeney and his assistant, Jack Lee, yelled at me in their Boston accents to "get those buckets away from those guys." So I tipped the buckets over, and the unappetizing mess spilled out on the ground. Val Jansante, an end, was standing there with a thick oatmeal paste in his hair and all over his face — glop that resembled vomit. He gave me a look I still remember and said with pure venom, "Kid, you're a mean little prick."

The players despised Sutherland's blocking sled, constructed of heavy wooden beams and equipped with large springs. The recoil of the springs made it almost immovable and sometimes knocked players to the ground. Their name for the sled was "Big Bertha." Two of them tried to set it on fire with lighter fluid one night, bungling the attempt.

Meanwhile, candidates to make the roster were leaving camp in droves. They would slip away at night after the lights in the Alliance College dormitories went out. As the exodus increased, Jock's assistant coaches stood guard by the doors. They appealed to the players' pride, but continued to torture them on the practice field. Most of these players were World War II veterans and not quitters. I heard a guy who had been in combat say that he ran harder for Jock than he did when the Germans were chasing him.

One player who liked all the hitting was Chuck Mehelich, a rock-solid defensive end from Duquesne. He was about 6 feet 1, all muscle and bone, and he couldn't have weighed much more than 190 pounds. Mehelich was born tough. If you played for Jock you started hitting as soon as you stepped on the practice field and you never stopped, and this was what Mehelich liked best. He could tackle with leverage and strike the rising blow. He made teeth rattle. "When Number 55" — Mehelich — "hit you," said Steve Van Buren, the Philadelphia Eagles' Hall-of-Fame runner, "you stayed hit."

Mehelich's teammates knew what that meant. Sutherland had a drill in which the defender lined up about seven to ten yards from the ball carrier, with no room for more than a single fake, or "juke." The good backs could get the defender off-balance with their juke, lower a shoulder, and run right through him. But what Mehelich did, he told me, was watch the ball carrier's belt. "They can fake with their head and shoulders and maybe even their hips, but not with their belly," he said.

With his eye on the belt buckle, Mehelich terrorized these guys. When it was their turn to go against him, the runners would cringe. One time Sutherland caught Steve Lach, an all-Southern Conference halfback from Duke, pretending to tie his shoe so that somebody else would move ahead of him in the line and face the hard hitter from Western Pennsylvania. As he dropped to one knee, Jock called out, "That's all right, Steve, we'll wait for you."

Mehelich had a successful pro career. Steve Lach didn't last very long.

Jock's scrimmages were ferocious. One player, unaware that his coach was a dentist, thought he could skip practice by claiming to have a toothache. Sutherland took him into an office, turned up the lights, and did some probing. "Is it that tooth?" "No, Doctor." "This one?" "No, Doctor — the one next to it, I think." Jock told the guy he'd be able to practice.

The trainer, Doc Sweeney, a tough, smart New England Irishman, had worked with Jock in Brooklyn. I remember watching him sew up all kinds of wounds, mostly to the chin or the hands. He would dose the cut with alcohol or iodine and put in the stitches right away. It was a little bit like a Civil War field hospital, but no bad infections resulted.

Jock's single-wing formation called for power, strength, and toughness, plus execution, execution, and even better execution. Offensive linemen had to pull out and block, which demanded quickness. Guards like Nick Skorich and Red Moore were not big, but they were tough, strong, and smart. In Jock's style of rock 'em, sock 'em football, there were injuries and there was pain, but his players developed great stamina. They were at their best in the fourth quarter, when the guys on the other side had started to wilt. "You might beat the Steelers on the scoreboard," a player from an opposing team once told me, "but they'd give you such a physical beating that you'd lose your next game."

Here's a story I heard from Jim Parmer, a fullback for the Philadelphia Eagles. He said the Eagles played the Steelers in the last game of the season one year and he was staying on the field with the defensive unit because Ebert Van Buren — Steve's brother and a regular linebacker — was hurt. Ebert sat on the bench wearing his helmet and a field cape which came down to the top of his football shoes while Parmer exhausted himself in his double-duty role. Parmer told me that in the second half he walked over to Ebert and said, "How about spelling me off? I'm dead tired." Ebert just smiled. He opened his cape, and Parmer saw that he was dressed in a white shirt, necktie, and blue serge suit with the pant cuffs tucked into his football socks.

"No way I'm going in there against those guys," Ebert said. "When this game is over I'm heading straight to the railroad station. And next week I'll be duck hunting, not lying in some hospital."

In Ebert Van Buren's three years with the Eagles they never closed the season with the Steelers, so it must have been another player in another season who wore the field cape over his street clothes and said that to Jim, but whatever their source was, the words summed up a prevailing attitude.

'He Never Changes'

Sutherland-coached teams owed their success to execution and conditioning, everybody said. Jock's message to his troops was always the same: One, keep it simple. Two, don't make mistakes. Three, wear down the opposition.

The star of the show was the left halfback, or tailback. He would take a direct snap from center and run inside or outside or maybe even pass now and then — mostly then. The fullback was primarily a blocker, although sometimes he would take the ball into the line. The quarterback was by necessity a big guy — a pulling guard in the backfield with brains enough to call the plays. On occasion the left halfback or right halfback would throw him a pass. Almost everybody played both ways. On defense, the halfbacks would be defensive backs; the fullback, quarterback, and offensive guards would be linebackers. In a system like this, it was easy to see the importance of conditioning.

Sutherland had his faults as a coach, and one of those faults was inflexibility. In Sutherland's system the tailback was required to take three steps before cutting. Not one step or two steps, but three — no more and no less. Bullet Bill Dudley, who had uncanny vision, quickness, and body control, liked to improvise. No matter how many steps he had taken, he liked to cut when an opening presented itself.

To Sutherland, this was heresy. He demanded adherence to his system the way the Pope hands down Roman Catholic dogma. If you did not run the play exactly as he had drawn it up, it was like not being properly baptized, married, or ordained. There's a story that Sutherland's unwillingness to bend — to allow the slightest departure from his blueprint — was why Dudley left town.

In a practice scrimmage, the story goes, Dudley took one step or two steps or four steps before cutting, but went through the designated hole and ran sixty-five yards for a touchdown. Sutherland, looking grim, called for the play to be repeated.

"We're going to keep doing this," he said, "until we get it right."

Dudley responded, "How was it for distance?"

Never happened. "It's just a story," Dudley would say whenever somebody asked. "You didn't talk to Doctor Sutherland like that."

There was no single cause for the personality clash between Dudley and Sutherland, just a steady accumulation of incidents.

In the Steelers' seventh game, a 14-7 win over Washington, Dudley cracked a rib or two, and for the rest of the year — some said at Jock's insistence — he played hurt. After beating Washington, the Steelers were 4-2-1. Of the four games that remained, they lost three. And Dudley was fed up.

As stubborn in his own way as Jock was, he threatened to quit football unless the Steelers traded him. He was AJR's favorite player; he had led the league in rushing, punt returns, and interceptions; he was voted its MVP. But AJR, feeling he must back up his coach, peddled Dudley to Detroit for two very ordinary backs and a number one draft choice.

Jack McGinley was present when Sutherland spoke to Dudley for the last time. The way Jack remembered it, Sutherland said, "Bill, I've coached great players, and you're a great player. But I don't have to have great players." In 1947, with Johnny Clement, a good but not great player, at tailback, the Steelers finished with an 8-4 record, the best in their fourteen-year history.

There were high hopes for the future — high expectations, actually. The Steelers' 5-5-1 finish in 1946 had been hailed by the public as a great leap forward. After the 2-8 record in 1945 and the Card-Pitts' 0-10 season, it was. But in 1942, with the last of the players who later went into the service, the Steelers were 7-4 and even the 1943 Steagles had won more games than they lost. Pittsburgh, however, looked upon Sutherland as a savior. No matter how exciting Dudley could be — and something good or spectacular happened whenever he got his hands on the ball — it was Sutherland who energized the fans. By now he had reached the status of a deity. If the great Bill Dudley was unable to follow protocol, he must go.

And so Dudley went. He played six more seasons in the NFL, three with Detroit and three with the Redskins.

Johnny Clement was called Zero because that was the number on his black and gold jersey. He had played in college at Southern Methodist and spent one season with the Chicago Cardinals before going into the Army Air Force. Like Dudley, he flew a lot of combat missions. After his football days he became a commercial pilot and died in a plane crash.

As I have said, the tailback position in the single wing created stars, and Clement played so well in 1947 that the Steelers did not miss Dudley. In that respect, Johnny Zero took Jock off the hook. He followed the offensive scheme with no deviations, and that made the coaches happy. Statistically, Clement had an excellent season. He finished second to Steve Van Buren of the Eagles in rushing, passed for more than one thousand yards, and accounted for eleven touchdowns.

While doing all this, he took a beating. Injured, he missed the Eastern Division playoff game with the Eagles, a 21-0 defeat. With Clement's backup, Gonzales Morales, hurt too, the Steelers had no offense.

For still another reason, it was not a good way to end the season, which no one knew would be Sutherland's last. Demanding to be paid for their extra week of practice, the players had gone on strike a few days before the game. They returned in twenty-four hours, without the extra pay, but Sutherland was outraged. The performance of his team against the Eagles, before a disappointed full house at Forbes Field, was in keeping with the atmosphere in the locker room.

Johnny Clement played one more season with the Steelers and one in the All-America Conference. I remember him as a kindly fellow with a soft Southwestern accent. At training camp he sometimes went fishing with the kids who carried water and helped the equipment manager.

As for Dudley, when his football career was over he sold insurance — a lot of it — and served in the Virginia state legislature.

Dudley played well for the Lions and Redskins, but never had a better season than his last with the Steelers, 1946. Even by the standards of the 1940s he was undersized. "Don't tell me I'm too small," he would say. "Tell me I'm not good enough." Nobody ever did that.

What Dudley lacked in size he made up for in toughness. He wore the old leather helmet with no faceguard, and in one game he came to the sideline with nothing recognizable as a nose. He went to the trainer's room, had some tape put on, and resumed playing.

Dudley was not fast but had a low center of gravity, which gave him uncanny balance. His other attributes were strength, quickness, soft hands for pass catching and punt receiving — his ability to put on a sudden burst of speed made him a threat to return any punt for a touchdown — and remarkable vision.

He was the master of the cutback. With Dudley the ball carrier, off-tackle plays would become reverses or inside plays; inside plays would end up as sweeps. This was the sort of thing that drove Jock Sutherland wild, but Dudley followed his instincts.

As a passer, he had no arm, yet the ball seemed to go where he intended it to go. If his receivers were covered, he would take off and run. He was also a fine defensive back — some said the best they ever saw. Coach Steve Owens of the Giants warned his quarterbacks that if they threw into Dudley's area they'd be fined. Dudley had great ability to run with the ball after an interception.

Kicking field goals and extra points, he used a pendulum stroke. He stood just behind the spot where the holder would place the ball, with his left foot planted and his right foot back, held in readiness. When the ball was centered and placed he would swing his leg into it without taking a step. That is why I call him a pendulum kicker. He had limited range — about thirty-five yards from the line of scrimmage — but in those days the goal posts were right on the goal line and he was seldom inaccurate.

"Could Dudley play today?" was a question I still heard in the 1990s. As a free safety and punt-return man, I think so. With his quickness, his ability to see the whole field, his sure hands, his moxie, and his toughness, Dudley would have earned his keep.

My brother Dan and I were standing on the sideline at a Steeler game one fall when Dudley got loose for a 65-yard touchdown run on a punt return. We cheered him every step of the way and were told by AJR to control our enthusiasm. AJR held Dudley in the same high esteem that we did, but on this particular day he happened to be playing for the Redskins..

Year after year he returned to the University of Virginia every spring to play in the annual alumni game. Old bones are brittle; in mortal fear of an injury, officials took to hiding his uniform. He coached for a while but preferred the insurance business. Settling down, he married a former Miss Virginia, who converted him in his old age to Catholicism. I was present at the ceremony and observed how happy his wife was. Afterward, Bill told me that AJR and Bert Bell would have been just as pleased.

I had a long conversation with Dudley in April of 1998 and it proceeded quite pleasantly until I asked him about Sutherland. To my surprise, his language immediately grew heated, not to say violent.

He told me that in 1946 Sutherland was losing his mind. As an example, he cited a play in the game against the Redskins. "We were supposed to go off-tackle down by the Washington goal line," he said. "The offensive guard — I think it was Nick Skorich — gave me a signal from the line of scrimmage with his hand: 'Run off of me instead of to the outside.' I did that. Nick made a hole, and I dragged a tackler through it for the winning touchdown. If I had gone to the outside, they'd have nailed me. There was nothing there." Dudley was getting more and more worked up. I am leaving out all of his F-words. "When we watched the game film," he said, "Jock stopped the projector on my touchdown run. He said, 'Bill, what play was called?' 'Off-tackle.' 'Well,' Jock said, 'you went to the inside.' I told him, 'Watch the play again, and you'll see Skorich wave his hand. That was his signal for me to go inside. Hell, we scored! We won the game!'"

Sutherland wanted the Steelers to win, but he wanted them to do it his way. That same season, 1946, the Chicago Cardinals were making a goal-line stand against the Steelers. With the ball on the one-yard line on fourth down, the Cardinals' safety, Marshall Goldberg — who had played for Sutherland at Pitt — told his teammates exactly what to look for. "He never changes," Goldberg said. The Steelers ran the play Goldberg knew they would, and he stopped it for no gain.

If Sutherland hadn't died after his second year in the NFL, would he have switched to the T-formation? Could he have coached the new, much more open type of game? AJR believed so, convinced that Jock was a realist ... a pragmatist. Like everybody else in football, he would have been forced to adjust. Sure, the hard-headed old Scotsman was set in his ways. But the college players coming into the league were schooled in the T, accustomed to the T, enamored of the T. Recognizing this, Sutherland would have done what was necessary.

There were those who agreed with that line of reasoning and those who did not. There were those who thought they knew what Goldberg knew: "He never changes." The question must remain unanswered, but here is one last thing to consider. It's a show-business truism I often invoke: an actor who plays a part too long will find it's the only part he can play. The mask becomes the face.

End Game

On March 22, 1948, one day after his fifty-ninth birthday, Jock Sutherland drove to Coatesville, in eastern Pennsylvania, for a coaching clinic. From there he proceeded south to observe spring football practice at Wake Forest and Duke, reporting to the Steelers' Grant Street offices by telephone. After that, silence. There were no further calls.

Shortly after daylight on the morning of April 7th a man got out of a 1947 Cadillac which was up to its hubcaps in a Western Kentucky swamp. He had been in the car all night. He took a suitcase from the trunk and carried it the short distance to a narrow country road. Muddied and confused, he started walking.

He was wearing a topcoat, a hat, a business suit, and a necktie. A milk-truck driver, making his early rounds, pulled up and offered him a lift. In these wet, dismal lowlands not far south of the Ohio River and not far east of the Mississippi, a stranger on foot toting a suitcase attracted attention.

Except in one particular, the man's conversation did not make sense. To the milk-truck driver, to the owner of a garage in Bandana, Kentucky (population 100), and to John Shelby, the county sheriff, he kept repeating, "I'm Jock Sutherland."

With none of them did the name ring a bell.

In response to the sheriff's questions, Sutherland wasn't able to say where he had been. Shelby asked him to empty his wallet. It contained hotel receipts showing he had gone from North Carolina to Atlanta to New Orleans, plus $329 In cash.

"You shouldn't be carrying all that money around," Shelby cautioned him. "Somebody might take it away from you."

The effect of the words was instantaneous. For a moment — no longer — Jock Sutherland's true self re-emerged. He was 6 feet 3, still a powerful wrestler given to impromptu matches on carpets and lawns with anyone big and brave enough to test him, and he put equal value on his money and his life. He said, "It wouldn't be as easy as you think."

It was his last coherent statement. Doctors at a hospital in Cairo, Illinois, across the Ohio River from Kentucky, diagnosed his problem as amnesia. Or mental exhaustion. Or a nervous breakdown. They were not sure which.

By now Sutherland's identity had been established. Back in Pittsburgh there were big black front-page headlines. It became known that for months the coach had complained of "excruciating headaches." Anxious friends flew to Cairo in a private plane belonging to Thomas E. Millsop, the president of Weirton Steel, and brought Sutherland home. Late that night at West Penn Hospital, surgeons discovered an inoperable brain tumor. The next morning – Sunday, April 11th – Sutherland died.

Mourners by the thousand filed past his open casket in Calvary Episcopal Church. Several eulogists said that football in Pittsburgh had "lost its heart and soul."

And Bill Dudley called Sutherland "the best coach I've ever had."

Chapter 16

Meeting Al Smith

AJR would take Kass and his friends to the Union Fishing Club on the North Side and to the Lotus Club on the South Side. As private clubs, they could keep selling liquor after midnight and on Sunday, when commercial establishments were shut down by the law.

Kass said that one night in the Union Fishing Club a customer sidled up to her and said that, as proof of his devotion, he would "kill" for AJR. She answered, "I hardly think that will be necessary." Such twisted loyalty frightened her, Kass said.

AJR needed no one to fight his battles. There was the time in the Union Fishing Club, Kass went on, that a "tough guy" – somebody he disliked – accidentally bumped into her chair. It was "no big deal," she insisted. But AJR jumped up, Kass said, and "beat the tar" out of the guy.

"He's no good," AJR later explained.

After football games on Sunday, we went to the Lotus Club as a family. The change in the Blue Laws put the Lotus Club out of business eventually, but for as long as it remained open AJR continued to go there. It wasn't much for atmosphere. Everyone praised the steaks and chops, but all I ever ordered was a sandwich and most of the time it came with stale bread. Yet AJR would invite football people to the Lotus Club, and when I'd see them years later on scouting trips they would ask about the place and speak of it fondly.

I never could figure that out.

Once after a game between the Steelers and the New York Giants, the two coaches, Jock Sutherland and Steve Owen, got their snoots full at the Lotus Club. They began to argue about blocking and tackling techniques and before very long were down on the floor, demonstrating. Both were big, strong guys and former linemen and they were slamming into each other. Jack Sell, the Post-Gazette sportswriter, said the roughhousing became so intense that it almost turned into a fist fight.

Fights in restaurants and bars were not unusual. AJR's most memorable fight brought him to the attention of the first Irish-Catholic – actually, Irish-Italian-Catholic – ever to run for president.

It happened at Luchow's, a fine German restaurant in New York City. AJR had spent the afternoon at a race track – Jamaica, perhaps, or Aqueduct or Belmont – and planned to eat by himself and afterward drive back to Pittsburgh.

Pulling up at the curb – pulling up onto the sidewalk, in fact – he gave the parking attendant a very large tip to watch his car, but locked it and kept the keys. In the glove compartment was $10,000.

When AJR went to Luchow's alone, he ate at the bar. The bar was informal and by custom off-limits to women. So that night all the drinkers and diners were men, and one of them stood out from the rest. He was being totally and purposely obnoxious.

AJR had seen him at Luchow's before. He used his size and intimidating presence to bully people. Usually he was drunk. On *this* occasion he was drunk. Spotting AJR, he made an insulting remark.

"Hey," said AJR, "I'm your friend. Have a drink." He ordered a doubleheader for the guy. Down it went in a single gulp. Then the hectoring resumed. AJR was taking a lot of lip.

He said, "Look, we're pals. Have another drink." A second doubleheader arrived and went the way of the first.

AJR's table was ready by now. He sat down to eat, and once again the pest was in his face.

Still playing for time, AJR said, "You need one more drink." One more was exactly right, because the third doubleheader incapacitated the guy. He tossed it off and slumped against the bar with his head down. AJR finished eating and called for the check.

He then walked over to the guy, said, "You're ready now," and flattened him.

As AJR was leaving the room, a man with a very prominent nose and thin white hair, parted in the middle, detached himself from the group he was with. "Young fellow," he said to AJR, "I've been watching you all night. I saw you setting up that bum. Good work. It was beautiful." He held out his hand. "I'm Al Smith."

Alfred Emmanuel Smith had been the governor of New York and in 1928 the Democratic candidate for president. (His campaign was a lost cause. He was a Catholic, he was wet — opposed, that is, to the Eighteenth Amendment — and he came from immigrant stock. The Republican, Herbert Hoover, swept the country.)

AJR told the Al Smith story three or four times in my hearing and never changed it. There are stories that improve with each telling. This one remained forever the same.

Duke

A JR and his brother Vince, called Duke, never could get along. In almost every large family there are siblings who have trouble connecting with each other, and this was true of the Rooneys.

The clash of personalities between AJR and Duke had its origin in their natures. Like three or four other Rooneys, Duke overindulged in drink on occasion, and AJR made it clear that he disapproved. His role as the family's alpha male was important to him. So for this reason, among several, Duke plainly thought that his brother was too controlling.

And Duke didn't like to be controlled. Thus when he worked for a time in the Steeler organization he was often at odds with his boss. After one misunderstanding he borrowed AJR's car and took off for Texas. When his money ran out, AJR flew down to wherever Duke was stranded and brought him home.

The smallest of the Rooney brothers, Duke was a pretty good amateur boxer. He followed Dan — Father Silas — to St. Bonaventure University but dropped out before earning a degree. AJR's political pull helped him to get a job with the Sanitation Authority and he was doing well there until his health failed. Upon hearing from Kathy, Duke's daughter, that a stroke had put her father in the hospital, AJR broke into tears. Down deep, his estrangement from Duke, which persisted right up to the end, was something he always regretted. At Duke's wake, he posted himself near the casket and remained there for every minute of the viewing.

Long after Duke was gone, my son Mike spent some time as AJR's unofficial chauffeur. "He reminds me of my brothers, who were *all* good regular guys," the Chief told me. In a roundabout way, he was extending to Vince the affection he felt for Red, Jim, Father Silas, and Tom.

I never found Uncle Vince to be anything less than a pleasant companion. He could tell a good story with humor and skill. All of us, including AJR, had the highest regard for Anne, Vince's wife. She worked as a volunteer at Divine Providence Hospital, and once when AJR had me drive him there to visit a friend we stopped at the information desk to ask for the room number. The person who gave it to us was Anne. We conversed for a few minute, and then on our way to the elevator AJR took my arm and said, "Do you see that woman back there?" He meant Anne. Obediently, I glanced over my shoulder for another look. "She's a living saint," he continued.

When AJR promoted you to the status of living saint, that was the ultimate tribute.

Duke and Anne were the parents of seven children, and they all grew up to be successful in life. One of the three sons, Vincent Timothy, played football at California University of Pennsylvania and became a scout in the NFL, first for the Steelers, when I was personnel director, then with the Detroit Lions and later the New York Giants.

If your children are your legacy, there is much to be said in my Uncle Vince's favor.

Dago Sam

Dago Sam Leone was Dad's oldest friend. He was very Italian, so Italian he must have come from the tip of the boot, or maybe even Sicily. He would speak of Italians he did not resemble as "American-looking."

Sam was the Latin Lover type, still rather handsome in middle age even though he wore Coke-bottle glasses with wire rims that made his eyeballs look like balloons. He had dark olive skin and the remnants of what he said was once an excellent physique. When bragging about this, he called attention to his "very flat breasts," as he described them.

By his own account, he was irresistible to women. But Sam never married. He told me once that, long-term, he wanted nothing to do with women who were not like our moms, his and mine. As far as other kinds of women were concerned, you never knew what to expect. He said that in a gambling house one night the wife of a close friend sidled up next to him and placed a note in his hand. The note expressed her desire to have sexual relations with him. Sam was shocked and disgusted, he said.

Despite his rather low position on the social scale, he could behave with unusual refinement. I am certain he kept his distance from the Mafia. Perhaps the most arresting thing about him was the way he spoke. He used his hands a lot, but told side-splitting stories without ever changing his expression. He had a high-pitched voice that got higher and higher the longer the story went on. He seemed to be grabbing you by the lapels and screaming, "What do you think of *that*?"

Like Uncle Jim, he sometimes would talk in a series of asides. When Jim and Sam were together it was like something from "Guys and Dolls." Actually, the characters in that Damon Runyon play could only hope to be as funny as these two. I had coffee one time with Jackie Gleason and went away thinking I had never met anyone funnier, but Dago Sam, in his own way, was Gleason's equal.

I can't do justice to the stories he told by paraphrasing them. You had to see and hear him to appreciate the humor.

One story involved an old friend, a carnival guy he hadn't seen for a while. They bumped into each other in a cigar store that was really a bookie joint. Sam wanted to know what the carnie guy was doing in Pittsburgh. He answered, "Sam, I've got the greatest job you ever heard of. The money is good, it's easy, and it's fun.'"

Now Sam was interested. Maybe he could get a piece of the action. Before saying anything else, the carnie guy suggested that they step outside, where no one would be likely to eavesdrop. When they were by themselves, he told Sam that he worked for a Christian evangelist, a faith healer whose prayer services in churches all over town and in places like the North Side Public Library attracted huge crowds. She cured her devoted followers of every disease known to medical science. "Cancer and carbuncles. Blood clots and bunions. Warts and welts," wrote the author of a *Pittsburgh Magazine* article. From near and far, the afflicted came. The evangelist stood before them on a platform and dealt with their illnesses as, one by one, they approached her. "I rebuke your cancer in the name of JEE-sus!" she would say.

The carnie guy's role, as he explained it, was to have some curable ailment. Deafness, for example. Invoking JEE-sus, the healer would give him the power to hear. Or he'd be a cripple, carried to her platform on a stretcher. "Stand up," she would order him. "Now you can walk. You are healed." And the carnie guy would do as she instructed him. He would get up and walk.

Dago Sam rejoiced in his friend's good fortune, but decided it wasn't his kind of scam, one reason being that he was too well known on the North Side to get away with such outright fakery.

Uncle Jim had plans of his own concerning Sam. If you converted a heathen to Catholicism, Jim believed, that was your ticket to heaven. So he worked on Sam like a missionary and took all the credit when Sam was baptized. I hope for Jim's sake he had the right information about the ticket-to-heaven business.

Sam told me before I was old enough to realize it myself that Jim drank too much, and not for social purposes. According to Sam, you had to pace yourself when you drank. Jim, he said, drank too quickly. He drank to get pie-eyed. Sam thought this was a shame.

Sam was also well aware of Jim's other great weakness, his attitude toward money. Once as they were going into a saloon, Jim borrowed ten dollars from Sam. Then even before they ordered a drink he handed the ten to the bartender. As a tip.

Sam said, "What did you do that for?"

"To ensure good treatment," answered Jim.

Sam went into the Army when the United States entered the First World War and discovered right away that he wasn't cut out for soldiering. At the camp in the South where he took his basic training, an officer asked if there was anyone in the outfit who knew something about horses. Looking for an escape from close-order drill, Sam stepped forward. The fact that he often bet on horses made him feel more than qualified. Of course, except at the race track, he had never actually been close to a horse. Unconcerned about that, the Army packed him off to a cavalry regiment — where his job was to clean out the stables. The worst part of it was that they assigned him to the stables where the mules were kept. Sam was eloquent in describing the foul toilet habits of mules.

Then came another opportunity. The Army sent out a call for soldiers who could speak and understand Italian. In World War I, the Italians were America's allies, but communication was a problem. Sam volunteered and was happy to turn in his shovel and broom. The North Side Italian language differed greatly from the mother tongue, and Sam's vocabulary had severe limitations, but he managed to get by as an interpreter and enjoy what was left of the war.

As unpleasant as his time in the cavalry had been, Sam kept on playing the horses. Back in civilian life, he would sometimes take the bus to Waterford Park in West Virginia. The bus company offered a round-trip package that included transportation from Downtown, admission to the track, and a program. One hot day, Sam made the trip wearing slacks and a golf shirt but no underwear. He bet on the Daily Double and his horses finished first in both races. The parimutuel ticket was in the pocket of his shirt, but before cashing it in, Sam took a detour to the men's room. He was carrying, in his pants pocket, ten dollars — just enough money to continue betting until the bus left for Pittsburgh.

In the men's room, however, Sam got into an altercation with somebody. How it started I do not recall, but one thing led to another and the altercation developed into a scuffle. The other guy took hold of Sam's golf shirt and ripped it right off his back. Just as suddenly as it began, the fight now came to an end, but Sam was left standing bare-chested and with rags for a shirt. Even worse, the pocket had been torn off and was nowhere to be seen. And the pocket contained the parimutuel ticket. Sam looked all over the men's room for his pocket. He got down on his hands and knees, poking around under the wash basins and toilet bowls, and he could find no trace of either pocket or ticket.

So now he was desperate. Times were different then. No matter how flat his pectorals might be, a man without a shirt or an undershirt could easily end up in jail. Sam appealed to a black guy who shined shoes in the men's room and had helped him look for the ticket. "Sell me your shirt." The guy probably lived near the track, Sam figured. He'd be able to sneak home in his undershirt, if need be, whereas Sam — half-naked — faced a bus ride from Waterford Park to Pittsburgh and then a walk through Downtown across the Sixth Street Bridge to the North Side.

He haggled with the guy, who gave in at last and agreed to sell his shirt, but set the price at ten dollars. So there went Sam's betting money. All he had now was his ticket for the bus, which would not leave the track until the last race was over. Busted, he spent the rest of the afternoon in total boredom — and wearing a shirt that made him look like a Federal Street wino.

Actually, Sam never dressed in high style. His clothes were old and baggy, in conformance with the way he lived. When AJR or Uncle Jim were not buying, he ate in lunchrooms — greasy spoons. He depended for an income on small-time card games and crap games, but that source dried up as his eyes began to fail. There came a day when Sam was in the crime news, arrested for running numbers. AJR said to him, "Sam, I didn't know that about you. How long have you been a numbers guy?"

Almost shrieking, Sam protested, "I'm not! I'm not! I was standing in a store on General Robinson Street and a guy puts these papers in my hand. He says, 'Hold these.' And then he takes off — out the side door. And a plainclothes cop is coming in the front door. He grabs me right away, and the stiff won't believe what I'm telling him."

For a guy with a reputation as a sharpie, and whose best friends were the real thing, Sam seemed to be on the receiving end of many a bad deal. In defiance of professional ethics, a dentist named Baum advertised an easy-payment plan. Sam needed work on his teeth, and Dr. Baum sold him a complete new set of uppers, a bridge, and maybe a couple of crowns. Now Sam could smile again, but he did not feel like smiling when Dr. Baum sent him the bill. It was clear that once more Sam had been taken.

He yelled and screamed — and refused to pay. Weeks went by, and then the upper plate started giving him trouble. Something was wrong with the fit; all Sam knew was that it hurt when he chewed. He returned to Dr. Baum. To his surprise, the dentist greeted him cordially. Removing the plate, Baum said he would have to examine it. Meanwhile, Sam should go sit in the waiting room. An hour later he was still cooling his heels. His patience running thin, he demanded an explanation. What was taking so long? Calmly, the dentist told him that he would not get his plate back until he paid every penny he owed.

"Try eating without teeth for a while," Baum said.

Sam did try, but found it was difficult, if not impossible. In the end he came across with the ransom money.

He lived to an advanced age, hanging around the Steeler offices in the Roosevelt Hotel and later Three Rivers Stadium and outlasting most of his contemporaries. The faces of AJR's friends, of the coaches and scouts and trainers kept changing. Sam the entertainer was a constant presence.

His stories amused every new audience, but the burden of the years was increasing. He worried about medical care. One winter day on his way to Three Rivers he was unable to make it through the snow. Stadium security rescued him. AJR learned that Sam could be admitted to a Veterans Administration hospital. Nothing doing, said Sam. He would stay on the North Side. He died a lonely old man, subsisting as best he could on Social Security and his World War I pension.

Chapter 17

Cum Posey

Our "colored" maid, Mary Roseboro, was about 25 years old when she first came to work at 940 North Lincoln Avenue in the 1940s. Mary may have had some American Indian in her. She was tall, with high cheekbones and a reddish-brown complexion. I never heard Mary raise her voice or complain. She was a kind, loyal Christian woman devoted to her church — ladylike but not at all prim. In fact, she had a good sense of humor.

She arrived every morning and went home every evening in a jitney. To the best of my knowledge, she never married. She had a boyfriend, she told Kass, but apparently did not regard him as husband material.

After Mary had been with us for many years, Kass gave her permission to bring an old friend who was senile to 940 North Lincoln. While Mary did her chores, this patient, elderly woman sat in the basement. From time to time, Mary would go down there to visit with her.

We knew that in Mary Roseboro someone out of the ordinary had come our way. She blended in; we considered her one of us; our problems were her problems. She was part of the chemistry, in short, that made 940 North Lincoln a special place.

Mary outlived Kass, AJR, and Aunt Alice. When she died at 75, the Rooneys who were left attended her wake in the Hill District. Talking with the funeral director, Evan Baker, Jr., I received confirmation of a story I had heard from AJR.

It concerned a friend from his days as an athlete, Cum Posey. Cum — short for Cumberland — was a light-skinned black man who had played baseball and basketball at Penn State and also at Duquesne. He could easily pass for white and often did, it was said. But after leaving college in 1911, he joined a black semi-pro baseball team, the Homestead Grays, becoming their manager. first baseman, and eventually their owner.

Cum was a tireless promoter. Recruiting talent from New York and Chicago, he was able to pay monthly salaries by 1922. The Grays drew good crowds against semi-pro white teams in the mill towns of Western Pennsylvania, and by 1925 they were playing home games at Forbes Field (although forbidden by management to use the locker rooms and showers). Eventually, Posey helped organize the professional National Negro League in 1928.

In 1930, he discovered and signed Josh Gibson, a 19-year-old catcher out of Allegheny Vocational School on the North Side. It was not too long before scouts, other players, and sportswriters were calling him the best catcher, black or white, in all baseball. Gibson hit prodigious home runs and hit lots of them — nobody knows exactly how many because the Negro Leagues took a casual approach to record-keeping. In any case, when Gus Greenlee, the Hill District numbers king, acquired a team called the Pittsburgh Crawfords in 1932, he raided Posey's lineup, making off with two future Hall of Famers, Gibson and Oscar Charleston, a first baseman.

Through the rest of the 1930s and the early 1940s, Gibson jumped back and forth between the Crawfords and the Grays as the two rival owners engaged in a bidding war for his services. Greenlee, with his numbers money, had the advantage. He built the Crawfords a 6,000-seat lighted stadium on Bedford Avenue in the Hill District. Both teams had a serious problem making ends meet, and this was where AJR came into the picture.

The Grays, like the white teams, went South for spring training. To economize, they traveled in two ancient Buicks, ate fat, greasy take-out food, and rented rooms where they could find them in the colored section of town. Posey still couldn't manage to pay for it all, so AJR made up the difference. For fifteen years — until the end of segregation in baseball put the Negro Leagues out of business — he advanced his friend "loans." As repayment, Posey once offered him part ownership of the Grays. "Forget it," said AJR. "You have your team and I have mine." Live and let live.

The undertaker Evan Baker substantiated this. He said that AJR was "a true saint." And he told me a story I had not previously heard.

It seems that Posey once had a political club that held regular meetings. Before one such gathering he confided to AJR that there was not enough money on hand for beer and sandwiches. AJR took care of both needs, calling the Bubbles and Sherman restaurant for the food and the Duquesne Brewery for a truckload of beer.

So many of the things our dad related to us had the flavor of half-truths or legends, but I learned over the years never to doubt.

Dan Hamill

AJR had a great friend named Dan Hamill, who owned the Pittsburgh Paper Products Company. Dan was a bachelor and the epitome of a Catholic gentleman. Two of his nephews and many of his friends were priests, and, like Dad, he gave a lot of money to the Church.

He was also a bit of a prude. Once he told AJR that he had found a wonderful place to eat supper — well off the beaten path on Evergreen Road, not far from North Park. It was in an old house up on a hill. So they went there together, and Dan was surprised that many of the patrons and many of the waiters spoke or nodded to the Chief.

He said, "Art, a lot of people seem to know you here."

Dad said, "Yep ... they do."

"How is that?" inquired Dan.

"Well," said AJR, "there's a gambling joint upstairs. This is a roadhouse."

That information did not upset Mr. Hamill, but a few minutes later Dad said to him: "Have you noticed all the pretty girls around here?"

Dan replied that he had.

"I've been in the gambling joint upstairs a lot of times," Dad continued "but never to the other part of the place."

"And what would that be?" asked Dan.

"Why, a notch joint," Dad told him. A notch joint was a house of ill repute.

Dan couldn't eat another bite, and he never went back to this restaurant he had liked so much. Nor did he ever allow the fact to slip out that he had taken Art Rooney to a "notch joint."

Another restaurant he crossed off his list was Klein's, one of the best places Downtown for fish. Dan would go there on Friday and order the clam chowder. There was no other clam chowder like it, he thought. After finishing a big bowl on a Friday during Lent, he happily discussed its merits with the cook.

"How do you make such good clam chowder?" he asked. "What is your secret?"

"Well," said the cook, "the ingredients are pretty much the same as the ingredients in all clam chowder. The difference with mine" — becoming confidential, he lowered his voice — "is that, for the starter, I use pork broth."

Dan's face turned white. "But it's Friday," he reminded the cook.

"Mr. Hamill," said the cook with a smile, "what you don't know won't hurt you."

Klein's that day lost a regular customer.

Like AJR in his later years, Dan was a total abstainer. There's a story about a request he made to a friend, a successful engineer named John Laboon, on a fishing trip. The weather was hot, and he asked Laboon to hand him a bottle of Coke. Laboon took a bottle from the cooler and surreptitiously spiked it with whiskey. One sip was enough to convince Dan he'd been tricked. With fire in his eyes, he sent the bottle flying toward Laboon's head, just missing the target. He was ready to slug it out until the rest of the fishermen pacified him.

Dan kept in shape by playing handball, often with AJR. One time in making a shot, he accidentally elbowed Dad, raking the side of his face. Although his eye was blacked and his mouth gashed, Dad thought nothing of it, having taken harder knocks in the boxing and football arenas, but Dan's remorseful apologies gave him a wicked idea. For the next few days, when people inquired about his bruises, he would say with a straight face, "Dan Hamill hit me," and leave it at that.

One of Dan's idiosyncrasies was walking backwards, even up a hill, for exercise. We thought this was strange, but in modern fitness centers people do many strange things. Dan may have been ahead of his time.

Possibly because he was lean, Dan looked tall. He had a silver-gray, almost white head of hair and sharp features. Going to the races with AJR was his only known vice. I doubt if Dan Hamill ever committed a bad deed, spoke a bad word, or entertained a bad thought in his life. He was squeaky clean.

His association with AJR was so close that the directors of St. Paul's orphanage asked them to be co-sponsors of an entire confirmation class one year. I like to think that the boys in that class remembered the occasion all of their lives. Far-fetched? Maybe not. At the Shamrock Hotel in Houston some time ago the bellhop who handled my luggage refused to accept a tip. I asked him why. Well, he'd been an orphan in the school at Hershey, Pennsylvania, he said; AJR and Bert Bell had visited the place a number of times (no doubt writing checks before they left), and he wanted to show his gratitude in some small way. I am sure that my dad and Mr. Hamill wrote a few checks for St. Paul's.

Unquestionably, Dan made money in the stock market as well as in the paper business. Before investing, he would get in touch with a firm's chief executive officer and pump him for information not found in the annual report. I understand that in 1929 he anticipated the crash. By the time the market collapsed he was out of it.

One year he was ordered to appear in the Downtown office of the Internal Revenue Service with all his books. "Why can't you come to my office?" he asked. "Because things just aren't done that way," he was told.

Don't be too sure, Dan thought. He called the Federal Bureau of Investigation and explained the situation to an old friend — J. Edgar Hoover by name. Soon afterward he heard from the IRS agent who had spoken to him earlier. "One of our men will be over to conduct your audit," the agent said. The next call Dan got was from Hoover, asking if everything had worked out all right.

Until television made professional football both popular and profitable, there were times when AJR needed help to meet the payroll. On one such occasion he went to Dan Hamill. In return for financial assistance from Dan, he offered him a piece of the team. "Also, I'll make you an officer of the company," Dad said.

Hamill answered with no hesitation. He said, "I'll lend you the money [$25,000], but I want no part of the ball club. The ball club's for you and your family. Pay me back when you can."

Dan Hamill was not a relative of ours, but the Rooney kids thought of him as a kindly, beloved old uncle.

Down on the Farm

In 1948, AJR's horse trainer, Jimmy McGee, talked him into buying a dairy farm in western Maryland, near Winfield. There would be no cows on the farm, and no milking machines. Instead, it was AJR's intention to breed and raise thoroughbred race horses. He converted the dairy farm into a stud farm.

On the side, Jimmy McGee had some roosters, which he entered in illegal cockfights. On visits to the farm many years later, AJR would ask the manager, Jim Steele, if any of the chickens running around the place were descendants of Jimmy McGee's contraband gamecocks.

McGee was the first manager, long before Steele, and a poor one. He thought that race-track guys could do the farm work, a colossal mistake. As a result of his hiring practices the work simply didn't get done. Everywhere you looked there were empty whiskey bottles, evidence enough that the men had other priorities.

McGee's prize stud was a stallion named British Buddy. He produced some big, strong, beautiful horses that were not especially fast. AJR was more successful at winning bets than at building up a stable — I was with him one day at a track in New York when he won an even hundred grand betting on a horse of his named for Pat Livingston, the *Pittsburgh Press* football writer — but he knew how to hold down overhead and managed to stay in business.

Jimmy McGee's real name, I understand, was Gray. He knew the horse business and he knew how to get a thoroughbred ready for a race. He also had a touch of the rogue in him. For a short while, he was a real good matchup with AJR. He made the mistake, however, of thinking that AJR needed him more than he needed AJR, and when Kass overheard him say that he had "big plans for Mr. Rooney — if Mr. Rooney's money holds out," his days at Shamrock Farm were numbered. Kass was not a meddling wife, but for that very reason her opinions carried a great deal of weight with the Chief.

The best money winners in Dad's stable were Air Patrol and Little Harp. These horses and several others of his he would send to the good Eastern tracks — Pimlico, Laurel, Bowie, Havre de Grace. The scrubs ran in claiming races at Charlestown and Shenandoah Downs. AJR knew horse flesh. No trainer could fool him by saying a horse was a good one when it was not.

Unlike John Galbreath, the owner of the Pirates, AJR never had a horse he could enter in the Triple Crown races or the big handicap races. There was a time in the 1950s, though, when it might have happened. A former trainer of his, a little fellow named Carl Hanford, was working for the stable owned by the DuPonts of Delaware. One day in a telephone call, he informed AJR that the matriarch of the family was ready to sell "a real nice horse" — a gelding — that for reasons of her own she didn't like.

"Mister Rooney," Hanford said, "I talked her into giving it one more race. If it doesn't win, I'll have to get rid of it. I think you should buy that horse, Mister Rooney. It's going to be something special."

"Sounds good, Carl. Anything you say," replied AJR, willing to accept the trainer's judgment.

But the horse won its test race, and Mrs. DuPont decided not to sell.

The horse was Kelso. Over a long career it won thirty-nine major stake races and purses adding up to nearly two million dollars.

I think there's a good chance that AJR had money riding on Kelso in most of these races — big money, if I know how he operated, and I do. Winning money on a horse like Kelso was more important to him than owning such an animal. Let the bluebloods in the racing business talk about improving the breed (not that Kelso improved the breed; turned into a eunuch by the veterinarian, all he could do was win races). Let the bluebloods pose for the television cameras with their Derby horses and garlands of roses, or their Preakness champions and fake black-eyed Susans. The engraved cups and the silver plates meant nothing to AJR. Kass, visiting the homes of his trainers, would notice on the mantel the trophies won by Air Patrol and Little Harp at events like the Atlantic City Stakes.

"Those things would look good in *our* house," she said once to AJR.

"Come off it, Kass," he told her. "What do we need with that stuff? For those people, it's different. Racing's their life! What I'm in it for is the money." He was in it, too, for the respect of the bookies, the turf writers, the trainers, the jockeys ... even the warm-up boys and hot walkers. "Yep, I like horses. But I like people more," I heard him say.

One of the people he liked was a "layoff guy" named Danny Shea. A layoff guy doesn't book bets, he places them. My wife Kay and I met Danny Shea on our honeymoon. All three of us were staying at the old Monmouth Hotel in Spring Lake, New Jersey. Mr. Shea, I perceived, was rather smitten with the beautiful red-haired math teacher who had married me. In an out-of-the-way spot in the lobby one day, he caught sight of us counting our money. He called me aside. "Artie," he said, "I know you're on your honeymoon, so I know you're probably having a cash crunch. To see you through this happy time, I can let you and Kay have a thousand dollars." When I assured Mr. Shea that we were merely taking inventory, he said there was no expiration date on his offer. If we ever needed help, I must let him know. I told this to Kay, and she was touched.

Years later I was able to find a place on the Steelers' training-camp roster for Mr. Shea's nephew, who had played at a small college in Connecticut. It puzzled AJR and I suppose the coaches as well that I would interest myself personally in a kid who had no real chance of making the team.

Despite the way he talked, AJR was openly on the lookout for a horse that could win the big races. The man he expected to find him such a colt, Tom Barry, had trained the Irish-bred Belmont Stakes winner, Cavan, and trained the horses the Chief entered in races at the major tracks. Nothing came of Barry's search for a horse that would put the Shamrock Stable in racing's top echelon except a strengthening of his friendship with AJR.

Barry himself was from Ireland, and he spoke in a soft Irish brogue. On the day that Kay and I met Danny Shea at the Monmouth Hotel, we met Tom Barry at the Monmouth Park race track. He won us over immediately by telling Kay that she was even more beautiful than she was reputed to be. His Hibernian charm so thoroughly disarmed her that by the end of the day she was confiding in him. She knew next to nothing about horse racing, she admitted. It was nevertheless very clear to her what AJR had to do if he was ever to make a splash as a stable owner. "Buy a great horse and get a good jockey to kick that great horse in the rear end."

She hadn't mentioned the need for a great or good trainer, but Barry was not offended. He chuckled and said, "Young lady, you have sized things up exactly right."

The first step in Kay's formula — buying the great horse — was the step that AJR could never negotiate. His contract jockey, a handsome little devil named Bobby Martin, could have ridden a great horse. My brothers Tim, John, and Pat looked upon jockeys as interesting characters. They were all about the size of pre-teen kids — little full-grown men who reminded me in that way of ponies. All seemed to have girlfriends and wives up to a foot or so taller than they were and without exception good-looking. There was a big, virile Steeler football player who lost his own wife to one of these pocket-sized Romeos. The dapper Bobby Martin, after leaving the Shamrock Stable, came to a bad end. Uncle Jim used to tell me, "That kid has larceny in his heart" — prophetic words. As a result of some shady business I never quite understood, he was barred from racing for life.

The Shamrock Farm was a no-frills place. It neither made nor lost money. AJR thought the land was as good as any in America, but his buildings — I have to be honest about this — were firetraps, including the farm house where all of us stayed. Again, AJR's strength was in betting on horses, not breeding them. He left the administration of the farm to his accountant, Fran Fogarty. A distant relative, Fogarty had been a hockey player at Duquesne University. During World War II, he escaped from a Nazi prison camp and worked with the French underground. He ran the Steeler front office day to day and negotiated contracts with the players, who did not then have agents. At Shamrock Farm, he audited the books, taking no guff from the trainers and hired hands. No one, but no one, put anything over on Mr. Fogarty.

After AJR's death, the farm became my brother Tim's responsibility. It was never a very opulent place — more like the kind of subsistence farm you would find in parts of Ireland. But for as long as he lived, AJR took pleasure in driving down there to relax. He liked to spend time with the mares and the foals and the yearlings. There were moments, I think, when he needed to get away from his football coaches. The horses were more restful; they couldn't talk back.

Chapter 18

Sutherland Clone

Almost by right of succession, John Michelosen took over as head coach of the Steelers after Jock Sutherland's death in 1948. He was Sutherland's protégé, dedicated to preserving all that the older man stood for. He believed in Sutherland's blood-and-guts philosophy, believed in his Spartan training methods, believed with all his heart in the single wing.

Recruited out of Ambridge, in the Beaver Valley, during the Great Depression, Michelosen had played on Sutherland-coached Pitt teams that in 1934, 1935, and 1936 lost only two games and won for the first time in the Rose Bowl. As a senior, he was the captain, becoming more and more Sutherland's clone. Once, the story is, when Pitt was protecting a lead against Notre Dame, running out the clock in the final minutes, a halfback broke loose and went all the way, twenty-one yards. Now Pitt would have to kick off — and give up the ball. Michelosen, the quarterback, collared the offending touchdown maker. "Dammit," he snapped, "the Doctor won't like this!"

Sutherland, for his part, considered Michelosen an extension of himself. He put him to work in 1938 as Pitt's assistant backfield coach, and when the blowup came, when Sutherland resigned as a protest against de-emphasis, they walked out together. Where Sutherland went as coach from then on — to the Brooklyn Dodgers in 1940, to the Steelers in 1946 — Michelosen went as second in command.

Johnny Michelosen was a man of honor, dignity, and character. But his uncritical devotion to Sutherland robbed him of individuality and in the end brought about his undoing. AJR had made him, at 31, the youngest head coach in the NFL. He was still the youngest coach when AJR let him go — not necessarily because of his undistinguished four-year record (4-8, 6-5-1, 6-6, and 4-7-1), but because of his refusal to abandon the single wing. He could not betray his teacher, Dr. Sutherland.

By the end of the 1940s the single wing was passé, and AJR knew it. Jock Sutherland had been special, but now he belonged in the history books. Pittsburgh's fans wanted to win, and they were seeing the Cleveland Browns twice a year. Paul Brown, Cleveland's coach, was revolutionizing the game. His best-known innovation — the messenger boy system of alternating two guards at the same position — enabled him to call every play, but he innovated in other ways too, and most of his innovations became standard procedure throughout the league.

It was Brown who developed the draw play, Brown who first used the fullback as both a blocker and a safety valve on pass plays, Brown who first saw the possibilities of the sideline spot pass as a means of gaining ground and at the same time stopping the clock, Brown who stationed his punter fifteen yards behind the line of scrimmage instead of ten, getting back the difference — and then some — at the other end of the field, Brown who hooked up the coaches in the press box and the coaches on the field by telephone. His players were quick and clever. They threw the ball all over the place. The Steelers would control the ball five to eight minutes to get a score; the Browns would come back, complete three passes, and kick a forty-yard field goal in two minutes.

The Browns were up to date. So were the other good teams, and every one of them, Pittsburgh fans noticed, was using the T formation. So why couldn't the Steelers? Of course it was more than just the T that went into winning. There was defense; there was talent. Get the best players and don't mess them up. To the fans, it looked as simple as that.

As rigid in his thinking as Sutherland had been, Michelosen couldn't bring himself to take the first step — junking the single wing. After all, it was Sutherland's formation. On the practice field, he paced back and forth with his head bowed, looking for answers in the grass.

For all their similarities, they were not much alike. Sutherland had great presence — intimidating presence. Michelosen did not. Sutherland was in some ways a hypocrite. Uncle Jim recalled from his Pitt days that on train trips Sutherland would carry a satchel into his stateroom. The players all knew what was in it — Scotch, in small bottles, and a small brass hammer. As Sutherland and his cronies finished each bottle, he would hammer it into fragments and flush them down the toilet. Michelosen, though secretive, never went to such lengths. He did not really have a façade.

Dismissed by the Steelers, Michelosen returned to Pitt as defensive coordinator under Red Dawson. When Dawson developed heart trouble in the middle of the 1954 season and quit, Tom

Hamilton, the athletic director, installed himself as head coach, but Michelosen did the actual work, and in 1955 he became the head coach officially. He kept the split-T formation Pitt had been using, having figured out a way to incorporate single-wing blocking. Some years later he went to a pro-style offense with an end split wide. Two of his teams played in bowl games and his 1963 team, overlooked by the bowls, had a 9-1 record. Meanwhile, a new chancellor, Edward H. Litchfield, was busily raising academic standards, and at last the time came when Michelosen no longer could recruit. By 1966 he was unemployed.

The San Francisco Forty-Niners hired him as a scout and later on made him their personnel director. Freed from the burden of living up to Jock Sutherland, he was finally able to relax and be himself. I saw him often then and enjoyed his company. Perhaps without the legacy Sutherland left him, he'd have been a better and happier coach.

Bach Is Back

In Shakespeare we learn what happens to actors. They strut and fret their hour upon the stage and then they disappear. The same thing was true of the Steelers' tailbacks. Bill Dudley's successor, Johnny Clement, had one good season, 1947, and one bad season, 1948, when he rushed for only 261 yards, and his hour came to an end. In 1949 the tailback was Joe Geri, a rookie from the University of Georgia.

Georgia's recruiters had dug him up in the hard-coal region of eastern Pennsylvania, but he arrived at the Steelers' training camp with a Southern accent. He ran, he passed, he kicked extra points, and he punted. At 5 feet 10 and 180 pounds Geri was just a little guy, and the battering he took wore him down, which explains why the 1949 Steelers lost five of their last seven games.

Even so, his statistics were respectable. In the single wing, the tailback is always the star. The following year he was better still. He rushed for 704 yards. Neither Clement nor Dudley nor Whizzer White ever had gained that many yards in one season. Disconcertingly, the Steelers' won-and-lost record did not improve. It was 6-6. Now the only single-wing team in the NFL, the Steelers were spinning their wheels.

AJR could not persuade his coach, Michelosen, to modernize the offense. Then in 1951 Joe Geri's production as the primary ball carrier fell off drastically. Michelosen responded by letting the other halfback, Ray Evans, do the passing, with indifferent success. The Steelers had a third-year player named Jim Finks who held all the passing records at Tulsa University. Michelosen used him as a defensive back.

Going into the last week of the season, the Steelers were 3-7-1. "Put Finks on offense" was the cry that went up from the fans. Michelosen kept him on defense. But injuries to Geri and his backup, Chuck Ortmann, knocked them out of the season-ending game with Washington, and Finks moved over to tailback (there was nobody else who could play the position). On a snow-covered field — not the kind running backs like — he completed thirteen of the twenty passes he threw, giving the Steelers enough offense for a 20-10 win.

AJR had seen as much of the single wing as he could take. Catching up with popular demand, he sent Michelosen packing. And then in answer to no demand whatsoever, he hired as Michelosen's successor Joe Bach, the coach he had fought with and fired in 1936.

By now they were fast friends. Bach's return to the Steelers, in fact, was viewed by the press and public as an act of nepotism once removed. Bach had been coaching at St. Bonaventure, Father Dan's school, but was out of a job, there being no team to coach after Father Dan, the athletic director, took a budgetary ax to the football program. Had AJR, possibly at the request of his brother, taken pity on Bach? Did he feel that he owed him a soft place to land? That seemed to be the perception.

The reality, I think, was different. Sportswriters are trained to be skeptics. What they failed to understand was the depth of AJR's respect for Joe Bach. "That bullheaded Dutchman is the best organizer I've ever had," he was quoted as saying. Bach was a take-charge guy, and in the 1930s AJR had not been ready for that type of coach. It seemed to him that Bach was taking charge of the whole organization. They clashed over that, and went at each other with their fists. Since then, both men had matured. Bach was less officious now, less insistent on having his way, and AJR had learned to make allowances.

It was clear to him now that a coach can't be one of the boys. Certainly Jock Sutherland had never been one of the boys. But where Sutherland simply laid down the law, Bach was a rah-rah guy. At Notre Dame he had listened to Knute Rockne's impassioned half-time speeches. Returning to the Steelers, he brought with him a watered-down version of Rockne's upbeat, inspirational approach. It was something the team needed after the negativity of the Michelosen years.

More important still, Bach was a strong advocate of adopting the T-formation. One of the assistants he hired was Gus Dorais, whose name is forever associated with the forward pass, which was legalized in 1906. It was called the *forward* pass to distinguish it from the lateral pass. Until Dorais started throwing to the aforementioned Rockne when they were Notre Dame teammates in 1913, football coaches regarded the forward pass with contempt. No one had ever heard of Notre Dame, a little backwater college in northern Indiana, but then the Irish came East and beat an astonished Army team, 35-13. They did it with Rockne, a short, stocky end, catching pass after pass from Dorais, a small, light quarterback.

Coached by Jesse Harper, Notre Dame lined up in the T, football's original formation, but shifted left or right into a box formation. Other teams were junking the T for the punt, short kick, single-wing, and double-wing formations. When Rockne succeeded Harper, he continued to use the shift, but also ran some plays without shifting. Dorais was on Rockne's staff and probably used the same offense in his years as a head coach at Gonzage (1920-'24) and Detroit (1925 –'42).

Not until 1940 did the T as we came to know it appear, worked out in its modern form by the Chicago Bears' coaches under George Halas. Clark Shaughnessy, an "advisor" to Halas, took the T to Stanford that year and rode it to an undefeated season. The Bears, in the meantime, were winning the NFL championship, and coaches everywhere (except in Pittsburgh) saw the T-formation as the new magic formula.

If Dorais was of any help to Bach, it must have been minimal. He was 60 years old, or close to it, and showing his age. He hadn't coached in some time. He was window dressing for the Steelers – living history, a well-liked old-timer who could talk about football's early days with the newspapermen.

Bach put Jim Finks at quarterback in the T, but the team did not immediately adjust, losing its first four games. As Finks gained confidence, so did everybody else. The Steelers won five of their next eight; they beat the New York Giants by a 63-7 score, getting off to a good start when Lynn Chandnois returned the opening kickoff ninety-one yards for a touchdown. All told that season, Finks threw twenty touchdown passes, including nine to Elbie Nickel.

Joe Geri played very little (his position had become obsolete) and in 1953 was traded to the Chicago Cardinals. With that team, his performance was so disappointing that Charley Bidwill, the Cardinals' owner, called AJR to say that he planned on having Geri tailed by a private detective. Mr. Bidwill suspected him of involvement in some kind of betting ring. AJR said, "No, Charley, he's not a bad guy, just a drunk."

In his last couple of years with the Steelers, Geri had taken up carousing and skirt chasing. I remember an incident at training camp. Joe saw me running laps and held up a hand. I stopped, and he said, "Artie, you run like a girl." Then he corrected my form. "Swing your arms like this. Bend your knees like that." He watched me do a few more laps, giving advice. I was now his pal. Two days later he took me aside on the practice field and called my attention to a good-looking girl among the spectators. He said, "Do me a favor, kid. Go over there and ask her if she'd like to have a date with Joe Geri."

I was too much the product of my home training to oblige.

After one season with the Cardinals, Geri reformed. He went into coaching and became a born-again Christian. At Chattanooga State in Tennessee, where he was wrestling coach and assistant football coach, he enforced a strict set of rules. No smoking. No drinking, No swearing. Like the private detective Bidwill wanted to hire, he would follow suspected miscreants in his car. He would count the cigarette butts they tossed out the window. Geri lasted twenty years at Chattanooga, so he must have been pleasing his bosses.

Back to Joe Bach. The Steelers under Michelosen had been accused of leaving their game on the practice field. He worked the players at least as hard as Sutherland had. Joe Bach's attitude was: Do the drills and be done with it. Joe had mellowed since his first time around with the Steelers.

He also had developed some physical problems – diabetes, for one thing. At first, AJR was not aware of it. When he saw what the effects were, he began to have doubts. In asking Bach to return, had he made a mistake? Maybe yes, maybe no. In appointing Walt Kiesling the No. 1 assistant to Bach, he most certainly made a mistake.

Poison Gas

I never have said that Kiesling turned the coaching staff against Bach. There was no need to. If the assistant coaches looked to Kies as their leader, rather than Bach, they did so without his collusion. But Kiesling was supposed to be Bach's right-hand man. He might have shown him the loyalty a head coach is entitled to expect. He did not. Nor did anyone else.

By the time AJR re-hired him, diabetes had changed Bach in ways that were plain to see. The take-charge guy became docile and compliant. Instead of calling the tune, he deferred to Kies and the other assistants, costing him their respect. They ridiculed Joe behind his back.

Kiesling was smart and experienced. He was also inclined to disparage any football man who knew less, in his opinion, than he did, an overcrowded category with Bach at its head. In truth, Bach was losing his grip. The game, it was clear, had passed him by, and Kiesling made certain that the whole Steeler family, from the owner right down to the trainers and equipment men, got the picture.

On the practice field, Bach would watch a drill for several minutes, demonstrate or explain something, and walk away. As soon as he was out of earshot — no great distance because Joe was getting deaf — Kies would say to the players, "Don't listen to that donkey."

He poisoned the team's attitude toward Bach, and the infection went deep. During a game in Bach's second season I was standing on the sideline next to Lynn Chandnois when one of our guys made a boneheaded play. "Saint Bonaventure!" Chandnois muttered disdainfully. St. Bonaventure was where Bach had been coaching, and to Chandnois it epitomized the bush leagues.

The Steelers opened the 1953 season as dark-horse contenders, but Jim Finks was playing hurt. A knee injury hobbled him from the start, and his passing suffered. His completion rate was so poor that Bach had him splitting time with the undistinguished Bill Mackrides. Of course Finks was not the whole Steeler team. Elbie Nickel was still a top receiver — whoever put the ball up, he could catch it. Chandnois excelled as a runner and kick returner. Jack Butler intercepted nine passes, turning three of those interceptions into touchdowns. It wasn't enough. The Steelers finished the season with a 6-6 record.

And the backstabbing continued at training camp the next year. My brothers and I, who were always around the team, might have passed the word along to AJR. What we told him instead was that Pittsburgh needed a coach like Paul Brown. Actually, AJR knew what was happening all along. At one point, he advised Bach to fire Kies. Bach refused. AJR, in keeping with the hands-off policy he adhered to, did not insist. Effectively, Bach's decision meant that he himself would leave and Kies would stay.

The end came for Bach at a squad meeting. Two days earlier the Steelers had lost a pre-season game, and he was showing the film. Within minutes one of the players ... there is no other way to say this ... farted. He farted explosively. A burst of laughter interrupted Bach's spiel. Bach was hard of hearing, remember, and the outbreak of levity puzzled him. As he started to speak again, another player erupted. Then a third. And a fourth. An epidemic of flatulence swept the room.

Players and assistant coaches were laughing and screaming, bent over double in their chairs. At last Bach realized what was happening. He turned on the lights and called out in his best Knute Rockne voice, "That's it!" The hilarity, but not the odor, died away. "Grow up! You're supposed to be college men," Bach snapped, shutting off the projector. The meeting was over; giggling and babbling, the players went back to their dormitory.

Unnoticed by all, AJR had come into the room at the height of the commotion. Standing in the back, he had seen and heard everything, and he understood now that Bach had lost control of the team.

On the following Sunday, the Steelers played another pre-season game, which resulted in another defeat. The game was at Forbes Field. Walking home with some of my brothers and friends, I saw AJR as he drove across the Sixth Street Bridge. He blew his horn at us. He looked grim, and not without cause. He was on his way, we found out, to do something distasteful — fire a head coach.

Again, there is no other way to put this: Joe Bach was farted out of the league. He might still have survived the farcical aborted squad meeting except for an earlier incident. In one of the first pre-season games, a player had gone out of bounds and careened into Bach near the bench, knocking him over. Bach was not seriously hurt, but the team doctor insisted on a precautionary checkup at a hospital. Only then did AJR learn that his coach was a diabetic. Whether Bach himself had known is unclear. At any rate, the doctors told AJR that diabetes could be a mood-altering disease, giving him more of an insight into Bach's loss of assertiveness and his consequent failure to lead.

AJR made him an offer. He could stay with the team as personnel director and head scout. At the time, 1954, personnel directors were a rare new species in the NFL. The Steelers, up to then, never had seen the need for one. A personnel director's work was a part-time occupation for front-office people with other responsibilities. Assistant coaches did all the scouting, most of which took place when the colleges were holding spring practice. AJR now was prepared to put Bach in charge of the scouting operation. There was also an implied guarantee. Barring the unforeseen, Bach could remain with the Steelers for the rest of his life.

Bach said that first he must talk with his wife. AJR asked him not to. "Take the job now and tell your wife later," he said. No, Bach replied. He and his wife had promised each other years before that they would always do things together. AJR could not dissuade him. He talked with his wife and called back the next day. He said that *they* had decided he would not stay with the team.

AJR, looking for a reason, concluded that Mrs. Bach's pride must have been hurt.

Bach never coached again. It took some difficult string-pulling, but AJR got him a job that Mrs. Bach's pride allowed him to accept. Recommended by Mayor Lawrence (at AJR's urging), he went to work for the state as a labor mediator and arbitrator.

He served the state well and seemed perfectly content, but you could tell that deep down he missed football. In the late 1960s an opportunity came along. Jack Butler by then was director of the Blesto Group, and he hired his old coach as a part-time scout. The irony here was inescapable. Bach had refused an opportunity to be a director of scouts, a job that would have paid him a good salary, and now he jumped at the chance to do the same kind of work at the lowest level and for very little money. Go figure.

Bach had two important qualifications to be a scout. First, he was well organized. Second, he was well connected. A scout needs friends who are college coaches, and Bach knew more coaches than he could count.

I saw him one Saturday up in north central Pennsylvania, where Lock Haven State College is located. Lock Haven was playing one of the Negro colleges, and we were there, as I recall, because the Negro team had a kid worth looking at. It was small-time football in a small-time setting, but Bach could not have been happier.

He had some age on him. My intention was to stay in Lock Haven overnight and rest up for the trip back to Pittsburgh, but Bach put me to shame by saying that *he* intended to drive back right after the game. He was looking forward to a Steeler game the next day and to a social affair preceding it. I thought, well, if an old-timer like Joe can drive all night, so can I. And I did. Bach drove back, I drove back, and on Sunday we both watched the Steelers.

On Monday Bach attended the Curbstone Coaches luncheon at the Roosevelt Hotel. He was there to receive an award for his contributions to football. When the speeches were over and the crowd was departing, he lingered on the dais to chat with Joe Tucker, who did the play-by-play for the Steelers' radio broadcasts. Suddenly he fell to the floor.

"Joe! Joe!" Tucker cried. "Are you all right?" There was no reply. Joe Bach had died of a heart attack.

'Get a Football'

Before Bert Bell replaced him as the NFL's commissioner, Elmer Layden brushed off the upstart All-America Conference with a curt piece of advice: "Get a football." The new league founded by the *Chicago Tribune's* sports editor, Arch Ward, did get a football. Its equipment was the same as the NFL's and its rules were the same. But there was one important difference neither Layden nor his employers foresaw: the All-America Conference had no color barrier.

Not so the NFL. Although AJR never mentioned this to me, the NFL practiced de facto segregation. Since 1934, when the old established owners forced AJR to drop Ray Kemp from his team, no blacks had played in the NFL. Giving Kemp his release was painful for AJR, but after only one year as a member of the club he did not yet belong to the in-group.

The All-America Conference came into being in 1946. World War II had ended and the culture was changing. In 1947 the earth seemed to shake because the Brooklyn Dodgers signed a black man, Jackie Robinson, to a major-league baseball contract. The year before, without fanfare, the Cleveland Browns of the All-America Conference had signed two black players, Marion Motley and Bill Willis.

Quickly, an NFL team, the Los Angeles Rams, added Kenny Washington and Woody Strode to its roster. The Browns' pair and the Rams' pair were the vanguard. By the time the leagues merged, in 1950, blacks were still few but no longer a rarity in football. Coaches began to realize that a great, untapped pool of talent existed. The Steelers, under Jock Sutherland and John Michelosen, had remained one hundred percent white, but when Joe Bach took over in 1952 he announced that his players would be judged on their ability, not their race.

And the word got around. Black players were showing up at pre-season camp in Olean uninvited. Bach at first made an honest attempt to give everybody a fair tryout, but there wasn't enough time, there wasn't enough space in the dormitory. He reverted to a policy of turning the walk-ons away.

I was 17 that year, a camp functionary. What I noticed about the black guys was that they were built well, moved with more fluidity than many of the whites, and were quick. The white players would tell me, "Yeah, yeah, they look good, but they don't have the smarts."

There were coaches who talked that way, too. For some time to come, an element in football clung to the idea that blacks did not have what were called the intangibles. In 1955 the Steelers drafted Willie McClung, who was black. An assistant coach informed me that Willie would absolutely never be good enough to make it. How could he tell? By Willie's walk. Willie did not have the stride of a football player.

Plodding, shuffling, or pussyfooting into his guard position, Willie McClung held his own in three full seasons with the Steelers, two with the Browns, and two with the Lions.

From Uncle Jim came a different appraisal of blacks. I heard him say that without them no football team would again be able to win. The statement at the time seemed radical. Could he have known there would be a day when all the best running backs, all the best defensive backs, most of the good wide receivers and defensive linemen, and most of the first-round draft choices were black?

The first black player drafted by Bach — the first to make the team — was Jack Spinks, a fullback. Spinks had played college football at Alcorn State in Mississippi. He had the ideal build for a football player and he could run. When somebody asked one of the coaches about Spinks, the coach answered as follows: "He doesn't even own a suit jacket to wear on road trips." Uncle Jim stood up and took off his own jacket, saying, "Here — he can have mine if that's all he needs to make the team."

Spinks made the team, but there were whites who continued to resent him. At practice one day, he took a swing pass or screen pass and ran right over the defensive back, a white player from one of the segregated colleges in the South, shaking him up both physically and emotionally. The defensive back called Spinks a lot of racial names and threw a football at him — hard — from point-blank range. Spinks returned to the huddle without a word.

After practice, AJR, who either had witnessed the incident or heard about it, took Spinks aside and said, "Jack, the guy who threw that football at you is a good kid, but the next time anything like that happens I want you to punch him out."

Spinks had a solid career in the NFL. He ended up playing guard for the New York Giants' 1956 championship team. By the mid-1960s, blacks were becoming established in the league. We had one who dated white girls. This surprised some of the players. However, he was not ostracized.

Willie Asbury, as he was listed on our draft chart, was a running back from Kent State. When he arrived at training camp I welcomed him, using his first name, or what I thought was his first name, as we talked. Noticing that he appeared to be uncomfortable with the way our conversation was going, I asked, "Is it Willie or Bill?" Swiftly, he answered, "Bill. It's Bill," and from then on he was more at ease. "Willie," I had suddenly realized, was a stereotypical black name. Asbury led the Steelers in rushing that year — 1966.

One of the blacks on the squad in 1952 was Willie Robinson, a North Side kid who had played for the Rooney Reds and then for Lincoln University of Pennsylvania. When his days as a Rooney Red were finished he was watching them play a Mount Lebanon team sponsored by Bob Prince, the broadcaster of Pirate games. Accompanied by his Steeler coach, Jock Sutherland, AJR was in the crowd. To his surprise — to the surprise of everybody, in fact — the "cake eaters" from suburban Mount Lebanon were pushing the tough North Siders all over the field. Suddenly one of the bigger Rooney Reds took off for the dressing room. He did not return. In his place — and wearing his uniform — here came Willie Robinson.

Whether Willie turned the tide I don't remember. What I do remember is that his dash to the rescue had Jock Sutherland, The Great Stoneface, roaring with laughter.

Willie Robinson was a speedster, as sleek and finely honed as a thoroughbred race horse. He took a realistic view of his opportunity with the Steelers. "The only thing these coaches know about Lincoln," he said, referring to his alma mater, "is that he was president."

It was true that the coaches were not too high on Willie. AJR allowed his coaches to coach, but before the first pre-season game he asked Joe Bach to let Willie run back a kickoff. The game was with Green Bay, and AJR went to Gene Ronzani, a former Steeler assistant who was coaching the Packers, and told him about Willie. "He's a kid from my neighborhood," AJR explained. "He isn't going to make the team. He won't be in there after the kickoff, and I'd like to see him get his hands on the ball. Could you kick it into his area?"

"Art," said Ronzani, "it's a pre-season game. I'll do better than that. I'll make sure he gets the ball and takes it all the way for a touchdown, if that's what you want."

AJR was appalled. "No! No!" he protested. "We can't do that. We have the integrity of the game to think about." Then he noticed Ronzani's broad grin. The offer had been meant as a joke.

Ronzani did tell his kicker to get the ball to Willie instead of to Ray Mathews, the other return man. The kick went into the end zone. Willie caught the ball and started up the field. Ray Mathews was screaming at him. "Down it, Willie! Down it! Come back!" But Willie was out to the one-or two-yard line. He skidded to a stop and backpedaled. Now he was back in the end zone, and the Green Bay coverage guys were all around him. The instant a Packer laid a hand on Willie, Green Bay had an automatic safety.

In the locker room afterward, Willie said, "Well, I wrote my own ticket home." He wasn't wrong. He drifted out of football and had to live with the nickname "Wrong Way Willie" for a while.

There were truly gifted athletes in the black schools back then, and most of them were pretty good guys. With some extra coaching and seasoning, many black players who were cut before the season started could have been standout contributors. The coaches at the black schools were competent but spread too thin. They could not give the players a lot of individual attention. So when the kids from these black schools and even the smaller white schools came to the NFL they needed special tutoring. They were not going to get it for several more years.

Pragmatism

In the late 1950s Tom Gallery, sports director of the National Broadcasting Company, made a deal with the Steelers and the Baltimore Colts to televise some of each team's home games on Saturday nights. It guaranteed them more money than other teams were getting from their regional broadcasts, but Carroll Rosenbloom, the owner of the Colts, refused to accept a fifty-fifty split.

He would take nothing less than two-thirds, he insisted. The Colts, having recently won a championship, were much the more attractive team to viewers and advertisers, went his argument. A team like the Steelers, whose ragamuffin status was beginning to look permanent, had to be content with the leavings.

Ed Kiely of the front office and my brother Dan, negotiating for AJR, were steamed. In no uncertain terms they let their adversary know what they thought of his arrogance. AJR, however, reined them in. As much as he liked their spunk, he could see that if Rosenbloom did not get his way the deal might collapse. With his gambler's mentality, he had worked the numbers: one-third would be better than nothing at all and still an improvement on the fee for a regional telecast. He could afford to pay better players — a Bobby Layne, a Big Daddy Lipscomb. Pride, he used to say, can be important, "but don't cut off your nose to spite your face."

The lesson was not lost on Dan, his heir apparent. Kiely and Fran Fogarty had some decision-making power, but Dan now surpassed them in authority. No playboy, no dumbbell, Dan kept his eye on the ball. "Out of my way or a leg off" was more than just a saying with Dan.

As for Rosenbloom, when reports that he was involved in serious unsavory activities began to circulate, the NFL appointed AJR a committee of one to investigate them. He learned that the accusations were undoubtedly true, but could pin nothing down. Hearsay evidence wasn't good enough. For example, a man in Las Vegas told AJR of having burned down Rosenbloom's house. He said that Rosenbloom had hired him to do it and used the insurance money to pay off gambling debts. AJR believed the man completely, but how could he ask the NFL to convict one of its own on the unsupported word of a professional arsonist?

Meeting with Rosenbloom in a hotel room somewhere, AJR laid out the case against him. Rosenbloom, he said, promptly fell to his knees and swore on the lives of his wife and children that all of these charges were false. For AJR, that was enough. As far as he was concerned, a man who would swear on the lives of his wife and children had to be telling the truth, and he pursued the investigation no further.

"But do you know what?" he would add when Rosenbloom's affairs were just a memory. "One year later, one year after swearing on the life of his wife, he divorced her."

In time, Rosenbloom became suspiciously curious about the Rooney family's race-track business, and AJR warned his sons not to answer any questions. "That Rosenbloom," he would say. "Lots of charm. Knows how to sweet-talk. But he'd hijack a deal in a minute."

Officially, Rosenbloom's death in the surf off the coast of South Florida was an accidental drowning, but rumors persisted that "frogmen" hired by the mob had pulled him down into the water and held him there. As with the stories about his gambling, there was only the most insubstantial proof.

Chapter 19

Boyz 'n the Hood

North Side kids thought it was great sport to give wrong directions to motorists who had lost their way. "Keep going for three blocks and then turn right and when you come to the first light, turn left." By the time the driver did that, he'd be nowhere near his hoped-for destination. I remember an old radio show called "Fibber McGee and Molly'.." One of Molly's signature lines after hearing a tall one from Fibber would be "'T'ain't funny, McGee." Nor was there anything funny about playing tricks on unsuspecting strangers. Small wonder people felt that North Side kids were nothing more than hoodlums.

Certainly there were high-class North Siders like Ray Utz, a distant cousin of mine who became a priest; like Larry McCabe, who got a Ph. D. and spent his adult life as a teacher; and like Mike Hayden, an Air Force general who was head of the CIA during the Bush 43 administration. On the other hand, there were also plenty of hooligans, and a lot of them ended up in the pokey.

Many North Side kids believed that the way to settle an argument was with your fists or by letting loose with a barrage of filthy language. It was not until I got to St. Vincent College that I learned the difference between vulgarity and profanity. One of my football teammates asked old Father John, a Benedictine monk from Hungary, for the loan of his car. Father John answered, "I will not loan you my car. I know what you want it for. All you American boys think about is fucking." We were shocked at the use of this forbidden (to us) power word by a pious monastic. "Well, boys," he said, taking note of our reaction, "I see you're ashamed for me. But the word I have used is merely vulgar. We should be able to express ourselves without vulgarity, yes. Now, you boys, I know, take the name of the Lord in vain. *That* is a sin. To call somebody a "fucking S.O.B." is not a sin. To say it in anger may be a sin, but the words themselves are not sinful. I have heard you boys say 'God damn you' to one another, and that is the sin of taking the Lord's name in vain."

Without a Father John to set parameters for them, North Side kids used vulgar language and profane language indiscriminately, and often it led to a hey rube. There was a fight between two of our schoolmates at St. Peter's that ended in a death. One of the grade school's best football players was involved; he went to the juvenile detention house in Morganza for all of his junior high school and high school years. Another boy who had a peripheral role in the fight was given a lesser sentence.

When my brother Tim played freshman football at North Catholic, the Morganza team was on its schedule. Tim said that the North kids expected the Morganza kids to disregard the rules against unnecessary roughness, so they decided to hit first and hit hard. From the opening kickoff to the final gun, Tim said, they punched, kicked, elbowed, and bit. Surprisingly, the reform-school players did not retaliate. Because as football players they were disorganized, grabbing and leaning instead of blocking and tackling, the game was one-sided in North's favor. "When it was over," said Tim, "we felt kind of sorry for them."

Later, the North kids learned that the Morganza players had been warned by their overseers that if they tried any rough stuff against decent Catholic kids from Pittsburgh they would pay for it. Also, the North kids found out, the work requirements at Morganza were so strict that the football team had little or no time to practice.

"All in all," Tim said, "it was a hollow victory for us."

The Rooney brothers' overseer was AJR. "Idle hands are the tools of the devil," so we were always kept busy with chores around the house — shining all of Dad's shoes, for example. Once, as a punishment, the good Brothers of Mary at North Catholic had two of our football teammates clean and shine the shoes of the marching band. Humiliated (football players feel vastly superior to band members), our friends saved face by using brown shoe polish on black shoes and by mismating the shoes — pairing a size nine with a size twelve and so on. We wouldn't have dared to try that with AJR's shoes.

At 940 North Lincoln Avenue, there was an old tin garage, a storage place for junk, in the back yard. By order of AJR, it was taken down. A permanent rubbish bin would replace it, but meanwhile, to prepare the ground for the pouring of concrete, a lot of earth had to be moved.

AJR decreed that his sons and any friends they could recruit would do the manual labor. The McCabe brothers, Richie and Jumbo; the Hart brothers, Billy and Jack; and Babe Hugo volunteered. AJR supplied us with picks, shovels, and a long steel instrument that looked like a spear, and we went to work. Before we could start, we had to carry some trash cans out of the way, and all hell broke loose.

Hordes of rats jumped out of the cans. They scurried for safety, but not as fast as we scurried ourselves. Our yells and the screeching of the rats brought Kass out of the house. She told us to forget about moving the dirt, she'd get an adult to do it. Our pride hurt, we shouted her down and started excavating. Soon we hit a tunnel, and out of it poured rats—big rats, little rats, medium-sized rats. We scattered, some of us heading for the back porch, others climbing up on the fence.

Once the rats had dispersed, Richie McCabe was the first to pick up a shovel and go back to work. He was soon followed by Jackie Hart. The rest of us followed his lead a bit later. When we got to the next tunnel and the next pack of rats came streaming out, we didn't run. We fought them, flailing at the rats with our shovels and picks. There were stones in the back yard, and we used them as heavy artillery. Digging again, we unearthed more tunnels, all full of rats. We were ready for them and won every battle. What it all added up to was more damn fun than we'd had the entire summer.

Rat hunts from then on became a part of our lives. The North Side, it seemed, was infested with rats. We would arm ourselves with clubs and broken pavement bricks and start down an alley at dusk. Someone would bring along a flashlight. In back of the big old rooming houses or the overcrowded one-family houses or the houses where the black families lived, the garbage was piled high. The bravest kid in the gang would shake the trash can; a rat would jump out and the brickbat barrage would begin.

Other rats would tumble out after the first one. The kid who shook the can was the bravest one in the gang because the hurlers of brickbats did not have perfect control. He was putting himself in harm's way. When a rat lay wounded, some kid with a club would beat it to death. Put these tough North Side kids on an uninhabited island and you'd have a re-enactment of what happened in "The Lord of the Flies" — everybody reverting to primitive savagery.

The rat hunts ended with the coming of television. AJR won our first black and white set, which had a screen about the size of a dinner plate, in a raffle. The neighborhood kids would flock to our house when their favorite shows came on — "Captain Video," studio wrestling, the Friday Night Fights. By the time the poorer families had television, everybody was mesmerized by it. We did get outdoors to play softball, touch football, and basketball.

In the softball games, AJR would do some pitching and take a turn at bat. Like Wee Willie Keeler, who said the secret of his success *was* to "hit 'em where they ain't," he could place a ball anywhere he wanted to. He would run to first base, but no farther. It was fun to have him actively taking part, but then pretty soon he'd be coaching us — or, rather, preaching to us on how to play the game.

When we played touch football, everybody demanded to be the quarterback or a receiver. Nobody wanted to block. The games started out as "touch" and invariably ended up with the players on defense tackling. The footballs and equipment — oversized but coveted — came from the Steelers. When we put on the helmets and pads, we meant business. We were going to hit. Actually, it was all mostly grab-ass, lean, and react, with lots of piling-on.

I am sure that sports— along with a good family life — helped to keep the Rooney kids and perhaps a few others out of trouble.

Hepburn

Whenever a new kid moved into the neighborhood, we initiated him into our gang. For this purpose, we had an old Steeler training table which we kept in the basement at 940 North Lincoln Avenue. The newcomer, shirtless, would lie on the table face down, with a few kids on both sides holding his arms and legs. By twisting his neck, he could see us heating a sharp table knife with a cigarette lighter.

As he watched, he became more and more apprehensive. He knew that something was about to happen. But what?

On another table, out of his sight, rested a piece of ice and a piece of bacon. Suddenly, when the knife was red hot, one of us would plunge it into the bacon, creating a sizzle and a smell — the smell of burning flesh? — while at the same time, somebody else would slap the piece of ice on the initiate's bare back. To the human senses, for a moment or two, extreme heat and extreme cold feel alike. The initiate would think he'd been stabbed.

At this point, everybody would laugh, ending the game.

But there was one kid, Hepburn by name, who could not quite appreciate the joke. Instead of joining in the merriment, Hepburn went berserk. He threw off the guys who had him pinioned as if they were rag dolls. No one could pacify him. He was turning the basement into a rumpus room when Aunt Alice McNulty flew down the steps. Taking immediate control, she chased us outdoors, where Hepburn, much calmer now, was made to see that we had meant him no harm.

Hepburn was 17 years old at the outbreak of the Korean War and his parents allowed him to enlist. Home on furlough, he came to our house in his Army uniform. He was toting the kind of knife used to kill people. Later in the week, the police picked him up for carrying a revolver. He told them he needed extra firepower in case his Army rifle failed him, and the cops took his word for it. We never saw Hepburn again. I hope he made it back from Korea.

To keep us off the streets of the North Side in the summer, Mom and Dad carted us off to the family cottage in the mountains near Ligonier. Defeating their purpose, we brought the streets with us.

World War II movies were popular back then, and a weapon called the flame thrower intrigued us. My brother Dan constructed a home-made flame thrower by filling an insect pump with lighter fluid and shooting the spray over a candle, which ignited it. After that he experimented with a bicycle pump, gasoline, and matches, and then with a fire extinguisher, which was close to the real thing. Whoever lighted the match was risking third-degree burns, but our contraptions usually worked. We set the woods near our cottage on fire before the protests of the neighbors forced us into tamer pursuits.

There was just one minor casualty from all this. Fooling with the lighter fluid, Tim burned a hand. I ask myself how we survived, and the only answer I can think of is divine intervention.

Doomed

In the summer of the twins' graduation from St. Peter's School a note came to AJR at the Steelers' office Downtown. It *was* neither handwritten nor typed, but put together with letters and words cut from newspapers and magazines and pasted on plain white paper. Unsigned, it demanded X amount of money to be delivered to a certain place at a certain time. If AJR did not comply, the note warned, his sons Pat and John were "DOOMED."

On or about the same date, the Heinz family — pickle and ketchup and baby food makers — received a similar communication. If a certain sum was not paid, its scion, young John Heinz, a future United States senator, would be done away with.

Dad and Mom took the threat seriously. They had a vivid recollection of the Lindbergh baby's kidnapping in 1934. Dad, according to Mom, put on a good front but was visibly shaken. He got in touch with the FBI. and then packed off the twins to our summer cottage in Ligonier, where they could be kept under family surveillance.

In July he sent them to the Steelers' training camp at St. Bonaventure. There were exhibition games scheduled that year in Shreveport, Louisiana, and Des Moines, Iowa. Dad took the twins along on the train rides with two of the older camp kids, Jack Hart and Richie McCabe, assigned to watch over them. Coaches, players, trainers, equipment men, and even the newspaper reporters helped out.

This was the summer an anonymous letter writer threatened *to* shoot the great Pirate home-run hitter, Ralph Kiner. As AJR's guest at Forbes Field for another pre-season game, he sat on the Steelers' bench, not far from the twins. "My God, look at that!" someone said "All three of them together! Perfect targets for a sniper!" Perfect targets to be sure, but the day went by without gunfire.

In the fall the twins enrolled at North Catholic. Rooney males all played football and they went out for the freshman team. Attempting to be inconspicuous about it, two plainclothesmen from the city police department shadowed them all day at school and looked on from the sidelines at football practice. Because the twins, wearing helmets and pads and dirty gray uniforms, were hard to distinguish from their teammates, some confusion arose. Another problem was that Tim and I practiced with the varsity squad, which used the same field, and there were times when the gumshoes seemed to be watching the wrong set of brothers.

Furthermore, they attracted suspicion. Here were these two big strangers who never missed football practice, rain or shine. Were they the would-be kidnappers, waiting for their chance? That was one school of thought. Another had them sized up as perverts.

The football coaches, until I explained what was going on, leaned toward the opinion that they were scouts for a rival team. To aggravate matters, one twin, John, lost interest in football and quit. You had to love the game to practice on Gardner Field, which was just oil-coated dirt under ordinary conditions and a slithery quagmire when it rained. And there were the smells — the disagreeable mix of odors from the rendering plants, the Heinz pickle factory, and an old abandoned brewery at the foot of North Catholic's perch on Troy Hill. So John turned in his equipment, and now with the twins split up for a part of each day, the bodyguards' work was twice as difficult.

The twins went to school and back home again on the jam-packed trolleys that served North Catholic, changing cars at the North Side Market hub, and the bodyguards would lose them in the crush. At a meeting with AJR and their boss, they complained that the job was too much for them. One even argued that if they themselves couldn't keep up with John and Pat, there was no chance the kidnappers could do it. In the end, the four parties worked out a compromise: the cops would continue to monitor the twins, but not as closely or obtrusively as before.

A month or two after the meeting, the FBI cracked the case. Its agents arranged a "sting" in West Park — a drop-off of the ransom money in the muzzle of the Civil War cannon near the statue of a soldier. An FBI agent and a Pittsburgh policeman hid out in the park on the appointed day and kept watch. Other agents and cops, men and women, blended into the normal flow of West Park pedestrian traffic. One pair was pushing a baby carriage (with no baby in it). Another couple sat on a bench and romanced — sweethearts lost to the world. An FBI man with a brush and trash can picked up litter. Two retired cops posed as an elderly couple out for a stroll.

The minutes went by and nothing happened. People came and went, making their usual daily rounds. The cops waited and watched, eyes fixed on the cannon. They saw two young girls approach it and stop. The agent in charge was exasperated. Why didn't they move on? If there was action, they'd be in the middle of it. Still the girls lingered, earnestly conversing.

"Damn! Someone get them away from the cannon!" the agent muttered. But now what was this? One girl walked up to the cannon and reached an arm into the muzzle. She pulled out the bait — a package that may or may not have contained money. And the FBI had the culprits. One girl was 12 and the other 13.

They were taken into custody and given psychological testing. They said the idea for sending threats to two prominent families came to them from something they had read. The older of the two was confined to a mental hospital for a period of time and then released. Neither the Rooney family nor the Heinz family ever knew what eventually became of her. The other girl's fate has also remained a mystery. To Mom and Dad, none of this mattered. All they wanted to do was forget the whole bothersome affair.

Man of Iron

My coach at North Catholic, Chuck Mehelich, was a taskmaster — after all, he had played for Jock Sutherland when Sutherland coached the Steelers. Mehelich was as tough as they come. In a game between the Steelers and Detroit, I saw him go down the field on kickoff coverage and put a thunderous hit on Leon Hart, who went from Turtle Creek to Notre Dame and won the Heisman Trophy. Considered the prototypical tight end, even though he also played defense, he was six inches taller and seventy-five pounds heavier than Mehelich, but a stretcher was needed to get him off the field. I intend to discuss this seismic event in fuller detail later on.

In addition to being tough, Mehelich was also inclined to be testy. The Steelers' center, Frank Sinkovitz, who also played linebacker, liked to encourage his teammates by patting them on the rump, which irritated Mehelich. During one game he warned Sinkovitz. "Don't do that to me again." A couple of plays later, Sinkovitz did it again. "Stop!" Mehelich growled. Still later, Sinkovitz patted him a third time. Wasting no more words, Mehelich uncorked a right-hand uppercut that missed contact with Sinkovitz's face mask — I don't know how — but not with his jaw. Sinkovitz played no more football that day.

Mehelich played so hard that by the end of his sixth season he was physically beaten down. The head coaching job at North Catholic was open, and AJR went to bat for him. No other endorsement was necessary. But lacking experience or the foresight to prepare himself — it would have been better if he had served an apprenticeship somewhere — Mehelich wasn't ready to coach.

There were times when he forgot that he was dealing with high school kids. Demonstrating some of the basics of defensive line play, he knocked our little nose guard, Jack Embersits, unconscious. (There were no lasting ill effects. After North Catholic, Embersits attended Yale, captained its 1952 football team, and returned as a graduate to be vice president for management operations and an officer of the Yale Corporation.)

Mehelich overdid the theatrics, I thought. Between halves of a game we were losing he called us quitters. At the climactic moment of his rant, worked up into a frenzy, he drove his fist through the blackboard in the locker room.

Sometimes in practice he scrimmaged with us, and one day, to our consternation, a third-string defensive end who liked to hit as well as Mehelich did, but had no other qualifications for the game, turned the tables on him. He blindsided Mehelich, knocking him head over heels.

Prizefighters will tell you it's the punch you didn't see that knocks you out. So blindsiding, I guess, doesn't count. The guy who really cut Mehelich down to size was not the blindsider, but our center, Larry Deer. Many years later he recalled his greatest day as a football player.

"It was near the end of the season," he said. "We were going through a tackling drill down on one corner of the field. The tackling dummy had two legs on it, simulating a runner, and must have weighed close to seventy pounds. Chuck liked to stand behind the dummy with his arms wrapped around it, and the tackler would get a ten-yard running start. At the moment of impact, Chuck would throw the dummy into him. On this particular day, as we were lining up to take turns, a red film seemed to cover my eyes. All the bullshit of that year gripped me in an uncontrollable rage. Going in low on the dummy, I hit it like a runaway freight train and put Chuck down on his ass."

Deer remembered that Mehelich got up, patted him on the back, and said, "Nice hit." There were two other things Deer remembered: the agonizing pain in his shoulder and a feeling of immense gratification.

If Mehelich lost status as a result of Larry's hit, my brother Tim unwittingly put him back on his pedestal. Mehelich gave a class in physical education, and Tim saw to it one day that several carpet tacks were placed in his chair. When Mehelich entered the room and prepared to sit, there was great anticipation. Suspecting nothing, he plopped himself down in such a way that penetration by the tacks was unavoidable. The tacks could not have failed to do their work.

Amazingly, though, Mehelich gave no sign of discomfort. He didn't jump. He didn't cry out. He didn't wince. He didn't change his expression.

From then on the students called him Iron Ass. They were totally and irreversibly in awe.

Baldy Regan

North Catholic High School, at the top of Troy Hill, was a streetcar ride from the part of the North Side where I lived. All the kids I knew, and many I did not know, boarded that trolley every morning, and one of the kids I did not know always sat next to me. He was cheerful, gabby, and undersized, and it got so I looked forward to seeing him. On the way up he would borrow his carfare from me — ten cents — never failing to repay it after lunch. Had he borrowed a dime in the meanwhile from somebody else? I never asked.

Nor did I ask him to tell me his name. This was at the start of our freshman year, and a lot of us were strangers to one another. Almost from the first day, though, everybody seemed to know my seat companion, and vice versa.

When the call went out for freshman football, we reported for practice at Gardner Field. I looked around on the first day and saw the kid who always borrowed a dime. He was there on the second day, too. The coaches never bothered to cut the squad. Three days of conditioning drills — calisthenics and wind sprints — took care of that. A lot of self-proclaimed tough guys quit of their own accord. My little friend, though, kept returning. When we ran the wind sprints, I noticed, he limped. It appeared to be a struggle for him, but he never dropped out.

On the fourth day, we were issued our hand-me-down uniforms and my friend was among the survivors. He had made the team. But then one night as we were riding home on the streetcar he told me that instead of playing he was going to be the student manager. The coaches, he said, had suggested it. He'd had polio, it seems, which accounted for the limp. No doubt for reasons having to do with liability insurance, a history of polio disqualified a kid from any contact sport.

We continued to ride the streetcar together. Meanwhile, I'd been hearing a lot of talk about a freshman called Baldy Regan. It was Baldy this and Baldy that. Baldy said this and Baldy did the other thing. Was there a kid in our class who was losing his hair? Nobody fit the description. I was too vain to ask questions. It would make me look like a know-nothing, I thought, but my curiosity got the better of my conceit. I put the question to a friend:

"Who is this Baldy Regan?"

He stared at me without answering. I asked him again. "Who is this Baldy Regan, anyway?"

"Are you kidding?" he said

"No! There isn't a bald-headed kid in the whole school. How would I know who Baldy Regan is?" My friend was still looking at me as if I had a screw loose. He said, "You sit with him every morning on the streetcar."

I was flabbergasted.

The mystery cleared up, I waited a few days, and then asked Baldy about the origin of his nickname. When he was in grade school, he said, his mother, to save money on haircuts, had made him tell the barber to shave his head.

So he was Baldy for the rest of his life, never Bernard (the name his parents gave him), and he always had hair, although his forehead receded as he aged. He did not remain small and thin.

As a North Catholic upperclassman, he was big enough to play on the baseball and basketball teams. Baseball and basketball players were allowed to have gimpy legs. What counted was ability, and he could throw and hit a baseball so well that he played with grown men in a twilight league. In basketball, he was good enough to make the first team.

He never gave up his job as the football team's manager, running and fetching for the coaches until graduation. He could get things and he could get things done. He was well-liked and smart and he passed all his courses, with help from a sympathetic teacher or two. Academics did not seem to interest him. He kept his grades just high enough to be eligible for baseball, basketball, and extracurricular activities.

Baldy's substitute for an older big brother was Mike Kearns, another North Side kid who lived on the edge of poverty and excelled at sports. Mike played football at North Catholic, and Baldy never missed a home game. Smuggled onto the team bus in the duffel bag Mike used for his pads, helmet, and uniform, Baldy saw some road games as well. The success of this arrangement depended on Baldy's small size. In later life, he added to his dimensions both lengthwise (to about 5 feet 10) and breadth- wise (in his fifties he must have weighed about 220 pounds).

Mike Kearns had been the end man, and therefore the star, of the minstrel shows at North Catholic. Minstrel shows in that long-ago time were still not seen as racist. To be the end man brought status and prestige. To be the end man and also a top athlete, as Mike was, made you the cock of the walk. Baldy, in a sense, outdid even Mike. In his senior year, he was the end man, the best baseball player, a good enough basketball player, and class president. His sports and theatrical achievements Baldy took in stride; being elected class president overwhelmed him. "Wow!" he exclaimed when the ballots had been counted. "Only in America!"

It was the first time I ever had heard him say that, but "Only in America" became his mantra, repeated on many occasions as a sort of all-purpose observation.

At the graduation ceremony each year, the tradition was for the senior class president to address the assembled students, teachers, administrators, and parents. Uncertain whether Baldy could handle such an assignment, a member of the faculty offered to pick a surrogate speaker. It would be Baldy's decision. If he did not feel up to making a speech, the teacher would ask someone else. Baldy wanted to know what I thought about that. No doubt he asked others as well. I told him I thought the faculty guy's suggestion was out of line. I said he had done a good job as president. He'd been in charge of the senior prom, which had gone off without a hitch. He'd been the end man in the minstrel show. Reciting lines in a stage production was just like giving a speech. "You can do it, Baldy," I said.

Baldy did it. His performance was smooth and free of gaffes and went over big with the audience.

When Baldy and I were seniors we made a trip to Shamrock Farm with AJR and my brother Tim. It was late in winter, when the hills and the fields were brown and the trees stripped of leaves, and there would be nothing much to do, but I could sense Baldy's excitement. He'd be the guest of Mr. Rooney, the owner of the Pittsburgh Steelers, and that was sufficient. As for AJR, he'd be taking Baldy's measure while giving no indication of it — not by so much as a word, a blink, a change of expression. That was his way with everybody he met. He'd be watching every move of this hot-shot kid he heard us talking up, and before the weekend was over he would know something important about him.

Baldy got the usual tour. We looked at the horses, and that was it. When we were back from the barns we watched television. AJR was the boss and decided what programs we could see. If he was talking on the telephone, the farmer and his wife, the caretakers of the place, controlled the set.

So that Baldy would not think we had brought him all the way from Pittsburgh to watch kiddy TV shows with the farmer's children or cooking shows with the farmer's wife, Tim and I suggested a walk. There were interesting things in the barns that we hadn't inspected — old tractors, a box of dynamite.

I don't remember what the dynamite was for, but we merely looked at it, removing and replacing the lid of the box with great care.

We took a second look at the horses. The colts and the stallions could be temperamental, so we gave them a wide berth, and almost all of the mares were in foal, or already had one. To my regret, it was not the breeding season. Watching the mares and the stallions get it on would have been an unforgettable experience for Baldy. We were left with nothing to hold our attention for long but an ancient lead pony from the race track. It belonged to one of Dad's trainers, who was boarding it at the farm.

All lead ponies were called Bill, or Billy. This one was in his stall, peacefully munching hay. We stood watching for a minute, and Baldy then asked if we could take the nag for a ride. I knew that Billy was at the farm for rest; I thought he might be injured or sick; so I said there probably weren't any saddles around, but Tim blurted out that he had seen one in a room near the stalls.

When we approached old Bill with the saddle and the reins, he gave us a sidelong look, showing the whites of his eyes. This was not a good sign, I had heard. He began to stamp his feet. Another bad sign. I could see that old Billy was nervous. He had been around horsemen all his life — people who knew what they were doing. And he was sure we were not that kind. Tim and I had taken riding lessons. We had ridden old nags on all the dirt roads of the Ligonier Valley. We had learned how to saddle up and how to put on a halter and reins. We could tell the front end of a horse from the rear, but that just about summed it up.

Old Bill made an effort to stay in the barn. He dug his hoofs into the ground, refusing to be led. Tim and I pulled at the reins. Baldy got in back and started to push. "Get away from there," we yelled at him. "Those horses can kick." Baldy just laughed. He was feeling giddy. All three of us were.

I was bigger and older than the others, so I said I would ride Billy first. It took me three tries, with Tim holding the reins at Billy's mouth, to get my foot in the stirrup. Billy then started to prance. I was hopping around on one foot, while Baldy and Tim laughed their heads off, before I could finally make it onto the horse's back.

Keeping a tight rein on Billy, which he fought, I galloped him up and down the road and across the meadow. I was never really able to hold him in check, but I didn't fall off (my football conditioning may have helped). When I returned, Tim and Baldy gave me a cheer. "Piece of cake," I said. "Nothing to it."

Now it was Tim's turn. Tim had the same trouble in mounting that I did, but, taking Billy up and down the road and across the meadow, he looked much better in the saddle. Maybe Billy was tiring or getting used to us and would not be too difficult for Baldy, who never had been on a horse in his life.

His approach, to say the least, was original. To avoid being dragged around the paddock with one foot in a stirrup and the other on the ground, as Tim and I had been, he got up on the paddock fence and declared he would mount from there. If we could bring the horse close enough, he would jump right onto the saddle,

We told him he was crazy. "You'll get hurt."

"No I won't. Bring him over here. I'll show you."

Baldy was as fearless as a rodeo rider. He made the leap onto Billy's back, somehow got hold of the reins, and jammed his feet into the stirrups. Then he was off. Heading out over the meadow, Billy never ran so fast. Baldy had on a white knit stocking cap, and soon it was all we could see of him, the cap bobbing up and down as Billy traversed hill and dale. We could hear Baldy's cries of either terror or elation.

Then they stopped. At the same time, we lost sight of the white knit cap. Had there been a spill? Had Baldy been thrown?

He was gone a long time. When he reappeared, it was not from the same direction in which he had started. We heard Baldy's cries before we saw him. Billy was still galloping. Baldy was still bobbing up and down, perpendicular one moment — sitting straight up — and horizontal the next — parallel from head to waist with the horse's neck. He did not have command. And yet, in a strange way, he did.

AJR, the farmer, the farmer's wife, and their kids were now on the back porch of the farm house, spellbound. Clotheslines were stretched across the farmer's back yard, and Billy headed for them. Baldy now demonstrated his athleticism. Just before reaching each clothesline, he ducked his head, bending over as far as he could. He had to do this three times. Next, Billy ran straight at the stone wall surrounding a little ice house. None of us were laughing, yelling, or cheering — not Tim, not me, not Dad, not the farmer and his wife, and not their kids. Billy dashed up to the wall and all of a sudden put on the brakes. He came to a dead stop — and Baldy did not pitch forward into the wall. A moment later he was off Bill's back and onto his own two feet.

"Wow! Only in America!" he shouted.

The farmer had Billy by the reins. "This horse ain't been ridden all winter," he said. "All of yez are lucky ya didn't get kilt."

On the way back to Pittsburgh we stopped at the Catholic church for a visit and at a hotel in Frederick, the nearest big town, for dinner. The hotel was old and elegant. College girls waited on tables. Our girl brought each of us a finger bowl filled with warm water, a slice of lemon floating at the top. While AJR asked her his usual question — "Where are you from?" — Tim and I, without being obvious about it, watched Baldy. He looked at his finger bowl and then did exactly what we thought he would do. He picked up a spoon and took a sip of the water.

When we were able to stop laughing we explained that the water was not for drinking. "Wise guys," he muttered, forgoing his customary "Only in America."

AJR had been watching Baldy from a different perspective than ours. "He's a fine guy," Dad said to us later. "Good little athlete. President of his class, isn't he?"

I said, "Yes, but he's real poor and there aren't any athletic scholarships for kids as small as he is."

Dad said, "Maybe something can be done."

He knew a Polish politician connected with Alliance College in Cambridge Springs, where the Steelers had gone for pre-season practice in the 1940s. The politician awarded a scholarship to Alliance every year. "I have a great kid," AJR told him, citing Baldy's qualifications, "but he's Irish, not Polish."

"Don't worry about it. He's in," the politician said.

Thus did our short trip to the farm pay off for Baldy in triplicate. He rode a horse for the first time. He learned about finger bowls. And now he'd be going to college.

He lasted just two semesters at Alliance, an extracurricular success, as always, but a failure in the classroom. He was into all kinds of activities and made a name for himself as the star of a one-man comedy hour on Alliance's campus radio station. He represented the college in a Golden Gloves boxing tournament in Erie and did all right. When a Polish jet pilot defected, stealing his fighter plane, and flying over the Steel Curtain to the West, the Cold War hero accepted an invitation to visit Alliance and spent more time with Baldy, it seemed, than with anybody else. Only in America. They shot enough pool at the student union to remind everybody of Fast Eddie Felson and Minnesota Fats, Baldy teaching the pilot English words and the pilot improving Baldy's Polish. In short, Baldy replicated his North Catholic High school career. It was a shame that he had to go to class.

He sold shoes for a while, and athletic equipment, and then through political influence (the district attorney, Ed Boyle, went to bat for him) he landed a patronage job as a county detective. Emerging from a take-out place in the Hill district with a box of fried chicken one day, he encountered three black men.

"Hand over that chicken," said the one in the middle.

"Brother," replied Baldy, "why should I do that?"

"Three reasons," the guy said, indicating himself and his two sidekicks. "Me, him, and him."

Baldy pulled out his service revolver, which he wore tucked into his waistband. He said, "Well, here are six reasons you can't make me give you that chicken."

The would-be poultry thief looked at the gun and shook his head. "Man," he conceded, "six beats three every time."

By the late 1970s, Baldy was a justice of the peace. During the week before Christmas every year, in his courtroom on the North Side, he gave a party that lasted from early afternoon into the evening hours. Judges, magistrates, lawyers, and doctors, City Council members, state legislators, captains of industry, newspaper reporters, and television personalities, Catholic priests and Protestant ministers, bank presidents, police inspectors, saloon keepers, high school teachers and college professors, working men and office girls, taxi drivers and jitney drivers came. Steeler football players came. Baldy, who never drank, remained sober. Once he performed a wedding, putting on his Benjamin Franklin glasses to read from the Bible. Always, he would break out the champagne (Chateau Luzerne), serving it in tall plastic cups from the Iron City brewery. The Santa Claus in full regalia would be David Barnett. "Wait a minute," he objected when Baldy first nominated him for the role. "I'm not the type." David Barnett was black. "Don't worry about the color scheme," said Baldy, settling the issue.

In the 1980s, his friends on City Council urged him to run for an open slot. He was elected, but not re-elected. His great popularity had peaked. Baldy, however, could be satisfied looking on from the sidelines. There was the time during his years as a magistrate when the lord mayor of Dublin came to Pittsburgh. Behind a police escort on motorcycles, he arrived at City Hall, where a big crowd had gathered to welcome him. Baldy, of course, was there. He turned to Jack Lynch, the county controller, and said, "Isn't it wonderful how everybody loves the Irish?"

"Baldy," said Lynch, "you know the lord mayor is Jewish, don't you?"

"Jewish? The lord mayor of Dublin?"

"That's correct."

For a minute Baldy was speechless. Then he smiled and said, "Only in America."

Chapter 20

The Survivor

In their first two decades the Steelers had some very good players, some moderately good players, and some fair players, but nothing to back them up. AJR, minimizing the importance of reserve strength, did not like to pay a lot for guys who sat on the bench. It requires supernatural luck to get through a season without injuries, and when the regulars are hurt the guys on the bench take their place.

There was no such thing as a taxi squad to draw from. The Steelers would start the season with thirty-three players and end it with twenty-six, twenty-seven, or twenty-eight. Guys who were playing both ways would be covering kicks. After all, reasoned AJR, that is what they were hired to do — play. If some of them got "nicked," so be it. Welcome to the ranks of the walking wounded.

Remarkably, when I came across these players twenty or thirty or forty years later, they all expressed affection for AJR, the Steelers, and the NFL. I think they put more into football than they ever took out of it, but that was not their attitude at all.

My opinion is that with better substitutes and some sort of taxi squad the Steelers of the '30s and '40s might have had more seven-win seasons and fewer three-win or two-win seasons. However, AJR's goal was survival, and he knew how to achieve it.

Other owners who had big ideas about winning and selling out their stadiums came and went. AJR, the Maras, and the Bidwills outlasted them all. They were proof that strong, dedicated individual owners could succeed where corporations and unwieldy partnerships fail. Only death released the hold of George Preston Marshall on the Washington Redskins. Tim Mara, Charley Bidwill, George Halas, and AJR established dynasties.

All of these founders had a passion for the game. They were pioneers with the vision to see what professional football might become and with the good sense to put restraints on free enterprise. By instituting the draft of college players, which gave the small-market teams equal access to this renewable source of talent and ready-made stars, and by consenting to an equal division of the television money that began to pour in after the mid-1950s — by, in other words, sharing the wealth — they increased it for one and all, the haves and the have-nots alike.

To survive, to make it through the lean years, AJR paid a price. The football fans in his own home town were not shy about blaming him for the Steelers' inability to win championships, or in most seasons even to challenge for one. In the public perception, he was cheap and he was dumb. Frugal he may have been — he had to be. He was anything but dumb. The Steelers of the 1930s were Depression babies. With smoke and mirrors, he weathered the hard times and then the manpower shortage of World War II.

The closest he came to bailing out was in 1940, when he sold the team to Alexis Thompson for $160,000 and engineered a deal whereby he still owned a third of it while Thompson ended up with the Philadelphia Eagles. As I have written, the transaction involved a switch of franchises between Thompson and the Eagles' owner, Bert Bell, and the need for AJR to share a certain amount of decision-making power with Bell and Barney McGinley. Five years later, when Bell replaced Elmer Layden as NFL commissioner, AJR had the resources to acquire most of Bell's stock and become majority owner once again.

Out of necessity he played it close to the vest. As generous as he was with the Church and with people down on their luck, he did not throw money around, the way Uncle Jim would have done, although there were times ...

Jamestown, New York, boasted a famous furniture maker patronized only by the rich. Condescendingly, this man escorted Kass, AJR, and Aunt Alice on a tour of his factory. "No point in your even looking at the dining-room pieces," he said. "They would be far too expensive for you. President Eisenhower has a complete set at his farm in Gettysburg, the gift of a wealthy admirer. But, as I say, there's no point in showing it to you."

"Let's look at it anyway," suggested AJR.

With his nose in the air, the man led these plebeians from Pittsburgh to the dining-room section. The set like the one that went to the Eisenhower farm was French Provincial — a table that seated eighteen or twenty people, twelve matching chairs elegantly upholstered in blue damask fabric, a mammoth breakfront for crystal, a long serving table, a pair of girondeles (lightly-carved "leaves" that stood two feet high) and a small buffet. The wood was an unusual blending of gray and brown. Kass could only agree that the pieces were dazzling. She gazed at the set lovingly and then turned to leave. But AJR, with a few words to their guide, stopped her in her tracks.

"We'll take it," he said.

Kay, my wife, called it the most beautiful set she ever saw. Dinner at 940 North Lincoln Avenue, with Kass's crystal glasses and figurines on the breakfront, her sterling silver tea set on the serving table, and a crystal chandelier fit for royalty over our heads, was from then on a special event.

Accidentally on Purpose

As far as his sons were concerned, AJR was a "sportsman" — the man who owned the Steelers, the man who promoted boxing matches, the man who owned the Shamrock breeding farm in Maryland and raced horses. We never thought of him as a gambler.

Oh, we knew that he made money by betting on horses. Otherwise, we'd have had to be blind and deaf. All I'm saying is that we disconnected ourselves from this part of his life. The Rooneys of North Lincoln Avenue were "pro football people." Both Mom and Dad encouraged us to think of ourselves that way. Either accidentally or "accidentally on purpose," as Mom would say, they shielded us from the gambling aspects of AJR's profession. Football was what the Rooneys were about. It monopolized our attention. Whether the Steelers won or lost was vitally important to us. The boxing matches at Hickey Park, Forbes Field, and the old Duquesne Gardens were not. The horses — the horses and the farm — existed in our minds as trappings, as accessories. They were things that belonged to us because AJR was a sportsman and had nothing at all to do with gambling.

We saw the horses on the farm; while we were kids, we never saw them race. Horse racing in Pennsylvania was illegal. The nearest track — Waterford Downs — was in West Virginia. Sometimes Dad raced his horses there. More often, he took them to places like Pimlico, Laurel, Bowie, or Aqueduct — hundreds of miles away. The Steelers were here in Pittsburgh, under our noses. We saw them play. We read about their games in the Pittsburgh newspapers. Every Monday there were stories and pictures. There were stories during the week. The papers' horse-racing coverage was limited. Pittsburgh reporters might go to the Kentucky Derby or the Preakness or the Belmont, but AJR's horses never raced in those events. To read about a Shamrock Farm horse you waded through the long, gray columns of agate type that appeared in a far corner of the sports section every day, captioned "Race Entries" and "Race Results."

When we were old enough to go to the track — you had to be over 16 — we made infrequent visits with AJR, and our interest was faintly stirred. We asked questions like "When are you going to get a top stakes horse?" John Galbreath, the owner of the Pirates, seemed not to have any other kind. In the 1960s two of his horses, Chateaugay and Proud Clarion, won the Kentucky Derby. Roberto, named for Roberto Clemente, the Hall-of-Fame Pirate outfielder, won the equally prestigious English Derby. AJR's best horse was Little Harp, named for a sandlot football player from the First Ward.

"Listen," he would tell us, "Little Harp has won more money than all of those fancy horses put together." We were not yet sophisticated enough to understand what he meant. Tim may have been, but not me. I knew that John Galbreath's horses raced for big purses. I knew that Little Harp raced for extremely modest purses. So how could this be?

Later on, it came to me. It wasn't the purses Little Harp won, but the bets Dad made on him that paid for a lot of our amenities.

I was slowly learning to add two and two.

New Digs

From the mid 1950s until Three Rivers Stadium went up on the North Side in 1970 the Steelers had their offices in the Roosevelt Hotel.

In some ways it resembled the Fort Pitt Hotel, where the Rooney-McGinley Boxing Club had shared the football team's headquarters. Both the Roosevelt and Fort Pitt were piles of red brick, undistinguished as architecture. The Fort Pitt, the older of the two, was a "railroad hotel," located near the Pennsylvania Station at the northeast corner of the Golden Triangle. It went back to the days before the Wright brothers lifted off at Kitty Hawk — back to the days when people dismissed the automobile as a plaything. There were marble floors and overstuffed chairs in the lobby, a coffee shop, and two attractive dining rooms. The boom in rail transportation during World War II extended the Fort Pitt's life span, but decline had already set in. When AJR moved to the Roosevelt, the Fort Pitt was a fleabag, long overdue for the wrecking ball.

There had been a partial move to the Union Trust Building on Grant Street some time earlier. In 1946, with the hiring of Jock Sutherland, AJR felt that changes must follow. He knew that his new head coach, a man of austere bearing, would be grotesquely out of place in the digs at the Fort Pitt among the fight managers, horse players, flunkies, and hangers-on who walked in and out through windows a step above the pavement — windows that were eight feet high. So with encouragement from Sutherland he split the football and boxing ends of the business, renting rooms for himself and the coaches in the tastefully ornate Union Trust.

His own private office was at ground-floor level, unobtrusively tucked away behind the ticket office. A meeting room and Sutherland's office, which he shared with his assistant coaches, were eight stories higher, inaccessible by design to the low-life element that frequented the Fort Pitt. But AJR's more respectable friends — among them Pie Traynor, the Hall-of-Fame Pirate third baseman now launched on a second career, sportscasting — also stopped coming around. Meeting Traynor on the street one day, AJR let him know that he was missed.

He said, "Where have you been, Pie? We never see you any more."

Traynor's answer became a staple for collectors of Steeler folklore. "You're too high up over there," he said. "I'm afraid I'll forget I'm not at the Fort Pitt and step out the window."

After Sutherland's death in 1948, AJR stayed on at the Union Trust for another four years. At the end of that time the boxing club turned up its toes. Free fights on television had destroyed boxing's customer base, and Uncle Jack McGinley, the club's promoter, matchmaker, treasurer, bookkeeper, and publicity man, was making a nice income with his partner Fritz Wilson in their Miller Beer distributorship. Accordingly, with no further reason to keep two offices open, AJR said goodbye to the Fort Pitt and skipped across town to the Roosevelt, on Liberty Avenue.

The Roosevelt, like the Fort Pitt, had seen better days but was ideally situated near the restaurant and theater district a few minutes' walk from the Sixth Street Bridge, the span that connected downtown Pittsburgh with the old First Ward. Among the glories of the Roosevelt was the Sylvan Room, moderately famous for its roast ribs of beef. The bellhops tended to be wise guys but could make themselves useful if properly tipped. Bag carriers like Wally, a personage of sorts in his tiny domain, were human surveillance cameras. They knew all the dirt about big shots and nobodies alike — knew all and told all. AJR inflated the bellhops' self-esteem by remembering their names. Quite often he remembered the names of their wives and children. If they needed help to get a relative into a nursing home, a hospital, or any other kind of institution, AJR was their man.

As they did at the Fort Pitt, the Steelers had offices with an entrance off the lobby. The Roosevelt's lobby and the Fort Pitt's lobby came from the same mold. They were big, dark, and high-ceilinged. AJR's private office in the Roosevelt was a windowless room with two adjoining desks, one for himself and one for Fran Fogarty. Neither desk lacked for telephones. AJR had three and Fogarty two, plus an adding machine.

Inconveniently, the command center Dad occupied was right next door to the men's room, and it was not uncommon for guests of the hotel to walk in unzipping their flies. The moment could be embarrassing for everybody concerned if AJR was talking business with a visitor he wanted to impress or with a newly-drafted football player from a large and prestigious university. Showing his best face (as he used to say), AJR would smile and make an effort to put such intruders at ease. Fogarty, when he was present, played bad cop to AJR's good cop. "Next door!" he would bellow. "Next door!"

Lunch in the Sylvan Room was always a prolonged affair. AJR, of course, would know the names of the waitresses, where they had gone to school, and what church they attended. The waitresses were apt to be from Irish or Italian Catholic parishes, but he quizzed the few Protestants among them with the same fatherly solicitude. Dragging in the name of someone's minister, he would show off his aptitude for finding a connection: "Played baseball against that fellow before he went to the seminary."

The waitresses were mostly middle-aged. AJR was "Mister Rooney" to them, a mark of unusual respect. The rest of us they addressed by our first names. If a waitress whose name was Peggy knew the customer well, she rarely bothered to take his order. "Fran," she would say to Fogarty, setting a plate of food down in front of him, "this is our special today. I know you'll like it." Or, conversely, "Fran, our special don't look too good today, so I brought you this." Like it or not, you ate it. If there were no empty tables, Peggy might seat you with a stranger. "This here's Mister Smith — he's one of our regulars," she would say.

For an evening news feature on KDKA, the television personality Marie Torre posed as a Sylvan Room waitress one day with a cameraman shooting unnoticed from a sort of shelf, or platform, high up on the wall at the far end of the room. A tall, big-boned woman, striking in appearance, she attempted to disguise herself with the aid of a hairdresser and makeup artist. The point of all this, a promotional stunt for KDKA, was to see how many people would recognize her.

I came to lunch that day with AJR, and as slow as I am on the uptake I immediately spotted the cameraman. We sat with Bill Burns, the KDKA news anchor, and he gave me the high sign: *Don't tip off your father.* To AJR, the name and renown of Marie Torre meant nothing, I am sure. Characteristically, he treated her with matter-of-fact politeness, as though she were Peggy or any other waitress. After twenty minutes or so, Burns and I spilled the beans — we let Dad in on Miss Torre's true identity. Without missing a beat, he called her to the table and said, "I have to tell you something — you could make your living at this, you're so good."

Unaccountably, I didn't notice whether AJR left a tip.

Bill Burns was about 6-1 or 6-2, a good-looking black-haired guy with a little wayward curl that fell down over his forehead. Women of all ages doted on him and men were not resentful, a tribute to his masculinity. Wounded in combat during World War II, he wore a brace on one leg and walked with a limp.

It was interesting to have lunch with Burns. One day a well-groomed matron came to our table, leaned over swiftly, and kissed him on the cheek. Then she apologized. Burns maintained his considerable aplomb. I expressed surprise at what had happened, and he said, "Oh, that was nothing." He told me that a woman came up behind him one time and started pulling at his hair with both hands. When he managed to get disentangled, the woman said to him, "I could have sworn you were wearing a wig."

Burns never joined us before 1 p.m. Two hours later he would still be drinking coffee with AJR and whoever else might have lingered — Jack Butler; my brother Tim, who worked in a nearby brokerage house; extroverted Mossie Murphy, assistant to Alex DiCroce, the man in charge of the restaurant. And many more. There were usually two tables — AJR's and another for late-comers. If Mossie Murphy arrived late, he would crash the Chief's table. Mossie liked to sit at the right hand.

One day when the gathering included prominent politicians and civic leaders, a large, ferocious-looking rat crawled out of its hole, scurried across the floor, and disappeared. Those of us consigned to the second table let out a cheer. "Rat!" we shouted. "Rat!" Alex DiCroce was indignant. There had NOT been a rat, he insisted. The rest of us argued; Alex stuck to his guns. At the high table — AJR's — the conversation had come to a halt. When our yammering ceased, and all was peaceful again, the rat came back for a curtain call. "Alex ... look!" we hollered. "Rat!" But in a flash it was gone, and Alex, defiant, said there was simply no way — simply no way — a rat could gain admittance to his ever-immaculate Sylvan Room. It was Tim, finally, who compelled him to face the truth. "Alex, you must be blind," he said. "That rat was as big as a kangaroo." Backtracking, Alex began to make concessions. He allowed that, well, they were tearing down a lot of old buildings near the Roosevelt. And rats do migrate. Rats were always looking for warmth and water. And food, someone suggested. Maybe they'd heard about "ribs at the Roosevelt," the sales pitch Alex used in his newspaper ads.

Just for the record, Alex got in the last word. "I can promise you," he said, "that the situation will be taken care of."

Although he did not have the title of manager until the 1960s or later, Alex seemed to run the whole place. He lived at the hotel with his family for many years. There were others, some of them football players, who lived at the hotel during periods of domestic turmoil. It was also a landing place for newcomers to the team. Fran Fogarty would book them into the Roosevelt and Alex DiCroce would see that they were made to feel at home. Downtown hotels still practiced de facto segregation, but the Roosevelt was an exception, at least where our players were concerned. White or black, most of them left after finding an apartment or a house; others were content to stay put. Dedicated hell-raisers could be counted on to get out quickly. They wanted distance between themselves and the front-office people.

Because anyone at all — a judge, a prelate, the mayor, the head of a corporation — might be coming to see him at the Roosevelt, AJR insisted on a dress code for his sons: jacket and tie, white shirt, shoes shined. And we were to keep our hair neatly trimmed. "Judge," he would say (or "Mayor" or "Bishop So-and-so"), "this is my boy Artie." I was always his boy Artie, never his son Art. Taking note of my girth, he would sometimes tell me to eat less or exercise more. What I hated about this was that his lectures came with the judge or the bishop or the mayor for an audience.

Again there were less distinguished visitors, too — the old Fort Pitt crowd, or its remnants. Patsy Scanlon showed up part of the time, Dago Sam Leone most of the time — more often, in fact, than Uncle Jim, who was still on the payroll for being "with Arthur," his duties as mysterious as ever.

John and Pat, the twins, had well-defined duties. Every Monday night and Thursday night during the football season they manned the Roosevelt Hotel ticket office, which faced the street. Monday and Thursday were the nights the department stores remained open, and AJR professed to believe that hordes of shoppers would be looking for Steeler tickets, never mind how pathetic the team was. His real objective, the twins felt, was to keep them away from their girlfriends.

With little else to do on the nights they sold tickets — there were precious few buyers — John and Pat sought diversion in an offshoot of baseball called whiffle ball. By rearranging the furniture in the executive suite, they were able to lay out a diamond. The player pool, consisting of themselves, various bellhops, any North Catholic classmates who happened to wander by, and walk-ons rounded up in the lobby, was sufficient now and then to put infielders and outfielders behind the pitcher and to have a batter always waiting to hit. At the ticket counter, meanwhile, wearing a Steeler shirt and a Steeler visor cap, stood a football-headed manikin rigged up from a coat rack. If Ed Kiely, the P.R. guy, or Fran Fogarty came around, the manikin and the whiffle ball players evaporated.

At some time during the twins' second season on the job it became apparent to AJR and to Fogarty that a night-time ticket office was uneconomical. Bad enough that the tickets weren't moving. John and Pat drew salaries, but their pay of four bucks a night for the two of them was the least significant expense; the trouble as Fogarty saw it was that the ticket sellers had to eat, and that these particular ticket sellers were running up a tab in the Sylvan Room.

As a cost-cutting measure, the night-time ticket office was closed. John and Pat were free once again to upgrade their social life. And the Roosevelt Hotel was a quieter place after dark, a portent of things to come. In the late 1970s, under the federal government's rental subsidy program, a real-estate company bought the rundown old hostelry and converted it into a high rise for senior citizens.

Chapter 21

Disciplinarian

Father Silas was always away when I was a kid. He spent eight years as a missionary in China, four in the Army as a military chaplain during World War II, and then eight years as athletic director at St. Bonaventure.

From time to time, though, he would be in Pittsburgh and might unexpectedly turn up at 940 North Lincoln Avenue. One night after dinner I was leading my three younger brothers in the rosary. We said the rosary every night at AJR's insistence. If he and Kass were not present, Dan, the oldest brother, led. If all three were out of the house, as on this occasion, the job fell to me.

I took it seriously, and on this particular night I felt that Tim was not showing sufficient respect for the prayers. I told him so. He took exception. We dropped our rosary beads and went after each other. I was having the best of it when he picked up a desk lamp and bounced it off my head. There was a fair amount of blood on me. As I made a lunge for him, the doorbell sounded. It was Father Silas, and we were instantly transformed into perfect gentlemen.

He was not taken in. Looking directly at me, but addressing all four of us, he said, "What are you guys up to?"

Together, we answered, "Saying the family rosary."

Slowly and cynically, Father Silas repeated, "Yes ... you are ... saying the family rosary."

We knew we'd been reprimanded. Father Silas had a temper, and we were fortunate that he had kept it under control.

One year when the Steelers were training at St. Bonaventure, a priest named Father McKean was draining the swimming pool. To his annoyance, the ball boys kept driving over the hose he was using. Many of these ball boys and assistant equipment men were Father Silas's nephews. Recklessly, Father McKean asked him to keep his "stupid, retarded relatives" out of the way. Father Silas hauled off and knocked his fellow Franciscan out cold. Years and years later, when Father Silas was dying at the Franciscans' retirement home in St. Petersburg, Florida, Father McKean spent a lot of time at his bedside.

Priestly garb was no protection if Father Silas thought a line had been crossed. Long after he no longer was with us, I happened to be at a Carmelite church in Niagara Falls, Canada. The pastor, a Father Jason Rooney — no relation — said he had taken a summer course at St. Bonaventure when Father Silas was there, and he proceeded to tell me a story. He and another priest, Father Rooney went on, were playing golf on the university's private course one day. "And we were taking a few divots," he said. "Father Silas came by on his tractor and saw that we weren't replacing them. He stopped and gave us holy hell."

Father Silas was a "good guy," Father Rooney said, "but tough. He wouldn't put up with any nonsense." Father Rooney remembered hearing that one of the football or basketball coaches made the mistake of giving Father Silas some lip one day and that Father Silas reached across a desk and belted him out. There were several other versions of this story. In one, Father Silas punched out a big football player for getting involved in some kind of trouble on the campus.

Could it be that he hit both a coach and a player? I know because he told me so that when he was father superior at St. Anthony's Mission in Boston in the late 1950s or early 1960s he in some way manhandled an alcoholic priest who was stationed there, injuring the man's ribs. Father Silas felt a lot of remorse about this.

Hard taskmaster or not, he was popular with his coaches. Ken Stilley, an assistant to Joe Bach at St. Bonaventure, said that Father Silas would show up at the end of their nightly meetings with beer for the whole staff, hidden discreetly under his cassock.

There were priests at St. Bonaventure who criticized him for eliminating football and building up the basketball program. Basketball required fewer scholarships and cost much less for uniforms, equipment, travel, and coaches' salaries.

"What are we going to do with our time on weekends in the fall?" one priest demanded.

"Do what you were ordained to do — hear confessions and say Mass," Father Silas told him, closing off further discussion.

He was not an easy man to oppose.

Summer Vacation

The summer following Jack Butler's rookie season AJR invited him to Shamrock Farm. Going over, Jack drove AJR's Buick; Tim and I, along with our dad, were passengers. We spent a night at the farm and drove to the Jersey shore the next morning, checking into a hotel. Jack, Tim, and I took a dip in the ocean, and then all four of us went to the race track, Monmouth Park. Jack placed some bets for AJR and put a few bucks of his own on the same horses. He won a little money. At the races the next day, after our morning swim, he was not so lucky. AJR told him, "I'm glad you lost. If you'd had two good days in a row, you'd think this was easy and get hooked."

After the races were over on the second day, we returned to the farm, stopping to eat at one of AJR's favorite restaurants. He liked a place that served good fish and steaks and was not too fancy. Usually there would be pictures of race horses on the walls. The owner was almost always an old race-track guy or a former athlete and he always made a fuss over AJR.

Back at the farm, AJR took Jack and me to the country store and bought us work clothes. All I needed were gloves, because I knew what was up and had work clothes in my luggage. AJR outfitted Jack with a straw hat, a pair of blue jeans, and some cotton shirts. Jack was mystified until AJR said, "You two can help bring in the hay." Addressing Jack, he added, 'This will get you in shape for the football season. I'll be back next week to pick you up."

For six endless days, Jack and I pitched hay with the farm hands. I was on the football team at North Catholic and though I welcomed the chance to build a few muscles the work exhausted me. Jack, who was older and stronger, handled it rather easily. As perplexed as he must have been — this had started out, after all, as a pleasure trip — not once did I hear him complain. We went to bed early and were up with the birds. The farm boys worked swiftly and efficiently, hardly seeming to expend any effort. I did my best to keep up with them, and with Jack, but I thought I was going to die.

On the seventh day, AJR reappeared, bringing Tim. When he left, I was with him in the car. Jack, to his surprise, remained at the farm with Tim and worked for another ten days. Returning once more, AJR picked them up and drove from the farm to our cottage in Ligonier, where, earlier, he had dropped me off. It was a Saturday night. On Sunday morning, after Mass, Mom fixed a huge breakfast for us, and Jack cleaned up everything on his plate, and then some. At first he was quiet and reserved, but once he saw that Mom was a true friendly soul they got to talking. He told her the farm had been "an experience" — boring at times but good conditioning for the football season.

Now he expected to be taken home. Instead, AJR drove him back to the farm with Tim for ten more days in the hay loft.

Forever after, when Jack went on trips with the Rooney boys and AJR, which happened often, he was careful to make certain that he knew in advance what the agenda would be.

For Tim and me, there were periodic visits to race tracks, most frequently Monmouth Park. New Jersey state laws prohibit race tracks from admitting minors, but Tim and I were big for our ages and nobody ever asked questions. In Boston once, however, we had to climb a fence. AJR was waiting for us on the other side.

AJR ran his horses at Monmouth as long as the season lasted and kept a stable there. We'd go to see the horses in the morning and have lunch in the track kitchen. Before the races started, AJR would drive to the clubhouse parking lot, leaving Tim and me in the stable area. If he was betting on the daily double or even had a horse in the third or fourth race we didn't mind. If, on the other hand, there was a horse he wanted to bet on in one of the later races, it could be a long afternoon. We'd watch the trainers ready their thoroughbreds for saddling; we'd go to the little grandstand overlooking the backstretch and watch the horses come flying by; we'd watch them being rubbed and washed down and walked to cool off after running.

Eventually all this would get tiresome and we'd wander into areas that, for unauthorized personnel, were off-limits.

"What are you kids doing here?" a security guard might ask.

We'd say that our father owned the Shamrock Stable and we were looking for him. "Well, get back where you belong," the guard would tell us. "And stay there."

When at last I arrived, a few years before Tim, at the magic age of 18, I was free to watch the races from the clubhouse or grandstand, and one of the many things I noticed was the number of pretty girls in the crowd. Always they seemed to be with an older, prosperous-looking man.

I said to Uncle Jim once, "Gee, a lot of these guys bring their daughters or granddaughters to the track."

He corrected me. "No, no. Never let them hear you say 'daughter' or 'granddaughter.' No. Those young, pretty girls are their nieces."

And then he laughed.

The Natural

Jack Butler spent his high school years at a Carmelite seminary in Niagara Falls, Ontario, and never had played football except in the way that kids do when he enrolled at St. Bonaventure University, no longer a candidate for the priesthood.

One of his several brothers was a priest, representation enough for the Butler family, he thought. The Butlers were from Pittsburgh and well known to AJR. Jack's father had been an all-around athlete and a sandlot teammate of the two oldest Rooney brothers. Father Dan, now the athletic director at

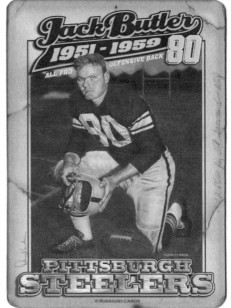

Jack Butler
(Drawing by Denny Karchner)

St. Bonaventure, guessed that Jack might have inherited the senior Butler's aptitude for football and urged him to try out for the team.

Well, why not? Asked by the coach what position he played, Butler was stuck for an answer, so he improvised. "Offensive guard," he said, prompted by the recollection that his roommate in the dormitory had claimed to be an offensive guard.

Practice started, and Jack worked hard at trying to block full-sized defensive tackles. "Wait a minute," said the line coach. "You're too small to be a guard, but you're tough and you're fast. What you look like to me is an end."

Butler played end for four years, both on offense and defense, and was outstanding. As so often happened if you played for St. Bonaventure, hardly anyone noticed. In the 1951 NFL draft he was overlooked entirely. Father Dan, knowing what the scouts did not, buttonholed AJR. "Give this kid a tryout," he said. One other team offered Butler a tryout, but he was from Pittsburgh, after all, and the Steelers took precedence.

At pre-season training camp, assistant coach Bob Davis observed that the newcomer was getting lost in the shuffle. Davis mentioned this to a visitor — one of Jack's brothers. Rookies, he said, had to assert themselves; they couldn't be shy. From that moment on, Butler was first in line for all the drills.

Cut-down day arrived, and either Jack or an end from Pitt would make the team. Head coach John Michelosen liked the Pitt man, perhaps out of loyalty to the old school tie, but fate took a hand in the guise of the Korean War. The Pitt man, it turned out, was prime material for the military draft. Butler, as the sole support of his widowed mother, had a deferment. Two of her other grown sons were married, with children, and one, as I have noted, was a priest. In this case, a draft worked to Jack Butler's advantage.

He made the team as a defensive back, not an end, although in special situations his coaches lined him up at wide receiver. The Steelers threw to Butler when they badly needed a score. Of the seven passes he caught in nine seasons, four went for touchdowns, and two of the four were game-winners. Jim Finks, who played quarterback from 1949 to 1955, declared he'd have been a better one with Butler catching his passes all the time.

Jack's soft hands were more useful, the coaches believed, on defense. To put his career total of fifty-two interceptions into perspective, NFL teams were still playing twelve-game schedules. In the history of the league, only two defensive backs up to then had been more prolific. They are Emlen Tunnell and Night Train Lane, Hall of Famers both. Butler should be in the Hall, too, but as I write this he is not.

And it's a shame. Let the record show that he played in four Pro Bowls and in one of those games was the MVP; that in a publication called "The First 50 Years of the NFL," Butler and Lane are named "the two best defensive backs of the 1950s;" that on the NFL's seventy-fifth anniversary, Butler and Tunnell were named the two best defensive backs of the 1950s; that on the all-time Steeler team picked in the fiftieth year of the team's existence, Butler and Mel Blount were the cornerbacks; that Pro Football Weekly, in 1998, included Butler among "the top one hundred players in NFL history."

Emlen Tunnell pronounced him "a defensive genius." Blessed with keen vision, he knew the whereabouts of every man on the field. While Butler was with the Steelers, Chuck Noll played for the Browns. Receivers, Noll said, hated to turn their backs on Butler. He was a vicious tackler with perfect timing. No sooner did the pass reach the receiver than Butler was there, jarring it out of his hands. Only great leapers — R. C. Owens comes to mind — could outjump him, and Butler would hit them so hard that from then on self-protection was paramount in their thinking, which precluded getting up in the air.

Self-protection to Butler was not important. By the end of each season, as others went down with injuries, he was filling in on special teams to cover kicks. He played with such abandon that a serious knee injury shortened his career.

Butler coached for a while in the NFL, with the Buffalo and Steeler organizations, and later became a scout. He was head of the Blesto group for more than thirty years, evaluating, over all that time, thousands of college players for the Bears, Lions, Eagles, Steelers, and Vikings. Great athletes who succeed in the administrative end of their sport are rare. Jack Butler was one of the few.

Chapter 22

Taskmaster

Ed Kiely, the Steelers' publicity director, would run bets for AJR at the race track. His orders were to hide out in the grandstand until it was nearly post time for a certain race and then go to the parimutuel windows as unobtrusively as possible. He would be carrying Dad's money in tens, twenties, fifties, and hundreds and take it to two or three different windows to conceal the fact that a single bettor was getting down big on one particular horse. I had done this for Dad myself, and it could be nerve-wracking. To blow your cover was simply not an option.

By watching the tote board, AJR could track the "smart" money — tell where it was going. Two-to-one shots didn't interest him. Rarely did he bet on a horse unless the odds were at least five to one. He might wait until the last minute and then toss his runner a bill. "Number eight horse to win," I can hear him saying. A man named Clark Gardner, an accountant who worked at our track in Yonkers, told me once that when AJR gave him twenty dollars to bet, a scant ninety seconds before the mutuel windows closed, he resolved to book it himself if he ran out of time. It could have cost Mr. Gardner a month's pay, but nobody ever wanted to displease AJR.

Ed Kiely had a habit of asking his boss questions, which required the most delicate judgment. There was a right time, a right place, and a right approach. If you asked a question undiplomatically you were going to be abruptly cut off. Kiely told my son Art that one day he was asking why AJR bet in such and such a way instead of some other way. AJR seemed exasperated, according to Ed. At last he said, "I don't know why I bet the way I bet. Why do you ask so many questions? I just do it!"

Ed persisted. He said that betting on horses was something he hadn't known about and he was trying to educate himself. Softening, AJR said, "Well, Ed, I've been at this so long I have a feel for it. But I'll tell you one thing. When I'm ahead of the game and playing with the track's money instead of my own, that's when I take more chances."

I left the probing questions to Kiely. Neither Dan, John, Pat, nor I dared to show any interest in wagering. We knew this about AJR: he didn't want his sons to be gamblers. Tim had thicker skin than the rest of us. He did ask questions, and the information he dragged out of AJR about everything connected with horse racing was useful to him later on, in his career as a breeder and track owner.

AJR could only teach by example. It was by example that he taught his five sons religion, morals, and character. He went to Mass every day. He made novenas. He went on retreats. We said the family rosary. He never told dirty jokes (though he could tell funny stories about his experiences, he was not very good at telling any kind of joke, tending to smother the punch line with laughter.)

Giving us baseball or boxing or field-goal kicking instructions, he was always impatient and brusque. If he had us fielding ground balls, and somebody ducked away from a hot one, he would say, "Get in front of it! Stop it with your glove!" After that, he would hit the ball harder and harder until he drove everybody off the field. Then if you went into the house, crying, Mom would come out and scream at Dad, calling him "a mean old bastard." He would shrug and tell her disgustedly that none of us could have lasted in The Ward.

When we boxed, it was much the same. He would put the gloves on and show us how to block with our shoulders or tuck our chins into our chests; meanwhile, he'd be throwing some pretty good punches without meaning to. We did our best to be somewhere else whenever it was time for a boxing lesson.

None of us developed into superior athletes, but all of us made the high school football and baseball teams. For Dad, this was insufficient. He would tell us how great he and his brother Dan were and how "near-great" Uncle Jim was.

He did not have much to say about Red and Duke as athletes. Tom, killed in the Second World War, belonged to a special category. Heroism on the battlefield transcended all other varieties.

After getting her fill of this, Mom would sometimes tell AJR he couldn't possibly have been a great athlete. "Why, you're a midget!" she would scoff.

Dad would then point to the evidence, his scrapbook of newspaper clippings. I wish I knew where it was. George Quinlan told somebody that one day when Dad was reading it, Mom said to him, "Why don't you burn that thing?" and he took her advice. From other sources, I have learned enough over the years to believe Dad was giving us the unadorned facts.

Out of His League

In his own world, AJR was a guy who knew the ropes, but as a handyman he could never have made it. At fixing things, or doing odd jobs around the house, he was useless. His working life had consisted of half a day in a steel mill. In those three or four hours, he had seen enough to realize that there were better and easier ways to earn a living.

At Ligonier one summer the heads of all the families in our vacation complex decided to build a wall and put in some steps near the part of the creek that was used as a swimming hole, and AJR, despite his unfitness for manual labor, felt called on to help.

He was making enough money at the race track to hire a construction crew and a bulldozer and finance the improvements himself, but this was a matter of pride. The other men who owned cottages were going to roll up their sleeves and get the banks of the creek shored up, so AJR, in a bathing suit and a pair of old shoes — and wearing his hat, a brown or gray fedora — joined the work gang .

Well, you never saw anyone who was more out of place. Men like our neighbor Mr. Duhon seemed to know by instinct where each rock and stone belonged and how to apply the cement. AJR did not have a clue. The athletic ability he possessed was in this case utterly wasted. He carried and lifted; he held things; he looked thankful when the work was completed.

Mom and the rest of us were happy, too. It was Dad's brain, not the sweat of his brow, that put the bread on our table and the clothes on our backs and the roof over our heads, not to mention the amenities and indeed the luxuries we enjoyed.

Easter Parade

After Mass on Holy Thursday every year, the whole family would pile into AJR's big old Buick Roadmaster for our annual trek to the Blue Grass country. The itinerary was always the same: an overnight stop in Cincinnati and then a tour of the thoroughbred horse farms around Lexington, Kentucky, the next morning. AJR would take a look at the yearlings his trainer had picked out and decide how many to buy for his Shamrock racing stable. It was important to be back in Pittsburgh for Mass on Easter Sunday; the return trip, therefore, might begin as early as Friday evening or on Saturday morning at the latest.

Seven people overloaded the Buick, so when Dan reached the age of 16 and could legally drive, we would split into two groups, with Dan at the wheel of the football team's station wagon, spelled now and then by his friend Billy Hart.

It was more fun to ride with Dan than with Dad and Mom. The radio would be playing and we'd wait for a tune called "The Saber Dance." Then we'd lower all the windows and Dan or Billy would step on the gas. At Easter time the air was usually cold and it would blow through the car ferociously. The cold air, the fast music, and the high rate of speed left us exhilarated.

Later, we'd catch hell from Dad for driving too fast, but our instructions were to stay fairly close behind the Buick so as not to get lost, and nobody drove faster than he did.

We were also ordered to say the rosary in the car. After all, it was Holy Week. Holy Week or any week, we were always expected to say the rosary on motor trips. On the way South we'd make stops at nine different churches. It had to be nine, just as there were nine First Fridays. Breaking the string was unthinkable. There was some kind of heavenly reward involved, but its nature is unclear to me now. I know we believed that if Catholics everywhere went to Mass and received Communion on the first Saturday of nine consecutive months, the Soviet Union would renounce Communism and convert to Christianity. When the government fell and the churches reopened in the 1990s I began to think that, hey, all those prayers must have worked. For certain the Rooney family by itself observed enough First Saturdays to ensure the salvation of a good-sized Russian city.

In hotels on these trips, our parents did their best to keep us from running wild. They remembered an experience in a Washington, D.C., hotel when the water bags we had thrown from the windows, aimed at passing targets on the sidewalk, brought an unhappy house detective to our floor. After that, we settled for pillow fights and simple rampaging from one connecting room to another.

If breakfast in the hotel restaurant got out of hand, AJR could silence us with a word and a look, the word a muffled roar. None of us ever wanted to be yelled at more than once by AJR. The ever-present likelihood of bringing down his wrath on our heads was one of several reasons we fought for a place in the station wagon.

By the 1950s all five Rooney boys were driving, and AJR was using us as chauffeurs. He subjected our driving skills and judgment to a drumbeat of criticism. We were either going too fast or too slow. "You know I want to get there for the first race," he would say. Or: "You know I want to get there for the kickoff." If, on the other hand, his driver had an agenda, safety considerations took precedence over making good time. "Hey, slow down," he kept saying to John the twin when John was taking him back to Pittsburgh from the St. Bonaventure training camp in Olean. He knew that John was in a hurry to keep a date that night with his girlfriend, JoAnn Wallace. It wasn't worth risking their lives for, AJR kept reminding him.

When we could turn over the driving chores to someone like Peezer Klingensmith we were always elated. Peezer Klingensmith had been a friend of Uncle Tom, the Marine who lost his life in combat during the Second World War. Temporarily out of a job — he was disputing an insurance claim with the railroad that employed him — he went to AJR for advice. "You can be my driver," AJR told him. "I need someone to take me to camp. The rest of the time, you can help our equipment manager." (Football season was about to begin, and the Steelers were back in Olean.) "Great," Peezer said." When do I start?" The answer — "Now" — startled him. He had barely enough time to go home and pack a gym bag before they were in the car.

It was late afternoon. Peezer drove out to Route 19 and headed north. "Wait a minute," AJR told him. "We're going to stop at the farm first." The Shamrock Farm was in Maryland, so Peezer turned east. They arrived after dark, ate dinner and went to bed, and were up at 5:30 the next morning so that AJR could attend early Mass before breakfast. After a tour of the farm, Peezer again started north. "What are you doing?" demanded AJR. There'd be a stop, he explained, at Laurel race track, farther east. He had a horse in the first race and wanted to get there early to talk with the trainer.

All the way to Laurel, AJR read the Racing Form, listened to the sports news on the radio, and filled the car with cigar smoke. From time to time, he issued directions "Hey, you missed the turn. Go back and take the first right." Peezer would have to slam on the brakes. A little later he would hear: "Stay on this road for ten miles and then make the first left. It's a shortcut. Save us a good ten minutes." They'd be on unpaved or badly paved farm-to-market back roads.

At the track, AJR entrusted Peezer with the task of getting his bets down. Exactly two minutes before post-time he was to bet part of the money at one window and the rest at another window. Peezer, who didn't even know what "post-time" meant, was in a state of high anxiety, aggravated by unmet needs. Because AJR was keeping him on the run he hadn't eaten since breakfast, nor been able to visit a men's room.

Peezer thought the day would never end. When at last the afternoon did, and he pointed the car toward Olean, he was ordered to take another detour. There was racing that night at Yonkers, "which is on our way," declared AJR disingenuously. "If you step on it, we can make the first race." It was hot, and AJR's Buicks were never air-conditioned. Feeling suffocated, Peezer stepped on it, speeding toward Yonkers through the twilight.

They missed the first two races but not the rest of the card, and then they were back on the road. "We'd better look for a place to stop," said AJR. It was getting on toward 11 o'clock. But each time they approached a motel, and Peezer took his foot off the accelerator, AJR would tell him, "No, not here — keep going." After a gasoline stop — it was now past midnight — AJR decided that pressing on would be the best thing to do. "I'll drive for a while. You grab some shut-eye," he said. He did drive — fast — over narrow country roads, and they pulled into Olean at 3:30.

The manager of the training camp found sleeping space for them in a dormitory. Breakfast was at 7:30. By 8 o'clock, Peezer was in the equipment room, helping Jack Lee. His stomach began to ache. He grew dizzy. At noon, Jack drove him to the hospital in Olean. Dehydration was the diagnosis, brought on by exhaustion and stress.

Soon after Peezer had recovered, he came to terms with the railroad and went back to his regular job. "I love your dad," he told me, "but I'm glad I'm not driving for him any more."

Chapter 23

Miss Hall

In the early 1950s I had my own special tutor, Miss Hall. Our classroom was an office in AJR's ground-floor suite at the Fort Pitt Hotel. Earlier, we had met at the Ursuline Academy, where Miss Hall lived, and later there were sessions at her next home, the Convent of the Little Sisters of the Poor near St. Peter's Church. In the years just before I enrolled at St. Vincent College, she would come to 940 North Lincoln Avenue.

Sometimes she worked with my brothers and me together, but at the Fort Pitt Hotel it was usually one on one. The Fort Pitt Hotel, an ancient pile of bricks, stood rather forlornly at the northeast corner of the Golden Triangle, within walking distance of the farmers' market in the Strip District. AJR's offices were accessible to the public by way of the lobby; for habitués, the summer-time entrance was an eight-foot-high window, its sill at the level of the street. In those days before air-conditioning, the window was always open during business hours from June to September. The hangers-on who came for the card games or race results simply stepped right in from the sidewalk and took the same route when they left, saving themselves a trip through the lobby.

If the card players were using the office where Miss Hall gave me my lessons, Fran Fogarty, AJR's accountant, would move them into another room. Margaret Hall was a fastidious schoolmarm, and I think the Damon Runyon types who foregathered at the Fort Pitt were unsettling to her at first. In time she became accustomed to them. With Uncle Red, Uncle Jim, and Fran Fogarty, she was never ill at ease.

During football season, or when the Rooney-McGinley Boxing Club was putting on an important fight, Miss Hall and I adjourned to the lobby, taking our books. There were comfortable armchairs in the lobby, and we could always find vacant ones side by side. It was actually more peaceful in the lobby, because AJR's cronies were constantly invading our usual space to get to the toilet or use the pay phone on the wall. AJR had had the pay phone installed as an economy measure. Too many people were making long-distance calls to their bookmakers or girlfriends on the phone in his private office. Calling from our classroom, they would lower their voices out of deference to Miss Hall, and though every word was audible she pretended not to hear.

In the time she spent at the Fort Pitt, a side of life opened up to her that must have been entirely new. Thus she advanced her own education along with mine. Miss Hall had been tutoring Rooneys and McNultys for years, going all the way back to the girlhood of Aunt Alice. A Bryn Mawr graduate, she attempted to whet our interest in the symphony and the theater but without making noticeable headway.

I remember she angered my mother by declaring the North Side to be no fit environment for growing boys. "You've already lost Tim," she told Kass. Dan by then was a freshman at Duquesne and the rest of us were going to high school, so we had probably reached a point beyond redemption.

Miss Hall was from Oil City, where her forebears had made money in — you guessed it — the oil business. She was extremely well-traveled. When she was paid for our lessons, she would pull up her skirt and tuck the bills away in a purse attached to her petticoat. Since the petticoat nearly reached her ankles, it was not a display of immodesty. She had learned to protect her money like this while traveling in Europe, she said. She encouraged us to see the world ourselves and to read good books.

Broaden your horizons, she was saying. How much of Miss Hall rubbed off is for others to judge.

A Done Deal

On matters of importance, I deferred to my dad without an argument. After graduation from North Catholic in 1953 I had a hard time deciding on a college to attend. I was a decent student, if far from outstanding. I had been a first-string tackle on the football team. In four years, I never had missed a day of school. For that I received an award. For never having earned a bad-conduct demerit I received a pat on the back. The University of Dayton had accepted me, but I dragged my feet. Inevitably, AJR grew impatient. One late-summer day when we were still at the cottage in Ligonier, he said to me, "Jump in the car. We're going over to Latrobe. I want you to take a look at Saint Vincent." Latrobe was only nine miles away. I was quite familiar with St. Vincent and said so, but AJR was the boss. He knew the football coach, Al DeLuca; we could talk. There was no point in resisting.

DeLuca seemed glad to see me. I was a big kid for my age and at least I had the general conformation of a football player. Also, North Catholic was in the upper tier of high school teams back then. He asked if I had applied at St. Vincent. I told him no, but I'd been accepted at Dayton. AJR glared at me. DeLuca said, "I'll get you over to the registrar's office," and ordered one of his players to show me the way. It seemed to be all cut and dried. The registrar, a tall white-haired man in a black cassock — a Benedictine monk — greeted me from behind a counter.

"Are you Art Rooney's kid?" he asked.

"Yes, Father."

"Where did you go to high school?"

"North Catholic, Father."

"Just a minute," he said, and went to a telephone. He dialed a number he apparently knew by heart and spoke to somebody in a low, inaudible voice. After just a few minutes he looked up and pointed a finger at me.

"You're in," he announced.

And I was.

Getting in had been easy, thanks to AJR. Surviving the next four years, and getting out with a bachelor's degree in history, I would be on my own.

'OK for Ginger Ale'

Phil Musick, a talented sportswriter for the *Pittsburgh Press* and later the *Pittsburgh Post-Gazette*, described the Steelers as "shot-and-a-beer guys" and the Dallas Cowboys as "sippers of daiquiris." The term "shot and a beer" was familiar to me, but I never had heard of the sweet rum drink called a daiquiri. Now that I have added the word to my vocabulary, I'm not sure it was the beverage of choice for the Cowboys, but that is neither here nor there.

Although I came from a family of saloon keepers and bartenders, I was slow to pick up the terminology of the trade. Having taken to heart my father's lectures on the evils of booze, I had tasted the stuff only on special occasions: Easter, Thanksgiving, Christmas, New Year's, and the birthday of a family member. Kass, who followed her own rules for alcohol consumption, irrespective of what AJR may have thought, felt that a sip of wine or beer on such holidays (champagne was a particular favorite) would act as a sort of inoculation for the five Rooney sons. "Just a sip, you understand, so it won't be a mystery to you." In mystery, there is allure, Kass believed. With some of her boys, and they know who they are, her prescription did not have the desired effect, but it worked for me.

It was with a sense of invulnerability, then, that in my freshman year at St. Vincent, I swaggered into a bar one night with two of my football teammates. Latrobe was more of a steel town than a college town, and the place we chose to patronize reminded me a little of Grandpa Rooney's saloon on the North Side. The customers all seemed to be loud-talking, tough-acting mill hands. Somewhat preppy in style, the clothes I was wearing made me a marked man. My St. Vincent friends, Tuck and Jimmy B., were dressed like everybody else. Still, no one paid me any mind. It may be that my physical dimensions — I was 6 feet 1 and weighed about 210 pounds — discouraged sarcastic comments.

The three of us did our best to be unobtrusive. We took our places at the long shellacked bar of blond mahogany and waited to be asked what we would have.

"Draft," said Jimmy B. The bartender looked at Tuck. "Shot and a beer, draft." My turn.

"Let's see your driver's license," the bartender snapped.

I did not immediately catch on. "Driver's license?" Why would the guy be interested in my driver's license?

"Yeah, your driver's license. Your I.D."

Tuck spoke up. "You're being carded," he informed me.

"Carded?" The word meant nothing to me. "I'd just like to have a ginger ale."

"Doesn't matter," the bartender said. "Show me some ID." He was a partly bald, slovenly looking fellow in a dirty white shirt. Tucker suggested I show him my driver's license. The bartender glanced at it. "OK for ginger ale," he said. He wasn't hostile, I decided, just worn down, like a quarterback who's been sacked a dozen times.

Jimmy B. was quietly putting away his beer. Both he and Tuck were very much at ease, blending right in with the mill hunks. Watching Tuck swallow his shot of whiskey and chase it with three or four gulps of beer, I felt like a tenderfoot. I was "brand new." With my ginger ale, I tried to imitate Jimmy B.'s way of sipping his beer. He had emptied his glass and was tipping it gently up and down, which captured the attention of the bartender. "Same," Jimmy said, keeping his voice low. The bartender looked over at Tuck. "Yeah," Tuck said, "same here."

Feeling left out, I blurted, "I'm OK." The bartender seemed not to hear. In an instant, he put a draft down in front of Jimmy and a shot and a beer at Tuck's place. Tuck took the shot of whiskey in his hand, looked at me, and said, "Boilermaker." He poured the whiskey into his beer and drained the whole glass in a few gulps, just as he had done before.

I started talking with Jimmy about the St. Vincent football program. Looking back, I think we must have been sorry excuses for football players, but we were young and hopeful and convinced that we had what it takes. I wondered if the bartender was listening to us.

Tucker patted the side of his glass, and the guy in the filthy white shirt brought him another shot and another beer. For Jimmy, he drew another draft. He now looked at me. I said, "I'll have another ginger ale, please."

This time Tucker not only poured his whiskey into his beer, but tossed in the shot glass too. "Depth charge," he announced, and gulped it all down — all except the shot glass.

Quickly, Jimmy and I finished our drinks and then we left. I still didn't know what a daiquiri was, but Tucker had expanded my vocabulary. I could now define 'boilermaker" and "depth charge." I had learned what it means to be a shot-and-a-beer guy. And I knew that drinking ginger ale in a steelworkers' bar doesn't quite make the right impression.

Chapter 24

Kiesling Again

After firing Joe Bach before the start of the regular season in 1954, AJR named Walt Kiesling head coach for the third time.

Before Bach's tenure he had sent Kies to study the T formation under the man who brought it back and modernized it, Clark Shaughnessy. Kies learned the fundamentals — he was a good football man — but imagination is a quality that doesn't rub off.

The Steelers under Kies were the same team they always had been. Like Jock Sutherland and John Michelosen before him, Kies was a grind-it-out guy. His approach was simplicity itself: establish the running game, control the ball, and play tenacious defense.

In 1942, when he coached the Steelers to their first winning season, this had worked. In 1954 and again in 1955 his teams won four of their first five games, but tapered off at the end of the season and had losing records. In 1956, with Jim Finks retired and little Ted Marchibroda from St. Bonaventure at quarterback, the Steelers were neither very much better nor very much worse, just not quite good enough, once more, to win as many games as they lost.

As was usual with Steeler teams in the 1950s, there were inadequate replacements for the starters. Kies had no other choice but to use his best players on kickoffs and punts. Selected offensive players would double up on defense; selected defensive players would double up on offense.

Kies was a man's man, popular with the assistant coaches and front-office people but not with the players — not, at any rate, until after they had finished their careers. Kies and Lynn Chandnois hated each other; the feeling between Kies and Jim Finks was something a bit closer to dislike.

Lynn Chandnois was an All-American halfback from Michigan State with size, speed, and strength. He could catch the ball and he could run. But Kies, the assistant coaches, and even some of his teammates were convinced that he lacked toughness. Kies thought that Chandnois would try only hard enough to get by, which may have been true. It was also true that his natural ability enabled him to do things that most other players were incapable of.

In back-to-back games one year, Chandnois returned kickoffs for touchdowns. After his second long runback, Kies said to AJR with a shake of the head, "Can you imagine that lucky bum — going all the way on kickoffs TWICE?" Gently, AJR told him, "Kies, when you do it once it might be luck. When you do it twice, it's talent."

Before a pre-season game in Oregon, Jim Finks got so upset with Kies that he walked out of camp. Their dispute was smoothed over, but Finks went on referring to Kies as "Krauthead."

One player Kies regarded with complete admiration was Fran Rogel, a tough little fullback from Braddock who had been with the Steelers since his graduation from Penn State in 1950. On the first offensive play in every game, following orders from Kies, the Steeler quarterback, whoever it might be, sent Rogel bucking into the line for one or two yards. The predictability of the thing became a joke. "Hi diddle diddle, Rogel up the middle!" chanted the fans, but they weren't amused.

The derision in the stands and in the newspapers got under AJR's hide. So did the taunts of Bob Drum, a 6-foot-3, 260-pound sportswriter for the *Pittsburgh Press*. Sitting at AJR's side in AJR's private box, and smoking AJR's cigars, Drum was the loudest critic of all.

Finally AJR resolved to break one of his rules. He called Kies on the telephone and demanded his presence at the Steelers' business office in the Roosevelt Hotel. Kies protested that he couldn't miss practice. "Just work it out," said AJR brusquely. When Kies found his way to the office, AJR waved him into a chair and said, "Now, I'm going to put in a play that I want you to call the first time we get the ball in next Sunday's game." Kies jumped to his feet as though lifting off from the top of a red-hot stove. Before he could speak, AJR said, "Sit down!" Seeing that AJR meant business, Kies complied. His boss then delivered the next hammer blow.

He said, "Kies, you are going to have the quarterback fake a handoff to Rogel up the middle and then throw a pass — a long pass — to an end." Kies opened his mouth to object, but AJR silenced him. "Kies," he went on, "you are going to do it!!!" The discussion, Kies knew, was over

At Forbes Field the following Sunday, on the first play of the Steelers' first possession, Jack Scarbath, playing quarterback, faked to Rogel and threw a bomb to Goose McClairen, a tall rookie end from an all-black school in Florida, Bethune-Cookman. Massed to stop Rogel, the New York Giants had left McClairen wide open. He gathered in the ball and crossed the goal line untouched. The crowd was on its feet, roaring with disbelief and delight. Up in his private box, AJR turned to Bob Drum with a what-have-you-got-to-say-now look.

But a penalty flag was on the ground. A Steeler end — the other one — had jumped offside. Touchdown nullified. The hubbub in the stands died away. And Drum, seizing on his moment of triumph, bellowed in AJR's ear, "Kies told him to do that! He told him to go offside! You can't control your own coach!"

AJR never called another play. From then on, as long as Kiesling coached the team, it was hi diddle diddle, Rogel up the middle on the first Steeler offensive play of every game.

Gary Glick the Bonus Pick

For a little over a decade after the Second World War, an NFL team determined by lot drafted a "bonus pick" every year, giving that team its choice of the best college football player — or college senior, anyway — in the country. In 1956, for the first and only time, the bonus pick went to the Steelers. Pretty much by common consent, the best college football player that year was Lenny Moore, a halfback from Penn State. Coach Walt Kiesling passed him up for an unknown defensive back, Gary Glick of Colorado A. & M.

Nobody in Pittsburgh ever had heard of Gary Glick and there was little awareness of Colorado A. & M. In time, Colorado A. & M. would change its name to Colorado State and play in a 30,000-seat stadium, but in the 1950s the football team played its home games before crowds of a few thousand in wooden bleacher seats.

Understandably, therefore, the coming of Glick to Pittsburgh met with widespread ridicule. Sportswriter Bob Drum mockingly called him "Gary Stick the Bonus Pick." Instead of drafting the best player, the Steelers had drafted a player to fill a certain position — a position where they felt they needed help. The fans did not appreciate this kind of thinking. Their reaction was: "Same old Steelers — taking a guy they could get for small change."

Lenny Moore, drafted by the Baltimore Colts, played on three championship teams and ended up in the Hall of Fame. Gary Glick turned out to be a serviceable, if unspectacular, safety. He was strong and steady and tough; he had decent movement, decent speed; he intercepted some passes and made some big plays. But the fans and the media wanted a game-breaker, which Gary Glick was not. After four years with the Steelers, he played an additional four seasons in Baltimore, Washington, and San Diego.

Gary Glick had long since departed when some media people, scouts, and coaches were sitting in the beer room at the Steelers' training camp in Latrobe, cooling off on a hot summer day. Sportswriter Jack Sell was making fun of the team's draft picks and harking back, as he always did, to Gary Glick. Don Joyce, a scout who had played for the Baltimore Colts, listened quietly. At last he said, "Well, Jack, I don't know how Gary played in Pittsburgh. I don't know about that bonus pick stuff. I do know this: He didn't ask to be drafted by Pittsburgh. He was tough and he played well in Baltimore. He helped us win. And he was a heck of a good guy. The Gary Glick you are talking about is not the Gary Glick I played with — a good player on a good team."

There wasn't another peep out of Sell.

'Foxy'

There are four things I can tell you about Fred Miller of the Miller Brewing Company.

    1. He was a proud Notre Dame alumnus.

    2. He was therefore interested in Notre Dame football.

    3. He was rich.

    4. He had Pittsburgh ties (the Miller beer distributors in Pittsburgh were his good friends Fritz Wilson, also a Notre Dame alumnus, and Jack McGinley).

Fritz Wilson recruited Western Pennsylvania high school players for the Notre Dame football coaches and generally kept in touch with ex-Notre Damers like Bill Walsh, drafted by the Steelers in 1949. After the 1954 season Walsh left the team to become an assistant coach at Notre Dame and after the 1955 season Jim Finks left the team to become an assistant coach at Notre Dame. Did Fred Miller and Fritz Wilson have anything to do with this? More than likely. To augment their Notre Dame salaries, Fred Miller gave the two Steelers part-time jobs with his brewery.

"He took the heart out of our team," said AJR. Walsh was an outstanding center and Finks ran the Steelers' offense.

Of course the loss of Finks was the more disturbing. In the T formation the quarterback makes everything work, and Finks had developed into a good one. His three years as a defensive back while John Michelosen was coaching the single wing undoubtedly tried his patience. But when his chance came, in the last NFL game Michelosen ever coached, the one in which Finks stepped into a tailback position denuded by injuries, he was ready. Operating out of the shotgun formation, he passed the Steelers to a 20-10 come-from-behind upset of the Washington Redskins.

Finks preferred baseball to football and played in the minor leagues until his career stalled. From the time he joined the Steelers as a rookie, sportswriters, camp followers, trainers, equipment men, and ball boys — everybody, in fact, but Michelosen — could see that his talents were made to order for the T. On Joe Bach's part, there was no hesitation in making him the quarterback. He was smart and had excellent vision. He could set up well and his experience as a defensive back helped him to read defenses. His arm was quite strong enough for the medium and medium-deep routes, but his forte was the accurate touch pass, thrown with an easy overarm baseball delivery. He was nimble enough to elude rushes and he ran with determination enough to pick up first downs. Though not a very big man — a shade over six feet tall and built on the scale of a dancer, a clothes model, a bullfighter — he was able to take hits. He played with cuts, bruises, broken bones, and even a skull fracture.

His personality resembled a politician's. He was temperamental — sometimes even childish, as when he walked off the field in Oregon — but also ingratiating. Everybody liked him and he in turn liked everybody, or seemed to. His teammates had a nickname for him — "Foxy."

I saw him show up the Steelers' No. 1 draft choice one time in a way that was oddly inoffensive. In 1955 the Heisman Trophy winner from Notre Dame, halfback Johnny Lattner, reported to the Steelers after the College All-Star game. Lattner was a great guy, but not a great NFL player. On his first day in camp, Walt Kiesling had him running "dummy" drills, in which there isn't any contact. He was following his blockers through the line and swinging the ball carelessly in one hand. Observing on the defensive side, Finks reached out quickly as Lattner ran by him and knocked the ball loose. It was neatly done and embarrassing to Lattner, but Finks, smiling at him, converted the incident into a friendly little lesson: Kid, he was saying, hang onto the ball.

Neither Walsh nor Finks remained long at Notre Dame. Walsh spent his life as a good assistant coach in the NFL, while Finks went into the management end of football. He was personnel director and later general manager of a team in the Canadian League, and then the Minnesota Vikings hired him as their general manager. He built the great Viking teams of the 1970s and did the same thing in Chicago with the Bears. After Pete Rozelle died, there was talk that Finks might succeed him as NFL commissioner, but the job went to Paul Tagliabue.

Finks was general manager of the New Orleans Saints when he died in his mid-sixties of cancer. For his work with the Vikings and Bears, he's in the NFL Hall of Fame at Canton, Ohio, elected posthumously.

Johnny U

In the 1957 college draft, the Steelers picked Len Dawson, a quarterback from Purdue, over the intimidating Syracuse running back, Jim Brown. Dawson, Coach Walt Kiesling announced, was "the quarterback of the future."

As it turned out Dawson was something less than that, but he did have a future in football. Kiesling himself did not. Before the start of the season, AJR replaced him with Buddy Parker, who had unexpectedly walked out on the Detroit Lions. Dawson, never more than an understudy to Bobby Layne with the Steelers, took the Kansas City Chiefs to the Super Bowl twice (in Super Bowl I, they lost to the Green Bay Packers; in Super Bowl IV they beat the Minnesota Vikings). Jim Brown, drafted by Cleveland, was a ground-gaining machine, the NFL's leading rusher in eight of his nine seasons.

Passing up Brown to take Dawson was a misjudgment much remarked on, but quickly forgotten in Pittsburgh. The gaffe for which Kiesling will always be remembered, little noticed at the time outside the Rooney family, had occurred two years earlier.

There are coaches who know how to build successful teams and there are coaches who don't. And there's an easy way to assess this. Chuck Noll — more about him later — told me what it is. If the coach of a team that is losing has cut a lot of players who are helping other teams win, that's the tipoff. The description comes close to fitting Kies.

Look at his track record. He got rid of Ed Modzelewski, a Maryland fullback from New Kensington who went to a better team, the Browns, and performed well. He had a chance to draft Jim Brown and he took Len Dawson. He had a chance to draft Lenny Moore and he took Gary Glick. He had a chance to draft Joe Schmidt in 1953, but took a lineman who couldn't make it through training camp.

Joe Schmidt was a home-town boy, an outstanding linebacker at Pitt. Injured during most of his senior year, he was still on the board after five rounds. Joe Bach was the Steeler's head coach at the time, but Kiesling picked the defensive players, and two Schmidt boosters, Ed Kiely of the front office and Pat Livingston, the *Pittsburgh Press* writer, were making a case for their man. AJR told them, "If you want this guy, keep your mouths shut. You're turning Kies against him. Don't you know how stubborn Kies is?" AJR was correct. In the sixth round, Kiesling took a nose guard from Clemson called Black Cat Barton — who couldn't make the team. In the seventh round, picking just ahead of the Steelers, the Detroit Lions drafted Schmidt and had themselves a Hall-of-Fame linebacker.

Kies underrated players like Lynn Chandnois, who was not, in his opinion, "tough," and overrated players like Fran Rogel, who had about one-tenth as much ability as Chandnois but would carry a football into machine-gun fire if that was the game plan. In most ways, Kies was a hard man to satisfy. At the mention of a player or coach he disdained — there were dozens — he would turn his head to one side and go through the motions of expectorating.

The year the Steelers drafted Johnny Unitas, 1955, was during Kies's third time around as head coach. Unitas had played quarterback for a small parochial high school on Mount Washington, St. Justin, and had beaten out my brother Dan, the North Catholic quarterback, for a place on the City of Pittsburgh's all-Catholic team. No major-college coach wanted Unitas, because he weighed only 130 pounds, but the University of Louisville gave him a scholarship and he bulked up enough to have a career that may have deserved closer attention. The only reason Kiesling drafted him was that AJR wanted some Pittsburgh kids on the training-camp squad.

It didn't take Kies long to decide he didn't think much of Unitas. "He's too dumb to play quarterback," Kiesling said — words that are still used against him. If Unitas's IQ failed to match up with — well, Kiesling's — it forever casts doubt on the importance of brain power in football.

Jim Finks was the first-string quarterback that year, with Ted Marchibroda backing him up. The number three man was Vic Eaton, a rookie as obscure as Unitas. His one advantage in their competition was the fact that he could punt. Pat Brady was gone, and if the Steelers kept Eaton there would be no need to pay a salary to a kicking specialist.

In the pre-season workouts at St. Bonaventure, Finks and Marchibroda took all the snaps. There was never enough time, it seemed, for Unitas. Kies would look at his watch and blow his whistle and the drill would be over. Meanwhile, the coach of the St. Vincent Prep team, Bill Rafferty, was telling me good things about Unitas. "We played against him," Rafferty said, "and even in high school his hands were so big he could wrap them around the ball. And he can throw from one goal line to the other."

I started watching Unitas with greater interest.

He was lean and raw-boned and bandy-legged, and, for someone his age, surprisingly stoop-shouldered. From what I got to see of him, he moved around in the pocket OK, but not with the niftiness of the shorter Marchibroda, who was being likened to Frankie Albert of the Forty-Niners and Eddie LeBaron of the Redskins, the most successful little guys playing quarterback in the NFL. All Unitas did was drop back, step up, and throw with a lot of zip. He never scrambled. Like all the great ones up to then — Sid Luckman, Sammy Baugh, Bob Waterfield, Otto Graham — his object was simply to get the ball to the receiver as accurately as he could.

His problem was that Kies had arbitrarily written him off. So when practice was over Unitas would throw to Tim, Pat, and John, and to some of the other kids who were helping out in camp. He'd have them running patterns — deep patterns, mostly — and put the ball in their hands, or, more often, bounce it off their heads.

Pat and John told AJR that Unitas was the best quarterback in camp but had not been given a chance to show what he could do. Tim had similar thoughts and put them into a twelve-page letter. After reading it, AJR remained skeptical. "Tim can be a wise guy," he said to Fran Fogarty. "I don't pay my coaches to be second-guessed."

Before the regular-season opener, Kiesling cut Unitas and kept Eaton. Unitas went to work on a construction job and played semi-pro football that year with the Bloomfield Rams for six dollars a game. Somehow the Baltimore Colts heard that this was a player they might be able to use, and for a 65-cent telephone call solidified their offense for years to come.

In every game Unitas played for the Colts, the kid who was "too dumb" to make it with the Steelers called his own plays. When Unitas died, at the age of 69, the great linebacker Sam Huff said, "One time when I was playing for the Redskins I called nine different defenses. Unitas beat all nine of them. Nothing worked against him." Pat Summerall, the placekicker for the Giants, said this: "Unitas was a gambler, and he had an unconventional way of calling plays. Tom Landry, our defensive coordinator, never could figure him out."

Though Finks, like Unitas, ended up in the Hall of Fame, it was not, as I have said, for his football playing. Marchibroda fell short of being another Eddie LeBaron, much less another Frankie Albert, but developed into a first-rate coach. Vic Eaton was the Steelers' punter for one less than memorable season and then disappeared.

Some time after Unitas had signed with the Colts, AJR was in a car with John the twin and Kiesling. They stopped at a red light, and John honked the horn at the driver of a car next to theirs. Just then the light changed, and the car alongside pulled ahead. "Who was that, John?" asked AJR.

"A guy who tried out with us — Johnny Unitas."

"Catch up with him," ordered AJR. John did as he was told. The cars were side by side again at the next light.

AJR was up front, in the passenger seat. He rolled down the window and called out to Unitas, "I hope you become the greatest quarterback in football."

By the time Unitas retired in 1973 with almost every passing record — most completions, most yardage, most 300-yard games, most touchdown throws — that is exactly what he was.

Chapter 25

The Teetotaller

In his late forties or early fifties, AJR gave up drinking entirely. He never in his life had indulged very heavily. He'd have a beer with the sportswriters or in the country-club bar after a golf match. As I have written earlier in these memoirs, he tolerated drinking by his friends and business associates, but preached against it to his sons with great vehemence.

To his sons and even his nephews, he would say, "Don't be saps. Stay out of those joints [any bar was a 'joint.'] Only jerks and losers go to places like that."

Of course, it didn't take long to figure out that "joints" had been a part of his and Father Dan's early environment.

Kass was an occasional beer drinker. At the advice of a doctor, Aunt Alice drank stout, to "build up" her blood. Stout is a popular Irish drink, but to me it always tasted like medicine or tar. Aunt Alice would drink a bottle or two of the stuff every day; then in late middle age she switched to beer.

On the big holidays, such as Christmas and New Year's, all of us had champagne — for my brothers and me, just a sip. Kass would also allow us to sip wine or beer, thus removing the lure of the forbidden. Her theory seemed to work for Dan and me, but not for the twins or our cousin Trish Fiske, who lived off and on at 940 North Lincoln Avenue.

Late in life, Kass switched from beer to Canadian Club highballs — two a day at the most. I saw her tipsy only once. It was a hot summer night. We'd been to Monmouth Park, where AJR had a horse running, a horse he had named for Pat Livingston, the sportswriter. Pat Livingston came in first and, as AJR would say, he "paid a buster." AJR won more on his bet than the purse for the race was worth. So we all went to a restaurant not far from the track, and we were all very excited. Instead of her usual highball, Kass ordered a martini. Apparently she drank it too fast. The bartender gave her another, and after taking one sip she said she could drink no more. Almost immediately, the alcohol turned her into a zombie. She stared straight ahead; she couldn't speak. We got her from the bar to the table, where some food and a cup of coffee fixed her up. That was it. She never had trouble with booze.

As for Aunt Alice ... well, let's just say that sometimes she overindulged.

Ladies Last

It never occurred to me until I had learned more about life, but at 940 North Lincoln Avenue our dinner-time protocol was that of a social order pre-dating the feminist revolution.

Only the males in the family were seated. The women—Mom, Aunt Alice, and when she happened to be staying with us, Trish Fiske — served them, having first prepared the meal.

It was certainly not a case of anyone being denied equal rights. For reasons of their own, I am sure that Mom and Aunt Alice wanted it that way.

Our dinners were always robust — salad, bread, sometimes soup; steaks or chops or spaghetti or stews; vegetables and potatoes in the old Irish tradition. When tea or coffee and dessert were set before us, Mom and Aunt Alice would take their places at the table with the menfolk. I never thought much about it, but up to then they had probably eaten on the run, at the kitchen counter.

Mom was a specialist at baking apple pies. All her fruit pies, in fact, were outstanding. She made a splendid coconut cream pie as well. How she learned to bake I don't know. Her mother may have taught her. More likely, she taught herself, just by following the recipes in a cook book.

Mom's cakes were good, but not in the same class with her pies. She liked to put sherry in her pies — Harvey's Bristol Cream. Just a dash was enough.

Kass earned considerable praise for a tossed mixed vegetable salad. The Italian dressing gave it that something extra, she said. The recipe for the dressing came from a bookie and fight manager who had been a professional fighter himself. Before he would tell Kass the secret of the blend, he ordered everybody else out of the kitchen. "This is just between the two of us," he said. Kass, though sworn to silence, let it slip that "a real good olive oil" and "a dash of white sugar" were two of the ingredients.

That is all she would ever say.

The Shamrock Room

Aunt Margaret's husband, Johnny Laughlin, borrowed money from Dad to open a little saloon on Western Avenue, and it prospered. John was a hustler. Once when he was remodeling, he continued to operate by setting up a makeshift bar. It consisted of two barrels and a plank.

Shutting down for any reason was something he hated to do. During a siege of the flu, unable to be up and around, he persuaded Aunt Margaret to tend bar. Though she could handle the job as well as he could, this was not a good business decision. Many of John's customers, as it happened, were alcoholics; on their way to work in the morning they would stop at his place for "a hair of the dog that bit them" and get a lecture from Aunt Margaret on the evils of drinking before noon.

"You should be thinking of your jobs and your wives and your kids," she would tell them. Then, reluctantly, she'd pour them a shot and a beer.

Johnny Laughlin was ambitious. He moved across Western Avenue into slightly larger quarters and added a kitchen. In addition to wet goods, he was now serving food. It was the kind of bar and grill that AJR called "a sawdust joint." People started going there to talk about politics and sport.

Encouraged, Johnny borrowed more money from AJR after the end of the Second World War and bought the warehouse-type building next door. Into it, he put an upscale restaurant he called the Shamrock Room.

AJR doubted the wisdom of this venture. The North Side, he said, was not the right location for upscale dining. He advised John to try Mount Washington, with its magnificent view of the downtown skyline. But John could be obstinate at times, and he had made up his mind to stay on Western Avenue.

To the rummies and hard-bitten working-class guys his old place had attracted, the new restaurant's dining room was off-limits. They had to go somewhere else or eat in the bar. Most of them could not have afforded the prices he now charged anyway, and though feelings were hurt and a few of the old regulars drifted away, his exclusion policy was all to the good. The Shamrock Room gave him a steady income for years, which meant that the Laughlins now had financial independence. The food was not bad — steak and chops and broiled chicken were the most popular items on the menu — and the knowledge that John was related to AJR drew a sports-minded clientele.

Dad would take his pals there for casual dinners, and every Christmas he threw a big ham dinner for the St. Peter's and Rooney Reds football teams. Billy Conn and some of the Steelers would say hello to the kids and sign autographs. In a modest way, the Shamrock Room acquired a name. Jack Palance, the movie actor, stopped by one night, a tall, scary-looking guy, and John introduced him to AJR. They talked about the fight game, Palance having started out as a boxer. (In a sparring session somewhere with Billy Conn, he failed to land a single blow. Conn, Palance said, "was like a feather in the wind.")

Just as AJR had foretold, the North Side was not the place for an upscale restaurant. The kind of patron his brother-in-law wanted would show up once or twice and seldom return after that. John's lunch business was good, but at night time, when a restaurant owner has a chance to cash in, the crowds did not come.

By doing a lot of favors for people and keeping up his political contacts, John stayed afloat in a deteriorating neighborhood longer than anyone thought possible. In the end, though, he was forced to unload the place and go to work as a lobbyist in Harrisburg.

John liked to eat and drink; over the years, he put on weight. He *was* in his seventies when the rich food caught up to him. Heart disease and a stroke were the official causes of death.

Chapter 26

Big Spender

So that Uncle Jim would have something to do — something constructive — AJR put him on the football team's payroll as coach of the punters. That year the Steelers had a marvelous punter named Pat Brady, and Jim watched him kick on his first day in camp. There were oohs and ahs from the spectators as the ball soared into the air, high and far. When practice was over, Jim spoke a few quiet words to Brady. Later, someone asked what he had said. In his familiar stage whisper, Jim answered, "I told him to keep doing what he was doing. I told him not to change a thing. Coaching," Jim added, "would only screw him up."

In effect, Jim had talked himself out of a job. Before the start of the regular season, Special Teams Coach Jim Rooney was ex-Special Teams Coach Jim Rooney and back in the job he had always had — "being with Arthur."

At some point, Jim and George Quinlan opened the Allegheny County Sportsman's Club, a place to meet and drink after 2 a.m. "We had a corporation," said Quinlan. "With zero funds. I'd ask Jim, 'How's your bankroll?' 'I've got four bucks,' he'd say."

Jim's accounting procedures were not widely accepted in the financial community. He believed that on Chinese New Year's Day all debts were wiped out. If you owed somebody, it was canceled. If somebody owed you, it was canceled. One of Jim's creditors was a guy named Sal, who kept hundred-dollar bills in his right hip pocket, fifty-dollar bills in his left hip pocket, and twenty-dollar bills in his vest pocket. When Jim was in need, he knew where to go. "Sal," he would say, "give me a couple from your right kick."

His rule was never to go to bed until he had spent or given away all his cash. "He'd give it to the bellhop," said Quinlan. "He'd give it to the hatcheck girl. He'd give it to the doorman. He'd give it to the elevator operator. Then he could sleep."

One day when Pop Rooney boarded a streetcar, the conductor, an acquaintance, told him of a strange occurrence. "A man in a blue suit handed me a ten-dollar bill and said, 'Keep the change.'" The fare at that time was a nickel. Conductors wore change belts with compartments for coins and currency. "What did the guy look like?" asked Pop. The conductor gave him a full description, and Pop said, "I know that fool."

It was Jim.

In the Fort Pitt Hotel, while drinking at the bar, Jim would smoke a cigar. When the cigar stopped burning, as it frequently did, Cap, the black waiter, would strike a match and re-light it. Jim would then hand him a dollar. Somebody figured out that for every cigar Jim smoked at the bar, Cappy made an average of eight bucks. Jim drank there maybe five days a week, so his smoking added forty dollars a week or roughly two thousand dollars a year to Cappy's take-home pay.

In restaurants, Jim sometimes tipped coming and going. He borrowed ten dollars from Dago Sam one night — they had not yet placed their order — and immediately gave it to the waiter.

"What's the idea?" demanded Sam.

"You don't want him to spit in our food, do you?" said Jim.

In Scranton a few days after AJR struck it rich at Empire City and Saratoga, Jim checked into a small hotel with Quinlan. The room clerk glanced at his signature and asked if he happened to be from Pittsburgh. Jim said that was correct. "Are you *the* Mr. Rooney from Pittsburgh?" asked the clerk. Jim acknowledged that he was. The clerk passed the word to the manager. *The* Mr. Rooney from Pittsburgh, who had just cleaned out the bookies at two race tracks, was a guest of the hotel.

"Show him to the presidential suite," said the manager. "Extend unlimited credit."

Uncle Jim Rooney
(McGinley Collection)

Jim threw a party that night, a big one that filled the suite and moved into the ballroom downstairs. There was music (a piano player). There were girls. Later in the evening, a friend of the family named Dan Odom checked in. "Mister Rooney from Pittsburgh is here," the room clerk proudly informed him. "He's having a big party."

Odom's eyebrows went up. "Are you sure you have the right Mister Rooney?" he asked. It was now the room clerk's turn to look surprised. "Is there more than one?" he wanted to know. Yes ... there was more than one.

Jim's friends had to smuggle him out the back door. AJR, of course, got the bill.

When he was flush, Jim's favorite drink was champagne laced with Hennessy brandy. At other times he drank Old Granddad bourbon with Miller's High Life beer. He would then buy a small tin of aspirin tablets and take all twelve at once to prevent a hangover.

"We had a guy at the Fort Pitt Hotel named Kalski," George Quinlan recalled. "He'd have a doughnut and a cup of coffee for breakfast — fifteen cents. One morning Jim came into the dining room at 10 o'clock, and Kalski said, 'Sit down, Jim — have a little breakfast.' And Jim had a tripleheader of Granddad and a bottle of Miller's — three dollars and something. The next day they took Kalski to the hospital."

Exchanging banter, Quinlan and Jim were like a vaudeville team. The subtlety of their humor, with its reliance on irony and understatement, demanded a certain amount of sophistication from listeners. Adolescents, by and large, tend to lack this requirement. So it was that when Richie McCabe and Jim Boston, training-camp ball boys at St. Bonaventure in the 1950s, drove with the garrulous old sidekicks to an exhibition game in northeastern Pennsylvania one Saturday morning, the Quinlan-Rooney act did not play well. After twenty minutes or so, McCabe looked at Boston and mouthed the word "Bullshit." Boston giggled. Soon there was open mockery. And sarcasm.

When Quinlan, the driver, pulled up at a wayside fruit store around noon, the kids in the back seat snickered. They knew what the game was. Camp manager that year, Quinlan had the meal money; he and Jim were sots; by economizing on lunch, they could finance a Saturday night bender. To the ball boys that seemed hilarious. A laughing jag seized them. They went into the fruit store doubled over with mirth. The customers, not knowing what to make of it all, stared at them. By contrast with the imposing natural dignity of Quinlan and Jim, their behavior seemed all the more mystifying.

Up the road a piece was a hospital for the deranged. Quinlan, looking grave, addressed the little crowd in the fruit store. "These unfortunate boys," he said, "are from well-to-do families in Pittsburgh. As legal advisors to their heartbroken parents, we have agreed, my friend and I, to bring them here for confinement and treatment at your justly renowned mental institution. We only hope they are not too far gone to be helped."

There were pitying glances and understanding nods. With all the feigned sincerity he could muster, Quinlan had cast the ball boys in parts which, to the naked eye, suited them perfectly. Richie McCabe was a tall, thin, geeky-looking youth; Boston — called "Buff," short for "Buffalo" — had a big balloon head on a large, ungainly frame. Strangers were apt to take him for a good-natured oaf.

Actually he was shrewd enough to be promoted from ball boy to the front office and entrusted with the job of negotiating player contracts, while Richie McCabe had a successful career as an NFL player and coach. But in taking on two such masters of repartee as George Quinlan and Uncle Jim they miscalculated badly. They were kids, yes. But they were North Side kids. And as North Side kids they should have known better.

Buff

Before there was air conditioning, people left their windows open in hot weather. Because our North Side neighborhood was a quiet one, voices traveled great distances on the soft summer breeze, allowing the nuns who lived at the Sisters of Mercy convent to learn, as one of them put it, all they needed to know about life.

Jim Boston grew up in this neighborhood. His friendship with the Rooney brothers was lucky for him and lucky for us. At an early age, he went to work for the Steelers, and from the 1950s into the 1990s he served the organization well.

Jim's parents owned a mom-and-pop grocery store near the police station. He was a pudgy, undersized, sports- crazy kid, always pleasant, always ingratiating. As soon as he was old enough to drive, he had the use of an old jalopy, a 1939 roadster his uncle had kept on blocks during World War II, when gasoline was in short supply. Jim ran the wheels off the thing, chauffeuring schoolmates all over town. He delivered AJR to the Duquesne Club one day and learned that no good deed goes unpunished. The Duquesne Club's members were the rich and the powerful. They arrived for lunch or for business meetings in shiny black limousines driven by uniformed flunkies. Boston's neighborhood pals seized on this. "Why doesn't Jim wear a uniform?" one would ask. With the callous levity of the young, another would say, "Because he can't find a chauffeur's cap big enough for his head."

At Steeler training camp when Boston was a ball boy, Jim Rooney made the remark that his head was the size of a buffalo's. Others repeated it. Jim Finks and Bill Walsh, two of the players, started calling him Buffalo. Then they shortened it to Buff, and the nickname caught on. He was Buff for the rest of his life.

Too small to play football, Boston became manager for the team at North Catholic High School. Before the start of the season, a ruptured appendix laid him low. During and after his long convalescence, a physiological miracle occurred. The rest of Jim Boston caught up with his head. Suddenly he was 6 feet 3, and growing sideways as well. The cops at the neighborhood police station started recruiting him for lineups whenever they had a crime, a suspect, and a witness or witnesses. Jim was always picked as the "perpetrator" — the guy who did it.

In spite of his bulk he was an excellent dancer and a pretty good pickup-game basketball player. He was not proficient at schoolwork. Because of his weak eyes, reading may have been difficult for him. He was smart, but lacked discipline and patience. AJR gave him a job as a ball boy, and he made himself useful in the trainer's room, the equipment room, and the ticket office. It seemed there was nothing he wasn't able to do.

Only once did he run afoul of AJR. At a pre-season game with the Philadelphia Eagles on a sweltering afternoon in Franklin Field, he was wearing a T-shirt and sweat pants. Jim had a nervous habit he appeared to be unaware of — lifting the front end of his T-shirt and putting it into his mouth, which left his ample paunch completely bare. His sweat pants, secured by a worn-out elastic band, kept slipping; Boston kept pulling them up tight, which outlined his genitals. Sitting with the Chief, NFL Commissioner Bert Bell found the display offensive. "Art," he said, "look over there by the Steeler bench. Who is that big fat kid with the thick glasses, the big belly, the big round head, and the big balls?"

From then on Boston had orders to tighten the waist of his sweat pants with tape and to wear two T-shirts or two sweat shirts — one to chew, as AJR explained, and one to cover his midsection.

Irish Brewmaster

George Quinlan said of himself, "I was born in March, a windy month, in Chicago, a windy city, and I'm a windy guy." Tall and gray-haired, distinguished in appearance, he looked like an actor, the kind of actor who is cast as a senator, judge, or district attorney in the movies. He was an expert story teller whose timing, voice inflection, and body language would have been right for the stage or screen, but his actual occupation during the years of Prohibition was something quite different.

"I was sent to Pittsburgh," he said once, "because I had a degree in brewing. I was an Irish brewmaster. "

At different times, Quinlan ran breweries in Millvale and Knoxville. "I was young," he said. "I could hustle and I think I had some belly." His partner was a man called Shine, from Panther Hollow. Quinlan told a story about Shine: "One day as he was getting ready to unlock the door from the outside and let me drive through from the inside with a truckload of beer, he heard an automobile coming. He thought it was the police, and he ran like hell. He ran away and left me locked in the damn brewery. I had to chop my way out through a window with a bung pick. An hour later I found Shine in Oakland, telling a bunch of guys about the Prohibition men. I asked him, 'Where the hell's the key?' 'Oh, I threw it in the river,' he said. So I went back to the brewery and chopped off the lock."

In Chicago, Quinlan had a brother on the police force and a brother who was killed by the mob. He had an uncle named Paddy McNamara who killed a guy in a saloon fight, pleaded insanity, and spent thirty-eight years in a Cook County mental institution. "He *was* insane," Quinlan said. "From whiskey. That was the curse of the Irish — drinking. In Illinois, you couldn't sell the Indians a drink, and I always thought they should put the Irish on that list, too. 'Don't you like the Irish?' someone asked me. I said, 'I love the Irish, and my love is intensified by knowing how weak some of them are, including myself.'"

Another uncle, Barney Birch, was a political boss. "Barney Birch made four trips to four penitentiaries and ended up with a ton of money," Quinlan said. Barney Birch introduced Quinlan to Al Capone. "I met him just twice. He had the whole second floor of the Lexington Hotel. A big, tough dago, and I didn't go for him. He weighed about 290 pounds, and he grunted. You couldn't understand him. He ended up with cirrhosis of the liver. I'm never proud to say that I knew Al Capone."

Quinlan was an Irish tenor. As a young man in Chicago he sang in Clark Street saloons. An Irish tenor named Dion O'Banion, an acquaintance but not a friend, also sang in Clark Street saloons. Later, O'Banion went into the racketeering business and died at the hands of Al Capone's gunmen. In 1926, Quinlan sang at Carnegie Hall in Pittsburgh and he sang on the radio. "I could sing in Italian and Hebrew," he said.

John McCormack gave a concert in Pittsburgh at the Syria Mosque. "In the second row that night," Quinlan said, "there were eighteen Catholic priests and a hoodlum named George Quinlan. Father O'Connor from St. Mary's of the Point was sitting next to me. He said, 'George, the honey has left John's voice.' I said, 'What do you think caused it, Father?' He said, 'The whiskey, George, the whiskey.' "

When Lily Pons, the French opera singer, gave a concert in Pittsburgh, Quinlan was introduced to her. "And she put out her paw," he said. "She expected me to kiss her hand. The only other French girl I ever met was a very beautiful movie actress" — who, for purposes of this narrative, shall be nameless. "She was brought into Johnny Laughlin's Shamrock Restaurant by Jackie Conn. We sat in a booth, and I asked her if she knew Jackie's brother Billy. She said, 'Yes, but Billy says bad things about me. He told some people in New York that I was a French pig.' 'Well,' I said, 'Billy makes very few mistakes.'"

During the run-up to the stock-market crash of 1929, Quinlan invested heavily. He said, "In 1928 I had a hell of a year. I made ninety thousand dollars. I took it all into Morris, Lloyd and Lynch. I went in there and started buying stocks. I couldn't even read the damn symbols. I bought five hundred dollars of this and four hundred dollars of that. I was a big shot. President of a brewery. Oh boy, was I something. And then the market crashed. I must have lost a hundred and fifty thousand dollars. I had RCA. I don't remember what I paid for it. I told my broker, 'Sell the RCA,' and he said, 'Who'd buy it?' I had Graham-Paige. Bought it for eight dollars. I sold it at sixty-five cents."

The repeal of the Eighteenth Amendment in 1933 completed the financial undoing of Quinlan. His illegal brewery — "Bootlegging may have been illegal," he used to say, "but it wasn't illicit" — shut down, and he worked for a while in the slot-machine business with Uncle Jim.

In the 1950s, when the Steelers prepared for the season at St. Bonaventure, Quinlan was camp manager. The job was not difficult. For the most part it consisted of keeping an accurate count of the camp population for the cooks and the mess-hall workers. Up to a point, the players, coaches, and newspaper reporters found Quinlan's stories entertaining. He did not have much of a formal education but had read a lot and knew how to express himself. By the last day of camp, however, his performance had usually lost some of its charm. I would say that most people dismissed him as an Irish version of Falstaff.

Undeniably, Quinlan had strong ties to the Rooneys of his generation. He knew Anne Jackson's father, the coal miner from Harmarville who believed in Communism. "Old Dan Rooney and I used to have arguments with him," Quinlan said. "Old Dan was one of the greatest men I ever met. His son Jim called him 'Square Paper.' No con. He never screwed anybody. He couldn't. He was a tough old man but an honorable old man and very outspoken. I remember one time after the Steelers lost a ball game he was on the front porch with Art and Jim. The Steelers had been slaughtered that day, and Art said it was terrible the way the people booed Kiesling. And his father said, 'Art, take Kiesling to the Duquesne Brewery and get him a job.'

"I met Art's brother Dan when he was studying for the priesthood. Dan was a great man. As a missionary, he had to learn Chinese. A lot of Chinks didn't think he understood it, but they were wrong. Dan didn't talk much about China. He didn't talk much about anything. He could have been an outstanding baseball player. He could hit. He hit a couple over the fence against the Homestead Grays. But he had no arm. All in all, Dan was a very strong character. He got in his rough work in life early. Ran a crap game, drove a beer truck. A pretty solid fella — quiet and very, very hot-tempered."

Quinlan and Uncle Jim were close. Quinlan told stories about Jim's proficiency as a fighter. "One night Jim got into an argument with Billy Conn's father-in-law, Greenfield Jimmy Smith, and Jim asked Jimmy Smith to get out of the automobile they were in. Jimmy Smith was tough, but he didn't get out of the automobile. Jim Rooney's daddy taught his kids to fight. He taught them all, and they fought with each other for the fun of it. I took Duke to the hospital one day after Jim knocked him unconscious.

"Jim could fight, Art could fight, and Dan could fight. There was a big, tough lieutenant of police named Henninger who hung out at an engine house on the North Side. He weighed about 200 pounds and he was flattening everybody. One day a young guy who weighed about 170 came in. He put on the gloves with Henninger, and *boom*! Henninger went out. The young guy was Dan Rooney.

"One time out at Forbes Field, Bert Bell got into an argument with Buff Donelli, and Buff was going to slug him. Father Dan was sitting three seats away, and he was wearing his collar. He jumped over the rail and grabbed Buff. And Buff didn't slug Bert Bell."

Quinlan recalled that when Uncle Jim was born — in 1905 on March 16th — his parents intended to name him Patrick James. "But nobody was hiring Irish Catholics at the time, and his mother said, 'We'd better call him James Patrick. If he's Pat Rooney, he'll never get a job.' The way it turned out, getting a job was the last thing Jim ever wanted to do."

Old age was not kind to George Quinlan. He was indicted for perjury when the police discovered — it must have been shocking to them — that there was illegal gambling at the Sportsman's Club, the after-hours place run by Quinlan and Uncle Jim. Although Jim was a full partner, the indictment did not mention him. Political pull? I'm not sure. At any rate, Quinlan was never brought to trial. AJR continued to send him money — a generous sum every Christmas — but they were never again very close. Another benefactor was Buck McArdle, a lawyer friend of Ed Kiely and Jack McGinley, who gave Quinlan a job as an investigator to keep him afloat. Bedridden after a stroke, he spent the last two years of his life in a rented room in Dormont.

"Doc," he said to the physician taking care of him, "how do I stay mentally alert? How do I keep from going nuts?" "Communicate, George," the doctor said. Quinlan had mistrusted newspaper reporters all his life, but now, using the telephone, he became friendly with two or three, including Kathy Kiely, Ed's daughter. A year or two before he died, Quinlan sent her a Christmas card. On it, he wrote:

With rheumy eyes, Sans teeth,
With concrete ears [he was partly deaf], *And one dead wing* [he was paralyzed on the left side],
I'm close to being a dead thing.
Merry Christmas to you and yours.
As for me, at 91 [actually, he was 81], *I'll take a small beer.*

Prankster

You either could not abide Owney McManus or you loved him. AJR was among his devoted friends. Although we did not get acquainted until Owney had seen his best days, I counted myself lucky to have known him, and so did my brother Tim.

Owney McManus was a round-faced little man with a red complexion, very Irish and very Catholic. There were those who appreciated his humor and his prank playing and others who found him abrasive. He talked a lot, and often it was possible to believe what he said. Until old age forced him to change his habits, he liked to drink. He liked women — his first wife died young — but practiced serial monogamy.

Owney was a World War I veteran. If he distinguished himself at all, it was on the troop ship going to France. The enlisted men, crammed below deck, mistook a loud noise for a torpedo hit from a German U-boat one night and panicked. In the bedlam, little Owney took charge. Fearful of being crushed in a stampede to the hatch, he shouted in the voice that in years to come would dominate many a bar-room argument, "Quiet! Take it easy! We haven't seen any water coming in! Let's get out of here one at a time! Don't do the Germans' job for them!" Reaching deck in an orderly fashion, the frightened recruits could see that nothing had happened. The ship was steady and the ocean was calm. And a lot of big, brave soldier boys who had lost their heads were embarrassed.

Anyway, that was the story.

Owney's saloon on Fourth Avenue resembled a fun house at times. Some of the games that he and his henchmen — and henchwomen — would play were elaborate, not to say juvenile and sadistic. If a stranger who looked like a rube walked in, a waitress from the bar might go to a room the boys kept in the nearby Pittsburgher Hotel. Owney would sidle up to the pigeon and ask if he wanted a girl. Often the answer was yes, and, following instructions, the fellow would go to the hotel room, knock in a certain way, and ask for "Gertie." Or "Mabel." Or whatever name Owney had mentioned. The waitress would let him in and close the door. A moment later it would fly open, and a man with a gun would be shouting, "So you're the guy who's trying to ruin my home life!" He'd be waving his pistol in the air. The waitress would shriek. And the "John" would take off and run down the stairs, not waiting for an elevator, and out onto the street, where Owney and his friends could see how successful their machinations had been.

A variation of this scam involved the firing of blank cartridges by the man with the gun and the sudden appearance of blood — actually ketchup — on the waitress's blouse.

In such ways did Owney and his pals get their kicks. The hotel-room caper had to be dropped after one victim, running for his life, tripped on the Fourth Avenue streetcar tracks and broke a leg.

In the year when a song called "Deep in the Heart of Texas" was popular, a cop named Al Quaill, who had been a middleweight boxer, patronized Owney's bar. Even if Al was off-duty, he carried his police revolver. "Deep in the Heart of Texas" always seemed to be blaring on Owney's juke box, and in one verse the lyrics went:

The stars at night
Are big and bright
Deep in the heart of Texas...

After the word "bright" there was a pause in the beat. From the juke box you would hear the sound of hands clapping four times, and people listening in Owney's bar would join in, either clapping or banging their glasses and bottles on the table. One night everybody did that except Quaill, who had tossed off a few stiff ones. Keeping perfect time with the others, he pulled out his revolver and fired four shots into the ceiling.

Furious, Owney ushered Quaill to the door. "You could have broken one of my overhead pipes!" he kept saying. The shots might have killed one of the customers, too, but McManus was only concerned about the pipes.

Another policeman — the beat cop working Fourth Avenue — often stopped in for a free meal. It was one of his perks, but Owney disliked the guy. McManus's was a ham-and-cabbage joint, and the cop was always asking for something exotic, like rabbit. One day when he asked for rabbit, Owney was prepared to teach him a lesson. A friend of his had ended the life of a stray cat, and a butcher carved it up. Owney cooked the pieces that looked like rabbit and served them to the cop, who complimented him on an excellent meal. "Best rabbit I've ever tasted," he said. "This place is finally getting some class."

One night around closing time Owney got into a drunken argument with a judge. The judge was attacking Mayor Lawrence, and Owney was defending him. Goaded beyond endurance, Owney picked up a whiskey bottle and hit the judge on top of the head. An ambulance came and took the judge to the hospital. Sobering up, Owney began to evaluate the trouble he was in. Would he lose his liquor license? Would the escapade put him out of business? Would it put him in jail? The next afternoon the judge walked into the bar. He had come to apologize, he said. He was a judge, and his actions had been injudicious. He'd made a complete fool of himself. As for his injuries, they were minor, a slight concussion and a lump on the head. Owney sighed with relief and agreed to let bygones be bygones.

Owney shocked me one day. He said he'd been playing golf at the Wildwood Country Club and his drive had hit the side of a car that belonged to a fellow club member, a Catholic priest, who happened to be in it at the time. He said the priest got out of the car and berated him. "Can you imagine that old S.O.B.?" Owney demanded. "What a miserable guy." Never before in my life had I heard a Catholic speak ill of a priest. I had been taught by my parents and the nuns and the brothers at North Catholic High School that you always showed deference to priests. It took me a long time to get over such a display of irreverence.

But Owney was no respecter of persons or of Roman collars. He made no secret of his antipathy for Father James Cox, the priest from the Strip district who in 1932 led an army of the unemployed in a march on Washington. It seems that as a shepherd of the Lord, Father Cox had once seen fit to criticize Owney for his lifestyle. Instead of listening meekly, Owney lashed back, pointing out to the noted clergyman some shortcomings of his own. McManus knew the dirt on everybody, Catholic priests included.

Owney did have a lot of friends who were priests, and he could impersonate a priest if need be. Once when AJR and a few of his pals were driving to Canada for a week or two of fishing, they ran out of booze in upstate New York. Prohibition was still the law, so replenishing their supply would be a problem. Opportunity suggested itself, however, as they passed a mom 'n' pop drug store with an Irish name over the door. "Stop here!" someone said. With a prescription from a doctor, you could legally buy whiskey at a drug store, and though the requisite medical OK was lacking, the man who had said "Stop!" had an idea. He went into the drug store and explained to the owner that he and some fisherman friends were driving to Canada but thought they would have to turn back. A priest in the group, who was over here from Ireland, had been suddenly taken ill. A bad cold. What might help was a bit of whiskey. They had no prescription, of course. On the grounds that this was an emergency, could the druggist possibly oblige them?

"Well, now," said the druggist. "A priest from Ireland, you say?" He could let them have a pint, but with one stipulation. He would have to see this priest and hand over the whiskey himself.

Owney, unaware he had been nominated for the role of sick priest, was asleep in the back seat of the car. Aroused from slumber to meet the druggist — "Father, I know you're not feeling good, but wake up!" the idea man said to him — he caught on at once. It was twilight and rapidly getting dark. Owney pulled up the collar of his coat. He started to cough. The fact is that in appearance he resembled Barry Fitzgerald, the Irish movie actor often cast in those days as a priest. He was introduced to the druggist as Father McManus. He coughed again and wiped his nose.

"Father, I think you might need this," said the druggist, offering the whiskey. Owney accepted it with a look of saintly gratitude. A pint wasn't much, but it would get the carload of Pittsburghers to Canada. "Bless you, my son," he said, and coughed. "I will pray for you." There was the hint of an Irish brogue in his voice. The druggist refused payment.

Owney was a dedicated Steeler fan. In the days when Steeler teams did not amount to much, he created a following for them with his Ham-and-Cabbage Specials to out-of-town games. Sometimes the trains Owney ran would be hooked onto the train that carried the players and coaches, arriving at the scene after an all-night trip. "Ham and Cabbage" was a metaphor. The only food served was the railroad's standard fare. Once when Owney showed up at the Pennsylvania Station in Pittsburgh with a ring of bologna, everybody hooted at him. But the club car turned out to be oversold for dinner, and the people who had laughed at Owney were begging for some of his bologna. He would share it only with Kass, who had said he was wise to bring provisions.

Owney and AJR were great card players. When they played at 940 North Lincoln Avenue, almost always with a priest or two in the game, Kass would cook for them. Owney at such times would be on his best behavior. In fact, when AJR was around, he refrained from off-color jokes and from pranks like the one involving the waitress in the hotel room.

Owney's girlfriend, Marie, co-habited with him for a while, and AJR disapproved. After this liaison came to an end, Owney courted a more conventional matronly woman who took an interest in the bar business and made suggestions to improve its profitability. For one thing, she helped him to cut down waste and employee theft. The woman's name was Jean, and eventually Owney married her.

Sometimes it almost seemed that Owney was more concerned with AJR's affairs than his own. He kept urging AJR to develop business interests other than the football team. "You have to think about your sons," he would say. "All five can't work for the ball club."

AJR would answer, "They're little boys."

"They won't always be," Owney reminded him. This was before AJR acquired the race tracks in New York and Florida. Did Owney plant the seed? I tend to think so.

Like Uncle Jim, Owney burned the candle at both ends, and his health began to wane before he was out of his fifties. He sold or closed his restaurant and moved to Fort Lauderdale with Jean.

Owney Junior had just finished law school at Pitt. In contrast to his old man, he was staid and strait-laced, a serious, hard-working, overachieving young guy. He had always been a special favorite of Kass, who feared that Owney Senior was bringing him up in a poor home environment — an apartment above the saloon in a household that included Marie. One summer while Owney Junior studied for his bar exams, Kass put him up at our cottage in Ligonier. Before too long he was on his own and doing very well, and his father may have been an embarrassment to him at times. He was married to a girl of similar tastes and temperament, and when they entertained corporate big shots Owney Senior could be present but with orders to stay in the background. The trouble was that Owney Junior's lawyer friends would congregate around Owney Senior and coax him to tell stories about the sports people he knew.

"What was I supposed to do?" Owney Senior asked. "Play deaf and dumb?"   For several years, Owney Junior was our football team's lawyer, but then the business became so big that one man no longer could handle all the legal problems – an entire firm was needed – and AJR had to replace him. Owney Junior was heart-broken.

Whether Owney Senior was still alive I don't remember. I know that his twilight years were anything but reposeful. He did stop drinking. As a diabetic with heart trouble, he had no alternative. He got some rest for a while and watched his diet. Though unable to break his cigarette habit, he succeeded in cutting back. But as soon as he realized that he was not about to die, he plunged into Fort Lauderdale politics. He was the Owney McManus of old, minus the booze and the pranks. Fort Lauderdale was full of transplanted Pittsburghers – former associates of Owney among them – and there were some, chances are, who found the moderated McManus more to their liking. Fort Lauderdale transformed him into something of a moralist. On a football trip to the Miami area, AJR was approached by the owners of the local jai alai frontons. They asked him to intervene for them with a tough little politician from Pittsburgh who was campaigning hard against a referendum to allow jai alai in Fort Lauderdale. (Jai alai is a Cuban court game similar to handball in which the players wear wicker baskets on their hands instead of gloves; in Florida there was lots of betting on jai alai, making supervision by each municipal government necessary.) AJR immediately guessed that the tough little politician from Pittsburgh was Owney McManus.

Without tipping his hand, he asked the jai alai promoters if they could get this fellow on the telephone. They could and did. Confident that Owney would recognize his voice, AJR took the phone and went straight to the point. All he said was, "I'm with the jai ali folks. They tell me you're giving them some grief. Well, they're OK guys. Lay off them ... OK. We understand each other." With that, he handed the phone back to one of the jai ali men and heard him say, "Yes ... Yes ... I'm glad you think that this can be worked out, Mister McManus. Thank you very much. I'll see you real soon." In the eyes of the jai alai guys from then on, AJR was a miracle worker.

Homesick after just a few years, Owney called Dave Lawrence in Pittsburgh. "I'd rather die around friends and family than down here," he said. "Can you get me a job?" Lawrence placed him in the state auditor's office.

Back where he belonged, he became an old uncle to the Rooney boys. One day at lunch time we brought him a sandwich from the Roosevelt Hotel, and he gave us a glimpse of his Merry Prankster persona. He picked up the telephone and called the cops who policed the Liberty Tunnel. "Hello," he began, "I'm calling about my airplane. Yes, my airplane. I landed it by mistake at the county airport last night. I meant to land it at the Greater Pittsburgh Airport, but the traffic controllers misdirected me. So I have to get my plane to Greater Pittsburgh, but I'm not allowed to fly there. I'm having it towed. Yes, towed. Now, wait a minute. Be patient. This is why I'm calling you. I got to your tunnel about three in the morning and couldn't get my plane through because the wings were too wide. Your guys told me to leave it there – park it off to the side – and come back and pick it up this afternoon, and they'd see what could be done ... What do you mean; you've never heard of anything like this? How about going outside to see if my plane is OK ... I'm not kidding, dammit! Please go out and see if it's OK. It won't hurt you to put your head out the door."

Glancing up at Tim and me, Owney chortled, "I've got the poor sap looking out the door. I hear him yelling at someone about an airplane that has to get through ..."

Another call Owney made was to the manager of the Hilton Hotel. Assuming a Polish accent, he demanded to know why the Hilton's American flag was not at half mast. An important public figure who was Polish had died – and Owney came up with a fictitious name full of Z's and K's. There were lots of Poles in Western Pennsylvania, he said, and they deserved as much respect as the Irish, who had their St. Patrick's Day parade. My brother and I were rolling on the floor.

When Rudy Bukich, a Steeler quarterback from the University of Southern California, asked AJR to finance a bowling alley, Owney took it upon himself to conduct an investigation. He visited many of the bowling alleys in Pittsburgh and took me along. His conclusion: "Bowling alleys are now like drug stores. They're at the point of saturation. That Bukich fellow is a pretty nice guy from what I hear, but how much does he mean to the Rooney family? If this thing works, he'll be sitting pretty. If it doesn't work he has used your money and contacts and good name. You are left holding the bag, while Rudy is still a nice guy and no longer around. He is back in Southern California."

It was a good lesson I have always remembered: what is the other guy bringing to the party?

In the 1950s Tim was a stockbroker. One day when I was in my early twenties I had a date to play golf with Tim and his boss and Owney. The three of them came to 940 North Lincoln in a car — I was still living at home — and when I did not make an immediate appearance, Tim ran up to the porch. He started giving me hell for causing a delay; I lost my temper; so did he; punches were exchanged, and Tim went down. The upshot of it was that they drove off without me — I no longer wanted to be a part of the golf outing.

A day or two later, I had a meeting with Owney. He told me that Tim and I must always remember who we were. If we insisted on fighting we should be careful to pick our spots. It was not a good idea to act like roughnecks in front of Tim's boss. This from an old brawler like Owney. I told him I hadn't meant to humiliate Tim. He was tougher than I was and a better fighter. It just so happened that I nailed him with a lucky punch. "Maybe," said McManus. "But when it ended you were standing over him. Don't sell yourself short."

We did not always appreciate Owney's words of wisdom. There were times when my brothers and I tested his patience with what Owney called "smart-ass remarks," but clearly he liked to be in our company.

As the old guard died off, AJR was going to five or six wakes every week, and in Owney he now had a companion. I was with them once when somebody said of the corpse that he "looked good." Owney shook his head in disgust. "NO ONE," he said turning to me, "looks good in the box."

The last wake he attended was his own. While playing pinochle with AJR and some others, he died of a heart attack. At the funeral home, I just had to say it: "No one looks good in the box." I meant this as a fond, sincere tribute to Owney, one of Pittsburgh's great unforgettable characters.

Chris

If you made a pig of yourself at the dinner table with Dad or one of his brothers present, they would say you were eating like Chris McCormick.

Chris was the guy who needed special accommodations at the Kenyon Theater because of his enormous rear end. So that he could watch the movies there in something like comfort he paid to have two seats in the back row converted into one.

Uncle Jim spoke highly of Chris. "Wonderful fella," he told me. "Must have weighed over four hundred pounds. He lived with his two sisters; they were almost as big as he was. They'd have Dan, Art, and me out to dinner on a Sunday afternoon. Dinner was one o'clock sharp. And, boy, did they put on a feed. Chickens. Roast beef. Ham. Everything king-sized. Huge bowls of mashed potatoes with lots of gravy. Huge pitchers of buttermilk. Different kinds of dessert. Filled you up for a week. They were real nice people, Chris and his two sisters."

Chris McCormick was a professional man — an accountant — but in all ways a rough-hewn North Sider. On Federal Street one night he got into a fist fight. An old sandlot football player named Jim Westerling gave me a blow-by-blow description. Come to think of it, no blows were actually struck, at any rate not by Chris. "He grabbed hold of the guy," Jim said, "and fell on top of him. Then he laid there, holding the guy down. He just about crushed the life out of that guy. Flattened him like a pancake."

As a mark of esteem, AJR named one of his race horses after Chris. I don't know how close their friendship was. I do know that Chris was part of the gang, included on at least one trip to a championship boxing match in New York. AJR used to talk about it. He said that after the fight, learning that their train would be late, he and the other Pittsburghers went for a midnight snack to a place near the Pennsylvania Station. Everybody ordered a big steak.

The moment the steaks arrived at their table, a friend from back home came rushing into the room. "Hey, Art!" he yelled. "You guys better get going! The train to Pittsburgh is ready to pull out!"

No one had had a bite of steak. But, leaping out of their chairs, they took off en masse for the station. AJR paid the bill on the run. Only Chris lagged behind momentarily. Snatching up the tablecloth, he twisted it into a bundle with the steaks inside, threw the bundle over his shoulder, and joined the stampede. No morsel of food would be wasted while Chris was around.

He died before his time, as gluttons often do. "Poor Chris," said Uncle Jim, ad-libbing a sort of epitaph. "His belly button exploded."

Part Two:
Bit Player
1956-1965
Chapter 27

Stagestruck

When AJR, pulling strings, got me admitted to Georgetown Law School in 1957, my history professor at St. Vincent College, Father Hugh Wilt, played devil's advocate.

"You can't spell," he reminded me.

"Your handwriting is unreadable." he reminded me.

I stared at him, puzzled. What did spelling and handwriting have to do with the practice of law? "But, Father," I said. "I'll have a secretary to type all my letters." His reply was: "Artie, you will find there are times when a handwritten note is more appropriate than a letter typed by a secretary."

He was pouring cold water on Georgetown Law School, and I didn't mind. AJR had a low opinion of lawyers anyway. And Uncle Jim told me, "They're a dime a dozen. All the lawyers I know are starving." (His acquaintanceship among lawyers must have been limited.)

There was something else that deflected me from the law. I remembered, or thought I remembered, a quote from Winston Churchill: "Youth is the time to take chances." Secretly, what I wanted to take a chance on was acting. I had just turned 21. "Go for it!" I could hear Churchill advising me.

I forgot about Georgetown Law School and started thinking about Carnegie Tech's renowned Drama School. Sure, actors were all fruits — sissy boys (my thinking back then had not yet begun to evolve). Even John Wayne. Well ... maybe not John Wayne. As Raoul Walsh, the director, once said, "The son of a bitch looks like a man." What was good enough for the Duke, I figured, was good enough for me. So I applied at Carnegie Tech and was told I'd be given an audition — or, in football parlance, a tryout. Did my name help? Possibly. Or possibly not. But, though I didn't know it at the time, the woman in charge, Edith Skinner, was a Steeler fan. I don't think that hurt.

Miss Skinner and two or three other instructors judged the auditions. I was asked to recite two short monologues — or were they soliloquies? — one from a serious drama, the other from a comedy. I chose a passage from "Macbeth" —"If it were done when 'tis done, then 'twere well it were done quickly ... " (Macbeth is about to murder Duncan) — and reporter Hildy Johnson's telephone call to his editor from the Ben Hecht-Charley MacArthur play, "The Front Page."

In the scene from "Macbeth," I took as my model the English actor Sir Ralph Richardson. I had a recording of Richardson as Macbeth and I copied every nuance of his delivery. Not very original, but it worked. I made a tape recording of my own interpretation and listened to it, and it seemed to be all right. I had to do this on the Q.T., because if AJR or my brothers were to overhear me, they would think I had gone queer.

With the Hecht-MacArthur scene, I was more comfortable. Having been around sportswriters all my life, I thought I could mimic their speech patterns and body language.

Waiting to go on, I was scared stiff. I was older by two or three years than the other applicants and self-conscious about it. The boys all had pimples, the girls had big noses. But they could act. Quite a few auditions preceded mine, and I was able to watch. I said to myself, "Boy ... those geeks are good!"

My turn came, and by then I had settled down. I started off with "Macbeth." There was a four-legged stool on the stage, and I put my foot on it, as I had seen professional actors do. I had a pretty fair theatrical voice, and I was letting 'er rip. So far, so good. Then my leg began to shake. I leaned on it. The shaking continued. I took my leg off the stool and tried to keep focused. At last it was over. I had remembered all the words, which was something.

Doing Hildy Johnson was easier for me. For some reason, though, I started to move sideways across the stage as I spoke my lines, forgetting that Hildy was supposed to be in a telephone booth. By a stroke of good luck, I finished before I ran out of stage.

All of us waited nervously for the verdict of the judges. The others, I saw, though more experienced than I was, were even less confident. Time passed. My name was called. I stepped before the judges to be told what I already knew: "You are more than raw!" But Miss Skinner said, "Your voice is a gift!" I was in!

Classes began, and a teacher named Bess Keeley made acting sound simple. "Just speak in a loud voice," she said, "and don't bump into the furniture." Alas, she was only kidding. Miss Skinner gave me constant encouragement. "You have a great voice. Learn to use it."

Another teacher took me aside and suggested I major in set design. "You *might* get a good job as an actor, but I say might. Major with me, and be *sure* to get a good job." Well, I hadn't passed up Georgetown Law School to be a set designer. All we seemed to do in those first few months, though, was build scenery.

By the end of the semester I'd had enough. I dropped out of school and left for New York City to study the Stanislavski Method of acting.

New York

AJR's first cousin, the actress Anne Jackson, was living in New York when I finished up at Carnegie Tech, and I wrote to her, inquiring about teachers. She gave me a list of names from which I selected the one with the most syllables in it, Tamara Daykahonova.

Madame D. had studied with the great Russian director Constantine Stanislavski at the Moscow Art Theatre. In 1917 she fled the Communist Revolution and came to America. Times were hard. She kept body and soul together, as she put it, by doing makeup — at first for just a handful of actors, then more, and at last for all the members of a cast. As her reputation grew, she found herself doing makeup by mail for entire theatrical companies on the road. Is such a thing possible, you ask? For the time being, let's not get into that.

Once Madame D. became established, she opened her New York actors' studio and made a nice living for years. She taught through improvisation, through character study. She expected us to interpret the playwright's intentions. We took diction lessons, dancing lessons, voice lessons. We learned to apply makeup.

Madame's husband — we knew him as "Mr. V." — was also a Russian. He escorted the whole class on trips to the great art museums of New York City. Right from the start, the old boy sort of took to me. He was impressed by the fact that I had gone to college and played football and that I read good books. I underestimated Mr. V., mistakenly supposing that he worked for his wife because that was the only job he could get. In truth, he had been a White Army general during the Russian Revolution, knew a lot about aeronautics, and held an important position with a big engineering firm on Long Island. Beyond all that, he had written a critically acclaimed paper on the Impressionist painter Gauguin. By the time I discovered these things, we were pals, and it was too late for me to be intimidated by Mr. V.

Madame Daykahonova gave me special attention. When I stopped going to dance classes — dancing, I thought, was "effeminate" — she did not object. Dancing lessons, she explained, were helpful to an actor because actors should be able to walk and move gracefully. (As Miss Keeley importuned us at Carnegie Tech, "Don't bump into the scenery.") Madame D. excused me from the class but made it clear I would not get my money back. She said I should take more interest in art, in classical music, in drama.

One day when AJR, Kass, and Ed Kiely happened to be in New York, I cut all my classes to go to Aqueduct with them. "I'm sorry," I told Madame D., "but my father has a horse of his running and he wants me to be there." Regretfully, she said she understood, but added in a meaningful way, giving my first name a vaguely Russian pronunciation, "Ar-tur, these classes are important."

The horse from the Shamrock Stables was the colt named for *Pittsburgh Press* writer Pat Livingston, and this was the day that AJR won an even $100,000 on him by placing bets at different windows through Kass, Kiely, and myself. As an afterthought he told me to bet "a couple of bucks" for Madame D. "She let you miss school. Show your appreciation."

I put twenty dollars on the horse for Madame D. It paid seven to one, so her winnings came to a hundred and forty. After that if she knew I was going to the track she would say, "Does your fart-er have his horse running good? Here's five dollars. Get it down for me."

I hated makeup class as much as I hated dancing. The makeup instructor, observing my indifference, gave me some good advice: "Even if you land an acting job on Broadway, you'll have to do your own makeup. To hire somebody would cost twenty-five dollars a night. That's one hundred and seventy-five dollars a week – a lot of money for an actor who plays supporting roles, even on Broadway. Instead of Broadway, chances are, you'll be acting in summer theatre learning the craft. You'd make a nuisance of yourself if you asked the other actors to do your makeup." So I didn't drop out of makeup class. My attendance record, however, was less than one hundred percent.

Makeup class was educational to me in still another way. The girls in the actors' studio were far from beautiful. They wore blouses and slacks or jeans and didn't bother much with their hair – just pulled it straight back and tied a ribbon around it. I thought, "Hey, these are just average-looking kids." I guess I expected actresses to be glamorous. But all of that changed as soon as they started going to makeup class. By the middle of the term, those plain little girls with the mouse-colored hair had started to remind me of movie stars. Cosmetics, I saw, could make a difference.

'Tommy, How Was I?'

My best friend in New York was Tom Bodkin, an old Pittsburgh associate of AJR. Tom had been a fighter, a fight promoter, and a referee. On Broadway, he worked in theatrical production. A theatrical company putting on a play would hire Tom as its business manager. His duties were similar to those of Fran Fogarty with the Steelers. That is to say, Tom paid the bills, negotiating with the actors, directors, stage hands, electricians ... everybody, in fact, who had anything to do with the show.

Thomas V. Bodkin was even older than my dad, which put him, I thought, in his dotage. In 1958, remember, I was not completely dry behind the ears. Actually, Tom was a big, well set-up man who looked almost handsome in his Homburg hat, dark blue suit, white dress shirt, and polka-dot tie. His clothes were well-tailored and up to date. Unlike other old men, and I include AJR, he disposed of his suits when they went out of style. AJR would keep a suit in his closet for thirty years.

I saw that with actresses and women in general, Tom's manner was urbane. My mother he addressed as Kathleen, never Kass, and she liked him a lot. An excellent raconteur, he put me in mind of George Quinlan, one difference being that Tom had more ... I don't know, call it self-respect. He believed that a man ought to work.

Tom's background in the fight game was something I had no inkling of. It was not until recently that I was able to fit the pieces together. Had it not been for Tom, writes James R. Fair in his biography of Harry Greb, "Give Him to the Angels," the great champion's career might have ended while he was still just a preliminary boy. In Greb's first year as a pro, 1913, he was matched with the more experienced Joe Chip. Tom Bodkin was the referee. In the second round, Chip had Greb badly hurt. Greb later said he was out on his feet. There were referees who would have let the fight continue until Chip had put Greb on the floor for a count of ten, writes Fair, but Bodkin alertly stopped it, awarding Chip a technical knockout. As soon as Greb got the cobwebs out of his brain, relates Fair, he told Bodkin, "One more hard punch could have ruined me. I won't forget this. Thanks."

Old newspaper clips reveal that Bodkin actually did count Greb out, but Jimmy Fair was an author with a lively imagination.

After Greb whipped Tommy Gibbons in his first big New York fight in 1922, Bodkin organized a parade for him in Pittsburgh. He then talked the manager of a burlesque wheel, Maurice Cain, into a thousand-dollar-a-week contract for Greb. (Cain threw in one hundred and fifty for Bodkin, to which Greb added another hundred dollars out of his thousand.)

They opened at the old Gayety Theatre, Downtown. Greb, reading from a script Tom had prepared for him, began his monologue by saying, "It was right here in Pittsburgh that I got my start in the ring by defeating ... "

The next week the show jumped to Detroit. Greb's monologue was unchanged except that he said, "It was right here in Detroit ... " Three or four other cities remained on the tour, each one, as Greb told the audience, the place where he had his first fight. In Montreal, where the tour ended, he lost his bearings.

"It was right here in Toronto ... " he started out, and was interrupted by boos. From behind the curtain, Tom Bodkin hissed, "You're in Montreal, you dope, not Toronto." When the boos stopped, Greb laughed and said, "Oops, I made a mistake. It was right here in Montreal that I won my first fight."

"He carried it off so beautifully," Bodkin declared afterward, "that the audience was taken in. They thought the whole thing was a wonderful gag."

Red Mason and sometimes George Engel managed Harry Greb in his role as a fighter, but Bodkin, for a time, managed Frank Moran, who was also from Pittsburgh and fought twice for the heavyweight championship, losing to Jack Johnson in Paris and Jess Willard in New York. In 1920, Bodkin arranged a fight for Moran with Denver Jack Geyer at Duquesne Gardens.

Among the spectators was Battling Nelson; from his seat far back in the auditorium the old lightweight champion plied Moran with advice. He dispatched an usher to Frank's corner at the end of each round with a note, telling his friend what to do. Moran put up with it for as long as he could, and then he sent back a reply. He said that if one more message came he would stop fighting Geyer, get down from the ring, and fight Nelson. There was no further help, and no need for any, from his counselor.

Nelson by this time was "strange in the head," a euphemism for pugilistica dementia, the ailment old fighters commonly develop in their fifties, sixties, or seventies. Just one year before, on the eve of the July 4, 1919 heavyweight championship fight between Willard and Jack Dempsey on the shores of Maumee Bay outside Toledo, Nelson's odd behavior gave rise to an oft-repeated story in which Bodkin played an important role.

As I heard it from Tom himself – there are several other versions — Tex Rickard, the promoter, had leased him the rights to the lemonade concession. It was hot weather that week in Toledo, and he figured to make a big score. On the night before the fight, he stored the lemonade in six vats, which he covered with gauze. To keep watch over these vats, he employed Battling Nelson. But the night was so unbearably hot that, looking for a way to cool off, Nelson got out of his clothes and took a dip in one of the vats.

Early the next morning, when Tom arrived on the scene, Nelson was crawling out of the lemonade. Tom was furious. "Has anyone else seen you?" he demanded.

"No one, Tommy. No one. That's the truth."

Thus reassured, Tom went ahead and sold the lemonade. Parched fight-goers — thousands of them — unknowingly slaked their thirst on Battling Nelson's bath water.

Bodkin's partner was a man named Billy McCarney. In addition to the lemonade concession, they also had the rights to sell sandwiches, ice cream, cigarettes, opera glasses (for the fans a long way from ringside), mildly alcoholic but still legal near beer, and, most important of all, seat cushions, and they subleased all of these contracts. The man who bought the seat-cushion concession planned on cleaning up, because Tex Rickard had built an 80,000-seat arena with green lumber, and the heat brought out the sap in the unseasoned pine planks, which fairly oozed.

Alas, the word got around, and people were showing up at the ticket office with cushions from home.

Jack Dempsey won the title on that historic July Fourth when Willard, knocked down seven times in the first round, failed to answer the bell for the fourth. In New York forty years later, Bodkin introduced me to Dempsey. We had gone to Dempsey's Broadway restaurant for lunch. "Come over here, Artie," said Tom, catching sight of the owner, "and say hi to Jack Dempsey. Jack, say hello to Art Rooney Junior of Pittsburgh. You know his dad ... " Dempsey, in his high-pitched voice, greeted me with "Oh, yeah, sure I do. Art Rooney. Hi, kid. Welcome to New York."

Bodkin seemed to know everybody. At Toots Shor's restaurant, he introduced me to Stan Musial, who recognized Dad's name with more alacrity than Dempsey had shown. Shor himself I had known for some time. AJR first met him when Shor was a bouncer in Philadelphia. Shor took me around his "joint," as he called it, while Tom had a drink. We stopped for a few minutes at Gordon MacRae's table. MacRae was a singer and a movie actor. Another time, Shor introduced me to Jackie Gleason, the best-looking fat man I ever saw — impeccably dressed and as funny in person as on television reciting a script. My brother Dan was with me, and Gleason asked, "What do you guys do?" Shor broke in to say, "Why they're here in town with the Steelers." Gleason responded quickly. "Well, how did I know? I thought they were here with a monkey act." Somehow it seemed hilarious.

Usually, Tom and I went to dinner at Moore's Restaurant. It was there that I met Joe DiMaggio, a polite, dignified man, comfortable, surprisingly, to talk with.

Thanks to Tom, I saw the big Broadway shows. At times, I had to sit on a wooden folding chair in the aisle, but the tickets were always free. He would take me backstage, and there I met Helen Hayes. "Art Rooney," she repeated. "What a great Irish name! And you're a nice-looking guy, too," she added graciously. I met the great English actor, John Gielgud. Is it possible, I asked myself that Tom Bodkin, graduate of the fight racket, could know John Gielgud, whose tastes were more, shall I say, on the decorous side? My doubts quickly evaporated. "Ohhh, Tommy!" cried the thespian, "its s-o-o-o-o good to see you! After all these years!" He then turned to me and said, "Tommy managed my first show here in America." Looking on in his dark suit, Homburg in hand, Tom was beaming.

Our meeting with Gielgud gave Tom an inspiration. I should study acting at the Royal Academy of Dramatic Arts in London. He knew a chap from the Academy who happened to be in New York. Very cultured, with an upper-class accent. We got together at Moore's, where Tom, all duded up as usual, proceeded to get drunk.

The Englishman was talking about the Royal Academy; Tom kept interrupting — and straying off the subject. He had some observations to make about the Royal Family, and they were far from complimentary. His friend at first dismissed them with a laugh. Tom persisted, and the Englishman's laughter began to sound forced. Then it ceased altogether.

Tom ranted on — "Elizabeth Rex? She's a prune!" — and the Englishman ignored him. Before we had finished our coffee, he rose to leave. "If you are truly interested in the Royal Academy," he said to me, "I shall see that your application is taken care of." As it happened, I was not truly interested. The whole idea had been Tom's, and I promptly forgot all about it.

AJR came to town with Jim and Dago Sam, and Tom gave them tickets to the show he was managing, Eugene O'Neill's "A Touch of the Poet." I had seen it four times and was certain that our visitors would hate it. They sat about ten rows back in the center section. best seats in the house. I attended a play that night across the street, intending to meet them afterward. Unaccountably, they were not in the crowd leaving the theatre. I went looking for Tom, who took a circuitous way to explain their absence.

He said that when the curtain came down on "A Touch of the Poet," Eric Portman, the star – who also happened to be English – had summoned him to his dressing room. "Tommy," he asked, "how was I tonight?"

"Real good — as usual. Why do you ask?"

"Well," answered Portman, "something happened to me tonight that never happened before. There were three gentlemen ... in very good seats ... who ... well, they just got up and walked out. They left at the first curtain, before the end of the first act. Tom, nobody — I mean *nobody* — has ever walked out on me before."

Tom assured Eric Portman that his performance had been up to snuff. "Those people who walked out," he said, "are not gentlemen. They are ignoramuses. I know them. They're from Pittsburgh, my home town. I should never have given them tickets. They are philistines, Eric. No culture at all. None at all."

In today's market, Tom's fifth-floor apartment, overlooking Central Park, would be worth several million dollars as a condominium. The antique furniture reminded me of 940 North Lincoln Avenue. Late one afternoon, as we sat gazing down at the park, he talked to me of his wife.

"A wonderful girl, Artie," he said. He spoke of how grateful he was for their life together, even though they never had children. He spoke of how well they'd been doing ... "Lots of money then. We had a nest egg — one hundred and fifty thousand dollars. And then she came down with cancer. It was deeply rooted. I went all over, looking for help. Nothing could be done. I ended up taking her to Mercy Hospital in Pittsburgh. She suffered a long time, Artie. I buried her out in Calvary Cemetery." His wife's illness, I gathered, had wiped out their nest egg.

Darkness had fallen, and we left for Moore's Restaurant. In the taxicab, he told me of another disappointment, the death of a friend. The man was an actor – "an entertainer,'" Tom called him. "I was his manager, Artie, and we almost hit it big – real big. Hollywood! Funniest man I ever knew. And a good guy on top of being talented. Broadway? He had it in the palm of his hand. This was in the 1930s. We had a radio show and a movie contract in Hollywood. 'Hollywood's the future, Tommy,' he said. 'We'll knock 'em dead out there, wait and see.'

"'But you're knocking 'em dead in New York,' I told him.

"'Never mind. Hollywood's the future.'

"He was right, too. Anyway, it was all set. We'd be going West in a few weeks. Meanwhile, we had some New York engagements to finish up. It was fall, and my friend owned a boat. We'd go for cruises up and down the East River, up and down the Hudson, with our wives. He loved that boat. But the weather that fall was brisk. A chilly wind always seemed to be blowing. He had the sniffles. It developed into pneumonia. Poor guy, he died real quick. We never even got to the railroad station.

"And do you know who took his place in Hollywood?" Tom said. "Do you know who it was?" He paused for effect. "Jack Benny!" The taxi pulled up at Moore's, and there were no more reminiscences that night.

Footnote: On the night before my wedding, Tom came to my bachelor party. Patsy Scanlon and Owney McManus were there – old fighters – and the three of them had a great time. Sadly, though, Tom was down on his luck. Too old to work, he could not pay the rent on his Central Park apartment. He spoke to AJR, asking him for advice. The Friars Club ran a home for retired actors in New York, and AJR suggested that he apply for admission. "It's just the place for you," Dad said. The actors' home took him in, and a few months later Tom Bodkin died among friends.

Mr. Lunt

When AJR had a horse going he tried to avoid people he knew. Casual acquaintances would pester him for tips. "Say, Art, if you've got something good at Monmouth Park today ... " His standard reply was, "Gee, one of our horses is almost ready, but there might be a last-minute change. Time is so short that if I had to get back to you I don't see how I could do it."

Better to travel incognito. On trips to New York with a race coming up – "cloak-and-dagger" trips, I called them – he would stay at an out-of-the-way uptown hotel. Under wraps in this place, he asked me to meet him there once. "Go to Moore's Restaurant," he instructed me. "A Mister Lunt will be waiting for you with a package." The name Lunt was a pseudonym which AJR had chosen on the spur of the moment. We were standing in front of a theatre where the husband-and-wife acting team of Alfred Lunt and Lynne Fontanne were appearing, and he had happened to glance up at the marquee. The "Mr. Lunt" who would have a package for me was a runner for a big-time bookmaker named Erickson. AJR had won a whopper of a bet from Erickson, and Mr. Lunt was going to give me the money.

I went to Moore's Restaurant and I found him. I was very nervous. Everybody was looking at me, I thought. Mr. Lunt turned out to be an undersized Irishman. He took me into the kitchen and counted out twelve thousand dollars. I started to leave, but he called me back. "Tell your dad the district attorney is shutting us down. We won't be able to handle your dad's business any more," Lunt said.

When I delivered the message, AJR cut through the double talk. "They're saying they can get along without me. I've been beating them too often this year. They'd rather take bets from suckers who don't know what they're doing."

I gave him the money, and he counted it. "Eleven thousand eight-hundred dollars," he said. "Lunt shorted you."

I felt like a fool. I flared up. I heard myself shouting, "That crook!"

"No. Lunt's a good man. I've known him for years. It's just a mix-up," said AJR imperturbably.

Sure enough. A month later we saw Mr. Lunt in Moore's Restaurant. He came to our table and handed me two hundred dollars. "Hey, Artie, I've been looking all over for you. I miscounted," he said.

I have no idea whether AJR resumed doing business with Erickson and Lunt, but he was one of their oldest customers. He told me the story of a wager he made with Erickson in the late 1940s.

They had gone to the men's room at a track in New York and were standing side by side at the urinal. Undistracted by the music of the waterfall, AJR bet $100,000 against $500,000 on a horse in the next race. He repeated this tale many times. "Oh, and my horse lost in a photo," he would add, making it sound like an afterthought.

It was his custom to name the horses he owned – quite a few of them, anyway — after football players and sportswriters. As an extension of this, he proposed to name a horse for a friend somewhat closer to God — Our Lady of Mount Carmel. Not unexpectedly, the Jockey Club disapproved. So AJR merely shortened the name to Mount Carmel. In his own mind and in his own way, he was honoring the Blessed Mother.

The foal developed into a speed horse and he quietly got it ready to win a big race at Aqueduct, in New York City, a race on which he would make a big bet. Meanwhile, at the Mount Carmel Church in New York, a weekend retreat was being held. After a devotional service and a sermon Friday night, the retreatants had time to themselves. There were horse players among them, and they used their leisure hour to study the Racing Form. In the next day's entries at Aqueduct, they noticed, was this horse named Mount Carmel. A horse from a stable called the Shamrock. Owned by a man named Rooney — without the shadow of a doubt an Irish Catholic.

It was like an omen. The horse players' excited talk spread to the other retreatants — confirmed non-gamblers, for the most part, but believers in signs from above. Somebody, it seemed clear, was telling them something. Even the reverend fathers caught the fever. The next morning — Saturday — New York City's bookmakers found themselves taking an unusually large number of bets on a long shot named Mount Carmel. Even so, the horse went off at good odds. And at the Saturday evening prayer service the retreatants got word of the miracle they anticipated. Praise be to Our Lady! Mount Carmel had won!

AJR later told me that for the next few years on his visits to New York, men would come up to him and say with an air of sly satisfaction, "Mister Rooney, I won a small bet" — it was always "a small bet" — "on a horse of yours one time. A horse named Mount Carmel." Having learned of the circumstances from several different sources, he would nod understandingly.

Best Man

I interrupted my stay in New York to be the best man for Tim when he married June Marraccini at St. Andrew's Church in Pittsburgh.

June Marraccini was an attractive brunette from Clairton whose family owned and operated a string of supermarkets. Tim had met her – and fallen hard – while both were attending Duquesne University.

The nuptials, performed on a typically bleak, gray, wet, cold day in March, were private. Except for a few family members, including the bride's parents and the groom's parents, the church was empty. Tim and June had chosen St. Andrew's, on Sherman Avenue in Manchester, because Father Jim Campbell, AJR's closest friend, was the pastor. Out of loyalty to him, AJR, Kass, and Aunt Alice had been going to daily Mass at St. Andrew's instead of St. Peter's.

A few hours after the exchange of vows, Tim and June flew to New York and checked in at the Manhattan Hotel, where Tim had reserved the honeymoon suite. The Steelers always stopped there on trips to New York, and management gave Tim a special rate. When I returned to drama school, on the following day, Tim called with an invitation to dinner. "Pick out a top restaurant," he said, and I suggested a fancy place I had been to as the guest of an NFL bigwig who was entertaining Dad and Mom.

From the lobby of the Manhattan, I buzzed Tim on the house phone. "Come up to the room," he said. When I got there, he had not yet put on a shirt and tie. June, I could not help noticing, was still in her negligee. As I have said, June was a good-looking girl – so good looking, in fact, that I caught myself staring. I was young and single, remember. "I think I should wait for you downstairs," I said to the unembarrassed newlyweds.

Laughing, June said she would only be a minute. "Only a minute" turned out to be twenty, but there was no great rush. A good table awaited us at the restaurant.

The next day Tim insisted on seeing my apartment, a fourth-floor walkup on West 90th Street at Central Park West. The "Central Park West" in the address was real-estate hype. Between Central

Park and my apartment stretched a full city block. We climbed the stairs and went in, and Tim shook his head. Although he held his tongue, his body language, which was eloquent, declared, "What a dump." Under oath, I'd have had to admit that I was not the most fastidious housekeeper. June, concealing her true reaction, appeared to be lost in thought. She said to us, "Why don't you two go for a walk? I'll stay here and read a magazine and maybe watch some TV."

So Tim and I sauntered over to Stillman's Gym on Eighth Avenue, where the heavyweight Tommy "Hurricane" Jackson was training for a fight. Stillman's, I perceived, was like the gyms we were taken to as kids, only more so. This shrine of professional boxing was airless, moldy, unhygienic, and malodorous. I attempted to identify the various smells. Stale sweat predominated, but with liniment in the mix, and cigar smoke.

Fighters sparred in each of two rings. Others skipped rope. Still others rattled the speed bags. A big guy worked on the heavy bag, making it thud. The managers, stubby middle-aged men in shapeless brown suits, all wearing wide-brimmed fedoras, monitored the activity. They looked a lot like the denizens of AJR's former offices in the Fort Pitt Hotel. At one end of the gym, close to the entrance, a concession stand offered sandwiches and coffee. Customers who did not eat the crusts simply threw them on the floor.

Hurricane Jackson was taking the day off, so in less than a half-hour we made our way back to the apartment. At the top of the stairs, Tim mumbled something to the effect that there was little or no difference in ambiance between the place I called home and Stillman's Gym. While I groped for an answer, I unlocked the door, and there was June, running the vacuum cleaner. She had my bedroom slippers on her feet and was wearing my trench coat over her slip.

Turning off the sweeper and glancing up from her labors, she said, "Well, I've done my best with this old carpet, but it needs professional help."

June's best, it seemed to me, had been pretty darn good. The improvement in the looks of the carpet was unmistakable, and she had dusted all the furniture. More wonderful still, the kitchen now sparkled. June had cleaned the stove and had washed the dirty dishes I habitually left in the sink.

In my head, I composed what I now understand was a thumbnail scouting report on the newest member of our clan. "No question about it," I was thinking, "my brother Tim has picked himself a winner."

I didn't know it at the time, but making assessments of that nature in a completely different field – some just as accurate and others less so – was to be my life's work.

Semper Fi

After three semesters at Madame D.'s actor's studio, I joined a summer stock company and worked at theaters in Delmont, PA, and Belle Vernon while waiting for my call from the draft board.

In the late 1950s every young man in America faced military service. My stint at Carnegie Tech had earned me a deferment, but having passed the physical examination, I was due to report for basic training in just a few months. Dan, Tim, and John were husbands and fathers by now and therefore exempt; not so Pat and I, the only remaining bachelors in the clan.

Fran Fogarty had a contact in the Army Reserve, but was told there were not any openings. Two years of training and active service lay ahead for me. .Then Fran or Ed Kiely or AJR – I'm afraid I can't be more specific – got in touch with Joe O'Toole, who handled problems of this kind for the Pirates in addition to his regular duties as traveling secretary. O'Toole said he could get me in the Marine Corps Reserve. It would mean boot camp – three months at Parris Island and three months at Camp Geiger.

"Hold off," people warned me. "An opening may turn up in the Army Reserve. You'd be nuts to go into the Marine Corps. Parris Island is hell. You couldn't take it down there."

The more they talked that way, the more determined I became to give it a try. I'd see if I was still tough. With O'Toole's help, I joined up.

I joined up and found out I had never been tough. The Marines, though, were tough. Every single one of them thought he was John Wayne. In truth, the guys at Parris Island were what John Wayne only pretended to be – the real thing.

My education started when I got off the train with the rest of the recruits in Yamassee, South Carolina. The troop handlers got into our faces, screaming their heads off. They herded us onto a bus and told us to sit up straight and be quiet. On the 45-minute ride to Parris Island, nobody spoke above a whisper. All the confidence I had acquired from my upbringing, from my years at North Catholic and St. Vincent, from my time in New York, and from the knowledge that I was a Rooney went out the window.

Three tanned, trim, closely-shorn drill instructors wearing starched khaki uniforms and wide-brimmed Smokey Bear hats met our bus. They screamed, they yelled, they barked, and they bellowed. It was "Move, move, move – that means you, Pimple Face. Come on, there, Fatso – get the lard out of your ass. Move! Move! What's-a-rnatter, Jelly Belly? You retarded? Move! Move! Move! This yer first time away from Mommy? Hey, you – Scurnbag! Down on the ground and give me some pushups. *How many?* You askin' me how many? Listen, boy, don't EVER talk to your DI that way. You say 'SIR' before you address me. And I want it loud and clear."

The DIs did their best to intimidate us, and they succeeded. We were "turds"– civilian turds, scumbag turds, idiotic turds, pimple-faced turds, every kind of turd, but always turds. We found ourselves standing at attention in a building of wood and tin and being hectored by a sergeant who was not a DI. He was telling us how to fill out a form of some kind. "Understand me?" he yells. Murmurs of assent. "I CAN'T HEAR YOU!" So we shout back in unison, "We understand you!" The sergeant hollers, "SIR, we understand you!" "SIR, we understand you!" we repeat.

After that we were ordered to take off our clothes and given sheets of brown shipping paper to wrap them in. Naked except for a towel worn amidships, we moved down the hall to the shearing room. Barbers equipped with electric clippers shaved off our hair close to the skull. From there we proceeded to the quartermaster building to be issued duffel bags (called seabags), underwear, socks, "utilities'" (green work clothes), and three pairs of shoes – high-top boots, low-cut boots, and dress shoes.

So it went until the processing was over. It was late September and beastly hot. We took an IQ test. Stripped down, we took our physical exams. As I waited in line, a tough-looking old master sergeant confronted me. "Rooney?" "Yes, sir." He looked like Victor McLaglen – not quite as big but even tougher. "I'm a friend of your Dad's," he said. "I was in China with your Uncle Dan, the priest, before the war. He's a great man. He used to put boxing matches on between the Navy and Marine guys. Good luck to you." I never saw him again.

The orthopedic doctor looked for a long time at my left leg, which was half an inch shorter than my right leg. Still another doctor came to look at me. They conferred, shaking their heads. One of them finally asked if I had participated in sports. "High school and college football," I said. They smiled, and the first doctor said, "Good. Once you get into shape, you won't have any problem with this program."

They measured and weighed me. I was a quarter of an inch over six feet tall and I weighed exactly 214 pounds. To a DI, the doctor said, "Moderate obesity. He'll have a tough time with training."

I couldn't believe my ears. No way was I fat. Big and strong, yes. But strength with the bar bells, I soon discovered, was not what these people wanted. They wanted stamina. They wanted lean and hungry guys who could run all day and never for a minute fall behind.

That "moderate obesity" tag clung to me. "Front and center, Fat Ass – double time," a DI ordered, and I was stood at attention before the senior DI and several others. They were sitting in judgment of me.

"How'd you get to be such a fat ass? Drink a lot of beer?"

"No, sir. Sweets, sir."

From the DIs, mocking laughter, laced with obscenity. I was a lazy rich kid, I could see. They could "set me back" – place me in a motivational platoon or a physical-fitness platoon, which would mean an extra month on Parris Island. But I passed inspection. They would not set me back.

"You'll have to work harder and eat less than anyone else in the platoon," they warned me.

"Sir, thank you, sir," I said, and I really meant it.

We were marched to the squad bay, yelled at every step of the way. Every morning at 5:30 our "alarm clock" sounded. A DI came into the squad bay and rolled a large, empty garbage can down the middle of the floor. We had from seven to ten minutes to make up our beds – tightly – answer the call of nature, shave, and get dressed. "Move! Move! Move!" the DI would be yelling, and then he would march us off to the chow hall, where we stood at attention until another DI called out, "Ready! Seats!" Somehow, I had no appetite.

On the second day, the training began — close-order drill, trips to the obstacle course. There was never any letup in the yelling, never any letup in the stream of derogatory language. The aim of the DIs was to separate us from any vestige of polite civilian life. They were vulgar, mean, sadistic, their object being to take away all your self-worth and rebuild you in the image and likeness of a U.S. Marine.

At night as we lay in our bunks, we prayed together. Our prayer was mandatory and got immediate feedback – not from the Lord, but from the drill instructor who had forced us to sing out in unison, "God bless my Marine Corps home." He would then scream, "I can't hear you turds!" So we'd do it again – and again and again, until many minutes after the lights had gone out.

Another DI gave us the "gung-ho" speech one night. Looking back, I'd compare it in tone to the opening scene of the 1976 movie "Patton," in which the pistol-packing World War II general, as personified by George C. Scott, stands on a stage with an oversized American flag behind him and delivers some plain talk to the men he will lead into battle. The Marine drill instructor was even more blunt. He told us what our rights were – we didn't have any – and what would happen if we ever disputed an order – first, we would get our posteriors kicked from one end of the squad bay to the other; after that, we would spend an unpleasant six months in the brig.

His unvarnished way of linking cause to effect certainly focused our attention. So did an accidental glimpse of what life in the brig could be like. We saw some prisoners on a work detail; they were guarded by a corporal armed with a shotgun – a shotgun that could have brought down an elephant. Their heads were shaved bald; on the back of each man's utility jacket, a large white "P" advertised his status. All this made it evident to us that crime does not pay. Boot-camp training lasted three months, and nobody in our squad bay with one exception, which I'll get to very soon, ever talked back to a noncommissioned officer or complained about the hardships and humiliations inflicted on us day after day.

I had thought before the Marines tried to reshape me that nothing could be more punishing than football practice at North Catholic High School and St. Vincent College, and that nothing could be more psychologically stressful than the demands of my teachers at these strict Catholic educational institutions. Little did I know. Football practice and final-examination week were child's play compared to the Marines.

The "obesity" tag I wore like a scarlet letter meant that I had my own private taskmaster. "I'm going to work with you every minute," one of the drill instructors said, and he kept his promise. From five o'clock in the morning until eight-thirty at night, he was on my case. "Give me five more pushups," he would shout when all the others had finished. "Do it again!" he would yell if I couldn't get over the wall on the obstacle course. And then if I failed a second time, he would call for help from the recruits next in line: "Boost that piece of crap over that wall." At the chin-up bar, he would warn me, "No jump starts." When I had chinned myself to the point of exhaustion, he would not let me quit. "Dangle there for a while!" he would bellow.

I had my own special diet: no bread, no dessert, no second helpings. To ensure that I wasn't cheating, the DI followed me through the chow line and monitored my tray. At the mess-hall door after every meal, he would frisk me for hidden cookies, hidden pieces of cake. I went from 215 pounds to 155, disconcerting the mess officer. "Are you getting enough to eat, private?" he asked. Glancing at my tray, he said, "Aren't you hungry? The DIs work you very hard. You need food. You need calories." Something seemed out of whack here. Marines didn't talk this way. They just didn't. Yes, I told him, I was getting enough to eat, and, no, I was not hungry. And that was the truth. I wasn't hungry, but I seemed to be constantly tired. Even so, I could now do eleven chin-ups — ten more than I had managed the first day. We had a chin-up bar in the squad bay, and at night, after lights-out, I used it on my own while the other recruits slept. I envisioned myself as a lean, mean fighting Marine.

But then came a fall from grace. My friends in platoon 172 took it upon themselves to save me from anorexia. At great personal risk, they smuggled contraband cookies and brownies out of the mess hall. They hid them in their pants pockets, their blouses, their utility hats. Proud of my new silhouette, I refused these offerings for a while; then my will power crumbled, and I gave in as haplessly as Adam taking a bite of the apple. In no time at all I weighed 170. It was amazing how rapidly I put on the pounds.

It was even more amazing that my stamina held up. Near the end of our stay at Parris Island, we were taken on a run with rifles at order arms. Sometimes at double time, sometimes at triple time, we ran the length and the width of the vast Parris Island drill field; we skirted its four sides; we ran up and down the company streets, every one of them. All this while the DI berated us, saving his cruelest sarcasm for the drop-outs.

I came perilously close to being one of them. Weakening, I slowed to a walk with the DI nearby, and he directed a stream of profanity toward me. I lost my temper. In a low voice, but loud enough to be heard, I cussed back. The adrenaline renewed my energy: I got back in line and continued to run. And the DI, to my astonishment, started laughing. His reaction seemed all wrong, but then it hit me. I felt accepted ... in some odd way, I now belonged to a brotherhood. There I was, running and cussing, letting a DI see my frustration, but not to the point of incurring his wrath. Just like the real Marines!

I had another small epiphany in judo class. On the teaching platform one day, the instructor came up behind me and encircled my neck in a choke hold. Instinctively, I grabbed his left arm with my right hand, bent over double, and threw him four or five feet into the air, head over heels. He landed on his back with a thud.

This was big trouble for me, I knew. I had made the instructor look bad. He jumped up, took me down with a swift move called a Yokoshiro leg toss, sat on my chest, and seized me once again by the neck. Until he abruptly eased his grip, I thought I was going to be strangled.

The next time we assembled for a lesson, he asked in a loud voice, "Where is the recruit who flipped me the other day?"

"That was Rooney," someone said. All heads were now turned in my direction.

"Oh, there you are. Well, congratulations, Rooney. Keep up the good work. If you last long enough, you may learn something."

Unexpected praise from an unlikely source. It was as near as I came to winning the Medal of Honor. Drill instructors, when you got right down to it, were not unlike human beings.

Some of them, anyway. When our platoon lost a tug of war to a rival platoon, the trip from the fitness field back to the squad bay was a silent death march. Our DI refused to call cadence, going on ahead. "Stagger back by yourselves, you quitters!" he sneered. As we passed the memorial statue of the flag raising on Iwo Jima, he stopped and called out, "See those guys raising that flag? Now, *they* were *Marines*! If they'd been quitters like you, guess what. Your mothers and sisters would be sleeping with Japs." When we arrived at the squad bay, he grabbed the scarlet platoon flag we carried with us and threw it into a urinal. Our platoon guide, putting loyalty to his mates ahead of hygiene, carefully fished it out.

For many weeks, the DIs had been talking about the real test that awaited us – the Slide for Life. On the appointed morning, we climbed into buses – "cattle cars," we called them – and traveled two and a half miles over the South Carolina countryside. The buses stopped in a wooded area, where a framework wooden tower three stories high rose up at the edge of a pond. From the top of this structure a bull rope extended downward at a 45-degree angle to a stake five feet high on the opposite side. I'd say the pond was about forty yards wide. Wearing light gear – helmet liners, utility belts and boots – we were to climb up the tower on ladders, take hold of the rope, curl our feet over it, and ease ourselves all the way down, hand over hand.

The instructors were patient and relaxed, but the possibility of falling was in everybody's mind. Just ahead of me at the top, an unusually large Chinese kid started down. Halfway across the pond he lost his grip. Arms waving and legs thrashing, he plummeted into the drink, going under with a tsunami-like splash. The rest of us let out a yell, half in derision and half in alarm, but he bobbed right up and dog-paddled his way to dry land.

Now it was my turn. I made the descent smoothly and quickly.

Thirty minutes later, as we prepared to get back on the cattle cars, I heard someone say to someone else, "Rooney fell. He couldn't do it." You can be sure that I lost no time in setting that knucklehead straight.

When our last march was completed, when the last round had been fired at the rifle range, when we had gone through our last inspection, I felt a sense of exhilaration. I hadn't washed out. A few days before graduation, I was called to the drill instructors' quarters off a corridor in the middle of the squad bay. A tall, trim, good-looking sergeant whose last name was Harms said to me. "Private Rooney, you and I are going over to the medical center, but first let me see you do some pull-ups."

He led me to the chinning bar, and I pumped out twelve.

"Not bad at all, Rooney," he said. "That's only average, but, for you, pretty good."

I cherished every compliment, even left-handed ones.

"Okay,' Harms continued, "I want you to put on your cleanest utilities – starched ones. Make sure your boots are shined. And gargle. You can't talk to the doc with stinky breath. I'll meet you when you're ready."

We marched all the way to the medical center in step, Private Rooney detoxified and wearing his clean utilities. Neither of us spoke.

My examination by the doctor was entirely oral. He started with a question for Harms. Had I kept up with the other recruits?

"Yes, Doctor. Private Rooney is one of our hardest workers," Harms told him.

The doctor then asked me how many pull-ups I could do. Before I could answer, Harms said, "Eleven, sir. And Private Rooney started with only one."

He was giving me a short count – I had just done twelve – but how could I not like the praise, coming, as it did, from a drill instructor?

That was it. There were no more questions, and we marched back to the squad bay, Harms and I, the way we had marched over – wordlessly and in step.

Years later I would hear that Sergeant Harms had been badly shot up in Vietnam.

Making it through Parris Island was the hardest thing I ever had done, and I felt emotionally and physically drained when I boarded one of the buses that would take the boot-camp graduates to Camp Lejeune, a stopover on the trip to our ultimate destination, Camp Geiger. Camp Lejeune is a long drive from Parris Island. It's in North Carolina. But the distance is short between Camp Lejeune and Camp Geiger, and our buses were almost luxurious – nothing at all like the Parris Island cattle cars. The DIs were still yelling at us, but with a difference. They called us Marines now, where before we'd been scumbags, and their screaming made no impression on me. I found a seat and flopped into it. I was worn out, yes, but I was saying good-bye to Parris Island and therefore at peace with the world.

A rather quiet Marine I knew as an acquaintance asked if he could sit next to me. I said, "Sure," and for an hour we rode with just the barest minimum of talk. The others in the bus were whooping and hollering, glad to have seen the last of Parris Island. I was too contented to be annoyed. Then the guy next to me spoke up.

"Hey, Rooney," he said, 'do you mind if I tell you something?"

"Go ahead."

"Well, I think you're the toughest guy I've ever met. And lots of others feel the same way. I couldn't believe what those DIs put you through, but you took it. You took it and you didn't break."

All I could manage to say was, "Thanks."

I knew I had never been tough. I'd been able to stick it out. But I wasn't tough.

Maybe, instead, I was the next thing to it – hardened. In consequence, the training at Camp Geiger, though arduous, was not the test of manhood for me that Parris Island had been. I thought of it as a harsh post-graduate course. In any case, my three months at Geiger passed swiftly. And at the end of that time, every notion of an acting career forever dismissed from my mind, I was ready, and more than ready, to come home and start learning the football business.

Chapter 28

High-Maintenance Coach

Buddy Parker was a truly brilliant coach whose Detroit teams were NFL champions in his second and third seasons, 1952 and 1953. In 1954 the Lions again won a conference title but lost to the Cleveland Browns in the playoff. Injuries and retirements then forced Parker to rebuild, which he proceeded to do without delay. After a 3-9 season, Detroit was once again a contender, finishing second to the Bears in the 1956 conference race.

Management rewarded Parker with a two-year contract extension, but two days before the first pre-season game in 1957 he flamboyantly resigned. At a "Meet the Lions" banquet, he made a speech that was startling in its content and brevity. "I'm quitting," he said, going straight to the point. "I can no longer control this team, and when I can't control a team I can't coach it."

What had brought this on was the sight of his star players drinking with the owners, a group of wealthy Detroit "socialites," at a cocktail party before the banquet. For obscure reasons, Parker disapproved of such fraternizing between bosses and hired hands. It was certainly not the drinking that bothered him. Emulating the team leader, charismatic quarterback Bobby Layne, the Lions did plenty of that.

Parker himself was a problem drinker. Alone or in the company of his assistant coaches, he drank under stress and he drank when the Lions lost. He drank as much, when the mood was on him, as Layne did, but he differed from Layne in his ability to handle the stuff. Once after an embarrassing defeat he put the entire team on waivers, infuriating Commissioner Bert Bell. When the Lions lost on the road Parker would be drunk by the time they arrived home, and often the results were unpredictable, as when he ordered assistant coach Buster Ramsey to get on the public-address system at Willow Run Airport in Detroit and announce the outright release of the players in Parker's doghouse at the moment.

As soon as he heard that Parker was now available, AJR made him an offer. Because of their mutual interest in horse racing, they were friends. Parker was a bit of a head case, yes. But he could coach. In AJR's opinion, he could do as much for the Steelers as Jock Sutherland had done. He could give the team the sense that it was going somewhere. He could bring hope and excitement to the fans.

Apart from all that, he was not a bad guy when he was sober. He was smart, with a sense of humor. He was close to his wife and son. His assistant coaches liked him, or seemed to. Parker was from Texas, but had gone to Centenary College in Louisiana. Few Centenary players ever make the NFL. Parker did, as an undersized fullback (about 5 feet 11 and 170 pounds) for the Lions and the Cardinals from 1935 to 1943.

In their contract negotiations, Parker made one thing clear to AJR: he would be a high-maintenance coach. When it came to bringing in players, he would need a free rein. He would need a taxi squad, which the Steelers had done without up to then. "The way I operate costs money," he warned. AJR said the money would be there.

In Detroit, Parker's salary was $30,000 a year. The deal he worked out with AJR, in all of its ramifications, netted him more than twice that amount. Parker brought two of his assistants to Pittsburgh, a payroll increase partly offset by a reduction in Walt Kiesling's pay. Off and on, either as head coach or assistant, Kiesling had been with the Steelers since 1939. Accepting a demotion, he would remain on the staff as an assistant until 1961. According to Pat Livingston, who covered the Steelers for the *Pittsburgh Press*, the hiring of Parker was actually Kiesling's idea "He cared more about Art Rooney's welfare than his own," Livingston said.

A man who believed in wasting no time, Parker immediately traded two first-round draft choices and linebacker Mike Matuszak to San Francisco for quarterback Earl Morrall and rookie lineman Mike Sandusky. From the Redskins he acquired scatback Billy Wells. In 1957, Morrall passed for 1,900 yards and eleven touchdowns and Wells led the Steelers in rushing, punt returns, and kickoff returns. Goose McClairen, the long-armed end, caught forty-six passes, third highest total in the

NFL. Jack Butler had eleven interceptions, which tied the club record. But the won-and-lost record that year — 6-6 — was no great improvement over 1956.

Giving Parker the benefit of the doubt, AJR was optimistic. His confidence in his coach was unshaken. So far, their relationship had been a good one. It was not to continue that way.

Garden Party

W hen Parker came over to Pittsburgh, one of the assistant coaches he inherited was Lowell Perry, who had been a member of the team, and a rookie at that, just the season before.

He was a wide receiver and defensive back from the University of Michigan, earmarked for success not only in football but in any occupation he chose to follow. I became a believer in Lowell Perry the first time I saw him return a punt. It was in a pre-season game in Toledo. Returning a punt is always a better measure of talent than returning a kickoff. With a burst of speed, Perry cut, juked, and hurdled tacklers all the way to the goal line. And what I saw was no fluke. That night and in subsequent games, Perry made other fine plays.

But what set him apart was more than just football ability. He had the indefinable quality known as class. He came from a black family of mostly professional people, and his behavior did credit to his upbringing. More than anything else, Lowell Perry was a gentleman. He was also something special as a football player, or might have been. Running with the ball in the sixth game of the season, against the New York Giants, he took a simultaneous hit from Emlen Tunnell and Rosey Grier. It shattered his hip.

The attending physician said he had only seen such injuries during naval engagements in World War II. Perry lay in the hospital for quite some time. His football career was over, but AJR enrolled him, at the Steelers' expense, in Duquesne Law School. He then broke the news to Walt Kiesling that Perry would henceforth be an assistant coach. Kiesling did not object; he went out of his way, in fact, to keep Perry involved as the season wound down and in training camp the next summer. It is accurate to say, I believe, that Perry was the first black coach in the NFL since Fritz Pollard's day, the early 1920s.

Buddy Parker wasn't known for his sympathetic treatment of black athletes. He could be abusive toward all of his players, but abusive toward blacks in a way that was shockingly racial. Taking over from Kies, he consulted with AJR about Perry. It would not be easy, Parker said, for Perry to coach while attending law school. He suggested making him a scout, which satisfied AJR — and Perry, too, as far as I was able to tell.

Perry's stay in Pittsburgh was a short one. He left to finish work on his law degree at Michigan. He did become a lawyer and also the manager of a Chrysler plant in Detroit. He kept in touch all this time with AJR, and when President Ford appointed him chairman of the Equal Employment Opportunity Commission in 1975 he invited his old boss to the induction ceremony in the Rose Garden.

The weather that May was perfect for a ceremony outdoors. Four months earlier, the Steelers had won their first Super Bowl championship, and everywhere AJR went he was recognized. ("It must be the cap or the cigar," he used to say.) So he was not especially surprised when the guard at the south gate of the White House greeted him warmly. The guard, it turned out, had grown up on the North Side.

Ushered into the Rose Garden, AJR and Ed Kiely stood in the back row of a semicircle while Perry took the oath. President Ford was at Perry's side, and he spoke a few words, recalling that, twenty-five years apart, both had played football at Michigan. Then the President stepped down to where the spectators were gathered. It was time to shake hands. Kiely, from the back row, heard an aide whisper to Ford, "There's Art Rooney!" As though he were blocking for the ball carrier in a short-yardage situation on third down (he played center at Michigan), Ford cut a path through the crowd.

"Art!" he said, "I've been wanting to meet you," and for the next five minutes (or maybe ten; AJR felt embarrassed about taking up so much of the President's time) they talked about football.

AJR had met every president since Franklin D. Roosevelt up to then. He liked Ford, he later said, the best of them all. Ford impressed him as "a regular guy, a guy you would meet walking down the street." He felt that Ford "really wanted to talk, that he was really interested."

Before they parted company, AJR mentioned Perry.

"You made an excellent choice," he said to the President.

And Ford answered, "I know I did."

I don't know how you evaluate EEOC chairmen, but I would bet that Lowell Perry was good at his job. At least I never heard anything to the contrary. He lived for only about twenty more years, dying of cancer in his sixties.

Bobby Layne

B uddy Parker once told me that above all else a football team needed a great quarterback and some topnotch pass catchers — along with that other indispensable component, "defense, defense, defense." Earl Morrall was not Buddy's notion of a great quarterback, so two weeks into the 1958 season Parker made a deal with his old team, the Detroit Lions. He traded Morrall and two draft choices for Bobby Layne.

Parker felt comfortable with the quarterback who had helped him win championships. Layne was now 31, with some wear and tear showing, but he could lift a team up by what appeared to be mostly will power. In 1958 the Steelers had lost their first two games. So had Detroit. The Lions without Layne continued to lose; the Steelers finished 7-4-1, their best showing in eleven years, and Layne was the difference. For his primary receiver, he had a talented rookie end from Georgia, Jimmy Orr, and in another deal with the Lions, Parker had added the veteran running back Tom (the Bomb) Tracy.

Layne was still a pinpoint passer who ran the two-minute offense at the end of a half with more skill and confidence than anyone else in football except perhaps Johnny Unitas over in Baltimore. Listed at 6 feet 2 and 190 pounds, he may not have been that big. He was certainly not that tall by an inch or more. But when you talked about Layne, you forgot inches and pounds. You talked about his competitive fire.

I remember a game between the Steelers and Lions when Layne was still with Detroit. He took a cheap shot from Ed Meadows, one of our defensive ends — and a guy his own teammates disliked — that left him motionless on the ground for several minutes. After first aid from the trainers, he wobbled off the field, but not before addressing a few words to Meadows. My brother John was on the sideline, close enough to hear what Layne said. He said, "You son of a bitch, somehow I'm going to get you for this."

Whether or not he ever did get Meadows I have no idea. I can only tell you I am positive he never stopped trying. Layne himself would have been no match for some of the real bully-boys in the NFL, but wherever he played he invariably had "protectors" around him — combat-ready infighters like Ernie Stautner, the hard-as-nails Steeler defensive tackle, who claimed that if the Marquis of Queensberry rules allowed him to wear boxing gloves on his elbows he would be the heavyweight champion of the world. Observe that in his warning to Meadows, Layne used the modifier "somehow." Revenge obtained by proxy is sometimes as sweet as the regular kind.

On or off the football field, Layne was a fearless tough talker. The year my brothers and I joined the Fraternal Order of Eagles, at the insistence of our dad, he also prevailed on Layne and Stautner and two or three other players to affiliate. The initiation rites were held in the old Arbuckle mansion off East Ohio Street on the North Side. No sooner had we assembled than a rumor began to circulate that the ceremony featured a paddling, with the inductees on the receiving end. I knew all the officers — they were all from the North Side — and I said to myself "Some of these old boozers would like nothing better than to brag that they smacked the Rooney kids and Bobby Layne and Ernie Stautner on the ass with a board." Thoughts of that nature must have also occurred to Layne. When the lights went out and we were ordered to move forward in single file, he was right behind me. Loud enough to be heard all over the room, he announced what he would do if "any of these bastards" laid a hand on him. We became Eagles that night without a single swipe from a paddle.

Layne was such a dedicated football player – during work hours, I mean; on his own time, he was dedicated to other activities — that he actually liked to practice, which is rare. At South Park one day in 1962 our first-round draft choice, a fullback named Bob Ferguson, arrived for practice a few minutes late.. I was serving my apprenticeship as a scout that year and I was standing near Layne on the field. As soon as Ferguson approached us, he got an earful in Layne's Texas drawl — high-pitched and rasping, a "whiskey voice" — about rookies who let their teammates down and were taking money from the owners under false pretenses.

Not only was Layne on time for practice every day, he made it a point to be at least ten minutes early, often bringing along a receiver or two and maybe a backfield guy to catch his warm-up tosses. And he would stay for fifteen minutes after practice was over, again with someone to run routes and catch the ball.

One sacrifice he would not make was to deny himself the pleasures of night life. He liked to keep late hours; he liked to party; he liked to drink. And when he did these things he wanted lots of company. Layne had an inner circle on the team, made up principally of the very best players. To be one of the favored few was a sought-after distinction. "Let's go bowling," he would say, but when the last pin had fallen, the carousing began. Jack Butler belonged to the gang but dropped out after one or two evenings that did not end until dawn. Butler was not a boozer, and for another thing he came to believe that the establishment of a clique, its members anointed by the quarterback, fostered dissension.

Layne had an off year in 1959, throwing twenty-one interceptions. In 1960 the Steelers were out of contention by October, and Layne missed part of the 1961 season with a shoulder injury. Then in 1962 he got it back together. The Steelers had their best season up to then, winning nine games and finishing second to the Giants in the Eastern Conference. Layne, though, went down with another injury and sat out the last three weeks. He never played again. Before the 1963 season he announced his retirement. He held the NFL career record for touchdown passes (196) and passing yardage (26,768) and would soon be elected to the Hall of Fame.

Len Dawson, drafted out of Purdue, was a backup quarterback during Layne's first two seasons, his presence barely acknowledged by Parker. He's in the Hall Of Fame now with Layne, but not for anything he accomplished as a Steeler. Traded by Parker and cut by the Browns, he flourished in the AFL and later the NFL. However, let's not get into that. In the short time he spent with the Steelers, something about him caught the attention of Layne, and Dawson became one of his Night Riders.

AJR was a hands-off owner, but there were times when he put aside his reluctance to interfere. Mom, answering the doorbell at 940 North Lincoln Avenue one morning, beheld an athletic-looking guy in a Steeler jacket. "He seemed so young," she said later, "young enough to be out in the back yard playing touch football with the twins." The kid was acting a little sheepish, she thought. "Mister Rooney asked if I'd drive him to practice," he said. It was Lenny Dawson, and AJR had a purpose in asking for transportation. On the long trip to South Park he delivered a lecture to Dawson on the evils of drink and on the importance of choosing the right companions. "You have a future," AJR told him. "Don't jeopardize it by getting into trouble."

Again I don't know how the story played out. What it illustrates best is AJR's ambivalent attitude toward Layne. He saw the good in Layne and admired him as a football player and competitor without condoning his lifestyle. He kept Layne on as an assistant coach after his retirement. Unaccustomed to being a second banana — actually, he wasn't even that — Bobby went back to Texas in no more than a year or two.

Layne put so much of himself into football that there wasn't a great deal left for anything else except drinking and mischief. He died before his time, of acute alcoholism.

Quarterbacks

At a football luncheon in New Orleans one year, AJR, who did not like to speak in public and always kept it short when he did speak, began with the following preamble:

"Number one, if you're going to ask me any questions I'm going to disappoint you, because I don't know that I'm able to answer your questions. So, better that you don't ask any. But if you insist on asking questions anyway, ask me about quarterbacks. I can tell you all about quarterbacks because in Pittsburgh we're experts on quarterbacks. We had Sid Luckman, we had Johnny Unitas, we had Earl Morrall, we had Len Dawson, we had Jack Kemp, and we had Bill Nelsen. Now, those are all quarterbacks you know about, and we traded them all. They were all with our ball club and we got rid of them. "

Morrall and Dawson, as I have said, were traded on Buddy Parker's watch. Morrall had some success in Baltimore. In 1968 he led the NFL in passing, was the league's Most Valuable Player, and took the Colts to the Super Bowl, where they lost to Joe Namath and the New York Jets. Four years later, in his football dotage at 38, he was sitting on the bench in Miami when a broken leg sidelined Bob Griese, the first-string quarterback. The Dolphins up to then had won all their games, with three left. Morrall kept them undefeated and won the playoff game for the division title. Then with Griese again at the controls, they knocked off the Steelers in the AFC championship game and the Redskins in the Super Bowl, becoming the first team in the history of the NFL to go undefeated in 17 games.

Lenny Dawson went from Pittsburgh to Cleveland and from Cleveland to the AFL. His old coach at Purdue, Hank Stram, picked him up for the Dallas Texans. In 1962 the Texans were league champions and Dawson was player of the year. They became the Kansas City Chiefs the following season, and, with Dawson still at quarterback, played in two of the first four Super Bowls, losing to Vince Lombardi's Green Bay Packers in 1967 and beating the Minnesota Vikings in 1970.

Another good quarterback whose existence Parker ignored was Jack Kemp. The Steelers drafted Kemp out of Occidental College in 1957. By 1960 he was in the newly created AFL, passing the Los Angeles Chargers, later the San Diego Chargers, to a divisional championship. In 1962, while Kemp was out of action with a broken hand, Coach Sid Gillman put him on waivers. Claimed by Buffalo for one hundred dollars, he was half of a Siamese Twin quarterback combination, sharing the position in the Bills' first two AFL championship seasons with Daryl Lamonica. Kemp is today better known as the long-time Republican congressman from upstate New York who ran unsuccessfully for vice president when Bob Dole headed the GOP ticket in 1996.

Johnny Unitas ... well, there is no point in beating a dead horse. Sid Luckman was the first great T-formation quarterback. He'd been a tailback in the single wing at Columbia. In 1938, the Steelers surrendered their draft rights to Luckman for Eggs Manske, an end with the Chicago Bears. Luckman was all-pro six times and quarterbacked the Bears to four championships. He of course is in the Hall of Fame. Eggs Manske's only distinction was his memorable nickname. After one season, AJR returned him to the Bears.

Parker had Bill Nelsen, too, finding no use for him, but it was Bill Austin, the coach from 1966 to 1968, who traded Nelsen to Cleveland. A believer in plain talk, Nelsen was on the outs with his backfield coach, Don Heinrich. The Steelers got Dick Shiner in the deal. He was a part-time starting quarterback on Austin's worst team and Chuck Noll's worst team. Nelsen, although not exactly another Unitas, prospered for a while with the Browns. They were divisional champions in 1968 and 1969, when he still had some cartilage in his knees.

To give Buddy Parker his due, he recognized the ability of the quarterbacks he unloaded, but correctly judged that they were not yet ready to pull their own weight in the NFL. Parker was a coach who wanted immediate results. He insisted on working with experienced players, and to get them he traded away prospects, he traded away slow learners, he traded away draft choices. For short-term gain, he was mortgaging the Steelers' future, as AJR eventually came to realize.

Chapter 29

Change of Scene

It was Buddy Parker who convinced AJR that the Steelers could not remain in Forbes Field. To begin with, there were not enough seats in Forbes Field; to make matters worse, the overhanging upper deck and the massive iron girders supporting it greatly reduced the number of good seats. Forbes Field was a baseball park, admired for its intimacy and charm, and for the view of Schenley Park beyond the ivy-covered outfield walls, but poorly configured for football.

During the Depression years of the 1930s it was not unusual for AJR to move a home game from Forbes Field to an out-of-town location — Latrobe, say, or Youngstown, or as far away, even, as New Orleans. Pittsburgh in the 1930s was more of a baseball town and a fight town than a football town. In the minds of the public, Pittsburgh's only football team was Pitt, never mind that Pitt sometimes lost to Carnegie Tech and Duquesne. Pitt had a stadium; Tech and Duquesne, like the Steelers, rented Forbes Field. Tech and Duquesne were Pitt's poor relations; the Steelers were more like the hoboes who knocked at back doors, begging for handouts.

Barney Dreyfuss, an immigrant German Jew, owned the Pittsburgh National League baseball team, the Plrates. In 1909, with his own money, he built Forbes Field (named for the British general whose expeditionary force chased the French out of Western Pennsylvania). Forbes Field, expansively described as "a symbol of civic pride and a monument to the national pastime," was nothing less than that, but for football games it contained only 12,000 seats with unobstructed sightlines, and on special occasions — an appearance by the Chicago Bears and Bronko Nagurski, or by the Washington Redskins and Sammy Baugh — 12,000 were not enough. It was then that Joe Carr, the Steelers' ticket manager, practiced his wiles.

"Right on the fifty-yard line," he would tell a customer, taking his cash. Sure enough, the seats might be at or near midfield; what Carr was certain not to have mentioned, though, was their proximity to a huge iron pillar obliterating most of the view. A misanthropic North Sider who radiated gloom, Carr had been on the payroll for as long as the Steelers had one. There were people he liked — just a few — and people he did not like. He saved the best seats for the people he liked and took vindictive satisfaction in putting those he did not like — almost everybody else— where they'd need a periscope for a glimpse of the action. A game with the Chicago Cardinals brought Marshall Goldberg's father from Elkton, West Virginia, to see his son perform in the Cardinals' defensive backfield. He went home with a stiff neck. Joe Carr had seen to it that his seat would be directly behind a pillar.

Carr's roots on the North Side gave him license to do as he pleased. If AJR was aware of how his ticket manager dealt with the public, he did not interfere. Whatever he knew or did not know, the question became moot with the hiring of Jock Sutherland in 1946. The new coach's mystique sold out the park for every game. When the good seats were gone, his worshippers clamored for bad ones. They happily paid their money for standing room. But by 1948 Sutherland was dead, interest in the Steelers back to normal, and the Forbes Field issue on the table once again

There were problems in addition to the sightlines. Parking was one. In the years before the Second World War, people came to the park by trolley car. But now they drove their automobiles — nobody seemed to be without one — and overcrowded Oakland, filling up with cultural, educational, and "health-care" institutions, couldn't cope. Such was the shortage of parking lots that enterprising residents sold space on their lawns, in their back yards, in their driveways. Two or three householders tore down their front porches to accommodate more cars.

Fran Fogarty, our business manager, complained of another aggravation. When Carnegie Tech played at Forbes Field on Saturday afternoon and the Steelers had a game on Saturday night, he spent the time in between searching the toilet stalls in the rest rooms and flushing out would-be gate-crashers. The only non-paying spectators Fogarty tolerated, aside from the players' wives and their girlfriends, were the hundreds of Catholic priests on the deadhead list.

Carnegie Tech games and high school games denuded the field of grass. When it rained there was deep mud. When the weather turned cold and the mud froze, razor-like ridges cropped up. I have told you how Johnny Grigas, the league's leading ground gainer, took one look at those ridges before the final game of the 1944 season and caught the next train home to New England — and how somebody else won the rushing title.

AJR would say, "Aw ... it's the same all over the league." He would say, "Other teams have to play here, too. At least we have the advantage of knowing where the bad spots are." He would say, "Don't lose any sleep over something you can't control." An attitude of hopelessness pervaded the front office. Naysayers like Walt Kiesling, Ed Kiely, and Joe Carr encouraged AJR to drag his feet. Until Buddy Parker tried it, no one could make him see that the team's financial future depended on finding a more customer-friendly playing venue. Television, in the late 1950s, was creating new fans for the pro game, but had not yet begun to generate big money. Gate receipts were still the critical factor.

Inconveniently, the one acceptable alternative to Forbes Field was Pitt Stadium. The political tug of war that would one day result in a new publicly-financed stadium for both the Steelers and the Pirates had only just begun. There were chances to move the franchise out of town. Because of AJR's loyalty to Pittsburgh, however, the only option was Pitt. And at Pitt a major obstacle presented itself.

Admiral Tom Hamilton, U.S. Navy retired, was Pitt's athletic director, and Hamilton saw the NFL as both disreputable and threatening. The followers of pro teams were in his opinion rabble; admitting them to the sacred grounds of Pitt Stadium was unthinkable. Furthermore, it would be an unwise business decision. Why help the Steelers compete for the football dollar and for media attention? The NFL itself, Hamilton thought, was like the camel peering into the tent. Once its nose was inside, the neck, legs, and hump would follow, leaving no room for the tent's original occupants — which of course would be exactly what happened. Tom Hamilton was a visionary. Over the next twenty years, in all the cities where professional football had taken hold, the college teams lost their support base, the general public. Already, New York was more devoted to the Giants than to Army or Columbia; Philadelphia preferred the Eagles to Penn; Chicago belonged to the Bears, not to Northwestern.

Admiral Tom was a big, bluff, strong-minded authority figure who commanded the aircraft carrier Enterprise in World War II. Very much accustomed to getting his own way, he reckoned without the political savvy of AJR. Pitt was an institution partly supported by state funds and therefore dependent on the good will of the State Legislature. Every Democrat in Harrisburg took his orders from Pittsburgh Mayor David Lawrence, soon to be governor, and AJR was by now the boss's best friend. One word from Lawrence set in motion a predictable chain of events, which ended with Edward H. Litchfield, Pitt's chancellor, converted to a-live-and-let-live point of view.

It was then that AJR, having cleared the way for the move from Forbes Field, started second-guessing himself. In 1958, Buddy Parker's second season, the Steelers played all of their home games at Pitt Stadium. The following year, and for the three succeeding years, they were back in Forbes Field. In 1963 there were games in both venues, but from 1964 until 1970, when Three Rivers Stadium opened, home sweet home was Pitt Stadium exclusively.

Pitt Stadium had 58,000 seats, all with good sightlines, and AJR needed the extra income this generated. He needed it because of Parker's contract. Clark Gardner, a financial advisor who worked for AJR, told me long after Parker was gone that his base salary with the Steelers had been eighty thousand dollars a year — top dollar at the time in the NFL — plus incentives. Gardner did not know what the incentives were. I did. But I had thought that Parker's base salary was closer to thirty thousand dollars. No, Gardner said – the eighty-thousand figure was correct.

Over and above that, Parker got a percentage of the profits, as Jock Sutherland had. The move to Pitt Stadium and a new TV contract with the National Broadcasting Company guaranteed that the profits would be higher than they ever had been.

And there were still more add-ons for Parker. This is hard to believe, but AJR cut him in on a percentage of his race-track and stock-market earnings, which were sizable. For one thing, he was betting heavily and successfully on the horses in those years. The real bonanza, though, was the killing he made in soy-bean futures, the result of a tip from Father Dan. There had been a huge crop failure in China, Dan learned. After the Communist takeover, the Franciscans had all left the country, but they were not without sources of information. Father Dan told AJR about the soy-bean shortage, and before the news could spread, raising prices all over the world, he invested enough for a hundred-thousand-dollar profit. The other Dan — my brother — raised the question of whether part of this money should go to Parker. He did not see how Buddy was entitled to it. AJR put the issue to rest by telling him, "Your word is your bond."

All in all, Parker made out pretty well with the Steelers. On AJR's side, there were no regrets, either, for the first couple of years. It is hard to tell at just what point misgivings began to set in. Parker was impulsive and eccentric. AJR had known that. Whether he foresaw the extent of the trouble this would cause is open to doubt. Personally, I got along with Parker very well. He was easy to talk to and friendly toward my brothers and me. Before his departure, I had started to learn the scouting end of the business, and he gave me some helpful advice. One thing he said was: "When you visit a college campus, conduct yourself in a way that will not keep anybody from wanting you to come back the next year." He saw that we needed more scouts and better scouts and was instrumental in the development of the Blesto concept, in which four or five teams would share the cost of tracking down and evaluating the NFL prospects among thousands of college players. It was ironic but typical that in his eight years with the Steelers he managed to trade away all of the team's high draft choices.

Footnote: AJR knew that Parker's first name was Raymond but always addressed him as Clarence. One day I asked why. "Because his middle name is Clarence," AJR said. I corrected him — something I did not often do. "I think his middle name is Kemp," I said. "Look it up to be sure." AJR looked it up and discovered that I was right. From then on he called the coach Buddy.

Uneasy Alliance

I think there was mutual dislike and mutual suspicion when the Steelers gained access to Pitt Stadium. The Pitt people seemed to think they were working with a pack of racketeers. Our own front-office people felt as out of place in Pitt Stadium as Irish Catholics in a Presbyterian church.

What Joe Carr felt was a loss of control. At Forbes Field he could parcel out the 12,000 seats with good sightlines to the customers he favored. At Pitt Stadium there wasn't a bad seat in the place. There wasn't a comfortable seat, either; all 58,000 were backless, but the fans who objected were the ones, for the most part, on Joe Carr's priority list.

They complained that their new seats were too narrow; that they were sacroiliac destroyers; that they bristled with butt-piercing splinters. They complained about the lack of cover: Forbes Field had a grandstand roof; Pitt Stadium was open to the elements. They complained about the climb up DeSota Street — called Cardiac Hill — from the bus stops, streetcar tracks, parking lots, and parking garages on Fifth Avenue.

For another thing, Pitt Stadium had no lights, which meant we could not schedule night games there. Joe Carr, making capital of all this, campaigned for a return to Forbes Field. Pitt Stadium had stripped Joe of his power. The old baseball park, with its vision-impeding iron posts and girders, its dankness and dirt, its odors of spilled beer and decay, was his source of power. He prevailed on AJR to authorize a survey — let the ticket buyers decide where we should play. And of course the outcome was never in doubt. Polling only his favored 12,000, ticket holders for life who bequeathed their seats to relatives when they died, Carr found that, overwhelmingly, the fans were for going back to Forbes Field.

AJR was taken in. After the 1958 season, we did not play at Pitt Stadium again until 1963, and then for only part of the schedule. In the end it was Dan who convinced him to make a clean break with Forbes Field. Joe Carr's hold on the Chief had been broken at last.

One of Fran Fogarty's concerns about the move to Pitt Stadium was the prevalence there of gate-crashing. Every male Oakland native, as Fogarty knew, having grown up in Oakland himself, considered free admission to the stadium almost a birthright. Working with Kenny George, the ticket manager at Pitt, Fogarty attempted to plug the leaks, aware that complete success would not be possible. A short, white-haired man, serious and strict, George had a reputation for tough-mindedness, but the equally tough-minded Fogarty won his confidence and, in the end, his cooperation.

On the upper administrative level, my brother Dan earned the respect of the Pitt people for his competence; AJR won them over with an irresistible combination of friendliness and good faith, proving once again that he was able to make connections with anyone. In doing so, he deliberately underplayed his sharp intelligence. High flyers who thought they were outsmarting AJR, and ended up being outsmarted themselves, rarely even knew how it happened.

A minor example of this was his psychological tussle with Beano Cook and Jim O'Brien.

Beano Cook, Pitt's sports information director, rubbed me the wrong way. In my view, he was too opinionated. Media members, I subsequently learned, admired him for his honesty and forthrightness. He said what he thought – overdoing it, I believed. But New York columnist Dan Parker called Beano "the greatest publicity man since Barnum – and, on second thought, Bailey too," and Frank Carver, who succeeded Tom Hamilton as Pitt's athletic director, pronounced him "the best press agent in the business." His allegiance, of course, was to college football. Beano's one stint with a pro team – the Miami Dolphins – coming after a decade or more at Pitt and a job with the American Broadcasting Company in New York, lasted just twelve months. Later, hired by the all-sports radio and television network ESPN, he developed into an on-the-air personality and something of a pundit.

Jim O'Brien, a brash Irish kid from Hazelwood, had been sports editor of the *Pitt News*. After graduation, he started a newspaper of his own, a tabloid called *Pittsburgh Weekly Sports*. Beano, Jim's patron, was listed on the masthead as co-publisher. It was a lively publication. O'Brien reprinted columns and articles by some of the talented young writers on big-city papers in the East, papers with sports sections more interesting than those of the stodgy, uncreative Pittsburgh dailies. He himself covered the local scene with a critical boldness absent from the *Press* and the *Post-Gazette*. The paper's style reflected Beano's journalistic credo. "I know what I like to read — controversy!" Beano would say. "I don't care if the writer is Ernest Hemingway — he's got to write some controversy."

Controversy, of course, makes for hard feelings, and O'Brien's bumptiousness offended both the objects of his scrutiny and the city's older, less adventurous sports reporters and sports editors, whose policy it was to sweep controversy under the rug. O'Brien was especially hard-fisted in writing about the Steelers. To my astonishment, that did not prevent Beano, his partner, from asking AJR for a favor. O'Brien, I believed at the time, was no more than a mouthpiece, putting into words what Beano, because of his affiliation with Pitt, couldn't prudently say on his own. Yet here Beano was, before a Steeler game at Pitt Stadium, coming uninvited into AJR's box and making what I thought was an outrageous proposition on behalf of *Pittsburgh Weekly Sports*. He wanted AJR to give the paper an exclusive story — no particular exclusive story, just the next big story that broke. It could be a story about a trade or a coaching change or a lineup shuffle — anything at all that the dailies wouldn't have.

To be truthful, I expected my dad to slug Beano. *Pittsburgh Weekly Sports*, remember, was a paper that consistently found fault with Dad's football team. But, instead, he was patient and courteous, explaining in a reasonable way that the *Press* and the *Post-Gazette* had large circulations, that their reporters covered the Steelers day in and day out, and that it could never be right to withhold something from them in order to make O'Brien's paper look good.

Beano persisted, showing none of the deference I had come to expect from people who had dealings with AJR. "Give us just one exclusive." Jack Butler was in our box, and I thought maybe *he* would punch Beano. Still under 30, Beano was six feet tall, or close to it, and weighed about 200 pounds. He was therefore, I thought, fair game. But though I knew Jack was steaming, he made no move — which left it up to me. I had recently finished my year in the Marine Corps and was still feeling gung-ho. Like Jack, though, I held off. Sucker-punching guys was not my style. And AJR, while never losing his composure, had made Beano see that he was pushing things a little too far.

I was surprised at how quickly Dad forgot the whole incident. No doubt to him, as to many others, Beano was a Pittsburgh character, outspoken and assertive but knowledgeable, humorous, and likable. As for me, after all these years, my temper still rises when I think of his demand for an "exclusive."

With good cause, Jim O'Brien continued to take shots at the Steelers. *Pittsburgh Weekly Sports* flourished for a time, but publishing on a shoestring entailed risk. There were rumors, finally, that the little upstart tabloid was going broke. As Ed Kiely told it, AJR made a telephone call to O'Brien.

"What would it take to keep your paper going?" he asked.

Whether O'Brien accepted the offer, only he and AJR ever knew. But from that day on, the coverage of the Steelers in *Pittsburgh Weekly Sports* was a bit more sympathetic. After the paper eventually did go out of business, O'Brien went to work for the *Miami Daily News*, then the *New York Post*, and at last the *Pittsburgh Press*. Halfway through the 1980s he unexpectedly turned up in Cook's old job, that of sports information director at Pitt. Another career change quickly followed. By the time he was 45, a mellowed 45, he was writing and publishing sports books, among them a laudatory memoir of AJR called "The Chief." Pieced together after his death, it's a collection of interviews with people who knew him. "I love and admire [AJR] more than ever," O'Brien writes at the end of the introduction.

A Pittsburgh character who ingratiated himself with me was Leo Chester Czarnecki, the Pitt athletic department's head groundskeeper. Thick-set, square-shouldered, and immensely strong, Czarnecki acquired his nickname — Horse — from Torn Hamilton, who watched him pull an iron-wheeled cart across the football field one day. The cart had a heavy tarpaulin in it. "Who's that horse?" Hamilton asked.

Czarnecki had a spiky blond crew cut and baby-blue eyes. He hit it off immediately with AJR, who always hit it off with people who were down to earth. Horse's humor was not for stuffed shirts. On the canvas-back chair he occupied at Pitt basketball games he stenciled a sign that read "Reserved: Field House Atzerverator." To those who inquired what "atzerverator" meant, he explained, "When

I carne here, they called me a janitor. I needed a more impressive title to scare off the walruses who plopped themselves down in my chair. So I threw a handful of alphabet cereal on the breakfast table and it spelled out atzerverator." In a year when the Pitt football team was scoring few touchdowns, Horse gave the offense some needed direction. Across the top of the goal-line markers he painted the words "Pay Dirt," with an arrow pointing into the end zone. A device that got better results was the sprinkler system he installed at the base of the goal posts to repel the mobs bent on tearing them down. Activated at the end of the game — if Pitt won — the sprinklers were more effective than the Pittsburgh police at protecting the goal posts from destruction.

Horse's greatest feat, the achievement that made his reputation, dated back to the big Thanksgiving Day snow of 1950. With the whole city immobilized, there was no way to disconnect the plumbing in Pitt Stadium. Commandeering a crew of five, Horse spent four days and four nights in the stadium's recesses, flushing toilets to keep the pipes from freezing.

"From now on," Hamilton told him, "you're a foreman."

As far as those of us with the Steelers were concerned, he was something much more than that — namely, Pitt's most successful good-will ambassador.

South Park

When the Steelers played their home games at Forbes Field they practiced there, too, on the outfield grass. With the move to Pitt Stadium, a difficulty arose. The stadium itself was out of the question as a practice site. Not even the university team practiced at Pitt Stadium but on a nearby field only eighty yards long, which was either unavailable to the Steelers or unsatisfactory.

As he usually did, AJR turned to his political friends for help. South Park, owned by the county, had a football field where the team from a small high school in the area played some of its games, and the Steelers became seasonal tenants.

Comprising almost two thousand acres of what once had been farmland, much of it reforested in the 1920s and 1930s, South Park was a pastoral extension of Pittsburgh's South Hills. With assistance from the Civilian Conservation Corps, a government-funded Depression-era haven for jobless young men, the talented landscape architect Paul B. Riis had planted and transplanted maples and oaks, beeches and dogwoods, cherry trees and pear trees. By the time all the work was finished, the park's attractions included a golf course, a "bathing" pool (four feet deep), tennis courts, baseball diamonds, nature trails, bridle paths, picnic groves, and dance pavilions. The county fair was held at South Park. Until attendance tapered off in the 1960s, half a million spectators came every year for the livestock judging and home-cooking exhibits, for the harness-horse races and high-school band competitions.

Once the summer was over, activity ceased. Off and on, the county's mounted police troop trained in one of the horse barns. The cow barns and sheep pens were empty. In 1927, a buffalo herd and a band of Native Indian caretakers had been trucked in from the West. No trace of either remained. There had been thirty-six buffalo all told, but Chief Wild Eagle's braves, instead of protecting the shaggy creatures, gunned them down for their meat and their hides. When all the buffalo were gone, the Indians went home to the Great Plains. Their reason for leaving, they said, was the weather. Winters on the prairie, which are famously long and hard, had not prepared them for Western Pennsylvania's icy Decembers.

So the Steelers worked out in isolation. Buddy Parker, obsessed with privacy, liked it that way. Parker and all or most of his assistant coaches lived in the South Hills, and they took the back roads to the park. One day a week, conveniently for Buddy, they met for a strategy discussion in his game room.

Halfback Ray Mathews, who also lived in the neighborhood, sometimes came to practice on horseback. Between workouts, he galloped his steed. Kicker Bert Rechichar kept a shotgun in his car and used it to wing pheasants until the chief of the county police, Monk Ketchel, reported him to AJR. Using Torn the Bomb Tracy's car, Bobby Layne was stopped by Ketchel for "irregular driving." Ketchel opened the trunk and found an entire arsenal of shotguns, rifles, and pistols — "enough hardware," he said, "to start a revolution."

All things considered, Parker's wild Steelers made Wild Eagle's wild Indians look like Cub Scouts. One of the quarterbacks working out with the team was a strong-armed walk-on named Dan

Nolan. He had an M-1 rifle for an arm, but never knew where his passes were going. Sometimes he bounced them off various body parts of the county police or their horses if they were anywhere near the practice field. For a night on the town, Mike Sandusky and Joe Krupa, veteran Steeler linemen, took Nolan with them as a safety valve. At their first stop, they informed him that he was not to imbibe. His job, they explained, was to drive them back to the South Hills, and he had to be sober. When Nolan tried to object, he could not make them listen. At the end of the evening, thoroughly soused, they handed him the keys to the car. He sat down behind the wheel, stepped on the accelerator, and took off, Krupa recalled, "like a bat out of hell." He rocketed across the Liberty Bridge and tore through the Liberty Tubes at ninety miles an hour. "Slow down! Slow down!" his terrified passengers shouted. Finding the brake at last, he pulled up on the side of the road. "Where in the hell," demanded Krupa, no longer under the influence, "did you learn how to drive?"

"That's what I've been trying to tell you," answered Nolan. "I never did learn to drive."

Nolan did not make the team. The next Krupa heard of him he had been ordained as a Catholic priest.

The Steelers' locker room at South Park was housed in a ramshackle clapboard structure of one and a half stories, painted white. During the heyday of the county fair, it had served as a first-aid station. At other times, the county stored supplies and equipment in the building or rented it out for parties.

County workmen did what they could to keep the place in repair, but it was close to falling down from old age. A small porch led to the front door; another door opened into the basement, where the players dressed. No more than three or four at a time could use the showers. Those who did not mind waiting played cards, but Parker had a rule against crap games. A "cheesy rug" — as Joe Krupa put it — camouflaged the cement floor.

The meeting rooms and the trainer's room were upstairs. There were three meeting rooms all told — one for the offense, one for the defense, and one for the whole squad. When the whole squad met, there was not enough space for all the players. Some had to sit outside in the hallway, along with a coach or two. The others huddled together on chairs that were too narrow for bulky tackles, guards, and centers.

In the absence of a kitchen and lunch room, the players chose to eat at the nearest fast-food joints instead of brown-bagging it. At least once a week, a local optometrist, a celebrity hound, drove to a good delicatessen and got take-out for Buddy Parker and his staff. Parker showed his gratitude by letting the guy hang around. He survived the Mike Nixon and Bill Austin administrations, but one of Chuck Noll's first moves was to bar him from the premises.

Steelers Andy Russell and Ray Mansfield, whose avocation in later life was after-dinner speaking, worked up a routine they often repeated. They told a story that went like this: Parker (they would say) complained to AJR about conditions at South Park and obtained a promise from the Chief to do something. After several days there were still no changes. So Russell and Mansfield took it upon themselves to remind AJR that the situation had not improved. "It's all being taken care of," he assured them. "Improvements are certainly in order. I know that you fellows have to put on the same underwear and use the same towels twice a day — once after the morning practice and again after the afternoon practice. We're going to end that. From now on when the afternoon practice is over, you two will change with each other. After the second workout, Mansfield, you put on Russell's underwear and use Russell's towel. Russell, you put on Mansfield's underwear and use Mansfield's towel."

The story was neither true nor very funny, but Russell and Mansfield liked to tell it, and I must say that it caught the flavor of our years at South Park.

Low Point

There was never a more passionate Steeler fan than Joe Chiodo, a short, wide-bodied tavern keeper from Homestead. At Pitt Stadium one rainy Sunday, I saw him shed his blood in defense of the team and its owners.

Chiodo's bar was on Main Street in Homestead, not far from the gates of the Homestead works of U.S. Steel, where many of his customers earned the money they spent at his place on whiskey, beer, and the specialty of the house, a "mystery sandwich," the mystery being that nobody knew what was in it. If you ordered one, you could only be sure that you never had eaten anything quite like it, or would do so again, for the contents differed each day.

"Sports bars," as such, did not exist back then, but Chiodo's came close to looking like one. Call it a cross between a sports bar, a junk yard, and the Hanging Gardens of Babylon. Suspended from the ceiling were all kinds of artifacts — everything from rare (and not so rare) antiques to the most ordinary household items. An equally eye-catching decorative touch was a collection of brassieres. How they ended up hanging from Joe Chiodo's ceiling I don't know. There was also a photo gallery. Pictures of sports figures covered every wall, football players predominating. Steelers past and present gazed down from these walls on the beer drinkers and mystery sandwich eaters.

For many reasons, Chiodo revered my dad. It would take me thirty minutes to list them all, but the one that he talked about most often was a commonplace courtesy the Chief seldom neglected. "When my father died," Joe would say, "Mister Rooney came to the wake. Can you imagine a guy like Art Rooney paying his respects to a poor Italian immigrant who could barely speak English?" What he probably didn't suspect was that Joe Carr or Ed Kiely or someone else in the Steeler office routinely checked the obituaries every day and notified AJR of wakes and funerals it might please him to attend.

Jack Butler nicknamed Joe Chiodo "The Little Tycoon" because he organized bus trips from his bar to our home games and also to certain games on the road. When we played in Cleveland, Washington, or Philadelphia, Joe and his busloads of steelworkers would form a boisterous Pittsburgh cheering section. For me at least, they revived fond memories of the Ham and Cabbage Specials run by Owney McManus to Steeler games in New York and to Billy Conn's championship fights. All the more unsettling, then, was the scene that took place on the Sunday Joe fought for our honor.

To start from the beginning: a crew from NFL Films was in town to do a segment on Chiodo's bar. Its uniqueness and its fame as a shrine to the Steelers was attracting a lot of attention from the media. When Karl Malden, the noted character actor ("Patton," "On the Waterfront," "A Streetcar Named Desire"), made a television movie about working in a steel mill, he chose to do his research at Chiodo's. All of this, I'm afraid, went to Joe's head just a little. Old customers who may have been a trifle uncouth found themselves barred from his place as undesirables. Joe's high-handedness in deciding who could or could not be served with a drink reminded me of no one as much as Pop Rooney.

On the day that NFL Films was in town, the camera crew finished shooting interiors — football fans juicing up for the game — and then the buses took off for Pitt Stadium, the movie people following in rented cars. What happened at the game ruined Chiodo's day and mine. The clouds hung low, the rain never stopped, the field was a swamp, and our football team, a very bad one that year, could not have been worse. Five minutes into the second half, most of the crowd had departed. Chiodo's guys — wet, cold, drunk, and unhappy — stuck it out. For shelter from the downpour, they huddled under the eaves of the press-box roof, growing mutinous. The foulness of their language matched the foulness of their mood. From our seats in the owner's box, we could hear all the words.

"Fuck the Steelers!" they were shouting. "Fuck the Rooneys!"

Only Chiodo himself was sober. Angrily, he tried to shut them up, and they turned on him. One yahoo lunged for his throat. He had a choke hold on Joe and wouldn't release it. I suppose the camera was recording the whole ugly spectacle. If so, it ended up on the cutting-room floor. No lasting harm came to Chiodo. Just in time, a few of the bus riders who still had some sense converged on his attacker and pulled him off. Joe was bloodied and bruised, but more embarrassed than hurt.

In all of our years at Pitt Stadium, this day was the low point.

Chapter 30

'Don't Knock Friendship'

Richie McCabe was a kid from The Ward, cut from the same environmental and educational swatch as the Rooney boys: St. Peter's grade school, North Catholic High School, the University of Pittsburgh. There was never a more unlikely looking football player. Tall and thin, he weighed 165 pounds at the most. He wore thick-lensed glasses that seemed to dominate his pale, narrow face. He was the temperamental opposite of the Cowardly Lion, the Bert Lahr character in "The Wizard of Oz." His courage and ferocity were all on the inside, camouflaged by a scarecrow exterior.

When we were kids at North Catholic, Richie played basketball for the neighborhood YMCA team. There was a game one night with a team from the Nike missile base at the Greater Pittsburgh Airport. One of the GIs singled out the scrawny kid with the thick glasses as someone he could push around. Richie let him have it with five quick punches, the last four landing on his hasty descent to the floor.

Intelligence and speed were Richie's main assets on the football field. From a distance, he could not see the goal line, but he knew where it was and how to get there. He played the game with a passion and learned the fine points so well that even at North Catholic High School he was telling his teammates what to do. The coach, Bob Hast, encouraged him to an extent. "Just don't get full of yourself," he would say.

Richie and my brother Dan played in the same backfield. "I was a hotshot offensive back — I thought," Richie said. "I could have gone to twenty or twenty-five schools." He went to Pitt — "and to be honest about it," he said, reminiscing, "I didn't do anything there. I mean I played — I played a lot — but I weighed 145 pounds and they never ran me around end. They ran me on dive plays and off tackle."

The Steelers, for old time's sake, took McCabe in the twenty-seventh round of the 1955 draft. No one gave him a chance to make the team, but deep down he felt he could play. When Dewey McConnell, the safety man, got hurt, Richie took his place in an exhibition game. He intercepted two passes, recovered a fumble, and scored a touchdown. He was the scrawniest defensive back in the NFL, but fast enough and tough enough to win a place on the roster in three of the next four years. Buddy Parker described him to AJR as "a player who makes a contribution." So AJR was a little surprised when Richie asked to be traded or released.

Pressed for an explanation, he said that he wanted to prove something. "Everybody in Pittsburgh is saying the only reason I'm on the team is my friendship with the Rooney family. I'd like to show them I can play for any team in the NFL."

"Look," AJR told him, "don't knock friendship. In this life you are lucky to make five really true friends — and that includes your wife. All the others are just acquaintances."

But Richie's heels were dug in. AJR traded him to Washington, and for one season, anyway, he proved he could play there. In 1960, he went to an AFL team, Buffalo, mainly because Jack Butler was on the coaching staff. It was the AFL's first season, and Richie described the caliber of play as a joke — better than college football, but not that much better.

He retired after two years. Bad knee. Back home in Pittsburgh, he found a teaching job at Mount Oliver High School, but what he really wanted to do was coach. "No one would have me — I couldn't even get an interview," he said. "The North Catholic job was open, my own school. I wrote a letter and nobody answered it."

Another two years went by and then Joe Gasparella, himself a former Steeler, invited Richie to be his assistant at Carnegie Tech — to "help out," as Joe put it.

"I'll be honest with you," Richie said. "I don't think Carnegie Tech can be helped."

But he accepted the offer and "turned out to be a good coach — a great coach," according to Joe. "He was very dynamic with our kids," Joe said. "He straightened some of them out, I'll tell you that. He had a little different vocabulary than we usually heard on our campus."

One day out of the blue a call came from Joe Collier, the Buffalo Bills' coach. He was asking McCabe to be his defensive coordinator, and it launched him on a second pro career. Coaches, especially assistants, change jobs a lot, and Richie was no exception. He went from Buffalo to the Jets to Denver.

The Richie McCabe I remembered was shy around girls, but in Buffalo he had married a secretary in the Bills' front office. Meanwhile, we were hearing good things about him from people like Babe Parilli, who had come here from the Jets to be our quarterback coach, and Joe Namath, the Jets' first Hall of Famer. In Denver, McCabe was the number one assistant to Dan Reeves. His future at this point looked as cloudless as a future could be.

And then, very quickly, the picture changed. He developed cancer. When he learned that it was terminal, he methodically called his friends to say good-bye. His call to me interrupted a meeting with some scouts. What he wanted to talk about, going all the way back to his childhood, was my mother. He said that from time to time when he was growing up, she would offer him money for a movie or a snack, knowing his family could not afford such luxuries. Always he had refused. The other kids would find out and make fun of him, he admitted to her at last. "Richie," she assured him, "it will be a secret between the two of us."

He asked if she ever had told me about this conversation. I said no.

Then Richie said, "I loved your mother very much."

They were his last words to me, almost.

Helping Hand

In the division of labor decreed by AJR, my brothers Tim, John, and Pat were not involved with the football team. They ran the horse racing and later the dog racing end of the family business. Because the tracks were so distant from Pittsburgh, outsiders seemed to be unaware of this. The Rooneys, they knew, owned the Steelers. As individuals, all five brothers were therefore accountable for every decision, no matter how trivial, made by either management or the coaches. Even the players' wives, or at any rate one player's wife, held to that view.

We had a wide receiver and kick returner from Michigan State, Gary Ballman, who was big and fast but lacking in the ability to improvise on the field. Buddy Parker used him sparingly, influenced, perhaps, by the perception then in vogue that Michigan State players were slow to catch on. As a Blesto scout put it, "You could toss them all into a bag and then throw Duffy Daugherty in" — Duffy Daugherty was Michigan State's highly successful coach — "and their IQs wouldn't add up to a hundred and ten."

However unfactual that may have been, Gary Ballman spent most of his Sundays on the bench.

Anyway, during Ballman's second year on the team, his wife was in the maternity ward at Mercy Hospital at the same time as my brother John's wife. One day after visiting JoAnn, John decided to call on Mrs. Ballman. He did not get quite the reception he anticipated.

Going straight to the subject of her husband's limited playing time, she gave him a thorough tongue-lashing. John listened quietly and departed.

The next weekend, for some reason, Parker had Ballman in the starting lineup, and he made some spectacular catches. On Monday morning, John was back at the hospital to pick up JoAnn and the baby. In the hallway or somewhere, he encountered Mrs. Ballman.

"Oh, Mister Rooney," she said. "How can I ever thank you enough for talking to Coach Parker about Gary? All he needed was a chance to show what he could do, and you gave it to him."

John had said nothing about Mrs. Ballman's complaint to anyone, Parker least of all, but told her he was glad to have been of service.

Gary Ballman became a good, productive player for the Steelers. The other wide receiver was Buddy Dial, which didn't hurt. Dial attracted double coverage every week, making it easier for Ballman. After the Steelers traded Dial to Dallas — handed him over for a draft choice we failed to sign — Ballman was still a decent performer but considerably less effective without his running mate.

Cannonball

On Interstate 95 in Florida where it passes through Jacksonville, there's a sign that says "Edward Waters College," with a big black arrow pointing west. Whenever I see it, I think of Cannonball Butler.

Edward Waters was a nineteenth-century Baptist minister, and the college that bears his name is affiliated with the Southern Baptist Church. No doubt the Rev. Mr. Waters was fully deserving of the honor his church bestowed on him, but as far as I am concerned the wording on that sign along Interstate 90 should be "Cannonball Butler College."

For those of us connected with the Steelers, it was Cannonball Butler who put Edward Waters on the map. In his senior year at Edward Waters, 1964, he played on an undefeated football team, scoring twenty-eight touchdowns. Against one opponent, Friendship College, he scored a touchdown every time he carried the ball, for a total of six. Edward Waters won that game 142-0.

Although our scouts had seen Cannonball only on film, we drafted him in the fourteenth round. He was not very big — just 5 feet 9 and 180 pounds — a matter of concern to some of our coaches. Ken Stilley, who signed Butler, advised them not to worry. Cannonball was compact, Stilley said, and would be able to block. In Buddy Parker's system, the halfbacks had to block, but what Cannonball did best was run. And he could run like ... oh, I don't know, like a shot out of a cannon, I guess you'd say. That was the reason for his nickname, after all. The nickname seemed to embarrass him a little, but nobody including his parents ever called him by the name he received at birth — James. "I have four sisters," he said, "and I'm the only boy in the family, so they call me Brother."

Getting back to the way he ran, his speed excited everybody at our training camp in Rhode Island. He got loose for some long runs in the intra-squad scrimmages, and against a minor-league team called the Rhode Island Indians he sprinted eighty yards for a touchdown.

Buddy Parker believed we had something. Cannonball, he said, was certain to be "a terrific running threat" for the Steelers. Parker wasn't around to see if his prediction held up (that was the year he resigned before the start of the season), but Mike Nixon, the assistant coach who succeeded him, liked Cannonball too. "Give him that much room in the open," Nixon said, holding a forefinger and thumb an inch apart, "and he's gone."

Nixon saved a place on the roster for Cannonball. "He's short, yes," Nixon told me, "but look at those shoulders and arms. He's all man. His thighs are huge. And he can cut on a dime. We have to get him into the game as much as we can. He may not be a starter, but there's so many good things he can do. We have to get the ball to him on pitchouts and screens and flares. He can outrun defenders to the corner. We have to use him on quick openers and draws. Why, he'll drive people crazy."

As it happened, the only people Cannonball ever drove crazy were the coaches and some of his teammates. Not that he was in any sense disruptive. Personally, he was quiet and well behaved. The trouble with Cannonball was that he lacked football intelligence. Despite multiple repetitions in practice, said his coaches, he simply could not remember the plays. After the 1967 season, Bill Austin, who had taken over from Nixon the previous year, traded him to Atlanta.

Cannonball's speed notwithstanding, Chuck Noll would have cut him in two weeks. Noll often said, "The dummies will kill you." When Noll took over as coach in 1969, he recognized the need for team speed. "But there was something we needed even more — team intelligence," he said. "And I saw that we needed it very badly."

Chapter 31

Owls Hoot, Eagles Fly

Even as an assistant coach, Bobby Layne continued to be the Steelers' off-the-field leader. He led them most often to Dante's, a popular hangout in Brentwood. A Detroit Lion teammate aptly summed up Layne's influence on everyone who ever played with him: "When Bobby said block, you blocked. When Bobby said drink, you drank."

If you drank all night, you blocked the next day — no excuses accepted. "Don't hoot with the owls unless you can soar with the eagles," Layne used to say. He applied this code rigidly to himself.

On his way home from Dante's one night, having hooted perhaps to excess, he met with an accident. "I was hit by a parked, swerving streetcar," he explained to the police. The next day was a game day, and Bobby soared. He soared even higher than usual.

Punter Frank Lambert, one of the more intellectual types to play for the Steelers, described the culture of the team as "hard-hitting, hard-drinking, blue-collar masculinity." Jim Brown, the punishing Cleveland running back, said, "I hear their coach puts beer on their bus. But when you play against them," he added, "your body is sore for days. They leave you black and blue."

Buddy Parker wanted players who could do that — tough guys in the mold of Ernie Stautner, John Henry Johnson (acquired from the Detroit Lions), and Big Daddy Lipscomb (acquired from the Baltimore Colts). Parker stocked his teams by trading draft choices; one of the few draftees who made the grade was Red Mack, a slight but ferocious pass catcher from Notre Dame. Mack's right hand was a lethal weapon. Teammate Lou Michaels, a defensive end/placekicker who was sixty pounds heavier than Mack, tested it twice. Both times the Notre Damer stretched him.

Parker's 1963 Steelers, even without Layne and even without Big Daddy Lipscomb, who had died in the off-season of a drug overdose, retained their character. Jim Brown called them the NFL's version of the Gas House Gang. The quarterback was Ed Brown, a big, shaggy-haired ex-Marine. Acquired from the Bears, Brown had been Layne's backup in 1962, and Parker had great confidence in him, or seemed to. He said that Brown "could throw the ball about as well as you'll ever see anyone throw it." That's an exact quote.

From the middle of the season until the final week, the Steelers were undefeated, winning a number of close games on fourth-quarter touchdown plays and getting a tie with the Eagles on Lou Michaels' last-minute field goal. All they had to do to be the Eastern Conference champions was close out the schedule by knocking off the Giants in New York. At home, they had beaten the Giants by thirty-one points.

This time they lost, decisively, and Myron Cope thought he knew why. In a story for Sport magazine, Cope blamed the Steelers' 33-17 defeat on Ed Brown's decision to give up booze. Brown dismayed the patrons at Dante's, Myron wrote, by taking the big game too seriously. It seems that "on the Wednesday preceding the showdown battle, he disappeared from his favorite saloon" and "went into training."

Consequently, according to Cope, he "lost his sang-froid," overthrew receivers all day, and "gave the most miserable performance of his career."

A neat theory, except for the fact that, resuming his old habits the next year, Brown gave a series of equally miserable performances. The Steelers descended to sixth place, and that was the end of Brown. Make of it what you will.

A Cuckoo's Nest

As Roy Blount described it in "About Three Bricks Shy of a Load," the Steelers' dressing room at South Park was "the basement of a dilapidated building [that] had six showers, four of which worked. The toilets didn't have seats; you had to sit on porcelain." The dressing area was dingy and cramped, with battered tin lockers. A network of bare pipes covered the ceiling.

At the start of his first year on the job, 1957, Coach Buddy Parker noted with disapproval that there was always a long line outside the trainer's room. Injuries couldn't explain it; it was early in the season, the team was in pretty good shape. Investigating, Parker discovered that the players were lining up to get rubdowns.

Parker's attitude toward rubdowns was similar to that of Luke Carney, an old boxing manager, who said, "A good fighter don't need a rubdown and a bad fighter don't deserve one." Parker at once had the door to the trainer's room padlocked. The next thing he did was tell AJR that the trainer himself should be fired. In his place Parker wanted a man with enough backbone to resist the players' demands and entreaties. In his opinion, they were being coddled.

Instantly, AJR thought of Doc Sweeney. A New England Irishman whose first name, like Parker's, was Raymond. Sweeney had been the trainer for the Brooklyn Dodgers when Jock Sutherland coached them. He had come to the Steelers with Sutherland in 1946 and had stayed on after Sutherland's death for as long as John Michelosen was coach. Tough and self-assured, he ran a tight ship. There was a story about his fearlessness that preceded him to Pittsburgh.

During his years in Brooklyn, the story went, he worked on the players with his shirt off, and one of the owners, Shipwreck Kelly, who was also the first-string tailback for the Dodgers, developed an annoying habit. He would sneak up behind Sweeney and slap him resoundingly on the back. Sweeney warned him to "cut out the foolishness." Kelly didn't listen. There came a day when he delivered one slap too many. Sweeney wheeled around and crashed a right to Kelly's jaw, putting him on the floor. To the surprise of everyone the trainer did not lose his job.

Sweeney was a bona-fide doctor, with a degree in osteopathy. In Maine, where he practiced, he was authorized to write prescriptions, deliver babies, and even perform appendectomies. It annoyed him to be called Mr. Sweeney or Ray instead of Doc. Then in his late forties, he was a bear of a man — six feet tall with massive shoulders and arms. As a trainer, he knew what he was doing and was tireless in doing it.

After Sweeney's return to Pittsburgh, I became his particular friend. At South Park, he would stand on the sideline and appraise various players in a word or two. This one had "lots to say" but wasn't much on performance. That one had talent but would never use it to the fullest extent. "There's something twisted in him." Nine times out of ten, Doc's assessments were right on the mark.

Parker, he quickly discerned, had much more wrong with him than just his addiction to alcohol. "He's a very backward person," Doc said. "Bipolar problems, I suspect." He considered Buster Ramsey and one or two others on the coaching staff a bad influence on Parker. They were "egging him on."

Ramsey, it seemed, was giving Sweeney "a lot of crap" in the meantime. "I came here to work for your dad and Parker — not that guy," Doc told me. "I've never taken anything from anybody, but I'm an old man now with no wife [she had died young] and two kids to raise, and I need this job."

He could stand for only so much, however, and one night when the team was on the road he resolved to have a showdown with Ramsey. He waited in the hotel lobby for Buster to come back from dinner, knowing the hour would be late. "I'm old and fat," Doc said to me later, "but Buster, I figured, would have a snoot full. I planned to go after him — invite him outside and let him have it."

It was not to be. When Ramsey arrived, half-drunk, his wife was with him. "Wonderful lady," Doc said. "Everybody liked her. And she hadn't been well. How did she ever marry a bum like that?" Instead of challenging Ramsey, Doc just said "hi" and went up to bed.

An incident in Dallas was "the last straw" for him, Doc said. The Steelers had gone there to play the Cowboys and were staying at the airport motel. Unlike the downtown hotels, the airport motel was not segregated. Neither were the Steelers, but black players and white players went their separate ways off the field. In Dallas on the night before the game, the blacks had gone off to a blacks-only night club and were late getting back to the motel. Ramsey, in charge of bed check, was "egging Parker on," as Sweeney related it to me, letting him know every few minutes that the black guys were not in their rooms.

"Buddy was drinking," Doc said, "and Buster was getting him upset. They came to my room and pounded on the door. When I opened it, Buddy says right away that he wants his hands taped. 'Like a boxer.' I ask him what for. 'I'm going to punch out Johnson and Lipscomb,' he tells me.

"Buddy and Buster were blaming John Henry Johnson and Big Daddy Lipscomb for keeping the rest of the black guys at the night club. There was no use arguing with Buddy, I realized that, so I taped his hands, but I taped them so tight that in twenty minutes the blood would stop circulating.

"Well, he's running up and down the hallway, punching his fist into his open hand and yelling, 'I'll beat the hell out of that black son of a bitch Lipscomb, and then I'll beat the hell out of John Henry.' This goes on for a full twenty minutes, until his hands went numb and he was back in my room asking me to 'cut the damn tape off.'"

Sweeney had worked with Jock Sutherland, a formal, dignified, larger-than-life sort of personage who tolerated no monkey business from either his players or his assistant coaches. The undisciplined ways of Buddy Parker were more than Doc could put up with. When Mike Duda, the president of California State College of Pennsylvania, offered him a trainer's job that also involved teaching, he jumped at the chance to leave the Steelers. He felt that California, PA, a little college town, would be the perfect environment for his children.

Footnote: After the Vietnam War ended, a cousin of mine told me that through the efforts of "a wonderful man who had once been connected with the Steelers" he was able to enroll at California State as a freshman and avoid being drafted into the Army. Immediately I knew that he was speaking of Doc Sweeney.

Up in the Air

The Steelers had played an exhibition game in Miami, losing to the Dolphins, and now their chartered jet was ready to take off. Fran Fogarty, who doubled as the team's traveling secretary, counted heads. Everybody was on board except Parker, the head coach, and Dick Plasman, his close friend and assistant.

They were not to be found. At the little building on the field where the aircraft was parked, away from the main terminal, there was no bar or restaurant. The plane's big motors were going, and Lou Kroeck of United Airlines, who always flew with the Steelers, warned Fogarty that the tower was pressing them to get on the runway.

Kroeck and Fogarty huddled with the pilot and his crew, after which Fogarty went to my brother John, who was 20 years old, and said, "Stand by. You are going to fetch the coach." The plane then taxied to a gate near the terminal, and the pilot lowered the back steps. Fogarty laid one hand on John's shoulder and placed the other against his back. "Go into the bar," Fran said. "That's where he'll be. Tell him he's got five minutes to get on the plane or his ass stays in Florida." With a gentle shove from Fogarty, John set off on his mission.

"I was scared to death," he later told me. After all, he was still just a kid. And Buddy Parker was a famous head coach with two NFL championships on his résumé.

As Fogarty had predicted, Parker was in the bar with Dick Plasman. Informed that the plane was about to take off, they made a beeline for the gate, with John at their heels. Actually, there was more time before takeoff than Fogarty, knowing Parker's habits, had led John to believe.

Parker had been downing whiskey, as he usually did after a defeat. When the plane was in the air, and the seat belt sign went off, he roamed the aisle, drunk. Jack Butler, Ray Mathews, and two or three other players were having a card game. "Ahh," said Parker. "Card players. Well, you'd better be card players, because you sure as hell aren't football players."

Somebody, for once, had the temerity or bad judgment to talk back. It was Mathews. "And you're the guy who was going to make us winners," he said. "Well, we haven't won yet." (He would soon be traded to the Cowboys, in those days a second-division team.)

Parker glared at Mathews, but held his tongue. Turning around and heading the other way, he stopped at the row where John Nisby and Billy Ray Smith, two big linemen, were seated. "Nisby," Parker sneered, "you're not black, you're yellow. Smith, you're always hurt. We got you from the Rams. You're supposed to be great, but you're a dud."

Nisby said nothing; Billy Ray spoke up. "Dammit, I *am* hurt," he protested. "And I didn't even play today."

"Just what I said — hurt and on your ass!" was Parker's comeback.

Smith had a bad temper. He started up from his seat, but Nisby restrained him.

Next, Parker turned on Ray Campbell, a quiet linebacker called "Soup," for obvious reasons. Since his days at Marquette, the Jesuit college had dropped football. "Campbell," Buddy screamed, "you're not even a player. That school you went to don't even have a football team any more. You're so bad you put them out of business."

Thus did Head Coach Buddy Parker comport himself when AJR was not with the team.

His most memorable scene was at the airport in Houston after a meaningless exhibition game with the Bears. First, though, a digression: To stop some hanky-panky that teams like the Bears and, yes, the Steelers were up to, the NFL had instituted a new rule. In those days it was possible to hide, stash, or stockpile a player by means of a phony, and temporary, "trade." Players would go from one team to another and be returned, by prior agreement, before the next game. Under the new rule, a team had to keep the "borrowed" player for two full weeks. Meanwhile, the player would take part in non-contact drills and calisthenics — nothing more. During games, he would sit on the bench but not play.

Two weeks before the exhibition game in Houston, Parker and George Halas, the owner of the Bears, had agreed to one of these bogus in-name-only exchanges. Consequently, there were two players on the Steeler bench who belonged to the Bears and two players with the Bears who belonged to the Steelers.

One of the Steelers in Bear's clothing was Rudy Hayes, a linebacker from Clemson. Immediately after the game, the so-called trade having been officially reversed, the four players turned in their gear and rejoined their original teams. Parker, living up to the unwritten code, had not used the Bears masquerading as Steelers, but Halas had used his Steelers on special teams. Near the end of the game the Bears went ahead by a field goal. The ensuing kickoff went to a Steeler who broke free and was seemingly on his way to a touchdown. At the Bears' 20-yard line, he had only one man to beat. That man was Rudy Hayes, and he brought down the runner with a desperate, diving, game-saving tackle.

An hour and forty-five minutes later, the team buses pulled up at the Houston airport. The Steelers' charter and the Bears' charter were sitting nose-to-nose on the tarmac, each with its back steps lowered. One by one, the players boarded the planes, Rudy Hayes and the other spurious Bear with the Steelers again and the two counterfeit Steelers back with the Bears. On the Steelers' plane, Buddy Parker, drunk already and brooding about the exhibition-game loss, was up near the front of the cabin. Looking around, he noticed Hayes, who had taken a seat toward the back and was trying to make light of his spectacular flying tackle.

"You traitor!" screamed Parker. "What are you doing on this airplane? Get off! GET OFF! Go over to the Bears' plane. You're no Steeler, Hayes. You cost us the game!"

Hayes was dumbfounded. With Parker standing over him, he got up out of his seat. Slowly, he moved to the back exit, looking at Parker over his shoulder, disbelief written on his face. He made his way down the steps, hesitated, and climbed the back steps of the Bears' plane. Going straight to George Halas, he explained his predicament.

Later, Halas said, "I thought my old friend Buddy had finally blown a gasket."

Halas escorted Hayes back to the Steeler plane, where he spotted Fran Fogarty with some airline people at the steps. "Do something with this young man; we're getting out of here," Halas said to him.

The ever-resourceful Fogarty solved the problem. He led Hayes up the steps once more and pushed him into a lavatory. "Stay here," he said, "until five minutes after we're airborne." Parker, his thoughts on the game, remained none the wiser, and the Steelers enjoyed a tranquil flight home.

Ordinarily Buddy watched himself when the Chief was on board. Only once did he lose control, but once was enough. The Steelers had lost a squeaker to the Giants, and the coach emerged from the airport bar with his usual post-defeat buzz. On the airplane, dropping into a seat next to AJR, he poured out a string of complaints. "I made an awful mistake when I came to this team," he said.

AJR had heard the stories about Parker. Abruptly, he ordered him to shut up. This was a side of AJR that Parker never had seen. Not another word was spoken until the wheels of the big aircraft touched down on a runway in Pittsburgh. Turning then to the Chief, who was looking straight ahead, Parker said, "We have to talk."

"Not now," the owner snapped. "You're in no condition to talk. I'll be in your office tomorrow at lunchtime."

That was all. They debarked from the plane and went their separate ways. Early the next morning, Parker called AJR and apologized. He said he knew he was out of line and would just as soon forget about their lunchtime meeting. "Let's put the whole thing behind us," he suggested.

"No," the Chief said. "It's important to get this straightened out. I'll see you today at practice."

On the long ride to South Park, I was AJR's driver. He asked me questions about Parker. The answers he got were consistent with his own observations. He rehearsed the speech he intended to deliver.

As it happened, the meeting was cordial. Parker was feeling contrite, and AJR was conciliatory but firm. He said to Buddy, "You walked out on a great championship team in Detroit. You're like the guy who had a beautiful wife. He loved her, but found her cheating. He took a walk — and pretty soon was wishing he hadn't. Deep down, he wanted go back to the woman he still loved. But he couldn't. It was too late.

"Buddy," the Chief went on, "you're in Pittsburgh now. Make the best of it. This is the only job you have. We're still friends, and believe me when I say I'd still like to have you as my coach. But I'm putting in some rules, and they have to be followed."

Henceforth, he continued, there would be no drinking on chartered flights. That meant everybody — from the head coach down to the equipment men. Assistant coaches, players, and front-office people, newspaper reporters, broadcasters, and invited guests traveling with the team were included. If a player or coach boarded the plane drunk he was fined $10,000. If a player or coach got drunk after the plane was in the air, he was fined $10,000. Anyone seen to be drunk while the plane was still on the ground would be left behind. He would be responsible for getting to the game or getting back to Pittsburgh on his own. For a second offense, players, coaches, and other employees would be fired. Everyone concerned had to sign a piece of paper acknowledging that he understood these terms and accepted them.

Parker did not object. He said that all of his coaches would sign the statement and that he would be the first. AJR promised to make sure that everyone else signed. Everyone did. On flights from then on, the Steelers were perfect gentlemen, the most circumspect team in the NFL. Even Buddy Parker was a model of good behavior

But in other ways — disastrously — he continued to make a fool of himself.

Chapter 32

Turmoil

Parker had many idiosyncrasies. The number thirteen was anathema to him. His fear of that number, in various manifestations, was almost comical. He refused, of course, to stay in a hotel room if the number on the door began or ended in thirteen, which was never a problem for traveling secretaries. What they were forced to guard against with equal vigilance, though, was assigning him to a room with a number that *added up* to thirteen.

His despair after defeats, even after defeats in exhibition games, often seemed almost psychotic. First he would look for a bottle, or a bar. Then came the ranting. Then, alone or with only his coaching assistants nearby, he would find a knife or a pair of shears, lie flat on his back, and cut off his necktie directly below the knot. Finally, re-playing the lost game in his feverish mind, and assessing blame, he would shake up the team, threatening cuts, trades, or lineup changes, and even, on occasion, putting them into effect.

Parker was a gifted coach, a gifted strategist. In 1964 the Steelers won five games, and coaching won two of them. He threw the Cleveland Browns into confusion with an unorthodox defense and got the Washington Redskins out of sync with an unorthodox offense.

But he relied too often on desperation measures, which became necessary, in part, because Parker created problems for himself. He made spur-of-the-moment decisions with a grand disregard for the consequences.

There was the Buddy Dial-for-nobody trade. In exchange for the draft rights to Scott Appleton, a tackle from the University of Texas, Parker sent Dial, his best wide receiver, to the Dallas Cowboys. What he failed to anticipate was that Appleton would sign with an AFL team — namely, the Houston Oilers.

There were other, less obviously misbegotten trades and releases. There was his stubbornness in the face of criticism from fans and sportswriters. Before Parker was ready to change quarterbacks in 1964, the fans wanted Ed Brown replaced, and the press backed them up. As the call for Bill

Nelsen increased, Parker's obstinacy mounted. Correctly, he reasoned that his knowledge of football was superior to the knowledge of the fans and the reporters. Therefore, if the fans and the writers preferred Nelsen to Brown, they must be wrong.

Brown's failures at the end of 1964 and in the early pre-season games the following year forced his hand. He gave in to the mob by starting Nelsen a couple of times, but what he really wanted to do was trade for somebody else's backup quarterback. All that deterred him was AJR's stipulation after the 1964 season that he and my brother Dan, who was taking over the day-to-day operation of the team, had to be consulted on personnel moves.

King Hill of the Eagles was the quarterback Parker coveted. "What would you think," he asked AJR, "of trading Ben McGee or Chuck Hinton for Hill?" McGee and Hilton were promising second-year defensive tackles from all-black schools in the South.

"I wouldn't do it," the Chief told him. AJR's thinking was: Why weaken your defensive line to get a second-string quarterback who might not be as good as the quarterbacks we already have? "But go ahead and do what you believe to be best for the team," he said.

Parker did nothing. But two weeks later, after the Steelers had lost an exhibition game to Baltimore, he proposed a different trade with a different team. Calling Dan's room in the training camp at the University of Rhode Island from his own room, he suggested trading McGee and a draft choice for two grizzled veterans, a lineman and a linebacker. It was late on a Saturday night, and Parker was drunk.

"Let's talk it over in the morning," Dan said.

"Are you questioning my judgment?" Parker asked.

"No," Dan replied. "But I don't believe in making trades in the middle of the night after a loss."

Parker then declared that he was quitting. Dan said, "I'll get back to you tomorrow morning," and called AJR in Pittsburgh.

Down through the years, after galling defeats, Parker had made a habit of quitting. "He quit twenty times," said AJR when the dust had settled. "He quit twenty times, and I got him back twenty times. This time I didn't get him back."

Accept his resignation, he said to Dan. So on Sunday morning Dan was prepared. The first thing Parker said to him was, "I don't think I can handle this team any longer." Dan said with finality, "I don't think so, either."

And that settled it.

The previous December Parker had signed a three-year contract extension. AJR agreed now to pay him for two of those three years. Roughly, the amount came to $160,000. If the Steelers had fired Parker, he'd have been entitled to his pay for the full duration of the contract — $240,000 or so, plus the extras it called for. But he quit, and legally they owed him nothing. Quitting turned out to be a luxury he could well afford.

Footnote: Parker flew home to Texas from the Greater Pittsburgh Airport. A newspaper photographer snapped a picture of him as he headed for his plane. It was leaving from Gate 13.

Power Struggle

B y the time Buddy Parker left the Steelers, my brother Dan and I were sold on building and maintaining the team through the draft. It was an unintended consequence of the way Parker operated. His way was to trade draft choices for veterans, or to pick up players who were not under contract to some other team. If there were bad actors, drunks, and oddballs among them, no problem. Using such misfits, he had won in Detroit, and he held to the view that what worked in Detroit would work with the Steelers. He was wrong.

Parker's attitude toward blacks — the fewer the better — was still another crippling mistake. Deep down I knew this, but I also knew that my opinions carried no weight. Too young and too green to speak with any authority, I held my tongue and bided my time.

Dan, on the other hand, was coming into his own. He had gone through a form of executive training — not that AJR or anyone else would have called it that. After starting out as a go-fer in what passed for our personnel department, he had worked with Joe Carr in the ticket department, with Ed Kiely in P.R., and with Fran Fogarty in the business office.

At Duquesne University, meanwhile, he studied accounting. And he had married Dad's secretary, Patricia Regan. His coming of age entitled him to certain perquisites. For one thing, he now had full use of the Steeler station wagon. That was nice — he had a wife and a kid to haul around, with other kids undoubtedly on the way. Better yet, AJR handed over the program concession to Dan.

The program concession had belonged since the 1930s to a man named Eddie Bernhardt, and losing it put his nose out of joint. From sales and advertising, the programs generated roughly $20,000 a year, half of it going to the team and half to the concessionaire. Eddie Bernhardt was a dapper little guy who tended to be officious and could rub people raw.

When Johnny Blood coached the Steelers, his exasperation with Bernhardt drove him to the point of committing ritualized murder. Bernhardt sat in on a meeting one day and attempted to do all the talking. Blood remained silent for as long as he could and then, picking up a yardstick, he cradled it in his shoulder, pointed it rifle-like at Bernhardt, and shouted, "Bang! Bang! Bernhardt, you little son of a bitch, you're dead!" A bullet from a yardstick Bernhardt could survive. Turning over the programs to Dan was a mortal blow. Did he need ten grand? Probably not. He worked full-time at a job in some other field. Far, far more than the money, he valued his Steeler connection. Deprived of it, he was visibly changed — perpetually downcast instead of cheerful to a fault. His visits to the office became much less frequent, and then, after a while, we saw him no more.

For Dan, gaining stature, the program concession was a springboard. Working with advertising agencies, local business people, and his NFL counterparts, he developed an identity of his own. He went from being Art Rooney's kid to a bright young guy who did his homework, asked intelligent questions, and offered original insights. He made some important friends — notably Pete Rozelle, an up-and-coming P.R. man soon to be tapped for the commissioner's job, and Art Modell, the Cleveland Browns' new owner. The three of them, forming a team, persuaded national advertisers to buy program space on a league-wide basis. AJR's oldest son was acquiring a reputation for wisdom beyond his tender years.

Buddy Parker, observing Dan's rise in the Steeler organization, felt threatened. By 1964 he was slipping over the edge. AJR continued to indulge him, moving the team's training base to the University of Rhode Island, for example, because of Parker's complaints about the "lousy practice fields" in Western Pennsylvania.

Down through the years the Steelers had been nomads. Under Jock Sutherland they had trained at Alliance College in Cambridge Springs. When Joe Bach was the coach, they trained in New York, at St. Bonaventure. There were summers when they trained at California State in California, PA, at Slippery Rock State, north of Pittsburgh, and even at West Liberty College near Wheeling, West Virginia. None of these places suited Parker. They were too close to Pittsburgh, too close to the fans and the media. Parker was publicity-shy. The fans in his mind were necessary evils, the media more like evils he could do without.

It was Ken Stilley, assistant coach and head scout, who suggested Rhode Island to Parker. The facilities and the practice fields, Stilley volunteered, were first-rate. Parker, convinced, told AJR, "It sounds pretty good. Maybe this is just what we need."

AJR was hesitant. He sent Stilley back for talks with the Rhode Island people and ordered me to go along, too. Stilley had been right about the facilities. They were clearly superior to anything we had seen up to then. Privately, I wondered about the practicality of it all. It would be a logistical nightmare, I thought, to get a jockstrap, much less a blocking sled, to Rhode Island, but the university was eager to have us as tenants and I knew that Buddy Parker's wishes would carry the day in the end.

He wanted greener pastures and he wanted them far away with no one looking over his shoulder. Dan would be there, having rented a house in Kingston, the university town, but AJR's other business interests tied him to Pittsburgh. Parker was free, as he supposed, free at last, and he gradually lost control of the team. More to the point, he lost control of himself .

It happened over the course of two summers, starting with the first week of practice in 1964, when perpetual troublemaker Lou Michaels badly beat up a smaller defensive back, Jim Bradshaw. Parker solved the problem by shipping Michaels off to Baltimore (where a few years later he was kicking field goals and extra points for a Super Bowl team), but the turmoil never really abated. There was the day police came, with questions about a player they identified as a Peeping Tom.

There were flare-ups and fights and disciplinary lapses that did not get into the papers, there was the unpredictable behavior of Parker.

A pre-season game with the San Francisco Forty-Niners was scheduled for a Saturday afternoon at the Brown University stadium in Providence. Long beforehand, Parker announced that the players would then be off until Monday. On Saturday, however, they lost the exhibition game, and he angrily rescinded their furlough. "I want you back tonight for dinner and meetings," he told them after the game. Rushing to a telephone, Fran Fogarty called the Rhode Island people with the news that in just a few hours there would be a football team to feed. Impossible, they said. There wasn't any food in the kitchen and the help had been sent home. There were no cooks, no waiters, no dishwashers.

Parker canceled his meetings and opened a bottle of booze. Only the injured players, then, would report back to camp, he told the squad. As he said this, he looked at John Henry Johnson, who had spent the whole game on the bench, explaining that his leg was sore. Treatment after a game for casualties was standard procedure, and John Henry Johnson by his own account was a casualty.

On the trip from Providence to Kingston, Parker got drunk. He went directly to his office and sent an assistant coach to John Henry Johnson's room. "Tell him I want him to see me right now," Parker said. The assistant coach returned in five minutes. He had knocked at John Henry's door and no one had answered. He had then tried to open the door. It was locked.

"He's hiding in there!" Parker exclaimed. "Go back. Break the lock. Kick the door down." Forcing his way in, the coach found an empty room. John Henry, it appeared, had gone AWOL. No doubt he was in the arms of some golden-hued temptress, all thought of football banished from his mind. Parker abruptly called for a large, rectangular piece of cardboard and a staff member adept at lettering and dictated the following manifesto:

TOO SORE TO FIGHT
BUT NOT TOO SORE TO FORNICATE

"Fornicate" was not the exact word Parker used, but close enough. Continuing to follow orders, the staff member took his artwork to Johnson's door and tacked it up as a sort of greeting. It would be the first thing John Henry saw when he returned from wherever he had wandered. Very quickly, Fran Fogarty learned of these developments and without wasting a minute he got in touch with Pittsburgh by telephone. "The coaches," he said starkly, "are running amuck."

AJR was by no means astonished. He had known for some time that Parker was on the verge of a crack-up. There had been an incident not long before that greatly disturbed AJR. The Steelers had played a pre-season game at Forbes Field, and some of AJR's North Side friends had arranged for a welcome-home dinner at the North Side Elks club, the mansion once occupied by the Arbuckle family, industrial pioneers. Its faded magnificence failed to impress Parker, who remarked in an aside that if this was the best the city could do there was not much hope for the old burg. That did not sit well with AJR, and his coach then rankled him further. On the front porch, as they were leaving, Parker delivered an ultimatum, or what sounded to his boss like one. With characteristic bluntness, he informed AJR, "I came here to work for *you*. I didn't come here to work for Dan."

Well, now. AJR had heard something like that from Doc Sweeney, but with Parker's stooge, Buster Ramsey, as the object of the trainer's disaffection. Whatever answer he gave to Parker carried no warning. But In the Roosevelt Hotel the next day a meeting took place, attended by AJR's sons and his front-office staff. His sons were full-grown now and eager to make themselves heard. At the dinner table after Steeler defeats we'd been trying to raise our voices for years. We would criticize the players, criticize the coaches, and criticize AJR. Shutting us up, he would bark, "That 's enough! There will be no talk of football at our table when we lose!" Soon afterward it became: "There will be no talk of football during the season." Then finally: "There will be no talk of football in this house unless I bring up the subject myself." The turn-around may have begun when all of us lobbied for Johnny Unitas, and AJR listened to Kiesling. The success of Unitas with the Colts was our wedge. From that time on, we had freedom of speech. When we sounded off, there were no more reprimands, as long as we did not overdo it. And Dan, the heir apparent, assumed a title also held by Jack McGinley — vice president. He was making decisions, preparing to take over the reins.

As for AJR, he appeared to be phasing himself out. At the meeting in his office he did a curious thing. In effect, he deputized the whole staff. As we all knew, he told us, every game the Steelers lost provoked a crisis. Parker, despondent, would offer to resign. AJR would talk him into changing his mind. Never again. The next time Buddy resigned, said AJR, it would be for keeps. If he resigned in the hearing of Fogarty, Ed Kiely, Dan, myself, or Jack McGinley, we were authorized to take him up on it. Our instructions were to say that his resignation was accepted.

The idea frightened me. I was 29 years old but everybody's junior, it seemed. Tell Buddy Parker good riddance? Somehow I couldn't see myself doing it. I'd have to run to a telephone and call AJR. But there was never the need. Routinely, the Steelers lost another exhibition game. Once again in the usual way Parker said he was quitting. Only this time he said it to Dan, not to the Chief. And this time, he picked the wrong guy.

Coming of Age

Dan's wife, Patricia Regan, was the older sister of Mary Regan, who succeeded her as Dad's secretary. Mary and Patricia were first-generation Irish girls from St. Peter's parish. Both had red hair. So did their sister Gerri, the Steelers' ticket manager after the death of Joe Carr.

Patricia and Dan had met in grade school at St. Peter's. A pretty fair quarterback despite his lack of size, Dan played football as a freshman at Duquesne, but in his sophomore year the university abandoned the sport. At North Catholic High School, Dan was a good student but not at the top of his class. At Duquesne, where he majored in accounting, his grades were never below A. Being married and the head of a family had changed Dan's priorities.

So obsessed was he with football that he coached the St. Peter's grade-school team just to keep his hand in. The players were dirt-poor North Side kids who loved the game with a passion and showed up for practice rain or shine. But his real career was in the administrative side of football, and it would take him all the way to the Hall of Fame.

Boots

A sidelight: Buddy Parker was the only coach in the NFL who had his own personal valet, or body servant. The go-fer was "Boots" Lewis, a medium-sized, old-looking, gray-colored black man who had evidently once been a shoe-shine boy. They had first met each other when Parker played football at Centenary College and Boots was a campus maintenance man.

It seems that he was also one hell of a craps shooter, which apparently struck a chord with Parker. They were together from the time that Parker got into coaching. The only real work that Boots ever did was to fetch and run for his boss — or, more accurately, fetch and walk. Boots had arthritis and always gave the impression of being tired.

Their partnership was an odd one if you took into account Parker's typically Southern racial views. In a way it harked back to the ante-bellum plantation days, with Boots as Old Black Joe and Parker in the role of benevolent white massa.

At training camp and on the practice field, Boots was a tolerated fixture. The football players, white and black, teased but did not torment him. To an onlooker, their bantering seemed affectionate, although Boots, no dummy, would not have agreed. The white players, he told Parker, didn't want him around and the black players accused him of being a spy. "I'm a man without a country," he said.

He accepted jocular remarks with good grace, but would let the players know, when they pushed him, that he was Buddy Parker's man, first and always. One year when the Steelers trained at Slippery Rock, in northwest Pennsylvania, Boots felt uncomfortable because the environment, he complained, was "too woodsy." On an early-morning errand for Parker, he imagined he heard a bear thrashing around, and Parker picked up on this. Finding a costume supplier somewhere, he rented a bear suit. One of the training-camp functionaries put on the disguise and made a juvenile attempt to frighten Boots. The joke fell flat when Boots refused to play the fool and pretend to be taken in.

At the time of Parker's resignation, Boots had a stroke and a heart attack. AJR paid the hospital and medical bills. Boots had some money put away and wanted AJR to be its custodian, for he trusted no one else. From his hospital bed, he would ask in agitation, "Where's mah munnah?" Reassured that "Mister Rooney" was holding it for him, he would settle down. When he was ambulatory again, AJR offered to keep him on the payroll for life. Showing more class than some of Parker's coaches, he said, "I worked for Buddy. When he goes, I go."

Friends in the scouting business would tell me years later that Boots was shining shoes in the Los Angeles International Airport. Many times when I flew in there I looked around but could never find him.

Logical Choice

Only two weeks were left before the start of the season when the Steelers parted company with Parker, so AJR could not afford to dilly-dally. The logical choice to replace Buddy as head coach was Mike Nixon, who had been on the staff, except for a brief hiatus, since the Jock Sutherland era.

Mike was AJR's man, not Parker's. As a stubby little halfback called Mike Nicksick, he had played for Sutherland at Pitt, for the Steelers when the Steelers were the Pirates, and during World War II for the Brooklyn Dodgers, the NFL team Sutherland no longer coached, having wangled a Navy commission. When Sutherland took over the Steelers, Mike returned also, as one of his assistants, and after Sutherland's death he stayed on, leaving in 1959 to become head coach of the Redskins. Two seasons later — unsuccessful seasons for Mike and the Redskins — he was out of work, and AJR obligingly brought him back to Pittsburgh. Somewhere along the way, probably out of deference to Sutherland, he had Anglicized his name. Sutherland liked to have ethnic Slavs and Italians on his football teams but wanted the public to think they were WASPs.

Parker's resignation, if that is the right word, took place on a Sunday morning. Notified by Dan in a telephone call, AJR told me to pack an overnight bag. We were leaving right away for Rhode Island, he said, and we were going to fly. En route, he bounced ideas off me, reviewing his options, running over in his mind the deal he intended to offer Nixon.

Simply put, it was this: the head coaching job is yours for the asking, but I strongly advise you to turn it down. If Mike accepted that advice, there would still be a vacancy to fill, though not for long, AJR was quite certain. Everybody he knew would have a candidate. In the Pittsburgh airport we had happened to meet an old friend, Bishop Vincent Leonard, and he suggested one. "Don't forget Ernie Hefferle," the bishop said. Ernie Hefferle had been an end at Duquesne (he caught the winning touchdown pass when Buff Donelli took the Dukes to the Orange Bowl), an assistant coach at Pitt, and an unsuccessful head coach at Boston College. He was just the man, Bishop Leonard seemed to think, who could clean up the mess Buddy Parker had left.

The good prelate was unaware of what AJR proposed to do. Whoever succeeded Parker would in all likelihood be nothing more than an interim coach. Once the 1965 season was over, AJR expected to make a complete overhaul — to "get the broom out," in Uncle Jim's borrowed metaphor, "and sweep the joint clean."

I was present when he talked to Mike Nixon. "I'm going to offer you this job," AJR said, "but I don't think you should take it. The situation is such that I don't think it can be turned around in one year. In that case I'd have to let you go. If you've been the head coach I don't feel I could keep you on with the new head coach. But if you tell me you don't want this job, I can pretty well promise that you will be with the Steelers for the rest of your working days."

Nixon listened impatiently. He had made his decision and could not be talked out of it. "Look, I'm from Pittsburgh, " he said in a placating voice. "To be head coach of the Steelers is something I've always dreamed of. I just can't bring myself to pass up an opportunity like this." Much more was said on both sides, but only to work out details. I remembered something Jack Sell, the *Pittsburgh Post-Gazette* sportswriter, once told me: "All football coaches are crazy."

Buddy Parker had lost the team, and it was impossible for Nixon to find it. With young Bill Nelsen at quarterback, the Steelers had a miserable season, winning only two games. John Henry Johnson was hurt most of the year and carried the ball just three times. Out came the broom, sweeping Nixon away with all the deadwood.

He coached for many more years in the NFL, but always as an assistant and never again in Pittsburgh. At the end of his career, when he was in player personnel, I would see him on scouting trips, a man with no regrets – or should I say with none that he confided to me?

Bargain Hunting

Rival football leagues had been competing for talent with the NFL as far back as AJR could remember. Always, he had managed to hold his own, but in the 1960s he was up against owners like Lamar Hunt, who was making a lot of money in the oil business and spending big sums on his AFL team, the Dallas Texans. Told that Lamar had squandered ten million dollars on the Texans, his brother Bunker drawled, "Gee, what a shame. Now he's only got a hunnerd and sixty-four million left."

There were other rich owners besides Lamar in the AFL. The Steelers traded Buddy Dial to the Dallas Cowboys for the draft rights to Scott Appleton and then couldn't sign him. They were outbid by the Houston Oilers. Our top draft choice in 1966 would have been Francis Peay, an offensive tackle from Missouri. If we selected him, he told us, he would play in "the other league." So the New York Giants, an NFL team with deeper pockets than ours, drafted Peay. We thought we still had a chance to sign Tom Mack, an offensive tackle from Michigan whose father was on the police force in Cleveland. On the telephone, he agreed to sign for the money we could offer. It would be an honor to play for the Steelers, he assured us. Alas, the team drafting just before we did took Mack. He remained with that team, the Los Angeles Rams, for thirteen years, earning himself a niche in the Hall of Fame

After Peay and Mack got away from us, AJR said, "Let's pick a guy we can sign." As it happened a guy we could sign was within arm's reach at the moment. His name was Dick Leftridge and he had dropped in to mingle with the pathologically curious draft-day crowd that assembled in our offices at the Roosevelt Hotel every year. Actually, the NFL had put Dick up at that hotel to hide him from the AFL. An underachieving fullback for West Virginia, he was big and easy-going and when he opened his mouth to laugh he displayed a shiny gold tooth. We knew of his reputation for irresponsibility and laziness, but we were desperate. And he did have the makings of a football player, if only some coach could get him to show a little interest.

Well, sure, he'd sign with the Steelers, he said, which was all we needed to hear. Bowing to the dictum that beggars can't be choosers, we went ahead and drafted him. "Steelers Go Shopping in the Bargain Basement" was the headline the next day in one of the newspapers. We couldn't dispute it.

Dick Leftridge played one season — not very well — and was never heard from again.

When it seemed that the NFL was losing the war for talent, Commissioner Pete Rozelle came up with a battle plan. Just before draft time in 1966, the league had hired "handholders." Each handholder or pair of handholders was assigned to a prospect, such as Leftridge. They were not to let him out of their sight. Kidnappers lure children with promises of candy and toys. The handholders lured football players with promises of lavish entertainment. Keep the player busy, show him a good time, and stash him away in a hotel room if necessary. He must not be allowed to see anybody or talk to anybody. Fence him off completely from the AFL's coaches and scouts.

Sometimes it worked and sometimes it didn't. While Jack Butler and I had one player on the telephone, an AFL representative was signing him to a contract. We took another kid to one of our games. He was not impressed with the team and he was not impressed with Pitt Stadium. Prudently, no doubt, we kept him away from the Roosevelt Hotel and our practice facilities at South Park. He signed with an NFL team other than the Steelers.

One of Butler's future Blesto scouts, Jerry Neri, was handholding a huge black lineman from Los Angeles State in a hotel room. The kind of portly Italian who looks and acts like a moody old man before he is out of his thirties, Neri had been a player and coach but never a handholder. Rooming for three nights with a Nubian behemoth, he said, was more than he had bargained for. Very quickly, they ran out of things to talk about, so from then on they watched television, listened to the radio, read the newspapers. Or Neri did. What the player did, mostly, was eat. Neri ordered freely from room service — gigantic breakfasts, double hamburgers for lunch, hot fudge sundaes for snacks, the biggest steak in the kitchen for dinner. In the end the player signed with the NFL. The downside was that he lasted only one season.

Combined, the two leagues spent seven million dollars in signing bonuses that year, a lot of money at the time. This, more than anything else, was responsible for the merger that took effect in 1970. Under its terms, the NFL would absorb the AFL. There would be two conferences in the league

— a National Football Conference, made up of teams from the NFL, and an American Football Conference, made up, for the most part, of teams from the AFL. To achieve balance, three NFL teams would have to be switched to this presumably inferior hybrid conference. Making it easier for them to swallow, the commissioner and the owners agreed on a "compensation fee" of three million dollars apiece.

Tempting, thought AJR. He asked some questions. If the Steelers and the Browns, traditional rivals by now, were willing to make the change (he was promised), they would be placed in the same division and continue to play each other every year. That assurance, plus the three million dollars, was incentive enough for both AJR and the Cleveland owner, Art Modell. When the two leagues became one, Pittsburgh, Cleveland, and Baltimore moved to the AFC.

One Steeler fan who found it hard to accept the new arrangement was Kass. "It's like a death in the family," she lamented. "Don't be foolish," responded AJR. "We've got three million bucks. We'll still be playing the Browns. And in five years no one will even remember the American Football League. It will all be the *National* Football League."

He was absolutely correct.

Chapter 33

Superman

One of Buddy Parker's more irrational moves in his last full year with the Steelers was the firing of Ernie Stautner as defensive line coach. In 1964, Stautner had worked very hard with the unschooled rookies and fading veterans at his disposal, but the Steelers lost nine games, and in 1965 he was gone.

Nineteen sixty-four was his first year as a coach after fourteen as an all-pro defensive tackle and future Hall of Famer. On the first day of pre-season practice, he gathered the Steelers' defensive linemen around him in a semi-circle and explained some of the fine points of line play.

"We hit with these," he said, thrusting out a huge pair of forearms. "That's where you get your power. Not from your legs or your belly or your head. If they'd let me use my elbows, I'd put on the boxing gloves with anybody."

The Steeler linemen, listening silently, accepted these last words at face value.

"The major thing about Pittsburgh Steeler football," Stautner went on, "is that we've always had the smallest line in the league. We'll be small this year, too, but we intend to be rough and tough. Everybody in the past has hated to play us, and it's still going to be the same way. There'll be times out there, especially for you rookies, when you'll forget all the things you ever learned, but remember this: with the snap of the ball, move. Move and be rough."

The fact that Stautner could stand in front of people like John Baker (6-6 and 270), Chuck Hinton (6-5 and 260) and Ben McGee (6-4 and 255), urging them to compensate for their lack of size by being rough, told a volume about the course of evolution, for when Stautner was a rookie in 1950 he reported to camp weighing 213. Although short for a tackle at 6 feet 1, normally in those days he weighed 220. What accounted for the seven-pound difference was that he and his brother-in-law, with one ax and one saw, had cut down a forest around Saranac Lake, New York, that summer and replaced it with a drive-in theater. There were few better ways back then to achieve a firm silhouette.

Even in that remote age, Stautner was not considered a full-grown tackle. He had gone to Notre Dame as a 219-pound freshman, and Frank Leahy had cut him from the squad. "You're too small and too slow," Leahy told him.

Without adding an ounce of weight or subtracting a tenth of a second from his time for the forty-yard dash, Stautner played four years at Boston College for Denny Myers, every minute of every game on both offense and defense unless he was hurt. John Michelosen, then the Steelers' head coach, drafted him in the second round.

All through the 1950s and into the sixties, he practiced what he preached about roughness and aggressiveness. Quarterbacks and their blockers thought they were being charged by a rhino.

When Stautner retired as a player — the truth was that Parker retired him — he claimed to be 38. Ed Kiely, the Steelers' publicity man, guessed that he was fudging by several years. Born in Bavaria, he had come to this country at the age *of* four with his parents, who were fleeing hard times. In the Germany of the 1920s, ruinous inflation had paralyzed the economy. By the time Stautner was 17, America was at war with Germany and Stautner was a U.S. Marine fighting against the Japs in the Pacific.

Coming into the NFL, he was all muscle and bone. He played with tremendous leverage and quickness. He was as quick off the line of scrimmage, in fact, as anyone who ever played the game. His first pop could devastate a blocker, and he rang the bell of so many opposing linemen with his slap to the head that the NFL ultimately outlawed that move. When he tackled, he tackled for keeps, hitting through the ball carrier and almost never losing his hold on the guy.

Stautner's habit of showing up late at training camp was annoying to his coaches and teammates. One year when he arrived a rookie named Ernie Cheatham had taken his place in the line. Both were ex-Marines. Both were from Jesuit colleges — in Cheatham's case Loyola of Los Angeles. Cheatham was much bigger than Stautner and seemed to be every bit as strong. Anticipation built up. Would this big, powerful West Coast kid teach Stautner a lesson when he finally straggled in from Saranac Lake?

The day of the showdown came, and Stautner looked lean and mean, not bulky and slow, as expected. He lined up opposite Cheatham in a scrimmage. Cheatham's foot was shaking the way my leg did when I recited Shakespeare at Carnegie Tech. The first time the ball was snapped, Stautner completely wiped him out. Cheatham played high, allowing Stautner to get leverage and upend him. The next few times it was more of the same. Stautner was still king of the hill. Before the season ended the Steelers had let Cheatham go. Baltimore then gave him a chance, but he quickly moved on into football oblivion. Cheatham rejoined the USMC and retired as a general.

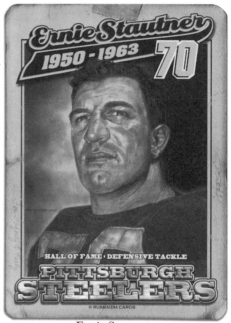

Ernie Stautner
(Drawing by Denny Karchner)

Another ex-Marine who came to the Steelers as a rookie years later decided that the best way to make his reputation was to pick out the toughest veteran on the team and challenge him to a fist fight. He saw himself winning the fight impressively and reigning from then on as the team's undisputed alpha male. As logic dictated, the kid chose Stautner to be his stepping stone. At a post-game party in the Roosevelt Hotel — Buddy Parker had a theory that post-game parties during the exhibition season created team harmony, with lasting results — he offered to take Stautner on. Both were well-oiled. Stautner at first could not believe the guy was serious. Realizing, finally, that nothing else would do, he followed him downstairs and into the alley between the Roosevelt Hotel's trash dump and the emergency exits of the Harris Theater. Those who saw the fight said it was evenly matched and vicious. The kid turned out to be a handful for Stautner. They kicked, they kneed, they head-butted, they rabbit-punched. They kept at it for thirty minutes or more, with the outcome in doubt until Stautner picked up a big metal garbage can — the whole can, not just the lid — and used it to beat the kid senseless.

Management, of course, meaning Parker and AJR, found out what had happened and who the instigator was and lost no time in sending the youthful tough guy on his way.

Implausibly, Stautner had a taste for the finer things in life. He aspired to play the piano. He took lessons one year, borrowed an old Steinway, and moved it all by himself into an unused office at the training camp. During lunch hour, when his teammates were trying to nap, he would practice. The man's fingers, misshapen from all the head slaps he had delivered, were less than ideal for making music, but he got to the point where he could pound out a current favorite or two. After pre-season games, he would play at the parties, with everybody present clustered around the piano for sing-alongs. Fran Fogarty's voice, trained in operettas at Duquesne University, rose above all the rest.

If the Steelers had a leader, it was Stautner, and then in 1958 Bobby Layne joined the team. Here were two living legends brought together. How would it work out? Was there room enough on one team for two such dominant personalities? The answer, as it happened, was soon apparent. Almost from the first day, Stautner subordinated himself to Layne, becoming his sidekick and bodyguard. Some people thought that under Layne's too powerful influence Stautner went over to the wild side.

In all of his years with the Steelers, there would never be a championship for Stautner. When Buddy Parker dropped him from the coaching staff, he immediately caught on with the Redskins. He remained at his next stop, Dallas, for almost a quarter of a century, a valued assistant to Tom Landry and to several of Landry's successors. After his NFL career was over, he returned to Germany, his native soil, as the head coach of a so-called spinoff team. He still spoke the language and he looked like an aging Superman. So the Germans idolized him. And why not? At last they had found a Superman who had won most of his wars.

McPeak

It was heavy weather for Steeler coaches in the 1950s as John Michelosen made way for Joe Bach and Bach made way for Walt Kiesling and Kiesling made way for Buddy Parker. Stability, such as it was, came from a small nucleus of veteran players, Elbie Nickel, Jack Butler, Ernie Stautner, and Bill McPeak among them.

McPeak, along with Stautner, anchored the defensive line. He played end, as he had at Pitt, and the coach who drafted him, John Michelosen, was a Pitt man, too. McPeak had something in common with Billy Conn. They were tough-as-nails Irishmen who misled people by looking like pretty boys.

Off the field, McPeak was a ladies' man. He liked a good time. In pads and a helmet, he attended strictly to business. He could make life miserable for blockers and quarterbacks and ball carriers. Nothing, in fact, gave him more pleasure, and if the inclination seized him he could make life miserable for a teammate.

Bill Krisher, an All-American guard on Bud Wilkinson's great Oklahoma teams, was a rookie with the Steelers in 1958. McPeak by then was past 30, a little overweight, a little slow, but hoping to play one more year and make it an even ten in the NFL. Buddy Parker, the head coach, considered that a dubious proposition. There was an opening for McPeak on the coaching staff, he said. Still a warrior at heart, McPeak dragged his feet, so Parker compromised. "For the time being," he told the old fire horse when training camp opened, "we'll call you a player-coach."

McPeak went along with the fiction that his title actually meant what it said, but perhaps he knew otherwise He may have therefore needed an outlet for the frustration he probably felt. At any rate, he took an immediate dislike to the inoffensive Krisher. Big and blond, as handsome as McPeak, Krisher was a nice enough guy. He was also a leader of the Christian Athlete movement on the team, and this, more than anything else, settled his hash with McPeak. The Christian Athletes were high-minded fellows intent on setting a good example for sinners. They met for prayer and meditation and were ready at all times to profess their faith in the Lord. McPeak, an acknowledged sinner, disdained them as pious frauds. From the first day of practice he took a special interest in Krisher. College All-American though he was, Krisher had run-of-the-mine ability. For someone like that to excel as a pro would require extra effort. I did not believe Krisher wasn't trying, but neither did I think he was going all-out. It may be that the adulation he received at Oklahoma had made him complacent. Or possibly football never was all that important to him.

So McPeak became his personal motivator. Krisher, he decided, would need some hands-on attention. I watched them one day when he lined up opposite Krisher for a one-on-one hitting drill, and the instruction he dished out was brutal. McPeak understood leverage and he knew all the tricks of the trade. In their first collision, he knocked Krisher's helmet off and bloodied his face. Krisher was ready for Doc Sweeney's ministrations, but McPeak said, "Let's do it again. I want you to work a little more on your blocking technique." Krisher put on his helmet and they did it again. And again. And again.

When Parker told McPeak to forget about playing and made him a full-time coach, which meant that he would have to turn in his pads, there was nobody happier than Krisher. He lasted out the season and then was gone, resurfacing two years later with the Dallas Texans in the AFL. By 1962 he was through with football entirely.

McPeak, after just three years as an assistant in Pittsburgh and then Washington, became the Redskins' head coach in 1961. The ex-Steeler and Pitt man he succeeded, Mike Nixon, left him with nothing much to build on, and five straight losing seasons brought his career to a turning point. He went into scouting and did a good job for the New England Patriots. When he retired, he was only 62. Three or four days later, with cruel and astonishing swiftness, he died of a stroke.

Return to Latrobe

As far back as the Depression years of the late 1930s, AJR made up his mind that St. Vincent College in Latrobe was the ideal site for his football team's pre-season training camp — ideal, that is, in all but one respect. The facilities were inadequate.

St. Vincent had two dormitories, but the Benedictine monks sponsored a retreat every August attended by large numbers of men from everywhere in Western Pennsylvania. Among those who never passed up this chance for spiritual enrichment was AJR. Since the retreat filled both dormitories, leaving no room on the campus for the football players, his solution was to practice at St. Vincent but to quarter the team at the Mountain View Inn, ten minutes west of the college on Route 30.

The Mountain View Inn looked out on the Chestnut Ridge of the Alleghenies in a setting of great natural beauty. On a clear summer day you felt that by extending your hand you could touch the sides of the ridge. But in rain and mist or even overcast the hills always seemed to be miles away. How much the players appreciated this, or what the coaches thought, I don't know. It may be that the coaches would have preferred a more Spartan-like atmosphere. Vacation resorts contrast oddly with the rigors of pre-season football practice.

The monks at St. Vincent, putting first things first, considered the football team a distraction while the retreat was going on. Accordingly, after one or two years, the Steelers began looking for other practice sites. They became nomads, moving from place to place. AJR, meanwhile, never lost hope of returning to St. Vincent.

At last the opportunity carne. In the 1960s the Benedictines built two new dormitories, and now there was room, with adequate separation, for both the football players and the retreatants. There was a new recreation center, a new gymnasium, and a weight room. There were new classrooms, new training and dressing facilities. St. Vincent had dropped football, and the stadium I once played in was torn down and replaced with science buildings. But there were two practice fields now instead of one.

St. Vincent's maintenance director, a Father Connell, worked out the logistics of our move with Fran Fogarty. I heard that the athletic director, my old phys ed teacher Dodo Canterna, gave me credit for selling the idea to Fogarty and AJR. The truth is that no selling was necessary. They both thought St. Vincent suited us to a T and they were right. We moved back there as soon as Buddy Parker was gone.

The Hypocycloid

From time to time people ask about the Steeler emblem that appears on the right-hand side of our helmets. It's a hypocycloid, defined in one of the dictionaries as a "curve traced by a point on the circumference of a circle rolling internally on the circumference of a fixed circle."

Do you get the picture? No? Let me try again. The Steeler hypocycloid — not a true one, perhaps — is a circle with a rim the color of gun metal and nothing on its circumference "rolling internally". The rim the color of gun metal encloses three diamonds against a white background. There's a yellow diamond at the top of the circle, an orange diamond on the right-hand side, and a blue diamond directly below the yellow diamond. That leaves a space on the left-hand side, which is filled with the word "Steelers" lettered in black.

Except for the lettering, this was the logo developed for the American steel industry. The diamonds represent ingredients of steel — yellow for coal, orange for iron ore, and blue for scrap metal. You say that coal isn't yellow, iron ore isn't orange, and scrap metal isn't blue? I'm only telling you what I myself have been told.

In 1962 Republic Steel of Cleveland took credit for suggesting this insignia to us. My own recollection is different. As I always heard it, the logo was John Reger's idea. Reger was a local kid, a linebacker from Pitt who made the team as a walk-on with only one year of college experience. By 1955, his first season, decorations had begun to appear on the helmets of other NFL teams — the Rams had their horns (very Hollywood), the Redskins their war bonnets, the Eagles their wings, and so on — and Reger proposed that we adopt and adapt the American Iron and Steel Institute's logo. The word to the left of the diamonds on that one was "Steel." Getting the AISI's permission to use the logo in the first place and to modify it in the second place took time. There was opposition to overcome and red tape to untangle. Nobody then foresaw the media exposure those Steeler helmets would bring to the AISI.

On the gold helmets the team had worn up to 1955 the logo did not stand out. Therefore, the color of the helmets was changed to black. Along with "What the heck is it supposed to be?" there's another question we get about the logo: "Why is it worn on only one side?"

Every other NFL team wears its logo on both sides. The answer is that Jack Hart, the Steeler equipment manager in the 1950s, was attempting to cut his work load. Hart had the job of attaching the logos — pasting them on — and of re-attaching them when they were knocked off during a game. Using one instead of two was a labor-saving device.

Chapter 34

Mama's Boy

After old Dan Rooney — Pop — passed on, Uncle Jim continued to live with his mother on Perrysville Avenue. One morning as he sat in his favorite parlor armchair, reading the *Post-Gazette* and smoking an after-breakfast cigar, she asked if he would please come to the kitchen and kill a fly. "It's a big one," she said. "It's driving me crazy."

Without looking up from the paper, Jim took a puff at his cigar. "Okay," he grunted. "In a minute."

A minute went by. Then another. And another.

Grandma Rooney reappeared in the parlor. "Jim! Are you coming?"

Jim was still absorbed in his newspaper. "In a minute." The minute turned into five. ..ten ... fifteen. Grandma Rooney called out from the kitchen, "Jim! Are you ever going to kill this fly?"

Jim stood up, tossed the paper aside, and placed the stub of his cigar in an ash tray. He took a step toward the front door. "I'll kill it tonight," he said, leaving the house.

Grandma Rooney lived to be 88. She died of a sudden heart attack, and Jim took it hard. He was now all alone, and he knew it. Teary-eyed, he said to me, "You can be a real tough guy, but when you lose your Mom ..." He stopped and looked away. Then he said it again: "You can be a real tough guy, but when you lose your Mom ... "

Leaving Perrysville Avenue, he moved to the Roosevelt Hotel, where the football team had its offices. By this time he was drinking heavily. On many a night some friend or acquaintance, with the help of a bellboy, would get him into the lobby and up to his room.

He returned once from McKees Rocks — don't ask what he was doing in McKees Rocks — by taxicab. Rummaging through his pockets to find money for the fare, he discovered that he had spent his last cent, or, more likely, given it away.

"See Arthur," he said to the driver

"Arthur" in some way learned about this – perhaps from the night clerk at the hotel, perhaps even from Jim. In some way he found out who the cab driver was and got in touch with him. "How much do I owe you?" he asked. "Look, Art," said the cabbie, "I've been driving Jim around Pittsburgh for years. When Jim had money, he always took real good care of me. So this one is on the house." As repeated over and over by AJR, the story became a part of Jim's legend.

Al Quaill, a cop who had been a pretty good middleweight boxer, described how Jim drank. "He drinks to get drunk," Al told me. "He doesn't enjoy drinking and he doesn't enjoy socializing when he drinks. He just drinks the stuff as fast as he can, for the effect."

That was also my own impression. I never saw Jim feeling euphoric when he drank. If he wasn't stone sober, he was either stupefied or delirious. Earlier in these memoirs, I wrote of a night on the road when he and I roomed together. I remember his screams that night. He'd cry out, "Ma-ma!" Then he'd mumble the Hail Mary. Then he'd be quiet for a spell, and I'd start to fall asleep, and suddenly there would be another shrill scream. My night with Uncle Jim sold me on the evils of booze.

In his cups he would borrow money from people. "Can you let me have five until I see Arthur?" "Can you let me have ten until I get a check cashed?" I don't think these loans were ever repaid. He hit me up only once or twice, but I was present many times when Jim put the arm on somebody else.

To him, asking people for money was like asking for a match, or asking what time it was. He put no value on money or on any other material possession. Everyone on the 1929 Pitt Rose Bowl team received a commemorative pin — something to remind him for the rest of his life that he had played in this important college football game. Getting off the train at Penn Station after the trip back home from Pasadena, Jim handed his pin to a girl he knew — not a special girl, just a student who was there to welcome the players.

I have said that I never saw Jim when liquor made him euphoric. I must now tell a story contradicting that statement.

The Roosevelt Hotel was where the Curbstone Coaches held their weekly football luncheon, a tedious affair at which the speakers always talked too long. The Steelers had a table in the back of the room, filled every Monday with front-office people who had to be at the luncheon or answer to AJR. One week Uncle Jim sat with us. He was wearing a dark suit and a necktie and looking his best. It took me a few minutes to see that he had a buzz on. Alex DiCroce, the hotel's banquet manager, came to our table with a guest — Guy Lombardo, the orchestra leader. They were friends of long standing. Alex, in fact, had worked in some capacity for Lombardo. Proudly, he introduced the musician to each of us, identifying Jim as AJR's brother and "a fine football player" for Jock Sutherland at Pitt. Lombardo was an ardent sports fan, according to Alex, and he appeared to be impressed.

"Jim," Alex said, "you know who Mr. Lombardo is. The big band leader. He has the New Year's Eve show from Times Square in New York every year." Lombardo's credentials meant nothing to Jim, who had not been sober on New Year's Eve since the night (or day) he lifted his first shot glass. In any case he was only half listening. Out of the corner of his eye, he was measuring the distance from our table to the door. His plan was to make an unnoticed getaway and hobble across Sixth Street to one of two or three bars he patronized.

But now he was being asked to acknowledge an introduction. "Coach Lombardi," he said after a pause, "it's an honor and a pleasure to meet you. You've been doing a great job with the Packers."

DiCroce and Lombardo were speechless. Finding his voice, Lombardo said, "No, Jim, I'm Guy Lombardo, not Vince Lombardi — the band leader, not the football coach."

Jim seemed oblivious to this distinction. He was still sizing up his escape route. Lombardo sat down, at a place near Jim, and everybody started to eat. Jim broke off a piece of his hard roll. Turning to Lombardo, he said, "Coach, I like the way you're using Paul Hornung. He's a triple threat. He can run, pass, and kick, and you're taking advantage of all these things." The rest of us, embarrassed, concentrated on our food. Lombardo forced a smile. "Jim," he repeated, "I'm the music man."

We tried to muffle our laughter. By this time Jim was into his soup. Looking up, he addressed Lombardo again as "Coach." We were laughing openly. Lombardo was laughing too. There were stares from the other tables.

His words drowned out, Jim had no more to say. He lurched to his feet and started toward the door. Passing Lombardo's chair, he said, "Coach, it was nice to meet you. Keep up the good work in Green Bay."

We watched him until he limped out of sight, and then we waited to hear from Lombardo. Not knowing Jim, what would he think? That he had somehow been played for a sap? That we'd been making him the butt of a practical joke? Not at all. He was flattered, he said, as soon as he could stop laughing, to be mistaken for the concert master of a championship football team — his *paisano*, the great Vince Lombardi.

Saying Goodbye to Pop

Some time after the fact I learned that the cause of Pop Rooney's death was prostate cancer. The adjective "prostate" had been omitted in all of the talk I had heard up to then — another example of the Rooney family's prudishness.

AJR, for one, never put a name to a private body part or to a bodily or sexual function. Instead, he employed euphemisms. I recall an incident when a daughter-in-law (not Kay) offended him by wearing hot pants (extremely tight, abbreviated shorts). "If you prance around like that," he told her, "you're going to get grabbed." By "grabbed" he meant raped. "And I'll be a character witness for the guy who does it," he added.

In the beginning, Pop Rooney's sick room was his upstairs bedroom in the old brick house on tree-lined Perrysville Avenue. The house was built on a terrace, and I never understood how Pop or, for that matter, Uncle Jim made the climb up the steps from the street to the big front porch. Perrysville Avenue had deteriorated a little, but Pop and Maggie were not pretentious people, a trait their son Arthur inherited. One of Pop's nieces, Helen O'Keefe, lived in Mount Lebanon and regarded the North Side as a slum area. "Well, they could certainly afford to live where they want to," she said of her uncle and aunt, "but they do have their ways, you know." Pop and Maggie, for their part, thought that Helen O'Keefe was someone who put on airs.

For a number of years before his death, Pop had suffered from what we now call depression. He had lost his youngest son — Tom — in the war. His son John had died in early middle age of alcoholism, and his son Jim had a drinking problem. Like Jim, Pop had a gimpy leg, the result of a fall. His brewery business had failed and he was too old for any other kind of work — too old and too infirm. All of these things had combined to make him "nervous," Maggie and the daughters, Margaret and Marie, would say. No one ever used the word "depression" back then. Not many people knew what it was.

Pop's grandsons were well aware that he was dying. Every few days we would troop into his bedroom — sent there, perhaps, to remind him that the bloodline would continue. This was old Irish stuff, I believe. Illness or maybe the pain killers he took had reinforced his natural cynicism. Walt Kiesling was still the coach of the Steelers, and Pop said to me one day, "That fella" - he had never been an admirer of Kiesling — "that fella should be tending bar in Milwaukee. And if it weren't for Arthur he *would* be!" Told that Luby DiMeolo had been made a United States marshal for Western Pennsylvania, he sputtered, "Luby? Why, if Luby can be a federal marshal, Jim could be a U.S. senator."

When they moved Pop to Mercy Hospital, all of us gave blood. We gave blood again and again, and afterward we would stop in his room to say, "Hello, Pop," and make a quick exit. In his bedroom at home we had lingered. Now it was best to get in and get out.

One day I noticed Margaret or Marie pouring him a stiff drink of whiskey. AJR was there. Driving us home, he said, "Boys, your grandfather was not a drinker. He was in the whiskey business and sold the stuff — but he never drank it. He'd take a sample out of the barrel and rub it on his hands. Men like your grandfather could tell the quality of whiskey from the aroma. If a customer offered to buy him a drink when he was tending bar, he would say, 'No, but let me pour you a drink." He'd give the man a free one to keep from having to take one himself."

And so Pop left his family and Pittsburgh. He died at Mercy Hospital, where many years later his son Arthur would die. It was a place where Rooneys came into the world and a place where they said goodbye.

Dan/Maggie Family Portrait – First Generation of the Rooneys
Top Row: Jim, Marie, Pop, Maggie, Father Dan (Silas) O.F.M
Bottom Row: Art Rooney, John (Red), Vince (Duke), Margaret
(Courtesy of Vince/Kathy Rooney Collection)

Second Generation of the Rooneys

Top row: Art Rooney, Bottom row: Art, Jr., Pat, Mom, John, Tim, Dan

(Dan Rooney Collection)

Rooney McGinley Military
Left to Right: Barney McGinley, Jack McGinley (US Navy),
Tom Rooney (USMC), Art Rooney
(*Jack McGinley Collection*)

Tom's grave
on Guam.
(*Courtesy of Carl
Wincalowicz*)

Father Dan (Silas) in field in France

(Vince/Jamie Rooney Collection)

Rev. Silas Daniel Rooney,
O.F.M.
(Jack McGinley Collection)

REV. SILAS DANIEL ROONEY, O.F.M.
Chaplain, United States Army

MAY 26, 1942

Dan, Art, Jr., AJR, Pat, John and Tim at Yonkers Raceway.
(Tim Rooney Collection)

AJR and Kass cir. 1975 at Yonkers Raceway
(*Tim Rooney Collection*)

Kay and Art Rooney, Jr. July 1, 1961, St. Paul Cathedral
(*Kay Rooney Collection*)

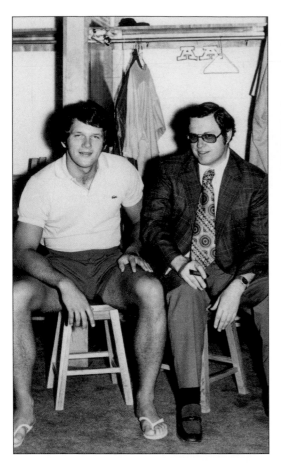

Upper left: Jack Ham
and Art Rooney, Jr.

Upper right: Art
Rooney, Jr., and
Jack Butler

Right: Art Rooney, Jr.,
and Sidney Thorton

(Steelers Collection)

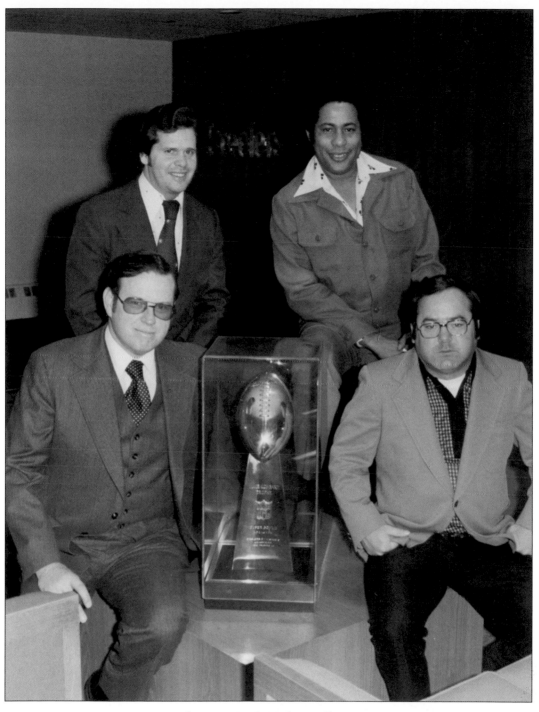

Back Row: Dick Haley, Bill Nunn
Front Row: Art, Jr., V. Tim Rooney
(*Steelers Collection*)

1986 St. Vincent Training Camp
(Left to Right): Dick Haley, Joe Krupa, Bob Schmitz, Art, Jr., Bill Nunn, Tom Modrak
(Steelers Collection)

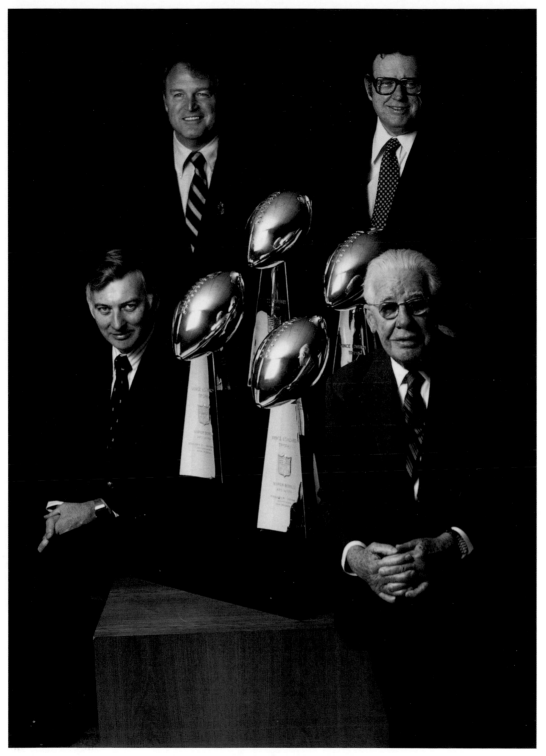

Back Row: Chuck Noll, Art Rooney, Jr.
Front Row: Dan Rooney, Art Rooney, Sr.
(Steelers Collection)

Franco Harris (above), Rocky Bleier (below)
Merv Corning Paintings (Art Rooney, Jr., Collection)

Terry Bradshaw (above), Mike Webster (below)
Merv Corning Paintings (Art Rooney, Jr., Collection)

John Stallworth (above), Lynn Swann (below)
Merv Corning Paintings (Art Rooney, Jr., Collection)

Joe Greene (above), Jack Lambert (below)
Merv Corning Paintings (Art Rooney, Jr., Collection)

Mel Blount (above), Jack Ham (below)
Merv Corning Paintings (Art Rooney, Jr., Collection)

Dan Rooney (above), Chuck Noll (below)
Merv Corning Paintings (Art Rooney, Jr., Collection)

ART ROONEY JR.
© MURRAY CARDS

Art Rooney, Sr. (above), Merv Corning Paintings *(Art Rooney, Jr., Collection)*
Art Rooney, Jr. (below), Merv Corning Paintings *(Art Rooney, Jr., Collection)*

Ham, Lambert, Russell, 1976
(George Gaadt Collection)

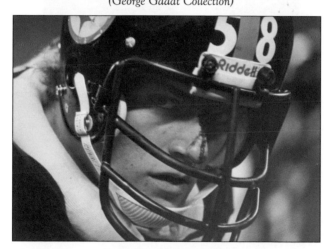

Jack Lambert, 1970s
(George Gaadt Collection)

Terry Bradshaw, 1970s
(George Gaadt Collection)

Right: Roy
McHugh

Below: (Seated)
Roy McHugh, Art
Rooney, Jr.,
(Standing) Dee
Herrod

(Meg Herrod Collection)

Art Rooney, Sr., and Rev. Silas Daniel Rooney, O.F.M. at Three Rivers Stadium.
(Steelers Collection)

2004 Rooney Boys at Southside Steelers Facility

Left to Right: Tim, Art Jr., Pat, Dan, John

(Steelers Collection)

Third Generation of Rooneys in Palm Beach, Florida, 2005
Front Row (Left to Right): Kyle Lewis, Jack Lewis, Alex Rooney, Heather Rooney,
Brian Rooney; Back Row (Left to Right): Susan Rooney Lewis, Mike Rooney, Kay
Rooney, Art Rooney, Jr., Art Rooney III, Christine Rooney, Art Rooney IV
(Kay Rooney Collection)

"There Will Never Be Another You"
Kay Rooney
painting by Merv Corning

Death in Dealey Plaza

Our ticket manager, Joe Carr, always seemed to have a radio turned on. Around 1 o'clock in the afternoon on Friday, November 22, 1963, he was listening to it as usual when a voice interrupted the regular programming to announce that President Kennedy had been shot.

Carr bolted from the ticket office (a very small room partitioned by a counter) into our main office, gasping out the news. Ed Kiely reacted like a newspaper reporter. He ran into his private office and picked up the phone to make a call. Steeler defensive back Brady Keys broke off a conversation with Mary Regan at her desk and started shouting obscenities. He was raging at "all the nuts in the world." There were others in the room, but names and faces elude me. All I know is that I followed Joe Carr back into the ticket office.

By the time we learned that the President was dead, a big crowd had gathered around the radio. No one spoke. After a little while, I walked to St. Mary of Mercy Church on the Boulevard of the Allies at Stanwix Street. It was full by then, and people were standing on the sidewalk outside.

The next day — Saturday — no college football games were played except for a few in the South. Blesto scout Will Walls came into the office and kept explaining to everybody that even though he had gone to college at Texas Christian he was really from Arkansas. Because the assassination took place in Dallas and because the man who had fired the shot lived in Dallas, Texans that weekend were being stigmatized through guilt by association.

With the whole country in mourning, Commissioner Pete Rozelle decided that the NFL would go ahead on Sunday with its full slate of games, a ruling he never lived down. AJR felt uncomfortable about it, and Buddy Parker was flat-out perturbed. The Steelers were playing the Bears at Forbes Field, and Buddy, who was paranoid anyway, expressed the fear that a sniper in the stands would be gunning for him. "Everybody in Pittsburgh hates Texans right now," he said to AJR, "and I'm the only Texan available."

A few minutes before the kickoff I was down on the field, talking with my brother Tim and Jack Butler, when we heard from one of the twins that a small-time Dallas racket guy named Jack Ruby had blown away Lee Harvey Oswald, the suspected assassin, in the Dallas police station. Will Walls later said that he had been in Ruby's strip joint two or three times.

The football game ended in a 17-17 tie, memorable still for a Hall-of-Fame play by the Bears' Mike Ditka. With up to half a dozen Steelers hanging onto him, he carried them a good twenty yards, maybe farther, before they could drag him off his feet. Ditka was an all-pro tight end drafted by George Halas out of Pitt. The game served one purpose, I thought. For a short while, at least, it took some minds off the national trauma.

Two weeks later, the Steelers played the Cowboys in Dallas. Fran Fogarty had a friend from Pittsburgh who was working and living there, and he offered to take Fran on a tour of Dealey Plaza, the assassination site. I went along with them, and so did AJR. Fogarty's friend pointed out the Texas School Book Depository and the window from which Oswald aimed his rifle. Our guide's small, nondescript car seemed to please AJR. The more unpretentious a car was, the better he liked it. When we returned to the hotel, he invited the Texan from Pittsburgh to dinner, but Fogarty had made plans for them that couldn't be changed.

For the rest of his life, AJR was ill at ease in Dallas. He never went back except on a "need-to-go" basis — a Steeler game of exceptional importance or for an NFL meeting at which major issues would be discussed. He conducted this partial boycott quietly. None of the other owners seemed aware of it. If the Steelers were playing in Dallas and it was just another game, there would be a wake or a funeral he had to attend, or business at Shamrock Farm to be taken care of, or a horse of his would be running in a race he couldn't miss, or it was time for his annual visit to the shrine of St. Anne.

I remember something Owney McManus once said: "There will never be a Catholic president, or if there is he will never finish his term." It may be that what happened to John Kennedy was for AJR sufficient proof.

Chapter 35

A Slight Misunderstanding

In the beginning and for many years afterward, the Steelers were just a hobby for AJR. His primary interest was betting on horses. The public tended to forget this, and his grandchildren, most of them, were ignorant of it.

For example, my son Artie. Delving into family history, he put a question to Kass:

"What did grandfather do before he owned the football team?"

"He had an office in town," Kass replied.

"What did he do at the office?" persisted Artie.

"Well," said Kass, "he had a lot of phones there."

"What did he do with the phones?"

"He answered them," Kass said, and that was the end of it.

When Artie was older, he found her to be a willing storyteller. The locale for one of her tales was Moore's Restaurant in New York, where she and her husband were having lunch. Tim Mara, the owner of the New York Giants and a bookmaker on the side, came to their table and informed AJR that such and such a horse was running at such and such a track. Would he like to place a bet?

Offhandedly, AJR told him, "Yeah. Fifty on it to win."

Kass was furious. When Mara left, she reminded her spouse that she was pregnant and that fifty dollars was money they'd need. It was risky to be betting so much on a horse race.

AJR said nothing for a while. He broke his silence when the lecture continued.

"Will you please stay out of my business?" he said. "And I'm not betting fifty dollars. I'm betting fifty *thousand*."

Pretty soon Mara returned. The horse, he told AJR, had won. Even for a bookmaker of Mara's stature, paying off on fifty G's was no small thing. AJR understood how he felt.

"I hate to do this to you," he said, "but I'll tell you what. If it's a boy, we'll call our baby Tim."

And that was how the Rooney brother in charge of the family's horse-racing business got his name.

A long time later, Tim Rooney's daughter Kathleen married Tim Mara's grandson Chris.

Cocoa Beans

At some point in his life — I am not certain when — it seemed to me that AJR began to bet more money on grain futures than on race horses. His partner was a man named Jerry Nolan, who worked in (or out of) the Chicago Board of Trade. AJR may have met him through one of his Chicago football pals, George Halas or Charley Bidwill.

Jerry Nolan was in on the soy-bean deal I referred to a while back. Down through the years the team of Nolan and Rooney brought off successful transactions by the dozen, but in the market, as in football and horse racing, sometimes you win and sometimes you lose. After AJR sold the cottage in Ligonier, which belonged to Kass, he promised to double or maybe triple her money in futures. He lost every cent of it — about $30,000. Most memorably, AJR and Jerry Nolan took a whacking from cocoa-bean growers.

Much of the world's cocoa comes from West Africa. However it happened, AJR got a tip that the crop there had failed, and he instructed Nolan to buy cocoa contracts. Accordingly, Nolan bought cocoa contracts the way Jim bought drinks in any bar. Then the two high rollers sat back comfortably and waited for the price to go up. Hadn't soy-bean prices gone up after AJR was told by Father Dan about the failure of the crop in China? They certainly had, but the analogy didn't hold. Where Father Dan's information had been accurate, the hot tip on cocoa turned out to be a scam.

Far from being scarce, cocoa that year was abundant. The native growers in Africa — Harvard Business School graduates, no doubt — were manipulating the market. Instead of taking their cocoa beans to the middle men, they stashed them away in their huts, to be sold when the price was right and not before — a time that never came. There was cocoa enough, from whatever source, for cocoa drinkers everywhere, it seems, and the cocoa market collapsed. The native growers lost their shirts

— or their dashikis, if that was the case. Meanwhile AJR and Jerry Nolan scrambled to unload their contracts.

No one was buying. "We'd better write this off as a loss," suggested Nolan. "Whatever we do, we can't take delivery of the beans." It was good thinking. But AJR and his accountant, Fran Fogarty, had one last card to play.

Fogarty called friends at the Hershey Chocolate Company and explained the situation. The advice he received was the same as Jerry Nolan's: Don't get stuck with those beans. You now own more cocoa — raw cocoa — than we have or are going to have here in Hershey, his friends added.

In the end, the Chief faced reality. There was no way out. He was stuck with the beans - or would have been if the seller had not agreed to take them back. Of course there was no refund. AJR had learned that cocoa can leave a bitter taste.

Branching Out

In the late 1950s or early 1960s AJR formed a business partnership with Dan Parish, a contractor and a friend of Mayor Lawrence. Dan Parish was from Youngstown, a self-made man who had Anglicized his Italian surname, Parisi. He told me once that he and his brother Mike got their start as cement layers. Many houses in Youngstown still had cellars with dirt floors; the Parisis, riding to work on streetcars, wearing unwashed overalls and carrying their equipment, transformed these cellars into basements.

By the time Dan Parish came into our lives he never wore anything but business suits. Well-mannered and intelligent, he was of average height and build and had a high, squeaky voice. Like Dan Hamill and Owney McManus, he prodded AJR to expand from football into other avenues. "Give your boys something to make a living at," he would say.

An earlier experience with a contractor named Martin Wise, whose wife was related to the McNultys, had left Dad with cause to be hesitant. The Chief was a third-interest partner, putting up the capital and using his political clout to get construction jobs. All seemed to be going well until Mr. Wise surreptitiously bought out the other equal partner. He now owned two-thirds of the business. To be a minority shareholder went against Dad's principles, a fact I am sure he conveyed to Mr. Wise when he ended their relationship. "I've done business with tough guys," Dad later said, "and all I ever needed was a handshake. This 'legitimate' businessman — married to a relative of my wife — turns out to be a sneak and a crook. If they're all like that, I want no part of them."

Dan Parish, of course, had Lawrence's endorsement, the ultimate seal of approval. With a man like Parish as his partner, AJR used to say, he could have made millions in the construction business. As it was, they got into the race track business. But first let me interject one last word about Wise: his health failed, his wife's health failed, their son developed a drinking problem, and they ended up losing their company.

AJR and Dan Parish, having reason to believe from what Lawrence had told them that legalized horse racing in Pennsylvania was a certainty, bought Randall Park, a dilapidated old track in Shaker Heights, Ohio, a suburb of Cleveland. When they applied for a license in Harrisburg, they theorized, a background in ownership would give them credibility.

I watched them research this deal with John Joyce, an associate of Parish, and couldn't help but be impressed. The football business, especially as conducted by AJR's generation, was in many respects like a game. AJR and his fellow owners thought of it as fun, and from a dollar-and-cents point of view this had always been a weakness, I felt. Getting ready to own and operate a track was different. Parish and Joyce could laugh at a good story, but levity had its time and place. When it came to working out the details, financial and otherwise, of starting a race track, they couldn't have been more in earnest. Business was business and they never forgot it. In the Steeler organization, after Jock Sutherland died, only Fran Fogarty took the same deadly serious approach. Among the Rooneys, only my brother Dan and later Tim seemed temperamentally fitted to run a tight ship.

AJR had no trouble adjusting as long as he left the grunt work to Fogarty and Dan — or even to Tim. Oh, he hollered and screamed now and then, but would ultimately defer to their business judgment. To people he had dealt with when there were no set rules, and who were taken aback to find that things had changed, he would say, "What you're asking for is the way I used to do it. But my boys — with their high-powered educations — tell me I have to do it the modern way." Not that he ever became rigid. When his instincts told him to deviate from business-school methods, he did so. And he would be right. And people loved him for it.

There had been no big money in pro football until the 1950s. AJR, along with pioneers such as Joe Carr (the NFL's first commissioner), Bert Bell, George Halas, the Maras, the Bidwills, and George Preston Marshall, had seen the game's potential long before the fans or the newspapermen wised up. With a common goal spurring them on, they had the foresight to pull in the same direction, so that when television gave their league a showcase and generated piles of cash they were able to agree on revenue sharing, which allowed small-market teams like the Steelers to compete with the Giants and the Bears and the Rams and with the handful of teams owned by men of unlimited wealth. However, this was not something that happened overnight. There were anti-trust issues for Congress or the courts to decide. And teams were making deals on their own with the networks, for example the one involving the Steelers, the Colts, and NBC. The league had not reached the point of "united we stand." But it was getting there. The days were not far off when the Steelers would be a valuable property.

Even so, and whether or not he realized it, AJR had a problem. As Dan Parish pointed out to him, there was only one football team and there were five Rooney sons. How to keep them equally occupied and equally happy, once they were ready to join the work force, was a question that would soon need an answer. Dan Parish now seemed to be offering one: throw a couple of race tracks into the mix.

'Not You, Art!'

AJR was a great one for writing postcards and thank-you notes. Over the years he sent thousands of them in his large, beautiful script. Msgr. Francis Rooney (no relation) once let me see a letter from Dad in which he stated that Catholic priests were his heroes.

All through his life Dad went to Mass and Communion every day. As I have said, I never once heard him use profanity and when it carne to sex he was puritanical. The only women in his life were the members of his extended family. In college, at Indiana Normal, he'd had a girlfriend, and later he dated Imogene Coca, the actress, but except for those two I don't believe that he ever spent time with women other than Kass, Aunt Alice, his mother, and his sisters.

The pastor at St. Mary's of Mercy on the Boulevard of the Allies, Downtown, was a tough old Irishman named Lawless. He ruled his congregation like a drill sergeant, issuing orders from the pulpit which he expected to be obeyed without question. At the early Mass on a Friday morning, he announced a re-routing of Communion traffic. Instead of coming up the middle aisle and returning to their pews by the side aisles, the parishioners were to reverse that procedure. "You're to approach the Communion rail by way of the side aisles and go back by way of the middle aisle," he instructed them. "In preparation for the big crowds on Sunday," he added, "we'll give it a trial run today." As our friend Father Bob Reardon told me the story, chaos resulted. Almost everybody started up the middle aisle, including AJR, who often attended Mass at St. Mary's and was always a big contributor at the offertory. Msgr. Lawless, standing behind the rail with the chalice, became incensed. At the top of his lungs, he shouted, "Up the side aisles, I told ya. Go back and start over." The parishioners were milling around — turning left, turning right, and bumping into one another. And AJR was in the middle of all this. Just then the monsignor spotted him.

"Art! Art!" he called out, "Not you, Art! Come right up the center aisle."

Some time later AJR confided to Father Reardon that he was never in all his days more embarrassed.

On a visit to New York City he was the unwitting cause of a traffic accident in St. Patrick's Cathedral. Toots Shor, the celebrated restaurant owner, was with him. A Jewish guy married to a Catholic, Shor attended Mass now and then but always as someone out of his element. He followed Dad into the cathedral and was looking around for familiar faces, since many of his customers were Irish or Italian. At this moment Dad genuflected. As his right knee touched the floor, his right foot became entangled with Shor's left foot. Shor was as big as an NFL tackle and he hit the deck with a thud.

At a testimonial dinner for AJR at the Hilton Hotel in Pittsburgh, the restaurateur did an encore. He went up to the dais and gave a speech extolling Dad's virtues, and then he started back to his table. Misjudging the steps, he crashed to the floor. The crowd let out a gasp. Falls like this had been known to kill people. But we underestimated Toots Shor. He was on his feet again in a minute, smiling and waving and proclaiming himself unhurt.

Could he have passed a sobriety test? I doubt it.

Two of a Kind

Exaggerating only a little, AJR used to say that his friend Davey Lawrence was a Democrat in Pittsburgh when nobody else was a Democrat. Because Senator Jimmy Coyne's Republican machine was unbeatable for a time, Democrats at heart, like AJR, grudgingly entered its ranks. In no other way could they escape irrelevance. Liberals who believed in giving a break to the poor, they worked from the inside. David L. Lawrence never joined them.

He studied politics at the feet of Bill Brennen, Allegheny County's Democratic chairman from 1901 to 1918. A lawyer who had been an ironworker and labor activist, Brennen hired Lawrence as a clerk-stenographer when Lawrence was 14 years old. At 29, he succeeded to the party leadership. "As a young guy," said AJR, "he ran errands. Later, he made the big decisions. And he was incorruptible."

Fastening onto that "incorruptible" tag in the years when Lawrence was mayor and then governor, my brothers and I would put a mock-serious question to Jerry Lawrence, his son: "How much graft money has your dad tucked away in Switzerland?" Having been close to Jerry Lawrence for most of our lives, we were sure we could take liberties that from anyone else would be a challenge to a fist fight. Jerry, as I have noted, had charge of the press-relations department at the Rooney-owned William Penn Raceway. "If I knew where that money was," he would answer good-naturedly, aware that the Rooneys were with him one hundred percent, "I'd be living high on the hog instead of working for you guys."

The local history books tell us how Lawrence and Richard King Mellon saved Pittsburgh from the ash heap in the 1950s and how they cleaned up the rivers and brightened the skies. So much has been written about Lawrence, in fact, that I can only put down the stories I heard from AJR and the things I observed at first hand. I understand that when AJR ran for register of wills, Lawrence made no objection. Realizing better than anyone the futility of such a race, he saw the potential for humor in it. Chances are Lawrence was not a man much given to laughter, but the combination of an inept candidate, AJR, and a buffoonish campaign manager, Owney McManus, must have tickled him. Certainly it was droll entertainment.

There is no doubt whatever that Lawrence enjoyed sports. In particular he liked baseball, football, boxing, and, after AJR had given him a sort of tutorial, horse racing. As mayor, Lawrence did what he could to help the Steelers. Several times a year he attended practice. On one such occasion, striking up a conversation with Jack Butler, he offered to get him a liquor license. Butler had no real intention of going into the bar business, "but here was the mayor of Pittsburgh," he said, "ready to be of assistance. I knew a lot of people who'd have traded one of their eyes for a liquor license."

I've described how Lawrence put pressure on the University of Pittsburgh to share Pitt Stadium with the Steelers. Tom Hamilton, Pitt's athletic director, was bitterly opposed to the idea. You'd have thought by the way he acted that he was selling his soul to the devil. Lawrence also played a part in making Three Rivers Stadium politically possible, and but for him we would not have had a harness-racing franchise.

Dad, Lawrence, and Dan Parish attended football games, baseball games, and boxing matches together, went out to dinner together, and played cards together. If I was present during their card games, the governor made an effort to include me in the conversation. He told me once, off the record, that obduracy on the part of our steel makers, who wanted the labor market all to themselves, kept the automobile industry out of Pittsburgh. With two such titans competing for workers, the cost of hiring them would be bound to escalate. As a result, Lawrence said, Pittsburgh lost out to Detroit. Something else that prevented us from being a diversified manufacturing center was our topography, he argued. There were too many hills and valleys and rivers, which are enemies of economical plant construction.

Being David L. Lawrence had its downside. I was in the visiting owner's box at a football game between the Steelers and the Browns in Cleveland when two rowdies nearby, spotting Lawrence and AJR, began to heckle them. They started on Dad, telling him what they thought of his lousy football team, but quickly shifted to Lawrence, calling him a crook and telling him what they thought of his lousy state. With us was Richie Easton, a *Pittsburgh Press* truck driver who was AJR's personal chauffeur at the time. Richie happened to be the strong, silent type. He took it all in for a while and then abruptly got to his feet. He was holding a pair of binoculars — mine. "If you don't shut up," he said to the two drunken loudmouths, "I'm going to shove these glasses right down your throats. And then," he went on, "I'm going to throw you out of your seats, all the way down to the ground."

In our boxes, we were maybe three stories high; the players below looked like ants. Sizing Richie up, the two louts could sense that he might be in earnest. For the rest of the afternoon, they held their tongues.

This time with Richie out of the mix, the same kind of problem arose at a College All-Star game in Chicago. Besides Lawrence, AJR's guests were two young owners of the Pick Hotel chain, husband, and wife. An adjacent drunk, overhearing Lawrence's name mentioned, took it upon himself to abuse the old politico unmercifully. Richie, as I have said, was absent, but sitting unnoticed a row or two back was the Pick Hotels' chief of security, who now intervened. He got hold of the pest by the coat collar and ushered him out of the stadium.

When his days in elective politics were over, Lawrence went to work for the Johnson administration in Washington and stayed on after JFK's assassination. He said that my dad would have loved the Kennedys because they were Irish Catholics. But they were also, in contrast with President Johnson, bluebloods. Lawrence himself preferred LBJ, "a real man of the people," and wished that AJR could have known him.

Lawrence's son Jerry, after leaving William Penn Raceway, moved up to an executive position — general manager of our track in Yonkers, New York. The governor's nephew, Tom Donahoe. was in the Steeler organization as director of football operations from the early 1990s until the turn of the century. In the end, he could not maintain harmonious relations with the coach, Bill Cowher, and resigned (one of them had to go, and it was Tom). Later, Tom became president of the Buffalo Bills. Both he and Jerry were great guys, and they excelled at what they did.

The Misfit

If I may repeat myself, AJR was a Democrat at heart, but out of loyalty to Senator Jimmy Coyne, he always had been and would continue to be a Republican. Most other Republicans in Western Pennsylvania were rich Presbyterians. AJR had money, but most of it came from betting on horses, and not even the Pope was more Catholic.

He differed greatly from your typical Republican in still another respect — his admiration for labor people. He spoke of Philip Murray, the steelworkers' revered leader — buried in the graveyard at St. Anne's Church in Castle Shannon — as a truly great man.

Grandma Margaret Rooney, herself born a Murray, was not related to Phil, but all the men in her family were coal miners, and AJR knew the head of their union, John L. Lewis. Returning from the race tracks in New York or from Shamrock Farm, Dad used to see John L. Lewis having dinner in a restaurant at White Sulphur Springs, in West Virginia, and they would talk. Despite his forbidding appearance — the shaggy black eyebrows gave him a sinister look — Lewis was never anything but cordial.

Then there was Pat Fagan, a coal miners official and a Pittsburgh city councilman. Pat Fagan would stop to visit with AJR at the Steelers' office in the Fort Pitt Hotel and later at the Roosevelt Hotel. He was a friendly, unassuming old guy.

Out of an interest in the Russian Revolution — I had a history degree from St. Vincent College — I asked him once if he had known Leon Trotsky. "Know him!" Pat said. "We ran that guy out of Western Pennsylvania. He was a Commie, and up to no good."

Not only labor leaders but politicians as well were looked on with favor by AJR. He introduced me to Jim Farley, who was Franklin D. Roosevelt's postmaster general and a man who reputedly never forgot a face or a name. Farley and Dad were busy conversing, and though Farley addressed his remarks to AJR, I could see that he was pleased to have somebody young and impressionable for an audience.

What he was saying surprised me. He claimed that FDR had lied to him several times, and that in consequence he watched his step around the President.

"I was careful never to be alone with Mr. Roosevelt," Farley said.

The Murrays and the Lewises and the Fagans, the Farleys and the Davey Lawrences — people of this sort, not football players and baseball players, should be our heroes, Dad told us. And then of course all priests were heroes - his friend Father Campbell in particular. If we modeled ourselves after men such as these, there was no way we could ever go wrong.

A Positive Product

According to John and Pat, AJR was against any and all forms of pleasure. We thought of him as a rigid disciplinarian but a fine man, the best we would ever know. His sense of honor was acute. He did not lie or cheat and he lived by the golden rule.

Publicity — favorable publicity, the only kind he received after the Steelers won their first Super Bowl trophy — was pleasing to him, but he knew how to act as though he disdained it. He liked sports and the people in the business of sports. He took a pragmatic view of the horse racing industry but believed that most sporting events, horse races included, were on the level. In many respects, he tended to be a romantic about sports, and I admit that I am one, too.

In moments of anger, he could tell someone off without cursing. People who aroused his ire were bums, or rotten bums, or dirty rotten bums, or greasers and the like. His epithets, although harsh, were safely within the bounds of the Second Commandment: "Thou shalt not take the name of the Lord thy God in vain."

He attended three institutions of higher learning — Indiana Normal, Georgetown, and Duquesne — and was none the worse for it.

His vocabulary neither changed nor increased. It was free of vulgarisms and free of obscenity. His slang never emerged from the 1920s. In fact it seemed quaint. He spoke Pittsburghese with a certain pride, although at some point he stopped saying "yinz." He pretended that words of more than two or three syllables were over his head, implying pretentiousness on the part of those who used them. He talked the way he did for a reason. Besides expressing his personality, it kept the people he dealt with off-balance. It gave them a misleading impression, which I think was the main idea. In practical terms, he was smarter and much shrewder than most intellectuals, and if the fact wasn't obvious to them, so much the better.

There were many Art Rooney wannabe's, copying this or that characteristic but failing to understand the uniqueness of AJR. My dad was tough — not the kind to back down from anyone — but soft on the inside, and on the outside too when it wouldn't be misinterpreted. He controlled his passions. He controlled his baser instincts. He had spiritual depth. Leadership came naturally to him, but he did not seek it out. Extremely generous, he could also be close with a buck. He appreciated humor, which he found in the give and take of life, but he could not tell a joke without messing it up. The men who tried to imitate him lacked the gift he was born with and cultivated — his ability to connect and interact. He was a positive product of his heredity and environment, profiting from the one and rising above the other.

Except for Father Dan, even his own brothers could never get a fix on exactly who Art Rooney was. Father Dan, like AJR, heeded the better angels of his nature. He was no less intelligent than AJR, and if a good big man always has the edge on a good little man, the superior athlete. He devoted his whole being, and not just a part of it, to the service of God.

Together, they made a phenomenal pair.

Chocolaholic

After Dad gave up booze he developed a gigantic appetite for sweets, in particular chocolate. He could eat it by the pound. If there's a connection of some kind — if chocolate addiction replaces alcohol addiction — medical science has not yet confirmed it. Kass was always able to combine chocolate and alcohol. While eating a Hershey bar, she would drink a glass of beer. "This is really good," she would say. I was never persuaded.

Dimling's and Reymer's made excellent chocolate candy here in Pittsburgh. The chocolate buttercups from Dimling's were irresistible. During the Korean War, people sent boxes of Dimling's candy to relatives in the service. The demand became extraordinary — and this was why Dimling's went out of business.

I am telling you the story as I heard it from Kass. Just when the orders peaked, according to Kass, the union boss at Dimling's called a strike. It dragged on for weeks. Angered, the owners closed all of their stores except one — the Downtown location on Liberty Avenue near the Stanley Theater. By the 1960s that store also was gone.

One day a man came into our offices in the Roosevelt Hotel and presented Dad with a large box of Clark bars from the Clark candy factory on the North Side. After he left, Dad told us that this was the candy chef who worked out the recipe for the Clark bar. The main ingredients seemed to be chocolate and peanut butter. At any rate, the Clark bar was now the company's best seller, but the man who created it had received nothing more than a bonus and a raise in pay, Dad said. Was he bitter about that? Yes, but in Dad's opinion, anyway, he had not been treated unfairly. "After all," Dad explained, "coming up with new ideas was part of his job. It was what the company hired him to do." Dad was a firm believer in capitalism.

Sometimes Dad went on eating binges. The once compact lightweight was rounder in the mid-section now; his face had a softer, more benevolent look. Every year for most of his life he paid a visit to the shrine of St. Anne de Beaupre in Quebec, and on all of these trips he stayed at the Chateau Frontenac. Because he tipped so well the staff gave him special attention. One time when Pat and his wife Sandy were with him, a huge silver tray full of chocolates, the best that Quebec could offer, was sent to Dad and Mom's suite. At a single sitting, he ate every piece except one. "He got woozy," Pat said, "and then all of a sudden he fell over backwards onto the bed." Kass called the head porter, who called the house doctor. "We thought Dad was down for the count," Pat continued. "He appeared to be unconscious. Then I saw him reach out and grab that last piece of chocolate and pop it into his mouth. I couldn't believe it."

Indulging Dad's taste for chocolate was only one of the ways in which the people who worked at the Chateau Frontenac expressed their deep affection for him. He took care of them, as they say – that was part of it. What weighed more heavily was his personal touch. By always having time for them, he made the doormen and the bellhops and the waiters and the busboys feel important. Returning from Mass in the morning, he would say to one or the other, "Come on and sit down and have a cup of coffee with me."

And he could do these things — I don't know what the secret was — without seeming phony. I'm a pretty good tipper myself, but it was always a fight to tip anybody at the Chateau Frontenac. "No, no, no," they would tell me. I was Art Rooney's son — in their minds his little boy, I suppose — and for that reason their services were not to be bought.

One of Dad's close friends was a police inspector from Lawrenceville named Ignatius Loyola Borkowski. Iggie's looks, which were unremarkable, belied his professional skill and intelligence. A bachelor with time on his hands, he put himself and his car at the Chief's disposal, becoming, in effect, an unofficial chauffeur. Dad always paid for the gasoline but never gave a thought to such broad-based incidentals as wear and tear. In time, as cars will, Iggie's broke down, and his suggestion that Dad should replace it led to a brief estrangement. They were pals again by the next Shrove Tuesday, when Iggie drove Dad to Sarris Candies, in Canonsburg, a confectionery noted for its unsurpassable chocolate and ice cream.

Predictably, Dad gorged himself. After eating all he could hold, he made it as far as the parking lot and then threw up profusely. Iggie got him into the car and to Mercy Hospital, back in Pittsburgh, at speeds you may be sure were illegal. Dad spent two days and two nights there, taking tests. "They dried me out like an alcoholic, and I don't even drink," he complained. The tests revealed that his sugar was high, but he continued to gobble up sweets. Alcoholics and chocolaholics have one thing in common: they don't know when to quit.

In the last decade of his life, Dad went to Ireland with Tim. Something about being on vacation stoked his appetite, it seemed, and he put away a lot of candy in addition to the regular fare. "One night he zonked out," Tim said. "I called a doctor." All of this happened in Waterville, a little seaside resort, but the doctor, a young guy, turned out to be very good. He made the right diagnosis. It was not an attack of diabetes, as Tim thought, but congestive heart failure. Dad was so full of liquid that his heart couldn't pump it out of his system. The doctor gave Dad some medicine, and it straightened him out quickly.

Meanwhile, Tim had called Pittsburgh. "This time Dad may not make it," he told us. Thanks to the young doctor, he lasted for another five years.

Generation Gap

Because AJR, Father Silas, and Uncle Jim were such outstanding athletes, my brothers and I felt like underachievers, and with good reason.

Three of us – Dan, Tim, and I — played football at North Catholic, and I lettered for two years at St. Vincent. Tim and Dan were good high school players. John went out for track at St. Mary's College of Emmitsburg, Maryland, and competed successfully in the pole vault. The unusual thing about this was that he never had vaulted before, since North had no track team. John could box, too. In that respect, he and Tim were most like their father and uncles. Pat, the other twin, was on the tennis team at St. Mary's.

In short, we had nothing to be ashamed of. Compared with our forebears, though, we did not measure up, and we knew it. More to the point, AJR knew it — and allowed his disappointment to show.

John's pole vaulting gave him no pleasure. It reminded him only of a track story that featured himself. AJR was a sprinter — exceedingly fast at short distances. So when one of his friends entered a marathon race of twenty-six miles and a fraction he agreed to be the "rabbit," he told us. He would set the pace for awhile, pulling along his friend to a start that might enable him to break the course record, and then he would drop out. "But when the time came," he said, "I felt pretty good. I felt good enough to keep going, so I ran some more and some more. In fact I kept on going and won the race."

We had learned over the years that when AJR talked this way he did not exaggerate. He really was as good at sports as he claimed to have been. Old newspaper clippings document most of what he said. Father Silas was almost his equal. And at football, if nothing else, Uncle Jim may have been the best of the three.

As for my brothers and myself, blessed with ordinary ability, we were doomed to fall short of the standard these older Rooneys had set. We not only failed to satisfy AJR, what was worse, we failed to satisfy ourselves.

Chapter 36

Liberty Bell

Pennsylvania legalized standard-bred racing in 1963. Standard-bred horses do not, in the technical sense, run. Harnessed to little two-wheeled carts called sulkies, they trot or they pace. The driver, equipped with reins and a whip, sits low in the sulky and maneuvers for position on the rail.

In the nineteenth century and during the first half of the twentieth, harness racing was popular at county fairs but nowhere else. Arc lights, which made night racing possible, parimutuel betting, and the invention of the mobile starting gate moved the sport off the fair grounds and into the big money. What the starting gate did was make it easier for the entire field of horses to get off at the same time. Uncle Jim and his friends — and AJR, too — still preferred thoroughbred racing, but that is beside the point.

Through their relationship with Dave Lawrence, who was governor by then, AJR and his partner Dan Parish obtained a license to operate at the Liberty Bell track, a newly-built facility in northeast Philadelphia, just inside Bucks County. It was owned by a group that included Jim Clark, as powerful a man in the Democratic party as Lawrence was. Besides Parish, the Chief's associates included Herb Barness, a real-estate developer from Philadelphia's Main Line. In John Macartney, they had a brilliant lawyer and spokesman.

The Kelly family of Philadelphia was also somehow involved. Jack Kelly, Sr., who started out as a bricklayer and worked his way up to construction-company owner, had been the gold-medal winner in single sculling at the 1920 Olympic games. A scull is a light racing boat propelled by one oar or two and by either one oarsman, as in single sculling, or four. Kelly's son, Jack Junior, was perhaps an even better sculler than his father but never an Olympic champion. Three straight times — at the games of 1948, 1952, and 1956 — he finished third and had to settle for bronze instead of gold.

The Kelly my brothers and I were most interested in, of course — not to deprecate scullers and their sport, as little as they excited us — was Jack's sister Grace. Jack merely looked like a movie star; his sister triumphantly became one. With her arresting blend of refinement and sex appeal, she was the actress every director wanted, and then she gave it all up for a royal wedding.

Monaco, the domain of her prince, a man named Rainier, wasn't much bigger than the Paramount lot in Hollywood - or, for that matter, the Beaver Valley steel town of Monaca — but the crown jewels and the palace were real. To our disappointment, none of us ever met Grace, who seldom returned to America.

Jim Clark was the principal owner of Liberty Bell. He got along very well with AJR and Dan Parish, who leased the track from him for fifty-day meets twice a year. All three men had come up the hard way, Clark as a one-time trucker. He now owned much of the stock — the majority of it, I believe — in the Philadelphia Eagles. Herb Barness had a smaller piece of the Eagles. He was a big help later on — the details are unimportant — to me and my family.

Politically, financially, and in the shifting sands of human relations, there was more to the Liberty Bell arrangement than I can put down on paper, but let me say this: AJR looked after our interests so shrewdly that fifteen years after his death the race-track business was as profitable to his family as the football team. Clark, Barness, and Macartney were out of horse racing entirely.

We operated at Liberty Bell as the William Penn Raceway. Without leaving Pittsburgh, I did some work for William Penn before the track ever opened, but horse racing never appealed to me. It fell to the twins, Pat and John, to represent the Rooneys at Liberty Bell, with Johnny Laughlin, Aunt Margaret's son, and Jerry Lawrence, the governor's son, as their associates.

Pat left a job selling copper for a Pittsburgh manufacturing company and served a brief apprenticeship at the Brandywine track in Delaware before making the move to Philadelphia. He was now a husband, having fallen in love with one of the copper firm's secretaries, Sandy Sully. John and Johnny Laughlin had been teachers, John at Plum High School, where he also coached track, and Johnny Laughlin at North Catholic. John the twin was married also, to his long-time girlfriend Jo Ann Wallace, a hot-shot basketball player from Spring Hill.

For Jim Clark's group, the Rooney-Parish participation was a sweetheart deal. To start with, it required us to make a two-million-dollar "security deposit." Clark's people ran the place and got about half of the profits. Even so, we made out all right, as AJR would remind us whenever we complained about getting the short end of the stick.

Pat and John and their families — they had children by now — lived in apartment complexes, huge places a few miles from the track. There was nothing ostentatious about these complexes, which suited Dad perfectly. Dad disapproved of ostentation. Mom disapproved of apartment living. She was happy when Herb Barness's real estate company put the twins and their wives and kids into nice big substantial houses.

John's first house had a back-yard swimming pool, and he tried to conceal it from Dad. A back-yard swimming pool was "putting on the dog." Also, Dad thought, swimming pools, and young children didn't mix. So whenever he came around, John and Jo Ann made sure that the curtains were drawn. If the kids raced in, dripping water, the parents would lie. They'd say the neighbors next door had a pool.

John's new Cadillac was harder to account for. Looking at it distastefully, Dad put John to a test.

"What kind of car is that?" he asked

"Oldsmobile," John replied

"Don't kid the kidder," Dad barked. "And don't be putting on the dog to impress these people in Philadelphia. That's a Cadillac."

Harness racing is such a sedate sport - compared with thoroughbred racing, anyway - that something I heard from John about the intensity of its patrons came as a shock. He said that deaths at the park from heart attacks and strokes were not uncommon. For every meeting, Liberty Bell had to hire a full-time physician and a full-time nurse.

Curious, John asked a doctor about typical last words. Before losing consciousness, what did these poor unfortunates usually say? Did they enter eternity with a prayer on their lips? With a farewell message to their loved ones? Hardly ever. Most often, according to the doc, they died wanting to know if the horse they had bet on had won.

When AJR was in Philadelphia, he would drive out to Liberty Bell early in the morning, right after Mass, and have breakfast at the kitchen in the backstretch — pancakes, bacon and eggs, and coffee. Then he would talk at length with the trainers, jockeys, grooms, warm-up boys, hot walkers, and miscellaneous flunkies. All of them spoke his language. They knew he was some kind of big shot but not much else.

Each year the racing people held an awards banquet which our Philadelphia contingent was expected to attend. At one such event a troop of dancing girls, stark naked except for G-strings, came out from the wings and ran into the dining area. They circulated among the tables, gyrating salaciously. AJR turned his chair around and sat facing the twins, Jerry Lawrence, and John Laughlin, Jr.

"He started a business meeting," Pat told me later. "He said, 'Pat, how are things going in the mutuel department?' Then he asked, 'What was the handle last week?' After that, he had questions for the others: 'John, are you getting top horses in here?' 'Johnny, how are the programs selling?' 'Jerry, what about the publicity department?'" On and on it went until the dancing was over. The twins, making a heroic effort, were able to keep their faces straight. Johnny Laughlin and Jerry may have been too frightened to laugh.

At another banquet one of the men who ran Liberty Bell made a disparaging remark about AJR from the dais. Del Miller, respected throughout the harness-racing world as both an outstandingly successful driver and the owner of the Meadowlands track near Pittsburgh, took umbrage. When the speaker passed Miller's table on the way back to his own, Miller got up and punched him, saying, "Nobody insults my friend Art Rooney."

All in all, his friend Art Rooney, and Art Rooney's sons, were doing pretty well. The football team was out of the red and phenomenal times in the racing business were not far over the horizon.

Foot in the Door

My aim all along was to work for the Steelers, preferably as a scout. The man in charge of our scouting at the time was Ray Byrne, better known as Digger. For more than one reason the name fit, because in addition to digging up football players, he buried the dead.

By profession an undertaker, he buried the dead in a grimly literal sense. When I say that he dug up football players I am using a figure of speech. Scouting methods in Byrne's day were primitive; to identify prospects, he dug through press guides, newspapers, and magazines.

Until the 1960s the Steelers were never able to spend more than a pittance on scouting. Assistant coaches doubled as scouts and there were one or two men on the road.

Byrne was the coordinator. He worked in the front office, too, helping Fran Fogarty with some of the minor bookkeeping chores. Byrne was short and slight, with the polite, deferential, gently accommodating manner that morticians acquire from daily inter-action with the bereaved.

I remember hearing him tell AJR on a train ride to Cleveland for the 1953 league championship game that Detroit University quarterback Ted Marchibroda, who had played at St. Bonaventure until Father Silas scrubbed the football program for economic reasons, was probably too short to be successful in the NFL. AJR, I could see, disagreed. Marchibroda's St. Bonaventure connection — and the fact that Father Silas was the school's athletic director — weighed heavily with AJR. Not that Father Silas had ever lobbied for Marchibroda. He told us that Ted was a good guy, nothing more.

In Cleveland, and again on the return trip, AJR discussed Marchibroda with Wellington Mara, the owner of the New York Giants. He then confronted Ray Byrne. "Ray," he said, "dooo ... you ... know ... who we are going to draft first? Well ... it's Teddy Marchibroda." He paused for a moment to let that sink in. "I just talked to Wellington Mara," he continued. "Wellington Mara knows more about drafting than anybody in the NFL, and he says if he gets the chance he will take Mar-chi-bro-da." For emphasis, AJR pronounced each syllable distinctly. "He will take Marchibroda *first*."

Byrne's job with the Steelers was only an avocation, but he treasured it. Meekly, he answered, "Yes, Mister Rooney."

The Steelers had given the Giants a 63-7 pasting that year, and perhaps this was Mara's revenge. They were friends, these two owners, but all's fair in love, war, and football. Drafted by the Steelers in the first round, Marchibroda proved to be an exciting, strong-armed little scrambler who was never quite good enough to unseat Jim Finks as the starting quarterback.

For several years after Byrne parted company with us — reluctantly but voluntarily; he and his family were moving away from Pittsburgh — we had no personnel director as such. My first job, given to me at the insistence of Kass, was in group ticket sales.

In a way, I was qualified for sales, and in another way I was not. Upon leaving the Marines, I had taken the first offer that came along: I sold advertising for WEDO, a radio station owned by Uncle Jim's old football teammate at Pitt, Eddie Hirshberg. Hirshberg seemed to think he could teach me all about salesmanship, but I knew better. Salesmanship was not in my blood. Football was. I believed I had a future with the Steelers.

I hoped it would also include a beautiful red-haired lady from Seton Hill College in Greensburg. She had the same first name as my mother, Kathleen, and my mother loved her. But what I needed now was a game plan. Step one would be to get out of radio, a move made more urgent by Eddie Hirshberg's desire to expand his business — acquire a station in Las Vegas and go on from there. In the picture he painted for me, I was to be his partner, with AJR putting up the capital. Somehow I couldn't see myself proposing this idea to my father. So I turned Eddie down.

In group ticket sales, I was a one-man department: no assistants, no office, and no secretary. I had the inescapable feeling that no one was taking me seriously. My job was to sell tickets in blocks, and I used the door-to-door method, visiting large corporations, small businesses, and even bars. It was hard going; the Steelers in those days were not exactly a hot item. In our thirty years of existence, there had been only four winning seasons. "Better things are corning," I would say. "Bullshit" would be the answer on the faces of the people I was trying to sell. Some of them even said it out loud, and I knew they were right.

Occasionally Art (Pappy) Lewis, our head scout, came with me to help with the sales pitch. Lewis had been a coach, most recently at West Virginia University, and Buddy Parker had brought him to the Steelers because college coaches everywhere knew him and liked him. He was a cracker-barrel humorist, capable of spinning tall tales.

Not long after we first teamed up, Pappy had a heart attack. I called the hospital to see how he was doing.

"Not too well," the nurse told me.

"Can I come to visit?" I asked

"If he gets better," she replied

"What do you mean by 'if'?" I wanted to know.

After a pause, the nurse said, "Well … he probably won't make it."

Pappy Lewis died the next day.

I no longer remember which of our scouts replaced him. It may have been Will Walls or it may have been Ken Stilley. I do remember that Stilley would come with me when I was making my rounds, just as Lewis had done, and we talked at great length about "recruiting" college players in competition with the new American Football League.

If we were ever going to win, I decided, we had to find more good players we could sign, the kind of players other teams were overlooking. We could not let a player like Johnny Unitas slip through our fingers because of a coach's misjudgment. In an operation like ours, there was no room for error. We could not afford to carry any deadwood. Given our limited financial resources, every player had to be a good one. You could lose with good players, yes, but without them you never could win.

Something else I decided was that I did not have the persuasive power to be a ticket salesman — not as long as we played our home games at Forbes Field. "These seats," a prospective customer would say. "Where are they?" When I told the unavoidable truth — "Behind a pole" — my prospect lost interest every time. I went to AJR and asked if I could work with the scouts. Reluctantly, he agreed.

"You're brand new," he told me, which was something he often said to all of his sons. "Brand new" meant green, naive, wet behind the ears. In my own opinion, I wasn't completely brand new. There were some big truths I was figuring out, and winning with good players, as simple as it sounds, was one of them. I had another idea that was mean-spirited and wrong. "Let's get so many good players," I would say to the other scouts, "that the coaches can't screw them up." As I matured, I put that one in mothballs. Football, after all, is a team endeavor. It was true, nonetheless, that you had to work very hard at your job and be self-reliant.

Starting out, I realized I was still an apprentice, with many things to learn from experienced old-timers like Stilley. Ken had been a lineman at Notre Dame. In the movies he'd have played a judge or a senator or the head of a corporation. Real life miscast him as the mayor of Clairton, a coal and steel town on the Monongahela River near Pittsburgh. Finding himself involved in a nasty campaign for re-election one year, he came to AJR for advice. A local bar owner, he complained, was bad-mouthing him all over town. "Close the guy down," AJR suggested. "He has to be violating some code or regulation or ordinance." Stilley was dumbstruck. That political power could be a weapon had apparently never occurred to him.

P.S. He was not re-elected.

Stilley helped me a lot while he was still with the Steelers and continued to help me as the first executive director of the Blesto scouting organization. He taught me how important good relationships are. There were college coaches and athletic directors who looked upon scouts as a nuisance. "Behave the right way when you go around to these schools," Ken reminded me, "and you'll always be welcomed back."

Stating the obvious, was he? Couldn't anyone with a brain have figured that out for himself? Well, yes, but it's surprising how rare a simple thank-you can be. I learned from Ken Stilley the value of sending follow-up notes and postcards. All right — so Ken was a politician, at least on a small scale. Was he giving me a lesson in the art of casting bread on the waters? A politician's trick? Or is there still such a thing as plain old-fashioned common courtesy?

In Charge

I am sometimes referred to — undeservedly — as the guy who invented Blesto. As a matter of fact, the idea came from Buddy Parker, Russ Thomas of Detroit, and Vince McNally of Philadelphia. When they were putting it together I attended all the meetings as a go-fer. While having fun, I enriched my knowledge of football.

Blesto was my big break. The following year, 1965, the Bears came into the organization and AJR put me in charge of the Steelers' scouting department. Our collaboration with the Lions, Eagles, and Bears gave us coverage from nine or ten scouts instead of three, and coverage was exactly what we needed. Just as crucial, it seemed to me, Blesto's executive offices were under the same roof as ours. Working and talking with so many capable scouts, I learned from the bottom up. They taught me the rudiments — everything from the importance of not leaving home without your foul-weather gear to the proper method of running a movie projector.

Besides me, our only scouts were part-time assistant coaches. They would coach a position in camp and then hit the road. Thanksgiving came and went before we saw them again. Although on paper I was now their boss, they answered to the head coach, not to me, an annoyance until the end of my tenure. As scouts, some of these coaches were good, some were OK, and others just simply didn't give a damn. They wanted to spend all their time on coaching, which was all right with me. Good riddance, I thought. We had coaches who were bad judges of talent and one coach who seemed allergic to work. On the day before the draft he would call somebody, get a recommendation, and then push that player real hard.

When I went on the road myself I kept my eyes and ears open and asked questions. Because of AJR, everybody treated me well. Constantly in the back of my mind was a small voice that said to me: Don't act like too much of a big shot.

In-house, there were changes to be made. Our bookkeeping was primitive. I had to fight for a full-time secretary. I angered a lot of people when I announced that scouting records were not to leave the office. And of course I heard the grumbling: "Artie's new job is going to his head."

Even if that was so, I intended to do things my way.

Will Walls

Will Walls
(Steelers Collection)

One of the more colorful Blesto scouts was Will Walls, a big, rangy guy, part Indian and all Texan. Or maybe not. After President Kennedy's assassination in Dallas, Walls disavowed his Texas heritage. "You know, Artie," he said to me once, "I'm really from Arkansas."

Wherever he was from, Walls had been the primary target for Sammy Baugh's passes at Texas Christian. Apparently the Indian blood that flowed in his veins qualified him for membership in a fraternal organization he belonged to — Wigwam Wisemen of America, who held their meetings in a telephone booth.

After college, Walls played for the New York Giants from 1941 to 1943. His next stop was Hollywood, where he presented himself for a screen test and earned a bit part in "Thirty Seconds Over Tokyo." Returning to Texas, he coached a junior-college team and helped to put on an all-star high school game; this enabled him to make contacts that were useful in his scouting career.

When Walls beat the bushes for Blesto, he averaged 50,000 miles a year on the road. He carried so much baggage — hot plates, coffee makers, movie projectors, still cameras, and what not — that the springs in his car gave way, and he drove at such a high rate of speed that he came very close to killing himself in a series of head-on crashes. An accident that sent him to the hospital knocked out all of his teeth and lacerated an ear. It may have given his face character — the producers of "Gunsmoke" had a part they thought he'd be right for, but Walls wasn't interested, which was television's loss.

In addition to the items listed above, Walls carried hundred-watt bulbs everywhere he went (the light bulbs in the hotel rooms were too dim to read by, he said), big bars of soap (the tiny wafers you got in hotels were next to worthless), and a .38-caliber revolver. It was Buddy Parker who advised him to include a still camera. Parker wanted a photograph of every top prospect — black prospects in particular. "If I'd known how ugly that Bob Ferguson was," he said to me once, "I wouldn't have drafted him." Ferguson was a fullback from Ohio State who played for the Steelers in 1962 and 1963.

I liked Walls a lot — almost everyone did — but learned to discount his reports just a bit. His judgments were sweeping and final. At the University of Colorado one day, we watched some film of a player we were checking out for the draft. "Artie," Walls said to me at the end of the reel, "did you see that feller flinch'?"

"Yeah, Will, I saw."

I was wasting my breath. To make sure that I saw, he ran the film again and again and again — ten times altogether.

"Once a flincher always a flincher. Remember that, Artie," he said.

On-the-Job Training

In the spring of 1965, Buddy Parker sent me on my first scouting trip — to an all-star game in Buffalo with Walls. We traveled in the ancient Packard he drove, and the trek took eight or nine hours (there were still no Interstate highways). Because I scarcely knew Walls, I wondered starting out what we would talk about — if anything. Walls, after all, was part Indian, and Indians were notoriously tight-lipped. In the cowboy movies I had seen as a kid, they muttered "Ugh" now and then but otherwise had little to say.

Walls lived up to the stereotype only part of the time, alternating between silence and loquaciousness. He was only part Indian, remember, his reddish brown complexion augmented by exposure to the sun. In his silent moments he fiddled constantly with the radio dial. When I relieved him at the wheel of the car, he practiced taking pictures with an unloaded camera. He would half turn around from time to time and fish something out of the back seat. As I have said, he carried enough equipment to outfit a department store.

His Packard went back to the 1950s, when ordinary cars were almost the size of the SUVs that became popular forty years later. At one point, in his deep Southwestern drawl, he said to me, "Art, big guys like us need these big boats. We've got to have cars with strong springs. There's pretty good safety in these babies, too. Ya know, I almost got kilt once — up in Colorado. I must of hit a deer; it happened so fast I couldn't tell. All I remember is that I laid there on the ground a long time. Another car was involved, and there were bodies all over the place, so I've been told. Like I say, I don't remember a thing."

The longer he talked, the harder he pressed down on the accelerator. "Pissant roads!" he grumbled. "They're nothing but wagon trails — farm to market. Gawdam!" We were doing about eighty.

I thought, "In a minute or two, I'm going to be dead! We both are! And me with a beautiful redheaded wife" - I had married Kay Kumer - "and a lovable little kid at home. I'll never see them again!"

Whoever looks out for daredevils — St. Christopher? — kept our four wheels underneath us.

And now Walls was back on the subject of his accident. "I heard someone say, 'This guy here is done for.' He meant me. I was alive, but I couldn't speak. I couldn't move. I was all broken up. My biggest fear right then was that they'd take me to the morgue and have me embalmed." He shook his head. "It was months before I could work again."

To lighten the mood — and take my mind off how fast we were going — I told a few stories about AJR. Walls smiled as he listened and once or twice actually laughed. He was quiet for a while, and then, out of the blue, he switched to a new topic: his football career. "I went to TCU. Over in Fort Worth, ya know. Played with Sammy. Caught a lot of his passes. Never anyone better."

"Sammy?" I was revealing my ignorance.

Walls sat still, scrutinizing the windshield. Then he said, "Baugh." That was all.

Uncomfortably, I recalled what AJR had been telling me: "You're brand new" — words I resented. I was 29 years old and full of myself. I was a college graduate. I had studied acting. I had lived in New York City. I had been through a course of Marine training at Parris Island. I was a husband and a father. How could I be brand new?

But I was. There are memorable football people, some of them great ones and others merely colorful, we know by their first names: Tuffy, Bronk, Fido, Peahead, to mention a few. And Sammy. Slingin' Sammy Baugh was a great one. Walls himself belonged to a subdivision of this species. When his fellow scouts spoke of him, they used both his first name and his last. Will Walls, they called him, never just Will or just Walls. The full name had a ring to it. "Will Walls" was both alliterative and assonant. He started talking again as we drove into Erie. "After TCU, I went to the Giants. Well Mara — Duke." He was using Wellington Mara's two nicknames. "Good man. Then I went out to Hollywood. Made some movies — mostly Westerns. Action things. Had a nice little part in a Wallace Beery movie."

He reflected for several minutes. "Spencer Tracy. Now, there was a good guy. And he could act." I thought of some Tracy films I had seen and of Tracy's reputation as a drunk. "Tracy had a deaf child," Walls was saying. "Brought his wife over to the sound stage one day to talk to me. Real nice lady." Another pause. "My mom and dad were deaf mutes," he went on. "I told them what they wanted to know. I can use sign language as good as any deaf person. Sometimes I run into a panhandler who's passing out a card that instructs you how to use sign language. I'll sign to them, and if they don't sign back I know they're phonies. I go after them."

Much later I saw this actually happen. Walls did go after the kind of impostor he was talking about, and the fraud took off on the dead run.

By then Walls had shown me how adversarial he could be. Checking us in when we arrived at our hotel in Buffalo, the desk clerk remarked that the place was sold out, adding, "You're lucky to get a room." Sharply, Walls answered, "No we aren't lucky. We made a reservation." The desk clerk had no further pleasantries to offer.

We were both laden down with Walls' paraphernalia but needed a bellboy with a dolly to get the rest of it to our room. Walls closely supervised the whole operation. "Here, Art," he said, "you take the tape recorder. I'll carry the cameras." Noticing my amusement, perhaps, he intoned, "You can't be overprepared."

Walls was in charge of the expense money, and I watched him reward the bellboy with a handful of small change. Having overheard the dialogue between Walls and the desk clerk, the bellboy concealed his disappointment. Accusingly, Walls said to him, "Damn hot in this room." The bellboy answered, "It cools off at night, mister. This is Buffalo, you know." Then he left, rattling the change in his pocket.

I had wanted two rooms, but Fran Fogarty, as usual, was squeezing nickels. At least there were two beds. Across the street from the hotel was a park; if Fogarty had known how to arrange it, we'd be over there in that park sharing a pup tent, I thought.

The first thing Walls did after stowing away all his gear was hook up a tape recorder to the telephone.

"Is that legal, Willie?" I asked.

"Who gives a fuck?" Walls said. "The law's got too much on its hands to worry about a pissant tape recorder."

He complained again about the heat. The hotel seemed to lack air-conditioning. "Ya know, Art," he said, "lots of times on trips like this I've slept in my car. And lots of times when I didn't sleep in my car I wished I had. You'll never know what hot is, Art, until you've tried to sleep in some of those West Texas fleabags. There were nights when I'd toss and turn in some poor excuse for a bed and then go into the bathroom and turn the shower on cold and jump in for a few minutes and then jump out as wet as a duck and run back into the room and take a flying leap into the sack. I'd do that all night — as many times as I had to. Then towards dawn I'd take the bed sheets into the shower with me. Wrap myself up in 'em and let the cold water soak through. Then I'd run back into the room and jump into the bed again and get about an hour's sleep."

The lobby, when we were ready to go down, was full of scouts, coaches, and football players. Buddy Parker had wanted me to tag along with Walls for a reason: "You'll be able to meet all these guys and do some networking." Walls knew all the coaches from the South and Southwest and introduced me to them. "Billy Bob, say hi to Art Rooney Junior. His daddy owns the Steelers, and he's going to be one of our scouts." A majority of the Billy Bobs were wearing cowboy boots. Privately, Walls told me that "every asshole in Texas" had a pair of cowboy boots. I was glad I never wore mine. When I got back to Pittsburgh I gave them to our equipment man, Pinky Freyvogel.

It surprised me, although it should not have, that many of Will's friends knew AJR. "Glad to meet ya, Rooney. Knew yer dad from when I was with the Eagles. He took us to a place in yer town called the Lotus Club. Art paid for everything. Good guy. Drop by and see us the first time you come to Southwest Texas State."

To the Eastern coaches, most of them, Walls was a stranger. Fortunately, I ran into Bill Daddio, the former All-American end from Pitt, who had just gone to work for Blesto. Daddio got me acquainted with his friends from the East and the Big Ten, giving Walls an opportunity to head for the bar with his Southern and Western pals.

I didn't know at the time how much booze he could tolerate. When we returned to our room at the end of the evening there seemed to be no cause for alarm. He allowed me to use the bathroom first, and I came back wearing my P.J.'s, ready for bed. Walls then used the bathroom and came back in only a pair of undershorts. "A real pro," I thought. So many of the coaches and football players slept that way. Later, to Kay's annoyance, I acquired the habit myself. It made me feel — I don't know — like a true NFL guy.

Just as Walls had done, I kicked off the bed covers and pulled up one sheet. Walls had a book or maybe some scouting reports and left his reading light on; I turned mine off and faced the wall. Our windows were wide open, admitting too much light from the street below, and I slept fitfully, dreaming of Queequeg and Ishmael at the Spouter Inn. Will Walls, a part-Indian Texas cowboy, looked as exotic to me back then as any Polynesian harpoonist. I knew that Daddio and Jerry Neri, of the Philadelphia Blesto contingent, had very little use for Walls. Buddy Parker liked him, but Parker also liked the bombastic Fido Murphy (who will make an appearance further on in this narrative).

After Walls turned off his light, all was quiet until about 1:45, when I heard him jump out of bed and quickfoot it into the bathroom. He moved with such lightness and speed I could see him breaking clear of a defensive back and snagging a pass from "Sammy." He did not, as far as I could tell, get under the shower. Returning, he literally dived into bed. He tossed, turned, farted, and went back to sleep. Maybe two hours later, he jumped out of bed again and made another trip to the bathroom. I thought, "His kidneys are processing all the liquor he's had to drink." He made one final bathroom run at 6, when I was just about to get up.

We had a practice to cover at 9:30. One of the all-star teams was working out at the Buffalo University field. The first player Walls pointed out to me was a big stud from Grambling, defensive lineman Alphonse Dotson, who had gone to the Kansas City Chiefs of the AFL in the second round of the draft. "I seen that feller play a few times," Walls said. "When the goin' gets tough, he's more of a Jane than a Tarzan." It was a half-speed workout — no pads, only helmets — but Dotson kept roughing up the guys in the offensive unit. "If he tries that cheap-shot shit against one of the Bears' kids," Walls said, "he'll get smacked in the choppers."

I made it a point to follow Dotson's career. He played a year in Kansas City, a year in Miami, and two years in Oakland, never with great distinction. Whether anyone ever smacked him in the choppers I couldn't say.

When we went to the other team's practice, the best-looking athlete I ever had seen caught my eye. A running back, 5 feet 11 and a little over 200 pounds, he was perfectly configured from head to foot. He was quick-quick, with absolute control of his movements. I mean he could cut without losing a fraction of speed. When this guy ran sideways, he was faster than Steeler backs like Tom Calvin and Popcorn Brandt going straight ahead. He caught the ball a few times on pitchouts and short curling routes; without breaking stride, he sucked it right into his hands. "Mister Smooth," I said to myself. His right name, I learned, was Gale Sayers. George Halas had drafted him out of Kansas.

Will Walls sidled over to me. "Look at him, Artie. He'll never hold up. All that dancing and jitterbugging — he'll get killed. The way I see it, he'll have to be a flanker. Bit of a risk there."

I was shocked. If this guy couldn't play in the NFL, who could? The Bears, who were not yet in Blesto, had taken him in the first round. This was my first look at Sayers in the flesh. What was I missing? Bill Daddio, standing nearby, had overheard Walls, and later he said to me, "Artie, I don't know what your man was looking at, but nobody has to be a scout to tell that this guy Sayers is special. What the hell — he was the best running back in the Big Eight, and the Big Eight isn't exactly a push-and-pull league."

A long time ago, I watched a comet as it streaked across a dark Hawaiian sky. Sayers' career in the NFL was like that comet — brilliant, but not long-lasting. For five years he set ground-gaining records; in his sixth and seventh seasons, he was hurt most of the time.

So, yes — in a way, Walls was right. Sayers didn't hold up — not like some of the indestructible if otherwise ordinary workhouse backs. But to say he didn't hold up is like calling Alexander the Great, who died at 32, a flash in the pan.

As Walls and I drove back to Pittsburgh, I thought about what I had learned on this educational tour, this field trip. I learned that big guys should ride in big cars. I learned who "Sammy" was. I learned that Spencer Tracy was a good guy and Spencer Tracy's wife a nice lady. I learned that beggars who claim to be deaf mutes are not always trustworthy. I learned how to survive on hot nights in West Texas fleabag hotels. I learned that Texans who wear cowboy boots are not necessarily cowboys. I learned that Will Walls could hold his liquor.

But what had I learned about my profession? I learned that two people looking at a football player don't always see the same thing. And what had I learned other than that? Not much.

Part Three: A Seat at the Table
1965-1969
Chapter 37

Kass

If Dad and Mom had a spat, Mom would jump in the car and drive to the summer cottage in Ligonier, an arduous trip in the days before Interstate highways. When you're driving a car you're in control, or imagine you are, and control was something Mom needed at such times.

She was one of the best drivers I knew. With Mom behind the wheel, there was no reason not to feel perfectly at ease unless her temper caused problems.

As I have said, she could cuss a blue streak. When another driver in some way annoyed her, she never hesitated to let the offender hear about it, and in language that will not bear repeating.

Before cars were air-conditioned, I must remind you, people drove with their windows rolled down except in the coldest months of the year. The comments Mom directed at lane-jumpers, tailgaters, cut-off artists, and slowpokes were clearly audible, and they sometimes provoked violent reactions.

Twice, as she related it to us — and I admit I have trouble believing this — paranoid drivers threatened her with guns.

The first time it happened was on the Manchester Bridge. There had been an exchange of words, and at the ramp to Galveston Avenue the man in the other car flashed a pistol. Mom planted her foot on the accelerator. Up the steep cobblestone hill she flew, outrunning her pursuer. She made a left onto Lincoln and was safe.

The experience left her "in a state," as she used to say. We were just as well pleased that Dad was not at home — he'd have jumped in his car and gone out looking for the guy with the gun.

Mom hated going through tunnels and always slowed down to a crawl. In the Fort Pitt Tunnel one evening she incited road rage in the driver behind her. After leaning on his horn for a while, he pulled out into the other lane, a serious infraction of the traffic laws. Mom had a passenger — Aunt Alice. "Kass," she said as the man in the other car passed them, "he's waving a water pistol at us." Kass had been watching him, too. "Water pistol, hell," she replied, setting Alice straight. "That's a real gun."

In a minute they were out on the Parkway West. Eager to get beyond firing range just as quickly as possible, they took the first exit the gunslinger passed up.

Call it flight at the end of the tunnel.

Mr. Marshall

Kathleen McNulty Rooney had a quiet elegance about her. The way she dressed and the way she furnished her house reflected it. There was no reason, ever, for AJR to complain about "putting on the dog." Mom's inborn good taste and the advice of a decorator kept her from overdoing things.

The decorator, a man named Bill Marshall, worked at the Joseph Horne Company, which at least in the judgment of my mother was Pittsburgh's finest department store. I was partial to Kaufmann's myself, but deferred to her superior expertise.

She had clerked at Horne's as a young girl and spoke of having waited on Lillian Russell, the extravagantly endowed stage actress whose career pre-dated the movies. Miss Russell and her husband, Alexander Moore, publisher, of the *Pittsburgh Leader*, lived for a while in the North Side neighborhood called Millionaire's Row.

Horne's was Downtown, near the Sixth Street Bridge, just across the river from the old First Ward. You could spend hours in Horne's, or even days if you were able to spend more than time. In the days before and just after the Second World War the department stores sold everything anyone could want. I remember the aroma that hit you as soon as you walked into Horne's. Overdressed, overcoiffed sales girls stood near the entrance and sprayed perfume on every woman in sight. Kids unaccompanied by adults received an entirely different kind of welcome. Floor walkers — store detectives, actually — gave them the bum's rush.

Marshall, the decorator, was a dapper young guy with a neatly trimmed mustache. Mom and Aunt Alice never used his first name. Present or absent, he was always "Mister Marshall." There were times when his objectivity took me by surprise. If Horne's did not have what Kass was looking for, he would send her somewhere else. "I think you can find it at Kaufmann's," he would say. Or perhaps he would tell her about "a little antique store in Squirrel Hill," where she could buy exactly the right table, exactly the right lamp, exactly the right chair.

Between them, Mr. Marshall and Mom had 940 North Lincoln Avenue looking like a place out of Architectural Digest. Dad, although he acted indifferent to all this, was proud of the results, I think. By the purchases Kass made, you could tell how successful, or unsuccessful, he had been at the race track. Years later, the broker he dealt with in the Chicago commodities market told my son Art that his own family went through decorating binges or periods of retrenchment according to the way Dad's investments turned out.

Mr. Marshall and Mom refurnished Dad's den to give it a very masculine look. There were leather couches and chairs, a bookcase filled with books on sports and religion, a telephone, a portable radio, and in later years two television sets — placed side by side so that Dad could watch the news and a football or baseball game at the same time. It was not unusual for both TV sets and the radio to be going while he talked on the telephone and kept up a conversation with a visitor. Inexplicably, he did not have any need for a desk.

When Mr. Marshall was in his eighties and officially retired he did some work for my wife Kay in Florida. "Your mother was a delight — lots of fun," he said to me one day. "She had taste. I didn't really know your father, in spite of all the time I spent at his house, but one thing about him I remember: he always paid in cash and right away."

After Mr. Marshall's wife died, he found a sort of replacement — a boyfriend, whose name was Don. Their relationship lasted longer than most marriages do. Sometimes Mr. Marshall and I talked about life. He said to me once, "Do you know what I'm most sorry about?" and I thought, "Here comes the baloney." But not for the first time, he surprised me. "I'm sorry I wasn't nicer to people," he continued.

Bill Marshall was about the last person I could have imagined saying this to, but I told him, meaning it, "You sound just like my dad."

Loyalty

In 1954, AJR's old friend and political godfather, Jimmy Coyne, lay dying in Mercy Hospital at the same time Kass was there for a rather serious operation. Every now and then Dad would steal away from Mom's room to visit Senator Coyne on another floor.

That didn't bother me, although I think I expected him to be constantly in attendance on Kass. What did make me angry was his focus on getting the race results every day. He borrowed a small portable radio from a nun and allowed nothing to keep him away from it when Joe Tucker came on with the sports news. Couldn't he give up the race results for just one or two evenings while Mom was recovering from surgery?

The nun who had loaned him the radio sensed my displeasure. She explained to me that when some men are worried about their loved ones — wives, children, parents — they try to hide their emotions. Feigning an interest in race results or baseball scores or the stock market, or in anything else of a similar nature, would be one way to do that, she said.

I was not entirely convinced.

Apart from his nearest relatives, Senator Coyne had few visitors other than Dad. Where were all the people he went out of his way to help when he controlled Republican patronage in Allegheny County? Dad wondered. It makes me think of something Dave Lawrence once said about AJR. I heard it from Carl Hughes, who covered the wartime Steelers as a young sportswriter for the *Pittsburgh Press*. He quoted Lawrence as follows: "Art was a Republican, and always able to do political favors until Roosevelt was elected and we Democrats took over. So when someone would ask his help he would write me a note: 'This is a good guy.' But when he really wanted to help someone the note would read: 'Dave, this guy will be with you when you lose.'"

"Art," Lawrence added, according to Carl, "will be with you when you lose." Then Carl asked me, "Could any of us ever have a testimonial greater than that?"

In later life, when he was president, chief executive officer, and chairman of the Kennywood corporation with responsibility for the four amusement parks it comprised, Hughes put loyalty, the kind exemplified in Lawrence's tribute to AJR, at the top of an ethics system he informally laid out for himself and for Kennywood's employees.

Senator Coyne drifted in and out of consciousness. In his lucid moments, Dad said, he would pray for his political enemies and for anyone he might have done injury to, inadvertently or otherwise.

Dad made sure that this message got back to his "boys," whose own prayers were only for their mother's quick recovery. We wanted her back home at 940 North Lincoln Avenue cooking our meals.

Chapter 38

Mr. Clean

Offensive linemen are the working stiffs of football – drudges unnoticed by the spectators. Have you ever seen an offensive lineman jump up and down and thump himself on the chest to celebrate a block? The notion is ludicrous. "Most people – most fans – don't even realize we're out there," said Charley Bradshaw, a Steeler offensive tackle who played from 1961 through 1966. "They don't even know our names."

With one exception, he might have added. They knew Bradshaw's name. They knew it well, but they seldom used it. Derisively, they called him "Mr. Clean." In any kind of weather he could play an entire game and never get his uniform soiled. The fans, accustomed to the down-and-dirty, give-no-quarter, all-or-nothing effort demanded of Steeler linemen by coaches like Walt Kiesling, Jock Sutherland, and John Michelosen, jumped to the conclusion that all Bradshaw did was stand around. They wanted to see football players with grass stains, mud, and preferably a little blood on their uniforms.

When Ray Downey, the Steelers' public-address announcer, introduced the offensive unit at the start of a home game, calling off the names one by one, there would be perfunctory applause for everybody but Bradshaw. What Bradshaw heard, Sunday after Sunday, would be boos, and with each game during the miserable twelve-defeat 1965 season, the boos increased in volume.

That Bradshaw had been chosen for the 1963 and 1964 Pro Bowls meant nothing to the fans. That his coaches – he played for Buddy Parker, Mike Nixon, and Bill Austin – consistently gave him the highest efficiency rating in the offensive line after watching game films meant nothing. That in a magazine poll of all the coaches in the league he was picked as the lineman who blocked straight ahead most effectively meant nothing. He was always on his feet, the fans complained, and so he obviously couldn't be giving the game everything he had. The logic of Austin's observation – "You're no good on the ground" – failed to register with them. "He should be putting the other guys on the ground," his critics argued.

Bradshaw "played tall," with his legs straight, and in fact he actually was tall – 6 feet 6, which made him easy to single out on the field, for his teammates in the line were mostly fireplugs half a foot shorter. What the fans did not perceive was that besides playing tall he played smart. He knew how to use his hands and he knew how to slide with the pass rusher, skills that could be appreciated by a quarterback in the pocket.

In or out of uniform, Bradshaw was destined to be recognized. Allowing for the difference in their ages, he was a dead ringer from the neck up for John Nance Garner, a much-photographed congressman who spent a single contentious term as Franklin D. Roosevelt's vice president. Garner had a shock of white hair; Bradshaw's hair was so blond it might as well have been white.

Besides looking like Garner, Bradshaw resembled a leaning tower. By habit he stood and walked with his head forward and his shoulders stooped, a posture he developed in the East Texas country town where he was born. "Back home," he explained, "all of my friends were little guys. I had to bend over to talk with them." Going off to Baylor University on a football scholarship, he fell for and later married a girl who was 5 feet 2.

Bradshaw accepted the hazing he took from the fans with good grace. "People watch the ball," he said. "Then they look back and see me standing up and think I wasn't blocking. I wish they'd watch me the whole play. One of these Sundays I'll get a bucket of mud and a brush and have the equipment manager paint me before the game. Then I'll roll back to the huddle after every down."

AJR used to say that when Bradshaw's playing days were over, no one would have to hold any benefits for him. While he was still with the Steelers, he earned a law degree and had an office in Houston. He was the only practicing attorney in the NFL. During the 1966 football season he appeared in Allegheny County Criminal Court, granted impromptu admission to the Pennsylvania bar by Judge Gwilym Price, Jr., under the jurisdictive equivalent of the free-substitution rule. Looking as immaculate as ever, he wore a sharply creased banker's gray suit, a radiantly white shirt, and a perfectly knotted tie. His client was charged with "malicious mischief" — throwing an empty beer bottle through the window of a doctor's office.

The switch from offense to defense was no problem for Bradshaw. Good offensive linemen "fire out," as the coaches then called it, and Bradshaw fired out in defense of the accused. With a series of objections, he kept the prosecution from showing that the window had cost fifty dollars or more. Mischief costing less than fifty dollars was not by definition malicious, which meant that it therefore was subject to a lighter sentence. Unable to produce a witness who could testify that the window had in fact cost fifty dollars or more, the prosecution asked for a delay of two hours in the trial. Judge Price, upholding Bradshaw's objection, denied the request, whereupon Bradshaw jumped up and asked him to dismiss the charges. The judge said, "I sustain the demurrer."

With that, Mr. Clean had won the case. And there wasn't a speck of dirt on his unwrinkled banker's gray suit.

Him Tarzan

In the first few Tarzan movies there was always a scene in which the ape man comes upon his future mate.

"Me Tarzan," he says.

"Me Jane," she replies.

The Tarzan series lived on, year after year. It never aged. Leading men and leading ladies were not as durable. Like Steeler coaches in the 1950s, new Tarzans replaced old Tarzans and new Janes replaced old Janes with clockwork regularity. The actor who played Tarzan had to be young, well-built, good-looking, and agile. It helped if he could swim (the best-known of all the Tarzans, Johnny Weissmuller and Buster Crabbe, won Olympic gold medals in the freestyle events). The Janes who came and went were held to the same high standards. Even in the Legion of Decency era, Tarzans and Janes swung from treetop to treetop, or splashed in the crystal-clear water of jungle lagoons, with hardly any clothing to impede them.

It was toward the end of the 1960s when Mike Henry took his turn at being Tarzan. Mike was a former Steeler and also a former Los Angeles Ram. As a linebacker he ranked in the middle of the pack. For good looks, he was up near the top. "Ruggedly handsome" would be an accurate way to describe him, an assessment concurred in by AJR's pretty secretary, Mary Regan. Hearing that Mike was to be the next Tarzan, she glanced up briefly from the letter she was typing and enhanced her reputation for laconic witticisms.

"Me Jane," she announced.

Mike Henry grew up in Hollywood — he came from a family of film cutters — and played college football at Southern California. The scout who discovered him was Fido Murphy, an outlandish character hilariously profiled in *Sports Illustrated* by a young Pittsburgh freelance writer named Myron Cope, for many years afterward the color man on Steeler radio broadcasts. After Henry's third season with the Steelers, Buddy Parker traded him to the Rams. He was now back in movieland, where another kind of talent scout discovered him. A screen test followed, and Mike was the next Tarzan.

Playing Tarzan does not require the acting skill of an Olivier or a Brando, but I saw Mike once in a somewhat demanding role. I forget the name of the film, but Jackie Gleason and Burt Reynolds had two of the leading parts. Gleason was a father and Henry his idiot son. He played off Gleason in a sure-footed, believable way, revealing a modest flair for comedy.

Most of the Steelers I have known, when they were through playing football, became coaches or teachers or salesmen or sportscasters. Just as Byron White was the only Supreme Court justice, Mike Henry was the only real movie star, if not for long.

Prematurely cast aside by the studios, he went into the old established family business — film-cutting.

Rock of Gibraltar

R ick Roberts, a black man who wrote sports for the *Pittsburgh Courier*, talked AJR into hiring Bill Nunn, Jr., another *Courier* sportswriter and the son of the paper's managing editor, as a part-time scout. I was pissed purple.

Nunn had near-perfect contacts. One of his beats for the *Courier* was college football — Negro college football. More than six feet tall, he had gone to a black college himself — West Virginia State — and had been an outstanding basketball player. He picked the all-star and the All-America football and basketball teams for his paper. I knew we needed a scout and I knew how important the black schools were to our future success. But I wanted to hire the scouts myself. He was not my guy.

Aware of how I felt, AJR got us together one night. Nunn seemed all right — well-spoken and polite. He did not try to B.S. me. I could see that he had a good attitude and I gave Dad a qualified OK — not that it mattered. Dad's mind was made up and could not have been changed.

Very quickly Nunn became a Rock of Gibraltar for me. Often I have wished I could say that I was the one who "discovered" him. He scouted part-time for us in 1968 and 1969 and became a full-fledged member of the organization in 1970. This I can claim to be my idea, but getting AJR and Dan to fall in line was no problem.

Nunn spent seventy percent of his time with me and the remainder in "community relations." He continued to work in the *Pittsburgh Courier* sports department, which he was able to do by doubling up. On trips to the black schools in the South he scouted football players for the Steelers and gathered material for his newspaper articles. Because the *Courier* appeared only once every week, he had some leeway in meeting deadlines. The Steelers and the paper shared his travel expenses.

I thought of the *Courier* editors and reporters I got to know through Nunn as pretty nice guys who seemed to like sports. It would be years before I developed a true appreciation of what a tremendous crusading newspaper the *Courier* was. Bill Nunn's merits, on the other hand, were obvious to me from the start.

At first it was only his contacts that made him valuable to us — his contacts and his insights — but as time went on I saw that he could scout football players of any color whatever — black, white, blue, green, you name it. In fact he tossed Dad an Irishman now and then, much to our amusement.

Like Jack Butler, he cut through all the baloney. There was a big murder case in Pittsburgh one year. "The broad did it," Nunn told me. I said, "Dammit, Bill, you're too cynical. She isn't even a suspect." "Just wait," Bill said. A few years later, big headlines in the morning paper confirmed what he'd been saying. The broad did it.

"It was there for you to see." Nunn said,

I found that to be a general principle. You could apply it to football players, to coaches, to scouts. The truth was always there for you to see.

We had this great young player Joe Greene — a defensive tackle, the cornerstone of our success. But he was also a loose cannon, thrown out of three games in his rookie year, infamous as far as the press was concerned for spitting in the face of a sportswriter, Pat Livingston. What could we do with this wild man?

Bill Nunn came up with the answer. We had a player named John Brown, a very good offensive lineman and a civilized human being. "Have Brown and Greene room together," Nunn suggested. "Brown is the one who can settle that kid down." He was right. Brown and Greene, both black, were the ideal color combination.

In the first few years after integration, color was all-important in the assignment of roommates at training camp. Black roomed with black; white roomed with white. A Hawaiian player, a rookie, stormed into the camp manager's office: "Get that black son of a bitch out of my room." The Hawaiian was moved in with a white guy. So now the white guy had a complaint; "Get that Chinaman out of my room." Everybody was angry at everybody else. So Bill Nunn took over the management of the camp. "From now on," he announced, "the rookies will be assigned to their rooms alphabetically, like it or not. Next year if you're on the team you can pick your own roommates. But while you're rookies you'll do as we tell you." It worked. There was no more turbulence.

Jake Gaithers, at Florida A. & M., and John Merritt, at Tennessee State, were two of the great coaches I met through Nunn. He advised me to take Merritt a box of my dad's cigars, which I did, and from then on we were friends. It was Merritt who told me, confidentially, "Never trust a black man with gray eyes." The task of checking out eye color wearied me so much that I soon gave it up. Nunn himself used to say, "Never draft or sign a big kid with small feet." I thought it made sense. On scouting trips, I would say in a deliberately casual manner, "By the way, Coach, what's the shoe size of ol' Smith over there?" At last I got tired of it. I said to Nunn, "Heck, Bill, I'm a size nine and I weigh two-fifty." I had left myself open for a counter punch. "From what I hear," Nunn drawled, "you couldn't run, either."

As camp manager, Nunn was in charge of the payroll. He made a trip each week to the Mellon Bank in Latrobe and withdrew enough cash to pay the coaches, players, scouts, equipment men, and ball boys. A coach from a black college was in the office one day when Nunn returned from the bank with a satchel full of money. Watching him empty the bag on a table, the coach was transfixed. When Bill had sorted everything out and left the room, the coach said to me, "You Rooneys would let him do that?" I knew what the sub-text was. "You Rooneys," he was saying, "would let a *black* guy do that?"

Of course he was black himself. I said, "Coach, that job is a pain in the ass."

He shook his head, and it was clear what his thoughts were: "You'd trust a *black* dude with all that money?"

Every one of us, I guess, has some learning to do.

Chapter 39

Dog Pound

Back home from a trip to the West Coast, I heard myself telling somebody, "I saw Fido out there, and he said he's seen Bow-wow." My wife Kay heard me, too. With a look of disgust, she said, "When are you going to get a real job?"

Fido Murphy and Bow-wow Wykevicz were scouts. Fido worked for the Steelers and the Bears and Bow-wow for the Eagles.

In Myron Cope's book, "Broken Cigars," a collection of his magazine stories, there's a profile of Fido, whose facial resemblance to a bulldog, Myron wrote, was not the origin of his nickname, as most people assumed. According to Fido, its derivation went back to the way he ran with the football as a halfback for Westbrook Seminary of Portland, Maine, in the early 1920s. His speed of foot was such that Boston sportswriter Bill Cunningham likened him to a greyhound, Fido explained. "And when we played in hostile territory after that," he went on, "the fans called me Fido."

If there's an explanation for Bow-wow's nickname, and there must be, I've never heard it.

Fido Murphy was a little guy, no more than 5 feet 8 inches tall. He claimed to have played football at Fordham when Major Frank Cavanaugh, noted for his heroism in the First World War, was the coach. "Cavanaugh called me 170 pounds of dynamite," Fido informed Cope. It was as a strategist and innovator, however, that, by his own account, Fido left a permanent imprint on the game.

Again according to himself, he invented the modern T formation while coaching at Samuel Johnson Academy in Connecticut. It seems that Marchmont Schwartz, an assistant to Clark Shaughnessy at the University of Chicago, saw the Samuel Johnson team play, and he let Shaughnessy in on the details of what Fido was doing. Shaughnessy then indoctrinated George Halas, and presto! Halas's Bears rode the T-formation to instant success.

The next thing Fido invented, as a consultant for the Detroit Lions, was the red dog, or blitz, and then he conceived the five-man line, middle guard and all. This was why George Halas hired him as a scout. Having given the Bears their offense, he told them how to prevent Sammy Baugh from completing short passes ("Back up your tackles and back up your secondary kids deeper. Baugh won't run, and if he overshoots the short stuff we'll pick 'em off.") Result: Bears 73, Redskins 0 in the 1940 title game. Later — still advising Halas — Fido imparted the secret of stopping the San Francisco Forty-Niners' shotgun offense. The Bears stopped it cold, winning by a shutout, but Shaughnessy, who was now their defensive coach, "again got credit for Fido's brainwork," related Cope with amused skepticism.

Revealing to Cope the source of his genius, Fido declared modestly, "It isn't that I'm smarter than everyone else in football. It's just that I know more."

Actually, there was sometimes a grain of truth in Fido's assertions. Buddy Parker once told my dad and me that Fido had "a real good eye for formations — where guys lined up and where they moved on the playing field." This was very important before game films came into use and were readily exchanged, Parker said. Up till then I had thought — erroneously, I now decided — that Parker kept Fido around just for laughs. I know that Fido had a feel for scouting quarterbacks. "Look at their feet, how fast they set up and move around and how well they escape the pressure," he told me. It was pretty good advice.

Overall, he was not an astute judge of talent. His scouting reports were always late and disorganized and his expense accounts exasperated the meticulous Fran Fogarty. I saw Fran take a punch at him one day in Parker's office. Like others who were present, I wanted to see Fogarty clean Fido's clock, but Parker quickly jumped to his feet and got between them.

For some time afterward, Fido went around telling people that Parker had saved Fogarty's life. Uncle Jim then took Fido aside and warned him that he was playing with fire. He said that Fogarty had fought with the French underground during World War II and had killed more Germans than Commando Kelly.

"Who is Commando Kelly?" Fido asked.

"A North Side kid who won the Congressional Medal of Honor for wiping out a whole German regiment. He killed a lot of those krautheads barehanded, and Fogarty is even tougher than Kelly was."

Fido swallowed all of this, even the exaggerations. From then on he was more prompt with his expense accounts (but not his scouting reports). He wrote friendly letters to Fogarty and spoke of him admiringly to mutual acquaintances. When Fran dropped dead of a heart attack several years later, Fido proclaimed that he had lost his best friend in football.

Fido lasted only two or three years with Blesto before Jack Butler sent him back to the Bears. Butler would have fired him, making no bones about it, but Fido was Halas's guy and therefore untouchable. This way, it was simply a case of goods being returned to the sender, and not even Fido took exception. He stayed with the Bears until his retirement, and wherever NFL scouts gathered, Fido would be there. After the Steelers had won a Super Bowl or two, he made a great point of introducing me to people. "Meet Art Rooney Junior," he would say. "I taught him everything he knows."

In truth, Fido did teach me a lot — how not to act, how not to present myself. It was typical of Fido that when Buddy Parker left the team he immediately called AJR with a recitation of Parker's shortcomings. Cutting him off, AJR handed me the telephone. "Fido," I said, "Buddy Parker was your sponsor, and now you're the first to tell us good riddance."

My portrayal of Fido may be a little one-sided. There were those who must have shared his good opinion of himself — for example, his wife. Fido's wife was an actress named Iris Adrian —"a Ziegfeld queen, the belle of Broadway," her husband told Myron Cope. For a guy with a mug like his to snag a Ziegfeld queen did not seem unusual to Fido, who saw nothing wrong with that mug. "The dolls loved Murphy in those days. He was a handsome devil," Fido confessed to Cope. As for Iris, she held her own, I understand, in the looks department. Her specialty as an actress was dumb-blonde parts. On the Jack Benny television show, she played a telephone operator with a Flatbush accent and an impudent tongue. She called Fido Raymond, or Ray, never using his nickname. He spoke of her always with pride, and they lived contentedly, as far as I know, in their Hollywood crash pad.

Bow-wow Wykevicz, a native of New Kensington, was tall, slim, and distinguished-looking. In the late 1940s, he surfaced on the Pacific Coast and ingratiated himself with Tommy Prothro, the coach at UCLA. Bow-wow would do anything for anybody. He ran Prothro's errands, baby-sat for him and his wife, and picked up their kids after school. Whenever he did a favor, he expected two in return. But Prothro genuinely liked Bow-wow and hired him as a scout upon leaving college football to coach the Eagles. The title, I suspect, was an honorific. Actually, he continued to serve Prothro as a glorified odd-jobs man.

Bow-wow had a bizarre sense of humor. From Los Angeles, he sent a telegram to his mother in New Kensington informing her of his death in an automobile accident. The next day he sent her a second telegram, instructing her to disregard the first.

While Prothro was still at UCLA, Bow-wow transported a Hollywood starlet to the coach's front door on his birthday, rang the bell, and ducked out of sight. The young lady was gift-wrapped in cellophane, a red ribbon securing the package. Underneath the cellophane, she was completely bare. Prothro's wife came to the door and let out a shriek. That Bow-wow remained a friend of the family indicates how much he could get away with.

For money or love, or maybe both, the bimbos he knew in the motion-picture business were willing to be his accomplices. He would get them to pose nude in some kind of football stance for a photographer, and then he would send the pictures — inscribed "To my dearest friend So-and-so: Hope to see you again when you come West. Yours ever, Trixie [or whatever]" — to various coaches of his acquaintance. How often such keepsakes fell into the hands of the coaches' wives I can only guess.

In communicating with AJR, and also with me, Bow-wow was much more discreet. Knowing the Chief's aversion to anything off-color, he sent us holy cards depicting St. Anne or the Blessed Mother.

Almost all coaches eventually lose their jobs, and after the Eagles got rid of Prothro, Bow-wow returned to his beloved California. His greatest triumphs were now behind him, but out there during his heyday he may or may not have been married to Hollywood columnist Sheila Graham. If there is proof that actual vows were exchanged I am not aware of it. Miss Graham writes extensively in her memoirs of a documented love affair with F. Scott Fitzgerald; she alludes only in passing to a "relationship," its nature undefined, with "a person who is not worth mentioning." Presumably this was Bow-wow. Those of us who knew him and followed his career would like to think so.

Brian and Brucie

With our drafting completed in 1966, we were signing free agents to fill out the roster when my telephone rang.

A man with a strong Italian accent introduced himself and said, "Why you not draft my son?"

I was taken aback. Still fairly new to the business, I never had heard a question like that from a parent. Without being rude, I tried to make our conversation a short one. It was no easy matter.

"Why you not draft my son? He's-a good-a football player," the stranger persisted. He seemed hurt. His tone of voice got to me, and I patiently explained that we were limited in the number of draft choices we could make. What was his boy's name? I asked.

Brian something. The last name I failed to catch.

Had anyone else drafted him?

No.

Where did he play?

Wake Forest

What position?

He ran with the ball.

It occurred to me suddenly that I was giving myself away. The mind of a scout who was worth his salt would be a repository for information like this. I came up with what I thought was a plausible excuse. I said, "I have to ask about these things because I'm not at my desk. So many names have been going through my head I'm in a bit of a fog right now."

He could fill me in, the man said. His boy had been a starter for the last two seasons at Wake Forest. He had run for a lot of yardage and had caught a lot of passes. Why had nobody drafted such a player? The man did not raise his voice and there was no animosity in it.

"Hang on for a minute while I get your boy's records" I said. I found the reports on Wake Forest, checked out a running back whose first name was Brian ("Very productive. An overachiever. Lacks size and speed. May have already reached his potential"), and went back to the phone, half expecting the line to be dead. But my caller was waiting.

"Well, the probable reason Brian was not drafted," I began, "is the lack of great size or speed …"

"Yes, but he's a top-a player." The man's pleading tone softened my response. I agreed that Brian had good credentials. "Let me talk with a scout who has seen him," I said, "and I'll call you back."

I spoke to the scout, Ken Stilley, the next day. He told me that in his opinion the kid should have been drafted in one of the late rounds, having led the nation in rushing with more than 1,000 yards in 252 carries. Then Stilley added, "He probably did reach his potential in college, but he's a fine individual and won't embarrass you in camp. Go for him." On the telephone again with the father, I said we would like to offer Brian a contract. Hardly able to contain his happiness, he promised to have Brian call me.

When Brian did call, he was somewhat apologetic. He respected his father greatly but explained how difficult it was for someone not born in this country to have a clear understanding of National Football League protocol. Fathers did not call personnel directors to lobby for their sons.

I told him not to worry about it. I said I liked what I heard from my scouts and would send him our standard free-agent contract. There would be a signing bonus of a few hundred dollars and another small bonus if he succeeded in making the team.

"Sounds good," he said. "I'll let you know my decision very soon." I had done this on my own, without consulting our head coach or anyone else, but I was comfortable with the thought that we were giving an opportunity to a young man who deserved it. For the rest of his life, whatever happened in camp, he could say that he'd had a tryout with the Steelers.

It wasn't long before Brian called back. He was grateful for our offer, he said more than once, but had made up his mind to sign with the Bears. I reflected that most free agents who accepted another team's offer rather than ours never bothered to let us know. I thanked him and wished him good luck.

The kid's full name was Brian Piccolo. He played in the Bears' backfield for four seasons and then died of cancer. Brian Piccolo had but a few months to live when his friend and teammate, the great runner Gale Sayers, was voted the Most Courageous Player award by the Professional Football Writers Association in 1970. Sayers had come back from a serious knee injury to lead the NFL in ground gaining. At the presentation ceremony, he said the award should have gone to Piccolo.

Sayers had much to tell about Piccolo in an autobiography he wrote with Al Silverman. Its title – "I Am Third" — was taken from a sign on the desk of his track coach at the University of Kansas, Bill Easton. Sayers had asked what it meant. "It means the Lord is first, my friends are second, and I am third," Easton told him. The book became the basis for a television movie – "Brian's Song" — its main theme the friendship between Sayers and Piccolo.

When Piccolo died, and when the movie came out, I thought of the telephone call I received from his father and of the question that haunted me: "Why you not draft my son?"

Brian's father and Brucie's aunt were two of a kind. Brucie's aunt was a cleaning lady who worked for my mother-in-law. "Tell Mister Rooney not to forget about my nephew, Brucie," she kept reminding her. In our occasional face-to-face encounters, the cleaning lady would ask if I had seen "Brucie" yet. Dismissing her as a pain in the neck, I resolutely ignored these entreaties.

Brucie, I gathered went to college at Davidson, in the Carolinas. Davidson was a member of the weak Southern Conference and not exactly a noted producer of NFL talent. Besides, how was it possible for anyone called Brucie to be a football player? Like Mr. Piccolo, my mother-in-law's cleaning lady would not be put off. She started hounding my wife about Brucie. At last for the sake of peace in the family I went to our scouting book, and found just a single entry for Brucie. I learned that Brucie played for Davidson, all right. A better way to put it would be that he did the field-goal kicking — "which accounts for his sissy name," I said to myself. Next I went to the report book and found another single entry for Brucie. Real prospects were written up six times, seven times, eight times. Brucie was a big, strong kid with a live leg, the report said, but "inaccurate."

"Tell your mother's cleaning lady that I looked up the scouting report on Brucie. The verdict is that he's not a good enough kicker for the NFL," I instructed my wife.

I heard nothing more about Brucie until the following spring. Pausing in her work one day, the cleaning lady told me that he had signed as a free agent with the Rams. I wished him the best of luck and got away quickly. A month later, with the season under way, my mother-in-law informed me that, according to her cleaning lady, Brucie made the team. "She must be mistaken," I thought. I checked out the rosters, and sure enough — a rookie free agent had won a job with the Rams as their field-goal kicker.

It was Brucie, and he played for several years.

He taught me something, a valuable lesson for a scout: listen to recommendations and follow them up — especially recommendations from cleaning ladies.

L. C.

Late in the football season of 1968 I was planning to scout a running back who played for Arkansas A. & M. Because I had a bad cold, I was tempted to stay at home and send for the team's game films. My wife had a cold and our kids all had colds, but though I caught hell from Kay for doing it, I flew to Little Rock, rented a car, and drove to the A. & M. campus in Pine Bluff.

The A. & M. coaches were considerate and friendly. First they let me look at the films, sitting in as I watched. I forget the name of the halfback I was down there to see, but they talked him up. "Look at that move," they would say. "Did you notice the way he broke that tackle? Run that play back again. See how big the defensive back is ... " They were certain the kid could play in the NFL.

I had another A. & M. guy on my list, a defensive end named Clarence Washington. "He's big and strong, and he has good movement," the coaches told me. "Let's watch him. He'll make it as a defensive tackle."

So we looked at the films of the defensive unit, and I liked Washington as a project. But somebody else caught my eye, a kid who appeared to be about 6 feet 6.

"Who's the guy making that pass rush?" I asked.

"Oh. That's L.C. We knew you'd spot him. He's special."

"L.C.? Spell that out for me."

"L.C. Greenwood."

I looked at my list, and he was on it. Too tall for his weight, the notation said.

"Well ... that's what they all say. He has growth potential, though. Wait till you see him in practice." The coaches were trying hard to reassure me.

On a dusty, hardscrabble practice field, we watched him in practice. He was so tall and thin he reminded me of the Masai warriors in the movie "King Solomon's Mines." But nobody pushed him around. Defensive tackles that tall aren't supposed to have leverage. Greenwood was different. He could break down and get under blockers.

This one could be a ruby — a sleeper — I said to myself.

When we met to prepare for the 1969 draft, our new head coach, Chuck Noll, said he was looking for guys who could make something good happen. I mentioned Washington and Greenwood from Arkansas A. & M., and we drafted them both. The halfback whose name I've forgotten did not fit into our plans.

Washington hung on for one season. Greenwood did more than hang on. He helped the Steelers of the 1970s win the Super Bowl four times and is nominated every year for the Hall of Fame.

Those initials — L.C— used to bother me. What did they stand for? L.C. himself would never say. Eventually I learned that they stood for nothing. In the South, somebody told me, it is not unusual to have initials instead of a first name and a middle name.

"L.C.," from then on, was O.K. with me.

Chapter 40

Lombardi Lite

When the time came to replace Mike Nixon as coach, there was certainly no shortage of recommendations. Everybody, it seemed, had a candidate. Even Nixon's old boss got into the act.

Buddy Parker had resigned in a huff, and he had done it abruptly at the worst possible moment — several weeks into the exhibition season — but AJR was still Buddy's friend. Buddy knew, as all of Pittsburgh did, that the Steelers were glad to see him go. A severance package of handsome proportions undoubtedly eased his pain. So, being helpful, he called AJR from Texas and told him about the coach at John Carroll, a Catholic university in Cleveland the size of Duquesne. "Get yourself a good young student of football who's an expert on defense," was Buddy's advice. "Look at what that young guy Don Shula has been doing with the Baltimore Colts. John Carroll has a defensive-minded coach named John Ray who's the same type. I'm not saying Ray is your man, but that's the kind of guy you want. He knows defense." Parker believed the importance of defense could not be overestimated.

I asked Ken Stilley about Ray, unaware that they were personal friends. Stilley concurred with Parker, telling me that Ray understood defense, was a man of good character, and would go places. (He later became head coach at Kentucky.) Stilley then made a prediction. He said that AJR would consult Vince Lombardi before he did anything at all and that Lombardi would recommend his former assistant, Bill Austin. "Remember this about Austin," Stilley continued. "Austin has a poor personality. He's a lot like Buster Ramsey, with one difference. Austin is not as smart as Ramsey." I relayed Stilley's warning to AJR. He said that with all due respect to Stilley, a capable scout, this was Vince Lombardi that he was going to call. There was no need for further discussion.

Ernie Stautner, meanwhile, applied for the job. After leaving Parker's staff, Ernie had caught on with the Dallas Cowboys. Jack Butler applied because I urged him to. Embarrassed about it, he asked for the job in a note I hand-delivered to AJR. "Tell that Butler to come over here and see me," he said. The Blesto offices in the Roosevelt Hotel were just a few steps away from Dad's, and, as fearless as he could be on the football field, the walk was a long one for Butler. Feeling responsible — the whole idea had been mine — I tagged along. AJR did not order me out. He said to Butler, "Jack, you're a top man and you're one of us. You have ability. But you need experience, and that knee of yours is so bad you can hardly stand. For you to think about coaching ... well ... this just isn't the time." Now Jack was even more embarrassed, but if he blamed me for putting him on the spot he kept it to himself. In hindsight, getting the brushoff from Dad was a lucky break for Butler. His promotion to the executive directorship of Blesto followed soon afterward.

Through Mary Regan, AJR placed a call to Lombardi in Green Bay. Nobody told this to Lombardi, but Dan listened in on Fran Fogarty's phone and I was hooked up at Ed Kiely's. Lombardi came on the line and greeted Dad heartily in his normal tone of voice — loud and gruff. Dad told Lombardi the purpose of his call, and the coach brought up a few names. In two or three minutes they were talking about Austin. Austin had left the Packers to take an assistant's job with the Rams the year before. "I didn't like that," Lombardi said, "but it was something he had to do. Talented people like Bill Austin get antsy when they're waiting for a head coaching position to open up."

At the end of the conversation, both Dan and I felt, as AJR did, that Austin was our guy. Lombardi had praised him extravagantly, had said we couldn't go wrong with Austin. And who would know better? Besides, Lombardi was Dad's old friend; he would never intentionally give us a bum steer.

Fleetingly, I thought once again of Ken Stilley's words. They lingered uncomfortably in the back of my mind. If Austin was a clone of Buster Ramsey ... But no — it couldn't be true. Vince Lombardi had spoken, and that was enough.

'Now Is Now'

B ill Austin was a big, blond, ruggedly good-looking guy, standing 6-1 or 6-2 and weighing 225-230 pounds. He had been an offensive lineman at Oregon State and had played for the New York Giants' championship teams in the 1950s.

His off-season hobbies were handball and aviation. Austin was pretty good at handball and considered it the ideal training for interior linemen. Handball compelled a player to stay low; at the same time, it sharpened his hand-to-eye coordination, Austin believed. Aviation seemed to fascinate him. He flew his own airplane and often spoke of his brother, a Navy pilot shot down in Vietnam. Once when Austin asked me for a scouting assignment, I sent him to a game at Bowling Green because the Bowling Green stadium was next to an airport.

It became apparent to us right away that, like his mentor Lombardi, Austin was going to be a control freak. In his own mind, he ruled the entire organization. Joe Bach had been the same way, but whereas Lombardi was a winner and Bach a nice guy, Austin fell short in both respects. His manner was sarcastic and he offered "suggestions" freely. Ticket sellers, publicity men, accountants, and most especially the personnel director — me — were the objects of his attention and criticism.

Not far into his first season, Austin had all of us on edge, including AJR, who did not like Austin's habit of chastising his players and assistant coaches in public. After Austin gave one coach a dressing down in front of his two young sons, AJR warned him never to repeat such an insensitive act.

The understanding between Dan and me that we would build the team through the draft meant nothing to Austin. His first move as coach was to trade our top pick to Green Bay for Lloyd Voss, a defensive tackle. Voss was hard-working and likable and still a pretty fair lineman, but the feeling was that Lombardi had given up on him. When the chance came to unload Voss, he took advantage of it. In fairness to Austin, we had not been able to sign the best available college players since the American Football League had come into the market, a state of affairs that would continue until the merger the following year. But I was still a personnel man first and foremost, and Austin's high-handedness put my nose out of joint.

Austin maintained that even with Blesto our scouting coverage was insufficient. I felt that our coverage had been good and would get better. When the Vikings joined the Blesto group in 1967 we would have more scouts in the field. "Next year is next year. Now is now," Austin said, and he had a point. To satisfy him, our assistant coaches were scouting college games on Saturday. It caused logistical problems because most of our own games were played on Sunday afternoon. The coaches resented the trouble this made for them, but Austin prevailed.

Our perceived shortage of scouts was the reason for the Bowling Green trip. The Steelers were not scheduled that weekend, and Austin had taken an interest in a guard named Jon Brooks who played for Bowling Green's opponent, Kent State. This Brooks was a top-rated blocker who would be a good fit, we thought, for Austin's "run-to-daylight" scheme, which required a lot of pulling by the guards.

Back in the office on Monday, Austin asked to see me. The trip had gone well, and I got my first look at a different side of him. There was nothing of the smart aleck in his behavior that day. It was man to man, scout to scout.

"Artie," he said, "I know that you and the Blesto guys are pretty high on Brooks, but he really doesn't have it as a top-of-the-line prospect. First of all, there's his size. He isn't tall enough for his weight, and most of his weight is in his thighs and ass. He can pop out on a man block. He comes off the ball well on the down block. The quick pass rusher who has some movement is going to be a lot of trouble for him. He's supposed to have good pulling ability. Check it out on the films again. He has nice short-pull quickness, but loses so much on the deep pulls ... and that's what we'll be asking him to do."

And so on and so on. When he was finished, Austin had convinced me of something without giving offense. The Blesto scouts were pushing Brooks hard, but I re-studied the films, as Austin wanted me to do, and they bore out his assessment. Brooks went to the Philadelphia Eagles in the second round of the draft. He had gained so much weight that somebody gave him a nickname — the S.S. Brooks, meaning he was as big as a ship. After his rookie season, the Eagles had no further use for him, nor did Brooks ever play again in the NFL. The scout who had been his staunchest supporter found himself in very hot water.

Austin tried to copy Vince Lombardi's methods the way that John Michelosen had imitated Jock Sutherland. His practices were long and hard. But a counterfeit is a counterfeit and never the real thing; he can't be. Just as Michelosen had not been another Sutherland, Austin was not a second Lombardi.

His first Steeler team ended up with a 5-8-1 record, a big improvement over Nixon's 2-12 and marginally better than Buddy Parker's 5-9 the year before, but insubstantial grounds for expecting Austin to be our messiah.

Battered and Bloody

Bill Austin never understood that conditioning and toughness were just a means to an end, and not ends in themselves. In his second year, 1967, the Steelers regressed, winning only four games, with one tie.

Austin looked and acted like a coach, but that was all. In one game, the Steelers lined up to punt with ten men. The quarterback was calling signals before Cannonball Butler, the fleet little running back, realized he was part of the coverage team. Frantically, Butler dashed onto the field. He crossed in front of the kicker as the ball was snapped, intercepting its flight. Like a guided missile gone wrong, it bounced off his helmet.

In the history of football, has there ever been a more ludicrous special-teams play?

Pat Livingston of the *Pittsburgh Press* had sized up Austin immediately and did not shrink from putting the coach's feet to the fire. Austin never forgot or forgave. A good while later, when Vince Lombardi was coaching the Redskins, and Austin was back where he belonged, coaching Lombardi's offensive line, Livingston strolled into the Redskins' dressing room after a Pittsburgh-Washington game at Pitt Stadium, and Austin saw red. Showing the speed that had made him one of the NFL's quickest guards, he had an arm around Livingston's neck in a split second and with his free hand he punched Pat in the ribs. Lombardi needed help to separate them.

If AJR had listened to Dan, Austin would not have returned for the final year of his contract. "Austin must go ... now!" Dan said, asserting himself with new forcefulness. "Not yet," answered AJR. "We'd be the laughing stock of the league. And remember," he added, "we'd have to pay the guy. We'd have to pay his assistants. In full. For not working. No way."

Austin's obtuseness had kept him from noticing that he was close to the edge of the cliff. He put a rule in, on his own, barring visitors from the dressing room before a game. AJR had not been notified. On a Sunday before the Steelers played the Giants at Yankee Stadium, he was with the New York columnist Jimmy Breslin and invited him into the dressing room, along with his kids. Austin, glaring at them, made it clear they were unwelcome. So they left, but AJR had some words with his coach the next day. "Bill, I didn't know the dressing room was closed," he began. "Otherwise, I wouldn't have taken Breslin and his kids in there. I keep the rules. Now, Breslin is a guy who can walk into any dressing room in the league. But he picked ours. Let me tell you this, Bill. I said I keep the rules, and I do — if I know them. But there's something I want you to remember: I own this team. I don't care if you're playing the biggest football game in the history of the world. I own the team. And if I want to, I'll bring Alexander's ragtime band into the dressing room. I hope I'm making myself clear."

AJR always told his five sons: "Treat everybody as you would like to be treated yourselves. But don't allow anyone to mistake kindness for weakness."

In Austin's last year, AJR hired a new trainer, Ralph Berlin from the University of Kentucky. The coach there, Charley Bradshaw, had played at Kentucky for Bear Bryant. That he patterned himself after Bryant was therefore not surprising. John Michelosen had played for Jock Sutherland and tried to be Sutherland II. Austin never played for Vince Lombardi, but he coached under Lombardi and mimicked Lombardi.

Charley Bradshaw was a stern-faced ex-Marine and a combat veteran of World War II. His biographer in the Kentucky publicity department described him as "inwardly tough." Bryant, of course, was inwardly tough and outwardly tough. Bradshaw's inward toughness found expression on the practice field. In his first year at Kentucky, twenty-nine players quit the squad. "Some things," he said, "have to be paid for in blood, sweat, and tears. And sacrifice." One Kentucky player sustained a broken neck in a hitting drill, and it proved to be fatal. Another owed his life to Berlin's prompt treatment before the ambulance arrived, but was permanently crippled. The new trainer came to Pittsburgh, then, wise in the ways of demanding coaches.

On a hot day at the Steelers' pre-season training camp, Berlin watched from the sideline as Austin put the team through a "grass" drill. In full uniform, the players jogged in place until Austin blew his whistle. Then they dropped to the ground and immediately jumped up again, repeating the process *for* what seemed like forever. After the grass drill came a nutcracker drill, sometimes called the Oklahoma drill. In the nutcracker, offensive players and defensive players line up and slam into each other. This one lasted longer than the grass drill.

Next on the agenda was a scrimmage, the first offensive unit versus the first defensive unit. It was uncommon in the NFL, once the exhibition season had begun, for teams to scrimmage, and the Steelers had played two or three games, but Austin had a point to make. He was teaching his guys to be tough.

Heard from up close, the sound effects of contact give you a keener appreciation of what a violent game football is. The animal noises, the grunts, the thud of pad against pad tell the story. Five minutes into the scrimmage Berlin was watching came a sound of a different character. A cry of "Trainer! ... Ralph! "sent him hurrying onto the field. A starter was down; it looked serious. Almost at once, Berlin called for the "wagon." Off went the injured player to the dressing room, and then the scrimmage resumed without a pause.

And soon another player was down. A nose-and-mouth injury, front teeth knocked out, blood pouring onto his uniform. More work for the ambulance/station wagon, but no halt in the scrimmage until still another player collapsed.

This time there were curses from the players ... intermingled with the calls for Berlin. "Damn fool!" "Fucking asshole!" "He's ruining our season before it starts."

Right there, Berlin later said, was where the bottom fell out of Austin's last season. The Steelers lost their first six games and their last five. In between those losing streaks there were two wins and a tie. While the defeats were piling up, I attended a dinner of some kind at the Roosevelt Hotel with AJR. He asked me suddenly if I knew the coach at Notre Dame, Ara Parseghian. I said I did, but not well.

"But he knows who you are?"

"I think so."

"Well, go call him now," AJR said, "and ask if he'd like to talk to me about coaching the Steelers."

I was startled. Stalling for time, I said I'd have to go to the office, look up Parseghian's number, and use our own telephone.

Dad said, "Don't worry about that. Do it now! Go to the pay phone." There was one in the room. "Call information in South Bend. You can probably get him at home." I protested that Parseghian's home number was undoubtedly not listed.

AJR cut me off. "Just try it! Now!" I went to the pay phone.

To my astonishment, the call went right through. Parseghian was at home. Yes, he recalled meeting me. "To talk to your father about coaching the Steelers? Well, I'm flattered," he said, "but, you know, I'm very happy at Notre Dame. I hope to spend all of my coaching days here ... " He was very nice. He sent his regards to Dad. The whole conversation was over in three minutes.

To AJR, it was not a rebuff. "Coaching's a shaky business," he said. "Today you're on top. Tomorrow you're looking for a job. It doesn't hurt to ask."

The search for Austin's replacement had begun. From that time on, it was Dan's responsibility, which suited me to perfection. I had a mission of my own — to get so many good players the coaches could not screw them up.

Austin's firing took him by surprise. The Steelers' final game that year was in New Orleans. The day before, in a conference room at the team's hotel, Austin met with his coaching staff — "to talk about next season," as one assistant put it. Minutes after the meeting broke up, Austin got the news that he was through. He'd be spending "next season" he knew not where.

The Steelers lost to the Saints, 24-14, and on Monday morning AJR announced Austin's dismissal. While answering questions from the media, Austin choked up.

A few weeks later, I met him on the street. He was finishing up some business in Pittsburgh, he said. He asked about my wife and kids. On one of the radio stations that evening, the host of a sports talk show interviewed Austin. "How do you think the Steelers will do next season?" the radio guy asked. "Well," answered Austin, "as long as Art Rooney Junior is working in scouting the team will get better and better."

I was completely dumbfounded. After all, the man hated me — or so I thought. Over the next dozen years, we would meet by chance here and there, and he was never anything but friendly and courteous. To this day I wonder if I had the guy wrong — misjudged him as a person, I mean. I know with certainty what kind of coach he was, because his record speaks for itself.

Chapter 41

Fran Fogarty

The Forgartys and the Rooneys were distantly related. Fran Fogarty's father, John Fogarty, had been the head groundskeeper at Forbes Field for many years. Temperamentally, father and son were somewhat alike — quiet, laconic, and undemonstrative.

Fran rarely smiled or raised his voice. He was short and stocky but athletic enough to have played on the hockey team at Duquesne University in the heyday of hockey as an intercollegiate sport. He went from Duquesne to the Army and eventually into combat against the Germans in France. He was either a first or second lieutenant. I don't know any of the particulars or what kind of outfit Fran was in, but at some point the Germans took him captive.

Here are the rough details as he told them to me:

The German soldier who captured him — when and where and what the circumstances were I can't tell you - was a big, good-looking guy who spoke almost flawless English.

"I was sorry to hear about Chicago," he said.

"About Chicago?"

"Yes, that it's bombed out."

He'd been misinformed, Fran told him. "Neither Chicago nor any other American city has been bombed by the Germans, by the Japs, or by anyone else." Instantly, the German soldier's friendliness evaporated. With anger in his voice, he accused Fran of "propagandizing." From then on, Fran kept his mouth shut, which was never much of a problem for him.

With other captured Americans, he was herded onto a cattle car. The doors slammed shut and the train began to move — headed toward Germany, the POWs assumed. Before it had gone very far, Fran noticed a GI with a pen knife at work on a screw in the floor of the car. Fran asked him what he was doing.

"I'm gonna get these floorboards up, so we can escape."

"Escape? Through the floor? Don't you know we'd be killed by the wheels?" Fran said. "If we're going to escape we have to make a hole in one of the doors."

And that is exactly what they did. How it was possible, using only a pen knife, to remove enough bolts or carve an opening large enough for a man to slip through I'm not sure. Nor do I know how many escapees there were. Nor do I know if they jumped from the train while it was moving, not to mention if they all made the leap without being hurt or killed. Nor do I know if it was daytime or nighttime. At any rate, they escaped from the train and got into the countryside. Whether Fran was alone or with others when the French underground picked him up is something else I don't know. Characteristically, Fran just never talked about it a lot, and so I can't even guess at how long he remained with the underground or whether he took part in any sabotage. I know that in some manner he worked his way back to the American lines and was personally interrogated by General Patton.

He came to work for the Steelers immediately after the war. You could see right away that he was tough and smart. He looked and listened but never blabbed. It always surprised people to hear him break into song, this taciturn little bookkeeper who would fight for a dime. In the musical shows at

Duquesne, he'd been a part of the cast and he remembered the words to some Gilbert and Sullivan airs. Actually, his voice was not bad.

He dealt with the coaches and scouts in ways that AJR was disinclined to, reviewing their expense accounts minutely. "That's too much for gas," he would say. Or "That's too much for meals." An item like "miscellaneous" was certain to raise his hackles.

And yet there were coaches and scouts and players who regarded him as their friend. Others, like Fido Murphy, hated him. He could be curt with all of them, but he was AJR's man, doing AJR's bidding. The joke was that when he visited Shamrock Farm he counted the horses, the cows, and even the chickens. (Speaking of chickens, they disappeared from the farm after Jimmy McGee left. McGee was the trainer who bred and fought gamecocks.)

When Fogarty first came on board, the boxing club was still in existence and we also had a piece of a motorcycle raceway out in Heidelberg. Fogarty kept the books for everything. The motorcycle raceway was meant to be a dog track, but the man who laid it out miscalculated. The distance between the turns was so short that in a practice race before the track was to open, the dogs couldn't negotiate them. They floundered all over the place. Dad's interest in motorcycles being limited, he relied on Fogarty to make decisions for him. Motorcycle racing was not a part of our sports conglomerate very long.

More and more, Fogarty got to be AJR's alter ego, even to the point of looking after his stock-market investments. If there were money matters to be straightened out between AJR and one of the other NFL owners, Fogarty was empowered to act. George Marshall (who called him by every name but his own) wanted to trade somebody in the Redskins' front office for Fogarty, the way he would trade a football player. "That fellow," he said to AJR, "is so good he could work for me!"

He was so good that with Dad's approval he had a say-so in every aspect of the business, and he worked anonymously. Sometimes in newspaper stories about the signing of this player or that player, Fogarty's name would appear. But never once in all the years he was with the Steelers did anyone write a column or feature story about him.

As you might expect, Fogarty knew Forbes Field like the back of his hand. The son of the head groundskeeper would have a certain familiarity with the place, but Fran's expertise exceeded the bounds of the ordinary. On the few occasions we had a sellout at Forbes Field, and needed temporary stands to accommodate the crowd, Fogarty was in charge of measuring the seat space. He believed that fans of professional football were wider in the beam than fans of high school or college football and he factored that into his assessments. If the weather was cold he made an allowance of two inches for overcoats and heavier clothing. In September and October the seats measured eighteen inches across. In November and December the figure was twenty inches. I remember hearing him call down from the end of a row at the top, "The guy who gets this seat better be half-assed — there's only fifteen inches left for him."

Fogarty's caustic side came out when he negotiated player contracts, but there were players he liked — Fran Rogel, Joe Krupa, and Jack Butler; anybody who gave one hundred percent. Not, heaven forbid, that they got more money than the others. His esteem for them paid off in respect, which was something.

After his wife, a fine lady, developed heart trouble, he made a thorough study of all the health-insurance plans, talked at some length with everybody concerned — the insurance agents, the team doctor, the Internal Revenue Service — and worked up a better deal for our players and front-office people.

The team doctor, John Best, looked like Robert Mitchum in a white smock. He was gruff; he smoked and drank. During a pre-season game a player was smacked in the mouth and had to be taken to the dressing room. Doc Best would need help, he could see, but the game was still in progress, requiring the presence of the trainers on the field. So Doc called for Fogarty and gave him a short set of instructions: "Don't worry about anything — just do as I tell you." With Fogarty's assistance, Doc gave the player some painkiller and stitched up his cuts. "Fran Fogarty," he told everyone afterward, "is by far the best nurse I've ever had, and I mean it. I'd like to have him in my operating room when I perform major surgery."

Is it any wonder we came to believe that Fogarty could do anything?

Among the many hats he wore was that of traveling secretary. For games out of town, he made the airline and hotel reservations and arranged for the ground transportation. His network of hotel managers and food-service people was vast. Fogarty and Lou Kroeck, the United Airlines representative, made an efficient team that functioned especially well during the years when our preseason schedule took us to places that were off the beaten path — places like Shreveport and Fresno, Salem, Oregon, and Omaha. One shot and you're out, never to return.

On all trips, there were petty thieves and petty politicians and venal policemen to deal with. In towns and large cities, the cops could be as worrisome as the thieves, stealing footballs and jerseys and anything else they could get their hands on. Of course, the politicians always wanted tickets. So did certain cops, and in some towns they expected to have their palms greased.

Getting seriously injured players back to Pittsburgh was another problem, and then along with the official team party you had the hangers-on and the relatives, not to mention the players' girlfriends. On occasion even a coach or two had a girlfriend to be looked after. Somehow Fogarty handled all this and made it look easy.

If sufficiently provoked, he would lash out at the hangers-on, unless their degree of intimacy with the Chief protected them. Special cases received special treatment. One year our first draft pick, Art Davis, a halfback from Mississippi State, was joined by his wife, a former Miss Mississippi, in a Southern tank town. Fogarty assigned me to pick her up at the hotel in a taxi, and he saw to it that our tickets to the game were the best available. "Forget about your other duties," he said. "Just take care of Mrs. Davis." Well, Mrs. Davis's personality and charm matched her looks. Her husband was never much of a football player, but in the matrimonial department he could not be faulted.

There were also women of a different type, for whom the players would demand rooms and tickets. "What am I," Fogarty would yell, "a pimp?" — and not without reason. Delivering tickets to one of these bimbos, he found the door of her hotel room ajar. He tapped it gently. "Mister Fogarty?" a voice called from within. "Come right in." Fogarty opened the door a little wider. "Mister Fogarty? I'm in the bathroom. Just bring the tickets in and put them on the dresser." He did so, and turned to leave, when "out jumped the devil," as he put it. The player's dream girl emerged from the bathroom in the skimpiest underwear obtainable. Fogarty flew out the door. "That girl was a photography nut," he explained to some of us later, too shocked to keep silent about it. "She might have had a camera with her. She might have been trying to blackmail me."

He did not hear the last of the ribbing for some time to come.

On another trip, Fogarty shared a suite with one of the coaches. There was a knock at the door. Alone for the moment, Fogarty opened it, and the coach's sweet patootie stormed in. She was looking for her boyfriend to complain about the way he'd been treating her. With nobody else to chastise, she turned all her wrath on Fogarty. She grabbed his briefcase, containing tickets, cash, keys, and documents, and flung it across the room. Papers and heavier objects landed everywhere. "She spilled all my 'brains,'" Fogarty said. Before the irate lady could trash the rest of the room, he hustled her out into the hall. Then and there in Fogarty's mind, that particular coach was finished. "He isn't our kind of guy," Fogarty declared to a few of us.

At the end of the season the coach got his walking papers.

Meanwhile, the winds of change were blowing hard. Dan, who had an accounting degree from Duquesne just as Fogarty did, and was taking over as a sort of chief executive officer, wanted a big national firm like Arthur Andersen to audit the books every year. Perhaps the time had come, Dan thought, for the Steelers to modernize their accounting procedures. And that was all right with him, Fogarty said. But how would it suit AJR to have a group of outsiders poking their noses into his football affairs and all of the other things he controlled?

Fogarty wondered about that. He'd been the man with the books for twenty years or more. Like it or not, though, professional football was becoming big business. In just another year the Steelers would be in a new, publicly-financed stadium. Fogarty did not live to see it. He appeared to be imperturbable, but the pressures he must have felt were building up. At the age of 51, on the day he attended his daughter's wedding, Fran Fogarty died of a heart attack.

Go-Between

Fran Fogarty's death left a void in the organization, which Ed Kiely proceeded to fill. From 1969 on, he was AJR's sounding board.

Ed had been an intelligence officer in the South Pacific during World War II and a reporter in New York City for the now defunct International News Service. He came to the Steelers as a public relations man. Other PR guys churned out statistics and bits of factual information for the sportswriters. Ed saw his job a little differently. Statistics, the condition of injured players, lineup changes, press releases, and so on were beneath his notice. Ed was much more of a big-picture guy. The commodity he chose to sell was not the team, it was AJR. And the place to do that, he believed, was on the road.

Long before everybody else caught on, he saw that AJR had a special brand of charisma. From over-familiarity, the Pittsburgh writers and broadcasters took the owner of the Steelers for granted. Among themselves, they agreed that he was down to earth, generous, straightforward, a man with a colorful, adventurous past. In the world he inhabited, high rollers, finaglers, cut-throats, and con artists had attempted to outsmart him and had failed. The reporters had heard all the stories, heard them too often. Where was the news value, anyway? And, besides, to mention Art Rooney in any favorable context was to infuriate large segments of the public.

This was because, year after year, the Steelers kept losing football games. As the owner of such a team, then, how could Art Rooney be the warm, intelligent, philanthropic, completely likable person the media sometimes dared to portray? It wasn't possible.

Even if Art Rooney did have good qualities, the disgraceful things that happened to his team on Sunday afternoons in the fall made them irrelevant, his detractors seemed to feel. Since about 1955 or 1956, pro football fans everywhere had been investing their own self-esteem in the fortunes of whatever team they identified with. Each defeat was a slap in the face, a personal affront. When the team lost, the fans lost. And who was to blame? Management, obviously. In the case of the Steelers, there could be no question about it. Management — in other words, AJR - was either too cheap to pay the salaries of good players or too dumb to recognize who they were. Too cheap AND too dumb, the chances were.

Aware of this attitude — how could he not be? - Ed Kiely ventured afield. Kiely was from Morningside, a Black Irishman, so-called, dark rather than fair, one of the Irish whose ancestry goes back, if the fabulists have it right, to shipwrecked sailors from the Spanish Armada, cast up on the shores of Ireland at the end of the sixteenth century. Ed's years in the Army and in New York City had given him an air of sophistication. He knew how to dress. He knew how to deal with maitre d's at high-priced restaurants. He knew how to meet people and he knew the kinds of people it was worthwhile to cultivate. If they were media people, they worked in New York. They remembered Ed Kiely from his time with the International News Service. They sat still for his presentation of AJR, and through him they got acquainted with the subject himself, and that's all it took.

At winning over the press, there was never a sports figure more effective than AJR. His secret was being one hundred percent natural. He genuinely liked people, even newspapermen, and they responded in kind. When Roy Blount, who prided himself on his objectivity, wrote an Art Rooney story for *Sports Illustrated*, his colleagues at the magazine — strangers to AJR — derided it as saccharine. Later, in his book "About Three Bricks Shy of a Load," Blount admitted having looked for discreditable things to say about the Chief to sort of balance the scales, but none of it turned out to be damning, and so the book merely added to the legend.

New York being the communications capital, if you could make it there you not only could make it anywhere, you could and did make it everywhere. Writers in the hinterlands take their cue from the writers in New York. Kiely understood this and expertly set the process in motion.

My first impression of Kiely, I have to say, was negative. He came across as condescending, I thought. Well read and well informed, he appeared to regard the coaches as his mental inferiors, "kidding them on the square" about their phys-ed degrees. In truth, there were coaches with master's degrees, whereas Kiely himself had left Pitt before earning a bachelor's degree.

For another thing, I felt that he considered me an upstart — the owner's son with no appreciation of what the older front-office people were contributing. He had the Walt Kiesling mind-set on Steeler culture: "Sure, we like to win as much as anybody does, but there are limitations to what we can do here, you know ..." Offering many good reasons why something could not be done rather than one good reason why something had to be done, the Kieslings and the Kielys were in my view holding us back.

"You're too tough on Kiely," AJR would tell me, and the longer I knew Ed the better I liked him. Whatever our differences may have been, I came to think of Ed Kiely as a real fine person and a gentleman.

By the 1970s, Kiely was out of publicity. His hand-picked successor, Joe Gordon, brought energy to the job — more than we ever had seen. Kiely, moving up in the hierarchy, became, in effect, AJR's right-hand man. When the Chief was into his seventies, Kiely read and sorted his mail and answered some of the letters. He wrote AJR's speeches and stood in for him, on occasion, at dinners and public affairs. "Art," I would hear him say, "you should look into this," or "Art, here's something you should take care of right away."

Around the NFL, people knew that Kiely had AJR's ear. Using him as a go-between, they could get things back to the Chief, and this was now one of his major functions. No further need existed to keep the name of Art Rooney before the public. Thanks in large part to Kiely, he was one of the best-known football men in America. Thanks to his own personality — and in no small measure to four quick Super Bowl victories — he was better known than he ever had been. His thoughts about this he kept to himself. He liked the good publicity but never once lifted a finger to encourage it, I am sure, having too much sense to believe that people came to the games to see the owners and not the football players.

Kiely's attractive, talented wife, Pat, was the first woman in Pittsburgh to anchor a television news show. She developed mental and physical problems and died before reaching old age. This was difficult for Ed, but he sent his daughter Kathy and his sons Tim and Kevin to excellent universities and all three had successful media careers, Kathy in journalism, the two boys in television.

After AJR's death in 1988, Kiely no longer had a niche in the organization, but he continued for a while to spend three or four days a week at his desk, not the last of the original front-office cadre but the last of the generation that followed.

Chapter 42

A Sense of Belonging

At our St. Vincent training camp one hot August day in 1969, the *Pittsburgh Post-Gazette's* Jack Sell flagged me down.

"Hey, Artie," he said, "I've been interviewing Bob Adams." I knew that to interview Bob Adams, a rookie tight end from a college called University of the Pacific, standing in line was not required. We had signed the kid as a free agent, and he had come to St. Vincent unheralded. But he was tough and smart and mature beyond his years and had caught Sell's eye in practice. "He told me you scouted him out in California," Sell went on. "He said you gave him a lot of encouragement." Which was true. When I heard that Adams was undrafted, I had called him and consoled him and offered him a contract. All of this seemed to astonish Sell. "You know, Artie," he said, "I owe you an apology. I thought you were on the payroll for family reasons. Because your dad wanted to keep you off the streets. I had no idea you actually worked — went out on the road as far away as the West Coast and scouted these guys, actually saw them play and sent in reports."

I could tell that the revelation pleased him. I was pleased that he was pleased, for Sell was a crusty old skeptic, but less than flattered to think that though I had been in charge of scouting since 1965 — four years — I was just now beginning to acquire some credibility with a sportswriter covering the team.

Adams turned out to be a good tight end, if not a great one. What he had that we liked was character - both off-the-field character and football character. As I define football character, it's a product of intelligence and heart, which are difficult for a scout to evaluate. All you can do is watch and wait.

You look for a moment of truth. Bob Ferguson came to the Steelers in 1962 with a big reputation that earned him a big paycheck — what we thought of as big money back then. In the Woody Hayes offense at Ohio State — "three yards and a cloud of dust" - Ferguson had been the ideal fullback. He could get three yards when they were needed, and there was nothing more that Buddy Parker wanted from him. Though he was built like a little bull, he couldn't block. He couldn't catch passes. But doing what he did best — hitting into the line of scrimmage — he kept his short, thick legs churning and was hard to drag down.

The fullback position appeared to be his for the taking. Then came a telltale incident. Ferguson skipped a meeting and was late the same day for practice, antagonizing Parker's quarterback, Bobby Layne. To antagonize Layne, the team leader, was bad news, but Parker gave Ferguson playing time the next week against Detroit, and at one point, after picking up his usual three yards, he broke free, which he did not often do. Coming on fast to meet him, linebacker Carl Brettschneider delivered a perfectly executed rising blow.

When his playing career had ended and Brettschneider was a scout for Detroit, we got to be friends. The hit on Ferguson, he told me, was "under and up." He meant that he came in under Ferguson's shoulder pads with tremendous momentum and leverage and drove them up into his face. The ball went one way and Ferguson another. According to Brettschneider, as Ferguson lay on the ground, dazed, he recited scripture.

Apparently convinced that the meek shall inherit the earth, he was never again much of a football player. Not far into his second season, 1963, Buddy Parker traded him to the Vikings. The year after that, he was back in Ohio, operating a skid loader on a construction job.

For the scouts who recommended Ferguson, it would not have been easy to foresee that one hard thump would be his complete undoing. Most often it's the intangibles, the psychological stuff, that scouts are unable to fathom.

I was in my first year on the job when we drafted Larry Gagner, and I agreed with all the reports, which told us he couldn't miss. A guard from the University of Florida, Gagner was big, fast, and strong. He was something else, too — over-impressed with his own ability, as we discovered too late. Florida played in a bowl game that year and lost. When Jack Butler met with Gagner afterwards to sign him, Gagner put the blame for Florida's defeat on his teammates. Because of their shortcomings, his valiant one-man effort had gone for naught, as he told it.

Wait a minute, Butler said to himself, do we know what we're doing here? In fact we didn't. Gagner made it through four full seasons with the Steelers (1966-1969), but, lacking heart for the pro game, he was never the player we expected him to be.

On our teams in the 1960s, journeymen like Gagner could prolong their careers by staying out of trouble off the field. That was about all it took. We had a veteran defensive tackle from a mid-level conference in the West, a big, good-looking guy, who, as big, good-looking guys sometimes do, got enmeshed with a girl. It was what in those days we called a predicament (I am trying not to be blunt). Even as late as the sixties, that sort of thing could be serious business. Compounding the offense, AJR had heard about it from the girl's employer, a close friend. He summoned me to his office and said, "That guy from out West. What a yegg. Is he any good? Can he play?" We were changing coaches, and I told my dad what I thought - that the guy had been getting by up to then on size and strength, but was too slow for the new system about to be installed. AJR said, "All right. We don't need him."

At St. Vincent that summer, the veteran defensive tackle failed to survive the cut.

Go-To Guy

Long before the end of the 1968 football season, AJR had made up his mind to get rid of Bill Austin. I therefore wanted no help from Austin or anyone on his staff in preparing for the 1969 draft.

Scouting had for years been a haphazard business with the Steelers. We relied for much of our information on assistant coaches, part-time bird dogs, and tips from old friends. This was work that belonged in the hands of full-time professional scouts. A man whose reputation and livelihood depend on the quality of his judgment will do a better job for you every time.

The reports of Jack Butler's Blesto scouts were available to us by now, but available also to the Bears, Lions, Eagles, and Vikings. Technologically, Blesto was miles ahead of us. Its computers broke down the information on prospects in ways and in combinations of ways that would answer many of the questions a personnel director might have. We were doing some of these things ourselves, but doing them "by hand," a slow, tedious, outdated process I was ready to junk.

Meanwhile, with Austin as good as gone and no one yet hired to take his place, I would be organizing, evaluating, interpreting, and then reorganizing the data we needed for the upcoming draft on my own. I had the Blesto material, yes. And Austin's assistants would be fanning out to the post-season all-star games. AJR, out of the goodness of his heart, was giving them a chance to network for new jobs. They would turn in reports; I would read the reports and debrief the coaches, yes. But their observations, I knew, would be of limited usefulness.

Nor did I want any input from the new coach, whoever it might be, and his assistants. I made this clear to AJR and I made it clear, profanely, to Dan. I was fully prepared and in charge. I had the prospects rated by position; more important, I had them rated, best to worst, regardless of position. Of course you didn't waste much time on the players at the bottom of the list — the rejects — but the rejects were part of it all. Dan Towler and Johnny Unitas were rejects who became all-pros. I had served my apprenticeship, I knew what I was doing. I was 32 years old and self-confident to the point of obnoxiousness.

But I'm getting ahead of myself.

My "go-to" guy for information and guidance would be Butler. He knew how to evaluate the reports of his scouts. In Butler's opinion, the critical factors in the makeup of a prospect were toughness, production, and NFL-type athletic ability, the little bit extra that separates the pro from the college player. Jack could look at a kid from Grambling or Alcorn or North Texas State and recognize that he had what it takes to make the transition, and he could look at an All-American from the Big Ten or Pac Eight and foresee a short, undistinguished NFL career. As Paul Brown said of the great Jim Brown, "When you have a gun, you shoot it." That was how I felt about leaning on Butler.

While it was true that the other Blesto teams I have mentioned also had access to Butler and his people, I perceived a difference between my attitude — I can't be modest about this — and theirs. Ralph Kohl, Butler's national scout, told me that some of the Blesto subscribers he worked for did not even know how to interview him.

"They'll ask me a question and then not wait for the answer," Kohl said. He described a meeting in the office of the Chicago Bears that opened with Abe Gibron, the head coach, asking about a player Kohl had scouted. Before Ralph could get two words out, George Halas, the Bears' owner, and Muggsy Halas, his son, interrupted him to offer their own opinions, Gibron countered with his, and the three men started shouting at one another. Presently Gibron's assistants chimed in, and the babble continued for ten or twelve minutes, becoming steadily more obscene. When at last the disputants ran out of breath, Gibron, turning to Kohl, said, "Good report, Ralph — nice job," and ushered him to the door.

"Don't get me wrong — I love those guys," Kohl said. "It's just that they're wasting their investment in Blesto."

There would be none of that in the Steelers' draft room, I resolved. We would prepare, prepare, and prepare some more. We would be organized and organized some more. The arguments and the bickering would take place at the draft development meetings. At the draft itself, unless Dan, AJR, or the head coach asked a question, only one voice would be heard — mine.

Looking and Listening

In the fall of 1968 I was doing double duty as a scout. Primarily, my job was to evaluate football players. Acting on instructions from AJR and Dan, I also scouted head-coaching prospects. Everywhere I went, I made discreet, low-key inquiries.

Even before the start of the season, we knew that Bill Austin would not be returning. Dan, in fact, had wanted to fire him at the end of the 1967 season, but AJR counseled patience. None of this had leaked to the media.

Meanwhile, in my conversations about coaches with other NFL scouts, I kept hearing one name again and again. It was that of a young assistant with the Baltimore Colts, Chuck Noll. The scouts all gave me the same feedback: "Real decent guy ... Smart as can be ... Gonna be a top NFL head coach some day ..."

I would sometimes ask my informants for the best two or three prospects, and the name Chuck Knox frequently came up. Knox, an assistant with the Detroit Lions, was a Western Pennsylvania guy from Sewickley. But whereas *most* of the scouts mentioned Knox, *all* of the scouts mentioned Noll.

Upton Bell, the Colts' head scout, and his brother Bert Junior recommended Noll in the strongest possible terms, not only to me but to Tim (a close friend of theirs) and to AJR. I don't doubt that Joe Paterno of Penn State was Dan's first choice and could have had the job if he wanted it, but when Joe indicated he was not interested, Noll's name went to the top of the list.

Subject to AJR's approval, Dan would make the final decision. As personnel director, I did not have a vote, but I was forceful about stating my views. I emphasized two things. I felt that our new head coach should be absolutely color blind and absolutely committed to building a team through the draft.

Bill, Ralph, and Rhoda

When I say I had no help from anyone in preparing for the 1969 draft, I am doing a disservice to three important friends — Bill Nunn, Jr., Ralph Berlin, and Rhoda Duffy.

Since 1966, Bill Nunn, Jr., had been covering the small Negro colleges in the Southeast and Southwest for the Steelers. He was not a football guy, but a newspaperman — sports editor of the *Pittsburgh Courier*. Moreover, he had not played football in college. His game was basketball, and he must have been pretty good at it. While Nunn was at West Virginia State, the team hardly ever lost, and he missed no chance to remind me that the Harlem Globetrotters had tried to sign him up.

I could not hold his résumé against him, not when I compared it with mine. After all, I had been just a so-so football player on a college team in the second or third tier, and I owed my job to my morn and dad. Joe Krupa remembered watching me tutor Nunn in his first year with the Steelers. "Artie, you taught him everything," Krupa said. If that is true, I would call it a classic case of the blind leading the blind. All I knew about scouting in 1966 I had learned from picking other people's brains, including Krupa's.

At our first meeting, Nunn told me that he never had been around a loser and was "not about to start now." I could have put that down to braggadocio, but he reminded me in certain ways of myself. We both had something to prove, Nunn and I. In a time of deep racial prejudice, Nunn was a black man, with all the baggage that being black entailed. And I, of course, was "the owner's son," which carried its own kind of baggage. We knew there were skeptics eager to see us screw up, and we were equally determined that it wasn't going to happen.

As the 1969 draft approached, I asked Nunn to help me get our Blesto reports in order. I still had my cubbyhole in the Roosevelt Hotel, and we met there one day. Ralph Berlin, the trainer, was lending a hand, too, as he sometimes did between the end of one season and the start of the next. I needed all the assistance I could get, having recently lost my secretary. Her departure was unexpected. Pleading stress and her forthcoming marriage, she had simply walked out. The timing of her resignation puzzled me just a little. Why had she not waited to collect her Christmas bonus? I wondered. Anyway, we were minutes into our task this January day when Berlin looked up from the files and said, "Art, a lot of reports from Blesto seem to be missing."

"Reports missing?"

"Yeah, we've got spring reports on a lot of these guys, but no follow-up reports in the fall."

Thoroughly nonplussed, I got in touch with Jack Butler. All the fall reports had been sent to us, he told me.

I said, "Well, they're not here."

As chief scout, I was constantly on the road. I took meticulous notes at the Blesto meetings. I took meticulous notes of my conversations with Nunn. But it just wasn't possible for me to keep an eagle eye on the Blesto reports that came to the office. That was the job of my secretary, the one who had left.

Instead of calling her to ask what she had done with those reports, I procrastinated. Frankly, I had been glad to see the last of her, and our relations were such that I was fearful of losing my temper. Berlin, meanwhile, took me off the hook.

His fetish for tidiness, acquired in the military, impelled him one day to declare that my office was a mess. "I'm going to sweep the floor," he announced. "Where's the broom closet?"

I pointed to a door in the corner of the room. Berlin pulled it open, and out tumbled all of the missing Blesto reports. In her haste to get to the altar, my secretary had streamlined our filing system.

The incident opened my eyes. I could handle the 1969 draft without any help from our coaches, but not without an efficient office manager, I now realized. A call to the Kelly Girls brought Rhoda Duffy of Homestead into my life.

Rhoda Duffy was not a "girl," but a mature married woman. She was with us until she retired, in 1978, and there were no further breakdowns in clerical procedure. Rhoda Duffy loved the Rooneys and she loved Bill Nunn and the feeling in both cases was mutual. Her presence gave me comfort because it proved that I could learn from my mistakes.

Chapter 43

Out of the Loop

The 1969 draft was scheduled for late January. In the middle of the month I attended a Blesto meeting somewhere and got back to our offices in the Roosevelt Hotel at a little after noon on the following day. Ed Kiely or Fran Fogarty — I am unable to be more precise — informed me as soon as I walked through the door that AJR and Dan were with Chuck Noll in the Sylvan Room.

Noll, it appeared, had the inside track for our vacant head coaching job, but neither my father nor my brother had bothered to clue me in about the interview. Just a few months earlier, neither Kiely nor Fogarty would have bothered to do so, either. Not without a feeling of gratification, I reflected that someone, at least, believed I had a stake in all this.

My determination to exclude the new coach, whoever it might be, from taking part in the draft was no secret. I had told AJR again and again that I wanted full authority in making our selections. Actually, I was hoping the draft would be out of the way before the new coach came on board.

AJR dismissed all my arguments. "I'm not saying the job is too much for you," he said. "I'm not saying you couldn't handle it alone, and handle it well. But there are other issues involved here. There'd be trouble from the press and the public. I've been in this business a long time. Just get it into your head that we are going to do things my way."

When I saw he was adamant about hiring a coach as soon as he could, and giving him a strong voice in the draft, my heart sank. If the new guy resembled Bill Austin — an iron-willed, hard-headed commanding-officer type with firm ideas of his own — all my work and preparation would go to waste.

The approach I favored was a simple one: Draft the best athlete available. The hell with drafting to fill a certain position. There were NFL coaches who looked at positions where they were thin and tried to reinforce them through the draft. There was no better way, I thought, to lose the prospective superstars and pack your roster with garden-variety talent.

Catering to the fans could be just as destructive. Terry Hanratty from Butler was the star of the 1968 Notre Dame team, a quarterback and a real nice kid. We had the No.4 pick in the first round, and if we listened to our fans we'd take Hanratty. But in no sense did I consider him the fourth best player — or even the fourth best senior — in the country. The draft was not a popularity contest; it was a mechanism, I believed, for improving your team.

Something else that concerned me was the ticklish subject of racism. I remembered dialogues from the past word for word:

"Yeah, well ... we've already drafted three of them in the first six rounds."

"But, Coach, this kid is special. I don't know why he's still on the board. We have him rated higher than our third-round pick ... Trouble? ... No, he's a kid who stays out of trouble ... Injuries? No, there haven't been any. And don't worry about the military. He's safe — he has a wife and a child to support. Eddie Robinson told me in confidence he's better than that other guy from Grambling who went to the Giants last year in the second round, and Robinson coached them both. This draft is like an auction, Coach. Knowing when to draft a player is one of the secrets. Let's go for him now."

"Well, you make it sound good, but I'm looking for a defensive end, not a linebacker. I like this kid at Alabama."

"Coach, we have the Alabama guy rated as the one hundred and tenth best player in the draft. The Grambling kid is our forty-sixth best player."

"Listen, *Artie*. I'm the one who'll be coaching these guys, the one who'll be out on the field with them every day. So we're taking the Alabama kid. Maybe your ace from Grambling will be there in the eighth round. We'll talk about it then."

(Head coach turns on his heel and exits stage left.)

This and other scenarios kept playing through my mind. AJR didn't get it. Dan did. He was committed, like me, to building through the draft. But he was also committed, like AJR, to a quick resolution of our search for a new head coach. And he had worked just as hard on his interviews as I had on the draft.

Knowing the game was up, I could do only one thing. Welcome or not welcome, I was going to barge in on the Sylvan Room meeting, see what was happening, and take a stand if I had to.

Elbowing In

AJR and Dan were surprised, just a little, to see me. They were with Noll at the big round table — the Chief's table, where he liked to hold court. AJR introduced me, and Noll stood up to shake hands. We were the same height, about 6 feet 1. He had the wide, compact, thick-necked build of an offensive lineman, fair skin, a broad face, and light brown hair. I knew how old he was — 36 — from my reading in press guides.

There were three empty chairs at the table, and I took the one next to Dan. On the face of a clock, I'd have been at seven, with Dan at six, Noll at five, and AJR at four. They picked up their conversation where I guess they had left off, chatting idly about Noll's boss, Don Shula. I wondered if AJR remembered the advice Buddy Parker had offered him before parting company with the Steelers. "Find yourself a good defensive coach like that Don Shula fellow over in Baltimore," he had said. Even then, in his second year as head coach of the Colts, Shula was impressing other football men. AJR began to cultivate his friendship, and now it was Shula's recommendation, more than anything else, that seemed to have sold him on Noll.

The way Shula described Noll, they were replicas of each other. "He's your kind of guy," Shula had told AJR. "Smart. Serious. Hard-working. *A good defensive coach.*"

The similarities went even deeper. Both Shula and Noll were Catholic (being Catholic raised your status with AJR). Both were from Cleveland. Both had played football at small Catholic colleges in Ohio, Shula at John Carroll, Noll at Dayton. In the NFL, both had played for their home-town team, Cleveland, and were coached by super organizer Paul Brown. As assistant coaches, both had been in charge of defensive units.

I listened for a while to the table talk. It had turned from Shula himself to the Colts' surprising defeat in their recently played Super Bowl game with the New York Jets. When would they finish breaking the ice? Noll, in his demeanor, was reserved, almost formal. Don Shula had called him AJR's kind of guy, but AJR liked people who were friendly and open.

I took a deep breath. This job interview, if that's what it was, appeared to be going nowhere. For weeks I had lost sleep over the draft. The fear that we'd end up with another Bill Austin, or for that matter another Buddy Parker, had me paranoid. It was time to end the sparring, time to forget about niceties. Plunging in heavily, I said, "Coach, what are your feelings about black players?"

Dan let me know with a frown that I had overstepped.

AJR assumed his poker face — not a good sign.

Noll said, "What do you mean?"

I said, "Well, some coaches seem to think you can have too many of them."

Noll's expression hardened. He said, "Look, all I want are top athletes who can learn. They can be black or white or any other color. If they can learn, I won't have any trouble coaching them." His voice, which was light but assertive, for the first time had an edge to it.

AJR was glaring at me now, but I couldn't be stopped. I told of my visits to black schools in the South and of the many great athletes and nice kids I had met. Noll answered that he, too, had been to the black colleges and also had met great athletes and good people. Almost baring his teeth, he said, "I don't believe in quotas. On any team I coach there'll be none of that. With me, the quality of the person is major, but I want athletic skills, too. I've seen films of the Steelers, and there's a need for team speed."

AJR and Dan nodded in agreement, and to lighten the atmosphere AJR tossed off a humorous anecdote. I sensed that the mood was changing, so I popped another question to Noll.

"How do you feel about building a team and maintaining a team through the draft?"

AJR and Dan squirmed in their chairs. I braced myself for a kick beneath the table from Dan, but it never came.

Buddy Parker, I reminded Noll, had traded away a big piece of our future for "now." He had done OK with that philosophy, but no more than OK, and only for a while. Then the wheels fell off.

Noll said exactly what I wanted him to say — that going with top young athletes who are coachable was the right path to take. As we soon would find out, primarily Noll was a teacher.

"When I was with Sid Gillman in the AFL," he said — Gillman had coached the Los Angeles Chargers, precursors of the San Diego Chargers — "we developed a lot of good players who came to us in the draft. I don't see a problem in doing that with Pittsburgh. You only have to be patient."

This put me at ease.

Then Noll added, "But I won't be selling out to the draft. There are times when a trade is the best thing to do."

Whoa! Could this guy be a Parker in disguise? I felt my paranoia returning. But there was more that I wanted to know.

"What do you think of the Blesto group?" I asked. "Jack Butler does a terrific job ... "

Noll cut me off.

"Scouting groups have their place," he said. "They can be very good at collecting basic information: height, weights, speed. They can separate the prospects in the draft according to ability. But you need your own people to look at these players and determine where they would fit into your organization. After all, Blesto is scouting for five or six teams. Practically speaking, their scouts can't be expected to know exactly what each team is looking for. It's asking too much."

Now I was really getting nervous.

"Well, Coach," I said, sounding argumentative even to myself, "we don't have enough scouts to cover all the players in the country — cover them in depth. I mean the down-the-line guys. There are sleepers out there in the sixth to eighth rounds, and they have to be dug out." I let it go at that, unwilling to put things more bluntly. In truth, we relied on Blesto for economic reasons. We couldn't afford the big scouting staffs the rich teams had. But to say that to Noll, with AJR listening, would be a mistake. Poor-mouthing was no way to present ourselves to this man.

Like the rest of the teams in the NFL, we used our assistant coaches as scouts. I felt that some of them were capable, or at least energetic; the majority merely went through the motions. I had never seen an assistant coach fired or even bawled out for writing a bad scouting report. The year that AJR put me in charge I was going over a draft list with Buddy Parker's coaches and one of them asked why we did not have Jim Grabowski of Illinois rated No.1 among the running backs. When I started to explain, he said curtly, "How can any back who gains a thousand yards in the Big Ten not be a star in the NFL?" Before I could continue, Dick Haley, an injured Steeler defensive back who was working that year as a part-time scout, spoke up. He answered the coach in two words: "Bob Ferguson." I repeated that story to Noll, and he almost smiled. He said, "I'm an assistant coach myself. I saw Jim Grabowski, too. And I didn't like him much, either."

As far as the Chief was concerned, my probing had gone far enough. "Chuck," he said, looking at Noll but intending his words for me, "our next coach will have his assistants involved in the draft as much as he sees fit. And the final say on the draft and on trades will belong to him and nobody else." Tacitly, he was telling me to shut up. This is Dan's show, not yours, he was saying. I was like the camel who got his nose into the tent. If AJR could help it, and he could, the camel's hump would remain outside.

From then until the meeting adjourned I was silent. Clearly my performance had been annoying to AJR.

There was only one more coach for Dan to interview — Nick Skorich, an assistant with the Browns and a former assistant with the Steelers who had played guard for Steeler teams in the late 1940s. Nick was head coaching material. When his chance came in Cleveland, he would prove it. But in his interview with Dan he eliminated himself by insisting on a deal that would make him the de facto general manager as well as head coach. As far as AJR and Dan were concerned, that settled it. Chuck Noll was their man.

Knute Knowledge

Chuck Noll's home town, Cleveland, was similar in many ways to Pittsburgh. Both were northern industrial cities in various stages of decay but energetically remaking themselves. Noll came from working-class people. So did the Rooneys. Though the family was now affluent, AJR's five sons had grown up in a working-class neighborhood, a neighborhood once populated by millionaires. AJR and Kass continued to live there, occupying a well-kept-up nineteenth-century mansion. He wanted us to believe we were "salt-of-the-earth folk," said John and Pat. By salt of the earth, he meant "poor," they explained. The twins weren't falling for that line of gab, but took care not to flaunt their subversiveness. It was the state of one's mind, not the state of one's pocketbook, that counted with AJR.

He sent his sons to a Marianist high school and to small Catholic colleges, in my case a Benedictine college. Charles Henry Noll, born in the same year as my brother Dan — 1932 — attended a Benedictine high school and a small Marianist college. He devoutly subscribed to what the Marianist Brothers taught, as did we, although some of us, in our habits of speech, did not reflect it. Our zeal for football, like his, matched in fervor the zeal we all felt for religion.

So in the ways I have just enumerated it was true, as Don Shula had said, that Noll was the Rooneys' kind of guy. In other respects we could not have been much more different.

The Rooneys were gregarious. They were story-tellers, always ready with an anecdote. Perhaps I should except Dan, who was more like Uncle George McNulty, we thought, than like his forebears on the Rooney side. But I'm straying off my subject — the disconnect between a few of us, anyway, and Noll.

Our new coach was all business. Aside from football, his main interests were music — classical music — food, and wine. He was focused and self-directed. In conversation, he tended to be didactic. His coaching associates called him The Pope, because he spoke with an air of infallibility. His manner discouraged small talk. AJR, who prided himself on being able to communicate easily with anyone, from presidents of the United States to Federal Street winos, confessed that in the company of Noll he was ill at ease. Beyond matters that concerned the football team, they had little to say to each other.

At the University of Dayton, Noll was a good student as well as a good football player. In jest, I once boasted to Noll and Jack Butler that the professors at St. Vincent never had cut me a break. "I had to earn my degree," I said. "You guys wouldn't know about that. You went to school on athletic scholarships." Butler saw at once that I was being facetious, but Noll promptly rose to the bait. Dayton, he informed me, was a serious institution of learning. He said he had earned his good grades by hard work. For Butler's entertainment, and my own, I pretended to be skeptical. The longer I kept the joke alive, the more staunch Noll became in defending the integrity of his school.

Playing linebacker and guard, Noll was a Little All-American at Dayton, and Paul Brown drafted him in one of the late rounds. In addition to playing linebacker for Cleveland, Noll was a "messenger guard." Brown called every play in every game and delivered them to the quarterback by way of Noll and another lineman. Alternating, they would run back and forth between the bench and the huddle. Noll disliked this role and disliked the term "messenger boy" so much that as coach of the Steelers he entrusted all the play calling to his quarterbacks.

On a red-eye flight from the West Coast, Paul Bixler, an assistant coach with the Browns, characterized Noll for me in the following words: "Hard-working. Undersized, but tough. Smart as can be. And opinionated! Lots to say about everything. This kind of got to P.B. [Paul Brown] at times. Noll wanted to know reasons. 'Why?' he would ask. 'Why?' It was always why? why? why?"

Noll put up with his messenger-boy job for seven years (1953-1959). Then the coach of the Los Angeles Chargers in the AFL, Sid Gillman, took him on as an assistant. Gillman was innovative, intense, scientific, and thorough. In breaking down every aspect of the game, he used so much film that his photographers became full-time auxiliary members of the coaching staff. Noll brought this approach to the Steelers. In addition to being a coaching tool, it helped him to evaluate personnel and it helped the scouts to see what he was looking for in the way of talent.

Gillman, Noll once told me, required his assistants to cut all the game film into segments for painstaking study. Each segment consisted of a series of plays, which the assistant coach had to analyze. He would then tag the film and "file" it. The "filing cabinets" were trash cans Gillman had collected — one for each coach. It was a very time-consuming process, Noll said, and one morning when the coaches came to work they found that a janitor had emptied all their trash cans. The game film they had so meticulously taken apart was gone forever.

Bobby Burns — one of Jock Sutherland's ancestors — had it right: "The best-laid plans of mice and men ... " Noll, when he coached in Baltimore and Pittsburgh, continued to edit and save film, but always remembered to place a large sign on each receptacle. And I think he avoided storing the film in trash cans.

The three years Noll spent with Don Shula put the finishing touches on his football education. To Bill Nunn, he explained how an assistant coach makes progress: "You take a step up the ladder, learn what there is to learn at that level and learn it thoroughly, and take the next step."

"That's easy to say," Nunn answered. "But guys like you bring a little bit extra to the learning business."

By the way, I never heard anyone call Noll the Pope, or use his other nickname, Knute Knowledge, except behind his back. A few of the Baltimore players, I understand, addressed him as Knute, omitting the rest of it. Neither AJR, Dan, nor I called him anything but Chuck, or Coach. For a while when he was winning Super Bowls I referred to him among my scouts as Charlemagne – Charles the Great in plain English — but it never caught on, for which I am grateful. In retrospect, I can see that I was being a smart ass.

I have said many times, and repeat it now, that my brother Dan was responsible for bringing Chuck Noll to the Steelers. My only contribution was to ask some coaches and scouts what they thought of him. When I muscled into the Sylvan Room interview, I expressed a lot of forceful opinions about coaching philosophy, but the way Noll reacted, I feel sure, had nothing to do with his hiring. He'd have landed the job regardless, I believe. The decision was Dan's, with AJR concurring, and for twenty-three years there would not be any need to look for another head coach.

Guardian of the Faith

Charles Henry Noll became the fourteenth head coach of the Pittsburgh Steelers on January 27, 1969. I do not include Greasy Neale, co-coach with Walt Kiesling of the wartime Steagles, or Phil Handler, co-coach with Kiesling of the wartime Card-Pitts, but I do include Bert Bell and Buff Donelli, co-coaches for part of the 1939 season. Kiesling, who was head coach three different times in three different decades, and Joe Bach, who reappeared as head coach in the 1950s after a sixteen-year hiatus, are counted only once.

Noll joined our ranks on the day before the 1969 draft. This was how AJR wanted it, and I tried to conceal my disappointment. It was how Dan wanted it, too, but I could argue with Dan. When AJR spoke, there was no appeal. Although, unofficially, he had handed over the reins to his oldest son, he was still very much the Chief, still very much in command. He made it evident to me now that Chuck Noll would be in charge of the draft and have the final word on the selection of players and on trades. As head of the personnel department, I would make out a draft list for him and offer advice. That was all.

The Steelers did not have a table of organization, but there were clear and distinct lines of authority. On football matters, Noll, like the coaches before him, was to have a free hand. Dan would continue to run the front office. In addition, he would hire (and fire) the trainers and equipment managers, subject to approval by Noll. I would hire and fire the scouts, subject to approval by Noll and by Dan. Left unspoken was something we all knew: Noll had more latitude than either Dan or I did, but every decision made by any of us was subject to approval by the Chief.

He had not yet started telling me, again and again, "There can be only one boss." That would come later — and when he said one boss, he meant Dan. But as long as the Chief lived, Dan was never completely autonomous. Always the Chief retained veto power. Even after his death I expected him to reach down from heaven and reclaim that power whenever it suited him. So as far as I was concerned I answered to only one man: AJR. My attitude, I'm afraid, was "Fuck everybody else" — a sure-fire recipe for trouble. I didn't worry about that. My focus was always on the draft, completely.

For years I had chafed at the public perception of the Rooneys: Nice people, maybe, but stupid and cheap. I resolved to do what I could to change all that. The family honor was at stake. If no one else realized it, I did. In 1969, AJR was preoccupied with our race-track acquisitions. He was constantly on the telephone, constantly on the move. Dan's responsibilities covered so wide a spectrum that he was barely a participant until the day of the draft. Only I could protect us from the ridicule that would follow if we took the wrong players for the usual wrong reasons, as we had done so many times in the past. I would not let it happen again. I would keep the faith.

Noll's answers at his first press conference as our coach, I had to admit, gave me hope. He repeated what he had said in our Sylvan Room interview: "I'm not looking for respectability, I'm looking to win a championship." From what he had seen in the Steelers' 41-7 loss to the Baltimore Colts the previous season, they needed help everywhere. When the Steelers' turn came in the draft, he would take the best player on the board, irrespective of his position. A No. 1 draft choice at any position couldn't help but improve us at that particular spot.

It was music to my ears. Bill Nunn, Jack Butler, and I had rated the players in the draft on their ability, as we judged it, also without regard to position. We rated them from one to one hundred and sixty, and from the top one hundred we wanted as many as we could get. The Steelers had never drafted that way; now our new head coach was calling it the approach he favored. But did he mean what he said? I thought of a bromide my mother used to repeat: There's many a slip 'twixt the cup and the lip.

This was how anxious I became: Noll had been working with Don Shula on the draft list of the Colts. Would he bring that information to Pittsburgh — a serious breach of ethics? I had seen Bill Austin do something similar. It could damage a coach's reputation. It could damage ownership's reputation. I need not have worried. Noll's conduct in such matters, as in everything else, was above reproach.

Our draft room — the press called it the war room — was in the Roosevelt Hotel on the eighth floor. While Noll was involved with the reporters, I went there with trainer Ralph Berlin, equipment manager Tony Parisi, his assistant, Frank Sciuilli, and my secretary, Mrs. Duffy, to make certain that all was in readiness. On draft day I would be in that room with Noll, Dan, Bill Nunn, Ed Kiely, Fran Fogarty, and maybe one or two other front-office people, all of us seated at three walnut tables arranged in the shape of a T and laden with telephones. A green cloth covered the tables. Berlin would be in Philadelphia, where the Blesto scouts were gathered. I needed him there to keep me informed about late-breaking developments such as trades, new injury reports, and, sad to say, the existence of previously undisclosed rap sheets, and to put me on the phone with various Blesto people as the need arose. Nunn would stay with me through the first day of the draft and then hop a plane for Atlanta. There he would be in place to sign undrafted free agents and our own late-round picks from the black schools. Leaving Philadelphia when the draft was over, Berlin would get in contact with players of that type in the Mid-Atlantic region and New England. The number of free agents we corralled by being first on the scene with cash in hand could be astonishing.

But now I was in the war room to work on our draft lists. We had them on large sheets of white poster paper mounted on easels that nearly reached the ceiling. The names had been blown up to gigantic proportions, a task we deputized to a company called Buhl Optics. If there were last-minute changes in height, weight, or 40-yard dash speed reported by Blesto — and there always were — Parisi or Berlin would print the information on a narrow strip of masking tape and place it over the existing numbers. If a player went up or down in our ratings because of last-minute developments, the name itself, along with the appropriate statistics, had to be printed on tape and moved, which meant that one other name, at least, had to be moved as well. Berlin was now making a change of this kind, standing precariously on a chair. Distracted by a phone call, I hadn't been watching him, and when I saw what he was doing, I flipped.

"You're taping over the wrong name!" I shouted. Then I shouted some more. And screamed. Berlin, who weighed about 200 pounds, lost his balance on the chair. For a long, suspenseful moment, I thought he would fall over backwards. So did everybody else in the room. When he righted himself, their attention shifted to me. I knew what they were wondering, or thought I did. Would I drop to the floor and start chewing on the rug, like Adolf Hitler in moments of lunacy?

With an effort, I got a grip on myself. I counted to ten and said, "Ralph, the first thing Noll will look at when he walks into this room are those charts. If he sees a lot of mistakes, if he sees all that masking tape, our credibility will be shot. Henceforth," I added, the calm executive once again, "keep that optical company open all night if you have to. Keep it open right up to the morning of the draft, but this work must be professionally done – I don't care how much it costs."

That was how the draft always affected me. It raised my intensity level and my blood pressure. It gave me acid indigestion. On two or three previous draft days, I had run to the nearest men's room and tossed up my lunch. Berlin, suffering, I would guess, from post-traumatic stress disorder, kept the optical company open on the night before the draft for years and years to come. The cost was high, yes, but we saved a few nickels on masking tape.

From the draft room, I went downstairs. Dan wanted to see me in my office, someone said. Noll was there, too, and the drabness of the place embarrassed me. On my blackboard was a list of the players I had rated by position and Noll now suggested that we review it together. I steeled myself for whatever might be coming, but with his first few words he stilled all my doubts.

Clearly we were on the same wave length. I would read off a player's name and his statistics and then say something about his athletic skills. Noll listened carefully. He was interested above all in "playing speed." He called it the Steelers' greatest need. We discussed that a bit heavily, I remember. We talked about quickness and body control. We talked about "production," a big factor with Jack Butler. When his scouts extolled a player's talent and "growth potential," Butler would ask impatiently, "Can he play the damn game? Does he have playing smarts? Is he aware of what's happening on the field or is it all just a blur?" And here was Noll, talking the same way, telling me now that besides lacking speed, the Steelers were deficient in "football intelligence."

We kicked production and playing smarts and football intelligence around, and then we got into the specific skills needed for each position. I seldom heard him say, "Well, we had this player rated this way with the Colts." He gave me his own impressions of the players he had seen, and they were not the impressions of the Baltimore scouts. He asked me some questions which I was pleased to be able to answer. I learned for the first time of his obsession with muscle building. If a player had a good frame, Noll said, we could get some solid poundage on him through diet and weightlifting. He said we'd need barbells – the Olympic sets manufactured in York, Pennsylvania. "This stuff works. You'll see that it does," he told me.

Another thing he stressed was "playing with leverage." Playing with leverage was more important than brute strength. "Play with your legs. Hit through. Get under and up into the other guy. Deliver a blow. Don't be taking a blow." This was Noll the teacher indoctrinating a new pupil. He spoke with such sureness and enthusiasm that I couldn't help but be dazzled. Dan, too, was dazzled. But not only by Noll. Turning to me after Noll had politely thanked us and left the room, he said, "You gave a memorable performance."

I was flattered. But what gratified me most of all was how my ratings of the eleven "best athletes" conformed so exactly with Noll's. One of the players on my list was Joe Greene, a defensive tackle from North Texas State. At the mention of his name, Noll actually smiled. Scouting for the Colts, he had watched Greene in spring practice. After the NFL season, he had studied North Texas game films. And he liked Greene as much as I did, he said. Greene was black; he had not been widely publicized; he might still be available when it was our turn to draft. In that case, Noll and I agreed, we would make him our first-round pick.

Later that same afternoon, Dan told me that Shula had called. "He wants to talk to you," Dan said. "Shula feels that since Noll is over here giving us the Colts' information on college seniors, we ought to reciprocate."

I blew my top — again. "Damn! Noll hasn't given us a thing! He doesn't have their draft papers and I don't want them anyway. He only talked about the players he's seen himself. Tell Shula to go to hell!"

"Back off a little," Dan said. "It'll be OK. Shula wasn't demanding with me. Just return his call. After all, Don was the one who recommended Chuck."

So I reconsidered. Shula had received me cordially on my visits to his training camp in western Maryland. It was part of my job to look at players we thought the other teams might be willing to trade, and some coaches were barely civil when I approached them. Shula was always friendly, and now our phone conversation was friendly. He started off by praising Noll in the same terms as before. Chuck was a good coach, a good man. He was smart and hard-working. I had heard all this, but I didn't mind hearing it again. Eventually Shula asked me about ten or twelve players in the draft. How did we have them rated? It wasn't really an interrogation, I felt. Rather, I had the sense that we were talking like fellow scouts. One player we discussed was Ted Hendricks, the tall, thin University of Miami linebacker the sportswriters had dubbed The Mad Stork. It seemed to please Shula that our evaluations of this Colt-to-be and future Hall-of-Famer neatly dovetailed.

I hung up feeling good about Shula, Noll, myself, and the upcoming draft.

Chapter 44

The 1969 Draft

On draft day, as usual, I was in our eighth-floor control center at the Roosevelt Hotel by 6 a.m. Nobody else had arrived. I checked out the phones to Blesto headquarters in the Philadelphia Eagles' offices. Jack Butler and Ralph Berlin were there. It was too early to call New York, where Commissioner Pete Rozelle, facing television cameras from a dais in Madison Square Garden, would announce the selections. We had my brother Tim in New York, sitting by a telephone to keep us abreast of developments. After one last inspection of the room, I ordered coffee, tea, doughnuts, and sweet rolls from room service.

One by one, Noll, Dan, Nunn, Ed Kiely, and the others drifted in. Sidney, the bellman, came with the breakfast cart. Alex DiCroce popped in to see if there was anything else we needed. Kiely was briefing Noll on our ground rules for dealing with the media guys, who still had access to the draft room back then (the next year I put it off limits). AJR always turned up late. He'd be in and out all morning, seldom speaking, seldom making his presence felt.

It was 8 o'clock — time for the draft to start — before I knew it. Buffalo had the first pick. Although inter-league play would not begin until 1970, the war between the NFL and the AFL had ended and twenty-six teams would take part in a common draft, the team with the worst record drafting first. In late October, it had seemed that the team with the worst record would be the Steelers or the Eagles. Both were winless. Both had looked bad in losing six games. Whichever team lost when they met at Pitt Stadium, the assumption was, would keep on losing for the rest of the season and thus earn the right to draft O. J. Simpson.

Even in 1968 the name O. J. Simpson was well known — almost as well known as it is today, if for a somewhat different reason. When in the late 1990s he went on trial in Los Angeles, accused of murdering his wife and a hapless acquaintance of his wife by cutting their throats with a knife, O. J. Simpson's fame turned to infamy, never mind that a jury perhaps swayed by racial bias acquitted him. In 1968, he was college football's premier running back, the holder of every national ball-carrying record worth talking about. He was so good that Jack Butler, after watching him play, did something unprecedented, something completely out of character. He asked O. J. for his autograph.

Blesto scouts graded players from zero to five in such categories, for a running back, as power, elusiveness, breakaway speed, blocking, and pass-catching ability. The lower the grade the better. Simpson scored a zero, or close to it, in every department. "He left a little to be desired as a blocker," Butler said, "but you wouldn't want him hammering on those big defensive ends all day and slowing himself up."

I knew what Butler was talking about. Simpson played for Southern California, and on a visit to the West Coast I had watched USC game films with a scout from the San Francisco Forty-Niners. We agreed that a coach who did not take O. J. first would have to be minus some buttons. Every scout in the country — every scout I knew of — felt the same way.

And so interest built up in that late-October meeting between the ragtag Steelers and the ragtag Eagles. Sports reporters dubbed it the O. J. Simpson Bowl. The winner will be the loser, they wrote. Joe Kuharich, the coach of the Eagles, was vexed about that. "All this talk is just nonsense," he told me. "Neither one of us is going to draft O. J. Simpson. We're not the two worst teams, and before the season is over we'll prove it. Wait and see."

I didn't believe him.

The game at Pitt Stadium went down to the wire. With the score 3-3, and 1:36 left to play, the Steelers lost the ball at the Eagles' three-yard line on an intercepted pass. From the looks of things, the game would end in a tie. But on fourth down at the 10, the Eagles ran the ball — for no gain. Seconds later, Booth Lusteg kicked a field goal for the Steelers. Final score: Pittsburgh 6, Philadelphia 3. The Eagles now had the inside track in the race to draft O.J. Simpson.

Feet propped up on a bench, hands joined behind his head, Kuharich leaned back in a Pitt Stadium folding chair and complacently discussed his fourth-down call. Had he been looking ahead, maybe, to the draft? Not at all. In fact, he was more convinced than ever that the Eagles would win some games. Bearing him out, they won two of their last seven. The Steelers, meanwhile, beat Atlanta by three touchdowns and then tied St. Louis before reverting to form. They finished the season exactly as they had started it, by losing six in a row, but their 2-12-1 record was better than the Eagles' 2-13, Atlanta's 2-13, or Buffalo's 1-12-1. My old pal Harvey Johnson had won the highly coveted booby prize for his Bills. And so it was that O. J. Simpson, much against his will, ended up in the AFL.

In our room on the eighth floor of the Roosevelt Hotel, none of us gave O. J. a thought. We were hoping that neither the Falcons nor the Eagles would take the player who had gone to the top of our list, Joe Greene. Buffalo drafted quickly, and we waited with mounting tension for Atlanta's selection. While Atlanta deliberated, Buff Boston, in an ante-room, was talking with Greene on the telephone. From having heard it so often, I knew Buff's routine. "Hey, Joe," he would say, "would you like to be a Steeler? ... You would? Well, that makes us real happy. Have you had any recent injuries in workouts? Playing basketball, maybe? Horsing around? ... Good. Say, how about the military? Any change in your deferred status ... No? And, uh — are you still single? ... Oh, you're married? Any kids on the way? ... You're a dad? ... Congratulations! ... Well, we think you could help our ball club, so stay close to the phone. And, by the way, have any of the other teams called you? ... New York? Which team in New York? ... Giants? OK. And, oh yes — you haven't signed with any team in the Canadian League, have you? ... OK. Thanks a lot. Just sit tight."

Atlanta drafted George Kunz, a two-way tackle from Notre Dame. We had rated him near the top of our own list, but Joe Greene was our man. Noll and Dan were talking to him now. As for me, I wasn't interested in talking to Greene, I was interested in talking to Butler, in Philadelphia. Once again, I demanded to know if his scouts liked Joe Greene as much as we did. "Art," Butler said — Butler never called me Artie — "we think he's a good pick."

The fear that seized me now was that the Eagles would take Greene. I thought of Tom Mack, and how in 1966 Los Angeles had beaten us to him. Years later we learned that Philadelphia was extremely interested in Greene, but, drafting third, they took a running back from Purdue, LeRoy Keyes. I looked across the table at Noll and mouthed the word "Greene." Everybody in the room was staring at us. "Let's go for him," Noll said, loud and clear. He nodded at Dan, who had our man in New York on the line, the receiver cupped to his ear. "Greene," Dan said, making it official, and soon, with dramatic pauses between his incomplete sentences, Pete Rozelle was speaking into a microphone, saying:

"Pittsburgh ...

"Fourth choice in the first round ...

"Joe Greene, defensive tackle from North Texas State."

For the first time in weeks, I could relax.

An excellent beginning. No confusion. No arguing, no discussion. In my meeting with Noll on the eve of the draft, we had worked out a procedure. We would follow our list, right down the line. The chemistry between us was good. Noll liked our setup, or seemed to. I had spent a lot of time making sure that we were organized, and, so far, nothing had gone wrong. I dreaded the possibility that in Noll's eyes we would look bad — look like bumblers.

For our first pick in the second round, Noll was leaning toward a player named Ernie Galloway, a big, fast defensive end from Texas Southern. Noll had been harping on our need for team speed, and Galloway was a No. 2 on my charts. But Philadelphia took him. We then switched to Hanratty, although in doing so we deviated from our plan. He was not "the best athlete available." We took him for one reason: pressure from our fans. I had not yet matured enough to keep from being influenced by them. Our choice of Greene in the first round had come as a shock to the fans. They had wanted Hanratty, had clamored for him, and so had certain members of the press corps. Hanratty's credentials were threefold: He was from Western Pennsylvania — Butler. He had played at Notre Dame. He had broken passing records that belonged to the storied George Gipp and then apologized for it, disarmingly. "I feel like I've broken my mother's most expensive set of china," he announced.

But Hanratty, at best, was a marginal second-round pick. I knew it, Noll knew it, and even AJR, as partial as he was to players with Irish names, as partial as he was to Western Pennsylvanians, and as favorably impressed as he had been when Hanratty came to Pittsburgh for a physical examination – he had undergone minor surgery – and a get-acquainted lunch in the Sylvan Room, knew it. Drafting quarterbacks, both the Bengals and Chargers had passed on Hanratty in the first round. The Bengals, predictably, went for Greg Cook, who was big and strong-armed and had played at the University of Cincinnati. San Diego, unpredictably, chose an Ivy League quarterback, Marty Domres of Columbia. If the Steelers had done that, said a radio reporter in our draft room, the fans would be rushing over to burn down the Roosevelt Hotel. The Bears, when their turn came, had called to make us an offer. They would be willing to take Hanratty if we agreed to trade a veteran for him. Thanks but no thanks, I replied. We could have waited to take him ourselves even longer than we did — until the second of our two second-round picks, at least. But I was still too unsure of myself to gamble. (Thirty years afterward, at an Ireland Fund banquet in Palm Beach, I ran into Don Shula. Harking back to the 1969 draft, he told me how lucky we were that Chuck Noll had been around to advise us. "You were going to waste your first pick on Hanratty," he said as though stating a fact. "Chuck Noll went over there and straightened you guys out." I repressed an impulse to straighten out Shula. In the end, all I said was, "Yep, we were real lucky.")

Hanratty was by no means a dud, but during most of his seven seasons in Pittsburgh, he stood on the sidelines with a clipboard. Our second pick in the second round was Warren Bankston of Tulane, a good running back with size. He would have been a better tight end. In the third round, we drafted Jon Kolb, a center from Oklahoma State who could also play tackle. He started on all four of our Super Bowl teams, as did L. C. Greenwood, the tall, skinny defensive tackle I had scouted at Arkansas A. & M. I can pat myself on the back for landing Greenwood in the tenth round.

One other player worth mentioning was our fifteenth-round pick, Kenny Liberto, a wide receiver from Louisiana Tech. Liberto ran disciplined pass routes. He had a good pair of hands. He made all the catches. But he was small and he was slow and he did not survive training camp. Why do I bring up his name? Well, in watching Louisiana Tech game films, we could not help but notice the quarterback who was throwing to Liberto. He had a cannon for an arm and a lightning-quick release. We were getting our first look at Terry Bradshaw.

Joe Who?

Eight of our seventeen draft choices remained with the team. That is a fairly large number, but I remembered what an assistant coach under Buddy Parker said to me once: "It isn't how many rookies you keep that's important, it's how many rookies who contribute — who help you win. You don't want stiffs replacing stiffs."

By that measure, the 1969 draft was still not a bad one at all. Joe Greene played for twelve years and made the Hall of Fame. L. C. Greenwood played for thirteen years. Jon Kolb also played for thirteen years and stayed on for ten more as an assistant coach. (Greene joined the coaching staff, too, after getting out of the restaurant business.) Without Greene, Greenwood, and Kolb, we would not have gone to the Super Bowl four different Januaries, returning each time with the Vince Lombardi Trophy. Terry Hanratty, Warren Bankston, running back Bob Campbell, defensive back Charles Beatty, and linebacker Doug Fisher had much less successful but not insignificant careers, and the same could be said of tight end Bob Adams, an undrafted, underrated free agent.

We were making a break with the past, I felt, building for the future through the draft. We were getting it all together, and Joe Greene was the cornerstone.

Not that anyone in Pittsburgh thought we had done the right thing by drafting him first. The headline the next day in the *Post-Gazette* was derisive: "STEELERS SELECT ... JOE WHO?" But then the know-it-all newspaper guys had not seen Joe Who? in action, as I had. Scouting North Texas State, I saw him dominate every third-down situation. He was 6 feet 4 and 275 pounds and seemed to push the entire offensive line back toward the quarterback on pass plays. In the 1960s Greene was big for a tackle, and though smaller linemen can often beat larger ones with quickness and speed, it was Greene's own quickness and speed, and not his size, that made him so hard to handle.

After his first couple of games as a Steeler rookie, the fans stopped calling him Joe Who? They adopted his North Texas State nickname, which he disliked. The school color at North Texas was green, and the defensive unit, collectively, was known as the Mean Green, and so of course its best player could not have escaped being Mean Joe Greene, no matter what.

The funny thing was that he thought of himself as a teddy bear. There was nothing ogre-ish in his looks or his manner, and on the football field he conversed in a pleasant way with the other team's center, sometimes asking hopefully, "You gonna run the ball at me?" True, he could show meanness under stress. Early in the 1969 season he leveled the New York Giants' quarterback, Fran Tarkenton, with an unnecessary forearm blow and the officials ejected him from the game. Other expulsions were to follow. The Steelers were losing every week — after beating Detroit to start the season, they lost thirteen times in a row — and he was taking it badly. He was like an uncontrolled oil-well gusher, spewing his talent into the wind. Near the end of one game, as our opponents came out of their huddle, he picked up the ball and threw it into the stands.

There was also the deplorable spitting incident. Greene let fly in the face of the *Pittsburgh Press* reporter Pat Livingston because Pat wrote a column defending the team owners' position during a short-lived player strike. For that, and for his other transgressions, Greene was suitably contrite, but he had to be reined in. I think he'd been spending too much time with Roy Jefferson, a militant member of the players' union. Previously, I have written how Bill Nunn put John Brown on his case, rooming them together in training camp. Older and wiser than Greene, Brown was a calming influence. A heart-to-heart talk with Chuck Noll did some good after Greene let his unhappiness show because the Steelers had cut Charles Beatty, a close friend. "You have a long career ahead of you," Noll said. "You will see many teammates and friends move on. I can understand your concern, but learn to deal with it."

Brown and Noll between them re-directed Greene's talent and energy. If he was never a perfect gentleman on the football field, Noll did not mind. "Make something happen," he liked to tell his players, and no one responded more willingly than Greene. To reach the playoffs for the first time, in 1972, we had to beat Houston, and he absolutely crushed his side of the Oilers' offensive line. The defense held Houston to three points, and our nine were enough to win. In that '72 season the Steel Curtain came into being, with Ernie Holmes joining Greene, L. C. Greenwood, and Dwight White as the final component of a fearsome front four.

There came a time when injuries and age reduced Greene's effectiveness, but he adapted. He mastered all the nuances of team defense. Greene was a special favorite of AJR. Their rapport had increased year by year. Often the Chief would hand Greene a fist full of expensive cigars, huge ones that were shaped like baseball bats. In Joe's mouth, they looked as insubstantial as toothpicks. But Greene was getting into his thirties, and AJR worried about him.

"Have you been watching Joe lately?" he would ask me.

"Yes," I would say.

"How is he doing?"

"OK."

"Just OK?"

"He's been great."

"Yes, he's still good. He still plays fine team defense, doesn't he?"

"Yes, he does."

"He should be able to keep it up for years. Don't you think so?"

"Yes, I think he can," I would say.

I wasn't lying, exactly — Greene did keep it up for a very long time. I never admired him more than in his last year at our training camp, but not because of his football playing. One afternoon my son Art was filming practice from the top of a high steel tower. Suddenly an electrical storm blew in. There was lightning, thunder, heavy rain. Everybody ran for cover — everybody except Art and me. And Joe Greene. He was standing at my side, shouting at Art, "Don't jump! Climb down quickly! Be careful!"

Art — concerned about his equipment — was calling, "I have to take care of the cameras. They cost a lot of money."

"Fuck the cameras!" yelled Greene. "You get off that tower right now!"

Placing his cameras on the platform he'd been using, Art Rooney III climbed down as fast as he could. The lightning flashed, the thunder pealed, and the rain fell in torrents, but one of our team cars was pulling up near the tower and all three of us hopped safely inside.

There was a scene in a movie about El Cid, the intrepid Spanish soldier who made life difficult for the Moors, in which he single-handedly killed a dozen would-be abductors of a prince of Castile. Call it far-fetched if you will, but Joe Greene, to me, was his modern-day counterpart. El Cid stood up to the Moors. Joe Greene, just as defiantly, stood up to offensive linemen and thunderbolts.

Our third draft choice, Jon Kolb, was a blond, open-faced, square-jawed country boy. At 6 feet 2 and 225 pounds, he appeared to be too short and too light to play center in the NFL, but he was strong, tough, durable, and willing to learn. On the surface, he had nothing in common with AJR. Kolb grew up in rural Oklahoma, AJR in a raffish urban neighborhood. Where they resembled each other was in their common philosophy of treating others as they would like to be treated themselves while allowing no one to mistake kindness for weakness. For Kolb, that was especially true on the playing field.

He was not an immediate success. In a game at Wrigley Field in his rookie season, Dick Butkus, the Chicago Bears' Hall-of-Fame linebacker, roughed him up shamefully — "kicked his ass," line coach Bob Fry told me — and it was shortly thereafter that Chuck Noll moved Kolb to tackle, where he gradually came into his own. His tenacity, consistency, discipline, and attention to physical condition made him an iron man.

Lifting weights tirelessly, he gained close to fifty pounds, and he mastered all the blocking techniques, the little tricks of the trade, as well as the textbook moves.

Here is one last thing to be said about Kolb: year after year, the fans and reporters took him for granted. There are not many higher compliments.

Chapter 45

The Media

Most of our fans paid little attention to the players we selected on the second day of the draft. Their names might come up in water-cooler talk at the office or in casual conversation over cocktails at the golf club or over beers and shots of whiskey at the neighborhood bar. Even the sportswriters and sportscasters who covered the draft seemed to feel that nothing of importance was taking place on the second day.

I noticed three of them on the far side of the room, forming a tight little group with AJR. There was Pat Livingston of the *Pittsburgh Press*, the first paid scout the Steelers had ever had. In 1946, just out of the Navy, Livingston went to work for Jock Sutherland. "You're my personnel director," The Great Stoneface informed him. "But Doctor Sutherland," protested Livingston. "I don't know a thing about scouting." "You'll learn, Pat, you'll learn," answered his boss. There was Jack Sell of the *Post-Gazette*, a North Sider of my father's generation. There was Joe Tucker, called The Screamer, the play-by-play announcer on our radio network for twenty-five years but who was then in poor health and semi-retired. All three were argumentative, Livingston as relentlessly as a trial lawyer (he had a law degree from Duquesne), Sell with sardonic amusement, Tucker if called upon to defend or denounce some coaching decision.

I noticed them standing with AJR, and I noticed something else: they were looking at our scouting reports. We had just drafted Doug Fisher, a linebacker from San Diego State, and now Livingston called over to let me know he approved. "Hey, Artie," he said. His voice came from deep in his throat, emerging in a series of barks. "Your reports on that Fisher were pretty accurate. You had him pegged as a late-round pick and he was right where you expected him to be."

Scouting reports were private information, but I wasn't touchy about it. I liked Pat Livingston. I liked Jack Sell. I liked Joe Tucker. I had nevertheless promised myself that from now on we would run a tighter ship, at least in the scouting department. John Troan, the editor of the *Press*, would never have opened his board room to Chuck Noll and Art Rooney and Art Rooney's sons while he and some department head were discussing the pros and cons of hiring a new reporter. I made a mental note to talk with Ed Kiely and Dan about changing our policy. More restrictions were needed on access to the draft room.

I wanted Ed and Dan in my corner before I approached AJR because I knew exactly what AJR would tell me: "This is the way I do business. It does us good to have the newspaper guys feel they're a part of the organization. It will all work out for the best." And so on and so on. Ed and Dan, to my relief, saw things as I did. There were more reporters now from the radio stations and television stations, more reporters from the papers in the Beaver and Monongahela valleys. Letting them all have the run of the place was impractical.

Surprisingly, when we put it like that to AJR, he gave us an unqualified OK.

AJR's liking for, and rapport with, sportswriters went back a long way. Like Richard Nixon, he had hoped in adolescence to be one.

Recall that his first mentor was Dick Guy, half sportswriter, half sports promoter. Why, then, couldn't AJR have become a sportswriter? He had an expert's knowledge, certainly, of football, baseball, and boxing. Developing reliable news sources would not have been a problem for him, either; he was born with the gift of putting people at ease, of getting them to talk. Could he have learned how to write — acquired the necessary skills and techniques? I believe so. There are different kinds of intelligence, and his may not have been literary, but America's press boxes were not overflowing with Hemingways, Joyces, and Fitzgeralds. Very few literary artists gravitate to the profession. But as much as I respected my dad's capabilities, I never thought he was tough enough to have been a good sportswriter.

Granted it contradicts all that we know about him to say such a thing. If anyone or anything ever intimidated AJR, it remains a secret. In moments of anger, he could and did use his fists. He had a frightening facility for taking the starch out of people with a scowl and a few caustic words. But these moments of anger were sporadic. He had a temper, and he lost it now and then. Hurting someone's feelings, or, worse, the feelings of that person's close relatives — his wife, his mother, his children — and doing it publicly, cold-bloodedly, was different. Sportswriters are not just reporters, but critics as well. They have to assess blame for the failures and mistakes and bonehead plays endemic in any type of sports competition. They have to write about the side issues that come up — scandals and scrapes and even felonies. Though less common back then, and more frequently hushed up, felonies occurred, and they had to be written about. I don't think my dad could have brought himself to be the instrument. He was too soft inside.

Let me give you an example of his thought processes. Back around the dawn of the twentieth century, two brothers who had murdered a grocer and a policeman sawed their way out of the Allegheny County Jail, assisted by the wife of the warden. Infatuated with one of the killers, she provided them with guns and joined them in their flight from justice. They headed north in a horse-drawn sled (it was January, and there was snow on the ground), but the sheriff and his deputies caught up with the unlikely trio. In the shootout that ensued, both brothers were fatally hit. More than eighty years later, Hollywood turned the escapade into a movie, which AJR refused to attend. "I knew that warden's family," he explained. "Some of them are still living. I think that movie will be embarrassing to them."

There was also the time he ordered Dan to remove a story that mentioned Tim Mara's gambling background from one of our game programs regardless of the expense. Mara was a bookmaker; it never had been a secret, but to say so in print wouldn't do.

Yet my dad's true vocation, he continued to insist, was sportswriting. What appealed to him about it was the life: sitting in the press box and eating free hot dogs while being paid to watch a baseball game or a football game. It pleased his fancy to believe that I enjoyed the same perks in my own job. "Scouting those Big Ten games must be great," he would tell me. The Big Ten, I would answer, allowed no scouts in the press box. At halftime, there was no free lunch. AJR never bought that.

For as long as I could remember, sportswriters and media people were always a part of his entourage. He named a few of his best race horses after sportswriters — Livingston, Sell, Al Abrams. He named one for Kathy Kiely, Ed's daughter, when she was only 14, too young to go to the track and see the horse run. Kathy grew up to become a fine journalist, a Washington correspondent for the *Pittsburgh Press*, the *Houston Post*, the *Arkansas Gazette*, and *USA Today* (though not all at once).

Sometimes Dad would talk about meeting big-name writers like H. L. Mencken, Ring Lardner, and Damon Runyon. Mencken never wrote about sports, but liked to bet on the horses, Dad said. Lardner and Runyon were sportswriters who graduated to fiction. AJR always spoke of them with awe.

He appeared to regard the local writers and broadcasters as cronies. Even though he would take them on junkets to the Kentucky Derby, to New York, or out to the Pacific Coast, he never gave the impression that he was buying them off. In Las Vegas one time, he sent Joe Tucker and me to a horse room with seven thousand dollars to bet. When we tried to get it down, we were told that four thousand dollars was the limit. Well, Tucker went into liftoff. He more than lived up to his nickname — The Screamer. At the top of his lungs, he shouted for the manager. "This is Las Vegas! The big time! You're supposed to take all the action!" Quietly, the bookmaker informed us it was almost post time. "Would you like to bet four thousand or not?" he asked. Tucker placed a bet for four thousand.

My dad's horse finished out of the money, so we saved him three thousand bucks — or, rather, the bookmaker did.

Dad, Tucker, Jack Sell, and I were staying at Milton Jaffe's hotel and casino, the Stardust, and Milton was picking up the tab. On the day we left for home, Dad won seventeen thousand dollars at a craps table in the Stardust. "Darn it!" he said. "I was trying to lose a little to pay Milton back for his hospitality, but then I happened to get on a roll. And craps isn't even my game."

In retrospect, I can see that the old-time writers and broadcasters knew things about AJR that the public did not know and that AJR would not have wanted the public to know. He was one of the most successful gamblers in the country, but to the people of Pittsburgh he looked like a loser, because the Steelers were losers, and the writers did nothing to enlighten them.

After Sell, Tucker, and Livingston had passed from the scene a generation gap existed between AJR and their successors, young journalism-school graduates with a more serious, businesslike attitude. No longer was AJR a friend and companion to the "newspaper guys," his all-inclusive term for print reporters and broadcasters alike. Instead, they regarded him as almost an object of worship. They were largely unaware of the past, unaware of a time when Art Rooney took the blame for everything that seemed wrong with the Steelers. Chuck Noll had turned the chronic losers into winners, and now the owner was receiving the accolades long denied him.

AJR's knack of remembering not only names but home towns and neighborhoods dazzled these journalistic tyros. As Ed Kiely put it, he could make the lowliest cub reporter feel like Red Smith. But there was never any personal relationship, never any hanging out. AJR's age and eminence discouraged familiarity. The new guys listened to his stories, but went to Joe Gordon or to Dan for information about the team. And there were many more beat reporters than ever before. Regional papers and radio stations had joined the two large Pittsburgh dailies and the three Pittsburgh television channels in providing their readers and viewers with constant, extensive Steeler coverage.

AJR, in his dealings with the press, was never adversarial. According to Ed Kiely, he would pick up the paper, read a story about the team that he didn't like, and fume. He would then denounce the author as a knucklehead, a dummy with no knowledge of football or anything else. Thirty minutes later, the knucklehead himself might show up, strolling into AJR's office unannounced, as Mary Regan allowed most reporters to do. AJR would offer a welcoming handshake, Kiely said, and compliment the guy on an insightful piece of reporting.

Still, AJR was sincere, I believe, when he said that he liked newspapermen. He liked to talk with them, and not about football, necessarily. I was discussing college prospects one day with Vito Stellino of the *Post-Gazette* when AJR made an unexpected appearance. "What's up? Whaddaya hear?" he asked Stellino. A tall, rather gaunt young man who resembled the illustrators' renditions of Ichabod Crane, Stellino had more than the usual sportswriters' understanding of X's and O's and was highly regarded by his colleagues and I think the coaches as well. He'd been taping our interview and did not turn off the recorder, I noticed, as AJR took a chair and began chatting with us.

Almost at once the conversation turned to boxing – I don't remember how. Boxing was not a sport that I followed very closely, but I had learned to appreciate the stories the Chief could tell about fights and fighters and managers. He was in rare good form – unaware of the tape recorder and hence not the least bit self-conscious – and Stellino seemed to be mesmerized. Even I was mesmerized, as often as I had heard all the tales. In fact, when AJR finished, I felt like applauding. He stood up to leave, said goodbye, and was out the door. I turned to Stellino. "Well, Vito," I said, "I got you one for the history books." I was proud of my Dad and happy to have been the agent for giving Vito, a nice guy who had treated me well in the *Post-Gazette*, access to a special kind of feature story.

But, alas, he was looking at me sadly. "There was only fifteen minutes on that tape," he said. "I used twelve of those minutes on your stuff, leaving only three, and Mister Rooney must have talked for half an hour."

After Stellino returned to Baltimore, his home town, Ed Bouchette became the *Post-Gazette's* pro football writer. One day in the 1980s he was typing up a story in the Three Rivers Stadium press room when AJR wandered in, chewing on a big fat cigar, the kind that looked like a baseball bat. He started talking about the old days, with no other purpose than to socialize with a newspaper guy. "At first," Bouchette said, "I tried to think of a way to cut your dad off. I was on deadline and in no mood for interruptions. But then I thought, this is Art Rooney, a man who's already a legend. He wants to give me some of his time. So to hell with my story. I'm going to take fifteen minutes, or even thirty minutes, and listen to him. That was what I did, and I don't regret it."

AJR was well up into his eighties now. Not long after the incident related by Bouchette, he asked if I would like to drive to the farm with him. "We could maybe take a few days and go on up to Quebec City," he said. "We could visit the Shrine of St. Anne."

"I'm sorry, Dad," I replied, "but I'm pretty busy right now. Let's do it some other time."

"OK, but time's running out on me, Artie," he shrugged – kidding on the square, as he would put it.

"Some other time" never came.

Unlike Bouchette, I do have cause for regret.

Al Abrams

Only once did I ever hear AJR address a harsh word to a newspaperman. The sports editor of the *Post-Gazette*, Al Abrams, wrote a notes column every Saturday that was captioned "A Whirl Around the World of Sports." It consisted of gossipy little items separated by dots. Abrams picked up his subject matter wherever he could find it. I know that Ed Kiely supplied him with notes and would write an entire column for him once or twice a year. But what I started to say was that in his notes column one week there appeared the following line: "Art Rooney's box at Forbes Field is filled at every Pirate game with priests and racketeers."

In the 1950s, when I was still in college, the *Post-Gazette* published an early, pre-dated edition, called the "bulldog," that hit the streets at about 6 p.m. Reading Abrams' Saturday column at home on a Friday night, while the rest of us watched television, AJR became very animated. "Why, that greasy bum!" we heard him say. He picked up the phone and called Kiely. "Have you seen the bulldog yet? Have you seen what Abrams wrote? He says my box at Forbes Field is filled with priests and racketeers. Do you have his telephone number? ... No, I won't wait till tomorrow. Give it to me right away. If you don't have it, get it ... OK. Let me write that down."

All eyes in the room are fixed upon him now, and he has noticed. We notice that he has noticed, and our heads swivel back to the television set. Now he is dialing Abrams. "Al? This is Art Rooney." His voice is hard, menacing. The eyes of his sons have switched again from the television screen to the Chief. "I just read your column in the morning paper. What are you talking about, priests and racketeers? That isn't funny. How do you think those priests feel? They read the paper too. You're way out of line, Al, way out of line." He is yelling into the phone. "I thought you had more sense than that ... Calm? I AM calm. And when I read something I know what it means. I'll talk to you later." The next sound heard is the receiver slamming down. We pretend to have been watching television all this time.

I had met Al Abrams as a kid, but our conversations had been brief and perfunctory. "How's school?" he would say. That sort of thing. Lebanese by extraction, Abrams was a short but substantial looking olive-complexioned man whose slicked-back, pomaded black hair was as shiny as the Guys and Dolls suits he always wore unless he was wearing a sport jacket. Dark, soulful eyes and sagging jowls gave him the melancholy expression of a basset hound.

A year or so after the telephone call, on a trip to the West Coast for a Steeler game, I was hanging around the hotel swimming pool with my brothers when Abrams turned up, dressed in a sport shirt, slacks, and loafers. Recognizing that we were Rooneys, he greeted us. His manner was as casual as his apparel. I admit I didn't know what to make of him. Al Abrams was the guy who had suggested in the paper that Art Rooney, Sr., was a racketeer, the guy Art Rooney had yelled at on the telephone. He was the best-known Pittsburgh sportswriter, a celebrity in his own right, the MC and organizer of the big Dapper Dan sports banquet, of which Owney McManus had said, "You could back up all the paddy wagons in town to the hotel where that affair is being held and you wouldn't have room enough for all the bums and con artists who deserve to be taken to the hoosegow." I recalled that AJR had named a race horse after Abrams. But AJR named his horses after all kinds of people. Should I give Al Abrams the benefit of the doubt or be hostile?

In a soft-spoken, good-humored way, he was telling us of a side trip he had made to Las Vegas. His outlook on Vegas, his outlook on life in general, seemed to be cynical and jaded, but indulgent. He reminded me of AJR's North Side friends, of the people he knew in boxing, of Uncle Jim, of Dago Sam. Over the next twenty minutes or so, Al Abrams completely disarmed us. From then on when I saw him he would always say, "Hi. What's up? How are things going?"

I decided he was not a greasy bum.

Jack Sell

Jack Sell and my dad played with and against each other on sandlot football and baseball teams in the early 1920s. Jack was a strict German Lutheran from the North Side neighborhood of Fineview. Higher than Troy Hill, Fineview looked down on the Allegheny River and the Pittsburgh skyline on the opposite side. He had a full head of iron gray hair and his perfectly tailored suits were the same color, which gave him a monochromatic look. He was stocky, like Pat Livingston, but several inches taller. Friendly but distant with the training-camp ball boys, he would take them on fishing trips to privately-stocked lakes near Olean. In the coaches' room at camp, he put away gargantuan amounts of beer without ever showing the effects.

Every Saturday night he went bowling, even when a Steeler game was scheduled. In Jack's day the *Post-Gazette* had no Sunday edition, and thus he was free to make a choice. That he preferred to go bowling amazed me. When I conveyed this to Ed Kiely, he said, "You have to understand Sell." Ed's theory was that year after year of covering Steeler teams that always fell short had left Jack professionally numb. He felt no emotional involvement with the team. Going to the games was a job, nothing more.

Jack's reporting on the Steelers was methodical and bland. Kiely and Dan often joked about it. I thought his straightforward, focused style of writing gave the reader the essential facts of a story without any attempt at fanciness, and AJR seemed to feel the same way.

Sell had a special relationship with the Chief. In fact, Sell, Tucker, and Livingston belonged to what I thought of as an inner sanctum. There seemed to be a tacit agreement among them that no one would break a story that made the team or the organization look bad. At our pre-season camp in Olean one year, I thought that Sell overstepped the line. Shockingly — to me and, I am sure, to the *Post-Gazette's* readers — something he wrote was actually quite critical of Walt Kiesling and his assistant coaches. On behalf of the whole Steeler family, I felt betrayed. The headline over the story seemed particularly nasty. Pat Livingston, noting my distress, explained to me that copy editors in the office wrote the headlines, sometimes distorting the information contained in the story itself.

"Take another look at what Sell wrote," Livingston advised me. "It's not as hard on Kies as the headline suggests. You have to remember, Artie, that we're supposed to do our jobs no matter how tight we are with your dad. Sell doesn't dislike the coaches. Just the opposite. But a reporter has to tell it like it is."

A few days later AJR drove up from Pittsburgh, and I saw him conversing with Sell as if nothing had happened. It was then that I first began to alter my thinking about sportswriters. Maybe Livingston had it right, after all. Over the years, for personal reasons, I came to appreciate Pat's sensitivity, but that is another story.

Jack Sell never covered our NFL championship teams. After the 1973 season, he retired — too old and too set in his ways to meet the changing demands of his job, or so it seemed to the *Post-Gazette* brass. The brass pushed him out, and he resented it. On January 12, 1975, he was our guest when we won the Super Bowl game for the first time. After that, I don't remember seeing much of Jack. One day in the mid-1980s, AJR collected Dan, Kiely, Uncle Jim, and me for a trip from Three Rivers Stadium up Fineview Hill to the Lutheran church. We were going to Jack's funeral, all of us. No questions or excuses accepted.

When my brothers and I were young, we had known Jack's son, Jack, Jr., a good-looking kid and a better athlete, I secretly felt, than any of us. Except for a blown-out knee, Jack, Jr., would have played college football. It sobered me at the funeral to observe how grief-stricken he was. The tears ran down his cheeks and he sobbed inconsolably. Tough old German Jack Sell, I reflected, had a gentler, less buttoned-up side invisible to us. It was there all the time but we were simply not looking.

The Screamer

In 1936, when the Steelers were still the Pirates, AJR hired a Jewish guy from Canada, Joe Tucker, to broadcast their games on the radio. Fitting in was no problem for Joe. He liked to play the horses, idolized AJR, took undisguised pleasure in the camaraderie associated with his job, exulted in each of the Steelers' rare victories, and agonized over their defeats.

A tall, jovial man verging on fatness, Tucker had no affectations, but took considerable pride in his tennis game. He competed in local amateur tournaments, always with success if you took his word for it. His great friend Jack Sell had a different story to tell. Assigned by the *Post-Gazette* to cover the West Penn championships (a bit of a comedown, he thought), Sell was on hand to witness Tucker's most embarrassing moment. A sizzling forehand drive from his opponent eluded Joe's racket, made contact with a most sensitive part of his anatomy, and left him writhing on the court in an anguished heap. Sell never tired of rehashing that incident.

Chronic bad luck at the race track provided Tucker with a punch line for one of his running gags. In the airport before traveling to a Steeler game, he conscientiously bought flight insurance — a $10,000 policy on his life, payable to Mrs. Tucker if the airplane went down. The ticket-sized receipt went into his pocket. When the plane landed safely, he would take out the receipt, tear it in half, and mutter to Livingston or Sell, "Another loser."

Because of his partisanship in the broadcasting booth, most listeners regarded him as a shill or a mouthpiece for AJR. He was in any case a loyal employee. He worked with a "color" man, usually Bill Burns, who interspersed comments during lulls in the play-by-play, and a "spotter" who helped him identify blockers, tacklers, ball carriers, pass receivers, and so forth. One Sunday in the absence of his regular spotter, he asked me to fill in. The lineups of both teams were spread out before us, and as each play developed my job was to point with a pencil to the names of the players involved. But though familiar with all the Steelers, and with the other team's personnel to at least some degree, I was still in my teens, and more of a fan than a professional observer. A spotter must not lose his concentration. Caught up in the fortunes of the Steelers, I frequently lost mine.

At halftime, Tucker gave me a cram course in the art of spotting. It was useless. By the middle of the third quarter, I had forgotten my lessons completely. Tucker did not reprimand me, or show any trace of annoyance. When he handed me my fee — ten dollars — I felt reluctant to take it, but I took it.

Tucker never asked me to spot for him again, but there were visiting broadcasters who did. All of them concluded, as Tucker had, that once was enough.

AJR's contract with the radio station allowed him to handpick the play-by-play announcer, and year after year it was Tucker. When professional football went national on television, the league and the network combined to pick the announcers. They looked first to the veterans of the radio booth, and Tucker perceived this as the chance he'd been waiting for. "Stay with radio," counseled AJR, but in television the money was bigger, the public exposure greater, the prestige of a higher order. Tucker left the Steelers to go with NBC and did not do at all well.

On a national telecast, the announcing must be objective. Screamer Joe, conditioned to root for the home team, failed to adjust. A second difficulty was that he found himself talking too much. Each play on television unfolds before the viewer's eyes. Detailed descriptions are therefore superfluous. Ray Scott, a Pittsburgh guy who also had learned his craft on radio, made the transition more smoothly than Tucker. His opportunity came when Bill Stern, another blabbermouth, had a meltdown on the air while broadcasting a Pitt-Georgia Tech game and couldn't continue. Ray Scott stepped in as his backup and revolutionized the calling of television games. He was terse and informative, never intruding on the action. "Let me set the defense: Left end, Jones, number ninety-two. Left tackle, Smith, number seventy-seven ..." "It was Sam Huff, from West Virginia, who made that tackle ..." From the day he took over for Stern, he was able to write his own ticket.

Tucker, with the help of AJR and Kiely, hung on for a while at NBC and did some telecasts for CBS, but they were using him mostly on color. His assignments began to come less and less often until at last there were none at all. Meanwhile, he continued to work in Pittsburgh for radio station WWSW, giving the race results and a commentary each night. To make extra money, he dabbled in stocks and bonds. Red Donnelly, a young announcer from Steubenville, was broadcasting the Steeler games on WWSW, with Tom Bender doing color, and there was never any thought of replacing them.

I was in AJR's office one day when Tucker came in and began to talk in a discouraged way about the turn his career had taken. AJR was surprisingly unsympathetic. He said, "Well ... I advised you to stay in radio. Remember what they called you? The Voice of the Steelers. You threw that away." This was where it seemed to me that AJR should have stopped. Instead, I heard him saying, "You're Jewish, Joe. A Hebe. Hebes are supposed to be smart. You should be the owner of that radio station by now."

What am I doing here? I wondered. I wanted to turn myself into a fly and buzz right out of the room. Tucker had not been looking for charity. He was an old and dear friend, almost a member of the family. His reception from the Chief put an end to all that. He got up to leave, and they mumbled something about seeing each other later. I walked out with Tucker and we paused for a minute. Smiling ruefully, he said, "Your dad doesn't get it. Owning the station because I'm Jewish ... Not all Jews are gifted businessmen, you know."

In the next few years, Tucker had a series of heart attacks. He and Frances, his wife, retired to Florida. With her encouragement, he wrote a couple of books about his time with the Steelers. "It helps him beat depression and his feeling of disconnectedness," she explained to some of us. AJR bought hundreds of Tucker's books and sent them to friends. Jack Sell once told me that he would never even think of writing a book. He said the risk of hurting people he had known well was too great. Tucker's books were harmless. As in his broadcasts, he was careful to avoid being critical of anyone. He wrote about himself and Jack Sell and AJR and Walt Kiesling, but not revealingly. The real Sell, the real AJR, the real Walt Kiesling, and even the real Joe Tucker were much more interesting and human than the cardboard characters in Tucker's books.

AJR used to tell me that his biography would have to be written twenty years after he died. "After all, I touched all the bases," he said. Tucker may not have touched all the bases — not the way AJR did — but they were running the bases together at times. If Tucker had just told his story, letting the chips fall where they might, he could have written a more interesting memoir.

Pat Livingston

I was 11 years old, or maybe 12, when I first met Pat Livingston. On the morning after a Steeler game in Washington, D.C., Kass, Aunt Alice, and all five Rooney boys — jammed into the family's Buick Roadmaster — were waiting for AJR in the driveway of a big hotel. A young, black-haired man came up to the car and spoke to Kass. He called her Mrs. Rooney. She introduced him to the rest of us, one by one, as Pat Livingston.

When the introductions were finished, he said, "Just a minute, I'll be back," and disappeared into the hotel. While he was gone, Kass said to Aunt Alice, loud enough for the rest of us to hear, "Pat works for the Steelers." In no time, he was back at the car with two bags of candy — Hershey kisses. AJR arrived, got behind the wheel, and we pulled away. Pat Livingston, I remember, stood in the driveway watching us depart.

I thought of him after that as the Candy Man. A few years later I came to know him as one of the toughest but fairest sportswriters ever to cover the Steelers.

In 1946 and 1947 Livingston was the team's press agent, a part-time scout, and an errand boy for Jock Sutherland. One day the frugal Scotsman sent him to pick up a suit at the dry cleaners'. Livingston returned with the suit and twenty-five cents in change from the dollar Sutherland had given him. Sutherland was not in the office, so Livingston put the change in an envelope and handed it to assistant coach John Michelosen, whose desk was next to Jock's.

Michelosen chuckled. "The Doctor won't want this quarter," he said. "Yes he will," Pat replied and went back to his own office. In a few minutes Sutherland appeared. "Did Pat come with my suit?" he asked Michelosen. "It's right here, hanging up," Michelosen told him. "Oh," Sutherland said. "Where's my change?"

To save carfare, Sutherland walked from the PAA in Oakland, where he lived in one room, to the Steeler offices in the Union Trust Building downtown, a distance of five miles. This was not out of character for him, but at the time of the dry-cleaning incident his behavior was growing bizarre. He accused Livingston of planning to keep the change he had put in the envelope. Years later Pat talked to me about it. The thing that seemed to bother him most was that both he and Sutherland had been Navy officers during World War II. "And now he's telling me I tried to steal his change — twenty-five cents. I knew it was time to move on," Pat said.

Shortly after that, he resigned. It was not until Sutherland's death from a brain tumor the following spring that we all learned the reason for the inexplicable way he had been acting.

Pat never used his Duquesne University law degree. The fact that his brother Tom was one of the most successful trial lawyers in Western Pennsylvania may or may not have been a factor. Shortly after joining the sports staff of the *Pittsburgh Press*, Pat got the Steeler assignment. He covered three winning teams in twenty-two years. As a beat reporter, he kept his eye on the story — on the performance of the players, on the way they were coached. He was willing to ignore a lot of off-the-field carrying-on by Buddy Parker, Bobby Layne, Ernie Stautner, and others.

I was present at our training camp in Latrobe on the day of the Joe Greene spitting incident, but all I saw was the aftermath. Interrupting a conversation we were having, Bob Reiland, an old high-school friend of my brother Dan, exclaimed, "Oh, this is terrible!" He was looking over my shoulder. I turned to see Joe Greene walking away and Pat wiping his face with a handkerchief.

At least a dozen people had been witnesses, but Pat made an effort to suppress the story. He prevailed on all the media people in camp to write nothing and say nothing about it. Even John Troan, editor of the paper he worked for, accepted Pat's argument that if the story were printed it would hurt his relations with the other players, shutting off valuable sources. The next day, after Greene told a *Press* columnist and a wire-service reporter that if he had it to do over again, he would, Troan changed his mind and wrote a blistering page-one editorial, which broke the media silence. There were follow-up stories in Pittsburgh and elsewhere without the consequences Livingston had feared. Not a single Steeler, including Greene, stopped talking to him.

Pat was a perceptive writer, I thought. In the 1950s and '60s, everyone said the Steelers were cheap and dumb. What Livingston saw was a lack of organization. He wrote long, analytical stories on how Paul Brown, in Cleveland, had organized his team from the ground up. Brown kept tabs on the training room, the equipment room, the conditioning program, the scouting, and the psychological and intelligence testing. He coached his coaches as well as his players. All of them knew where they stood, knew what Brown expected from them.

He did not throw money around. Instead, as Livingston pointed out, he emphasized doing things right. My brother Dan and I read Pat's stories about Paul Brown closely and often discussed them. We felt that AJR's approach was in many ways not compatible with Brown's, but when AJR decided at last to modernize his operation he asked a former Brown, Don Shula, for advice, and hired another former Brown, Chuck Noll, as his coach. The system Noll installed was a lot like the one that Pat Livingston had touted a decade before.

Pat encouraged me in my work and was kind enough to compliment me now and then in his columns. In my office one day we were talking about the way that new and sophisticated scouting methods had become commonplace since Sutherland's time. "That stuff," Pat said, "is baloney."

I challenged him to a test. We turned down the lights and turned on the movie projector and watched a University of California quarterback. Using our current scouting forms, each of us graded him as a prospect. It was serious business, lasting forty-five minutes. Little was said, other than, "Run that one back again ... " When we were finished, I turned up the lights and pushed our final scouting form at Livingston. "We've scouted the same quarterback," I said. "Let's each write him up and see what we have."

It took us another twenty-five minutes. And our reports were almost identical. We agreed that the prospect could improve with time and play in the NFL, that he should develop eventually into a starter, although perhaps not a starter for a winning team, that he was worth a second look. Both of us rated him a second- or early third-round draft choice. We compared what we had written about his size, speed, quickness, body control, toughness, football smarts, position skills, running ability, release, vision, awareness, throwing accuracy, and arm strength. Pat wrote much better than I did, but, over all, our conclusions were similar. Our final summing-up was similar, too.

"Well, Pat," I said, "this shows me that even a newspaper guy can do what I do. I guess you learned something from Sutherland after all. Come out for a plate of spaghetti and some chocolate cake with me and Kay and the kids. She'd love to have you. You'll be an Irishman eating home-cooked Italian food served by a red-headed German girl while a bunch of half-Irish, half-German teenagers are running around. "This plain-talking reporter who'd been barred from the Steeler locker room, pushed or thrown out of the Bears' locker room, and punched in the ribs while being held in a headlock by one of Vince Lombardi's assistant Redskin coaches was a mellow fellow in our dining room that night.

After Pat became the sports editor of his paper in 1972, Phil Musick covered the Steelers. Pat continued to write columns about the team, but seemed to be more interested in golf.

On a perfect summer night in 1980, AJR and Kass marked their fiftieth wedding anniversary with a party at 940 North Lincoln Avenue. Only two media people were invited — Bill Burns and Pat Livingston. Dad and Mom were still in good health. Chuck Noll had given them a winning football team and I don't think they could have been happier. Pat by then was calling Mom "Kass" instead of "Mrs. Rooney." She said she never read anything that Pat or Jack Sell had to say about AJR for fear of jeopardizing her friendship with them. If what they wrote wasn't "nice," she would prefer not to know it.

I thought that Pat would write a column about the anniversary celebration. He chose not to. He had come to the party as a friend and not to report on it. From AJR and Kass on down, all of us Rooneys had a true affection for Pat.

In my case, it went back to the Hershey kisses.

The Mighty Atom

Toward the end of World War II, the pro football writer for the *Pittsburgh Press*, Les Biederman, went into the Army, and Carl Hughes, a kid just out of Geneva College, took his place. Carl was from South Fork, in Cambria County, where Barney McGinley had once tended bar. McGinley and AJR were still promoting fights, and Chet Smith, Carl's boss, informed him that in addition to covering the Steelers and Pitt, he was now the paper's boxing writer.

"But I've never seen a fight in my life," Carl protested.

"Don't worry about it," Smith advised him.

Carl never had written a news story, either, but he turned out to have quite a flair for the job. His reporting uncovered the fact that without an OK from the university the Pitt coach, Clark Shaughnessy, was moonlighting on Sundays as a consultant to the Washington Redskins. Incensed, Shaughnessy called the editor of the *Press*, Ed Leech, and demanded that Hughes be fired. Leech's response was to give Carl a five-dollar raise, increasing his pay to the munificent sum of thirty dollars a week.

AJR, unlike Shaughnessy, took a liking to Carl. In the 1920s the world flyweight champion, a Welshman named Jimmy Wilde, had been known as The Mighty Atom. Carl Hughes was Welsh and also diminutive in size. Accordingly, AJR bestowed Jimmy Wilde's nickname on Carl, abbreviating it later on to "Atom."

When the Steelers played out of town, AJR would take the writers and broadcasters to dinner. In Detroit one Saturday night, he piled them all into a taxicab and asked the driver to recommend a good place for fried chicken. As Hughes told the story, the driver said there was only one good place but added, "No use going there, because you couldn't get in." AJR said, "Well, take us to that place anyway. I'll make it worth your while."

Grunting "OK," the cabbie drove them to what appeared to be an ordinary house — a private residence - deep in the black ghetto. The writers and broadcasters exchanged looks with one another, but followed AJR up the steps of the front porch to the door. AJR rang the bell. Nothing happened. He rang again. Another long wait. He rapped on the door with his knuckles. No one came. He rapped a second time, harder. At last a door panel which was little more than a peephole slid open. A black face peered out. "Whaddya want?"

"Some fried chicken," said AJR.

"We don't let strangers in."

"Do me a favor," AJR told him. "Go tell your boss that Art Rooney is here. If he doesn't know who Art Rooney is, ask him to call Gus Greenlee in Pittsburgh." Gus Greenlee, as I have said before, was the numbers king of Pittsburgh and the owner of the city's Negro League baseball team, the Crawfords.

The sergeant at arms disappeared. In a minute a different man came to the door and pulled it wide open. He was short and fat and beautifully dressed and he had a big cigar in his mouth.

"Art Rooney!" he said. "Come right in! You look exactly how Gus Greenlee described you to me."

The fried chicken, according to Hughes, was excellent, and the dinners were all on the house.

The Groundling

Tom Birks, the pro football writer for the *Pittsburgh Sun-Telegraph*, was an untidy man in his sixties who came from somewhere in the British Isles and talked with a Scottish or North of England burr. Tom never flew with the team to out-of-town games. Instead, he would travel by railroad or bus or drive his own car, sometimes missing out on important stories.

"Mister Birks," I once asked him, "why do you refuse to fly?"

"Young man," he replied, "when I was a cub reporter I had to cover an airline crash. This was in the early days of aviation. When I got to the scene, I looked at all the mangled, compressed corpses, and the body parts lying around, and said to myself, 'From now on I'm staying close to the ground.'"

I wished I had not been so curious.

Mort Sharnik

In the early 1960s, Mort Sharnik of *Sports Illustrated* showed up at our training camp in Rhode Island and asked Ed Kiely if he could speak to "Mister Rooney." Whether or not Kiely knew of Sharnik's reputation as a top-flight investigative reporter I have no idea. If he did, it might have given him pause. In any case, he arranged the interview. Off and on, Sharnik and my father talked for several days. Before their last meeting broke up, Sharnik said, "Mister Rooney, you are known by football people as a good loser. I don't believe it. From what I've seen and heard about you, I think you are anything but a loser."

After I got to be friends with Mort, he told me that AJR choked up with emotion. He clenched his teeth, biting off the end of his cigar. And then with his voice cracking he said, "I hate losing! I've won as a baseball player and a baseball manager. I've won as a football player and a football coach. I've won as a boxer. And you know that I've won at the race track. With the Steelers, I'm trying to win. Just remember that. I'm trying! I hate losing!"

That particular story never made *Sports Illustrated*, but Mort kept in touch with the family. "It's only a matter of time before Art finds a winner," he would say. Art did find a winner, and Mort was with us as a friend, and not in his capacity as a *Sports Illustrated* writer, at all of the Steelers' Super Bowl games.

He accompanied us one time to a mid-season game between the Steelers and Bengals in Cincinnati. A constant theme in the sports pages just then was quarterback Terry Bradshaw's supposed lack of intelligence. The Steelers won that day in Cincinnati, but not because Bradshaw had distinguished himself, and in the dressing room afterward the writers were subjecting him to an unending string of blunt, not to say insulting, questions. Before the interview was over, we were ready to board the bus for the airport. "Wait a minute," Mort said. He took a few quick steps to Bradshaw's locker and penetrated the crowd to introduce himself. "Terry, I'm Mort Sharnik from *Sports Illustrated*." On such and such a play, in such and such a situation, Mort went on, "I thought you did exactly the right thing." Bradshaw looked up, and Mort proceeded to ask him questions of a much more positive nature than the ones he'd been getting from the other reporters, who were taking it all in and writing it all down.

After they scattered, Sharnik and Bradshaw stood by themselves for a while, talking and laughing and having a good time. Mort then rejoined us, and I gave him a quizzical look. He smiled, shrugged, and said, "Well, you've been telling me that Bradshaw just needed some self-confidence. So I thought I'd try to make him feel good."

Part Four: New Broom
1970-1973
Chapter 46

Three Rivers

On April 25, 1968, after twenty years of political bickering, ground was broken for the city's new baseball and football stadium. "Hallowed ground," the speakers kept calling it — this clearing in a junk yard on the north shore of the Allegheny River where Exposition Park and Pop Rooney's tavern once stood. Five civic leaders with five silver spades dug five little holes in the hallowed ground, and Pittsburgh had started building a $28 million playpen for the Pirates and Steelers.

AJR was one of the ground breakers. For public- relations purposes, there were goal posts on the site, and he placekicked an extra point, with my brother Dan holding the ball. It was pure symbolism — getting the project off on the right foot, so to speak. Afterward, AJR told reporters that he had not tried a placekick since 1921, when his sandlot team, the Hope-Harveys, played the Canton Bulldogs. As I don't have to remind you if you've been reading this memoir closely, a Canton lineman blocked that kick, allowing Jim Thorpe to pick up the ball and run for the only touchdown of the game.

It takes forever in Pittsburgh to get something done, and Three Rivers Stadium, as the structure would eventually be named, had been pie in the sky since the late 1940s. There were vague plans for a stadium during what came to be known as Renaissance I, the massive cleanup and construction project launched by Mayor Dave Lawrence and banker Richard King Mellon, but bridges, tunnels, the Hilton Hotel, the Gateway Center office-building complex, and Point State Park had priority. Finally in 1958 the University of Pittsburgh, gobbling up real estate in Oakland, bought the Pirates' outdated ball park, Forbes Field, with the object of tearing it down. Pitt needed land for classroom buildings and a library, so Forbes Field had to go — not right away, but eventually. Pirate owner John Galbreath, in consenting to the sale, was sending Pittsburgh a message: without a new, taxpayer-financed, state-of-the-art facility, the Pirates might pick up and leave.

For both the Pirates and the Steelers, there were greener pastures elsewhere. America's population was shifting to the South and the West, creating boom towns that hungered for major-league baseball and professional football, and they were offering unheard-of inducements to established but troubled franchises. Among these inducements was the latest and gaudiest in free public housing: new stadiums at no cost. AJR, who spent his entire life in the same North Side neighborhood, wasn't tempted. "We're Pittsburgh guys," he admonished his sons. "I want you to keep the team here. But if the time ever comes when you see that you can't make a living," he added, "get out."

There was never the need. Just the mere possibility that one day it might come to that — that Pittsburgh would find itself without a baseball team or a football team — concentrated the minds of the politicians. Lawrence, the expediter, was in Harrisburg now, his energies channeled into governing the state, and though the Lawrence wannabe's attempting to fill his shoes squabbled endlessly over every little detail, they agreed in principle that a stadium should be built. How, and with whose money, were more difficult questions to deal with.

The Republican county commissioner, a dentist named Bill McClelland, was the main obstructionist. Getting him to play along with the two Democratic commissioners was like pulling teeth — harder than pulling teeth, in fact, because McClelland held out to the end. A private business, he insisted, should pay for its own workplace. Maybe so. John Galbreath, with his real-estate millions, could have managed it; AJR's resources were not as great. In any case, when the give and take was over, and the last speech had been made, the politicians found a way out. They floated a bond issue.

The site of the new stadium, within walking distance of 940 North Lincoln Avenue, was never a point of contention. AJR could not have been better satisfied, but his knowledge of past events made him apprehensive as well. "We'll be right in the middle of a flood plain," he warned the architect,

Dahlyn Ritchey, repeating the old story of how he almost drowned in Exposition Park on the long-ago day when Squawker Mullen upset the canoe. No cause to worry, Ritchey assured him. All the new dams on the Allegheny River had made flooding a thing of the past. AJR worried anyway. Not two years after the stadium opened, Tropical Storm Agnes careened into the area, the Allegheny overflowed its banks, and again there was high water. "A once-in-a-life-time occurrence," Ritchey explained, to the Chief's amusement.

Ritchey's first model for Three Rivers, presented in 1966, was a gem — graceful and crescent-shaped, with a multi-level concourse around it, and open at one end. It offered a view of Mount Washington and the skyline nearest the Point. Everything about it seemed right except the price tag — $38 million. Go back to the drawing board, the Stadium Authority instructed Ritchey.

The cheaper design he came up with, a concrete cylinder indistinguishable in any way from the cookie-cutter stadiums going up all over the country, lacked intimacy, lacked character, lacked charm (which Forbes Field had in abundance, despite its shortcomings). None of this bothered me. I felt that any new stadium would solve our problems if only we could put a winner on the field. The seating capacity was the same as before — 52,000 for baseball, 59,000 for football — but there were fewer seats close to the action and fewer seats covered by a roof. One other thing: with the usual overruns, the cost turned out to be more like $40 million than $28 million, the estimate. Adding the cost of new roads to the total, it came to at least $55 million. Thirty-three years later, when the stadium itself had ceased to exist, the bond issue was still unredeemed.

Both the Steelers and the Pirates wanted a glassed-in restaurant from where diners — and drinkers — could watch without leaving their tables, but they differed on its placement. The Stadium Authority listened to Galbreath, with the result that the Allegheny Club, as it was called, overlooked the football field between the twenty-yard lines — premium seating space — instead of from an end zone. AJR would tell his people, "Do you know how many good football seats we lost?"

Even so, Three Rivers was a better stadium for football than for baseball. Oval-shaped now, rather than crescent-shaped, it gave every football fan the best possible view for his money. Some of the baseball seating might as well have been in Saskatchewan. Dan, looking at the model, spoke for us all (with the exception of Joe Carr) when he said, "We're pleased." We preferred Three Rivers to Shea Stadium in New York, to the stadiums in Washington and St. Louis, and for sure to the circular Atlanta stadium.

Long after we had moved in, knowledgeable people would say to me, "The Steelers have the best of it. This place was built for football, not baseball." Undeniably true. However, John Galbreath and his son Dan owned the corporation that held the lease, collected all the rent from the motorcycle races, rock concerts, and circuses held at the stadium, and owned the air rights, which meant that only the Galbreaths could develop the adjacent land. They developed nothing — and they were builders. Eighty-one baseball games and only ten football games were played at the stadium every year, and yet the football team generated almost as much revenue as the baseball team.

No ... the Pirates, not the Steelers, had the best of it.

In the months before construction began, we were hearing loose talk about financial and political shenanigans. Innuendos like "How much is Davey Lawrence getting out of this? ... Nothing? ... Aw, come on." A suggestion that the stadium bear his name met with ferocious resistance. Inevitably, I suppose, the Rooneys and the Galbreaths were said to be the owners of the land Three Rivers would occupy. A title search disposed of that particular canard, but revealed something else: much of the housing property displaced by the stadium had belonged to families we knew from St. Peter's parish — the McCabes, the Yuhaszes, the Boyles, and various others. Just for the record, the buyouts they received did not make them rich.

On the site of their demolished houses, a scrap heap had risen: piles of gravel and coal and rusty wrecked cars, all destined to be bulldozed into stadium landfill. And rising weirdly above the bleak panorama was the unfinished north end of the double-decked Fort Duquesne Bridge — "the Bridge to Nowhere," *Post-Gazette* writer Mel Seidenberg called it. In time the bridge would carry Pirate and Steeler fans across the Allegheny River to the parking lots. For now, it hung uselessly above the shore, dead-ending in the sky because the Urban Redevelopment Authority had run out of funds. Drivers who were either drunk, insane, or recklessly macho would maneuver their cars onto the bridge and keep going until they plunged into space. There were not as many deaths as you might expect.

Predictably, work stoppages and slowdowns kept the stadium from being finished on time, and featherbedding expanded the construction costs. Under the terms of the labor contract, if a delivery truck arrived at the gate to the chain-link fence surrounding the work site, it could not pass through. Only the builders' trucks were allowed to transport cargo from that point on, and the driver had to be paid for an eight-hour day. Once when Burrell Cohen, the project coordinator, arrived at the gate on foot with a package under his arm, a package that weighed about a pound, he was halted. A union truck driver relieved him of the package, took it through the gate, and handed it back. For that, he received a full day's pay.

Outsiders who had business at the work site were being systematically shaken down by the gatekeeper, a man named Brown. He was charging people an admittance fee. Everybody knew what he was doing, but for reasons I can't explain he was able to get away with it. One day when I intended to show a few friends of mine how the work was coming along, Fran Fogarty called ahead to alert the construction foreman. I had a name that opened doors – I was Art Rooney, Jr., the son of Art Rooney, Sr. – but Brown, I had heard, was an arrogant little bastard and no respecter of persons. Afraid of being turned away at the gate with my friends looking on, I requisitioned a football from the Steeler equipment manager and presented it to Brown in lieu of payment, I am sorry to say. Admittedly, though, we were treated quite well on our tour of the work site.

Either the union bosses or the Stadium Authority eventually put an end to Brown's scam. He was arrested, tried, convicted, and sent to jail. Later on, there was trouble with the painters. Jim Lally, a labor leader and city councilman, was also a member of the Stadium Authority. The painters who had been on the job, Lally told me, tried to "blackmail" the Authority shortly before the stadium opened. Instead of giving in to their demands, the Authority took Lally's advice and hired a crew of painters from the union hall to replace them.

Our move to Three Rivers would be total. The team would practice there, abandoning South Park. Executives, coaches, secretaries, scouting department, and the ticket office would be headquartered there.

Overseeing all this was Dan, who could look for no help from the rest of us. On the eve of the changeover, we had lost our irreplaceable business manager, Fran Fogarty. to a fatal heart attack. AJR, at 69, had become very involved in our race tracks. Ed Kiely's P.R. duties kept him sufficiently occupied. And, speaking for myself, I was focused on player personnel and only that. I headed for Latrobe when training camp opened, hit the road at the start of the season, and did not return home, except for fresh laundry, until after Thanksgiving.

In short, my older brother had his hands full. Overworked and on edge, he discovered one day that Joe Carr and his assistant, Jim Boston, had messed up the ticket manifesto. Season ticket holders at Pitt Stadium expected comparable seating at Three Rivers, and something had gone wrong in making the switch. Dan was irate. He wanted to fire Carr and he wanted to fire Boston. AJR was at Liberty Bell, with John, and Dan put in a call. "Our whole organization will look stupid," he raged. "The public thinks we're incompetent as it is. We are seen as incapable of making a move like this, and now here's the proof."

AJR de-escalated him. Joe Carr, he reminded Dan, was like an old family retainer. Not only that, but he was still in mourning for his son, who'd been killed in Vietnam. Allowances had to be made. Jim Boston needed self- discipline, but he was bright. Jim and Joe were our kind of people, North Siders. Give them a break this one time. Everything will be OK. We can get this straightened out. Just make it clear that there will not be any further mistakes.

Joe Carr, Jim Boston, and everybody else in the ticket office were out in the stadium counting seats the next day. Dan was there, too, riding herd. Joe Carr remained on the job until he retired, but with gradually decreasing responsibility. Buff Boston was made traveling secretary and acquitted himself to Dan's satisfaction in the unenviable task of keeping owners, players, coaches, and influential hangers-on appeased. He also negotiated contracts, in the process dealing with players, their agents, their wives, and even their mothers-in-law. His years with the Steelers taught him to be a diplomat.

The move into Three Rivers was a definitive moment in our history. Under the iron hand of Jock Sutherland, we had known success for a time in the 1940s. Just his name was enough to fill the stands. When he staggered out of a Kentucky swamp, ready to die of a brain tumor, the Steelers died with him, on the field and in the counting house. Three Rivers Stadium brought back the crowds and the fan interest. Season-ticket sales took off, and never thereafter was the stability of the franchise in doubt.

It's trite to say this, but in 1970 we turned things around. In 1970 the balance between major-league baseball and professional football had shifted; more Americans now preferred football, and Three Rivers positioned us to catch the incoming tide. The new stadium was the showcase we needed. The product itself, the football team, soon would be worthy of its packaging. Dan, who was now in charge, and Chuck Noll, the young coach he had hired, were giving us fresh, imaginative leadership, with AJR presiding over the transition. At last the stars in the heavens were lining up perfectly for us — either that, it seemed to me, or the coal dust was blowing the right way.

Chapter 47

Golden Boy

In the fall of 1970, convinced from our scouting reports that Terry Bradshaw, the quarterback at Louisiana Tech, would be a first-round draft pick, I flew down to Shreveport, rented a car, and drove to the Tech campus in Ruston on Interstate 25, not far south of the Arkansas border. I was traveling east and passing through hill country, a rustic landscape of cow pastures and ponds grotesquely overhung with pipelines. There is oil in Louisiana, and natural gas. The traffic consisted mainly of pickup trucks. They were arsenals on wheels, a rifle or shotgun in every rear window. Up North, it was getting cold; in Louisiana, green leaves still clung to the trees, and for comfort I turned on the air conditioner.

Grambling, where Eddie Robinson coached, is just outside Ruston, so I stopped there to say hello. "Wait till you see this guy Bradshaw. He's the greatest thing going," Robinson told me. Thus reassured, I drove into Ruston with pleasant expectations.

At the Holiday Inn, the desk clerk recognized my name. "Rooney," he said. "The Pittsburgh Steelers. Pro scouts have been coming through here for weeks. Everybody wants a look at that big blond kid over at Tech."

The Tech coach, Maxie Lambaugh, received me affably. Two months earlier, for a Steeler exhibition game in Shreveport, I had taken care of his whole staff's ticket needs. Lambaugh set up a movie projector for me, and in a stifling room with just a chair and a table for furniture, I watched game films of Bradshaw. Nothing in them surprised me. I had seen him on film in his junior year and I knew what the Blesto scouts thought. Jess Thompson had called him a "dinger" — a pro all the way. Jim Palmer declared that he "had it all — size, mobility, quick release. And a cannon for an arm." In high school, Palmer noted, Bradshaw had been a javelin thrower and in fact held the national record. Will Walls compared him with "Sammy" — to Sammy's disadvantage. He said that, for strength, Bradshaw's arm was actually superior to Baugh's.

At practice the next day I examined the flesh-and-blood Bradshaw. He was big, all right — 6 feet 2 or 3, 215 pounds. And he could move. Even in the NFL, he'd be a quarterback who ran like a halfback. As for the quick release, it was something to behold. He got rid of the ball *right now*. And for sure he could lay it out there. At the same time, he was not a "mad bomber." Arm strength, Chuck Noll and backfield coach Don Heinrich maintained, was less important than accuracy and the quick release; Bradshaw's accuracy gave me no qualms. His short and medium passes were catchable and his deep throws came down in "the area of reception" (scoutspeak for "close enough to the target"). He could use some fine-tuning, that much I recognized, but the basics were solidly in place. I learned at first hand about the strength of his arm when an incomplete pass ricocheted off the ground and hit me on the leg. Two days later, the black and blue mark had not yet disappeared.

A Tech student manager, tall and dark-haired, was gathering up footballs and putting them into a bag. Student managers, if they're not afraid of the coach, will tell you things that you otherwise never would hear, so I introduced myself. "What kind of a guy is this Bradshaw?" I asked. He paused in his task and straightened up. Beaming, he answered, "Wonderful guy."

The kid was so willing to talk that I decided to probe him for headshrinker stuff. I remembered a few questions from Psychology 101 at St. Vincent. Did Terry respect his father? Very much, which meant he'd be coachable. Did he drink? He'd take a beer, and I had no objections. Most good athletes don't abstain. What about girls — did he like them? Absolutely! Nothing wrong with that, either, nothing at all.

I asked about Bradshaw's character, and the student manager described to me an All-American Boy, possessed of so many virtues I couldn't help but be skeptical.

"You sound like a relative," I said.

"I'm his brother."

His name was Gary. Two years older than Terry, he'd been a football player himself, he said, until he fell from a tree, breaking his back. I thanked him for his help and sought out the team's quarterback coach, Mickey Slaughter.

Chuck Noll had made a point of asking me to interview Slaughter, an acquaintance from the days when Noll was an assistant on Sid Gilman's San Diego staff and Slaughter played quarterback for the Denver Broncos. A persistent story that Baylor and L.S.U. had stopped recruiting Bradshaw because of his SAT score was troubling to Noll. Were we wasting our time on a physically gifted dunce? If not, it seemed odd that a quarterback with NFL potential, "a pro all the way," had chosen a middle-of-the-pack college like Tech in preference to a Southwest or Southeastern conference school. Sure, the Denver Broncos had drafted Mickey Slaughter out of Tech, but that was in 1963, when Denver was in the AFL and the AFL was still very much a fledgling league. So, to ease Noll's concerns, I asked Mickey Slaughter about Bradshaw. "Listen," he said, "don't believe the rumors. The guy's plenty smart enough to figure out a pro team's offensive schemes."

I went back to Pittsburgh completely satisfied. Everything I had seen, everything I had heard, made me a full-throated member of the chorus, singing Bradshaw's praises with Thompson, Palmer, and Walls. Not that I envisioned him yet as a Steeler. Somebody else would draft him ahead of us, I was sure. In our opening game, Noll's first as the Steelers' coach, we had beaten Detroit; now we were losing week after week, but there was still no way, I believed, that we could possibly end up with the NFL's worst record and thus get the No. 1 pick.

Bad guess.

In November, when we lost to the previously winless Chicago Bears, my brother Dan, for one, saw the writing on the wall. We finished the season 1-13. So did the Bears. To decide which team drafted first, there would be a coin toss in New Orleans during Super Bowl week.

On December 10th, Jack Butler's Blesto scouts, meeting in Pittsburgh, arrived at their final evaluation of one thousand college seniors. Bradshaw, the ratings said, was most likely to succeed, making him the theoretical No.1 pick.

Or so I believed. Our coach, Chuck Noll, was not as certain. One thing that bothered Noll was the quality of the competition Bradshaw had faced — Northeast Louisiana and Southeast Louisiana, Northwest Louisiana and Southwest Louisiana, McNeese State and East Carolina, not exactly seedbeds of professional talent. The post-season all-star games, Noll predicted, would test Bradshaw's mettle. At the Senior Bowl game in Mobile, he'd be playing for Don Shula, running the Baltimore Colts' offense, or one that resembled it, against top-flight pass rushers and top-flight defensive backs. "We'll see how he picks up the teaching," Noll said.

"Gawwd," I replied — under my breath. I was like a kid who has fallen madly in love and is getting disagreeable feedback from his parents. (My own parents, happily, were just as smitten with Kay as I was.)

At the North-South Bowl, in Miami, and the All-America Bowl, in Tampa, Noll's assistants had scouted Bradshaw. The head man himself went to Mobile. Noll was a Doubting Thomas. He had to see to believe. He attended three practice sessions, watching Bradshaw run the forty-yard dash in 4.7 — fast time for a quarterback — while pulling a hamstring. Shula, considerate as ever, offered to send him home, but Bradshaw refused to hear of it. He played the whole game, and Noll was impressed. Still he reserved judgment. Noll could be maddening.

What decided the issue, for me, was the I.Q. test. I.Q. tests for football players were not yet standard procedure, but Jack Butler sent Dick Haley to Mobile, and Haley persuaded Bradshaw to take one. Actually, Bradshaw was more than willing, Haley said. There were twenty-five math questions and twenty-five that dealt with vocabulary. Bradshaw measured up, or I don't think we'd have drafted him. Given Noll's priorities, the I.Q. test was important.

Questions about Bradshaw's reputed lack of brainpower followed him throughout his career. Jim Palmer had seen him as Li'l Abner, the Al Capp cartoon character from the mythical redneck village of Dogpatch. For a fact, there were similarities. Bradshaw had deep-set blue eyes and a square-jawed, snub-nosed, ingenuous face suggestive of Li'l Abner; he had the same massive upper torso, developed through weightlifting and summertime ditch-digging. The analogy ended there. Bradshaw was neither dumb nor naive. He carne from a Deep South back-country culture unfamiliar to Eastern sportswriters, so they misunderstood him, or some of them did, baffled by his cracker-barrel witticisms. Sometimes to amuse himself, Bradshaw played games with the sportswriters, giving different answers to different reporters when they asked him the same silly question. Bradshaw knew, if the writers did not, that what football players say to newspapermen is seldom of any great consequence.

Even among his fellow athletes Bradshaw was known as a dimwit. Hollywood Henderson's infamous gibe — "He couldn't spell 'cat' if you spotted him the 'c' and the 't'" — appeared in newspapers all over the country during Super Bowl week in 1979. Henderson played for the Dallas Cowboys, whose coach, Torn Landry, was a certified football genius. In the championship game between Dallas and the Steelers, Landry called every play for his quarterback, Roger Staubach. Bradshaw, for the most part, relied on his own oft-disparaged intellect. Amazingly (or maybe not), Bradshaw came out on top. When his playing career was over and his blond hair was gone, he raked in more money as a public speaker and television personality than he ever had made in football. (It may be that the ability to spell "cat" is overrated. As one for whom spelling has always been a struggle, I'd like to think so.)

The coin flip took place on the day before the Senior Bowl game. Under the eyes of witnesses gathered around a cloth-covered table, Commissioner Pete Rozelle tossed a 1921 silver dollar into the air. Ed McCaskey of the Bears called out "heads" and made a face when the dollar came up tails. Dan, smiling broadly, said, "I have no idea who we'll take."

There was never any doubt what the Bears would have done. In a conversation about Bradshaw years later, Ed McCaskey told me, "That coin flip made such a difference to both of us."

I lobbied hard for Bradshaw with Dan and with Noll. Buddy Parker had always preached that when you're putting together a football team you start with the great quarterback. To me, it made sense. Whatever Noll may have thought was not clear; in any case, he wanted to think some more. There was game film, he said, to be studied and re-studied. And if we did take Bradshaw, what then? Already the telephones were ringing at the Roosevelt Hotel, bringing trade offers. AJR had decreed that the final say on the draft belonged to Noll, and presumably this meant he was free to make deals, but the Chief himself, I noticed, was taking every call, which terrified me.

I was violently opposed to any kind of trade. We were notorious — weren't we? — for giving quarterbacks away. I could roll the names off my tongue: Luckman, Unitas, Dawson, Kemp, Morrall, Nelsen. We had cut them all loose or traded them and they all had won championships elsewhere. Would history repeat itself with Bradshaw?

The owners and general managers who took us for fools, and were making ludicrous offers ("Same old Steelers"), worried me only a little. But there was one proposal, from our old friend Frank Wall, general manager of the Atlanta Falcons, that struck me as halfway worth considering, and AJR seemed to be interested. Wall was offering multiple draft choices and a handful of veterans for Bradshaw, veterans who were close to being stars. Instead of calling Noll or Dan, he talked to the Chief directly, and it gratified AJR's ego. It seemed to me that they talked every day.

Back from my last scouting trip before the draft, I went into crisis mode. I had to make my dad see that we must not even think of letting Bradshaw go. But for that I would need one-on-one time, and AJR was never alone. He shared an office at work with Fran Fogarty; if he and Fogarty were not together, he and Kiely were together. During business hours, it was impossible for me to isolate my dad. Newspapermen, hangers-on, close friends, acquaintances, the Catholic clergy, and even complete strangers had seemingly unfettered access to him. He was almost incapable of turning people away, convinced it would hurt their feelings. To hurt anyone's feelings — anyone's, that is, except his sons' — was unthinkable. I could ask for a private meeting, but it would bring out all of his stubbornness. The approach had to be an oblique one. And then it came to me — the solution. He liked to be chauffeured to and from work. I therefore volunteered to transport him. Each morning I picked him up at 940 North Lincoln Avenue and drove him across the river to the Roosevelt Hotel; in the late afternoon I returned him to Kass. Twice each day, for fifteen minutes at the most, the

Chief was my captive audience. There were no cell phones back then, and no car phones. I prayed for heavy traffic on the Sixth Street Bridge.

Sometimes John the twin, who in 1970 was a schoolteacher, would be with us, but he sat in the back seat and kept his mouth shut. On our first trip, I decided to go slow with the Chief. I said, "Dad, Noll is not saying that Bradshaw's a bad first-round pick. He's saying we have to weigh everything out. These quarterbacks we have now" — Terry Hanratty and Dick Shiner — "are not the kind who can take us to a Super Bowl. I think eventually Bradshaw could do that." AJR remained noncommittal. It seemed clear that I was not getting through, and I knew the reason why. "He's warming up to the Atlanta deal," I said to John.

Gradually I began to harangue him. His response was to chew his cigar and say very little. And then one morning as we were headed toward the Roosevelt Hotel, I made a spur-of-the-moment suggestion. I said, "If Frank Wall is serious, if he really wants Bradshaw, ask him to throw in Claude Humphrey with the rest of those veterans he's offering."

Claude Humphrey was a dominating defensive linemen for Atlanta, one of the new breed of NFL player the small black colleges in the South had been developing. In Humphrey's case, it was Tennessee State. AJR had hoped we could draft him and was not unaware of the impact he had made in his first two years as a pro. "Ask the Falcons if they're willing to trade Humphrey," I repeated. From the way the Chief looked at me, I was certain I had caught his attention.

When we were back in the car at quitting time, the first thing he said was, "I heard from Frank Wall again today."

Faking coolness, I said, "You did?"

"Yes. I asked if he'd let us have Humphrey. He didn't answer me right away."

Get to the point! I was thinking.

"Then he said, 'Art, we can't do that.' He said, 'You don't win championships by getting rid of your great young players.' And I told him, 'That's what my son Artie says about Bradshaw.'"

So there would not be a deal with the Falcons, I understood, and I was elated. But now a different concern replaced my fear of losing Bradshaw to Atlanta. I disliked what I was hearing from Noll. He spoke of "offers" from other teams, offers he would have to evaluate after taking into account the views of his assistant coaches.

Wait a minute, I said to myself. Had he forgotten our agreement to build through the draft? In a state of agitation, I took up the matter with Dan. Calmly, he reminded me that Noll had the right to keep or trade draft choices. "Well, I know how to settle that," I blurted. "We were one-and-thirteen last year. Fire him! If he refuses to go for Bradshaw, fire him!"

In hindsight, I can't believe I said that.

Temperate words from Dan brought me back to my senses, but I was not giving up. With only twenty-four hours left before the draft, I appealed once more to the Chief. I was driving him from 940 North Lincoln to the Roosevelt Hotel as usual, with John in the back seat. Many years afterward, John's recall of the pitch I made that day was better than mine. As he told it, I said, "Dad, you gave me a job to do, and I've worked at it. Now I am telling you that we've got to keep Bradshaw, regardless of what the coaches decide. Who are you going to believe — them or me?"

The Chief's answer — if there was one — left me in the dark. But as soon as we arrived at the Roosevelt Hotel, he went to the eighth floor. The coaches and Dan were up there. John, for some reason, tagged along, and he told me what happened. First, the Chief called everyone together. Then he delivered a speech. He said, "I've given this draft a lot of thought. Here's what we are going to do with our first choice: we are taking Terry Bradshaw. And we are NOT going to trade him." There was no further discussion. Case closed.

All I could think of when John brought me the news was "Mission accomplished."

Control Freak

On draft day, having decided in advance that we would use our first pick to take Bradshaw, we could immediately start thinking about the sixteen rounds that were left. Steeler drafts in years gone by had been a disorderly process. Under Buddy Parker and Bill Austin, a lot of mischief could happen. Their assistant coaches were the source of the trouble. We'd be ready to go ahead with a selection when one or the other of them, barging into the draft room, would call out excitedly, "We can make a trade for so-and-so!" I promised myself I'd put an end to these disruptions.

For the most part, that is what I did. Chuck Noll was all business, which suited me perfectly; I was all business myself — to a fault. There was this routine I fell into of writing down in chalk on a blackboard the names of the top four athletes in the draft, regardless of position. I had a long list of players ranked numerically, and as names disappeared from the board I added new ones. Meanwhile, we'd be discussing our options, but even after Noll took over, an assistant might interrupt to bring up the name of some marginal prospect, and I'm afraid I would let my annoyance show. "Hey," I would tell him, laying down the law, "we've already decided this."

In the eyes of the coaches, I suppose this made me a control freak. One year on draft day when I was out of the room, an assistant took the liberty of putting a few names on the board. I considered it an act of insurrection. Demanding silence, I announced, "Only one person can write on this blackboard — me!" There were hoots of derision from the coaches. "Listen," I continued, "you guys will be allowed to write names on this board when you allow me to call the plays during our games." With that, I grabbed an eraser, wiped the board clean, and chalked up my own names, three of which duplicated the names I had just taken off.

For the rest of the draft, the coaches carried on like schoolboys tormenting a teacher. They would write down players' names on pieces of paper and contrive to let me see them. One taped his names to the inside of his coat lapel and flashed it at me whenever I walked past. Another attached a list to the sole of one shoe and sat across from me with his feet on the table. It was all in good fun, no hard feelings on either side. They were making their point just as I had made mine, but with humor rather than passion.

The 1970 draft was even better than the one the year before. In Bradshaw, we now had a passer, and Noll's first thought was to give him a target. Unexpectedly, Ron Shanklin from North Texas State — Joe Greene's school — was still on the board in the second round. We'd been watching him for three years and none of us doubted that Ron was our man. Though never a great player, he turned out to be a very good one, voted the MVP by his teammates in 1973. The following season, Ron was a starting wide receiver on the first Steeler team to play in and win the Super Bowl. He made the Pro Bowl, too, but by that time Noll had Lynn Swann and John Stallworth, rookies with Hall-of-Fame skills, and he traded Shanklin to the Bears. When his playing career was over, Ron did some scouting for me. He was still a fairly young man when he died.

In the third round, we improved the defensive backfield. Noll was certainly not a disciple of Buddy Parker, but in some ways their values were similar. Your first need, Parker always said, was a quarterback who could throw, and then you had to get him some receivers. "Everything else is defense," he would add.

A cornerback we liked, Mel Blount, played at Southern University, an all-black institution in Louisiana. He was tall, handsome, and ebony-colored, with sharply-sculpted features and no hair on his head, and he could run about as fast as the quarter horses he liked to ride. One of Southern U.'s assistant coaches, Ron Brown, told me that Blount was (a) a great defensive back, (b) the very best horseman in Louisiana, and (c) a fine person. The first two of these claims turned out to be indisputably true, and I never doubted the third one, although I differed in that respect from certain NFL players — ball carriers, tight ends, and wide receivers who in years to come would let their feelings be known. Having taken hits from Blount, they feared and despised him. In time, his aggressiveness prompted a change in the rules. So successful was he at bumping receivers to keep them from running their pass routes that the NFL officially made this tactic illegal.

The drafts of 1969 and 1970 and the signing of Jim Clack, a free agent, added seven players to the roster who would start against the Minnesota Vikings in Super Bowl IX. The draftees were Joe Greene, L. C. Greenwood, Jon Kolb, Terry Bradshaw, Mel Blount, and Ron Shanklin. Greene,

Blount, and Bradshaw were future Hall of Famers. Eight players in all from the 1970 draft made the roster, which included four eventual Super Bowl starters Noll had inherited from Austin — Andy Russell, Ray Mansfield, Sam Davis, and Rocky Bleier.

We were getting our act together.

Labor of Love

Bradshaw's "legal representative," a lawyer from Shreveport named Robert Pugh, was tall and lean, with strawberry blond hair and a soft Southern drawl. "Please un-da-stand," he informed us. "I am not an agent. I want the best for my client, of course, but I think we can work something out that is fair to both sides."

Doing business with Mr. Pugh was a pleasure. He took an immediate liking to AJR, and said so unabashedly. "Youah fathah," he told me, "is truly special. I am honored to call him mah friend." AJR was equally honored. He made a generous offer to Bradshaw, who quickly accepted it, and the signing took place in an atmosphere of mutual good feeling.

Our association with Mr. Pugh continued for many years. A large glass case in his Shreveport office held autographed Steeler footballs, photos of Bradshaw, photos of AJR, and personal letters from AJR. When our Philadelphia lawyer, John Macartney, got us into the oil and gas business in Louisiana, Mr. Pugh represented the family down there. To judge by the difficulty we had in persuading him to send us a bill, he was doing it as a labor of love.

Our team physician, Dr. John Best, performed surgery on Bradshaw to remove a calcium buildup on his hamstring. It was "no big deal," according to Best, but required a stay of a few days at Divine Providence Hospital. Thinking a visitor might be welcome, I went to see Bradshaw. He's alone in a strange city, I said to myself. Up here in the frozen North, where the faces are all unfamiliar. But I needn't have worried. There was somebody else in the room — an attractive brunette with a honeysuckle accent and a million-dollar smile. She was fluffing his pillows and paying him all sorts of little bedside attentions.

"Terry," I said, "you sure have a nice girlfriend. Is she from back home in Shreveport?"

With a straight face, he answered, "She certainly is. Let me introduce you. Mister Rooney — meet my mom."

Chapter 48

Sunrise

Except to get a line on rookies (and veterans who were dealing with injuries), exhibition football games, or, to use what is now the preferred nomenclature, "pre-season" games, are meaningless affairs, quickly forgotten. But on August 21, 1970, the Steelers and the New York Giants played a pre-season game of transcendent importance to the Rooney family. It was our first game ever at Three Rivers Stadium.

Never mind that the Pirates had been installed there for more than a month — had opened the place with great fanfare on July 16th (losing, by the way, to Cincinnati). Still another month would pass before our first regular-season game at Three Rivers (with Houston; and we, too, were destined to lose). Nothing mattered except that at last we were putting a team on the new civic stadium's brilliant green Tartan Turf. Nothing could detract from the moment; nothing could detract from the excitement we felt.

It was perfect summer weather. Pat and John flew in from Liberty Bell. Tim came up from Palm Beach. The two Kathleens, looking gorgeous, were dressed for an opening night. I had a bounce in my step which I hoped was not evident. It wouldn't do to look "brand new" — AJR-speak for acting like a rube. Never wear your emotions on your sleeve. Never show dejection. Never show jubilation.

The crowd came early and filled the tiers that rose up to a clear, deep sky. When darkness came and the lights burned bright, 59,000 spectators gazed down on the dazzling scene. Of course, the circumstances called for the Steelers to win, and they did.

There was confusion — on our family's part, at least — about the parking. AJR, it goes without saying, had spaces reserved in Stadium Circle, a step or two away from the door to the Steelers' office suite. Of these, there were not enough. Less privileged Rooneys parked where they could — in the lots for the general public, which were teeming with cars, on the streets around 940 North Lincoln. Kay, though, was able to do neither. August 28th would be my mother's 66th birthday, and Kay had the cake for a party in Kass's private box. Pulling up at the gate to the preferred-parking area, she turned on her smile for the guard.

"I'm Kay Rooney. We're having a surprise party for my mother-in-law, Mrs. Art Rooney. I have to deliver this cake ... A parking pass? No, sir, I don't have one. But what am I to do with this cake? ... Oh, yes sir. You're very kind, sir. Just tell me where to park and I'll drop off the cake and come right back and move my car. Thank you so much."

"Well, you see, sir," she explained three and a half hours later, "my mother-in-law wouldn't hear of my leaving her box with the party and the game going on. I'm s-o-o-o-o sorry. Thank you for understanding."

Kass's box, No. 341, was on the fifty-yard line (where else?). It had a carpet, or rug, a wet bar, leather swivel chairs for fifteen people, a counter at each row for programs, purses, and so on, and, most special of all, a private rest room. Only this box and Pirate owner John Galbreath's box had private rest rooms. A black waiter dressed in a tuxedo served the birthday cake with glasses of champagne. This was Sidney, a bus boy at the restaurant in the Roosevelt Hotel. Sidney looked magnificent, and he went about his work with the aplomb of an English butler. He bowed and scraped; he hovered over Kass. Sidney added much to the elegance of the occasion, but after his first year on the job a nondescript woman attendant succeeded him. It seemed to AJR that, with Sidney, we were "putting on the dog." Sidney was too flamboyant — and too free-handed with the liquor. He poured such generous drinks that by the time the game ended Box 341 was like a night club at 2 a.m. Get rid of him, ordered AJR.

Box 341 was the owner's box, actually, but AJR sat with Richie Easton and Father Mark Flanagan or Father Jim Campbell in a bare-bones box near the press box. A priest named Reardon sat in my box, an open-air eight-seater next to the visiting owners' box. Father Flanagan and Father Campbell did not have long to live. After both had died, AJR approached me and said, "That Father Reardon — does he keep his mouth shut?" Father Reardon, I told him, was as quiet as a mouse. "All right, then," said AJR. "From now on, he can sit with me."

Impressed by his elevation from my box to AJR's, Father Reardon's friends started calling him Monsignor, or so he alleged.

Iggy Borkowski, who sometimes occupied the fourth chair in AJR's box, said that sitting there was no fun. "You're not allowed to say a word." AJR himself rarely spoke. "The only time I ever heard him sound off," said Father Reardon, "was to second-guess Chuck Noll. 'Chuck's a good man,' he began. 'A fine coach. But he's bound and determined to set up the run. No matter what, he has to establish the ground game. Even with a passer like Bradshaw throwing to the best receivers in the league. He'd rather prove that we can run than win the game.'"

My box was close to the press box, where fat Harry Kalson served up the best Jewish hot dogs I ever have tasted. More than once I missed a big play near the end of the half because I left my seat early for a good place in line at the hot dog grill. Never first in line — that would be too obvious — but up toward the front.

AJR never had women in his box, and neither did I except in emergency situations. At one game, a young lass came into my box and said her boyfriend had told her she'd be "warmly received." Her boyfriend, it turned out, was the *Sports Illustrated* writer Roy Blount, who was working on a book about the Steelers. It was December; she was lightly dressed. Until a good-hearted usher brought her a folding chair, she sat, looking uncomfortable, on a cold concrete step.

Box 341 was on the other side of the field, but Kay always came with binoculars, and she spotted my visitor. That night at home, we had a dialogue. If a sportswriter's girlfriend could sit in my box, asked Kay, why was it off-limits to her? I pointed out that Dan's wife, Pat, never sat with her husband in his box, an argument Kay rejected. Finally I said, "Look — when I watch a football game, I'm at work. Does your father take women to his wool mill?" (Roy Kumer owned the Pittsburgh Wool Company). Kay had no answer for that, but made it clear she did not accept my analogy.

Only one other woman ever made it into my box – the girlfriend of a scout for the Kansas City Chiefs, Lloyd Wells. Lloyd flagged me down one Sunday to complain that she had been barred from the press box. "You're a big shot, Rooney," he said – smiling. "Whuddaya gonna do about it?" What I did about it was have an extra chair sent to my box. Both Lloyd and his girlfriend, I should note, were African- Americans. Perhaps I should mention also that the girlfriend was very beautiful. Conscious of Kay's binoculars, I placed her next to Father Reardon, an arrangement that pleased my other two regulars, Bill Nunn and Jack Butler. "She's a very sweet girl," said Father Reardon after the game, "but it bothered me a little that she didn't stand up for the national anthem."

Lloyd Wells ended up in Muhammad Ali's retinue, by the way.

Inevitably, I suppose, Kass's box, 341, became a catch-all location for guests of the management who did not have a seat – governors, mayors, bishops, college presidents, state legislators, movie actors, Hall-of-Fame football players, Hall-of-Fame coaches, and, yes, a Supreme Court justice, Whizzer White. Not only the VIPs, but even the no-names, Kass said, had to be treated with respect, because you never knew. The mild-mannered priest might be in charge of marriage annulments somewhere, and in a large family like the Rooneys it didn't hurt to have a friend in court. The politician you never heard of might be voting on a race-track bill that affected Liberty Bell.

Other than AJR, and sometimes Dan, the most tireless proponent of using Box 341 for our overflow was Joe Gordon, the Steeler publicist. Joe was a can-do guy. If you had to rush somebody to the airport, Joe could get a taxi or limousine right away. If you had to transport a whole football team, Joe could have a bus at the door in five minutes. There were those who resented his aggressiveness. I had some negative moments with him myself when my scouting agenda clashed with his drive for publicity, but I could be aggressive too, and I made allowances. Joe was Dan's hire and extremely loyal to him. He had come to the team while Three Rivers was under construction, and very soon we realized that he belonged in the top rank of P.R. men. One guy in his corner was AJR. Gordon had been a baseball player at Pitt and spent hours with the Chief talking about the Pirates, talking about the Wheeling Stogies, talking about long-ago sandlot teams.

But on Sunday afternoons during the football season, he made life difficult for Kass. Mom, Kay, and especially Aunt Alice valued their privacy. The guests who were showing up for the free lunch and free booze at halftime upset them. After Sidney's departure they had a security guard posted outside the box. AJR considered this "uppity." The guard followed Sidney into oblivion, and halftime became an open house. Decorative fixtures – Steeler memorabilia – began to disappear. Visitors walked away with Steeler cocktail glasses, a black and gold Steeler throw rug, a waste basket with the Steeler insignia. Old-time Steeler photographs vanished from the walls. One of Kay's touches was a supply of Steeler-embossed hand soap for the private john. It lasted approximately two hours. Returning from an inspection tour, she announced that "even the goddam soap" had been taken.

"This is your father's fault," Kay and Kass would tell me. But the problem, Kass knew, could only be controlled, never eliminated. Even during the off-season, Box 341 was perceived as a hospitality suite. One year on May 10th, the eighth or ninth birthday of our son Art, Kay had a party in the box, and almost before she knew it there were strangers present – middle-aged men, helping themselves to the hot dogs. If AJR had sent these men to the box from his office below, it seemed odd. Were they friends of his? Kay had no clue, so she asked. Well, ma'am, someone explained, they were friends of a friend of Mr. Rooney. They were friends of Dago Sam.

Politely – she said "please" – Kay invited them to leave.

Dan replaced the missing photographs with new ones and had them securely bolted to the wall. The centerpiece was an oil painting – AJR and Father Silas in their Wheeling Stogie uniforms. The Wheeling Stogies played baseball, not football, a discordant note in keeping with AJR's notion of irony. Bolted down like everything else, the painting was safe from the pillagers – souvenir hunters, let's call them. The new cocktail glasses, a gift from Charley Affif, liquor salesman and former middleweight boxer, they disdained as lacking in uniqueness. A plain gray wall-to-wall carpet had replaced the black and gold Steeler throw rug, and there were no fancy emblematic waste baskets. Box 341 had been stripped of its ornamentation.

There came a Sunday when Kass was gone, too. I looked across the field and saw Kay, with her red hair shining in the sunlight. Beside her I saw Aunt Alice. The third chair was vacant. I lowered my binoculars and pretended to watch the game.

A Link to the Past

Our post-office address at Three Rivers was 300 Stadium Circle. We had an office suite on the ground floor that followed the curvature of the oval-shaped superstructure for something like three city blocks. If you walked from Dan's office past the other offices, past the dressing rooms, and on through the runway to the field, and then walked back, you were exercising.

I remember one day the scouts used a gently curving stretch of corridor to measure the forty-yard dash speed of Jim Haslett, a linebacker prospect from Indiana University of Pennsylvania. Haslett's entire playing career was with the Buffalo Bills, but we added him to the coaching staff during Bill Cowher's regime, the final step in his progression to the head coaching job at New Orleans.

A commercial decorator, hired by the Stadium Authority and Dan, picked out the gun-metal gray carpeting and palomino brown furniture. There were no windows in any of the rooms — none — but the incandescent lighting was easy on the eyes. AJR tried to hide his satisfaction with the looks of the place by protesting that, for his taste, everything was too fancy.

"I'm just a yinz guy," he would say.

"Now that you've arrived," the decorator would answer, "your new home should reflect your higher status." AJR reveled in that kind of talk.

His own private office had dark wood paneling, a black couch, modernistic chairs, and potted plants. AJR wanted pictures on the wall — photographs. The decorator quietly demurred. "It's really not that kind of an office," he suggested. AJR paid no attention, insisting, "I want my old friends around me." Up on the wall went Johnny Blood and Whizzer White, Jack Butler and Ernie Stautner, George Halas and Big Kies — and, directly overlooking AJR's desk, Honus Wagner. Another baseball player in foreign surroundings. To his own surprise, I have no doubt, the decorator approved of all this. The office, he said, mirrored AJR's personality.

Flesh-and-blood old friends were less numerous at Three Rivers. Hangers-on found the atmosphere inhospitable. Uncle Jim was still a fixture and Dago Sam too, but not many others. Patsy Scanlon and Doc Sekay dropped in now and then.

Mort Sharnik, my *Sports Illustrated* friend, remarked to me once that our digs at the Roosevelt Hotel reminded him of Times Square — the crossroads of the world. Three Rivers was off the beaten track, which suited Dan and me perfectly. Good riddance to all the characters, we thought. The environment now was more businesslike, a change I considered long overdue. On scouting trips I had visited big universities with big budgets, and I saw how important ambience could be. Neither Dad nor even Dan seemed as sensitive to this as I was. The Union Trust Building had been an improvement on the Fort Pitt Hotel, and the Roosevelt had been an improvement, if only a slight one, on the Union Trust Building, but the two hotels were dumps and we knew it. Because we had to, we made jokes about them. We made jokes about our practice field at South Park and the dilapidated frame house where the players changed into their workout gear. But now that was all in the past. We were moving up in class.

And at first it was too rich for my blood, I'm afraid. Glancing disdainfully at AJR's picture gallery, I said to Dan, "We'll get so many good players he'll forget about these guys." Well, I give myself credit for being half-right. We did get good players, Super Bowl-quality players. But I was a jackass, I confess, for minimizing a legacy that meant more to my dad than I could understand.

Backwater Moses

I always see, in my mind's eye, Pitt Stadium and Forbes Field as gray, cold, wet, gloomy places and Three Rivers Stadium glowing with color, the Tartan Turf a vivid green, the plastic seats a painter's palette of blue, orange, and yellow (for yellow, an ex-Marine would say gold; yellow is not a shade the Marine Corps recognizes). In reality, of course, there were dismal days and nights at Three Rivers, and the stadium itself was a huge gray pile of concrete, as dreary in the rain as a penitentiary. So much of life is perception.

Three Rivers stood for hope. It stood for the future. It stood for a new beginning. After that first exhibition game, the team's outspokenly confident, awesomely athletic, ruggedly handsome rookie quarterback came out with a manifesto. Everybody, he said, was to forget about the past, forget the losing seasons, forget that in 1969 our 1-13 record had been the worst in professional football.

That was then, this was now. We were starting from scratch — a new team in a new decade in a new stadium. The Steelers would get the job done, for sure.

Terry Bradshaw was young and immature then, with a full head of blond hair. (Later on, he'd be middle-aged and immature, with some remnants of blond hair behind his ears.) Cynics in the press and cynics in the stands often ridiculed his artless big talk. But Bradshaw was on to something, never mind that it would be 1972 before the Steelers and their fans caught a glimpse of the Promised Land envisioned by this backwater Moses from Shreveport, Louisiana.

The biggest believers were Dan Rooney and Art Rooney, Jr. There were two things the people knew about the Rooneys — they knew we were dumb and they knew we were cheap. What Dan and I knew was that the Rooneys had something to prove. It became a shared passion. Let the skeptics make fun of Terry Bradshaw. The Steelers would get the job done, he said, and we took those brave words as a challenge.

We would see to it ourselves that they got the job done.

The Allegheny Club

The Allegheny Club in Three Rivers Stadium, which took up space that otherwise would have been occupied by four hundred of the best seats for football, was where the baseball team, the Pirates, wanted it. The Pirates — or, rather, John Galbreath, the Pirates' owner — called the tune when it came to the design of the new facility. AJR was so desperate to have a stadium of any kind that he never questioned either the location of the club or whether there should even be one. Three Rivers, after all, was a publicly-funded stadium, and the Allegheny Club, after all, was a private eating and drinking place, accessible only to dues-paying members and their guests.

It never occurred to the Chief, I am sure, that inside of five years, with thousands of would-be customers on the waiting list for season tickets, the Steelers would need those four hundred seats and need them badly. A sellout at a Pirate game was as rare as an eclipse of the sun. But the Pirates played eighty-one times at Three Rivers every year and the Steelers played ten or eleven times – twelve at the most.

One wall of the Allegheny Club, on the side overlooking the field, was a huge sheet of virtually unbreakable glass. With unobstructed sight lines, diners watched the game from tables placed on terraces. It was a tastefully decorated place and had a breathtaking view of the stadium's interior. Visitors were bound to be impressed.

In the first few years of the club's existence, a strict dress code was enforced. Steeler scouts grumbled that when they brought a draft-eligible player to lunch, and he was wearing a sport shirt with no jacket, the maitre d would turn them away. "You have to be dressed like a U.S. Steel executive," one scout complained.

Mom, Aunt Alice, and Kay dressed for the Allegheny Club like U.S. Steel executives' wives. The upscale atmosphere suited them. So did the service and the menu. It pleased them to see AJR's likeness — and mine and Dan's — among the mahogany-framed portraits of sports celebrities on the wall of the corridor between the foyer and the restaurant. No Rooney men ever patronized the well-stocked bar.

The restaurant's back windows looked out over the conjunction of the Allegheny and Monongahela Rivers and up to Mount Washington on the opposite side. Kay preferred this view to the view of the playing field. A decorative touch that appealed to every Pittsburgher had historical connotations. It was a section of brick wall from Forbes Field. With the score tied in the ninth inning of the seventh and last game of the 1960 World Series, Bill Mazeroski of the Pirates hit a pitch from Ralph Terry over that wall for the home run that beat the New York Yankees.

The Allegheny Club was where Kass — "Mrs. Art Rooney" — became a personage of sorts. To the functionaries and waitresses, she was someone special — "the owner's wife." Aunt Alice, the more diffident of the sisters, found such attention uncomfortable. At lunch, she ordered the same thing that Mom ordered, or that Kay ordered. Kay once asked me if Aunt Alice could read. I said, "Sure." "How do you know?" Kay demanded. After a moment's reflection, I said, "Show her something negative about the Rooneys or Terry Bradshaw in the newspaper. You'll learn that she can read, all right."

Aunt Alice had met Terry Bradshaw when he came to see AJR at 940 North Lincoln Avenue. Printed allegations that Bradshaw was "dumb" infuriated her. "The dumb one," she would say, "is the simple son of a bitch who wrote that story." Now, this was a woman who went to Mass and Holy Communion every day and who wore out rosary beads and prayer books.

The Allegheny Club did not show a profit for some time. Our representative on the board of control was Ed Kiely, who had turned over his P.R. duties to Joe Gordon and who liked to work at the upper levels of the power structure. "Hey," he'd report to AJR, "we might have to come up with some dough to keep this place afloat." AJR would hit the ceiling. We were underwriting the club's indebtedness on exactly the same basis as the stadium's principal tenant, the Pirates. "These guys ..." the Chief growled. "They're too darn high-toned. They should hustle up some business in the off-season, when there aren't any games." Parking at such times was plentiful, and where else in town, apart from the Duquesne Club, were the amenities superior?

What was needed, decided AJR, was a manager with pizzazz. He thought of Alex DiCroce, who ran the Sylvan Room at the Roosevelt Hotel. Kiely and Dan were pushing for him, too. Alex took the job, filled the club's open dates with weddings, banquets, and corporate parties, and pulled it out of the red.

He was equally skillful at human relations. If AJR was in the club, Alex knew when he could take a visitor to his table and when it was best not to bother him. AJR, regardless of the circumstances, would never be less than courteous, Still there were moments when a private business discussion might be going on. Alex had a feel for these things.

With the waitresses, busboys, bartenders, cooks, and bottle washers, AJR was his approachable self at all times. He knew their first names; he knew the intimate details of their lives. They brought him their family snapshots to look at, brought him news of a son or nephew in the military, kept him up to date on their relatives' health problems. "How's your mother?" he would ask a waitress. "Did that medicine do her any good?"

The Allegheny Club's membership cards were numbered according to rank. My recollection is that John Galbreath — who could have walked into the dining room without being recognized — had Number 001 and AJR Number 002. The mayor, Pete Flaherty, rated 003. My number, in which I took a certain vainglorious satisfaction, was 009. I felt like a big shot.

But then the system had to be changed. Low numbers were easy to remember. On nights when the bar was crowded, a patron ordering drinks would call out his number and name. Even in a high-class joint, and the Allegheny Club was high class, there are always unscrupulous people. The next time the bartenders were busy, someone of this type, having overheard a number and name, might call out, "Johnson, oh-oh-seven" (let's say), and in the hubbub get away with it.

Of course it was only a matter of time until new cards were issued. From 009, my number went to something like 2761, ending an ego trip I had rather enjoyed.

Whatever may have happened to AJR's number, he probably gave it no thought.

Chess Board

P. T. Barnum or someone said that people will come to see the elephant, but to keep them coming back the elephant had better learn to do tricks. So it is with a new stadium. For a year or two, the fans will buy tickets just to see it. After that, they demand a winning team.

To build a winning team, you need good players, good coaches, and good management. I mention management third, but management's job — to put all the pieces together — is by no means the least important.

Management is responsible for scouting, drafting, and signing the players, an ongoing process. The pipeline must never run dry. Management hires the coaches. And management must give them the tools they require to do their work — first-rate practice facilities, first-rate locker-room facilities, and first-rate training facilities.

Everything, in other words, that South Park notably lacked.

With plenty of justification, Steeler coaches had complained about South Park for years. "You play as you practice," they insisted. And at South Park, they argued, practicing in the rain or the snow was impossible. There was too much mud. Too much slop.

Uncle Jim gave the faultfinders no sympathy. "Players and coaches are all the same," he would say.

"They're looking for a reason to flop. A reason to fail." Chances are he was quoting Jock Sutherland. But in Chuck Noll's system, the condition of the practice field really mattered.

It was linebacker coach Denny Fitzgerald who clarified this for me. We were going over my list of college prospects one day. "Art," he said — only the old-time coaches still called me "Artie" — "those linebackers you're looking at — they'd better be able to think on their feet as well as move. We change our damn defensive scheme three times a week. For the players, it's like a chess board. They have to be smart enough to pick up the changes and get to the right place on the chess board."

Finding the right place in the mud could be difficult.

Three Rivers Stadium, with its artificial turf, was ideal for Noll's version of chess. There were other advantages, too — the spacious locker-room area, for instance. The locker room at South Park was a joke if not an outright disgrace. Three Rivers had locker rooms with carpeting thick enough to serve as a bed. There were players who took naps on it, recovering from an arduous workout. The atmosphere was so pleasant and home-like that AJR would go there to relax. Wearing his cashmere sweater and chewing on an unlit cigar, he would circle the room with his hands behind his back. He might stop for a conversation with someone, but not necessarily. For AJR, the locker room was a quiet retreat.

In the trainer's room, Ralph Berlin had a taping table big enough to hold three football players, even if they were linemen. The whirlpool tubs – there were two — occupied an area up against the wall. Hot-water treatment for injuries was popular with the players but disdained by the team physician, Dr. John Best. In his deep voice he would cackle, "I suppose it helps if you think it helps."

Ralph Berlin's office, which adjoined the trainer's room, contained a desk, his locker, and two examining tables. Over two large windows separating the office from the rest of his domain he had hung a heavy pair of draw-string curtains. I asked about them one time. "Why the curtains, Ralph? Why the need for so much privacy?" "Well," he told me, "I had a player in here whose chin had been split open from contact with a helmet, and he needed a lot of stitches. Blood all over the place. It was halftime, so Big John" — Dr. Best — "sewed his face up right there on that table. One of the other players, his best friend on the team, was looking through the window, and his eyes got as big as saucers. I thought for sure he was going to faint. So I went over and pulled the curtains together, but it was locking the barn door after the horse is out. Do you think that guy was worth a damn in the second half? Ever since then, I keep those curtains drawn when I'm working on an injured player."

The weight room was Noll's innovation. He imported a body builder and judo expert from New Orleans, a guy named Lou Riecke, to install the equipment. Lou was small but of course muscular, a one-time Olympic silver medalist in weightlifting. The silver medal matched the color of his perfectly coiffed silken hair. Noll wanted free weights – dumbbells and barbells — "not those useless machines." Free weights, Noll thought, built what he called "gross strength." He said that when he coached as an assistant with the San Diego Chargers in the AFL, a lot of "skinny-assed kids" the NFL had rejected were able to gain from fifteen to twenty pounds through a combination of weightlifting and diet. "And they'd be just as fast. We'll do it here, too," he promised.

He was right. But, ever the teacher, Noll always had to demonstrate. Lifting more than he could handle, he damn near ruined his back. That was Chuck, a man who would stop at nothing to prove a point.

Bean Counters

After Fran Fogarty had been taken from us, my brother Dan talked AJR into signing on with the nationally known, highly respected accounting firm of Arthur Andersen. This was thirty years, more or less, before Arthur Andersen's fatal involvement in the Enron scandal, a house-of-cards collapse that left thousands of defrauded investors holding the bag when the high-tech stock-market run-up of the late 1990s came to an end.

Fogarty had been "a one-man dog," answering only to AJR. Arthur Andersen's representative, Dixon Rich, worked more closely with Dan, the former Duquesne University accounting major. Dan knew how to speak the current language.

AJR, you should understand, was still the big boss. Over many years of dealing with race-track sharpies, his common-sense approach to money and finance never had failed him. He was dismissive, even scornful, of people who needed accountants and lawyers. Give him Fogarty, who could keep the books straight and smell a rat. Doing business with a handshake satisfied AJR.

Which was good enough for the old days, perhaps, but now things were different. The NFL had grown beyond recognition. There were all kinds of rules to comply with — federal, state, and local. You had the IRS looking over your shoulder. Dixon Rich treated AJR with the greatest respect, cluing him in on the discussions he was having with Dan, but to put it plainly, the Chief had become a sounding board.

It was Dan's job to supervise the numbers crunchers in the office. Besides the Arthur Andersen people — Dixon Rich, an assistant, and a secretary — we had a "controller." The way it looked to me, a controller was a sort of super accountant. Buff Boston had been acting as Dan's liaison with Arthur Andersen, and he could not have been more relieved when Dan hired our first controller, Terry Jacobs.

All of us liked Terry. Our compensation for accepting membership in the supposedly inferior American Conference after the merger between the NFL and the AFL had been three million dollars, a considerable sum at the time, and Terry wanted to put this money into a real-estate tax shelter. High finance was out of my line, but he and Dan would ask me to sit in on their conversations with the real-estate people. I'd stay for thirty minutes — forty-five at the most — look at my watch, and say, "I have some reports to make out and some game films to watch," an excuse that did not fool anybody. Dan being all business, Terry had the notion that the real-estate guys were eager to talk football with me. At lunchtime, when they moved from the conference room to the Allegheny Club, he would urge me to come along, and I did now and then, but mostly then. I never looked at myself as a public-relations man or a greeter. If I could make a contribution, it would be as a scout.

After leaving us for opportunities elsewhere, Terry remained a friend of the family and continued to work on the real-estate end of our business. His successor as controller, Bob Quinn, devoted all his time to the football operation. Recommended by Dixon Rich, Quinn came to the Steelers from Arthur Andersen. He was the second in a series of people who held the controller's job for two or three years and then departed. The anxiety-and-stress quotient must have been higher than I realized.

We were slow, for some reason, to computerize. Although Dan was a believer in modern business methods, he "outsourced" the work that could most efficiently be done by computers. At the risk of antagonizing everyone, I begged, pleaded, and even groveled a bit for an in-house system. In the scouting department, I told AJR, we needed computers for the ever-increasing volumes of information we were gathering, but he appeared not to listen. He'd shake his head as if to say, "The kid wants another new toy."

It was like Christmas morning when at last he gave in.

Our oldest scout, Will Walls, scoffed at computers. "What a crock," he would sneer. But computers eliminated much guesswork. They quantified everything, helped us put a number beside a prospect's athletic potential. Will Walls belonged to the past; whether we like it or not, the world keeps spinning on its axis. Still, I considered myself fortunate to be a scout instead of a bean counter. A scout's activities, it seemed to me, were part of the main show. Scouts went places, saw people, and evaluated football players. Accountants sat behind desks and juggled figures. Ours, overseen by Dan, kept the business office running like a fine machine. Because of them, the Steelers got value for every dollar they spent. And yet, compared with Dan, I thought I had the best of the bargain.

Chapter 49

VIPs and Others

D ad's partners at Liberty Bell — rich men, patricians, swells — gathered in the track's VIP room and took in the races from there. It was also where Dad stopped for dinner on his way back to Philadelphia after watching the thoroughbreds run at Delaware Park. His driver would be with him and sometimes an extra guest, a horse-player friend he had casually invited. The bigwigs in the VIP room thought this was presumptuous. The VIP room was for VIPs, and neither Richie Easton nor Iggy Borkowski — AJR's drivers — qualified. The others, guys from Delaware Park, were even less welcome.

Nothing of this was ever put into words. The job of weeding out undesirables belonged to the black doorkeeper, a man who resembled the butler on a Cream of Wheat box. He had the tuxedo, the gray hair, the dignified, forbearing look. Known as "Mr. Lee," this well-turned-out functionary was a bit of a snob, but AJR's method of dealing with such people never failed. It was called "duking" them, and from years of experience he duked with great skill.

AJR's business partners were not the only ones who could see that the tone of the place was being lowered. Even Kass sometimes noticed. Addressing no one in particular, she might ask, "How did that stiff get in here?" whereupon a woman at the next table would be as likely as not to whisper, "Shhh! He's a friend of Mister Rooney's." To the annoyance of the waiters, Iggy Borkowski had a habit of going to the bar and pouring himself a drink. His explanation to my brother John, our man on the scene at Liberty Bell, would be that after driving AJR from Pittsburgh to Philadelphia to Camden, New Jersey, (where Delaware Park was located) and back to Philadelphia, he needed the sedative of alcohol.

There were times when AJR traveled by himself and other times when he would fly. One of the Liberty Bell stockholders, Herb Barness, had a private plane, but AJR would not allow our own corporation such a luxury. He patronized the commercial airlines or, when that wasn't feasible, chartered a small four-seater.

In one of these light planes, he was caught in a heavy storm with a pilot who seemed to be panicking. "You could see the fear in his eyes." And you could hear it in his voice as he said, "We're in trouble, Mister Rooney. It looks real bad up ahead. I believe we should turn back."

The guy was in no shape to make life-or-death decisions, AJR realized. Soothingly, he told him, "I flew as a young man. Here's how I look at it: We know what we've been through. What's up ahead might be better. At least there's a chance. There'd be no chance, though, if we turned and went back. Keep going."

Dad said that the weather ahead was not good, but neither did it keep them from landing without mishap. A few years later, flying the attorney general of Pennsylvania somewhere, the same pilot crashed. The pilot, the attorney general, and all of the other passengers were killed.

AJR said, "I never did think that fellow had any judgment."

Like the social committee at Liberty Bell, AJR categorized people. It was just that his standards were different.

People Person

A JR was drawn to politics and politicians. He followed elections closely and looked forward with great interest to election day. Always he was backing some local candidate and supporting him financially, too. His contributions, I think, were modest except when a particular issue excited him, and then he would dig deep.

He liked aldermen, constables, and ward heelers. He liked state legislators. He liked justices of the peace. He made all of these people feel like big-timers, and when some of them actually did get to the big time they remembered that AJR had been their friend when they were nobodies.

Whatever came along he could handle. He took care of himself, took care of his family, took care of his extended family, and took care of his friends. He abided by certain rules. If you asked for a favor, you gave one in return. He was a great one to send postcards – postcards to say thank you, postcards to say hi. He sent them from places like the shrine of St. Anne, in Quebec, to places like race tracks. His handwriting was wide open and beautiful. In that way it resembled his sisters' handwriting and did not at all resemble his sons'. It may be that our father's generation learned penmanship as part of the educational process, but in his case I think it was something more. As a young kid, I would find doodles and signatures on his scrap paper. Penmanship was an art that he practiced.

He remembered names and he remembered home towns. Bumping into the most casual acquaintance, he would always have something to say. "Oh, you're from St. Clairsville, aren't you? ... I used to play baseball over in Wheeling ... We played in St. Clairsville a few times ... Is that landmark still there? ... Our second baseman, Joe Doakes, was from St. Clairsville ... Did you know him? ... " And so on and so on. If a bond of some kind existed, he could find it.

In later years I'd be with him at Steeler training camp. He wanted me within earshot whenever an obscure new player approached him. As the player drew near, he would ask, "What's this kid's name?" I'd say, " Walter Smith." And Dad would call out to him, "Hi, Walt," or "Hi, Smitty," and throw out his hand as though greeting a top draft choice or a veteran. As likely as not, the player would soon be cut. Then on more than one occasion when I made the rounds of the colleges to scout spring practice I would hear from the coach that Walt Smith had told him what a fine gentlemen Mr. Rooney was.

In his old age I asked AJR to drop in on practice at St. Vincent. He said he would do it after the cuts were made, because then there'd be fewer names to remember, and remembering names was important to him.

AJR was a "people person." There was nothing phony about it. He actually *liked* people. They say in drama school that if you play a part long enough the mask will become the face. With AJR, it was different. You got exactly what you saw.

In the 1940s, when AJR was in his heyday as a horse player, the walls of his office in the Fort Pitt Hotel were covered with a hodgepodge of photographs. There was a big one of Twenty Grand, the great Kentucky Derby winner, inscribed in AJR's flowing hand, "Champion of Champions." AJR said that in 1931, the year Twenty Grand won the Derby, he had made more money betting on the horse than on all of the other races that year put together.

When the Steelers moved their headquarters to the Union Trust Building and then the Roosevelt Hotel and eventually to Three Rivers Stadium, AJR took the pictures along, too – everything from autographed photos of big shots to little plastic-framed group shots of a Cincinnati sportswriter's children. The sportswriter, Pat Harmon, had ten or eleven kids; one of the daughters grew up to be a television actress, best known for her role as the mother in "Everybody Loves Raymond."

In our splendid new digs at Three Rivers Stadium, the disorder of Dad's office seemed incongruous. The haphazard arrangement of the pictures drove a lot of us nuts, but meant nothing to AJR. What did mean something was that they were there.

At home, the pictures on the walls of his den were neatly hung. Kass saw to that. There was a story behind every face. These were photographs of people he liked. How well off they were, or how high in the world, was of no account. The people he did not like were bums, yeggs, and con men. I said to him once, repeating something I had heard in a movie, that an honest man couldn't be conned. "Bunk," he replied. He disliked mean people and people who had no compassion. Once in AJR's presence the head Steeler coach berated an assistant in front of the assistant's kids. At the end of the (losing) season, without a touch of remorse, AJR told the head coach he was fired.

This was the same coach who embarrassed John Baker, a huge black defensive end, with hundreds of fans watching a training-camp drill. In the off-season Baker worked at a North Carolina penitentiary, and one day the coach yelped at him, "Baker, if you don't get off your backside you'll be back in that prison." AJR was furious. He thought that to the fans it must have sounded as though Baker had been a jailbird. In truth, John Baker was a high-class fellow who went back home at the end of his playing days and served for years in the elective office of sheriff.

Insensitive people like this coach were the kind that AJR had no use for.

Going To Bat For Joe

In the beginning, AJR liked to deal with Jim Clark. They worked out any problems between Liberty Bell and our William Penn Racing Association on a man-to-man basis, bypassing the lawyers. This arrangement suited them both; unfortunately, Clark was in failing health and died at about the time the track started flourishing. From then on, Liberty Bell's lawyers and John Macartney handled almost everything, with Macartney reporting to AJR.

A company owned by the Sullivan family of Lowell, Massachusetts, printed our tip sheets and programs. The Sullivans did the printing for almost every important race track from Narragansett, near Boston, to Pimlico, in Maryland, and had a special tie with the Rooneys. Old Joe Sullivan, the patriarch of the clan, was a cousin of Billy Sullivan, the Boston Patriots' owner. Joe had loaned Billy the money to buy the franchise and had placed his own son, Walter Sullivan, on the Patriots' board.

The Sullivans transported their printing presses in an eighteen-wheel tractor trailer, moving from track to track. After the last race at Liberty Bell one night, Walter Sullivan, Pat the twin, and a Liberty Bell employee whose name I've forgotten went pub-crawling, with Walter at the wheel of his monstrous rig, which happened to be a new one. They stopped at every after-hours bar within a ten-mile radius of Liberty Bell, Walter said. "We had a devil of a time parking," he added, "but somehow we managed."

In later years, both Walter and Pat joined Pathfinders, an Irish-American temperance organization.

While Billy Sullivan's football team prospered, Joe Sullivan's printing business fell on hard times. With the advent of computers, the race tracks the company serviced could do their own printing. The Sullivans no longer were needed, and a Liberty Bell official, speaking for the William Penn Association as well as for Liberty Bell, told them so, bluntly.

"Wait a minute," said AJR. "Who gave you the right to make decisions on behalf of William Penn?" He went on to tell the official that Walter Sullivan, big truck and all, would continue to do the printing for the Rooneys. Economically, it wasn't feasible to bring the rig and the presses into the park for only one race meet, so Liberty Bell had to back down and the Sullivans stayed in business a while longer.

AJR had a soft spot for the Sullivans because of old Joe's generosity to Father Silas and other Franciscan missionaries. In the 1930s, Joe Sullivan had made a practice of giving each Franciscan five thousand dollars on the eve of his departure for a foreign land. Throughout Massachusetts, many a Catholic priest said Mass before an Italian marble altar paid for by Joe. He was AJR's kind of Catholic.

When the old man died, the Chief saw to it that all five Rooney brothers attended the wake and the funeral. His loyalty to the Sullivans was a lesson to us, one of many.

Keeping Up Appearances

AJR never lost his love for Shamrock Farm. It was one of many ways in which we differed. As far as I was concerned, Shamrock Farm belonged in the same category as Parris Island. When I took my kids to the farm for a visit, we stayed at the nearest hotel.

Shamrock Farm was on a beautiful piece of land, its rolling hills and pastures sectioned off with black wooden fences. The springs and streams fed the water supply of Baltimore, a half-hour drive to the east on Interstate 70. On Interstate 270 the farm was just a forty-minute drive from Washington, D. C. AJR always predicted that easy access to these interstates and to a good state highway, 26, would make the price of the farm soar. It never happened.

My brother Tim shared Dad's interest in the farm and in horses. The only horses on my radar were the two-legged kind to be found up the road on the football team at the University of Maryland. In football terminology, a horse is a guy who stands well over six feet tall, weighs at least 250 pounds, and runs about a 4.7 forty.

At judging horses, buying them, breeding them, and selling them, Tim had better success than the Chief did, and nothing could have pleased the Chief more. At one of our William Penn or Yonkers meetings in the 1970s, he was going on and on about Tim's expertise. Our lawyer, John

Macartney, listened quietly, smiling. When Dad paused for a moment, Macartney interrupted. He said, "If Franco Harris, Terry Bradshaw, Joe Greene, and some of your other football players had four legs instead of two, they'd be Kentucky Derby winners, maybe even Triple Crown winners."

I had scouted and recommended those guys, and I could not help showing the satisfaction I felt at hearing Macartney's indirect praise. As we left the meeting room, he fell in step with me and said, "Artie, I meant every word of that." I was momentarily too flustered to make an adequate response.

In its austerity, Shamrock Farm resembled Jimmy Coyne's farm in the hills north of Pittsburgh. Coyne sold his land for a lot of money. Property values in Carroll County, Maryland, never went high enough to make selling a worthwhile option for AJR or his heirs. Coyne, a born rustic, liked to plow and plant and harvest and look after the livestock. AJR thought of Shamrock Farm as a place to get away from it all. On his visits, he never lifted a finger. The Rooney womenfolk avoided the farm as much as possible.

One of AJR's earliest pair of custodians, Charles Clayton and his wife, resembled the stern-faced couple in "American Gothic," the painting by Grant Wood that shows a man wearing overalls, holding a pitchfork and standing side by side with a woman in an apron, the two of them guarding, or seeming to guard, their farmhouse, a narrow white clapboard structure with a high-pitched roof. Clayton was called Johnny Bill, never Charles. By any name, he was not much of a caretaker. Shamrock Farm's buildings and grounds suffered greatly from inattention. Tim, embarrassed by the looks of the place, pushed for improvements, but Fran Fogarty, AJR's financial watchdog, held fast to his purpose of spending no money that didn't absolutely have to be spent, and AJR backed him up.

Despite the rumpled suits, the cloth caps, and the studied air of unpretentiousness, AJR was not without vanity. The role of gentleman farmer was one that he liked. It was how he wished to be seen by his NFL colleagues. To appear unsophisticated in the eyes of these people — "brand new," as he always put it — would have bothered him much more than he wanted you to think.

One of the few NFL guys who had actually set foot on Dad's farm was Harvey Johnson, the Buffalo Bills' head scout and a close personal friend of the owner, Ralph Wilson. In their dependence on one another, they reminded me of Walt Kiesling and AJR. Twice when Wilson fired his head coach, Johnson filled in as interim head coach. He then would return to the personnel department. On the side, he dabbled in thoroughbred racing. With a man named Breezie Reed, he bought a filly they thought could "run some." After racing the horse at two of the Maryland tracks, Bowie and Laurel, they put her up for the winter at Shamrock Farm.

Johnson was something of a story teller. He had a resonant tenor voice that could penetrate the thickest wall. The more he got involved in a story, the higher his voice would climb. One tale he was fond of went like this:

In 1972, after a 1-13 season as interim coach, he was back in scouting. Arriving at War Memorial Stadium in Buffalo for a meeting, he found himself confronted by a rent-a-cop behind a locked gate. The cop asked Johnson for his I.D. card.

"I don't have one," Johnson told him.

"Then I can't let you in," the cop said.

"But I'm Harvey Johnson."

"You're who?"

"Harvey Johnson, the head scout. I'm here to attend a meeting."

"You're who?" the cop repeated.

At this point, Johnson lost his temper.

"Were you working here last season?" he yelled at the cop.

"Yeah."

"Well, do you remember the head coach who fucked up the whole team?"

"Yeah, yeah."

"Well, that asshole was me!" Johnson yelled. "Now, open this damn gate!"

"Yes, sir, Mister Johnson. I remember you now," said the cop.

It was in his usual uninhibited, clamorous way that Harvey accosted me at a Blesto gathering the year he had boarded his filly with the Claytons.

"Hey, Artie," he said, "when's the last time you were over to your dad's horse farm?"

"It's been quite a while, Harv. My brother Tim is into that stuff."

"Well, you'd better get over there and take a look." His voice was in the fortissimo register already. "You know that filly that belongs to Breezie Reed and me? The one we took to your farm? We only took her there because of your dad. Great guy. But that farm! It's a pig-sty!"

I glanced around. Everybody in the room was tuned in. "Breezie and I went over to see that horse," Harvey continued. "Hell! The fence rails were down! Horseshit everywhere you looked! And our filly had lost weight.

"I want you to tell your dad about it. I can't believe he knows how bad the place is," Johnson finished, every syllable reverberating.

Of course, as soon as I got back to Pittsburgh, I dutifully reported what Harvey had said. AJR looked stricken.

"Who was there — who heard him say that?" he demanded.

"A lot of scouts and some general managers — all the football people."

I could see that Dad was upset.

Not too long afterward, renovations began at the farm. Johnny Bill Clayton and his wife were sent on their way, replaced by a couple named Shaw. Dad was now listening to Tim's recommendations. They had the Winfield Volunteer Fire Department burn down the old, dilapidated farmhouse and the old, dilapidated cow barn. "Good practice for our boys," said the fire chief. Fran Fogarty was gone, and our real-estate advisor, Terry Jacobs, closed a deal with an advertising firm to put up a larger, contemporary farmhouse.

Don't ask me about the particulars. Preoccupied with football, I paid no attention.

A little later, new stables were constructed, attracting more business from horsemen with brood mares. Shaw, the new tenant, had worked at other stud farms and knew horses — unlike Clayton. A couple of new stallions, one named for St. Bonaventure, the other for Pat's son Christopher, helped pay the bills.

Tim, justifiably, took credit for all the refurbishment. He had forced AJR to recognize that changes were necessary. Everybody said so. But if you want my opinion, raucous ol' Harvey Johnson had quite a bit to do with it, too.

Chapter 50

Man of LaMancha

By 1970, the year we moved into Three Rivers Stadium, I was representing the Steelers at the Blesto meetings. I had had my first shouting match with a Steeler head coach (Bill Austin). I had argued with my wife over the inordinate amount of time I was spending on the road. And I had clashed with my brother Dan over territorial rights.

The Steelers' front office had always been understaffed. During my first few years as personnel director, I worked without an office or a secretary. Buddy Parker's departure left his back-room cubbyhole in the Roosevelt Hotel vacant, and I lobbied for it. To Dan, it may have seemed that I was making a power grab. Once installed, I asked for help with my correspondence and filing.

There was nothing at all grand about this hole in the wall I had seized. Sports Illustrated writer Mort Sharnik came calling, took a look at my new digs, and said it confirmed his belief that the Steelers ran a no-frills operation.

I introduced Mort to some of our office fixtures — Uncle Jim, Dago Sam, Patsy Scanlon, Doc Sekay, our eccentric team dentist, and Radio Rich, a toothless, jobless, mentally challenged sports nut who walked in on us one day with a transistor set clamped to his ear and soon had the status of a permanent hanger-on. Mort was mesmerized. "This place," he told me, "is like something right out of a Damon Runyon story."

The thought made my father uneasy.

"Hey," he cautioned me in a private conversation, "I don't want these press guys talking to Jim or Sam or any other Damon Runyon character." They were loose cannons, he was saying.

My brother Dan's view of the Steeler organization was much broader than mine. He looked at all aspects of our business. My one concern was to build a good scouting system. I became obsessed with player procurement: "Build through the draft." And I was obstinate about that — pigheaded, some people thought. But I knew I was right and would take on anyone who differed with me. Mort Sharnik would say, "You're on a quest." I didn't know the definition of "quest" and was too proud to ask. So did I look it up in the dictionary? No. I learned the meaning years later at a Broadway musical — "Man of LaMancha."

Don Quixote would say it was an honor and privilege to be on a quest, and that is how I felt about my job in the Steeler scouting department. Pursuing my aims single-mindedly, I antagonized the entire front office and coaching staff. AJR would tell me, "Nobody likes you." I wanted to be liked — I really did. But if not being liked was the price of doing what had to be done, I was willing to pay it.

Soft Sell

In the spring of 1969 I arrived at Wake Forest on my swing through the South with a list of prospects from Blesto and instructions to look up Beattie Feathers, an assistant coach. Although we never had met, I knew all about him. Thirty-five years earlier, as a rookie from Tennessee in the backfield of the Chicago Bears, Beattie Feathers had gained 1,004 yards, averaging 8.4 yards a carry. At a time when there were fewer games, and when officials stopped the clock less often, reducing the number of plays, and when running backs also played defense - back in those days, to gain one thousand or more yards was extraordinary, and no one before Feathers had done it.

He was now in his late fifties, but I expected to see a big, rugged, powerful-looking guy. Instead, he just missed being undersized. He was affable in his greeting and said he remembered AJR. I had been told he would give me a good appraisal of the Wake Forest players on my list, and he discussed each one thoroughly. Then he asked with an air of puzzlement, "Why did you leave off our best prospect?"

"Your best prospect?" Now it was my turn to be puzzled. "And who might that be?"

"His name is Jimmy Clack," Feathers said. "Nobody drafted him. Even though he won't be back next fall, he's working out with the kids who will be." Clack, Feathers told me, was a center. "He's too tall for his weight - six-five — and that's what scared you guys off. But take a look at him. He's strong and he's as smart as they come. Heck, Jimmy won the Bill George Award as the best blocker in the Atlantic Coast Conference. Played basketball and track, too. Fine student. You can watch him on film when you're lookin' at the other seniors."

I had heard this type of story before. It would turn out in the end that the player was a relative of the coach — maybe a son-in-law. Or else the kid had a police record. Drugs were not yet a problem back then, but he may have been a boozer. Whatever it was, you could be sure that a coach who talked in such flowery terms about an undrafted player almost certainly had a hidden agenda.

Feathers, though, didn't sound like the kind of guy that Ken Stilley referred to as "a high ambassador of bullshit." From his matter-of-fact tone, I did not get the impression that he was making a sales pitch. "You can check Jimmy out for yourself on film," he repeated.

This, I thought, was the least I could do, if only as a courtesy to one of the game's most respected old-timers. Feathers set up a movie projector — when I traveled by air, I did not bring my own — and put on a game film. As we sat there watching it, he quietly called attention to everything Clack did. Coming from other coaches I could name, but will not, this might have been aggravating. But Feathers remained low-key, and I saw with my own eyes that Clack was good. In fact, he was more than good. He was dominating.

Still, I did my best to resist going overboard. Once when I was praising an undrafted player to Jack Sell, the old *Post-Gazette* football writer, he asked me why no one had wanted him, suggesting that there had to be a reason. This was now the question I put to myself about Clack. What bothered me was that besides being undrafted he had failed to catch on as a free agent. Why? You needed bodies — cannon fodder, if you like — for training-camp scrimmages, after all.

We watched another film — Wake Forest-North Carolina. Playing opposite Clack was a tackle expected to be an early-round selection in the upcoming draft, a tackle named Smith. As Feathers kept pointing out to me, Clack won every round of their contest. His height was not a handicap because he went in low, getting up and under the Tar Heel. After taking care of Smith, he would then go looking for others to block.

"Coach Feathers," I said, "there has to be something I'm missing. I haven't seen anything not to like about this guy."

"Well, Jimmy is on the practice field now. I'll go over there with you," Feathers answered. Tall and skinny, just as Feathers had described him, Clack was in shorts and a T-shirt. His legs were muscular and he had a deep chest. He was all smiles — a yes-sir and no-sir lad. Chuck Noll had warned me to watch out for Southern kids who said yes sir and no sir. "That's just the way they're brought up — it doesn't mean anything," he said. However, as far as I could determine, Clack seemed genuine. He made it a point to let me know he had been a basketball player, and I remembered that Noll was partial to basketball players, basketball being a movement sport. Noll wanted offensive linemen who could maintain a block while they were moving.

Clack's playing weight during the 1968 season, he told me, had been 215 pounds. He knew that 215 was too light for the NFL, but he was lifting barbells and other weights, he said. He went on and on about that, which would have been pleasing to Noll.

I watched Clack run a little, and noted that he was fluid, showing quickness and body control. Something else I observed was the way he got along with the other players. He was very much a part of the gang, and I liked that.

As soon as the workout ended, I said to him, "Jim, would you like to sign a contract with the Steelers?"

"By golly, yes!" he answered, a wide grin creasing his face. Before Jim Boston and Bill Nunn took over the job of negotiating with our late draft choices and free agents, I always carried a blank Steeler contract with me; this was the only time I ever used one. Agents had not yet begun to proliferate, and we could deal with most players directly. All that was to change. Even the free agents would say, "Well … you'll have to see my agent." In the late 1960s and early '70s, Dan or Fran Fogarty signed the high-enders; the rest of us had parameters within which we could operate. We might offer someone like Clack five hundred dollars to sign and another five hundred on top of his salary — eleven or twelve thousand a year — if he made the team.

Clack, to the best of my recollection, did not receive a bonus. I placed the contract on the roof of a parked car, handed him a ballpoint pen, and in just a few seconds the ceremony was over. The only thing we guaranteed him was a tryout, and he was happy to sign for that. Despite his lack of bulk, he could be assured of fair treatment from Noll, who believed in the benefits of diet and weight training. Noll wasn't looking for redwood trees — he favored short, compact linemen with mobility and quickness — but I once heard him say of a player, "Hey — he's a midget!"

In any case, Clack's performance that summer in pre-season camp made a strong impression on Noll. Clack wasn't ready for the NFL, but Chuck farmed him out to a minor-league team in Norfolk, Virginia, the Neptunes. His coach there was George Hughes, a former Steeler, in whom we all had the utmost confidence.

The next year Clack returned to us heavier and stronger. George Young, head scout for the Dolphins at the time, saw him doing his stuff in an intra-squad game at Jeannette and said to me, "Arthur, are you guys trying to hide that kid?" You couldn't hide a good prospect from a top scout like Young, but before the season started Clack disappeared into the Army.

Fran Fogarty, making use of his contacts in the National Guard, got him assigned to a local unit. It may be that, unlike Rocky Bleier – there'll be more about him as we proceed — he was thus spared the fate of the Vietnam veterans I saw when we played a pre-season game in Norfolk, the site of a large military hospital. Sailors and Marines were looking on from wheelchairs or gurneys, some of these young kids bandaged like mummies while others had missing arms or legs.

After his year in the Army, Clack was bigger and stronger still, but with no loss of quickness. Once the game was under way, he knew how to "make things happen," Noll used to say. Noll's system was intricate, featuring traps, sweeps, down blocks, and slides (to pick up pass rushers), but it gave Clack no trouble, and in 1971 he cracked the starting lineup. He could play anywhere in the offensive line except at tight end. In fact, he started at guard in two Super Bowl games, IX and X.

Clack remained with the Steelers until 1977, when he was traded to the Giants. There he developed into a team leader and had five more good seasons. Not bad for a kid the pros would have ignored without the understated intercession of his college coach.

Frank and Peahead

Most NFL scouts headed south early in March, checked out the teams in the Southeast Conference, and worked their way north, from Florida up into the Carolinas and Virginia. By the end of the month they would be in Pennsylvania, New York, and New England, fanning out from there to the Midwest, to Texas, to the Rocky Mountains, to the Pacific Coast.

As late as the 1970s there were still assistant coaches who doubled as scouts. Some had bright futures; you could pick out the assistants who would one day be head coaches. Some of the scouts were real sharp guys also. I can think of three — George Young of the Colts, Ron Wolf of the Raiders, and Bobby Beathard of the Chiefs – who became general managers and Hall-of-Fame nominees.

Scouting was a chance for me to meet and establish friendships with such men. I had a passion for my work, and I could not understand why there were scouts who felt differently. I recall a cold, wet spring in Utah; I was sitting in a darkened room with two other scouts I did not know well, watching game films. One of the two started whining about the unpleasant weather, about the unpleasant reception the coaches we came to see had given us. Then the second scout chimed in, saying, "Yeah, you're right. While you and I are out here in the boondocks seven days a week, the personnel directors sit around drinking coffee and talking on the phone. They don't hit the road until Thursday. They're home again on Sunday and back in the office Monday morning."

Well, I happened to be a personnel director myself. It was Tuesday, not Thursday, and I was four thousand miles from my wife and kids. Like the two complainers, I preferred sunshine to rain. Like the two complainers, I had not been made to feel welcome by the coaching staff at this college. I thought, "Hell — I don't have to worry about competing with these guys. It doesn't matter how smart or how experienced they are. They don't like their jobs. And I couldn't be more satisfied with mine."

There were coaches who looked down on scouts and there were coaches like Frank Howard of Clemson who went out of their way to be cooperative. When I met Frank Howard he had been at Clemson for years and was also the athletic director. Even the unfriendliest coaches provided us with game films, a room, and a movie projector. Howard did more than that. He allowed us to watch practice; he allowed us to interview his assistants; he allowed us to time his players in the forty-yard dash.

We were timing the forty at Clemson one spring on a day that began with the air damp and raw. Then the sun came out, and by mid-afternoon it was warm. I took off my trench coat and draped it across my shoulders like a cape. I put on my sunglasses. To complete the picture, I may have been smoking one of Dad's big cigars; Howard did not forbid smoking or even chewing on his practice field. In any case, I was making myself conspicuous, a violation of scouting protocol. Cape effect, shades, and cigar (if there was one) had not escaped Howard's attention.

"Rooney boy," he said, "is that the new look for the well-dressed scout these days?" My answer came from out of the blue, unpremeditated. "Only if his father owns the team." Howard laughed uproariously. Given their cue, his assistants laughed uproariously too. (When Howard laughed, his assistants laughed; when Howard frowned, his assistants frowned.) Even the other scouts and the Clemson players were chuckling. I felt like Bob Hope. As we walked off the field when practice was over, another scout fell in step with me and said, "I think Coach Howard likes you."

I did what I could to keep on the good side of Howard. At Christmas I would send him a box of expensive cigars. He had long been out of coaching but was still athletic director and still an important figure on the campus (Clemson had named its big new stadium after him) when I asked if he could help a nephew of mine, Pat Rooney, enroll at the university as a freshman.

Sarcastically, he demanded to know if Pat could at least read and write. I vouched for the young man's literacy. "Well, then, Rooney," Howard assured me, "I'll get him in. Hell, boy, the president here is one of my former student managers. He'll do what I tell him."

Howard had a penchant for practical jokes. His friend Peahead Walker, at one time the coach at Wake Forest, but a scout for the New York Giants when I first encountered him, told me of a joke Howard pulled that he did not soon forgive. Arriving with his Wake Forest team for a game at Clemson one year, Peahead recalled, he stepped off the bus to find a pair of South Carolina state troopers waiting for him.

"You're under arrest," one of them said.

While Walker's players and assistant coaches looked on with their mouths hanging open, the no-nonsense enforcers of the law hustled him into their patrol car and drove away. At the local police station, he was put in a cell, screaming, "What's going on here? I'm Coach Walker! I have to be with my team! Call the president of the college — Wake Forest! Call the governor of North Carolina! Damn! I just know that old bastard Howard's behind this! Take my word for it, there'll be hell to pay! You jackasses! I'll have your jobs!"

Back at Clemson Stadium, meanwhile, the Wake Forest squad was out on the field, loosening up. At last the troopers let Peahead out of his cell, explaining that — ha-ha — it was all in good fun. They got him to the stadium just before the kickoff. He spent the entire first half yelling across the field at Howard, calling him names I would rather not repeat.

"Aw," Howard retorted, only making matters worse, "your players and coaches didn't miss you."

In football the rule is that anything goes, and Peahead himself was not above practicing trickery. As you may or may not know, Wake Forest is located in Winston-Salem, North Carolina. Its original campus, in the Raleigh area, was nothing special, I understand. I heard that Peahead would show high-school prospects the more opulent Duke University campus in Durham, giving them the impression that this was an extension of Wake Forest. When they turned up the next fall to enroll, they'd be puzzled.

"Gee, Coach," they would say, "this place looks different from when we visited last spring."

"Well, son, it is different," he would tell them. "See, you have to prove yourself here before you can go to our big main campus as a sophomore."

Walker and Howard had thick cornpone drawls. Howard was a big man, Peahead quite a bit smaller. His tasteful clothes, silver hair, and courtly manner gave him the air of an ante-bellum aristocrat. Recruiting coal miners' sons and steelworkers' sons from Western Pennsylvania, he exuded Southern charm. Mamas and grandmas never doubted him for a minute when he said, "Ma'am, if this fine boy of yours comes down to play football for us at our splendid college, we'll take real good care of him."

Peahead was partial to Western Pennsylvania football players but resented it, he told me, when Wake Forest recruited a Western Pennsylvania golfer one year.

"This fellow would take a short cut across our practice field to the golf course every day," Peahead said, "and he seemed to know a lot of our kids. He'd stop and talk with them, interrupting their work, and I could see that they were just a little bit jealous because of how easy he had it. He was getting a free ride just to hit that little white ball while the football players were taking bumps.

"So do you know what I did? I told him he couldn't cut across the football field any more. I said, 'You're distracting my players. From now on, use the same path to the golf course that everybody else uses.'

"Good Lord! If I'd a known he was going to be Arnold Palmer, I'd have asked if I could carry his golf bag."

Peahead's wife bought a parrot to keep her company in the house, and he hated the squawking creature. In Mrs. Walker's absence one day, he found a way to silence it. He poured a fraction of an ounce of Kentucky bourbon into the bird's drinking water.

It had a tranquilizing effect, and Peahead continued the treatment. Half-stewed, Polly was much less of a nuisance. As time went on, Peahead became fond of the parrot. Surreptitiously, he started teaching it a new vocabulary — locker-room talk. At first it was just "hell" and "damn." Kindergarten stuff, Peahead thought. He added "shit" to the bird's repertory, then "son of a bitch." When Mrs. Walker got wind of what was happening, she was horrified, but Polly's language lessons could not be unlearned and Peahead now had a drinking buddy, so to speak.

Most parrots live a long time. This one died fairly young — perhaps of acute alcoholism, though I hope not. It is horrible to imagine a parrot in the throes of delirium tremens, and I know that Peahead would have been devastated. I heard him say to someone, "I have lost a real friend."

Several years later, at an NFL meeting on the West Coast, the owner of the Giants, Wellington Mara, came to me and said, "I just had a telephone call from New York. Peahead Walker is dead. I know you liked him."

It was true, and I thanked Mara for remembering. Somehow, all I could think of for the next few hours was Peahead getting that parrot drunk and teaching it to swear.

'Why Do You Hate Me?'

For professional reasons, politicians, traveling salesmen, and football scouts must be able to woo. Politicians court voters. Salesmen shine up to their customers. Scouts curry favor with college coaches.

Getting off on the right foot makes everything else so much easier. Whenever I could, I laid the groundwork beforehand. In 1969, we played an exhibition game in Baton Rouge, Louisiana. Southern University, a small black school, is in Baton Rouge, and I took care of the coaching staff's ticket needs. It paid off. Later, I got good information on Southern U.'s gifted defensive backs, in particular Mel Blount.

It was equally important not to aggravate a coach. For the preservation of harmony, there were times when you had to bite your tongue. The head coach at Texas A. & M., Gene Stallings, was a Bear Bryant disciple who patterned himself after his teacher. On my first visit to College Station he invited me into his office, indicated that I should sit down, and proceeded to tell me why the Rooney family had no one to blame but itself for seven losing seasons in seven consecutive years under four different coaches: it was our slipshod organization.

Recollecting that I was a guest – an intruder, almost – obligated to Stallings for the access I needed to do my job, I managed to curb my temper. Besides, what he was saying made sense. So instead of arguing with him I listened in silence until he had come to the end of his lecture and led me out onto the practice field.

What awaited me there was a demonstration of Bryant-like efficiency: so many minutes allotted to this drill, so many minutes to that one. At intervals timed to the second, a horn sounded. Groups of players and coaches would then disintegrate; new groups would form somewhere else. The players' jerseys were color-coded – one shade for the offense, another for the defense, a third for the injured, a fourth for the teams of specialists. There was no lost motion, no indecision, not a tick of the clock wasted in idleness.

On one side of the field stood a tower reaching into the sky. From this lofty eminence Stallings surveyed the scene and issued orders, like an admiral on the bridge of an aircraft carrier. He headed for it now. "Come along, Rooney," he said. "I'll show you what we're doing." I followed him to the base of the tower and we started our climb up a ladder of sorts. Stallings went first, as easily as a steeplejack. For five feet, ten feet, twenty feet, I was right behind him.

And then I missed a step. I lost control and was falling backward. Stallings, informed by some sixth sense that I was in trouble, glanced down at me over his shoulder. I saw his face – he was thinking: "Oh, my God!" Racing through my own mind were thoughts of a broken leg, a broken back, a fractured skull. But then I felt two strong hands firmly placed on my rear end. They were pushing me up and in. A young graduate assistant had been right on my heels. Maintaining his balance – I can't imagine how – he pushed until I recovered mine.

Quite literally, the guy saved my ass.

I made it to the platform above, all in one piece but embarrassed – so embarrassed that while Stallings pointed out the players he regarded as NFL material, detailing their strengths and weaknesses, I couldn't concentrate. Though I had risked life and limb to get my interview, his words went unheard.

Texas A. & M. 's facilities were magnificent. Not so the facilities at the small black colleges, and yet these segregated schools, back in the days of separate but unequal, held the same attraction for scouts that the Klondike had held for an earlier generation of prospectors.

Future all-pros were to be found in such places, and I valued all the help I could get with their coaches. Accordingly, when John Baker, a one-time Steeler defensive end, offered to ride shotgun for me on a trip to North Carolina A. & T. one year I gratefully accepted. Based in Raleigh, Baker was the county sheriff. AJR had given me orders to look him up, and as we talked in his office I mentioned casually that the all-black college a few miles down the road in Greensboro would be my next stop. "I'll drive you over there," he said, jumping to his feet. "I know all the coaches."

I knew the head coach, Hornsby Howell, myself. Hornsby was a guy who made life easy for scouts, but with the tall and impressive Baker at my side, dressed completely in black and wearing his star, the A. & T. people outdid themselves. It was all the more dumbfounding, then, to be shunted off from the others by one of Hornsby's assistant coaches and asked in aggrieved tones, "Why do you hate me?"

I had no idea how to answer. "Hate you?" I said. "I don't even know you. Why should you think I hate you?"

"All white men hate all black men," he explained.

I said I would like to hear why he believed that.

"Because you're afraid of two things about us," he said. "First, you think we enjoy sex more than you do. Second, you're afraid we'll take jobs that would otherwise go to white men."

"Well, Coach," I said, "if you enjoy sex so much I admire you for it. And I'm not a bit worried that you're going to take my job. My daddy, you see, owns the football team I work for."

Instantly, this made us friends. From then on, I couldn't get away from him. He asked where I was staying, and I named a motel in Raleigh. He said, "Well, give me a call the next time you're here. They have a lot of these big furniture conventions in North Carolina, you know, and sometimes it's hard to find a motel room. If there aren't any vacancies, you can always stay with me and my wife. We have a nice house just off the campus."

There would never be the need to call on his hospitality, but I was flattered and touched.

Scouting at colleges like A. & T., where usually I would be the only white man in a room full of blacks, never made me uncomfortable. I liked the ambience; I liked the humor you always could count on; I liked the coaches. Before the word got around, I heard about Mean Joe Greene at a small black college in Texas. The coach there had films of North Texas State, and he said to me, "Hey, Rooney, you'd better see this. North Texas has a defensive tackle who is gonna be great!"

At one school I visited, there was plenty of film on hand, but no projector. The only projector the coaches had was being repaired.

"When will you have it back?" I asked.

"Oh, it's been ready for two or three days now. We're waiting for the check from the accounting office, so we can pick it up."

Where I was from, I said, we'd call that getting it out of hock. I asked how much the repair bill would come to.

"Thirty-five bucks."

I was with Jerry Neri, a scout for the Detroit Lions, and I suggested that each of us could throw in seventeen-fifty to reclaim the darn thing. I said we were eager to look at the films.

Everybody waited for the head coach to answer. "OK," he said after a pause, "but there's one other problem. We're all too busy to go after it. Now, if you two guys are that interested ..."

So Neri and I drove to the repair shop. We felt that back in the coaches' office they were laughing at us, but we also knew that if we left without watching the films, another Sam Davis, Ernie Holmes, or L. C. Greenwood might forever remain undiscovered.

Mormon Country

At St. Vincent College in the summer of 1969, Bill Nunn and I spent hours at a time with Chuck Noll. He repeated to us again and again that there were three things he looked for in a football player — athleticism, intelligence, and character. Our job was to learn how to recognize these qualities. Even though there are nuances to be considered, almost anyone can tell if a prospect has the requisite physical ability. Identifying character and intelligence — football intelligence — is not quite so simple.

When Noll and his assistant coaches studied film, he invited us to sit in. As they endlessly dissected the performance of each player, we watched and we listened. He was cloning us, in a sense — transplanting his vision and his values. Or trying to.

That year in camp we had something like one hundred players. All wore jerseys with numbers, which made life easier for Nunn and me. In the future Noll would order Tony Parisi, the equipment manager, to get rid of the numbered jerseys and substitute plain ones. It seems that at practice one day a Steeler coach had noticed a little-known scout from another pro team looking on. "We don't want those guys to spot the talented young players we're bringing along," Noll explained to me.

"And turn down any requests you may get for practice games," he added. "Hell, they film those scrimmages and see who our best young free agents are. Then they grab them on waivers for a hundred bucks."

I was miffed, because practice games were helpful, I believed. In retrospect, though, taking into account the overlooked free agents and late-round draft choices who developed into starting players for us, perhaps Noll was right. As usual.

Every year after Labor Day, I hit the road. As head scout, I followed Wellington Mara's advice: Do a good, accurate job when you visit the colleges in the spring and then hold a meeting with the other scouts to map out an itinerary for the fall.

For myself the routine was to stay on the road until Thanksgiving. I had permission to take Kay with me, and when I was going to sun-belt places like California, Arizona, or Florida late in the season I frequently did. AJR insisted that I attend every Steeler game, both at home and away. He also instructed me to telephone Kay every day and telephone Kass once a week at a minimum. Returning to Pittsburgh for our games allowed me to recharge my batteries, keep the home fires burning, and catch up on administrative work. I had no office help except for a secretary, which meant that she had to be competent (over the years, not all of them were).

Making it to the games away from Pittsburgh became a chore, but I obeyed Dad's orders unthinkingly. As I have said, I felt that I worked *with* Noll and Dan, but *for* AJR, and for AJR alone, an attitude that would get me into trouble. Years were to pass before AJR began telling me, "There can be only one boss." What could he mean by that? AJR was my boss. Did he suppose I needed reminding? It hadn't registered with me somehow that by then he was in his eighties, and slowing up. At the start of the Noll era he was still very much in charge.

So was I, in my own mind, when I took off from Latrobe that September and headed west. There were colleges in Utah worth visiting, and I planned on hitting them all. At Utah State, my first stop, the head coach was not at all friendly. "Hell, man," he grumbled, "we haven't played a game yet." Practice was about to start, and he grudgingly permitted me to watch. He considered my presence an imposition, I could see. We were sitting in his office and he was puffing on a cigar. It looked like a burning piece of rope and smelled the same way. So from the inside pocket of my sport jacket, I whipped out a Bance Aristocrat.

"Here, Coach, try this," I said. "It's one of my dad's cigars, and he smokes the best. Before I go on the road, I grab as many of these as I can."

The coach's face lit up like the smoldering end of the weed in his mouth. "Hey, thank ya," he said. "Ya can't buy or steal a good cigar in Utah. Mormons, ya know." The coach himself was from Los Angeles, where his wife, a nurse, had stayed on to work in a hospital. "She sends me a box of my regular cigars once a month, but they haven't come yet," he said, tossing aside his rope and striking a match for the Aristocrat I had given him.

After that, I received special treatment.

I got my Bance Aristocrats from a guy named Jake who ran a cigar stand in the Jenkins Arcade, a Pittsburgh landmark on Liberty Avenue back then. Jake sent the bill to AJR, and he always paid up without a word. Tobacco, as compared with booze, was the lesser of two evils, he believed. As a parting gift for the head coach at Utah State, I entrusted a box of Aristocrats to one of his assistants. "Pretty smart move, Rooney," he said. "As long as Coach stays here, or wherever else he goes, you'll be welcome."

Actually, this was more of an R.A.K. — a random act of kindness — than a calculated smart move. I was never a guy who consistently made smart moves. I remember giving Rip Engle, the Penn State coach who preceded and groomed Joe Paterno, a tin of licorice. Mike Nixon, scouting for the Philadelphia Eagles, happened to be in State College at the time, and he told me, "That was very nice. And very smart. Old Rip loves his licorice." Which I hadn't known.

The coaches in Utah much preferred contraband cigars. I discovered, to my chagrin, that not many natives were so disposed. At Brigham Young I found myself with time to kill and wandered around the campus smoking a toby. I have told you what tobies are — black, tightly-rolled cigars that give off the odor of musk. AJR bought them for twenty-five cents apiece at a cigar store in Squirrel Hill, and I helped myself to his ample supply. I thought of tobies as a good change of pace. AJR liked to bite a toby in two and chew it, one half at a time. I did my chewing bit by bit. The taste was acrid, but not unpleasant.

Because a religious convocation, attended by all the students and faculty, was going on in the field house, I had the Brigham Young campus all to myself. It's at the foot of the mountains on the Provo side of the boundary between Provo and Orem. I walked for thirty-five minutes and then slowly headed toward the athletic department's building. Approaching the field house, I lit another toby; I had smoked and chewed the first one down to a stub. Just then the convocation let out, and I stopped to take in the scene — scores of clean-cut Mormon kids streaming in my direction from the exits. In the warmth of a sunlit September afternoon, I stood there puffing and spitting, smiling and saying hi to the fresh-faced boys and the uniformly pretty girls passing by.

But hold on — something was wrong. They were giving me sour looks. They were glaring at me. Instinctively, I reached for my fly; it was zippered up completely. Puzzled by this show of hostility, I continued on my way to the football coaches' domain. And when I told them the story of my misadventure, including the detail of the cigar, they spelled out what should have been obvious to me. "Certainly they were glaring at you," one assistant coach said. "These are Mormon kids. Smoking is against their religion. You were lucky they didn't run you off the campus." The head coach, as it happened, was a friend, an old NFL guy. "Look here," he said, pulling open the bottom drawer of his desk. "See all these ash trays and matches? This is where I have to keep them. If I didn't hide this stuff, I'd be in trouble."

I scouted football players in Utah that year, and maybe we signed one or two. I don't remember. What I do remember are the inconsequential occurrences.

Driving into Ogden, where Weber State is located, I looked at the fuel gauge and saw that I was low on gasoline. Against my better judgment, I had rented a sports car — a Cougar. Getting into and out of the damn thing was a chore, for I had gained a lot of unneeded weight. "You can't eat like the football players unless you work as hard as they do," one of our trainers had warned me. At the filling station in Ogden I wedged myself out of the door, putting a heavy strain on my clothing, unscrewed the gas cap, and then dropped it. I bent to pick it up and heard a ripping noise. All the way down to the crotch, I had split the seat of my pants. Underneath, I was wearing white skivvies, which now were on public display. I finished gassing my car and, red in the face, went inside to pay up, all the while cursing the Avis gal who had talked me into renting a Cougar.

"Mister," said the guy at the cash register, "there's a tailor and dry cleaner right across the street. They can help you."

I was almost too embarrassed to say thanks.

Weber State had a player the Blesto scouts regarded as a "keeper." Although I scouted him, I do not recall his name, his position, or whether he ever made it to the NFL. I don't remember the names of his coaches. But I can tell you about Weber State's student manager.

We were watching the team practice, and he was talking up the prospect, as student managers tend to do. But then the next thing I knew he had changed the subject. He was giving me the most intimate particulars of his personal life.

He came from a strict Mormon family, he said. His grandfather had died and left him more than five million dollars. There was a caveat, however. The will provided that by his twentieth birthday the kid would have to be married — and married to a good Mormon girl. No wedding, no dough. The grandfather's money would in that case go to the Mormon church. He was 19, the kid said, which didn't leave him much time. Plus he did not have a steady girlfriend.

He knew he could easily find someone who met the will's specifications and would jump at the chance to marry five million dollars. That was by far the least of his worries. The thing that bugged him — the thing he resented — was the sense of being manipulated, of being squeezed. He was ready to tell the lawyers who drew up the will and the matchmakers in his family to go to hell — where it's possible he suspected his grandfather might be.

As he spoke, I asked myself what to make of all this. Was he giving me a line of bull? I didn't think so. As far as I could determine, the kid seemed sincere. I believed he was telling the truth.

Any last doubt evaporated when he turned to me and said, with anguish in his voice, "Mister Rooney, what should I do?" Unprepared for such a question, I thought it over carefully. I understood how Solomon must have felt when people with large problems came to him. Then I offered my advice. I said, "Kid — you'll have to solve this one yourself."

I never did find out if he took the money.

Emergency Landing

Intent on leaving no stone unturned, domestic or foreign, I decided to take a look at the Canadian League. Football players were where you found them, even in Canada. In addition to the home-grown talent, such as it was, you came across promising American players the NFL had somehow overlooked or players at odds with their NFL teams as an aftermath of failed contract negotiations.

Because of the fierce winters in Canada the football season started while we were still in our summer workouts and it finished around Thanksgiving time, when the NFL division races were just heating up. The Canadian League's equivalent of the Super Bowl was a championship game called the Gray Cup.

Canadian teams played on fields that were wider and longer than ours. Instead of four plays to make a first down, there were three, enhancing the importance of punters and punt returners. Our great punter Pat Brady, who came to us in 1952 and played only three seasons before an injury put an end to his career, was scouted in Canada.

The early onset of cold weather required Canadian teams to play twice a week. I planned to spend a day in Montreal, meeting with coaches and front-office people, catch a mid-week game the following night, and fly from Montreal to Southern California, where I could scout USC on Saturday afternoon and San Diego State a few hours later. AJR had instructed me to fly first class on long trips; interpreting these directions liberally, I booked a first-class flight to Montreal as well as to Los Angeles. Any flight that took me west of Cleveland, east of Harrisburg, or south of Morgantown was to my way of thinking a long trip. My duties as our team's personnel director encompassed more than scouting. I had to study reports, organize reports, and write reports, and I could get a lot of work done on airplanes. In first class, this part of the job was much easier.

The Montreal team was called the Alouettes, alouette being the French word for skylark. Everybody in the organization seemed overjoyed to make my acquaintance. They were bringing people out of the woodwork for me to meet, and some of them said things like "I met your father at the Frontenac in Quebec City," or "I knew your dad from the race track in Toronto." I even attended a party they were having that night, a sort of old-timers' reunion. It was a positive first trip for me, and I resolved to get up to Canada once a year or to send one of our scouts. I wondered if Jack Butler might be willing to expand his Blesto group's Canadian coverage.

On the morning after the Alouettes' game, I boarded a Canadian-Pacific flight to Los Angeles. Canadian planes were very comfortable: upholstered leather seats, excellent meals, flight attendants who looked like the actresses selected for "nice-girl" parts in the movies. This was before the feminist revolution, when there was no such thing as a homely or middle-aged stewardess. The ones with Canadian-Pacific were wholesome rather than seductive, and slim enough to fit their uniforms well. They indulged all of our wants with perfect propriety.

I had a seat on the aisle. Shortly after takeoff, I got my charts out and brought them up to date on the players I had scouted since the start of the season, discouraging conversation from the nice but talkative elderly couple in the two seats to my left. I then reviewed statistics on the players I'd be watching in California. I remember a flight on which a stewardess asked me what I was doing. When I told her, she asked how often I flew. I said, "I'm on nine or ten airplanes every week." Not even airline crews traveled that much, she exclaimed. "Our union rules don't allow it."

I laughed and replied, "Just routine."

On this flight to the West Coast, we were zipping along at about thirty-five thousand feet. I could hear the sounds of lunch being prepared in the galley — heavy silverware and expensive china clinking, stewardess talk in modulated, ladylike voices. Lunch was always elaborate on the Canadian-Pacific, and today we were having prime roast beef. I gave the attendant my drink order — ginger ale — and settled back in anticipation.

Across the aisle from me sat a pleasant-looking gray-haired gentleman. A conservative banker, I guessed. The stewardess, however, informed me that he was the Canadian-Pacific Airline's chief pilot, en route with his wife to a conference in Los Angeles. Minutes later, the man left his seat and walked up the aisle to the cockpit. While the door was open, I saw him shake hands with the pilot and pat him on the shoulder. Soon afterward, he was coming back, all smiles. Before sitting down he paused and said something to the stewardess, holding her by the arm.

I returned to my scouting reports. When I looked up again, I saw the stewardess bending over his seat, talking earnestly. She moved on, and he took his wife by the hand, whispered briefly into her ear, got up, and made his way to the cockpit once more. My only thought, meanwhile, was, "When are they going to serve lunch?" The carts with the food had been out in the aisle, but now they had disappeared.

Then I noticed that the plane was descending — not abruptly but gradually. We were slowly losing altitude. I looked at my watch. We had been in the air for just a few hours. No way we were close to Los Angeles. We'd been flying due west and had not yet turned to go south. The airplane dropped through the clouds and even from my seat on the aisle I could see that the ground below us was flat. We were still over Canada's great wheat plains. North of us, I saw the skyline of a city. But what city? Winnipeg? Saskatoon? Wherever we were, it seemed clear that a landing was imminent.

Next I became aware that the pilot who looked like a banker was still in the cockpit. And now the flight attendants were going from seat to seat, saying politely but firmly, "Put everything away. Fold up your tray. Carry-on luggage under the seat, please."

I said to one of the girls, "We're not in California."

Smiling, she answered, "I know. We're in Saskatchewan."

Over the airplane's P.A. system came the voice of the captain. "We must make an unscheduled landing in Saskatoon. Follow the instructions of the cabin attendants without question. I will speak to you again in a matter of moments." The attendants, moving about serenely, were giving soft-spoken orders. They reminded me of the nuns at St. Peter's School. "Do not remove the personal belongings under your seats for any reason. Seat belts must be tightly fastened."

Through the porthole I caught a glimpse of ambulances, police cars, and fire trucks gathering on the runway. Red lights were flashing. The flight attendants, patrolling the aisles, kept reaching down to tug at loose seat belts. "This must be tighter. Stay calm. Everything will be OK." There were no smiles. The passengers, unnaturally silent, asked no questions.

A different voice on the P.A. system, that of the co-pilot: "We're about to land. So far, everything looks good. We will slow the airplane with our engines. Do not be alarmed. Continue to follow the instructions of the cabin attendants." We touched down softly and smoothly. The pilot reversed the engines and we came to a sudden stop. An attendant's firm voice was urging us to our feet. "Leave your belongings and proceed to the nearest exit." We did as we were told, but the chief pilot's wife, I observed, went straight to the cockpit, where her husband was waiting.

On our shuffle toward the first-class service exit, I stepped back to let a woman of mature years go ahead of me. Curtly, the flight attendant said, "Keep your place in line, sir. Continue to move forward." When I arrived at the exit, another attendant was saying, "Step out onto the slide. Then sit. And do not grab hold. Just slide. Do not hesitate." Lemming-like, we followed one another through the door. The slide was rubber, I noticed, and slick. I went down to the bottom swiftly. When I hit the tarmac I heard someone calling, "Don't bunch up. Step away from the slide." The voice was masculine. In contrast to the voices of the flight attendants, it sounded panicky. "Get away from the airplane!" It was coming from a man in a green uniform — a policeman, I thought, or maybe a soldier "Run!" he was shouting. "Get away from the airplane!" Huffing and puffing, I joined a stampede that included weak-kneed old men and women in high heels.

It was more like a marathon than a sprint. The terminal buildings and hangars were off in the distance. If the airplane exploded, nothing else would go up.

The cop's voice now directed us to buses that were parked with their motors running. They were not as far away as the hangars but safely removed from the plane. The one I boarded took off when it was only half-full. The driver, it seemed to me, was in a god-awful hurry to leave the area. Only then did I notice that my heart was beating faster than normal, and not from our gallop across the runway.

It was a two- or three-mile ride to the terminal, a cookie-cutter affair of cement, glass, and marble which appeared to have been recently built. Two policemen at the entrance directed us into a roped-off section. I asked and received permission to visit the men's room and the cigar stand. Both were nearby. When I returned, I had a gift for AJR: Havana cigars, unobtainable in the United States because of our differences with Castro.

Later I went to a pay phone and called home. When Kay answered — she'd been getting lunch for the kids — I blurted, "Guess what just happened to me ... "Interrupting, she said, "Are you all right?"

"Yeah, but my plane just made an emergency stop in Saskatoon, Saskatchewan." Everything, I repeated, was fine, and she said, "Thank God. You damn nut, you — flitting and flying all over the place. You need your head examined."

Which ended the conversation.

I still didn't know why our flight had been aborted, but I could guess. Although Canadian politics held no interest for me, I had read newspaper stories about the clash over language and customs between the French-speaking Roman Catholics and the English-speaking Protestants in Quebec. Quebec is a province in which the French make up the majority. Elsewhere in Canada, the non-French outnumber them overwhelmingly. The French in Quebec wanted secession. In fact, they had forced a referendum on the issue, or would do so shortly (it failed by a narrow margin). Outside of being a Roman Catholic myself, I couldn't see that I had a dog in this fight. I understood, however, that the French Roman Catholics were inclined to be passionate in their beliefs and belligerent when it came to asserting them, and I assumed that some out-of-control separatist faction had planted a bomb in our airplane.

After a wait of three hours in the terminal, we learned that it was all just a hoax. There'd been a phone call while the plane was in the air, an anonymous warning that we would all be blown to bits. But now security people had gone through every piece of luggage on our plane, and no explosives were found. We boarded another plane, identical to the first one, and resumed our flight. There was lots of drinking. Then lunch, or by this time dinner, was served: succulent roast beef, fine china, fine wines. The drinking continued almost all the way to California. So did the excited babble. We were veterans of a slide-for-life, and eager to talk about it.

In Los Angeles the next day I searched the newspapers for an account of the bomb threat. Nothing. It was not a story. Among the people who'd hit the slide with me were men and women in their sixties and seventies. Some, I imagine, had heart problems; a few of the women could have been pregnant. In our first-class compartment, I had seen a man with an artificial leg. He'd had a hell of a time, he told me later, getting up on his feet after our slide. But to the newspapers this was not a big deal. And when I told of my adventure back in Pittsburgh, or on subsequent scouting trips, I could sense that most listeners were bored. Other scouts always seemed to have a story of their own that topped mine.

In later years, I did not, as I had planned, make annual expeditions to Canada. I returned, I think, twice, but when our staff became larger I sent a scout up North every year. I never was able to persuade Jack Butler that Blesto's time would be well spent in Canada beyond an occasional visit. In the end, I came to agree with that judgment. We were sold on developing our Steeler teams with college talent from the good old U.S.A.

The relative danger quotient of airplane travel in the U.S. and Canada had nothing to do with this decision. Now that it has shifted dramatically, though, I sometimes recall with a certain wistfulness a half-hour of suspense in the clouds above Saskatchewan and fifteen harrowing minutes on the tarmac in Saskatoon. The threat, I had believed at the time, was real. But fortunately for me and my fellow travelers, those French-Canadian cultural rebels were pussycats by comparison with Osama bin Laden's homicidal and suicidal Islamic fundamentalist hit men.

Chapter 51

Training Camp

Midsummer, for as long as I can remember, has meant training camp. It's a time when the Steelers come together to hit and hurt, a time when nervous, untested rookies measure themselves against veteran pros — veterans in their prime, veterans just hanging on. It's when the baseball season goes into retreat and Latrobe is the capital of Steeler Nation.

There are rigid specifications for a training camp, and St. Vincent College in Latrobe fills the bill. It's off the beaten path — rustic but not without amenities, removed from big-city distractions but accessible to the Steelers' fan base. In searing heat or soaking rain, zealots in gold and black crowd the hillsides that overlook the practice fields. They come in two major sub-species — critics and followers. The critics are there to judge and to argue, firm in the belief that their knowledge of the game is more profound than that of any coach. The followers seek a religious experience. They hunger for a blessing of some kind from the demi-gods in shoulder pads: a word, a smile, an autograph. A *Post-Gazette* reporter named Rebekah Scott has written that training camp is the start of their "liturgical year." For everybody concerned it's a time of renewal and preparation and hope, like Advent.

The followers, during the years I was personnel director, included a group of decorous middle-aged women, all good friends, it appeared. They did not seem to want any attention but attracted it anyway from the players, coaches, and scouts, who would greet them with a wave or stop to chat. There was something different in their behavior that set them apart from the hero worshippers and autograph hounds.

Back in 1933, when AJR took his first Pirate team to the wilds of North Park for pre-season training, it was largely a non-event. Public and press barely noticed. Early on, AJR realized that colleges offered better facilities, and he switched to St. Vincent in 1934 or 1935. As I have written, he put the team up at the Mountain View Hotel, which was closer to Greensburg than Latrobe. Room and board at the Mountain View, like everything else in the 1930s, was cheap, because, for one thing, no one had money. After the Second World War, when the Mountain View was thriving, AJR would speak of a lost opportunity. "The owner of that place," he said, "tried to give it to me for back taxes. I wasn't interested, and look at it now."

There were years when he shopped around for a camp. He moved from St. Vincent to St. Francis, a small Catholic college in Loretto. The first camp I can say I remember was in Hershey, where the sweet smell of cooking chocolate permeated the town. It comes back to me now as I write this. And Hershey had a wonderful amusement park.

It was too much of a resort town for Jock Sutherland. He preferred Alliance College in Cambridge Springs, an hour north of Pittsburgh near the Pennsylvania-Ohio state line. Sutherland's camps made Parris Island look like Club Med, but in any camp brutality is the norm. With my brothers, I watched the vicious hitting from up close. We saw the players bleed, saw them sweat, heard them swear, listened to the screaming of the coaches, and thought nothing of it. This was routine training-camp stuff, all in the day's work. "Smash-mouth football," people called it approvingly, and we were hardened to it, excited by it. I can still hear one of Sutherland's assistants yelling, "Get those kids the hell out of here! They're gonna get run over!" It happened once to Tim, who was knocked flat.

In the 1950s, while Father Dan was athletic director at St. Bonaventure, the Steelers trained nowhere else until Buddy Parker took over as coach. He said that Olean, New York, was too far from Pittsburgh. He said the weather up there was too cold. "We need the hot sun to get these guys in shape," he complained, and that was it for St. Bonaventure. Owney McManus accused him of being devious. "It's not the location or the climate he doesn't like, it's the monks," McManus said. "All those Franciscans in their long brown cassocks."

Parker coached the Steelers for nine years and moved the team around like a band of gypsies — from St. Bonaventure to West Liberty College in West Virginia, where the practice field was "too dry," causing "shin splints and sore legs," and then on to California State of Pennsylvania, where the facilities were unsatisfactory, and then on to Slippery Rock, where "the people in charge" weren't friendly enough, and finally all the way to the University of Rhode Island. There at last Parker found contentment of a sort. He liked the dressing room and the trainers' room, he liked the coaches' offices, he liked the thick green grass on the practice field, and most of all he liked the isolation. When the Steelers took leave of Parker, they also took leave of Rhode Island. Our coach the next year, 1966, was Bill Austin, and he rejected Rhode Island as "too far away and too cold."

We had heard that song before, I remember thinking.

So back to St. Vincent we went, and the union now looks to be permanent. The Benedictines are good landlords, and I am sure they can use the income. Over and above the rent, the Rooneys as a family have paid for a million-dollar campus renovation program — money well spent, I would say. St. Vincent, after all, is my old school.

All of us — the old-timers, I mean — have our favorite training-camp stories. It was Ralph Berlin who told me about the unsigned free agent recommended by the Lord.

On Saturday nights and Sundays when Chuck Noll was coach, the players were not required to stay on the campus. Until a team meeting Sunday night, their time was their own. Noll and his whole staff would normally absent themselves too, and even Bill Nunn, the camp manager, sometimes went home to Pittsburgh, leaving Berlin at the head of a skeleton crew. There would be no one else around except a handful of players with injuries that needed attention and a dozen or so rookies with nowhere to go.

Late one Saturday night, Berlin was in Nunn's office when a neatly dressed young black man walked in. He was wearing a white shirt with a button-down collar, dark slacks, and loafers. Calmly and pleasantly, he announced that this was where he'd been "ordered to report."

"Well, the coaches and scouts have gone home for the weekend, but maybe I can help you," said Berlin. "Are you a player?"

"Oh, yes sir. A very good one. By the grace of God."

A strange way to put it, Berlin thought. Neither Nunn, Noll, nor anyone else had told him to expect a late-arriving prospect. "Well, who sent you here?" Berlin asked. It was not unusual for AJR himself to promise tryouts to the relatives and acquaintances of his friends. Even Tip O'Neill, the Speaker of the House in Washington, had once called the Chief about a football player. So Berlin took care to be polite, but the answer he got was unsettling.

"The Almighty One sent me," the kid said. "He who is ..." He was not allowed to finish the sentence.

Berlin, breaking in, said, "Wait a minute. Just what are you talking about?"

"God Almighty has sent me to play for the Steelers."

"God Almighty?"

"Yes, and I am his humble messenger."

"OK, OK," said Berlin. "Look — come back tomorrow evening when the coaches and scouts are here."

God's humble messenger was not to be so easily dismissed.

"He told me to come NOW!"

It crossed Berlin's mind that religious freaks can be dangerous. "I'm just the plumber," he said, using his standard disclaimer. "Please come back tomorrow, when everybody is here. I'm just the guy who answers the phone."

"NO!!!" God's messenger thundered. "He said TONIGHT!"

With all the diplomacy at his command, Berlin now asked him to step outside the office while he put in a call to his bosses. The ruse worked. Berlin then called the state police. They arrived within minutes and led the young man away. He was screaming, "I am the Paraclete of Kaborgia — God's messenger and prophet! I am here to take my place as a Pittsburgh Steeler!"

The next day when Bill Nunn returned, he asked Berlin casually if anything had happened over the weekend.

Shrugging, Berlin answered, "Nothing out of the ordinary."

The best trash talker in camp one year was a huge defensive lineman from a small black college in the South. "I'm gonna send you to your grave!" he would yell as he started after a ball carrier.

He lasted two scrimmages before being cut.

"Hasn't made a single good hit since he got here, you know," explained an assistant coach. "He should go back home and become an undertaker," the coach suggested.

A Greyhound bus took the players who were cut to the railroad station or the airport. They called it "the Big Grey Dog."

A free agent from one of the black schools came to St. Vincent with a label. Our scouts had pronounced him "the fastest wide receiver in the Southwest." He was every bit of that, but nothing more. He could not catch a pass or be taught to catch one. Embarrassed by his failures, he went out one night and got drunk. When he returned to camp, he wandered out onto the practice fields instead of going to his room. All alone in the night, he just stood there, surrounded by darkness and empty real estate. Teammates implored him to end his self-imposed isolation and get some sleep. It was simply no use. So then a few of the camp assistants were told to corral him. Even drunk, he was much too fast to be caught. The coach, Bill Austin, now sent for his four fastest rookies and told them, "Go get that guy." Working in concert, they encircled him, bagged him, and dragged him back to the dormitory.

Before noon the next day he had a window seat on the Big Grey Dog.

At Texas Southern one year I scouted a football player who could jump over cars. I saw him warm up on a Volkswagen and then jump over a Cadillac. He'd take a running start from the side, lift off, and easily clear the top. Even if the car was in motion he could do this.

The gazelle was a wide receiver, with good moves and good hands. Though not very big, he was fearless. Nobody drafted him, so I suggested to Bill Nunn that here was a free agent we ought to sign. "Who knows, we might get lucky," I said. Nunn had some doubts, but went along with the idea. To get him, we outbid two other teams.

He did not have a successful training camp. Yes, he could run, and yes, he could jump for the ball. What he could not seem to do was free himself from defensive backs. As he came off the line of scrimmage, they would bump him, and then bump him some more, disrupting his patterns. No fool, he sensed that his days in camp were numbered. Once, rather pathetically, he offered to jump over my car, or even Noll's car, to attract the attention of the coaches. They would see that he was an athlete and allow him more time to develop. But the coaches had made up their minds, and soon he was climbing aboard the Big Grey Dog.

Later I heard that Norm Van Brocklin of the Atlanta Falcons had given the car jumper a tryout. For the same reason we did, I can only assume, the Dutchman let him go. I mentioned to Chuck Noll once that the kid was an exceptional athlete. Again I described how amazing it had been to see him jump over cars.

Noll answered me tersely.

"Save that kind of stuff for the halftime show," he said.

Noll had little patience with car jumpers, but would willingly take a chance on a basketball player. I know we drafted a couple and invited several others to camp. Noll also liked wrestlers. "They work low and understand leverage," he would say. Late in his coaching career, he drafted a wrestler named Carlton Haselrig from the Pitt campus in Johnstown. Haselrig developed into a good offensive lineman but had problems with alcohol and drugs. A Pitt basketball player who got away from us was Sam Clancy. The Seattle Seahawks drafted Clancy and turned him into a capable defensive end. None of the basketball players Noll or I brought to camp ever actually played a down in the NFL.

What most of them seemed to lack was the temperament needed for football. By temperament, I mean a form of toughness. I remember a tough-looking basketball player from Gannon College in Erie who worked in a gin joint up there as a bouncer. He was 6 feet 4 and 240 pounds, not quite big enough for the NBA but adequate for professional football. The day he reported to camp he had a black eye, a fat lip, and various other facial bruises, sustained the night before when he broke up a fight in the gin joint.

My heart soared. Here at last was a prospect with the smooth agility of a basketball player who would not shy away from physical contact. Could we have found a defensive end — another Sam Clancy? The way he handled himself in the drills was encouraging. He moved well and picked up his assignments easily. Then the hitting began. This was rookie camp; the big boys were not yet in practice togs. Our basketball player's stance was too high, natural for a kid of such limited experience, but he did not back down, even while getting the worst of it. He may just be OK, I thought. And then one day after lunch he came looking for me in Nunn's office, where I was talking on the phone. "*Mister* Rooney!" he exclaimed when I put down the receiver. "You gotta get me out of here! They're bouncing my ass around like a basketball. I can't see where they're coming from!" I tried to explain that this was part of the learning process. He refused to listen. I never again wasted time on a basketball player.

Two or three years after we discarded John Unitas, one of the free-agent quarterbacks in camp was a kid from the University of South Carolina whose name I forget. Like most rookie quarterbacks, he did not immediately distinguish himself. After the first week, though, he was showing a lot of arm strength and making accurate throws. Still later, he was firing pinpoint passes. He could see the whole field and put zip on the ball or lay it out softly. Everybody in camp was impressed.

But then that old Gray Dog began yelping. Cutdown time came, and we were forced to release him. My brother Dan drove the kid to the bus station, listening all the way to his cries of anguish. "How could they cut me? Did you see me in practice these last two days? How could they do it?" the unhappy victim of oversupply kept asking. I suppose he went home to a job teaching school or selling insurance. A lot of ex-jocks made a pretty good living as salesmen. But for those with real talent, like the quarterback from South Carolina, not to play football was the same thing as going into exile.

With the creation of more teams through expansion, more young players got better and longer looks from bigger coaching staffs. In fact, when the Steelers became valid contenders, a lot of our cuts were picked up by other teams. The feeling was that we had more talent than we could use. Because of Chuck Noll's reluctance to part with the aging stars of his great teams from the 1970s, sometimes we did. I directed our more promising castoffs to the New York Giants, where my friend George Young was the general manager. Once before a game between our teams, the coach of the Giants, "kidding on the square," thanked me for my help.

The Giants didn't always listen to me. When I saw that Dwaine Board, a rookie defensive end from North Carolina A. & T., was about to be cut, I hurriedly called Young and said, "Offer us something for this guy — a used jockstrap, your last pick in the draft two years from now, anything at all. He's good."

Young said, "Well, Arthur, our team has improved so much that we may not be able to find room for him. I'll talk to the coach."

"Hey, George," I persisted, "I'm telling you not to pass on this guy."

The Giants passed on him; the Forty-Niners did not. Board was a starter on their championship teams in the early 1980s and ended up as a coach.

Driving from Pittsburgh to Latrobe on treacherous Route 30 one day, I got a little past Greensburg when a torrential rainstorm came up. Unable to see very far, I slowed to a crawl. A car with a man, a woman, and two children in it passed me. It was not going unusually fast, just too fast for conditions. A few minutes later, at the bottom of a hill, I saw the wreck of this same car ahead of me. The driver had skidded into a bridge abutment. I stopped and got out. It was raining so hard that the instant I stepped onto the concrete I was soaking wet. The woman I had noticed sat motionless in the passenger seat. I saw that she had bounced off the windshield and was obviously dead. The man behind the steering wheel was unconscious, but moving a little and groaning. The kids in the back seat, boys of about 10 and eight, appeared to be in shock.

Looking me in the eye, the younger one pleaded, "Save me, save me." I said, "Stay in the car. You will be OK." With the rain still coming down, I knew that nothing would catch fire. Just then Warren Bankston, a Steeler fullback, pulled up in his car. I told him, "Go back to the gas station over the hill and ask them to call an ambulance. This is bad." As he drove away, some people came out of their houses off the highway and stood in the rain. "Call an ambulance," I shouted.

Very quickly, an ambulance arrived. Then another one. Paramedics were bending over the woman and shaking their heads. They put the injured man on a stretcher and whisked him away to a hospital. The little boy in the back seat who had begged for my help continued to follow me with his gaze. He kept repeating, "I don't want to die," and I kept assuring him he was not in any danger. He talked to me that way until he and his brother were removed from the wreck and carried off in the second ambulance.

In the paper the next day I found the story of the crash on an inside page near the back. It was short and to the point. The mother had been killed. The father and one of the sons – the older one – were seriously hurt.

Just a few years later Route 30 took the life of a red-haired Steeler rookie named Randy Fritsch, a big lineman from a school in Missouri. The minute I heard about it, I thought of the little boy who lost his mother on that same stretch of road and was looking in desperation for a guardian angel.

I was far away on a scouting trip when the Benedictines at St. Vincent held a memorial Mass for Fritsch, but somebody told me that Fats Holmes, one of the football players who were present, had received Holy Communion. Fats was not a Catholic. Later that season, he joined some Catholic teammates at a Mass in a hotel room the night before a game on the road. Being on fairly good terms with Fats, I whispered to him as we took our seats that in order to receive Communion you had to be a baptized Catholic. He nodded and said he understood. When it was time for the distribution of the Host, he did not participate. Immediately after Mass he grabbed me by the arm. "I have to talk with you," he said. Fats had been having emotional problems and I was not sure what to expect. Just a few days earlier, he had said something odd to Bill Nunn: "Please tell Artie not to forsake me." But we went to my room, and all he had to say was, "I know I am not a Catholic, and I know I am not to receive Holy Communion. But Randy Fritsch was a real nice kid and I thought if I received Communion for him that one time, God would not get mad at me."

"Ernie," I said, using his alternative nickname, "I think you are right."

One hot day as I was heading for afternoon practice, I noticed a car pulling up in the parking lot near the dormitory that housed the camp manager's office. Two young men in dark suits and conservative ties got out and went into the building. The only people I knew of who dressed so circumspectly in the summertime were Mormons doing missionary work and plainclothes law-enforcement officers. These men, some instinct told me, were not Mormons.

Bill Nunn, the camp manager, almost never was late for practice. On this day more than an hour had gone by when he appeared. He came over to where I was standing and said, "We've got trouble." Indicating one of our linemen, a big white kid, he explained, "I have to talk to that guy and to Noll."

My response was a single word: "Cops."

Nunn's response to my response was also a single word: "Yup."

I watched him go down to the practice field and walk up to Noll. They talked for five minutes or so. There were lots of hand gestures and shrugs. Noll kept taking his visor cap off and putting it back on. They parted, and Nunn spoke briefly to the lineman he had pointed out to me. A whistle blast signaled that practice was over, and the players now headed for their weightlifting stations – all except the lineman, who was trudging up the hill toward the locker rooms in Kennedy Hall. Nunn and I, meanwhile, headed for his office, walking swiftly. On the hill, I was huffing and puffing.

The men in the suits, Nunn told me, were narcotics police. They were there to pick up the player Nunn had talked to and take him away for questioning.

"In cuffs?" Nunn said he had asked them.

"That's the procedure," they replied.

"Hey, you can't do that," Nunn objected. "His teammates down there on the practice field aren't gonna like it."

"Mister Nunn," one of them said, "that's the law. If anyone tries to interfere, we can handle it."

"Are you telling me you could handle Joe Greene and the front four?" Nunn asked. "Look," he went on, "let's use our heads here. The kid you want is not a violent criminal. Let him shower and change clothes and meet you down in the parking lot. I promise you, it'll be OK."

There was much more palaver, Nunn said, including a telephone call to Dan in Pittsburgh, before the drug agents reluctantly gave in. Nunn and I watched them wait in the parking lot while the player, showered and dressed, slowly made his way to their car. He got into the back seat with one of the lawmen. The other one slid behind the steering wheel and drove off. It was all done so quietly that nobody other than Nunn, Noll, and I knew what had happened. This was Nunn at his best. He had managed the situation perfectly.

AJR never forgot a player's name. Ralph Berlin told me about a kid on the injured-reserve list who spent the whole season in the trainer's room and was there one day when the Chief came in. Berlin introduced them. Eventually the player was cut, never having appeared in a game, and he dropped out of sight. A few summers later, finding himself near Latrobe, he drove to camp for a visit with his old friend the Plumber. While they were talking, Berlin said, AJR came by. He recognized the ex-player at once and called him by name. He asked how his wife was, referring to her also by name. He then wanted to know what the fellow had been doing and listened to the answer with evident interest.

After AJR went on his way, the former player was awe-struck. "Imagine him remembering me. And I was just an injured-reserve guy!" he exclaimed.

AJR came and went unpredictably, never remaining in camp for more than a day or two. He knew what he wanted from the coaches and from everybody else, and his word was law. I remember a punter sent to camp by a friend of his, a horse trainer. AJR made it clear to me and to scout Dick Haley that the kid was to get a fair tryout. Just to be sure, he sat on a bench a short distance from the practice field and watched.

No walk-on ever received a more thorough inspection. One of the scouts snapped the ball to this guy. Haley and Nunn recorded the hang time of his punts with their stopwatches. Other scouts with notebooks stood in various locations and jotted down their impressions. One of them marked the line of scrimmage, the goal line, and the spot where the ball came down with towels. In no way were we mocking the Chief by such overkill. As Haley put it, we were just making sure that his orders were carried out.

The punter, by the way, was a dud — a humpty-dumpty.

Over time, the Chief's visits became a great deal less frequent. He would customarily drop by on his way to or from the race track or Shamrock Farm, generating excitement among the media hordes, players, and fans. "Art Rooney is here!" went the buzz. "That's him over there. Look at the cigar!" Instead of his cloth cap from Ireland, he'd be wearing a Steeler visor cap. The collar of his shirt would be open and his tie would hang loose. To protect his weak eyes, he'd be wearing sunglasses. He would pull off his cap from time to time and run a hand through his bushy white hair.

Like his football team and its training camp, he was now an institution. Taken all together, they created a way of life for the Rooneys.

The Spectator

During batting practice and infield practice before Pirate games, AJR liked to sit behind the visiting team's dugout on the third-base side of the field. The Pirates all knew him or recognized him; to most of the visiting players and management people, he was an elderly guy in a tweed cap who chewed incessantly on a cigar and seemed to have the run of the place.

AJR never met a stranger. Especially if the people around him were baseball men — scouts, ex-managers, and the like — he would start a conversation. At some point he would say, "Want a cigar?" and since most of the old ball players were addicted to tobacco, having picked up the habit of chewing it early in life, they would seldom refuse. An instructor at the Pitt dental school — I'm not sure how he knew this — told my son Art III, "Your grandfather has no enamel on his teeth. He wore it off with his chewing." No doubt the baseball guys who sat with AJR at Three Rivers Stadium observed that he could spit cigar shreds and tobacco juice with the best of them.

Something else they must have noticed was that he could talk baseball. He could talk about Honus Wagner and Pie Traynor from the old days; he could talk about Branch Rickey; he could talk about the Pittsburgh Crawfords and the Homestead Grays. He knew all the technical stuff, too. One day the New York Mets' first-base coach said to the team's manager, whoever it may have been at the time, "See that old-timer over there behind the dugout? The one with the cap and the cigar? That guy knows more about baseball than most of our players do. He knows as much about the game as we do." The manager replied, "Why, that's Art Rooney. He owns the Pittsburgh Steelers. He used to play and manage in the minor leagues."

When the Steelers were practicing, AJR would get right down on the field. He knew how important it was to stay alert. Keep two big steps away from the sideline. Never take your eye off the ball. But one day his attention wandered. He took his eye off the ball for some reason. And *wham!* A quarterback overthrew a receiver, and the receiver, Mike Collier, heading for the sideline and reaching for the ball, crashed into the Chief at full speed and sent him flying.

Instantly, a crowd of players, coaches, and functionaries surrounded their fallen leader. Trainer Ralph Berlin was kneeling at his side. Collier stood dumbfounded, not knowing what to say or do. The usually imperturbable Chuck Noll never had looked more agitated. There were cuts on AJR's face and head. Berlin applied bandages and tape. The injuries, he could see, were not serious. He helped the Chief back to his office. Mike Collier followed them, eager to apologize. AJR cut him off.

"Don't worry, Mike. I'm OK. I've been around a long time, but I forgot one of the rules.
"I took my eye off the ball."

Chapter 52

Shakedown

"The majority of you," Chuck Noll warned his squad of about one hundred on the first day of pre-season practice in 1969, "will not be with us very long. Keep your bags packed."

New brooms sweep clean, and Noll was a new broom. The 1968 Steelers, he knew, both from first-hand observation and the films we had watched together, were lacking in speed, "athleticism," and "football intelligence." There would be a complete overhaul, it was clear. "We need better athletes to fit the schemes I intend to put in," he kept telling me.

If you spend much time around coaches, you'll hear them talk about their "schemes" — football jargon for the various components of a particular offense or defense. Noll had three teachers – Hall of Famers Paul Brown, Sid Gillman, and Don Shula; mixing and matching, he took the schemes they had taught him and tinkered with them, refined them, added things, subtracted things. What emerged was a system of his own.

To make it work required a certain kind of player. He wanted top athletes who were smart. By definition, a top athlete is strong, tough, coordinated, and fast. For Noll's purposes, you could be a top athlete with only a moderate amount of football intelligence, or you could be a very smart player with moderate athletic ability, and make the team. If you were unacceptably deficient in either or both of those qualities, he immediately crossed you off his list.

Historically, up to then, our principal sources of talent had been the major conferences and the major independents. But from everything I had seen I knew that more top athletes were to be found somewhere else — in the small black colleges of the South. And though the players from these colleges may not have been as thoroughly tutored as the white players in the Big Ten, Pac Ten, Southeast Conference, and so on, where integration was just getting into gear, they were teachable.

So I brought them to camp by the carload, and Noll welcomed them. His prejudices — and they were keenly felt — had nothing to do with skin color. "I'm prejudiced against bad athletes," he said to the scouts. "I'm prejudiced against slow guys, dumb guys, bad actors. Get us people who can think on their feet, who are tough, strong, fast, people of good character, and I will teach them. I will teach them."

And teach them he did. His practices were not brutal, in the Bill Austin tradition, but St. Vincent College never had seen their like for intensity. There in the foothills of the Allegheny Mountains, where I had lost a front tooth in the service of the St. Vincent Bearcats, the black players more than held their own.

One of the white guys from the South, looking around, exclaimed, "Have you ever seen so many blacks?"

From the first day it was evident that Noll played no favorites, black or white. Clendon Thomas, who was white, had been an All-American halfback at Oklahoma, one of the quick, slashing runners coached by Bud Wilkinson in the 1950s. AJR liked him a lot, liked him for his personality and attitude and liked him because they could talk about horses. To Dad it was all the same that Thomas raced quarter horses, not thoroughbreds. He had come to the Steelers in 1962 from the Los Angeles Rams, and Buddy Parker asked him to make the switch from running back to defensive back. The rangy Southwestern type, Thomas was not ruggedly built and had taken a pounding as a ball carrier. He changed positions uncomplainingly and continued to give his all for the team. When tight ends were in short supply, he played some tight end. Nature had not designed him to be a tight end, but he made the adjustment willingly.

By 1969, when Noll arrived, Thomas had been in the league for eleven seasons. On our first day at St. Vincent, unaware that different rules were now in effect, he set out for the practice field wearing a railroad engineer's cap. It was his trademark — like Billy Johnson's white shoes and Harp Vaughan's headband, a sartorial touch that set him apart. Very quickly, he learned that Noll made no distinction between eleven-year veterans and rookies.

Stopping him before he had taken a dozen steps, Noll said, "We all wear the same uniforms here, Clendon."

I could hardly believe what I was hearing. I said, "Hey, Coach — this is one of the good guys. Cut him a break." But I said it to myself.

I realized later that Noll was setting a tone. All of our players were starting out from scratch. Veterans, as well as newcomers, had to prove they belonged on the team. And Thomas, despite his skills and versatility and know-how, no longer could get a jump on the ball, no longer had the speed to cover the younger, faster, more agile wide receivers. I am unable to tell you what Thomas may have been thinking when Noll warned his players that most of them would not be around long, but before we left camp he was gone.

A defensive back still in his prime, Marv Woodson, was another short-term guy. In 1964, Woodson had been a high draft choice. In 1968, he played in the Pro Bowl. None of this helped him to master Noll's defensive schemes, and he suddenly found himself in New Orleans.

His departure, like that of Thomas, was uncontroversial. Thomas, the fans knew, could not last forever, and they never had thought of Woodson as a star. It was Paul Martha's failure to please Noll that grieved and disappointed them.

Martha was a home-town hero, a celebrated high school player from Wilkinsburg who became an All-American halfback on a 9-1 Pitt team famous for missing out on a bowl bid. The reason was simply that on November 22, 1963, an assassin in Dallas murdered a president of the United States. Anticipating an invitation from the Orange Bowl, Pitt had turned down the not quite as prestigious Gator Bowl and maybe some other bowls too. A game on Saturday, November 23, remained; it was with Penn State, and Pitt was heavily favored. Then the rifle shot that killed John F. Kennedy transfixed the entire country. All college games on November 23, except a few in the South, were postponed. It was two whole weeks before Pitt and Penn State could reschedule their game, and the Orange Bowl, meanwhile, had settled on Auburn and Nebraska. In refusing to take it for granted that Pitt would beat old rival Penn State, the Orange Bowl was only being prudent. Pitt won the game, all right, but by the ultra-thin margin of an extra point.

I throw that in as an almost forgotten bit of Pittsburgh lore. What I started out to tell you was that we drafted Paul Martha in 1964. At Pitt, he had been a breakaway runner, but running backs in the NFL had to carry enough weight to absorb punishment, and Martha was as sleek as a greyhound. So for Buddy Parker he caught passes and returned punts, or tried to. Alas, his hands were made of stone, and he ended up playing defensive back.

In the 1960s I subscribed to the theory that superior college running backs who were too light or too slow to be great athletes could make it on defense in the NFL. Chuck Noll changed my thinking. He convinced me that you needed great athletes on defense to stop the great athletes on offense. Paul Martha had played defense as well as offense at Pitt and was certainly not without athletic ability. He was fast and he was smart; he got to the right spots on the field. But Noll, after one season, gave up on him, explaining, "He's not a tough enough hitter."

When we traded Martha to Denver, AJR, along with most of our fans, was sorry to see him go. An unmistakable rapport had developed between them, partly because of their Pittsburgh heritage. AJR called him "The Star." In football matters, however, Chuck Noll made the decisions, and AJR adhered to his policy of rigid non-interference.

Noll's assertion that Martha did not have the will to make shattering tackles was not for publication, but, somehow, Martha got wind of it. The slur was uppermost in his mind when Denver came to Pittsburgh in 1971 for a late-season game with the Steelers. On that day, Martha hit everything in black and gold that moved. He was the second coming of Jack Butler, and, due in no small part to his ferocity; Denver beat us, 22-10.

As time went on, the Steelers acquired defensive backs with the athletic traits Noll demanded — defensive backs like Mel Blount, Glen Edwards, and Donnie Shell from the small black colleges in the South. Martha had his moments both on the field, with Denver, and off the field. He married the daughter of the chairman of U.S. Steel, obtained a law degree, and was president for a while of the Pittsburgh team in the National Hockey League, the Penguins.

I don't think he ever forgave Noll, but his friendship with AJR ended only when the Chief passed away.

Senior Citizen

At Noll's first training camp, one of the few returning Steelers whose efforts seemed to satisfy him was Ben McGee. Five years earlier, before the start of the 1965 season, McGee had played an unwitting role in the philosophical clash between Buddy Parker and Dan Rooney that culminated in Buddy's resignation.

McGee was a 6-foot-4, 255-pound defensive end from Jackson State, in Mississippi, this at a time when weight training, steroids, growth hormones, advances in nutrition, and various other factors had not yet produced a race of behemoth linemen. With help from assistant coach Ernie Stautner, he had shown considerable promise in 1964 as a rookie. But Parker wanted to trade him, along with a draft choice, for two more experienced players.

Dan (as I have written before) counseled patience, telling Parker, "We can't continue to mortgage our future by trading away young guys for players nearing the end of their usefulness." The upshot of it was that McGee stayed with the team and Parker left, his departure unmourned by either Dan or AJR. Noll was McGee's fourth coach, and his last. He played through the 1972 season, in which the Steelers won more games than they lost for the first time since 1963.

A holdover running back who looked "interesting" to Noll was Don Shy. He was big, strong, and fast, and could catch passes. Shy had come to us well schooled in the pro sets used by Don Coryell at San Diego State, but in his first two seasons he was inconsistent. Though capable of making big plays, he lacked the steadiness a coach likes to see.

I had urged Bill Austin to draft Shy despite the reservations expressed by Ken Stilley. The fact that Shy had been a track man prejudiced Stilley against him. "Beware of those guys, they're in the training room all the time," he warned me. Then he added, "You can't coach heart."

"What about Bob Hayes?" I asked. "I've never heard anyone say that Bob Hayes doesn't have heart." Hayes, of the Dallas Cowboys, had won the 100-meter dash in the 1964 Olympic games, lowering the record to ten seconds flat, and yet there were few wide receivers as productive or as durable.

"Hayes is an exception," Stilley argued. "He's a football player first and a track man second."

Noll said, "We're looking for exceptions," and went on thinking — at least for a while — that we had one in Shy. Upon closer inspection, he changed his mind, and Shy spent the season in New Orleans. His accomplishments there were so minuscule that the Saints got rid of him, too.

Noll initially misjudged Shy, overestimating him (as we both did), and he initially misjudged Dick Hoak for the opposite reason.

Hoak had been one of our running backs — usually our primary running back — since 1961. He was dark and somber-looking, short, chunky, and slow. Every summer in training camp, he had fought off competition for his job. "We know what you can do," the coaches would tell him. "Now we're trying to see what these other guys can do."

"These other guys" were rookies like Don Shy — younger, bigger, faster, and flashier than Hoak. They would come to camp, get their opportunity, and fail. By the time the season started, unspectacular, reliable Dick Hoak would be the first-string running back. In his eighth season, 1968, he was the Steelers' old man — the player with more seniority than anyone else on the team.

And the stereotype he never could shake — "too small, too slow" — had become a burden. Normally, Hoak kept his mouth shut, but finally one day he spoke out. To a reporter, he said, "I'm tired of this stuff about not being big enough, not being fast enough. A lot of guys who can run fast don't know where they're going. You have to get to the hole in the first four or five steps, and then it's not how fast you run, it's what you do when you're there."

He was making what, for him, was a speech. "That's the big thing about some of these kids coming out of college," he went on. "They're not that smart. It takes a little brains to play this game. Plays are changed at the line of scrimmage, you have to recognize different defenses. If you don't know where you're going, it doesn't do you any good. In a football game, you never run in a straight line. You never run a forty-yard dash, and usually you're following a guard. On most of your plays you have a guard pulling out in front of you, and if you go full speed it doesn't help you."

At full speed or half speed, Hoak always knew where he was going. Hoak always got to the hole in four or five steps, and it was always the right hole. We had drafted him out of Penn State, where Fran Rogel once played, and in some ways he ran like Rogel, with tenacity and a willingness to sacrifice his body, scratching for tough yards when they were needed. But, slow or not, surprisingly, he could make the occasional breakaway run – seventy-seven yards against the Saints, eighty yards against the Giants, seventy-six against the Eagles, seventy-six against the Forty-Niners.

It was not Hoak's fault that penalties wiped out all of those runs except the one against the Saints. On the way to the goal line, Hoak said after the New Orleans game, he resisted an impulse to turn around and look for a yellow flag.

Hoak had other credentials more highly esteemed running backs did not. He could block, he could pass — at Penn State, he had been a quarterback — and he could catch the ball. So why did he have to keep proving himself, year after year — with Parker, with Nixon, with Austin, and now with Noll?

"I know you like him, and he's a good player," Chuck told me on the second or third day in camp, "but he's far from a great player." And then he said something that put my nose out of joint. He suggested I go to the next Pro Bowl game "and see what a great running back looks like."

Come again? I hadn't said that Hoak was a "great" running back. In the NFL at the time, there were not too many of those. But I knew he was better than Noll gave him credit for being, and now I seemed to hear our coach imply that I did not have the know-how to recognize a great back, never having seen one.

Well now. I had been a scout for five years and had a fairly high opinion of my ability to assess and evaluate. I had seen Jim Brown, an old teammate of Noll's in Cleveland. Most people, I thought, would agree with me that Jim Brown had been a great back. Besides, didn't Noll realize that Hoak himself had played in the Pro Bowl the previous January? That he was one of our all-time statistical leaders, right up there with John Henry Johnson, a Hall of Famer (and another great back I had seen)?

I never did get to the Pro Bowl. Kay, I am sure, would have welcomed a winter-time trip to the West Coast, but my work kept me busy. Meanwhile, Hoak's good showing in camp silenced Noll on the subject of who was and who wasn't a great running back. Hoak played two years for Chuck and then retired — voluntarily. He had run out of gas, he explained.

Lindley Military Academy, in Wheeling, West Virginia, hired him as its coach in 1971. From AJR down to Jack Hart, the equipment manager, everybody in our organization hoped that Noll would bring him back to fill the next vacancy on his own staff. Never once did Noll acknowledge that he might. But when rumors of an offer to Hoak from Pitt began to circulate, Noll immediately called him. They quickly came to terms without haggling, and more than three decades later Hoak was still with the Steelers, an assistant to Bill Cowher.

He had seen Buddy Parker go berserk, Mike Nixon and Bill Austin flop, Noll briefly flounder and then win four Super Bowls, Bill Cowher win a Super Bowl, AJR become a demi-god, and Steeler football arouse passions that in 1961, his first year with the team, were beyond imagining. Through it all, he remained as unobtrusive as ever, a model of dedication and efficiency.

The Agitator

Aplayer whose days were numbered when Noll took over as coach was Roy Jefferson, his best wide receiver. "We aren't going to have any troublemakers on this team," Noll had promised AJR, and Jefferson made trouble. Though never quite openly insubordinate, he was a "tester" — assistant trainer Bob Milie's term for a player who tested his coaches. Jefferson tested Bill Austin, Noll's predecessor, by asking sarcastic questions in team meetings; he tested him by demanding water, ice, and wet towels on the practice field when he saw that teammates were suffering from the heat. Here, I believe, Jefferson had a point. Austin, like a majority of coaches in the 1960s, thought of dehydration as a training aid; Noll came to realize how dangerous it was. But Jefferson, right or wrong, could be a pain in the ass with his yelling and screaming and carrying on.

He had come to the Steelers in 1965 as Buddy Parker's top draft choice, a number two pick from the University of Utah. Normally, Parker traded his top choices for over-the-hill veterans. What predisposed him in Jefferson's favor was the strong recommendation of Fido Murphy, our West Coast scout. For some reason Parker had great confidence in Murphy, and certainly Fido did not overestimate Jefferson. The kid's physique — his nickname was "Bird Legs" — belied his strength. He was tall and fast, with exceptional body control, and he ran the kind of routes that caused directional problems for cornerbacks. After Jefferson had been in the league for a while, Ray May, a teammate, described how he came off the line. "Man, he's slithering like a snake. Everything's moving — his arms, his feet, his head, his legs. He's running in seventeen different directions," May told a writer for *Sport* magazine, Tom Dowling.

That Jefferson had gone to college in Utah was strange. When you think of Utah, you think of conservative white Mormons. Jefferson was a black guy from inner-city Los Angeles — an anti-establishment black guy. I'm not sure how he adjusted out there in Salt Lake City. With the Steelers, he was always an agitator.

Parker, who accepted blacks grudgingly, did not have much inter-action with Jefferson. The year we drafted him, Parker resigned before the start of the season. I don't recall any problems with Mike Nixon but there was friction all the time between Jefferson and Austin. Given Austin's facade of toughness, and his blunt way of dealing with black players, it surprised me how much he put up with from Jefferson.

Noll sort of bided his time. Jefferson, he knew, was not a good influence on Mean Joe Greene and the other young blacks. Still he did not intervene. At St. Vincent, Jefferson flouted minor regulations — parking his car in a no-parking zone (Noll and Dan scrupulously obeyed the rule), tossing aside his helmet during practice. In meetings, as he had with Austin, he tried to play word and mind games with Noll, coming out second-best more often than not. And then in Montreal, before an exhibition game, he went too far. Noll fined and suspended him for missing curfew.

Dispassionately, Jefferson agreed that justice had been served. It was not, however, the end of his complaining. The season got under way, and he said the quarterbacks never threw him the ball "when it meant something." From her seat in Pitt Stadium, his wife kept statistics. They demonstrated, Jefferson said, that the quarterbacks passed to him "mostly in the second half, when we've already lost the game."

After winning their opener from Detroit, the Steelers were losing every week. Losing teams are not happy teams, and Jefferson burned with discontent. When he "did something good," the fans, the press, and the coaches ignored him. When he "messed up" — dropped a pass — he was castigated. Of course he saw prejudice as the reason.

At the end of the season, Noll traded him to Baltimore for two fourth-round draft choices.

Objectively, it made no sense. We were giving Jefferson away. But Noll — and Dan, too — wanted nothing more to do with the guy. "It's not a black-white thing," Dan told *Sport* magazine. "But with Roy around, there would have been confusion. Uncertainty. Chaos."

There was no connection, Dan said, between the trade and Jefferson's role as a militant leader in the player strike the previous July. The underlying problem, he thought, was pretty clear: "Roy wants to be in the limelight. He wanted to be the Steeler superstar. And the truth is, if we had kept Roy, he wouldn't have been number one. Joe Greene and Terry Bradshaw" — the Steelers had just drafted him

— "were going to get more publicity than Roy. We talked about it, and Roy was not pleased with the lack of attention he was getting in the press."

Whatever. The end result was that Jefferson went to the Colts, and in 1970 he caught fewer passes than he'd caught the year before with the Steelers. The explanation was that everybody double-covered him, helping the other receivers. The Colts won their division title, and Jefferson caught passes when it meant something, twice for winning touchdowns with time running out. It didn't hurt a bit that Johnny Unitas was throwing to him.

After the 1970 season, Baltimore traded Jefferson to the Redskins. He was with them until he retired, in 1977, and Washington never failed to make the playoffs during his time there. In 1972 they got as far as the Super Bowl, losing to Miami.

The Steelers by then, without Roy Jefferson, had been to two Super Bowls themselves — and had won both of them.

Trip Ticket to Texas

Right from the start, my choice of an occupation baffled Kay. The way it looked to her, I was Don Quixote chasing windmills, but now I had the guidelines I needed. Chuck Noll's specifications made it easy to identify the particular type of player he wanted, and Blesto's scouting reports were my compass and my map.

They led me to places like North Texas State, where in 1969 we had found our number one draft choice, Mean Joe Greene. The head coach there was Rod Rust, formerly an assistant at Stanford and destined to join Noll's staff toward the end of the 1980s. He could not have been more helpful to the Steelers and to Art Rooney, Jr. Other coaches gave us access to game films. Rust gave unlimited access. He allowed us to meet and talk with his players.

North Texas State under Rust was one of the first Southwestern schools to break the color line in football, hastening the move toward integration. From the Rio Grande Valley to the cane brakes of Georgia to the Florida Everglades, a vast pool of talent had been going untapped. North Texas State's success was helping to change all that. Coaches and administrators were facing a new reality. In order to stay competitive, you hauled down the Confederate flag.

Tipped off by Blesto, I knew that, for NFL scouts, North Texas State was a happy hunting ground. In the 1968 lineup, there were others beside Greene: defensive back Charles Beatty, wide receiver Ron Shanklin, and defensive end Cedric Hardman, to name three. All were black; all were prospects who couldn't miss. In 1969 we drafted Beatty along with Greene. In 1970 we drafted Shanklin. We'd have drafted Hardman, too, if the Forty-Niners hadn't taken him first. North Texas by then was no longer our little secret.

On my occasional visits, Rod Rust always put me at ease. Everywhere I went I presented myself as a working stiff, and not as the pampered son of the man who owned the Pittsburgh Steelers. At North Texas this was no problem. I had the run of the place, thanks to Rust. I could roll up my sleeves and watch game films with the players — let people see that I knew what I was doing. Alas, there came a day when my self-assurance betrayed me.

A player I was looking for did not seem to be in the film. Surrounded by members of the squad, I decided to show off my knowledge. "Where's so-and-so?" I demanded. For an answer, I heard a ripple of nervous laughter. Then a voice drawled, "Have you really been scouting him?" "Sure I've been scouting him," I replied. "Hey! We've got some good reports on that guy." More laughter — laughter with an undercurrent of strain. In the darkened room, I could not distinguish faces. I asked, "Is there something wrong?"

"No, sir. Not at all."

Those Texas kids, black or white, always said "yes, sir" and "no, sir."

I let it drop for a while. The film kept rolling, and I mentioned a good play by one of the guards. It prompted a humorous jibe or two from his teammates. And then I asked again, "Where's so-and-so? I can't find him."

Silence, broken only by a cough.

"Is he still on the team?" I persisted.

"No," someone finally said. "Just before the start of the season, he was killed in an automobile accident."

I had my answer.

After that, for what seemed like a long time, the only sound was the whirring of the movie projector. Then, with muttered excuses, the players started to leave, scraping their chairs. "Gotta go see the trainer," the first guy remembered. Another said quickly, "Me, too." A third one bailed out with, "Time for my class." And there were those who said nothing at all. In a matter of minutes, I found myself alone, staring blankly at the screen.

The embarrassment of that moment comes back to me now whenever I think of North Texas.

Chapter 53

Growing Pains II

September, 1970. A new season, a new stadium, a new quarterback. A new feeling of hope for the fans. Filled to the top row, the stadium dazzled them. Initially, so did the quarterback. Their satisfaction with the stadium never waned; but soon they were disillusioned with the quarterback.

In every Steeler crowd, maybe half of the ticket buyers are men who played football in high school. One and all, they consider themselves expert appraisers of talent. And they perceived after two or three games that Terry Bradshaw, his strong arm and quick release notwithstanding, simply wouldn't do.

By the time we were 0-3, the verdict was in, and it was scathing. The talk was the same wherever you went. "Yeah, he's big and he can move, but he doesn't see the field. He doesn't know where his receivers are. He doesn't know where the defensive backs are" ... "Chuck Noll can't allow that guy to keep on calling his own plays. He doesn't understand the offense" ... "What do you mean, calling his own plays? The center calls the plays. Ray Mansfield has to do it because Bradshaw's too dumb." ... "That country bumpkin is killing the offense, and he's killing the defense, too, with all those interceptions."

There wasn't any letup, and it only got meaner. And though Bradshaw came across in his lighter moments as a classic self-confident extrovert, he was not cut out to take criticism. This unflawed physical specimen with the gleaming blond hair and square-jawed good looks was insecure. He wanted to be loved. He wanted to be admired. Instead, he was booed and reviled. The coaches in the stands called him a redneck ... a hick. He was not one of our own, like Terry Hanratty. The minute he opened his mouth, you could tell. Guys who said "yinz" and "dahntahn" made fun of his locutions and his accent.

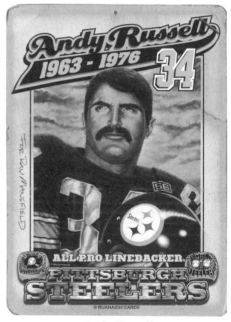

Andy Russell
(Drawing by Denny Karchner)

The hostility toward him bewildered Bradshaw. He was not unpopular with his teammates, but none were close friends or companions. He did have a girlfriend, Melissa Babish, a minor celebrity in Pittsburgh. Just a year or two before meeting Bradshaw, she had reigned as Miss Teen-Age America. In short order, they were married. It didn't last. From the Chief came some fatherly counsel. "Terry," he said, "marry a girl from Shreveport. A farm girl. A girl who milks the cows. A girl who believes you're the most important man in the world."

"And you are," the Chief always added. When all of Western Pennsylvania seemed to be down on Bradshaw, AJR would remind him that "everyone has bad days. I do," he said. "Your coach does. Babe Ruth struck out a lot. Man 0' War lost a race. Jack Dempsey lost a couple of fights. Forget those yeggs who are booing you. They don't know how lucky they are to have you in Pittsburgh. You're a once-in-a-lifetime player."

Bradshaw's staunchest supporters were Kass, Aunt Alice, and Mary the maid. He was often a dinner guest at 940 North Lincoln Avenue. No one could say a word against him. Especially after the breakup of his marriage, he may have needed all the solace he could get.

Terry Hanratty predicted — correctly — that Bradshaw would be married "at least three times." Over the next thirty years or so, he was married three times and divorced three times. His second wife, Jo Jo Starbuck, was a figure skater, the star attraction of the Ice Capades.

Certainly Bradshaw's best friend in the Steeler organization was AJR. They talked about football; they talked about boxing; they talked about horses. Bradshaw shared a passion for quarter horses with Mel Blount, who was also from Louisiana. As soon as they could afford it, each of them had a stable of sorts. AJR invited Bradshaw to Shamrock Farm and gave him a thoroughbred horse for breeding purposes.

Like many others, including even AJR, Bradshaw could not communicate easily with Noll. The coach's extracurricular interests — music, wine, food — were too sophisticated for Terry. Noll dismissed the allegations that Bradshaw was "dumb," but considered him "flighty." AJR believed, as I did, that he suffered from low self-esteem. Looking back, I wonder how I could have felt sorry for him, considering all the things he accomplished.

Bradshaw liked cigars, and he conducted bold raids on AJR's well-stocked brown humidor, following my example. The humidor sat on the front edge of the Chief's desk. When the Chief was out of the office, Bradshaw would walk past a dismayed Mary Regan and fill his shirt pocket with the choicest Havanas. Mary's boss knew what both of us were doing, but did not make an issue of it. "Once in a while is OK," he allowed me to understand. Placed beside the humidor was a stainless steel sculpture of two upraised hands with the fingers intertwined, an award from a human-rights organization. It stood about twelve inches high. One day Bradshaw stopped for a moment as he started to leave with his cigars. He took a crisp dollar bill from his wallet and tucked it into a space between the fingers.

The dollar bill, or a dollar bill, stayed there for years. Every time somebody filched it, AJR would insert a new bill of his own. When people asked why those metal hands were holding that dollar bill, he would eagerly tell them the story.

Getting to Know Chuck

Even though our cultural interests overlapped to some extent, encompassing music, theater, and the fine arts, I can think of only one non-football conversation I had with Chuck Noll. And I'd just as soon forget it.

Noll, like almost every other coach I have known, was conservative politically. I considered him slightly to the right of Attila the Hun. On a day in 1971, when the Vietnam War was still very much in the news, he made an unexpected foray into my office while Bill Nunn, Dick Haley, and I were going over scouting reports with our charts spread out on the floor. He appeared to be highly agitated, and since the draft was coming up in a week or two I wondered if we had somehow displeased him. But no. His concern was about the massacre at My Lai — not the massacre itself, but the public's reaction to it.

Three years earlier, American soldiers under the command of Lieutenant William Calley had slaughtered more than five hundred noncombatants suspected of having ties of some kind to the Viet Cong. They were mostly old men, women, and children, and now Seymour Hersh, the great investigative reporter, had broken the story. It was all over the airwaves, all over the newspapers, and Noll was disturbed. He thought that Calley and his men were being maligned. "You have to see their side of it," he argued. "Strange things happen when you're at war. In the stress of the moment, any of us might be capable of doing what Calley did. I know I could have done it myself."

I was shocked. I said, "Bullshit! You're too good a person to shoot down women and children and unarmed old men in cold blood. I don't believe you."

Without replying, he turned to leave. Apparently I had offended him. Before reaching the door, he stopped and called back, "If that's what you think, you don't know me very well."

"Like hell I don't know you!" I shouted. Now we had both lost our tempers. He started for the door again, and I yelled, "Watch out! You're stepping on our charts!"

He instantly countered with, "No, I'm NOT stepping on your charts!" It was beginning to sound like a playground squabble. I don't know what kept me from saying, "You are too!"

Later, I reflected, "Why did he get mad? I was showing him esteem. No way in the world he could have shot those helpless villagers."

I suppose that war stirs the passions like nothing else, not even football. It makes us say ridiculous things.

Tempest in a Teapot

The 1971 draft was our first in Three Rivers Stadium. Nothing about the draft room itself was different. Same wall charts, same easels, same T-shaped table, same telephone bank, same swivel chairs. The most important chart was our list of the 220 best players regardless of position.

There was one innovation. Our accountants had informed us that it would actually be less expensive to leave the telephones connected the year round than to keep installing them for the draft and taking them out afterwards. Tony Parisi, our street-smart equipment manager, foresaw trouble with the new arrangement: everyone from the coaches and players to the go-fers and janitors would be placing long-distance calls at the team's expense, he predicted. I forget who came up with the solution, but it was really quite simple. Between drafts, we would hide the phones — there were four or five — in the space between the layers of the ceiling. It worked well over the years except for one glitch. At times the draft room served as a meeting room, and it had not occurred to us that people are apt to dial wrong numbers. It happened more than once, inopportunely, when Chuck Noll was addressing his squad. To the mystification of the players, the unseen phone in the ceiling would ring for minutes at a time.

Once during a draft at the Roosevelt Hotel we used a magic marker to cross out the names of the players who'd been selected and were horrified to discover that the lines had bled through the chart and onto the wall. Never again, I vowed, but after the first draft in our beautiful new home, sure enough: there were black, red, and gold ink marks on the wall. Parisi and his helpers were able to cover them up with paints that blended in with the wall paint.

We had an expensive gray rug in the draft room. To protect it from cigar and cigarette smokers, Parisi placed ash trays everywhere and would personally pick butts off the floor. His tender loving care went for nothing when, as AJR had warned the stadium architects, the flood waters came. In the spring of 1972 they invaded our magnificent offices and destroyed every rug we owned.

The area for the scouts at Three Rivers consisted of a reception room and work station for our secretary, Rhoda Duffy, a room for Bill Nunn and later Dick Haley, and my T-shaped office. After the boiler room I inhabited at the Roosevelt Hotel, I felt that I was now in the Taj Mahal. Behind my desk and chair, next to the bookcases filled with scouting reports, was a pair of big, square boards. On one, I had the names of all the players in the NFL, listed alphabetically. On the other, they were grouped by position, listed as we rated them in the order of their ability. Stuck to the board magnetically, these names were moveable.

Draw curtains covered this board when it was not in use, but eventually I started leaving the curtains open. The players who came to my office wouldn't look at the board anyway, I reasoned. And then one morning a young linebacker stopped by for a chat. During our short talk he did not, as far as I could tell, even glance at the board. Getting up to depart, though, he casually reached out to his own name — it was close to the top but slightly askew - and straightened it. As he left, he gave me a quick little smile.

On or off the football field, nothing escaped Jack Ham.

From then on I made sure that the curtains were drawn.

In the scouts' office were two blackboards, one on each of the side walls, and a white screen on the wall at the far end. We wrote on the white screen with dust-off magic markers except when we absent-mindedly used regular magic markers. The dust-off markers left no trace on the wall behind the screen; the regular markers created a mess. It was Mrs. Duffy's job — and she hated it — to find a solvent that removed the permanent ink.

Our unintentional vandalism greatly disturbed AJR, who was proud of his new domain. I had a habit of dropping cigar ashes on the rug, and he constantly took me to task for my carelessness. Worse yet, I would rest a burning cigar on the edge of my vast, gorgeous desk, with its blond wood top, and forget about it while taking a phone call. Another of my sins during a phone conversation was to write the names of prospects on the desk top instead of using a scratch pad.

"Who do you think you are, anyway?" the Chief would roar. "Cigar burns! Scribbling on the desk! Ashes on the rug!" He never called me a slob or an ignoramus, but that is what he was thinking, I knew. He would end these tirades with what I felt was a non-sequitur — "Get a haircut!" maybe, or "Go on a diet!"

I've been told that years after I left the organization the names and the cigar burns were still on that desk. Somehow, my conscience remains clear. Any damage I may have done, it seems to me, was an unfortunate but forgivable side effect of the zeal with which I went about my work.

When I reported what was going on to Kay, she bought me an enormous ash tray for the desk. Dan, who considered himself the guardian of our office furniture, was displeased with my carelessness but at the same time consoling. "A tempest in a teapot," he told me. "Remember, the Chief always gives us hell about the little things, but cuts us a break on our major crimes."

'What About Ham?'

The Steelers' 5-9 record in Noll's second season gave us the eighth first-round pick in the 1971 draft. My only scout was Bill Nunn, a full-time employee by now. Necessarily, I looked at all the prospects myself and relied a great deal on Blesto. After the NFL season, our coaches got involved, evaluating prospects at the all-star games and on film. This was around the time when I came in off the road and went to Blesto meetings with Noll. Between Christmas and New Year's, working both at home and in the office, I reorganized the scouting reports and studied game films endlessly.

We drafted at the end of January back then, which for most teams was too soon after the season. Physically and mentally exhausted, the assistant coaches who doubled as scouts had a hard time refocusing. Not so Chuck Noll. For him, the transition was seamless. He never preached to his assistants, but would tell them, "The more you can do for the club ..." and let the sentence tail off. As his coaches understood, he was saying, "Get off your asses and do something useful." Noll led by example. With the head man so fully energized, how could the others lay back?

I had always felt driven, but I know that because of Noll I felt more driven than usual. Bill Nunn and Jack Butler seemed to share this attitude, and Butler's intensity rubbed off on his scouts. In my opinion, we were the only team getting its money's worth out of Blesto. I interviewed the scouts and I interviewed Butler. Every piece of paper that came across my desk from Blesto I scrutinized thoroughly. I made a pest of myself, badgering the scouts for more and more information. "I'm a slow learner," I'd say. "Would you do me a favor and discuss that report with me again? Can I take you to dinner tonight and talk about some of these players?" I would ask to spend a few days on the road with a scout. When we looked at a player, I'd say, "Would you take this kid on the first or second round if your job depended on whether or not he was worth it?" I became a pain in the neck to everyone everywhere, but the Blesto people didn't mind. "Artie," they would tell me, "you're the only personnel guy who's listening to us."

Mort Sharnik, the *Sports Illustrated* writer, thought I was "on a quest." "You have a passion," he said. Actually, I was afraid of being typed as the boss's lazy son. I dreaded failure. For years we had been "the same old Steelers." Scouting was a low-priority job. Uncle Jim could have handled it — his football résumé was much more impressive than mine — but early in life he had formed an antipathy to work. Ray Byrne, the Digger, acquired his expertise from magazines and newspapers. Byrne was an undertaker, a bookkeeper, and an organizer, but not a scout. With just one assistant, a dedicated football man beating the bushes, Byrne could have made a difference. But he and Uncle Jim belonged to the past. Now, thanks to Mom and Dad, it was my turn.

Just before our first draft meeting in my still new office, Chuck Noll buttonholed me.

"Artie," he said, "my coaches and I have a big request to make."

"Sure, Coach. What can I do for you?"

"Please limit yourself to just one of those big green baseball-bat cigars a day."

He was serious. So was I.

"I'll try, Coach," I promised. "I'll try."

And I did.

Our meetings always began the same way. Alternating, the assistant coaches, Nunn, and I would read the scouting reports aloud. Noll did not read, but took notes. One thing I never failed to notice was the difference in reading skills the coaches exhibited. Some coaches read the reports very well; others read poorly, even the former school teachers among them. As the years went by, and we hired more coaches and scouts, I proposed a change in the routine. Let the scouts do all the reading, I suggested to Noll. And let the coaches take notes, but only about the players they would be supervising. If a scout read a report about a cornerback, for example, only the defensive backfield coach would take notes. The other coaches need not even be in the room. The offensive line coach could make better use of his time watching films of offensive linemen; the backfield coach could make better use of his time watching films of halfbacks and fullbacks. And so on.

Noll did not like this idea. He said, "We all have to be part of this as a team." I agreed in principle but said I had observed during these meetings that some of the coaches always seemed to lose interest unless they were directly engaged. Their minds tended to wander.

Flaring up, Noll demanded, "Just who is not paying attention?"

"Hey, I'm not a squealer," I said. "But look around."

There the matter rested until the following year. We covered only two positions a day at our draft meetings, one in the morning and one in the afternoon, which meant some hours of near boredom for certain coaches. In the middle of one report, a coach who was not a bad guy and no dumbbell started nodding. Soon his chin dropped down to his chest. He had dozed off for all of us to see. Over the next couple of days, the same thing happened again and again. He would catch himself, stay alert for a few minutes, and then stop fighting it. To the horror of his colleagues, he started to snore. No one laughed. We were all too embarrassed. Noll, characteristically poker-faced, kept his eyes on the scout who was reading the report. At last I nudged Rip Van Winkle, waking him up, and said, "Please don't sleep on my time."

I was to learn shortly afterward that the coach had narcolepsy; he would fall into deep slumber at any time of the day without warning. Properly medicated, he was soon back to normal. Meanwhile, he had settled the issue between Noll and me. "Come to think of it," Noll admitted, my suggestion made sense. Henceforth only the coaches whose positions were being discussed would attend the draft meetings.

Noll himself missed a full week of meetings in 1971. Late on the morning of the first day, Dan walked into the room and asked if he could see Chuck alone. While they were gone, we continued, at Chuck's request, with our work. He returned after fifteen minutes or so. "I've received some bad news," he announced. "My father has just passed away." There was silence, and then an outpouring of murmured condolences. "I'll be leaving right away for Cleveland," Noll said. "Just go on without me."

I considered it a tribute to Noll that his absence did not set us back. The meetings were conducted as smoothly as if he had been on the scene: no short cuts; no joviality. When he was with us again, Nunn and I brought him up to date, and now we were ready for draft day.

Anticipating, I had written the name of Frank Lewis, a wide receiver from Grambling, on the blackboard and underlined it three times. Both Nunn and I had seen him on film and in games. We liked him a lot, and so did the Blesto scouts. He was very fast, with stop-and-go movement besides. He could see the whole field and knew the location of everybody on it. We had talked with Eddie Robinson, Grambling's long-time legendary coach, and everything he told us was positive. Lewis, he said, was a nice kid, a quick learner, easy to coach. These traits, along with his athleticism, made him exactly the kind of player Noll wanted. Grambling was not far from Shreveport, Terry Bradshaw's home town, and I had visions of Lewis and Bradshaw working out together in the off-season. The thought of Bradshaw throwing to Lewis and Ron Shanklin, the wide receiver we had drafted in 1970, excited me.

While the seven teams picking ahead of us announced their selections, I was on the edge of my seat. Our own turn came, and no one had taken Lewis. With a nod of assent from Noll, I reached for the phone, becoming aware, in the same instant, of a voice that bounced off the walls. It belonged to an assistant coach, who was calling out, "Hey — what about Jack Ham?"

I went rigid. Jack Ham, from Penn State, was the player we hoped to draft in the second round. Turning on the assistant coach, I said, "Look: we have worked on this list together. So now I suggest that we take these players the way we have them rated. If Ham is out there in the second round, we'll grab him. But first we're taking Lewis."

For the record, I have said that no one we ever drafted was more of a disappointment to me than Lewis. If I could, I'd retract those words. Actually, Lewis turned out to be everything we expected. He worked hard in practice. He was never seriously hurt. He made some important plays in big games. Once when we were up against a good Houston team in the Astrodome, the Oilers' head scout came rushing through the press box, headed for the Houston coaches' booth and shouting at the top of his voice, "He's coming into the game! Back 'em up, back 'em up! He's in the fucking game!" Noll had inserted Lewis, and the head scout was spreading the alarm. Look out! he was warning the Houston defensive coaches. Back up your cornerbacks and safeties. If Lewis gets behind them it's a touchdown.

The scout was right to be fearful of Lewis. Speed kills, and Lewis had speed in abundance. He was a starting wide receiver the first time we went to the Super Bowl. Eventually, though, we traded both Lewis and Shanklin. The more productive wide receivers we drafted in 1974, Lynn Swann and John Stallworth, had made them expendable. Sitting on the bench, Lewis was wasted. With Buffalo in 1981, near the end of his career, he had a Pro Bowl year, catching seventy passes. I took this as vindication for Nunn and myself. A great athlete and a good guy, Frank Lewis was one of my favorite Steelers.

Getting back to 1971, we drafted Ham in the second round. My hunch that he would still be available was correct after all. Inexplicably, the coach who had thought we should draft him ahead of Lewis was urging us now to take a linebacker from Bowling Green, Phil Villapiano. I looked at the guy to see if he was being facetious. Villapiano became a very good player for Oakland, but Ham made the Pro Bowl eight years in a row and is now in the Hall of Fame.

After we had taken him, my good friend Upton Bell, director of player personnel for the Baltimore Colts, had a question for me: "Where are you going to play the guy? He's an undersized linebacker and an oversized strong safety." I had seen Ham in games, I had seen him on film, and I had seen him practice, and I felt sure he had the size to be a linebacker. I had not, however, seen him in street clothes. We had an orientation meeting for rookies and free agents in the Downtown Hilton that year, and just as we were ready to get started I heard a knock at the door of our suite. I opened it, and there stood a slight-looking young man wearing a blue zipper jacket, a white shirt, blue slacks, and loafers.

"Is this the Steelers' room?" he asked.

"Yes," I said. "What do you want?"

"I was told to come here."

"Yes?" This time I made it sound like a question. "Do you have a message for us?"

Bashfully, the kid said, "I'm Jack Ham."

Upton Bell's question came back to me. Could this be the linebacker we had picked in the second round?

The next morning, when the rookies took their physical examinations at Three Rivers, I watched them being weighed and measured. They were wearing only shorts. It would be going too far to call Ham emaciated, but from the waist up he was certainly fat-free. Though his frame seemed big enough, he'd be a project for Noll and Lou Riecke, his strength coach, I told myself. Then I looked at his legs. They were long and muscular.

Before the start of the season, Ham pumped iron and put on twelve pounds, mostly in the shoulders and chest. I came to regard him as the perfect football player for the 1970s. He was a wonderful athlete with exceptional leverage, excellent vision, and unerring anticipation. Moving to the ball, he could not be blocked. He covered passes with the agility and speed of a defensive back.

The first time Ham played in the Pro Bowl, it happened that Noll was his coach. During the week devoted to practice, my cousin Tim Rooney, who was helping Noll as a go-fer, found himself on an elevator with some of the players. They were speaking freely of their discontent with Noll's hard-to-grasp defensive scheme, and Tim, under the cloak of his anonymity, was an interested listener. "Nobody," said one guy, "can make this coverage work. It's too complicated." Another player, Tim reported, promptly took issue with that. All he said was, "Ham. Ham will make it work." To which the first guy responded. "OK. OK. Ham. It'll work."

After Ham's eleventh year with the Steelers, a foot injury sent him to the team's orthopedist. "You can continue to play," he was told, "but you'll be slower." Ham tested the foot, and sure enough — he'd be able to play but had lost a full step. Unwilling to lower the standard he had set for himself, he retired.

We came out of that 1971 draft with twelve players who would make the team. Seven of the twelve were starters in Super Bowl games. Four would play in the Pro Bowl. One — Jack Ham — would become the fourth Hall of Famer we drafted in Noll's first three years. All in all, our 1971 draft was one of the best in the history of the league — the fourth best, actually, according to a recent poll of the statistical wizards who evaluate such things.

We had two picks in the fourth round. Both made the team. We had four picks in the fifth round. Three made the team. Our three picks in the eighth round included Fats Holmes, who made it big. Our eleventh and thirteenth picks made the team, and one outstanding free agent, Glen Edwards, was a starting defensive back for seven years, MVP of the 1974 team, and a Pro Bowler in 1976 and 1977. Edwards had come to the team from Florida A. & M. as a running back. He was tough, fast, and smart, but trouble off the field. After the 1977 season, we traded him to the Forty-Niners.

The eleventh-round pick was Mike Wagner, a defensive back from Western Illinois. "Hey," Noll said to me, "how come this guy is still on the board after ten rounds?" I suggested that early in the season he'd been hurt. Noll said, "If he's smart enough maybe we can do something with him." An accounting major, Wagner was smart enough. But I confined myself to saying that he hit hard and seemed to be a nice kid. Noll laughed. "Nice kids make good son-in-laws, but I'd rather have tough guys." Wagner was tough enough, it turned out, to play in our first four Super Bowls and also a couple of Pro Bowls.

Let me sum it all up: Fifteen of the players who were starters on one or more of the Super Bowl teams had been drafted since Noll's arrival or signed as rookie free agents. You could call that striking it rich.

One of our fourth-round picks, Gerry Mullins, from Southern California, was an offensive lineman who could be plugged in almost anywhere. In a career that lasted nine years, Moon played guard, tackle, and tight end. The other fourth-rounder, defensive end Dwight White, was one of my lucky scouting finds. Blesto, for some reason, hadn't rated him high, but in my opinion he was everything Noll looked for in a player. Moreover, White's coach at East Texas State had spoken well of his attitude and intelligence. White used his intelligence after ten seasons of football to start a successful career as a stockbroker.

Fifth-round pick Larry Brown was a tight end from Kansas, a better blocker than pass catcher at 6 feet 4 and 225 pounds. But in Super Bowl IX he caught a touchdown pass from Bradshaw that finished off the Minnesota Vikings. Eventually Noll moved him to an offensive tackle position, and in 1983, his thirteenth season, Brown went to the Pro Bowl. He played one more year and then ran a chain of restaurants after dropping out of dental school at Pitt. Neither the public nor the press ever gave him his full due. Nominated for the Hall of Fame, Brown fell short of receiving enough votes for induction.

Players like Steve Davis, a running back from Delaware State; Mel Holmes, offensive tackle from North Carolina A. & T.; and Craig Hanneman, defensive end from Oregon State, were cut before we ever went to a Super Bowl. Hanneman, a big farm boy, was born tough; the other defensive linemen — Joe Greene, L. C. Greenwood, Dwight White, and Fats Holmes — simply happened to be better football players. Hanneman earned his place in Steeler lore on the afternoon of November 11, 1973. The Steelers were beating the Oakland Raiders in Oakland for their eighth victory in nine games, and Hanneman was in his usual place on the sidelines. Next to him stood Roy Blount, who'd been gathering material for a book about the team. As the Steelers scored the touchdown that assured them of a 17-9 win, Hanneman uttered the words that gave Blount's opus its title. "We're about three bricks shy of a load," Hanneman said. It could not have been put more strikingly, Blount thought. With all the bricks in place the following year, the Steelers began their Super Bowl run. Hanneman, sad to say, was by that time a New England Patriot.

Fat Man

My first glimpse of Ernie Holmes in the flesh was on a rainy night in Texas in 1970. I had seen him on film and he had caught my eye (he'd have caught anybody's eye). So, for an up-close look, I flew down to Houston and drove my rental car to Jepson Stadium, where his team, Texas Southern, played its home games, usually under the lights. On this night Texas Southern was playing … oh, forget who Texas Southern was playing. It's beside the point. Arriving at Jepson Stadium, I found a seat in the stands. There were no booths for pro scouts, and the raindrops kept falling on my head. As I waited for the kickoff, thoroughly wet and thoroughly miserable, I heard a baritone voice calling, "Hey, Artie!" It was Red Almond, a Washington Redskin scout and the only other white guy in the stadium. From the track that encircled the field, he hollered, "Come down here. I've got something important to tell you."

Red had gone to college at Mount St. Mary's with my twin brothers John and Pat and our cousin Johnny Laughlin. The information he had for me concerned the Texas Southern coach. Aware that two scouts would be in the stands, he had changed the numbers on the jerseys of all his seniors. His motive was anger — not at us, but at his players. Unhappy with the way the season was going, he had labeled the whole team "a bunch of quitters."

"What a jackass," Red growled. The teams on the field, their pre-game loosening-up exercises finished, had gone to their respective benches. "Come on," Red urged me. "Let's walk over to the Texas Southern bench and see if we can figure this out."

The first guy to spot us was Holmes. Waving his arms to get our attention, he pointed to his number and shouted, "Fats! This is me! Fats!" All of the other seniors were doing the same thing — pointing to their numbers and calling out their names.

But I was interested mostly in Fats. He showed his enormous strength that night. I remember a luncheon in the Allegheny Club for Bill Nunn's black college all-stars at which Muhammad Ali was the main attraction. Americans were still fighting in Vietnam, and his refusal to put on a uniform still rankled with supporters of the war. To show how he felt, an NFL scout who had been a colonel in the Army boycotted Nunn's Steeler-sponsored affair and ate his lunch in Ed Kiely's office. I wasn't too crazy myself about having Ali for a guest, but I shook his hand and called him "Champ" and I must say that he was certainly a presence. I'm digressing, however, so let me start over. Fats Holmes crashed the luncheon in order to meet Ali (they engaged in a duel of wits, which Fats lost) and Kay was on hand with Susie, our three-year-old daughter. Fats, in greeting us, picked Susie up and held her in the palm of one hand. I do not exaggerate. He was that big, that powerful. The instant he put Susie down, Kay swiftly hustled her out of sight.

To become a functioning part of the Steel Curtain, the Steelers' front four, Fats needed guidance. He got it from Bill Nunn and assistant coach George Perles. They curbed his flamboyant individualism. Fats himself looked to Joe Greene for leadership. One time when his feelings were hurt — Greene had ordered him off the field for freelancing instead of playing within the defensive scheme — he refused an order from Perles to go back in. "Not till Joe tells me it's OK." Somehow, Perles got word to Greene, and he came to the sideline. Pointing a finger at Fats, he bellowed, "Get your ass in here!" Did you ever see an elephant fly? The elephantine Holmes fairly flew off the bench.

During the 1976 season there was a stretch of five games in which the Steeler defense did not give up a touchdown. Houston then pushed one across, and an argument broke out in the dressing room over who was at fault. Fats and his idol Greene exchanged angry words. None too soon, trainer Ralph Berlin alerted Noll — "It was getting real bad," he told me — and Noll had to step between the combatants. It may be that Fats now considered himself a rival of Greene. Frank Gifford, the Hall-of-Fame running back turned broadcaster, was calling him the best defensive lineman in the NFL. There even came a time when Noll, who measured his words, would say that for two years, 1976 and 1977, Fats was a better lineman than Greene, L.C. Greenwood, or Dwight White.

That is possible. But he was also a very troubled soul, an alcoholic with bipolar disorder. On a memorable afternoon in the off-season one year, news reports came in over the radio that a Steeler player had gone berserk; from his car; he was firing a revolver at truck drivers on the Ohio Turnpike. "Couldn't be true," we told ourselves in the Steeler offices. "Must be a case of mistaken identity."

The news flashes continued; in fact, they got even worse. The Steeler was now shooting at a state police helicopter. A bullet had gone through its floor and hit the pilot on the foot.

More details quickly followed. The rampaging football player was being chased by the cops across Ohio. One by one, the tires on his car were blowing out. Now he had left it on the Turnpike and had disappeared into some woods. Then came the news of his capture. He was being taken to jail in Youngstown, but not in handcuffs, which were too small for his wrists, the police said. For the first time, they gave him a name: Ernie Holmes.

Dan, Joe Gordon, and our lawyer, Jack McGinley, Jr., were swinging into action. Mrs. Duffy, my secretary, put in a call to the Youngstown jail and got me on the line with a lady cop. I wanted to be sure that the man they had locked up was Fats, and not an impostor. What did he look like? I asked. The description she gave me was as thorough and exact as a scouting report; when she finished I knew there had been no mistake.

Doc Best, our representative at the court hearing for Fats, got him committed to Western Pennsylvania Psychiatric Hospital in Pittsburgh. An early visitor, Buff Boston, told us, "He's there with all the nuts — and he's one of them." The assessment seemed harsh, but I welcomed it. Nothing less than an insanity plea could keep Fats from going to prison. I went to see him after Boston did, and he was moved by my gift of a prayer book. He appeared to be the king of his unit. The other patients looked up to him, and he related quite well with the nurses and orderlies. He told me that during the car chase in Ohio one of the pursuing state troopers had a "direct bead" on him with a pistol. Fats, who was out of his car, heard the trigger snap, he said, "and nothing happened." A truly lucky misfire.

According to one of his doctors, Fats was a man who "behaved like the people around him." Good company influenced Fats for the better, bad company influenced him for the worse. After his release from the hospital, he was put in the custody of his girlfriend.

Fats was a Steeler for several more years. In January of 2000 he came to our twenty-fifth anniversary Super Bowl party weighing 415 pounds. From the dais, he talked incessantly of having found redemption in "Christ Jesus our Lord," belaboring this theme until his teammates induced him to shut up by tapping with knives, forks, and spoons on their water glasses. At this same party, the only player I asked to sign my team picture was Fats. Yet for all he contributed to the success of the front four, it was painful to think of how great he might have been except for his personal problems.

Far less physically gifted than Fats, another player we drafted in 1971, Al Young, was his opposite also in level-headedness and character. Young was a wide receiver from South Carolina State. He developed sickle cell anemia, which affects mostly black people, after just two years with the team and never played again. Looking for a way to keep Young in the organization, I offered him a chance to become a talent scout. He thought about it, and even scouted some games for us, before deciding that what he really wanted to do was work with adolescents as a teacher and coach.

"Do you know what I mean?" he asked. I said I did.

Chuck Noll had assured us when we interviewed him for his job that he placed no importance on the color of a player's skin. Could there now be the slightest doubt? In that 1971 draft, three of our first five picks and seven picks altogether were from schools in the South with all-black enrollments. I know that Bill Nunn and I helped to bring that about, but Noll had the final say. As our draft picks and free-agent signings demonstrated, his commitment was to winning with the best players available. Down through the years, I have never heard him even hint that he deserved any credit for this. And I can say just as much for myself. At least I think I can.

Frank O'Harris

The Blesto scout was telling me about a sophomore running back at Penn State who had the talent to be a big-time star. His name, as I heard it, was Frank O'Harris.

Ordinarily, I paid little attention to scouting reports on sophomores. We had a thousand seniors to think about, after all. But as the 1969 season moved along, everyone kept praising this Frank O'Harris. Penn State's opponents couldn't contain him.

"One for Dad," I said to myself. There weren't that many good Irish players any more. I felt we should keep an eye on this guy.

But then I saw his name in print, and it wasn't actually Frank O'Harris. There was no capital "O." There was no apostrophe. Thus rearranged and altered, the letters spelled Franco Harris. No way he was Irish, I realized, not with a first name I had seen on spaghetti cans. His mother, I learned, was Italian — an Italian war bride — and his ex-GI father African-American. Franco Harris came from a town in New Jersey. He was tall, maybe 6 feet 2 or 3, and he weighed about 215 pounds. He could run over tacklers or run away from them. But he was still just a sophomore and hardly more than a blip on my radar screen.

I did not scout Franco in person until his senior year, 1971, when I made the drive from Pittsburgh to State College twice, first with my family and later with Dick Haley. Even though it was always a distraction, taking Kay and the kids along on scouting trips eased my conscience. As I have said, I was spending too much time on the road. While Kay kept the kids occupied — she took snapshots of them climbing all over the granite Nittany Lion sculpture - I slipped away to meet with the coaches in their office, study film, and then watch practice.

It was early in Joe Paterno's long run as Penn State's major domo. Our relations with him were excellent, as they had been with Rip Engle, his predecessor. In fact, when we were looking for a coach after ridding ourselves of Bill Austin, Paterno had been Dan's first choice. He was interested, too — very much — but his roots in Happy Valley were too strong and too deep and he decided to stay put. It was only after Paterno turned down the job that Chuck Noll moved to the head of the list.

When I talked to Paterno and his assistants about Franco Harris, I was in for a surprise. None of them really bad-mouthed Franco, but they diverted the conversation to one of the other running backs, Lydell Mitchell. I watched a game film and saw that while Mitchell was a pretty good player in a big-time program he did not have his teammate's size, power, speed, or mobility.

For a close look at Franco, I cadged an invitation to practice. On a gorgeous fall day, the hills that enclosed the campus were blazing with color. Somehow this background seemed perfect; it was just the right setting to view an athlete who might have been carved out of marble by, oh, Michelangelo, let's say. Later, describing Franco to Kay, I remarked, "There's something classical about him."

"That's nice," she replied, "but can he play?"

I was certain of it. "He has all the tools," I said, "and he's made the big plays in big games."

Pure football talk. There never was much of that between Kay and me. On the drive back to Pittsburgh, we stopped at a famous eating place called Erculani's and found that we didn't like it at all; neither did the kids, who wanted hamburgers instead of Italian food. Situation normal again, I thought. Afterward, in the car, the kids fell asleep, and Kay brought up the subject of my job. I was being consumed by it, she felt, and the evidence backed her up.

Scouting had gotten to be an opiate with me. Always there was more to do — more players to check out, more coaches to interview. Though we had hired Dick Haley to relieve me of certain duties, psychologically I was not yet prepared to give them up. I would have to achieve a balance between work and family — I knew that. The strain that my long and frequent absences were putting on Kay had become a matter of great concern to everyone most important to me. Kass and Aunt Alice were saying rosaries, making novenas, attending Masses every day. They were asking God to show me the light.

AJR was more direct. I should be going to Mass every day myself, he let me know. If he and Kass and Aunt Alice could do it, what was my problem? Unconvincingly, I tried to explain that in most parts of the country, and particularly in the South, where the football players I was tracking seemed to be concentrated, Catholic churches were few and far between. Of course, when Jerry Neri was traveling with me, excuses were not acceptable. Jerry Neri would drag me to Mass. In the Northwest that year, during Lent, we never missed a day. The church he took me to might be a one-room wooden building in the boondocks or a chapel in some college or university's Newman Club quarters. No matter where it was, this hard-bitten little Blesto scout would find it. "I know about you and your family," he would tell me. "So get your ass in gear."

Before my next and last trip to State College, the one with Haley, AJR cautioned me to avoid Route 22. "It's a death trap since they made it three lanes," he said. "That middle lane is supposed to be a passing lane. They should call it a suicide lane. All the nuts and drunks think they can pull in and out whenever they want to. Take the Turnpike. Or, better yet, fly."

I did neither. Winter comes early in the Allegheny Mountains, and I had driven Route 22 in November snowstorms — real white-outs; this time it was merely cool and damp. We had some rain, and in places the road was slick, but we arrived safe and sound on a game day.

Our seats in the press box were good ones. Harris, we knew, had been having a sub-par year. He was lackadaisical in practice, the coaches complained. As on my earlier visit, they dwelt on the abilities of Mitchell. A coach in the press box, cupping a hand over his mouth, confided to me that Harris "sulked." "He's moody, Won't work hard." I decided to trust my own instincts.

Afterward, when Haley and I were by ourselves in the car, we agreed that Harris was still an outstanding NFL prospect. Taking into consideration the things a scout looks for, there was just no comparison between Harris and Mitchell. Somehow Harris gave you the feeling that here was a great football player. Mitchell for some reason did not.

On New Year's Day, from a seat on the bench, Harris watched Penn State beat Texas in the Cotton Bowl. He'd been late for practice one morning, and Paterno removed him from the starting lineup. Stubbornly, I continued to think of Franco as the guy we should draft in the first round if we could.

The Steelers had won more games than in 1970, but it was still a losing season. Even so, we would pick rather late — thirteenth. Chuck Noll attended the Blesto winter meetings and listened to all the scouts give their lengthy presentations. He took a few notes but asked no questions. He did ask questions, under his breath, of Haley, Nunn, and me, making sure he was not overheard. It was all very hush-hush, an approach that, for reasons of my own, I disdained. I had a whole list of questions for the scouts, and I asked them openly. My manner was low-keyed but persistent.

After the first couple of days, Noll said he wanted a word with me — in private. "I like the way you've prepared for this meeting," he began. "You've put a lot of time into it. But you're tipping off the people who are here from the other teams. All they have to do is listen to the Blesto scouts answer your questions. You're doing their work for them."

Without showing disrespect, I nodded and turned away. Chuck's perception that other personnel directors were eavesdropping was correct. I could not have cared less. Whether or not we had an audience, I continued to interrogate the scouts. I was unabashedly out to prove something — that I did not owe my job to nepotism. Call me obstinate. Call me hard-headed. Say I was putting my own interests ahead of the team's. But more than anything else I wanted my competitors to realize that Art Rooney's son was not a lazy, over-indulged rich kid. If I was doing their work for them, let them all see that no one had to help me do mine.

Was I being immature? Perhaps. Was I being smart? Maybe not. Was I antagonizing Noll? I suppose so. But as the coming years were to demonstrate, we ended up with a better draft than any of the other Blesto teams could claim. In fact, our 1972 draft was one of the best in the NFL.

Back in Pittsburgh, Nunn, Haley, and I studied and re-studied our reports. We shuffled our ratings and carne up with a new list of top players for every position and another new list of our top two hundred regardless of position. It took us a full week. For two weeks after that, we met with Noll and his assistant coaches every day, which resulted in more new lists.

We moved to the draft room for "discussions," as Chuck called them. I called them "heated" discussions.

"You know, Art," he said to me, "this all has to be like your teeth."

"Teeth?" I didn't get it.

"Yes, teeth. I have read," he explained in his best professorial tone, "that all animals — humans included — must work their upper teeth against their lower teeth. It has the same effect as exercise. Keeps the gums healthy and the teeth themselves firmly in place. It's like our scouting meetings, where we have a clash of opinions — weigh the pros against the cons, so to speak. It keeps us sharp."

"Oh," I replied. "Yes. Like your teeth."

After chewing on it for a while, I guess I could see what he meant.

I have said that our discussions were "heated." When we got around to discussing the running backs and fullbacks, they were more than heated. Pure emotion took over, especially in my own case. Let's say I was carried away.

Even before the Blesto meetings, Noll had made it plain to the scouts that he was biased against big backs. "If they're more than 6 feet 2 and 220 pounds," he said, "they can't change direction.

They're not flexible enough at the hips and knees. And their forward lean is too pronounced, because they lean from the waist instead of the hips and legs. Give me the strong short guy – 5 feet 10 and 205. Short guys have balance, quickness, control. They hit it in tough. They can bounce to the outside and cut back. They can set up the arm tackle with a sudden move. Put 'em in a pass pattern and you have a guy who can run after making the catch. All those big guys can do is run straight ahead. They're one-dimensional."

It seemed to me that Noll preferred two good backs who could run and catch to a backfield with one great runner and a fullback who does all the blocking. "Two backs who produce fifteen hundred yards between them and catch sixty passes are just as valuable as one star," he maintained. It made sense. Years later, I would hear George Young of the New York Giants, the winners of two successive Super Bowls, echo Chuck's remarks.

Coming up in the same draft as Harris was a good little big man at the University of Houston. Short, strong, productive, and willing to give his all for the team, Bobby Newhouse had every virtue that Noll said he admired in a running back. I liked him a lot myself, but I happened to like Franco more. That was where we differed — vociferously.

Noll seemed just as concerned about Franco's height as with the reports about his moodiness and his aversion, in the eyes of some of the Penn State coaches, to hard work. While our draft talks were going on, I got support from an unexpected source — my good friend George Young. A big, corpulent, erudite man with two master's degrees, he said to me one day on the telephone, "Arthur, you sound gloomy. Are you having trouble with Chuck? Is he giving you a hard time again?" George and Chuck were friends, too, by the way. In need of a sympathetic ear, I explained that Chuck and I were at loggerheads about the relative merits of Newhouse and Harris. Young answered, "Well, that argument, tell him for me, was settled more than six thousand years ago when Socrates said, 'A good big man will beat a good little man every time.'"

The epigram sounded more like something from the mouth of a twentieth-century fight manager than that of an ancient Greek philosopher, but I repeated it to Noll. "Just like George," he said with a chuckle, and went on arguing with unabated fervor that Newhouse belonged at the top of our list.

Sometimes Noll would put us on notice that no matter how high we may have rated a certain player he wasn't going to draft him. Never once did he say this about Franco, which gave me hope. Though our discussion of running backs ended with Noll unshaken in his support of Newhouse, and though we would start to evaluate offensive linemen the next morning, the game wasn't over.

On the previous evening I had called Jack Butler and asked him to compare Newhouse and Harris. He must have thought I was losing my marbles. We had talked about them as prospects again and again. What Jack didn't know was that on this occasion he was being tape-recorded. After my conversation with Jack, I proceeded to call every Blesto scout who had seen Newhouse or Harris or both. My plan was to add their opinions to the tape and put together an audio for Noll and his staff.

I talked to Alex Bell, Ralph Kohl, Jess Thompson, and Will Walls. Bell, the former head coach at Villanova, had scouted Harris for two years. "Take him if you get a chance," he urged me. Kohl had scouted both Franco and Newhouse. "Don't worry about the squabble between Franco and Paterno," he said. "Franco will be a better pro than Newhouse because of his size." I had not told Bell or Kohl about the tape recorder; I did tell Jess Thompson (I'm not sure why). He didn't mind. Thompson scouted the Southwest Conference for Blesto and knew a lot about Newhouse, but had watched Franco play only once — in a post-season all-star game. He was therefore unwilling to compare them. "Well, would you take Newhouse with the thirteenth pick?" I asked him. He hesitated. "Need gets into it," he said. Then he added, "Bobby won't let you down." Walls, like Thompson, was more familiar with Newhouse than with Harris but had scouted them both. When I asked him the same question I'd put to Thompson — was Bobby Newhouse a legitimate thirteenth pick? – he answered, "Uh ... say hi to your dad, Artie." It was all I needed to hear, but I pushed for just a little bit more. "If your life depended on it, Will?" Cornered, he said, "I don't know." I told him, "OK, Will, thanks. You've been a big help."

Taping these guys, the ones who hadn't given their consent, was unlawful, I suppose, but nothing to bring up in the confessional. Still, I am glad I did not let the newspapers in on it for a good long time.

On the morning after my phone calls, Mrs. Duffy was in the scouts' office, passing out lists of offensive tackles. Besides Noll and his staff, Haley and Nunn were present. Haley, on paper, was our personnel director now, but he had taken no part in the debate between Noll and me. The fact that I presumed to argue with Noll surprised him, I think. I am not putting Haley down. He was new on the job and had a newcomer's reluctance to assert himself.

These morning meetings started with coffee and doughnuts. Before we had drained our cups, I took out my tape recorder and placed it on my desk. It was plugged in and ready to go. Addressing Noll, I said, "Chuck, I've come up with some more information on Franco and Newhouse. How about giving it a listen?"

He nodded, more expressionless than usual. For thirty minutes, the whole room listened quietly. The voices of the scouts were unnaturally loud and clear. When it was over, no one spoke for what seemed like a long time. Finally Noll, betraying no emotion, said, "You asked the Blesto scouts leading questions. They had to answer in the way that you wanted them to. Let's move on here." He was telling me his mind had not been changed. "OK, Coach," I said, but I still had a card to play.

Dan Radakovich was a Western Pennsylvania guy who had been on Noll's staff in 1971 but resigned to take a coaching job in college football. Because of a misunderstanding of some kind – I can't be more specific because I don't know the details – it turned out that the job would not be open, and he was helping me now with the 1972 draft, watching game films and writing reports.

What I wanted him to do for me was make the case for Franco with Noll. My interviews with the Blesto scouts may have eaten away at Noll's certainty just a little. But in spite of his denials, were the stories about the trouble between Franco and the coaches at Penn State in the back of his mind? The label they had fastened to Franco was that of a shirker. The "intangibles," so-called, had always been supremely important to Noll. He wanted players who were "teachable," who worked hard to improve themselves, who came to practice and meetings on time. If this was his problem with Franco, I thought that Radakovich, who had been on the Penn State coaching staff when Franco was a junior or sophomore, might be qualified to offer a second opinion.

We had talked about Franco previously, and I knew what Rad would say: "He's not a troublemaker. He's not a bad guy. He comes from a good family. There were some misunderstandings with the coaches – he has some sensitivities – but this is a good person. If you draft him you won't regret it."

Rad did speak to Noll, and it made a difference, I could sense. It wasn't anything Noll said, it was everything he did not say. On draft day, the first twelve teams to make their selections were agonizingly deliberate, but at last it was our turn. "The Steelers are on the board." To my relief, with some apprehension mixed in, Franco was still out there. I waited for Noll's decision. Would it be "Let's go somewhere else"? We had fifteen minutes to decide, but Noll didn't vacillate. From his seat at our T-shaped table, he was looking at me. "Let's take the big back from Penn State," he said.

I held myself in check. Jim Boston was on the phone, maintaining contact with NFL draft headquarters in New York. Calmly, I said to him, "Franco Harris." It was like touching a match to a short-fused Roman candle. "FRANCO HARRIS!" Boston thundered, splitting eardrums at both ends of the line. "RUNNING BACK FROM PENN STATE."

Joe Gordon raced out of the room to notify the media. Dan left with Boston to call Franco. As for me, I put on an act. Hiding my elation, I glanced at Haley and then at Nunn in lieu of a thumbs-up. I then called Jack Butler. "Good move," he said, and that was about the extent of it. At Gordon's request, I spoke with a newspaper reporter. I took pains not to gloat, and I excused myself quickly. We had eighteen more players to draft.

Before the 1970s were over, Franco Harris gave us reason to congratulate ourselves on our astuteness that day. By serving as Franco's advocate, it was Radakovich, I still believe, who converted Noll to the cause. Rad himself was not loath to suggest the same thing. He told a story to the effect that AJR had kept him around as an odd-jobs man for no other purpose than to lobby Noll. I don't remember it that way, but if I'm wrong – if AJR really did play the role of silent manipulator – then all I can say is "thank God."

Bad Rad

Tall, lean, and blond, a center in his playing days, Radakovich had coached our offensive line. "Bad Rad," we called him — a tribute to the hard work he demanded from his charges. He had a genius IQ and the absent-mindedness that extraordinary brain power sometimes engenders.

Bad Rad lived in a neighborhood where the streets and the houses looked pretty much the same, and one night returning home (as he thought) from practice he let himself in through the unlocked kitchen door and sat down at the table with his playbook, his mind on the following Sunday's game plan. The next thing he knew, a small boy he never had seen before was staring at him from a few feet away.

"Mommy," the kid called out, "there's a strange man in our kitchen."

Seconds later, Mommy appeared. "What are you doing in our house?" she demanded.

Slowly, Rad began to realize that he had made a mistake.

Even in his own house, Rad found himself out of bounds once, to use a football metaphor. This was in Cincinnati, one of his coaching stops. The Radakoviches had house guests, another married couple, the husband a former Penn State teammate of Rad's. They were using the master bedroom, where Rad and his wife normally slept. Doing their best to be hospitable, host and hostess moved into the guest room. Not long after dinner, the friend's wife, tired out from a day of traveling, excused herself and went to bed. An hour passed and then Rad said good night. "Gotta get some sleep for our game tomorrow," he explained.

He did get some sleep, but it was soon interrupted. Not half an hour later, his friend was standing over him and shaking him awake. "Hey, Rad," he was saying. "You're in bed with my wife."

Whenever Rad told the story, and he told it many times, he was careful to emphasize that he had gone to the master bedroom out of habit and forgetfulness, an understandable lapse.

"Nothing bad happened," he would say.

Turning Point

Historians of the Second World War point out that before the U. S. Navy destroyed the Japanese fleet at Midway, American forces never had won a battle, and that from then on they were never to lose one. Franco Harris was the counterpart of Midway for the Steelers.

Before he came to Pittsburgh, we had not had a winning season since 1963. After he arrived, the Steelers went thirteen years without a losing season.

In the second round of the 1972 draft, the Dallas Cowboys took Robert Newhouse, the "fine little running back" from Houston. He had a praiseworthy career with a great team but was never a Hall-of-Fame-type player. Franco Harris did make the Hall of Fame. In his first season, he gained more than one thousand yards, was the NFL's Rookie of the Year, and was voted MVP of the Steelers by his teammates. In his third season he was the MVP of Super Bowl IX, a 16-6 win over the Vikings. He rushed for one thousand or more yards eight times and played in nine straight Pro Bowls. I found it interesting that Harris and Jack Ham, who were teammates at Penn State, had parallel careers with the Steelers.

The second player we took in the 1972 draft, Gordon Gravelle of Brigham Young, was a tall, smart offensive tackle. After five years with the Steelers, he lasted another three seasons with the Giants and Rams. Gravelle and our No.5 pick, defensive tackle Steve Furness of Rhode Island, became Super Bowl starters. Furness got his chance when we shipped Ernie Holmes to New England after the 1977 season. Eventually we traded Furness to the Detroit Lions, but not until 1981. Like Joe Gilliam, the exceptional but ill-starred quarterback we drafted the same year, Furness died young, of coronary problems. After his playing days were over, he had taken up coaching and served for a time under Bill Cowher.

While they were with the Steelers, no player we took in that 1972 draft would ever experience a losing season. Except for defensive back J. T. Thomas, who came on board in 1973, and Jack Lambert, who arrived in 1974, the starters on both offense and defense in our first Super Bowl game were now in the fold, and Franco Harris was the catalyst.

Footnote: Our third pick in 1972, a tight end from Clemson named John McMakin, showed up at Latrobe as a raw-boned, crew-cut Southern kid who yes-sirred and no-sirred everybody in camp. Returning in 1973, he was unrecognizable. He had hair that was longer than Robinson Crusoe's. He carried a purse, hanging from his shoulder by a strap. I was in Bill Nunn's office when McMakin checked in. Poker-faced, Bill sent him off to a room in the dorm. Then he said to me with a look of disgust:

"That guy won't even make the squad this year."

Nunn's vehemence took me by surprise. I said, "Gee, Bill, he did very well as a rookie."

Nunn said, "Well, look at him now. He's in the 'cute' bag. That long hair. That purse hanging over his shoulder. Last year John was a biter and scratcher. Not anymore. He thinks he's a finesse guy. He won't make it."

As usual, Nunn was right.

He went up another notch in my estimation.

The Kid from Idaho

On draft day, AJR was forever getting phone calls from cronies all over the United States, cronies bent on giving him tips. This kind of intrusiveness made me more paranoid than ever. I wanted no help from friends of my dad, and I wanted no help from the assistant coaches, who always seemed to be pushing some overlooked player of rare ability. "We know about that guy, we have detailed information on him," I would say, stamping out another brush fire. On draft day I had to have order, and now as the fourteenth round of the 1972 draft came to an end, here was AJR with a tip from an old pal — in his race-track lingo "a tip right out of the barn."

"A kid from Idaho — Idaho U.," Dad was telling me. "Plays linebacker. And the best part of it is, he's an Irish kid."

The name was Linehan — Ron Linehan. "My friend out there knows athletes, and he says this guy is a steal," continued AJR.

I thought of times in the past when the Chief had accused me of "just throwing darts at the names on the board." He would stand then and listen to my lecture about the work we put in on our draft list. The reaction I got was always the same. First he would shake his head. Then he'd puff at his cigar, chuckle sarcastically, lock his hands behind his back, and walk away.

In the fifteenth round, I did not draft the Irish kid from Idaho, making Bill Nunn and Dick Haley nervous. "Hey, Artie," said Nunn, "your dad owns the team." Haley said, "I think you'd better cut him a break."

I dug in my heels a little deeper. An important principle was at stake: my independence. In the sixteenth round I drafted a wide receiver — Nate Hawkins by name — from Nevada Las Vegas. One pick was left.

AJR returned to the room and stood with a cigar in his mouth and his hands behind his back, staring at the board. It was almost too much for Nunn and Haley. Even Chuck Noll felt the tension. He was glaring at me. One of them — either Nunn, Haley, or Noll — said to me under his breath, "Last round. Loosen up."

When our turn came to draft, I was tongue-tied. In a quiet voice, Noll said, "Linehan."

Just as softly, I repeated, "Linehan."

He was our seventeenth pick.

At training camp the next summer, Linehan did not make the cut. Neither did Nate Hawkins.

AJR kept his thoughts about this to himself, and so did I.

Chapter 54

Paper Promotion

By 1972, the Rooney family — primarily Kass - had decided that Art Rooney, Jr., personnel director and head scout of the Steelers, was spending too much time away from home.

"It's endangering his marriage," Kass said to AJR.

At her instigation — the word is not too strong - he came to my office in Three Rivers Stadium for a talk, father to son.

"You're on the road too much," he began.

I knew what he was getting at, but my job had become a passion, an addiction, a cause. "Same as you," I replied, "when you were following the horses."

"That was different," he said.

"How so?"

"I had to make a living for your mother and your brothers and you. The race track was where I worked. Anyway, I got home more often than you do. When I gave you this job, I didn't mean for you to be gone as much as you are."

I played my trump card. "Dad, this job is important. It's the most important job in the organization. You cannot win without good players. And I'm the one who's supposed to make sure we have them."

AJR wasn't buying it. "You're forgetting Blesto, aren't you?" he said. "Jack Butler does a fine job there."

"Yes, he does. But Blesto is rating players for half a dozen teams — not just the Steelers. Chuck Noll has specific things he's looking for, and the Blesto scouts aren't as familiar with them as I am."

I had hit on an argument that gave him pause. He puffed at his cigar, thinking of how to respond, and then he said, "OK. I understand. Maybe you need some extra help. Besides Blesto."

Extra help was the last thing I wanted. "We have Bill Nunn," I reminded him.

"Yes, and he's good. But Nunn only scouts the Negro teams."

I said, "He's ready to start looking at all the teams." It was no use. AJR put an end to the discussion.

"You still need more help. I'll talk to you later."

Even Noll had been urging me to cut back. After scouting a college game on a Saturday afternoon, or sometimes on a Saturday night, I would fly to wherever the Steelers were playing. If their game was on the road I'd return to Pittsburgh with the team. At least twice Noll suggested that I was covering too much ground. "You don't have to be flying all over the map. You can study film, read scouting reports, go to the post-season all-star games." I would listen patiently and say, "I do study film. I study enough film to go blind. I do read scouting reports. I do see the post-season all-star games. There's more to it than that. If you're a scout, you have to watch practice. You have to talk with the coaches and trainers." From the Dick Guy Book of Clichés, I resurrected a mixed metaphor. "You have to touch all the bases ... leave no stone unturned."

Down deep, no matter what I said, I knew that further resistance was foolish. My parents were correct. What sense would it make to put a football team ahead of my family life? Could there be a way, I wondered, to have both? There had to be a middle ground somewhere.

Extra help. That was the answer. On the Blesto staff was a young guy scouting the Southeast. He was from Western Pennsylvania, which, for AJR, always seemed to be a definite plus. At Pitt, during John Michelosen's tenure, Dick Haley had been a halfback, playing both ways. Buddy Parker drafted him in 1959 as a defensive back and traded him to the Redskins, who traded him to the Vikings, who traded him back to the Steelers in 1961. His pro career was over by 1965 and then he had gone into scouting.

I had traveled with Haley and considered him very organized. He was also, I thought, a terrific person. Given my choice, the assistant I would have picked was Jack Butler, whose lofty status as Blesto's executive director of course ruled him out. Even with Haley, we had a problem. So many NFL teams had been raiding Blesto for talent that a sort of gentleman's agreement among the owners became necessary: no Blesto scout could be hired away from Butler unless the move was a promotion.

Thus if we offered Haley a job, it could not be as an ordinary scout. To make it look right, we'd have to give him a title.

But what title? The only title in the scouting department — personnel director — belonged to me. It was Kass, I believe, who came up with a solution. Dick Haley would join the Steelers as personnel director, and my new title would be vice president. There were two other vice presidents — Jack McGinley and Dan. On paper, at least, I was now their equal.

Exactly how much my brother and my father had to do with all this I'm not sure. Forever after, I would say that I owed my new title to my mom, infuriating Kay.

"Don't say that! You *earned* the position," she would tell me.

"I'm kidding," I'd answer. To myself, I would add, "On the square."

Until Haley got his bearings, I continued to do my job the same as before. In other words, I spent too much time away from home. After that first season, though, I changed my modus operandi. (If AJR could read that sentence, he'd say I was putting on the dog.) I traveled less and coordinated more, letting Haley do the bulk of the field work.

He remained with the Steelers for nineteen years. As a matter of fact, he outlasted me.

Cousin Tim

After the 1972 draft, I pestered AJR, Dan, and Chuck Noll to let me branch out. I wanted a subdivision within the scouting department to evaluate and keep track of the players on other teams in the NFL.

It would help us make trades and, even more important, avoid trades. For reasons like injuries, poor performance, and undisciplined behavior, teams were always looking to unload somebody.

As I expected him to, AJR raised objections. "We hardly ever make trades," he pointed out. Our philosophy, after all, was to build through the draft. Although he never actually bought into the idea, he allowed me to hire a couple of scouts.

My first pick was Chuck Klausing, the dean of high school and small-college coaches in Western Pennsylvania. He agreed to take the job and then, on the grounds that he could not give up coaching, reversed himself, and I understood. If a football man preferred coaching to scouting, it was all right with me — just as long as he did not give the impression that to be a mere scout was somehow degrading.

The scout I ended up with was my cousin Tim Rooney. AJR seemed to hesitate when I mentioned Tim. There were limits, he believed, to the number of family members the Steeler organization could accommodate.

"I know that," I replied. "But Tim would be working somewhere else in the NFL except for the fact that he's a Rooney. The other teams ask me why the Steelers don't hire him. It makes them question his ability."

For once, I had struck the right note. "If he's the guy you want," said AJR, "then it's all right with me. Our name shouldn't keep him from getting a decent job."

Tim was an assistant coach at Villanova. I called him immediately and said that if he'd like to be a full-time scout for the Steelers he should get to Pittsburgh as soon as possible. The time was about 10 a.m. At 4 in the afternoon, Tim walked into my office.

I expressed surprise that he was able, on such short notice, to catch a plane.

"Catch a plane? No way," Tim said. "I jumped right into my car and hit the Turnpike. I thought if I waited too long you might change your mind."

Tim's work for the Steelers was first-rate. After seven years, he left to become head of the Detroit Lions' scouting department. From Detroit, he went to the New York Giants.

The way I look at it, the lift that Tim needed to start his very successful career as a scout came from AJR. Tim was Duke's son, remember. And AJR's relations with Duke had been anything but brotherly. They disliked each other, in fact. Tim, of course, wasn't Duke, but AJR's ability to disassociate father and son said something I had always believed about his essential good will. It was not just a job he was offering Tim; he was giving him a chance to start a new and more satisfying life.

'He's Got an Agent!'

Franco Harris got off on the wrong foot with AJR by immediately hiring an agent. AJR liked to negotiate contracts directly with the player, one on one. But now we were hearing that Tony Rossano, a Western Pennsylvanian from New Castle, would do all the bargaining for Franco.

Rossano was a friend of Bill McPeak — had played football with him at New Castle High School, I believe. He followed McPeak to Pitt, but was never more than a bench-warmer. After college, they kept in touch. McPeak spent nine years with the Steelers and Rossano went into coaching. When McPeak became coach of the Washington Redskins, he found a place for Rossano on his staff.

Jack Butler's opinion of Rossano, in contrast with McPeak's, was unfavorable. I'd be leery of anyone who failed to meet with Butler's approval, and yet in some respects Rossano impressed me. I liked his "go-get-'em" attitude and I respected his knowledge of football. These same qualities may have been apparent to the San Francisco Forty-Niners, who made him their head scout in the 1980s.

In 1972, AJR had not yet accepted agents as a fact of life. When he saw that there was no getting rid of them, he tried to adapt. Sitting across the table from an agent, while Dan did the negotiating, he could turn on his Irish charm, although not without difficulty. Whether Irish charm prevented any agent from getting the best deal possible for his client I couldn't say.

As time went on and there was still no agreement between the Steelers and Rossano, AJR's testiness increased. I was with him one day at 940 North Lincoln Avenue when the telephone rang. The call was from Dan, about Franco. Greatly agitated, AJR began shouting. As soon as he hung up, I got the full benefit of his anger. He swiveled around in his chair, gave me the kind of look I had come to dread, and spoke just two words. "Franco!" he said. "Rossano!" Nothing else. Making Franco our No. 1 draft pick had been entirely my doing, and now I had to answer for Rossano's intransigence.

Faster than Joe Greene could slash between two offensive linemen, I was out the front door and headed for home.

One of Chuck Noll's innovations was a get-acquainted session with our rookies every spring. They would come to the city, visit Three Rivers Stadium, take a physical examination, meet Noll and the other coaches, get a brief tutorial on the system he'd be using, and listen to him talk about the training program he expected them to follow. They'd meet the Chief, they'd meet Dan and Ralph Berlin and Tony Parisi. They'd go to dinner that night at LeMont, a restaurant on Mount Washington with a panoramic view of the Golden Triangle. They'd watch our highlight film – action shots from the previous season. (The fact that cynics had stopped calling our highlight films "lowlight" films attested to the progress we were making under Noll.) The next morning, on the Tartan Turf at Three Rivers, there'd be a light non-contact workout.

When the rookies from the class of '72 checked in, only Franco Harris was missing. "He's late," someone said, but then a scout, my cousin Tim Rooney, summoned Noll to the telephone. The call was from Dan, who had heard from Rossano. It seemed that, instead of being late, Franco wasn't coming at all.

According to Tim Rooney, Noll gave vent to his outrage in a voice that may have reached Happy Valley, where Franco was holed up. He then slammed down the receiver. The tour of Three Rivers, the physical exams, the introductions, the lectures, and the dinner on Mount Washington proceeded with Franco still absent. But in the morning, lo and behold, there he was at the team's workout.

Like every other player, he was wearing a light gray sweatsuit. I saw him standing alone for a minute or two, which gave me an opening to say something. It wasn't much — just that he'd be doing the things we knew he could do best. With that, our conversation was over, interrupted by a call from Dick Hoak, the backfield coach, for Franco to walk through a play.

I don't know how it happened that Franco came in for the workout that morning. Dan, I assume, got to Tony Rossano. The give and take between them continued in the days that followed until they finally settled on a contract. I could not have been more relieved. If we were going to win — if we were going to be successful — we had to sign our top picks. Dan understood that. His antipathy toward agents equaled AJR's, but he knew when to compromise and when to stand firm.

With help from Jim Boston, Dan had been our chief negotiator even before Franco's signing, but in more ways than one it turned out to be a watershed moment.

Vindication

I had stuck my neck out for Franco, and no one allowed me to forget it. Later that spring on a tour of the Southwest, I traveled with another scout, an outspoken, abrasive type. We were watching practice one day at Arizona State when he told me, for no apparent reason, that drafting Franco had been a terrible mistake. "He won't be there when things get tough — he's a front-runner," the scout said.

After nine years on the road, I could listen to such blowhards without wanting to fight.

At St. Vincent, in July, Franco dispelled the myth that he saved all his effort for game day. He practiced as willingly and intensively as Chuck Noll and the other coaches could have wished. When the team finished running a play, he would keep going downfield for twenty more yards. In the post-practice conditioning drills, he skipped rope for what seemed like hours. He was good at it, too, as graceful as any heavyweight boxer with the exception, perhaps, of Muhammad Ali. And though Franco was not an effusive person, his teammates accepted him as one of the gang.

It helped that Dick Hoak, another Penn State man, was the backfield coach. Franco and Hoak had confidence in each other and were temperamentally alike — quiet and retiring. Typically, Chuck Noll treated Franco with even-handed reserve. Noll was first and foremost a teacher; his players were members of the student body. In a Chuck Noll classroom, there were no teacher's pets.

I watched the early exhibition games nervously until Franco's first breakaway run. Then I said to myself, "He can do it." But how consistently? Consistently enough, it turned out, to satisfy Noll. When the regular season opened, Franco was the team's starting fullback.

All great athletes have uncanny vision. It was why Franco could see a hole when it opened up and could sense the location of every other player on the field. Cutting back to a hole was easy for him because of his quick feet. He could pick his way through the debris of a broken field and turn on a burst of speed that would take him all the way to the goal line. Instead of blocking, he positioned himself in front of the runner (or the quarterback), and most of the time, anyway, his size kept the tackler at bay. Used primarily as a runner himself, he seldom was called on to block. At catching the ball, we were to learn that we had a miracle worker in Franco.

Size and quick feet are an unlikely combination. Here's a training camp story: Franco had a brother, a defensive back named Dino, and we gave him a tryout one year. On his first day at St. Vincent he was working with the other rookies in a basic drill for defensive backs — backing up and turning — when Franco sauntered over to take a look. Maybe somebody dared him to join in the fun. At any rate, that was what he did, moving his feet so adroitly and swiftly that the rookies, Dino included, were made to appear hopelessly inadequate. Sabotaged by his well-meaning older brother, Dino's NFL career never got off the ground. The brothers' DNA, although it came from the same source, differed in crucial respects.

Quick feet, vision, strength — these were the qualities that would take Franco Harris to a coveted destination, pro football's Hall of Fame in Canton, Ohio.

The French Connection

As successful as he was at squeezing through holes, Franco needed a teammate who could block, and in Frenchy Fuqua he had one. Of Frenchy's myriad skills, the ability to impede big defensive linemen or to mow down linebackers, safeties, and cornerbacks was most eye-catching.

He came to the Steelers in a trade with the New York Giants, a trade engineered by Chuck Noll. Frenchy was short but well put together. He was quick and hard to knock off his feet. He was strong — much stronger than he looked.

His Frenchness, as he explained it, derived from an earlier incarnation. He'd been of royal birth — a count, no less — but while sun-bathing in the nude on the French Riviera one day, he fell asleep and woke up as a black man.

Disowned by his aristocratic relatives, he carne to the United States.

That was Frenchy's story, related in a broadly humorous vein to anyone who asked about the origin of that nickname.

He spoke with a faint lisp. "My French accent," he called it. He wore a cape and a wide-brimmed hat. His accessories included a cane with a silver handle. But to appreciate Frenchy's sartorial uniqueness, you had to look at his feet, as everyone did. Frenchy's shoes – black pumps with four-inch high heels of transparent unbreakable glass – were twin aquariums. Each of those heels was full of water, and in each of them swam a pair of goldfish.

The fish had short lives. Inexpert marine biologists, Frenchy and his shoemaker did not understand that fish need fresh water and oxygen. In two or three days, the little fellows would be belly up – dead. Others replaced them and met the same fate. Over the course of a single football season, the casualty rate was enormous.

As far as I know, Frenchy never did get the problem resolved.

Play of the Century

With few exceptions, the twenty-two starters on the 1972 team were players we had either drafted or signed as free agents. The Steelers were now ready to roll, and it was Franco Harris who got them under way. No Pittsburgh team since 1963 had won more games than it lost. From 1972 until 1985, no Pittsburgh team would lose more games than it won. Let me put that another way: in the nine years before we drafted Franco, there were no winning seasons; from the beginning to the end of his career as a Steeler – twelve years in all – there were no losing seasons.

Right from the start he was clipping off one hundred yards a game. By NFL standards, his blockers were undersized but quick, smart, and durable. Through a process of addition and subtraction, Chuck Noll had rectified the Steelers' most obvious deficiencies: team speed and team intelligence.

The 1972 team won eleven of its fourteen regular-season games, putting us into the playoffs for the first time since the Jock Sutherland era. In a matchup at Three Rivers Stadium, our opponent was Oakland, which worried me sick. The Raiders had a lineup of skilled, veteran bruisers, capable, I thought, of making us look bad.

To my considerable relief, we held our own. With time running out, Oakland led, but by the narrowest possible margin, one point. I was ready to accept an honorable defeat. So was AJR. Leaving his box, he headed for the elevator. He would get to the Steelers' dressing room before the usual tidal wave of newspaper reporters and radio/television crews and be there to offer condolences and congratulations. This team, he intended to say, had played better and won more games than any other in the history of the franchise.

I was still in my own seat, watching the game clock: only twenty-two seconds left and no way to keep it from moving. The Steelers had the ball at their own 40-yard line and were lining up for one last play. I whispered a Hail Mary.

Certainly we needed help from on high, for whatever call Terry Bradshaw had made wasn't working. He dropped back, looking frantic. Not a single receiver was open. Dodging pass rushers, he scrambled to his right. An Oakland defensive end got a hand on his jersey. Pulling free, Bradshaw stopped and anchored himself and zipped a bullet pass in the direction of the one teammate he could spot, diminutive Frenchy Fuqua.

The Frenchman leaped skyward, his back to the Raiders' goal line. Simultaneously, and just as the ball arrived, Jack Tatum, the NFL's most fearsome defensive back, slammed into him. *Oof!* The ball now reversed its direction. It traveled in an arc toward an oncoming Steeler – Franco Harris.

Instinctively, Franco had started downfield to block for the pass catcher, if any. As his backfield coach, Dick Hoak, pointed out later on, in the heat of action he was always around the ball. Stretching forward now, and bending from the waist, he scooped this one up no more than eight or ten inches above the turf.

Between Franco and a touchdown there were forty-two yards. Knees pumping in a race with the Oakland defense, he angled toward the extreme left corner of the field. At the ten-yard line or thereabouts, he stiff-armed his last pursuer. With exactly five seconds on the clock, he was loping into the end zone.

On the most written-about, talked-about, argued-about play in the overcrowded annals of football, a play that Franco's employer, imprisoned for the moment in the press-box elevator, did not see, the Steelers had won a landmark victory, 13-7.

To the present day, the ending remains controversial. Had the pass from Terry Bradshaw bounced off the person of Tatum or Frenchy Fuqua? Under the rules then in effect, if Fuqua last touched the ball, Franco's touchdown was illegal. Referee, umpire, and back judge conferred on the field, after which the referee called the press box to speak with the NFL's supervisor of officials. And then, dramatically, he lifted both arms.

The roar of the crowd must have shattered many eardrums. In a downtown bar, The Interlude, a man named Michael Ord climbed onto a chair and silenced the other patrons, who were whooping it up. "This day," he announced, "will forever be known as the Feast of the Immaculate Reception."

A few hours later, preparing to do a commentary on the eleven o'clock news at radio station WTAE, Steeler broadcaster Myron Cope received a telephone call from a friend of Ord's. Did the name Ord had given to Franco's catch strike his fancy? Cope hesitated — "for fifteen seconds," as he subsequently acknowledged. Shared with his listeners, would the phrase be perceived as offensive — "sacrilegious, even?" He decided it would not, and over the next days and weeks, not only Cope's large audience but football fans everywhere were repeating the words gleefully.

AJR was one of the holdouts. To him, a pun on the doctrine that the Mother of God had been born without original sin violated good taste and by extension the Fourth Commandment. But gradually his attitude softened. He learned to accept the fact that the Immaculate Reception had changed the Steelers' image. It had made them "winners." More to the point, it had changed their owner's image. He, too, now was a winner. Besides, if everybody insisted on using a blasphemous term to describe a football play, there was nothing, after all, that he could do about it.

In the American Conference championship game the following week, the Steelers again played well, but lost to the undefeated Miami Dolphins, 21-17. Significantly, Miami went on to win the Super Bowl, beating the Redskins, 14-7, for a clean sweep of their seventeen games.

Franco Harris ended the season with more than one thousand yards rushing and was Rookie of the Year. I wasn't shameless enough to go around reminding people of the trouble I'd had in convincing Chuck Noll of Franco's merits, but on one occasion, anyway, Noll himself raised the subject, at least indirectly. Not long before the 1973 draft, Noll, some assistant coaches, and I were checking out the fullbacks available. One of them, Chuck Foreman, had impressive credentials, most of us thought; watching him on film, we were all the more surprised when Noll abruptly stopped the projector.

"I'm not crazy about this kid," he said, "but I suppose I'm wrong." He got to his feet and then continued. "Just like I was wrong about that big fullback from Penn State last year."

As we looked at each other, withholding comment, Noll left the room. An assistant coach broke the silence. "Art," he said to me, "that's as close as you'll ever get to hearing Chuck say, 'You were right and I was wrong.'"

I allowed myself just a flicker of gratification. Another new draft was in the offing, and all of us had work to do.

Fighting Back

By the time Rocky Bleier was a senior at Notre Dame in 1967 all the NFL scouts had sized him up. He was captain of the team, a guy who consistently made good plays, not a great athlete but not a bad one. His quickness and speed were OK rather than eye-opening. He ran the forty-yard dash in 4.8 seconds. We saw him as "an overachiever who had reached his physical potential." If he gained the twelve pounds he needed as a pro, we thought, his time in the forty would be 4.9 instead of 4.8. Not up to par for an NFL running back.

We were lucky to have Don Heinrich, our backfield coach, scouting Bleier. A quarterback for the University of Washington and later the New York Giants in his playing days, Heinrich had been a scout when Bill Austin hired him, and he knew what to look for. In the hours we spent over scouting reports, I gained an appreciation of Heinrich's acuteness. He stressed what we called in the jargon of our profession the intangibles — toughness, intensity, character, football smarts. Discussing a prospect, he would ask, "How much does he love the game?" He believed that regardless of how talented a player might be, "if football is not the most important thing to him, he will let you down somewhere along the line." This sort of thing may sound like hogwash, but it helped us to evaluate Bleier.

Rocky's glass, you could say, was only half full talent-wise, and, for most scouts, half-full was not enough. Heinrich chose to analyze the contents of the glass, not to dwell on how much was in it, or how little. "Yes, the kid's limited," he told me. "But let's look at it this way: He was playing big-time college football and was in on all the action; he produced; he is willing to sacrifice his body. If this kid gains the twelve pounds he needs for the NFL and stays at a four-eight forty, he will be a valuable special-teams guy and can play some as a running back, though he will always be pretty much of a straight-ahead runner. He catches the ball in a crowd and I think he can learn to block. He won't embarrass us for lack of effort. We've done worse. Let's try to get him as a late draft choice."

We drafted Rocky Bleier in the sixteenth round. Exceeding expectations (a habit of his, we were to learn), he lifted weights that summer at Notre Dame and reported to training camp not twelve pounds heavier, but twenty pounds heavier. And, at 205, he still ran a 4.8 forty. His toughness impressed Bill Austin, and his attitude — infectiously positive — impressed all of us.

For the first eleven games of the 1968 season, he made a significant contribution on special teams. But America was at war in Vietnam, and the lives of young men were being put on hold — or in some cases violently extinguished. The Steelers, like every other team in professional sports, tried to keep their personnel on the home front. This was Fran Fogarty's job, and he did what he could for Bleier, working through friends in the military. Late in November, the National Guard unit in nearby Washington, Pennsylvania, found an opening. Bleier was in.

But then his home-town draft board in Appleton, Wisconsin, was heard from. What Bleier had done at Notre Dame, and what he might possibly do for the Pittsburgh Steelers, made no difference whatever to the woman who served as its chairman — or chairperson, if you prefer. Special treatment for athletes, she believed, was grossly unfair. Men without athletic ability and men without connections were doing their part to the fullest extent, and so should Bleier. Period. Ordered to report for induction into the Army irrespective of any arrangement with the National Guard, he missed the last three games of the NFL season.

He went into the Army uncomplainingly, let it be said. On a moral and ethical level, he agreed with the draft board's point of view.

He did have a grievance, a minor one. In accordance with league rules, he was entitled to be paid for only eleven games. Believing that the Steelers shouldn't dock him for his time in the Army, he took up the matter with Fran Fogarty while on furlough in April. When he arrived at our offices in the Roosevelt Hotel, AJR had greeted him with a handshake and then wandered off. Instead of chaining himself to a desk, he liked to circulate. Fogarty, ever mindful of the balance sheet, told Bleier there was no way he could be compensated for the entire season. They argued about it a little, back and forth, and Fogarty, as usual, was adamant. Suddenly, from the next room, a voice rang out.

"Give him anything he wants!"

Stubbornly, Fran held his ground. "We can't do that, Art," he protested. "The league won't allow it."

"Then give him his bonus."

Bleier's contract called for a bonus of $1,500 if fifty percent of his playing time was at running back. He hadn't come close to earning it, but the Chief ordered Fogarty to write out a check.

From Fort Gordon in Georgia, where he had taken his basic training, the Army shipped Bleier to Vietnam, a private first class in an infantry battalion. Four months later, in a firefight with North Vietnamese Communist troops, he was hit twice, taking a rifle bullet through his left thigh and hand-grenade shrapnel that did severe damage to the ligaments, tendons, muscles, and bones in his right foot.

A fellow GI, a black man whose name he never learned, half-carried him to the helicopter evacuating the wounded. He was flown to an aid station and then to a military hospital in Tokyo. There he asked a doctor the question that had been on his mind all along:

"Will I be able to play football again?"

"No," the doctor said. "It's impossible."

To accept that verdict was the impossibility for Bleier. He wrote a letter from Tokyo which AJR read to me aloud, something I never before had known him to do. In the letter, Rocky said he'd been badly hit. "But don't worry, Mr. Rooney, I'll be back. I'll be back as good as ever," he promised.

His optimism, I thought, sounded genuine. AJR, who had been around a lot longer than I had, was more experienced at reading between the lines. "Yeah, Rocky, you'll be back," he said in a disconsolate voice, and tossed the letter onto his desk.

A few years after the war ended we heard from the helicopter pilot who evacuated Bleier to the aid station. Rocky's foot, the pilot said, had appeared to be hanging onto his leg by the tendons alone. The medics had given him morphine and he started babbling, telling everybody he would soon be playing football again. "I admired Rocky's spunk, but couldn't see how he'd ever walk again — walk normally," the pilot told me. "As for playing football ... I thought the chances against that were a million to one."

October 26, 1969, was Steeler Alumni Day. Before the game with the Redskins at Pitt Stadium, Rocky limped onto the field, and the crowd of 46,500 gave him a standing ovation. He was many pounds underweight and using a cane. Not for a minute believing it, AJR told him, "I'm sure you're coming back to the team," adding, "I'll take care of the rest."

It would be another thirteen months before Bleier was eligible for discharge. At Fort Riley, in Kansas, he underwent an operation on his foot. He ran laps on the track (it was agonizing, he said). He lifted weights. He ran the steps of the Kansas State football stadium with weights attached to his ankles. A friendly personnel officer hastened his release from the Army and by the summer of 1970 he was in Pittsburgh, determined to resume his football career.

Training camp opened with the NFL players' union on strike, creating a dilemma for Rocky. His decision was not to cross the picket line, and it seemed to inflame every Steeler fan. Pittsburgh always had been a union town, but though a small percentage of talk-show callers praised Rocky's stand, the majority excoriated him. He was showing ungratefulness to his team and to AJR. Letters to the newspapers were similar in tone. Almost nobody thought that Rocky would ever play again, but the Steelers were giving him a chance. It was known that AJR had assumed the full cost of his rehabilitation. On Myron Cope's popular radio show, he appeared one night as the union's spokesman. Driving Dad home from the office, I listened to the calls and was shocked. The comments phoned in were blistering. I glanced at AJR and saw that he was greatly disturbed. At last he began to talk. He said he could not understand why Rocky's teammates had put him in such an awkward position. "All the work and pain he has to go through ... " To a degree, the Chief blamed Cope, one of our broadcasters. He "shouldn't have let Rocky do this."

I went into the house with the Chief instead of dropping him off. The first thing he did was call Joe Gordon, our publicity guy, and ask him to get in touch with Rocky. "Tell him I'd like to speak with him," AJR said. Minutes later (Gordon worked fast), Rocky was on the phone. In my life with my father there were times when I took him for granted, times when I was furious with him, and times when I held him completely in awe. Hearing what he said to Bleier, I was in awe. He let Rocky know he had listened to Cope's show. "I thought you handled yourself very well," he said. He went on to tell Rocky he owed the Steelers nothing and should do what he felt was right. One thing he should not do was worry about the opinions of the herd.

I remember wondering at the time how I could ever live up to the standards my father had set for me. To this day, years after his death, I wonder how he would feel about the things I have done and have not done. In the end, Bleier reported for practice. At a meeting of the Steeler veterans, he had asked for, and received, permission to join the rookies in camp because of his "special circumstances."

As it turned out, that was the easy part. Though he had gained back all his lost weight, he was slower, even, than the linemen, limping and running flat-footed. He could not get up on his toes, he said, because it hurt too much to bend them back. After watching him for a while, I said to my brother Dan, "He's going to get hurt. He can't protect himself. One of these afternoons when he's really tired, he's going to get killed on a sweep."

Doc Best, our team physician, felt the same way. So did Ralph Berlin, the trainer. "Why is he doing this to himself?" some of the other players were asking. Rejecting advice to quit, advice to have another operation, Bleier told his well-wishers, "There's only one man whose opinion counts." That man was our coach, Chuck Noll.

In short order, Noll made up his mind. He called Bleier into his office and said he was putting him on waivers.

"Driving home that night, the tears blinded me. I could barely see the road," Bleier wrote in his autobiography, "Fighting Back."

Early the next morning Rocky's telephone rang. It was Dan. He had talked things over with his father, he said. The Steelers were putting Rocky on the injured reserve list instead of on waivers. And now it was AJR who suggested a second operation.

"How soon do you want me in the hospital?" Bleier asked.

Doc Best performed the surgery. There were two Doc Bests — the martinet who cracked down on inattention or levity in the operating room and the big, loud, jovial, chain-smoking, two-fisted drinking man. Diagnosed with cancer and told that only the removal of his prostate could save him, he declined, explaining, "I intend to leave this world with all the parts I came in with." Ultimately, he did leave this world with all his parts, but he was spared sufficient time to work on Rocky, and the Doc Best who went about it was the skilled orthopedist. The military surgeons had left some shrapnel in Rocky's foot. Best dug it out. In therapy sessions, he pulled and stretched Rocky's tendons and ligaments. Ralph Berlin pulled and stretched. This second, more painful round of treatment and exercise, Rocky said, was sometimes pure hell. But his foot had begun to improve.

AJR gave instructions that Bleier should receive a full year's salary — $19,000. That taken care of, he said to me, "Rocky's got a long way to go. I want you to keep him busy. Make him one of your scouts. In case his foot doesn't get better, let's see if we can find a place for him in the organization."

Rocky's conditioning program and the frequent team meetings he had to attend cut drastically into his time, but on weekends I could send him to college games. His scouting reports, a bit ragged at first, quickly improved. Rocky didn't mind being kidded. "I can tell who your friends are," I would say when he reported on Notre Dame players. "You're making them all sound like Heisman Trophy winners." Half-serious, I would advise him, "If your comeback doesn't work out for you, Rocky, you can always be a scout. Don't look down your nose at scouting. It's the scouts who make this game go. Hell, anybody can play."

In "Fighting Back," Bleier wrote, "I laughed with Art because he knew what I was thinking — that I'd rather be a third-string special-teams player than the greatest scout in the world."

After the season was over, Rocky sold insurance in Chicago and worked out hard at the YMCA. My brother Dan tried to discourage him from returning to the team, but he insisted on giving it a try. He asked to report with the rookies that July, and Dan consented. On the first day, loosening up, Rocky pulled a hamstring. At the urging of Noll, Doc Best advised him to retire. Rocky paid no attention. He wrapped up the hamstring and played in a few of the exhibition games. Noll then put him on the taxi squad. Reactivated to fill a vacancy created by an injury, he was hurt in his first game. He appeared in only three games all season and failed to distinguish himself on special teams. AJR, people said, was keeping him around for three reasons: he was Irish, he went to Notre Dame, and he was a war hero.

Dick Haley asked, "Does anyone actually think he can play? He can't run. He can't do anything." And I am quoted in Rocky's book as saying, "Last year he was a cripple. This year he's just bad."

Over the winter, Rocky practiced yoga. He ran up the fire escape on the side of the apartment building he lived in — eight stories, bottom to top — eight times in a row every day. He worked at the conditioning program Ralph Berlin had given him: five consecutive 350-yard runs in sixty seconds apiece with twenty-five seconds of rest in between.

In July, when training camp opened, I couldn't believe what I was seeing. Rocky looked big. He looked strong. We lined him up to run the forty-yard dash and I was even more surprised when I checked my watch: 4.6 seconds. He was two steps faster than he'd been at Notre Dame. I checked with the other scouts and the coaches. Everyone had either 4.6 or 4.65.

I said, "I've never seen anything like this." How could a guy who'd had most of his foot destroyed pick up so much speed? "Guts ... perseverance ... good physical therapy ... Doc Best," I told myself. "And the prayers of all those nuns and moms and grandmoms throughout the United States."

Rocky again was a special-teams player in that 1972 season, but with a difference. He tackled and ran back kicks like a whirlwind. We drafted Franco Harris that year, improved from 6-8 in 1971 to 11-3, and won our division title before losing in the playoffs to Miami. Harris was the rookie of the year. Terry Bradshaw was learning to be the kind of quarterback Noll wanted. Through the draft, we were building a defense to match the offense.

And, with Rocky Bleier an unexpected addition, our Super Bowl lineup was gradually taking shape.

Chapter 55

Airlift

First Dan and then Noll flew their own airplanes, small twin-engine four-seaters. On short trips to NFL meetings, they would ask other members of the Steeler organization to be their passengers. I never flew with Dan unless he had a co-pilot, but I would and did fly with Noll even when his co-pilot was his wife, Marianne.

Noll liked to fly to the Blesto physicals in Philadelphia because the football team's offices in Veterans Stadium happened to be near the airport. Each time, he offered to take the scouts along. Bill Nunn and Dick Haley begged off. Not me. I thought that flying with Noll was an excellent way to save time. Since Noll kept his plane at the Allegheny County Airport, there would be no standing in line at the much larger Greater Pittsburgh Airport.

The Blesto physicals were held in mid-winter, but if the weather was clear it never worried me. Returning to Pittsburgh, a trip of about an hour and a half, I would take a back seat and work on my reports. Meanwhile Noll would be busy on the radio or occupied in making instrument adjustments. There was no small talk. None was needed.

The first of these trips was uneventful. On the second, I noticed that Noll kept in contact with the radio tower as we approached the airport. By now I had made many landings with Noll, but this one seemed different. Although weather conditions were perfect, he started to curse. We descended almost to the runway, and then he pulled up and gained altitude. The twin engines were making a racket.

"I missed the [expletive deleted] approach," he said to me over his shoulder. "I'll have to go around again." This had happened previously to me with other pilots, and it was never a big deal. However, Noll was berating himself the way I had heard him admonish Terry Bradshaw for bonehead decisions on the football field.

I wasn't especially frightened, but I did what the Sisters of Mercy at St. Peter's School had trained me to do. I said a hasty Act of Contrition. I said it silently: I had no wish to distract Noll as he circled around for a second landing attempt. After my Act of Contrition, I started in on the rosary. I was halfway through the Sorrowful Mysteries when he brought the plane down very softly.

Noll sometimes said that any flight you could walk away from was a good one. He may have said it this time. I don't remember. What I do know is that this was a flight we never talked about afterward.

Uncle Miltie

On AJR's trips to Las Vegas, there were times when Kass went along. "In small doses," as she put it, Kass enjoyed the company of Ruth Jaffe, Milton's wife. Milton owned a piece of the Stardust Resort and Casino, and Ruth could dish the dirt about the big-time performers who came to Las Vegas. Her gossip entertained Kass, but only up to a point. "Too much of a good thing," she would say after one of Ruth's talkathons.

When Ruth and Milton first moved to Las Vegas they lived in a suite of rooms at the Stardust. However exciting that was, Ruth told Kass, she wanted them to have "a place of their own," and they found one away from the Strip. Even after Ruth's death, Milton remained there. AJR would see him often, stopping off on his way to or from the West Coast, where football and race track meetings were most frequently held. The NFL, for obvious reasons, never met in Las Vegas itself, the nation's gambling capital, but the players' union would meet there in spite of the league's disapproval. Under the terms of the bargaining agreement there was nothing the league could do about that.

With Ruth gone, we thought that Kass might curtail her visits, but she liked to see the shows, for which Milton obtained tickets, refusing to be compensated for them, and she liked to play the slot machines. Milton was always happy to have her around. Reminders of Ruth seemed to comfort him somehow.

AJR, Milton's old partner, took an academic interest in the show-business side of Las Vegas, but what drew him to the place was the gambling. When any of his sons were in town, he and Milton would go their own way, hanging out with friends from the Pittsburgh-Youngstown-Steubenville area — friends like Nick the Greek — while one or more of the boys and their wives looked after Kass.

I remember an evening at a Ziegfeld Follies-type show in Las Vegas with Kass, Kay, and the Butlers, Jack and Bernie. Up on the stage was a chorus line of beautiful girls – every one of them bare-breasted. We of course had expected something like this, but seeing it in the flesh, so to speak, was a little overwhelming. Though we tried to act blasé, our jaws fell open. Kass, with a chuckle, guessed that not even George Jaffe, Milton's brother, would let the strippers at their burlesque house in downtown Pittsburgh display quite so much of themselves.

It got so that Kass preferred the games in Las Vegas to the shows. On one of the last times she went out there, AJR gave her a hundred dollars for the slot machines, already a major attraction on the Strip. To women especially, the blinking lights and the sound effects seemed irresistible. As Kass told the story herself, she was merrily feeding coins into her favorite machine when she dropped one. Bending down to retrieve it from the carpeted floor, she noticed an alligator shoe on the foot of the person playing next to her. A tuxedo trouser leg grazed the top of that shoe. It was just barely visible beneath a long fur coat — mink, Kass thought, or maybe sable.

She looked up to see who was wearing this outfit. A smiling, wavy-haired, middle-aged man with powder and rouge on his face. In a singsong effeminate voice, he said to Kass, "Don't you just love these toys! My mother always loved to play them."

Kass was too startled to reply. The man pumped the handle of his slot machine a few more times and then walked away. And Kass went running to AJR, who was having a conversation with Nick the Greek.

"Art!" she exclaimed. "Art! I've been playing the slots with Liberace!"

AJR was not in the least surprised. He immediately understood what had occurred.

"Milton Jaffe," he said, "put him up to that."

A Kiss from Mary Ann

Clint Eastwood, the old cowboy actor, made a boxing movie called "Million Dollar Baby" that was popular with the critics and the public. It took me back to a time when AJR and the McGinleys promoted fights at Forbes Field, Hickey Park, and Duquesne Gardens and when the drivers who picked up my brothers and me after school were often ex-pugs or their managers.

"Do you remember those days?" I asked Tim.

"Sure do."

Tim then wanted to know if I remembered Gus Camp, a middleweight club fighter in the 1920s. Camp, Tim thought, was on the after-school pickup crew. "Nice guy. Owned a bar. When Dad's office was in the Fort Pitt Hotel, Gus would drop in to say hi once in a while."

I remembered Camp well. And I knew a story about him.

Frank Moran, an Irishman from the North Side who boxed twice for the heavyweight championship, losing to Jack Johnson in Paris and to Jess Willard in New York, had a fight coming up at Duquesne Gardens with somebody named Jack Geyer. Moran was approaching the end of his career but still carried a knockout punch in his right hand. He had a name for his right hand — "Mary Ann." Opponents who were kissed by Mary Ann became instantly weak in the knees.

As George Quinlan told it, with the date of his appearance at Duquesne Gardens impending, Moran needed sparring partners and there were none to be had. He was his own manager, usually, but on this occasion was being handled by Luke Carney, who in years to come would manage Pittsburgh's colorful welterweight champion, Fritzie Zivic. Looking around in the gym one day, Carney spotted Gus Camp.

"Wanna make ten bucks?" Carney asked.

"Doing what?" Camp replied.

"Boxing a couple of rounds with Moran."

Moran was 6 feet 2 and weighed 215 pounds; Camp weighed 160.

"He'll throw the right hand and kill me," Camp objected.

"I'll tell him not to use the right."

Camp then agreed to spar. They got into the ring, and he was having an easy time of it. Moran was a fighter who could hit with only one hand; deprived of that hand, he looked helpless. All the punches were being landed by the smaller, quicker Camp.

At the end of the round, Moran went back to his corner unhappy.

"You're letting that guy show me up," he said to Carney.

"Use the right hand then," Carney answered. In round two, Moran did. Camp hit the deck, unconscious. Carney, in an access of guilt, bent over the stretched-out fighter and passed smelling salts under his nose. Gradually, Camp came to.

"Gus!" Carney said. "Are you all right? Shall I call a doctor?"

Camp's eyes were now beginning to focus. He lifted his head a few inches. "Hell, no," he said. "Call a priest."

This was one story that Tim never had heard. There were dozens of others like it, and AJR knew them all.

On Second Thought

After Ralph Berlin had been with us for several years, he approached me about changing jobs. Since coming to the Steelers as trainer during the Bill Austin regime, he had done a little scouting for me. Now he was interested in scouting full-time, as long as extended road trips would not be necessary. I expressed my willingness to give him a try. Berlin was easy to work with, a subscriber to the doctrine passed on to Chuck Noll from his mentors Paul Brown and Don Shula: "Whatever it takes."

All the things a trainer must do were wearing Berlin down. His knees hurt, making it difficult for him to tape ankles, which required a lot of stooping, and to help injured players get back on their feet before they limped off the field. He was not in a position, financially, to retire, and he loved football. Scouting, therefore, would be an ideal situation for him, he thought.

"You can scout the Mid-Atlantic Conference teams — Bowling Green, Kent State, Miami, Ohio U., Youngstown, Marshall," I told him.

Initially, it worked out fine. His reports were well written and he got them in on time. He knew the technical aspects of the game. His opinions were OK. And he represented the Steelers in a high-class way. Early on, I advised him to keep at it. He had the makings, I said, of a first-rate scout. His response to this, I must admit, was unexpected.

"Thank you, Arthur," he said, "but scouting is not for me. Too much time on the road. I'll stick to taping ankles and taking care of the wounded as long as I can."

All told, Berlin was with the Steelers for more than twenty-five years. From time to time, he continued to give me help when I needed it. In retirement, he helped Dan, working at part-time jobs in the scouting and ticket departments and also on occasion as a driver.

"The Plumber," he called himself. "Jack of all Trades" or "Handy Man" might have been closer to the mark. There was nothing he couldn't do, it seemed, and nothing he couldn't do well.

'That One's a Cop'

If I had followed through on my youthful ambition to be an actor, I could have played any character part. Without makeup. Without a disguise.

Do you doubt that? Read on.

In New Orleans one time on the morning of a football game, I went to the hotel coffee shop with my brother John and assistant coach Woody Widenhofer. The place was packed. We spotted three open seats at the counter, but only two of them were together. John sat with Woody, and I took the single. The counter was in the form of a square, and I could see, but not hear, John and Woody. Seated next to Woody was a young woman, attractive in a rather flashy way. I saw him turn to her and say something, and I saw that she answered him. Later, John filled me in.

"Woody whispered to me, 'Watch this, '" John related. "Then he said to this lady, 'How much?'"

According to John, she told him to keep his voice down, explaining, "I can't talk now. That one over there is a cop."

"She meant you," John went on.

"And you do look like a cop," he said. "An Irish cop from the North Side."

It must be that I have an air of command. At Parris Island one day, I walked into the squad bay wearing my summer dress uniform — khaki pants, shirt, and tie. Someone shouted, "Officer on deck!" and everyone else snapped to attention.

Almost immediately, one of my fellow enlisted men, recognizing me, called out, "Aw, that's no officer; it's just that damned Private Rooney."

A long time afterward, when Kay and I were in Aspen, Colorado, for a wedding, I was pointed out to my brother Tim by another guest. We were outdoors, near the ski slopes. "See that big guy with the redhead?" said Tim's acquaintance. "The one with the Irish cap on? That's Victor McLaglen's son."

Victor McLaglen was an old-time character actor with an unmistakable Irish brogue. A heavyweight boxer in his younger days, he co-starred with John Wayne in "The Quiet Man." They engaged in a memorable bare-knuckle fight, which McLaglen would have won in real life.

The man who told Tim that McLaglen was my father went on to say that I had used this connection to land a job as a Hollywood movie director.

At another gathering, somebody confided to my nephew Sean Rooney that he had seen me often on television. I mostly played cowboys, the man said.

Sometimes even Kay could be fooled.

At a big social affair in a high-class nightclub, she told me I looked very handsome in my new tuxedo.

I'm as willing to accept compliments as most people are, but this was overdoing it.

"Dear," I replied, "I look like the bouncer."

A Special Relationship

When "On the Waterfront," a movie about union racketeering, played the Stanley Theater in 1954, Billy Conn went to see it. The scene that everybody remembers from "On the Waterfront" is the one in which Marlon Brando, as the washed-up prizefighter Terry Malloy, has a long conversation with his older brother Charley, the union's lawyer, in the back seat of a taxicab. They discuss, among other things, Terry's ill-starred boxing career, and Charley says, "Kid, when you weighed 168 pounds you were beautiful. You could have been another Billy Conn."

At that point, according to Conn himself, someone in the audience at the Stanley called out very audibly, "He's a big enough bum as it is."

Conn had a mordant sense of humor and was capable of inventing a story like that. And yet it has the ring of truth; in the way they treat their celebrities, Pittsburghers are notoriously irreverent.

Conn was anything but a bum in the ring. Light-heavyweight champion of the world at 21, Conn beat every good fighter he ever went up against except one – the great Joe Louis. On the other hand, he fastidiously avoided work, which was something he had in common with AJR if work is defined as the drudgery of a 9-to-5 job. AJR made his living with his wits; Conn earned more than a half-million dollars with his fists; he sustained himself and his family from then on in ways that were not clearly visible.

He was prudent enough, I believe, to have invested wisely. And AJR once said that he had "made a ton of money" for Conn by giving him advice at the race track. It was a favor he rarely did for anyone else, which tells a great deal about the special relationship between them.

Another of Conn's special relationships was with Milton Jaffe, his business manager. Jaffe owned a piece of the Stardust Casino in Las Vegas and would pay Conn handsomely to go out there now and then and make himself agreeable to the customers. Conn being Conn, this was sometimes difficult for him.

The newspaperman Gene Collier wrote in Conn's obituary that he was "as blunt as a fist." It's a statement for which plenty of documentary evidence existed. In the early 1970s, thirty years after Conn's first fight with Louis, AJR was taking him on a tour of Three Rivers Stadium. He introduced Billy to several white players in the locker room, and they admitted they never had heard of him. Irritated, Billy called over to a group of black players in another part of the room: "Hey, blackies." In unison, their heads swiveled toward him. "Do you know who Joe Louis was?" he asked. The black players nodded. Conn turned again to the white players. "And you knuckleheads don't know who I am," he said.

Conn was from East Liberty, and like everybody else who grew up in tough big-city working-class neighborhoods before World War II he used all the ethnic slurs so common back then. There was nothing malicious about it – it was just the way people in that time in those places talked.

An example: While waiting for the bell on the night he won the light-heavyweight title from Melio Bettina, who was from Beacon, New York, Conn noticed a group of the champion's home-town Italian fans in the front row at Madison Square Garden. They had unfurled a banner imploring Bettina to "Bring Back the Bacon to Beacon." Conn looked down at these high-spirited partisans from the camp of the enemy and said, "There's gonna be a lot of hungry dagoes in Beacon tonight."

He was just as irreverent toward the Irish. On his only visit to the land of his ancestors, a newspaper reporter said to him, "Billy, you're a god over here. Everybody loves you. Now, what do you think of Ireland?"

And Billy answered, "I'm glad my mother didn't miss the boat."

Then of course there was also his unforgettable "What's the use of being Irish if you can't be dumb?" – this after he was foolish enough to slug it out with Louis in the thirteenth round of their first fight.

Billy Conn was a Pittsburgh guy. He could have settled in Las Vegas with a well-paid sinecure at the Stardust. Instead, after just a few weeks out there, he could hardly ever wait to get home. He believed that God had in mind the same fate for Las Vegas that was meted out to Sodom and Gomorrah. Returning for the last time, he announced he was home to stay,

But then he always had felt drawn to home in whatever part of the globe he happened to be. Johnny Ray, his manager, sent him down into the Ozark Mountains of Arkansas to prepare for a big fight, and he took no pleasure in the scenic splendor, the pure air, the company of the birds and bees.

"Why, Billy," admonished Nate Liff, who was training him, "this is God's country."

"God's country?" said Billy. "I wouldn't give you an alley in Pittsburgh for it."

Conn took $17,000 from his purse for the first Louis fight and bought a house in an upscale section of Squirrel Hill. For the rest of his life, he lived there with Mary Louise. Their four kids, three boys and a girl, grew up in that house. His purse from the second Louis fight, $325,000, plus the money that Milton Jaffe, AJR, and other financially-wise pals were able to funnel in his direction, enabled him to keep the wolf from the door without scrimping.

His aversion to anything like actual work had been apparent from the time he was 13 years old. William Conn, Sr., who worked as a steamfitter at Westinghouse, took him to the plant in East Pittsburgh one day and said, "This is where you're gonna be as soon as you're old enough, son."

"It scared the hell out of me," Billy later recalled. Soon afterward, having left Sacred Heart School in the eighth grade by request of the nuns, he presented himself at Johnny Ray's gym and asked to be taught how to box.

"You've got to be nuts to be a fighter," Conn said at the end of his career, "but it was better than working in a mill."

Or working almost anywhere at all. Budd Schulberg offered him a supporting actor's role in "On the Waterfront" – Schulberg had written the screen play – but Conn turned him down, saying "One stink bomb is enough." In 1941, after his first fight with Louis, Billy had gone out to Hollywood and played the part of a fighter based on himself in a movie called "The Pittsburgh Kid." The film was so bad, Conn thought, that when people he didn't like came to his house he made them watch the video.

Conn may have been a wooden actor but his boyish good looks impressed casting directors. There were offers from several studios – they wanted Mary Louise to audition for them as well – but Conn wasn't interested, so neither was Mary Louise. He did have a role, for which he received no screen credit, in "Gentleman Jim," a film about the nineteenth-century heavyweight champion, Jim Corbett. The only parts of Conn the audience could see were his legs from the knees down. Errol Flynn played Jim Corbett, but his footwork in the fight scenes was not quite satisfactory, so the director substituted Conn's.

Unlike other ex-pugs, Conn was never reckless with money. Whether or not he had it, he turned to AJR or to Milton Jaffe for advice. Once when Conn lost his driver's license, AJR used his political influence to regain it for him, but declined to pay the twenty-five dollar fine. "I've done enough for Billy," he told the magistrate. "Let him pay it himself." Weeks went by, and Billy still wasn't driving. AJR called the magistrate to ask what had happened. He was told that Billy had refused to fork over. AJR simply shrugged and wrote the magistrate a check.

On the other hand, there was this: Over the Mediterranean Sea during the war, Billy was in an airplane that developed engine trouble. He made a promise to the Lord that if the plane landed safely he would give five thousand dollars to Father Silas for the Franciscans' missionary work and a statue of the Blessed Virgin to Sacred Heart Church in East Liberty. The plane landed with no casualties, and Billy was as good as his word. The five thousand dollars in cash went toward the construction of a church and a school in China.

Billy's gruffness masked a streak of sentimentality. He was devoted to Mary Louise. When he spoke of his mother, his eyes filled with tears. Told that Father Silas had died, he said, "I know this: I've got a friend up in heaven today." Father Silas and AJR, he confided to Aunt Marie, had kept him from being what that real or imaginary movie critic in the Stanley Theater suggested he was — a bum.

As for AJR, he smiled from ear to ear when he talked about Billy, regardless of how exasperated with him he might have been at the time. And yet it amused the Chief that Milton Jaffe, in his will, left nothing more than a fountain pen to Billy. They had flown to Las Vegas for the funeral together, Billy anticipating a five- or six-figure windfall.

A few years later, Billy died of a fighter's occupational ailment as destructive to the brain cells as Alzheimer's — pugilistica dementia. But in his early old age, shortly before going to the Veterans' Hospital where he ended his days, he made the newspapers and newscasts one last time. He was in a convenience store with Mary Louise when a hold-up man came in. Billy knocked him down with a left hook, whereupon the guy crawled to the door, scrambled to his feet, and ran off into the night.

Chapter 56

Horse Sense

Our experience with Ken Phares reminded me of a story that Kass used to tell about one of Dad's race horses. We were kids the first time I heard it. According to Dad's trainer, this particular horse was unbeatable. It couldn't lose. Kass did not believe in sure things, and she said so. "Take my word for it," the trainer assured her. "This horse can't lose. No way it can lose." Still not convinced, Kass said she could think of a way. "Suppose it breaks a leg," she suggested.

At this point in her narrative, Kass would say to us, "And do you know what happened to that poor animal?"

We could guess, but we always asked, "What?"

"Broke its leg. Right in the middle of a race. In front of where we were sitting that day. One of those big green horse vans came onto the track, and a man with a pistol got out. He went up to that horse and shot him in the head, the poor thing — shot him dead. Then they got him into the van and off the track and the races went on just as usual."

Ken Phares, a defensive back from Mississippi State, was our second selection in the 1973 draft. Phares was a "can't-miss" prospect. He had size, speed, and mobility. He liked to hit. In the draft room, we were still congratulating ourselves when AJR came around. "Hey, you guys," he said, "I just had a phone call from a good friend of mine in Atlanta. He's a top sportscaster who used to be a coach, and he said we never should have drafted this Phares kid. He said that Phares has a real bad knee. It kept him out for part of the season and may not hold up very long."

We immediately pulled our scouting reports on Phares and showed them to the Chief. They were unreservedly positive. The player's coaches all downplayed his knee injury. There was no reason to worry about it, they insisted.

AJR barely glanced at the reports. "I can read this stuff," he said, "but my informant is very well connected. He'd never give me a bum steer."

"It's OK, Dad. It'll be OK." I was telling him we could do without advice from outsiders. Ken Phares came to camp in perfect condition. He looked, moved, and conducted himself exactly the way our scouts had promised he would. The team doctors examined his knee and pronounced it as good as new. "A nice repair job," they agreed.

So what happened? On the second play of the first drill in which he took part, Phares re-injured his knee — badly. He never played football again.

And the Chief? He reminded us frequently of the mistake we had made. Our successful 1972 season meant that in 1973 we would draft near the end of each round. The system set up by Bert Bell, with AJR backing him all the way, ensured parity. It prevented the more prosperous teams from cornering the market on talent. Drafting lower now, we had to juggle our rating list just a little, but still we came up with a couple of worthwhile picks.

In the first round, ahead of Phares, we drafted cornerback J. T. Thomas from Florida State. A fine athlete with leadership qualities, J. T. was a starter on our first two Super Bowl teams. He missed the 1976 season because of illness - sickle cell anemia — but returned to the starting lineup, this time as a safety, for one more Super Bowl. The season after that, Thomas was a Pro Bowl selection. In the 1980s, like so many of his fellow ex-Steelers from the Super Bowl years, he distinguished himself as a businessman and community leader.

Besides Thomas, three other players we drafted in 1973 made the team. Two of them, Dave Reavis, defensive tackle from Arkansas, and Glenn Scolnick, wide receiver from Indiana, didn't last long. Scolnick, nicknamed "Tomatoes," was a vegetarian. He could catch the ball and was fast, but lacked the physicality to cope with the bump-and-run defense, which made me wonder about the muscle-building power of spinach.

Our eighth-round pick in 1973, linebacker Loren Toews, was more typical — a meat eater, or so I presume. Toews (pronounced Taves) hung around for ten years and started in one of our Super Bowl games. I blush to say that the scout who called my attention to Toews was not a football scout, but a Boy Scout, perhaps 16 years old. Seated high in the stands, I was watching the 1972 intra-squad game at the University of California when the kid approached me. The Boy Scouts of Berkeley were acting as ushers, their good deed for the day.

'What are you doing'?" he asked, taking in my notebook, binoculars, and other paraphernalia.

I told him I was scouting talent for the Pittsburgh Steelers.

"Oh. Are you watching a player named Toews? He's my brother."

I consulted the Blesto list I always carried. Loren Toews was on it. Six feet two and a half, 205 pounds. Blesto had him rated as a "prospect," nothing more.

From then on I took pains to notice what Toews was doing. He made a few stops. He could hit and move and he played with confidence.

I put the guy's name on my "must-watch" fall list. During the season I happened to catch the California-Oregon game in Eugene. Toews was bigger and just as fast. He had a faculty for being in the right place at the right time. I gave him a decent "can make it" grade.

When I got back to Pittsburgh, Dick Haley said to me, "You know that Toews kid you liked last spring'? I had a chance to see him. He's OK. We have to look at him again."

I chuckled and said, "I just did look at him again."

We had found ourselves a sleeper — an undersized, underappreciated player who would not go high in the draft All we had to do was put some more weight on the guy. He was one of the late picks we made in the 1970s who contributed to those Super Bowl wins.

Footnote: Toews' brother Jeff, the Boy Scout, grew up quickly. The University of Washington recruited him out of high school as an offensive lineman, and from 1979 to 1985 he played in the NFL for Miami, sometimes going up against Loren.

California

Few title or not — in our table of organization I was now a vice president — I continued to think of myself as a scout, first and foremost. And to the detriment of my marriage, I continued to spend weeks at a time away from home. Partly to placate the various family members who were telling me to get my priorities straight, I decided, in the fall of 1973, to take my wife and our five-year-old, Susie, on a scouting trip to the West Coast.

We would fly to San Diego, where Don Coryell had installed a pro-type offense at San Diego State, drive from there to Los Angeles — Kay could visit relatives, and I could scout UCLA and USC — and then proceed north on U.S. A-1-A to San Francisco, arriving in time to catch a Stanford home game in Palo Alto. Berkeley was nearby, too, and there I'd be able to learn if there were any decent prospects at "Cal" — the University of California.

Kay and Susie would be free to take in the sights. San Diego had mountains spilling into the Pacific and a breathtaking coast line, its somber browns and brilliant greens a perfect match for the blue of the ocean and the sky. There were fine hotels and many good restaurants and a harbor that was home to the U.S. Navy's Pacific fleet. In Los Angeles a tangle of freeways awaited us, but the drive to San Francisco is a scenic wonder, and San Francisco itself offered us Telegraph Hill and the Golden Gate Bridge. Berkeley, in those days of student unrest over Watergate, Vietnam, civil rights, and whatnot, was an interesting freak show, a gathering place for the nonconforming rebellious young in all their ragtag, bearded and long-haired, unwashed outrageousness.

I was their staid sartorial opposite, dressed at all times in a dark suit, white shirt, and conservative necktie. Other scouts, our own included, went to work in more casual attire. They were not the obedient offspring of AJR. No Rooney, the Chief insisted, must ever appear in public looking slovenly.

Some years before, on my first trip out West, Jerry Neri had sent a friend of his to pick me up at a USC practice scrimmage. These practice scrimmages were major events. I was watching from the bleachers, one individual in a crowd of at least two thousand, but Neri's friend, a man I never had met, identified me at once. "Rooney!" he called out. "Hey, Rooney!" "He'll be the only guy wearing a suit," Neri had told him. "He dresses like he's going to the office."

In about my fifteenth year on the job, I at last felt secure enough to switch from a suit jacket or dark blue blazer to a golf shirt. When it came to those "athletic shoes" with foam-rubber soles and white canvas tops, I drew the line.

Jerry Neri lived in Los Angeles and was well acquainted with all the coaches in the area. Of course by 1973, introductions were the last thing I needed. Don Coryell at San Diego State was a football genius, highly regarded for his passing schemes. "Our receivers will know what they're doing when they get to your camp," Coryell had assured me, "but don't let their training fool you. They still must have talent to compete in the NFL." A friendly tip that I found to be useful. John McKay, at Southern California, hailed from Western Pennsylvania. His parents, West Virginians, had farmed him out to relatives in rural Greene County when he was still in his teens because Western Pennsylvania's brand of high school football was superior.

McKay and I had some reference points in common, and perhaps for that reason he gave me a lot of help. I recall that on my West Coast visit in 1973 we sat on a bench not far from the USC practice field and discussed the seniors on his team who were pro prospects. One player he talked about — "a wonderful person who comes from a good family and is just big and fast enough to be a winner for you" — was Lynn Swann.

McKay drove around in a golf cart, and he asked me to hop aboard. "I'll show you the kids," he said. Out on the field, he would stop the cart to instruct a player in some technique and for brief consultations with an assistant coach or a trainer. Meanwhile he'd be calling my attention to the seniors, Lynn Swann in particular. I noticed how smooth in his movements Swann was and how well he could jump. Most especially, I liked his cheerful, spirited demeanor.

I felt out of place on the golf cart — a little embarrassed, in fact. When practice was over, two of the assistant coaches had some fun with me. To be a passenger in the USC counterpart of Air Force One meant that I had "arrived," one of them said.

On our second day in Los Angeles, I watched USC film and met with McKay's backfield coach, Craig Fertig. When I told him that Kay and Susie and I would be driving to San Francisco, he said we had to stay at the elegant Del Monte Lodge in Monterey. "I know the manager, I'll call him for you. It's a tough place to get into," he said. That it was, but Fertig delivered on his promise. By the time we checked out of our hotel the next morning, we had a room, thanks to Craig, at the Del Monte Lodge.

So far the trip had been a success, but now our luck changed. A few miles north of Los Angeles, Kay became very ill. Under the circumstances, going on to San Francisco in our rental car was out of the question. I turned around and drove to the airport. How easy it was before September 11, 2001, to travel by air. At the ticket counter, I asked about a night flight to San Francisco. We could rent a car there, I figured, and backtrack to Monterey. "Won't be necessary," the airline agent informed me. A direct flight to Monterey was leaving in half an hour. "A Hertz car will be waiting for you there," the agent said.

By this time, Kay was feeling better. At the Del Monte Lodge, we were affably greeted and shown to a spacious room. It had a wood-burning fireplace, a king-sized bed, and a rollaway bed for Sue. Flying from Los Angeles instead of driving had been a good idea. There were still a few hours of daylight left, and Kay suggested going for a ride. The scenic Seventeen Mile Drive would take us past Pebble Beach and one of the world's most beautiful golf courses.

All of it lived up to our expectations. There were oohs of appreciation from Kay. So we agreed to take a trip after breakfast the next morning — south to the Big Sur. On the two-lane highway, up in the mountains, we came to a bridge that crossed a deep, wide gorge. At the bottom of the gorge, a stream rushed into the ocean. Kay said, "You're driving too fast." The altitude and the sheerness of the canyon walls were making her queasy. I lost no time in putting the gorge behind us.

A few miles farther on, we stopped for lunch. Kay couldn't eat, which worried Sue. "Mommy's not feeling well, Daddy," she announced. Still we drove on, with stops here and there to take snapshots. I was ready to turn around and head back to the lodge when Kay said, "Stop here! This is a great place for a picture." Though I could see nothing special, I pulled off the road and got out of the car. "Where's the picture?" I asked. "Over there," Kay said, directing me to an ordinary-looking rise in the ground.

Dutifully, I walked to the little hillock and took a shot of a nondescript view. When I returned to the car, Kay was ensconced behind the steering wheel.

"Hey!" I objected.

"I'll drive," she said.

"You're too sick to drive."

"No I'm not. I'll get us back alive. No way do I want you driving Susie over that bridge again. This isn't Indianapolis."

Actually, Kay handled a car better than I did. We crossed the bridge — the Bixby Bridge, it was called – at a moderate rate of speed and arrived at the lodge safe and sound.

That night was a downer for Kay, so much so that I canceled out of the Stanford game and called off the rest of my scouting trip. On our way to the San Francisco airport, we drove past the Stanford campus. Because the Steelers were good customers of United Airlines, booking a mid-day flight to Pittsburgh, non-stop, was no trouble.

On the way home, it struck me that Susie's concern for Kay was greater than my own. I'm ashamed to say it, but I gave as much thought to the scouting opportunities I had missed as I did to the condition of my wife. I must further confess that during her illness and convalescence I went about my work with just as much intensity as before. Kay had good doctors, I told myself. They were taking good care of her.

Besieging heaven for Kay's recovery, Kass and Aunt Alice renewed their novena campaign. One day Kass lectured me. "Your wife is not *well* ... don't you see that?" she said. "Don't you appreciate what it is to wake up in the morning beside a woman as nice and as beautiful as Kay?" Kass thought, and so did AJR, that perhaps I should leave my job with the football team and move with Kay and the kids to Palm Beach. There I could work at the dog track we had recently acquired. Even Father Silas joined the chorus. The man who was running the dog track, he told me, was very old. Soon there would be an opening for me. "In just a few years," he said, "a smart guy like you could be ready to take over down there." I wasn't flattered; I wasn't interested. Football still was my passion. "Anyway," Father Silas went on, "you've done a great job with the team. But there will be problems in the future about who's in control, I believe. Keep that in mind."

In the years to come, after Kay had recovered, we made return trips to the West Coast again and again. Susie and Art and Mike would be with us. We'd drive from San Diego to San Francisco and even farther north, most of the time with me at the wheel and most of the time with no adverse comment from Kay. But on side trips out of Monterey, whenever we approached the Bixby Bridge, she would say, "Look, kids. This is the place where your father almost killed Sue and me, going ninety miles an hour over this dangerous bridge."

Lambert

L ate in the fall of 1973 I decided to take a look at a Kent State linebacker named Jack Lambert. Just 110 miles west of Pittsburgh by way of the Pennsylvania and Ohio turnpikes, Kent State was an easy trip. I could eat a leisurely breakfast, see the kids off to school, skim through the morning newspapers, watch an early newscast on television, call the office, and kiss my wife goodbye before departing. Once I arrived, there was time to interview the coaches, study films, watch practice, and still get home (a little late) for dinner.

Kent State football teams did not compete at the top level but played some top-level opponents and had to be scouted. As my old drama coach in New York, Tamara Daykohonoa, used to say, "For every ten students I accept, only one has a true chance of making it as an actor. But I do not accept people who have no potential. That would be dishonest. I look for people with the capacity to act and re-act with each other. If they can do that much, I will take them."

That is roughly the way it was at Kent State. In fact, a shocking event connected with the Vietnam War had served indirectly to upgrade the university's football program. In the spring of 1970, National Guardsmen assigned to keep order on the campus had fired point-blank into a group of war protestors, killing four of them and wounding thirteen. Subsequently, in the hope that success on the football field and basketball court might divert the student body's attention from matters of life and death in Southeast Asia, Ohio government officials earmarked more money for Kent State athletics. Anyway, that is how I heard it from one of Chuck Noll's assistants, Denny Fitzgerald, who had been a Kent State coach at the time of the shooting.

Jack Lambert, as a senior, was the Kent State captain. The question about him had nothing to do with ability or toughness. It was whether he could put on enough weight for the NFL. Lambert stood 6-3 or 6-4 but was all sinew. Dick Haley, my cousin Tim, and even Ralph Berlin had scouted him. One and all agreed that he could get to the ball, had moxie, and was mean as hell.

The definitive story about Lambert came from Tim. It seems that the Kent State quarterback missed bed check or something and would not be allowed to play in one of the season's biggest games without doing penance. He must run, roll, and crawl the length of the practice field, one hundred yards, one hundred times. Sure that he wasn't up to it, the quarterback demurred. If he sat out the big game, Kent State undoubtedly would lose, and thus fail to qualify for post-season bowl consideration. Kent State never had gone to a bowl; as far as Lambert was concerned, missing out on this one could not be tolerated.

"Look, asshole," he said to the quarterback. "Do the drill. I'll do it with you. It may be tough, but not as tough as it's going to be if you don't do it or don't finish it. Because I'll kill you."

Taking Lambert at his word, the quarterback did the drill. At about the halfway mark he stopped to puke, and from then on he had to be dragged and pulled by Lambert, but he completed the ten thousand yards. As he lay on the ground, totally exhausted, Lambert looked down at him and snarled, "I think I'll kill you anyway, but not until later. Right now I'm too tired."

Whether the quarterback lived to win the big game I don't know.

On my visit to Kent State in 1973 I studied film, talked to the coaches, and watched practice, just as I had planned to do. Heavy rains that week had soaked the practice field, so after wading around in the mud for a while the players moved over to the cinder-coated stadium parking lot and worked out in shorts. There was just enough activity to give me a good look at the prospects on our list, primarily Lambert.

I liked the depth he was able to get on his pass drop. I liked his peripheral vision and his lateral movement. I liked his awareness; he was quick to anticipate both the pass and the run. I liked his leadership qualities – the way he communicated with his teammates and coaches. In short, I was feeling that my time had not been wasted. And then something really memorable happened.

Coach Don James was putting the team through a touch-tackle drill. Cutting through the line, a running back broke free. Lambert went after him but appeared to be a step and a half short. So instead of reaching out to make the two-handed touch, he launched himself into the air and got his two hands on the ball carrier's back. The ball carrier, stumbling, kept his balance. Lambert went face down into the cinders.

For the rest of the workout he was picking cinders out of his epidermis. His face, arms, and legs were scraped. Not by a single outward sign did he show that any of this bothered him even slightly. All business every minute, he concentrated on doing his job.

There was nothing more I needed to see.

Inducting Sinatra

Notwithstanding injuries to Terry Bradshaw, Franco Harris, and Frenchy Fuqua, the Steelers returned to the playoffs with a 10-4 record, good for the wild-card berth, in 1973. The playoff game was in Oakland against the Raiders; late in December. A week beforehand, to escape the cold weather in Pittsburgh, Chuck Noll took the team to Palm Springs.

He had done the same thing the year before, when the Steelers ended the season with a must-win game in San Diego. Acclimated to temperatures in the high seventies or low eighties, they had beaten the Chargers easily, 24-2, despite a major distraction — Frank Sinatra's appearance at practice during the week.

I wasn't there, but I heard about it and read about it and can piece together all the details.

Unquestionably, Steeler broadcaster Myron Cope, inspired by his involvement with a Franco Harris fan club, orchestrated the whole thing. The fan club, called Franco's Italian Army, consisted of twenty or so members headed by Tony Stagno, a baker, and Al Vento, a pizza maker. I know that Franco thought of himself as a black man, like his father, but his mother, you may recall, came from Italy. In any case, Stagno, Vento, and their followers attended Steeler games wearing battle helmets. One guy proudly waved an Italian flag. Stagno and Vento were generals in the Army, Stagno with five stars and Vento with four. Cope, the only non-Italian so honored, was a one-star general. Under orders from Stagno, he had gone to Palm Springs on a mission.

"Frank Sinatra lives there, you know," Stagno reminded him. Cope's job would be to track down the singer, bring him to practice, and induct him into the Army as still another general of the single-star variety.

Nothing, it turned out, could have been easier. Cope spotted Sinatra one night in a high-class restaurant and sent him an invitation, delivered by a waiter, to be present the next day at practice and receive his commission. With surprising affability, Sinatra joined Cope and his friends at their table and agreed to cooperate.

After Sinatra left the restaurant, Cope excitedly called Stagno in Pittsburgh. He must fly to Palm Springs with Vento as soon as possible, Cope urged him. This the commanders did, arriving just in time to officiate at the induction ceremony. They were wearing their battle helmets and carrying baskets laden with Italian wines and foodstuffs. Sinatra was on hand, taken in charge by Cope, newspaper photographers trailing along as they moved toward the sideline. Out on the practice field, Noll had become aware that he was losing the attention of his players. He looked unhappy. Cope then did the unthinkable. Boldly setting foot on Noll's turf — sacred ground — he shouted, "Franco! Get over here!" Sinatra was waiting. Stagno and Vento were waiting.

Franco glanced uneasily at Noll. "Can't do it, Myron, I'm practicing," he apologized. First things first. The onus now was on Noll: would he humiliate Cope and openly "diss" Frank Sinatra? The suspense seemed to last forever; then he ended it by echoing Cope. "Get over there, Franco," he said, and the ceremony proceeded with much fanfare.

Allow me now to digress. At some point that day, Sinatra met AJR and was much taken with him. They were to meet again and again over the years. Sinatra made a ritual of sending gifts to his friends, and for AJR it was always a fine box of cigars, dispatched like clockwork every six months.

Getting back to the Italian Army caper, its effect on the team had been harmless, but sideshows of that nature did not amuse me. So when Noll opted again for a week in Palm Springs before the playoff game with Oakland the next year, I was looking for reasons to be worried. A newspaper photograph of two Steeler players at poolside, hovering lasciviously (I assumed) over a voluptuous young miss wearing a barely noticeable bikini, turned the trick.

I asked myself unsettling questions. Was a pleasure resort the right place to get a team ready for so important a game? In such an atmosphere, did the players have their minds on football or on babes? Strange business, it seemed to me, with puritans like Dan, AJR, and Chuck Noll on the scene.

Months later I was to learn that my suspicions were groundless — even silly. The girl was no temptress but a child-woman of 15 or 16, physically mature for her age. Her parents, it turned out, were not football fans; unaware that the team was in Palm Springs, they had booked themselves into the same hotel. Moreover, my informant told me, they kept their daughter under non-stop surveillance. And in the second place, Palm Springs was actually quite staid. When they weren't on the practice field, there was little for the players to do.

Not knowing this, and looking on from a distance, all I could do was judge by what I took to be the evidence. There was still another reason — the big one — for my foul mood that week and beyond. Noll and his coaches had gone to Palm Springs with every last one of our movie projectors. When I was told about this, I blew my stack. "Don't those people realize that life has to go on for the scouting department?" I bellowed. Here we were, three weeks before the draft, without an essential tool.

All we could do was rent and borrow projectors — if possible. Dick Haley scrounged one from Pitt, trading on the fact that he had played there, but we were still far short. Seething, I bought an expensive Bell and Howell projector and had a nameplate attached to the top of it. "For the personal use of Art Rooney, Jr.," the nameplate proclaimed. "Not to be taken from the scouting department." For months and years to come, this would rankle the assistant coaches.

My grievances against Noll peaked on game day. We lost to Oakland disgracefully, 33-14, and I blamed this catastrophe on the frivolous week in Palm Springs that existed solely in my mind. Two days after the trouncing, Noll walked into the room where I met with the scouts. He was rubbing his hands together in what struck me as a self-satisfied way. His first words — something to the effect that he and his assistants were ready now to do some real work on the 1974 draft — lit my fuse.

"Coach," I blurted, "that was some performance your team gave in Oakland Saturday. We were not just defeated, we were embarrassed. I never imagined I'd see a Chuck Noll team play so poorly."

Taken by surprise, Noll was speechless. All of my scouts were speechless. Mrs. Duffy, my secretary, was speechless. Breaking the quiet that hung over the room, someone finally mentioned the scouting assignments for the post-season bowl games we were to cover.

This set me off once again. "Coach," I resumed – I never called him Chuck — "some of your assistants take scouting seriously and do a good job and some of them have a so-so attitude and do just a so-so job. Still others don't give a damn, and it shows in their reports. I'll give you an example. One of your coaches wrote that a prospect he had seen at a bowl game was 'a little fat guy who rolled around in the mud.' Period."

With that, Noll found his tongue. He came up close to me, baring his teeth. "Tell me who that coach is," he said. "Just tell me which of my coaches doesn't give a damn about scouting, and I'll fire him. Right now."

We were practically face to face. I said, "Coach, I'm not going to tell you. The coaches are your responsibility. The scouts are mine."

Noll turned on his heel and left the room. Dick Haley, Bill Nunn, Tim Rooney, and poor Mrs. Duffy were looking down at the floor. As for me, I was shaking with rage, indignation, and self-righteousness. I had never stood up to Bill Austin like this. Now I was making amends.

Of course I came to regret my impetuosity. There's a time and a place for letting off steam. This was neither. But then I had always been one to hold things in when I should have spoken up and to lash out intemperately when I should have kept my mouth shut. I was right about the assistant coaches — I still believe that — but my treatment of Noll was inexcusable. Reflecting on it, I remembered how I felt when AJR would reprimand me in front of scouts, coaches, secretaries, and whoever else happened to be listening.

There's a postscript to this. Years later, Noll hired an assistant coach with dubious credentials. I knew the guy's history at second hand, but kept it to myself. Noll in time grew dissatisfied with his work; during a conversation between us in my office one day, he said so, and this was my cue to lay out the information that had come to me.

"Art," Noll said, "when you hear something like this, you should tell me right away."

I repeated that our areas of authority did not overlap.

Half an hour later, the coach with the problems in his résumé no longer was employed by the Steelers. I thought of how Noll had promised to fire any coach I accused of taking scouting assignments lightly.

And I said to myself, "He'd have done it."

One thing more: never again did Noll take a team to Palm Springs or anywhere else for a week of warm-weather practice.

Weights and Measures

After Kenny Phares went down on the second play of his first practice at St. Vincent, we looked to our medical staff for some answers. In addition to a serious knee injury, we were told, Kenny had rheumatoid arthritis, which "never really gets better." On top of that, "the problem migrates from one part of the body to another."

There was more to understanding sports injuries than we knew at the time, it seemed. When we lost Kenny Phares we not only lost the money invested in him, but the draft pick as well — a high one. Our investment in scouting and draft selection was now so substantial that it made a lot of sense to have better information about injuries. Scouting reports and interviews with trainers were not enough. I don't mean to say that the college people were intentionally deceiving us. But they were not our employees, after all, and there was no incentive for them to be as uncompromisingly forthright as we might have liked.

The situation with Phares and others like him convinced us to spend a little more money on physical examinations. Why couldn't the fifteen or so top prospects who were injury risks come to Pittsburgh every year for checkups? It would be more work for trainer Ralph Berlin and my secretary, Rhoda Duffy, not to mention the front office, but everybody pitched in with great enthusiasm. The outcome was so pleasing that we added more players to the invitation list and set up a branch in Los Angeles, where Kay's cousin, Dr. Don Gaylor, a Pitt medical school graduate, put together a team of orthopedic and neurological surgeons to examine the West Coast prospects with physical problems.

And we didn't stop there. We arranged to swap injury information with the other four Blesto teams. Television revenue and sold-out games at Three Rivers Stadium made all of this possible. AJR never liked to throw money away, but Dan argued persuasively that money for such a purpose was well spent. As Dan reminded him, he always had said that the most overpaid player a team could have was the guy who "sat on the oak." The medicals were helping us avoid that.

Not long after the other Blesto teams had adopted our idea, Carl Peterson, personnel director of the Eagles, suggested, rather forcibly, that Blesto as a group bring *all* of the top-rated prospects to a central location for physicals, I.Q. tests, and psychological evaluations. Blesto bought into the concept, and in deference to Peterson the central location we agreed on was Philadelphia. Two or three years later, we moved the operation to Detroit, where the new domed stadium gave us room to bring in even more players and work them out. My cousin Tim Rooney, by that time the head of player personnel in Detroit, got together with Peterson and Dick Haley, and the three of them organized a series of drills: a long jump, a high jump, a change-of-direction run, a bench press to measure strength, and of course the forty-yard dash — all in addition to basic drills set up by the coaches for quarterbacks, receivers, defensive backs, and linebackers. The running backs had their own set of drills, and it was easy to make a judgment on the kickers.

Many college administrators protested that we were taking these "student-athletes" away from the business of getting an education. So, to appease them, we compressed all of our testing into a single long weekend, a tremendous organizational feat for the scouts, coaches, trainers, doctors, and secretaries (who never received enough credit).

Meanwhile, the rest of the teams in the NFL had also started a camp, and league officials agreed with the colleges that too much time was being demanded of the players. The solution we reached was to combine the other teams' camp with the Blesto camp, which eliminated duplication. We now had a supersized operation. There were media people who called it a "meat market" and others who likened it to the slave markets of the antebellum South. In my opinion, that was baloney. We were not putting price tags on slaves, but appraising young men who were going to be extremely well paid.

The testing was done in mid-winter, making it necessary to move back the draft until spring. I had always felt that a hard-working, knowledgeable, well-organized scouting department — ours, for example — could outdraft the teams that were slower to prepare, but now we were all on equal terms. Even the late starters could get their act together with an additional two months of leeway.

Another result of the testing was that scouts and coaches were putting more stress on athletic skills, so that the camp itself had become a showcase for players with exceptional speed and agility. Jack Butler of Blesto, for one, thought it was misplaced emphasis. "You'd better evaluate a kid on how well he plays the game of football rather than how well he hops, skips, and jumps in his underwear," Butler said. And Chuck Noll repeated the line he had used about the rookie who could leap over cars. "These workouts," he said, "are all well and good in their place, but are we looking for football players or auditioning for the half-time show?"

After a while, I started to feel that Butler and Noll had it right. During a film study of the workouts, I told Dick Haley, "I could send you guys to scout the Olympics. You'd see the greatest athletes in the world there, but half of them will be girls and the men won't like football."

Not that it makes any difference, for these mid-winter circuses are now a permanent part of the landscape, their popularity undiminished by the passing of time.

Name Game

In the early 1970s, Blesto, under Jack Butler, entered the computer age. With the help of high-tech professionals at companies like Sperry Rand, Butler developed a program that could take the information his scouts had assembled on a football player, put the various pieces together, and measure his potential as precisely as technology allowed.

I said to Butler, "That's fine, Jack, but how did you pay the bills for all this? Sperry Rand guys don't work for nothing."

"We got lucky," he told me. "One of the top men with that outfit has a Pittsburgh background and loves football. He was so interested in our scouting procedures he gave us a special deal."

"Hey, Jack," I reminded him, "don't forget what the Chief always says. If something looks too good to be true it probably is. What is the catch here? What does your Pittsburgh friend want in return? And just who is he, anyway? You haven't told me his name."

"It's John Butler," Jack said.

"No, I asked you what *his* name was, not your own."

"His name and my name are the same: John Butler."

For a long time I wondered if Butler — Jack Butler — was putting me on. But a year or so later — this would be 1975 — Jack called me and said, "Remember that John Butler guy who helped me computerize our scouting? You asked if there was going to be a payback. Well, the answer is yes. His company wants to do a TV commercial for an NFL game, a TV commercial with a Blesto angle. When they shoot it, I'm going to be a consultant."

I heard from Jack later that the set for the commercial was a mockup of an NFL draft room. "You can't believe the detail that went into it," Jack said. "Everything was absolutely authentic except the names on the charts. The names of the players and the schools were made up. I think it'll work."

As an afterthought, I asked if all the teams in the Blesto organization had given Jack permission to do the commercial.

"Yes, quite a while ago."

I said, "You didn't ask *me*."

"I didn't think I had to," Jack sort of explained.

There were actually two commercials. One was a full minute and the other a half minute. The actors, pretending to be coaches and scouts at a draft meeting, were sporty looking guys, a little too pretty for their roles. One actor yelled, "Pittsburgh is up!" Another one, playing the guy in charge, but too sharp-looking to be Chuck Noll or me, said, "Hold on. We're looking for the best athlete available." He was hunched over a computer, with everybody else crowded up behind him as a name appeared on the screen.

"Here it is!" the Noll/Rooney figure exclaimed. "Defensive back ... Six-two ... Two hundred pounds ... Four point six forty ... Butler — Jack Butler ... Saint Bonaventure University."

"Yep, that's our man," said an actor who was playing an assistant coach. "Jack Butler. He'll be great."

All in all, it was not a bad commercial. The next time I saw Jack, I had only one question: "'Best athlete available.' Did you give them the idea for the name?"

The look on his face said, "How could you think such a thing?"

Out loud, he said, "No, not at all. The name wasn't supposed to be mine. It was the other Jack Butler's. The guy from the computer company. *John* Butler, he calls himself. But that was supposed to be him, not me."

"Oh. My mistake," I said, but not out loud.

Chapter 57

A 'Yeah, But' Player

To the old-timers in my department, the Blesto computer program was an irritant. The younger scouts acknowledged its usefulness, and my own point of view was the same as theirs. If aircraft and automobile companies could test products still in the planning stage on simulated tracks and landing strips, why couldn't we do something like that with football players?

Computers were not infallible, however. Where they sometimes went wrong was with players you couldn't pigeonhole — players like Mike Webster, a center from Wisconsin. The Blesto computer took into account the intangibles Webster possessed. It gave him high marks for desire, toughness, stamina, effort, awareness, and football intelligence. But his height, 6 feet 2 1/2, his weight, 225 pounds, and his forty-yard dash time, 5.25, were substandard. With a center that small and that slow, the computer said, you could not win a championship.

I'd have said so myself, I am sorry to say, and the Blesto scouts would have concurred. Mike Webster was not a "computer player," a guy who jumped off the screen. Neither was he an obvious reject. He was simply the kind of player who might easily get lost in the shuffle.

But this time good fortune attended us. I thought of AJR and his belief in the importance of luck. An assistant coach at Wisconsin had kept in touch with our defensive line coach, George Perles. I've forgotten the Wisconsin man's name. It was Irish, I know. And I know that he called Perles to tell him about Webster — "the best offensive lineman in the Big Ten if not the whole country."

I had an up-and-down relationship with Perles. To be frank, I considered him a Neanderthal type. In the coffee room at Three Rivers Stadium one day, he told me bluntly that the only reason Chuck Noll put up with me was the fact that my father owned the team. Mustering all the self-control I was capable of, I answered without raising my voice. I said, "George, I have learned a lot from Chuck and from each of his assistants, but I don't think it's one-sided. I can offer them a lot in return."

In the back of my mind — I can't shade the truth here — was the realization that if I blew up at Perles and we duked it out, he'd have taken me. Enviably, AJR was always sure that, like John L. Sullivan, he could lick any man in the house.

Perles and Noll complemented each other. Perles was outspoken and passionate, Noll understated and cerebral. "Football," Perles would tell his defensive linemen, "is a violent, emotional game, and it has to be played that way." He deserves a tip of the hat for developing L. C. Greenwood, Fats Holmes, and Dwight White, three of the components in our Steel Curtain, and later John Banaszak, Steve Furness, and Gary Dunn, starters, like the others, on Super Bowl teams. I omit any mention of Joe Greene. Sister Mary Vincent from the Little Sisters of the Poor could have coached Joe Greene.

Perles lacked the temperament to be of much use as a scout. He hated those long days and nights alone on the road. Mike Webster, in a sense, was dropped right into his lap. Before the 1974 draft, George's friend at Wisconsin sent him game films, and we were able to judge Webster on the way he performed against Big Ten players we had earmarked as prospects. Not only did Webster hold his own with these guys, he was dominant. Dick Haley and our offensive line coaches agreed that while he came up short when we looked at his numbers, there were "compensating factors" — namely, the intangibles I have referred to, plus the unbelievable leverage he could generate.

What we had here, we thought at first, was a late middle-round pick who could hang on for a while as an adequate special-teams player. He would be what we called an "exception," just as bumblebees are exceptions. The laws of aerodynamics tell us that bumblebees are not built to fly. Yet, somehow or other, they do. Another law, one that football scouts ignore at their peril, says you can go broke taking chances on exceptions. The trick is to spot the real thing, which of course requires superior drafting know-how.

I think an awful lot of NFL teams had a "yeah, but" attitude toward Webster. "Yeah, he was good in college, but he's just not big enough for the pros." This kind of talk played into our hands. We could hold off drafting him until a very late round. Given the general feeling of apathy toward Webster, even a free-agent signing might not be out of the question. But then we saw the films from the post-season all-star games.

Dick Haley would run into my office after watching them. "Ya gotta see this Webster!" he'd exclaim, and see him I did. I saw him knock a prospective first-round pick, 275 pounds of muscle and beef, halfway back to where he came from. "Look at Webbie get up under his face mask. *Wham!* He hits like Rocky Marciano," Haley chortled.

My cousin Tim Rooney came around with a reel of film, and we expressed our amazement at Webster's complete mastery of blocking techniques. "Look at his feet!" Tim enthused. "Look at him slide! He pops one rusher and slides over to pick up another guy. Do you know how many years of NFL experience a center needs to make that move look so easy?"

"Great work," I replied, "but let's not go overboard yet. We can still get the guy in the late middle rounds."

As it turned out, he was the fifth player we drafted. Though I believed my own words, I couldn't wait any longer.

Senior Bowl

Senior Bowl week in Mobile, Alabama, was not the ideal time to scout a football player, and Mobile itself was not the ideal environment.

There was Mobile's weather, as fickle as a Southern belle. A January day in Mobile could be springlike; it could be oppressively hot; it could be cold, wet, and windy. Old-timers packed their bags to be ready for anything. I had a big fleecelined coat that I sometimes wore to practice when the temperature dropped. A sudden storm rolled in from the Gulf of Mexico one day and it covered my coat and me with ice. Twenty-four hours later, I thought I would die from the heat. On one of Chuck Noll's first visits, a wind came up, the sky clouded over, and a freezing rain started to fall. Noll took his staff to an Army-Navy store and the whole gang returned wearing galoshes and waterproof jackets.

The competing all-star teams practiced at different sites — a Catholic military school and a field near the Senior Bowl stadium. Our understanding was that the coaches would stagger their practices so that the scouts in attendance could see both teams twice a day. Because of the weather, it didn't always work out that way. Rain could muddy a field and make it necessary for a practice to be moved. Then the scouts and the visiting coaches would have to scurry around in search of the new location.

Still another impediment was the presence of agents and news media. When the players weren't practicing, their agents would whisk them away or the sportswriters and sportscasters would be after them. Getting time with the players alone was always difficult. Renting a car was difficult. Finding a place to park was difficult. As necessary to the success of these post-season all-star games as publicity is, and as much a part of professional football as agents had become, my perspective was that of a scout, and the sheer profusion of such supernumeraries, as I thought of them, made a scout's job anything but pleasurable.

There were distractions unconnected with football, too — distractions like Wentzel's Oyster House. We were drawn to Wentzel's at lunchtime every day by the blue points, the clams, the fish sandwiches, the cold beer — I took a pass on the beer — and the likelihood of hearing football stories from 350-pound Don Joyce, a scout for Blesto and later the Indianapolis Colts. Without ever repeating himself, Joyce could hold us spellbound all week. In the early evening hours, we assembled at the Senior Bowl's nightly cocktail party for NFL people only. The "bar food" at these functions was so abundant that the scouts would pocket their meal money and hang around to pig out. Then at the end of the week came the super pig-out — a mammoth fish fry, called the Seafood Jamboree, at which tons of aquatic creatures and gallons of truly excellent gumbo would be consumed.

Royal entertainment, without question. "But is that why we are down here?" I asked myself. It went against the work ethic I had carefully developed. As much as I enjoyed the Gulf Coast cuisine, the shop talk, and the companionship, my conscience hurt. I could have been studying game film, after all.

At the 1974 Senior Bowl, the Steeler contingent was interested in one player above all the others, a wide receiver the public never had heard of. Nor, as far as I could tell, had more than a handful of scouts become aware of him. His name was John Stallworth, and he played in obscurity at Alabama A. & M., a little-known black college.

But not in total obscurity. Bear Bryant, the football coach at Alabama's state university and in that part of the country a figure of Olympian proportions, was threatening to break the color line. Without black players, Bryant realized, Alabama no longer could win. Though it would take a little time, he therefore intended to recruit them. To everybody's surprise, he had publicly regretted that there were no John Stallworths catching passes for the Crimson Tide.

The Blesto scout who alerted us to Stallworth's potential was Joe Bushofski, a teammate of mine and Tim's at North Catholic High School and later the head coach at North Catholic. In college, Joe played at North Carolina State. Joe and his brother Jack, another North Catholic guy, had parallel careers as scouts. Both worked for Blesto after I recommended them to Jack Butler, and both ended up as personnel directors in the NFL, Joe with the Detroit Lions, Jack with the Baltimore Colts and Carolina Panthers.

Joe's report on Stallworth at the fall Blesto meeting in 1973 placed him among the top wide receivers in the nation, and we immediately got Bill Nunn on the case. Because of Nunn's connections with black college coaches, he could get access and information denied to most other scouts. The films he brought back included a game in which Stallworth was a one-man highlight show. He appeared to be a tall, skinny kid who caught every ball that was anywhere near him. Our time for Stallworth in the forty-yard dash was 4.6; he looked a bit faster than that. He separated himself from defenders quickly and made over-the-shoulder catches on the dead run.

Chuck Noll took a look at the films and pronounced Stallworth a definite first-round pick. "If he's going to the Senior Bowl, there's no way of hiding him," Noll said. "Everybody will see how good he is. These scouts for the other teams in the league aren't idiots, you know." Dick Haley and I counseled restraint. "Let's calm down a little," I suggested. "At this point, we can get him on the third or fourth round." Noll shook his head. Stallworth, he repeated, was a first-round pick.

Alabama A. & M.'s coach had exacted a promise from Nunn to return all the game films we had seen. The coach wanted to circulate them among the other NFL teams for Stallworth's sake. The films would move him up in the draft-selection process. Nunn sent back all except one — the film in which Stallworth evoked memories of Don Hutson, an end from Alabama who played for the Green Bay Packers from 1935 to 1945 and set pass-catching records that remained in the books for decades. It seemed to me that every time I walked past our projection room, Nunn and Dick Haley, or Haley and Chuck Noll, or Nunn and Lionel Taylor, the receivers coach, or all of the above would be watching that film. In the interest of complete truthfulness, I must admit that I joined them on occasion. Even AJR would sometimes be in the audience. In later years, when we had the technological ability to do it, we'd have made a copy of the film and returned the original to Alabama A. & M. As it was, we kept the damned thing until the eve of our departure for the Senior Bowl, when I at last said to Nunn, "Look, Bill, you promised that coach you would send back all of those films. If we hang onto this one any longer, we'll be getting a bad reputation." I then repeated the same warning to Haley.

Well, Senior Bowl week came and went, and I noticed one day that we still had the film. Nunn and Haley were looking at it again. In college at St. Vincent, I learned about "pragmatism" — the theory that whatever works is OK. I also learned that getting away with anything you could was *not* necessarily OK. Going back on our agreement with Stallworth's coach was the first and last time we were guilty of such a trick during my tenure as head of the scouting department.

Noll's fear that the Senior Bowl game would be a showcase for Stallworth, revealing the extent of his talent to every other team in the NFL, turned out to be groundless. I was reminded of AJR's belief in the importance of luck. He used to say that no matter how smart you were, no matter how well-prepared, it could all go for nothing if luck was against you. This time, luck was on our side. Uncertain of what to do with Stallworth, his coaches kept moving him back and forth between two positions — wide receiver and cornerback — so that he never had a chance to display his pass-catching skills. Having already observed them on film, we didn't mind. We could see that Stallworth in the flesh was a gifted athlete, and when our emissaries talked to him they liked his good-natured acceptance of the way he had been misused. Evidently he was not a prima donna.

Hall-of-Fame Haul

In the NFL, success had a downside. To ensure parity — balanced competition — losing teams drafted early, winning teams drafted late. The Steelers, under Noll, had started to win. Accordingly, the first player we selected in the 1974 draft would be the twenty-first who was picked overall.

Personnel directors lived by the saying "Don't screw up when you have those real early choices." In making some real early choices since 1969, the year we drafted Mean Joe Greene, we hadn't screwed up. But now all of a sudden we'd be "reaching" — taking a chance on a player with what Noll aptly referred to as "impediments." As AJR put it, we would have to get lucky.

As he also put it, you never counted on luck. He spoke from the perspective of a horse player. For a visit to the race track, you prepared as if there were no such thing as luck. Approach a draft the same way, was his counsel. To borrow again from Noll's terminology, we'd be looking for "exceptions" — players deficient in size and/or speed but with qualities not as easy to assess, qualities like intelligence, tenacity, an instinct for the game.

Everyone liked Lynn Swann, a graceful wide receiver from the University of Southern California. His lack of height — he was barely 5 feet 9 — and his time in the forty-yard dash, 4.65, worked against him. When our turn in the first round came, he might still be available.

Interested, I spoke to Jack Butler about Swann. He said that Howard Slusser, Swann's agent, had agreed to let a Blesto scout time him in the forty in Los Angeles a week before the draft. Butler did not like Slusser. In Jack's opinion, the agent was overbearing and glib. The adjectives I'd have used were "sharp" and "verbal." Slusser's clients esteemed him, I understood; he delivered for them in contract negotiations. Slusser was a short, red-haired guy on the somewhat corpulent side. AJR had a favorable opinion of him, but was uncomfortable with the presence in his stable of "too many Steelers." Trouble would come of it, he predicted. As it happened, none did, other than "mental aches and strains." Dan and Jim Boston dealt with Slusser honestly and fairly, and AJR treated him like a human being, this at a time when NFL owners in general looked upon agents as vermin. The result was that we never lost a player represented by Slusser. Many of them, in fact, helped us win championships. "Tell Howard for me," I said one day to his good friend Jim Boston, "I wish we could give him a Super Bowl ring."

Blesto's Howard White re-timed Swann in the forty at 4.54, nearly a tenth of a second faster than his previous best time. One of our assistant coaches had said of Swann, using a commonplace putdown, "He's small, but he's slow." He was still small, but no longer slow. He now had a timed speed to go with the playing speed we knew he possessed from our studies of USC film. Later, if we asked Swann to run a forty in training camp at St. Vincent, he'd consistently do 4.61, but in a match race with John Stallworth, losing by a nose (as AJR would say), he'd run a 4.55 to Stallworth's 4.54. Swann had what we called competitive speed. The fact that his extracurricular activities included ballet dancing was something we were willing to forgive. Ballet dancing is good for a player's footwork and equilibrium.

In Swann, Stallworth, Jack Lambert, and Mike Webster, we now had identified four good draft picks we believed the rest of the teams had underrated, or, in Stallworth's case, overlooked. In previous drafts when we had singled out such players, they would disappear from the board while we waited to claim them. On this occasion the stars in the heavens were properly aligned for us. We took Swann in the first round and Lambert in the second. Someone — I forget who — suggested an alternative second-round pick, a linebacker from the West Coast. Assistant coach Woody Widenhofer saved the day. He stood up and said, "Look, this West Coast guy is a fine player. No question. But our defense, don't forget, is very, very sophisticated. Both of these guys will take a long time to learn it, but Lambert, while he learns, will be a heck of a player on special teams. The other linebacker ... I don't think so. Let's go for Lambert." Providentially, Widenhofer's logic prevailed.

I had fought for six years to keep our assistant coaches out of the draft process. Now at last I could see the merit in Noll's argument that pulling together was necessary. "Coaches, scouts, trainers, everybody, even the secretaries and equipment men ... we all have to work as a team," he would say. I remembered how an assistant coach named Walt Hackett insistently beat the drum for Moon Mullins in 1971. At tight end, the position he played for Southern California, Mullins was not a prospect. "Never mind that. He'll make an outstanding offensive guard," Hackett kept telling us.

At offensive guard, Mullins became a starter. He would continue to be a starter on our Super Bowl teams. I remembered how Don Heinrich encouraged us to draft Rocky Bleier in 1968. And how Dan Radakovich gave me so much support in my lobbying on behalf of Franco Harris. Maybe, after all, there were times when it paid to listen, regardless of the source.

The third-round pick we had traded brought us defensive tackle Tom Keating from Oakland. In the fourth round, as Haley and I had promised, we were able to get Stallworth. Selling our head coach on the idea that we could wait that long had been no easy task. "If he's not there," I said to Haley, "we're going to hear some screaming." When Stallworth fell into our clutches, I was not too polite to gloat.

So far, so good, I said to myself. Drafting twenty-first and without a third-round pick, we had timed the big auction perfectly. With our second fourth-round pick, the result of a trade with New England, we chose a defensive back from UCLA, Jimmy Allen. Jimmy Allen was a street kid from Watts, the black ghetto in Los Angeles. As remote as Watts is from the surfboard culture, swimming, rather than football, may have been his best sport. He was good enough, I had heard, to consider trying out for the U.S. Olympic team, but football punched his ticket to UCLA, where the long arms that propelled him through the water bedeviled pass receivers. He was tall and flexible, with a hawk's eye for tracking the ball and magnetized fingers for snatching it out of the air. And, by the way, he could also return kicks.

Allen's most striking personal characteristic was fearlessness combined with a hair-trigger temper, evident for all to see in the mess hall at St. Vincent on one of his first days in camp. He had taken his place at the table when Mean Joe Greene, the toughest Steeler of them all and the one most universally deferred to, reached out in a spirit of playfulness and grabbed something from Allen's tray — a shrimp, or a piece of fruit. Instantly, Allen lifted his tray and banged Greene over the head with it. Allen's lunch flew in every direction. He'd have mixed it up with Greene then and there except for the intervention of teammates. In any case, the rookie had served notice that he was not to be trifled with.

Allen was a part-time starter and a full-time contributor on the championship teams of 1974 and 1975. After the 1977 season, we traded him to Detroit, where he distinguished himself one year by intercepting ten passes. Eventually, the ghetto reclaimed him. In the 1980s I heard that he had dropped out of sight, a homeless vagabond.

Luck remained with us as the draft moved into the fifth round. We had rated two or three offensive linemen ahead of Mike Webster, but now they were off the board. That much conceded, luck played no part in the choice we then made. "Catching lightning in a bottle," someone called it. I disagree. Our decision to take Webster was the result of considerable spadework. After George Perles had mentioned him to us, we studied film and asked questions. For very long stretches of the next twelve years, Mike Webster was the NFL's most dominant center.

Distressingly, and for reasons I will not at the moment explore, he came to the same end as Jimmy Allen.

The first five rounds of the 1974 draft produced a result we could not have imagined. Of the five future Hall-of-Fame players in the draft, the Pittsburgh Steelers came away with four — Swann, Stallworth, Lambert, and Webster. Dave Casper, the Oakland Raiders' tight end, was the fifth. Chuck Noll pronounced it "a draft of exceptions." There was Swann, who was "too small and too slow;" there was Stallworth, a hidden jewel from a small agricultural school in the South; there was Lambert, whose "growth potential" raised questions; there was Webster, the unappreciated overachiever.

The credit for this draft does not begin and end with the scouting department. Dan Rooney and Jim Boston got the players signed. Chuck Noll and his assistant coaches brought out the best that was in them. Finally, as an old talent hunter once reminded me, I owe a debt to their "mamas and papas." Why did they grow up to be football players at all? Because they had the right genes. and, in most cases, because they had the right training at home. In football, as in the construction business, everything starts with the bricks and mortar.

Add-Ons

In the remaining rounds, we drafted sixteen players. Three of them — Jim Wolf, defensive end from Prairie View; Rick Druschel, offensive lineman from North Carolina State; and Charley Davis, defensive tackle from Texas Christian — survived the weeding-out process at St. Vincent and were with us for one season.

One season isn't much, but what a season it was. They suited up for a Super Bowl game, something to cherish for the rest of their days, something to tell their children and grandchildren. Twenty-five years later, at an anniversary celebration, I spoke with Druschel, a successful coach and athletic director in the Western Pennsylvania high school world. He expressed profuse gratitude to me and to Dan and to our entire organization for "a year that changed my life." It made me feel that scouting for the Steelers had been a worthy occupation.

We drafted still another player from North Carolina State in 1974 – Alan Sitterly, who had gone to high school at North Catholic. Our scout Tim Rooney told me a story about Sitterly. It seems that his coach at North Catholic decided one day that Sitterly's toughness needed testing. He tossed the player into his car and drove him to North Park. There, on one of the dusty back roads, he tied Alan Sitterly to the car's rear bumper and dragged him around the park for the next sixty minutes. Thus inured to the bumps and bruises of football, Sitterly more than held his own at North Carolina State.

It has been said that our 1974 draft was the best in the history of the NFL. And beyond the draft, there were free-agent signings of consequence. We had picked up two free agents in the 1960s who opened my eyes to a way of improving the team that required a lot of intensive bird-dog work, but was cheap. Both were from schools below the radar. Sam Davis, offensive lineman, had played at Allen University in Columbia, South Carolina; Jerry Simmons, wide receiver, came from Bethune-Cookman on the east coast of Florida. By the time that Chuck Noll was in charge, we were making a real effort to dig up more athletes of their caliber. Noll, I had learned, would spend as much time with promising free agents as with top-five draft choices. Exhilarated, I put my scouts on a year-round free-agent alert.

Noll didn't want any "stiffs" in camp — third cousins of front-office people, politicians' nephews, "friends of friends." We had moved away from cluttering St. Vincent with "nice-guy" candidates for the team. Pre-season practice was for prospects only, and this, on occasion, put AJR's nose out of joint. At his insistence, we'd be forced to make an exception now and then. He was the Chief, after all; he paid the bills. Moreover, every one of us had been guilty to some degree of bending the same rule. "Just this once," we would tell ourselves, and grant a tryout to somebody's kid, saving a friendship.

On a warm summer day in the 1980s, Kay and I were cooling off on the porch when a neighborhood kid named Peckish, like our son Art a former wrestler at Mount Lebanon High School, showed up. He also had wrestled at the University of Cincinnati and punted, he said, for the football team, and now he was proposing that I allow him to try out for the punting assignment with the Steelers. I admired young Peckish; he was as tough as old shoe leather, I had heard. But to punt for the Steelers was something else. I suggested reasons why Peckish would be wasting his time. And then Kay jumped in.

Right in front of the fellow, she called me "the meanest old coot" she had ever known. "Give the boy a tryout," she said. "It won't hurt anything, and he'll be better than those other hopeless cases you bring to camp."

Peckish got his tryout. Hard-edged from wrestling, he was in wonderful shape. Whether or not the coaches knew that Kay was his patron, they let him dress for the first pre-season game. It was at Three Rivers Stadium, and he kicked the ball once when the third- and fourth-stringers were on the field.

By the following afternoon his football career was over. He was free, as Noll always put it, to "get on with his life's work."

Several months later, driving to a restaurant one evening, Kay and I came to an unexpected four-way stop. Just ahead of us, a work crew was repairing the road, and we took our place in a long line of cars, Kay at the wheel of her big black Caddy. We were stuck for an agonizing length of time, inching forward slowly as a man with a red flag moved the cars through, one by one. Suddenly he caught sight of Kay. He approached us, smiling. "Hello, Mrs. Rooney, how are you?"

Only then did we recognize him: Peckish.

Vigorously waving his red flag, he held up all traffic for a minute, pulled us out of line, and sent us through.

Deluded would-be punters like Peckish turned up in camp every year. One of them, a young married man, had resigned from his job as the pro at a nearby golf club. How he obtained a tryout I never knew. He had a beautiful wife who came to watch him punt. While he chased his fantasy, she would stand by her parked car and gaze out over the practice fields, and her eyes would be full of affection for him. But then at times I would catch a look that betrayed the dismay she had to be feeling. The punter had no chance of making the team, and she realized it. "You crazy nut," she seemed to be thinking, "why have you walked out on a steady job and a decent paycheck for this?"

Greenfield Jimmy Smith's grandson, also named Jimmy Smith, was another of our undrafted free agents. I forget who his sponsor was — Billy Conn, perhaps. Billy was married to the grandson's aunt, Mary Louise. Young Smith had been a linebacker at Penn, in the Ivy League. He had the Irish pugnacity of his baseball-playing granddad, along with fiery red hair, but was not exactly NFL material. Few Ivy Leaguers then were, or now are. Young Jimmy was smart, and not without talent, and the coaches were willing to "get a picture" of him, as Noll used to say. "The question is," Woody Widenhofer asked, "will he be tough enough?"

During practice one day at St. Vincent, Widenhofer got his answer. One of our first-round draft choices, Baylor running back Greg Hawthorne, decided that the one hundredth and last kid invited to camp, an Ivy Leaguer in the bargain, could be pushed around, and he gave Smith a late bump. Then a second late bump. It was one too many.

Football fights are usually just pushing and shoving, and only an idiot would take off his helmet in order to fight, but the story I heard was that Greenfield Jimmy Smith's grandson flattened Greg Hawthorne. It may even be true. Smith never denied it and Hawthorne never talked about it. Noll, when I asked him one time, professed not to remember the incident. All he would say was that Hawthorne, a superior athlete who lasted five years with the Steelers, could have used some of Jimmy Smith's combativeness.

Jimmy did not make the team. Instead, he made money — as a banker. I ran into him once, I forget where. He still had his red hair, all of it. He was wearing a banker's blue suit with a red tie. "Jimmy," I said, "I got you that tryout, and you made me look bad by beating the crap out of my first draft choice." Jimmy smiled and said, "Thanks for the tryout."

In the space I occupied at the Roosevelt Hotel I received word one day that a lawyer had come to see me. Envisioning a lawsuit of some sort, I felt a small, brief tremor of apprehension. The man who presented himself might have been 35 years old. He was very good looking and unusually well dressed. "What can I do for you?" I asked. For an answer, he recited his curriculum vitae in a nutshell: college, law school, the bar exams, a job in a law firm. He was happily married with two children. Yet none of this had brought him fulfillment. "You see, in college I played football," he said. "And it was always my ambition to play for the Steelers. I've stayed in good physical condition, and I think I could help the team."

I spent the next fifteen minutes talking sense into the guy.

When someone applied for a tryout by mail, I never failed to answer. Recently I became aware that a letter of rejection I wrote in 1965 had turned up on eBay, the network auction site. It was written by hand; I did not yet have a secretary. As Kay pointed out, my penmanship back then was the same barely legible scrawl that it is today, but at least there were no misspellings.

Re-reading the letter, I looked for some trace of historical value. None was evident to me. The name of the person who had asked for a tryout did not at first glance ring a bell. Then I came to my closing sentence: "Drop by to say hello some day." Inviting these romantics to look me up was something I had resolved never to do. Why, in this case, I changed my policy I don't recall. This particular letter of application may have struck a chord with me. At any rate, as a result of my suggestion, a short, heavy-set guy in his early-to mid-twenties came walking into my office.

The first thing he said to me was that he always had been a big Steeler fan. I asked him about his background. He'd played college and semi-pro football in Ohio, he said. He spoke of his semi-pro team reverently, the way I had heard old-timers reminisce about the Canton Bulldogs and Jim Thorpe. He went on to say that he was also a wrestler and a judo expert, which had been an advantage to him in football. "Leverage, you know." He was sure he could help "turn the Steelers around."

"Well," I replied, hoping to discourage this kind of talk, "our roster is pretty well solidified, and, anyway, I don't know what kind of shape you are in, or how fast you are. We time our players now in the forty-yard dash. Speed in today's game is very important."

He understood that it was, he said. Being timed in the forty-yard dash was something he would welcome. "Let's go outside and get it done right now," he said.

I did a double take and saw that he was serious. He was proposing to run the forty-yard dash on Sixth Street, downtown, in street shoes, in the middle of a weekday afternoon.

Stalling, I said, "Gee ... it's hardly the time or place. There's too much pedestrian traffic ... "

"OK. But let me show you what kind of an athlete I am. That desk of yours ..." He was sizing it up. "I think it'll hold me. I'll do a squat jump from the floor up onto your desk. I'll do it ten times."

He was slipping out of his blazer. "Hey, wait a minute," I protested. "This desk isn't built for gymnastics. I'm afraid you'd wreck it." In truth, I was afraid he might wreck his knee or his ankle. With the promise that I'd get in touch with him later — in a few weeks, maybe — I persuaded this bulldog to be patient.

I never saw him again.

By the way, my letter on eBay was sold to the highest bidder for eleven dollars and six cents.

Part Five: Full Speed Ahead
1974–1980
Chapter 58

Jefferson Street Joe

In the eleventh round of the 1972 draft we took a young black quarterback from Tennessee State, Joe Gilliam. The main reason, as I recall, was that Bill Nunn kept insisting, "He's a steal."

Nunn had Chuck Noll convinced, too. Gilliam's father coached the defense at Tennessee State and was known for his football savvy. He had handed down a lot of it to Joe, we had heard. "Gilliam," Babe Parilli once told me, "is smarter than either Bradshaw or Hanratty." Parilli was the Steelers' quarterback coach and therefore qualified to judge, I suppose.

Not five minutes after we drafted Gilliam, my telephone rang. A football man I regarded as well informed was on the line with a warning. "Don't you know this guy's into drugs?" I let it go. With an eleventh-round pick, what did we have to lose? Gilliam wasn't getting big money. We could take a chance.

They called him Jefferson Street Joe, for the street that wended its way through the Tennessee State campus in Nashville. He was tall and thin and he played with a sort of devil-may-care flamboyance that seemed to captivate Noll, who discouraged such tendencies in Bradshaw. He moved around quickly in the pocket; he got rid of the ball quickly; he had a strong arm, good peripheral vision, uncanny anticipation.

Gilliam made the team, but spent his first two seasons watching Hanratty start when Noll was dissatisfied with Bradshaw. There were sports reporters who wrote that Gilliam's talent exceeded Hanratty's *and* Bradshaw's. They were half-wrong, anyway — Bradshaw was our best quarterback but the fact that he continued to struggle reinforced the belief that Noll should be using Gilliam.

By 1973, the Steelers' defense was among the best in the league. All the offense had to do was control the ball. Its overriding mission was: don't get the defense in trouble with too many interceptions. Ron Shanklin and Frank Lewis, a player we had drafted in 1971 for his speed, were top receivers. Franco Harris was a big, powerful, deceptively fast running back. In the offensive line there were quick-thinking men with quick feet. For Bradshaw, then, it should have been all so simple: give the ball to Franco; throw short, high-percentage passes, going deep only in rare situations; do those two things and let the defense kick hell out of the other guys' offense.

But to Noll's ill-concealed annoyance, Bradshaw was making it complicated. He appeared to be throwing passes blindly. As the interceptions multiplied, critics asked if by any chance he was color-blind, or needed glasses. An ex-coach said to me, "Everything on the field is a blur to Bradshaw."

Only Kass, Aunt Alice, and Mary the maid seemed to give him their unquestioning love. Even AJR began to have doubts. Meanwhile Gilliam, the third-stringer, was looking better and better to Noll.

When the players' union called a strike before training camp opened in 1974, Gilliam saw his opportunity. He was one of the few veterans who crossed the picket line. Surrounded by rookies and a scattering of older guys, marginal players in fear of losing their jobs, he performed with confidence and style in the early exhibition games, and he was lucky as well. Three of the incoming rookies, wide receivers Lynn Swann and John Stallworth and center Mike Webster, were earmarked for the Hall of Fame. Another rookie, Randy Grossman, would in time be the starting tight end. And Rocky Bleier was in camp, recovered now from his war wounds. Though he considered himself a defector, his striking teammates did not. They knew that after four years of painful rehabilitation, Bleier had reached the make-or-break point.

With four exhibition games left, the strike ended. Bleier hadn't broken. Swann and Stallworth had established themselves, foreshadowing the ultimate departure of Shanklin and Lewis. Rookie Jack Lambert at middle linebacker and rookie Donnie Shell at strong safety had made the defense even more frightening. And Terry Bradshaw no longer was the No.1 quarterback. Joe Gilliam had replaced him.

Along with the other veterans, Bradshaw had to feel some bitterness toward Gilliam. Did they use the word "scab" in referring to him? I don't know. What I do know is that Bradshaw went back to his religious roots. In college, he had belonged to the Fellowship of Christian Athletes and was youth director at his Baptist church. Even earlier, he felt called upon to enter the ministry, but decided in the end that God would rather have him play football, as he expressed it. Now that he wasn't playing at all, he consulted God once more through the scriptures. He carried around a Bible almost constantly, looking into it whenever he could. He would come by himself, Bible in hand, to the stadium every morning and lift weights. No later than 8 o'clock he would be in the coffee room, wearing sweats. After drinking a cup of tea — Constant Comment — he would head for the field and throw passes to anyone he could find, usually ground-crew workers or front-office people. "Run as fast and as far as you can, and I'll get the ball to you," he would tell them, and off they would go. He reminded me of Johnny Unitas in Olean.

During our mornings in the coffee room, I felt I was learning what made Bradshaw tick. We never were pals, but I frequently spoke with his parents and I knew his three brothers at least casually. Craig, the youngest Bradshaw, was a quarterback at Utah State in the late 1970s, and one day Terry asked me — just kidding, or maybe kidding on the square — not to write Craig off without taking a look at his scouting reports. I assured him I would do as he asked, but when I took up the matter with Noll, his reaction was: why bother? We weren't going to draft Craig, he said. I answered, "No, we're not. But I gave my word to Terry. Let's look at the reports." And we did.

The Houston Oilers drafted Craig, but kept him for only one season.

Terry by then – the late 1970s, remember — was a certain Hall of Famer but still having problems with Noll. In the weight room one day I was watching some of the younger players work with barbells when Terry came up and stood next to me and started talking about his coach in the most unflattering terms. They were oil and water, these two, incapable of understanding each other. Terry believed, erroneously, that Noll disliked him, which made it mutual, he said. As he spoke, he kept his eyes on the weightlifters. So did I, but my attention was focused on Terry's diatribe. When he had finished, I said, "You know, Terry, I haven't gotten along with Noll myself. I don't worry about it, though, because we're here to do a job, and with players like you, we've won big. Because of that, people really think I know what I'm doing. Try to look at your own situation the same way. You're a great player on a great team. That's the important thing — getting a job done, being part of it. Whether we like our boss or not is beside the point. Furthermore, whatever you might think, Noll's not a horrible guy. He's just tough."

Bradshaw had listened in silence. Now he said, "See ya later" — that was all — and drifted away. I was left with the impression that my attempt at imparting wisdom had been a failure.

Some time later, I caught him being interviewed on television one night. The interviewer was asking about the team, about Noll, about the Super Bowls he had played in, and Bradshaw's answer left me dumbfounded but gratified. He repeated, almost word for word, everything I had told him in the weight room.

But the rift between Terry and Noll lasted for years. After his retirement, in fact, Bradshaw nursed a grudge against the Steeler organization as a whole and the entire city of Pittsburgh, a grudge that lasted for years. Launched on his second career, that of broadcaster, motivational speaker, pitch man, comedian, and movie actor, he never came near us. He boycotted player reunions, he refused to accept honors and awards. During much of that time, we have learned, he was suffering from clinical depression. And then, declaring bygones to be bygones, he returned for a testimonial dinner, a lovefest attended by most of his surviving Super Bowl teammates and by Noll. It was Bradshaw who had made the first move, and he of course was the star of the televised reconciliation. He gave a virtuoso performance, by turns sappy and droll, flippant and serious, plain-spoken and sentimental. As a student of acting, I had always seen in Bradshaw this talent for show business. I am glad it has served him well.

Lucky Strike

The NFL players' union called it a "work stoppage." Our fans, Western Pennsylvanians, were more concise. They had a word for what happened that went back in history, a word that went back to the railroad riots of 1877 and to Homestead in 1892. The word was "strike."

Nobody died, nobody bled. The players' union, after negotiating for weeks with the club owners in that summer of 1974, turned down their proposals for a new collective bargaining agreement. A peaceable boycott of the training camps followed. Peaceable or not, the fans didn't like it one bit.

How could these "pampered athletes" hold out for more money? They were lavishly paid (the fans thought) for playing "a kids' game" six months a year. The argument that football is a dangerous occupation, that football players risk serious injury, was unacceptable to Western Pennsylvanians. And why wouldn't it be? Coal miners and steelworkers risk serious injury and worse. The fatality rate was higher and the wage scale lower than in the NFL. So *gittahta* here, the fans said. In bars and on talk shows, the players' defenders were few.

When the training camps opened, the union miscalculated fatally by allowing the rookies to report. Imagine the plumbers' union calling a strike and letting the plumbers' apprentices go to work. A scenario just as unlikely was playing out in the NFL. While the veterans picketed, the rookies who came to camp were trying to take their jobs. And many of these rookies could play. That is why they'd been drafted or signed as free agents. They were not quite finished products, but they were getting there.

Our own rookies, it turned out, were the best of the lot. Draft scholars — the people with strange one-track minds who devote their entire lives to studying and analyzing and researching this subject — still say that our 1974 draft never has been surpassed.

On the first day of camp, the veterans set up their picket line at the entrance to our training facilities. The AJR who had dealt with his players face to face would have talked them into moving away from the main gate by appealing to their common sense and loyalty. But now things were different. The pickets included "union representatives" — agitators, some called them. We turned the problem over to our downtown law firm. That we could do this was entirely because of Dan. He had replaced Fran Fogarty with a team of accountants, and he had replaced lawyer Owney McManus, Jr., the son of AJR's longtime crony, with what amounted to a legal department of our own — after considerable soul-searching, I should add. Invoking arcane labor laws and, for all I know, the Constitution of the United States, our counselors got the picket line transferred to an unpaved farm-to-market road that wound its dusty way through corn fields and a cemetery to the back door of St. Vincent College. From then on, there was absolutely no contact between the strikers and the pared-down football team, or, for that matter, the front-office people and coaches.

Chuck Noll, in public, was stoic and noncommittal. "I try very hard not to worry about things I can't control," he would say in response to questions from the media. On the subject of the absent veterans, he would say, "I can only coach the players who are here." And coach them he did. When Noll could coach — that is to say, teach — he was never happier. With a camp full of rookies, he could teach to his heart's content. The veterans, as far as Noll was concerned, had ceased to exist. Out of sight, out of mind. There was work to be done (two-a-days in the hot sun, weightlifting sessions, flexibility drills); there were meetings to be held — meetings with the players, meetings with the assistant coaches, meetings with the scouts. From all appearances, Noll and his coaches had gone to football heaven.

We were well prepared for the strike. Along with our draft picks, we had signed an unusually large contingent of free agents and walk-ons, giving the coaches enough players for full-scale practices. Most of the other teams, it was clear, had taken the threat of a boycott less than seriously. The decision to go ahead with the pre-season schedule, using rookies and any veterans who crossed the picket lines, took them by surprise. Caught shorthanded, personnel directors went looking for bodies.

The Steelers' only need was at quarterback. Woody Widenhofer had sold us on drafting Frank Kolch, a marginal prospect from Eastern Michigan, one of Woody's coaching stops, but after showing up for the indoctrination get-together, he refused to sign a contract. Perhaps he knew that we needed arms. So when Jim Trimble, a scout for the New York Giants, called and asked if we had a running back we could spare — the Giants were desperate for one — we sent them Doug Kotar, a rookie free agent, in exchange for a quarterback named Leo Gasienica. Kotar was from Canonsburg and had played at Kentucky. In letting him go, we presented the Giants with a back who served them well until a brain tumor seven years later ended his football career and his life. And Leo Gasienica? In the short term, he helped to alleviate our quarterback crisis but is chiefly remembered for something else.

It was late at night when he reported to camp, and my cousin Tim had to find him a place to sleep. There happened to be a dormitory room with two beds and only one occupant – another rookie, Tim supposed – and that was where he stashed Leo. Morning came. Leo woke up first. He went to the lavatory and showered and shaved. When he returned, ready to dress for the day, his roommate was up and moving around. The first thing Leo noticed about him was his age. He must have been 60 at least. "This is no football player," Leo realized. He then did a double take. At Rutgers, Leo had majored in literature. "Hey, I've seen you before – your picture, anyway," he blurted. Then it came to him.

"You're James Michener! I've read your books!"

The best-selling author was doing research for a scholarly work about the cultural role of sports in America. Upon meeting him earlier in the week, AJR, who had *not* majored in literature at Indiana Normal or Georgetown or Duquesne, had taken him for an ordinary "newspaper guy."

Assigned by Bill Nunn to room with another player, Leo demurred, asking if he could stay with Michener. "It's as close as I'll ever get to a famous writer," he explained. And with Michener's enthusiastic approval, the arrangement continued for as long as Michener remained at St. Vincent.

Besides Leo, there were two or three others in camp who could at least throw the ball, and we had some promising receivers: John Stallworth, Lynn Swann, Randy Grossman, Nate Hawkins, Reggie Garrett. Those last three, under different circumstances, might have been more appreciated. Chuck Noll had nothing but praise for this crew. The only real quarterback, though, was Leo. And then, unexpectedly, Joe Gilliam reported to camp, breaking ranks with the strikers, and our troubles were over.

This was the same Gilliam who had made an impassioned pro-union speech at the outset of the strike, excoriating management. It appears that after giving the matter some thought, he had seen on which side his bread was buttered. Noll watched him throw and was visibly excited. He walked with a light step on the first day Gilliam practiced. And Bill Nunn, who had scouted Gilliam and recommended him to us, was all smiles.

Gilliam's sharp passing changed the tenor of the workouts, and Gasienica's presence kept him from wearing out his arm. Stallworth and Swann were going deep for the first time and making beautiful over-the-shoulder catches. Not only Nunn and the coaches were pleased. The other scouts, ecstatic, couldn't believe their eyes. "Did you see that?" they were asking one another. Training-camp blossoms often die with the first frost, but this new fleet corps of receivers looked like hardy perennials.

(With defensive backs Jimmy Allen and Donnie Shell putting hits on them, life for the receivers wasn't easy. Jack Lambert's Kent State teammate, tight end Gary Pinkel, made a good catch one day, and then, *wham!* A killer hit by either Allen or Shell – here, again, my memory fails me — knocked him senseless. The crash could be heard from one end of the practice field to the other. Up went the cry for first aid — "RALPH!" — and out trotted Berlin, pumping his bad knees. Just for the record, Pinkel did not make the team. In another end of the business, he did make it, becoming a good assistant coach at the University of Washington and elsewhere.)

Someone else in camp who could throw a football was Lionel Taylor, the receivers coach. Taylor had a drill in which the receivers would form a circle around him. Picking up footballs from a collection at his feet, he would fire them at the players. He would go clockwise to start with, and then throw passes randomly, so that no one could tell whose turn it might be. From time to time he would call out a warning: "Keep your eyes on the ball, not my face." With either hand, he would throw hard passes and soft passes, behind-the-back passes and between-the-legs passes. He could put a tight, perfect spiral on the ball or make it travel end-over-end, like a placekick. His dexterity was amazing; it reminded me of the Harlem Globetrotters' famous Meadowlark Lemon and his sleight-of-hand tricks with a basketball.

A player who muffed a pass dropped out of the circle. When only three or four players were left, the competition became intense. The eliminated players would cheer for their particular friends, creating a hubbub. At last it would come down to Taylor and one survivor – often enough, but not always, Stallworth or Swann. It might be Grossman, it might be Hawkins, it might be Garrett. It might even be, and this was not out of the ordinary, an unknown free agent. Draftee or long shot, the last man would stay on the firing line until one of Taylor's passes eluded his grasp. Or until Taylor himself, soaked with sweat after fifteen strenuous minutes, called an end to the drill.

I tried to guess, as I watched Joe Gilliam, what Bradshaw and Hanratty were thinking. How resentful did they feel? Gilliam's — what would you call it, naked opportunism? — must have rankled. Noll did not say so, but I could sense that Gilliam had moved ahead of Hanratty and now was the second-string quarterback. Then came the first pre-season game, and after Noll and the other coaches had made their evaluations, there could not be the slightest doubt: even Bradshaw's job was in jeopardy.

"Pre-season game" was the new terminology. The league's marketing geniuses had decided that "exhibition game" conveyed the wrong message. Football was serious business now. We were charging the same price in the pre-season as in the regular season, combining both sets of games in one inseparable ticket package, and how could you ask the fans to dig that deep for "exhibitions"? In the second place, or maybe the first place, the television networks were voicing concern. The networks had to think about ratings. And that word "exhibition," was a turnoff, the networks believed. Who would tune in to watch an "exhibition"? Not as many viewers as profitability required. So there was general agreement that the word wouldn't do. Orders went out to eradicate it. None of which meant that in "pre-season games" the coaches would not pull their starters very quickly and let the players on the fringe compete for jobs.

A Very Good Year

Some teams, I believe, thought the strike would be settled before the pre-season games got under way or that the pre-season schedule would be cancelled. The picketing players held to this view, I am sure. But on July 27, the annual Hall-of-Fame game took place as usual at Canton, Ohio, the officially designated birthplace of professional football. From St. Vincent, I watched on television as the Cardinals and Bills, traveling by bus, approached Fawcett Stadium. The whole thing resembled a military operation. Police cars escorted the buses and stood watch at the overpasses. Helicopters looked down on the side roads for union members lying in wait with sabotage in their hearts. But nothing happened. There were no disruptions. When the Cardinals' rookies kicked off to the Bills' rookies (or it may have been the other way around), I knew there would be a pre-season.

The Steelers' first game was with the Saints in New Orleans. Joe Gilliam was spectacular, and, as AJR used to say in his race-track vernacular, we won going away, 26-7. Back in Pittsburgh, we trounced the former Monsters of the Midway, the Chicago Bears, in front of a large, enthusiastic crowd. The Steeler aerial circus, with Gilliam once more the ringmaster, ran up the score. It stood at 50-21 when AJR got up from his seat looking embarrassed and sought out his old friend George Halas to apologize. "But Dad," his sons reminded him, "what about all the times that Halas did the same thing to us?" AJR took a savage bite out of his cigar. "Aw, you wise guys ... you ... you just don't get it," he growled.

We understood this much: the Steelers' image was improving. Fast. For two years in a row, Chuck Noll had put us in the playoffs. And now the early success of this makeshift team of rookies and retreads was attracting favorable attention. As I had learned to expect, much of it rubbed off on the family. After the Saints and the Bears, we played the Eagles. In Philadelphia. Where our race-track operation had not been well received by the power structure. Initially, the Main Line bluebloods had been disposed to regard us as agents of Davey Lawrence, the evil, conniving political boss whose object in life was to grind them under his heel. Worse, even, than being interlopers, we were hoodlums and racketeers. Not any more. AJR had become "Mister Rooney," no longer a shady character but a "sportsman," welcome now in the most elevated circles. "Funny thing," he said thoughtfully. "Wherever I go around here, people are asking me all kinds of questions. What do I think of this, what do I think of that. As if I was some guy whose opinion mattered, a guy with the inside dope. And you know something? I'm starting to give them answers."

Our newly acquired popularity had its drawbacks. All of our friends wanted tickets to the game. Free tickets, of course. And not just any free tickets, but good ones. The job of satisfying their demands fell to Jim Boston and Dan. I was glad, once again, to be the scouting director.

Buffered by the return of the veterans – the union had given in and the strike was over – we won from the Eagles in overtime, 33-30, and Gilliam was still the big story. Every night on the talk shows you heard the admonition: Bradshaw had better watch out. One fine old veteran, linebacker Henry Davis, didn't last long. Davis lost his job to Jack Lambert and was cut. Other experienced players who were kept on the roster found themselves suddenly demoted. To his evident chagrin, Bradshaw was one. The unwritten rule that an injured player kept his starting position did not, as far as Noll was concerned, apply here. It was one thing to be hurt, something entirely different to strike.

The next game we played was with the Giants, and there were scouts all over the place. I could guess what they were thinking: *The Steelers have too many good young players. They can't possibly keep all these guys. And who knows? Maybe Gilliam will be available. He's too good to be a number three.*

Our game with New York was a 17-7 win. Against the Giants' regulars, Gilliam performed as brilliantly as he had against rinky-dink defenses. We beat the Redskins in Washington, 21-19, and the Cowboys in Dallas, 45-15, for a 6-0 record. Gilliam was still the ace. He had played every minute on offense, and now, for the first time ever, we had finished the pre-season undefeated. It would happen again, often enough, but never with such an overabundance of rookies in the lineup. Six of those rookies plus Rocky Bleier became starters on Pittsburgh teams that won Super Bowls. They were Swann, Stallworth, Grossman, Webster, Lambert, and Shell. To paraphrase some lyrics from an old Frank Sinatra tune, 1974 was shaping up as a very good year.

The Only Thing

My scouts and I, although buoyed by the success of our young players in the pre-season games, kept reminding ourselves that it didn't mean a whole lot. Pre-season results can be misleading.

So we were not uncontrollably euphoric. We thought we had a playoff team, yes. After winning a division title in 1972 (our first in forty years) and landing a wild-card berth in 1973 despite some truly inopportune injuries, we expected something similar in 1974. The playoffs were now a sort of benchmark for us, and of course I felt good about it. This was my tenth year in the scouting department; I had shown that I belonged, that I was not just the owner's son, an undeserving rich kid. The respect I had wanted from my peers was coming to me now, along with words of caution from tutors like George Young. "Arthur," George said to me once, "you have done well. But please remember – the only real prize is the Super Bowl. And getting to the Super Bowl is not enough. You have to *win* it."

The gospel according to Vince Lombardi. Chapter and verse. Winning isn't everything, it's the only thing.

Looking back, I still don't see how we managed to go all the way. The players' strike helped us by hastening the development of our rookies, but it also created a huge problem — the quarterback controversy that was almost the team's undoing. Joe Gilliam's arm strength and pizzazz, so evident from his first day at St. Vincent, seemed to have Noll entranced. Bradshaw, consigned to a backup role, couldn't believe what was happening. He sulked and popped off to the media. Hanratty, the new low man on the totem poll, accepted the situation dispassionately. Aware of his limitations, Hanratty was content to be the backup to the backup.

In 1974, we did not yet realize that Bradshaw suffered from clinical depression. Knowing about it, we could have dealt more understandingly with his moodiness and his juvenile behavior. That he did not completely blow his cork was due not only to his reliance on Holy Writ but to AJR's influence, I thought. AJR studied people the way he studied race horses. He talked with Bradshaw, listened to him, kept him from forcing a showdown with Noll.

The first game of the regular season, at home against Baltimore, was a 30-0 win. So far so good for Gilliam. Next, it was off to Denver, where Gilliam's exposure to the thin mountain air seemed to bring on an attack of giddiness. He forgot that, with Franco Harris, we had a powerful running game, and he never stopped throwing passes, too many of them caught by the guys in the wrong uniforms. We should have won easily; instead, we were lucky to get a tie. The score was 35-35 after a fifteen-minute overtime, the limit back then under the rules.

Inevitably, Gilliam was now the focus of talk-show debate. Noll's assistant coaches had questions of their own. "Damn it, anyway," one of them grumbled, "we can't throw away a victory like that." The subject came up in meetings with their boss. George Perles and others lobbied for a shutdown of the aerial circus. "Those interceptions can kill you," they said. "Control the ball with the run."

The Oakland Raiders came to Pittsburgh and shut down both the aerial circus and our running game. Oakland 17, Steelers 0. Making his third start, Gilliam couldn't get the offense in gear. Still Noll kept him at quarterback, a move that paid off in road wins over Houston and Kansas City. Then at home against Cleveland, Gilliam misfired on thirteen of his first eighteen passes, and Noll replaced him with Bradshaw. We won the game, 20-16.

After that, no one knew whether Bradshaw or Gilliam was the starter until Noll made up his mind with the season nearly over. Let me just say that Bradshaw won out in the end by subordinating his ego. Gilliam threw far too many passes, and they were deep passes, mostly. He was hell-bent on showing off his arm. Bradshaw gave the ball to Franco and threw medium-distance passes to his agile receivers. Bradshaw kept the defense off the field, adding to its effectiveness as the best defense in the league. After the Cleveland game the Steelers beat the Falcons and the Eagles, with Bradshaw now the starter, but lost at Cincinnati, and once again it was Gilliam's turn. Wins over Cleveland and New Orleans followed, but then we lost to Houston, 13-10, and that was the end for Gilliam. Noll reinstated Bradshaw with the promise, "I'm sticking with you for the rest of the year, no matter what happens."

What happened was that the Steelers won their last two regular-season games, knocked off Buffalo and Oakland in the conference playoffs, and, in their first trip to the Super Bowl, overpowered Minnesota, 16-6. The defense put pressure on Fran Tarkenton, intercepting three of his passes and deflecting four others. Franco Harris, meanwhile, rushed for 158 yards, a Super Bowl record.

I never have figured out whether Gilliam started on drugs — hard drugs — before Noll benched him or afterwards. We knew that in college he had used marijuana. As a Steeler, no doubt he continued to use it. He remained with the Steelers through the 1975 season, nothing more than a supernumerary until the meaningless final game. Bradshaw was banged up and the Steelers had their divisional championship won, so Gilliam relieved him against the Los Angeles Rams on the road. At once it became apparent that he was high on drugs. Noll took him out, and he never again played in the NFL.

His life after football was that of a junkie. He died at 50 of natural causes brought on by his addiction.

Not the Howling Type

After the win over the Vikings in the Super Bowl game in New Orleans you'd have thought that AJR, instead of Franco, was the MVP. In the locker room, where he accepted the championship trophy from Commissioner Pete Rozelle with television looking on, the print reporters scrambled to get near him. He was irresistible copy, the lovable loser transformed into a winner at the age of 73. The reporters threw questions at him. They were smiling and laughing, reveling in the occasion and all but ignoring Dan.

AJR, wearing his overcoat, a yellow cashmere polo shirt buttoned at the neck, and a checkered woolen cap brought back from Ireland by Tim, was affable but poker-faced. The reporters kept asking him how he *felt*. Unexcitedly, he said he felt good. The reporters weren't satisfied. They wanted emotion, they wanted exuberance. "Well, at the end of the game," one of them prodded, "did you let out a little howl?" AJR explained that he wasn't the howling type. "If you were standing alongside of me at the race track," he said, "you wouldn't know I was betting." The reporters were acting nonplussed. The millions watching on television ate it up.

Later, talking with friends, the Chief unburdened himself. He said, "It may not look like it, but I'm every bit as happy as a guy who hollers and whoops and jumps up and down. I just hoped I could get through this without starting to cry."

A lot of other people had started to cry — people in the television audience. As unlikely a sentimentalist as mean old Bear Bryant had tears in his eyes. Coach John McKay of USC told me so; he watched the game with Bryant. I know that more than a few stragglers in the Sugar Bowl were blubbering.

My description of the locker-room scene is gleaned from the accounts of it I have heard and read. I had watched the game from the stands, and for some time afterward I remained there with Mom, Kay, Jack Butler, and Bernadette, Jack's wife. New Orleans in January can be as frigid as any Northern city, and Mom, shivering, said she could use a shot of whiskey. From out of nowhere, bottles and flasks appeared. On this day, anyway, the Pittsburghers in our vicinity were not going to let Mrs. Arthur J. Rooney feel the cold.

A confession: I had learned from my sixteen years of Catholic schooling never to try to barter with the Lord. But I bartered with Him in the fourth quarter. "Let us win this game," I proposed, "and I'll give up ..." Give up what? An image of the Chief came to me. Ah! Cigars! "I'll give up cigars," I said to the Lord. "For a month." And I kept my word.

Bud Carson, our defensive coordinator, said after the game that he had looked for me at the trophy presentation. Then in words I have never forgotten, he continued, "If any one guy deserved to be in that locker room, it was you." I told him that, on the contrary, I thought I belonged with Kay. "Making up for all the time I spend on the road every year." Bud Carson had nothing to say about that, but I can tell you what Kay's reaction was. "Well, sweetheart," I said as the final minutes of the game ticked away, "wasn't it all worthwhile?" Looking beautiful in her mink coat, she turned the question over in her mind. It didn't take long. Flatly and firmly, she answered, "No."

The Kipling Ideal

From the Sugar Bowl, all of us returned to our hotel in the Latin Quarter. As AJR was about to enter his suite, his bodyguard, 6-foot-3, 270-pound Joey Diven, said, "Just a second, Mister Rooney," and flung himself through the door like an undercover narcotics agent leading a drug raid. One by one, he gave the sitting room, the bedrooms, and the bathrooms a quick eyeball job. No interlopers were lurking under the beds or behind the shower curtains. The Chief didn't know what to make of all this. As puzzled as the rest of us were, he was staring at Joey.

"Mister Rooney," Joey explained, "I wasn't worried about crooks or bad guys. It's those crazy fans. So many of them want to shake your hand I thought I'd better check the place out. To be on the safe side."

AJR's ticket for the game dangled from his lapel. He tore off the ticket and flipped it onto a desk. Picking it up, I asked if he wanted me to save it for him. He did not. The ticket was marked: "Super Bowl IX. Official. Art Rooney." A week or so later, I asked him again if he'd like to have it. He said no, I could keep the darned thing. "Would you sign it?" I asked. He took a pen from his pocket and wrote "Art Rooney" on the ticket. Back in Pittsburgh, I had it sealed in plastic.

Not long afterward, I gave this memento to a doctor, Frank Reda, who had taken care of Kay. Thirty years went by. The doctor was now an old man. One night when Kay and I attended a party at his house, he gave us a look at his curio cabinet. And there, among his precious possessions, was AJR's Super Bowl ticket.

The Chief's apparent lack of emotion after the game carried over into the victory celebration, a large but private gathering in the ballroom of our hotel. There was absolutely no change in his demeanor. I thought of Kipling's famous verse:

If you can meet with Triumph and Disaster

And treat those two impostors just the same ...

Well, then, according to Kipling, you're a man.

I doubt if AJR was a really devoted reader of Kipling, but he embodied the Kipling ideal. In victory or defeat, in good times or bad, there was never the slightest difference in the face he presented to the world. His claim that if you stood right next to him at the race track you wouldn't know if he'd made a bet was accurate. More than once I had seen him win a hundred thousand dollars on a single race and give no sign of elation or even satisfaction.

But now as we made our way to the victory party, he could not help looking pleased. For the first time since the end of the game he was smiling ... letting his humanity show.

I wondered if Kass was responsible. Had she told him to lighten up? She was capable of it, certainly. But on reflection I think it was just the sense that he had of knowing exactly how to behave.

Chuck Noll's reaction to the game was similar to AJR's, and Chuck's wife Marianne resembled Kass in the way she conducted herself. They were cheerful, but low-keyed. Neither the owner nor the coach was a back-slapper.

At one point in the evening, Chuck and Marianne came to our table and asked if they could join us. Kay and I were with Mom and Dad. "Sure, sure. We'll make room. Sit right down." Noll's chair, as it happened, was next to mine, and a funny thing happened. Here was the man who had taken our team to the pinnacle of football a few hours earlier, and I could not find the power to speak. I was tongue-tied. Struck dumb. Don't ask me to explain it. I can't.

Most of us went to bed early that night. At 5:30 a.m., we'd be leaving for the airport. At 6:45 a.m. I'd be thirty thousand feet above the ground and thinking very hard about the 1975 draft.

All Hail

For the trip to New Orleans with sixteen of his friends, Mike Kearns had rented a big mobile trailer. I don't know the route they took. I don't know who drove. I don't know when they left Pittsburgh or how long it took them to get to their destination. I asked Mike only one question: "Was anyone in the expedition sober?"

At least two of the travelers were — a young man named John Clayton and his mother. They will reappear in this narrative later on. Mike Kearns himself was among the imbibers. It was his last real alcoholic fling. He gave up drinking shortly afterward, cold turkey, and never again swallowed a drop.

Mike's luggage on the trip included a huge cardboard sign reading: "A.J. Finally Has His Day." He took this sign into the Sugar Bowl and kept it under wraps, I don't know how, until the outcome of the game was no longer even slightly in doubt. Then he broke through security and got down onto the sidelines and, holding the sign aloft, circled the field. He was wearing a steelworkers' hardhat, which he had painted black and gold. Rising from its crown was a battery-powered, spinning red light. All the television cameras recorded Mike's one-man victory parade for the viewers back home.

The initials "A.J." referred, of course, to the Chief. Every Pittsburgher understood this, and many others in both the crowd at the game and the television audience could deduce as much from the context of the message on the sign.

A bigger, more boisterous celebration awaited us all the next day. As soon as our plane, dubbed Steeler One, landed at Greater Pittsburgh Airport, we were herded into buses. Along the Parkway West, between the airport and Downtown, it seemed that every inch of space was packed with cheering, waving Steeler fans. Car horns were blowing in the outbound lane of the Parkway. In the distance, we could hear the whistles of railroad trains. Our escort of fire trucks and police cars sounded their bells and sirens.

In the press of humanity there were small children, teenagers, fathers, mothers, and grandparents. Thousands among the tens of thousands wore black and gold, and thousands fanned the air with Terrible Towels. Conceived, designed, and popularized by broadcaster Myron Cope, the black and gold Terrible Towel was the Steelers' new battle flag.

The day was cold and bright, with some snow on the ground. When our buses emerged from the Fort Pitt Tunnel, we entered a black and gold sea. Daredevils were hanging from the girders of the Fort Pitt Bridge; people were massed in an unbroken line between the exit and Market Square. They screamed, they shouted, they lifted clenched fists above their heads. It was Rome welcoming Caesar back from the wars. And we were part of it, every one of us – not only the coaches and players, but the scouts, the trainers, the equipment men, Dan, Jim Boston, Ed Kiely, Joe Gordon, the secretaries and, most of all, AJR. He was having his day and then some, smiling and waving but at all times keeping his composure. As for Kass, I can only say she was beaming.

In Market Square, the coaches and players climbed up onto a platform and surveyed the noisy, ebullient throng. Cope, the master of ceremonies, called Chuck Noll to the microphone and demanded an ovation. "All hail the Emperor Chaz!" he cried out, and the Emperor's subjects broke into a roar. The celebration continued with speeches and ovations for the stars of the game. At last the platform emptied, and slowly, reluctantly, the worshippers dispersed. It would be six months before the coaches and players returned to Latrobe, and I know they could hardly wait. And neither, to be honest, could I.

Prize Catch

On the 1974 Steeler team that defeated the Minnesota Vikings in the Super Bowl there were five undrafted free agents. Five may not seem like a lot, but it's an extraordinary number, believe me. Remember also that nine of the players we drafted that year were with us all season. Probably no team before or since ever went to a Super Bowl with fourteen rookies.

Ray Mansfield and Sam Davis in the offensive line, Rocky Bleier in the backfield, and linebacker Andy Russell were the only significant leftovers from the Buddy Parker and Bill Austin regimes. The 1974 team was almost entirely put together by Chuck Noll through the draft, a few trades, and free-agent signings.

Two of the free agents — Reggie Garrett, wide receiver from Eastern Michigan, and Dickie Conn, safety from Georgia (and no relation to Billy) — played very little. Marv Kellum, linebacker from Wichita State, was not a starter but contributed. Randy Grossman, tight end from Temple, became a starter eventually. In 1974 he was our go-to guy in tough-yardage situations. He could track the ball, separate himself from defenders, and twist his body into unbelievable shapes to make a catch. His hands were like grappling hooks. If the ball came anywhere near them, it was his.

After eight years with the Steelers, Grossman got into the investment banking business full-time. Intelligent and affable, he rode the economic boom of the 1990s to a successful career. AJR, foreseeing how well he would do, always said, "They'll never have a tag day for Randy." (Tag days were once a staple of Pittsburgh's downtown civic life. Awarded a tag day by City Hall, a charitable organization would post collectors on every street corner to hand out lapel tags in exchange for donations.)

Our prize free agent in 1974, and, along with Jack Butler, one of the two best free agents the Steelers ever signed, was Donnie Shell. In his four years at South Carolina State, an all-black school in the lowlands near Charleston, Shell had had two head coaches, a man named Banks and a man named Jeffries. Both had praised him to our scouts, using nearly identical words: "He'll knock a ball carrier's jock off." He was also, they told us, a high-class individual.

For a linebacker, Shell lacked size. He was only six feet tall, or a little over, and 205 pounds. In the NFL he would have to be a defensive back. Bill Nunn tried to get him on our draft list, but without success. The transition from linebacker to safety would be "too tough," everyone said.

In the draft, there were no takers for Shell. Afterward, as in previous years, Nunn headed South with a briefcase full of contracts and blank checks. His job was to sign draft picks and free agents in the area, including Shell. None of us, except possibly Nunn, held out much hope for him, but Noll, we knew, was a brilliant developer of talent. Given the athleticism Shell possessed, and his reputation for being coachable, there was always a chance.

Shell signed, as we expected he would. Then fate took a hand. Just before training camp opened, the players' union called its strike, and the rookies had the place to themselves, opening the door for Shell. In short order, he proved himself to be a top special-teams man while developing into a very good defensive back.

In many ways Shell reminded me of Jack Butler. Both were free agents who had played college football in the sticks, so to speak. Butler, like Shell, was a "projection" — a defensive end and receiver at St. Bonaventure but a defensive back in the eyes of our coaches. Both he and Shell were hard hitters.

I remember a ferocious hit Shell delivered on the Houston Oilers' powerful fullback, Earl Campbell. The Steelers were playing Houston in the Astrodome in 1978. As Campbell bulldozed his way through the line, Mean Joe Greene got a piece of him. Campbell managed to stay on his feet, but was slightly off-balance when Donnie Shell came up fast from the secondary. Dipping his hips, he exploded "under and up." It was a textbook rising blow into Campbell's neck and jaw. Knocked flat, the NFL's most punishing runner was through for the day. I had seen Mike Ditka make a pass reception and shake off four Steelers who had climbed onto his back, an unforgettable Hall-of-Fame play; I had seen the hit Chuck Mehelich put on Leon Hart; but nothing that ever happened on a football field is more vivid to me than Shell's hit on Campbell.

Butler, in a nine-year career, had fifty-two interceptions; Shell had fifty-one in thirteen years and many more games. Butler played in four Pro Bowls, Shell in five. The fact that Shell made it to four Super Bowls, as against none at all for Butler, doesn't mean a thing. It was Shell's good fortune to have exceptional teammates; Butler came along at a time when the Steelers were also-rans. Like Butler, Shell remained in football after his playing days, a front-office executive with the Carolina Panthers.

Barefoot Boys

There was a time in the early 1970s when our trainers, to make things easier for themselves on road trips, taped the ankles and feet of the rookies before we left the hotel. They would then be able to give the veterans more attention at the game site.

I remember an incident in an Alabama hotel during John Stallworth's first year. Bob Milie and Ralph Berlin were taping the rookies in the lobby. Walking through on my way to the team bus, I caught sight of Stallworth, alone and half-hidden in a corner by the door.

I stopped and asked why he was not with the other players, who were clustered around the trainers some distance off in an open part of the lobby.

He glanced at his bare feet and told me politely that he would prefer not to be seen in so public a place without shoes on.

"I don't want to look like I'm from Alabama," he added.

I said, "Hey, it's no big deal. All of those other barefooted guys are being taped over there in full view. And, anyway, you *are* from Alabama."

"I know it," Stallworth answered. "I just don't want to *look* like I'm from Alabama."

An unimportant happening that told me a lot about Stallworth. His sensitivity was a trait I admired.

Stallworth became a successful businessman, the president and CEO of an information technology company based in Huntsville – Huntsville, *Alabama*. The firm had 650 employees with offices in nine cities and yearly revenues way up in the millions.

Chapter 59

Too Much Too Soon

Late in 1974 our Philadelphia lawyer, John Macartney, apprised the Rooney family of a business opportunity that had nothing to do with football.

Macartney had worked out a deal that would give us an excellent chance to acquire the Avis Rent-a-Car company. Avis was then a subsidiary of the International Telephone and Telegraph corporation, which had somehow run afoul of the anti-trust laws. The courts had ordered IT&T to divest itself of certain holdings, Avis chief among them. And IT&T had to get this done by a certain date; otherwise, outside receivers would take over Avis.

From our point of view, the timing could not have been worse. The "certain date" would coincide with the Steelers' preparations for Super Bowl IX. But Macartney wanted us to think very hard about branching out from football and horse racing into other entrepreneurial ventures.

He had talked to "the right people" at IT&T, he confided, and had found them receptive. He said that AJR's reputation for integrity was already well known to these movers and shakers. Macartney, who was also a mover and shaker, had set up the necessary financing with the same banks that had handled our Yonkers Raceway acquisition, and AJR was his hole card.

For estate-tax reasons, AJR himself would not be officially involved in the transaction. If everything fell into place, ownership would reside with his five sons and Macartney. By this time, Macartney was one of the Chief's "boys," as my father always referred to my brothers and me. No one believed for a moment, of course, that AJR would not have a key role to play.

Macartney belonged to the exclusive Sailfish Club in Palm Beach, and all of us met there with the general manager of Avis. I've forgotten this gentleman's name, but he did not come across as an "old-money" guy. Rather, I deduced that he had made his considerable pile the old-fashioned way, by earning it. Still, there was something Ivy Leaguish about him. "Did you dig that fellow's suit — classic

Brooks Brothers," said Pat to me after the meeting. "It might be ten years old or six months old. Doesn't show its age."

Like Macartney, this man was low-keyed and focused. He knew what questions to ask us, and he knew what the answers ought to be. Mainly, he was interested in our intentions. Were we determined to keep Avis in business? AJR quietly made it clear that we did not have a hidden agenda.

I remained perfectly silent until the confab was winding down. Then I mentioned to our inquisitor that I had been using Avis cars for years and that my dealings with the company had been very satisfactory. On his part, there was no reaction to this until I went on to say that as the head of the Steelers' scouting department I rented Avis cars in the spring, fall, and winter, and even on summer vacations now and then. I pinpointed the cities and towns where the Avis service had been good and also some places where the service had been not so good. When I observed that most of the company's young female employees were ladylike and attractive, and added that the turnover rate among them must be high because of their desirability as marriage partners to the young, single, upwardly mobile businessmen who travel in rented cars, the Avis man broke down and laughed. Up to then, and we'd been talking for three hours, he hadn't cracked a smile.

"That's an inside thing at Avis," he said. "The young ladies we hire do tend to be pretty. And they do get to meet successful young businessmen. But more often than not they end up marrying the guys who deliver the cars."

My playful little digression was an ice-breaker. Since I was such a good friend of Avis, this very professional higher-up continued, he would send me a special credit card.

He kept his word, and one time when I used it, an Avis station manager said to me, "Hey, where did you get this? Are you some kind of VIP?"

The way things turned out, our meeting at the Sailfish Club led to nothing. With the Super Bowl coming up, we didn't have time to make a concerted pitch for Avis. Macartney stayed hot on the deal and kept telling us it was far from dead, but we just couldn't give it our full attention.

In the lobby of our hotel in New Orleans on the day before we played the Vikings, my brother Dan told me Macartney had called. "He said, 'If you mean to go through with this, you have to do it now. Tomorrow at the latest, or Avis will be in the hands of a New York law firm acting as receivers or controllers.'" In Dan's opinion, all we could do was hold off. AJR had waited forty years to be in a championship game, and the Avis deal would take "too much away" from his moment. I said, "I agree. The Super Bowl is more important to Dad than Avis."

Just then I heard myself being paged. It was Kay. She said, "Get up here to the room right away. John Macartney is on the phone and desperate to talk to you." When Macartney and I spoke he repeated his words to Dan. I then repeated what Dan said to me and what I said to him. Macartney answered, "I thoroughly understand. But please believe me when I say we can get Avis now. Next week we'll be dealing with an outside controller."

Tim, Pat, and John looked at this dilemma the way I did, the way Dan did. The Super Bowl came first. We told Macartney to hold off, and sure enough, the court turned Avis over to an outside controller, a New York law firm.

A month or so later, Macartney invited me to New York for a meeting with the head of this firm, who turned out to be a stuffed shirt. After we had cooled our heels in his waiting room for a while, he listened to Macartney's proposal. "We have enough money. Our business concept is good," Macartney assured him. The stuffed shirt was completely unresponsive.

During our wait for the meeting, I had noticed a collection of elegant model railroad trains in a big glass case. I asked the receptionist about them. The law firm, she explained, was the outside controller for a railroad that happened to be in financial trouble.

I said, "Oh? How long have you been the railroad's controller?"

"About fifteen years."

As Macartney and I left the stuffed shirt's office, I nodded in the direction of the model trains, reminded John of my conversation with the receptionist, and said, "I don't think these people will be in any hurry to let us take Avis off their hands."

I was right about their way of operating. They held onto the reins for many years, and we never came close to getting another smell of the deal.

"How much," I once asked Macartney, "would Avis have meant to us money-wise?"

He said, "Oh, if we had held it for just a couple of years, with the old guard at Avis running the business – if we had held it for two years and then sold it, the six of us – you and your brothers and I – would have made at least a million dollars apiece."

Winning that first Super Bowl had its price.

Standing Up to the Chief

Something else important in the strike year of 1974 took place on the administrative side of our business. My brother Dan became much more active in league affairs.

The players' union had been gaining strength and giving ownership a lot to think about, and one thing that helped Dan when it came to dealing with labor problems was the legacy of AJR. Going all the way back to the 1930s, AJR's reputation with the players was that of a straight shooter. Joe Krupa, the one-time Steeler Pro Bowl tackle who joined my scouting department on a part-time basis after his playing career was over, summed it up for me one day. The trade that sent him to Los Angeles in the mid-1960s heightened his appreciation of the time he had spent in Pittsburgh, he said. Los Angeles was a first-class operation, but Krupa found the personal touch lacking. "Your father," he said, "always treated me like a friend. With Mister Rooney, you always knew where you stood." Dan wisely built on that trust; he knew where the players were coming from and would listen when they voiced their concerns.

Like Tim, Dan spent more time with AJR than I did, or than the twins did. Dan's link to the Chief was the managerial responsibility they were sharing; Tim's was their mutual interest in the horse racing business, local politics, and the stock market.

At standing up to the Chief, Tim was braver, even, than Dan. Tim's arguments with the Chief never seemed to end until the Chief told him, "Get out of here!" Tim would then disappear for a while, but he always returned to the wars. "He has a hide like an elephant," said John (or maybe Pat). "He can take what the Chief dishes out and come back for more."

I held Tim in awe. The thought of displeasing the Chief terrified me. When I was unlucky enough to cross him, I retreated to my office or hurriedly arranged a scouting trip. In my dealings with AJR, with college coaches, and with NFL general managers, I wanted no trouble. I wanted above all to be liked. With Noll and his assistant coaches, and with anyone who got in my way when I was trying to do my job, I could take off the gloves. I surprised even myself at how roughly I sometimes treated Noll. I couldn't figure Noll out. My verbal attacks on him seemed to make no impression. He actually thought I was too diffident, too unassertive. "Polish up those brass balls," he would tell me.

As good as the advice was, I just couldn't bring myself to slug it out with the Chief. "Artie doesn't talk to me," the Chief would say to my brothers. It was true. I seldom did. But I listened to him, and I listened to him closely.

Folk Hero

The start of AJR's elevation to folk-hero status is hard to pinpoint. Perhaps it went back to a luncheon he gave at the Allegheny Club before the Steelers' first football game in Three Rivers Stadium.

He was saying thank you to the people who in his opinion got the stadium built – the politicians, the bankers and lawyers, the newspaper editors and broadcasting executives. The main speaker was Howard Cosell, the newest television celebrity. Due in no small measure to his obtrusive personality and crisp judgmental attitude, Monday Night Football on the ABC network was attracting a larger audience every week. Ed Kiely, I assumed, had been responsible for his presence on the dais. Kiely had a way with the media stars from New York. His goal was to make the whole country aware of AJR, and to make the country aware you first had to make New York aware. Home-town coverage of the Steelers could meanwhile take care of itself. In Kiely's view, the local writers and broadcasters had no need of a P.R. guy to feed them information and attend to their every wish. They were being paid by their employers to do a job. Let them do it.

Whoever persuaded Cosell to be on the program, granting that any persuasion was necessary, the words he spoke were his own. He spoke in his familiar New York staccato, high-pitched and nasal. He spoke with authority, and he spoke of AJR in terms that were almost effusive.

The public up to then had known the man called the Chief as the owner of a chronically unsuccessful football team and some race horses that didn't amount to much. He had bet on more winners than would ever come out of his Shamrock Stable. But Cosell now spoke of him as "one of America's most distinguished sportsmen," deserving of honor, a man who had turned down every chance to name his own price for moving the Steelers to some other town. Pittsburgh was where they belonged and Pittsburgh was where they would stay. Such loyalty, Cosell went on, put the money-hungry baseball owners to shame. To the shakers and bakers in the Allegheny Club that day, this was a new way of looking at AJR. Perceptions were being changed almost tangibly. You could feel it.

Four years earlier, the speakers at his sixty-fifth birthday party were preaching to the choir when they showered AJR with accolades, and even in that audience you had his mother attempting to keep everybody's feet on the ground. Using Father Silas as her mouthpiece, she reminded the crowd of mainly long-time friends that AJR was "not yet a saint."

Canonization, or something very nearly like it, would come later, in stages. Cosell's talk was the beginning; the Immaculate Reception — the miraculous catch and run by Franco Harris that won a playoff game with the Oakland Raiders — greatly accelerated the process; the first of the four Super Bowl championships, and the televised presentation of the Lombardi Trophy, with AJR looking humble and almost sad instead of elated, set his transformed image in concrete.

During the bad times, the public used to believe that the Steelers lost because AJR wanted them to lose. Losing was less expensive than winning. It kept the payroll within bounds. Every Steeler failure, every Steeler defeat, was AJR's fault. But in the 1970s all of that changed. The Rooneys weren't dumb or cheap any more, and AJR, as I have said, was a folk hero, a folk hero so accessible that anyone at all, it seemed, could walk past Mary Regan, his personal secretary, barge into his office, and settle down for a conversation.

A cub reporter from the *Pittsburgh Press*, 24 years old, recorded his first impression of AJR. "There is something captivating," he wrote, "in meeting so great a man with so little sense of his greatness." Another young sportswriter said it was like visiting Mount Vernon and finding George Washington still in residence. Not only did the great man welcome you like a friend, you learned that he knew your uncle or your grandfather and could tell you a funny story about him.

Now and then the rumors linking AJR to the rackets resurfaced. At a New Year's Eve party, a local business executive was talking to me with a drink in his hand. His friends in New York, he said, regarded AJR as a "mystery man." Here in Pittsburgh, he went on, he had heard that mob money financed the Steelers and the racing stable. I held my tongue, even though his, loosened by liquor, was flapping irresponsibly.

Somebody else, an old retired guy who had married into money, cornered me at another gathering. He and his friends, he confided, just knew that AJR had made his money on the fringes of the law. He then revived the shopworn accusation that AJR had saddled Pittsburgh with losing teams as a cost-control measure. Next, in the belief that he was giving me a compliment, he said the Steelers had started winning in the 1970s for one reason only: because Dan and I were calling the shots.

Politely, but coldly, I said it surprised me to hear a purported gentleman spreading such mischievous gossip. His wife, who was listening, looked hurt. I felt sorry for her, mainly because she was stuck with this viper until one of them died.

There were times when it seemed that everybody in town had the lowdown on AJR. A retired North Side police detective told Rob Ruck that AJR was in the numbers business. Even Kay's dentist spoke of this as a fact. During my courtship of the beautiful redhead, he shared his information with her parents. AJR, he assured them, was the "numbers king" of Pittsburgh, raking in one thousand dollars a day. Not long after our marriage, Kay reported this to me. With a straight face, I reminded her that one thousand dollars a day, or three hundred and sixty-five thousand a year, wasn't much when you considered the overhead.

It is true that AJR had friends and maybe relatives who were numbers men, but he was not in the business himself. He told his sons he was not, many times, and I believed him. He was in the slot-machine business and he never denied it. He and Milton Jaffe operated the Showboat, where you could gamble illegally and buy liquor illegally, and there was never any secret about it. If he indeed had been in the numbers business he'd have said so, without hesitation.

For his book about AJR called "The Chief," Jim O'Brien interviewed Frank Bolden, entertainment editor and later city editor of the *Pittsburgh Courier*. Bolden referred to numbers writers as "digitarians." It was more respectful, in his opinion. As to whether AJR had been a digitarian, Bolden considered it unlikely. The reason people thought so, he explained, was AJR's association with Senator Jimmy Coyne. In Coyne's organization, there were digitarians, all right, but AJR wasn't one of them. Bolden seemed to be positive about that.

Rob Ruck's North Side police detective may have come to a different conclusion. During my freshman year at North Catholic High School, a teacher asked a silly-sounding hypothetical question: "Is it a sin to break a numbers writer's pencil?" At supper that evening I posed the same question to Dad. "Of course it's a sin," he answered emphatically. "Some good men write numbers for a living. They have to take care of their kids like everyone else."

AJR believed that human beings are weak by nature and that attempts on the part of government to legislate morality always fail (Prohibition comes to mind). People will gamble, he said, no matter what. Consequently it was better to have a lot of small-timers writing numbers on their own than for one powerful crime boss to be soaking up all the cash. When crime became big business, the corruption of elected officials was certain to follow.

In my civics classes at North Catholic High School and St. Vincent College, theories such as this were never discussed.

The snobs who liked to insinuate that AJR's fortune came from the numbers underestimated his prowess as a horse player. The fights he promoted gave him an income for many years, and in the 1970s television revenue and sellouts at Three Rivers Stadium turned the Steelers into a money maker. Shamrock Farm, a hardscrabble, no-frills place, probably didn't pay for itself, but whatever losses there may have been were negligible. Fran Fogarty, you can be sure, took advantage of every tax-saving opportunity. Overall, the racing operation more than broke even because AJR knew how to bet.

According to Pat Livingston, AJR made his money in the Chicago grain market. I disagree. He had one big score in soybean futures, but the grain market wasn't something to be counted on. By the time he was in his seventies and eighties, the football team and our race tracks — Liberty Bell, Yonkers, and the Palm Beach Kennel Club — kept the wolf a long way from the door. His days as a plunger were over.

My brothers Pat and John, as adults, often said that AJR got the best out of life. Everything he wanted, he had — the football team, the boxing club, a hideaway horse farm where females did not intrude, his own stable of thoroughbreds running at nearby tracks, the jockeys in Shamrock silks, the horses named for particular saints and for his friends, not all of them saintly; pals like Kies and Father Jim Campbell to hang out with; brothers like Jim, for all his faults, and Father Silas; a great wife who believed him when he told her the Depression hadn't ended; five sons he put through the Catholic educational system from grade school to graduate school (no Ivy League costs there, and we all stayed out of the pokey). Never less than one hundred cents for every dollar he spent. On a higher plane, faith in God. And almost everybody loved him.

Who could ask for anything more?

Don't Kid the Kidder

Nineteen seventy-two was the year of the Immaculate Reception and the year of AJR's de facto canonization. Overnight, Pittsburgh embraced the Steelers and their suddenly popular owner. Forgotten were four decades of almost continuous ineptitude. Under Chuck Noll the Steelers had started to win, and there were no more losing seasons until 1985. The public's scorn gave way to a Terrible Towel-waving giddiness. Steelermania was born. And though the fans could appreciate Noll, and though they knew, or at least were told, that Dan was responsible for bringing him here, and though a few sportswriters mentioned that the scouting department had helped put the pieces together, the accolades went to AJR.

Reviled for so long as a bumbling loser, he was now unexpectedly a civic treasure, a man who had weathered the bad times with fortitude and grace, never losing heart, refusing all inducements to move the franchise. Sometime in the late 1960s, thanks mainly to television, professional football had supplanted baseball as the national pastime, and the Steelers were now the champions of the

NFL. In the glare of the television lights, AJR gave a virtuoso performance. He was always himself, plain-spoken, humble, and unaffected. He had a down-to-earth type of charisma, he connected with everybody, high or low, and America ate it up. All over the country, sportswriters and broadcasters — on cue, it almost seemed — were calling him as though with one voice, "the most beloved figure in sports."

His humility and unaffectedness were real, but let there be no mistake — he liked this new perception of himself. His wife knew it; his sons knew it; Ed Kiely knew it. My brothers and I caught on slowly; Kass was never fooled for an instant.

Of course, when she heard that Johnny Laughlin, Aunt Margaret's husband, had referred to AJR as a prima donna, she sprang to her husband's defense. "Prima donna, is it?" she said, sounding like the Maureen O'Hara spitfire character in "The Quiet Man." "Coming from that one! Everything he has he got from Art." But she saw very clearly, and his sons gradually learned, that the accusation was not totally false.

We are all prima donnas in the sense that we want recognition and approval. It was obvious to me from my scouting work that even the greatest football players need a certain amount of praise. It's a universal trait. AJR simply happened to be adept at masking this need.

When Pat Livingston or Ron Cook of the *Post-Gazette* or someone from out of town wrote a favorable newspaper story about him, he read it with evident enjoyment. When he expected to be on television, he watched. One night at the supper table, as the 6 o'clock news came on, he demanded silence. He'd been filmed that day with Governor Dave Lawrence and Mayor Joe Barr at the funeral of an important politician, and their exit from the church was shown twice – the second time when we were having dessert. "Wait!" he ordered us, putting a stop to the table talk. "Here it comes again." But we were much more interested in Mom's great apple pie. He pushed back his chair and jumped to his feet in a swift athletic move not often seen in an overweight fellow nearing 60. "Well, if you people don't care about this, I'll watch it myself in the front room," he said as he stalked to the door.

He was passing up a slice of the best apple pie ever baked for his cameo appearance on the news.

As soon as he was out of hearing range, we looked at one another and laughed. Even Kass was amused — something rare. It was her habit at such times to remind us that, collectively, we would not make a patch on our father's ass. (Kass rarely sugarcoated anything.) This was one night she kept quiet.

"Don't kid the kidder," AJR always said, and though his foibles entertained us, we were careful not to let on. We felt we could recognize his human failings with no loss of respect. There was genuine affection between us, and yet we were not a demonstrative family. AJR was a Rooney. His love for Kass and his love for his "boys" — that was what he called us, his "boys," never his sons — did not have to be constantly proclaimed. We were sure of it, as Kass was. His brothers, except for Dan and Tom, might have wondered at times where they stood. He loved them all, I believe, including the three reprobates - Jim, Red, and Vince.

When I was in New York City studying drama, AJR would come in from Pittsburgh. We would meet at his hotel and go to Moore's Restaurant in a taxicab, an exciting trip through the night-time sounds and sights of Manhattan. One night on our way to the restaurant he suddenly reached over and took my hand, an overtly intimate gesture so uncharacteristic it shocked me. I was 23 years old; I thought, "My God — he's dying! Or, no — Mom's dying! He's getting ready to tell me. Or, wait — maybe it's Aunt Alice who's dying. Or else — could it be? — he's lost the Steelers."

But we finished our ride without speaking, and then he released my hand. It was over — for me, an uncomfortable experience. And it was never to happen again.

Yankee Doodle

From 1921 through 1964, the New York Yankees won twenty-nine American League pennants and almost as many World Series championships. In 1964, a television network, the Columbia Broadcasting System, bought the team. It made no sense, except that owning the New York Yankees was a can't-lose proposition.

The Yankees had two inherent competitive advantages — the biggest fan base and the biggest TV market. Their minor-league farm teams routinely delivered an endless supply of talent to the parent club. When age caught up with Babe Ruth in the 1930s the Yankees had Lou Gehrig; when Gehrig passed on just a few years later, they still had Joe DiMaggio; when DiMaggio turned up lame at the outset of the 1950s, Mickey Mantle was ready. The Yankees' pre-eminence seemed as permanently fixed as Manhattan Island itself. Then the ownership of the team passed to CBS, and everything changed.

Overnight, the Yankees stopped looking like a dynasty. Instead of winning pennants, they were thrashing around in the second division. In 1966, before the two major leagues split up into divisions, they ignominiously finished tenth. Improvement after that was only marginal, and, by 1974, CBS wanted out.

It could not be admitted, of course, that the difficulties of operating a baseball team were more than the network's top brass could handle. After all, CBS had its image to think about. The official line, therefore, was "conflict of interest." CBS was in the news business as well as the entertainment business; to get rid of a team it "reported on" became necessary "for the good of the game."

And bringing it off without fanfare was desirable. Quietly, somebody from the network got in touch with AJR. He was now a man of acknowledged prestige and integrity. Years of picking winners at the race track — and of not picking coaches who were able to win football games — didn't make you an "American sportsman." It took a Super Bowl victory, televised and publicized and celebrated as never before, to do that. The owner of the football team that won the Super Bowl was deemed worthy of owning a tradition-rich baseball team like the Yankees.

"Make a legitimate offer for the ball club, and it's yours. You'd know how to run it," he was told.

The Chief spent some time in deep thought. Would his background as a horse player make such a venture controversial? Until John Galbreath bought the Pirates, baseball had been off-limits to anybody connected with a sport whose lifeblood was the parimutuel window. And Galbreath made his living in real estate, not at the race track. Owning thoroughbreds was his avocation. If he ever placed a bet — and who could doubt that he had? — it was not as a professional gambler. AJR, as everyone knew, had built his fortune on gambling.

There was also the NFL rule against owning more than one major sports franchise. You could not own two football teams in the same league. You could not own two football teams in competing leagues. You could not own a football team and a baseball team, or a basketball team, or a hockey team. You could own a football team and a racing stable, but the NFL preferred that you did not.

AJR wore two hats, but he was careful about donning a third one. Milton Jaffe, his old business partner, approached him once as a representative of the casino owners in Las Vegas. How would he like to be the commissioner of gambling out there? There'd be a lot of money in it and also a lot of power, Milton promised. AJR turned him down. "I'm a Pittsburgh guy," he said. "And I'm a football guy." He wasn't tempted.

Neither did the offer to buy the Yankees interest him for long. It never got out of the conversational stage.

Later, the Chief second-guessed himself. "I didn't use my head," he told me. "I had three boys" – always, we were his "boys" — "who weren't involved in football. I could have bought that team for Tim, John, and Pat."

The price tag on the Yankees was six million dollars, a pittance. When John Macartney learned that the Chief had taken a pass, he shook his head. "We could have borrowed six million from a small local bank," he lamented. Not long afterward, George Steinbrenner, a filthy rich shipbuilding impresario, bought the Yankees. He paid, as I recall, eleven million dollars. By the turn of the century they were worth well over a billion.

Postscript: Sometime during the late 1960s, Tim and I had dinner one night with AJR at Toots Shor's restaurant on 52nd Street. AJR left us money enough to pay the check and went off to take care of some business. Shor carne to the table, said that dinner was on him (he insisted), and called for his car. We were going to the ball game, he said.

The game was at Yankee Stadium, where we were ceremoniously ushered to a V.I.P. box. An attendant served hors d'oeuvres, and though we protested that we were not at all hungry, having so recently finished our dinners, Shor wasn't listening. "Both of you bums eat something," he said, using the epithet he reserved for friends, friends of friends, or relatives of friends. "Act like this is a big deal."

After watching us force down the snacks, he took us on a tour of the private boxes and introduced us to people whose names he was sure we would recognize. "Meet Art Rooney's boys from Pittsburgh," he'd say.

For the Yankees, these were the lean years, and the occupants of the boxes made up a large share of the crowd. Tim and I, adept at counting heads, thought that no more than three thousand paying customers were present. Shor seemed to read our minds. In a barely audible voice, he muttered, "CBS has really screwed this up. Now, I ask you, how could anybody screw up the Yankees?"

We watched a couple of innings and returned to the restaurant. It was my first and last visit to the House That Ruth Built, which I also like to think of as The House That Art Rooney's Boys From Pittsburgh Almost Fell Heir To.

Chapter 60

Overcoming Oakland

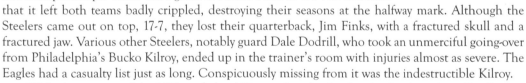

Traditional rivalries come and go. From the 1930s into the 1960s, geography ordained that the Steelers' bitterest rival would be the team at the other end of the state, the Philadelphia Eagles. When Jock Sutherland's Steelers had a shot at the Eastern Division title in 1947, it was the Eagles who beat them in a playoff game.

Mostly, however, the Philadelphia-Pittsburgh rivalry was for blood, not championships. There was a game at Forbes Field in 1954 so ferocious that it left both teams badly crippled, destroying their seasons at the halfway mark. Although the Steelers came out on top, 17-7, they lost their quarterback, Jim Finks, with a fractured skull and a fractured jaw. Various other Steelers, notably guard Dale Dodrill, who took an unmerciful going-over from Philadelphia's Bucko Kilroy, ended up in the trainer's room with injuries almost as severe. The Eagles had a casualty list just as long. Conspicuously missing from it was the indestructible Kilroy.

With the merger of the NFL and the AFL, putting the Steelers in the American Conference and the Eagles in the National, the rivalry died. Cleveland became the team the Pittsburgh fans chose to hate. Pre-game and post-game brawls between Pittsburgh fans and Cleveland fans resulted in more mayhem than anything that happened on the football field. The rivalry with the Browns has persisted, in a way, but with much lower intensity since Art Modell, who owned the Cleveland franchise, moved it to Baltimore, filling a vacancy created when the Baltimore owner moved the Colts to Indianapolis. For a couple of seasons there was no team in Cleveland. The league then brought forth the expansion Browns, who were too weak, at least in the beginning, to be thought of as anyone's deadly enemy. And the original Browns, transformed into Baltimore Ravens, don't arouse the same passions as they did wearing Cleveland uniforms.

Rivalries in professional football can't be shuffled around, or arbitrarily called into existence. Paul Brown was so dominant a personality that as coach and general manager of Mickey McBride's new All-America Conference team in 1947 he selected the uniform colors and agreed to the nickname — Browns — suggested by a fan. His accomplishments and renown, as much as the cultural resemblances between Cleveland and Pittsburgh and their accessibility to each other by automobile, gave our rivalry with the Browns its special cachet. But when Modell, weary of playing second fiddle to Brown, unceremoniously fired him, and Brown became the owner and coach of a startup team in Cincinnati, the Bengals, not much of his name's magic rubbed off. As far as Pittsburgh was concerned, the Bengals were just another opponent. Their games with the Steelers at Three Rivers Stadium drew capacity crowds, but only because all Steeler home games drew capacity crowds.

Paul Brown had a cold formality that not even the Chief could penetrate. The Chief was affable toward Brown, but had to work at it. George Halas, George Marshall, the Bidwills, and other owners were friends. Brown was never more than a respected business acquaintance.

This absence of a close relationship embarrassed the Chief once in a California airport. It was back before the days of credit cards. AJR paid for everything by cash, whatever it was, and he always carried several thousand dollars in his kick. On this occasion, after an NFL meeting in Los Angeles, he discovered that he was carrying less than one hundred. His traveling companions, Ed Kiely and Fran Fogarty, couldn't help. They were running almost on empty; when you traveled with AJR, money was not a necessity. But this time the Chief had broken his own rule, which was never to be caught with "short paper." By his own extravagant standards, one hundred dollars and change would not get the three of them back to Pittsburgh. And their flight was about to take off. What could he do?

Looking around the airport, he spotted Paul Brown. There was no other choice. He would have to approach Brown and ask for at least two hundred bucks. It would not be like going to Halas or Marshall or Charley Bidwill or Milton Jaffe. For favors, you went to your pals, and Brown was not exactly a pal. In truth, he may have been nobody's pal. The Chief tried to imagine what Brown would be thinking about these unpolished, unsophisticated Pittsburgh guys. Nothing irked the Chief more than to be taken for a rube, for a greenhorn right off the boat. But, with an effort, he swallowed his pride. "Hey, Paul ..." It must have been excruciating to put that request into words.

"Brown was real good about it," the Chief told me later. As far as I could make out, he did not see the incident as humorous. I thought it was like the time he mistakenly poured vinegar on his pancakes and pretended he liked them that way. To admit the truth wouldn't do. It would be humiliating. Taking money from Brown was humiliating, too, all the more so because the Steelers, in their rivalry with the Browns, were the underdogs then, just as they had usually been with the Eagles.

By the 1970s, when the Oakland Raiders were up there with the Browns as the team we most wanted to beat, as well as the team our fans most wanted us to beat, the situation was different. The Raiders had great teams, yes, but so did we. In Buddy Parker's time as coach, we could beat the great teams now and then. After Chuck Noll had the players he wanted, our chances were never worse than even.

The man who built the Raiders brick by brick was Al Davis. Like Paul Brown in Cleveland and Cincinnati, he controlled the entire operation, including every insignificant detail. Like Brown, he was a student of the game, whose knowledge did not derive from first-hand experience on the playing field but from sharp observation. Ted Dailey, one of the ends on the 1933 Steeler team, was a coach at Syracuse University when Davis attended school there. "He came to practice every day, just to watch," Dailey told me. "And he watched with an eagle eye." After graduation, Davis applied for a high school coaching job. "You know, a lot of guys named Davis played football here," Dailey went on. "What Al did, he wrote on his application that he was 'Al Davis of Syracuse.' In his interview they asked if he was *the* Al Davis of Syracuse. And he finessed it. He didn't say yes and he didn't say no. That was clever. He got the job."

Cleverness served him well wherever he coached from then on. One place was The Citadel, in South Carolina. "Al was just an assistant," said a scout I knew, "but you'd have thought from the way he talked and the way he acted that he ran the whole show." It led to better job offers elsewhere.

Davis was from Brooklyn, but he picked up his Southern accent at The Citadel. A Southern accent is for some reason one of a football coach's most valuable assets. Players from the South find it reassuring and Northerners imitate it.

Along with his Southern accent, Davis picked up organizational skills. He knew how to put a team together. Chuck Noll had coached with Davis in the AFL and said he was not to be underestimated.

The guy was a fitness freak. He brought his barbells with him to league meetings, and I saw him a time or two when he was bare from the waist up and wearing sweatpants. He was fairly tall, about 6 feet 1, and moderately well-built.

AJR "kind of" liked him, or did until Davis began to sue the NFL whenever he wanted to move his team from Oakland to Los Angeles or vice versa. After that, the Chief would say, "You know, there is something sinister about Al." Davis used to wear a black leather trench coat, and AJR once said to him, meaning no harm, "You look like one of those storm trooper guys in that coat." Davis was Jewish, and he told AJR later on that the remark had been hurtful. AJR said, "Gee, Al, I'm sorry. I never thought about that."

AJR looked with favor on the coach Davis hired in the 1970s, John Madden. I liked him, too. Madden was from California, but he reminded me of guys I had played with at North Catholic. In college, he'd been a defensive tackle of barely enough promise to be signed by the Eagles. He spent an entire season on the injured-reserve list and made the best of a bad situation by studying game films. Norm Van Brocklin, the Eagles' veteran quarterback, noticed how focused and intent Madden was, and gave him a lot of useful advice.

When Madden went into coaching, he never had played a down in the NFL. During the off-season, he worked as a sporting-goods salesman, and somehow this added to my good opinion of him. It was what a regular guy would do, I said to myself. Jack Butler had sold cemetery lots between seasons. I was happy for Madden when Al Davis made him the head coach of the Raiders, but I wondered at the same time how he would ever manage to survive. Already Davis was known as a hard man to work for. He was a martinet, a second-guesser, a tyrant.

Madden did more than just survive. He thrived; he won championships; he made it to the Hall of Fame. I credited Al Davis with brilliance for having picked so successful a coach.

It was during Madden's time with the Raiders that our rivalry grew discordant, even violent. On the evening before a playoff game at Three Rivers Stadium, a Raider tight end, returning to the hotel from somewhere, roughly pushed his way through several dozen Steeler fans who were gathered near the entrance. He may have given some lip to a Pittsburgh cop assigned to the job of keeping order. At any rate, the cop used his billy club on the player, hitting him upside the head and heaping fuel on a raging inferno. When the Raiders played in Pittsburgh or the Steelers played in Oakland, there was always the threat, sometimes acted upon, of fisticuffs or worse.

The football teams were evenly matched. In the 1970s and early '80s, the Steelers and Raiders split even in ten games. One year the Raiders beat us to go to the Super Bowl; another year, we beat the Raiders to go to the Super Bowl.

After a Monday night game we had lost to the Raiders by three points, I sat with Dan and Danny Ferens, our No. 1 numbers cruncher, in the Oakland press box, motionless. We were not sore losers, we were stunned losers. Sportswriters passing our seats offered condolences. "Tough one," they'd say. "Get 'em next time." We were giving our well-wishers one-word answers. Don Meredith, the former Dallas Cowboy quarterback who was doing commentary on the Monday night broadcasts, said hi as he passed us, but stopped and turned around after taking a few more steps. He walked back and stood in front of us and said, "It's all over, boys. They're not gonna play any more. You may as well pack it up." With that, he continued on his way once again.

Dandy Don's summation had broken the spell. All three of us started to chuckle. We slowly got to our feet and went to the locker room.

On the night before our playoff game with the Raiders in 1974, I attended a big party in an Oakland hotel, everything paid for by the NFL. I was with a fair-sized contingent from Pittsburgh, but the Oakland mob outnumbered us by at least ten to one. Their whole organization seemed to be present, from the guys who picked up jockstraps in the dressing room to Al Davis himself. It was while talking to an Oakland scout at this party that I realized how overconfident the Raiders had become. The scout was Al LoCasale, Davis's administrative assistant. Davis was Big Al and LoCasale was Little Al. He was short, gruff, smart, talkative, opinionated, "a bit of a rogue," as my brother Tim's friend, Father Duggan, characterized him. "We have a problem," this scout was telling Tim and me. "We can take only so many people to the Super Bowl, and it's gonna be tough to leave the others behind. A lot of people have worked hard all year and deserve to go. But we can't take them all."

I saw the disdain Oakland felt for us in such an unwary admission, but let it pass. Tim's reaction was more like outrage. Until LoCasale had left us, he held his tongue. Then he said, "That little friend of yours, saying, 'Who can we leave behind?' Those S.O.B.'s think they have the game already won. I'll tell you what. If *we* win tomorrow ... not *if* we win, but *when* we win ... we'll take everybody on our payroll."

He paused and then added, "Like 'Giant.'"

I was mystified. I said, "What do you mean, like 'Giant'?"

"'Giant,' the movie," Tim explained. "Remember the movie about the Texas oil people? With Jimmy Dean? Liz Taylor? Rock Hudson? Remember how they flew to the big party in Dallas? Remember all those planes coming in at the airport? We'll do the same thing. We'll charter a bunch of planes and take everybody we can think of to New Orleans."

We actually did do something like that. Tim chartered a big jet for our New York and Philadelphia people and a smaller one to fly from Palm Beach. And we put a lot of people on commercial flights and private planes leaving from Pittsburgh.

First, of course, we had to beat the Raiders, which we were able to get done. The score was 24-13, maybe not as one-sided as Tim could have wished, but clear-cut.

Happily for the Raiders, it solved their problem. They flew no jets to the Super Bowl and therefore left no one behind.

Best to Worst

I hold these truths to be self-evident, that our 1974 draft, as people who study these things have concluded, was and still is the best in the history of the NFL, and that our 1975 draft was a bust.

Think it over.

The first four players we picked in 1974 are now in the Hall of Fame. Conversely, except for Dave Brown and Mike Collier, who were used as kick-return guys, nobody we drafted in 1975 made the roster.

Yes, I know: in 1975 we drafted last. Super Bowl champions always do. But in 1974 we drafted very late and found riches at the bottom of the barrel.

Jack Butler pointed out that 1975 was not an auspicious year to be a brand new Steeler in training camp. Both on offense and defense, the lineup was set, full of talent not yet at its peak. On the team that had beaten the Minnesota Vikings in the Super Bowl, only Ray Mansfield, the center, and Andy Russell, an outside linebacker, were anywhere close to retirement.

If I went along with that, I'd be rationalizing. I know what a rationalization is because the Benedictine monks at St. Vincent explained it to me. It's "a good reason for the real reason" — plausible enough, that is, to sound convincing.

The real reason our 1975 draft turned out to be a dud was not that there weren't any openings for newcomers. It was not that our scouts hadn't worked hard. We were just as well organized and just as well prepared as in 1974. We collected as much information, fine-tuned it as carefully, and presented it to the coaches in as orderly a fashion. The real reason we drafted so poorly was the absence of the passion I had brought to this task since the hiring of Chuck Noll. In 1974 and the five previous years, getting ready for the draft had been an obsession with me. In 1975, the flame did not burn quite as high. I did what I had to do, yes; there was nothing I shirked, nothing I overlooked. It was just that I was somehow less than fully engaged. Success breeds contentment, it breeds complacency. Was I resting on my laurels? Possibly. I can't be sure.

In fairness to my staff, not everybody we drafted was a stiff.

Our first pick, Dave Brown, had been an All-American defensive back at Michigan. There's an adage to the effect that you can't judge a draft until after the third season. Dave Brown was gone after one season, taken by Seattle in the 1976 expansion draft. On his last day in Pittsburgh, he came into my office for a handshake. He thanked me for the Super Bowl ring he was wearing and for giving him a chance to be a Steeler. In a ten-year career with Seattle, Brown intercepted sixty-two passes, five more than Hall of Famer Mel Blount's lifetime total with the Steelers. After his playing days, he remained in Seattle as an assistant coach.

Mike Collier, a running back out of Morgan State, looked like a steal as our fourteenth-round selection. Collier was the player who ran out of bounds in practice one day and accidentally pancaked a spectator – AJR. That is the only thing he's remembered for. We cut him before the start of his second season. Later, he caught on with the Buffalo Bills and played for another three years – returning kicks.

Our second-round pick, Bob Barber, defensive end from Grambling, washed out in training camp, but played for a few years with the Green Bay Packers. Our third-round pick, Walter White, tight end from Maryland, found a haven in Kansas City after we cut him. Until an injury laid him low, White was productive, catching 160 passes for sixteen touchdowns in four seasons.

But that was the extent of it. Except for Collier, the players we drafted from the fourth through the seventeenth rounds quickly dropped out of sight. Bob Barber was an example of what Chuck Noll referred to as the superior athlete with an "impediment," the superior athlete who "lacks something." Performers of this stripe can make the big play, but not consistently. "Yes, we see the problem," Noll would say, and try to correct it. The problem was usually an "intangible" – insufficient toughness, insufficient "football intelligence," insufficient zest for the game. I don't recollect how Barber fell short, but Noll clearly regarded him as one of the "exceptions" he was always talking about, a player whose undoubted natural ability could be brought to full flower with coaching and a customized strength program. Alas, in Barber's case the "impediment" was too deeply ingrained.

So many high draft picks turn out to be disappointments that some NFL teams — the New York Giants were one — looked for help in the realm of the behavioral sciences. The man who was running things for the Giants, my good friend George Young, hired a psychologist to interview his players, and, with George's permission, I asked the guy to visit our training camp.

Jack Butler, for one, didn't think much of this idea. "More paper and pencil testing?" he asked. Any scout with a lick of sense, Butler thought, could glean as much information as he needed by poring over game films and talking to the people who knew the player best — coaches, trainers, equipment men. You had to talk to these people selectively, Butler added. There is always a "right" coach, meaning the coach who is most insightful. It's the job of the scout, Butler stressed, to identify that coach. He may or may not be the coach at the top, but stay away from assistants who merely parrot what the head man is saying.

The shrink the Giants sent to us, Neil Goldberg, did not dispute Butler's assertions. "You have first-rate scouts; your record proves it," he told me. And they collect valuable data, tons of it, he conceded. All the same, he went on, there was information in our files that we might not know how to interpret, information we were probably misreading.

Predictably, our scouts were not pleased to hear this. Our West Coast guy, Bob Schmitz, was openly scornful, arguing, "I played here with Bobby Layne. At practice sometimes, he'd be half-loaded. He drove his car into a streetcar one night, and played the next day. And won the game." Schmitz's point seemed to be that Layne would have flunked any psychological test ever conceived. Therefore, everything we were hearing from Goldberg was hogwash.

To which the headshrinker responded, "I'm only saying you'd get more out of the information you've compiled if you knew what to look for and listen to, and if you asked better questions of the coaches." He explained how we could learn invaluable lessons about a player from his body language, his tone of voice, his willingness or unwillingness to make eye contact. This was just the tip of the iceberg, or the Goldberg, if you prefer. Every word, every gesture, every quirk, it seemed, was loaded with meaning. To hear Goldberg tell it, a player's psyche was just as important as his physical dimensions and his time in the forty-yard dash.

I told the good doctor we'd get together with him later. And we did. Some of his ideas could be helpful to us, I thought. "Bullshit," grumbled Bob Schmitz. All Jack Butler said was, "How much are you going to pay for that stuff?"

Again I dredged up a maxim I had learned from the Benedictines: If you could state a problem correctly, you were well on the way to solving it. Our problem was that, because of "intangibles," too many high draft choices never became the football players we expected them to become. Every team in the league had this problem. Decades later, it still exists. Despite the efforts and advice of all the behavioral gurus, high draft choices continue to fail.

Not even the Benedictines have an answer for everything. The way it turned out, the best new player we acquired in 1975 was a free agent who looked like a misfit. A linebacker from Eastern Michigan, he was "too big," the scouts said, for his position. They meant he did not have the agility to cover pass receivers. On the other hand, he was "tough as hell," and could put a good rush on the quarterback, shedding blockers right and left. Let's bulk this guy up with a barbell program and see how he looks in a three-point stance, someone suggested.

We gave my cousin Tim a blank contract and dispatched him to Ypsilanti. He called back quickly to tell us, "The kid won't sign. Says the Steelers are loaded and he couldn't make the team."

With Eastern Michigan prospects, our trouble shooter, if we needed one, was Woody Widenhofer. Woody called the player on the telephone and went into his spiel. He said that as someone with Eastern Michigan connections, having coached there, he would personally see to it that the kid got a chance to show what he could do. We'd move him from linebacker to defensive end. The coaches would work with him patiently. He'd be a special project. Five minutes into the conversation, John Banaszak was ours.

Of the twenty-one players we selected in the 1975 draft, nineteen never played for the Steelers. Banaszak was on the team from 1975 through 1981. He suited up for three Super Bowl games and started at defensive end in two. Impressed with Banaszak's progress in his rookie season, Jack Lambert remarked to a teammate, "Those scouts of ours must be pretty smart guys to dig up a free agent that good."

In my twilight years, I accept all compliments even if they're only half-true, so let me say I am grateful to Lambert for his comment. I am even more grateful for his kindness in overlooking the nineteen draft picks who flopped.

The Steel Curtain

In the years between 1972 and 1980, the Steelers under Chuck Noll redefined defensive football. His formula was so simple: Run the ball. Play the hell out of special teams. Keep Terry Bradshaw from getting a case of happy feet, throwing off balance, and putting the ball up for grabs. Let the Steel Curtain do the rest.

There was never a better defense than the Steeler defense of 1975. When I use the term Steel Curtain I include the linebackers, the cornerbacks, and the safeties along with the front four. Many times when the offense fumbled or the kick returners left us in bad field position and we had to punt, the defense pulled the fat out of the fire. Joe Greene and the other linemen could destroy an opponent's offense. Collectively, our linebackers were unsurpassed. Andy Russell had lost a step but couldn't be faked or fooled. Jack Lambert played with controlled ferocity. Jack Ham was a coach's dream. If there were flaws in his game, I couldn't name them. The defensive backfield looked to Mel Blount, big, strong, and frightening, for inspiration and leadership.

This was the kind of football that Pittsburghers admired. It was in the DNA of all who had breathed the soot-filled industrial air of Western Pennsylvania. Bradshaw kept the defense out of trouble and made judicious use of his fleet and elusive receivers. Lynn Swann alone caught eleven touchdown passes. In the 16-10 win over Oakland for the AFC championship, defensive back George Atkinson put a hit on Swann that knocked him out. Swann left the field in the arms of Joe Greene, who picked him up like a baby. He had a brain concussion, and spent the next few days in a hospital bed. Would he be able to play in the Super Bowl? No one knew.

Getting back to the regular season, Franco Harris scored eleven touchdowns on runs, equaling Swann's total on pass catches, and gained 1,246 yards, a Steeler record. Rocky Bleier was Franco's blocker and picked up important yardage as a change-of-pace runner. Blount led the league with eleven interceptions. The Steelers lost to Buffalo in the second game of the season and then won eleven straight. (Eleven, you will notice, seems to have been our lucky number.) We finished the regular season 12-2, and beat the Colts as well as the Raiders in the playoffs.

The venue for Super Bowl X, Pittsburgh vs. Dallas, was the Orange Bowl in Miami. By contrast with New Orleans, Miami seemed cut off from history and tradition. Miami and New Orleans were very different cities. Early twentieth-century real-estate speculators cleared away the tropical jungle and filled in the mangrove swamps to create Miami, from then on a haven for snowbirds drawn to the sun. Pre-Katrina New Orleans was redolent of its Creole past, a collection of old neighborhoods, unchanging and faintly mildewed, wrought-iron balustrades enclosing the second-floor balconies. Miami in January was warm, New Orleans close to frigid. The skies over Miami were bright and cloudless, New Orleans was overcast. Everything in Miami looked white, or salmon-colored. Even before the levees broke, everything in New Orleans looked brown.

New Orleans was a long trek for Steeler fans. They could get to Miami in a hop, skip, and jump. And Miami was full of Pittsburgh expatriates, pensioners who remembered when the Steelers were chronic also-rans, fair game for ridicule and scorn. They had joined in the vilification, but now they decked themselves out in black and gold and trumpeted their undying loyalty.

The NFL had booked the football team and its front-office cohort into the Miami Lakes Hotel – partly owned, we understood, by Don Shula, coach of the Dolphins. For reasons I couldn't make out, the players all seemed to dislike it. Fats Holmes was dissatisfied with the hotel and everything else about Miami, "a place," he declared, "where old people come to play golf and die." If Fats could maintain his bad temper until kickoff time it might be helpful, I said to myself. He might re-direct his animus toward the Cowboys.

One day in the hotel restaurant my brothers John and Tim were sitting with Senator Ted Kennedy and some other people when Jack Butler and I walked in. I heard John mention our names, and immediately a rich baritone voice called out, "Hi, Art. Why don't you guys join us?" We accepted Kennedy's loud invitation willingly, and for the next half-hour fielded questions about football. Surprising me, Kennedy seemed to know without being told, although John did tell him, that I was head of the Steelers' scouting department. A big, Irish-looking guy whose hair was still dark and whose waistline was still well contained, the Senator reminded me of the scouts and assistant coaches I usually hung out with.

While we were talking, my son Artie appeared. Running up to the table, he asked if he could rent a motorbike, and Kennedy beat me to the answer. "Don't let him do it, Art. My brother Jack rented motorbikes in Bermuda when he was just that little guy's age. There was an accident, and one of Jack's friends was terribly hurt."

No motorbike for you, Artie, I said.

The conversation switched from football to stories about the Kennedy who'd been president. When it was time to break up, I called for the check. "Hold it!" The resonant baritone again. "I'm paying!" Best not to argue, I decided.

The next day a little earlier, here came Kass, presenting me with a crisis to handle. It seemed that AJR had set up a luncheon for still another Kennedy – Ethel, Bobby Kennedy's widow. Somehow Ethel and the Chief had met and hit it off. To Kass's consternation, he would not attend the luncheon himself – league business prevented it – and neither would Dan. "Your father got me into this, and I don't know what to do," Kass was telling me.

I attempted to put her at ease. Nothing to worry about, I said. We made a reconnaissance excursion to the dining room. It was ready for the party, with everything in order. "All you have to do, Mom, is sit there and smile."

All right, she said, but I must be at the luncheon, too, in the place right next to Ethel Kennedy. I asked what I'd have to say that might interest the lady.

"Oh, you'll know what to say. You read a lot of history books. Talk about history."

A better idea came to me. "Mom, you can be on one side of Ethel and we'll put George Young on the other side, with me next to George. George has three history degrees and he used to be a teacher. He can keep this luncheon going until it's over."

"Damn!" George said upon hearing my plan. "Why, hell, I've never even voted for a Kennedy. I don't like their ideology."

Many football people are staunch Republicans, but George, though he didn't talk like one, was a Democrat.

"Well, you're going to sit next to Ethel. Turn on the charm," I instructed him.

It worked out. I could hear them go back and forth, and Ethel seemed totally engaged. There was animation, there was laughter, and there were serious moments as well. "We have to meet again and continue our conversation," Ethel said to George as we were leaving.

Kass was relieved and happy. And George, forgetting he did not like the Kennedys' ideology, was ecstatic. He had met the wife of a figure in American history and had held his own. But then he always held his own, in any company.

The Steelers, it seemed to me, had a sound, no-frills way of doing business. The Dallas Cowboys were glitzier. The package they sold included a leggy chorus line of cheerleaders. In their calf-high boots, ultra-short skirts, and skimpy tops, they were part of the show, an important part. AJR had done away with the Steelers' cheerleaders after just a few years. We gave our people football, and that was enough.

On game day, while the Cowboys loosened up before the kickoff, their cheerleaders did some rehearsing. I stood on the field with Dan, watching them. Up close, they looked like the girls you might see on any college campus, only prettier.

"In thirty minutes," said Dan, "a preacher will give the invocation, a band will play the Star-Spangled Banner, and then the game will start."

"That's how it is all over the South," I reminded him.

"Yeah," Dan agreed. "Football in the South is sex, prayer, patriotism, and violence."

Kay, my son Art, and I sat with Mom and Dad in our box near the rim of the stadium. AJR, uptight and irritable, was wearing his game face. In the first quarter, Art III began to film the action with a brand new, motor-driven, 35-millimeter Nikon camera. The click-click-click of the shutter was continuous, and AJR could endure it for only so long. Then he swiveled his head and snapped, "No more pictures!" If Artie never had understood why everyone called his grandfather the Chief, he did now.

AJR liked to watch football in silence. Once in a great while he would make a pronouncement of some kind. Or he would ask me a question and answer it briefly himself. Mom and Kay sat dutifully quiet, "seen but not heard," as Kass would say. In spite of his desire to concentrate on the game, AJR wanted us with him. I was like a dictionary – there to be consulted, but only if necessary. Which suited me fine. I was into the game as much as the Chief was.

Early in the first half our punter, Bobby Walden messed up a kick, and the Cowboys scored. Their object was to shut down our running game. At times they succeeded, but Franco Harris and Rocky Bleier combined to gain 133 yards, enough to keep the defense honest and give us opportunities to pass.

Of the first ten Super Bowl games, this was the best-played. At one point Jack Lambert exhorted his teammates as no one else could, shouting, "We're supposed to be tough guys, but they're bringing it to us!" He then made an effort to change the momentum. When our stubby placekicker, Roy Gerela, missed a field goal we badly needed, a Dallas defender mockingly patted him on the helmet. Lambert flew at this Cowboy, knocked him to the ground, and stood there screaming over him. It got us going again.

Roger Staubach, the Dallas quarterback, took a pounding. We sacked him time after time. Chuck Noll had warned Bradshaw that he could not throw short passes. The Cowboys' defense prohibited short passes. "Go at 'em deep," Noll ordered him, but Randy Grossman got into the clear for a touchdown pass of a mere seven yards. Lynn Swann, meanwhile, was having a Hall-of-Fame day, completely recovered from Atkinson's hit. Defensive back Cliff Harris persisted in thinking that he could get into Swann's head and intimidate him, but Swann said after the game that he never had felt so loose. He caught only four passes, but they were long ones. A jumping, twisting catch at a critical moment silenced the trash-talking Harris. Another catch by Swann went for a touchdown. By vote of the sportswriters, he was the game's most valuable player.

In the last few minutes, the Cowboys made it exciting. With a four-point lead to protect, Noll put his trust in the defense. It was the only time I ever had seen a "prevent" defense work. We covered their receivers downfield while giving them short gains. On the last play, Staubach passed into the end zone, and Glen Edwards came up with an interception. The final score was 21-17.

Two officials from the NFL stepped into our box. They'd be taking AJR to the dressing room for the presentation of the Lombardi Trophy. One of them asked if I was coming along. "Naww," I replied. My heart was still beating too fast.

At our second victory party in twelve months, the Chief and Chuck Noll were just as low-keyed as at the first one. Celebrations in the end zone after touchdowns were anathema to Noll. "Act like you've been there before," he would counsel his young receivers and running backs. That was the approach he took now. It was also the Chief's approach. They "acted like they'd been there before." Following their lead, so did I.

Everybody who missed the victory party in New Orleans, and everybody who did not, seemed to be in the crowd at this one. I don't know why, but when I think of that party I think of John Troan, editor at the time of the *Pittsburgh Press*. With swarms of people around us, he happened to be alone for a moment, and I spoke to him. "Art Junior!" he said, recognizing me. We could not have met more than once or twice before, and then very briefly, but Troan remembered. Something else he remembered, and repeated to me, was the story of how AJR had picked him up on the Pennsylvania Turnpike when he was hitch-hiking home from a Naval base in Maryland during World War II. AJR always had liked John Troan.

Again we had a victory parade from the Greater Pittsburgh Airport, witnessed by cheering thousands. I rode in a limousine with Kay, Art III, Kass, and AJR to 940 North Lincoln Avenue. No sooner had we settled down than Artie said to me, "I'm bored. There's nothing to do here."

He was taking Noll's strictures about keeping one's cool a step too far. Bored? Nothing to do? "This," I told Artie, "is a time in your life you'll never forget."

In February, Kay invited Dad, Mom, and Aunt Alice over to Mount Lebanon for a big roast beef dinner. When the dishes were put away, Artie set up a screen, got out the slide projector, and displayed the "transparencies" he had taken from our box in the Orange Bowl. AJR, who had been so abrupt with the kid when the camera was running — "Put that thing away!" — watched intently. Time after time he would ask for a replay. "Can we see that one again?" Was he perhaps showing remorse for his treatment of Artie in Miami? I couldn't say, but for one evening, anyway, he made the youngest Art Rooney feel like a big shot.

Chapter 61

Wising Up

Credibility comes with success. When the Steelers were chronic losers, the reason had to be that the Rooneys were dumb. As soon as we started winning championships, our IQs climbed up to the Einstein level. We were geniuses, all of us, including Tim and the twins, whose connection with the football team was marginal.

Almost overnight, the sports world readjusted its outlook on the Rooneys. For close to forty years, we'd been hopeless bumblers. Now we had the know-how to rescue floundering franchises.

CBS renewed its offer to sell us the Yankees, this time sounding out Tim. Again there was no deal. Shortly afterward, we heard from Ned Irish, the man who popularized basketball in New York City by promoting college doubleheaders in Madison Square Garden and later became the founding owner of the New York Knicks. The San Francisco team in the National Basketball Association was for sale, and AJR could buy it to be overseen by Tim and the twins. Basketball before Irish got involved had been outside the scope of the national media. Now even the pro game was going big-time, but not fast enough to suit the Chief.

He dispatched his brother-in-law, Jack McGinley, to an NBA contest in Cleveland. McGinley talked to people and crunched a few numbers and concluded that the NBA at the time did not have the venues, the marketing, or the television exposure to make it a powerhouse professional sport. Owning a franchise in the league, McGinley advised the Chief, would be fiscally unwise.

But that was many years ago. The franchise we could have acquired, the Golden State Warriors, survived and eventually prospered.

NASCAR got in touch with us. NASCAR was wasting its time. We did buy a soccer team, the Philadelphia Spartans. The twins and even the Chief had some fun with it, but when our losses in just a few years reached half a million dollars there was nothing to do but bail out.

Football and horse racing were the only things we knew about. John Macartney discouraged me from buying a Mount Washington condominium with a spectacular view of the downtown skyline. My plan was to be a landlord, leasing it for "good money," as I explained to Macartney. "Good money," he said, "is nice. But it's not big money. Put up a whole condo building and lease it. You spend as much time and effort on those little deals as you do on big ones." We explored the subject no further.

In search of a big-money proposition for us, Macartney went on a wild goose chase to Zurich and Jakarta. He was bent on getting us into the oil business. In Conoco tankers, we would transport oil from Indonesia. He came home without a deal but with a nasty case of malaria. Having been infected before, as the pilot of a PT boat in the South Pacific during World War II, he was only too familiar with malaria. That little foray cost us about one hundred thousand dollars, an unexpectedly high price for a sniff of oil. Big deals, we were learning, didn't come cheap.

Our next purchase, Green Mountain Raceway in Vermont, set us back millions. Like the soccer team, it turned out to be a dud. We tried to race the year round, but winters in Vermont were brutal. Think of Napoleon's retreat from Moscow, and you get the idea.

AJR was against the Green Mountain project from the get-go. The job of running the place, a thankless one, went to Pat. Later, he added our dog track in Florida to his responsibilities.

And there was trouble at the dog track, too. The dog owners were making demands that we considered unreasonable. Looking for a way to deal with them, we consulted Macartney, and he predictably had a brainstorm, another one. "Buy your own greyhounds from all over," he advised us. "They breed them in Ireland, you know. Race your own dogs, and you won't have to fool around with outsiders."

We tried it. The operation was a success, but the patient eventually died. The dog men proved to be hard-fisted adversaries. They planted explosives under the car hoods of people they didn't like, someone warned us. That kind of talk could be largely discounted, but it would have been foolish to ignore the risk we were taking.

We had a meeting at Green Mountain to discuss the whole dog-track issue one day, and I remember it for a single irrelevant incident. Macartney tossed his keys to young John McNulty, who was up there learning the business. "Go fetch my car, will you, John?" Macartney asked. Unthinkingly, John headed for the door. Then he stopped and turned around and tossed the keys back to Macartney. "Start your own car," he said.

We operated the dog track independently for a couple of years and then returned to the old status quo. Nobody's car was ever blown up.

Business deals, I reflected, were like the draft. Sometimes you had a good one and sometimes you had a bad one. And, whichever it was, you worked hard.

Thanks But No Thanks

More and more often, AJR would be required to attend a function of some kind at the Duquesne Club, where the coal and iron barons of the nineteenth century, Pittsburgh's WASP aristocracy, isolated themselves from Catholics, Jews, and of course Negroes. Women were admitted only as guests — women with the proper ethnic and socio-economic credentials. Irish males could be doormen or porters or waiters. Italians, and maybe one or two blacks, toiled out of sight in the boiler room.

With the passing of the years, the Duquesne Club lowered its barriers just a bit. Hesitant steps toward ethnic, religious and gender diversity were taken. One thing remained constant: members still had to have money. But new money, as well as old money, was perfectly acceptable now.

And so the membership committee offered AJR a chance to join. Never one to forget or deny where he came from, he refused the bait. What he could not avoid, for business reasons, was the need to be present from time to time at the small, exclusive civic luncheons and dinners for which the Duquesne Club provided a venue. On one such occasion — a meeting of NFL and NBC officials, as I recall — he directed Buff Boston to chauffeur him there in a broken-down Oldsmobile on loan from Buff's uncle. As they pulled up in front of the club's majestic sandstone building, a uniformed factotum hurried down the steps. With practiced ceremony, he opened the jalopy's battered door. AJR was a man who had a fine sense of irony.

The Duquesne Club went in for dark, austere, wood-paneled elegance. Murky portraits of dead capitalists hung on the walls. Up the street a few blocks stood the William Penn Hotel, where gatherings a shade less important than the ones at the Duquesne Club took place.

Having left a meeting at the William Penn on a bright spring day in the late 1970s, AJR obeyed an impulse. Instead of jumping into a taxi, he decided to walk. But he was getting along in years and the Steeler offices at Three Rivers Stadium were no short distance away. Approaching the Sixth Street Bridge, he began to tire.

A passing bus slowed down. The Steelers had lately won their fourth straight Super Bowl, and AJR was a frequently photographed, incessantly feted, easily recognized folk hero. In the middle of a block, the bus driver came to a stop and opened his door.

"Mister Rooney — where are you going?"

"Over to the Stadium."

"Wanna ride?"

AJR did not deliberate. "Don't mind if I do."

Climbing into the bus, he said, "I hope this won't take you out of your way." The driver glanced over his shoulder. There were maybe half a dozen people on the bus. "Would you folks mind if I dropped off Mister Rooney at Three Rivers Stadium?" he asked them.

Their answer was a chorus of no's and not at all's, and then the riders were calling out, "Hi, Mister Rooney," or, more boldly, "Hi, Art." The Steelers' mantra that year was "One for the thumb," and undoubtedly someone invoked it.

Across the Sixth Street Bridge on Federal Street, the driver turned left, making a detour. A few minutes later he was in Stadium Circle, parked at the door to the Steelers' suite of offices. "No charge, Mister Rooney," he said.

I don't have any documentation for this, but the passengers, I'm inclined to think, gave the driver – and AJR – a round of applause.

Bidwill's Burg

The Chief called Chicago "our kind of town." He said it was "Pittsburgh — only bigger." Carl Sandberg called Chicago "the City of the Big Shoulders, Hog Butcher to the World," and so on. All of us felt a kinship with Chicago, one reason being that it was Charley Bidwill's home town. Charley Bidwill owned the Chicago Cardinals. He owned a piece of two race tracks, Sportsman Park and Hawthorne. He was AJR's kind of guy.

Chicago had the Board of Trade, where fortunes were made and lost in the blink of an eyelash. Chicago was where "killers could kill and go free to kill again." The Chief knew the stock traders; he knew the killers — a few of them, anyway. He himself was a sportsman — a horse player, a football guy, an investor in grains and soybeans.

Aunt Harriet had lived in Chicago when she was married to Max Fiske. "It's where the wind always blows. That's why they call it the Windy City," she told me. Chicago, I concluded, was many things to many people.

My first look at Chicago came when I was 13 years old. Dad and Mom took me there, leaving all of my brothers at home with Aunt Alice. How come? If I ever knew, I've forgotten. We traveled by train, on the Pennsylvania Railroad. "*Dinner in the diner, wake in Carolina ...* "Over the radio, I had heard Tex Benecke sing "Chattanooga Choo Choo," with just a slight change in the lyrics, I imagined myself waking in Chicago. I thought the telephone lines that whizzed by our coach were bull ropes, attached to the poles to keep them from blowing away.

AJR was taking us to the Chicago All-Star game, the brainchild of Arch Ward, an enterprising Chicago sports editor. Every summer since 1934, the champions of the National Football League had played a collection of the previous fall's best college seniors. Ward's paper, the *Chicago Tribune*, sponsored the game. Everything over expenses went to charity.

This annual extravaganza was popular with football fans and the NFL owners for the first thirty years of its existence. The game in Soldier Field was a showcase for the league, the owners thought. But after about 1960, with the NFL in the ascendancy and baseball losing its dominance as the national pastime, their attitude changed. They became paranoid about the injury factor, and so did I in my role of personnel director. In what the league now perceived as a glorified exhibition game, top draft choices could get hurt; high-priced established veterans could get hurt. Beyond that, the game was no longer competitive. From 1934 to 1958, the College All-Stars frequently won; from 1958 until the promotion was discontinued in 1977, the pro champs lost only once.

The pro champs were always the Chicago Bears or the New York Giants or the Green Bay Packers or the Detroit Lions — any team but the Steelers. On that first exciting trip to Chicago, in 1949, I saw the Philadelphia Eagles manhandle the All-Stars, 38-0, before a typically large crowd in mammoth Soldier Field.

It would finally be our turn in 1975. We represented the league in the last two All-Star games ever played, winning both. The score was 21-14 in 1975, with Joe Gilliam passing for two fourth-quarter touchdowns. In 1976, we were leading 24-0 toward the end of the third quarter when a storm from Lake Michigan hit. The special effects were spectacular: thunder and lightning, torrential rain, cyclonic winds. Play was suspended, and the crowd, wet and unruly, spilled onto the flooded field. After about fifteen minutes of anarchy, Commissioner Pete Rozelle called the game.

George Halas was still alive in 1976, but so many others of the old guard were gone. What I remember with most pleasure about that All-Star week was a visit to City Hall. "Come on," the Chief said to Dan, Tim, and me. "Mayor Daley wants to meet us. Put a tie on."

Ed Kiely and Jack McGinley were with us when we entered the mayor's office, which looked as spacious to me as Soldier Field. Richard J. Daley, a short, heavy-set man in a smartly-tailored business suit, got up from his high-backed chair with green leather upholstering, walked with a firm step around a shining mahogany desk, and offered his hand to the Chief. The Chief then introduced the rest of us, one by one.

Daley at the time was the best-known mayor in America. In Chicago, he was all-powerful; in the Democratic Party he still had great influence, even after the tumultuous 1968 presidential convention. The Democrats met in Chicago to nominate Hubert Humphrey that year, and Daley's police turned the streets of the Loop into a battleground, beating up demonstrators against the war in Vietnam, beating up newspaper reporters, beating up innocent bystanders.

De facto leader of the Illinois delegation, Daley himself created an uproar on the floor of the convention hall, jumping up in the middle of Senator Abe Ribicoff's nominating speech on behalf of George McGovern and shouting something at Ribicoff, his exact words in dispute to this day. Were they obscene, as lip-readers watching on television claimed? "I've never used language like that in my life," he insisted irately.

Daley's hold on his followers survived the convention. It even survived his depiction in Mike Royko's 1970 best-seller, "Boss." Royko, a newspaper columnist as king-like in Chicago as Daley was, described how the mayor had built up an unstoppable political machine through deception, dirty tricks, patronage, and vote-buying.

Well, I can only speak for myself, but I found this ruthless manipulator to be not without wit and charm. He made us all feel like big shots. He asked intelligent, pertinent questions about our lives and our various enterprises, and he listened to our answers with what seemed to be genuine interest.

A year or two later on, Dad and Mom sat next to him at a dinner of some kind. Mom's take on the mayor was as favorable as mine. "He's so nice. Made me feel at ease. Talked about you kids. It was like being with Davey Lawrence or Joe Barr [the genial ex-Congressman who served as mayor of Pittsburgh after Lawrence moved up to the governor's office]."

I rest my case.

Chapter 62

A Different Approach

Before the 1976 draft, AJR called me into his office for a lecture. "Chuck Noll," he began, "is the best coach in the NFL. We could never get lucky enough to find another coach as good as Chuck is, and if by some chance we did find a guy like that, we couldn't afford him. Don't cause Chuck to leave us. In your dealings with him from now on, I want you to just take it easy."

I said, "I understand," and that was it. Nothing more remained to be said.

AJR's edict reinforced a conclusion I had already formed in my own mind. I had been thinking for some time that my turbulent confrontations with Noll had to cease. Every year when we prepared for the draft, our discussions would turn into disagreements and our disagreements would turn into altercations, in which I was always the aggressor. The Chief, Dan, and even Noll himself would tell me, "You take everything personally." And it was true. But how did they expect me to take things? They were like the Mafia figures in the "Godfather" movies, explaining actions that issued from lethal differences of opinion with the phrase, "It's just business." To get your own way, you did what you had to do, they seemed to be saying, but in an unruffled, dispassionate manner.

Unruffled dispassion wasn't my style. I had too much McNulty in me.

But losing my temper with Noll would get me nowhere, I could see. His was the last word when it came to the draft. AJR had made that exceedingly clear. My job, then, was to collect, organize, and evaluate information and present it to the coaches in a thoroughly professional manner. A modus operandi of this sort would be something that could go on for decades.

By 1976, friends and media people were referring to me as "the guy who drafted Franco Harris over Chuck Noll's objections." I didn't want that. Rather, I aspired to be known as the guy who put together the best scouting system in professional football or any other sport. We had the basics in place for such a system: Blesto; Dick Haley as head scout; cousin Tim Rooney tracking NFL players along with some of the college players; Bill Nunn scouting everywhere instead of just the African-American institutions (which is what the black colleges were now being called). Haley, Tim, and Nunn winnowed out the top seniors, and I made it a rule to look at them all.

We had an unfulfilled need — another scout to cover the West Coast with Bob Schmitz. A Steeler linebacker in the 1960s, Bob Schmitz had come over to us from Blesto. I thought there were just too many teams in California, Oregon, and Washington for one scout to keep tabs on. Building up our coverage had been a long, hard fight. When I first took charge of the scouting department in 1964, it was not uncommon for our scouts to turn in one-line reports. Sarcastically, the assistant coaches would say things like, "Hey, Artie, what did that scout of yours do — stop at a gas station when he was driving by the campus and call somebody on the telephone?" Now we were getting reports so comprehensive it created a different kind of problem. A professor from Penn State, a statistical expert, went through our files and said to me, "You have more information about these players than the mind can take in. It all runs together and just becomes words, words, words. Break it down. Computerize."

Three years were to pass before I could sell this idea to the Chief, Dan, and the accountants. Tom Modrak, who joined the scouting department in 1979, said to me that the best thing I ever did was set up our computer program.

Again in 1976, we drafted dead last, but with much more success than the year before. "Don't screw this up!" I kept telling myself. I was able to control my intensity, avoiding passionate encounters with Noll. As in 1975, players we had our eye on disappeared from the board one by one — all but Bennie Cunningham of Clemson. A powerful tight end, he lasted until the end of the first round, and we snapped him up.

We were looking for a tight end who could block like a tackle, and Cunningham, we thought, might be the type. As it turned out, he developed quickly, allowing Noll to make a move he had long envisioned. He shifted Larry Brown to tackle. Brown had started two Super Bowl games at tight end. In Super Box XII, against Dallas, he'd be lining up next to Cunningham.

At Clemson, Cunningham had been a good pass-catching end. We expected him to develop into an equally good blocker, and he did. But in the nine years he played for some great Steeler teams, he thought of himself as a pass receiver who blocked, and not the other way around. One summer at St. Vincent, Bill Nunn began suggesting that Cunningham's true position, when you considered his ability to block, might be tackle. Getting wind of it, Cunningham was incensed. The next day Nunn attended a controlled scrimmage. He stood behind the huddle, watching, and Cunningham went after him. He chased Nunn around the field, shouting, "Bill, you just keep your mouth shut. No more crap about moving me to tackle. I'm a tight end, Bill. I'm a tight end." Back with his teammates, he would line up and run through a play or two, and then it would start all over, Bennie advancing, Nunn retreating, Bennie commanding Nunn to mind his own business.

At last Nunn removed himself to another part of the field, and Bennie now focused his wrath on me. "Mister Rooney, he works for you. Get him in line. None of this offensive tackle stuff. I'm a tight end."

He certainly was, and he finished his career as a tight end.

Ironically, when critics suggested in years to come that we had wasted a first-round draft pick on Cunningham, Nunn was his stoutest defender. "On a passing team like the Raiders, Bennie would have been all-pro," Nunn declared.

We had two second-round picks in 1976. First we took Ray Pinney, from the University of Washington, who became one of the good Steeler centers whose game Noll improved. Like Jimmy Clack and Jon Kolb before him, Pinney could play any position in the offensive line except tight end. Although not overly strong, he used his head. He knew all the tricks, and it kept him on the team for eight years. The second round also yielded us Mike Kruczek, quarterback from Boston College, who played for the Steelers through the 1979 season, but more about him later.

In the sixth round, we drafted Gary Dunn. He'd been a linebacker at Miami, where his father was president of the university, but Chuck Noll turned him into a nose tackle. Dunn was a stalwart on excellent Steeler teams for the rest of the decade, including two Super Bowl winners.

All in all, I was satisfied with our choices. The draft had gone smoothly, and I had not clashed with Noll. I thought we were back on track.

Bottom Line

AJR lived to see his 1974, 1975, 1978, and 1979 teams win Super Bowl games. Which of those four, then, did he consider the best Steeler team of them all? When he was asked, he would answer: None of the above. Or words to that effect.

AJR thought his 1976 team was the best.

The 1976 team lost four of its first five games. One of those defeats, in the season opener, came at the hands of our hated and hateful rivals, the Oakland Raiders, which was doubly hard to take because of off-the-field repercussions from the 1975 AFC championship game between the two teams.

To recapitulate: There had been bad blood between us for several years. It reached the boiling point in that title game when Oakland defensive back George Atkinson slammed into the Steelers' Lynn Swann just as Swann caught a pass on a cross-over pattern. "It was a quote-unquote *legal* hit, up around the head," Atkinson told Frank Deford of *Sports Illustrated*. And it put Swann in the hospital with a brain concussion.

For a time, he considered getting out of football, citing far too many "intentional acts of violence." Earlier in that '75 playoff game, another Oakland defensive back, Jack Tatum, had flattened Swann in the end zone, hitting him from behind when he was "nowhere near the ball." Swann played the second half in a daze, he said.

Built like the ballet dancer he might have been, rather than the all-pro football player he was, Swann risked annihilation every week by running pass routes over the middle that exposed him to blind-siding defensive backs. He could take deliberately vicious hits and still hang onto the ball. Nonsensically, Atkinson accused him of being "gutless." Chuck Noll, meanwhile, had been talking to reporters about a "criminal element" in the NFL. "Are you referring to Atkinson?" somebody asked. Correct, answered Noll. He was also referring to Tatum, his listeners inferred, because Tatum and Atkinson were two of a kind.

Atkinson sued Noll for defamation of character, and in cross-examination when the case went to court, Noll was led to admit that, by his own criteria, Steelers Mel Blount and Joe Greene were part of the criminal element, too. Well, now. If Greene had any objections, he kept them to himself. Blount, however, was ticked off. He threatened a lawsuit of his own against Noll, with the Steelers as co-defendants. He'd been bickering with the team about a raise he did not think was sufficient. Eventually, Blount dropped the idea, but I blamed our slow start in 1976 on the distractions resulting from the controversy itself, the trial in San Francisco, and Blount's displeasure at being tarred with the same brush as Atkinson.

The trial took place while the Steelers were encamped in Latrobe. During Noll's absence to testify, George Perles took charge of the team, and though Perles was a competent football man, we missed the head coach. But even after the trial, in which Noll was acquitted of slander, we could not get untracked.

Our fourth defeat of the regular season left me shaken. Besides losing away from home to the Browns, we lost Terry Bradshaw — for how many weeks or months, no one was sure. Turkey Jones, a 6-foot-9 Cleveland defensive end, had corkscrewed Bradshaw head-first into the turf. Only luck and Bradshaw's great physical strength saved him from a broken neck.

When he boarded our flight back to Pittsburgh on a stretcher, a crisis arose. Where on that crowded airplane could we put him? Ernie Holmes had the answer. He picked up the stretcher with Bradshaw still in it and carried the whole cargo — Bradshaw, remember, weighed about 220 pounds — to the last row of seats. Depressing the armrests, he gently laid the stretcher across the row. At Greater Pittsburgh Airport, Doc Best had an ambulance waiting, and off Terry went to the hospital.

In the coffee room at Three Rivers Stadium Monday morning, I said to receivers coach Lionel Taylor, "Four out of five down the tube. Have you ever known a team to recover from a start like this? We won't make the playoffs." Too despondent to answer, Taylor could only give me a vacant stare.

Bradshaw missed the next six games. Rookie Mike Kruczek replaced him and engineered a miraculous turnaround. The Steelers won every game he started. All he did, really, was give the ball to Franco and Rocky. In our first game without Bradshaw, a 23-7 win over Cincinnati, Kruczek handed off to Franco forty-one times, an NFL record. After Bradshaw's return, the Steelers kept winning. The Cleveland game was the last one they lost in the regular season. They finished 10-4, with five shutouts in their last nine games. In the four that were not shutouts, they held their opponents to twenty-eight points. Over one stretch, the defense did not allow a touchdown for twenty-three consecutive quarters. Eight of the starters on that 1976 defensive unit went to various Pro Bowls and four ended up in the Hall of Fame.

For years people asked me if Kruczek deserved to be a second-round pick. I always said we were drafting for the type of guy we needed at the time. Kruczek had good size, and he moved fairly well. Terry Bradshaw felt that he lacked a strong arm. Maybe so, but he could get the ball to receivers on short and medium pass routes. And he was intelligent — a student of the game.

Bradshaw considered Kruczek his friend. I hope he was right, because Bradshaw needed friends. Once at a practice I was watching, Bradshaw delivered a very poor pitchout to a running back, who fumbled it. Another player, a second-stringer, walked over to Kruczek on the sideline and mockingly pantomimed Bradshaw's awkward underhand toss. Kruczek turned his back and walked away. He wasn't interested in making fun of Bradshaw.

I recalled that incident years later when Bradshaw spoke warmly of Kruczek in a television interview. A couple of paragraphs back, I referred to Kruczek's size. Bradshaw used to call him the strongest quarterback in the league, a believable assertion. "Mike followed the weightlifting plan Noll gave him to the letter," Ralph Berlin told me. "Golly, he could push those barbells around."

As either a person or a passer, there was not a bit of Joey Gilliam in Kruczek. In the six games he started, he put the ball in the air only eighty-five times for an average of fourteen passes a game. None went for touchdowns, but fifty-one were complete. Do the arithmetic: it's not a bad percentage. Of course, he had two Hall-of-Fame receivers, Stallworth and Swann, plus the speedy Frank Lewis and short-yardage specialist Randy Grossman.

Mostly, though, he simply did as he was told, which was to keep the defense out of trouble by handing off to Franco and Rocky. When the defense took the field, it was always fresh. Franco and Rocky each gained more than one thousand yards rushing in 1976. "A lot of the credit," said Bleier long afterward, "goes to Kruczek."

The offensive line was pretty efficient, too, I reminded him.

Kruczek played very little while backing up Bradshaw. He stayed in Pittsburgh long enough to get a couple of Super Bowl rings and spent one final season with the Washington Redskins. Thereafter, at the college level, he went into coaching. Let Kruczek's detractors remember two things: (1) we had a number of more talented second-round picks who did not even make the team, and (2) he kept us in the hunt in 1976.

The Steelers ended the regular season looking unbeatable. In their last two games, they shut out Tampa Bay and Houston while totaling sixty-three points. A large contingent from Western Pennsylvania followed them to Baltimore for their AFC playoff game with the Colts, who never knew what hit them. On the third play of the first quarter, Bradshaw threw deep to Lewis, who took advantage of double coverage on Swann to break free. The play covered seventy-six yards for a touchdown.

Bill Nunn and I had been waiting six years to see Bradshaw hook up with Lewis like that. Bradshaw said afterward that he couldn't believe Noll would allow him to cut loose so early in the game. AJR was just as surprised. Noll's concern with establishing the run before he would let Bradshaw pass reminded him too much of how Walt Kiesling stifled his quarterbacks.

Bradshaw had a marvelous day against Baltimore, completing fourteen of eighteen passes for three touchdowns and 264 yards. Two of his touchdown passes went to Swann. Franco Harris gained 132 yards in two and a half quarters, and the offense as a whole amassed 526 yards, a divisional playoff record. The defense sacked Baltimore quarterback Bert Jones five times and forced two interceptions.

At the line of scrimmage, the Colts were calling Dwight White a "bush-leaguer." Bad mistake. White gave their linemen and backs such a going-over that Dick Szymanski, the Colts' general manager and a close friend of mine, came to me several times with complaints about his allegedly "dirty play." I let it pass.

The final score, by the way, was 40-14.

Only a few hundred stragglers from an original crowd of 60,000 witnessed the afternoon's most exciting moment. Twenty minutes after the game, a pilot who'd been buzzing Memorial Stadium in a single-engine Cherokee flew it right into the empty upper deck. "Look, it's a bird," wrote Glenn Sheeley in the *Pittsburgh Press*. "It's a Terry Bradshaw pass. It's the Steelers soaring toward the AFC championship game with their tenth straight win." And then: "No, it's a plane." Somehow the pilot survived.

At the time of the crash, I was just outside the press box, talking with Mort Sharnik. June, my brother Tim's wife, was with us, waiting for her husband, who had detoured into the press box to say hello to a Baltimore sportswriter he knew. She was seven or eight months pregnant. Fearing an explosion, Mort and I grabbed her, each of us taking an arm, and hustled her all the way down to the parking lot, three ramps below. "My feet hardly touched the ground," she said later. Tim, who'd been looking all over for June, was more annoyed with us than grateful. "There wasn't any danger," he insisted.

On Monday, when Ralph Berlin turned in his casualty report, we got the butcher's bill for that tenth straight win. Franco Harris had taken a cheap shot in the ribs from Joe Ehrmann, a Baltimore defensive tackle, and would miss the AFC championship game in Oakland the following Sunday, the day after Christmas. Bleier was hurt, too. Even Roy Gerela, the team's placekicker, had not come back to Pittsburgh unharmed. Worse luck that we were going to play Oakland, of all teams.

Before fanning out to the post-season college all-star games, our scouts spent Christmas at home every year. It was one of my steadfast rules. Kay and I and our kids and my in-laws exchanged gifts that year on Christmas Eve in our new house on Washington Road in Mount Lebanon. After a big breakfast the next morning, I flew to San Francisco with Jack Butler, Tim, and Harry Harvey, a devout Steeler fan who drove and trained harness horses. On our cab ride from the San Francisco airport to Oakland, I assured my three companions that the dining room at the Hyatt Hotel would be open. It wasn't. In fact, every good restaurant in town seemed to have closed its doors, so we settled for a fast-food Christmas dinner at Denny's. The team had been served an early catered dinner in private.

Bleier and Gerela, as well as Harris, had to sit out the game the next day. Oh well, I said to myself, maybe Bradshaw, his three great receivers, and the defense could pull us through. Maybe Reggie Harrison, who had done well as Franco's replacement in limited action against the Colts, would amaze everybody. Full of confidence, he vowed to take up the slack. Then there was Noll, our equalizer. Surely he would think of some answers. He always did.

During our pre-game warm-up, I noticed Al Davis and his coach, John Madden, watching Ray Mansfield kick field goals. They looked skeptical. I imagined I could hear them telling each other, "This is some kind of trick, a mind game." If only it was. What Davis and Madden saw was what Davis and Madden got. Without Harris and Bleier, we did not have an offense. The Oakland defensive line easily wrapped up Harrison. All the Raiders had to do was defend against the pass. Putting up little resistance, we lost, 24-7. Mansfield, by the way, kicked our extra point.

Monday morning, Butler and I rented a car and drove to Stanford University in Palo Alto, where the East and West college all-star squads were practicing. As I accepted condolences from the other scouts and the coaches on hand, I spotted Davis and Al LoCasale some distance away. I started toward them, and a few of my well-wishers called out, "Don't do it, Artie! Come back!" They knew what my intentions were. Disregarding them, I continued on my walk of shame. I went up the field a way and cut over to the other side, where Davis and LoCasale were standing. First I held out my hand to Davis. "Congratulations, Al." Then I nodded to LoCasale, including him, too. Davis, the bad loser, proved he could be a gracious winner. "We beat a great Steeler team," he said. Then he said it again. "A great team."

Great, but just how great? AJR, as I have written, called it the best Steeler team of them all. I know of coaches, players, and media people who agreed with him. Ralph Berlin said he agreed.

I beg to differ. Injuries and luck are part of the game. In 1976, the Steelers had too many injuries and not enough luck. I repeat: injuries and luck are part of the game. To me, the best Steeler teams were the teams that won Super Bowls.

Fear of Flying

Lionel Taylor's only phobia — the only one as far as I knew — was fear of flying. He especially feared to fly with Chuck Noll. I had flown with Noll myself and appreciated Taylor's point of view, but my scariest minutes in an airplane occurred on a flight in a private four-seater from New Orleans to Jackson, Mississippi.

Everett Marks, a Louisiana oil man, was with me. About halfway to our destination, an electrical storm caught up with us. There was thunder, there was lightning, there was wind. Marks ordered the pilot to turn the plane around and go back to New Orleans. The pilot obliged, but now we were flying into the teeth of the storm. We were low enough to see a two-lane asphalt highway, and Marks screamed at the pilot to set the plane down on the road. "Like hell," he called to us over his shoulder. "I could wreck the plane. That would cost you guys a lot of money." To say nothing of our lives, I said to myself. Out loud, and profanely, Everett Marks expressed the same thought. I don't know how, but we made it back to New Orleans and landed on the airport runway.

But I was talking about Lionel Taylor, the second black coach AJR had ever hired. Chuck Noll brought him in for the 1970 season. He had a fine way with the players and was popular, in fact, with everyone, which meant that the satisfaction was mutual, because Taylor liked the Steelers as well as the Steelers liked him. His only complaint, as far as I could see, was Noll's insistence on taking the other coaches with him when he flew his own plane to NFL meetings or on scouting missions. Taylor was not alone in feeling like this, I can assure you.

At any rate, in January of 1977, Noll flew most of his staff to the Senior Bowl game in Mobile in a small chartered plane. Whether Chuck took over the controls, as he sometimes did, I'm not sure; I never asked. I know that on the way to Alabama they met with foul weather. It was like hitting a stone wall, someone told me. The passengers were lifted out of their seats, and Dan Radakovich dropped the cigarette he was smoking. "Put it out!" the others yelled at him. Then they yelled, "And don't even think about lighting up another one!"

When Noll and his shaken assistants checked into our motel after "a white-knuckled, sweaty-palmed, nail-biter of a flight," as one coach described it, I happened to be in the lobby. There were those who tried to make light of the experience, but Lionel Taylor was still upset, and he let it show. He took me by the arm and led me outside, where we could not be overheard. "Art," he said, "the Rooneys have always been more than fair to me. You have a first-class organization." He stopped, almost breaking down. With a tremor in his voice, he resumed, "But I don't like those plane trips. Why do I have to travel that way — because the head coach tells us, 'Let's go'?"

With that, Lionel turned on his heel and strode back into the lobby. I hadn't uttered a word, but it made no difference. What could I have said? Here was this strong ex-football player, a fearless pass-catcher who had set receiving records with the Denver Broncos, in such an obvious state of distress that he could hardly hold back the tears.

Before the next season, instead of renewing his contract with the Steelers, Taylor joined the staff of the Los Angeles Rams. No doubt he had personal and professional reasons for doing so, but I can't help but think the plane ride to Mobile was a factor.

His replacement, Tom Moore, was a true, hard-working professional, the first coach to show up at Three Rivers Stadium every morning. Once when we pulled into our parking places at roughly the same moment, I jumped out of my car and ran to the door for no better reason than to say I was there before Tom.

Lionel Taylor's departure and the retirement of Andy Russell and Ray Mansfield would alter the makeup of our 1977 team. I hated to see them go. Russell, like Jack Butler, deserved a Hall-of-Fame nomination and never got one. Mansfield was a team leader who had the ability to laugh at himself. He died before his time — of a heart attack in the Grand Canyon, where he and his son Jim had gone for an extended backpacking hike. The end came at sunset, while Ray was taking in the gorgeous view.

There was tragic irony connected with the death of Everett Marks, my companion on the aborted flight we were certain would be the last for both of us. A few years later, Everett and his wife, Mary Anne, were killed when a flight taking off from the New Orleans airport suddenly lost altitude and crashed.

Total Recall

One of our three choices in the fourth round of the 1977 draft was Ted Petersen, a center from Illinois, 6 feet 6 with a frame that would carry 285 pounds. He was Chuck Noll's kind of athlete: intelligent.

To be a center, you had to be smart. Everything starts with the center, he's the switch that turns on the motor. Often he must call the offensive blocking schemes. On every play, he must know what his teammates in the line are expected to do. Petersen, in that respect, was the equal of Steeler centers like Bill Walsh and Ray Mansfield and Mike Webster. Perhaps I also should mention Tunch Ilkin and Jimmy Clack, who were centers when they came to us.

On a day almost thirty years after we drafted Petersen, I met him for lunch at the St. Clair Country Club. A Steeler alumnus who had chosen to remain in Pittsburgh, he was athletic director at Upper St. Clair High School, where high academic standards and success in competitive sports co-existed. As soon as we sat down, he started talking about the 1977 draft. "I want to congratulate you on that draft," he said, and I accepted the compliment gratefully. I have learned it's the only way. As I remembered it, nine guys we drafted that year made the team, a team that had won two of the last three Super Bowls, and three of those nine – Robin Cole, Dirt Winston, and Cliff Stoudt – became starters.

Cole and Winston were linebackers. Cole, our first-round pick, developed into a Pro Bowl player. Stoudt, one of Terry Bradshaw's successors at quarterback, took the Steelers to the playoffs in the 1980s.

The player we drafted in the second round, Sidney Thornton, unearthed in one of those Louisiana colleges named for a point on the compass, had many good games and made occasional big plays, but was never going to beat out the running back ahead of him, Franco Harris. In the third round, having given up a player to the Jets, we drafted twice, coming up with Tom Beasley, who turned out to be a good support guy in a strong defensive line, and Jimmy Smith, a wideout and kick returner from Michigan, as friendly an environment for wideouts and kick returners down through the years as you will find. How good was Smith? Let me just say that he made Frank Lewis expendable.

And now to hear Ted Petersen recall these old teammates, the names and all the circumstances rolling off his tongue, gave me a lift. At one point, he switched the conversation to Chuck Noll and his emphasis on fundamentals. "He was always on my tail about run blocking, pass protection, weightlifting," Petersen said. Noll's inscrutable exterior mystified Ted. "I never quite knew what he was thinking. Maybe he liked me and maybe he didn't. I couldn't tell."

"If he didn't like you," I said, "he wouldn't have pushed you so hard. You were his prototype offensive lineman."

I had noticed that Petersen's back was giving him trouble, a legacy of his days with the Steelers. "Comes and goes," he said now in answer to my question. "When I played, it hurt all the time. This back cut short my career."

Nodding sympathetically, I told him what Walt Kiesling used to say about injuries. They hurt like hell initially, but then you put some ice and heat on them and ran them off and forgot them. "But after you're retired," Kies would go on, "the pain comes back. About the time you hit 50 you're hurting constantly. You remember when you got that injury, and then you remember where you got it, and a little while later you remember the name of the bastard who hit you." Petersen forced himself to smile. "My Uncle Jim," I went on, "used to say that betting on the horses was a hard way to make easy money. Well, professional football is like that, too." Uncle Jim was the philosopher I quoted most often.

The talk of injuries turned Petersen's thoughts to Laverne Smith. "Remember him?" he asked me. "The fast kid from Kansas? He was our other fourth-round pick in 1977."

"Yes, a great talent," I said. "We hoped he would be a guy who could change off with Franco." But Smith was unlucky. "He took a bad hit. Busted up his wheels. Never the same runner again."

Our third fourth-round pick in 1977, Petersen remembered, was Dan Audick, an offensive guard from the state university in Hawaii, a state that exports a lot of pineapple but very few football players. "Hawaii, beautiful Hawaii. I'll bet you scouted Audick yourself," Petersen said.

"Unfortunately, no. Bob Schmitz went out there. My only look at Audick was in a game on the mainland. In person, I mean. Of course I saw him on film. And, oh yeah – Audick was in one of those all-star games we scouted."

"Noll cut that guy, and then he played in the league for eight years – mostly with the Raiders," Petersen recalled.

"The Raiders," I said "Our hated rivals."

"We took three guys in the fifth round," Petersen resumed. His mind seemed to work like Google or America On Line.

"Cliff Stoudt, he was the first!" I blurted, my competitive instincts coming to the fore. "Noll and Bill Nunn went to Youngstown State to watch him play, and they went in Noll's plane. Hell, you could *drive* to Youngstown in an hour and a half. Anyway, Noll and Bill were favorably impressed. Stoudt was a big tall kid, like you, and he had a strong arm. No dumbbell, either. But he lacked something."

I have trouble defining exactly what it was that he lacked. Consistency at placing his long passes, I'd say to start with. Beyond the physical demands of a quarterback's job, the ability to generate a feeling of confidence is needed, and there again he fell short. Our fans, with the fervor of a lynch mob, loathed him, and one reason seemed to be that he wasn't Bradshaw. He escaped them by jumping to the USFL – the United States Football League – one of those fly-by-night conferences that seemed to come and go for so many years.

As I said, Stoudt passed his audition with ease, but what Nunn and even Noll recalled most vividly about their visit to Youngstown was the return flight. Nunn likened it, I remember, to a World War II bombing mission over Berlin, the turbulence was so bad.

"Steve Courson, fifth round." Petersen said, bringing us back to the 1977 draft.

I cut him off. "We don't have time to talk about Steve Courson."

"OK, Mister Rooney."

"Call me Art."

"OK, Art. But Steve has matured." I did not respond. Moving on, Petersen said, "After Courson, we took Dennis Winston — Dirt. From the University of Arkansas. Gosh, he was tough."

"Sure was."

We had covered the first six rounds, and I mentioned again how remarkable it was that nine of our draftees made the team.

"Ten," Petersen said, correcting my arithmetic. I'd forgotten Dave LaCrosse, a linebacker from Wake Forest who hung on as a special-teams player. We kept a walk-on that year, too – Tony Dungy. I had scouted him myself at the University of Minnesota. Dungy was a quarterback, but Tom Moore, the assistant coach who signed him for us, said he could be a defensive back, Tony's lack of speed notwithstanding. With the Steelers, he played both positions, and he used his time here constructively, asking good questions and increasing his knowledge of the game. Although he would not like to hear me say so, I felt all along that his abilities were more suited to coaching than to playing. After three years in the league, two with the Steelers and one with San Francisco, and a year on the coaching staff at Minnesota (the university), he came to us as an assistant to Noll. It was easy to see, at least for me, that he was cut out to be a head coach, and in fact he got to be one, first at Tampa Bay and then at Indianapolis, where his assistants included Tom Moore. Under Dungy, the Colts were Super Bowl winners in 2007.

We parted, Ted Petersen and I, with no discussion of the season we had in 1977, which uncannily resembled the 1976 season. The team lost four of its first eight games, then won five of the next six. Our 9-5 record put us into the playoffs, but we made a quick exit, losing in Mile High Stadium to Denver, 34-21. Red Miller, the Broncos' head coach, and George Perles, our defensive coordinator, were long-time antagonists, and they almost got into a fist fight down on the field before the kickoff. The game itself was played in the same spirit, with lots of hard hitting and some intermittent displays of good old-fashioned animosity. The Broncos beat us, you might say, at our own game, Steeler football.

Steroids

My thoughts about Steve Courson are so mixed that I can only express them on paper. In conversations like the one with Ted Petersen, I don't trust myself to be sufficiently even-handed.

Anyway, by the time we scouted Courson intelligence tests had become a part of the process, and he passed them with high scores. Athletically, he measured up just as well. He could run, jump, and change directions with great agility for an offensive lineman. But he was flighty and lacking in common sense, it seemed to me, and prone to make questionable decisions. Electing to use steroids was the worst decision he ever made, and one that he came to regret.

Like too many others gone astray in the drive for excellence, he believed that he needed an edge. Weight training and large intakes of protein were not enough. To improve his performance, he juiced himself up.

What the source of his advice was I never knew, but at pre-season training camp in 1984, which would have been Courson's eighth year with the team, Chuck Noll perceived that something was wrong and told us to get rid of him. "I don't want the guy around here," Noll said. We traded Courson to Tampa Bay, and he played for another two years.

The steroids eventually ruined his health. A decade or so after his retirement, he confessed to having taken them and revealed that he was suffering from damage to his heart. He was on the waiting list for a transplant, he said, but time went by and there was no further word about a transplant, and finally Courson announced that his heart had repaired itself, crediting the improvement to radical changes in his lifestyle.

When Courson made public his use of steroids, he said there were many other users in the NFL. Some of them, he added, naming no names, had played for the Steelers when he did. He wrote a book; he appeared before Congressional committees. I was surprised at how well he expressed himself, I admit, having always considered him a blowhard.

Even before the trade, Noll banished Courson from training camp. On the day of his departure, my son Mike, a teenager then who washed the players' cars for pocket money, saw Courson climbing into his SUV. Mike always had liked Steve; whether he knew what had happened is doubtful. At any rate, he chose this moment to remind him of a promise. "You said you'd give me a ride in your truck. Let's do it now."

"Sure, kid," answered Steve. "Hop in." Later Mike said that Steve gave him a tour of the St. Vincent campus. They drove to the Benedictine cemetery and down the steep hill to the terrace from where our fans watch the workouts and then out onto the practice fields and on up to Kennedy Hall, the building that houses the dressing rooms and showers. There Mike got out, saying, "Great ride, Steve. Thanks a lot."

"OK, Mike, take care of yourself," Steve told him and was off down Fraser Purchase Road and onto Route 30 — out of our lives, we mistakenly thought, for good.

I had been taught about redemption in grade school at St. Peter's, high school at North Catholic, and my four years at St. Vincent College. The Good Thief stole heaven on the cross next to Christ. I wish I had known Steve Courson after he turned his life around with strict diet, exercise, and medical care. He became an advocate of clean living. He lectured young people on the dangers of drugs and steroids. He wrote about it and led by example.

Steve died trying to save his old Labrador retriever from a falling tree. It could have been a teammate or a child. He reached out to a friend in danger. Courson saved the dog and lost his own life.

Were there Steelers besides Courson taking steroids during the Super Bowl years? I couldn't say yes and I couldn't say no. Certainly Mike Webster was open to suspicion. What I can say unreservedly is that Chuck Noll would not have knowingly tolerated steroid use. In meeting after meeting, attended by assistant coaches, scouts, and trainers, he inveighed against steroids in the strongest language. The marching orders he gave to our scouts went something like this: "Guys who take that crap are destroying themselves. Their balls will fall off. They have to grow beards to hide the blemishes and lesions on their faces. I don't want anybody like that."

He felt the same way about drugs. Every rookie we signed went directly from the Greater Pittsburgh Airport to Divine Providence Hospital, where he took a physical examination that included a urine test for steroids and controlled substances. One year when my other son, Art III, was studying dentistry at Pitt, he had a summer job with the team that required him to pick up the new players and take them to the hospital. Then he monitored the tests.

His instructions were to stand by and watch the players urinate into plastic cups and make sure there was no switching of samples. After one week of this, Art came to me and said he had had enough. He was pissed off, if you will pardon the expression. "This job is dehumanizing, Dad. It's not respectful to me or the players," he said.

I asked if he knew why having an overseer was necessary. "You're a medical person," I reminded him.

"Yes," he replied, his demeanor turning one hundred percent professional. "That is true. I do understand the motivation for what you are doing. But my focus is on dentistry. The mouth. May I suggest that you engage a urologist for this work?" Then and there, Art's duties as a urine watchdog came to an end.

The Little Architect

After the 1977 season, two more staff members defected. Offensive line coach Dan Radakovich and defensive coordinator Bud Carson followed Lionel Taylor to the Rams. Their reasons for leaving were unclear, at least to me. Perhaps they believed they were putting themselves in a better position to become head coaches. Or maybe they looked at the way the Steelers had regressed since their two straight Super Bowl victories and jumped to the conclusion that the wheels were coming off. Possibly the California weather seduced them. No doubt they were getting upbeat reports from Taylor on life in the Golden West. I could only guess.

Bad Rad's departure bothered AJR, who predicted, "He'll be back." For the next twenty years Rad wandered all over the coaching landscape, professional and college, going from job to job. Like Ulysses returning home from Troy, he did come back to Pittsburgh as an assistant to Joe Walton at Robert Morris University, but AJR had not lived to see it. Lionel Taylor meandered around the NFL for a while and then came to rest at Texas Southern University. He was still the head coach there when he retired. Essentially, Taylor and Radakovich were nomads. The Bud Carson case was not quite the same.

In my opinion, this bright and able football man left the Steelers at least partially because of a power struggle he was losing, a power struggle with George Perles, the coach who was closest to Chuck Noll. Perles coached the defensive line and I thought he resented the credit that went to Carson for certain innovations in the development of the Steel Curtain, the name the sportswriters gave to the Steeler defense in its entirety. My own impression was that Chuck Noll developed the Steel Curtain, but Carson, I would say, contributed. Woody Widenhofer, a good friend of Perles, sarcastically referred to Carson as "the little architect" of the defense. If Bud had a fault, and I think he did, it was an inclination to be impatient with young, physically gifted players like Mel Blount who had not yet mastered all the techniques.

Los Angeles was not the last stop for Carson. In fact he ended up, several jobs later, as head coach of the Browns. Losing him, I believed, was a blow to Noll. With Tom Moore and Rollie Dotsch as their replacements, Taylor and Rad could be spared. Dotsch had some theories about offensive line play that were not in accord with Noll's, but it never became a problem. Noll was the boss; nobody disputed it, least of all the affable Dotsch. Taylor and Radakovich versus Dotsch and Moore was a wash. The assistant Chuck really missed, whether or not he would say so, had to be Carson. Perles and Widenhofer could install Noll's defensive system and get it operative, but the new defensive backfield coach, Dick Walker, seemed unable to communicate with the four very exceptional Pro Bowl performers he inherited. All he had to do was oversee their conditioning and make sure they understood the game plan every week; it was still too much for him. Even so, he remained on the staff for four years, and to say that three of them were good ones for the team would be understating it.

Moore, Dotsch and Walker had one thing in common: George Perles and his ally Widenhofer were the employment agents who had orchestrated their hiring. I don't mean to imply that this was harmful, necessarily. But Perles and Walker were not very good at evaluating talent, which made the work of the scouts more difficult. Dick Haley and I had to be constantly on the lookout to keep them from getting into mischief.

We would see the effects of their meddling in future drafts.

Chapter 63

Too Many Cooks

In 1978 the league moved the draft from early in the year, late January, to spring. The thinking was that playoff teams would have more time to prepare and coaches would have more time to assess the condition of veteran players who had suffered injuries late in the season.

Selfishly, I didn't welcome the change. The early draft, I had always believed, gave us an edge. We made some hurried decisions, and hurried decisions could result in mistakes, but I felt that we were always more successful than the teams that did not put manpower and, yes, money into the draft. I was proud of the organization we had developed. In my opinion, only Dallas and Los Angeles had scouting departments equal to ours. Never mind that the public considered us penny-pinchers. We outspent most of the other teams and got more bang for the buck than all of them. The proof was in how well we had done with low-end selections and free agents.

With the draft moved back to April, Chuck Noll seized the chance to get his assistant coaches more deeply involved. He dispatched all seven on a two-week mission to scout the college teams engaged in spring practice. A saying among coaches went like this: "If we have to cook the stew, we should help pick out the ingredients." That was how it seemed to Noll, and he insisted on sending his kitchen workers to the produce market.

Each assistant coach would visit nine or ten schools and in that way get to observe almost all of our top-rated prospects. Ordinarily at this time of the year our scouts would be looking at younger players, rather than the ones we had already evaluated, but to monitor the situation I assigned a scout to each coach as a traveling companion. As I have said before, some of the coaches were very good at scouting and some were OK; the others, and there is no reason to name them again, did not have a feel for the job.

And so it was that in spite of the scouting department's reservations, we wasted a second-round pick on Willie Fry, defensive end from Notre Dame. Our scouts had him rated considerably lower, but the assistant coach who visited Notre Dame was susceptible to the mystique of the place and to the sales pitch of the Notre Dame staff. Swayed by his report, Noll remained a believer until Fry's weak performance in training camp gave him buyer's remorse. Before the season was under way, he traded Fry to San Francisco.

Our first pick that year was a cornerback, Ron Johnson, another Eastern Michigan guy. One of our regular cornerbacks, the competent and experienced J. T. Thomas, had been diagnosed with sickle cell anemia, obliging us to shore up the position. Johnson, like Thomas, was strong enough to cope with the supersized receivers who could trample "pissant corners" (as Bud Carson called them) and fast enough to keep up with the more elusive type. Thomas made a complete recovery; meanwhile, Johnson was in the starting defensive backfield and even after J. T.'s return he more than earned his keep as a backup.

In the third round, we drafted again for insurance purposes. Punter Bobby Walden, a holdover from the Bill Austin era, had retired; his legs were gone. To replace him, we took a chance on Craig Colquit from Tennessee, and he was our punter for the next four years.

Of the players we drafted in rounds four through twelve, four made the team. Larry Anderson, a cornerback and kick returner from Terry Bradshaw's old school, Louisiana Tech, came to us in the fourth round. Our eighth-round selection, running back Rick Moser, was a long shot. Moser had played at Rhode Island, a school not noted for its football tradition. He hung around long enough to pick up a couple of Super Bowl rings. In the eleventh round we took another cornerback, Nat Terry from Florida State. His time was even shorter than Moser's, one year, but he, too, experienced the euphoria that goes with a Super Bowl appearance.

We drafted a Pitt player, Randy Reutershan, in the sixth round. Reutershan was a wide receiver, but Noll preferred to use him as a special-teamer and part-time defensive back. Shortly before my wife Kay turned 40, Noll flip-flopped Randy to his original position, wide receiver, and I saw my chance to requisition the number 40 jersey he had worn as a defensive back and give it to Kay for a birthday party I was planning. We had recently cut a free agent named Kay, and the idea was for Tony Parisi, our equipment manager, to take Reutershan's name off the number 40 jersey and substitute this guy Kay's.

One thing worried Parisi. "You know how upsetting it is for women to hit 40. They don't like to broadcast it," he reminded me. "So, remember — this came from you, not me. Old Tony isn't looking to get on the wrong side of Kay."

But it pleased Kay to see her name on the black Steeler jersey with the big gold 40 front and back. Reutershan was a sort of streamlined fellow, and Kay looked just fine in the still loose fit. Her red hair blended perfectly with the jersey colors and the flaming fall foliage.

Then came an unexpected hitch. Chuck Noll had changed his mind again. Reutershan was being returned to the ranks of the defensive backs and would wear his old number once more. There was no time before the next game to dig up another number 40, so Parisi would have to come to the house and retrieve Reutershan's jersey.

I broke the news to Kay. She had surprised Parisi by raising no objections to the advertisement of her age, and now she startled both of us. She said a birthday gift was a birthday gift; no one was taking it from her – not Parisi, not Noll, and not Reutershan. I explained that league rules left Parisi and the team with no choice. As a defensive back, Reutershan could not wear his receiver's number, 87. Kay refused to listen. "This jersey is a present," she said. "It's mine! The Rooneys own the team, and I'm a Rooney. Let Randy Reutershan wear 87. All he does is go down under kicks anyway." The beautiful redhead's temper was flaring. She had her own set of rules, and they superseded the NFL's.

It took a lot of persuasion, but at last I got her out of Randy Reutershan's jersey. Tony Parisi returned it after the game, and it has been in Kay's possession ever since.

There's an unhappy postscript to this story. With the 1979 season barely under way, an automobile accident put an end to Randy Reutershan's football career. Kay was saddened even more than I normally would have expected her to be. After all, they had worn the same jersey, she and Reutershan, in the glorious season of 1978.

Never Better

To this day I call it the greatest of all Steeler seasons. In 1978 there were questions about the team after an indifferent showing in the exhibition games. As no one seemed to realize, Chuck Noll was reconfiguring his offense. This was to be the year he turned his quarterback loose. The receivers, he knew, if no one else did, were better than ever. John Stallworth was showing himself to be as talented as the flashier Lynn Swann and now for the first time as productive, and Jimmy Smith was an able replacement for the departed Frank Lewis. Injuries limited Bennie Cunningham's effectiveness, but Noll was letting Terry Bradshaw throw the bomb, ignoring the tight ends as never before. What came of it was twenty-eight touchdown passes.

In every way, it was Bradshaw's finest season. Possessed of new-found confidence in the huddle, he quieted the chatterers. He alone would decide whose pass play he would call. The countrified Southern boy with the unruly temperament had become a team leader at last.

Don Shula had told me that the Mel Blount Rule, as it was now being referred to – the restriction that kept defensive backs from manhandling pass receivers running their routes – would not cramp the defensive unit's style. I think it did, but only a little. The new guy, Ron Johnson, was fresh clay, easily molded. There was less freelancing now, and more cohesiveness. As for the linebackers and front four, they had lost nothing physically and were bringing one more year of experience to their work.

The offense was at its pinnacle, I thought; the wide-open passing game kept defenses off balance for Franco and Rocky. We looked unstoppable, in short, and for the first seven weeks of the season, which started auspiciously with a 28-17 thumping of the Buffalo Bills (who had O. J. Simpson in their backfield), that was the case.

To my bemusement, AJR seemed embarrassed by the fact that in going undefeated over that seven-game span, we had beaten Cleveland twice. The win at Three Rivers Stadium, 15-9 in overtime, was our ninth in a row in games there with the Browns. We never had lost to them in Three Rivers, and it seemed to weigh heavily on Art Modell, the Browns' owner.

Starting from scratch, Modell had become successful in the advertising business (radio and TV commercials). He was smart and sharp-witted and he openly worshipped AJR. At a league meeting one year the Chief was seated at our table, a rosy-cheeked, white-haired, benevolent-looking patriarch. Just as he deposited his chewed-up cigar in the ash tray, Modell approached him and, bending over, cupped the older man's face in his hands. That was Modell's greeting. For an instant I thought he was going to kiss the Chief on the forehead.

Any doubts I may have had about Modell's good faith vanished then and there.

The Pittsburgh-Cleveland game at Three Rivers was our fourth of the season. Just when the Browns appeared to have it won, a 36-yard field goal by Roy Gerela tied the score, 9-9. The game went into overtime, and Bradshaw called one of the "gadget" plays which Noll half-reluctantly allowed him to use now and then. Designated in the playbook as "fake 84 reverse gadget pass" (I had to look that up in an old newspaper story), it was nothing more groundbreaking than the ancient "flea flicker." Bob Zuppke, if I'm not mistaken, originated the flea flicker at the University of Illinois in the 1920s. For all I know, he may have copied it from some even earlier coach. Anyway, at the Browns' 36-yard line, Bradshaw handed off to Bleier, who handed off to Swann, who lateraled to Bradshaw, who floated a high-trajectory pass to the overlooked Cunningham, all by himself in a corner of the end zone. And that was the death blow. Flea bites can sometimes be fatal.

Modell, I understand, was in agony, but he pulled himself together, concealing his chagrin, and said something congratulatory to AJR and Dan. I could be wrong, but I think that in this moment of what should have been elation, or satisfaction at least, the Chief felt genuine sadness for his friend. "Art," he said consolingly, "you beat the tar out of us for fifteen years. Things are just evening up." Maybe. My own point of view was that nothing could ever atone for what Paul Brown's Cleveland teams did to us in the late 1950s and all through the '60s.

I was never very adroit at either winning or losing graciously. It just isn't part of my nature. I liked Bum Phillips, the Houston Oilers' coach and the best of the good ol' boys; he wore boots and a ten-gallon hat, and he spoke in the lazy idiom of the cowpuncher. Besides, he knew football. I liked him, but when his Oilers handed us our first defeat of the season, 24-17 at Three Rivers in another overtime game, I was in no mood to tell him the better team won, or that losing to nice guys didn't hurt.

Actually, the better team had not won, as events were to prove. Our record after the loss to the Oilers was 7-1. We lost one more regular-season game, 10-7 at Los Angeles, and won all the rest to finish 14-2. In the Astrodome on December 3rd, we hogtied Earl Campbell and squared accounts with the Oilers, 13-3. That was the game in which Donnie Shell flattened Campbell with one of the hardest hits ever delivered. Running smack into Campbell in the open field was like meeting a locomotive head-on and derailing it.

We were to play Houston a third time in the AFC championship game, and win much more easily.

At 77, AJR was feeling the effects of age. His over-all health seemed OK, but his hearing had deteriorated and his vision was poor. Cataract surgery on both eyes had not been altogether successful. I remember that after the first operation he was flat on his back in Mercy Hospital for a week with his head immobilized between sandbags. For the rest of his life he would wear Coke-bottle glasses and complain that his peripheral vision was gone. "I can see the games better on TV," he said, and had one installed in his box at Three Rivers. Meanwhile, he was spending thousands of dollars on unsatisfactory hearing aids. At NFL meetings, he could read the printed agenda but only pretended to hear what was being said.

Although he delegated more work to Dan now, he wanted the rest of us to know that he was still very much in charge. His state of mind worried Kass. "Your grandfather," she told us, referring to Pop Rooney, "went into a funk at about your father's age and never really got out of it." AJR, deaf to the conversation at the dinner table, would silently recite the rosary, using a metal wheel the size of a man's ring. It contained only one decade – ten beads. He held it under the table cloth as he prayed. If the others at the table were laughing, he would smile; if the others looked serious, he matched his expression to theirs.

The way the football team was performing brought him out of his depression. Nobody called it that, but the term was not then in general use. Depression had certainly darkened the last few years of Pop Rooney's life. AJR overcame it. He could see, after all – not perfectly, but well enough to manage. And perhaps he had found a good ear doctor: his hearing seemed to improve.

Early in the season he had watched all the road games from Pittsburgh, but he accompanied the team to Kansas City the week after Houston had beaten us. More encouraging still, he invited Ed Kiely and me to have dinner with him at the Kansas City Hilton the night before the game with the Chiefs, which was not at all customary.

An invitation from AJR wasn't an invitation, precisely. It was more like an order, meant to be obeyed without demurral. I was scouting a college game in the afternoon – Kansas was playing in nearby Lawrence – and had arranged to meet George Young for dinner. He, too, was scouting in the area. Turning down AJR would have been unthinkable, but I could mention my appointment with George, and I did. For a very long second or two, AJR thought about this. Then he said, "George Young. Oh, yeah, the scout ... your friend." Reaching a verdict, he continued. "Well, bring him along ... George is OK."

At dinner, although I sat between them, AJR seemed to hear Young's every word. He asked questions, laughed at the stories George told, and left no doubt that he was having a good time.

Wins over Kansas and New Orleans sent us to Los Angeles with a 9-1 record. Our expatriate coaches – Taylor, Carson, and Radakovich – had Los Angeles ready for us, and though the Steel Curtain did well, our offense did not. Lionel, Bud, and Bad Rad knew what to expect from Noll and Bradshaw.

If they tried to conceal the pleasure they took in the outcome, I was not aware of it. On the other hand, Perles, Widenhofer, and their confederates smoldered for the better part of a week. As for Noll, he was his usual imperturbable self. My respect for the Rams' scouting department tempered my own disappointment. However, I still viewed L.A. as a team that would never win a league championship in spite of the great talent its scouts routinely identified, and this failure, I thought, could be summarized in a single word. "Chinatown, Jake," a detective says to the Jack Nicholson character in the cult movie called "Chinatown" to explain why municipal crime went unpunished in the Los Angeles of the 1930s; "Tinseltown" was the reason I gave for the Rams' chronic failure to end up on top. Partying with the Hollywood crowd was not the best way to condition one's self for a game of football.

Again the following Sunday the Steeler offense could muster just seven points, but the defense held Cincinnati to six. In the Bengals' own stadium, we had beaten them by twenty-five points. At Three Rivers, they put up the kind of fight we had come to expect from a team with Paul Brown in command.

Paul Brown and AJR were men of contrasting personalities, but with the passing of time the similarities between them increased. As club owners and in all of their business dealings, both got full value for their money ("one hundred cents for every dollar spent"). Both were devoted family men. And Brown, like AJR, had two sons working in positions of responsibility for his football team. Mike Brown was the assistant general manager and Pete Brown the personnel director. If Pete and I happened to be scouting the same team, we would often get together for lunch or dinner. From Pete and from all that I observed on my own, I learned that Paul Brown the driven perfectionist had a mellower side: he could be an indulgent father.

The week after the Cincinnati game, the Steelers flew back to the West Coast and pummeled San Francisco, 24-7. San Francisco had a young coach named Bill Walsh – sarcastically dubbed "The Genius" by envious rivals – but a few more years would elapse before his brain power came close to bearing fruit.

Our win over Houston in the Astrodome the following Sunday all but made it certain we'd have the home-field advantage in the playoffs. Any questions on that score were answered in the last two regular-season games, a victory at Three Rivers over Baltimore and one in Mile High Stadium over Denver. The traveling our team had done since the second week in November — two flights to California preceding the long trip to Denver — seemed to worry Noll. "We've spent so much time in airplanes we can't get ready for the games," he said. The notoriously thin air in Denver worried him, too. His recourse was to "get out there early and acclimate ourselves." He had the right idea, but the 21-17 score was a little too close for comfort.

We had ended the regular season with our best won-and-lost record, and now there would be a rematch with Denver to start the playoffs — Denver, the team that eliminated us in 1977. I blamed myself to some extent for that defeat. One play near the end of the game did us in — a 34-yard touchdown pass caught by Jack Dolbin, a free-agent wide receiver I had unsuccessfully tried to sign. Back in 1970, when I visited Wake Forest and corralled Jimmy Clack, he told me about Dolbin, an undrafted teammate. "He's faster than fast," Jimmy said. I looked at film of Dolbin and watched him romping around on the practice field and offered him a contract. Politely — all Southern kids were polite — he insisted on a bonus that was five hundred dollars more than I had offered, and Dolbin ended up with the Broncos. In the aftermath of our playoff defeat, I reconsidered one of the certitudes I had been taught. Holding out for "one hundred cents on the dollar" is not invariably good economics.

Pittsburgh in late December is cold and forbidding — good Steeler weather. On the next-to-the-last day of 1978, an icy rain was falling and the temperature had descended into the lower thirties. In the back of my open nine-seat box in Three Rivers Stadium, I could see the gray-brown shank of Mount Washington and the roiling black waters of the Monongahela-Allegheny-Ohio confluence. I had come to the game bundled up. So had Bill Nunn, but the rain and the frigid air chilled our bones. Jack Butler, always the stoic, made only one concession to the cold. He wore gloves. His sport jacket and raincoat were more suitable for September, and he was characteristically hatless. Into this bleak environment came the Broncos, looking out of their element. "We felt like turning around and jumping on our buses and going back to Denver," defensive lineman Bernie Chavious confessed later on to his old South Carolina State teammate, Donnie Shell.

Three Rivers in December could do that to a team. The fans, dressed in black with just a sprinkling of gold, set up a din. They roared and screamed and stamped their feet till the stands shook. The kickoff, and what followed it, only intensified the noise. The thumping, cheering, and howling just never let up.

Two weeks earlier in Denver, the hard-charging Steeler pass rush had put Craig Morton out of commission. Replacing him, fleet-footed Norris Weese gave us fits. Again the Steeler defense knocked Morton out of the game; again he made way for Weese, and I nudged Bill Nunn. "We'd be better off with Morton still in there." Nunn, it turned out, was thinking along the same lines. When Weese led the Broncos to a touchdown, we threw up our hands. But then the defense started getting to him. Joe Greene forced a sack. He blocked a field-goal try. There were two or three Denver fumbles and six sacks of Weese all told.

And Jack Dolbin? He wasn't a factor. Bradshaw passed for 272 yards. John Stallworth had ten catches for 156 yards and a touchdown. Lynn Swann caught a touchdown pass in spite of double coverage all afternoon, and Franco Harris ran like Franco Harris, scoring twice. What all of this added up to was sweet revenge, 33-10.

Our third meeting with Houston, also at Three Rivers, would be for the AFC championship. It was cold again — even colder than the week before — and raining again. Jack Butler had a cap on, a cap he had got from Ireland. I wore my fur-lined trench coat, a tassel cap borrowed from Tony Parisi, and my good-luck talismans, the high-top shoes in which I had watched our Super Bowl wins over the Vikings and Cowboys. The shoes and a pair of heavy woolen socks did not keep my feet warm.

In the run-up to the game, the normally easy-going Bum Phillips had been almost belligerent. He publicly declared war on the Steelers. Houston would get even, he promised. But as they waited in the rain for the kickoff, the Oilers seemed anything but warlike. Rather, they stood petrified during the minute or so it took a brainless Steeler fan, naked except for a Terrible Towel loin cloth, to burst out onto the field and race through their kick-return formation, waving another Terrible Towel above his head.

The rain, the slush, and the cold affected both teams, the difference being that the Steelers found ways to adapt. There were twelve fumbles, and the Steelers recovered almost all of them. Earl

Campbell fumbled three times. Franco Harris fumbled three times. Rocky Bleier fumbled three times. But when Harris and Bleier weren't fumbling they were ripping off pretty good gains, whereas the Steelers held Campbell to sixty-two yards.

In common with everybody else, he was slipping and sliding on the drenched Tartan Turf. Dan Pastorini, the Oilers' quarterback, complained that he couldn't get a grip on the ball, his hands were so numbed from the cold. We intercepted four of his first six passes in the second half, but by that time the game was as good as over. Scoring seventeen points in the last forty-eight seconds of the second quarter, the Steelers had leaped ahead, 31-3. At the finish it was 34-5.

The one-sidedness of the game provoked some late hits by the Oilers, which in turn led to some scuffling, but good ol' Bum Phillips discouraged any talk of animosity between the two teams. "Aw," Bum said, "you couldn't do a lot out there 'cause it was wet." Still, Jack Ham, the best outside linebacker in the NFL, was hitting so hard that he cracked his helmet. Ham started fast, dumping Campbell for a two-yard loss on the first play from scrimmage. He recovered two fumbles, intercepted a pass, and accounted for one of the sacks on Pastorini.

So we were back in the Super Bowl for our third appearance in five years. "And this time," Kay informed me, "we're taking all three of our kids."

"What about their schoolwork?" I asked.

"I talked to the principal. The principal and their teachers feel that this is an educational and life experience that can't be passed up. The teachers just wish they could go with us. I don't know how many times I've heard one of them ask if we needed a baby-sitter."

I said I'd work things out, but I didn't have to. So many Rooney grandkids and so many young children of other people connected with the team were looking for an "educational and life experience" that Joe Gordon and Buff Boston made special arrangements to include them all in our traveling party. Once we arrived at the Super Bowl site— Miami — their entertainment needs would be provided for.

Aunt Alice was staying in Pittsburgh, she told us, impervious to the coaxing of Kass, AJR, and just about everybody else in the extended family. "Not me! I don't like those crowds," she kept repeating. Uncle Jim felt the same way. A few days before the game, an elderly woman approached him in the coffee shop of the Webster Hall Hotel, where he had taken a room. "Why, Mr. Rooney," she said, "I thought you'd be in Miami for the Super Bowl." Jim's answer, as he related it to me in cadences echoing W. C. Fields, went like this: "My dear friend — I don't think you appreciate the marvels of modem technology. I am now at a stage of life where travel wearies me and big crowds annoy me and unnecessary hoopla drives me up the wall. On Super Bowl Sunday, you will see me having breakfast in this room. Then a limousine sent by Arthur will whisk me to the Allegheny County Airport, where the corporate jets land and take off. I will board one, sent by Arthur, fly to Miami, proceed to the Orange Bowl in another limousine, and watch the game in Arthur's box. Afterward, another limousine will take me back to the Miami airport and another corporate jet will fly me home. That night you may see me right here at this table, having a late-evening snack. Ah, these modern-day marvels."

"And do you know what?" he went on. "That lady believed every word of it."

Earlier in the week, as I was driving to work, I noticed cut-out figures of all the Steeler players, AJR, and Chuck Noll in the windows of the Washington grade school building on Washington Road in Mount Lebanon. The cut-outs were the work of the school kids. AJR's had a big cigar in its face. The hold of this football team on Pittsburgh and all of its suburbs was astounding, I thought, but how were Susie, Mike, and Art III going to cope with the attention they were getting because of it? How were they going to keep their heads screwed on right? Next, I wondered what AJR would do in my place. It wasn't long before I had a general idea. I was driving him, along with Kass and Aunt Alice, to our house for dinner, and I stopped to let them see the cut-outs. As tickled as one of the kids would have been, AJR made me park there illegally for minutes on end while he gawked at those silhouettes — chewing on a long green cigar.

Foster, the grade school that Susie and Mike attended, was not to be outdone by Washington. The kids in Susie's class designed and put their signatures on a banner, a huge one containing black and gold images of individual Steelers. We were to take this banner to Miami with us, I learned, and make certain to have it placed where the television camera would pick it up. "Well," I told Susie and Kay, none too enthusiastically, "I'll deal with that problem when the time comes."

To myself, I added, "But not if I can find a way out."

Spelling Lesson

In the media buildup for Super Bowl XIII, the Steelers were portrayed as rough and ready guys from a shot-and-a-beer town, the Cowboys as slick and sophisticated. Football teams in the eyes of the public took on the properties of the metropolitan centers they happened to represent. Pittsburgh was steel mills and coal mines; Dallas was office buildings populated by the millionaire businessmen Big Oil had created.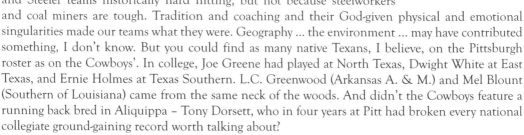

Journalistic hot air, signifying nothing. Our players were tough, yes, and Steeler teams historically hard hitting, but not because steelworkers and coal miners are tough. Tradition and coaching and their God-given physical and emotional singularities made our teams what they were. Geography ... the environment ... may have contributed something, I don't know. But you could find as many native Texans, I believe, on the Pittsburgh roster as on the Cowboys'. In college, Joe Greene had played at North Texas, Dwight White at East Texas, and Ernie Holmes at Texas Southern. L.C. Greenwood (Arkansas A. & M.) and Mel Blount (Southern of Louisiana) came from the same neck of the woods. And didn't the Cowboys feature a running back bred in Aliquippa – Tony Dorsett, who in four years at Pitt had broken every national collegiate ground-gaining record worth talking about?

Both teams were loaded with Pro Bowlers and future Hall of Famers, and both teams had cultivated their own gardens. Of the forty-five players on the Steeler squad, we had drafted all but three – the place-kicker, a second-string tight end, and a second-string linebacker. Dallas was our mirror image, the prototype drafting team in the National Conference.

The Super Bowl team that Chuck Noll put together in 1974 was no longer intact. We had eleven new starters – six on offense and five on defense. We had a different punter. All in all, there were twenty-three new faces. Dallas was back in the Super Bowl for the third time in four years. Most conspicuously absent from the team we had beaten in Super Bowl X was Bob Lilly, the Hall-of-Fame tackle. For both teams, the dynamics were moving forward.

At Super Bowl X in Miami, AJR had asked – that is to say, ordered – Kay, Art III, and me to keep him company in the owner's box. This time, to our relief, we three plus Susie and Mike were seated with the Steeler entourage in the stands. We were ten rows up from the twenty-yard line, high enough for a good overview of the action but close enough to the Steeler bench to see and hear what was going on. For Kay and Susie, the first order of business was to get the Foster School's banner displayed in a location where the television cameras would be sure to zoom in on it. Kay had the banner tightly rolled up, and now she handed it to me, saying, "You and Artie have field passes, and Mike can be helpful without going onto the field. Here is some masking tape." We marched down the steps and went to work, unfurling the banner and taping it to the barrier between the field and the crowd while Kay called down instructions from above. It was, Do this, do that. And, No, not that way, it will never hold. Standing in the aisle, all she needed was a bullhorn.

I was mortified but obedient. At these post-season games, I felt superfluous, my self-importance shredded. As Kay liked to put it, when we went to the Super Bowl the coaches coached and the players played, but the scouts were as useless as tits on a bull.

"Where did you learn that language?" I demanded.

"From the North Side Rooneys," she answered. "Before we met, remember, I was a convent girl at Seton Hill."

Packed in the former convent girl's luggage, I knew, was a pair of lacy, vulgar, salacious black panties, with the obscene exhortation PULL 'EM DOWN PITTSBURGH lettered on the backside in gold. Bernie Butler, Jack's wife, had a pair in her luggage, too; so did the wives of my brothers. Would I be obliged, as a corrupter of innocence, to bring up the matter in confession?

Art III had a problem of his own. Neither his camera nor his field pass obscured the fact that he was 14 years old. Nobody mistook him for Neil Leifer, the *Sports Illustrated* photographer, least of all the security guards. "Hey, kid, where'd you get that field pass?" they would ask. Then they'd pick up the name on the badge, an attitude changer. "Oh, from your granddad!" The tone of voice would sweeten, suspicion giving way to solicitude. "Need film or anything? Just let me know."

Names can be magic, but I could now open doors on my own. Having mastered the technique of looking as though I belonged, I wandered around unchallenged, even venturing onto the Cowboys' side of the field. At one point, talking with a fellow scout, I stood near the Dallas cheerleaders, oblivious, I thought, to their manifest charms. Ten minutes later, back in the stands, I was shocked to hear Bernie Butler suggest something different. Giving me a look, she said, "I saw you checking out those cheerleaders." My rejoinder, I'm afraid, was brusque. "No, you didn't. I was over there on serious business." How sharper than a serpent's tooth is a false accusation.

That's what I thought at the time. Reliving the moment as I write this, years and years later, something tells me that Bernie was correct. These are memoirs, and I have to be truthful; involuntarily, I may have stolen a peek or two.

Now for the game itself. The Steelers kicked off, and Dallas started feeding the ball to Dorsett. When Dorsett was at Pitt, he weighed 170 pounds; in the NFL, he couldn't possibly take the punishment a running back must absorb, it seemed to me. I envisioned him as a combination running back/wide receiver, a speedier Frank Gifford, a more compact Lenny Moore. Gale Sayers was Dorsett's size, and crashing into gargantuan defensive linemen week after week had shortened his career. Dorsett, however, surprised me. In his first two NFL seasons he had gained more than 2,300 yards in heavy traffic. And now with Super Bowl XIII barely under way, he was penetrating the Steelers' line and racing around their flanks. In four plays he moved the ball deep into Steeler territory.

But then the Cowboys got cute, or rather, their coach did. Tom Landry called a reverse. Messing up the handoff to Drew Pearson, Dorsett lost the ball. Defensive tackle John Banaszak fell on it, and the day's first change of momentum had occurred. It was not to be the last.

In a drive that covered eighty-one yards, Terry Bradshaw quickly passed the Steelers to a touchdown. On the last play, from the Dallas 28, his target was John Stallworth, who made a move that fooled the Cowboys' defensive backfield and left him open in a corner of the end zone.

We had seen the best first quarter in Super Bowl history. The second quarter was no less exciting. It started with Bradshaw throwing an interception. On our next possession, he fumbled, and Dallas tied the score. He fumbled again, under pressure from the insufferable Hollywood Henderson, and Dallas took the lead when Mike Hegman picked up the ball and ran thirty-seven yards for a touchdown.

Henderson, the trash talker, was putting his athleticism where his mouth was. On the sideline, he yakked at the camera. Bradshaw needed help, and he got it immediately from Stallworth, who turned a fairly short pass into a 75-yard touchdown play. And then toward the end of the half, with the Cowboys driving again, Mel Blount made a Hall-of-Fame move. One of Roger Staubach's receivers was open in the end zone until Blount came out of nowhere to intercept the pass. A penalty on the play put the ball in Cowboy country, and Rocky Bleier, never known for his leaping ability, went up high to make an impossible-looking catch for another Steeler score. Meanwhile, on the Cowboys' bench, Staubach and Landry were discussing with evident acrimony the reason for Blount's interception.

I watched the first half in near silence, trying hard to concentrate on the game and resenting the flow of questions from the boisterous Steeler fans in our vicinity. Butler and I were the authorities here, it seemed. My curt one-syllable answers got a rise out of Kay. "Be more pleasant! This is fun! Fun!" I begged to differ. "Fun? Like hell it's fun! It's life and death!"

The Steelers were out in front. 21-14, but still there was reason to be wary. Dallas had blanketed Franco and Rocky on the ground. And from the locker room came alarming news; leg cramps would keep Stallworth from returning for the second half. Far worse from Susie's perspective, a strong wind was ripping the Foster School's brown paper banner to shreds.

The third quarter was a vicious slugging match. Dallas got down to our 10-yard line, where, on third and three, Staubach threw a little too low to his tight end, Jackie Smith, all alone in the end zone. Smith was a hard-luck guy. He'd been a first-rate player on a third-rate team, the St. Louis Cardinals, before a serious neck injury bumped him into retirement. Offered a chance to come back, he saw the Cowboys as his ticket to a Super Bowl. Balanced against that was the very real risk of permanent disability, of life as a paraplegic. He took the gamble. And now a Hall-of-Fame career had come down to one play. Staubach, as I said, threw low, but the pass was catchable; Smith had hung on to many a throw just like it. This time, though, instead of using his meat-hook hands, he encircled the ball with his arms. Bouncing off his chest, it fell to the ground, and the Cowboys had to settle for a field goal. Going into the last quarter, Pittsburgh led by four points.

"Luck," I remember hearing Chuck Noll tell his players, "is being prepared to take advantage of your opportunities." If good luck is being prepared, then bad luck is its opposite. In the biggest game of their season, the Cowboys couldn't do what they had to do. They missed a shining opportunity, but for some of our Dallas friends there was much more to it than that. General manager Tex Schramm, in particular, never stopped talking as though Jackie Smith's failure to bear-hug a football was an undeserved stroke of misfortune.

The way I looked at it, there were fifteen minutes left in the game, more than enough time for the Cowboys to regroup. The fourth quarter had everything. There was suspense; there was controversy. Lynn Swann made a catch to put beside Rocky Bleier's. Hollywood Henderson got his come-uppance. The Steelers stretched their lead to eighteen points and ended up winning by only four, the margin they started the quarter with.

And yet the final result was decisive enough. Landry and Schramm, in the aftermath, talked incessantly about luck – about the unforced incompletion in the end zone, about a fourth-quarter call that went against the Cowboys. Swann, going out for a pass, tripped over the legs of a Cowboy defender. An official just a few yards away did not react. Another official dropped a flag, calling pass interference. Landry and Schramm yelled bloody murder. The tripping was not intentional, they screamed. Doesn't matter, the official informed them. According to the rules, even accidental tripping is not to be countenanced. The penalty stood. I thought that by harping on a legitimate call and a dropped pass, Tom Landry and Tex Schramm detracted from their own team's valiant performance.

The interference penalty prolonged a 94-yard Steeler drive that ended with one of the most memorable runs in a Super Bowl setting. The incentive for it was a routine late hit on Bradshaw by Hollywood Henderson — who else? All afternoon, the Cowboy linebacker's over-the-top behavior had been an irritant to the Steelers. Franco Harris, in his own quiet way, was seething. In itself, the roughing up of Bradshaw with the ball dead was nothing too far out of the ordinary by NFL standards. But Henderson couldn't leave it at that; he added a few expletives, which was going too far. Face to face with Hollywood, Franco was telling him off. Observers who thought they knew our mild-mannered fullback were stunned. Open displays of anger, or emotion, were foreign to his nature. Bradshaw, seizing the moment, discarded a play he intended to use. He could see that Franco was bursting with adrenaline and changed the call to a tackle trap. Our quick, almost undersized offensive linemen were excellent blockers "in space," by which I mean on the move. As the team advanced to the line of scrimmage, I caught a glimpse through my binoculars of Franco's face. I've been to Florence, in Italy; I have seen Michelangelo's David. This may sound nutty, but Franco just then was David ready to slay Goliath. At the line of scrimmage, everything went perfectly. Franco took the handoff and bolted straight up the middle on a 22-yard touchdown run. Nothing could have stopped him, and nothing did.

OK, an official helped out by partially shielding Franco from a tackler. It was still an extraordinary feat. Bobby Newhouse, the fullback we might have drafted in Franco's place, was watching from the Dallas bench. Could Newhouse have made such a run? Never in a million years.

Momentum brings luck, as Chuck Noll has probably said. On the subsequent kickoff, Roy Gerela lost his footing and squibbed the ball directly to the Cowboys' all-pro tackle, Randy White, who had a cast on one hand. A split second later, Tony Dungy was climbing all over him, and White fumbled. Dirt Winston recovered for the Steelers. Up in the stands, our fans were pummeling one another in a demonstration of pure joy.

Without delay, it got better. The graceful Swann jumped up for a pass, reached it with his fingertips, and came back to earth with a touchdown. The difference between this catch and Bleier's was that from Swann you half-expected these miracles of levitation. They were the rule, not the exception, or seemed to be. On the sideline, Bradshaw slapped backs and high-fived, but cut the celebration short when he remembered how Staubach had rallied the Cowboys in Super Bowl X, keeping them in the game until the very last play. The same thing could happen again, and it did — passing on almost every play, Staubach took Dallas eighty- nine yards to a touchdown.

With under two and a half minutes remaining, the Cowboys were eleven points behind. So, predictably, they tried an onside kick. And Dungy, the opportunist who had made an accidental onside kick work for the Steelers, gave us a scare. He fumbled, and Dallas recovered. Starting from the Pittsburgh 48-yard line, Staubach threw nine passes in a row, and Dallas had still another touchdown. After the extra point kick, the score was 35-31.

Time was nearly up. Dallas of course took the onside-kick route, but Rocky Bleier put a death grip on the ball, and the Steelers just waited for the clock to run out.

Bradshaw was the game's MVP. His seventeen pass completions in thirty attempts were good for four touchdowns and 318 yards, a Super Bowl record. Impatient with any talk of statistics, the gentlemen of the press, gathered in the Steelers' locker room, wanted human-interest stuff. Relentlessly, they asked about Hollywood Henderson, attempting to draw Bradshaw out. "He said you couldn't spell cat," a persistent fellow reminded him. "Maybe not," answered Bradshaw, "but there's one word I can spell, and that's w-i-n — win."

On a chartered bus outside the Orange Bowl, waiting to make the trip to the hotel, where we all would attend another victory party, I felt contentment. In the afterglow of a game like the one we had just witnessed, how could any Pittsburgher — any Pittsburgher with the right kind of values — be susceptible to life's petty annoyances? It wasn't all that hard, I soon learned.

The bus was almost full, and still the driver sat there, making no move to depart. My fellow passengers seemed to be on a timetable. They were eager now for the evening's festivities. Voices were raised, demanding, "Let's get the show on the road!" The driver sat motionless, ignoring them.

I became aware that Merle Gilliland, the president of PNC Bank, had left his seat and was standing next to mine. "Say, Art," he said, bending over confidentially, "can't you do something about this? Can't you show your authority?" Beneath his banker's self-control was an unmistakable note of urgency.

Stirring myself, I got up and walked to the front of the bus and said to the driver, as nicely as the circumstances allowed, "Hey, let's pull out of here. We're nearly full."

"Sorry. I have my orders." His tone was polite but determined.

"Who gave you the orders?" I asked.

"That big guy. The one they call Buffalo, or Buff."

"Yeah, Buff Boston. He works for me."

The driver said nothing. He was forcing my hand.

"Listen," I told him, "if anyone asks you for an explanation, just say that Art Rooney Junior said to get out of here."

He turned on the ignition and hit the gas pedal. We were on our way to the hotel.

Have I mentioned that names can be magic? Tranquility restored, I went back to my seat and resumed my enjoyment of the afterglow.

Chapter 64

Father Jim

Father Jim Campbell was a golfer and pinochle player. He liked sports. He liked to hunt and fish. He liked a good smoke but never tasted alcohol except each morning at Mass. Originally from Scranton, in Pennsylvania's hard-coal region, he entered the lives of the Rooney family when his order assigned him to St. Peter's Church.

Father Jim was much loved by the poor people of the parish. He had dark hair and looked like an athlete and became a dedicated horse player and stock-market investor, but AJR used to say that you never could mistake him for anything other than a priest. Long after I got to know him, he told me that he was trying to make enough money to support himself in his old age. If he could help it, he would never be a burden on his friends, his family, or the diocese.

As it happened, the problem never arose. He died at the age of 60, his financial situation unclear, at least to me. With AJR telling him how to bet on the horses and stock market, I am sure there were more ups than downs for Father Jim, but like all good priests he gave so much of his money to the poor and unfortunate it is hard to say if any was left.

It seemed to me that in Father Jim's day the pastors of Catholic churches remained on the job too long. They would do magnificent work in their prime, but grow old and feeble as the years went by. Some who were lucky had a dynamic young assistant like Father Campbell. Those with enough sense would let the young assistant take over. Others, due to bullheadedness, lack of intelligence, or simple jealousy, would cling to their authority. This was the case at St. Peter's.

World War II allowed Father Jim to get out from under a boss who had outlived his usefulness. He served in the Philippines during MacArthur's campaign to recapture the islands, and when at length he came back to St. Peter's the setup was different. A fine old Celt named MacPherson was now the pastor, and he loosened the reins on Father Jim.

In time there came a transfer to St. Andrew's in Manchester, a tough blue-collar neighborhood. St. Andrew's and St. Peter's were equidistant from 940 North Lincoln Avenue, so Dad, Mom, and Aunt Alice started going to daily Mass at Father Jim's church. Manchester back then was similar in many ways to the old First Ward. Father Jim understood his parishioners and knew how to communicate with them.

A man who worked at the bingo game (every Catholic church had a bingo game) got drunk one day – not for the first time – and Father Campbell gave him a temperance lecture. "How long are you going to make a fool of yourself and break the hearts of your family?" he demanded. Contrite, the fellow took the pledge; he swore to Father Campbell that he would never take another drink as long as he lived.

Of course in no time at all he came to work drunk again. Father Campbell told him he was fired. The boozer asked why.

"Because you're not trustworthy. You took the pledge and went back on your word."

"Oh, that?" said the drunk. "I took the pledge, all right, but it wasn't official. It didn't count."

"What do you mean, it didn't count?"

"When you made me say I'd never drink again, you weren't wearing your collar, your Roman collar."

If Father Campbell had an answer, it is lost to posterity.

Father Campbell was a man's man, but, like AJR, he frowned on off-color jokes. When you were with him, said AJR, you knew you were with a priest. Even so, he willingly went along with the cloak-and-dagger games that AJR's race-track companions had to play. Once on the train from New York City to Aqueduct, Father Jim and I rode in one car, AJR in another. You could not be seen with Dad because professional gamblers, eager to know how he was betting, would in that case follow you to the parimutuel windows. On the train that day, Father Jim tried to recruit me for Holy Orders. He urged me to think very seriously about the possibility of going into a seminary. I was flattered. I also reflected that never before, in all likelihood, had there been a conversation such as this on a train that was headed for a race track. Here we were, our pockets filled with money to bet on a horse, a man of the cloth and a teen-age boy he regarded as suitable material for the priesthood, earnestly discussing the religious life.

We were having dinner after the races at Moore's restaurant in New York. Now, AJR was a people person. If he had met someone two or three times he was just as apt as not to call him a friend. At Moore's he spoke of a certain public figure as a friend. Father Campbell interrupted him, which no one else except Mom ever did. He fired a series of questions at AJR: "How well do you know this man? ... How long have you known him? ... Under what circumstances did you meet?"

AJR was flustered. "Because that is a bad guy – a killer," Father Campbell went on. Defensively, AJR was saying, "Well, I don't know him that well ... I was introduced to him at the track ... " Father Jim interrupted again. "I should hope so. Don't ever say that guy is your friend! Forget that you ever met him!"

There was a silence, and then, mercifully, one of us changed the subject. We relaxed and enjoyed the rest of our meal.

It was the only time I can ever recall hearing anyone aside from Kass give AJR such a talking-to, but the Chief told me later that on their long drives together he and Father Campbell would now and then have a difference of opinion. If the argument grew heated, Dad said, Father Campbell would turn off the radio in the car and suggest that they recite the rosary.

AJR and Father Campbell were together so frequently at the race track and ball park that Kass felt left out. She often said she begrudged the time they spent with each other. Had Father Campbell realized this, he would have quietly backed off, I am sure. His sensitivity would not have allowed him to become a problem. It was exactly this quality that enabled him to work so successfully with the down-and-out poor of St. Andrew's. He understood their problems, but could not be deceived or imposed upon.

To raise money, he had started a street fair with Las Vegas-type games of chance. Schooled by AJR, he knew how to run them. All went well until a fleet-footed thief grabbed a stack of bills from a table one night and took off. Father Campbell gave chase. He was neither young nor swift; by one account, a heart attack felled him while he was still in pursuit. Another story, less plausible, is that through perseverance he ran the guy down, subdued him, brought back the money, and *then* collapsed.

The heart attack took years off his life. Transferred to St. Margaret's in Greentree, a prosperous neighborhood that was growing in size, he had a difficult time adjusting. He felt closer, he told me, to the poor folks at St. Peter's and St. Andrew's than to the well-off parishioners at St. Margaret's. Thinking, perhaps, of his Greentree flock, he said that as people got older they became less susceptible to boozing and to sins of the flesh but never seemed to lose their love of money. For all that, he was every bit as popular with the rich as with the poor.

Father Campbell knew when the end was near. In a conversation between us at Three Rivers Stadium one day, he confided matter-of-factly that his heart was worn out and he was operating on reserve, as he put it. A few weeks later I was driving out of the stadium as Father Campbell was driving in. We stopped and lowered our windows and he asked how I was doing. He asked about Kay and the kids and then he asked me to say hi to Kay. That was his way of sending her his love and his way of saying goodbye to us both. He did not last much longer.

Doc Sekay

Art Sekay, commonly referred to as Doc, was a man of compact build and average height or less. He had a round, partly bald head, a bulbous nose, a thick neck, heavy shoulders, and the beginning of a paunch. He wore ill-fitting clothes in need of cleaning and pressing. At a football convention in Florida, Sekay was standing outside the Hollywood Beach Hotel when I drove up with relatives in the car. My mother-in-law said, "Look ... there's a bum near the entrance."

Just then Doc happened to spot me. I waved and said hi. He waved back, calling, "Hi, Artie ... I'll see you later." My mother-in-law was astonished.

"Who is that?" she asked.

"He's our team dentist," I replied.

In all candor, Doc's appearance and behavior could not have inspired much confidence in the people who sought his professional help. The constant use of chewing tobacco had worn down his own teeth and stained them a bilious yellow. When he was not chewing tobacco he was smoking cigars.

He had played football at Pitt, where Jock Sutherland, also a dentist, was his coach, and, like other Pitt players, Sekay had gone on to dental school, graduating near the top of his class. "When he puts his mind to it," one leading dentist told me, "Doc can be one of the best. He has great strong hands." At the mechanics of the business, Sekay was more than adequate. At the hygienic end, his methods were sometimes alarming.

Whenever he dropped an instrument on the floor – and though his hands may have been strong, they did not exactly stick to the tools of his trade like glue – he would pick it up, wipe it off on his smock or a pair of dusty curtains that hung on the window of his office, and go immediately back to work. That was what happened when Soup Campbell, a Steeler linebacker, needed Doc's ministrations.

Another time, Jack Butler's son John was having a tooth capped by Sekay. While affixing the cap, he dropped it, and the cap just disappeared. Sekay told John to get out of the chair and help him look for it. John was crawling around on his hands and knees. The search continued for I don't know how long, and then Sekay found the cap in the tread of one of the football shoes he always wore. He pried it loose and stuck it back – unsterilized – in John's mouth.

Doc was a low-handicap golfer, and his second-floor office in a building on Forbes Avenue in Oakland wasn't far from the nine-hole course in Schenley Park. He did a good business with young people for some reason, and if the weather was fine, and he had a teen-age boy in the chair, he might say to him, "Hey, kid. Would you like to learn something about golf?" Unaware of what Sekay was getting at, the kid would usually nod, or say, "Sure." Sekay's bag of clubs would be handy, and saying, "Come on," he would lead the way to the golf course and play two or three holes with the kid as his caddie.

Sekay always said he could beat any other dentist in town who played golf, and do it with three clubs – a driver, an iron, and a putter.

His football background – he and Uncle Jim were teammates at Pitt – was why AJR selected him to be the team dentist. Furthermore, AJR had a weakness for characters, and in that respect Sekay certainly qualified. He was completely without tact. During Chuck Noll's first season, 1969, Sekay was in my office telling me the new guy coached "sidewalk football." In the middle of his tirade, Noll walked in. I introduced them, and Sekay took up where he'd left off, directing his comments this time to Noll. Instead of taking offense, Noll listened politely and then suggested that the three of us have lunch together. Afterward, I said to Doc, "Well, what do you think of Chuck Noll now?" They had seemed to hit it off over lunch. "He's no dumbbell," Doc conceded, "but I still think he coaches sidewalk football."

Doc never played much at Pitt before his senior year, but he considered himself an authority on football and did not have to be pressed for his opinions, which were mostly negative. Fran Fogarty attributed Doc's sour attitude to his own lack of success as either a player or coach. Where and when he coached, I couldn't tell you; he'd been a part-time assistant somewhere, I think. I know that he spent more time on the golf course than as a coach or a dentist.

John Michelosen, a fellow Pitt man, he dismissed with the phrase "dumb-ass." Buddy Parker he sort of liked. Buddy was one of the few. Jack Barrett, a craft-union boss who knew Sekay, said the only people he liked unreservedly were AJR, Jack Butler, a local high school coach named Joe Moore, and me.

Sekay was in the military during World War II and resented it when his number came up for service during the Korean War also. He went back in as a lieutenant colonel, but rank was not important to him. In company formations he would wear his cap with the bill turned around. Saluting, he would bring up his hand to the back of his head. "What is the meaning of this?" asked the company commander. "I'm saluting the enlisted men," answered Sekay. "They deserve a salute more than the officers do."

Doc told me that when a soldier came off the front line for dental work he would pull one of his teeth, whether or not it was sound.

"Why would you do that?" I wanted to know.

"Because if one of these kids had an extraction it kept him out of combat for twenty-four hours. Any other procedure, they went right back to their unit. I gave a lot of kids an extra day of life."

I heard from Fran Fogarty that while Doc was in Korea both his wife and his daughter died and that Army red tape kept him from returning in time for either funeral, which embittered him further.

AJR was patient with Doc, but only up to a point. Complaints from the players about his unkempt looks, slovenly behavior, and disregard for sanitation at last became so numerous that the Chief had to act. He instructed Fran Fogarty to give Doc the word that his services were no longer required.

The last time I saw Doc – we met by chance on the street one day – he said he was working in the office of another dentist. "All I have to do," he told me, "is put on a white smock, wash my hands, and pull teeth."

He asked me where I was going. When I said, "To the bank," he reached in his pocket and brought out a large roll of bills. "How much do you need? I'm making a ton of money," he said.

I told him, "Thanks, Doc, but I'll be OK."

A year or so later I was reading Doc Sekay's obituary.

Butch

Butch was a big kid from the First Ward who seemed to have a future in football. A standout lineman at North Catholic High School, he attracted the attention of college scouts in his junior year. He attracted the attention of the girls in the neighborhood, too. With pretty little Betsy Sue, the attraction was mutual.

Soon they were going steady. Not long afterward, Betsy Sue was in an unwanted condition. Butch did not hesitate to do the right thing. Without a second thought, he married the girl.

At North Catholic in those days, there were certain inflexible rules. The Marianist Brothers could have expelled Butch; showing lenience, they encouraged him to save them the trouble. He transferred to Allegheny High School and continued to play football so well that two or three college coaches with scholarships to offer came calling. All bets were off, though, when they learned that a wife and child would be part of the deal, with still another child on the way. (College athletic departments had not yet begun to change with the times. In fact, the times themselves had not yet begun to change. Butch was ahead of the curve.)

So Butch went to work instead of to college. His father, a dispatcher for the Exhibitors Trucking Line, got him a job as a driver. In due time, he was driving a Pepsi-Cola truck. Pepsi-Cola drivers doubled as salesmen, and Butch had a salesman's personality. When the money started coming in, he, Betsy Sue, and their kids moved from the First Ward to an upscale part of the North Hills.

Betsy Sue had gone through nursing school and worked at various hospitals. Her salary helped pay for the arrival of a third child – born, unfortunately, with a physical disorder. In their search for a cure, the parents traveled far and wide, consulting with specialists and spending every dime of their savings.

One thing kept Butch's spirits up. As a First Ward kid who'd played football at North Catholic, he was not unknown to the Rooney family, and his connections landed him on "the chain gang," a highly coveted distinction.

The chain gang performed, and still does, at Steeler games. It consists of only three men. They carry a ten-yard length of chain attached to sticks at either end, the chain that is used to measure for first downs. At the top of one stick are the down markers – metal signboards numbered one through four, which are flipped after every play. Stick holders wear the uniform required by the NFL – white cap, white shirt, white knickers, black knee socks, and football shoes.

Butch gloried in this job. It brought him prestige, and the envy of his friends. It was a time when the Steelers were winning Super Bowls, and he had what is called high visibility. A lower profile, as it happened, might have kept him from getting into trouble.

When the Steelers played at Three Rivers Stadium the game officials went to their private dressing room for the fifteen-minute halftime intermission. The chain gang and the field crew had soft drinks and sandwiches in one of the two baseball dugouts. But soft drinks and sandwiches were not Butch's notion of a satisfying snack.

He started venturing into the stands and making his way to the concession area for a brewski or two and a hot dog or two. Butch liked people and liked to talk. It was not too long before friends and complete strangers were competing for the honor of buying him his beer and his dogs. He never once got drunk or out of line. It is natural, however, for people to spread tales, and the tales people spread about Butch were reaching NFL headquarters in New York – tales to the effect that officials at Steeler games were consorting with the fans and guzzling beer in the stands. Was it any wonder they were blowing so many calls? An investigation resulted, and the finger of blame pointed at Butch.

He must be fired, the league office insisted.

It was a staggering blow – the loss of psychic income more damaging to him than anything else. The Steelers had a great team, elevated to demi-god status, and Butch was a part of it. And now his comedown had turned him into a laughing stock. At work and at the neighborhood bar he patronized, Butch endured joke after joke. Outwardly, he affected indifference. "I'll make more money pushing soda pop than some of these football players will when their careers are over and they're has-beens," he said, fooling no one. Privately, he berated himself. To go up in the stands the way he did had been stupid. And he felt he had let down the Rooney family.

But it was true just the same that his soda pop business was thriving. His route was in the Hill District, and black people sure liked their Pepsi. They drank more soda pop, Butch used to say, than all of the other ethnic groups combined.

Betsy Sue, meanwhile, continued to work as a nurse. All three children went to college. The son who was born while Butch and Betsy Sue were still in their teens finished pharmacy school at Duquesne and found a well-paying job with one of the big drug-store chains. Butch himself was putting on too much weight. Betsy Sue worried about it and pestered him continually to diet, but life couldn't be better, he thought.

And then on a cold March night he was roused from his sleep by a telephone call. His son the pharmacist had died from an overdose of prescription drugs.

Butch was in shock. He could not understand it. Over and over he said that this was a boy who never had been a problem. Increasingly, he leaned on Betsy Sue, the more resilient of the two. He was drinking no more than usual, but seeking comfort in food.

Spring departed and summer came. At a family picnic on the Fourth of July, Butch again ate too much. Getting up from the table to greet a relative, he checked himself for a moment, collapsed into his chair, and lurched forward. His face in his third helping of fried chicken, baked beans, and potato salad, he was dead of a massive stroke. Those who really knew Butch, his closest friends, were convinced there had been a much deeper cause.

What he died of, they said, was a broken heart.

Political Pals

Even after Jimmy Coyne's downfall in the 1930s the North Side continued to be an assembly line for politicians, with the difference that now they were Democrats. Tom Foerster and Pete Flaherty, the most successful, had close ties with AJR. Foerster made some noise as a state legislator, but for most of his career was a county commissioner.

Finding ways to keep AJR's name before the public seemed to be Tom's avocation. He was a tireless organizer of award banquets and testimonial dinners. Pete Flaherty got his start as the attorney for the Steelers. Successively, he became a city councilman, mayor of Pittsburgh, deputy United States attorney general, and, like Foerster, a county commissioner.

Bob Colville — public-safety director, district attorney, and judge – had been another North Side kid who regarded AJR as a patron. Jim Flaherty, Pete Flaherty's brother, preceded his older sibling as a county commissioner but returned, after one term, to the practice of law. Jim was a sort of maverick commissioner, teaming up with the Republican minority commissioner, Bob Peirce, to neutralize Foerster, the chairman. There was never any kind of association that I know of between Jim Flaherty and AJR. Foerster, a big, curly-haired endomorph, had been a football player, a tackle, at North Catholic High School and Slippery Rock State Teachers College. While serving in the State Legislature he coached his neighborhood kids team, the Perry Atoms, and a Catholic grade-school team that competed with my brother Dan's team at St. Peter's. Torn distinguished himself in the legislature by working hard for the passage of environmental and conservation laws.

In the shifting power struggles of county government, he was always at the center of things, gaining, losing, or vying for control. The politics could often be tortuous. After Jimmy Carter's election to the presidency, everybody knew that he would offer Pete Flaherty a job in his Justice Department and that Flaherty would resign as mayor to accept it. In circumstances such as these, the president of City Council served out the departing mayor's term. At the time Flaherty left, the president was Jeep DePasquale, head of the ushers' union at Three Rivers Stadium. Foerster and his henchmen forced or persuaded Jeep to step aside for Dick Caliguiri and forced or persuaded Caliguiri to promise he would not be a candidate in the next primary election. Caliguiri kept his word; he did not run in the primary, and the nomination went to Foerster, as planned. But then in what looked to the Democratic power structure like a double-cross, Caliguiri ran as an independent in the general election. Having done well in his year as the incumbent, he won from Foerster hands down

It was never quite clear why Foerster wanted to be mayor, given the influence he could exercise, and the good he could do, as chairman of the county commission. He was largely responsible for

Allegheny County's community college system and for the billion-dollar expansion of the Greater Pittsburgh Airport in the 1990s — not a bad legacy.

Pete Flaherty came from a typical Irish family in what AJR considered "the right" part of town. He had a sister who married Jimmy Smith, the son of Billy Conn's father-in-law, Greenfield Jimmy Smith. Pete, a World War II veteran, went to a Pittsburgh girls' college, Mount Mercy, and to Notre Dame Law School as a beneficiary of the GI Bill. Right from the start, AJR recognized his potential.

What impressed the Chief most after Pete came to work for the Steelers was the *way* he handled a sensitive assignment at Shamrock Farm. It seems that the wife of the tenant farmer had been taking retarded children to live there in return for monthly payments from the state. In AJR's view, a house full of retarded kids was an accident waiting to happen. At the same time, he wanted them taken care of. He turned the problem over to Flaherty, who talked to the woman and gave her a lease on the farm house for a dollar a year with the understanding that as soon as she was able to move somewhere else and take the kids, she would do so. The lease, I suppose, put AJR in the clear if there was trouble with the state in the meantime. Flaherty's kindness and tact made the solution he came up with as agreeable to the woman and her husband as to everybody else.

Tall and somewhat shambling in the Jimmy Stewart manner, with an unruly forelock and photogenic blue eyes, Pete had uncommon political charisma. As mayor, he proved to be a ruthless cost cutter. He cleaned the deadwood out of City Hall and stood up to the featherbedding truck drivers' union. When Pete was in office in the 1970s other cities like Pittsburgh were going bankrupt. He kept it from happening here. But as "Nobody's Boy" — the label under which he campaigned — he made enemies, and his reclusive personality turned off many friends who at least by their own lights had helped him.

Being nobody's boy meant a freeze in his relationship with AJR. As disappointed as he may have been, AJR understood. He looked upon Pete as "one of our own" — Irish, Catholic, born and raised on the North Side. Enough said.

Chapter 65

A Kindly, Aging Guy

At his specialty, betting on horses, AJR was as good as they come. He knew every betting system, knew every scam, and knew all the schemers at all the tracks. I am quoting Pat Lynch, turf writer for the Morning Telegraph. He knew the horses, AJR did, knew the jockeys, knew the trainers, knew the touts, knew the bookies, knew the guys the bookies went to when they were looking to lay off a bet.

He considered race tracks his second home. At race tracks he could always feel good about himself. At race tracks his name commanded instant respect.

But at NFL meetings, with a new generation of businessman-owners taking over — sharp and self-important entrepreneurs — AJR the race-track legend seemed to be oddly diminished. He was looked on, it appeared, as just a kindly, aging guy in a rumpled dark suit — a little too nice and a little too easy-going to stay in the swim.

Certainly he appreciated irony and certainly he could laugh at himself. He understood where talent and where luck came into play. But maybe this was too much. AJR prepared for a horse race as thoroughly as Paul Brown prepared for a football game. In a world far tougher than the NFL, not only had he survived — he had flourished. To see how little that counted with men such a world would have eaten alive must have nettled him, and yet it's hard to be sure. If he ever felt patronized no one could tell. Behind his gambler's poker face, his feelings were not for public display. Even the way he dressed was part of the mask.

But he could put almost anybody, stuffed shirts not excepted, at ease. I recall a business luncheon in fancy surroundings — a private dining room in the William Penn Hotel if I'm not mistaken — at a time when we were starting to look at things other than football. On this occasion we met with some people from the Consolidated Coal Company, good ol' West Virginia boys who had risen in the corporate hierarchy and were now big executives dressed for the part and acting the part and very much aware of their hard-won eminence. In just a few minutes, the Chief softened them up.

Exactly as he did with everyone — waitresses, bus boys, parking attendants, elevator operators — he asked one of the men where he was from. Reluctantly, the coal company honcho mentioned a little town in the West Virginia panhandle. "Been there," said AJR. "You know, I used to play center field for the Wheeling Stogies in the Middle Atlantic League. When we played in your town we got into a big fight. My brother Dan — he's a priest now — was our catcher, and he laid out a guy on the other team. You had a big, fat sheriff, I remember. I'll never forget him."

Interested suddenly, the coal company man forgot he was wearing a Brooks Brothers suit and broke in to say, "He died just this year, that sheriff did. I knew him well." Then the others chimed in with their own reminiscences. Three of the four, it turned out, had played baseball in West Virginia themselves, and now they were dredging up ancient games and ancient anecdotes, kindred spirits, for the moment, with AJR, and he was having as much fun as anyone else at the table.

His stories were contagious — they got the ball rolling. They were never about sex and he always mangled the punch line, if by some chance there happened to be one, but people listened. At Toots Shor's Restaurant in New York, AJR and Bert Bell would start telling football stories and keep on going until Shor chased them out of the place at two or three in the morning with just the waiters and a handful of sportswriters still hanging in and eager for more.

This was AJR the spellbinder. At home we got AJR the sermonizer — hellfire and brimstone. And we listened as raptly as the waiters and sportswriters did. We listened because we had to. For us, there was no other choice.

Dirt

Trainer Ralph Berlin recalled that when the Steelers played home games at Pitt Stadium, AJR would spend the hours before the kickoff in their dressing room, seated on an equipment trunk and absorbed in conversation with Horse Czarnecki, the Pitt groundskeeper. Much of the time he'd be laughing and gesturing, waving his cigar like a band leader's baton, Berlin said.

AJR would have liked to bring Horse to the new stadium with us, but Czarnecki by that time was a permanent fixture at Pitt. In any case, the same ground crew that worked at Forbes Field had moved to Three Rivers with the Pirates.

Headed by Eddie Dunn, who had learned the business under John Fogarty, Fran's dad, the ground-crew members were spirited, obscene, opinionated, inbred (nepotism dictated the hiring), and unionized. They could make life difficult for an employer, but AJR was on good terms with all of them. He knew their relatives, he knew their politics, and he knew their frailties, which he excused.

AJR had the common touch. The hot walkers and stable boys at the race tracks we operated in Philadelphia, Vermont, and Yonkers idolized him. So did their counterparts at our greyhound track in Palm Beach. This rapport between AJR and people who worked with their hands for low wages was something that Pat, John, Tim, and I used to discuss. Our father's attitude seemed to be "We're all in this together, but some of us are luckier than others." He understood how these "others" felt and could make them see that he understood. The odd thing, of course, was that he never had worked a day in his life. He worked a half-day, in a steel mill, and then quit.

My relations with the ground crew lacked the same intimacy as my father's. One time when he invited the whole bunch, wives and all, to a week of Super Bowl fun in Miami, we were lining up after a pre-game party to get on the bus. Kay, our kids, and Father Bob Reardon were with me. As the bus door swung open, one of the young ground-crew guys jumped ahead of us, bumping my little girl Susie out of his way. I followed him onto the bus, grabbed him by the neck, and pinioned him against a support pole. Neither of us said a word — we just looked at each other — and after a few seconds I released him.

Father Reardon, I think, was in shock. My kids were very obviously in shock. I expected AJR to castigate me. Ground-crew guys were sacred cows, and I had over-reacted. For whatever reason, he let me off the hook. I was reprimanded instead by one of the ground-crew wives. At the end of the bus ride, when we were filing into the hotel, she came up beside me and said, "You have to understand that we're people. We have little kids just like you do." It was then that I experienced full remorse. I said to myself, "You'll never be the man your father is."

The sequel to this embarrassing incident was strange. From then on, the ground-crew guys would go out of their way to say hi, and the new head man of the crew, Dirt DiNardo, made a special effort to strike up conversations. "Come around and hang out with us," he suggested. I was still too mortified to take him up on it.

One of the football players — L.C. Greenwood, I believe — gave DiNardo his moniker. Dirt was a loud, heavy-set, dark-skinned Italian, quick to speak up in any situation. AJR liked his boldness and humor, and he spent as much time with Dirt as he had with Horse Czarnecki. Once when Dad and I were returning by air from a trip to Yonkers, the stewardess asked for our drink orders. I said, "Coke." I'm a total abstainer. Dad, who had been on the wagon for years, said, "Ginger ale and Canadian Club." He then told the stewardess to bring me some Canadian Club too. When she had left us, I gave him a look. He said, "We're in first class. The booze comes with it. Always pick up the drinks." They were served in small three-ounce bottles with the seal unbroken. "Bring them home to me." For Mom and Aunt Alice, I thought he was going to explain. But no. He said, "I'll give them to Steve."

Steve? Who was this Steve, I asked.

"Steve DiNardo — Dirt. On your scouting trips, you travel all over the country. Always pick up the booze for Dirt."

Of course I complied. If I neglected to — purposely at times — more than likely I would hear from AJR.

"Did you get the whiskey for Dirt?"

One day at Three Rivers when I took a free agent onto the field for a workout, Dirt and his crew were rolling up the big, heavy tarpaulin. At one end, I noticed a little white-haired guy with a cigar in his mouth. AJR was in his seventies then, and pushing as hard as everybody else. It staggered me to see my father engaged in what could only be called manual labor.

He would sometimes watch practice from the vantage point of Dirt's tractor, contentedly smoking his cigar. The tractor had two massive wheels in back and two small ones in front, behind a power brush for removing snow from the field. Dirt's proudest moment with the tractor came on a December afternoon in 1978, when the Steelers played the Baltimore Colts in a blizzard. Ordered by the officials to keep the yard lines visible, he did just that, racing back and forth across the Tartan Turf and leaving pale green strips on the snowy surface. He worked during timeouts and he worked while the game was going on. The teams would be at one end of the field and DiNardo at the other. He was more of a threat to Baltimore's defensive backs than Terry Bradshaw was, sometimes coming within a foot or two of mowing them down. They shouted at Dirt, and Dirt shouted back. "I've got a job to do!" he let them know.

Dirt was never shy about protecting his territory. After a cold-weather playoff game with the Oakland Raiders at Three Rivers, Al Davis, the Raiders' owner, accused him of conspiring with AJR to let the Tartan Turf near the sidelines freeze. The purpose of this nefarious scheme, Davis said, was to make it difficult for the Raiders to run their sideline pass patterns.

Dirt's professional pride would not allow him to forget such an affront. The next time the Raiders came to Pittsburgh, he took his revenge. Waiting until John Madden, the Raiders' coach, had led his team onto the field for a Saturday workout, Dirt gruffly ordered them to "get the fuck off." Madden was about the size of the legendary Bigfoot and accustomed to being spoken to with a lot more civility. "Do you know who I am?" he demanded. "I don't give a fuck who you are," answered Dirt. "My men have some work to do on this field." The Raiders didn't practice that day until Dirt and his crew were finished with their chores.

Madden went to AJR for a rundown on Dirt and concluded that feuding with him would not be productive. "I'll win the guy over with kindness," he said. From then on when the Raiders played here, Madden always took time for a visit with Dirt and brought his name up frequently at press conferences, referring to him as "my good friend." Apparently it was more than just fence-mending. Years afterward, when he was a well-known member of the Monday Night Football broadcasting team, if Madden encountered someone with a Steeler connection he would ask to be remembered to Dirt.

In their game uniforms — shimmering yellow acetate shirts and white duck pants the first year at Three Rivers — the ground crew looked like a mariachi band. These outfits were provided by the Pirates. When the ground crew was actually at work they wore castoff Steeler regalia — T-shirts, old game jerseys, old warm-up jackets, discarded tassel caps. Tony Parisi and Jack Hart, the equipment managers, had instructions to be generous with the ground crew. While AJR was alive, it would not have surprised me to see them show up in Steeler helmets and knee pants.

Even the trainer's room was available to the ground crew if one of them needed first aid. Bumps and bruises went with the job, and the Steelers' trainers worked on these men as conscientiously as they attended to the players.

At least once a year, AJR would have a party for Dirt and his boys in their quarters at the stadium. He would buy the best ham for the cooks at the Allegheny Club to bake, order Jewish rye bread and New York cheesecake from a place in Squirrel Hill, and supply the booze, large quantities of it. To imagine John Galbreath doing something like this would be impossible.

For heavy-lifting chores at 940 North Lincoln Avenue, Dad would send DiNardo and some of his men to help Mom, Aunt Alice, and the maid, Mary Roseboro. I saw them in action just once — at Christmas time. Mom, impeccably dressed and ladylike, was still a North Sider, issuing crisp orders as they put up the tree. "Barry, you're tall," she would say. "Please put the star up on top ... Now, that looks just right ... Steve, don't worry about the bulbs. Mary will take care of it ..." And so on. Dirt and the others, striving to be gentlemen, kept their voices carefully subdued.

Sometimes on summer nights if AJR saw the lights on at the stadium and knew the Pirates were out of town he would hop into his car and make the short drive from North Lincoln to see what was happening. Usually Dirt and the gang were getting ready for an event of some kind — a rock concert, perhaps. Cigar in hand, AJR would watch them set up the stage. And then he might stay for the performance, looking on from the dugout with the crew. "Hey, Dirt," he might say, "what kind of music is that?" Or, "Say ... what's that sweet smell? The more I sniff it, the better the music sounds."

After AJR's death, I made a sentimental journey to my boyhood home and took ten cigars from his humidor. I gave five of them to Ralph Berlin. The other five were for Dirt DiNardo.

Chapter 66

High Noon

After the 1978 season Chuck Noll's mantra, reiterated time and again in his conversations with the press, was: "This team has not peaked." Noll said what he thought and thought what he said, but I didn't see it that way.

Granted, we were still getting stellar performances from our best players, nine of them future Hall of Famers and two others good enough to be nominated for the Hall several times. The center, Mike Webster, never seemed to age, and his career was not yet half over. Franco Harris had lost a step for sure, but was still a quick, powerful runner with the savvy derived from years of big-game experience. He was still cranking out the thousand-yard rushing seasons that would make him, next to Jim Brown, the most productive ball carrier in NFL history at the time of his retirement. Rocky Bleier had been a thousand-yard runner in 1976 and was coming off an excellent Super Bowl game. Terry Bradshaw, maturing late, had come into his own. There was never any question about his talent. As long ago as 1969 we had known what Bradshaw could do, and now he was doing it. At the other end of his passes, John Stallworth and Lynn Swann were the best receiving tandem in the NFL. The foundation of our defense, Mean Joe Greene, was showing a few cracks, but the combination of Greene, L. C. Greenwood, Dwight White, and John Banaszak gave us a truly formidable front four. In the defensive backfield, there was Mel Blount, whose disruptive pass coverage had forced a change in the rules. Blount was as good as ever - better, in fact; he had learned the principles of team defense and was playing with more discipline. Mike Wagner gave us stability at the safety position. Like Blount, and like Donnie Shell, he could rattle a pass catcher's teeth. Going on down through the roster, I could talk about Moon Mullins and Sam Davis, who had started all three of our Super Bowl games at guard; Hall-of-Fame nominees Larry Brown and Jon Kolb; backups like Ted Petersen, Steve Courson, Jimmy Smith, and Sidney Thornton.

But so many of these players were now more than 30 years old. AJR believed, as Noll did, that they hadn't peaked. I was the lone Doubting Thomas, and it made me uncomfortable. More than anything else, I wanted to be wrong. It was not that I expected our team to dry up and blow away, following the example of other Super Bowl winners in the past. I thought that, with no important changes, we could have good teams, playoff teams, or winning seasons, at least for another five years. Meanwhile, I told myself, Noll would be artfully rebuilding, piecing together his next Super Bowl team. If we could draft and develop three good players a year we would stay on track.

It sounded good. The fallacy was that three new quality starters a year would keep the machine running but not allow us to win big. To win really big, you needed three *great* new players every year, people who could not just make the good plays consistently, but make the great plays consistently – and do it in big games. It would come as a bonus that great players elevate the performance of good players – "catapult" them, Lynn Swann used to say.

As winners, we'd be drafting late. In the NFL, this was a fact of life, and not, in my opinion, an excuse for mediocrity. There were other ways, I thought, to explain the difficulty of staying on top. I knew that on the good teams the players lost their edge. Successful and well paid, they went into every game a little too complacent, taking it for granted they would win. Players on championship teams forget how they got to where they are. A scout from a great team in decline once told me that when your players show up with Wall Street Journals instead of The Sporting News tucked beneath their arms, you know you're in trouble. I wondered if the agents who hustled endorsements for their players understood that endorsements could be a pitfall. These were the things that Noll called "distractions." "We have to get back to the basics," he would say.

And draft even better than we had been, I added silently. I asked Doc Best if a football player past 30 was over the hill. He shook his head. "Naw. That idea is a lot of bunk, especially for quarterbacks. With a good training program, a guy can go on and on. But I'll tell you something that happens to those nine-and ten-year vets. Since high school, they've been taking hits; they enter the injury phase of their careers. Formerly, they would get banged up on Sunday, rest, shake it off, and be practicing again on Wednesday. But now they need more time to recover. Instead of practicing three or four days a week, they're practicing one or two days. And then before you know it they're hardly practicing at all. They play on Sunday, and that's it. There's an old saying, Artie – 'practice makes perfect.' Pretty soon those guys are missing a game here and there. Then they're missing more than just a game; they'll be out for several weeks. They're hurting like hell every day, and they don't like football any more, don't like the whole package: summer camp at St. Vincent, the practices, the meetings, the aches and pains. The money's good and the attention's good, but the price is too high. They chuck it in – or they *should* chuck it in."

Too many Steelers had reached that stage, it seemed to me, but there I disagreed with Noll, and I hoped Noll was right. My job would be to draft the way we had from 1969 through 1974 while sticking to Noll's guidelines; my scouts were to look for the kind of player Noll could motivate, the ones with football smarts and recognizable, if unrefined, athletic ability. It was easy to say, "We want the great athlete." The great athlete who had fully realized his potential was out of our reach; we were drafting at the bottom, remember. Consequently, we had to hold our mistakes to a minimum and reel in the players Noll and his assistants could teach. Noll was a football genius; with superior playing schemes, he could make us win and win big. So our work was cut out for us in the upcoming 1979 draft.

It would be more challenging, even, than I thought. Jack Butler kept urging me: "Go after guys who are tough and who play with consistency. Toughness and consistency can't be taught." In other words, leopards don't change their spots. Still, we believed that if a kid had exceptional athletic ability, coaching would bring out whatever else may have been lacking.

We continued to rely on Blesto as the base of our scouting system, but Blesto's past success was taking a toll. Too many of the scouts who had made it possible were leaving the organization for better-paying jobs with NFL teams either affiliated or unaffiliated with Blesto. Butler kept bringing in promising young scouts, molding them into the finished product, and then losing them. Blesto, nonetheless, continued to be a valuable tool for us.

I have said that pushing back the draft from late January or early February to the beginning of spring was not advantageous to the Steelers, the Rams, or the Cowboys. These were the three teams, I thought, with the most highly developed scouting systems. In my opinion, the time, money, and resources we put into scouting had given us an edge. Now the rest of the field had a chance to catch up with us. They were getting their coaches involved.

So were we, and in our case this was causing problems. Noll and his assistants were swamping us with their reports. Added to the necessity of scouting the post-season all-star games, there were meetings with Noll and his staff to attend. All of this called for substantial amounts of time – time we had previously spent on the road, on interviewing coaches, watching practices, comparing notes, picking up information. In the staff meetings, there were questions to be answered – questions from Noll and his coaches, questions, even, from AJR and Dan. Much more film had to be watched, much more information had to be processed.

In my mind, the ancient bromide that too many cooks spoil the broth was sounding more and more like a priceless bit of wisdom. I was now making judgments that were based more on other people's opinions than my own. Whether this was good or bad, I didn't like it. I was spilling out answers like the history major I had been at St. Vincent in the early 1950s. When I talked about a prospect it was not with my former fervor. I was repeating what others had told me. In the years when I was free to spend weeks on the scouting trail, weeks that began on Labor Day and kept me busy until after Thanksgiving (at the sacrifice of my family life, I'm afraid), I could speak from first-hand, personal observation.

Even so, I was ready to go to war for my beliefs. Only now I had to be temperate. I was part of a team effort. Never mind that I had no respect for the input from certain assistant coaches. "No complaining," I said to the scouts. "Let's just get the job done. We're after the best athletes we can get who are smart enough and coachable enough to pick up Noll's system."

One week Noll requisitioned Dick Haley and Dick Hoak and flew them to Texas in his private plane. For us, this was something new, a departure from our modus operandi. The reason, it seemed, was the presence at Baylor of a running back who could be the perfect fit for us. His name was Greg Hawthorne. He had the football intelligence Noll demanded. He was in every way a solid citizen. And he was the best athlete likely to be available when our turn came to draft. Here was a player who just might be one of the great ones we would need very soon as replacements for worn-out parts.

Hawthorne stood 6-2 1/2 and weighed 218 pounds. He was fast – a sprinter on Baylor's track team. With his fleetness of foot, he could get outside on sweeps; with his size, he could go up the middle and move the pile. One thing kept him from being an early first-round pick: a chipped bone in his hip. Because of it, he had missed a large portion of the 1978 season. Noll was flying to Waco with Haley and Hoak to see for himself how serious the injury might be.

Auditioning in T-shirt and shorts for this jury of three, Hawthorne was impressive. He demonstrated running ability and catching ability. He ran flawless pass routes. Hawthorne was a lad who excelled in the world of drills. The game films we studied – films, for the most part, from 1977, his last full season – revealed that he could make good plays with consistency and great plays every so often. Will Walls used to say, "If a guy can do it once, he can do it all the time." I had decided that this was malarkey, but now we all seemed to be falling for it, especially Noll. Woody Widenhofer argued that except for Hawthorne's hip he would be a high first-round choice. Well, we all make misjudgments.

The trouble was that Hawthorne was only the forerunner. For the next few years, drafting late, we'd be taking flashy kids who were not consistent when we might have helped ourselves more in the first and second rounds. Noll had always wanted a running back with the speed to get off tackle, the size to hit for the tough yardage inside, and the hands to catch all kinds of passes. He wanted a running back who could beat the strong safety in man-to-man coverage, and Hawthorne appeared to be the guy. He appeared to be a mixture of Paul Hornung and Frank Gifford.

Noll had seen all these things in Preston Pearson, and when Pearson was with the Steelers he lived up to expectations but not consistently. Pearson seemed to think that blocking for Franco Harris was somebody else's job – Rocky Bleier's, to be precise – and there were too many times when he failed to hang onto the ball. His shortcomings made him expendable, and after the 1974 season we shipped him to Dallas, where he did quite well, becoming a good, productive player on a championship team. Noll may have come to believe that he had given up on Pearson too soon; if so he never admitted it. And yet I'd swear he was hopeful that in Hawthorne we'd be getting another Pearson. This would undo the mistake he may have feared we had made.

All right, I'm speculating; in any case, Hawthorne was the first player we drafted. I didn't argue. In the second round we took a linebacker from North Carolina State. Purely as an athlete, Zack Valentine resembled the "perfect" linebacker, Jack Ham. And we thought he might grow into a pass rusher on the order of Dwight White. Could be a real good one, we assured one another. *Should* be a real good one. We were wrong.

Our third-round pick was the one the so-called shoulder-pad incident – a violation of a widely disregarded rule — had cost us. The shoulder-pad incident will be fully explained as we move along. Suffice it to say for now that we had put the whole thing behind us. Certain sportswriters guessed that the penalty imposed by the NFL kept us from taking, as our third-round choice, Joe Montana. Montana was a Western Pennsylvania kid who had quarterbacked Notre Dame. He threw a soft short and medium-range pass that was very accurate and very easy to catch. It was also easy to intercept. Dick Haley had him pegged as a third-round selection, but I must tell you again that we were drafting last. When the Steelers' turn came in the third round, Montana was long gone. The Forty-Niners had taken him.

Why, then, hadn't we moved the guy up to the second round? Because we didn't have him rated that high. Neither, may I point out, did the Forty-Niners or any other team. At Notre Dame, Montana had been the quarterback who came off the bench. The Notre Dame alumnus who recruited him was Fritz Wilson, Jack McGinley's partner in the beer business; Carl Hughes remembered that every week during the football season, Wilson would get a call from Montana's mother. "Why isn't Joe playing?" she would ask. Sure, Montana's in the Hall of Fame now, but in 1979 this was largely unforeseeable.

With our two fourth-round picks, we went for Russell Davis, a fullback from Michigan who had size, strength, and willingness, and Calvin Sweeney, a fast wide receiver from USC who made the difficult catches look easy. In that respect, he was similar to Lynn Swann. Unlike Swann, he also made the easy catches look difficult. Sweeney gave us one good year out of eight with the team. Davis, envisioned as a replacement for Rocky Bleier, lasted four years but never came close to taking over the role. During much of that time, he was on the injured reserve list.

Rounds five through twelve yielded just two players who were helpful to us – Dwayne Woodruff, defensive back from Louisville, and placekicker Matt Bahr from Penn State. Woodruff became a longtime starter who was our MVP one season. In later life he practiced law, ending up as a judge. Bahr replaced Roy Gerela, whose performance had deteriorated with age. Bahr's kickoffs left something to be desired, but he converted field-goal opportunities from forty yards or less with great accuracy. As long as we had Bahr, we could almost count on getting three points whenever our still tenacious defense forced turnovers or punts in enemy territory.

Along with Zack Valentine, two other rookies hung around for one season. They were linebacker Tom Graves of Michigan State, an eighth-round pick, and running back Anthony Anderson of Temple. The 1979 team won another Super Bowl championship, and these three supernumeraries were part of it. They had their big winner's bonuses, their Super Bowl rings, and a wealth of recollections to share with friends and family for the rest of their lives.

Greg Hawthorne played five years for the Steelers but reminded no one of Paul Hornung or Frank Gifford. For that matter, he did not even resemble the Preston Pearson who disappointed us in Pittsburgh, let alone the Preston Pearson who played so much better for Dallas. His story was the same as it had been at Baylor: too many injuries, not enough consistency. Taking him off our hands, the Patriots thought he could be a tight end; the experiment lasted until 1989 with only moderate success. AJR had taken a liking to Hawthorne and wrote a letter of recommendation to the Sullivans, the Patriots' owners. Learning of it, Hawthorne from then on was one of the Chief's worshippers, an ever-growing multitude.

Calvin Sweeney led the Steelers in receptions one year. Sweeney and Hawthorne were great guys but not great football players. We got rid of the likable Bahr, after just two seasons, because of a rap pinned onto him by one of Noll's assistants: "He's killing us with those short kickoffs." Bahr's subsequent NFL career went on for another sixteen years. His older brother Chris, also a kicker, played for fourteen years.

We failed to achieve our goal of drafting three new starters every year, three new starters who could play for a winning team. In my time with the Steelers, we never again drafted a Hall-of-Fame player. We had some very good players, such as Louis Lipps, wide receiver from Mississippi Southern, but no catapults, to borrow Lynn Swann's figure of speech. Gabe Rivera, the defensive tackle we drafted out of Texas Tech in 1983, might have been such a player, but an automobile accident in his rookie season left him permanently crippled. Other than Lipps and Rivera, our first-round picks over the seven years after 1979 were either average players or not even that. There were top-level performers on those teams of the 1980s, but not enough of them to put us into a Super Bowl.

Nineteen seventy-nine was to be our last hurrah during the reign of Chuck Noll, but a cherished last hurrah that continues to resonate.

Sidney

Running backs don't last long in the NFL. Wear and tear comes with the job. It is doubly burdensome to be a running back who blocks when he doesn't have the ball, and by 1977 Rocky Bleier's exertions were beginning to tell.

Bleier's history was well known: Drafted out of Notre Dame in 1968. His rookie season cut short by a call from the draft board in Appleton, Wisconsin. Horribly shot up in Vietnam. More than two years of arduous rehabilitation. His unlikely return to the Steelers, detailed so well in "Fighting Back," a blockbuster autobiography. He had not reached the end of the line, but it behooved us to look ahead. Sidney Thornton, our second-round draft pick from Northwestern Louisiana, was the running back we hoped would be his successor.

Chuck Noll worked him into the lineup gradually. Filling in at first for Franco Harris now and then, he did not do badly at all. He would block, or perhaps I should say at times he would block. He could hit the line hard and break a tackle. He made some big runs — when he found the right hole. On the debit side, he was too much inclined to fumble.

There were other things we learned about Sidney. "He's not the sharpest knife in the drawer," I'd been warned. But on a ninety-minute flight from Louisiana to Pittsburgh, he conversed with me quite sensibly. When I reported this to Dick Haley, he laughed and said, "Art, you could talk to anyone that long." Any good listener, I think Haley meant.

"Let's see if he has football smarts," Haley added. Well, Thornton did have football smarts — sort of. What he also had was a propensity to get hurt and to pick up avoidable illnesses. For example, food poisoning once caused him to miss a stretch of games.

"What did you eat?" Ralph Berlin demanded.

"Oh, just some pizza. I had it in the ice box."

Berlin couldn't see any harm in eating a little reheated pizza. As an afterthought, he asked, "How long was it in the refrigerator?"

"About three weeks" said Thornton, clearing up the mystery.

Sidney always seemed to have a sprained ankle; for big running backs, sprained ankles can take a long time to heal. In desperation, he consulted a voodooist from the bayous of his home state. The witch doctor was an old woman. She concocted an emollient for Sidney to use, its main ingredient being human urine. Whether Sidney applied the stuff to his ankle was something I never wanted to know.

It was Sidney of whom Chuck Noll aptly declared, "His problems are great, and they are many."

Mr. Peepers

Between the end of one football season and the start of another, coaches have too much time on their hands. In the way that nature does, Coach Noll abhorred a vacuum, and he filled the empty days with sessions like the one he instituted in the spring of 1970, he invited (read: ordered) all the rookies and free agents, together with the quarterbacks, the players who had been on the injured reserve list during the previous season, and the players whose chances of making the team were in question, to an "indoctrination period" at Three Rivers Stadium. For the better part of a week, the rookies and free agents would acquaint themselves with our offensive and defensive schemes, the quarterbacks and bubble players would learn the new plays Noll intended to put in, and the injured reservists would undergo conditioning tests.

Noll was always in search of a "good picture," as he put it, and this, he believed, would provide one, but not if all of these guys were simply "running around in their underwear" — i.e., wearing T-shirts and shorts instead of football gear. Inconveniently, NFL rules prohibited any kind of equipment at these mini-camps except helmets. The idea was to discourage contact, which league rules also prohibited. In Noll's mind, the regulations made no sense. To put twenty or thirty football players on a football field and expect them to refrain from bumping into one another was unrealistic. On his own, he decided to stretch the rules and allow them to wear shoulder pads. Pittsburgh was not the only team to hold a mini-camp in the spring, and most of the others ignored the shoulder-pad rule, so why not the Steelers? With helmets and shoulder pads, the players would feel protected, Noll reasoned. They would move faster, show off their skills to better effect.

In the spring of 1979, I watched the first day's workout with Dick Haley and Bill Nunn. As we were leaving the field, I said to Haley, casually, "Of course, we're breaking a rule with the shoulder pads." All of us knew this. All of us knew that other teams broke the rule. And all of us felt, as Noll did, that we could not let these others get the jump on us, regardless of how trivial the advantage might be.

Admittedly, a rule is a rule. But the NFL, it seemed to me, had been turning a blind eye to the rule against shoulder pads. Don't ask, don't tell. So I did not think our rule-breaking was anything really scandalous.

I was at the Blesto meeting in Florida with my fellow scouts when I heard about the controversy that erupted. A young reporter from the *Pittsburgh Press*, John Clayton, had been present at one of the "indoctrination" workouts — or perhaps he had merely caught a glimpse of the players on their way from the locker room to the field. At any rate, he started to ask questions. Was there not a league rule against shoulder pads? There was? Then why were the players wearing them? Because other teams did it? To find out what the official attitude was — like Noll, he wanted a "good picture" — Clayton put in a call to the commissioner's office in New York, and the fat was in the fire. Once notified that the Steelers were wearing shoulder pads, the commissioner's office would have to take steps.

I think that in 1979, Dan, Noll, and I regarded sportswriters who came to practice as our "guests." What was seen there was to be kept there, we thought. Later on, I realized how immature that notion is. When I was sounding off on the subject, Bill Nunn said to me, "Art, I was a newspaperman myself. Newspapermen have a job to do, just like coaches and scouts. The people connected with the team may be their friends in a way, but you can only protect your friends up to a point. Then you're risking your own job, because if you sit on a story as a favor to the owners or the coaches or the players, somebody else on some other paper will report it."

AJR either had already learned this or knew it instinctively. He would tell me, "Don't talk to the press. You don't have a knack for it, like I do. All you're going to do is get in trouble." I think he was mostly right, but partly wrong. Talking freely to the press has hurt me in some ways and helped me in others. Wherever the truth lay, I resented the implication that I was "brand new," a slur I'd been hearing from AJR all my life.

Noll and Dan, aware that Clayton was going to write a shoulder-pad story, attempted damage control. If the story got into print, there'd be "hell to pay." The NFL would have no choice but to impose the proscribed penalty – a fine and the loss of a draft choice. Indirectly, through Pat Livingston, they contacted the editor of the *Press*, John Troan. Troan was a Steeler fan. He was immensely fond of AJR. He respected Noll and Dan. But he stood behind his reporter. The story would appear in the next day's *Press*. "If it's a bad rule," he suggested, "then the NFL ought to change it."

Not long afterward, we were fined — I don't recall the amount — and deprived of our third-round choice in the 1979 draft. I was furious. I did not blame Noll, I blamed Clayton. An outsider, a newspaper guy, was impeding my effort to keep our team on top through the draft.

The story and its repercussions turned a spotlight on Clayton. Outraged Steeler fans attacked him for his perfidy. So did a majority of the radio and television sportscasters. The newspaper guys all defended him: he had handled the situation in a fearless, professional manner.

I had known John Clayton a long time. As a high school kid, he covered our pre-season training camp for one of those shopping center "green sheets." It wasn't much of a paper, but Clayton obtained access to the practice field and locker room. His mother, I remembered, drove him to St.

Vincent every day. If the perception that he was still a mama's boy embarrassed him, he gave no hint of it, and his *sang froid* impressed me. I was even more impressed by the willingness of his mother to encourage his ambition.

Nothing about Clayton's looks was impressive. A pipsqueak, he was short and thin. He wore glasses. He was nerdy-looking, a youthful Mr. Peepers. I imagined him as the smartest kid in his class at school. He was always respectful and asked intelligent questions. After graduation from Duquesne University — his choice of a college gave him a leg up with the Rooneys — he landed a job at the *Press*. Over time, I found out that I had underestimated this guy.

The *Press* underestimated him, too. Taken off the Steeler beat after Troan had retired and Russ Brown had succeeded Livingston as sports editor, Clayton moved on to a newspaper in Tacoma, Washington, and became a stringer on the side for the cable television network ESPN. He had a face made for radio, as they say, but established himself in just a few years as ESPN's most knowledgeable pro football correspondent. Nobody else in his field was breaking more big stories than Clayton, whose competence has earned him a place in the writers' wing of professional football's Hall of Fame.

From the shoulder-pad incident, I learned the truth of something AJR had observed — that newspaper and radio-TV reporters no longer conformed to the Jack Sell-Joe Tucker-Pat Livingston mold. Among the newer breed, the competition was fierce. No longer did anyone worry that something in the paper might make us look bad. It was "out of my way or a leg off." If the reporters smelled a story we wanted to cover up, they'd "gang up on us — operate in packs," I heard Dan complain.

"They'll ask the trainer a question about an injury the coach would rather conceal from our next opponent. Ralph Berlin will throw them a bone. He'll say just enough to get off the hook. What they do then is take the little bit of information Berlin has given them to Tony Parisi. 'Player A has a knee problem. will he suit up for practice?' Tony, he figures they already know how bad the guy's knee is. So he tells them, 'I can't say much, but no — the player won't dress.' Then with that information they go to Dick Haley. 'We hear that this guy has a bad knee. Won't dress. Might need surgery.' Haley thinks they know the whole story, so he confirms it. The only thing I'm saying is: be careful. They're tricking us into giving them stories we don't want in the paper."

Dan's new rules cramped my style. In dealing with reporters I tended to say more than I should. Wariness wasn't my strong suit. It would be better, I decided, if I simply kept my mouth shut, never the easiest thing for me to do.

My anger at John Clayton subsided when I saw that AJR was treating him like an old and trusted friend. I followed the Chief's lead and became very comfortable with Clayton. Meanwhile, though, deep inside, a little voice told me to watch my step. Clayton's agenda was different from mine, after all, and I don't think I ever forgot it.

At the draft meeting that year, we referred to the pick we didn't have in the third round with a mixture of ruefulness and humor. There were those who called it the shoulder-pad pick and still others who called it the John Clayton pick.

'A Great American Sportsman'

Even before our third Super Bowl victory, AJR was everlastingly in demand for speeches and public appearances. He liked the attention but pretended not to. His "speeches" rarely lasted more than three minutes. He knew how to get to the point quickly and he knew how to infuse his remarks with humor in perfect taste.

Sometimes it seemed that he lived to accept honors and awards. He was constantly being asked to attend some banquet or luncheon, if only to stand and take a bow. Invitations came from civic organizations, social organizations, fraternal organizations, and athletic organizations. The Catholic Youth Association sold one thousand tickets every year to an awards banquet called the Art Rooney Dinner. Even today, with the name unchanged, it's the CYA's biggest money-maker.

AJR was at the same time gregarious and shy. He overcame what I think was a natural reticence by seeming genuinely interested in everybody he met. After his rise in the public eye to a level just short of deification, the mere sight of him could overawe the unsophisticated — young football players, young sportswriters and broadcasters, many ordinary people aware of his status as a legend.

Then he would show, with the ease of a skilled actor, his unpretentious side. "How are ya?" he would say. "What's your name? Where ya from?"

Displayed to strangers familiar with the name but not the image — strangers who never had seen the man on television or pictured in a newspaper — this unaffected informality was sometimes confusing. At Three Rivers Stadium, AJR had a habit of leaving his office and wandering around sort of aimlessly, his arms behind his back, a cigar in the corner of his mouth. More often than not he'd be wearing a dark cashmere polo shirt with a necktie. The polo shirt would have a pocket in it for his matches and hearing aid. He was in the lobby one day, emptying an ash tray, when a brand new Steeler rookie walked through the door. The player didn't recognize AJR. He was there to see Dan, or maybe Chuck Noll, and asked for directions. AJR, after telling him where to go, detained the kid briefly for the usual interrogation – "What's your name? Where ya from?" and so on. Later, when the rookie was told he'd been greeted by Art Rooney, he exclaimed, "My God! I thought I was talking to the janitor!"

AJR would not have been offended by this. Still, there was something in his demeanor that commanded the utmost respect. Old friends addressed him as "Art," new friends and everybody else as "Mister Rooney." Just once did I hear him called, to his face, "Chief." A newly-employed secretary committed that indiscretion. She never repeated it.

The polo shirt with the inappropriate necktie was my Dad's only sartorial eccentricity. On formal occasions, he wore a necktie that never called attention to itself with a well-fitted white dress shirt and a conservative dark suit. His pants were always creased, his shoes were always shined, and he was always neatly barbered. Kass, his superintendent in such matters, saw to that. Once when my wife happened to read a description of me as "an overweight man who has little regard for grooming," she took me to task. "Where did you come from?" she demanded. "You look too much like your father to be a bastard. There's a missing gene in you — the grooming gene!"

If Fran Fogarty had been the watchdog of AJR's purse, Mary Regan and Ed Kiely were the guardians of his time. Given free rein, their boss was accessible to everybody, from bankers and cardinals and high-ranking politicians all the way down to street beggars. In the absence of Mary Regan, anybody known or unknown could walk right into his office. Mary Regan — Patricia Rooney's sister— converted her desk into a checkpoint.

Mary was a good-looking redhead. Politely or tartly, depending on the circumstances — depending, sometimes, on her mood — she turned away bores, pests, and callers who lacked the proper credentials. Her standards of admission were rigorous, and only AJR could change the red light to green. Peering out from his office while a disappointed visitor pleaded for a hearing, he would give the nod, the safe-conduct, the sign of approval: "He's OK, Mary, he's OK." Usually, though, Mary Regan's word was law. "Sometimes I don't know if Mary works for me or if I work for her," AJR used to say.

Ed Kiely found his proper niche as the Chief's indispensable alter ego after Joe Gordon took over the public-relations job in 1969. Ed liked to deal with the upper echelon; responding to the needs and demands of the media was never one of his strengths. During the last ten years of AJR's life, Kiely was often his stand-in, chauffeur, and traveling companion. "We were more like friends than anything else," Kiely told a reporter a long time afterwards. "He was still the boss, but we had grown really close. His kids said I was like part of the family" That was correct. Kiely knew the Chief's mind and in certain situations could speak for him. The Chief was therefore enabled to pace himself. Once he had reached his late seventies, the celebrity whirl became exhausting, but it pained him to refuse invitations. Using Kiely as a surrogate lessened the guilt he invariably felt.

He was still making decisions on issues connected with the football team and the horse-racing business. When it came to horse racing, my brother Tim was a big help. In addition to running Yonkers, he supervised Shamrock Farm. AJR was breeding and raising standardbreds as well as thoroughbreds there. He would sometimes describe Tim as an "ignoramus," but proudly relate, in the next breath, that son number three had made and given to charity thousands upon thousands of dollars.

My own relations with the Chief were not as close as Tim's or Dan's and not as contentious as Tim's. In that respect, I felt like Ensign Pulver, the lowest ranking officer on the World War II Navy tub created by author Tom Heggen as the setting for his novel "Mr. Roberts," which became a Broadway play and then a Hollywood movie. Ensign Pulver tried very hard to avoid being noticed by the captain of the ship; in the same way, I wanted as little as possible to do with the Chief.

And yet at times, when we traveled together, I thought we achieved a kind of intimacy. He entrusted me with two of his possessions, and I treasure them. One was a limited-edition copy of Richard Nixon's autobiography, numbered and inscribed to "Art Rooney, a great American sportsman." Admittedly, Richard Nixon had his flaws, but he was a twice-elected president of the U.S.A. My other prized memento is a key to the city of San Francisco, presented to the Chief by Dianne Feinstein, San Francisco's mayor at the time and later a U.S. senator.

When he was alive I wondered often what AJR thought of me, and I wonder what he would think of me now.

Distractions

Chuck Noll hated distractions. They caused his football players to lose focus, which caused them to lose concentration. And without concentration the learning environment was in jeopardy.

Distractions came with success, and distractions were the enemy. After the Steelers' third Super Bowl win, Joe Greene and Terry Bradshaw had bit parts in movies. A distraction. These two and other marquee players — Swann, Stallworth, Lambert, Ham, and Blount — were getting offers to endorse commercial products on television. A distraction. Less publicized players, including part-time starters and special-team guys, were making paid appearances in the Tri-State area. A distraction. Loaner cars and golf outings were suddenly available for everybody: assistant coaches, trainers ... all the way down the pecking order. Another distraction.

Media guys were almost as worrisome as the advertising people. They hounded anyone with the team who would talk to them — even me. I was one of their favorites, in fact, because I said things. My attitude was that we had nothing to hide. And, besides, publicity was an agent of the NFL's popularity. It made no difference. The Chief, Noll, and Dan considered me a blabbermouth. Even some of the media guys wondered if I knew what I was doing. "You're so candid," one of them told me. A friend with my best interests at heart said, "Hey, you don't owe those reporters anything. Be more circumspect." So I was a big distraction, too.

I've told you how AJR seemed to welcome certain distractions (although not the one he attributed to me) and how Kiely and Mary Regan protected him from them. They grew concerned about the infirmities that come with the years. The Chief had some health problems (eyes, ears, gall bladder), but professed to be in "pretty good shape." Physically and mentally, he was better than pretty good. It would have angered the Chief to know that people who worked for him thought that he had to be watched over. His astuteness in all matters personal was unimpaired. Let me give you an example: The distillers of Smirnoff vodka had a proposition they brought to Ed Kiely. They wanted a distinguished looking older man with a recognizable name to appear in a magazine ad pushing their brand of booze, and AJR was made to order for the part. All he had to do was pose for one of America's leading photographers and be well recompensed. A sum in five figures was mentioned.

I think he felt honored — or maybe just amazed. "But I don't drink — haven't for years," he reminded Kiely. "I don't really approve of drinking. You know that. I'd be a real hypocrite, doing this."

So Kiely told the ad men, No sale.

Ask him to reconsider, they answered. "We'll give all the money to any charity of his choosing."

The Chief was tempted, but wouldn't budge.

Of course, Kass looked after him as much as she could. He made an effort to attend the horse owners' and dog owners' conventions, viewing it as part of his job, and Kass would go along to make sure that he took his medications and always had clean shirts to put on. Her own health, I'm afraid, was something we tended to forget about.

Chapter 67

Last Hurrah

On the St. Vincent practice field in the rainy, sweltering summer of 1979, the heat would build up all through the day, creating a mist that obscured the Chestnut Ridge of the Allegheny Mountains off to the east. Then the wind would start blowing and the thunder would crackle. The thunder reminded me of the artillery exercises at Camp Lejeune, but the Emperor, Chuck Noll, made light of it. "Thunder never hurt anyone," he would say. I'd been hearing that from Noll for ten years. Lightning was a different story. Even Chuck Noll feared lightning. With thunder came lightning and rain, and then the crowds on the hillsides would scramble for safety and Noll would lead the charge to the Kennedy Hall gym, where his players took refuge from the wicked atmospherics.

Sometimes it rained or drizzled for two or three days without a break. Then the fields so carefully tended by Benedictine Brother Pat Lacey would turn to mud, causing Noll and his assistants distress. Time was short, and you couldn't practice in such conditions. Buff Boston would canvass the area high schools in search of a dry field. If none could be found, Noll would herd his players into the St. Vincent gym. Looking ahead to the regular season, he foresaw difficulties but remained unshakeable in his conviction that even with twenty-two Steelers above the age of 30 the team had not peaked.

New rules designed to protect the quarterback would help rather than hurt, Noll thought. Despite the changes of a few years before, designed to protect pass receivers, the defense had caught up with the offense. The NFL was now a television league, and the millions of fans who watched from their living rooms preferred high-scoring games to the knock-'em-down, drag-'em-out trench warfare of professional football's formative years. The quarterback was the star of the show; to keep him on the field, the rule-makers imposed penalties for late hits, penalties for spearing, penalties for blows to the head. Disgustedly, Jack Lambert grumbled that quarterbacks ought to wear dresses. He was too young to remember Charley Seabright, the quarterback in Jock Sutherland's single wing. Seabright was just a glorified pulling guard; all he did was call the signals and block. Well, Noll had Terry Bradshaw, who could throw the ball a mile. With Bradshaw feeling safe in the pocket, how many passes would Lynn Swann and John Stallworth and Jimmy Smith and Ben Cunningham be able to haul in?

One of Bradshaw's idiosyncrasies — his latest — bothered Noll. Bradshaw had taken up country western singing. He was more than raw, but I liked his stage persona. Having been exposed to the theater in my youth, I saw that he had a talent for self-abasement. Right: self-abasement. He could laugh at himself, which tends to draw laughs from the audience. I thought the critics who said "Boy, does he stink" were missing something.

Lynn Swann's aborted career as a ballet dancer never had been an issue, but now he was missing practice for a reason that forced even Noll to hold his tongue. He was suing the San Francisco Police Department for racial harassment. A few years previously, with his brother and some friends, he'd been accosted by the police without provocation, he charged. The case had come to trial, and no one was saying that Swann should be in Latrobe. He remained on the West Coast to testify — persuasively, it seemed, for the verdict went against the cops. In his absence I expected some of our young wide receivers to strut their stuff, just as Swann himself had done as a rookie in 1974 when the veterans went on strike and skipped the first few weeks of the pre-season. I was disappointed. Nobody came to the fore.

Center-guard-tackle Ray Pinney, a bright light in the offensive line, suffered complications after an appendicitis operation and was lost for the season, but there were no other ailments or injuries of any real consequence and, despite the wet weather, the team left St. Vincent pretty well prepared for the season.

Everybody said it had been a hard-hitting camp. Compared with Sutherland's camps, and John Michelosen's and Bill Austin's, it had been a walk in the park. Noll was a coach who believed that pre-season camp should be a learning experience. He kept his players constantly on the move, but nothing was left on the practice field, as in Sutherland's day, or Michelosen's or Austin's. After all these years, the players were sold on Noll's system. It was tested and successful. His veterans were experts at putting his schemes into practice; in addition to being great athletes, they were artists at the game of football, pliable and smart.

Twenty-two veterans — the over-thirties, for the most part — had played in the 1974 Super Bowl, and they were not yet ready for the ash heap. I would like to mention also that everybody on the roster was home grown, which gave me a lot of personal satisfaction. Not one of these players in his pro career ever had worn a jersey other than Steeler black and gold. To the best of my knowledge, this had never happened before in the NFL. Nor has it happened since, I think it is safe to say.

Our pre-season record was 3-1. We took the measure of the Bills, Jets, and Giants (thereby winning the championship of New York state) before losing by two points to the Cowboys. Our first-round draft choice, Greg Hawthorne, came to life against the Giants; at a critical moment he made a spectacular catch. "See? See?" I exclaimed to our scouts. "He has what it takes." Again, I had made a bad guess.

We won our first four regular-season games. Three of the four were what AJR and the sportswriters called cliffhangers. The other, versus the Oilers in Houston, was a romp. During the 1979 season the Steelers played seven close games and won five of them. Great teams with great players could rise to the occasion.

Houston had replaced the Oakland Raiders as our designated bitterest rival, but there was nothing like enmity between the Oilers and the Steelers. In 1977, after a win by the Oilers over one of our division opponents had put us into the playoffs, every Steeler chipped in to buy every Houston player a handsome briefcase. Our games with the Oilers were hard-hitting but relatively clean. There may have been more rough stuff, actually, in our loss that year to the Eagles, one of four regular-season defeats. The first four times we got the ball we gave it back on fumbles, and Philadelphia won by the margin of a field goal.

Our 12-4 record did not impress a segment of Steeler fans, who asked what had become of Noll's aerial circus. Bradshaw was still completing passes, but not with as much regularity as in 1978. What did the fans want? I asked Nunn. How we won and by how many points never concerned me. As Al Davis used to say, "Just win, baby, just win." And in 1979 we won when it mattered.

The loss to the Eagles came in our fifth game. It was a setback Noll blamed on mistakes and injuries. Recovering, we proceeded to blow out Cleveland, 51-35, but in Cincinnati the next week there came a relapse. Nine Steeler turnovers added up to a 34-10 embarrassment. For the second time in three weeks, the offense had disappeared, and AJR joined the multitude wanting to know why. Earlier in the season he had questioned Noll's game plan. "Chuck will establish the run if it kills us," he grumbled to a crony in his private box. After the Cincinnati debacle, he said the Steelers had become a "herky-jerky" team, alternating good games with bad games. Then they went out and won their next four.

The aerial circus was back against Denver, with death-defying catches by Stallworth, Swann, and Smith. Bradshaw that day passed for more than three hundred yards in a 42-7 victory. Dallas, the team we had beaten in Super Bowl XIII the previous January, was in Pittsburgh the following week, and the Steelers came out on top in an epic defensive struggle, 14-3.

One week after that, the offense was reasserting itself when Bradshaw took a blow to the head and had to be pulled from the game with Washington — through for the day, it appeared. Shortly afterward, the Redskins fumbled on their own four-yard line and Pittsburgh recovered. Off the bench, where he'd been attended to, hustled Bradshaw. He threw a touchdown pass to Randy Grossman, and the Steelers were back in overdrive. At halftime their lead was 27-7. In the locker room during the intermission, Bradshaw's eyes were glazed, but Noll sent him out for the second half, in which the Steelers outscored the Redskins 14-0.

"I want a tough quarterback," Noll used to say, and in Bradshaw, he most certainly had one. Mike Webster, I understand, called every play for Bradshaw from the second quarter on. In thirty-two minutes of action, Bradshaw passed for 311 yards and four touchdowns, and I doubt if he remembered doing it.

His head was clear enough in our game the next week in Kansas City. We won it easily, 30-3. Bradshaw passed for three touchdowns, and Sidney Thornton, a.k.a The Bull, broke off some big runs as the backup to Bleier and Harris. Thornton's career would eventually fall apart, but in 1979 he answered our needs.

Military historians say an army is no better than its reserve strength, and this was a year in which the Steelers had to call upon every available man. It became difficult, because of injuries, to keep our Super Bowl warriors on the field at the same time. We were thinnest in the offensive line, where the battle-hardened Old Guard was showing signs of erosion. The Old Guard included old guards — aging ones, anyway; younger guards — Ted Petersen and Steve Courson — were fast acquiring game experience. "Make good things happen" was Noll's oft-repeated battle cry; young linebackers Robin Cole and Dirt Winston were making things happen, and so was Tom Beasley, a backup who played tackle or end. Like Petersen and Courson, all three had been drafted in 1977 or 1978. J.T. Thomas, who played a lot of safety and wing that year off the bench, was of a slightly earlier vintage.

Going into the San Diego game out West, the Steelers' passing attack looked unstoppable. San Diego stopped it, and stopped the run, too. The Chargers had our offense well scouted. Instead of moving up their defensive backs to deal with Harris, Bleier, and Thornton, they dropped them even deeper than usual and intercepted Bradshaw five times. Their own offense, meanwhile, tore the Steel Curtain apart in a 35-7 stunner.

A humbled Pittsburgh team was back in Three Rivers Stadium the next week to play the Browns, who never had won there and came to town with blood in their eyes. Although he was sacked seven times and had L. C. Greenwood putting pressure on him all afternoon, Brian Sipe, an underrated quarterback, kept the Browns in front most of the way. When the score was 20-6 and later 30-20 the Steelers seemed to be out of it. But great players will find a way to win. Greenwood, Joe Greene, and Jack Lambert never let up. Franco Harris, taking hit after hit, gained 151 yards on the ground, all in short chunks, caught nine passes for an additional eighty-one yards, and scored three touchdowns. Steve Furness, the extra man in the front four, had the best day of his career up to then. But three-point plays were the difference. Near the end of the fourth quarter, rookie Matt Bahr tied the score with a field goal and near the end of the fifteen-minute overtime he kicked the game-winner, his third of the season.

This was a game that had everything, not excepting great defense in spite of the 33-30 score. Pat Livingston, who'd been covering the Steelers for thirty years, expressed amazement at the behavior of the normally raucous, Terrible Towel-twirling crowd: as the suspense intensified in regulation time and then in overtime, a hush came over the stadium. When the final gun sounded, Lambert threw his arms around Bahr and hoisted him into the air. Bahr didn't weigh much, even for a kicker, but it was all Lambert could do to lift him up. Lambert, Greenwood, Greene, and Harris had played themselves into exhaustion, and 35-year-old Sam Davis said he felt like a zombie. George Perles was drained just from watching. I was worn out myself, voiceless and happy and dazed. Leading Houston by one game in the Central Division, we were ready now for the stretch run.

The hangover all of us thought was coming did not materialize. Before another home crowd the next week, the Steelers got even with Cincinnati, 37-17. Lynn Swann's five catches were good for 192 yards and a pair of touchdowns. Then it was on to Houston. The Oilers had to beat us to stay in the race, and they did, 20-17. For the first time in his life, the great Earl Campbell battered our defense, rushing for 100 yards. The Houston people — owner, management, coaches, and players — celebrated the outcome in Super Bowl style. From several different sources, I heard the locker-room scene was something out of a Cecil B. DeMille spectacle.

But the season wasn't over. One week later, at Three Rivers Stadium, a 28-0 whacking of Buffalo gave us our sixth straight division title. Houston, with an 11-5 record, got into the playoffs as a wild card. The home-field advantage, though, would be ours.

We'd be playing without Jack Ham, whose season ended in the Buffalo game when an ankle injury put him out of commission. Jack Ham, it was generally agreed, did not have a weakness as a linebacker. He would play three more years but never again at the same high level of proficiency. Filling in for him, Robin Cole and Dirt Winston helped to shut down the Bills. Our defense forced them to punt ten times, an NFL record, and their total yardage for the game was not quite the length of a football field. When it came to giving up yardage, the Steelers that year were the stingiest team in the American Conference.

Ten of our players made the Pro Bowl, seven were named to the all-NFL team, and Franco Harris had his seventh straight thousand-yard season, tying Jim Brown's record. Had the Steelers finally peaked? As a matter of fact, we were on the way down, but there was still another Super Bowl to be won.

Over the Hump

On the last day of 1972, at Three Rivers Stadium, Chuck Noll's first Steeler playoff team had lost to the Miami Dolphins in the AFC championship game, 21-17. The Dolphins were coached by Don Shula, the man who had hired Noll to be an assistant on the coaching staff of the Baltimore Colts and later recommended him to AJR when we were looking for a successor to Bill Austin. Noll's young team gave the Dolphins all they could handle, but Miami was on its way to a 17-0 season climaxed by a Super Bowl victory and came up with the big plays.

Now the situation was different. After seven years, almost to the day, Shula's current Dolphins would be the Steelers' first opponent in the 1979 playoffs, and this time the edge in experience and skill belonged to Pittsburgh. The pupil had a great team, the teacher merely a good one. Fog enshrouded Three Rivers Stadium at the kickoff; by the time it lifted, at the end of the first quarter, the issue was decided. With Stallworth and Swann catching touchdown passes from Bradshaw, Pittsburgh had the lead, 20-0. From then on the Dolphins held their own, but the final score, 34-14, correctly measured the disparity between the two teams.

Except for a missed extra point by Matt Bahr, the Steelers came close to playing mistake-free football. Said the normally low-keyed Noll: "We were outstanding in all areas of play." He did not exaggerate. The Dolphins, according to their coach, were overmatched. "We never challenged them," Shula conceded. "They totally dominated us." The Steelers, he said, were "the best team of the 1970s." He was taking the whole decade into account and not admitting that his 1972 Dolphins were inferior to any single championship team of Noll's.

"Everywhere we looked," a Miami player said to Bob Milie, the Steelers' assistant trainer, "we saw future Hall of Famers." With so many of our future Hall of Famers hurt, I was pleased, as a scout, to see our recent draftees perform well. On the Steelers' first-quarter touchdown drives of sixty-two, sixty-two, and fifty yards, Steve Courson was a terror getting out on sweeps and traps. And Sidney Thornton, with the help of a killer block by veteran guard Sam Davis, pounded the ball across for one of our scores.

It was amazing only in retrospect that a few of the most self-confident Steelers — Joe Greene, Mike Webster, Robin Cole — had been sleepless with worry before the game, and not entirely without reason. On certain Sundays, the 1979 Steelers underachieved. To put it bluntly (as Joe Greene did), they were blown out a couple of times and had no business losing the other two games that got away from them.

The four defeats, and Greene's relentless harping on the subject, concentrated their minds for the playoffs. Something else that may have helped was the outcome of the Houston-San Diego game. The Oilers, like the Steelers, had finished the regular season with certain key starters out of action. But they upset San Diego, 17-14, giving the home-field advantage to Pittsburgh in the AFC championship game. If the Chargers had won, a flight to the West Coast would have been necessary. Out there during the season, remember, San Diego had beaten us, and though our records were the same, 12-4, that head-to-head result would have broken the tie.

So Bum Phillips, the Oilers' coach, had it right: Pittsburgh was the door to the Super Bowl — the pearly gates, so to speak. And Houston stepped onto the threshold when defensive back Vernon Perry, who had intercepted four passes in the Oilers' win over San Diego, picked off one of Bradshaw's with the game barely under way. He ran it back seventy-five yards for a touchdown. There was a time in Bradshaw's career when a reversal like this would have rattled him. Not now. Before the first half was over, Bradshaw had hit Cunningham and Stallworth for touchdown passes, and the Steelers were out in front, 17-10.

The Steel Curtain, meanwhile, was taking care of Houston. Slanting and stunting on their pass rush, the Steelers gave Dan Pastorini no room to operate, and they stopped Houston's running game in its tracks. In seventeen carries, Earl Campbell gained only fifteen yards. Except for two field goals and Perry's runback, the nearest thing to a score the Steelers allowed was a pass caught by Ray Renfro deep in the Pittsburgh end zone. Out of bounds, was the call, disputed by the Houston players and coaches.

Meanwhile, our offensive line was a fortress protecting Bradshaw. And the running game produced a touchdown when Rocky Bleier, back in the lineup because Sidney Thornton was ailing, crossed the goal line from four yards out after the Steelers had recovered a Houston fumble. Final score: Pittsburgh 27, Oilers 13. The Oilers had lost to the Steelers for the second time in three games, prompting Bum Phillips to declare that, on this day, no other team in the NFL could have done any better against Pittsburgh.

What was there to fear, then, from our opponents in Super Bowl XIV, the Los Angeles Rams? Their record was 9-7, and no team with seven defeats had ever lasted this long in post-season play. They had won the NFC championship game without scoring a touchdown, but their defense was impregnable, holding Tampa Bay without a score of any kind, and their offense moved the ball just enough to get Frank Corral within range for three successful field-goal attempts. That defense, coached by ex-Steeler Bud Carson, was one of the best in the NFL. Let me give you a for-instance: in a 24-0 win over the Seahawks, it had held them to minus seven yards. There was also this to consider: the Super Bowl game would be in the Rose Bowl, home territory for the Rams.

Carroll Rosenbloom, the team's owner, had died several months before the start of the season in a drowning accident. While Georgia, his wife, watched from the beach, the 75-year-old daredevil had gone swimming in rough surf off the coast of southeastern Florida. He never returned alive. Officially, "the undertow got him," but there were far-fetched rumors of foul play. In any event, his widow, a blond former showgirl, inherited the team. Steve Rosenbloom, her stepson, was the executive vice president who ran things, but Georgia quickly replaced him with Don Klosterman, on the face of it a more capable football man.

Ray Malavasi, promoted from assistant the year before when the elder Rosenbloom fired George Allen after two pre-season defeats, remained as coach. In 1978 the Rams got to the playoffs and almost made it to the Super Bowl, losing to Dallas for the conference title. In 1979, although Malavasi had heart problems, and a broken finger sidelined Pat Haden, their first-string quarterback, they reached the playoffs as a wild card, and this time they beat Dallas, 23-21. With under two minutes left in the fourth quarter, Haden's backup, Ray Ferragamo, completed his third touchdown pass for the winning points.

Partly because of Carson, I did not underrate the Rams. When it came to understanding defenses he was just about as good as they come. Still, we were ten-point favorites, and deservedly so.

Beating Bud

We'd be playing Los Angeles in the Rose Bowl, twenty or thirty miles of freeway travel from the Coliseum, which had been the Rams' home field since Danny Reeves moved his team out of Cleveland in 1946. Reeves was long gone, but his pioneering spirit had changed the face of professional football. Where once there were no teams west of Chicago or south of Washington, D.C., by 1979 the league was far-flung.

There also had been an unintended consequence — the disappearance of a de facto color line. In agreeing to take Reeves as a tenant, the board that ran the Coliseum had insisted on an unusual quid pro quo, that the Rams must offer contracts to Kenny Washington, who had been an All American halfback at UCLA, and Woody Strode, an end from the same school. Washington's NFL career lasted only three years and Strode's was even briefer, but they were Southern Californians, popular with the fans, and their signing opened up the NFL to other non-white players. By the time of Super Bowl XIV, blacks, or African-Americans, as the preferred usage now has it, were well-represented on both teams, although not in the numbers we have since grown accustomed to see.

Forget that the Rose Bowl is in Pasadena: this would of course be a home game for the Rams. It was Chuck Noll's wish to keep the Steelers in Pittsburgh, working out in cold weather, for half of the two-week interval between the end of the playoffs and the Super Bowl itself. As usual, he wanted no distractions. "Enjoy yourselves," he told his players when they reached the West Coast, "but remember what we're here for. Don't blow it."

The logistics of transporting the team and its support structure and getting everything set up at the Super Bowl site fell to Dan, Joe Gordon, Buff Boston, and Dennis Thimmons, our controller, but they were experts at it by now. My own preoccupation was with the 1980 draft. Following Noll's lead, I gave a talk to the scouts: Have a good time for the few days we'll be out here, but re-focus quickly after the game.

What was driving me nuts, and the same thing went for everybody else connected with the organization, were the calls from our friends, if the word fits them, for tickets — tickets that in many cases, we knew, would end up in the hands of agents and scalpers. They could be sold for ten times their worth and then sold again for twenty times their worth, while fans who had backed us all season long were shut out.

I was fuming about this. Unabashedly, one of our assistant coaches approached me and asked for "help" in obtaining tickets. In his mind the Super Bowl was a "once-in-a-lifetime chance" to "make a nice buck" for his family. The coach was not a sleazeball, just an ordinary nice guy who didn't get it. I discussed the situation with Dan, who told Dennis Thimmons to wise up the poor sap. Dennis explained to the coach that scalping tickets was illegal; he mentioned the IRS; he mentioned our loyal ticketless fans. The coach did not take this well, and for some time afterward the displeasure he felt was directed toward me. It may be that he changed his outlook when a man of importance in the Rams' front office went to jail as a tax cheat for Super Bowl scalping.

Game day was sunny and bright — normal, in other words, for Southern California. Driven onto the field in a 1933 model touring car, 1933 because that was his first year in the league, AJR called the coin toss. He was famous now, the biggest winner in sports, and universally beloved, and yet he managed, as he always did, to look humble. Affection poured down from the 103,000 spectators; an estimated sixty million others were watching the telecast. In all the pre-game hoopla, Dad was a necessary presence. Seemingly reluctant, seemingly embarrassed by the attention, he went along with it, never for a minute fooling his wife or his sons. These were the best years of his life, we knew, a sort of grand culmination of all that had gone before.

The Rams won the coin toss. AJR was consistently successful at the race track, but ten years earlier, in New Orleans, we'd had better luck with Dan making the call. I'm talking about the coin toss between the Steelers and the Bears for the first selection overall in the 1970 draft. The prize then was Bradshaw, who'd be starting his fourth Super Bowl game as the Steelers' quarterback. Could we have come this far without him? The answer, I suggest, is self-evident.

Up in the stands, near the middle of the stadium, I nervously awaited the kickoff. The Super Bowl is a spectacle, a pageant, and rightfully so, but I was saying to myself, "Get it on, get it on." There had been enough ritual, too many bells and whistles. Even the panoramic background scenery was losing its charm for me. How long can you look at palm trees and eucalyptus trees and mountains that change to a different shade of purple every few minutes?

I had on my game face; I was ready for the action to start. In our section of seats there was lots of black and gold. We'd been placed with an assortment of Pittsburgh-area big shots and just a tiny sprinkling of AJR's hangers-on. Mom and Dad were seated above us, in one of the VIP boxes. A limousine and a chauffeur had been provided for their transportation to the game, but AJR had insisted on riding in the team bus with the players. ("I guess he wants to get his ankles taped," Bernie Butler theorized.)

When Kass found out that she would be in the limousine all alone, she decided to join the rest of us in the Rooney family's bus and ordered Kay to telephone her father and stepmother and any other relatives who had tickets to the game and have them come to the Newport Beach Marriott, where AJR had reserved a suite. "Now, don't argue with me," Kass said. "We've got that big car, and it's going to waste. Tell your folks they might as well use it. The driver will take them to a parking place right next to the entrance gate." No question about it, Kay was always Kass's favorite daughter-in-law.

In an offhanded way, I'd been wondering about the silver-foil trim attached to all the seats. Now I saw what the purpose was. The sun, on its downward arc, had reached a calibrated point at which the angle of the rays lit up the stadium and the silver foil. I admired the stage-managing. A brilliant effect had been achieved, but it temporarily blinded me. "When, oh when," I muttered, "will the bullshit come to an end?"

In due time, was the answer. The Steelers took the field without their two most seriously injured starters. Jack Ham and his wife were watching the game from AJR's box; Mike Wagner had a seat outside with the rest of us. Twenty-two holdovers from Super Bowl IX were still in uniform, but outnumbered now by the players we had added since 1974. To me, this meant that the scouts had been doing their job. The draft was the pipeline that kept our tank full.

Chuck Noll's game plan was for Bradshaw to stretch the field. The three assistant coaches who had defected to the Rams – Bud Carson, Lionel Taylor, and Dan Radakovich – would know how to stop, or at least hinder, our running attack. The best way to respond, Noll felt, was to put all our chips on Bradshaw. Throw the ball downfield, let Stallworth and Swann do the rest. How well the three of them executed would determine the outcome. No defensive scheme was a match for perfect execution, and Noll had full confidence now in Bradshaw's ability to deliver. As for Stallworth and Swann, there never had been a time when they were anything less than consummate pros.

On the first possession after the kickoff (another short one by Matt Bahr), Los Angeles had to punt on fourth down. And then, game plan or no game plan, the Steelers ran the ball. It was business as usual, with Franco and Rocky biting off yardage. There was one pass completion, thirty-two yards to Franco. But all-pro defensive end Jack Youngblood made a couple of good stops, and we settled for a field goal from Bahr.

Two weeks earlier, when the Rams beat Tampa Bay for the National Conference championship, Youngblood had broken a leg. "Damn! The guy's inhuman," I said to no one in particular. "How can he keep this up?" He couldn't – couldn't possibly, I assured myself. I was wrong, It turned out, but meanwhile the Rams were completing a 59-yard touchdown drive on which their ball carriers punctured the Steel Curtain. What was going on here?

Larry Anderson, a second-year special-teams player from Louisiana Tech (since finding Bradshaw there, we had kept going back), reversed the momentum for us with a 45-yard kickoff return, and now Bradshaw mixed up his play-calling. On a 53-yard drive that ended with Franco bucking over from one yard away, the pass supported the run and the run supported the pass. Just three minutes into the second quarter, we had taken the lead, lost it, and taken it back.

Negative thoughts entered my mind. How could I have expected anything other than the kind of game I was watching – a tough one? These Rams were the same team, pretty much, that had beaten us the year before in a regular-season game. We never had won from them here in their home surroundings. I wondered if Bud Carson was right when he said that the Rams (meaning himself) had our number.

Bahr's next kickoff carried to the 10-yard line, a bit of an improvement. The runback took the ball to the 19. Five and a half minutes later, Frank Corral kicked a field goal. Pittsburgh 10, Los Angeles 10.

Another long kickoff return by Anderson, this one for thirty-eight yards, gave us a chance to score again before the half. It had been a sub-par second season for Anderson, but he was having his greatest game, both as a runner and tackler on kickoffs, a game of the kind he was never to replicate. Anderson was a guy who could make both good plays and bad plays; against the Rams he was making only good plays. This latest one, though, got us nowhere. The offense couldn't muster a first down, and another field goal by Corral gave Los Angeles a 13-10 lead.

Believe me when I say I felt relief. But for a dropped pass or two, it could have been 17-10. After the field goal, Anderson took the kickoff past midfield again, but the half ended before we could score.

A group of singers and dancers – hundreds of them, it seemed, all vibrantly youthful and excessively clean-cut – performed during the long intermission. Among them, I now recalled, was the daughter of a friend who had asked me to look for her. Finding a needle in a haystack might have been easier.

"Help me out," I said to Kay.

"All right, but you'll have to describe her for me."

"Well ... she's pretty and she's athletic."

"Pretty and athletic? Every one of those girls is pretty and athletic. You've been sent on a fool's errand," Kay said.

I forgot about looking for the daughter of my friend. These young entertainers were full of what the French call *joie de vivre*, but I thought they never would get off the field. We were three points behind in a game that could go either way, and I was anxious to see what tactical alterations Noll had in mind.

Down in the Steeler locker room, Joe Greene and Jack Lambert were berating their teammates on the defensive unit. "We're letting them push us around!" The offense had problems of its own. Almost every time Bradshaw audibled – changed a play at the line of scrimmage – the Rams knew exactly how to adjust. This was Bud Carson's doing, some of our assistant coaches believed: the Rams knew our signals; Carson had cued them in. My own guess was that unaided anticipation on the part of the Rams' defensive players was hurting us more than any signal stealing.

Either way it was no time to panic. Right on schedule, the sun descended into the Pacific, the lights in the stadium came on, and the second half started. And now the Steelers, I could sense, had fire in their eyes. Los Angeles kicked off, and Larry Anderson did it again: another nice return, thirty-seven yards. Five plays later, Bradshaw went deep. From the Rams' 47, he launched a touchdown pass to Swann, who went up high, splitting two defensive backs, to make the catch. So here it was at last: Noll's game plan remembered.

But Malavasi had a game plan of his own. In fact, it resembled ours; a pass good for fifty yards, Ferragamo to Billy Waddy, put the ball on the Pittsburgh 24, and the Rams then caught us off-guard. Ferragamo handed the ball to Lawrence McCutcheon, but instead of blasting into the line he swept right, stopped, and threw a touchdown pass to Ron Smith. Our defensive backs, looking for the run, had been overly aggressive, and Smith got behind them in the end zone. It had taken the Rams less than a minute to cover seventy-seven yards in four plays.

Shockingly, Corral missed the extra point. With Los Angeles leading by only 19-17, a field goal would put us ahead once again. This time we started a little deeper, from our 28, and moved to a first down on the 44. Then came one of those "what-if?" plays. Bradshaw fired a pass that missed the intended receiver; its trajectory took it straight into the arms of defensive back Norm Cromwell, a Hall of Famer to be. And he dropped the ball.

Afterward Cromwell said that all he could see in front of him was "green grass and the goal line." All I could see, in a flashback to Super Bowl XIII, was Jackie Smith, the Dallas Cowboys' most dependable receiver, dropping a pass in the end zone. Fate, once again, had been kind to us, by which I don't mean to say we were not a better team than either the Cowboys or the Rams. Norm Cromwell and Jackie Smith, excellent players, dropped the ball in big games, but that's why we call them games. As Kass once reminded AJR when he boasted of having bet on a sure thing at the race track, there is no such thing as a sure thing. The horse could break a leg, she cautioned. That's what the horse did, and they shot the poor animal. At least Smith and Cromwell lived to tell about the passes they dropped, Kass said.

Time and again you've heard the old truism that everybody makes mistakes. The difference between the Steelers and the Rams in Super Bowl XIV was that the Steelers overcame their mistakes. It's what great teams usually do. In any case, not long after the failed interception Lynn Swann caught a short pass over the middle and was knocked silly. Our doctors would not allow him to finish the game. A bad break. Swann had been making routinely fantastic catches. Injured earlier, his sub, Theo Bell, was already out of the game, leaving no one to take Swann's place except Jimmy Smith, who was taking Bell's place as our punt-return man. Carson's defense had been stuffing our run. "Now all we have to do," he was telling his guys, "is shut down Stallworth." He made it sound easy. Too easy.

Despite the near interception and an interception by Eddie Brown that changed the flow of the game temporarily, Bradshaw kept throwing the bomb. Time was when an interception like Brown's would have unsettled him, but when the Steelers got the ball again, on their own 27, he was calm and efficient, setting up play-action passes with the run. We were soon on the Rams' 16, close enough now for a go-ahead field goal. Then on third-and-ten, instead of setting it up with a safety-first thrust into the line, Bradshaw threw toward the end zone, where Stallworth was open, and Rod Perry intercepted on the four.

Damn, damn, damn! Why didn't we kick the easy field goal? Why didn't we play the percentages? Now, with the fourth quarter under way, we were still two points down.

But the Rams were slowly fading. Under pressure from Robin Cole, Jack Lambert, and Steve Furness, their offensive line, a very good one, was beginning to crumble. Ken Clark, their punter, pushed us back with a 59-yard kick, but we still had time. On second-and-eight, with the ball on our 27, Sidney Thornton dropped a pass. "Get Rocky in there," I grumbled, sending a telepathic message to Noll – whose mind was on something else.

"Go for the big one," he instructed Bradshaw, calling for a play that had not worked in practice, a pass to Stallworth on a hook-and-go route. Bradshaw, I later heard, was dubious; even Stallworth wasn't sure they could bring it off. But Bradshaw put the ball in the air and Stallworth caught it. He caught it at the Rams' 32 and never broke stride as he kept on going into the end zone. The pass and run covered seventy-three yards. After Bahr's extra point, our lead was 24-19.

Bud Carson, I understand, did some powerful emoting on the sidelines. The sportswriters still referred to Bud as the architect of the Steel Curtain. Bud was a smart coach, but the Steel Curtain's only architect had been Charles Henry Noll — who was proving himself now to be an architect of some distinction when it came to offensive football, too. The pass to Stallworth was Noll's call; nobody else, not Bradshaw, not Stallworth, and not the assistant coaches in the spotter's booth, had a whole lot of faith in that call, but it worked. Bud Carson said it shouldn't have worked. "All we needed to do was double-cover Stallworth," he explained after the game. His defensive plan, he said, had provided for double coverage. Somehow, the Rams were remiss. They didn't execute. Or simply got beaten on a game-busting play by a Hall-of-Fame quarterback, a Hall-of-Fame receiver, and a Hall-of-Fame strategist.

It was odd, when you think about it, how Super Bowl XIV had come to be viewed by so many of the actual participants as a duel of wits between Carson and Noll. Noll himself was caught up in it: "I know how to beat Bud," he had said to Marianne, his wife, before leaving Pittsburgh. Not "I know how to beat the Rams," but "I know how to beat Bud." Coaches don't win or lose games; players do, we are told. Undeniably, however, coaches have their moments. The hook-and-go call was one such moment, and something similar happened with five and a half minutes of the fourth quarter remaining. Los Angeles had the ball on the Steelers' 32, first-and-ten. Wendell Tyler had been running hard; Ferragamo was hitting his passes; our five-point lead appeared to be none too secure. In front of the Steeler bench, linebacker coach Woody Widenhofer shouted to Lambert. "It's coming, Jack – this is it!" "It" was a pass from Ferragamo to Ron Smith. Lambert, judging the trajectory of the ball with scientific exactitude, intercepted. And up at the top of the stadium, AJR got to his feet and headed for the elevator. "Where are you going, Dad? The game's not over," called out Dan. "Yes, it is," answered AJR. "Lambert just ended it."

That was not how it looked from where Kay and I were sitting. Five minutes in a football game can be a long time. Bradshaw handed off to Franco and then to Thornton for a net gain of three yards. Third-and-seven on our own 33. "OK, run the clock out," I urged Bradshaw silently. But somebody had other ideas. Again he went deep to Stallworth, on the same hook-and-go pattern that had given us our come-from-behind touchdown. Again there was no double coverage.

This pass took us to the Rams' 22, from where Bradshaw threw to Jimmy Smith in the end zone. The defensive back climbing all over Smith was flagged for interference, and though it took three tries from the one-yard line, with Rocky and then Franco and then Franco again hitting straight ahead, the penalty set up a touchdown.

Now it was Steelers 31, Rams 19, and it stayed that way. In a dying-gasp effort, Ferragamo passed the Rams to the Pittsburgh 27 before J. T. Thomas dumped him seventeen yards behind the line of scrimmage, effectively ending the threat, if that's what it was.

Larry Anderson got the game ball for his 162 yards on five kickoff returns, a Super Bowl record. Bradshaw, though, for the second straight year, was the MVP. In football, as in warfare, it's the bomb that can do the most damage. And yet this best of all Super Bowl games up to then was in one sense a vindication of Noll. Bud Carson was sure he could double-cover Stallworth. Noll had a hunch his old assistant was mistaken about that. So where did all this leave Ray Malavasi - Carson's boss? Out of it, I guess you'd have to say.

For Noll and his assistants and each of our players, the winner's share of the Super Bowl jackpot was thirty-two thousand dollars. Neither Dan nor I, after previous Super Bowls, ever had taken a cent, but now I went to him and suggested that perhaps we owed something to our wives and kids. I never asked how it happened – did Dan argue the case with AJR? – but both of us received a full share. To this day I don't know if the Chief ever cut himself in.

Filling In

Alex DiCroce was in charge of the post-game party at the Newport Beach Marriott, and he had told me ahead of time that Kay and I would have our own table. I reminded him that after Super Bowls IX, X, and XIII, we had sat with Mom and Dad. "I know," Alex said, "but you're as much a part of the Steelers' success as your father is, or as Dan is. You should have your own table, and I'll see that it's right next to the Chief's." Whatever distinction there was in being put at a separate table pleased me, of course, but not half as much as Alex's compliment did.

In any event, we sat with Dad and Mom after all. It was Kass's idea. Dad's race-track cronies spent their winters on Florida's east coast; very few of them had come to Pasadena, which meant that his table would not be full, Kass said. And he wanted no walk-ons. The solution Kass proposed was for Kay and me and the friends we had asked to sit with us — the Butlers and the Youngs — to occupy the empty spaces. That would leave Kay's father and step-mother and her other relatives to keep an eye on young Susie at our table. Meanwhile, Art III and Mike would be happy to pal around with their numerous cousins. It worked out, I think, to the satisfaction of everybody concerned.

These victory parties were elegant affairs. There was music, good food, and – yes — lots of liquor. But no one ever got boisterous. No one misbehaved. The presence of AJR and Noll had a moderating influence, I believe. All the wives and girlfriends looked beautiful to me. All the children did credit to their parents.

We flew back home to another big welcome. Once it was over, I quickly turned my thoughts to the draft. So many of our players were getting long in the tooth. They were still superior athletes, with great experience and moxie, but age was catching up with them. Since 1974, I had drafted many good players, but no great ones. It was time to rectify that.

Nowhere To Go But Down

I didn't' know it then, but we were full of ourselves, dangerously so. Winning inflates the ego. Everybody seemed to be on a high, everybody except the head coach, Chuck Noll. Like the traveler in Robert Frost's poem, Noll had miles to go before he slept, but it was not in his nature to pause and reflect on where a change of direction might take him – or to revel in Super Bowl glory.

As for AJR, he had reached his destination in life, by this time content to play a largely ceremonial part in the Steeler hierarchy. Over the previous six years the fans and the sportswriters had coroneted, then canonized him. The former vagabond scatback, amateur boxer, minor-league batting and base-stealing marvel, ward boss, sandlot football impresario, up-by-the-bootstraps NFL pioneer, and immensely successful race-track plunger had become a "great American sportsman," so designated by nobody less than a president of the United States. Expunged from the Chief's past were his rough beginnings – the days of hey rubes and fist fights, of illegal booze and illegal gambling aboard the Showboat, of speakeasies and all-night card games, of an easy familiarity with hoodlums like Bill Duffy and Owney Madden. In the public consciousness, nothing remained of that time but mythology — nostalgic recollections of the NFL and its origins. With George Halas and George Marshall and Johnny Blood and Whizzer White, AJR was a symbol of an age perceived as golden and romantic.

The Chief's reputation was important to him, and carefully guarded. He wore his persona like a monk's habit. Puzzled over a quotation attributed to the philosopher Jacques Maritaine - something to the effect that artistry is "the habit of practical intellect" – I asked my teacher at St. Vincent, a Father Erik, for amplification. "Well, a habit, you see, is like a cloak," he said. "A habit is what I'm wearing right now. It's my costume. An artist wears a habit, too - the habit of practical intellect." I was now more confused than ever, but looking back, it seems clear that AJR wore humility and charm like a habit. Not that there was anything phony about this. The public now saw him as warm, kind, benevolent, and upright, and he was all of these things, a man of truly countless good deeds. Once again I repeat something that my drama school instructors used to say of an actor perpetually cast in the same role — "the mask becomes the face." In the end there is no distinction between actor and character. They are one.

In private, however, AJR was still the Chief. He could be humble and charming and generous, but also a dictator. If it was Dan who now ran the football team, Dan who made the day-to-day administrative decisions, they were not irreversible. AJR retained veto power. And it was AJR, unless he waived the privilege, who accepted our championship trophies from Pete Rozelle, the NFL commissioner, while Dan stood quietly in the background, a secondary figure.

When I say that all the Chief's sons feared his reprimands, I speak from experience. As vice president in charge of personnel, I had some status, I supposed, in the organization. Thus when AJR ordered me to appear in his place at a public function I had no wish whatever to attend, I offered the valid excuse that I was trying to spend more "quality time" with my neglected wife and children. Such opportunities for me were rare; even as the scouting department's "coordinator," I continued to go out on the road. But AJR was unsympathetic. In front of the whole office staff, he gave me a fiery dressing down.

Of course I went to the affair. I spoke. Word that I had done well filtered back to the Chief. Genially, he observed, "You should do more of this." Although the topic never was alluded to, my years at drama school in New York had cost him a lot of money. If I could now use my training, it would be a return of some kind on the Chief's investment, but I was quiet about this. My interest in acting, I knew, had made me, for a spell, the family's black sheep. "Don't ever mention it," Kay often counseled me. All the time I had logged in Madame Daykahonova's version of the Actors' Studio was in Kay's opinion – and AJR's – something best hushed up, like a jail sentence.

I was wise, as it turned out, to abandon any notion of a theatrical career. Working for my father had its drawbacks; but in no other job could the rewards have been as great. Just the personal associations that were open to me enriched my existence. By virtue of being Art Rooney's son, I was frequently in contact with the social, political, and economic elite, but I'm talking about something else.

I wasn't comfortable with the elite; I preferred ordinary, grass-roots football people – scouts and coaches, administrators, team doctors and trainers. Most but not all of my friends had played the game. Those who hadn't included even sportswriters. I liked to entertain, both at home, where Kay was unsurpassed as a hostess, and at our club. When I entertained at the club, Kay excused herself. She knew the story-telling would last for hours, with waiters and bartenders gathered around to hear the yarn-spinning, a mixture of fable and fact.

There was also the work itself. Since 1974, we had won four Super Bowls, and I think I can claim without boastfulness that the scouting department was entitled to some of the credit. Since the move to Three Rivers Stadium in 1970, there had been only three losing seasons. But now it was 1980, the start of a new decade, and I recalled, from the scriptures, a warning, a reminder that mortality spares no one. With the passing of the years, certain changes occur. Muscles weaken, strength wanes, reflexes atrophy. As reluctant as we were to recognize the truth, our football team was getting old.

Part Six: Winding Down
Chapter 68

Executive Privilege

On a wet, chilly morning in February of 1980 the Pittsburgh Steelers, reigning Super Bowl champions, and the Pittsburgh Pirates, reigning World Series champions flew in a chartered jet to Washington, D.C., for a visit with President Jimmy Carter.

Pittsburgh, at the time, had a sports-page moniker – Title Town, U.S.A. Unable to choose between Terry Bradshaw, the Steelers' quarterback, and Willie Stargell, the Pirates' first baseman, *Sports Illustrated* had designated both as its Sportsmen of the Year. For the magazine's cover, they posed side by side in their uniforms, outlined against the silhouette of a steel mill.

Never mind that by the end of the 1970s steel mills producing steel were hard to find around here. Closed forever, all but the Edgar Thomson Works in Braddock awaited the wrecking ball. Gone from the river banks was the flare of the open-hearth furnaces that lit up the night with a demonic red glow. The U.S. Steel Building stood watch just as always over the Golden Triangle, but it had a new name – the USX Building. What did X mean, anyway? It was certainly not a synonym for steel. And who remembered that the decoration on the side of the Steelers' black helmets, three stars enclosed in a circle, was the industry's insignia?

We had won four Super Bowls, but the invitation to the White House was our first. Kay and I would be going in Chuck Noll's twin-engine six-seater with Buff and Janet Boston. On the big chartered jet, with a football team and a baseball team to accommodate, extra seating was limited. AJR, down in Florida with Kass, elected to pass up the trip. He made decisions like this on a unilateral basis. The thought that his bride of forty-nine years might perhaps take some pleasure in seeing the White House, in meeting the President, would not have occurred to him. In my inner ear, I could hear him saying, "Kathleen, you don't want to go to that thing, do you?" And it would not be a question, but a statement. "I've been to the White House, Kass," he would say. "It's nice but a real hassle. Let's stay here. We'd be taking away attention from the team."

On the day of our departure a low-hanging fog was in the air. Kay, under the best of conditions, did not like to fly. "If we have to go – and, frankly, I'd rather not – let's drive," she proposed.

"Kay," I said, "it's too late to drive. We wouldn't get there in time."

"Then go by yourself." was her answer.

In the end, after much vacillation, she relented. Chuck Noll's little plane took off from the County Airport. We had a pilot from the Westinghouse Corporation, a good one named Ralph something. The fog was still heavy, but Ralph said the sky would be clear above four thousand feet. As we fastened our seat belts, Kay whispered to me, "Headline tomorrow in the newspapers: 'Art Rooney Junior and Steeler associate Jim Boston killed when airplane crashes in Allegheny Mountains.'"

We rose above the clouds at three thousand feet and were flying in sunshine – but not for long. Over the Chestnut Ridge of the Alleghenies we were back in pea soup. Kay and Janet Boston were getting panicky. Even Buff, by nature a fatalist, had started to sweat. Our plane was bouncing around like one of those teacup-shaped bumper cars at Kennywood Park. Ralph the pilot, jabbering non-stop, gave us his word that there was no cause whatever for alarm. To myself, I said, "Right. You can be sure if it's Westinghouse."

Kay wasn't buying any happy talk, especially not from Ralph. We'd been holding hands. Now she released hers and dug the fingernails into the flesh just above my knee. "You!" she hissed. "You made me come on this goddam pissant excuse for an airplane!" The Bostons were quiet but looked paralyzed. They could both use a drink, I thought, and I was worried about Kay. The buffeting worsened the closer we got to Washington, but finally Ralph turned around and said, "Not long now until we land. We only have to get clearance."

Descending through fog, we could not see the ground. And then all of a sudden there were lights. We landed almost gently, and I recalled one of Noll's original epigrams: "Any landing is a good one if you can walk away from it."

On the tarmac, Kay said, "I don't care how we go back to Pittsburgh as long as we don't fly. I don't care if we rent a car and drive. I don't care if we take the train. I don't care if we go by Greyhound bus. I don't care if we hitchhike. I don't even care if we walk every step of the way. But I'm not getting back on that goddammed airplane." She paused to let her ultimatum sink in. Then she added," Do you understand me?" I did. When a redhead lays down the law, there is no ambiguity.

On the buses that were to take our group to the White House, we learned that President Carter, who was having a busy day, would not be able to see us at the appointed time. So, first, there would be a tour of FBI headquarters in the building named for J. Edgar Hoover. The explanation that Carter was in a meeting that had not yet broken up evoked cynicism on our bus. "Overtime meeting my ass," someone chirped. "We're going to the FBI building so they can check us out. They think there might be subversives in our midst. Buff Boston looks like a bomb tosser for sure. Once they eyeball Buff, they'll think he's gonna blow up the White House."

Everybody laughed, but those were innocent times. After September 11, 2001, remarks of that nature ceased to be humorous.

Actually, the tour was quite interesting. And before very long we were back on the road. As soon as we got to the White House, I headed, with many others, for the restroom. It was all black marble and polished brass. Just like the Duquesne Club, I reflected. When we had reassembled, a White House guide took us through the corridors, which were lined with the portraits of the presidents ... Washington, Jackson, Lincoln, Wilson, FDR, Harry Truman, Jack Kennedy. The furniture was French Provincial and the trimmings were gold – one of Thomas Jefferson's legacies, I suppose. Jock Sutherland's Pitt Rose Bowl champions had been here in the 1930s, having their picture taken in the Rose Garden with Herbert Hoover. Uncle Jim was in that picture, as big as life. And now it was our turn. There's a lot to be said for being a winner, I told myself smugly.

I had left home full of nonchalance. Now my mouth was hanging open and my head was on a swivel. There was so much to see and to think about. Big-time football players accustomed to the hoopla that went with Super Bowl games and their victorious aftermath were gawking and chattering like schoolboys. With smiles on their faces, they were taking it all in. So was I. So was Kay. So was everybody.

We were ushered into a room for coffee or tea and pastries (the best I have ever tasted, and I'm a connoisseur of sweet stuff). There were presidential seals on the cups, saucers, and silverware and predictable jests about taking them home with us for keepsakes. One of the wives – a lovely strawberry blonde – suggested a perfect place for the women to stash away the cups. I am sure you can guess where it was.

"Too obvious," someone said, and I recalled a story Dick Szymanski, one-time general manager of the Baltimore Colts, had told me, confirming George Young's account of the same incident. Once when the Colts were Super Bowl champions, the governor of Maryland, Spiro Agnew – later the only vice president forced to resign from office for taking bribes – invited them to dinner at his official residence in Annapolis. Toward the end of the evening, Agnew and several members of the Baltimore coaching staff adjourned to the billiards room, where they were sipping brandy, smoking cigars, and shooting pool. All had removed their jackets except for one coach. Agnew urged him to loosen up. "You look uncomfortable," he said. "Maybe if you take off your coat you can make a few shots. Ha ha." So, feeling pressured, the coach took off his coat. Where to put it? He spotted an empty chair and was draping the garment over the back of it when, *crash*! Knives, forks, and spoons, each one bearing the Maryland state seal, fell out of the pockets, landing with a clatter on the hardwood floor.

"It was embarrassing," said Szymanski. He didn't tell me how Agnew reacted. When it came to thievery, of course, Agnew turned out to be fully as inept as the Baltimore coach.

President Carter, standing next to a tall Marine captain at the end of the White House reception line, looked diminutive. He was wearing a beautifully tailored dark suit. When Kay and I, moving forward, found ourselves facing the Marine officer, he said to me, "Your name, sir?" I gave him the information. Turning to the President, he passed on our IDs in an undertone.

Jimmy Carter now addressed us in his Georgia drawl. "Come over here, Art," he said, smiling toothily, "and have your picture taken with me. And bring Kathleen." He shook my hand. As we posed for the photographer, he put his arm around Kay, at the waistline. When the picture session was over, we exchanged a few pleasantries and Carter returned to the business of welcoming his guests.

The greeting and smiling all done with, he led us to a stage at the far end of what appeared to be a ballroom. There we all gathered for a group photo with Carter. Then Chuck Noll and Dan gave him an NFL football with the players' and coaches' signatures on it. The Pirates gave him a memento of some kind, too, but I don't know what it was. When Carter left us, he had our football cradled in his arm.

To Kay's delight, the Steelers returned to Pittsburgh by bus, and two of the seats were for us. It was a warm, pleasant ride. At one stop along the way, Noll and Dan, noted oenophiles, bought a case of expensive wine, and when we stopped at another place for dinner they had the waiters bring the wine to all the tables.

On the bus as we were pulling into Pittsburgh, Kay spoke privately to me. In a whisper, she said, "You may not believe this, but it's true," and waited for me to respond.

"What's true?" I asked.

"Well ..." Again she hesitated. "Well, when we had our picture taken with President Carter, he ..."

"Yes, go on."

"He pinched me on the backside."

I have to admit I was speechless.

"On the upper part of my bum," Kay went on.

As she had predicted, I couldn't believe it. "You're nuts!" I exclaimed.

"It's true," Kay said.

"No! Not the President!"

"It's true," Kay repeated. "Now I'll say no more about it. But it's true."

And there, for the time being, we let the subject drop.

Several years passed. In my office at Three Rivers Stadium early one morning, I was talking about the draft with one of our coaches. We were drinking coffee. The conversation somehow shifted from football to our White House visit in 1980. The coach put his cup down and said, "You know, that Carter was a feisty little guy."

Feisty? I nodded as though I understood.

"Can I tell you something?" the coach said, leaning toward me confidentially. "When we were getting our picture taken, he pinched my wife on the ass."

I said, "Oh, my God!" Then I jumped up and ran to the telephone and dialed our number at home.

"Darling," I said when Kay answered, "you once told me a story I didn't believe, but I believe it now. And I apologize for ever having doubted you."

Some time later I got to thinking about the label our coach had for Carter – "feisty" – and a different, more suitable adjective occurred to me, one that, like "feisty," ends with a "y."

It was "horny."

Change or Die

When Moon Mullins signed a long- term contract sometime during the 1970s he announced to his teammates (I overheard him say it), "I'm a Steeler forever." Mullins was a man of his word. After the 1979 season, Chuck Noll arranged a trade that would have sent him to the Cleveland Browns; instead of going along with the deal, Mullins retired. He had played for the Steelers since coming into the league and would play for nobody else.

We had drafted Mullins in 1971 out of Southern California. For nine years, Mullins and Sam Davis, an undrafted free agent from Allen University in South Carolina, gave us quickness and mobility at the guard positions. Davis, the team's "old man," was a survivor of the failed Bill Austin regime, but, like Mullins, he possessed the attributes needed to jump out in front of the ball carrier on Noll's sweeps and traps. And now he, too, would be gone – finished as a player because of injuries accrued over thirteen backbreaking seasons.

We owed them a debt, Mullins and Davis, and their departure would leave a void. They took so many intangibles with them. But a football team is an organism, and an organism cannot remain static.

It must change or it must die. Baldly stated, Mullins and Davis were worn-out parts. Replacements had to be ready, supplied by our scouts.

So in the 1980 draft we were looking for offensive linemen. In the fifth round we took Craig Wolfley, from Syracuse, and in the sixth round Tunch Ilkin, from Indiana State. Ilkin was a center, but adaptable enough to play tackle. In that way he was similar to Ray Pinney, our second-round choice in 1976. Although Pinney had been a center at the University of Washington, Noll used him mainly as a fill-in for Mullins and Davis.

Wofley, Ilkin, and Pinney had long, productive careers with the Steelers, maintaining the standard of offensive line play established by their predecessors. Wolfley, in fact, made one of those Steeler all-decade teams for the 1980s. Ilkin had a more difficult time of it. He was cut before the season started, but when Rollie Dotsch, his position coach, expressed misgivings to me about this, I instructed one of our scouts, Tom Modrak, to keep us from losing track of Ilkin. Tom called Tunch every week and urged him to stay in shape. With just a few games remaining, his chance came. An injury left us short-handed in the offensive line, and Ilkin rejoined the team. He was a Steeler for twelve years, captaining the offensive unit at the end of his career, and he played in two Pro Bowls.

All in all, the 1980 draft was not a bad one. We took a quarterback, Mark Malone of Arizona State, in the first round. A fellow scout I knew and respected had a theory about Malone: his above-average passing ability, according to this scout, blinded us to the fact that he was playing out of position. Malone was a reasonably good quarterback who never developed into a great one. As a halfback, the scout said, he could have been another Frank Gifford or Paul Hornung. (I'd heard that before about, oh, any number of talented individuals whose accomplishments fell short of their potential.) "If Malone hurt his arm," the scout told me in all seriousness, "it would be the best thing that could happen to him."

Actually, my friend may have had a point. Terry Bradshaw was going to be our quarterback for another three years, but, recognizing Malone's versatility, Noll found ways of getting him on the field from time to time. When we played Seattle during Malone's second season, Noll lined him up at wideout because his ranginess and speed created coverage problems for the defense. While the Seahawks were wondering what to do about this, Malone, who was positioned off to the right – something like Army Coach Red Blaik's "lonesome end" — caught a pass from Bradshaw and streaked down the sideline all the way to the end zone, a distance of ninety yards. Years and years later, it was still the longest pass play in Steeler history.

Malone never hurt his arm, but he did hurt his knee, badly. With his mobility diminished, quarterback from then on was the only position he could play. After taking over from Bradshaw's successor, David Woodley (obtained in a trade with Miami), he finished the 1984 season strongly, and we won a playoff game for the first time in five years. Against Indianapolis the next season, he tied Bradshaw's single-game team record by passing for five touchdowns, but that, I am sorry to say, was his high-water mark.

Four other players from the 1980 draft made the squad. Linebacker Bob Kohrs, who had been Malone's teammate at Arizona State, lasted six seasons, but always seemed to have an injury of some kind. Aside from Wolfley and Ilkin, we made our best pick that year in the eleventh round. Continuing our search for a running back to replace Rocky Bleier, we drafted a kid from Baylor, Frank Pollard. Faster than Rocky, he could block just as well and catch just as well. In Kass' phrase, Greg Hawthorne, the Baylor running back who had been our first-round pick the year before, "lived in hope and died in despair," by which I mean that he ultimately disappointed everyone, himself included. Pollard never had a thousand-yard rushing season, but came close a couple of times in a nine-year career. He was an unselfish player who could have been a starter on our great teams of the 1970s in a role similar to Bleier's. In the role that circumstances forced him to take, one that was similar to Franco's, he could not quite fulfill the requirements. In other words, Pollard just wasn't a franchise player, but of course there are not too many of those.

Making late picks has been likened to throwing darts at the draft board. During my tenure as head scout, we had remarkably good luck with late picks. "Why do your scouts do so well from the fourth round on down when the top picks tend to be so-so?" Dan used to ask. Well, it wasn't by throwing darts at the board. We rated our late picks as carefully as the ones higher up, and it frequently paid off. In the NFL, drafting toward the end of every round is the price you pay for success, and no matter how well you may do, it isn't often you get the real superstars.

To state the obvious, great players are the stuff that great teams are made of, and great teams win the close games. In 1980, a lot of our great players were either aging or hurt – sometimes both. The result was that Cincinnati beat us twice by one point, Cleveland beat us by two points, and Houston beat us by six. We finished the season with a 9-7 record, missing out on the playoffs for the first time since 1971.

Golden Anniversary

For Mom and Dad's fiftieth wedding anniversary – June 11, 1981 – the late-spring day was picture-perfect: golden sun, pale blue sky, air that sparkled like Waterford crystal. The only reminder of how Pittsburgh had looked when the couple first met was the soot-blackened exterior of St. Peter's Church. No farther away than Terry Bradshaw could throw a football were the main-line tracks of the Pennsylvania Railroad, and decades of smoke from the coal-fired locomotives had left the building blocks of the church – originally some color no one remembered – with a coat of obliterating grime. Since the anniversary Mass would be at St. Peter's, a touch of old Pittsburgh was not amiss, for, in fundamental respects, AJR – and by necessity Kass – had kept to the old ways. They had aged with St. Peter's and the old crumbling neighborhood that once had been Millionaire's Row, content to stay on at 940 North Lincoln Avenue, the well-preserved architectural relic dating back to a time when houses like theirs were called mansions.

On this milestone anniversary there would be a twilight garden party, "orchestrated," as Kay put it, by Dan, with his usual thoroughness and efficiency. But first the Rooneys and McNultys and McGinleys and Laughlins and Millers, brought together from wherever life had taken them, converged on St. Peter's for the Mass. The occasion demanded it; any such gathering without this expression of our Catholic faith was unthinkable. From the time of Maggie and Pop, Rooneys had gone to Mass at St. Peter's, and to St. Peter's a penitent AJR and his bride had returned for the wedding that authenticated their mysterious civil union of the year before.

This detour from the straight and narrow was now long forgotten. At the anniversary Mass, Bishop Vincent Leonard, Father Bob Reardon, and Monsignor Bassom Pierre officiated. Father Reardon had obtained a papal blessing from John Paul II – Dan's inspiration – and he solemnly read its text from the altar. Father Henry McAnulty, speaking with his expected eloquence, put into words what so many of us felt about the man and the woman we were honoring.

Accustomed to being made much of, AJR, I must say, was not exactly carried away. For one thing, a year in advance, there had been an "anticipatory" anniversary party for family and close friends in the rectory of Duquesne University's Holy Ghost fathers, which occupied the entire fourth floor of the on-campus Holy Childhood Building. "We have the octave of Christmas and the octave of Easter, so why not an octave for Kathleen and Arthur's anniversary?" said one of the good priests who taught at Duquesne – AJR's alma mater of choice. It may be that events too long foreshadowed become anticlimactic. Unless they don't. Either way, AJR had been bluntly dismissive when asked if he and Kass were planning to renew their vows at the anniversary Mass, a tradition his daughters-in-law favored. "Certainly not," said the Chief. "The vows we took the first time still work. Vows don't wear out."

Whatever Kass may have thought, with those words the issue was settled. And then to a priest who spoke of the papal blessing as something a bit special, AJR replied rather airily, "Well, you know, Father, I've heard from all kinds of important people about this – cardinals, bishops, governors, mayors, top business executives. I've had cards, letters, phone calls, and they've come from all over." Repeating this dialogue later, with an understanding smile, the priest was a little bemused. AJR's cloak of humility had parted, revealing the pride that lay hidden.

It was a pride his accomplishments justified, a pride his wife and five sons were aware of and happily shared. Through the exercise of self-discipline, he concealed this minor weakness from the world at large, but he was human, and at rare moments it surfaced.

For Kass, however, his seeming contrariness on this day of all days was too much. Back home after the Mass, with only Kay and another relative in the room, she started to sob. And then, with sudden vehemence, she exclaimed, "I'll divorce that little bastard yet!" Kay, astonished, cried out,

"What are you talking about? You've been married for fifty years!" "It's not too late, dear, it's not too late," answered Kass, and now the three women were laughing, the built-up tension of a stressful episode released.

For the garden party, the immense back yard at 940 North Lincoln was strung with Christmas lights and Chinese lanterns provided by Kay. Votive candles flickered on the twelve large circular tables that were spaced around the lawn. The tablecloths and napkins – black and gold, of course – came from the Allegheny Club. Kay, recalling the affair a long time later, wrote that "Kass looked elegant in her azure blue cocktail dress. She wore a necklace of gold set with a cluster of diamonds that Sandy and Pat gave her and a diamond pin that Art and I gave her the year before."

Her anniversary gift from the family was a set of twelve gold and white Picard serving plates, with an inscripted "R," hand-painted, in the center of each. On the back were the words "Kathleen and Art" and, under the names, the dates: "June 11, 1931-June 11, 1981," (It was Kay, by the way, who drew the design for those plates and who ordered them from the upscale jewelry store Bailey, Banks and Biddle.)

Aunt Alice, Kay said, "looked great in her traditional black." Kay herself was never more beautiful. Her red hair, I remember, caught the rays of the setting sun. Aunt Alice and Kass – I'm quoting Kay again – were "coiffed to perfection" by Angie, the hairdresser. Angie was present as a guest – partly to keep an eye on Alice and Kass, in case their plumage should need attention – and Mary Roseboro, too, was a guest, a guest who insisted on pitching in to help the caterers. "Mary," we kept urging her, "please sit back and enjoy the party," but she could not leave the serving and "redding up" to Alex DiCroce's staff. In her own mind, Mary was still the Rooney family's loyal and vigilant maid.

Two media people were there – Bill Burns the news anchor and Pat Livingston the sportswriter, but with an unspoken condition attached: no publicity. AJR wanted nothing on the society pages. None of us did. The guest list of dozens included few outsiders. Relatives and the Steeler gang predominated. The most notable absentee was my brother Tim, who felt that his duties at Yonkers Raceway during the biggest week of the standardbred season took precedence, a decision I am sure he came to regret. June, Tim's wife, and their children represented his branch of the family. I remember seeing only one politician – Tom Foerster, the longtime county commissioner. Most of AJR's old political friends were under the sod.

His grandchildren – regiments of them – seemed to be everywhere. In the early afternoon they had stormed through the house like a herd of frightened antelopes, racing in from the back yard and up the back steps, gathering speed as they rushed from one end of the upstairs hall to the other before risking their slender necks in a bouncing descent of the steep, carpeted main stairway, a pastime my brothers and I invented as kids. We had torn up the back yard with our war games, football games, and hockey games, churning it into mud when the weather was wet, but now, as Kay said, it looked amazingly pristine.

Under Kass's garden canopy, Bob McCartney, our young film director, had set up a projector and screen for a continuous slide show – still pictures and moving pictures of the Rooney family, going all the way back to when AJR and Kass were honeymooners. Probably there was music of some kind; after all these years I'm uncertain. The dinner, I know, was an appetizing buffet. Afterwards, the conversational hum and laughter were stilled as Mom and Dad cut the wedding cake, and then came the singing of "Happy Anniversary." Finally, Kass opened the gifts. One gift Kay admired was a gold Picard serving bowl with scenes painted on it. Kass, she said, "seemed thrilled by it all." AJR was embarrassed by all the attention but smiling, his earlier show of offhandedness put aside.

Nobody drank too much, and the grandchildren, sequestered in a corner of the yard, were peaceable – or maybe just exhausted. I found myself thinking of North Side garden parties from the storied past, the kind the Fricks and the Phippses and the Thaws and the Joneses and the Mooreheads and the Byerses — the custodians of high society at the turn of the twentieth century — must have staged. Ours, I imagined, was just as grand. And in conformance with AJR's wishes, we hadn't really "put on the dog."

I know that this night, for Kass, was as good as it would get. She had made her marriage last through fifty years, not all of them golden. To hear me say this would displease her, but it's true. Though she had threatened, out of pique, to "divorce that little bastard," AJR was, in her opinion, the greatest man who ever lived.

Some time before, in this same comfortable house, there had been a fiftieth anniversary party for Maggie and Pop. The old saloon keeper soon would pass on. Maggie was nearing the finish line, too, but not quite as fast. How much longer, I asked myself, would Mom and Dad be around?

With an effort, I turned away from such thoughts. Maggie and Pop had looked old. Tired. Mom and Dad were still full of life. Snap out of it, I said to myself. In a few more spins of the earth, the football team would be encamped at St. Vincent, starting a new season. Nineteen eighty was a disappointment, but 1981 would be different. We had hope. We were winners. We were Rooneys. All was well.

Slipsliding

In retrospect, my parents' golden wedding celebration was the best thing that happened to the Rooney clan in 1981. The football season turned out to be a downer. In clusters now, we were losing important pieces of the mechanism that had brought us our championships. Nineteen eighty was the last time around for Rocky Bleier, Dwight White, Mike Wagner, and Steve Furness. Bleier, White, and Wagner retired; Furness, disposed of, was picked up by Detroit. He would play only one more year. We got rid of Matt Bahr as well – his weak kickoffs, anathema to the coaches, had shortened his time with the Steelers – but Matt, unlike the others, was still in his prime. Super-accurate field-goal kicking would keep him in the league for another ten seasons.

The loss of Bleier – and, to a lesser extent, of White, Wagner, and Furness – took away part of our ambience. I remember something that Lovey Young said on the night before we played a pre-season game in 1981 with the New York Giants. Lovey and her husband, George Young, the Giants' general manager, were having dinner with Kay and me, and Lovey remarked that the team's younger players, not all of them rookies, seemed to be over-awed by the Steelers. She had heard them talking about Joe Greene, Jack Lambert, and Mel Blount as if they belonged to a race of superhumans. "Our guys are licked before the game starts," Lovey said, and perhaps this was true, for on the following day the Giants lost to us. But even then they were on the way up, while the Steelers, with their fading superstars, were on the way down.

Rocky Bleier's value to the Steelers derived just as much from its inspirational nature as from anything he was able to do on the field. A player who was neither big, fast, nor agile, one whose battlefield wounds might have crippled him for life, he epitomized strength of will. To no one's surprise, he prospered as a motivational speaker when his football career was over. I thought that, if so inclined, he could have been an exceptional coach. Frank Pollard, our second-year running back from Baylor, filled the bill as Rocky's replacement, but only by the measuring stick of performance. To the fans and the media, what Bleier stood for could not have been duplicated.

Dwight White, after leaving the Steelers, was an overnight success in the brokerage business. He revealed an unsuspected talent for making shrewd transactions in stocks and bonds. With White gone, only Joe Greene and L. C. Greenwood remained from the original Steel Curtain; at the end of the 1981 season they would follow White and Ernie Holmes into retirement. Furness, a late comer to the brotherhood, had started at defensive tackle in Super Bowl XIV and many other big games. Then there was Wagner, a total player who used his head, heart, and athletic skills to "make things happen."

We would miss all four of these veterans, miss their experience and attitude. That Matt Bahr would also be missed was largely unforeseen. Coaches make the mistake of thinking kickers are where you find them. Well, the kicker we signed in 1981 couldn't kick, requiring the expenditure of quality scouting time to find a new one.

Dick Haley and I had always maintained that we could stay near the top by drafting three new starters of top-flight ability every year. We thought that any other team with a core of good players could do this, too. There was nothing wrong with the concept, nothing obviously wrong, but in the 1981 draft, picking seventeenth in each round, we came up a player short. I can offer no excuses for the 1981 draft, none at all. I bungled it.

Our first-round selection, Keith Gary, a defensive end from Oklahoma, seemed to have all the tools. We thought he could step in right away and fill one of the holes in the line; and the truth is that he played some good games. His trouble was inconsistency. Along with the good games, there were just as many not so good games. As for the rest of our top four, all of them rated among the top one hundred in the draft, they were not worth a hill of beans, and the same could be said for my analysis of the information about them delivered to me by our scouts.

Summing up, I did not do my part to keep our defensive front four intact. The two rookies who became starters were linebackers – Bryan Hinkle, from Oregon, and David Little, from Florida. Continuing a trend, we took Hinkle in the sixth round and Little in the seventh. Our best picks of late seemed to come, as Dan had observed, from the middle of the pack, or even lower. Little had good bloodlines: he was the younger brother of the Dolphins' great offensive lineman, Larry Little. In his eighth year with the Steelers, 1988, David was the team's MVP, and three years later he went to the Pro Bowl. Hinkle was MVP in 1986; both he and Little were still on the roster in 1992, when Bill Cowher succeeded Noll as head coach.

Again in 1981 we failed to make the playoffs. Another sign of regression was that we lost as many games as we won. And again we lost the close games, the kind we had won in our playoff years. In six of our defeats, a touchdown or a field goal was the difference. Football indeed is a game of inches. It is also a game of intensity and focus, a game in which the hungry prevail. To complete the metaphor, age dulls the appetite. Our players from the years I speak of would be upset with me for saying this, but they were swiftly becoming superannuated.

Their coaches wouldn't like to hear that, either, which makes it none the less true.

What is equally accurate, and the blame falls on me, is that our draft did not help the situation. For example, Swann, Stallworth, and Cunningham were still catching passes, but not quite as many as before, and the wide receivers we drafted in the fourth and fifth rounds were absolute duds. Under certain conditions Noll would use Ray Pinney, a center, guard, and tackle, as an emergency receiver, lining him up at tight end. In one game, he actually caught a touchdown pass.

Speaking of Pinney, Joe Gordon overheard him remark at the end of the season that an 8-8 record "wasn't too bad." When Joe repeated that to me, saying, "It shows how far the attitude of those young guys has slipped," I shook my head in consternation but made no reply. After all, I had drafted those young guys. A lot of them, like Pinney, were good players. They were not, however, the game-breakers we needed.

In the first forty years of the franchise's history, an 8-8 record would have been satisfactory, or even at times something to celebrate. But the 1970s had changed that way of looking at things. The 1970s had raised our expectations, and in 1980 and 1981, we failed to meet them.

Chapter 69

Patchwork

Retirements were changing the face of our team. After the 1981 season Joe Greene and L. C. Greenwood, the last two charter members of the Steel Curtain front four, retired. John Banaszak, a backup and sometime starter at defensive tackle and defensive end, retired. So did J. T. Thomas, who had given us years of service at defensive back. From the offensive unit, we lost Jon Kolb, a durable, highly valued tackle, and Randy Grossman, one of the better pass-catching tight ends.

Joe Greene's jersey number also went into retirement. Greene's 75 and Ernie Stautner's 70 were the only numbers that would never again be worn by a Pittsburgh player. Selecting jersey numbers for retirement is a ticklish business. Rosters are so large that to retire every number that belonged for a while to a Hall of Famer would cause a shortage. Greene, though, was a special case. Starting in 1969, his rookie season, he'd been the cornerstone (if I may mix a metaphor) of the Steel Curtain front four. The day we drafted Greene was the day we turned the franchise around.

But now he went home to Texas and opened a restaurant – three "family-style" restaurants, actually. Chuck Noll's advice to every departing Steeler was: "Find your life's work and get on with it." Joe Greene's life's work, as he soon discovered, was not the restaurant business. Which left football, something he knew about. In 1987, at the suggestion of Joe Gordon, Noll made room on the coaching staff for him, and he remained with the team as long as Noll did. Moving on in 1992, when Bill Cowher took over from Noll, he was with the Dolphins for a while and then the Cardinals. Finally Dan brought him back for the second time – not to coach but to be a scout.

Even without Greene and the others, we were not quite ready for the graveyard. We still had Terry Bradshaw. We still had Franco, who had lost a step but reported to pre-season training camp in fine fettle. We still had Stallworth and Swann. We still had Mike Webster. We still had Larry Brown, one of the most underrated offensive tackles in the NFL. We still had Ben Cunningham. We still had two of the top linebackers in the game – Jack Ham and Jack Lambert, plus Loren Toews. We still had Mel Blount, Donnie Shell, and Ron Johnson in the defensive backfield. We still had Gary Dunn in the defensive line. Frank Pollard had become an able replacement for Rocky Bleier. Ray Pinney was becoming a Noll-type offensive lineman – smart, quick, versatile. And we had filled one of our greatest needs by acquiring a place-kicker, Gary Anderson.

We had wanted Gary Anderson since we scouted him at Syracuse, but on draft day in 1981 we fell into an easily avoidable trap. "We can get this guy on the next round, we're the only ones who have him rated this high." we kept telling ourselves. It's a mistake that coaches and personnel directors repeatedly make. The waiting game had worked when we drafted Stallworth, but Buffalo beat us to Anderson.

"We'll have to trade for him," I said to Dick Haley. "Hold on," he answered. Anderson was a prospective free agent, and Haley believed we could sign him. "No. We have to trade," I insisted. "Trust me," Haley said. Haley got his way and, just as he had foretold, Anderson signed with us in 1982. In his second season he was our MVP. He remained with the Steelers until 1994, when Cowher changed kickers, and was one of the most consistent performers in the league for many years afterward with other teams.

The credit belongs to Dick Haley for landing this prize catch.

We prepared for the 1982 draft in the same manner and the same spirit as always, but with more people involved – assistant coaches, that is to say – and more gadgetry. Computers had become an indispensable help in sorting and qualifying the raw information we gathered. I was trying to set up models that would give us a complete list of draft-eligible players who met certain minimum height and weight standards and minimum time standards in the forty-yard dash. In addition, we were looking for such things as growth potential, body control, prehensile hands (which wide receivers must have), quickness off the ball (a requirement for pass rushers), the ability to block and to shed blockers, strength, toughness, and so on, all hard to measure. Counting free agents, we had seven hundred or more names in the computer. Fewer than half were legitimate prospects.

As a result of our 8-8 record in 1981, we'd be picking twelfth. With the thirteenth pick in 1971, we came up with Franco Harris. With the twenty-first pick in 1974, we drafted Lynn Swann. We were therefore not without hope. We thought we could possibly draft someone who could lift the whole team, who could make the big play when the occasion demanded. And Walter Abercrombie, we believed, was such a catalyst.

He was still on the board when our turn came, and we grabbed him. Walter Abercrombie would be the third Baylor running back we had drafted in four years. In the first round of the 1979 draft, we had taken Greg Hawthorne, who underachieved. In the eleventh round of the 1980 draft, we had taken Frank Pollard, who overachieved. Abercrombie, it seemed to us, had Greg Hawthorne's talent and Frank Pollard's intangibles. "Can't miss" was a phrase I had learned never to use. But Abercrombie could run, catch, and block. He could make the big play. He was consistent. He was productive. He was a splendid athlete with all the intangibles.

Of course, there is always a "but." In his senior year, Abercrombie had hurt his knee. Accordingly, our medical people gave him an especially thorough physical examination, which he passed to their satisfaction. His knee, they informed us, was "playable." And they were right. Abercrombie played six years for the Steelers and seven years in the NFL. He made some big plays and some good plays. There were years when he was our second-best rusher and pass receiver. But none of this made him another Harris. As Rocky Bleier's successor in the backfield, Frank Pollard was everything we expected, and more. As Franco's successor, Abercrombie fell short by about the distance from Pittsburgh to Waco.

Watching game films of Abercrombie after he left the team, I noticed something that escaped me while he was with us: he favored his "playable" knee. George Allen, a Hall-of-Fame coach, once said to me, "The good ones" – the good running backs – "have that burst." When Abercrombie ran, he couldn't shift to a higher gear. He could not turn a good run into a great run.

Our second-round pick, offensive tackle John Meyer of Arizona State, had two sound knees when we drafted him, but only one by the end of his first and only training camp. Seriously injured, he never played a down for the Steelers or for any other pro team. In the third round, we had much better luck. Mike Merriweather, linebacker from Pacific, became a team MVP and a Pro Bowl player. Our fourth pick, defensive back Rick Woods of Boise State, was a Steeler for five years. He started at times and could make an interception. We drafted a number of other players who were able to contribute, but the 1982 crop wasn't among our better ones.

We did have some luck with free agents. Besides Anderson, there was Keith Willis, a defensive end from Northeastern University in Boston, where scouts seldom ventured. He played nine years for the Steelers. In six of those years we won more games than we lost and in four of those years we went to the playoffs. Willis was one of the guys who popped up in our computer listing of lower-rated players deserving of consideration. Bill Nunn made a trip to Boston, watched him work out, watched a few game films, and told us he looked like a prospect.

In camp, he confirmed Bill's judgment. Little else of a positive nature was happening. Before the season started, George Perles, who had the title of assistant head coach, bailed out on us. Perles always had wanted to be the commander-in-chief somewhere, and one of the fly-by-night teams in a brand new – and short-lived – pro league gave him the opportunity. Then came an offer from his alma mater, Michigan State, and Perles bailed out on the pro team to be the Spartans' head coach. Perles did well at Michigan State. He had a series of winning seasons and took the team to the Rose Bowl one year. Even the most successful coaches usually end up being fired – they're fatalistic about that – but when Perles left Michigan State he left on his own terms: he retired.

The Steelers missed Perles. He provided a sort of counterbalance, I thought, to Chuck Noll's cerebral approach. George was a down-and-dirty type of guy, by which I don't mean to say that he taught dirty football. I mean that he implanted a rambunctious mind set. Particularly in the NFL, line play is hand-to-hand combat, and Perles had the temperament to coach it as such. He also helped Noll choose assistants. Perles lobbied for Woody Widenhofer, Tom Moore, and Rollie Dotsch. They were three of the best we ever had. I thought the best assistant that Noll himself actually hired, aside from Perles, was Tony Dungy.

Rollie Dotsch left the Steelers to go with Perles, his mentor, but did not make the move to Michigan State. He became the head coach of the pro team and was doing very well when he suddenly died of a heart attack. He was one of the true gentlemen in the coaching profession. Paul Uram, our conditioning coach, also departed with Perles. After that, I lost track of him. We did not have to search very far for a conditioning coach. Jon Kolb, newly retired from the playing ranks, was eager to take the job and made a seamless transition.

On the other hand, the defection of Perles and Dotsch left us high and dry, at least temporarily. And it strengthened the impression that the Steelers were falling apart.

Momentum Killer

After going undefeated in four exhibition games, the Steelers opened the regular season of 1982 like anything but a team on its deathbed. They outfought the Cowboys in Dallas, 36-28, and won from Cincinnati at Three Rivers Stadium in overtime, 26-20. Terry Bradshaw was still throwing touchdown passes. Franco Harris was still breaking tackles. Gary Anderson had given us a field-goal threat. There was nothing to suggest our imminent demise. Then the Players Association called another strike.

The timing of the walkout was calculated. The players had learned their lesson in 1974, when they went on strike before the training camps opened. It was shortsighted strategy. Draftees and free agents reported as usual. A handful of veterans, worried about losing their positions, crossed the picket line. Others who had gone along with the strike began to lose heart, and two weeks into the season the insurgency collapsed.

For this strike, the planning was better. With the rookies assimilated, the union had everyone on board. Team owners, unable to fill out their lineups, suspended the schedule. They did not have a choice. Over an eight-week period in September, October, and November no games were played while negotiations with the union proceeded acrimoniously.

The players were asking that fifty-five percent of the league's gross revenue be earmarked for salaries. I remember hearing three of my brothers — Tim, John, and Pat – declare that if the owners gave in, then the NFL could just fold up its tent. "It'll kill the league," they told Dan and me. "The race-track owners gave the horsemen a percentage, and now we have a business where the return on investment is hardly enough to make it worthwhile." In the end, the football players got a percentage, but not the fifty-five percent they demanded. That would come later, as the outcome of a strike in 1993. The NFL not only survived, but seems to be doing fine.

During the 1982 strike, AJR continued to pay the coaches, scouts, and front-office people their full salaries. The coaches studied film; the scouts carried on as they always had. There was work, I suppose, for the front-office people, but I didn't have time to pay attention.

In the talks between the owners ad the Players Association, both sides listened closely to Dan. He was taking a first step toward the leadership role he would one day assume. Unmistakably, he was now his own man, a person of true consequence in the affairs of the NFL and no longer merely Art Rooney's son. The pride the Chief took in him was barely containable.

It eclipsed by far the confidence he placed in his second-oldest son. While the strike was still going on, he called me into his office and told me to say nothing to anyone about it. "Let Dan make all the statements to the media," he said. "The strike is his show. You butt out of it."

Since I hadn't butted in, I was taken aback. I knew the importance of the part Dan was playing. I knew the limits of my authority in the Steeler organization, or thought I did. No newspaper, television, or radio reporter had asked me to talk about the strike and I hadn't intended to volunteer anything. Whether I'd have answered a question about the strike I couldn't say. I believed in being open and honest with reporters, but I didn't tell them everything I knew.

This was not quite the way the Chief would have put it. He thought I talked too much, that I couldn't hold my tongue. He never exactly said so – not in as many words. He didn't have to; he could make his opinions clear without getting into specifics. The Chief himself was a master at talking to the media. He never let anything out unless he wanted it out. Or almost never. Once in a while he slipped up. Usually, though, if that was his purpose, he could beguile a reporter who was digging for something and send him away satisfied with a humorous story. Dan tried to do this, but lacked the Chief's ability to disarm. Although he and the Chief took pains not to lie, they were good at misleading – or "disassembling," as George W. Bush would say, losing another struggle with the English language.

They were more in control of themselves than I could ever be. My big mouth helped my relations with the press, but got me in hot water now and then. One thing I came to realize: the Chief's insistence that Dan should be the spokesman for the whole organization made sense. During the strike, when I went to a college football game on a scouting trip, I sat in the stands, not the press box. That way, there was no chance I would absentmindedly give a sportswriter a quote.

While the owners and the Players Association were scratching out a new collective bargaining agreement, Paul Martha, now a Pittsburgh attorney, rendered valuable service as an intermediary. In my view, the strike hurt both sides, since the revenue lost was gone forever, but the players ended up with a minimum salary guarantee, higher training-camp and post-season pay, and an increase in medical, retirement, and health-insurance benefits.

With a rejiggered schedule, the season resumed on November 21st. Our October 24 game with Cleveland, wiped out by the strike, would be played on January 2nd. The remaining bypassed games, seven in all, were simply canceled.

Back in action, we had an easy time beating the Oilers in Houston and were now 7-0, including those four pre-season wins. But the layoff had cost us our momentum. We had an aging team that lost three of its last six games.

Because of the shortened season, the format for the playoffs was different. For one year only, the league held a sixteen-team tournament. The Steelers qualified as one of the eight teams from the American Conference by winning the postponed game with the Browns but lost in the first round of the tournament to San Diego, 31-28. On our own field, we let an eleven-point lead slip away in the fourth quarter.

Disappointing, yes. But 1982 was another winning season. We had not had a losing one since 1971. We were keeping our heads above water.

Special Delivery

What bothered me almost as much as the way our defense crumbled after Bradshaw's touchdown pass to Stallworth had given us a 28-17 fourth-quarter lead in that 1982 playoff game was the performance, leading up to it, of the Steelers' ticket people.

Unaccountably, they hadn't prepared.

I mean they hadn't printed playoff tickets beforehand. The news that our win over Cleveland on January 2nd had put us into the tournament seemed to come as a big surprise.

So when our season-ticket holders started calling for their seats, there was utter confusion.

Quickly, the utter confusion gave way to pure bedlam.

In poured the howls of displeasure.

"You don't have my tickets? What are you telling me? Is this a joke of some kind?"

And "How can you do this to me? I've been with you since the days when you were bums and losers. I sat behind the girders at Forbes Field. I walked up Cardiac Hill to get to Pitt Stadium. I sat in the rain and snow and watched you disgrace yourselves. And now I can't get tickets to a playoff game?"

And "You Rooneys will never change. You've been giving us the shaft for fifty years."

On and on it went in the same tones of outrage. Where was the good will I thought we had earned with ten winning seasons in the past eleven, with four trips to the Super Bowl and four Lombardi Trophies?

Day and night in the frigid January weather there were long lines that almost encircled Three Rivers Stadium. Inside, the scouting department worked day and night on the 1983 draft. On rare occasions, I caught a glimpse of the freezing ticket buyers and wondered if somebody in the organization was getting hot coffee to them while they stood out there in the cold. Preoccupied with the draft, I did not take the trouble to check. I had my father's strong bent for the random act of kindness but not his disposition to act on it.

In this case, the only Rooney who acted was Dan. He ordered coffee for the people in the cold at least once.

Crisis management dictated that everybody in the front office deliver tickets door-to-door, in person. We were to do this for any customers who lived in our neighborhoods. Three houses down the street from ours there resided a sour-visaged old guy of the curmudgeonly type. He never smiled, never spoke, never, in fact, made eye contact. That he was one of our fans greatly surprised me, but, tickets in hand, I rang his doorbell on a cold, dark night near the end of the week before the game.

The next thing I knew, he was standing in the entranceway. "I have your playoff tickets," I blurted, and his face suddenly lost its rigidity. With his left hand, he grabbed the tickets. With his right hand he grabbed mine, and started pumping it. I thought he would never let go. Meanwhile, he was actually smiling. "Our tickets! Our tickets!" he shouted to his wife. "Our playoff tickets are here! And Art Rooney's kid delivered them!"

Then he was saying to me, "Thanks, neighbor, thanks. Come in! Have a drink. Or, if you don't want a drink, a cup of coffee. Gosh, I've heard so many nice things about the Rooneys, and now I know they're true."

I was flabbergasted. I did not stay for coffee, but it took me a while to break away.

"Thanks," he kept saying. "This is great. Good luck in the playoffs."

From then on, whenever I saw him, he gave me a smile and a big hello, I returned his friendliness to the best of my ability, thinking that in all the time I had lived near this fellow I misread him. He was not anti-social, just reserved, or maybe shy. AJR would have quickly penetrated his shield. He'd have made the guy believe there was nobody else whose company he preferred.

Was my father born with that gift, or did he work to acquire it? Either way, it was something I felt I never would have.

A Night with the Stars

On October 9, 1982, one year and four months after the fiftieth wedding anniversary of my parents, we celebrated another significant milestone, the fiftieth anniversary of the day that AJR put up $2,500 to buy a franchise in the National Football League.

October 9th was Kay's birthday, as it happened, a coincidence important only to me. The strike called by the Players Association had been going on for three weeks. Even so, there was no thought of postponing the big public shindig we had scheduled for that date at the David L. Lawrence Convention Center or the private party the night before at LeMont Restaurant up on Mount Washington.

The party at LeMont would honor the all-time Steeler all-star team selected in a poll of its readers by the *Pittsburgh Post-Gazette*. More than a third of the players voted onto that team – Terry Bradshaw, Franco Harris, Jack Ham, Jack Lambert, Mike Webster, John Stallworth, Larry Brown, Mel Blount – were participants, willing or otherwise, in the strike, but everybody came except a handful who did not live nearby. Only AJR could have dealt with the social awkwardness inherent in such a gathering. His person-to-person skills, as I knew they would, instantly put the strikers at ease.

If there was any disharmony at all, it had to do with the fiftieth-anniversary team's makeup. No one could even quibble about many of the selections – Bradshaw, Harris, Joe Greene, Blount, Lambert and Ham, Stallworth and Swann, Jack Butler, Ernie Stautner, L.C. Greenwood, Pat Brady as the punter. And Bill Dudley belonged – there was general agreement about that – but where? As a running back? He led the league in rushing one year, after all. Conveniently, he led the league also in pass interceptions. So Dudley ended up in the defensive backfield, leaving room on the offensive unit for John Henry Johnson as well as Harris.

My own feeling was that, while John Henry Johnson was a true Hall-of-Famer, he did not do as much for our teams in the 1960s as Rocky Bleier had done for the teams that won Super Bowls. When we drafted John Henry in 1953 he refused to sign with us and went off to Canada. His best years in the NFL, actually, were with San Francisco and Detroit. He came to Pittsburgh in 1960 and had two exceptional years and two good years. Then he got hurt, and after that he did nothing.

In the voting for center, there were pockets of support for Chuck Cherundolo, who played both ways in the 1940s, and Ray Mansfield, a favorite with the fans and the media. But Mike Webster was beyond any doubt the logical runaway choice. And though without Ben Cunningham our Super Bowl record might have been 2-2 or 2-0 instead of 4-0, Elbie Nickel deserved to be the tight end. Nickel paid a price for every pass he caught, but in a career that lasted eleven years he caught more passes than any other Steeler tight end and seldom missed a game or even a down.

It is no easy matter to judge an offensive lineman's performance except by looking at film and then rerunning it. So the choice of Jon Kolb and his teammate Larry Brown at the tackle positions reinforced my belief that no fans anywhere knew as much about football as ours did. The third linebacker, with Lambert and Ham, was Andy Russell, an equally pleasing selection. Russell, like his good friend Ray Mansfield, came to the Steelers in the 1960s, when times were tough, and played on into the Super Bowl years. That Russell, Mansfield, and Jack Butler have never even been nominated for the Hall of Fame is an injustice I don't understand.

To be with all these men who were sharing a special award for excellence was exhilarating. At the risk of going overboard, let me say it reminded me of certain Marines I got to know at Parris Island, veteran instructors who had fought in places like Guam, Iwo Jima, Guadalcanal, and the Chosen Reservoir. They seemed to be saying, "We have been there, and we survived." So did the Steeler all-stars. I hope the analogy I am making is not too far-fetched.

LeMont Restaurant on Grandview Avenue offered better-than-adequate food and a stunning view of the rivers and the Downtown skyline. Next to the view from Nob Hill in San Francisco, the urban panorama that lies before you is unrivalled in all of America. Whenever we drafted a player we wanted to impress, we took him to LeMont.

On the night of the party the skies were clear and everything sparkled. I looked around me and took in the magic. There I was with these Hall of Famers – the Chief, Johnny Blood, Bill Dudley – plus future Hall of Famers like Dan, like John Henry Johnson and so many of the still-active all-stars. There were also the players I knew would be nominated for the Hall. I'd be nominated myself one day. How lucky I am, I thought, to be Art Rooney's son and to have some involvement in the creation of what the Steelers had become – a championship team and a civic institution.

There were no formal speeches, but at the end of the dinner Andy Russell, who was always so at home on occasions such as this, tapped a fork on an empty glass. The clink-clink-clink brought us all to attention. "Let's go around the room," he proposed, "and give everyone a chance to tell what it means to be a Steeler – everyone who wants to, that is." Almost everyone, as I recollect, did want to.

Fittingly, AJR went first. With the simple straightforwardness for which he was known, he spoke of his good fortune in having guided his team through the lean years we thought would never end. He said that every player and coach connected with the Steelers in times gone by had helped us get to the top of Mount Washington on this night.

Johnny Blood, still looking like a movie star pushed into grudging retirement or like a U. S. senator at the zenith of his career, gave us a refresher course on the history of the NFL. Bill Dudley expressed his affection for AJR. Speaker followed speaker, each with a perspective of his own. Smart enough to keep quiet, I sat back and listened. Waiters and busboys and I think a few of the cooks listened too, from inconspicuous vantage points along the fringes of the room. They were all as transfixed as I was.

Each all-star left the restaurant with a foot-high bronze sculpture of a defensive player colliding with a ball carrier. The artist had somehow compressed all the dynamism and force of a spectacular open-field tackle into his creation. The image of Chuck Mehelich's hit on Leon Hart in a game at Forbes Field came back to me.

Hart was with the Detroit Lions, a huge tight end from Turtle Creek who had won the Heisman Trophy at Notre Dame. Mehelich weighed 180 pounds at the most. Knocked end over end, Hart was carried off the field on a stretcher. Mehelich got up and walked to the bench, his eyes glazed. Then he staggered into the arms of the trainer and a helpful equipment man. Snapped in two by the violence of the tackle, the leather belts attached to Mehelich's hip pads, the belts that held them in place, were dangling free. That scene, for me, epitomizes Steeler football.

I was so moved by the sculpture's symbolism that I thought of finding out if there were replicas left over, so I could buy one. It would nicely enhance a collection I had started – water-color paintings of our greatest players, past and present, by Merv Corning, a talented West Coast artist. Then I dismissed the idea. You don't buy an award meant for someone who has earned it.

My paintings had been put on display at the LeMont affair, and Joe Gordon told me that after it was over he spotted a female guest walking out with the likeness of Rocky Bleier. These paintings are originals, not copies, and my investment in them was more than sentimental; there had been times in the not-so-distant past when their cost put a squeeze on my finances.

Joe stopped the woman before she got to the door.

"Where are you going with Rocky?" he asked.

"I'm taking him home," she explained. "I just have to. I want him to be mine."

"Impossible, lady. He belongs to Art Rooney Junior," said Gordon – and, thanks to Joe's protectiveness, he still does.

I continued to collect Merv Corning's work, by the way. I have an excellent study of AJR, one of Chuck Noll, another of Billy Conn, and a beautiful portrait of Kay, with her glorious red hair accentuated.

Only the still-new David L. Lawrence Convention Center could have held the crowd that attended the big open reception on the night after the party at LeMont. I remembered how, when Lawrence was alive, public outrage killed a suggestion that Three Rivers Stadium be named in his honor. Now that he had gone to whatever place in the hereafter is reserved for politicians, it was OK to put his name on the convention center. But that was how we treated the American Indians – first we tried to exterminate them and then we gave Indian names to cities and rivers and national parks and sports teams and everything else under the sun.

Howard Cosell – "Mr. Monday Night Football" – emceed the televised celebration at the convention center. He introduced Myron Cope as "the diminutive one" (Cope loved it) and he introduced all the football players. His introduction of AJR was effusive. AJR repeated much of what he had said the night before and expressed hope that the strike would soon end. He introduced Kass, who looked elegant.

But of course she always did.

Burglarized

There was excitement afterwards, of a different kind, for the Art Rooney, Jr. family. When we returned to Mount Lebanon, Kay and I were worn out; our two sons, Mike and Art III, were hungry. While they snacked on her apple pie in the kitchen, Kay went upstairs, with Sue. In a minute, she called down, "Art, get up here immediately. Something's wrong." As she was putting away her long strand of pearls, she had made an unsettling discovery: her short strand was missing. Then she had looked into her jewelry boxes. They were empty. Everything in them was gone, including her Super Bowl X necklace. The only other such necklaces belonged to Kass, Mrs. Noll, Patricia Rooney, and Aunt Marie McGinley. The thief had even taken some of my cufflinks. I'd had the foresight to stash my Super Bowl rings in a safe-deposit box at the bank. My St. Vincent class ring had not been worth stealing, apparently. It was untouched. "Thanks, pal, you son of a bitch," I said between gritted teeth. Under Kay's bed was a jackpot the burglar had overlooked – her best silverware, lots of it.

Some on-the-spot detective work revealed that the guy was a second-story man. He had climbed up on top of an awning and entered Art III's room in the back of the house. We guessed that he had turned on the TV and watched the convention-center doings to judge how much working time he would have.

The stolen jewelry, by the insurance company's estimate, was worth about twenty thousand dollars. There had not been any cash in the house. On the window sill where the thief broke in, Art III had left a Rubik's Cube he'd been trying unsuccessfully to master. Now, glory be, it was solved.

The police identified the burglar when they picked him up later for another crime. Among the many houses he had looted was one that belonged to a relative of Kay's. The bum never confessed but went to jail for a short time. Kay's jewelry – and my cufflinks – were never recovered.

For the rest of the year, when the Steelers had a game at Three Rivers Stadium, we hired an off-duty cop to watch our house. AJR said, "You're locking the barn door after the horse has been stolen." And then he said, "You fancy dudes in Mount Lebanon who put on the dog, you're asking – just begging – to be taken."

Chapter 70

Put in Our Places

Like all of us, AJR had his faults. When he said hurtful things to Mom, I sincerely hated him. He appeared to believe that since he was the linch-pin of the family it gave him certain prerogatives. If he saw the need to be brusque with the rest of us, that was his right.

Father Silas, of course, who worked for Christ Almighty, was exempt from this sort of hazing. Father Silas would not have put up with anything like that except perhaps from the head of the Franciscan order and most certainly from the Pope.

I have said that when Dad and Mom had a spat, Mom would drive all the way to Ligonier, cooling off. After one of these blowups, when there were visitors in the house, she asked me to come with her as she started out the door. Instead of driving to Ligonier, she got no farther than St. Peter's Church. There, sobbing and crying, she remembered her guests and turned back.

AJR's wrath could be shattering to Pat, John, and me. In the Steeler offices he might put you down in front of an intern or a secretary. Only Tim was bold enough to talk back.

I made a suggestion once that I thought was in Mom's best interest, and her reaction surprised me. Because Dad was out of town so much, I told her, she should have her own credit cards and belong to a country club. To Kass, this sounded like criticism of Dad. She fastened me with a look and said: "You and your four brothers put together would not make a patch on your father's ass."

And she was right.

Ordinarily, AJR did not berate his football players, but I was in the office one day when he picked up a telephone and called Steeler guard John "Bull" Schweder a "no-good greasy bum." It seems that Bull was asking questions about the team and its finances, which Dad thought was none of his business. Another time, on a street corner, he took a swing at a heckling fan. It was perhaps just as well that the punch did not connect.

I don't want this to be one-sided. Dad could compliment your work and make you feel super. He was an exponent of the R.A.K. — the random act of kindness. The part-time workers at Three Rivers Stadium — the press-box crew, the security people, the spotters for the radio announcers — were frequent beneficiaries of these R.A.K.'s. Let me give one example. Hearing that Ralph, a member of the ground crew, was in Palm Beach on vacation one winter, and knowing that he was seriously ill with kidney trouble and liver trouble, Dad invited him to dinner at our dog track. He also invited Curt Gowdy, a big-time television sportscaster. "Ralph's with our organization," Dad said to Gowdy after introducing them. As far as Gowdy knew, Ralph might have been the trainer or he might have been the controller — the man in charge of investments.

"Mister Rooney made me feel like a million bucks," Ralph said.

He could make perfect strangers feel the same way. Checking out of a motel in Frederick, Maryland, I found a note to call the head of security. It crossed my mind at once that my car had been stolen. But no. The man wanted to tell me about the time he had gone to Pittsburgh for a Steeler game at Pitt Stadium in the 1950s.

"My young son was with me, and we were waiting for the ticket window to open when this guy came by," the cop said. "He was short and portly. Had a big neck. Glasses. Big cigar in his mouth. He was wearing an old topcoat. And a hat. Somehow we got to talking. The guy asked my boy where he was from. 'Frederick, Maryland.' 'Frederick? I have a farm near Frederick.' The ticket window opened and I pulled out my wallet. 'Save your money,' the guy said. 'Come on with me.' Well, he took us through the gate and down to the field. When we got there, the boy and I hung back. This older man said, 'Come on,' and we followed him out to where a few of the players were loosening up early. He introduced us to them and he introduced us to some of the coaches. Then he pointed to a section of the stadium and said, 'Go up there and find yourselves a couple of seats. There'll be a lot of them open, because we're not sold out.' That man was Mister Art Rooney."

Certainly Dad mellowed with age. In the 1970s and 1980s there were only occasional eruptions. One that I recall took place in the coffee kitchen at Three Rivers Stadium when Myron Cope, the color man on Steeler radio broadcasts, learned what it was like to displease AJR. A streaker, naked except for a jockstrap, had been making a spectacle of himself at our games, dashing out onto the field and running around madly until the cops chased him down. Myron seemed to regard this as harmless entertainment. On Steeler broadcasts and on his radio talk show, he mythologized the guy – "When will he strike next?" – and other media people picked up on it.

AJR, meanwhile, was smoldering. He blamed Myron, the most popular and most listened-to sportscaster in town, for egging the halfwit on. The chance to say so before an audience came one morning in the coffee room, a gathering place for coaches, scouts, and front-office workers. Myron was with them, shooting the breeze, when AJR strolled in. He was wearing his gray cardigan sweater with a white shirt, sharply-pressed dark slacks, and well-shined black loafers, a fashion plate now in contrast to the way he had dressed before our move to these bright new surroundings. He poured himself a cup of coffee and then, without preamble, gave the unfortunate Cope a blast right out of the old days.

"Myron," he began, "you're making a hero out of that streaker. What you're doing is just going to encourage other nuts. They'll be trying the same thing. The cops will be after him, and it could easily cause a riot one of these Sundays. I thought you had better sense than that."

Simply repeating the Chief's words doesn't fully suggest how withering they were. It was the tone of his voice and the look on his face that conveyed the extent of his anger. Having spoken, he turned on his heel and quickly walked back to his office. Myron called after him, "Mister Rooney ..." but Mister Rooney paid no attention.

The coffee room fell silent. Ten or fifteen seconds that seemed like an hour went by, all of us staring into our cups, and then I said cheerfully, "Well, Myron, welcome to the family. The only people he talks to like that any more are his sons!"

'Gone'

On a morning two or three weeks after the Steelers' anniversary party and a day or two before the end of the players' strike, I was at Three Rivers Stadium as usual – the strike hadn't changed my routine – when Mary Regan came into my office, looking perturbed, and said, "You'd better get over to your dad's house right away."

Then she continued, "Your mom hurt herself on the steps."

Kass was 78, and visibly slowing down. She was no less elegant, no less ladylike. At the anniversary party, beautifully dressed as always, she had sparkled, making all of us proud. Though she had instantly recognized such long-absent friends as John Blood McNally, Bill Dudley, and Ernie Stautner, her short-term memory was failing. She had stopped driving her car, the big, high-powered Buick replaced for her every two years by AJR. Now she relied on the chauffeurs he recruited: Iggy Borkowski, Richie Easton, and her favorite, Ed Kiely. Ralph Berlin helped out between football seasons, and of course there were always sons and grandsons.

"Hurt herself on the steps," Mary Regan had said. I made the trip from Three Rivers Stadium to 940 North Lincoln Avenue in less than five minutes. That Victorian stairway was treacherous. When my brothers and I were young, and addicted to racing back and forth in the upper hall, a barricade had been placed at the top to keep us out of danger. Kass, while descending those steps, had twisted an ankle. Instinctively, she reached for the banister, saving herself from a fall to the ground floor. And now she could not stand, or move from the steps, where I found her awkwardly seated.

Aunt Alice, I think, was the one who had called Mary Regan. AJR was at home, but seemed helpless. "These damn steps!" Kass said to me. They were steep, the distance between them hard to judge. From Aunt Alice, or AJR, or Kass herself – I'm no longer certain – I learned that Ralph Berlin was on his way. Kass would be getting the same quick first aid as a Steeler disabled on the football field.

Ralph Berlin and Kay arrived in a dead heat. Kay had just sent the kids off to school when Aunt Alice called her at home. Nobody – not the fastest driver on the NASCAR circuit – could have made better time between Mount Lebanon and the North Side. Berlin was his capable self. With help from the rest of us, he moved Kass off the steps and into a chair with rollers. He called the paramedics. Then he called Dr. Paul Steele, the football team's orthopedic specialist.

It took the paramedics a full twenty minutes to get to the house, greatly annoying Kay. When the ambulance left for Divine Providence Hospital, where Dr. Steele was waiting, all of us piled in except AJR. "Aren't you coming?" asked Kay. To her consternation, he answered, "No, I'm not much good in situations like this."

At the hospital, Dr. Steele ordered X-rays. They revealed a broken bone in the lower part of Kass's leg. All the while she was calm – "mostly mad at herself for causing such an uproar," Kay remembers. Dr. Steele ordered a cast. We did not get a look at it until some time later, and Kay was not pleased. It covered the entire leg from the foot (every bit of it) to the upper thigh.

"All this for a turned ankle?" Kay said to Dr. Steele.

"We have to immobilize these older people," Steele replied. There was also a fracture, he reminded her.

The top of the cast cut into Kass's leg, making her "miserable," she said. So the next morning, Kay asked Dr. Steele if he could shorten the cast "by at least five or six inches." He shortened it by one and a half inches.

More confident in Dr. Steele than Kay was, I believed Kass to be in good hands. In about a week and a half, she was out of the hospital. Dan engaged round-the-clock private nurses, and Mary Roseboro moved in to help with the work. In Dan's opinion, Mom, AJR, and Aunt Alice had all reached the stage where they "needed keepers." The house was extremely crowded, but Dan could organize and operate anything, it seemed to me.

Thanksgiving arrived. There would be no big family dinner for upward of fifty-five people at the St. Clair Country Club, our traditional way of celebrating. Kay, who'd been visiting Kass every day, cooked and delivered to 940 North Lincoln Avenue a sumptuous repast of turkey breast, stuffing, giblet gravy, cranberries, mashed potatoes, corn, peas, and a pumpkin pie with fresh whipped-cream topping.

By this time the football strike was over and the Steelers were to play the Seahawks that Sunday in Seattle. Saturday, on my way to the airport for the flight to the West Coast, I made a stop to see Kass. She was in bed in my old room, with its view of the back yard, the garden, and the church steeples on Western Avenue. I thought she looked old and gray, but otherwise "not bad." Dan thought differently. He told me on the plane that, to him, she looked "like death." I knew that Kay was apprehensive, too. She and Susie also had gone to see Kass on Saturday, and Kay was overcome with "a strange feeling." Would this be the last time? she found herself wondering.

I watched the game in Seattle from the Kingdome press box with Dan. At some point, I was called to the telephone. "Art, this is Jim Laughlin. You mom is in bad shape. She's been taken to the hospital ..." He stopped talking. Then: "Wait." Another few seconds of silence. "I'm just getting something ... She's gone, Artie. She's gone."

After a heart attack at home, Mom had died in the operating room while Dr. George Magovern was installing a pacemaker.

Dan was now beside me in the Kingdome press box. "Let's get out of here," he said. We waited below, in a private office, until the game was over. On the long plane ride home, players, coaches, trainers, and equipment men came to us with murmured condolences. I thought of what Uncle Jim said to me after Grandma Rooney had died: "You can take a lot, Artie, but when it's your mother ..."

Now I understood. Completely. All I can say is that my dad never meant as much to me as Kass did. I thought of them differently. He was Art Rooney. She was Mom.

Devlin's

At Devlin's Funeral Home, we were in for a shock. As Kay expressed it years later, in writing, the Devlins "had actually laid Kass out WITH THAT !@#$% CAST STILL ON HER LEG!!!!!"

Kay spoke to the head mortician. She told him to get the cast off or he would never again bury anyone from the Rooney family. "Kass *hated* that thing." she added.

"We don't have a saw," the man replied.

"Then you'd better *find* one," Kay said.

"Which they did, by God," she wrote in her reconstruction of the incident.

Kay still feels that by impeding Mom's circulation the cast was what hastened her death.

So many flowers were sent to Devlin's that nobody knew where to put all the baskets. It was customary, in cases like this, to send the extra flowers to nearby hospitals, but AJR had a different solution. In another room at the funeral home, the 93-year-old father of a firefighter he knew was laid out. At AJR's behest, this room was soon full of floral arrangements with cards bearing well-known names – names of football players and coaches. When the players and coaches came to pay their respects to Kass, they were urged by the Chief to visit the old man's casket and sign the condolence book. All the Rooneys in sight were requested to do the same thing, and they knew the request was an order.

A random – and typical – act of kindness. Even in this hour of grief, it was second nature with the Chief to think of others.

St. Peter's Church was too small for the crowd at Kass's funeral Mass. There were twenty or more priests and concelebrants. Friends of Kass and the Chief from every NFL team came, and they joined the long procession to the North Side Catholic Cemetery, a cortege of automobiles that stretched out for miles.

As I was pulling away from the church with Kay and the kids, I caught a glimpse of Mort Sharnik, the *Sports Illustrated* writer from New York, standing alone on the sidewalk bordering West Park. He looked lost. I stopped at the curb and called out to him. "Need a ride?" He did. "Squeeze in," I suggested, and after hesitating a little, he complied. "You're with the main mourners," I told him, " but don't be embarrassed. We're all glad to see you."

Once we had put him at ease, he told us of having said to a taxi driver at the airport that morning, "I'm here for Mrs. Rooney's funeral, but I don't know where it's going to be." The driver said, "Don't worry about it," and took him straight to St. Peter's Church.

I thought of how many lives of strangers my parents had touched. Mort, as though reading my mind, said, "Your mother was such a wonderful lady."

Later he reminded me of a promise I had made to write down everything I could recall about the Rooney family. "Your mother is gone," he said, "and soon a lot of others will be gone. Believe me, your memory will grow dim. Do it for all your kids. Do it for your grandchildren. Do it for your nephews and nieces."

Here is one last memory – Kay's – from the cemetery. She noticed AJR wandering off, away from the crowd at the gravesite, and going behind a tree – in order to cry without being seen, Kay presumed. "But then my Art walked down to find him 'taking a whiz,'" she continued. "Strange what comes to mind when one thinks back."

A Time to Grieve

For about a month after the funeral, our family would drive to 940 North Lincoln Avenue every evening to visit AJR and Aunt Alice, who continued to make her home there for as long as she lived. AJR had promised Kass he'd "take care" of Aunt Alice, but in some respects it was just the reverse: Aunt Alice took care of him. None of us ever knew her actual age, but she was well over 70 – old enough, Dan said, to need help. AJR, who was 81, believed they could get by with only Mary Roseboro's assistance; artfully, Dan persuaded him that some of the extra staff people who were looking after Kass should be kept on.

With his wife gone, AJR spent more time than ever at Three Rivers Stadium. The Steelers, more than ever, became his family, Mary Regan more than ever his protector, Ed Kiely more than ever his right-hand man. His infirmities increased, but his mind remained sharp. He was still the Chief, and everyone knew it.

At Three Rivers, his routine seldom varied. Every morning he walked the gray carpets, from the kitchen past Dan's office and the accounting department, down past the scouting department, out to the front desk and Joe Gordon's office, on through the meeting rooms and the coaches' area, then into the dressing rooms to play a hand or two of poker with Ralph Berlin and any players being treated for injuries. Even now I encounter players who speak of these card games as the most vivid memory they retain of their days with the Steelers. They are players whose injuries cut short their careers, who may never have worn a uniform on a Sunday afternoon. AJR embodies the whole experience for them. "He always remembered my name," they tell me, finding it hard to believe.

There was never any change in the way he dressed: red, brown, or tan polo shirt, with or without a necktie, cardigan sweater, dark gray slacks. The big green cigar, protruding at an angle from the corner of his mouth, was an unneeded badge of identity. "Doing your laps, Mister Rooney?" asked the people who passed him in the corridor. And unfailingly his answer was the same: "Yep. At my age, it's all you *can* do."

In good weather, he would venture out on the field to watch practice, or to chat with Dirt DiNardo and the grounds crew, getting them to talk about themselves and their families. When he asked how the wife and kids were, he really wanted to know.

At home, he would sit every night in his black leather reclining chair, one leg dangling over the side. An arm's length away, he kept the blue cashmere lap robe we had bought for him in Scotland. The big brass spittoon that Mary Roseboro still attended to would be on the floor at his feet. Two television sets would be blaring. Yes, blaring: his deafness had increased. While he listened to the news, he'd be saying the rosary.

Alice, who always before had remained in the kitchen with Kass, now sat in the den, keeping him company. Sometimes Dan and his family would be there. Aunt Margaret's son Jim seemed to be always around. He referred to himself as AJR's driver and "go-fer."

Kay and Susie, and I would stay for a half-hour, stretching it out at times to forty-five minutes. Susie had a special way with her grandfather. Somehow she knew how to comfort him, silently holding his hand. Years later, she endeared herself in much the same fashion to Kay's father, Roy Kumer, who was then in his nineties. How did she do this – establish such an easy rapport with these two strong men? I could only wonder. It was not a skill she inherited from her dad. Communication with the Chief was always difficult for me. As a mark of his fondness for Sue, he gave her Kass's rosary, the one she had held in the coffin.

Friends and relations were allowing the Chief time to grieve. There were interruptions in our visits while he answered brief telephone calls. When it was Jack McGinley or Ed McCaskey of the

Bears on the line, the conversation would last a while longer. Over time, the telephone calls gradually lengthened and AJR's life returned to normal. He listened more closely to the televised news and sports. On visits, we found ourselves drifting back to the kitchen, where Alice had resumed spending most of her time. We no longer made the trip every evening. Then AJR's name began to reappear in the newspapers. He was back in circulation. "I'm going to the farm with Iggie and Richie," he would say. Or, "I'm flying to New York to see Timmy."

The mourning period had come to an end.

Chapter 71

'Let's Take Rivera'

I don't have much to say about the fourteen players we drafted in 1983. No, the player who stands out in my memory, and I am not alone in feeling this way, is a guy we could have taken but didn't.

Dan Marino was eligible that year. Pittsburgh born and bred, Marino grew up in lower Oakland and played quarterback at Central Catholic High School. He was good – very good. Another game he played well was baseball. The Kansas City Royals, convinced that he had the makings of a big-league third baseman, drafted him early, but Marino chose to play college football. At Pitt, a short walk up the hill from his working-class neighborhood, he passed for 8,597 yards and seventy-nine touchdowns in three and a half seasons. Both were all-time Pitt records and still are.

As a freshman, Marino became Pitt's starting quarterback in the seventh week of the season. The Panthers then won their last five games and beat Arizona in the Fiesta Bowl. In his sophomore year, Pitt won ten of eleven games and then beat South Carolina in the Gator Bowl. In his junior year, Pitt won ten of eleven games and then beat Georgia in the Sugar Bowl on Marino's 33-yard touchdown pass with thirty-five seconds to play.

When Marino was a senior, Pitt lost two regular-season games, while winning nine, and lost to Southern Methodist in the Cotton Bowl, 7-3. It was one of the few times ever, possibly the only time (I haven't researched this), that a defense had kept Marino from throwing any passes for touchdowns. He appeared to have slipped just a little but was still the best quarterback by far in the 1983 draft. He was 6 feet 4 and solidly built, a dropback passer in the NFL mold who didn't move around much in the pocket. He didn't have to: he could put a lot of zip on the ball and he could get it away instantaneously. His arm may have been as strong as Bradshaw's. He could pinpoint receivers and his passes were easy to catch.

But we were hearing rumors about Marino, rumors we didn't like. Word had gotten around that he was sniffing cocaine. Other scouting directors would say to me, "Hey, Artie, what's the story on Marino? Is he or is he not a cokehead?" There's no proof of it, I'd tell them. But I resolved to find out, if I could.

As it happened, one of the players on our injured-reserve list was Steve Fedell, a linebacker who had been Marino's teammate at Pitt. He was smart and proud-spirited. Told he'd continue to be paid while he was hurt, he said to my brother Dan, "I don't want money for doing nothing. Give me a broom. At least I could sweep the floors." Dan then suggested to me that Steve might be useful as a part-time scout. Rocky Bleier had helped in that way while recovering from his war wounds, Dan reminded me. I made a phone call or two, learned only good things about Steve, and put him to work. He was an excellent judge not only of football talent but of character, it seemed to me, and so I asked him about Marino.

"Is he into dope? No," Steve said. Marino's only fault, he told me, was excessive loyalty to certain friends of long standing – friends who were not good guys, according to Fedell. I thought of how AJR remained close for a long time to the hangers-on he collected the way a ship collects barnacles. They were people he knew from the race tracks, from the fight game, from the North Side, from Las Vegas. Father Silas would shake his head and say, "It's amazing how much good there is in these men" – he never used the word "hoodlums" – "but there's something flawed about them. They can't take that big step, the big step away from their impediments." AJR could step away. He could separate himself from dubious companions and do it with such finesse that there were no hard feelings.

I don't think he knew Marino at all, but he loved him – saw some Billy Conn in him, perhaps. I didn't know Marino, either. I had watched him work out for us on a windy day between the 1982 football season and the 1983 draft, but our conversation afterwards was brief, and I remember only one thing he said to me: "I'd sure like to play for the Steelers." I may have replied that we'd sure like to have him. Certainly Tony Dungy, our defensive coach, was impressed with Marino's arm strength. I have said that the day was windy. Actually, the wind was more like a gale, and Marino was firing missiles into its teeth.

Just as Steve Fedell had assured me, the rumors about Marino were untrue. Three or four weeks before draft day, the Chief called me into his office. Two men wearing dark suits and nondescript neckties were with him. Neither of them cracked a smile. They were very tough-looking in an unmistakable Irish way and I immediately recognized them as cops – plainclothesmen. I could see the clear-enough outline of their shoulder holsters. "Close the door," the Chief ordered. I did as I was told. Then he said to the detectives, "This is my boy Artie; he's in charge of our scouting." He introduced his visitors, but their names have slipped my mind. "These men," he went on, "have something to tell you about Danny Marino."

It was this: "We've been looking into the rumors about him, and we find no evidence that he is using, selling, or transporting hard drugs like cocaine. There aren't any maybes about this. He may have puffed on some marijuana. Most college kids nowadays do."

The one who did the talking asked if I understood. Wondering what he had said that I could possibly misinterpret, I nodded. AJR then dismissed me with the injunction, "Say nothing about this to anyone except Noll and Haley." I did tell Noll and Haley – and no one else.

Steve Fedell came with me to the Senior Bowl game in Mobile, and we kept an eye on Marino during practice. He appeared to be moody and distracted. Is it any wonder? I thought. When you're the subject of innuendo and scandal mongering, when you're constantly under a microscope, what does that do to your peace of mind? One day when we were watching from the stands he walked off the field looking disgusted and headed for the North team's bus. He climbed inside and sat there alone until Fedell joined him. As Steve told me later, he said to Marino, "Hey, Danny, you can't behave like this. No matter how you feel. This is your showcase. The scouts and coaches from the pro teams are down here to learn who you are."

These words from an ex-teammate may have done Marino some good. I saw him that night in the hotel lobby with Don Shula, who was coaching the Miami Dolphins by then, and he was noticeably more cheerful and relaxed.

We had the twenty-first pick in the first round of the draft, our penalty for having won twice as many games as we lost in 1982. Dick Haley wanted to move us up by trading this first pick and a couple of extra picks we had somehow acquired in the middle rounds. By doing so, we could get a higher-rated player, but Noll and I felt that we needed every pick available to us. We were looking for smart, coachable players with the capacity to improve, players we could develop into the kind you must have to keep winning. There was always a supply of gifted natural athletes who had not performed up to their ability. To think we could bring out the qualities in them that were lying dormant may have been arrogant, but, damn it, the concept had worked wonders for us in the past, so why would it not continue to be successful?

One reason, hindsight informs me, was that the other teams in the league were pulling even with us. They were doing as good a job of identifying these overlooked diamonds in the rough and either scooping them up in late rounds or signing them as free agents. Maybe, in fact, they were doing a better job. Perhaps we had lost an edge we once had, but in 1983 it was not yet completely evident.

Ordinarily when we were picking as far down as twenty-first, we watched the players we had rated one, two, and three disappear from the board. But as the teams drafting ahead of us in 1983 made their picks, we didn't see this. There were three players we wanted badly, and everybody was passing them up. One of these was Marino. Another was Gabe Rivera, nose tackle and defensive end from Texas Tech. The third was Dave Rimington, a center from Nebraska, who in our opinion was one of the best offensive lineman in the draft. Team after team left them unclaimed, and our optimism grew steadily. "Hey," Noll said to Haley and me, "it looks like we've got a shot at one of these guys."

It turned out that Noll was correct. All three still could be had when our turn came. AJR was hoping we'd take Marino, I knew. Noll seemed to lean that way too. He spoke of Marino in superlatives, stressing his size, his strong arm, his quick release, the accuracy of his throws, his excellent field vision. "He has it all," Noll said. "He's going to be a good one."

I agreed with every word of this, but I was low-keyed about it. On draft days in the past, I had been an unabashed partisan. It would be the end of the world, I believed in 1970, if we did not draft Terry Bradshaw, the end of the world in 1972 if we failed to take Franco Harris. This time I controlled my emotions. Don't let the fact that Marino's a Pittsburgh guy influence your judgment, I said to myself. Go about your job in a professional, impersonal manner.

Haley and I huddled with Noll. The first thing he said was, "Let's decide between Marino and Rivera." Our information was that Rimington had been playing with two bad knees, and though he had played very well it was still a negative. It explained why twenty other teams had stayed away from him, we surmised. "He'll have a short pro career," Noll predicted, with perfect foresight. The Cincinnati Bengals drafted him, and in three years he was finished. "Both of you know how I feel about Marino," Noll continued. "He's a marvelous talent. But look – we're overloaded with quarterbacks. We have Bradshaw. We have Malone. We have Stoudt." Cliff Stoudt had been with us since 1977, but all he needed, Noll thought, was a chance. Furthermore, it might come a little sooner than anyone expected, for though Mark Malone was next in line after Bradshaw – now a thirteen-year veteran – Malone, too, had a bad knee. Bad, but not alarmingly bad. "It could be OK," Noll allowed.

"Anyhow," he said, having finished his review of our quarterback situation, "let's go the way we started." The way we started, back in 1969, was by drafting a great defensive lineman, Mean Joe Greene. "Let's take Rivera."

I didn't argue. I didn't ask questions. I didn't prolong the discussion. Chuck Noll had given his reasons for making Gabe Rivera our number one pick, and I thought they were sound reasons.

So without further ado we drafted the defensive lineman from Texas Tech instead of Danny Marino.

And the whispered allegations that Marino was using drugs had nothing to do with it.

Déjà Vu All Over Again?

Twenty-six of the twenty-eight teams in the league had kissed off a chance to take Marino when the Miami Dolphins drafted him. We were one of those twenty-six, but here in Pittsburgh there was no great outcry; picking Joe Greene before Hanratty back in 1969 had been more of an issue with the fans. Multiple Super Bowl championships can do a lot for a team's credibility.

The parade of great quarterbacks spurned by the Steelers is a long one, and Marino fell into step right away. In the very first game of his rookie season, he passed for more than three hundred yards. From that time on, in seventeen years with the Dolphins, Marino did not often *fail* to pass for three hundred yards.

The analogy I draw between Marino and Johnny Unitas is that both were home-grown and both might have played for the Steelers instead of for Don Shula. We drafted Unitas, yes, but cut him before the start of the season and then watched him break the following NFL records as a Baltimore Colt: most passing yardage, most completions, most touchdown passes, most 300-yard games. When Marino retired, he held all the records Unitas had set and thirteen others besides, which I hope you will not expect me to list.

Of course, the relative ability of football players from different eras cannot be measured entirely by the statistics they leave behind. Changes in the rules, the help a player gets from his teammates – these and other factors, lots of them, contribute to the breaking of records. Unitas is still thought of by many NFL historians as the quarterback who could do the most to win a game for his team. With Unitas at quarterback, the Colts were league champions in 1958 and 1959, before championship games were called Super Bowls. The one time Marino took Miami to the Super Bowl was in 1984, his second season. He dueled it out with the Forty-Niners' Joe Montana, still another product of the Western Pennsylvania quarterback hatchery, and Montana prevailed, 38-16.

Bradshaw, just in case you've forgotten, was the winning quarterback in Super Bowls IX, X, XIII, and XIV. (Don't ask me why Super Bowls get the Roman numeral treatment, a prerogative once reserved for popes, emperors, and kings.) When we drafted a defensive lineman instead of Marino, we had no idea that Bradshaw would start only one more game for the Steelers. During the 1982 season, even in our post-season loss to San Diego, he had played as well as ever, or almost as well. For a quarterback, he was not yet an antique – just 33 or 34 years old. The elbow on his throwing arm had been giving him pain, but our orthopedic specialist, Dr. Paul Steele, counseled that surgery would be foolish. Cortisone shots in the affected area, coupled with a program of physical therapy, should keep him playing for several more years, Steele believed. We called upon our highly-regarded neurosurgeon, Joe Maroon, for a second opinion, and he backed up Dr. Steele. Cortisone shots and therapy were all that was needed; Bradshaw could "play through the pain."

Bradshaw himself was not convinced. At home in Louisiana, he went to a Shreveport doctor who sold him on undergoing surgery. I heard about this from our trainer, Ralph Berlin. "If you let me operate," the doctor promised Bradshaw, "you can be playing pain-free for a long time to come."

What the operation actually did was wipe out the first three months of the 1983 season for Bradshaw. He was back in the lineup on December 10th for our game at Shea Stadium with the Jets – a game we had to win to reach the playoffs. In the first quarter, he efficiently directed two long drives that ended with touchdown passes. On the second touchdown pass he blew out his arm and never played again for the Steelers or any other team.

Crack-Up

Gabe Rivera was friendly and likable, a Mexican-American from Crystal City, Texas, who spoke with a barely perceptible Spanish accent. At Texas Tech, he acquired a media nickname – "Senor Sack." Getting to the quarterback – bringing him down, making him scramble, or forcing him to throw a hurried pass – was his specialty. He measured 6 feet 2 or a little over and weighed 290 pounds. In 1983, even for a defensive lineman, that kind of size was extraordinary. Despite his bulk, he was quick off the ball; no one could hold him up at the line of scrimmage – at any rate, not for long. Keeping low to the ground, which wasn't easy considering how big he was, he used his strength to shed blockers on the move.

The 1983 season opened, and week by week Senor Sack was showing improvement. We were all quite content with the No. 1 draft choice we had made. In Bradshaw's absence, the inheritor of the quarterback job was Noll's favorite, Cliff Stoudt. Mark Malone's trick knee had so impaired his mobility that all he could do now was back up a few steps and throw the ball. Stoudt, when he had to, could pivot away from tacklers or sometimes knock them over. He was tall, maybe 6 feet 5, and no beanstalk. For another thing, he had a better arm than Malone did. In his own estimation, his arm was the equal of Bradshaw's. For a guy who had spent his first six years in the league as an understudy, he did not lack self-confidence.

Calvin Sweeney was more of a realist. "I'm not a Hall of Famer like Swann and Stallworth," he would say, just in case there was any question about it, which there wasn't. But with Swann gone and Stallworth on the injury list, fun-loving Cal became our go-to pass receiver.

The running game, though, was our bread and butter. Franco Harris, for the eighth time in twelve seasons, would gain one thousand yards. Frank Pollard continued to run and block effectively and Walter Abercrombie was everything Noll had hoped he would be as a runner and pass catcher – maybe not quite everything, but close. Right here let me say that a tenacious offensive line (Webster, Brown, Wolfley, Ilkin, and Cunningham) undergirded the success of the running game.

After seven weeks, our record was 5-2. I thought, "Hey – this could be the start of something big!" On October 16th, in a 44-17 win over Cleveland, Stoudt at one point completed thirteen passes in a row. He was taking pressure off Sweeney by throwing just as often to Cunningham or Harris. I had to admit it: he reminded me of Bradshaw when Bradshaw was coming into his own. In another way, too, he mirrored the youthful Bradshaw. He was throwing a lot of interceptions – momentum killers.

They hadn't hurt us all that much because of the defense. There were times when Mel Blount or Donnie Shell or the upstart Rick Woods, our 1982 fourth-round pick from Boise State, would get us back on offense with an interception. Jack Lambert was still hell on wheels, a threat to the other team's quarterback whether leading the pass rush or climbing all over a receiver. In the defensive line, Gary Dunn and Keith Willis were having good years. And Gabe Rivera – Senor Sack – was doing his part and more.

To sum it all up, the future looked promising. Then came a blow from which we never fully recovered.

Friday night, October 21st. It was raining a little. Enough to make the streets slick. Gabe Rivera was having "one for the road" at a popular North Side tavern owned by a man named Wiggins. Before that, he had evidently had five or six for the road somewhere else. I knew that Gabe liked to drink, and I should have factored that little item into the data we had used in reaching our decision to draft him, but I didn't. His appetite for food bothered us more. Told he must keep his weight under 300 pounds or thereabouts, and that one way to do it would be to substitute fish – tuna, perhaps – for a Tex-Mex diet rich in saturated fat, Gabe went along with the program. He started to eat tuna — by the can. He was eating, we learned, twenty-eight cans of it every day. I fear that his consumption of alcohol was equally unrestrained. When one of our assistant coaches came into the Wiggins place on the night of October 21st with a friend, he saw that Gabe had a snoot full and told him he'd better get home. The team was flying to Seattle the next day, but first there would be a light practice.

Bitterly, the coach blamed himself for letting Gabe drive, for letting him go out to the parking lot and wedge behind the wheel of his modified sports car. Gabe was used to driving on the Texas prairie, where the roads are straight and flat. Speeding along Babcock Boulevard, he came to a hill. At its crest he lost control of his car, and it hydroplaned.. No doubt he was going too fast; no doubt the asphalt was wet; no doubt all the alcohol had deadened his reflexes. He skidded out of his lane and crashed head-on into a bulkier car driven by an elderly man. The force of the collision sent Rivera through the large rear window of his car, which had no back seat. Except for minor cuts and bruises, the driver of the other car was unhurt.

The paramedics called for a helicopter. Alive, but badly injured, Gabe was lifted in and flown to Allegheny General Hospital, a few miles away. One of the orderlies at the hospital told me, "I helped carry Gabe from the chopper to the emergency room. He was huge – so big we had to call for extra guys."

Instead of getting on the plane to Seattle the next day, I stayed behind with AJR to monitor Gabe's condition. The previous November, I had gone with the team to Seattle while Kass was in Allegheny General. To my everlasting sorrow, she died there before we got back to Pittsburgh.

On our way to see Gabe, the Chief had me park his Buick near the hospital's main entrance. We started walking, and a flower vendor reached out and thrust a bouquet into AJR's hands. "Mister Rooney," he said, "please give these fall flowers to Gabe." AJR seemed embarrassed. He carried the bouquet to the hospital entrance and then turned it over to me, explaining, "The nurse can take care of this."

Right away we were told that Gabe had a very severe spinal-cord injury. In the recovery room, mingled with the smell of the antiseptics, was another pungent odor. Blood. Gabe Rivera's blood. We saw him hoisted up in his bed, motionless. Several nurses bustled around him, doing busy work. He was wearing one of those ridiculous, bib-like hospital gowns - light blue, I think - and he was conscious but heavily tranquilized.

"Gabe," a nurse said to him, "Mister Rooney is here to see you. And his son, too." I had spoken with Gabe a number of times after the draft and the pre-season camp, but AJR seemed to know him better than I did. The Chief went out of his way every year to make himself acquainted with all the rookies. Approaching the bed, he took this helpless hulk of a man by the hand.

"Remember me, Gabe? I'm Art Rooney. And this is my boy Artie." On the opposite side of Gabe's bed, I had taken his other hand. It was immense, and he was hanging on tight. AJR kept talking. "We came over to make sure you're OK. The nurses say that you're not in pain now."

Dazedly, Gabe was staring at AJR, looking into his eyes. He glanced over at me with what I thought was a faint, fleeting sign of recognition. He would not let go of our hands. Did he realize, I wondered, how alone he was, a long way from Texas in this dark, cold, strange northern city? He must have sensed that we were his lifeline, or that AJR was.

"Gabe, your mom will be here very soon," the Chief was saying to him softly. "And I'm here. I'll make sure you're OK." Again, he added, "That's Artie over there. This is a good place here - very good. They'll look after you. I'll make sure that they do." The Chief's voice was low and assured. At this sort of thing no one equaled him. For the hundredth time I was tremendously impressed. If I had gone to see Gabe by myself, I would have been absolutely tongue-tied.

Gabe's mom did come very soon. His wife came, too. When Gabe left the hospital, weeks later, we knew he would never walk again. He was paralyzed from the waist down but had movement in his arms and upper body. Dr. Huber, our team intern, told me, "In cases like this, you never regain the use of your legs. Lots of work is going on in the area of paraplegics, but the big breakthrough is still years away. There is no hope for Gabe as an athlete."

Nor was there much hope, in Huber's opinion, for Gabe's marriage. Top athletes who are permanently and totally disabled at the outset of their careers have a difficult time adjusting, Huber said. "They're young, strong, and active. It takes a lot of mental and emotional resilience to keep going on. Rivera faces a complete change in life-style. His mother can help – she's a comparatively young woman – but often the changes in the husband are too much for the wife. His marriage is in real jeopardy."

I talked with Dad and Dan about Rivera's situation and suggested that he could work with me in the scouting department, as Rocky Bleier and Steve Fedell had done. Both Rocky and Steve rendered valuable service and could have been successful in the administrative end of football had they so desired. I thought I could teach Rivera to be a capable scout. He was in a wheelchair, but there were reports to analyze and masses of film to review. Even by watching games on television you could learn a great deal about a prospect. Even by getting on the telephone it was possible to collect information. Gabe came to my office four times, as I recall, and would stay for a half-hour or forty-five minutes. Then he would have to leave for a doctor's appointment or physical therapy. Of necessity, we were taking it slow, but he appeared to be bright and willing. Together, we went through our scouting manual, and I gave him a tutorial in the jargon we use.

I met his mother and his wife. The mother, as Dr. Huber had noted, was young-looking, the wife tall, fair-haired and attractive. She had married Gabe while both were in college. On one of her visits she brought their little boy. I was upbeat for a while, and so was Gabe. But in the end Dr. Huber was correct. Rivera, preoccupied with his physical condition, lost interest in being a scout – or, rather, just sort of stopped coming around – and when the doctors at the hospital had done all they could for him, he went home to Texas.

AJR bought him a customized van, which he learned to drive but eventually wrecked. His marriage, as Dr. Huber had feared, did not endure. But he pulled himself together, married again, and has a job down in Texas working with kids. The last I heard, he was getting along surprisingly well.

Destry Rides Again

The Steelers beat the Seahawks, 27-21. Forgive me if I'm being sentimental, but they won it, I think, for Gabe Rivera. After beating Tampa Bay, San Diego, and Baltimore, they took a seven-game winning streak and a 9-2 record into their November 20th date with the Vikings at Three Rivers Stadium. Minnesota was a team they should have been able to handle. But something happened. Maybe the rest of the league, by this time, had us figured out. Whatever it was, we lost, 17-14. Then the Lions embarrassed us in Detroit, 45-3. The following week, Cincinnati – a team we had beaten earlier, rather easily – won the return game at Three Rivers rather easily.

For reasons that were hard to fathom, the bottom was falling out. It wasn't just the loss of Rivera – Senor Sack – although without him the pass rush had suffered. Both the run blocking and pass blocking were less efficient. Our wide receivers were not getting open and Cliff Stoudt was being hurried. Often his only recourse was to take a sack. Or to dump the ball off to a running back. There were so many broken plays that Stoudt ended the season as our third leading ground gainer with 479 yards. Interceptions increased, and so did fumbles. Inside the 20-yard line, the offense stalled so consistently that Gary Anderson, the field-goal kicker, was our leading scorer that year.

None of which meant we were out of the running for a playoff spot. We had two games left, with the Jets in New York and with the Browns in Cleveland, and the Central Division of the AFC was so weak that no one could catch us unless we managed to lose both. Providentially, the one guy who could spark us – Terry Bradshaw – would be ready to play against the Jets. It seems that where ice packs, heat pads, pain killers, cortisone shots, and Aunt Alice's novenas had done him no good, a myna bird worked its magic.

The myna bird was a pet he had taken in. Perching on Bradshaw's sore arm, his little feathered friend had brought about a miraculous cure, he announced. Not since another Louisiana native, Sidney Thornton, bathed his sprained ankle in a bucket of piss, provided for him by a witch doctor, had we witnessed such a marvelous recovery.

Having Bradshaw back lifted our flagging spirits. Against the Jets, he'd be making his first appearance on a football field since the previous January, when, through no fault of his, we lost to San Diego for the AFC championship. It was Wyatt Earp getting off the train to clean up Dodge City. Or maybe it was "Destry Rides Again." (For those of my readers with a limited frame of reference, I'm invoking a 1939 Western with Jimmy Stewart in the title role). But could one player, even if that player was Bradshaw, make a difference?

The game with the Jets would be the last in Shea Stadium before their move to the Meadowlands (formerly just a swamp) in New Jersey. While the two teams warmed up, I wandered around taking in the scene. Many of the players I was gawking at, Jets as well as Steelers, I had scouted in college. Now I was feeling anxiety. The Jets had won their last three games. The Steelers had lost their last three and were floundering. Mike Webster had said that the Jets' defensive line was the best in the league.

So much would depend on whether Bradshaw was the gunslinger of old. He'd been doing just fine in practice, although his elbow continued to bother him. The operation in Shreveport the previous March was a mistake that could not be undone. And now at last the time had come to see if old Number 12 still had it.

Lining up to take the first snap, he was nervous, I could sense. But then he threw his first pass, a completion to Ben Cunningham, and it was just as if he never had been on the shelf. "We're going to have some fun," he said to his teammates. Of his first six passes, he completed three. On the last of these, it was third and ten. He scrambled and threw a touchdown pass to Gregg Garrity, a rookie from Penn State and a Pittsburgh kid. Something for Gregg to tell his grandchildren.

My elation was tempered by a change in Bradshaw's delivery. Early in the drive he'd been throwing without effort. Now there was evidence of pain. On our next possession, we ran much more often. From our 29-yard line, Harris and Pollard moved us to the New York 10. Once on third down, Bradshaw hit Pollard with a screen pass for a seventeen-yard gain. From the 10, in the face of a heavy blitz, he passed to Sweeney in the end zone for a touchdown, and though we didn't at the moment suspect it, that was the last pass he ever threw.

He went to the bench looking troubled. His arm was now useless. Cliff Stoudt came in and played as he did before going into a three-week slump. With the ground game churning out yardage, the Steelers added to the 14-0 lead Bradshaw had given them. Our offensive line played its best game of the season and Sweeney caught a second touchdown pass. The final score was 34-7.

We came back from New York on a high, thinking Bradshaw would be ready for the playoffs if not for our last regular-season game with Cleveland. "I proved I can do it. I proved I can throw the football," he assured everybody. He threw no footballs in practice that week and he threw no footballs against the Browns the following Sunday. This time Stoudt, who had regained his form in the win over the Jets, was not the same quarterback, and we lost to another team we had beaten earlier.

My reaction was: Oh, well. A meaningless game. Surely the extra week of rest would be all that Bradshaw needed to play on New Year's Day in Los Angeles against the Raiders. We were shutting our eyes to reality.

Whacked Out

On New Year's Eve, an old fried of AJR's, a man named Ray Heffernan, invited all the Rooneys to a fancy dinner party at a fancy Hollywood restaurant. Heffernan lived in Rye, New York, but took his family to Pasadena for the Rose Bowl festivities every year. He had made a lot of money in the shoe business and was putting on the dog with a will.

Before we had finished our dessert, we found ourselves in the middle of an elaborate costume party. Dozens of after-dinner guests, presumably Heffernan's, streamed into the restaurant. They had raided the wardrobe departments at the movie studios to outfit themselves, it appeared. One guy was dressed like General MacArthur, right down to the corncob pipe and the sunglasses. Another fellow came as the Little Tramp, Charlie Chaplin: derby hat, mustache, too-tight jacket, baggy pants, oversized shoes with holes in them, and a cane. And he could waddle like Charlie Chaplin. There were John Wayne impersonators, of course, and women from the court of Louis XVI, the Hollywood version, with piled-up blond hair and low-cut gowns that showcased their boobs. Unfortunately, Kay, who had chosen to stay in Pittsburgh, missed the fun.

Explaining to our host that we had to make bed-check, we left for our hotel before the new year arrived.

As it turned out, Ray Heffernan's party was the highlight of our trip. For the game with the Raiders, we had Stallworth back in the lineup. We did not have Terry Bradshaw, whose myna bird had lost its healing power. He could barely raise his arm to comb what was left of his hair, and neither all the king's horses nor all the diocesan holy oil from St. Anne's in Quebec would have helped. It was over for him. We would have to face the Raiders with Stoudt.

And for part of the first quarter, it looked as though Stoudt might be up to the task. Our tried and tested formula was working: establish the run; pepper the other guys with passes when they tried to clog the holes with linebackers and cornerbacks; rely on the defense to get the Raiders' offense off the field. We drove to their 17-yard line. Fourth and inches. Chuck Noll took the field goal, which was automatic with Gary Anderson kicking. I thought it was sound football. Watching from the press box in the Los Angeles Coliseum, full to the brim with more than 90,000 spectators, I felt we had made a good start.

The coach of the Raiders, Tom Flores, looked at it differently. If we were satisfied with three miserable points, he had us where he wanted us. To Flores, it proved that the Raiders could stop our ground game. Our passing game didn't worry him much, not with Stoudt instead of Bradshaw under the center. The next time we had the ball Lester Hayes picked off a pass from our 18-yard line and sauntered into the end zone.

It was only the beginning. On touchdown drives of eighty, seventy-two, fifty-eight, and sixty-five yards, Marcus Allen cut through our defense like the future Hall of Famer he was, and the Raiders whacked us out, 38-10.

Would it have mattered if a vigorous, strong-armed Bradshaw had been in there? Yes, I believe so.

We'd have lost by fewer than twenty-eight points.

Chapter 72

The Blacklist

The NFL had a blacklist of restaurants and bars with connections to the mob, real or imaginary. They were off-limits to everyone in the league — owners, front-office people, coaches, and players. In the NFL, there was always this fear of a betting scandal. The best way to keep from being tainted was to avoid all the places where gamblers hung out, or were likely to hang out, or were thought by the sportswriters to hang out.

Neither Dan nor I felt that such a precaution was unreasonable. AJR understood why prudence might be necessary, but would jokingly say, "You should see the kind of yeggs I came up with." He said that the restaurants on the list, or at least some of them, were by his standards forbiddingly upscale.

Of course, AJR was so sure of himself, and so sure of exactly who he was. In fact, when the NFL commissioner's office was in doubt as to whether a particular place belonged on the index, it would frequently ask for his advice.

I have to say that sometimes I thought it was Dad who needed guidance. I remember being apprehensive once when he suggested a family dinner at a restaurant in Bethel Park called The Living Room. Appointing me the host, he said, "I hear they have fine steaks. Take us all out there next week — your mom and Kay and Aunt Alice and me."

I said, "Well, Dad, people do say it has fine steaks and chops. Pat Livingston and some of your other friends go there a lot. But the owner, you know, is Tony Grosso."

Tony Grosso was a numbers guy who had recently served time.

"I realize Tony Grosso is the owner," Dad replied, and that was the end of the discussion.

So we went to The Living Room and enjoyed ourselves. The maitre d' and the waiters made a fuss over Dad; he knew, or seemed to know, a few of the patrons; the service was good and the steaks were good and the fruit plate served for dessert looked like the work of an artist. Pat Livingston was nowhere in sight.

AJR asked the maitre d' if "Tony" had been around. "Not lately, Art. He comes in once in a while, but he don't own the place any more. His wife does."

AJR just nodded. The information came as no surprise. On the way to the parking lot, he said, "I was never close to Grosso at all. He was sort of a loner who did his own thing. Those guys" — the real bosses, Dad was saying — "keep guys like Tony in line. They're the ones who have control."

We walked another five yards before Dad spoke again. "So his wife owns the joint, does she? Hah!"

He never said, "Don't go back there," but his vocal inflections got the message across.

For obvious reasons — just because something's a stereotype does not mean it's false — most places on the index were Italian-owned. Out on Route 88, beyond the South Hills, I knew an Italian restaurant where the food was not only good but cheap. Kay and I and the kids would go there early; we liked the spaghetti. There was nothing sinister about this joint, which was called, if I'm not mistaken, Mama Lena's. It was bright and clean, a nice place to take the whole family.

On our first few visits, no one recognized us, but then one night a presentable young guy at the cash register noticed the name on my credit card. He said, "You must be Art's son."

I admitted I was and added a word of praise for the food.

While he was thanking me, the man who owned the place walked through the door, and the other one introduced us. I was accustomed by now to being Art Rooney's son. Kay was accustomed to being his daughter-in-law. Artie and Mike and Susan were accustomed to being his grandchildren. Reflected glory is sometimes hard to put up with, but it's better than reflected notoriety, better than having someone like — oh, John Dillinger, let's say — for a relative.

The boss was now telling me, "A lot of sports people come in here, but they don't come this early."

I said, "Well, ya know, with the kids, we don't like to eat too late."

"Sure. Sure. Come back. You're always welcome."

And we did go back, bringing Kay's parents with us now and then. In the Steeler offices one day, someone who overheard me talking about the place said it was on the forbidden list — "a real den of iniquity," as I later told Kay. "The hell with that," she said. To her way of thinking, the list was far too inclusive. "Anyway," she went on, "the devil shows up after nightfall, you know. By that time, we're in and out."

At her insistence, we kept returning. "Good to have you," the owner would say. "We like families. Next time bring the Chief. We'll make something special."

Though my demeanor, I hope, didn't show it, I was nervous. All through dinner I'd be looking over my shoulder for gangster types, characters I could spot from having watched Francis Ford Coppola's "Godfather" movies. In the meantime, Kay was losing patience with me. "There is absolutely nothing to worry about," she said. "Nobody else in Pittsburgh goes to supper as early as we do. We open the place up."

So we continued to eat at Mama Lena's, opening the place up and leaving while it was still almost empty. But finally one evening when we arrived we had company — a table of at least a dozen men in the back of the room. All but one of them were young: early twenties to mid-thirties. Two, as I recall, were black; only a few looked Italian. I thought, well, the Mafia recruits all kinds and all ages these days.

The one older man — short, round, bald, and definitely Italian — was in charge. This guy did all the talking, it seemed. He laughed, he pointed, he gestured. Yep, I said to myself, he's the "don;" we have to get out of here.

Our orders came, and I urged the kids not to dawdle. "We'll get dessert at the Tasty Creme," I told them. In an undertone, I said to Kay, "The NFL was right about this place. Let's move."

I called for the check and paid in cash to save time. Pushing the kids ahead like a sheep dog, I started for the door, with Kay right beside me. We were almost free when a voice cried, "Stop!" and the owner of the joint came running after us. "Mister Rooney!" he was shouting. "Wait a minute! I want you to meet my friends."

"God deliver me," I said — again to myself.

The owner was grabbing my arm. "I wanna innerduce you to these fellows. They're special people." He dragged me toward the T-shaped table where this loud, fat take-charge guy was holding court. "Tommy!" the owner said. "Tommeee! This is Art Rooney's kid, Art Junior. Art, this is my good friend Tommy."

Possibly he mentioned Tommy's last name. If so, I didn't hear it. All I could think of was the need to get out of the restaurant. Tommy, I knew, would be asking about our football team, digging for information that guys who make bets always want. Instead, he was saying, "Your dad's a great guy!" Then he added, "I like this place. Every time we're in town I bring my boys here. The food's good, and it's out of the way."

I forget how I answered — unintelligibly, no doubt — but my interior monologue went like this: "His 'boys!' All of these mob guys call their henchmen their 'boys.'"

Tommy, still in control, was introducing them to me, one by one. Hardly listening to the names, I heard them say, "Hi, Rooney," or "How ya doin', Art?" or "Good to see ya" — things like that. I do remember thinking that, gee, in appearance and manner they were not much different from our Steeler football players. One of the mob's more pernicious aspects was its ability to change with the times.

As quickly as I could, I broke away. Kay and the kids hadn't waited inside. They were already out in the parking lot. The genial Tommy was calling after me, "Say hi to your dad!" And then, regretfully, it seemed, "I thought those boys of yours might have liked to meet the players."

The "players"? What the hell was he talking about?

My pal the restaurant owner escorted me to the door. "Great guy, that Tommy Lasorda," he was saying. "Always comes in here when the Dodgers are in town. Brings a whole bunch of his players with him, too."

Not until I got into the car and was pulling out onto the highway did the realization hit me: Tommy Lasorda! Manager of the Los Angeles Dodgers! I had not, after all, stumbled upon a meeting of the Cosa Nostra.

The first thing Kay said was, "Who were those men?"

"Oh, nobody," I told her. "Just some friends of my dad."

One of AJR's favorite Italian places was the Rosa Villa. It was near Three Rivers Stadium on General Robinson Street, where he had lived as a young man above his father's saloon. By the 1970s, General Robinson Street was the last of the First Ward's "bedbug rows," the name used by Aunt Alice for all the narrow, grimy, alley-like passageways that criss-crossed the neighborhood in the days before urban renewal. They reminded Ed Kiely of "something right out of Dickens." The decrepit three-story houses were all much the same: soot-covered red brick, rotting wooden doorframes, "stoops" made of dirt-darkened stone. Their owners were slum landlords, who fed off the poor.

I remember how astounded Aunt Alice was when she learned that her uncle, George McNulty, had bought a row of these squalid houses for "investment purposes" during the Hoover depression of the 1930s. Aunt Alice's brother John said that George spent nothing on their upkeep. "All he did was pick up the rent." To be sure, there was never any love lost between John and George. After World War II, with the clearing of ground for a housing project, George's bedbug row disappeared. With the building of the stadium, the others disappeared — all except the one on which the Rosa Villa still proudly stood.

About once or twice a month over this relatively short stretch of cobblestones — "hobblestones," AJR called them — he would take a carload of front-office people to the Rosa Villa for lunch. Separated from the slum houses by a parking lot, the restaurant was not in bad shape. Even so, I never went inside without looking for rats. The First Ward's rat population, I always thought, probably exceeded its bedbug population. My brother Dan disliked these trips to the Rosa Villa for a different reason entirely. He believed we were taking a chance — patronizing a place that would not have met the standards of the NFL.

The building itself had a gray stucco exterior. Not far from the front door was the cash register. A room to the right contained a mahogany bar with eight or ten stools, but we never ate there. We went to the main dining room beyond the cash register. We never seemed to need a reservation. The woman at the cash register, Frances LaQuatra, would greet AJR and ask about Kass. In turn, he would ask about "Joey," her son. Frances LaQuatra was a little past middle age and neatly but not stylishly dressed. She gave the impression of having known Dan and me a long time. When I first started going to the restaurant, I could not quite place her, but then one day it came to me. Frances LaQuatra was Mike Hogan's wife.

I remembered Mike Hogan from years gone by. But why did his wife and his sons – Joey and Jack LaQuatra – have a name that was different from his? Eventually Kass cleared it up for me. "Hogan," it seemed, was Mike's ring name. He had boxed as a pro, and AJR had been his manager. Back in the 1920s and '30s, Italian, Slavic, and Jewish boxers often adopted Irish-sounding names. Irish boxers, in the opinion of managers and promoters, were the ones who pulled in the ticket buyers.

Although vaguely aware that Mike Hogan had boxed, and later refereed, I thought of him only as an older acquaintance. Jack and Joey had boxed, too, using their own last name, but now only Joey, the head of a laborers' union, was still alive. Looking back, I think I understand why Frances LaQuatra would remark so often to AJR that her son Jack had been my age: to this well-mannered, self-contained woman, I represented something — a link with the past.

There were booths in the Villa Rosa's dining room, but we always sat down at a big round table near the swinging doors to the kitchen unless the Rosa Villa "family" was occupying that table. When this was the case, Dad would quietly walk over and pay his respects and then join the rest of us at another large table on the opposite side of the room. Nothing was ever said about this, either by him or by anyone else.

If the second table was occupied, Frances LaQuatra would leave us for a minute while she spoke to the men who were eating there (it always seemed to be men). They would immediately get up and move to the bar, some with napkins tucked into their belts or shirts and carrying cups of coffee. As they passed us, they would nod deferentially to AJR, unresentful at being displaced. Then while AJR protested to Frances LaQuatra that he was putting everybody to a lot of unnecessary trouble, a waitress and maybe someone from the kitchen would come by with the unfinished lunches of the men now waiting for them on barstools.

Whether the Villa Rosa was a mob hangout I never learned. Nor did I ever learn exactly who the owners or their customers were. What I took from my visits there was the feeling that AJR could be many things to many different kinds of people. Like St. Thomas More, he was a man for all seasons.

Richie Easton

Every time we added a race track to our holdings, AJR offered his friend Richie Easton a managerial job. Richie always declined. It was not his lack of a formal education that gave him pause, but the fact that he needed only a few more years of driving a delivery truck for the *Pittsburgh Press* to retire with a good pension.

Richie was tough and smart and a true friend of my Dad. He had been in the Navy during the Second World War. Married, with two sons, he made sure they attended college. One of them, Dick, chose the academic life as his profession, becoming an English instructor at Washington & Jefferson. The other, Tom, was the owner of a prosperous surveying business.

Because of a conversation we had with Richie at a Dapper Dan sports banquet, my son Mike enrolled at Washington & Jefferson. Richie asked Mike where he planned on going to college and Mike replied that he didn't really know. "How about W. & J.?" Richie suggested. Mike expressed doubt that he could pass the entrance examination for W. & J. Richie, who was fond of Mike, said, "Well, let me look into that."

I could tell what Mike was thinking: "This is Granddad's old friend, a guy who drives a truck. How is he going to help me at Washington & Jefferson?" As it happened, there was no further discussion of Mike's future that night; hovering over us, the waitress at our table spilled a whole dish of Ranch/Roquefort salad dressing on Richie. He was wearing a gunmetal gray suit and the salad dressing now covered most of it. Flustered, the waitress took a napkin to the mess with results that were far from satisfactory. After a hurried trip to the kitchen, no doubt for a consultation with her boss, she returned and told Richie apologetically that there was no good way to rub out the stains.

"Send us the cleaning bill," she added. Richie got to his feet, slowly. He was a dignified, rugged-looking man with an abundance of silver-white hair. I knew him to be normally unexcitable, but I remembered how he had dealt with two obnoxious hecklers who were bothering AJR and Governor David L. Lawrence at a football game in Cleveland, and I felt apprehensive for the waitress. But all Richie said was, "Sure," and, excusing himself, he left the banquet room and headed for home.

It was four or five weeks before Mike and I saw him again. We had forgotten about his offer to intercede at Washington & Jefferson. "You haven't applied," he said to Mike. "Why not? Do it, Mike. Do it."

The urgency in his voice spurred Mike to act. He mailed in an application. Soon afterward, a caller from the W. & J. registrar's office invited him to come down for an interview. I drove Mike to Washington, Pennsylvania, where the college is located, and when the registrar greeted us, Richie Easton's son Dick was at his side. As soon as the necessary introductions were made, Dick left the room, and the registrar asked if he could talk to Mike alone. Their conference lasted twenty minutes at the most. The registrar then informed me that Mike's application had been accepted.

In due time, he was a Washington & Jefferson graduate. All the way through, Professor Dick Easton guided him step by step. For all this, of course, we had Richie to thank.

During his last few years at the *Pittsburgh Press*, Richie spent more and more time with AJR. Wherever AJR went – whether to Shamrock Farm, the races, Steeler games, or pre-season training camp — you could always find Richie. When he retired he took a part-time job in the Steeler ticket office. If he actually sold tickets, that was nice, but driving AJR to wakes and funerals came first.

He outlived the Chief by five years or so, continuing to work in the ticket office. As he aged, he complained of hip pain — due, he supposed, to the jostling a truck driver takes. At last he allowed a doctor to examine him, and the doctor's diagnosis was bone cancer. Tough, loyal, reliable Richie Easton lived for another six months. When he died, he was 74.

Tom Murray

Someone uniquely different among AJR's innumerable race-track companions was Tom Murray, a bank executive who worked for First Boston Corporation. Tom seldom bet. He liked to watch thoroughbreds run for the spectacle of it. The sight of these large, powerful, magnificent animals thundering toward the finish line in a pack was like nothing any other sport could offer, he thought.

Educated at Georgetown, Tom had more class than most of the Damon Runyon types who clustered around AJR. In a time of discrimination against Irish Catholics, he rose to the upper levels of the banking business, the exclusive domain of WASP aristocrats back then. If you were good at your job, and Tom was good at his, you could beat the odds. He'd take a nip of the bottle now and then, and it sometimes interfered with his work.

In appearance, he resembled Edward Everett Horton, a dapper Hollywood actor who played fussbudget parts in some of the Fred Astaire-Ginger Rogers movies. Tom had perfect manners. In restaurants, he unfailingly got to his feet when a woman approached the table, and he could open a car door for a woman without seeming awkward. His diction and grammar were meticulous. AJR, contrasting himself with his friend, would say, "Tom's a gentleman; I'm a 'deeze, dem and doze' guy." Murray, in turn, would say that AJR was a "true" gentleman.

Tom lived to be 92. Not too long before he died, my son Art spotted him one day at the Pittsburgh Athletic Club. He was living by himself in an apartment in Oakland. His neighbors, mostly Pitt and Carnegie Mellon students, kept his mind young, he told Art cheerfully. I hadn't seen Tom in years, so I called him on the telephone.

His voice was unchanged – a bit high and nasal – and his mind, sure enough, was still keen. We got to reminiscing about AJR, and Tom was reminded of a race-track story I never had heard.

"This must have been in the late 1950s or early '60s," he said. "One of your dad's horses was running at Pimlico, and he asked me to fly to Baltimore with him. Your dad was a good guy to travel with, because he always paid for everything, airline tickets and all.

"On the flight over, I noticed a couple of rugged-looking men sitting behind us. They didn't have much to say to each other, and nothing at all to anyone else.

"At Pimlico, your dad and I went to the clubhouse. In the cheap seats not far away, I saw the same two guys I had seen on the airplane. Shortly before the race your dad's horse was entered in, his trainer came to our box and said in a loud stage whisper that the horse wasn't feeling well, but could run. Your dad got up and left with the trainer after telling me to stay put.

"Near post time, the two guys from the airplane came over to where I was sitting. One of them said, 'I heard that trainer say the horse was sick. What's up?' Now I was scared. The guy said to me, 'We're with Art, too. We have two thousand dollars of his to bet on the horse. When is he coming back?' I told him, 'Well, if Art gave you two thousand dollars to bet, you'd better follow his orders.' The two guys looked confused. They stood there for a minute and then started off in the direction of the parimutuel windows.

"I had fifty dollars of my own money I'd decided to bet, but I didn't know if I should. Where was your dad? Finally I said to myself, 'Well, the hell with it. I'll take a chance.' I went to the window and put my fifty dollars on the sick horse to win.

"As it turned out, he wasn't sick after all. He won going away and paid over thirty dollars. For my fifty I collected more than fifteen hundred. Not bad interest for a conservative banker.

"When the Chief showed up I told him it was one of the most exciting things that ever happened to me. I said I was perplexed, though, when the trainer told him the horse was sick. Your dad then explained that if the trainer had announced for everyone to hear that the horse was in top shape he would have gone off at even money instead of 30-1.

"I thought, but didn't say, 'Those two friends of yours – the ones I advised to do as they were told – bet two thousand dollars for you. That's sixty thousand dollars you won today.'"

Many an old-timer could attest to AJR's genius for beating the horses. When I talked to Tom Murray, he was one of just a handful who were left.

Out of Time

After Father Silas retired – or "semi-retired," as he liked to think – he spent a lot of time at 940 North Lincoln Avenue and not much time with his sisters, Marie McGinley and Margaret Laughlin. They were openly displeased about this, but the house on the North Side had two advantages over theirs: it was larger, offering more room than ever now that all five sons had flown the coop, and it was only a short distance from Three Rivers Stadium. When the Pirates played or the Steelers played, Father Silas always sat with AJR in his private box. Gently, he turned down invitations from his sisters with the explanation that his presence as a house guest would be an imposition on them, which was part of the truth, at least.

At the behest of AJR, he attended many funerals and wakes. I went, too, if I knew the surviving relatives. I remember that on the ride to a wake for Phil Musick's father – Phil Musick covered the Steelers for the *Pittsburgh Press* – AJR and Father Silas got into a low-keyed argument about just what position an old baseball teammate of theirs had played.

"He was a second baseman," said AJR.

"No, he played shortstop," contradicted Father Silas. They went back and forth like this until we arrived at the funeral home. After paying our respects, Father Silas and I returned to the car. AJR had lingered on the sidewalk to converse with an old friend or acquaintance. While we waited for him, Father Silas said to me, "Your dad is confused. That fellow was a shortstop."

Presently AJR beckoned to Father Silas, and the twosome on the sidewalk became a threesome. A few minutes went by, and then AJR broke away. Father Silas and the other man continued to talk. AJR got into the car, and the first thing he said to me was, "Your Uncle Dan is losing it a little bit. That guy was a second baseman."

AJR grew increasingly more protective of his brother, whose health was deteriorating. Mom's niece, Kathy Milligan, lived at 940 North Lincoln for a while, and one day by accident she left a razor blade in the soap dish. Picking up the soap, Father Silas grabbed the razor blade as well and cut his hand. Kathy Milligan was a good kid, and AJR always treated her with great consideration, but when he heard what had happened he went berserk. He told Kathy off as only he could do. It left Kathy, Mom, and Aunt Alice in what I think was a state of shock.

Father Silas had a need to feel productive and busy. He was always reading newspapers, periodicals, and books. With AJR, he watched sports on television, and of course they attended the games at Three Rivers. Father Silas was even a spectator from time to time at the Steelers' daily practice sessions. Every year in late fall he headed for Florida, spending a part of the winter at AJR's Palm Beach condominium and the rest of it at the Franciscan friary in St. Petersburg, where some of his fellow missionaries from China were then in residence. Father Silas was the designated driver, taking people to the doctors, to restaurants, and to the airport.

He never lost his aptitude for driving. He told me once that he had picked up "two hitch-hikers, teen-aged girls," and had given them a ride to their homes in the North Hills. "When you do that," I said, presuming to give my uncle some useful advice, "you can't really be sure of what you're getting yourself into." He replied that they were just a couple of kids. "I knew they were OK with me," he said, "but I didn't know what might happen to them if they were with somebody else."

My cousin Jim Laughlin and I were sitting with Father Silas one day at our dog track in Florida, the Palm Beach Kennel Club. He was into his late seventies by now. He said, "You know, boys, I've been ready to meet my maker for twenty-five years." Taking off his wristwatch, he handed it to Jim. "Here. I won't need this any more. I've run out of time," he said.

It was not too long before the meeting with his maker occurred. Just short of his seventy-eighth birthday, Father Silas died at the friary. At his bedside was the priest who had been such an unruly alcoholic in their days together at St. Bonaventure that Father Silas had seen fit to apply discipline with his fists. Now the same priest was giving him the last rites.

The Franciscans offered to bury Father Silas at their cemetery in Paterson, New Jersey. AJR said, "No. At St. Bonaventure. More of us can visit his grave there."

I missed the funeral. It was on the day of the Senior Bowl All-Star game, which I was scouting, and I asked AJR what I should do. "Stay for the game," he said. "Your uncle would want you to do your job." My cousin Tim Rooney, also a scout, was at the Senior Bowl, too, and I know it eased his conscience to receive a dispensation from AJR.

It was so cold that winter in Olean that the Franciscans postponed Father Silas's burial until spring. A few years later, on a beautiful summer day, I visited the gravesite, which was near the golf course he had kept in such good condition. Lining up the family around the gravestone, I prepared to take a picture, but my daughter Sue, a junior in high school, objected. She said, "Dad ... stop! That is so Polish! Besides, Father Dan wouldn't like it."

I did not take the picture.

Before leaving, we toured the campus. An aged Franciscan approached us and asked if he could be of any help. I told him we knew our way around, and he asked what my name was.

"Art Rooney Junior."

He backed off a couple of steps, beaming.

"Then you're Mike's family'?"

At first, I thought he meant my son. But Mike was a name the Franciscans used in referring to Father Silas. They used it more often than Silas or Dan. I said, "Yes. We're from Pittsburgh."

The old friar reached out and took my hand.

"Welcome!" he said. "Welcome home!"

Chapter 73

1984

Going into the 1983 season, we had a quarterback glut. For that good reason, we did not make Danny Marino our first-round draft pick. With Bradshaw coming back, with Cliff Stoudt coming back, with Mark Malone coming back, we chose to strengthen our defensive line. That's where the need was, we thought, not at quarterback. At quarterback, we were set.

But now it was 1984 – 1984, a year made synonymous with doomsday by the crystal-ball gazing George Orwell. And our quarterback cupboard, if not exactly bare, was understocked. Suddenly we were left with only Malone, whose damaged knee would impede him for the rest of his career.

First, Cliff Stoudt had defected to the United States Football League. Stoudt believed, as most of us did, that Bradshaw would return for another season. Two or three more years on the bench was a prospect that did not appeal to him. So when Rollie Dotsch's team, the Birmingham Barons, offered him more money than he was getting from the Steelers, Stoudt had no difficulty in making up his mind.

If we were unprepared for Stoudt's departure, we were staggered by what was to follow. Bradshaw announced his retirement. Sure, we knew that his elbow was hurting. But, blindly, we had viewed it as something temporary. A little more rest, and the elbow would come around. Wasn't time the great healer?

Not in Bradshaw's case, we were to learn.

More than the media did, and more than our fans did, I regretted the loss of Stoudt. Before our playoff game with the Raiders, I was telling a sportswriter that if Stoudt had a decent day we could win. "Well, he won't have a decent day," the sportswriter said. "He's the worst quarterback in the NFL." Believe what you want to, I thought, but give Stoudt receivers like Swann and Stallworth, instead of the ones at his disposal, and then make a judgment. The fans were just as harsh as the writers. Toward the end of the 1983 season they'd been booing him. Then in 1984 the Pittsburgh team in the USFL, the Maulers, drew the only big crowd in their three-year history – 60,000, it was said – for a game with Birmingham at Three Rivers Stadium, and all of those people, if their behavior was any indication, had come to boo Stoudt. In his defense I would say we had a pretty good season in 1983 with Stoudt as our quarterback for all but a part of one game. He played well for Birmingham, too, and, after the upstart league folded, began a second career in the NFL as a backup.

As for Malone, the bad knee would prevent him from ever being more than a journeyman quarterback.

Bradshaw left Pittsburgh feeling terribly unappreciated. To his way of looking at it, he was mishandled by Noll and underrated by the fans. A couple of years after his retirement, Dick Haley bumped into him at the Dallas-Fort Worth airport. Bradshaw told Haley that he could have returned to football in 1985 – had been making practice tosses without any discomfort, in fact – but was glad to be out of it; he preferred his new life as a television personality. For a long time afterward he did not attempt to conceal the bitterness that was eating at him. He appeared to hold a grudge against both his ex-coach and Pittsburgh as a whole, never coming back for Steeler reunions, spurning invitations to return for any purpose at all.

Then came the open acknowledgement that he had suffered since early youth from clinical depression. Going public seemed to change his entire outlook. There ensued a dramatic re-enactment of the prodigal son's return, Pittsburgh version. Old grievances were buried, palsy-walsiness reigned. He buried the hatchet with Noll, he participated joyfully in a television talkathon with some of his old teammates.

Let me say that I like Terry Bradshaw. I have felt a kinship between us dating back to the 1970 draft. So I lobbied hard to make him our number one pick. He gave me some trying moments, Bradshaw did, but in the end he more than justified my confidence in him. He was a once-in-a-lifetime player. Without him we would not have won our first four Super Bowl games – or even have had the opportunity to win them, I've heard it argued.

AJR could not understand my failure to see in Danny Marino the same gifts of nature I thought were so evident in Bradshaw. "Never pass up a great one," I had preached, and AJR kept reminding me of it. My part in letting Danny Marino slip away was a malfeasance I was not to be allowed to forget.

The USFL

A few words now – or maybe a few hundred – about the USFL.

The first Steeler to defect, a year before Stoudt and Ray Pinney, who went to Birmingham with him, was Jimmy Smith. On almost any NFL team other than Pittsburgh, Smith could have been a starting wide receiver. In Pittsburgh, Stallworth and Swann had kept him on the bench. By 1985, Smith was back in the NFL with the Raiders, who were still in Los Angeles.

The USFL played its games in the spring and summer, avoiding direct competition with the NFL. Its commissioner, Curt Simmons, had been the president of ESPN and was able to land two big television contracts, one with his old network and the other with ABC. Simmons, the networks, and the founders of the USFL were betting that America's appetite for professional football was insatiable.

In every decade since the 1930s, AJR had seen rival leagues such as this one come and go. A professional football team must have a place to play, and my recollection is that no team in either the NFL or the USFL had a stadium of its own. Since the stadiums in the cities where the two leagues would be going head to head – all the big ones, anyway – were leased by the NFL, what the people behind the new league were trying to do, my dad believed, was position themselves for an anti-trust suit. Their aim, reasoned AJR, was to force a merger, as the American Football League had done in the 1960s.

There was a lawsuit, all right, and the USFL won it, but no merger resulted. The jury awarded the plaintiffs the sum of one dollar – one whole dollar – in damages. Ultimately, two USFL cities, Jacksonville and Carolina, ended up getting expansion franchises in the NFL.

Most of the new teams in the USFL drew fairly well while the league was still a novelty. Initially, no team was to spend more than $1.2 million on salaries or try to sign more than ten of the top-rated college players, but neither promise was kept. Right off the bat, a USFL team gave Herschel Walker, the swift, powerful running back who had won the Heisman Trophy, five million dollars to leave the University of Georgia after his junior year.

Walker was very good, but the team that signed him was not. Attendance throughout the league began to decline, and so did the television ratings. Players who had left the NFL were returning en masse. Every team in the USFL lost huge amounts of money. At the end of its third season, 1985, the league went out of business.

The ill will I felt toward George Perles and Rollie Dotsch, the coaches I blamed for luring Cliff Stoudt and Ray Pinney to the USFL, had long since dissipated. AJR's animosity was focused on the owner of the Maulers, Edward DeBartolo, Sr. We regarded DeBartolo Senior as an NFL colleague. On paper, the younger DeBartolo, Ed Junior, owned the San Francisco Forty-Niners, but he was still, at the time, a front man for his father. Now DeBartolo Senior had bought a USFL team – the Pittsburgh Maulers – and moved it onto the Steelers' turf, Three Rivers Stadium.

AJR felt betrayed. He was angry. Furious. Livid: He got up at a meeting of NFL owners and excoriated DeBartolo. I wasn't there, but I heard about it at second hand. His remarks, as they were reported to me, went like this.

"I'm going to talk about class. There is class among bank robbers, class among pimps, class among whores. But what Ed DeBartolo has done is completely without class. How can this man belong to our league and screw one of his partners?"

Not the kind of language the Chief ordinarily used, but I know he was boiling over.

His outburst reminded me of how Franklin D. Roosevelt denounced Mussolini – a bit more gracefully, it is true – after Italy declared war on France while the Germans were driving toward Paris in 1940. "The hand that held the dagger," FDR proclaimed, "has struck it into the back of its neighbor."

Postscript: Once the USFL ceased to exist, the Rooneys and Ed DeBartolo, Sr. resumed diplomatic relations. There never had been a rift between the Rooneys and Ed Junior.

Departures

Mel Blount's retirement coincided with Bradshaw's. We had drafted them together and now they were leaving together. Blount was the best defensive back who ever played for the Steelers, but defensive backs don't last as long as quarterbacks do, and his time had come.

There were also involuntary departures. Chuck Noll unloaded two of his most experienced offensive linemen, sending Ted Petersen to the Browns and Steve Courson to Tampa Bay. As I have said, I think Chuck knew that Courson was using steroids. One of our younger offensive linemen, Rick Donnalley from North Carolina, had the skills and the physical requirements to be the prototype of a Steeler guard, but Noll sent him packing for "failure to produce." He spent the next two seasons with the Washington Redskins and two more with Kansas City. We had drafted worse players than Rick Donnalley.

In the 1984 draft, we scored big with our first-round pick, Louis Lipps, a wide receiver from Southern Mississippi. Lipps had it all – great athletic ability, great hands, great field vision, and great speed. And he could "make things happen," as Noll used to repeat – and repeat and repeat. I believe that Lipps could have played on any of our Super Bowl teams, holding his own with Stallworth and Swann.

Our second-round pick was a rugged tight end from Wyoming, Chris Kolodziejski. When we took our new players to LeMont for a get-together dinner that year, I sat next to Chris, and he opened the conversation by saying, "Well, Mister Rooney, Jenna said she would get you to draft me, and here we are."

"Jenna?" I was puzzled.

"Yes. You know. Jenna, your niece. Lives in Santa Monica."

I wracked my brain. Then it came to me. He meant Gina – Gina Valdivia, whose mother was a first cousin of Kay's. Chris had been one of Gina's high-school boyfriends in Los Angeles, and she boasted to him that her "uncle" was the Steelers' personnel director. She would get the old boy to draft him. Never once had I heard Gina mention Chris Kolodziejski, but as soon as I caught on I went along with her tall tale.

In his rookie season, Chris played an outstanding game against the Forty-Niners in San Francisco. Afterward, the offensive coordinator, Tom Moore, came up to me and said, "We've got a keeper." He meant Chris – "Kolo," Moore called him. And Moore was a guy who measured his words. But in that same San Francisco game, Kolo had gone down with a severe knee injury, foreclosing from then on his usefulness as a football player.

The supply of quarterbacks in the draft was so limited that we waited until the seventh round to take one. Scott Campbell was a little guy from Purdue, a school that was famous then and is famous now for turning out quarterbacks. Chuck Noll liked his mechanics, and so did I, but good mechanics were not enough to compensate for his short stature. Talent-wise, Campbell reminded no one of undersized wonders like Davey O'Brien, Frankie Albert, and Eddie LeBaron. It was remarkable, I thought, that we kept him around for two years.

Knowing that Campbell was a long shot and fearing that Mark Malone could not be counted on because of his knee problems; Noll traded our third-round pick to Miami for David Woodley. As if we needed another reminder of the mistake we had made the year before – as if AJR needed another reminder – Woodley was the quarterback whose job Dan Marino had taken.

Trading for a quarterback was something we hadn't done since the tenure of Bill Austin, but Noll was desperate. When Bill Nunn scouted Woodley at LSU, he turned in a favorable report, and in fact Woodley had quarterbacked Miami to the Super Bowl in his third year as a pro. Then Marino came in and made him expendable. On film, Woodley looked better than OK to all of our scouts, myself included, but we failed to allow for the demon that possessed him - alcoholism. After his second season with us, he was finished at the age of 27. Let me say this: for as long as he lasted, he served the team capably.

One of the players we drafted before Campbell was Terry Long, a guard out of East Carolina. He played well as a starter for a couple of good Steeler teams, but did so, we were to learn, with the help of steroids. When Long tested positive in 1991 (the NFL had started to crack down), Noll suspended him. All through as a Steeler after two unsuccessful attempts at suicide, he pulled himself together and started a business. His Value Added Foods Group was a chicken-processing plant on the North Side with thirty employees, but in 2005 he died of "inflammatory meningitis" after swallowing antifreeze. Long was 41. An inordinate number of offensive linemen who played for us in the 1970s and early '80s had unusually short life spans. Ray Mansfield died in the Grand Canyon on a backpacking trip with his son. Jim Clack died at 49. The early deaths of Steve Courson and Mike Webster were highly publicized. Webster's family, in a lawsuit against the NFL Pension Fund, claimed that head injuries sustained as a football player were partly responsible for his health problems and put the onus on steroids as well. There was testimony from two doctors that Webster "experimented" with steroids. Courson, after his troubles became public, let the whole world know he'd been using them. And Clack told the author Roy Blount that steroids had helped him add muscle and weight.

There were also the quarterbacks who died prematurely. Joe Gilliam was addicted to cocaine, David Woodley, as I have said, to alcohol. Drugs, booze, and steroids. All three were anathema to Noll and to AJR, but in spite of our best intentions we did not go unscathed.

Unhappy Ending

On the eve of the 1984 season, I thought we had a pretty good mixture of youth and experience and were still on the right track. I thought we could pull something off that you did not often see in the NFL. We had an excellent chance, a kind of sixth sense told me, to rebuild a great team without hitting rock bottom.

One thing that gave me hope was our success in the pre-season games. Winning three out of four didn't mean much; what mattered was that we looked good doing it. Mark Malone and David Woodley kept the offense moving, and I came to believe that our two-quarterback system might work. In 1983, Cliff Stoudt's pass receivers had a hard time getting open and a hard time catching the ball when they did get open. Malone and Woodley were throwing to a fully recovered John Stallworth and to a young guy with Stallworth-like ability, Louis Lipps.

Replacing the worn-out parts in our Super Bowl machine was an ongoing process. Through it all, there had not been a losing season. I felt sure that for the rest of the 1980s we could keep this up – make the playoffs habitually and perhaps, with any luck, return to the Super Bowl one more time.

At St. Vincent, however, we had a distraction – the absence of Franco Harris. In twelve seasons, all with the Steelers, he had rushed for 11,950 yards, a total second only to Jim Brown's NFL record of 12,312. But now he was holding out. He wanted a two-year contract extension, and we had offered him only one year. As productive as he had been in 1983, for a running back he was entering old age. I thought that this time around we could expect him to rush for maybe five hundred yards at the most instead of his usual thousand or more. In 1983, though he was hitting the holes with as much precision as ever, he had lost some agility. Cutting back was a problem for him now, and on sweeps he was being forced out of bounds more and more. In Franco's favor, he knew the offense thoroughly; he knew what the blockers could do; he was a good pass receiver and his competitive flame burned with the same intensity. I believed that even as something less than a full-time player he could still help us win.

All of us – Dan, AJR, the assistant coaches, the other players, the medical staff, and the fans; all of us, that is, except Noll – desired what I thought of as a Hollywood happy ending for Franco. As for Noll, he seemed to feel that Franco's happy ending had already occurred. His 1983 stats – 1,007 rushing yards, thirty-four pass receptions, five touchdowns – closed the books as far as Noll was concerned.

He commissioned Dick Hoak, Franco's predecessor as a Penn State and Steeler running back and his coach from the time we had drafted him, to deliver a message: "Tell Franco to retire."

Respectfully, Hoak declined the privilege. "Chuck," he said, determination in his voice, "that has to come from you. Either from you or the Rooneys. We're talking about a Hall of Famer here."

Objection sustained.

With Noll, there was no room for sentiment. Whether or not Franco Harris overtook Jim Brown was irrelevant to Noll. What always came first was the team. Personal records counted for nothing. In fact, the nearer Franco got to Brown's record, the greater the harm. Press, fans, and even Franco himself would be focused on the record, creating difficulties. There would be pressure to play Franco when it was not the best thing for the team and not the best thing for Franco. I remembered what the coaches said about L.C. Greenwood toward the end of his career: "Let's get him out of there before he gets hurt. L. C. can't protect himself well enough any more."

In camp, we appeared to have made a lucky ninth-round pick. Rich Erenberg, who had played college football at Colgate, a seldom-visited way station for pro scouts, was showing considerable promise as a running back. Erenberg looked so good to Noll that while the team was still at St. Vincent he got rid of Greg Hawthorne, sending him to the Patriots. It raised the question: if we didn't need Hawthorne, why did we need Franco, for whom the clock was so obviously ticking?

To make the contract negotiations even stickier, Franco had an inexperienced agent. The agent and Franco's wife seemed to be unaware that his pursuit of the ground-gaining record was of secondary importance in Noll's mind to the object of winning games. Between these two and the coach there was little or no communication. Still, I felt it could all be worked out. And would be.

I was wrong for two reasons: Noll's strong belief that Franco ought to retire and the reluctance of AJR and Dan to throw away money on a player the coach didn't want. And yet, by accepting our terms, Franco could have stayed for a graceful fadeout. He could have had one final season with the Steelers.

On a morning in August Dan told me that he and the Chief were meeting that day with Franco and his agent. Dan said he was pretty certain that Franco was going to sign. Pleased, I took off for St. Vincent, where I had some business of my own to attend to – a discussion with Haley and Tom Modrak about moving Hawthorne. After that, I went up the hill to Bill Nunn's office, and while Nunn and I were talking, our assistant P.R. guy, John Evenson, rushed in.

"Art," he said breathlessly, "there's something I want to tell you before the press comes after you …"

I broke in on him. "Yes, I know – we traded Hawthorne."

That wasn't it, Evenson started to say.

"Oh." Again I thought I could see what was coming. "Yeah, Dan told me this morning. We signed Franco."

"No, no." Evenson was more excited than ever. "Dan and your father gave Franco his release!"

I reached for the telephone and got Dan. He said our differences with Franco could not be bridged. I talked to AJR, who ordered me to keep my mouth shut when the sportswriters came around. "All you can say is that you have nothing to say."

For the rest of the afternoon I had media people shooting questions at me.

"What's your reaction? You were the one who brought Franco here."

"I'm sorry. I have nothing to say."

That was the way it went, over and over.

The Hollywood ending for Number 32, the man who, along with Joe Greene, started us on our way to greatness, the man who never played on a Steeler team that lost more games than it won, was not to be. A free agent now, Franco went out to Seattle. Having missed training camp, he was physically unprepared for the season. And of course, he was unfamiliar with Coach Chuck Knox's offense.

In his first two games, he did not do a thing for the Seahawks. The season was in its third week, and the Steelers were idle (they had played a Thursday-night game with the Jets in New York), when Kay and I met AJR for dinner on Sunday evening at the St. Clair Country Club. Because the Chief liked his privacy there, we'd have asked for a table in a secluded part of the dining room, but this time he insisted on eating with the crowd that was clustered near the television set. The Seattle game was being shown. AJR's eyes were getting weak, and when the Seahawks had the ball he would leave our table and his dinner and put his nose right up against the screen. To his unconcealed disappointment, Franco performed miserably. He looked lost.

Seattle let him go before the season was over.

With Frank Pollard, Walter Abercrombie, and Rich Erenberg running the ball, the Steelers got to the playoffs, vindicating Noll's judgment.

On a weekend afternoon in late January, I drove to 940 North Lincoln Avenue for a visit with my dad. I walked into his den, and there was Franco. He had come, as I had, to see the Chief. His young son was with him. Franco stood up and gave me a warm greeting. He introduced me to the kid. I thought, "What a special guy."

And then I corrected myself. I was in the presence of two special guys. Franco Harris and Art Rooney, Sr.

Against the Odds

I have an abiding affection for our 1984 team. In the face of what seemed like endless bad luck, it persevered. It overcame injuries, overcame obstacles, bounced back from defeat. And went to the playoffs for a third straight year.

AJR reacted to all this rather sourly. The team's performance, he complained, was "herky-jerky." The Super Bowl seasons of the 1970s had accustomed him to a steady diet of success. Bumping along – taking two steps forward and one step backward, and then repeating the process again and again – was not the kind of advancement he liked.

Right from scratch with that 1984 team, there were holes to be filled, beginning with the great void at quarterback. Mark Malone, getting his chance to start after four years as a backup, was far from the sprightly athlete we had drafted out of Arizona State. He reminded me now of Mike Kruczek, the stand-in who kept us winning while Bradshaw was sidelined in 1976: big, strong, mechanical, admired by his teammates for bringing out the best that was in them. (Kruczek's teammates, it is worth mentioning, included nine or ten Hall of Famers in their prime). Another difference: where Kruczek lacked exceptional inborn talent, Malone at one time had a ton of it. The injury to his knee would linger. He no longer could escape the rush, no longer could pick up yardage by running with the ball, which had been his most striking asset. He had a pretty decent arm, but not a gun. To see him work by the numbers – drop back, step up, throw – was disheartening.

Still, he got through the season, completing fifty-four percent of his passes for a respectable 2,137 yards and sixteen touchdowns. Stallworth and Lipps had plenty to do with these totals, of course. The silky Stallworth, our MVP, was never better, catching eighty passes. Lipps caught forty-five and was Rookie of the Year. When Malone alternated with Woodley, there was never a fall-off in production. Woodley had played for one of Chuck Noll's mentors, Don Shula; because their systems were so much alike, he made the transition easily.

In the sixth game of the season (our record going in was 3-2), we went up against Shula's Dolphins at Three Rivers Stadium. It was Dan Marino's homecoming party, and I can't honestly say that I had a good time. Unperturbed by our blitz, Marino picked us apart, 31-7. We were to play the Forty-Niners in San Francisco the next week, and I left for the Coast as soon as I could, not only because Kay was going with me, but to distance myself from the Chief.

October that year in northern California was golden. Jack Butler also had brought his wife, and the four of us took in the sights: the vistas from Nob Hill, looking out on the Bay; the Golden Gate Bridge; the cable cars; Fisherman's Wharf; Berkeley ("So many weirdos," declared Kay); Palo Alto and Stanford ("Beautiful!"); a Stanford football game. There were marvelous restaurants to go to, and wine to be sipped on a tour of the Napa Valley.

San Francisco itself was not yet as iniquitous as Sodom and Gomorrah, but getting close. Our trip coincided with an early gay-rights parade, and we joined the onlookers. Bernie and Kay were bemused, I guess you would say, by the spectacle. "Nothing like that in Pittsburgh," one of them observed.

Our game with the Forty-Niners was at Candlestick Park, better suited, unlike Three Rivers Stadium, to baseball than to football. The sky was blue and the sun was shining, but a cold wind blew in from the Bay. It goes without saying that we were underdogs to the reigning Super Bowl champions. Their Joe Montana was another Western Pennsylvania quarterback we had chosen not to take in the draft. Would he burn us the way Marino had done? I was understandably nervous.

Montana had shown that he knew how to win. The Steelers, looked upon as has-beens even though we'd gone to the playoffs the previous two years, were given no chance. What worried me as much as the Forty-Niners' proven ability to dominate was the fact that we entered the game banged up. Louis Lipps was hurt; Larry Brown was hurt; Ben Cunningham was hurt. Even Stallworth was limping. All four would play, but Brown and Cunningham couldn't do much. After Chris Kolodziejski's injury, Noll had to alternate Weegie Thompson, a slightly built wide receiver, and Tunch Ilkin, whose position was tackle, at tight end – Thompson in passing situations, Ilkin when the play called for a block. With Ilkin at tight end, a retread named Steve August filled in at tackle. He was so unfamiliar with the offense that Mike Webster finally told him to forget about the blocking assignments and simply "come off the ball."

Early in the first half, Terry Long hobbled off the field, and Emil Boures, who had been a center at Pitt, and a lowly-regarded center at that, went in to play guard. Even Blake Wingle, a late-round pick from UCLA in 1983 and a bench rider ever since, logged some important minutes at guard. And who was that guy Noll kept putting in at tackle, taking out for repairs, and putting in again? Why, if my eyes did not deceive me, it was Ray Snell from Wisconsin, another no-name.

Everywhere you looked, there were no-names, but this was to be a day on which these rag-tag offensive linemen would excel. Their blocking cleared the way for Frank Pollard to grind out 105 yards. The Steelers' offense controlled the ball most of the day and when this happened Montana could do nothing but watch. Mike Webster was a dynamo, leading the charge of the offensive line and urging his teammates on. An inspirational force if there ever was one, he elevated their level of play.

Stallworth used all of his guile to snooker the Forty-Niners' defensive backs, lining up first on one side and then on the other, designing and calling a pass play that resulted in a touchdown, a touchdown made possible by one of the jumping, twisting catches for which he was known. In attempting to cover him, the Forty-Niners' Eric Wright drew some holding and interference penalties at critical times in the game.

The Steelers won it, 20-17, on two long, time-consuming touchdown drives and Gary Anderson's field goal, set up by the defense when linebacker Bryan Hinkle smartly intercepted one of Montana's arrow-like passes and made a dodging, darting runback of forty-three yards. It was the only game the Forty Niners lost that season – a season in which they repeated as Super Bowl champions – and Chuck Noll put the victory right up there with some of our big ones in the 1970s.

From then on, there were ups and downs, and to reach the playoffs again we had to win our last two games. Which we did, just barely, edging a rival from way back, the Browns, and a hated adversary of more recent vintage, the Raiders, out in Los Angeles.

We took a 9-7 record into the post-season. Our first opponent, Denver (13-3), had John Elway, a future Hall of Famer, at quarterback, a thousand-yard rusher in Sammy Winder, and the home-field advantage. The Denver fans, who were just as crazy as ours, were hollering their heads off in Mile High Stadium long before Elway's short touchdown pass gave the Broncos an early lead. But the Steelers came back. The defense shut down Winder and got us out of trouble that was caused by Malone's two fumbles in Steeler territory and a blocked punt. We drove for a touchdown, Denver scored again, so did we, and the teams traded field goals.

Finally Eric Williams, a second-year safety from North Carolina State, made the play of his life. He slipped between Elway and the intended receiver for an interception; his return put the ball on the two-yard line and then it was Pollard up the middle for the game winner. Pittsburgh 24, Denver 17.

So many of the players we had acquired since our last trip to the Super Bowl were producing for us now. I began to think that we might be able to pull this off: beat Miami for the AFC championship – and, after that, who could tell? In Super Bowl competition, the Steelers never had lost. But we had gone about as far as we could go. For the game with Miami in the Orange Bowl, another vast crowd was on hand: 76,000-plus. Again, no one gave us a chance. Even though we had defused Montana, even though we had defused Elway, the explosive offense engineered by Marino would be too much for us, the know-it-alls decided. And they were right.

On a bright, warm sixth of January, Malone had a good day (312 yards passing and three touchdowns), and we moved the ball on the ground. When we got near the goal line we pushed it across, scoring in every period. Near the end of the first half the game was even, but while Malone was having a good day Marino was having a better one: twenty-one completions, 421 yards, and four touchdowns.

When the Dolphins had the ball it was quick-strike football, reminiscent of our games with Paul Brown's Cleveland teams in the 1950s. Back then, the Steelers would keep the ball for up to ten minutes and score a touchdown; then Otto Graham would take to the air, and the Browns would have a touchdown in two minutes. Cleveland's touchdowns came with less exertion and more frequency than ours did, and the same thing was true in Miami. We were zinged again by Danny Marino, 45-28.

It would be eleven more years before Pittsburgh went to another Super Bowl and twenty-six years between Lombardi Trophies.

Chapter 74

Overrated

After the 1984 season, the leaves continued to fall from the tree. Jack Lambert, Ron Johnson, and Larry Brown called it quits. Just four players were left from our Augustan Age, the 1970s: John Stallworth, Mike Webster, Donnie Shell, and Gary Dunn. Ben Cunningham remained on the team, but had reached the injury phase of his career. For some time now, he had not been much of a factor.

Yet in my estimation, we were on our way back. It would take a while longer – four years, maybe five – but we could win while rebuilding and possibly return to the Super Bowl. The 1984 season had convinced me of that.

There was still only one route to take. We couldn't trade for the players we needed, nor hope to shuffle them out of the deck. We had to draft them, as we had done since Chuck Noll took command. The difficulty was that again in 1985 there would be nineteen teams drafting ahead of us.

To get the special athletes who could make the big play we'd have to reach. When at last our turn came, the best available bet seemed to be Darryl Sims, a defensive end from Wisconsin. I had seen him play and had scrutinized him on film. In height, weight, speed, and quickness, he certainly measured up. Put to the test in actual competition, he could and did make big plays – once in a while. He was similar to a lot of other guys we'd been drafting for the past several years, the kind we believed we could somehow reconstruct. We could transform him, we thought, into something a bit closer to an L. C. Greenwood, a Steve Furness, or a John Banaszak. We were kidding ourselves, of course. No matter how full of wisdom our coaches were, no matter how inspirational it was to play on the same team with future Hall of Famers wearing Super Bowl rings, you could not take a Darryl Sims and train him to be consistent.

Chuck Noll would tell me that Sims was "flashy," meaning volatile, unstable, erratic: an on-again, off-again performer. Joe Greene, now a member of our coaching staff, said he was overdrafted, someone you'd hope to get in the fourth round. After watching Sims in a few exhibition games I doubted if he was even that good. I recalled that Moon Mullins and Dwight White were fourth-round draft picks, and Sims was no Mullins or White. He put in two mediocre years with the Steelers and another two years with Cleveland.

Because Larry Brown's departure left a vacancy in the offensive line, we had to draft a tackle, so Mark Behning of Nebraska was our second-round pick. Defensive linemen in the NFL were getting bigger every year; the mammoth power rushers coming into the game could run right over standard-sized tackles and guards, and Behning, we felt, had the strength and the heft to deal with them. He was a big ol' boy. Pass blocking had become more important; too, with more teams stressing the pass instead of the run, and here again Behning filled the bill. The officials were letting blockers "lock on" to the rusher with their hands and arms, which appeared to be a tactic for which Behning was well adapted.

No such luck. He turned out to be a slow learner, easily got discouraged, and gave it all up at the end of his first year.

In sum, our 1985 draft was almost a washout. Of the thirteen players we took, only five made the team, and there was no long-term help from any of them except maybe Harry Newsome, who was our punter for the next five years. A defensive back we cut, Liffort Hobley of LSU, caught on with the Miami Dolphins. We drafted a center from Wisconsin named Dan Turk. In 1974, we drafted a center from Wisconsin named Mike Webster. Nineteen eight-five would be Webster's twelfth year with the Steelers. Dan Turk played two years for the Steelers and ten more in the NFL, most of that time on special-teams duty with the Raiders.

Our sixth-round choice in 1985, Gregg Carr, was a linebacker from Auburn who had the same characteristics as Jack Ham, Loren Toews, and Bryan Hinkle. He could move and he was smart. Too smart, as it turned out. After improving in each of his first four years, he left us to study medicine.

I thought of what Will Walls said to me once when I was breaking in as a scout: "Pass 'em up if they're too smart. Before very long, they'll find better things to do than play football."

Breakdown

Granted the 1985 draft was a disappointment. Still I expected us to play at the same level as in 1984 – to win more often than we lost and find a way into the playoffs. We were upbeat in camp, especially after a 42-27 spanking of the Tampa Bay Bucs in our first pre-season game.

I know, I know. Pre-season games are meaningless. But I was looking at how we had finished the 1984 season, with that gritty performance out in Los Angeles and the playoff win over Denver. There'd be a carryover, I was sure. We were getting some traction.

On this score I had enough confidence to let the word out wherever I could find any listeners. Once we had started playing for keeps, the feeling only grew. We hammered the Colts, 45-3, in our opening game. But if the 1984 season had been herky-jerky, the 1985 season was like a roller-coaster ride at Kennywood Park. We were up and down, up and down. We'd win one and then lose one. There was a stretch where we lost three games in a row, split the next two, *won* three games in a row, and then – going into another death spiral – *lost* three games in a row for the second time.

Up and down, up and down. To avoid our first losing season in fourteen years, we'd have to come on strong and win our last two games. But where the 1984 team, needing two wins at the end of the season for a playoff spot, was able to get the job done, this one couldn't make it to .500.

At home, we won from Buffalo, 30-24. Then we lost on the road to the Giants, 28-10. Which left us with a 7-9 record.

For me the Steeler dynasty ended on that cold December Sunday in the Meadowlands. Here we were – not even in contention for the playoffs. The incentive was to keep our heads above water. And we couldn't do it. Oh well, some would say – winning exactly as many games as you lose is like kissing your sister. If so (I'm no authority), I'd have settled for that.

There were individual Steelers who performed well statistically in 1985. Frank Pollard missed becoming our fourth thousand-yard rusher, joining Franco Harris, John Henry Johnson, and Rocky Bleier, by less than the distance it takes to make a first down. Walter Abercrombie gained 851 yards and caught twenty-four passes. John Stallworth caught seventy-five passes and Louis Lipps fifty-nine. Lipps led the league in punt returns. Dwayne Woodruff made five interceptions.

Add it all up and it still comes out to a sub-.500 record.

We lost a few games we should have won. Close ones. Good teams win the close ones. We had some injuries, but every team has injuries. In 1984 we overcame our injuries; the 1985 team lacked the bench strength to do the same thing. Lambert and Brown were gone, and we missed their leadership. But it was time for new leaders to take their place, and none did. Our drafts in recent years had failed to produce these new leaders. The assembly line was malfunctioning.

Since 1980 we had reached for players who could have been great but were not. Most of them, I am sorry to say, were not even solid, steady contributors. There were no Randy Grossmans or Bryan Hinkles or John Banaszaks among them. Forget the Pro Bowlers and potential Hall of Famers. There was not a Keith Willis, a Loren Toews, a Frank Pollard, or a Rocky Bleier in the bunch. All of these overachievers I have mentioned, none of them big names in college, were drafted below the fourth round or signed as free agents. Our aim was to acquire at least three players every year who could be starters on a winning team, and we hadn't been doing it, not consistently.

We had to go back to where we started.

We were losing sight of a big part of Noll's strategy to get what he needed in young players: football character and grit. One of his first acts as head coach was to trade Roy Jefferson, a fine athlete and performer, to the Colts for almost nothing. Noll said he would not work with players whose personal goals were put above team goals.

We had to continue looking for superior athletes who were coachable, but we had to reemphasize character – character for our game. We had been picking up too many players without the burning desire to win.

And it wasn't being instilled.

Since 1980 we had drafted at least a dozen players in the first four rounds who were useless to us. If even half of them had measured up to the low-end picks we made every year in the 1970s, then beyond any doubt we could have kept on winning.

The Long Goodbye

Bill Nunn wanted to retire. He was adamant about it, saying the only reason he had not retired earlier was his loyalty to the Rooneys. After one last look at the college teams he scouted in the spring every year, his days as a full-time member of the Steeler organization would be over.

One year earlier, in the spring of 1985, it had looked as though Dick Haley would be leaving us. Officially, Haley was our "director of player personnel." My title, since shortly after Dick came on board was "vice president in charge of personnel." Somehow, there was not any overlapping. I ran the scouting department and Haley was my No. 1 assistant. I liked Haley as a person – as a gentleman and a family man – and had great respect for his astuteness as a scout.

But now he was mulling an offer to be the top personnel guy for the Detroit Lions. In a way, it flattered me to hear that. Since 1980, I had not been pleased with our drafting. At the time of the offer to Haley, we had nonetheless gone to the playoffs for three straight years, and the Detroit people, at any rate, must have thought we were doing something right.

Haley was taking the offer seriously, he said. I advised him to meet with the Lions' executives, carefully weigh their proposal, and take a week to decide. A week but no longer. If he left, we'd have to find a replacement, with time growing short.

After Haley left my office, I went down the hall and conferred with Chuck Noll. If Haley had a chance to better himself, Noll said, there was little we could do about it, or should. He expressed satisfaction with the work of our scouts. Finally, we agreed that of the people on our staff who might fill Haley's shoes, Tom Modrak would be best qualified.

Modrak scouted the other pro teams for us. Like Haley, he was personable, responsible, and a hard worker. He knew football. He knew how we operated. When the week I had given Haley to make up his mind went by without a decision, Dan and I spoke to Tom. Would he be interested in Haley's job? His answer seemed "different," to say the least.

"Is this a situation," he asked, "where if I say no I'll be fired?"

Not at all, we assured him.

"Well, in that case," he said, "I'd just as soon stay as I am."

Replacing a good man like Haley would be no easy matter, I could see.

Another five or six days passed before Haley informed us he had made up his mind. He was turning down the Detroit job.

I was relieved, but henceforth, I promised myself, if the possibility of losing a deputy as important as Haley arose, there must be someone available who was ready to move up. And by the time I found out we'd be losing Bill Nunn I knew where to find such a person.

Young Tom Donohoe had been a successful high school coach in Western Pennsylvania. Now he was scouting for Jack Butler in the Blesto organization and responding very well to Butler's tutelage. I went to Nunn and asked if he might let Donohoe tag along on his next scouting trip; when they returned, he could tell me what he thought.

Nunn was exactly the right man for this assignment. They were gone for a week, and then he handed in his report. It confirmed what my instincts had told me: "One of the best new scouts Jack Butler has developed in years and years."

Donohoe was a grandson of David L. Lawrence. The only significance this had from the Steelers' point of view was to give Tom some identity. It had nothing at all to do with whether or not we would hire him. With Jack Butler's approval, hire him we did.

Another Blesto scout I added in the spring of 1986 was Jesse Kaye. Jesse would scout the central states, Donohoe the Eastern Seaboard, and Bob Schmitz the West, while Haley and I would look at the top picks wherever they were. Modrak, besides checking on the NFL teams, would help scout the colleges selectively.

I had a talk with Dan about Nunn. I said, "Hey, we can't let this guy get completely out of the organization. He can do special scouting assignments on a part-time basis and earn every cent of what we pay him." Dan sort of chuckled and said he'd been thinking along the same lines. Something would be worked out.

Nunn's post-retirement plans were to spend the winters in Florida with Frances, his wife. They were going down there for a week to get the lay of the land, so I arranged for them to stay in AJR's

Palm Beach condominium on the ocean. Long-range, I had a schedule in mind for Bill. He could scout the Florida schools for us from mid-October until the end of the season, help with the draft when he came back to Pittsburgh, and scout some Northeastern colleges in the early fall before heading south again.

This, more or less, was how everything fell into place. The Nunns bought a condominium of their own and spent the winters in Florida for the rest of the 1980s and the first part of the 1990s. Three of my brothers – Tim, Pat, and John – had winter homes in Florida, too, and so did our cousin Artie Laughlin. All four came to look upon Bill as their football guru. Eventually, Bill and Frances tired of the snowbird life and sold their condominium at a profit. As a full-time resident of Pittsburgh once more, Nunn continued his part-time work for the Steelers, remaining on the job into a hale and hearty old age.

During all these years our friendship would go on, but we were not any longer professional associates.

Aftermath

On Monday, December 22, 1985, the day after our season-ending loss to the Giants, Dan called me into his office. At once, we began to discuss the game and its consequence — our first losing season in fourteen years.

Both of us were upset. I had been certain we would make it to the playoffs again. I felt that with Louis Lipps in our offense and also returning punts, the 1985 team should have been superior to the 1984 team. Chuck Noll referred to players like Lipps as "weapons." This was a team that had outscored its opponents, 379 points to 355, and yet the striking power mostly generated by Lipps was not reflected in our over-all performance and 7-9 record.

To a considerable extent, I felt responsible. After the Battle of Gettysburg, somebody asked a general on the losing side to explain the Confederate Army's defeat. "There were many reasons," he said, "and I contributed to them." So it was with me. I had been the one, after all, who promised to get so many good players into black and gold uniforms that the coaches would not be able to mess things up. I had matured since making that unwise (and unfair) assertion, but our failure in 1985 to win as many games as we lost could in large part be laid at my feet. Our scouting department had not given our coaches the players I had said we'd provide.

I knew this better than anyone else, but now my brother Dan was saying it to me, and his words were hard to take.

Our discussion became an argument. Then a heated argument. When I left Dan's office, I was angry and remorseful. The anger was directed mostly at myself – in the first place because we no longer were drafting players of the kind who had kept us going to Super Bowls, and in the second place for losing my temper. I resolved not to do that again, and I never have.

In a little over two weeks – on January 11 — Art III was to marry Christine Swanson, a tall, lovely blonde he had known since grammar school. Art had a degree from Boston College in biology and was in his third year of dental school at Pitt (where some of his instructors, he told me, remembered Jock Sutherland and Art Sekay). Christine was a Duquesne University graduate. Certain family members, among them Kay's father, Roy Kumer, thought that marriage and dental school combined would be too much for Art to handle. Kay and I had some misgivings, but Art was a good student and in fact would receive two awards on graduation day.

Father Bob Reardon tied the knot for the young couple at St. Louise de Marillac Church in Upper St. Clair. There followed a bounteous reception at LeMont arranged by Christine's parents. The wedding put a cap on a very pleasant Christmas season, and my spat with Dan seemed a thing of the past.

Last Draft

With the wedding out of the way, I turned my thoughts full-time to the draft. We'd be picking ninth, which gave us our best shot since 1971 at getting good quality. In 1971 we drafted a Hall of Famer (Jack Ham), four Pro Bowlers, and four other really good players. "Let's get solid performers who can help us over the long run," I now told my scouts.

We came up with three.

Our first pick, John Rienstra, was a big offensive lineman from Temple. For five years, he made steady improvement. Then we traded him to Cleveland, where he played for another two seasons.

After Rienstra, we drafted Gerald Williams, defensive tackle from Auburn. Gerald Williams played nine years with the Steelers and two more with Carolina.

Bubby Brister, the quarterback we selected third, had played college football at Northeast Louisiana. In temperament, he was similar to the Louisiana Tech quarterback we had drafted in 1970, Terry Bradshaw. Both were flippant and temperamental. What Brister lacked, for the most part, was his predecessor's ability.

By which I don't mean to imply that he couldn't play, just that Bradshaw was a quarterback with skills you don't often see.

All Brister had to be was himself, not the second coming of Bradshaw. He'd been a minor-league baseball player and threw a pass from behind his right ear, with lots of zip on it. He could move around behind the line of scrimmage, avoiding defensive linemen and linebackers. Although he was not by any means a dumbbell, Noll found it best to eliminate things from the playbook for Brister – to keep the offense as basic as possible.

In 1988, the year that Brister replaced Malone, the Steelers had their worst record since 1970, Bradshaw's rookie season, losing eleven of sixteen games. The following year, for the first time since 1984, they got to the playoffs. They beat Houston in overtime, 26-23, before losing to Denver by an even closer score, 24-23. Bubby played well against Houston and played well against Denver until he lost his composure near the end of the game.

The 1989 season was Brister's high-water mark. He lost his job to Neil O'Donnell after Bill Cowher succeeded Noll in 1992. That same year, his refusal to enter a game in relief of O'Donnell earned him a one-way ticket to the Steeler boneyard. His words to Joe Walton, the offensive coordinator – "I'm not mopping up for anybody" – became Bubby's epitaph.

His epitaph in Pittsburgh, that is to say. The repercussions of the incident taught Brister humility, and he ended his playing days as a backup, first with the Eagles, then with the Jets, and finally with the Broncos – mopping up when the need arose.

His NFL career covered fifteen or sixteen seasons and brought him a Super Bowl ring as the backup in Denver to John Elway.

A tight end who came to us in 1986 out of Santa Clara but never made it through training camp ended up with no fewer than four Super Bowl rings. Noll cut Brent Jones before the season started. He was a pass-catching tight end, not a blocking tight end, the only kind Noll liked to use. The misfit caught on with San Francisco and flourished for ten years in Coach Bill Walsh's "West Coast" offense, with its premium on passing.

Another tight end we released, Cap Boso of Illinois, signed with the Bears and had a six-year pro career. Boso was our eighth-round pick. I didn't know it at the time, but I would never again be involved in the drafting of a player whose name you will find in the NFL Encyclopedia.

Out

There was a different atmosphere that summer at Latrobe. We had finished the 1985 season with our worst record in fourteen years. It took away some of our charisma, some of our swagger.

And there was trouble right at the start. Frank Pollard went down with an injury, leaving us short-handed in the offensive backfield. For very little – almost nothing – we acquired Earnest Jackson from the Eagles, a small stroke of good fortune. Jackson was not a bad pickup. Twice with San Diego and once with Philadelphia, he had rushed for more than one thousand yards.

Our performance in exhibition games – one win, three defeats – was not encouraging. Then in our first three regular-season games, we lost to Seattle, Denver, and Minnesota. Two more defeats followed an overtime win over Houston. We lost to Cleveland by three points and to Cincinnati by two.

Back in July or August, I had been told by Dan that he wanted to meet with me in October to discuss some organizational ideas for the scouting department. "That's fine. I'll be ready," I said. Meanwhile, my scouts and I met with Noll, as usual, to hear what he felt was needed in the way of player personnel for 1987.

On October 14th, the day after the Cincinnati game, Dan let me know it was time for our get-together. In preparation, I sat down with my secretary, Bev Zavodni, widely regarded as the very best secretary in the entire Steeler organization, and developed three or four sheets of talking points. When I entered Dan's office, he was looking rather pale, I thought – pale and serious. Occupying leather-upholstered chairs with ultra-modern cast-iron silver frames, we faced each other on opposite sides of his desk. I don't know why, but I was sharply aware of the furnishings in Dan's office that day: the desk in the shape of a football flattened on the topside; the document for which AJR had paid $2,500 in 1933 – the Steelers' NFL franchise – hanging in a frame on the wall behind the desk; the familiar gray carpeting. Dan barely glanced at my outline, which I had set down in front of him. He pushed it aside and said, "This is not what I want to talk about."

I waited.

Then he said, "I want you out of the day-to-day business."

He continued to speak, but I don't remember his words. There was something about my going into one or another of the family's various enterprises, where I could write my own paycheck. The message I most clearly retained was that I was finished with the football team. Out.

Since my terrible display of temper the previous December, I had vowed never again to lose control. And on this occasion, as on all other occasions ever since then, I succeeded. When I left Dan's office, I walked down the hall to AJR's office, passing Mary Regan, who kept watch outside his door, without a word. Calmly, I told the Chief what had happened. I couldn't make out if the news surprised him. He did not know it was coming, he said. He told me to go back to the scouting department and "do my job." When we parted, he said evenly, "There can be only one boss."

Back in my office, I reviewed the events of the previous half-hour. Do my job, AJR had said. But how? There was no way I could concentrate on football, study film, evaluate scouting reports. So I sat. And I thought.

I have no recollection of what Kay and I said to each other that night.

The next day, for the first time ever, I closed the door to the personnel department. I called my three younger brothers Tim, John, and Pat. They were surprised but not shocked to hear that I had been fired. I went to see Dad again. I never had seen him looking more frail and tired. Sadly, he told me, "I can't make things happen any more." Later, he repeated, "There can be only one boss."

And of course that boss was Dan. Who wanted me out. That was it. Humpty-Dumpty sat on a wall, Humpty-Dumpty had a great fall.

It would be a change of lifestyle for me and Kay and the kids. I was concerned just a little about our future financial well-being until AJR called me at home and said, "You will never have to worry about money."

For the remainder of the 1986 football season, I went through the motions of "doing my job." The Steelers ended up with a 6-10 record. Our fans were not chanting their "one for the thumb" mantra that year.

On January 8th it was publicly announced that I would have nothing further to do with the scouting department. I was to stay on as vice president, but without any duties except to attend meetings of the board. Dick Haley succeeded me as head of the scouting operation. He remained with the Steelers until Chuck Noll retired after the 1991 season. Haley then took a job with the New York Jets and Tom Donohoe moved up to become scouting supervisor of the Steelers. Later, Jesse Kaye and Bob Schmitz joined Haley in New York and Tom Modrak left Pittsburgh to accept a very good offer from the Eagles. Modrak ended up with the Buffalo Bills, but Schmitz stayed with the Jets for fifteen years and then retired.

Kay and I got on with our lives. Nothing was more important to us than family and religion, and the Steelers were family. Beyond the pain of separation, my job had been more than a job; it had been a passion. With Kay's help, eventually I refocused.

A couple of NFL teams sounded me out: would I be interested in continuing to work? Jack Butler, Bill Nunn, and my high school coach, Rip Scherer, advised me to disregard these overtures. "You set the standard here," they told me. "Let the guys who follow you try to live up to it."

In 1993 Chuck Noll was elected to the Hall of Fame in Canton, joining seven of the players he had coached. Over the next nine years, Mike Webster, Lynn Swann, and John Stallworth were chosen. Dan Rooney was elected in the first year of the new century, joining AJR.

Other Steelers coached by Noll – L. C. Greenwood, Dwight White, Donnie Shell, Jon Kolb, and Larry Brown – have been nominated to the Hall of Fame. For whatever it may be worth, two Steeler scouts have also been nominated:

Bill Nunn and Art Rooney, Jr.

Chapter 75

Vigil at Mercy

Dr. Ted Gelet still made house calls – for one patient only: AJR. During the horribly hot summer of 1988 he examined the Chief in his offices at Three Rivers Stadium. "Art," the doctor said after looking him over, "everything seems to be pretty good."

For some time now, the Chief had been wearing a pacemaker. Toward the end of May he'd had a blood clot removed from an artery in his upper left arm. But he had cut down on cigars (to one a day, and he chewed only half of it). He was laying off sweets (except in moments of weakness). He had cut down on salt. "How many years will this buy me?" he asked Dr. Gelet. "A few," he was told. "A few? I guess that means three." The tradeoff, he concluded, wasn't worth it.

And yet for the most part he followed orders. He was living alone now, except for a daytime practical nurse and a nighttime practical nurse; Aunt Alice had died in 1986. The practical nurses were holdovers from Mom's last days. "I don't need help," AJR had insisted once she was gone, but he did need help, all of us knew, only that was not the way to make the case. "You need help for Alice," Dan explained, and AJR, never the easiest man to be taken in, was taken in.

Or pretended to be taken in. Again after Alice's death, he argued against keeping the nurses on, but Dan overrode his objections once more, this time encountering less resistance.

Mary Roseboro still cooked, dusted, and vacuumed, and Aunt Margaret was often on hand to see that AJR did not over-exert himself. "Remember," Dr. Gelet had warned him, "these are the dog days. Don't go outside in this heat. Before you get into your car, make sure that your driver has turned on the air-conditioner. Your car must be cooled off completely, because a car can be just like an oven. Go straight home when you leave the office. In the office and in your house, have the air-conditioner going full-blast. What I'm telling you is very important."

Not important enough, though, for AJR to change his most ingrained habits. There were wakes to attend, and funerals. There were sick friends in hospital rooms to be visited. And he could not miss Mass for even one day. If hot weather was a danger, he had to risk it.

On August 17th, Kay, Mike, Susie, and I retreated to the Laurel Mountains. Kay's father, Roy Kumer, was generous in letting us use his lakeside house in Deep Creek, Maryland, and we had gone there for relief from the deadening heat of the city. While Susie and Mike, who were college students by now, zipped around the lake in a speedboat, Kay and I immersed ourselves in the cool, shallow water near the shoreline.

In the evening, we had a cookout. Darkness came, and we went inside. After skimming through the newspapers, I looked at my watch. Eight-thirty – for us, almost time to turn in. Then the telephone rang. It was Dan.

He spoke calmly, but in tense, clipped tones. "I'm calling about Dad. He had a dizzy spell at the office this afternoon. We called 911 and got him to Mercy Hospital. At first he wouldn't go, and then he said he'd drive. We talked him into the ambulance. On the way to the hospital, he almost fell asleep. The doctors gave him tests. A brain attack of some kind. Don't rush home now, but come back tomorrow."

When I told all this to the family, Sue was the most upset. Granddaughter and grandfather had developed a close relationship. I called Art III in Pittsburgh. Art was a dentist, not a physician, but with more than just a layman's knowledge of medicine. AJR, he conjectured, had suffered a stroke. He advised us not to wait. "Come now. Right away."

By 10 o'clock we were speeding westward on Route 40. The gas tank in my oversized Cadillac was less than half full, and all I could think of as we passed a series of darkened service stations was how AJR would reproach me now for "putting on the dog." Cadillacs were gas-guzzlers. Everybody knew it. At the foot of Chestnut Ridge, to my immense relief, a station owner in the act of turning off the lights allowed me to pull in and fill up. Laconically, he said, "You just made it."

We were home before 1 o'clock and, after a short night's sleep, at the main entrance of Mercy Hospital by 6.

Already the television people were setting up their equipment. Mercy Hospital's information director, a competent young woman, told us that calls had been coming in from all the news organizations. A nun who worked in the intensive care unit spoke of how AJR had apologized for "causing trouble." He was "out of it" now, she said, but "not in a full coma."

We approached his bed. I said, "Dad, this is Artie," and took his hand. I felt him put pressure on mine. His eyes were closed, but he turned his head toward me. Holding his other hand, Kay said, "Art, I am here, too." He turned his head now in Kay's direction. She relinquished his hand to Susie, who took it in both of her own hands. Later, Susie recalled how white everything was – the walls, the bed, his hair. Everything but his eyes, which he suddenly opened. And his eyes, she said, were blue.

"So blue. Just those blue eyes looking up at me."

When he closed them, he was never, as far as I know, to open them again.

In the next day or two, my brother John and his wife flew in from Philadelphia, my brother Tim and his wife from New York, my brother Pat and his wife from Palm Beach. Rooneys and Rooney relatives from everywhere flew in. People from all walks of life and from every ethnic group came to the hospital: the rich and the poor, upright citizens and low-lifes, priests by the dozen and bishops, too. An Army private who was stationed in Iceland showed up. On the second day, as I sat with my four brothers in a restricted section of the hospital lunchroom, the information director came to our table.

She said, "There's a man out there who says he must see Art Junior and Dan. Just has to. He's quite insistent. A nice-looking fellow. Well-dressed. He says he is one of your dad's best friends."

Maybe, I suggested, it would be a good idea to show him in. She glanced at Dan, who simply nodded.

In a minute, she was back with our visitor, a clean-cut, middle-aged black man who was wearing a suit and tie. He greeted me in a familiar way and Dan somewhat formally. I thought I recognized him, but from where? He had excellent manners. He appeared to know Dad very well. "He was always nice to me," the man said. "You, too, Art Junior," he went on, and I searched my memory. Where had I seen this fellow? He'd been a boxer, he said. A football player. A cop. For some reason, he used the word "airport," and then I remembered. This was Jerry the redcap – a porter at the Pittsburgh International Airport. Without his uniform on, he might have been almost anyone.

AJR, he had said, was one of his best friends, a declaration we had long been accustomed to hearing. Most people, when they first met the Chief, felt instantly connected. By the second or third time, he was someone they had known all their lives.

Dan and I were urging Jerry to sit down, have some coffee, have a sandwich. We introduced him to Tim, John, and Pat. "This is Jerry, from the airport. Real good friend of Dad's." Jerry volunteered to make himself useful to us in any way he could. Did we need a driver? Whatever it might be, all we had to do was just ask.

We heard a hundred Art Rooney stories that week, all of them touching or humorous. Ron Cook of the *Pittsburgh Press* assembled two full pages of Art Rooney stories. He interviewed relatives and friends; he interviewed people the Chief had helped in a financial way – more often than not without being asked. It's a common journalistic practice to gather obituary material on important public figures who are getting along in years, and Cook had started this project earlier in the summer, careful to state his purpose when he asked somebody for an interview. Art III was still attending Pitt Dental School when Cook interviewed him. Wearing his starched white laboratory coat, he sat with Ron in the end-zone seats at Pitt Stadium. Ron tried to interview Mary Regan, but she turned him down with the utmost decisiveness. "For an obituary? While he's alive and not even sick? God forbid!"

Mary was loyal and wonderful and as Irish as Aunt Alice.

My brothers and I had sealed ourselves off from reporters. "Not now," we would say when somebody with a microphone came near. The information director did her best to protect us from media people, well-wishers, gawkers, and pests, and she was mostly successful. The gifts pouring in, hand-delivered or mailed, were something else. There were holy medals, scapulars, prayer cards, pictures of the saints. Somebody sent me rose petals from the shrine to St. Rose of Lima. Or was it the shrine to St. Theresa of Avila, the Little Flower? The rose petals were too fresh to have come from any great distance. I delivered them to the head nurse in the intensive care unit. They would end up in the trash, I supposed. Then I noticed on one of my visits that she had pinned them to the top of Dad's bed, with a scapular and a likeness of St. Rose completing the arrangement. Smiling, I said to myself, "God bless these good people at Mercy Hospital. They're looking out for Dad's spiritual welfare along with his bodily needs."

Dr. Oliver Turner called on me at home. Retired now, he had been AJR's personal physician in years gone by. He was a former chief of staff at Mercy Hospital and still had the run of the place. He had read Dad's charts and talked to his doctors and nurses, and he gave me the kind of report any football scout would have envied for its thoroughness and professionalism. The details were harrowing, the prognosis even worse. There had been a stroke, extensive bleeding, and total destruction of the brain. "You and your brothers should know this," he said.

(As time went by, Dr. Turner and I got to be pals. I called him Ollie, the difference in our ages notwithstanding. He told me something I never had known – that in the weeks after my dismissal from the football team AJR had come to him and said he was worried about me. My "mental outlook" and health were much on his mind. "He asked me to look after his 'boy,'" Ollie confided.)

Like Father Silas before him, AJR was ready to meet his maker. He believed in the sacraments and he believed in the promises of the Roman Catholic Church, and now his hour had come. Very early on the morning of August 25th, the five Rooney brothers and their wives were called into a meeting room and told that the Chief could only be kept "going" (not living) by artificial means. All of us agreed that survival without consciousness was not an acceptable option, and we were taken to his room for a last good-bye.

We gathered around the bed in a shuffling semi-circle. As we stood there, the silence became heavy. Then Dan's wife, Patricia, spoke some necessary words. "Let's all hold hands and say a prayer for Art." We said an Our Father, a Hail Mary, and a Glory Be. Patricia Rooney impressed me that day. She gave us an image to take away from our last few minutes with the Chief.

Reunited

And so once again the Rooney-McNulty clan would be making the trek out U.S. Route 19 to West View, where the Devlins had moved their funeral home from a deteriorating North Side. Three times in the previous six years the Devlins had buried family members – first Kass, then Dan's daughter Kate, who departed too young, and most recently Aunt Alice.

I remembered how Alice used to talk of the "three-two plan – three days in Divine Providence Hospital and two days at Devlin's." That is the way it was with Alice herself and Kass, but we had taken AJR to Mercy Hospital, not Divine Providence, and he had lingered there for a week. At Devlin's, he was to stay for only a short while and then be transported to St. Peter's Church for a full day's visitation before the funeral.

Visitation at Devlin's was restricted, supposedly, to the immediate family, a dictate that proved impossible to enforce. Kay, when she arrived there, noticed a black limousine in the parking lot and caught a glimpse of "a sinister-looking old fellow" heading towards it. The old fellow was Ed DeBartolo, Sr., who had driven over from Youngstown.

On arriving, he had greeted me with a hug and described AJR as "a most special man, a man of his word." Had I misjudged Mr. D., as I had misjudged so many other things in my fifty-three years? It was possible.

Something else Kay noticed at the funeral home was that "every politician in Pittsburgh" seemed to consider himself immediate family. Politicians, gate-crashers, and relatives we'd never heard of joined the unending line that filed past the casket. The Devlins were overwhelmed. But AJR had been going to wakes and funerals for decades, and now it was payback time.

This wake and this funeral would be the biggest in the history of Pittsburgh, surpassing Davey Lawrence's sendoff in 1966. Bursting with flowers, Devlin's and the church looked like the Phipps Conservatory. In AJR's opinion, flowers were the way to memorialize the dead. "I don't want any of that 'in lieu of flowers, contributions to this or that charity are suggested,'" he had said after Mom died. In his lifetime, he gave more to charity than many a nonprofit foundation ever did, but he was thinking of all the flower-store owners he knew; a wake was their chance to "make a few bucks," he explained. So it was somehow fitting that only hours after he died, a florist on Western Avenue converted the front window of his store into a shrine to the Chief, whose portrait, enlarged and bedecked with lilies and black and gold ribbons, looked out on the street from an easel.

As for what he might have thought of the sentence that concluded his voluminous newspaper obituaries – "The family requests that donations be made to the St. Vincent DePaul Society" – I refuse to guess.

The doubleheader wake was Dan's idea. He called the transfer of the casket from Devlin's to St. Peter's a "removal ceremony." As verified for us by Monsignor Charles Owen Rice, a native of Ireland, removal ceremonies are an old Hibernian custom. This one, fortuitously, gave my brothers and me a chance for some time to ourselves; from Devlin's, we took a detour to 940 North Lincoln Avenue, John and Pat in one car, Dan, Tim, and I in another.

When John, driving the lead car, went through a red light a momentary crisis ensued. An officer in a patrol car, his siren blaring, ordered John to pull up at the curb. Driving the second car, I pulled up behind them. The policeman asked John for his driver's license. He looked at it, handed it back, and poked his head through the window of the car. First he shook John's hand, then he shook Pat's. He did not write a ticket. John drove off, and I followed with Dan and Tim. As we passed the cop, who was standing outside his patrol car, he waved.

The visitation at St. Peter's was open to all. What we saw there, once again, was true diversity: the young and the old, the rich and the poor, the black and the white, the high and the low. Friends and people who considered themselves friends converged on the church. A woman named Flo Swinski told a *Pittsburgh Press* reporter, "I didn't know Mister Rooney personally, but I've read and heard so much about him I felt he was part of my life." She was dressed in black and gold. There were men and women in shorts (the August heat), there were men in coats and ties, and there were all kinds of people in blue jeans. They arrived in their cars; they arrived on foot and by bus. A few, like Ed DeBartolo at Devlin's the night before, came in chauffeured limousines.

By the time the doors opened at 2 p.m. a line had encircled the block. It was Friday, a work day. Police estimates were that three thousand people came in the afternoon and two thousand more at night. More than half of the two thousand remained to say the rosary.

The newspapers listed the NFL owners who attended the wake, the funeral, or both. There were eight or nine, plus the commissioner, Pete Rozelle, and the supervisor of officials, Art McNally. My close friend George Young was among the mourners. Al Davis – hard-crusted Al Davis – referred to the Chief as "someone I loved." Billy Sullivan of the Patriots added, "This may be sacrilegious, but I'll say it anyway: God was having a good day when he made Art Rooney."

Our coaches and players – all of them – came on Friday afternoon and went directly from the church to the airport. There was no thought of canceling their game the next day in New Orleans. "Mister Rooney," said Chuck Noll, "would expect us to play." Superdome officials arranged for a likeness of the Chief to be shown on the scoreboard during a minute of silence preceding the kickoff.

At least two dozen Steelers of an earlier vintage, the majority from the Super Bowl years, joined the throngs at St. Peter's, and there was even an original Pirate – Angelo Brovelli, a quarterback on the 1933 team. George Perles, Noll's one-time top assistant, who was still the head coach at Michigan State, flew in from East Lansing.

The Chief liked politicians, having been one himself on the ward-boss level, and there were plenty of those: Governor Bob Casey; former governor Dick Thornburgh, by that time the U.S. attorney general; County Commissioners Tom Foerster and Pete Flaherty; Mayor Sophie Masloff; Sheriff Gene Coon, on crutches (hit by a car as he was crossing a highway at night, he had recently lost a foot); County Controller Frank Luchino, who was Jack McGinley's good friend; and many smaller fry.

Jimmy the Greek Snyder came from Las Vegas. All of AJR's special cronies – the ones still living – were there. The kids from St. Peter's grade school came in a body. Two of them – boys – entered the church eating ice cream cones. It was in tune, everyone thought, with the spirit of the occasion.

There was talk of moving the service from St. Peter's to the cathedral in Oakland. We wouldn't hear of it. Jack McGinley said, "If we buried Art from another church, I don't think he'd go." St. Peter's Parish went back to 1849. The church building itself was one hundred years old. Throughout his long life, AJR had gone to Mass there. His parents had gone to Mass there. During the bleak Depression days of the 1930s the Chief raised money for St. Peter's in every conceivable way. "No one who lives in this parish," went a saying attested to by many of his neighbors, "will ever go hungry as long as Art Rooney is around."

To accommodate the funeral crowd on Saturday morning, the North Side farmer's market was canceled so that its parking lot could be used. Flags in the city flew at half-mast. A small airplane circled above the church, trailing a banner that read:

"BLESS YOU CHIEF – GLASSPORT."

The funeral was scheduled for 11 o'clock. According to the *Pittsburgh Press*, Blanche Furtwangler, a North Side native who lived in Bellevue, came in by bus to be first in line. She arrived three hours ahead of time. "I only knew Mister Rooney to say hello," she told a reporter, "but I felt like I'd known him all my life." The church's main sanctuary, which had a seating capacity of 1,100, was packed. "Standing room only," as Joe Carr would have put it. An overflow crowd of three hundred watched the service on four wide-screen television sets in the basement.

Only the closed-circuit camera was allowed upstairs. Anxious to save room for family, friends, and VIPs, Ed Kiely restricted the television stations to before-and-after coverage outside the church. As much as he might have wanted to, he could not show favoritism even to our friend from KDKA, Bill Burns. Three radio stations, their announcers unencumbered by camera crews and ponderous equipment, carried live broadcasts of the service.

The funeral Mass was extended to eighty minutes. Two soloists, both women, led us in four hymns. "On the altar," recalls Kay, "were what seemed like one hundred priests, bishops, and archbishops." Actually, there were four bishops, one auxiliary bishop, and two priests – Father Henry McAnulty, who may or may not have been Mom's distant relative, and Father Daniel Dixon, the pastor of St. Peter's, a man with the dimensions of an offensive tackle long retired. Bishop Vincent Leonard and his assistant, Bishop Donald Wuerl, gave eulogies. Bishop Wuerl had cut short his vacation, hastening back to Pittsburgh when he learned of the Chief's stroke.

Art Rooney was not a saint, just a near-saint, declared Bishop Leonard from the pulpit. "A devil's advocate," he said, "could have a field day with a man who took his wife to the race track on their honeymoon. He knew good people and he knew evil people, but he never let the evil embrace him."

One of the Chief's most frequently quoted remarks – that there never had been a Steeler he didn't like – made a deep and lasting impression on him, Leonard continued. He himself could not have said the same thing about some of his fellow bishops and priests, the old prelate admitted with a smile.

Our son Art III was one of the readers and did a good job. When the service was over, all of us filed out behind the casket. AJR had wanted an inexpensive one; in this respect, we disregarded his wishes. Six of the Chief's grandsons were pallbearers.

As we headed for the cars, I looked around. There were people I had not seen in years. So many, from so far away. The funeral cortege, by Kay's estimate, was "four miles long at least." Close to St. Peter's, the crowds on each side of the street stood shoulder-to-shoulder, three deep. Farther along, they gathered at every corner, silently watching. I caught sight of familiar faces here and there. All the way out Perrysville Avenue, people in Steeler jerseys were waving Terrible Towels. It reminded Kay of our trips from the airport to town after Super Bowl wins. Down in New Orleans, the Steelers and the Saints were going at it. I turned on the radio and listened for several minutes.

Near the gate to the North Side Catholic Cemetery the masses of spectators thickened again. An old man standing next to his car – stiffly at attention – held his hat over his heart and saluted the hearse as it passed. Resting on the car's hood was a large framed photograph of AJR. The old man, the salute, and the photograph form a tableau still emblazoned in my mind.

The graveside ceremony was brief. A few final words from Bishop Leonard. A sprinkling of holy water. Spoonfuls of earth tossed onto the casket. And AJR reunited with Kass. On their granite tombstone, three feet wide, were carvings of the Savior and a shamrock.

For the funeral luncheon, we adjourned to the Allegheny Club, where the solemnity of the morning gave way to lightheartedness. Among the guests were two women from Philadelphia, well dressed, well coiffed – and mortal enemies, or so I had heard. But now with their heads together they were all smiles and giggles, chatting away like schoolgirls. John and Pat knew the two women, and I asked if it wasn't true that they despised each other.

"Yes," answered Pat, "they certainly do."

John said, "But not today."

Bishop Leonard had declared from the altar that AJR was not a saint. And yet ... for canonization, according to the Catholic Church, it must be shown that a saint-in-waiting has performed three miracles. If that is true, I reflected, AJR had made a start. It was one down and two to go. Under the spell of his aura, two very dedicated antagonists had buried the hatchet.

Yes, indeed – I had witnessed the Chief's first miracle.

940 North Lincoln

Not long after the funeral, the five Rooney brothers met at 940 North Lincoln to decide what should be done with the old place. Tom Foerster had told us that Allegheny County wanted to make the house a historical site. The County Community College, the Catholic Diocese of Pittsburgh, the Holy Ghost fathers from Duquesne University, and two or three charitable foundations also had expressed an interest in taking it over.

For our part, we agreed that we would prefer to see it turned into rubble than fall into disrepair and perhaps become a crack house or worse. "Don't sell the old homestead after we're gone – burn it!" Kass used to say. I envisioned a sort of Viking funeral pyre – a real spectacle.

When we finally got down to business, Tim and I offered to buy the house from the estate, turn the ground floor into an office for the family enterprises, and keep the bedrooms upstairs in good repair so that relatives from out of town could use them on visits. In the end, it was Dan who bought the house. He and Patricia fixed it up and eventually moved in from Mount Lebanon. They are still there as I write this, happily ensconced.

Mary Roseboro and Georgia Flaherty, one of the housekeepers who attended to AJR, Aunt Alice, and Kass, continued for many years to be a part of the ménage.

What all of this caused me to realize was that I had come to think of the house as a person, almost. I was intensely concerned with its well-being. I gave the fifteen thousand dollars Dan paid me for my share of the purchase price to Bishop Wuerl, who had succeeded Bishop Leonard as head of the diocese. It was his to use as he pleased. Tim, Pat, and John did something similar.

Having been left one million dollars by the Chief, none of us needed the money. A stipulation of the will was that we should each give one-fifth of our two hundred thousand to charity. I divided my own share among worthy recipients in Western Pennsylvania.

A short time before his death, AJR had told me that he was handing down equal shares of the football team to his sons, but that he wanted Dan to run it. He was very emphatic about who was to be in charge. People I knew – some of them relatives – predicted that our joint ownership of the Steelers would fall apart in from five to seven years. They assured me family businesses never endure. This one, I think it is safe to say, did.

Mary Regan, AJR's loyal secretary, and Ed Kiely, his loyal lieutenant, remained with the Steelers until they retired of their own volition. Mary's great value was her ability to judge character, to weed out the frauds and the phonies who ingratiate themselves, or try to, with prominent figures like the Chief. She had the additional advantage of being Dan's sister-in-law, which gave her a personal investment in the welfare of the organization. And, like Kiely, she never lost track of people. Where AJR and later Dan might have been at a loss, she knew the whereabouts and the circumstances of friends and acquaintances and one-time business associates who had slipped off the radar screen. I always said I would like to have Mary Regan's Rolodex. Ed Kiely helped to settle the Chief's affairs and made himself useful in other respects. Just his presence on the scene was an asset to the Steelers. Like Jack McGinley, he connected the team's past with the here and now.

Chuck Noll retired after the 1991 season. He had a playoff team in 1989 and two other teams after 1987 with winning records. Bill Cowher, his successor, twice took the Steelers to the Super Bowl and came home with the trophy in 2006.

As I write this, the Chief's five sons are healthy, wealthy, and wise. Or healthy and wealthy, at any rate. All of us are married to the wives we first accompanied to the altar. Good things have happened to us. We give the credit for that to AJR and Kass.

Bishop Wuerl, at AJR's funeral, said in his eulogy that everyone he addressed had walked "in this big man's shadow." I walked in the big man's shadow during the last fifty years of his life, and I walk in his shadow even now.

Epilogue

At a time when life was mistreating Uncle John McNulty, I heard Uncle Jim say to him, "Your luck is going to change. And when it does," he continued, "I hope you are at the race track." Then he added, "And I hope I am with you."

In the grip of an impulse to wish someone well, Jim could do so with style. He liked and felt grateful to Kay, who remembered to send him a gift on his birthday and on other occasions and who frequently invited him to dinner, along with Grandma Rooney. Spotting Kay one day in the lobby of the Roosevelt Hotel, where he had taken a room after the death of his mother — they had been living together in the house on Perrysville Avenue — he limped across the distance between them to greet her. "Kay," he said in his best confidential stage whisper, "I don't know what you want in life, but I hope you get it."

His wants for himself, beyond the next drink, were hard to fathom. He led a solitary existence, an aging and lame alcoholic with no one looking after him. AJR was now a very old man; Uncle Dan, like Grandma Rooney, was gone; Margaret and Marie were getting no younger and in any event had families of their own to keep them occupied.

Small accidents bedeviled him. Crossing the streetcar tracks near the Roosevelt Hotel, he tripped and fell. An elevator door slamming shut too fast broke his arm. AJR, alarmed at these signs of decrepitude, made arrangements for the Passionate priests at St. Paul of the Cross Monastery to take him in.

St. Paul of the Cross overlooked the South Side from a hilltop. The dwindling number of priests in the Passionate order left them with enough vacant rooms for an old folks' wing. AJR, having gone to many retreats at St. Paul's, was friendly with the administrators and a generous contributor to fund-raising drives.

Uncle Jim's one request was for a large-screen television set, which AJR provided. Jim always preferred to watch the news and the sports in privacy, rather than in the monastery's common room. He had to do without booze unless Iggy Borkowski, John Joyce, or one of his other friends came to see him. Off they would then go, all three of them, for a visit with AJR and the rest of us at Three Rivers Stadium and maybe to watch a few innings of a Pirate game. Nothing wrong with that, you might think, but when Jim went back to the monastery he would usually have with him a bottle of contraband whiskey. Taken to task by AJR, his suppliers stoutly denied their complicity.

Physically, Jim thrived in his new surroundings. Mentally, he had started to slip. One day when Jim Laughlin drove AJR to the monastery, they arrived to find him having soup with some other old men in the dining hall. Suddenly one of them fell face forward into his lunch, dead of a heart attack. Seemingly unconcerned, Jim went on spooning up his soup.

The incident depressed Jim Laughlin for days, and AJR began to talk about the grim possibility of living too long.

Uncle Vince was the fourth of the brothers to die. Accompanied by John Joyce, Jim showed up at the wake. His hair had turned white and he looked old and pale. He knelt at the casket. He asked for "Arthur." No one else who was present seemed to interest him. He was worried about "Arthur," he said, having heard he was going "balmy." As it happened, "Arthur" was still fully functional — he remained so, in fact, until the day of his fatal stroke.

Uncle Vince's wake was Jim's last appearance in public. On one of my visits with Kay to the monastery, he informed us as though it were news that his brother Tom had been killed by the Japanese. At other times, his language would turn into gibberish.

Six months went by. Perhaps a year. I no longer was working out of Three Rivers Stadium. A newspaper story appeared, stating that I had been absent from the Steeler office for weeks. Someone called me from St. Paul's. Uncle Jim was frantic. He had to see me. A telephone call would not suffice. He was demanding that a taxicab be sent for him so he could get to me. It was urgent. He could not be settled down. He had to see me in person.

I told Kay about this, and we drove to St. Paul's, bringing candy for Uncle Jim. The Passionist brother who took us to his room said he never had seen him so upset. He thanked us for coming quickly. But, face to face with us, finally, Jim was perfectly calm. He smiled all the time we were there. He thought Kay was our daughter Sue. He told us again that his brother Tom had been killed in the war. As before, he ended up babbling nonsense.

Some time later word came to me that Jim wasn't going to make it. He'd been taken from St. Paul's to a hospital on the South Side. I decided to put off seeing him until the next day, but then for some reason I changed my mind. I found him alone in his room. He was dying, the nurse said. He would be moved to a hospice to wait for the end. I stayed for a while and talked to him. He looked at me blankly, and I told him who I was. I used his Irish name – Seamus – but there was still no response. I said some prayers and then departed.

I was the last of the Rooneys to see Jim alive. He died at the hospital before they could move him. On a glorious summer day he was buried at the monastery. A second cousin, Father Utz, officiated at the funeral Mass. Laid out in a blue suit, Jim was a handsome corpse. His sisters were there, along with nephews, nieces, and friends, and everybody said nice things about him. "He must have been made of steel," someone marveled, "to live as long as he did after putting away so much liquor."

It was indisputable. He was into his eighties and had outlasted all five of his brothers. And now he would be "with Arthur" again. Believe it.

***

Soft lights. Subdued Christmas decorations. White table cloth, good silver. Trusted old friends.

The waitress asked for our drink orders, and Kay said, "I'll have a highball – C.C. and water with a lemon twist. Kass drank that all the time. I guess I got that from her."

Dee Berlin, responding to the memory, said, "Yes, yes – I'll have the same thing. Kass was so special. She'd say, 'Hi, Dee, it's so nice to see you,' and you knew she meant it. She made me feel special, too."

"Dee, you are special." Kay said. She patted Dee's hand. Meanwhile Ralph Berlin was telling the waitress, "Scotch and water for me." Now it was my turn. "Too cold outside for a soft drink," I said. "What I'd like – if you have any – is one of those non-alcoholic beers."

The waitress assured me it would not be a problem.

I explained to the others that I had tried the stuff before and it wasn't bad. "In fact it almost tastes like the real thing." Not only tastes like the real thing but looks like the real thing, I could have added. My St. Clair Country Club friends – and the dining room seemed to be full of them – would think I had given in to John Barleycorn.

Ralph Berlin said, "We went to see 'The Chief' – that play about your father. It brought back old memories. Kay, did you ever hear that one of my first jobs with the Steelers was to fish your Uncle Jim out of Frenchy's, across the street from the Roosevelt Hotel? He was over there tying one on, and Fran Fogarty said, 'Hey, Berlin. Go get Jim. Get him up to his room.' Jim had a room in the hotel."

Ralph was smiling. "I came here to be the trainer, but I soon found out there were lots of other things I had to do."

There were indeed. He was the odd-jobs man in our organization, or, as he himself put it, "the plumber." "I'm just the plumber," he took to saying, and "The Plumber," in time, became his more or less self-bestowed nickname.

The drinks had arrived. We lifted our glasses and wished one another a Merry Christmas. Ralph took a swallow of Scotch. He said, "I knew all those people Gene Collier wrote about: Father Dan ... Dago Sam ... Patsy Scanlon ... Remember Patsy Scanlon, that little old white-haired bookie, Art?"

"I sure do. He could fight. Patsy Scanlon boxed some world champions."

"So many characters," Ralph said. "We were lucky to be a part of it, Dee and I." Helped along by the Scotch, the reminiscences started to flow. "The Berlins were Philadelphia people. Somehow we got out to Los Angeles. The Depression was on. My father must have thought he could get a job out West. We lived in Watts, Kay – that's the tough black section of L.A. Heck, I never really got to know my dad. The war started, see ... and he was gone for five years. He came back and died. Went to the Vets hospital and died. I knew I should feel bad, but he'd only been back about a year, and I couldn't grieve.

"Art" – Ralph never called me "Artie" – "I felt more sorrow when my dog was killed by a car."

In our relationship of thirty-five years, I never had heard Ralph talk this way. The guy was an ex-Marine. His coach at Iowa State in the late 1950s had called him one of the toughest interior linemen on the team. But now on this cold December night almost half a century later, the season, the warmly festive atmosphere, the Scotch, and most of all, perhaps, the sentiments awakened by the play he had recently seen were having an unexpected effect.

"Your dad," he said to me earnestly, "was the father I never had."

We were starting on our second round of drinks. "Remember all those years you sent me to work those Blesto draft meetings in Philly? Sometimes your dad would drop by. He liked to hang out with the scouts and coaches from the Eagles. 'Ralph,' he said to me once when he was there, 'I need a cab — I'm going to the airport.' I was waiting at the phone for a call from Pittsburgh, but I grabbed one of the Blesto scouts and told him, 'Take over for me here. If Art or anybody from Pittsburgh calls, they'll let you know what to do.' And I picked up the Chief's bag and said to the receptionist, 'Call Mister Rooney a cab. He's going to the airport. '

"Well, the next thing you know, here comes Leonard Tose rushing out of his office — the owner of the Eagles himself. The receptionist must have tipped him off. 'Arthur,' he says, 'I hear you'd like to go to the airport. My driver is outside with the limousine.' And the Chief says, 'No, no. Berlin here will take care of it.' And Tose said, 'Arthur, I insist.' He snatched the Chief's bag out of my hand and gave it to this guy in a chauffeur's uniform, cap and all. 'Take Mister Rooney right to the gate,' he tells the driver. 'If that isn't possible, park right next to the entrance and get Mister Rooney to his gate.' He turned to the Chief. 'The police know our limousine, Arthur. Give my regards to Kathleen and have a good flight.'

"I am now going to tell you the difference between your dad and phony big shots like Leonard Tose. While the driver was putting his bag in the trunk, the Chief said to Tose, 'Do you know our trainer, Ralph Berlin?' 'Oh, yes,' Tose says, 'I've seen him around here before.' The truth is he hadn't even known I existed. And after our introduction, if you can call it that, he never looked at me again.

"I'll tell you another thing about your dad. When former players of ours — guys who'd been with us for only one season, or maybe half a season — would drop by the training room years later to say hi, the boss would sometimes happen to come in. And nine times out of ten he'd remember the player's name. I'll never know how he did that."

I said, "Neither will I, Ralph. I saw that, too. It was certainly not a talent passed down from the father to the son."

"Oh, Art, you have a wonderful memory — all of those stories about the old days," said Kay, letting the air out of my false-modesty balloon in the gentlest way imaginable. "He's a Civil War expert, too," she informed the Berlins.

As much as I liked the attention, I felt I was upstaging Ralph. To keep him going, I said, "I interrupted you," and that was all it took.

"Another time in Philly," he resumed, "I shared a room with the Chief at this big fancy hotel. In the morning your dad says to me, 'I plan on going to Mass, but I don't know this section of town very well. Go down to the desk and ask where the Catholic church is. And, while you're at it, see if you can find out the schedule for the Masses.'

"I was so excited about doing this job that instead of stopping to check with the head bellman I ran right out into the street and started asking whoever passed by. People were on their way to work, and to judge by the clothes they were wearing, they all seemed to be going to construction jobs. There must have been a lot of construction around the hotel. Anyway, I was asking them, 'Where's the Catholic church? What time are the Masses?' and they're looking at me like I'm a nut. I'm getting no answers, but at last I see a cop. I ask him where the church is, and he points to it.

"'Right across the street.'

"Well, it was easy to miss, that's all I can say. It didn't look like a church. It looked like an old library or bank. It had gray stone columns, and there were empty lots on both sides — empty lots full of rubble. I go inside. There was nobody there except a priest in one of those long black robes. He had a big old black dog with him — a Labrador or something. I said, 'Hey, Father — when's the next Mass?'

"'Not till noon.'

"Oh, my. I said, 'Gee, Father, my boss wants to go to Mass. My boss is Art Rooney from Pittsburgh.'

"'Art Rooney? The man who owns the Steelers? I'll say a special Mass for him. Right here.' He indicates a side altar close to where we're standing.

"'What time, Father?'

"'Right now. As soon as he gets here.'

"Fifteen minutes later we're having the Mass. The priest is up on the altar and I'm in a pew with your dad. Two Catholics and a Lutheran. And oh, yes — the black dog. I don't know if the dog was a Catholic or not."

Ralph said he had been to so many Masses and funerals with the Chief that he knew some of the prayers. "But of course I kept my mouth shut. I was only the plumber. Still, you'd be surprised at how much the same the Lutheran services are to a Catholic Mass."

That night Berlin went with the Chief to a testimonial dinner for a Philadelphia boxing promoter named Herman Taylor. They left from Liberty Bell with my brother John in his Cadillac (the car which he had tried — without success — to make our dad believe was an Oldsmobile). "The dinner was at a restaurant in South Philly," Ralph said, "and John had some trouble finding it. When we finally got there, the parking lot was full and all the parking places on the street were taken. South Philly is all Italian, and a little Mediterranean guy was standing in front of the restaurant. He recognized your dad. 'Park here,' he says, waving us up onto the sidewalk. He put us right up against the steps to the front door.

"Inside, it looked like a Mafia joint. The place was packed with Italians. Everybody made a fuss over your dad, which was old stuff to him. He did his thing, the same as always, and he knew just the right time to leave.

"When we got out to the car, John said, 'I'm still lost. If you can get me to Broad Street, I'll know where I am. From Broad Street I can take you anywhere in Philly.'

"The Chief said, 'Ralph, you're from Philly. Where's Broad Street?'

"I couldn't answer. I was as lost as John, I had to tell him.

"Then the Chief saw some kids pitching pennies on the sidewalk. He goes to the biggest kid, whips a five-dollar bill out of his kick, and says, 'This is yours if you can get us to Broad Street.'

"The kid grabs the bill. He says, 'Get in your car and follow me. It's not far at all.' With the three of us close behind him, he runs down the middle of the street, takes a couple of turns, and there we are — right on Broad Street. In no time, John has us back at the hotel.

"'Mister Rooney, you da man,' I said to myself. Believe me, I was in awe of that guy."

"Ralph," Dee said, "tell the one about Rico's."

I remembered Rico's well — an old roadhouse off McKnight Road.

"We'd go to dinner there — Dee and I and your dad," Ralph said. "One night Joe Greene came with us. Well, when Mister Rooney showed up at Rico's, he owned the place. We got the best table, and the only thing we ordered were the drinks. Your dad would have ice tea. Then they just brought out the food. Salad. Hors d'oeuvres — all kinds. The good stuff — crabmeat, shrimp. I had no idea what it was. Then pasta. All kinds of fish and veal. When we finished eating, your dad didn't wait for the bill. He left a tip — a good one — and then stood up and said, 'We're going.'"

Dee broke in to say, "Joe Greene was so surprised."

Kay asked, "What did he do?"

"Do?" said Ralph. "He got up and walked out with the rest of us — still looking baffled.

"But the best — the very best — was on a trip out West with the football team. We went to this restaurant, Saturday night before the game. There were five or six of us. The bill comes, and the Chief grabs it. 'Mister Rooney,' I said, 'I have the Steeler credit card.'

"'Not when I'm here.' He puts his hand in his pocket — and comes up empty. 'What a sap,' he says. 'I forgot to bring my money.'

"'We'll have to use the card,' I tell him.

"'No way!' He says to the waiter, 'I'll give you an I.O.U.' and pulls out a ballpoint pen. He takes his napkin — a big white linen napkin, because this was a nice place — and writes in big, bold letters on the napkin: 'I.O.U. — X amount of dollars.' Then he signs it 'Art Rooney, Pittsburgh Steelers, Three Rivers Stadium, Pittsburgh, PA., 15212, telephone 412-323-1200.'

"What a man!" Ralph said. "The father I never knew."

After Marie McGinley's death in 2003 the only surviving Rooney of AJR's generation was Aunt Margaret Laughlin. At the age of 90, suffering from congestive heart failure, she made a special effort to see the play about her brother by Gene Collier, a Pittsburgh Post-Gazette columnist, and Ron Zellers. In reality Collier wrote the script, or most of it; Zellers' contribution was to get the play on-stage. Called "The Chief," it had a successful month-long run at the O'Reilly Theater on Liberty Avenue, downtown. There was only one part — the title role — played by a very good local actor named Tom Atkins, who delivered an unbroken ninety-minute monologue.

With her son Jim, Aunt Margaret attended a matinee. She was so moved by the performance of Tom Atkins, she said afterward, that she laughed and cried all through the show. When it was over, she attempted to meet the actor backstage, unsuccessfully. So as soon as she returned to her house on the North Side she wrote Mr. Atkins a letter. Her calligraphy was like AJR's — strong, but at the same time flowing and elegant. Both learned the art of penmanship from the nuns at St. Peter's School. Atkins responded at once, with a telephone call. "We had a nice, long, warm conversation," Margaret told me. From Atkins later on, I heard the same thing.

Aunt Margaret died in her ninety-first year. Late one night she asked her son Jim to fetch some ice cream from the kitchen. "And don't forget the chocolate sauce," she called down the steps while Jim was on his way. Aunt Margaret liked to have the last word. If "Don't forget the chocolate sauce" qualifies, she had the last word right up to the end, for when Jim returned with her bedtime snack, chocolate sauce and all, his mother had left us.

Jack McGinley, Aunt Marie's husband, was the next to go. He died in 2006. Jack McGinley, along with men like Father Silas and Byron White and Jack Butler, had been someone I was taught to emulate, or try to. They were models of upright behavior.

With AJR's death in 1988, his sons had become the patriarchs of the family. In March of 1987, sensing that his time was short, the Chief wrote a formal letter addressed to all five of us. After expressing his "love and respect" for our wives and children, he told us we should "make every effort" to buy back all of their stock in the football team, the stock we had put in their names. If we failed to do this, he predicted, there would be lawsuits and strife "down the road." He wanted us all — sons, wives, and children — to be fairly treated, and this was the best way to ensure it.

As we always had done, we honored the Chief's request. We bought back the stock. Twenty years have gone by, and we are all still in business together. Through some trying times, we have kept the ability to communicate with one another. Even more to be celebrated, the same thing holds true for our wives.

Lately the third generation of Rooneys has entered the picture. Dan's son Art joined him some time ago in the day-by-day operation of the Steelers. None of Dan's brothers are involved. In accordance with AJR's wishes, however, all five of us own the same amount of stock in the team as I write this and we are all on the board of directors. In the table of organization, I'm the only vice president listed. We have kept the Steelers and our other businesses under family ownership since the 1930s and are hopeful this third generation can hold things together as successfully.

I don't play golf. I don't play cards. I never have hunted or fished. But in one respect I'm a hobbyist:: I value my collection of Merv Corning art - the water color paintings I've commissioned of great Steeler players from the 1970s and earlier. Merv Corning died in 2006. Portraits of athletes were his specialty, and he was preeminent in his field. I was fortunate to have counted him as a friend.

One of the advantages of a more anchored existence is the time I've been able to spend with my family. Almost from the day I was married, my work as the football team's personnel director obsessed me. I was committed to building up a first-class scouting organization, and nothing seemed more important. Perpetually on the move, I touched down often at home, but only between trips and eager to be off again, insensible to the burden this was putting on Kay. Alone, she was taking care of our children.

Art III was the oldest, then came Karen, Mike, and Susie. Karen, born in 1964, was a strikingly beautiful child - blue-eyed, with her mother's red hair. But with good cause we were troubled. We had noticed, when she was still in the cradle, that Karen did not respond to the sound of our voices, or indeed to the ordinary sounds of a busy household. Pediatricians advised us not to worry. As time passed, all would be well. We were to learn, instead, that Karen's hearing problem was permanent, and "profound." We were to learn as well that there were problems of a far more serious nature, with "strong features," said the doctors, of that mysterious affliction known as autism.

We needed help. Thank heaven for the Sisters of Charity at DePaul Institute, the good nuns of the order that taught at Seton Hill College when Kay was a student there in the late 1950s. Kay's mother had recently died, but Kass and Aunt Alice gave us their support. And yet the stress on Kay, as our daughter's condition worsened, was enormous.

Desperate, we were taking Karen to specialists everywhere, not only in Western Pennsylvania, but in Washington, D. C., Philadelphia, the Menninger Clinic in Topeka, Kansas, and Children's Hospital in Baltimore. And in all of these places we were told the same thing. Our daughter could not be "cured." She would require full-time professional care for the rest of her life.

Throughout this ordeal my extended absences on football business frequently left Kay on her own, coping heroically. In the words of an old song, she was "the wind beneath my wings."

Karen, now in her forties, is in good physical health. She receives the best and most devoted attention that one of the topmost facilities in America can provide. There she will live out her days, visited often by her parents for as long as the fates allow.

Before his death some time ago, Roy Kumer, Kay's father — who lived to be 95 — gave Kay a fine piece of property next to his lakeside home in Maryland, and on it I have built her a weekend retreat. We go there in the spring, summer, and fall. From January to April, we're in our Palm Beach condominium in the ocean-front building where AJR and Kass spent a part of each winter. I can still see them walking up Grace Trail every morning on their way to St. Edward's Church for early Mass.

And now I am following in their footsteps. It's a ritzy neighborhood for sure, but if I'm putting on the dog, so was the Chief. I look around and say to myself — sometimes I even say it out loud — "Thank you, Dad. Thank you for making all of this possible."

1974 PITTSBURGH STEELERS

Bottom Row: Field Manager Jack Hart, Terry Hanratty, Roy Gerela, Terry Bradshaw, Joe Gilliam, Rocky Bleier, Dick Conn, Mike Wagner, J. T. Thomas, Ron Shanklin, Preston Pearson, Equipment Manager Tony Parisi.

Second Row: Head Coach Chuck Noll, Glen Edwards, Donnie Shell, Franco Harris, John Fuqua, Andy Russell, Steve Davis, Ed Bradley, Bobby Walden, Frank Lewis, Jim Allen, Defensive Coordinator Bud Carson.

Third Row: Offensive Backfield Coach Dick Hoak, Mel Blount, Jim Clack, Loren Toews, Mike Webster, Marv Kellum, Jon Kolb, Ray Mansfield, Sam Davis, Jack Lambert, Jack Ham, Defensive Assistant Bob Widenhofer, Flexibility Coach Paul Uram.

Fourth Row: Defensive Line Coach George Perles, Jim Wolf, Ernie Holmes, Steve Furness, L. C. Greenwood, Gordon Gravelle, Gerry Mullins, Rick Druschel, Dave Reavis, Joe Greene, Receiver Coach Lionel Taylor.

Top Row: Offensive Line Coach Dan Radakovich, Charlie Davis, Dwight White, John Stallworth, Randy Grossman, Reggie Garrett, Larry Brown, Lynn Swann, John McMakin, Trainer Ralph Berlin.

*With many good wishes
for the holidays and the coming year*

Mother - Dad - Grandmother &
                                    Grandfather
We are grateful to you for
your kindness to us. We
are proud of you. You have
made us very happy by
the way you live your life.
Be good and Stay a close
Knit family -

PITTSBURGH STEELERS
300 STADIUM CIRCLE
PITTSBURGH, PA. 15212
412/323-1200

March 18, 1987

Mr. Daniel M. Rooney
Mr. Arthur J. Rooney, Jr.
Mr. Timothy J. Rooney
Mr. Patrick J. Rooney
Mr. John J. Rooney

Dear Sons:

Time is starting to run out on me. I am concerned,
just as you are, about my Will, particularly my Stock in the
football club. I would like to reach some kind of an understanding so that there will be no questions or complications
regarding my Estate.

You are all fine men; I love all of you and I am
proud of you just as your Mother was. I love and respect your
wives and children. I believe that you should make every effort
to buy the football Stock that is in their names. I want them
all to be treated fairly. I believe if this does not happen,
down the road, there's going to be nothing but lawsuits. I do
not want this to happen. I want you to start working on this
immediately and try and come to a fair conclusion.

With all my love,

Dad

Managers/Coaches/Scouts

Dan Rooney
HOF 2001

Bert Bell
1941 HOF 1963

PITTSBURGH STEELERS

Bill Nunn
1967

Walt Kiesling
Pittsburgh Pirates
1937 HOF 1967

Art Rooney
HOF 1964

Coach Buddy Parker
1957

Art Rooney Jr.

PITTSBURGH STEELERS

Dick Haley
1972

"Jock" Sutherland
1946

Chuck Noll
1969 HOF 1993

Johnny "Blood" McNally
Pittsburgh Pirates 1937
HOF 1963

Design by Kathy Rooney, www.krooney.net